LEGAL RESEARCH, ANALYSIS, AND WRITING

Third Edition

LEGAL RESEARCH, ANALYSIS, AND WRITING

Third Edition

WILLIAM H. PUTMAN
JENNIFER R. ALBRIGHT

DELMAR
CENGAGE Learning

Australia • Brazil • Japan • Korea • Mexico • Singapore • Spain • United Kingdom • United States

DELMAR
CENGAGE Learning

Legal Research, Analysis, and Writing, Third Edition
William H. Putman and Jennifer R. Albright

Vice President, Careers & Computing:
  Dave Garza

Director of Learning Solutions: Sandy Clark

Senior Acquisitions Editor: Shelley Esposito

Director, Development-Career and Computing:
  Marah Bellegarde

Managing Editor: Larry Main

Senior Product Manager: Melissa Riveglia

Editorial Assistant: Diane Chrysler

Brand Manager: Kristin McNary

Market Development Manager: Erin Brennan

Senior Production Director: Wendy Troeger

Production Manager: Mark Bernard

Senior Content Project Manager:
  Betty L. Dickson

Art Director: Riezebos Holzbaur Group

Senior Technology Project Manager: Joe Pliss

Media Editor: Deborah Bordeaux

For product information and technology assistance, contact us at
Cengage Learning Customer & Sales Support, 1-800-354-9706
For permission to use material from this text or product,
submit all requests online at **www.cengage.com/permissions**
Further permissions questions can be emailed to
permissionrequest@cengage.com

Library of Congress Control Number: 2012940893

ISBN-13: 978-1-133-59190-0

ISBN-10: 1-133-59190-6

Delmar
Executive Woods
5 Maxwell Drive
Clifton Park, NY 12065
USA

Cengage Learning is a leading provider of customized learning solutions with office locations around the globe, including Singapore, the United Kingdom, Australia, Mexico, Brazil, and Japan. Locate your local office at
www.cengage.com/global

Cengage Learning products are represented in Canada by Nelson Education, Ltd.

To learn more about Delmar, visit **www.cengage.com/delmar**

Purchase any of our products at your local bookstore or at our preferred online store **www.cengagebrain.com**

Notice to the Reader

Publisher does not warrant or guarantee any of the products described herein or perform any independent analysis in connection with any of the product information contained herein. Publisher does not assume, and expressly disclaims, any obligation to obtain and include information other than that provided to it by the manufacturer. The reader is expressly warned to consider and adopt all safety precautions that might be indicated by the activities described herein and to avoid all potential hazards. By following the instructions contained herein, the reader willingly assumes all risks in connection with such instructions. The publisher makes no representations or warranties of any kind, including but not limited to, the warranties of fitness for particular purpose or merchantability, nor are any such representations implied with respect to the material set forth herein, and the publisher takes no responsibility with respect to such material. The publisher shall not be liable for any special, consequential, or exemplary damages resulting, in whole or part, from the readers' use of, or reliance upon, this material.

Printed in the United States of America
2 3 4 5 6 7 8 16 15 14 13

BRIEF CONTENTS

CONTENTS

PART III THE SPECIFICS OF LEGAL ANALYSIS {303}

CHAPTER 9 Legal Analysis—Key Facts {305}

CHAPTER 10 Legal Analysis: Issue Identification—Spotting the Issue {325}

CHAPTER 11   Legal Analysis: Stating the Issue   351

CHAPTER 12   Case Law Analysis—Is a Case on Point?   371

CHAPTER 13   Counteranalysis   391

PART IV LEGAL WRITING 413

TABLE OF CASES

PREFACE

Paralegals and law clerks are increasingly called upon to perform substantive legal research, analysis, and writing tasks. These tasks range from drafting interoffice legal memoranda summarizing the research and analysis of issues involved in a client's case to preparing drafts of appellate court briefs. This text provides the student with in-depth knowledge of the fundamentals of legal research, analysis, and writing.

The impetus for this book came from student requests for comprehensive information regarding many of the difficult areas of legal research, analysis, and writing, such as:

- How to conduct statutory research and analysis
- How to conduct case law research
- How to research secondary authority
- How to conduct electronic research
- How to cite authority
- How to brief cases
- How to identify the issue
- How to state the issue
- How to determine if a case is on point
- How to identify the key facts in a case
- How to conduct counteranalysis
- How to prepare an interoffice memorandum and court brief

The text is designed for use in research and writing classes. It can be useful in schools that have separate research and writing courses, where the first course focuses primarily on research with an introduction to writing, and the second course focuses on writing with research as a secondary component. For the research course, the instructor would use Chapters 1 through 13. For the writing course, instructors would use Chapters 9 through 19. Where both researching and writing are combined in one course, instructors can select the chapters appropriate for such a combined course.

The text is designed to cover the topics of legal research, analysis, and writing in general. It is organized to provide students with comprehensive information about difficult areas of analysis and writing. The text is divided into the following four parts.

Part I: Introduction to Research, Analytical Principles, and the Legal Process. Part I is composed of two introductory chapters. The first chapter presents an overview of the legal system and the legal process, as well as a summary of the basic legal principles involved in the process, such as authority, precedent, stare decisis, and so on. The second chapter introduces legal analysis and the IRAC analytical process.

Part II: Legal Research. Part II consists of six chapters that provide in-depth coverage of legal research and the research process. It begins with two chapters on primary authority; that is, chapters on statutory and case law. Next are two chapters on secondary authority. A chapter on computers and legal research followed by a chapter on legal citation complete Part II.

Part III: The Specifics of Legal Analysis. Part III covers matters essential to the analysis of a legal problem. It begins with a chapter on a principal component of a legal question (legal issue), the key facts, which are facts critical to the outcome of the case. Next are chapters on identifying and writing legal issues:

- Identifying the issue—The identification of the legal issue presented by a fact situation

- Stating the issue—How to present the issue

Part III concludes with two chapters on topics fundamental to legal analysis:

- Case law application—The analytical process used to determine if a court opinion applies to a legal question

- Counteranalysis—The process of discovering and considering the counterargument to a legal position or argument.

Part IV: Legal Writing. The focus of Part IV is on legal writing and the legal writing process. It covers the application of the principles presented in the previous chapters to the drafting of legal research memoranda, court briefs, and legal correspondence, with chapters on the following topics:

Fundamentals of writing

- The legal writing process in general

- Office legal memoranda (two chapters)

- Court briefs

- Correspondence

CHAPTER FEATURES

Each chapter is designed to help students completely understand and apply the concepts presented in the chapter. Chapters include the following features.

Hypothetical

Each chapter begins with a hypothetical that raises a question or questions involving the subject matter of the chapter. Following the hypothetical is a presentation of the principles, concepts, guidelines, and information concerning the subject matter. After the discussion of the subject matter, the principles and information discussed in the chapter are applied to answer the question or questions raised in the hypothetical.

The use of the hypothetical at the beginning of the chapter creates student interest in the subject matter of the chapter. The answer to the hypothetical toward the end of the chapter allows the student to see how the subject matter ties together and is applied.

Key Points Checklist

Each chapter has a list of key points that may be used as a quick reference and checklist when applying the concepts presented in the chapter. This checklist allows both the instructor and the student to make sure nothing is missed when reviewing or applying the principles presented in the chapter.

In-Depth Coverage of Topics

The greatest advantage of this text, for both teachers and students, is its comprehensive and in-depth coverage of topics not thoroughly covered in most texts. These topics include:

- Issue stating

- Issue identification (issue spotting)

- Case law analysis (whether a case is "on point")

- Counteranalysis
- Statutory analysis
- Office legal memoranda preparation

Examples

A major advantage of the text is that every principle, concept, and so on is followed by an example that illustrates it. One of my students requested that there be "plenty of examples." This text has plenty of examples. These examples help the instructor teach principles and concepts and help the student understand them.

Internet Resources

Each chapter contains a list of Web sites related to the chapter topic. This allows access to additional information on chapter topics from the Internet.

Assignments

There are assignments at the end of each chapter that range in difficulty. The assignments require students to apply the principles and techniques presented in the text. For example, among other assignments, there are eight case brief assignments in Chapter 4 (the cases are presented in Appendix A) and nine office legal memoranda assignments in Chapter 13 (based on the facts and law presented in the assignment and the court opinions in Appendix A). The answers to all the assignments are presented in the Instructor's Manual.

Appendices

The text has three appendices and a glossary of terms. Appendix A consists of court opinions that are necessary for the chapter assignments. Appendix B presents the brief of the appellee in a case filed in the United States Court of Appeals for the Tenth Circuit. The legal research, legal analysis, and initial drafts of this brief were performed by a paralegal who works in the Criminal Division of the United States Attorney's office for the District of New Mexico. Appendix C is a list of the Web sites presented in the text.

Readability

The text is written in a manner that a lay person can understand. The text avoids legalese, illustrates concepts with examples, and presents the subject matter simply and clearly.

New Features in This Edition

The major changes in this edition are to the legal research chapters of the text—Chapters 3 through 7. Chapters 3 through 6 are updated in regard to the increased use of online and electronic sources in legal research. Chapter 5 (on secondary and other research sources) is updated to reflect the use of *Shepard's* online and Westlaw's KeyCite to update and validate research. Chapter 7, on computer-assisted legal research, is rewritten to reflect changes to Westlaw, focusing on WestlawNext; it includes information about the new LexisNexis interface. In addition, new assignments are added to Chapters 3, 4, and 5.

Unlike other areas of the law, such as criminal and constitutional, where there are continuous changes in the case and statutory law, the process of legal analysis and writing remains essentially the same over time. Therefore, there are few substantive changes in the legal analysis and legal writing sections of this text.

However, there are additions. Chapter 17 includes two memo assignments. New assignments also are added to Chapter 9 (on key facts), Chapter 10 (on issue identification), and Chapter 19 (on correspondence). In response to requests for additional material, there are additions to the "Word Selection," "Grammar," and "Punctuation" sections of Chapter 14 (on the fundamentals of writing). In addition, Chapter 8 (on legal citation) is updated using

the 2010 version of *The Bluebook: A Uniform System of Citation*, 19th edition, and the 2010 version of the *ALWD*
   Citation Manual: A Professional System of Citation, 4th edition.

SUPPORT MATERIAL

The text is accompanied by the following support materials designed to assist students in learning and instructors in teaching.

Paralegal CourseMate

Legal Research, Analysis and Writing, Third Edition, has a Paralegal CourseMate available. Paralegal CourseMate includes:

- an interactive eBook, with highlighting, note-taking, and search capabilities
- interactive teaching and learning tools, including:
  - Quizzing
  - Case studies
  - Chapter objectives
  - Assignments
  - Flashcards
  - Web links
  - Crossword puzzles
  - PowerPoint® presentations
  - And more!
- Engagement Tracker, a first-of-its-kind tool that monitors student engagement in the course

To learn more about this resource and access free demo CourseMate resources, go to **www .cengagebrain.com**, and search by this book's ISBN (9781133591900). To access CourseMate materials that you have purchased, go to login.cengagebrain.com, enter your access code, and create an account or log into your existing account.

Instructor's Manual

Each chapter has several exercises ranging in difficulty. The Instructor's Manual provides complete answers to each exercise, general guides for instructors, and suggested additional assignments. Among other things, the manual includes 11 examples of briefs of court opinions, 14 examples of office legal research memoranda, and 2 examples of appellate briefs. The manual also provides a test bank of true/false and multiple-choice questions for each chapter. A test bank answer key is also included.

INSTRUCTOR
RESOURCES

Instructor Resources

Spend less time planning and more time teaching. With Delmar Cengage Learning's Instructor Resources to Accompany Legal Research, Analysis and Writing, preparing for class and evaluating students have never been easier!

This invaluable instructor CD-ROM allows you "anywhere, anytime" access to all of your resources.

- The **Instructor's Manual** contains various resources for each chapter of the book.
- The **Computerized Testbank** in ExamView makes generating tests and quizzes a snap. With many questions and different styles to choose from, you can create customized assessments for your students with the click of a button. Add your own unique questions and print rationales for easy class preparation.
- Customizable **PowerPoint® Presentations** focus on key points for each chapter. (PowerPoint® is a registered trademark of the Microsoft Corporation.)

To access additional course materials (including CourseMate), please go to login.cengage.com, then use your SSO (single sign on) login to access the materials.

WebTUTOR™

WebTutor™

The WebTutor™ supplement allows you, as the instructor, to take learning beyond the classroom. This online courseware is designed to complement the text and benefit students and instructors alike by helping to better manage your time, prepare for exams, organize your notes, and more. WebTutor™ allows you to extend your reach beyond the classroom.

WebPage

Come visit our website at http://www.paralegal.delmar.cengage.com/, where you will find valuable information such as hot links and sample materials to download, as well as other Delmar Cengage Learning products.

SUPPLEMENTS AT-A-GLANCE

SUPPLEMENT:	WHAT IT IS:	WHAT'S IN IT:
Paralegal CourseMate CourseMate	Online interactive teaching and learning tools and an interactive eBook. Go to login.cengage.com to access.	Interactive teaching and learning tools, including: ▪ Quizzing ▪ Case studies ▪ Chapter Objectives ▪ Assignments ▪ Flashcards ▪ Weblinks ▪ Crossword puzzles ▪ PowerPoints® presentations ▪ Interactive eBook ▪ Engagement Tracker
Online Instructor Companion Site	Resources for the instructor accessible via Cengage Single Sign On	▪ Instructor's Manual with answers to text questions, CourseMate assignments, and test bank and answer key ▪ Computerized Testbank in ExamView, with many questions and styles to choose from to create customized assessments for your students ▪ PowerPoint® presentations
Instructor Resources CD-ROM INSTRUCTOR RESOURCES	Resources for the instructor, available on CD-ROM	▪ Instructor's Manual with answers to text questions, CourseMate assignments, and test bank and answer key ▪ Computerized Testbank in ExamView, with many questions and styles to choose from to create customized assessments for your students ▪ PowerPoint® presentations
WebTutor™ WebTUTOR™	WebTUTOR™ supplemental courseware is the best way to use the Internet to turn everyone in your class into a front-row student. It complements Cengage Learning paralegal textbooks by providing interactive reinforcement that helps students grasp complex concepts. WebTUTOR™ allows you to know quickly what concepts your students are or aren't grasping.	▪ Automatic and immediate feedback from quizzes and exams ▪ Online exercises that reinforce what students have learned ▪ Flashcards ▪ Greater interaction and involvement through online discussion forums

Please note that all Internet resources are of a time-sensitive nature; URL addresses may often change or be deleted.

ACKNOWLEDGMENTS

I wish to gratefully acknowledge and express my deep appreciation to a number of individuals who took time and effort to assist in the development of this book. Without their expertise, suggestions, and support, this text would not have been remotely possible. I am particularly indebted to the following individuals:

Pamela A. Lambert, Esquire, who reviewed the text for intellectual and legal content and consistency. Her legal expertise, analytical skills, and input were invaluable. Pam's encouragement and positive attitude helped me through the rough spots.

Kate Arsenault, who reviewed the text for general readability. Kate's patient support and encouragement helped ensure that the text would be completed.

Hon. John J. Mitchel, who provided invaluable assistance on the appellate brief chapter.

Leigh Anne Chavez, Esquire, for assistance with several hypotheticals and ideas in general.

Robert T. Reeback, Esquire, for the ski resort hypothetical.

Dai Nguyen, Esquire, for her encouragement and assistance with hypotheticals.

Kathy Campbell, paralegal, for her assistance with office memos.

Sheila McGlothlin, a paralegal, for her support in the overall development of the text.

Shelley Esposito, Melissa Riveglia, Diane Chrysler, and all the individuals at Delmar Cengage Learning who helped with the development of the third edition. Their encouragement, suggestions, patience, and support were essential to its completion.

Thomson Reuters, for permission to publish all the cases in this text.

Finally, I would like to thank the reviewers who provided very valuable comments and suggestions for the text:

Miriam Joan Allen-Hart
Palomar Community College
San Marcos, CA

Hannah Barnhorn
Dayton Area Campus—National College
Kettering, OH

Regina Dowling
University of Hartford
West Hartford, CT

George W. Kent
Keiser University ecollege

ABOUT THE AUTHORS

William Putman received his Juris Doctor degree from the University of New Mexico School of Law and has been a member of the New Mexico Bar since 1975. For 10 years he was an instructor in the Paralegal Studies Program at Central New Mexico Community College in Albuquerque, New Mexico, and the Paralegal Studies Program at Santa Fe Community College, in Santa Fe, New Mexico.

He is the author of the *Pocket Guide to Legal Writing,* the *Pocket Guide to Legal Research,* and the textbooks *Legal Research, Analysis and Writing; Legal Analysis and Writing;* and *Legal Research.* He also authored the legal writing column in *Legal Assistant Today* (James Publishing Co.) for two years, and published several articles on legal analysis and writing in the magazine.

Jennifer Albright was the Director of the Paralegal Studies and Judicial Studies programs at Central New Mexico Community College for six years. She was a full-time instructor in both programs for nine years. Currently she is an adjunct faculty member in Legal Assistant Studies at Phoenix College. Jennifer received her Juris Doctor degree from the Southern Illinois University School of Law.

PART I

Introduction to Research, Analytical Principles, and the Legal Process

OVERVIEW

Part I presents two introductory chapters designed to provide a review of basic information fundamental to legal research, analysis, and writing. Chapter 1 is an overview of the legal system and the legal process, including a summary of basic legal principles and authorities involved in the process. Chapter 2 introduces legal research, analysis, and the research and analytical process.

CHAPTER 1

Introduction to Legal Principles and Authorities

Learning Objectives

After completing this chapter, you should understand:

- The main sources and types of law
- The basic structure of the state and federal court systems
- The hierarchy of the various sources of law
- The types of legal authority
- When and how legal authority applies

Renee works in a clerical position at the Addison law firm. Last fall she entered the paralegal program offered by the local community college. Renee is an excellent employee. The firm, in support of her continued education, pays her tuition and allows her to leave work early so that she can attend a late afternoon class. The firm recently reassigned Renee to work in the paralegal division and directed that she be assigned some substantive legal research and analysis tasks.

Two weeks ago, Renee started working on a gender discrimination case. In that case, the client, Mary Stone, worked for a company for 11 years. She always received excellent job performance evaluations. Her coworker, Tom, asked her on several occasions to go out with him. Ms. Stone always refused his invitations. The last time he asked her out was about a year ago. After she refused, he told her, "I'll get even with you." Nine months ago, Tom was promoted to the position of department supervisor. After his promotion, he did not ask Ms. Stone out again. On her evaluation three months ago, he rated her job performance as "poor" and stated that she was uncooperative and abrasive. He recommended that she be demoted or fired. Ms. Stone feels that she has been discriminated against, and she wants the "poor" evaluation removed from her file.

Renee's assignment is to locate the pertinent state and federal law governing gender discrimination and any other relevant information on the subject and prepare a memo summarizing her research and how it applies to the case. Renee located a federal and a state statute prohibiting discrimination in employment on the basis of gender, a federal and a state court case with facts similar to those in Ms. Stone's case, and two law review articles discussing the type of gender discrimination encountered by Ms. Stone.

While analyzing the law and preparing her memo, Renee realizes that she must determine what part of her research applies and how. She asks herself, "In which court should the claim be filed, federal or state? If a complaint is filed in state court, which statutes and court opinions must the state court follow? Why?" This chapter presents general guidelines that assist in determining when and how legal authorities apply. The Application section at the end of this chapter presents guidelines to answer Renee's questions.

I. INTRODUCTION

As they become more aware of the capabilities of paralegals and legal researchers, attorneys increasingly assign them substantive legal research, analysis, and writing tasks. **Legal research** is the process of finding the law that applies to a client's problem. **Legal analysis** is the process of determining how the law applies to the problem. The goal of this text is to provide comprehensive coverage of the legal research, analysis, and writing process. Emphasis is on in-depth coverage of many difficult areas of legal research, analysis, and writing, such as:

- Issue and key fact identification
- Issue statement (how to write the issue)
- Location of statutory and case law
- Location of secondary authority
- Statutory and case law analysis
- Counteranalysis
- How to effectively conduct legal research and analysis

Before considering these areas in subsequent chapters of the text, it is necessary to have a general understanding of the law and the legal system and some of the basic doctrines and principles that apply to legal analysis. This is essential because legal analysis involves a determination of how the law applies to a client's facts, which in turn requires a knowledge of what the law is, how to find it, and the general principles that govern its application. This chapter presents an overview of the legal system and fundamental principles that guide its operation. The definitions, concepts, doctrines, and principles addressed are referred to and applied in the subsequent chapters of the text. A familiarity with them is essential when studying those chapters.

The term *law* has various definitions, depending on the philosophy and point of view of the individual defining it. Law can be defined from a political, moral, or ethical perspective. For the purposes of this text, **law** is the body of enforceable rules that govern individual and group conduct in a society. The law establishes standards of conduct, the procedures governing the conduct, and the remedies available when the rules of conduct are not obeyed. The purpose of the law is to establish standards that allow individuals to interact with the greatest efficiency and the least amount of conflict. When conflicts or disputes occur, law provides a mechanism for a resolution that is predictable and peaceful.

The following sections focus on the various sources of law and the principles and concepts that affect the analysis of these sources.

II. SOURCES OF LAW

The legal system of the United States, like the legal systems of most countries, is based upon history and has evolved over time. When America was settled, English law governed most of the colonies. As a result, the foundation of the American legal system is the English model, with influences from other European countries.

In England, after the Norman Conquest under William the Conqueror in 1066, a body of law called the *common law* developed. The common law consisted of the law created by the courts established by the king. When colonization of America took place, the law of England consisted primarily of the common law and the laws enacted by Parliament. At the time of the Revolution, the English model was adopted and firmly established in the colonies.

After the Revolution, the legal system of the colonies remained largely intact and remains so to the present time. It consists of two main categories of law:

1. Enacted law
2. Common law/case law

A. Enacted Law

As used in this text, the term **enacted law** means the body of law adopted by the people or legislative bodies. It includes:

- Constitutions—adopted by the people
- Statutes, ordinances—laws passed by legislative bodies
- Regulations—actions of administrative bodies that have the force of law

Laws established by two governing authorities govern society in the United States: the federal government and the state governments. Local governments are a component of state governments and have the authority to govern local affairs. Each governing authority has the power to enact legislation affecting the rights and duties of members of society. It is necessary to keep this in mind when analyzing a problem, because the problem may be governed by more than one law. The categories of enacted law are addressed in the following subsections.

1. Constitutions

A **constitution** is a governing document adopted by the people. It establishes the framework for the operation of government, defines the powers of government, and guarantees the fundamental rights of the people. Both the federal and state governments have constitutions.

United States Constitution. The United States Constitution:

- Establishes and defines the powers of the three branches of federal government: executive (president), legislative (Congress), and judicial (courts)
- Establishes the broad powers of the federal and state governments and defines the relation between the federal and state governments
- Defines in broad terms the rights of the members of society

State Constitutions. Each state has adopted a constitution that establishes the structure of the state government. In addition, each state constitution defines the powers and limits of the authority of the state government and the fundamental rights of the citizens of the state.

2. Statutes

Laws passed by legislative bodies are called **statutes**. Statutes declare rights and duties, or command or prohibit certain conduct. As used here, *statute* includes any law passed by any legislative body: federal, state, or local. Such laws are referred to by various terms, such as *acts, codes, statutes,* or *ordinances.* The term *ordinance* usually refers to a law passed by a local government. Statutory law has assumed an increasing role in the United States, as many matters once governed by the common law are now governed by statutory law.

> **For Example** Criminal law was once governed almost exclusively by the common law. Now statutory law governs a large part of the criminal law, such as the definition of crimes.

Because statutes are usually designed to cover a broad range of present and future situations, they are written in general terms.

> **For Example** Section 335-1-4 of a state's Uniform Owner Resident Relations Act provides, "If a court, as a matter of law, finds that any provision of a rental agreement was inequitable when made, the court may limit the application of such inequitable provision to avoid an inequitable result." The statute is written in general terms so that it covers a broad range of landlord–tenant rental situations and provisions. It is designed to cover all provisions of all rental agreements that may prove to be inequitable. The general terms of the statute allow a court a great deal of flexibility when addressing an issue involving an alleged inequitable lease provision. The court "may limit the application . . . to avoid an equitable result." How and to what degree the court limits the application of the lease provision is left to the court to decide.

3. Administrative Law

A third type of enacted law is **administrative law**. Legislative bodies are involved in determining what the law should be and enacting the appropriate legislation. They do not have the time and are not equipped to oversee the day-to-day running of the government and implementation of the laws. Legislatures delegate the task of administering the laws to administrative agencies. The agencies are usually under the supervision of the executive branch of the government.

When a law is passed, the legislature includes enabling legislation that establishes and authorizes administrative agencies to carry out the intent of the legislature. This enabling legislation usually includes a grant of authority allowing the agency to create rules and regulations necessary to carry out the law. These rules and regulations have the authority of law. The body of law that results is called *administrative law*. It is composed of the rules, regulations, orders, and decisions promulgated by the administrative agencies when carrying out their duties.

Administrative law is usually more specific than statutory law because it deals with the details of implementing the law.

> **For Example** The Environmental Protection Agency, in order to implement the Clean Air Act, adopted various regulations setting air quality standards. Many of these regulations establish specific numerical standards for the amount of pollutants that may be emitted by manufacturing plants. The Clean Air Act is written in broad terms, but the regulations enforcing it are specific. For example, the regulations define the exact amount of pollutants a new automobile may emit.

Enacted law covers a broad spectrum of the law. The process of analyzing enacted law is covered in detail in Chapter 3.

B. Common Law or Case Law

In a narrow sense, **common law** is law created by courts in the absence of enacted law. Technically, the term includes only the body of law created by courts when the legislative authority has not acted.

> **For Example** The courts have created most of the law of torts. Tort law allows a victim to obtain compensation from the perpetrator for harm suffered as a result of the perpetrator's wrongful conduct. From the days of early England to the present, legislative bodies have not passed legislation establishing or defining most torts. In the absence of legislation, the courts have created and defined most torts and the rules and principles governing tort law.

Case law encompasses a broader range of law than common law. Case law includes not only the law created by courts in the absence of enacted law, but also the law created when courts *interpret* or *apply* enacted law.

Often the term *common law* is used in a broad sense to encompass all law other than enacted law (i.e., law enacted by legislatures or adopted by the people). This text uses the term *common law* in the broadest sense to include case law (often called judge-made law). Throughout the remainder of this text, the term *case law* is used primarily instead of the terms *common law* or *judge-made law* and should be interpreted to include all law other than enacted law.

As mentioned, the case law system in the United States is based on the English common law, and much of the English common law has been adopted by the states. William the Conqueror established a king's court (Curia Regia) to unify the country through the establishment of a uniform set of rules and principles to govern social conduct throughout the country. The courts, in dealing with specific disputes, developed legal principles that could apply to all similar disputes.

With the passage of time, these legal principles came to embody the case law. The case law process continues to the present day in both England and the United States, with new rules, doctrines, and principles continually being developed by the courts.

> **For Example** One hundred and fifty years ago, there was no remedy in tort law for strict products liability (liability of manufacturers and sellers for harmful or dangerous defective products). The tort was developed by the courts in the 20th century to address the needs of a modern industrial society.

The ability to research and analyze case law is an essential skill for a legal researcher. The researcher usually needs court opinions to determine how a law has been interpreted and how it might apply to specific fact situations and problems such as those of the client's case.

1. Role of the Courts

Disputes in our society arise from specific fact situations. The courts are designed to resolve these disputes. When a dispute is before a court, it is called a *case*. The role of the court is to resolve the dispute in a peaceful manner through the application of the law to the facts of the case. To accomplish this resolution, the court must identify the law that controls the resolution of the dispute and apply that law to the facts of the case.

When there is no enacted or case law governing a dispute, the court may be called upon to create new law. If the meaning or application of an existing law is unclear or ambiguous, it may be necessary for the court to interpret the law. In interpreting and applying existing law, courts often announce new legal rules and principles. The creation of new law and the interpretation and application of existing law become law itself.

The result reached by a court is usually called a *decision*. The court's written decision, which includes how it ruled in a case and the reasons for the decision, is called an **opinion**. The case law is composed of the general legal rules, doctrines, and principles contained in court opinions.

2. Court Systems

A basic understanding of court systems is necessary for anyone analyzing a legal problem. The approach to a problem and the direction of research may depend upon whether relief is available in federal or state court or both. This section presents a brief overview of the court systems.

There are two parallel court systems, the federal court system and the state court system. A factor common to both systems is the concept of jurisdiction. An understanding of this concept is essential to understanding the operation of both systems.

a. Jurisdiction

The types of cases that can come before a court in either system are determined by the jurisdiction of the court. **Jurisdiction** is the extent of a court's authority to hear and resolve specific disputes. A court's jurisdiction is usually limited to two main areas:

1. Over persons by geographic area—personal jurisdiction
2. Over subject matter by types of cases—subject matter jurisdiction

(1) Personal Jurisdiction **Personal jurisdiction** is the authority of the court over the parties to resolve a legal dispute involving the parties. The jurisdiction of state courts is limited to the geographic boundaries of the state or to matters that have some connection with the state.

> **For Example** New York state courts do not have authority to decide matters that take place in the state of Ohio. Their authority is limited to the geographic boundaries of the state of New York. State courts in New York have jurisdiction over an Ohio resident if the resident is involved in an automobile accident in New York State.

In addition, personal jurisdiction requires that both the plaintiff and the defendant be properly before the court. Assuming the correct court is chosen, a plaintiff properly comes before the court by filing the pleading that starts the lawsuit (the complaint in a civil case or an indictment, information, or complaint in a criminal case). A defendant is properly before the court when the defendant is notified of the lawsuit, that is, correctly served with a copy of the complaint (service of process).

(2) Subject Matter Jurisdiction **Subject matter jurisdiction** is the court's authority over the types and kinds of cases it may hear and decide. In regard to subject matter jurisdiction, there are basically two types of courts in both the federal and state court systems:

1. Courts of general jurisdiction
2. Courts of limited jurisdiction

Courts of general jurisdiction have the authority to hear and decide any matter brought before them, with some limitations. The United States District Courts are the courts of general jurisdiction in the federal system. They have the authority to hear and decide all matters posing federal questions (involving the United States Constitution or federal law) or cases in which the parties are citizens of different states and the amount in controversy exceeds $75,000. All states have state courts of general jurisdiction that have authority over state matters. The courts of general jurisdiction are the main trial courts in both systems.

Courts of limited jurisdiction are limited in the types of cases they can hear and decide. There are courts of limited jurisdiction in both the federal and state court systems.

> **For Example**
> 1. The authority of the United States Tax Court is limited to matters involving federal tax law.
> 2. Most state court systems have courts whose authority is limited by dollar amount. Such courts are limited to hearing and deciding matters where the amount in controversy does not exceed a certain amount, such as $10,000. These courts are called by various names: small claims, magistrate, and so on. Some state courts are limited to hearing specific types of cases, such as matters involving domestic relations or probate.

(3) Concurrent Jurisdiction **Concurrent jurisdiction** exists when more than one court has the authority to deal with the same subject matter. In such cases, the plaintiff may choose the court in which to file the case.

For Example	
	1. In diversity of citizenship cases (disputes between citizens of different states) in which the amount in controversy exceeds $75,000, the matter may be tried in either federal court or the state court of general jurisdiction. Both the federal and state courts have authority to try the case; they have concurrent jurisdiction.
	2. A state court of limited jurisdiction, such as a county court, may have authority to try cases where the amount in controversy does not exceed $10,000. Such cases may also be tried in the state's court of general jurisdiction, such as a district court, which has authority to try a claim of any dollar amount. These courts have concurrent jurisdiction over claims that do not exceed $10,000; that is, the matters may be tried in either court.

Jurisdiction is a complex subject. An exhaustive and detailed treatment of jurisdiction is the subject of many texts and is properly addressed in a separate course of study. The brief discussion here is designed to acquaint the student with the fundamentals.

b. Federal Court System

The federal court system is composed of three basic levels of courts.

(1) Trial Courts The **trial court** is the court where the matter is heard and decided. The testimony is taken, other evidence is presented, and the decision is reached. The role of the trial court is to determine what the facts are and how the law applies to those facts. A trial is presided over by a judge and may include a jury. If the trial is conducted before a judge and a jury, the judge decides **questions of law** such as what the law is or how it applies. The jury decides **questions of fact** such as whether a person performed a certain act. If the trial is conducted without a jury, the judge decides both questions of law and fact.

The United States **District Court** is the main trial court in the federal system. This court has jurisdiction over cases involving federal questions. This includes matters involving the United States Constitution, federal laws, treaties of the United States, and so on. The United States District Court also has the authority to try diversity cases. These are cases involving disputes between citizens of different states where the amount in controversy exceeds $75,000. Each state has at least one United States District Court (see Exhibit 1-1).

In addition to the United States District Court are other federal courts whose authority is limited to specific matters, such as the United States Tax Court, the United States Court of International Trade, the United States Court of Federal Claims, and the United States Bankruptcy Court.

(2) Court of Appeals A party aggrieved by the decision of a trial court has a right to appeal the decision to a **court of appeals** (also referred to as an *appellate court*). The primary function of a court of appeals is to review the decision of a trial court to determine and correct any error that may have been made. A court of appeals only reviews what took place in the trial court. It does not hear new testimony, retry the case, or reconsider the evidence. A court of appeals reviews the record of the lower court and takes appropriate action to correct any errors made, such as ordering a new trial or reversing a decision of the trial court. The court of appeals in the federal system is called the United States Court of Appeals. These courts are also called *circuit courts*. There are 13 federal courts of appeals (see Exhibit 1-1).

Exhibit 1-1 *United States Circuit Courts of Appeals and United States District Courts.* Source: http://www.uscourts.gov/court_locator.aspx

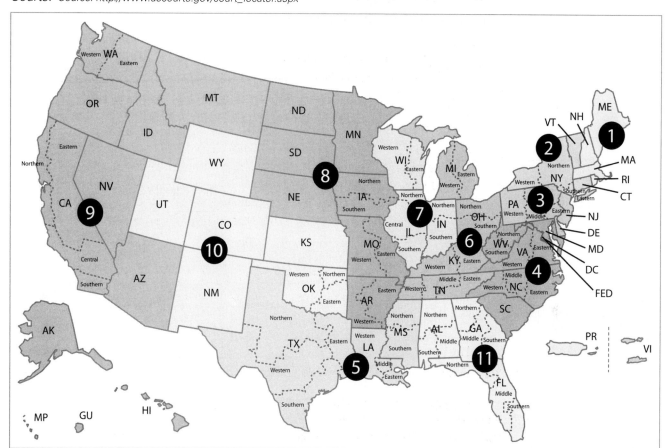

(3) United States Supreme Court The United States Supreme Court is the final court of appeals in the federal system. It is the highest court in the land. With few exceptions, an individual does not have an absolute right to have a matter reviewed by the Supreme Court. A party who disagrees with the decision of a court of appeals must request (petition) the Supreme Court to review it. The request is called a **petition for writ of certiorari**. The Supreme Court has discretion to review or not review a decision of a court of appeals. If the Court denies the petition, the decision of the court of appeals stands. If the Court believes that the matter involves important constitutional issues, if the challenged decision conflicts with federal court decisions, or if there is a conflict between the opinions of the courts of appeals, then the Supreme Court may grant the petition and review the decision of the lower court.

The organization of the federal court system and the various federal courts is presented in Exhibit 1-2.

c. State Court System

Every state has its own state court system, and each has unique features and variations. The names of the courts vary from state to state.

For Example	The highest court in many states is called the supreme court. In New York, however, the highest court is called the court of appeals.

Because of the unique features of each state system, it is essential that you become familiar with the court system in your state. Like the federal court system, most state court systems are composed of three basic levels of courts.

Exhibit 1-2 *Organization of the Federal Court System.*

© Cengage Learning 2014

(1) Trial Courts All states have trial courts where the evidence is presented, testimony taken, and a decision reached. Usually there are trial courts of general jurisdiction and trial courts of limited jurisdiction. The court of general jurisdiction is often called a *district court.* There are various courts of limited jurisdiction, such as probate courts, small claims courts, domestic relations courts, magistrate courts, and county courts.

(2) Courts of Appeals Many states have intermediate courts of appeals that function in the same manner and play the same role in the state court system as the federal court of appeals does in the federal system.

(3) State Supreme Court Every state has a highest appellate court, usually called the supreme court. This court is the highest court in the state, and its decisions are final on all questions involving state law. In states that have intermediate courts of appeals, the state supreme court often operates like the United States Supreme Court in that there is no automatic right of appeal. Like the federal Supreme Court, the state supreme court grants leave to appeal only in cases presenting important questions of state law. In those states where there is no intermediate court of appeals, a party who disagrees with a trial court's decision has a right to appeal to the highest court. In either system, state or federal, all individuals have at least one opportunity to appeal the decision of a trial court to a higher court.

3. Precedent and Stare Decisis

It is apparent, when you consider the number of courts in the state and federal court systems, that the courts address an immense number of legal questions and problems. Often, similar legal questions and fact situations arise in the same court system or in different court systems. If a court in an earlier case has developed a legal doctrine, principle, or rule that helps resolve a legal question, then later courts addressing the same or a substantially similar question should be able to look to the earlier decision for guidance. Why should a court go through the process of determining how a matter should be decided if an earlier court has already gone through the process and developed a principle or rule that applies? The efficiency of the court system is greatly enhanced because courts do not have to "reinvent the wheel" in every case—they may rely on legal doctrines, principles, or rules developed over time in previous cases.

Reliance on doctrines, principles, or rules to guide the resolution of similar disputes in the future also makes the legal system more stable, predictable, and consistent. If the law governing a specific subject or legal question is established in an earlier case, then individuals can rely on a court addressing the same or a similar question to base its decision on the principles established in the earlier case. Outcomes can be predicted to some extent, and stability and consistency can become part of the court system.

Two complementary doctrines have developed to provide stability, predictability, and consistency to the case law. These doctrines are precedent and stare decisis.

a. Precedent

Precedent is an earlier court decision on an issue that applies to govern or guide a subsequent court in its determination of an identical or similar issue based upon identical or similar facts.

> **For Example** The state's highest court, in the case of *State v. Ahrens*, held that bail must be set in all criminal cases except when a court determines that the defendant poses a clear and present threat to the public at large or to an individual member or members of the public. If a case before a subsequent court involves a situation in which the defendant has made threats against the life of a witness, *Ahrens* applies as precedent and can serve as a guide for the court's determination of the question of whether bail must be set.

A case that is precedent is often called "on point." Chapter 12 discusses the process and steps to follow when determining if a court opinion may apply or be relied on as precedent.

b. Stare Decisis

The doctrine of **stare decisis** is a basic principle of the case law system that requires a court to follow a previous decision of that court or a higher court when the current decision involves issues and facts similar to those involved in the previous decision. In other words, similar cases will be decided in similar ways. Under the doctrine, when the court has established a principle that governs a particular set of facts or a specific legal question, the court will follow that principle and apply it in all future cases with similar facts and legal questions. In essence, stare decisis is the doctrine providing that precedent should be followed.

> **For Example** A statute of state X prohibits employment discrimination on the basis of gender. In the case of *Ellen v. Employer, Inc.*, an employee was fired because the employee was homosexual. The supreme court of state X interpreted "discrimination on the basis of gender" as used in the statute to include discrimination based on an individual's sexual preference. The doctrine of stare decisis requires that in subsequent cases, the supreme court of state X and all the lower courts of state X follow the interpretation of the statute given in *Ellen v. Employer, Inc.* In other words, the lower courts must follow the precedent set in *Ellen v. Employer, Inc.*

The doctrine of stare decisis, however, does not require rigid adherence to the rules or principles established in prior decisions. The doctrine does not apply if there is a good reason not to follow it. Some of these reasons include:

1. The earlier decision has become outdated because of changed conditions or policies.

> **For Example** In *Plessy v. Ferguson*, 163 U.S. 537, 16 S. Ct. 1138, 41 L. Ed. 256 (1896), the court adopted the "separate but equal doctrine" that allowed segregation on the basis of race. In *Brown v. Board of Education of Topeka*, 347 U.S. 483, 74 S. Ct. 686, 98 L. Ed. 873 (1954), the Supreme Court refused to follow *Plessy* and overruled it, holding that separate educational facilities were inherently unequal and denied equal protection of the law.

2. The legislature has enacted legislation that has, in effect, overruled the decision of an earlier court.

> **For Example** The state supreme court, in *Stevens v. Soro, Inc.*, ruled that the phrase "on the job" in the Workers' Compensation Act means that an employee is "on the job" from the moment the employee leaves for work until he or she arrives home. After the decision, the state legislature amended the act, defining "on the job" to include only the time the employee is on the premises of the employer. The amendment in effect overrules the prior court decision, so courts are not required to follow that decision in subsequent cases.

3. The earlier decision was poorly reasoned or has produced undesirable results.

> **For Example** Review the gender discrimination example presented in the beginning of this subsection. Suppose the supreme court of state X, in a later case, decides that the reasoning in the court's decision in *Ellen v. Employer, Inc.,* was incorrect and that the term *gender discrimination* should not be interpreted to include discrimination on the basis of sexual preference. The court can overrule *Ellen* and is not bound to follow it thereafter (nor are lower courts of state X).

When a court follows the doctrines of precedent and stare decisis, the court can be relied on to reach the same decision on an issue as an earlier court when the cases are sufficiently similar. Without these doctrines, a similar case could be decided in an entirely different manner based upon the unique beliefs of the individual judge and jury. The result would be little or no consistency in the case law, and chaos would reign. Later in this chapter, we discuss when a decision of an earlier court may or must be relied on by a subsequent court (see the sections addressing authority).

III. HIERARCHY OF THE LAW

A hierarchy of authority exists between the two primary sources of law: enacted law and case law. When a question arises concerning which source applies in a case or there is a conflict between sources, a hierarchy governs which source will apply.

In general, within each jurisdiction, the constitution is the highest authority, followed by the other enacted law (legislative and administrative law), then the common or case law. This means that legislative acts and court decisions must not conflict with the provisions of the constitution. A court decision may interpret a legislative act, but it cannot overrule an act unless it is determined that the act violates the constitution.

The United States Constitution separates the powers to govern between the federal and state governments. This separation of powers is called **federalism**. The **supremacy clause** of the Constitution (Article VI) provides that between federal and state law, federal law is supreme. If an enacted law or court decision of a state conflicts with a federal law or court decision, then the state law or decision is invalid to the extent it conflicts with the federal law or decision.

> **For Example** A state passes a law declaring that it is illegal to burn the American flag. The state supreme court upholds the statute. Both the state statute and the state supreme court decisions are invalid because they conflict with the Constitution of the United States. The United States Supreme Court has ruled that the freedom-of-speech provisions of the Constitution include the right to burn the flag. The federal law is supreme, and the state law is invalid to the extent it conflicts with federal law.

IV. AUTHORITY

To analyze the law, in addition to knowing the sources of law, you must become familiar with the concept of authority, principles relating to authority, and the various types of authority. **Authority** may be defined as anything a court may rely on when deciding an issue. It includes not only the law but also any other nonlaw source that a court may look to in reaching a decision.

This section discusses the two types of authority and the two roles that authority plays in the decision-making process. The two types of authority are:

1. Primary authority—the law itself
2. Secondary authority—nonlaw sources on which a court may rely

The two possible roles that authority may play are:

1. Mandatory authority—the authority a court must rely on and follow when deciding an issue
2. Persuasive authority—the authority a court may rely on and follow, but is not bound to rely on or follow

The following subsections first address the two types of authority (primary and secondary), then discuss the role of authority, that is, the value or weight a court must or may give to authority (mandatory and persuasive authority). See Exhibit 1-3.

A. Types of Authority

1. Primary Authority

Primary authority is the law itself. It is composed of the two main categories of law, enacted law and common law.

> **For Example** Primary authority includes but is not limited to constitutions, statutes, ordinances, regulations, and court opinions.

Courts refer to and rely on primary authority first when resolving legal problems.

2. Secondary Authority

Secondary authority is any source a court may rely on that is not the law, that is, not primary authority. Secondary authority consists of legal resources that summarize, compile, explain, comment on, interpret, or in some other way address the law.

Secondary authority can be used in several ways:

- To obtain a background or overall understanding of a specific area of the law. Legal encyclopedias, treatises, and periodicals are useful for this purpose. See Chapters 5 and 6.

Exhibit 1-3 *Types and Role of Authority.*

Types of Authority	
Primary Authority	The law itself, such as constitutions, statutes, ordinances, administrative agency rules and regulations, and court opinions
Secondary Authority	A source a court may rely on that is not the law, such as legal encyclopedias, *American Law Reports (ALR)*, *Restatements of the Law*, treatises, and law review articles
Role of Authority	
Mandatory Authority	A source of law a court must rely on when reaching a decision, such as an enacted law (statute, ordinance, etc.) that governs the legal question being addressed, or an opinion of a higher court in the jurisdiction that addressed the same or a similar legal question and facts
Persuasive Authority	Any authority a court is not bound to consider or follow but may consider or follow when reaching a decision, such as an opinion of a court in another state on the same or a similar issue, or a secondary authority source (encyclopedia article, legal dictionary definition, etc.)

© Cengage Learning 2014

For Example If the researcher is unfamiliar with a specific area of law, such as defamation, then a treatise on tort law will provide an overview of the area. The treatise will also include references to key court cases and enacted law (primary authority) concerning defamation.

■ To locate primary authority (the law) on a question being researched. *American Law Reports (ALR)*, legal encyclopedias, and *treatises* can be used for this purpose. See Chapter 5. All secondary authority sources include references to primary authority.

■ To be relied on by the court when reaching a decision, which usually occurs only when there is no primary authority governing a legal question or it is unclear how the primary authority applies to the question. Treatises, law reviews, and restatements of the law are relied on for this purpose.

There are literally hundreds of secondary sources. An in-depth discussion of all of them is beyond the scope of this text; therefore, only some of the major secondary sources are summarized here.

a. Annotations

Annotations are notes and comments on the law. A well-known annotation is the *American Law Reports (ALR)*. The *ALR* is a series of books that contain the complete text of selected court opinions, along with scholarly commentaries explaining and discussing issues raised in the case. The commentaries also include an overview of how the issues are treated nationally, focusing on the majority and minority views, and a list of cases from other jurisdictions dealing with the same issues. The *ALR* is useful for obtaining an in-depth overview of the courts' treatment of specific questions and issues. These annotations are also useful as an aid in locating court decisions dealing with specific issues.

b. Law Dictionaries

Legal dictionaries include definitions of legal terms (and usually a citation to the authority for the definition) and guides to pronunciation. The two major legal dictionaries are *Black's Law Dictionary* (West Publishing) and *Ballentine's Legal Dictionary* (Delmar Publishing).

c. Law Reviews

Law reviews are scholarly publications usually published by law schools. They contain articles written by professors, judges, and practitioners and include commentaries written by law students. The articles usually discuss specific topics and legal questions in great depth and include references to key cases on the subjects. These reviews are useful as a source of comprehensive information on specific topics.

d. Legal Encyclopedias

A *legal encyclopedia* is a multivolume set of books that provides a summary of the law. The topics are arranged in alphabetical order, and the set includes an index and cross-references. The two major legal encyclopedias are *Corpus Juris Secundum (CJS)* and *American Jurisprudence* (now *American Jurisprudence Second*) (*Am. Jur.* or *Am. Jur. 2d*), both published by West Group. An encyclopedia is a valuable source when seeking an overview of a legal topic.

e. Restatements of the Law

Published by the American Law Institute, the *Restatements of the Law* present a variety of topics and discuss what the law is on each topic, or what it should be. Following a presentation of the law is a "Comment" that explains the rule of law presented, discusses why the rule was adopted, and gives examples of how the rule applies. The *Restatements* are drafted by authorities and experts in specific areas and are often relied on and adopted by legislatures and courts.

f. Treatises

A *treatise* is a single- or multivolume work written by an expert in an area that covers that entire area of law. A treatise is a valuable resource because it provides a comprehensive treatment of a specific area of law, reference to statutes and key cases in the area, and commentaries on the law.

B. Role of Authority

After the types of authority have been identified, it is important to understand the role these sources play in the decision-making process. Not all authority referred to or relied on by a court when deciding an issue is given equal weight. Authority is divided into two categories— mandatory authority and persuasive authority—for the purpose of determining its authoritative value, or the extent to which it must be relied on or followed by a court (see Exhibit 1-3).

1. Mandatory Authority

Mandatory authority is any source that a court must rely on or follow when reaching a decision (e.g., a decision of a higher court in the jurisdiction on the same or a similar issue). Primary authority can be mandatory authority because courts are required to follow the law itself. As discussed earlier, primary authority is composed of enacted law and case law. Secondary authority can never be mandatory authority. A court is never bound to follow secondary authority because it is not the law.

Not all primary authority, however, is mandatory authority. Primary authority becomes mandatory authority only when it governs the legal question or issue being decided by the court.

The factors involved in deciding when enacted law and case law are mandatory authority are briefly discussed here.

a. Enacted Law

Chapter 3 details the process for determining whether an enacted law applies to govern a legal question or issue before a court. The three-step process presented in that chapter is summarized here.

STEP 1: *Identify all the laws that may govern the question.* This requires locating all statutes or laws that might possibly govern the legal question.

> **For Example** Some legal questions and fact situations, such as gender discrimination, are governed by both state and federal law and on occasion by more than one state or federal law.

Once you identify the laws that may govern the question, determine which of these laws applies to the specific legal area involved in the dispute. This requires an analysis of the law.

> **For Example** In the preceding example, an analysis of the law may reveal that even though both federal and state law govern the question of gender discrimination, the federal law requires that the matter be tried in state court before being pursued in federal court. The federal law, therefore, does not apply until the remedies available under state law have been pursued in the state courts.

STEP 2: *Identify the elements of the law or statute.* Once you determine the specific law or laws that govern the question, identify the elements of the law or statute, that is, the specific requirements that must be met for the law or statute to apply. It is necessary to identify the elements before moving on to step 3, which is determining whether the requirements of the law or statute are met by the facts of the case.

> **For Example** Mary bought a toaster at a local store. It did not work when she plugged it in. The store owner refused to replace the toaster or give her a refund when she returned it. The legal question is whether Mary can get a new toaster or her money back. Assume that, after performing the first step of the analysis, you determine that article 2 of the state's commercial code is mandatory authority because article 2 applies to the sale of goods and a toaster is considered goods. Article 2 provides that a warranty is created if:
>
> 1. The transaction involves the sale of goods.
> 2. The seller of the goods is a merchant.
>
> These are the elements of the statute. These elements must be identified to determine what the section requires for the warranty to exist. It is necessary to identify these requirements before it can be determined how the section applies to the client's facts. The statute further provides that the seller must replace the item or refund the purchase price if the item doesn't work.

STEP 3: *Apply the facts of the case to the elements.* The final step is to apply the facts of the client's case to the elements to determine how the law or statute applies. If the elements match the facts raised by the legal issue, then the law applies and governs the outcome. Even if some of the elements are not met, the law still applies, but the outcome may be different.

> **For Example** Referring to the previous example, the warranty exists if the two elements are met. In this case, the first element is met because a toaster is considered goods. The second element is met because the store owner is considered a merchant because he routinely sells toasters. The elements are met and Mary is entitled to a new toaster or a refund.
>
> If the transaction does not involve the sale of goods, such as the sale of land, or the seller is not a merchant (the toaster was purchased at a yard sale), the elements of article 2 are not met, there is no warranty, and Mary is not entitled to a new toaster or a refund.

After you determine that an enacted law governs a legal question, the law is mandatory authority, and a court must apply the law unless the court rules that the law is unconstitutional.

b. Case Law

For a court opinion to be mandatory authority (often referred to as *mandatory precedent*) that binds another court to follow the rule or principle of law established in the opinion, two conditions must be met:

1. The court opinion must be on point.
2. The court opinion must have been issued by a higher court in that jurisdiction.

> **For Example** If the highest court in state A defines malice as used in the state's murder statute, then all the lower courts in state A (intermediary and trial courts) are bound to follow the highest court and apply the highest court's interpretation of the term in cases involving the statute.

In regard to this example, is the highest court in state A, in later cases, bound to follow its own earlier definition of malice? No. The highest court is always free to overturn the opinion and change the definition. The court will follow its earlier decision unless it overturns it or in some way amends it. The lower courts do not have this option.

What if the decision of the highest state court is different from the decision of a federal court? If a state court decision conflicts with the Constitution or federal law, then the state court must follow the dictates of the federal law. State courts usually have the final say over interpretations of state law. If a federal court is addressing an issue involving state law, then the federal court usually follows the interpretation of the state law rendered by the state's highest court.

Chapter 12 presents an in-depth discussion of case law analysis and the process involved in determining whether a case is on point.

2. Persuasive Authority

Persuasive authority is any authority a court is not bound to consider or follow but may consider or follow when reaching a decision. When mandatory authority exists, persuasive authority is not necessary, although its use is not prohibited. Persuasive authority consists of both primary authority and secondary authority.

a. Primary Authority as Persuasive Authority

On occasion, courts look to enacted law as persuasive authority.

> **For Example** A court, when interpreting a term not defined in an act, may apply the definition of the term that is given in another act. Suppose the term *gender discrimination* is not defined in the state's fair housing act but is defined in the state's fair loan act. The fair loan act is not mandatory authority for questions involving the fair housing act because it does not govern housing. It can, however, be persuasive authority. The court may follow or be persuaded to apply the definition given in the fair loan act.

Primary authority represented by case law is often used as persuasive authority (often referred to as *persuasive precedent*). Even though case law is primary authority, it may not be mandatory authority in a specific situation if it does not apply to govern the situation. The court is not required to follow such authority. A court may, however, be guided by and persuaded to adopt the rule or principle established in another court opinion.

> **For Example**
> 1. The courts in state A have not addressed a legal issue. Therefore, there is no mandatory authority that state A courts must follow. State A courts may consider and adopt the rules and reasoning of federal or other state courts that have addressed the issue. It is not mandatory that state A follow the primary authority of the other federal or state courts, but state A may be persuaded to adopt the primary authority of these courts.
> 2. Neither the legislature nor the courts of state A have adopted strict liability as a cause of action in tort. State A's highest court can look to and adopt the case law of another state that has adopted this tort.
> 3. A trial court in state A has written an opinion on a legal issue. A higher court in state A is not bound by the lower court opinion (it is not mandatory authority), but it may consider and adopt the rule and reasoning of the lower court.

When there is no mandatory authority that a court is bound to follow, as in the preceding examples, the court may look to and rely on other primary authority as persuasive authority.

b. Secondary Authority as Persuasive Authority

As discussed earlier, secondary authority is not the law and, therefore, can never be mandatory authority. When mandatory authority on an issue exists, it is not necessary to support it with secondary authority, although it is permissible to do so. Secondary authority should not be relied upon when there is mandatory authority. In such situations, the mandatory authority governs. If there is no mandatory authority but there is persuasive primary authority, the secondary authority may be used in support of the primary authority.

> **For Example** The courts in state A have never addressed a certain issue. The courts in state B have addressed the issue. The rule of law established by the state B courts can be persuasive primary authority for state A courts. Secondary sources, such as *ALR* commentaries and law review articles, may be submitted to a state A court in support of the persuasive primary authority from state B. Secondary authority also may be submitted to the court for the purpose of opposing the adoption of the persuasive authority from state B.

Secondary authority has its greatest value in situations in which there is no primary authority, either mandatory or persuasive. This situation is rare, however. Few matters have never been addressed by either some legislature or some court. As noted earlier, secondary authority is also valuable because it is useful in locating primary authority. Some secondary authority is given greater weight or considered to have greater authoritative value than other secondary authority.

For Example A court will more likely rely on and give greater weight to a *Restatements of the Law* drafted by experts in the field than to a law review article written by a local practitioner in the field.

Always locate the available primary authority and exhaust all avenues of research in this direction before turning to the location of secondary authority. There are two reasons for this:

1. Courts will look to and consider primary authority before considering secondary authority.

2. Primary authority will often lead to key secondary authority sources.

For Example
1. A court opinion addressing an issue may include references to key secondary sources such as *ALR* citations.

2. State statutes are often annotated, and the annotations usually include references to *ALR* and legal encyclopedia citations that address the area of law covered in the statute. The annotations also include references to law review articles that address specific issues related to the statute.

V. KEY POINTS CHECKLIST: *Legal Principles and Authorities*

✓ When analyzing a legal question or issue, always identify the primary authority (the law) that governs the question. First consider primary authority, then look to secondary authority. As a general rule, courts will rely on primary authority before considering secondary authority.

✓ When you are searching for the law that governs a topic, always consider all the possible sources of law:

1. Enacted law—constitutions, statutes, ordinances, regulations, and so on

2. Case law

✓ Remember that there are two court systems operating in every jurisdiction: state and federal. A legal problem may be governed by either federal or state law or both. Both sources of law and both court systems must be considered when analyzing a problem.

✓ Keep in mind the hierarchy of primary authority. Constitutions are the highest authority, followed by other enacted law, then by case law. When there is a conflict between federal and state law, federal law governs.

✓ The doctrines of stare decisis and precedent provide that doctrines, rules, or principles established in earlier court decisions should be followed by later courts in the same court system when addressing similar issues and facts. Therefore, when researching a question, always look for and consider earlier cases that are on point.

✓ Courts are required to follow mandatory authority; therefore, always attempt to locate mandatory authority before searching for persuasive authority.

✓ Do not rely on persuasive authority if there is mandatory authority. No matter how strong the persuasive authority, the court will apply mandatory authority before persuasive authority. Secondary authority is never mandatory authority.

VI. APPLICATION

The following example illustrates principles discussed in this chapter. The example addresses the questions raised in the hypothetical presented at the beginning of the chapter.

Renee's research on the subject of gender discrimination identified the following authority that might apply to the issues raised in the client's case:

1. Title VII of the Civil Rights Act of 1964, which prohibits employment discrimination on the basis of gender

2. Section 59-9-4 of the state statutes, which prohibits employment discrimination on the basis of gender

3. *Erik v. Coll, Inc.*, a federal court case with facts almost identical to Ms. Stone's, which held that the conduct of the employer constituted gender discrimination in violation of Title VII

4. *Albert v. Conrad Supplies*, a state supreme court case with facts almost identical to those presented in Ms. Stone's case, which held that the employer's conduct violated the state statute

5. Two law review articles addressing gender discrimination, which concluded that the type of conduct encountered by Ms. Stone constituted gender discrimination. One article addressed the question in the context of Title VII, and one article focused on the question in the context of the state statute.

Renee's assignment is to prepare a memo that includes a summary of her research and an analysis of how the law applies to the client's case. She realizes that she must organize and analyze her research before she can draft the memo. After reviewing the principles and concepts presented in this chapter, she proceeds with the following steps.

STEP 1: *Identify and separate primary authority and secondary authority.* This step is important because the court will rely on and consider primary authority before referring to secondary authority.

1. Primary authority:

   ▪ Enacted law—Title VII and Section 59-9-4 of the state statutes

   ▪ Case law—*Erik v. Coll, Inc.* and *Albert v. Conrad Supplies*

2. Secondary authority: the two law review articles

STEP 2: *Organize the presentation of the primary authority.* Because the highest authority in the hierarchy of primary authority is the enacted law, followed by the case law, Renee organizes her summary of the law with a presentation of the enacted law first. (She did not locate applicable constitutional law.)

1. *Enacted Law.* In regard to the enacted law, Renee determines which law applies to govern the situation. It is possible that both the state and federal laws apply and that a potential cause of action exists in both federal and state court. It is also possible that the federal law requires that the state remedies be exhausted before a claim in federal court can be pursued. This means that the federal law requires that any remedy available under state law be completely pursued before a claim can be brought under federal law. It is possible that the federal act does not apply to the specific legal question raised by the facts of the dispute, or the federal act may apply exclusively and there may be no possible cause of action under the state law. All of these possibilities must be considered when she analyzes the enacted law.

   Once Renee concludes this part of the analysis, she must identify the elements or requirements of the law or laws that do apply. She then applies the elements to the facts of the client's case to determine how the laws apply and what remedies are available. In her memo, she will include a summary of the law and her analysis. Chapter 3 provides guidelines to follow when analyzing enacted law.

2. *Case Law.* Renee next addresses the relevant case law. She first determines whether the cases are on point. A case is on point if there is a sufficient similarity between the key facts and legal issue addressed in the court opinion and the client's case for the court opinion to apply as precedent. If a case is on point, it provides the present court with guidance in resolving a legal question or issue.

If the enacted law is clear and there is no question about how the enacted law applies to the facts of the client's case, then there is usually no need to refer to case law.

> **For Example** A client is ticketed for driving 90 mph in a 60-mph zone. The statute establishing the speed limit at 60 mph is clear, and there is no need for case law to interpret the statute. A speed of 90 mph is clearly in violation of the statute.

Even if there appears to be no question about how the statute applies, always be sure to check the case law for possible interpretations of the statute.

If Renee concludes that federal law exclusively governs the area, then the state case, *Albert v. Conrad Supplies*, does not apply. If she concludes that only state law applies, then the federal case does not apply.

Once Renee has analyzed the case law, she includes in the memo a summary of her case analysis, discussing whether each case applies and how.

STEP 3: *Organize the presentation of the secondary authority.* The secondary authority is summarized last in the memo because it has the least authoritative value. In the client's case, there is primary authority, so the secondary authority will be used, if at all, in support of or opposition to arguments based on the primary authority. Renee includes a summary of each law review article, emphasizing those aspects of the articles that focus on questions and issues similar to those in the client's case. Even if the articles will not be used in court as secondary authority, a summary is included in the memo because it may provide Renee's supervising attorney with information that proves helpful in the case.

Renee's understanding of the primary and secondary sources of law, and the hierarchy of the sources, is an essential aid in her organization of the research, analysis of the issues, and preparation of the memo. Chapter 15 through Chapter 17 provide useful information concerning the actual preparation of legal memoranda.

Summary

The process of legal analysis and legal writing requires a determination of what law applies to a legal question and how it applies. To engage in the process, you must have an understanding of the law and the basic doctrines and principles that govern and guide the analysis of the law.

The two primary sources of law in the United States are:

1. Enacted law

2. Case law

Enacted law, as used in this text, consists of constitutions, laws passed by legislative bodies, and regulations adopted by administrative bodies to aid in the enforcement and application of legislative mandates. Case law is composed of the law created by the courts in two situations:

1. When there is no law governing a topic

2. Through interpretation of enacted law where the meaning or application of the enacted law is unclear

There are two court systems in the United States: the federal court system and the state court system. Although there are differences in each system, they have basic similarities. Both systems have trial courts where matters are initially heard, trials held, and judgments rendered, and both have courts of appeals where the judgments of trial courts are reviewed and possible errors corrected.

To provide consistency and stability to the case law, two doctrines have evolved:

1. Precedent
2. Stare decisis

Precedent is an earlier court decision on an issue that applies to govern or guide a subsequent court in its determination of identical or similar issues based on identical or similar facts. The doctrine of stare decisis provides that a court must follow a previous decision of a higher court in the jurisdiction when the current decision involves issues and facts similar to those involved in the previous decision.

The two sources of law, enacted and case law, are called primary authority. Primary authority is the law itself. Any other authoritative source a court may rely on in reaching a decision is called secondary authority. Secondary authority is not the law but consists of authoritative sources that interpret, analyze, or compile the law, such as legal encyclopedias and treatises. Courts always rely on and look to primary authority first when resolving legal issues.

If primary authority governs the resolution of a legal question, it must be followed by the court. This type of primary authority is called mandatory authority. Secondary authority can never be mandatory authority. Any authority the court is not bound to follow but that it may follow or consider when reaching a decision is called persuasive authority. Both primary authority and secondary authority can be persuasive authority.

The remaining chapters of this text address the application of the basic concepts and principles presented in this chapter. Each concept and principle plays a critical role in legal analysis and writing.

Quick References

Administrative law	5	Opinion	6
Authority	13	Personal jurisdiction	7
Case law	6	Persuasive authority	17
Concurrent jurisdiction	8	Petition for writ of certiorari	9
Constitution	4	Precedent	11
Court of appeals	8	Primary authority	13
District court	8	Secondary authority	13
Enacted law	4	Stare decisis	11
Jurisdiction	7	Statutes	4
Law	3	Subject matter jurisdiction	7
Mandatory authority	15	Trial court	8

Internet Resources

http://www.findlaw.com
> This site is considered one of the best sites for finding legal resources in general.

http://www.uscourts.gov
> This site offers information about federal court justices, statutes, state laws, and links to other sites.

http://www.law.indiana.edu
> Indiana University Law School Library

http://www.law.cornell.edu
> Cornell University Law School Library

http://www.law.villanova.edu
> This site is a state court locator.

http://www.access.gpo.gov
> This is the official site for the Government Printing Office.

http://gsulaw.gsu.edu
> This site provides an index to legal sites on the Web, including links.

Links to documents that help you evaluate Web sites:
> "Evaluation of Information Sources/internet"
>> **http://www.vuw.ac.nz/staff/alastair_smith/evaln/evaln.htm**
>
> "Evaluating Internet Resources: A Selective Bibliography"
>
> The Virtual Chase
>> **http://www.virtualchase.com**

Exercises

Additional assignments are available on the CourseMate.

ASSIGNMENT 1

What is the name of the court of general jurisdiction in your state? What is the name of a limited-jurisdiction court in your state? What is the subject matter jurisdiction of this court? This information is available in your state statutes.

ASSIGNMENT 2

Describe the differences between a trial court and a court of appeals.

ASSIGNMENT 3

When is a court opinion considered precedent?

ASSIGNMENT 4

Facts: The researcher is analyzing a problem involving the sale of goods on credit in state A.

Authority: The following authority has been located concerning the problem:

1. State A's Uniform Commercial Code Act
2. State A's Consumer Credit Act
3. State B's Uniform Commercial Code Act
4. A federal statute—Consumer Credit Act
5. *Iron v. Supply Co.*—a decision of the highest court in state A
6. *Milk v. Best Buy, Inc.*—a decision of the highest court in state B
7. *Control Co. v. Martin*—a decision of an intermediary court of appeals in state A
8. *Lesley v. Karl Co.*—a decision of a trial court in state A
9. *Irene v. City Co.*—a federal case involving the federal Consumer Credit Act
10. Regulations adopted by state A's Corporation Commission that apply to consumer credit and the sale of goods
11. *Restatements of the Law* defining sales, consumer credit, and other terms related to the problem
12. An *ALR* reference that directly addresses the issues in the case

Assume that all the cases are on point, that is, they are sufficiently similar to the facts and issues involved in the problem to apply as precedent.

Questions

a. Which authority is primary authority, and which is secondary authority?

b. Which authority can be mandatory authority? Why? What would be required for any of the sources to be mandatory authority?

c. Which authority can be persuasive authority? Why?

d. Assuming that all the primary authority applies to the issues raised by the facts of the client's case, list the authority in the hierarchical order of its value as precedent; that is, authority with greatest authoritative value will be listed first, followed by other authority in the order it will be looked to by the court.

ASSIGNMENT 5

Facts: Your client is the plaintiff in a workers' compensation case. She was injured in 1993 in state A. In 1995, her employer destroyed all the business records relating to the client. The destruction of the records was apparently accidental, not intentional. They were destroyed, however, while the client's workers' compensation claim was pending.

Authority: You have located the following authority, all of which is directly related to the issues raised by the facts of the client's case:

1. *Idle v. City Co.*—a 1980 decision by the highest court of state A in which the court created a cause of action in tort for the wrongful destruction of business records. The court ruled that a cause of action exists if the records were destroyed in anticipation of or while a workers' compensation claim was pending. The court also held that a cause of action exists if the destruction was intentional or negligent.

2. A 1989 state A statute—a law passed by the legislature of state A that created a cause of action in tort for the intentional destruction of business records. The statute provides that a cause of action exists if the destruction occurs in anticipation of or while a workers' compensation claim is pending.

3. *Merrick v. Taylor*—a 1990 decision of the court of appeals of state A. The court of appeals is a lower court than the state's highest court. The court held that the term *intentional*, within the meaning of the 1989 statute, includes either the intentional destruction of records or the destruction of records as a result of gross negligence.

4. *Davees v. Contractor*—a decision of the highest court of state B interpreting a state B statute identical to the 1989 state A statute. The court held that the term *intentional*, as used in the statute, includes gross negligence only when the gross negligence is accompanied by a "reckless and wanton" disregard for the preservation of the business records.

5. A 1991 federal statute—the statute is identical to the 1989 state statute but applies only to contractors with federal contracts.

6. An *ALR* reference—addresses specific questions similar to those raised in the client's case.

Questions

a. Which authority is primary authority, and which is secondary authority? Why?

b. Which authority can be mandatory authority? Why? What would be required for any of the sources to be mandatory authority?

c. Which authority can be persuasive authority? Why?

d. Can *Idle v. City Co.* be authority at all? Why or why not?

e. If *Idle v. City Co.* is authority, to what extent?

f. Discuss the impact of *Merrick v. Taylor* in regard to the 1989 state A statute.

g. Discuss the authoritative value of *Davees v. Contractor*.

h. Assuming that all the primary authority applies to the issues raised by the facts of the client's case, list the authority in the hierarchical order of its value as precedent; that is, authority with greatest authoritative value will be listed first, followed by other authority in the order it will be looked to and relied on by the court.

CHAPTER 2

Introduction to Legal Research and Analysis

Marian has worked as Robert Walker's paralegal for the past four years. She conducts initial client interviews, manages the case files, and performs basic research. Robert, a solo practitioner, always determines the merits of a case and performs the substantive research. Marian started law school last fall and now works only part time at the law firm.

Robert called Marian into his office one morning. "Marian," he said, "I'm going to hire another paralegal to do your assignments." Robert continued, "Now that you are in law school, I want you to take over some of the more substantive legal work. I want you to start performing the legal analysis of some of the new cases and determine what, if any, possible causes of action exist. Your new responsibilities will be to study the cases and provide me with memoranda of law identifying the legal issues and analyzing how the law applies to the issues. This will free me to concentrate more on trial work. Start with Mr. Lietel's case."

Marian remembered the initial interview with Mr. Lietel. Jerry Lietel has a hot temper. He got into an argument with his neighbor, Tom Spear. Mr. Lietel's temper got the best of him. He punched Tom, and a fight ensued. Steve Spear, the father of Tom and a retired deputy sheriff, came out of the house and announced that he was placing Mr. Lietel under citizen's arrest. After a short struggle, Steve Spear subdued and handcuffed Mr. Lietel. After Mr. Lietel was handcuffed and had ceased resisting, Steve Spear kicked him about six times, cracking one of his ribs. Mr. Lietel incurred medical bills and lost two days of work. Since the incident, Mr. Lietel has had a lot of trouble sleeping, and he is taking sleeping pills on his doctor's advice. He is fearful of Steve Spear whenever he sees him.

Jerry admits that he punched Tom without provocation and that the citizen's arrest was probably justified, but he wants to sue for his medical bills and the loss of work.

Marian realizes that this, her first analysis assignment, is very important: the quality of her product will determine whether she continues to be assigned this type of substantive legal work. She asks herself, "What's the best way to approach a legal problem? What is a systematic way to analyze a client's problem that will produce the best result in the least amount of time?" The Application section at the end of this chapter presents an analysis of Mr. Lietel's case and the answers to Marian's questions.

Outline

Learning Objectives

After completing this chapter, you should understand:

- The definition of legal analysis
- Legal research and the elements of legal analysis
- How the elements of legal analysis apply in specific situations
- The importance of focus and intellectual honesty
- When and how legal authority applies

I. INTRODUCTION

As discussed in the preface, the focus of this text is on the process of analyzing legal questions raised by the facts of a client's case, legal research, and the process of communicating research and analysis in written form. This chapter presents an overview of the process of legal analysis and some concepts and considerations involved in that process.

Most cases begin like the Lietel case. A client relates a set of factual events that the client perceives entitle him or her to legal relief. The client seeks a solution to what he or she believes is a legal problem. The problem may be as simple as the need for a power of attorney or as complex as a question involving multiple parties and several legal issues. The problem may be one for which there is no legal remedy, or it may not be a legal problem at all.

> **For Example** An individual is fired in retaliation for disclosing a defect in the employer's product. The state where this occurs does not have a statute prohibiting retaliatory discharge, nor have the state courts adopted a cause of action in tort for retaliatory discharge. Therefore, it may be that no legal remedy for this type of discharge is available under state law. It is possible that the client's only recourse is political; that is, the client may have to attempt to get legislation passed prohibiting retaliatory discharge, or to exert social pressure through the media.

The purpose of legal analysis and legal research is to analyze the factual event presented by the client and determine:

1. The legal issue (question) or issues raised by the factual event
2. The law that governs the legal issue
3. How the law that governs the legal issue applies to the factual event, including what, if any, legal remedy is available

Once this is accomplished, the client can be advised of the various rights, duties, and options available.

II. LEGAL ANALYSIS DEFINED

Before addressing the steps involved in the legal analysis process, it is necessary to understand what is meant by *legal analysis*. The term has different meanings, depending on the context of its usage (the type of legal analysis being performed).

> **For Example** The term *legal analysis* can refer to, among others, statutory analysis (discussed in Chapter 3), case law analysis (Chapter 12), and counteranalysis (Chapter 13).

In this chapter, **legal analysis** is used in a broad sense to refer to the process of identifying the issue or issues presented by a client's facts and determining what law applies and how it applies. Simply put, legal analysis is the process of applying the law to the facts of the client's case. It is an exploration of how and why a specific law does or does not apply. Legal research is the part of the legal analysis process that involves finding the law that applies to the legal question raised by the facts of a client's case.

III. LEGAL RESEARCH AND THE ANALYSIS PROCESS

A **legal analysis process** is a systematic approach to legal research and analysis. It is an organized approach that helps you develop research skills. It makes legal research easier, saves time, and helps develop research skills.

The most common approach to legal analysis involves a four-step process:

STEP 1: *Issue.* The identification of the issue (legal question) or issues raised by the facts of the client's case

STEP 2: *Rule.* The identification of the law that governs the issue

STEP 3: *Analysis/Application.* A determination of how the rule of law applies to the issue

STEP 4: *Conclusion.* A summary of the results of the legal analysis

An acronym commonly used in reference to the analytical process is **IRAC**. It is composed of the first letter of the descriptive term for each step of the legal analysis process. The use of the acronym is an easy way to remember the four-step legal analysis process—*i*ssue, *r*ule, *a*nalysis/application, and *c*onclusion.

The research component of this process involves steps 1 and 2. Steps 3 and 4 of the process involve the analysis of the research results once the research is complete. The subsequent sections of this chapter address steps 1 and 2 in detail. Steps 3 and 4 are summarized in this chapter and then discussed in detail in Chapter 15 in the legal writing section of the text.

Before the legal analysis of a case can properly begin, however, the following preliminary preparation must take place:

1. All the facts and information relevant to the case should be gathered.
2. Preliminary legal research should be conducted to gain a basic familiarity with the area of law involved in the case.

A. Facts and Key Terms

1. Facts

It is important to keep in mind the crucial role the **facts** play in the analytical process. The four steps of the analysis process involve the facts of the client's case, and the facts play a major role in each step:

1. *Issue.* The key facts are included in the issue. The issue is the precise question raised by the *specific facts* of the client's case. A properly stated issue requires inclusion of the key facts. This is discussed in detail in Chapters 10 and 11.

> **For Example** Under the provisions of the state battery law, is a battery committed by an individual, *present at the scene of a battery, who encourages others to commit the battery but does not actively participate in the actual battering of the victim?* The key facts of this issue are italicized.

2. *Rule.* The determination of which law governs the issue is based on the applicability of the law to the facts of the client's case.

> **For Example** If the issue involves oppressive acts by a majority shareholder against the interests of minority shareholders in a closely held corporation, then the facts govern the determination of which corporation statutes apply. Only those statutes that address acts by majority shareholders can apply. In most states, this is limited to a few statutes.

3. *Analysis/Application.* The **analysis/application** step is the process of *applying the rule of law to the facts*. It obviously cannot take place without the facts. Without the facts, the law stands in a vacuum.

> **For Example** The client was ticketed for driving 65 mph in a 55-mph zone. The client believes that the speed limit was actually 65 mph and that the officer made a mistake. A determination of whether the client violated the law requires the application of the rule of law to the facts of the client's case. Was the speed limit where the ticket was given 65 mph or 55 mph? The *facts are essential* to the process. Without the facts, one cannot make a determination of how the law applies.

4. *Conclusion.* The **conclusion** is a summation of how the law applies to the facts, a recap of the first three steps. It too requires the facts.

In every case, the analytical process involves a determination of how the law applies to the facts. In court opinions, courts determine how the law applies to the facts presented to the court. Very often students pay too little attention to the facts, focusing on what the law is and what it requires. They ignore the crucially important role the facts play.

In a sense, cases are fact driven—the facts determine the outcome of the case. Often, if a single fact is changed, the outcome is different. The application of the law results in a different conclusion.

> **For Example** In a murder case, the degree of the offense can depend on a single fact. First-degree murder requires specific intent. It requires not only that the defendant intended to shoot the victim but also that the defendant intended the shooting to kill the victim. If the facts of the case show that the defendant intended to shoot but not kill the victim, the offense is not first-degree murder. The defendant's intent is a fact, and changing this single fact changes the outcome of the case. The application of the law results in a different conclusion. The offense is not first-degree murder but a lesser offense.

With this in mind, the analysis process should begin with a consideration of the facts of the client's case. *Identify and review the facts at the outset.* This preliminary step should include the following:

1. Be sure you have all the facts. Ask yourself if you have all the interviews, files, statements, and other pieces of information that have been gathered concerning the case. Are the files complete? Are facts or information missing? As discussed in the murder case example, a single fact can determine the outcome of a case. If key facts are missing, your analysis may result in an erroneous legal conclusion.

2. Study the available facts to see if additional information should be gathered before legal analysis can properly begin.

3. Organize the facts. Group all related facts. Place the facts in a logical order, such as in the sequence in which they occurred (chronological order) or according to topic (topical).

4. Weigh the facts. The value of some factual information, such as hearsay, may be questionable.

5. Identify the key facts. Determine which facts appear to be critical to the outcome of the case. Chapter 9 discusses the importance of key facts and the process for identifying key facts.

2. Key Terms

Most legal research sources, such as statutory codes, legal encyclopedias, legal treatises, and digests, contain one or more indexes. These indexes are a list of terms that help to locate information. To effectively use an index, you must identify the relevant terms in the client's case. These **key terms** help guide the researcher in the area being researched. If you are researching electronically, such as through the Internet, searches are conducted using key terms.

Key terms are identified by reviewing the case file and listing all the terms relevant to the legal questions raised by the facts of the case. When preparing this list, keep in mind the following:

- Parties involved (e.g., private citizen, corporation, public official)
- Place (e.g., public or private property)
- Actions or omissions that form the basis of the case (e.g., negligence, intentional acts)
- Defenses available (e.g., self-defense)
- Relief sought (e.g., money, injunction)

Key terms may be broad terms you use as a guide to perform preliminary research to gain a familiarity with the area of law governing the client's case, or narrow terms if you are already familiar with the area of law and want to focus your research on a specific aspect.

> **For Example** The client's case involves a question about child custody and the researcher is unfamiliar with this area of law. The researcher decides to read about the topic in a legal encyclopedia. The first step is to list all the terms that the subject "child custody" might be indexed under, such as *divorce, marriage, custody, parent and child, child custody, children,* and *domestic relations.* By listing the terms, you focus the search in the index and avoid having to scan the entire index. The topic will be under at least one of the search terms.

Because the key term may not be indexed in the way you think it should be, it is important to think of all the terms or categories that may apply. One role of legal education is to teach key terms and the categories where they fit.

> **For Example** A legal education teaches that, in general, unintentional harmful acts are categorized under tort law as negligence, the act of striking someone is categorized under both civil and criminal law as battery, and child support is under the umbrella of domestic relations.

Key terms may include key facts from the client's case. This often occurs when the researcher is familiar with the general area of law and is seeking the specific law that governs the client's fact situation.

> **For Example** The assignment is to locate the federal law the client may be charged with breaking. The client placed a bomb made of nitroglycerin under a bridge. Assume these are the key facts. The researcher, based on her legal education and previous experience, knows that the general research topic is "federal criminal law" and the subtopic is "explosives." By identifying the key search terms *nitroglycerin* and *bridges,* the researcher is guided to the specific law within the general area of "federal criminal law" and "explosives."

It is recommended that a list of key terms be developed while you are reviewing the case and identifying the key facts. If you are unfamiliar with the area of law, use a list of terms related to the general topic of the case to perform general research and become familiar with the area of law (see the preceding child custody example). Once you are familiar with the area of law, identify the key facts and the legal issue before conducting research.

B. Preliminary Research

Before conducting any research, check the office research files for previous memos or research that may have addressed the issue(s) you are researching. This may obviate the need for further research.

It may, however, be necessary to conduct some basic research in the area(s) of law that govern the issue or issues in the case. You may be unfamiliar with the area of law in general or with the specific aspect of the area that applies in the client's case. You may obtain a general overview of the law by reference to a legal encyclopedia or a single-volume treatise. If the specific question or area is known at the outset, use of an *ALR* reference or a multivolume treatise may be appropriate.

C. IRAC Analysis

Once the facts have been gathered and reviewed, follow the four steps of the IRAC legal analysis process (see Exhibit 2-1). It is important to keep the following considerations in mind when performing these steps.

Exhibit 2-1 *Steps in the IRAC Legal Analysis Process. Source: http://www.uscourts.gov/court_locator.aspx*

STEP 1: Issue	Identify the issue (legal question) or issues raised by the facts of the client's case.
STEP 2: Rule	Identify the law that governs the issue.
STEP 3: Analysis/ Application	Determine how the rule of law applies to the issue.
STEP 4: Conclusion	Summarize the results of the legal analysis.

1. Issue

Identify the issue (legal question) or issues raised by the facts of the client's case. The **issue** is the precise legal question raised by the facts of the dispute. The first and probably most important step in the analytical process is to identify the issue. You must identify the problem before you can solve it. The issue is the starting point. If it is misidentified, each subsequent step in the process is a step in the wrong direction. Time is wasted, and malpractice may result.

For Example A client complains that the individual who sold and installed the tile in his bathroom installed it in a defective manner. After a few months, the tile began to fall off the wall. The person who installed the tile gave no oral or written warranty covering the quality of the installation or the quality of the tile.

The researcher assumes, without conducting research, that the entire transaction is a sale of goods covered by state statutes governing the sale of goods. The researcher makes this assumption because the transaction involved the sale of goods—the tiles. Under the sale of goods statutes is a section creating an implied warranty that goods are merchantable when sold, which in this case means the tiles will not fall apart.

The statute as interpreted by the state courts, however, does not apply to the service portion of such transactions, which, in the client's case, is the installation of the tile. Based on an incorrect assumption, the researcher identifies the issue as a question of whether the implied warranty of merchantability was breached. The identification of the issue is incorrect because of the erroneous assumption. The question is not about the quality of the tile but about the quality of the installation. Research on the existence of an implied warranty of merchantability is misdirected.

The case may be lost because the issue is incorrectly identified. The laws governing the sale of a service are different from those governing the sale of goods. A lawsuit claiming breach of an implied warranty of merchantability will probably not prevail because the implied warranty of merchantability statute does not apply.

The client does not pay to have the wrong question answered. The subjects of issue identification and presentation are of such importance that Chapters 10 and 11 are devoted to them. Some important considerations involving issues are discussed briefly here.

a. Multiple Issues

The client's fact situation may raise multiple legal issues and involve many avenues of relief. The implied warranty example involves one issue, but there may be several issues in a case. You should be aware of and keep in mind that one set of facts may raise multiple issues and include multiple causes of action.

For Example Mr. Elvan rear-ended the client's car at a stoplight. After the impact, Mr. Elvan exited his car, approached the client's car, and started yelling at the client, threatening to hit the client. He grabbed the client's arm but never struck him. As a result of the incident, the client's car was damaged. The client suffered whiplash from the collision and a bruise on his arm from being grabbed, and since the wreck, he has been upset and has had trouble sleeping.

The client may have several causes of action against Mr. Elvan: a claim of negligence arising from the rear-end collision, civil assault for his conduct of approaching the client in a threatening manner, battery for grabbing the client, and intentional infliction of emotional distress for his conduct after the collision. Each of these potential causes of action may raise legal issues or questions that must be addressed. This example is referred to in this chapter as the rear-end collision example.

b. Separate the Issues

Analyze and research each issue separately and thoroughly. If you try to research and analyze several issues at once, it is easy to get confused and frustrated. If you find information relevant to another issue, make a reference note and place it in a separate research file.

c. Focus on the Issues of the Case

Keep your focus on the issues raised by the facts of the client's case or on those issues that you have been assigned to research.

For Example In the rear-end collision example, assume that there was a passenger in the vehicle with the client and that the passenger is represented by another law firm. Although there may be many interesting issues involving potential legal claims available to the passenger, the passenger is not the client. The focus should be on the issues in the client's case. The issues involving the passenger are outside the scope of the problem and should not be allowed to become a distraction.

Avoid getting sidetracked and wasting time on interesting aspects or issues of a case you were not assigned to address.

> **For Example** Suppose that, in the rear-end collision example, you are assigned to research the assault issue. Do not research the other issues or clutter your analysis with issues you were not assigned to address. Stick to the assignment. If you come across useful information that is relevant to another issue, note it and give it to the person assigned to address that issue.

2. Rule

Identify the law that governs the issue (legal research). The second step in the IRAC analytical process is to identify the **rule of law** that applies to the issue; that is, to solve the client's problem you must find the law that applies to the problem. This is the legal research component of legal analysis. The three-part process presented in Exhibit 2-2 is recommended for conducting legal research.

Exhibit 2-2 *Three Parts of Step 2: Rule.*

PART 1	Locate the general law that governs the issue—usually statutory or case law.
PART 2	Locate the law that interprets how the general law applies to the specific fact situation of the issue—usually case law. Reference to secondary authority is necessary if there is no primary authority that applies or if additional authority is needed to help interpret the primary authority.
PART 3	Update research to ensure that the source you are reading has not been amended, repealed, revoked, overruled, modified, or otherwise changed.

© Cengage Learning 2014

The first part is locating the general law, such as a statute, that governs the question. The second part is locating the law, such as a court opinion, that interprets how the general law applies to the specific fact situation of the issue. The third part is to update the research sources.

> **For Example** The client is a divorced parent who does not have custody of her child. The father, the custodial parent, was recently convicted of possession of a small amount of cocaine. The client wants to obtain custody of the child due to the father's drug conviction. The issue is: "Under the state's child custody law, may a change of custody be obtained due to a custodial parent's conviction for possession of cocaine?"
> The first step of the legal research component of the legal analysis process requires locating the state statute that governs the modification of child custody. Assume that the statute provides that custody will not be changed unless there has been a substantial change in circumstances that affects the welfare of the child. The statute does not define or give examples of a "substantial change in circumstances." The second step requires locating a court opinion (case law) that answers the question of whether a custodial parent's conviction of possession of drugs is a "substantial change in circumstances" within the meaning of the statute. The third part is to update the research sources to ensure that the source is current law.

Chapter 3 through Chapter 7 present detailed instructions on how to research specific types of primary and secondary authorities, such as statutory law, case law, and treatises. A summary of the three-part research process follows.

a. Part 1: Locate the General Law That Governs the Issue

This requires the identification of terms that you will use to search for the law that governs the issue. Ask yourself, "What type of law applies to the question raised by the facts of the case?" This may be enacted law or case law.

(1) Enacted Law The legal issue may be governed by enacted law, such as a constitutional provision, statute, ordinance, or regulation. Ask yourself, "What terms will I use to search a statutory index or computer database to locate the law that applies to this issue?" List all the possible terms that might encompass the relevant law. Search the enacted law index or database using the search terms you have identified.

Review the annotations to the statute for cases that interpret the statute in fact situations similar to your case. Also, check the annotations for secondary sources such as encyclopedias, *ALR* annotations, and law review articles that discuss the statute. To avoid having to look up the law more than once, save the relevant research concerning the rule of law as you go along. This should include the proper statutory citation, a copy of the relevant portions of law, case citations (if any), and references to secondary sources.

> **For Example** In the child custody example, think of all the terms for the laws governing child custody. Laws involving child custody could be indexed under "family law," "domestic relations," "divorce," "marriage," "child custody," "custody," or "parent and child." The laws governing changes in custody should be indexed under one of these terms.

(2) Case Law Rules or principles established by the courts may govern the issue. In such cases, there may be no statutory law that applies. As with searching for enacted law, ask yourself, "What terms will I use to search a case law digest or computer database to locate the law that applies to this issue?" List all the possible terms under which the court opinions governing the issue may be categorized.

> **For Example** An individual, while not paying attention, runs a stop sign and hits the client's vehicle. The client is suing for the damage caused to her vehicle. Lawsuits between individuals arising out of accidents are governed by tort law. Most tort claims are based on case law, that is, the law defined by the courts in court opinions. Think of all the terms under which the court opinions governing automobile collisions may be categorized. The opinions may be listed under "negligence," "automobile collisions," and other topics.

Search the case law digests or computer databases using the search terms you have identified. Chapter 4 addresses the research of issues governed by case law. Chapter 7 presents techniques for conducting research using computers.

b. Part 2: Locate the Law That Interprets How the General Law Applies to the Specific Fact Situation of the Issue

The rule of law that governs the issue may be written in such broad terms that it is necessary to look to another source, such as case law or secondary authority, to determine how the law applies to the specific fact situation of the issue. Ask yourself, "What terms will I use to search a case law digest or computer database to locate the court opinion that interprets how the general law applies to the specific fact situation raised by the issue?"

> **For Example** In the child custody example presented at the beginning of this subsection, it is necessary to find case law that addresses the question of whether a drug conviction is a "substantial change in circumstances" within the meaning of the statute. Think of all the terms or phrases that may help locate cases that interpret the statute in this fact situation. These terms may be *child custody, custodial parent and drug convictions, change of custody and drug convictions,* or *change of custody and parental misconduct.*

Chapter 12 addresses how to determine when a court opinion applies to a specific fact situation.

When looking for primary authority, be sure to conduct counteranalysis. That is, always look for authority that may present a counterargument in response to your analysis of an issue. If you find a case on point in support of your position, look for other cases that have a different holding.

Role of Secondary Authority Although it is essential to locate the primary authority that governs an issue, be sure to note important secondary authority as well. The court may rely on secondary authority if there is no primary authority or if it is unclear how the primary authority applies. Sources such as *ALR* annotations, legal encyclopedias, and treatises often discuss and list the statutes and cases related to a topic. Reference to such sources ensures that you have found all the law related to the issue being researched. Also, secondary authority sources such as *ALR* annotations are helpful in locating counterarguments when performing counteranalysis.

c. Part 3: Update Research

Update all research to ensure that sources are current. Statutes must be checked to determine if they have been repealed or amended, cases checked to ensure they have not been reversed or modified by later cases, and secondary sources checked for additions and amendments.

When conducting research, follow a **research sequence**. First, locate the primary authority that governs the issue. As mentioned in Chapter 1, the courts refer to and rely on primary authority first when resolving legal problems.

When researching primary authority, look first for the enacted law, that is, the constitutional provisions, statutes, and so forth that govern the issue. There are two reasons for this. One, the constitutional or statutory provision may answer the question, so that reference to case law is not required.

> **For Example** The issue is, "How often must stockholder meetings for a corporation be held?" The statute provides that meetings must be held at least once annually. The statute answers the question; there is no need to find case law interpreting the statute.

Two, the annotations (summary of court opinions and other references that interpret the law) that follow the constitutional or statutory provision may include an opinion or a secondary authority source that interprets the law in a fact situation similar to the facts of your issue. Therefore, you will not need to spend time researching other sources for relevant case law.

For Example The issue is, "Does a majority shareholder of a corporation engage in oppressive conduct when he or she refuses to issue dividends?" The corporation statute prohibits oppressive conduct but does not define what constitutes oppressive conduct. The annotations that follow the statute make reference to a court opinion in which the court held that the refusal to issue dividends was oppressive conduct. The researcher does not have to research other sources for a case that interprets the statute.

The second part in the research sequence is looking to secondary authority, if there is no primary authority that applies or if additional authority is needed to help interpret the primary authority (see Exhibit 2-3).

Exhibit 2-3 *Sequence for Conducting Research.*

First—Locate the primary authority that governs the issue	Step 1: Locate the constitutional or statutory law. The constitutional or statutory provision may answer the question raised by the issue, making reference to case law unnecessary. Also, the annotations (summary of court opinions and other references that interpret the law) that follow the constitutional or statutory provision may include an opinion or secondary source that applies that law to a fact situation similar to the facts of the issue.
	Step 2: Locate the case law. This is necessary when there is no constitutional or statutory law or when the law must be interpreted. In this situation the case law rules or principles established by the courts govern the issue.
Second—Locate secondary authority	Reference to secondary authority is necessary if there is no primary authority that applies or if additional authority is needed to help interpret the primary authority.

© Cengage Learning 2014

See Chapter 15 for an additional summary of the research process.

3. Analysis/Application

Determine how the rule of law applies to the issue. Once you have located the rule of law, you must analyze the law to determine how it applies to the facts of the client's case. In other words, you apply the law to the legal issue. This is a three-part process (see Exhibit 2-4).

Exhibit 2-4 *Three Parts of Step 3—Analysis/Application.*

PART 1	Identify the component parts (elements) of the rule of law.
PART 2	Apply the elements (the component parts) of the law to the facts of the client's case.
PART 3	Consider the possible counterarguments to the analysis of the issue, i.e., conduct a counteranalysis of the analysis.

© Cengage Learning 2014

An in-depth discussion of this step in regard to statutory law and case law is presented in Chapter 3 and Chapter 12, respectively. The role of the key facts is addressed in Chapter 9. Counteranalysis is discussed in Chapter 13. Therefore, only a brief summary of this step is included here.

a. Part 1: Identify the Component Parts (Elements) of the Rule of Law

For the rule of law to apply to a fact situation, certain conditions established by the rule must be met. These conditions or component parts are called the *elements*. You must identify the requirements (elements) of the rule of law before you can apply the rule to the issue raised by the facts of the client's case.

For Example Section 93-85A of the state statute governing the execution of a will provides: "The execution of a will must be by the signature of the testator and of at least two witnesses as follows:

1. The testator, in the presence of two or more witnesses:
   a. signifies to the witnesses that the instrument is the testator's will, and
   b. signs the will or has someone else sign the testator's name at the testator's specific direction.
2. The attesting witnesses must sign in the presence of the testator and each other."

To determine how the statute applies to a client's facts, first identify the elements of the statute. The elements of the statute follow:

1. The testator must indicate to two or more witnesses that the instrument is the testator's will.
2. The testator must sign the will or have someone sign it at the testator's specific direction.
3. The witnesses must sign.
4. Steps 1 through 3 must be done in the presence of the witnesses and the testator.

This example is referred to in this chapter as the wills example.

b. Part 2: Apply the Facts of the Client's Case to the Component Parts

Once you have identified the elements of the rule of law, match or apply the facts of the client's case to the elements and determine how the rule applies.

For Example If the client's case involves a question of whether a will was validly executed in accordance with the statute presented in the wills example, match the facts of the client's case with the elements of the statute to determine if the execution was valid. Assume the will was signed by someone other than the testator, and not at his specific direction. The testator never specifically directed the person to sign the will, but was aware of what was happening and did not object. When this fact is matched to the element of the statute requiring that a will be signed by the testator or someone at the testator's specific direction, the requirement of the element may not be met.

Once the facts of the client's case have been matched to the elements of the rule of law, you may determine how the rule applies in the client's case.

> **For Example** In the preceding example, one could reach a conclusion that the element allowing a signature by "someone else" at the testator's specific direction was not met. Although the testator was present, he did not specifically direct the other person to sign the will. One could also conclude that additional research is necessary to determine how the courts have interpreted "specific direction" as used in the statute.

In some cases, the way the rule applies is clear from the face of the rule, and there is no question how the rule applies. All that is required is the application of the elements of the rule of law to the facts to determine how the law applies in the case.

> **For Example** An 18-year-old client wants to know if she is eligible to run for the position of probate judge. Section 34-214 of the election code provides that the minimum age for candidates for the position of probate judge is 21 years. It is clear from Section 34-214 that the client is not eligible to run.

In many cases, it is not clear from the rule of law how an element applies in a specific fact situation. In such instances, it may be necessary to refer to court opinion where the court, in a similar fact situation, interpreted how the law applies.

> **For Example** The rule of law defines *slander* as the "publication of a false statement of fact concerning the plaintiff that causes damages." In the client's case, the client's neighbor orally communicated to another neighbor a false statement of fact concerning the client. While visiting her neighbor's house, she falsely stated that the client was a thief. The statement damaged the client.
>
> The answer to the question of whether an oral communication to one person constitutes "publication" within the meaning of the statute is not clear from a mere reading of the statute. You must refer to case law to determine how the courts have interpreted the term *publication.* You must then apply the courts' interpretation of the term to the client's case. If the courts have defined *publication* as "communication to any third person," then the communication to the neighbor is slander.

This example is referred to in this chapter as the slander example.

c. Part 3: Consider the Possible Counterarguments to the Analysis of the Issue (Conduct a Counteranalysis of the Analysis)

Once you complete the analysis and application of the rule of law, consider any potential counterarguments to the analysis or application. This involves the anticipation and consideration of any argument an opponent is likely to raise in response to the analysis. (Chapter 13 addresses counteranalysis.)

> **For Example** Refer to the wills example in which the testator did not specifically direct a third party to sign the will, but was aware of the signing and did not object. It can be concluded that the element of the statute allowing a third party to sign the will at the testator's specific direction was not met. Although the testator was present, he did not specifically direct the other person to sign the will.
>
> The counterargument is that this element of the statute is met because the equivalent of "specific direction" took place. The testator was aware that the third person was

signing on his behalf and did not object. The failure to object is evidence that the signing took place at his specific direction.

Undertake research to determine if this counterargument has support in the case law. You should consider and address the counterargument in this step of the analysis process.

4. Conclusion

Summarize the results of the legal analysis. The final step in the analytical process is the conclusion, the result of the analysis. As discussed in step 3, part of the analysis/application process is a determination of how the rule of law applies to the client's facts. This determination is, in effect, a conclusion. Therefore, the conclusion step in the analytical process is a summing-up and commentary that may include:

a. A recap of the determination reached in the analysis/application step.

b. A consideration or weighing, based on the analysis, of what action a court may take or how a court may rule upon the issue.

c. The identification of additional facts or other information that may be necessary because of questions raised during analysis of the problem.

d. The identification of further research that may be necessary in regard to the issue. Further research may be required because the necessary research sources are not readily available, because the analysis is preliminary owing to time constraints, or because the factual investigation of the case has not been completed.

e. The identification of related issues or concerns that became apparent as a result of the research and analysis.

IV. GENERAL CONSIDERATIONS

The process of analyzing a legal problem can at times be difficult, especially for a beginner. In addition to the steps addressed in the previous section, the following general considerations and guidelines will prove helpful when researching and analyzing a legal issue.

A. Focus

Focus is critical when performing the steps of the analytical process. Focus has several meanings, depending on what part of the process is being performed. At the broadest level, it means to concentrate on the specific task assigned, to analyze only the issue or issues assigned.

> **For Example** Referring to the rear-end collision example, if the assignment is to analyze the question of whether a cause of action for civil assault is present, stay focused on that issue. Answer only that question. If you come across information relevant to another issue, note it, but do not pursue it. When you have a break or at the end of the day, give your notes to the person assigned to analyze that issue. Valuable time may be lost, and work may be duplicated, if you research and analyze the other issue or interrupt your work to discuss the information with the other person.

When identifying the issue, focus on the facts of the client's case. Ask yourself, "What must be decided about which of the facts of the client's case?"

When identifying the rule of law, focus on the facts of the case and the elements of the rule of law. This will help you quickly eliminate rules of law that do not apply.

For Example The fact situation involves a credit purchase by the client. There may be several rules of law that govern the transaction, such as the state's usury laws, the state sale of goods statutes, and the federal truth-in-lending laws.

The interest charged in the transaction in question was 1 percent and the usury statute provides that interest rates in excess of 20 percent are void. If you keep this fact in mind when locating the laws that might possibly apply to the transaction, you can immediately eliminate the usury statute from consideration. The interest charged does not violate the usury statute, so that statute clearly does not apply. It does not have to be considered when analyzing the problem in step 3.

When analyzing and applying the rule of law in step 3, focus on the client's facts and the issue or question being analyzed. It is easy to get sidetracked, especially when reading case law. Interesting issues may be addressed in a court opinion that are close but not directly related to the issues in the client's case. Stay focused. Ask yourself, "Is the issue being addressed in this opinion really related to the issue in my case? Is it on point?" The guidelines and principles addressed in Chapter 12 are helpful in this regard.

If you do not stay focused, after you have completed your research, you may have several cases in front of you that are only marginally related to the specific issue you are analyzing. A lot of time can be wasted reading cases that are not really on point.

Focus on the work. Avoidance and procrastination are deadly. When you are stuck or having a difficult time analyzing or researching an issue, it is sometimes easy to procrastinate, to avoid working on the problem. You may find excuses for not working on the problem, such as working on an easier project. The way to overcome this is to *start*. Do not put it off. If you are at the research stage, *start researching*. If you are at the writing stage, *start writing*. Do not be discouraged if the results seem poor at first. Focus on the problem and begin. Often the barrier is beginning.

B. Ethics—Intellectual Honesty

Rule 1.1 of the American Bar Association's Model Rules of Professional Conduct requires that a client be represented competently. This means that it is your ethical duty to possess and exercise that degree of knowledge and skill ordinarily possessed by others in the profession. One aspect of competence requires that a legal problem be researched with intellectual honesty. **Intellectual honesty** includes researching and analyzing a problem objectively. Do not let emotions, preconceived notions, personal views, or stubbornness interfere with an objective analysis of the client's case. Do not assume you know the law. Check your resources. Just because you "feel" a certain outcome should occur, do not let that feeling prevent you from objectively researching and analyzing the issue.

For Example The person who interviews clients in a law office has a personal history of domestic violence. When he was a child, there was domestic violence in the home. He thus has a strong aversion to domestic violence and harbors a prejudice against perpetrators of domestic violence. He interviews a client who complains that, the night before the interview, her husband hit her in the face with his fist. She states that he has beaten her frequently and savagely throughout their 10-year marriage. The client appears to have been severely beaten. She has two black eyes, and her face is swollen around the eyes.

The interviewer is outraged and upset by what happened to the client. As a result of his outrage, he fails to conduct a thorough and objective interview. He does not ask questions to elicit the details of the events of the previous night. He assumes the battery was unprovoked and does not ask questions concerning the reasons the client's husband hit her. His emotions and personal feelings cause him to focus on punishing the husband.

The interviewer knows that in addition to the remedies available under the criminal law, a civil cause of action for domestic battery is available under the state's recently passed domestic violence statute. He recommends that the supervising attorney file a civil complaint for domestic battery under the domestic violence statute. Relying on the paralegal's record for thoroughness, the supervising attorney directs that a complaint be drafted and filed.

A few weeks later, the husband's counsel, a friend of the supervising attorney, calls concerning the case. "Why did you file this complaint?" she asks. "My client was acting in self-defense. He hit his wife after she stabbed him." As it turns out, the client decided to kill her husband rather than face a future of continued beatings. She took a kitchen knife and stabbed him in the chest. In self-defense, he hit her once, and the blow caught her between the eyes, causing the two black eyes and facial swelling.

Had the interviewer not lost his objectivity, he would have conducted a thorough interview. Probing questions concerning the events of the night in question would have revealed all the facts, and the lawsuit might not have been filed.

This is an extreme example, but loss of objectivity occurs in varying degrees. Personal prejudices, personal beliefs, or sympathy for the client can combine to affect objectivity, which may lead to a failure to conduct an objective, critical analysis of the case, to not vigorously pursue potential opposing arguments, or to discount opposing authority.

Remember, the client may not be telling the whole truth. This may not be intentional. It may be the result of forgetfulness or a personal tendency to discount or downplay the importance of adverse facts. In this example, the client may have been so focused upon the years of abuse, and the desire to escape from further abuse, that she truly considered the stabbing insignificant when weighed against her past experiences.

Pursue the analysis of all legal issues with intellectual honesty. Identify all the facts affecting the case. Locate all legal authority concerning the issues, including any authority that may negatively affect the client's position. Ignoring adverse authority will not make it go away. It must be addressed. The importance of counterargument and counteranalysis is detailed in Chapter 13.

For additional rules of ethics, refer to the National Association of Legal Assistants (NALA) Code of Ethics and Professional Responsibility and the Model Standards and Guidelines for Utilization of Paralegals, available at http://www.nala.org; and the National Federation of Paralegal Associations (NFPA) Model Code of Ethics and Professional Responsibility and Guidelines for Enforcement, available at http://www.paralegals.org.

C. When to Stop Researching

One of the more difficult problems is to determine **when to stop** researching. This occurs in two situations. The first is when to quit researching a specific source if you find nothing. The second, and more common, situation is when to stop researching after finding several legal sources that address the research topic. In other words, when is your research complete? Both of these situations are discussed in this section.

1. When to Stop Researching If You Find Nothing

One of the more difficult problems is when to stop looking if your research fails to produce any results.

> **For Example** The assignment is to locate law identifying elements of the tort of emotional distress. The first step is to locate the statute governing emotional distress. In many jurisdictions, torts such as this are not governed by statutory law, but by case law. How do you know when to quit looking in the state statutes for the statutory law?

There are several different approaches to take in this situation.

a. Look to Another Source of Law

In the previous example, there may simply be no statutory law that governs the question. Then, once you have conducted research using all the possible terms the statute may be categorized under, it is time to look to another source, such as case law. It may be that the subject is covered by federal rather than state law. If you have exhausted all possible avenues of research under a specific source, look to another source.

b. Reconsider the Issue and Search Terms

It may be that your issue or search terms are stated so broadly or narrowly that your search turns up nothing.

> **For Example** The issue is stated as: "Is a will valid when the testator wrote 'invalid' on the title page of the will?" The researcher finds nothing when looking in the statutory index under *wills, testator,* and *validity*. A simple rephrasing of the issue to, "Is a will validly revoked when the testator wrote 'invalid' on the title page of the will?" might improve the research results. Expanding the search terms to include *revoked* or *revocation* may lead to the answer.

In this regard, it may be necessary to consult the person who gave you the assignment for guidance or to make sure the assignment is clear. In addition, reference to a secondary source such as a treatise may help you reframe the issue or identify additional search terms.

c. Reconsider the Legal Theory

It may be that you have incorrectly analyzed the question and are searching in the wrong area of law. Review the question to see if another area of law may be involved. It may be necessary to consult a secondary source such as a legal encyclopedia for an overview of the law that compiles all the ways a topic may be addressed.

> **For Example** The client runs a small business and a competitor induced a customer of the client to breach a contract with the client. Because the matter involves breach of contract, the researcher looks to state contract law for remedies that may be available against the competitor and finds nothing. The matter, however, is governed by the state's tort law: the tort of interference with contractual relations. Reference to contract law in a legal encyclopedia will reveal that third-party interference with a contract is often governed by tort law.

d. Matters of First Impression

It may be that the issue you are researching has not been addressed in your state. That is, it is a matter of first impression with no law on the subject in your jurisdiction. If this is so, refer to a secondary source such as a legal encyclopedia, treatise, or *ALR* annotation to identify how other jurisdictions have answered the question. The results of your research should not simply inform the supervising attorney that the state has not decided the matter. It should include the various ways in which other states have addressed the question.

2. When to Stop Researching after Finding Several Legal Sources

A more difficult problem is to know when to stop researching after finding several sources. There may be an endless variety of sources that address a specific question you are researching. There may be a statute, case law, encyclopedia references, *ALR* annotations, law review articles, and so on. There is no simple answer to the question of when to stop. Learning when to stop becomes intuitive with experience. The following considerations may help you determine when to stop.

a. Stop When You Have Found the Answer

The first research step is to find the primary authority that answers the question. If the authority clearly answers the question, then stop researching, as the answer is simple.

> **For Example** If the question is, "What is the statute of limitations for filing a claim for breach of a written contract?" the statute will clearly provide the answer. Reference to case law or secondary authority is not necessary. The only task remaining is to update and Shepardize the statute to determine if it has been amended or repealed.

There may be case law directly on point that answers the question being researched. If this is the situation, then you must Shepardize the case to determine if it is good law and identify any cases that may criticize or affect its application. In addition, check the appropriate digest for other cases that may analyze the issue differently. Also, check a secondary source such as an *ALR* annotation on the topic for authority that may provide a different analysis. Include any cases that are on point in the research.

b. When You Find Several Authorities on the Research Topic

Keep the following factors in mind if you locate several authorities that address the research issue.

(1) Primary Authority (Constitutions, Statutes, Cases) Always try to find a mandatory primary authority source(s) for each issue. If you have several cases that address the topic, use the mandatory authority cases. If you have case law that is mandatory authority, you do not need persuasive authority such as cases from other jurisdictions.

If you have several mandatory authority cases, select the case that is most on point, that most clearly analyzes the law, and is most recent. Courts, or the person reading your research, do not have time to read through numerous cases addressing the same legal arguments. Select only the lead case or cases.

(2) Secondary Authority You do not need to include secondary sources in your research if the primary authority clearly provides the answer to the issue. However, you may wish to include secondary authority sources to support your research if they specifically address the research topic. A reference to an *ALR* annotation or law review article on the issue allows the reader to review a comprehensive analysis of the topic if additional reference is desired.

If there is no primary authority on a topic, then reference to secondary authority is necessary. The more specific the secondary authority source, the better.

For Example If you have a legal encyclopedia citation that generally addresses the question being researched and an *ALR* annotation that specifically addresses the question, the *ALR* annotation is preferable.

Courts often refer to *Restatements of the Law, ALR* annotations, law review articles, and treatises when relying on secondary authority.

c. Other Factors Governing When to Stop

Time and economic factors may govern how thorough your research should be and when you should stop. The assignment may be governed by a short time constraint, or you may be informed to not spend too much time on the project because the potential claim is small. The assignment may be to draft a three-page legal memorandum. Each of these situations limits the amount of research to be performed.

When this occurs, first locate the primary authority that answers or addresses the question, that is, the enacted law (statute, etc.) that applies and the case law that is on point. Follow the research sequence presented earlier in this chapter until you run out of time.

Discuss the amount of research time you should spend on the project when it is assigned. If you find that you are running out of time or the project is more complex than you anticipated, consult your supervisor.

V. KEY POINTS CHECKLIST: *Legal Research and Analysis*

- ✔ Always pay attention to the facts. Keep them in mind when performing each step of the analytical process. The analysis process involves determining how the law applies to the facts. Make sure you have all the *facts* at the outset.

- ✔ Before beginning the IRAC process, perform preliminary research to become familiar with the area of law involved in the case.

- ✔ Remember IRAC. An easy way to remember the legal analysis process and what to look for when reading a court opinion is to use the acronym IRAC: *i*ssue, *r*ule, *a*nalysis/application, and *c*onclusion.

- ✔ When conducting research, locate the primary authority that governs the issue first. If there is no primary authority that applies or additional authority is needed to help interpret the primary authority, then look to secondary authority.

- ✔ When conducting legal analysis, address one issue at a time. If the assignment involves several issues, consider each issue separately. Complete the analysis of one issue before proceeding to the next issue. By doing so, you will be more efficient and avoid confusion.

- ✔ Remember counteranalysis. Always look for authority or arguments counter to your position.

- ✔ Stay focused. Concentrate on the specific issue you are assigned to analyze and the facts of the client's case, and keep asking yourself, "What must be decided about the facts of this case?"

- ✔ Maintain intellectual honesty. Do not lose your objectivity. Do not let personal beliefs or feelings interfere with a thorough legal analysis.

VI. APPLICATION

The steps of the analytical process are illustrated here through their application to the hypothetical presented at the beginning of the chapter.

Marian's new assignment requires her to analyze the Lietel case, identify the issues, and determine if Mr. Lietel has any cause of action against Steve Spear. Marian realizes that she must first familiarize herself with all the information concerning the facts of the case. She reviews the case file and all interviews that have been conducted. Next, she reviews the notes from the legal research and analysis course she took when she was studying for her paralegal degree. She notes a four-step approach for analyzing a case:

STEP 1: *Issue.* Identify the issue (legal question) or issues raised by the facts of the client's case.

STEP 2: *Rule.* Identify the law that governs the issue.

STEP 3: *Analysis/Application.* Determine how the rule of law applies to the issue.

STEP 4: *Conclusion.* Summarize the results of the legal analysis.

A. Battery Issue

Step 1. Identify the Issue(s)

Assume for the purposes of this problem that there is no question concerning the lawfulness of the citizen's arrest by Steve Spear. He had authority to make a citizen's arrest.

Marian, based upon her education and experience as a paralegal, quickly identifies two possible civil causes of action that Mr. Lietel may have against Mr. Spear:

1. Battery

2. Intentional infliction of emotional distress

From her training, Marian knows that the best approach to legal analysis is to address and completely analyze one issue before proceeding to the next one. She decides to begin with the battery issue.

Marian knows that the issue is the legal question raised by the facts of the client's case; therefore, the statement of the issue must include reference to the law and the facts. She identifies the issue as follows: Under the state's tort law, does a civil battery occur when an individual encounters resistance while making a lawful arrest, uses force to overcome the resistance, and kicks the person being arrested several times after the resistance ceases?

Step 2. Identify the Rule of Law

The second step is to identify the rule of law governing battery. Marian first looks for any state statute that defines civil battery. Based upon her familiarity with tort law, she is fairly certain that civil battery is defined in the case law, and there is no applicable statutory law. She researches the statutes, however, to be sure that the state legislature has not enacted any legislation concerning civil battery. Her research reveals that there is no statute. She finds that the case law definition of *battery* adopted by the state's highest court is: "A civil battery is the unprivileged, intentional, and harmful or offensive contact with the person of another."

Step 3. Analysis/Application

The third step is a determination of how the rule of law applies to the facts of the client's case. This is a three-part process:

■ Part 1: Identify the component parts (elements) of the rule of law.

■ Part 2: Apply the facts of the client's case to the component parts.

■ Part 3: Consider the possible counterarguments to the analysis of an issue (i.e., conduct a counteranalysis of the analysis).

a. Part 1: Identify the Components (Elements) of the Rule of Law

After reviewing the definition of battery, Marian identifies the following elements that are required to be present for a battery to occur:

1. Unprivileged
2. Intentional
3. Harmful or offensive
4. Contact

b. Part 2: Apply the Facts of the Client's Case to the Component Parts

If the elements of the case law are met or established by the facts of the case, then a cause of action exists. Elements 2, 3, and 4 appear to be clearly established by the facts of the case. Mr. Spear's actions of kicking Mr. Lietel were clearly intentional and harmful and did contact Mr. Lietel's body. Admittedly, Mr. Spear was making a lawful citizen's arrest, and he did encounter resistance. Did the continued use of force after resistance ceased constitute a battery? Was the continued use of force unprivileged?

The case law definition of battery does not provide sufficient guidance for a determination of whether the conduct was unprivileged. Marian must, therefore, refer to additional case law to determine what constitutes "unprivileged" contact. She looks for a court opinion that is on point—an opinion with facts similar to the client's facts in which the court addressed the question of the use of force in making a lawful arrest.

Assume that she finds the case of *Art v. Kelly*. In this case, an off-duty police officer, while making a citizen's arrest, continued to use force after the arrest had occurred and resistance had ceased. The court held that whenever a lawful arrest is made, either by a citizen or a law enforcement officer, the privilege to use force in conducting the arrest ceases when resistance ceases. Any continued use of force is a civil battery.

Applying the rule from *Art v. Kelly* to the facts of the case, Marian concludes that the requirements of the first element are met. Although Mr. Spear may have been privileged to use force to overcome resistance when making the citizen's arrest, the continued use of force after resistance ceased constituted a battery under the rule announced in *Art v. Kelly*. Marian concludes that a cause of action exists for civil battery. Mr. Spear's actions of kicking Mr. Lietel after Mr. Lietel had ceased resisting constituted unprivileged, intentional, harmful contact with Mr. Lietel.

c. Part 3: Conduct a Counteranalysis

Before proceeding, Marian should conduct a counteranalysis, identifying and addressing any counterarguments to the analysis.

> **For Example** Suppose Marian found a court decision involving an arrest by law enforcement officers holding that some continued use of force after resistance ceases is permissible if the situation is extremely heated. The court reasoned that law enforcement officers are not perfect, and if the situation is extremely heated, the brief continued use of force is privileged. In Marian's analysis, she would have to include the case in her memorandum and discuss how it does or does not apply to the facts of the client's case.

Step 4. Conclusion

The final step in the analysis of the battery issue is a conclusion. When applying the rule of law to the facts of the case in step 3, Marian reaches a conclusion that there is a cause of action for civil battery in Mr. Lietel's case. Law firms vary with regard to what should be included in the conclusion. Marian's conclusion could include, among other things, any or all of the following:

- A summary of the analysis

> **For Example** "The case law defines battery as the nonprivileged, intentional, harmful, or offensive contact with the person of another. In the court opinion of *Art v. Kelly*, the court stated that when a lawful arrest is being made, the continued use of force after resistance ceases is unprivileged. Mr. Spear's actions of kicking Mr. Lietel after Mr. Lietel had ceased resisting constituted unprivileged, intentional, harmful contact with Mr. Lietel. Therefore, a cause of action for civil battery is available in this case."

- A weighing or consideration, based on the analysis, of the merits of the cause of action.

> **For Example** "There is strong support for a battery claim in this case. The testimony of the witnesses supports Mr. Lietel's statements that Mr. Spear kicked him after he was subdued. All the elements of the cause of action are established by the facts of the case. Under the rule of *Art v. Kelly*, Mr. Spear's continued use of force was clearly unprivileged."

- An identification of additional facts or information that may be necessary. In this case, the statements of additional witnesses or other information may be required.
- The identification of further research that may be required. Further research may be necessary because part of the research could not be performed due to time constraints (the memo was due) or the research sources were not readily available.
- The identification of other issues or causes of action that became apparent during the analysis of the case, which is not necessary in this example because Marian's assignment is to identify all possible causes of action and issues. Suppose Marian's supervisory attorney believed that only a battery claim was present in this case and Marian's assignment was to address that issue. If her analysis of the battery issue revealed other possible causes of action, she should mention those possibilities in her conclusion.

B. Intentional Infliction of Emotional Distress Issue

When performing step 1, Marian identified intentional infliction of emotional distress as a possible cause of action. After concluding her analysis of the battery claim, she follows the same steps in analyzing the possibility of an intentional infliction of emotional distress claim.

Step 1. Identify the Issue

As with the battery issue, Marian knows that this issue is the legal question raised by the facts of the client's case; therefore, the statement of the issue must include reference to the law and the facts. She identifies the issue as follows: Under the state's tort law, does intentional infliction of emotional distress occur when an individual, who encounters resistance while making a lawful arrest, kicks the party being arrested six times after the resistance has ceased, causing the party to have trouble sleeping and be fearful whenever he sees the individual?

Step 2. Rule of Law

Marian's research reveals that there is no statutory cause of action for intentional infliction of emotional distress. The state case law does establish a cause of action for intentional infliction of emotional distress. There is no cause of action for negligent infliction of emotional distress. Intentional infliction of emotional distress is defined in the case law as intentionally causing severe emotional distress by an act of extreme or outrageous conduct.

Step 3. Analysis/Application

a. Part 1: Identify the Components (Elements) of the Rule of Law

Marian's review of the case law reveals four elements:

1. Extreme or outrageous conduct
2. Intent to cause severe emotional distress
3. Severe emotional distress is suffered
4. The conduct causes the distress

b. Part 2: Apply the Elements to the Facts of the Client's Case

Marian's application of the elements to the facts of Mr. Lietel's raises several questions about whether the requirements of intentional infliction of emotional distress are met in this case:

1. Was Mr. Spear's conduct "extreme or outrageous"?
2. Mr. Spear obviously intended to kick Mr. Lietel, but did he intend to cause severe emotional distress?
3. Was the harm suffered by Mr. Lietel "severe emotional distress"?

The answers to these questions are not apparent from a reading of the definition of intentional infliction of emotional distress. Marian turns to additional case law for guidance and locates the case of *Addik v. Garay*, which appears to answer her questions. In the case, Mr. Garay and Mr. Addik got into a fight at a party. Garay knocked Addik down and, while Addik was down, kicked him multiple times yelling, "I'm not gonna kill you, but you'll remember me in your dreams. You'll never forget this." Addik was so affected by the incident that he had a nervous breakdown and was out of work for two months.

The court, addressing Addik's claim for intentional infliction of emotional distress, ruled that public humiliation, such as that suffered by Addik, constitutes "extreme and outrageous conduct." Ruling that the requisite intent was present, the court held that there must be some *specific conduct* indicating an intent to cause emotional distress. The mere intentional act of kicking was not sufficient to evidence an intent to cause emotional distress, but Mr. Garay's statements while kicking Mr. Addik were specific conduct indicating an intent to cause emotional distress. The court went on to rule that the emotional distress suffered must be severe: The mere loss of sleep is not sufficient. Instead, severe harm, such as loss of work or medical expenses, must result.

Applying the guidelines presented in *Addik v. Garay*, Marian concludes that there is probably not a cause of action for intentional infliction of emotional distress in Mr. Lietel's case. Mr. Spear's conduct of kicking Mr. Lietel in public is sufficiently extreme and outrageous. It is questionable, however, whether the requirements of elements 2 and 3, intent and severe emotional distress, are met by the facts of the case. There was no conduct by Mr. Spear evidencing a specific intent to cause emotional distress. The act of kicking alone was not sufficient evidence of such intent, according to *Addik v. Garay*. If Mr. Lietel's loss of work and medical expenses resulted from the battery and were not related to the emotional distress, then there is no evidence that Mr. Lietel suffered severe harm as required by *Addik v. Garay*. Fearfulness and loss of sleep are probably not sufficiently severe to meet the *Garay* standards.

c. Part 3: Counteranalysis

In this part, Marian would identify and address any authority or counterarguments to her analysis. We will assume that she did not identify any counterargument to her analysis of the emotional distress issue.

Step 4. Conclusion

As with the battery issue, Marian begins her conclusion with a summary of the analysis.

> **For Example** The case law definition of *intentional infliction of emotional distress* is the intentional causing of severe emotional distress by an act of extreme or outrageous conduct. In the case of *Addik v. Garay,* the court ruled that:
>
> 1. Public humiliation by kicking constitutes outrageous conduct.
> 2. The act of kicking alone is not sufficient evidence of intent—there must be additional conduct evidencing an intent to cause severe emotional distress.
> 3. Severe harm must result from the severe emotional distress.
>
> In Mr. Lietel's case, there is no evidence of the required intent, and it is questionable whether there was severe harm. Therefore, a cause of action for intentional infliction of emotional distress does not appear to be present.

Marian may include some other items in her conclusion similar to those presented in the conclusion to the battery issue.

> **For Example** Marian may identify additional information that is needed. She may note that the client and witnesses should be reinterviewed to determine whether Mr. Spear said anything while he was kicking Mr. Lietel.

Summary

Most clients enter the law office with a problem that must be analyzed and solved. Legal analysis of the problem involves the identification of the legal issues in the client's case and a determination of what law applies and how it applies. The commonly used legal analysis format involves four steps:

1. Identification of the legal issue or issues
2. Identification of the rule of law that governs the issue
3. Analysis and application of the rule of law to the facts of the case. This step is composed of three parts:
   a. A determination of the elements or requirements of the rule of law
   b. A matching of the facts of the client's case to the elements and a determination of how the rule of law applies to the facts
   c. A counteranalysis that addresses any counterarguments to the analysis
4. A conclusion that summarizes the previous steps. The conclusion may also include a weighing of the merits of the case and an identification of other information or avenues of research that should be pursued.

The four steps of the analysis process can be easily referred to and remembered by the acronym IRAC: *i*ssue, *r*ule, *a*nalysis/application, and *c*onclusion.

It is important to keep three general considerations in mind when engaging in legal research and analysis:

1. Focus
2. Intellectual honesty
3. When to stop researching

Stay focused on the task. Focus on the facts of the client's case, and analyze only the issue or issues raised by those facts. Avoid being distracted by interesting or related issues that need not be addressed.

Perform analysis with intellectual honesty. Always look for the correct answer, even though that answer may not be in the client's favor or in accordance with your beliefs. Do not let preferences, prejudices, or politics interfere with your duty to objectively and honestly analyze the legal question. Base the conclusion on an objective analysis of all the facts and law and include both the supporting and opposing positions.

Quick References

Internet Resources

The following sites may provide useful support information to paralegals engaged in legal analysis.

http://www.nala.org

This is the site for the National Association for Legal Assistants (NALA). The NALA site provides a wealth of information, ranging from articles on the profession to education and certification programs for paralegals. It includes information on court decisions affecting paralegals and links to other related sites.

http://www.paralegals.org

This is the Web page for the National Federation of Paralegal Associations (NFPA), another national paralegal organization. The Web page provides links to a wide range of sites of interest to paralegals: research sources, publications, products, and so forth.

http://www.paralegaltoday.com

Paralegal Today is a magazine geared toward the needs of paralegals. It often includes helpful articles on legal analysis and writing.

Using http://www.google.com as a search engine and "IRAC legal analysis" as a topic can identify several hundred Web sites (too many to list here) related to the topic "legal analysis and the IRAC process."

Exercises

Additional assignments are available on the CourseMate.

ASSIGNMENT 1

Describe in detail the steps of the IRAC legal analysis process.

ASSIGNMENT 2

Client's Facts: The client found a check written out to cash in the amount of $750. The check was completely made out when he found it. He took it to the bank, signed it on the back as instructed by the teller, and cashed it. He was subsequently arrested and charged with forgery.

Rule of Law: Section 30-236 of the state penal code defines *forgery* as "falsely making or altering any signature to, or any part of, any writing purporting to have any legal efficacy with intent to injure or defraud."

Section 45-3-109d of the state commercial code provides that when a negotiable instrument is made out to cash it is a "bearer instrument." The section goes on to provide: "A bearer instrument refers to an instrument that is payable to anyone possessing the instrument and is negotiable by transfer alone, it is the same as cash." Note: A check is a negotiable instrument.

Assignment: Based on the information presented in the problem, prepare a complete and detailed analysis of the question of whether there is sufficient evidence to support a charge of forgery.

ASSIGNMENT 3

Client's Facts: The client is charged with burglary. He broke a window, entered his neighbor's garage, and took three cases of beer. The garage is a separate building located about six feet from the neighbor's house.

Rule of Law: Section 2397 of the state penal code defines *burglary* as the breaking and entering of the dwelling house of another with the intent to commit a crime.

Case Law: In the case of *State v. Nelson,* the court ruled that "a dwelling includes outbuildings close to but not physically connected with a dwelling house, if such buildings are capable of being fenced in."

Assignment: Based on the information presented in the problem, prepare a complete and detailed analysis of the question of whether there is sufficient evidence to support a charge of burglary.

ASSIGNMENT 4

Client's Facts: The client is the president of an extremist group that believes that the followers of Islam should be deported to Islamic countries. At their ceremonies, the organization members burn a large replica of the Koran while singing anti-Islamic songs. The organization's letterhead and literature are embossed with a picture of a burning Koran being stepped on by a spiked boot. The local library has books by members of the American Nazi Party, the American Communist Party, and the Ku Klux Klan. The library refuses to include the organization's literature among its materials. The client claims this violates the organization's constitutional rights.

The law firm handles cases involving the violation of constitutional rights.

Assignment: The researcher is assigned the task of identifying and analyzing the possible causes of action that the client may have against the city library.

a. Discuss and describe in detail the steps you should follow when conducting the legal analysis.

b. Assume there are possible causes of action based on freedom of speech under the First Amendment and equal protection under the Fourteenth Amendment. For each issue, describe in detail each step of the analytical process.

c. Discuss factors that may possibly affect a researcher's objectivity and how those factors could affect the legal analysis of the problem.

ASSIGNMENT 5

Client's Facts: The client was cited for passing in a no-passing zone. Frustrated by a slow-moving vehicle on a two-lane highway, the client admits that he passed the vehicle entirely in a no-passing zone—that he began and ended the passing maneuver in an area where the center of the road was marked with two solid stripes. There was no oncoming traffic, and he made the maneuver safely.

Rule of Law: The state's motor vehicle code, Section 293–301, provides that it is a violation of state law to pass a vehicle in a no-passing zone. In the statute, a no-passing zone is defined as that portion of the road marked by two solid lines painted in the center of the road. Passing zones are indicated by single, eight-foot stripes down the center of the road.

Case Law: The only relevant case on the subject is *State v. Roth.* In that case, Mr. Roth was cited for improper passing. He began the passing maneuver in the last 30 feet of a no-passing zone and completed it in a passing zone. There were no oncoming vehicles. Evidence presented to the trial court established that the last 30 feet of the no-passing zone should have been marked as part of the passing zone. Mr. Roth appealed his conviction in the trial court. On appeal, the state's highest court held that the purpose of the state motor vehicle code is to ensure safety on the public highways. The court ruled that Mr. Roth's passing maneuver was clearly made safely, and in light of the evidence that the no-passing zone was improperly marked, a strict reading of the statute was not appropriate. Mr. Roth's conviction was set aside.

Assignment: The researcher is assigned the task of analyzing the likelihood that the client's ticket can be set aside.

a. Based upon the information presented in the problem, conduct an analysis of the client's case and prepare a complete and detailed analysis of the problem.

b. Repeat assignment a, assuming the following facts: The client began the passing maneuver approximately 20 feet from the end of the no-passing zone and completed it in a passing zone. There was no oncoming traffic, and the client completed the maneuver safely.

c. Repeat assignment a, assuming the following facts: The client began the passing maneuver in a passing zone, but completed it in a no-passing zone.

d. What additional information, if any, may be necessary for a complete analysis of the preceding problems?

ASSIGNMENT 6

What should you do when you do not find anything while researching a specific source? After finding several legal sources that address the research topic, what considerations should you keep in mind concerning when to stop researching?

PART II

Legal Research

OVERVIEW

Legal research is the process of locating the law that applies to the question raised by the facts of the case. Legal research and analysis are interrelated, and performing legal research usually involves the use of analysis principles. It is helpful, however, to have an understanding of legal research sources and the legal research process before studying the legal analysis process.

Part II covers legal research and the research process. It begins with two chapters on primary authority, specifically statutory and case law, followed by two chapters on secondary authority. It concludes with a chapter on computers and legal research, and a chapter on legal citation.

CHAPTER 3

Constitutions, Statutes, Administrative Law, and Court Rules—Research and Analysis

Learning Objectives

After completing this chapter, you should understand:

- The meaning of statutory law
- The components of a statute
- How to find constitutional, statutory, and administrative law and court rules
- How to analyze a statute and apply it to specific problems
- The role of legislative history and canons of construction

Alan attended one year of paralegal classes before being admitted to law school. After his first year, he obtained a part-time job with a law firm. Initially, Alan's assignments had been the preparation of deposition digests. He is good at preparing deposition digests but wants to be involved in projects in the early stages of the litigation process. At his request, he was assigned to work exclusively with Ms. Tilton, who is a litigation attorney specializing in corporation and contract law.

His first assignment from Ms. Tilton is to determine if Mrs. Jackson has a cause of action against Beauty Care Beauty Salon for breach of warranty under the sales provisions of the state's commercial code. Mrs. Jackson went to her hairdresser, Beauty Care Beauty Salon, to get their "special long-term hold" permanent. Once a year for the past three years, she asked for the "special" permanent. Beauty Care made no warranties about the permanent. It did not provide Mrs. Jackson, either orally or in writing, any statements concerning the quality of the permanent. The receipt she received for the permanent listed a $20 charge for the permanent kit and other products, and an $80 charge for the services of the beautician.

This year, three days after Mrs. Jackson was given the permanent, her hair, which had been blonde, turned a light green. Five days later it broke off approximately 1 inch from the scalp—not a good result.

Alan, based on his paralegal and first-year law school courses, is aware that Mrs. Jackson has a possible tort negligence claim and other possible causes of action against Beauty Care. His assignment, however, is to determine if there is also a possible breach of warranty claim under the state's commercial code.

Alan has not worked with statutes since he took a paralegal research course. Several questions occur to him: "How do I find the commercial code statutes? Does the Commercial Code Sales Act apply? Is this a sale of goods within the meaning of the act? If this is a sale of goods, which warranty applies? How do you analyze a statute?"

I. INTRODUCTION

This chapter focuses on how to research and analyze enacted law and court rules. As discussed in Chapter 1, enacted law includes constitutions (governing documents adopted by the people), laws passed by legislative bodies, and the rules and regulations adopted by administrative agencies.

Laws passed by Congress or state legislatures are generally called *acts* or *statutes*. This body of law is commonly referred to as **statutory law**. Ordinances are laws usually passed by local governing bodies, such as city councils and county commissions. Administrative agencies, under the authority granted by legislative bodies, adopt rules and regulations that have the force of law. Courts adopt rules that regulate the conduct of matters brought before the court. For the sake of clarity, throughout this chapter the discussion and examples focus upon laws passed by legislative bodies, that is, statutory law. Note, however, that the principles presented in the chapter also apply to the analysis of constitutions, statutes, administrative law, and court rules.

Statutory law is a major source of law that a researcher must become familiar with when researching and analyzing the law. Statutory law has assumed an ever-increasing role in the United States. With the passage of time, the body of statutory law has expanded greatly. Many matters once governed by case law are now governed by statutory law.

For Example	Criminal law was once exclusively established and regulated by the common law; today, most criminal law is governed by statutory law.

Consequently, with the growth of statutory law, more and more legal problems and issues are governed by it. Because an ever-increasing number of legal problems and issues require the interpretation and application of statutory law, researchers are more frequently called upon to engage in statutory analysis. **Statutory analysis** is the process of determining if a statute applies, how it applies, and the effect of that application.

Because most statutes are designed to cover a broad range of present and future situations, they are written in general terms. As a result, a researcher is required to engage in statutory analysis to determine whether and how a statute applies in a specific fact situation.

The focus of this chapter is the process of statutory research and analysis. It begins with a presentation of the anatomy of a statute, follows with a discussion of the process of statutory research and analysis, and ends with general considerations involving statutory construction and analysis.

II. ANATOMY OF A STATUTE

Before you can analyze a statute, you must be familiar with the basic structure of statutory law, the component parts. Assume, for the purposes of illustration, that you are interested in whether a contract for the sale of goods must be in writing, and the governing law is the Indiana Code. Exhibit 3-1 shows selected portions of the Indiana Code concerning commercial law. Exhibit 3-2 presents the section of the *United States Code Annotated (USCA)* concerning ransom money. To the left of sections of the codes (in the margins) are terms that describe the components of the codes. The following text discusses each descriptive term and that portion of the statutes referred to by the term.

Not all of the statutory components included in the discussion following the Indiana Code and the *USCA* are included in every statute. Some statutes, for example, may not have a definitions section. It is important, however, to discuss the components so you will be familiar with them if you encounter them in other statutes.

Exhibit 3-1 *Indiana Code—Commercial Law. Michie, Burns Indiana Statutes Annotated (1990), cited material is from Title 26, 1992 replacement pamphlet. Reprinted with the permission of LexisNexis.*

Number of title ———————

TITLE 26
COMMERCIAL LAW

Number of article ————

ARTICLE.
1. UNIFORM COMMERCIAL CODE, chs. 1-10.
2. COMMERCIAL TRANSACTIONS, chs. 1-6.

ARTICLE.
3. WAREHOUSES, chs. 1-7.

ARTICLE 1
UNIFORM COMMERCIAL CODE

Number of chapter ————

CHAPTER.
1. GENERAL PROVISIONS, 26-1-1-101 — 26-1-1-208.
2. SALES, 26-1-2-101 — 26-1-2-725.
2.1. LEASES, 26-1-2.1-101 — 26-1-2.1-532.
3. COMMERCIAL PAPER, 26-1-3-101 — 26-1-3-805.
4. BANK DEPOSITS AND COLLECTIONS, 26-1-4-101 — 26-1-4-504.
4.1. FUND TRANSFERS, 26-1-4.1-101 — 26-1-4.1-507.
5. LETTERS OF CREDIT, 26-1-5-101 — 26-1-5-117.

CHAPTER.
6. BULK TRANSFERS, 26-1-6-101 — 26-1-6-110.
7. [WAREHOUSE RECEIPTS, BILLS OF LADING AND OTHER] DOCUMENTS OF TITLE, 26-1-7-101 — 26-1-7-603.
8. INVESTMENT SECURITIES, 26-1-8-101 — 26-1-8-408.
9. SECURED TRANSACTIONS, 26-1-9-101 — 26-1-9-507.
10. EFFECTIVE DATE, REPEAL, SAVING PROVISION, 26-1-10-101 — 26-1-10-106.

CHAPTER 1
GENERAL PROVISIONS

PART 1. SHORT TITLE, CONSTRUCTION, APPLICATION AND SUBJECT-MATTER OF THE ACT

Number of section ————

SECTION.
26-1-1-101. Short title.
26-1-1-102. Purposes — Rules of construction — Variation by agreement.
26-1-1-103. Supplementary general principles of law applicable.
26-1-1-104. Construction against implicit repeal.
26-1-1-105. Territorial application of the act — Parties' power to choose applicable law.
26-1-1-106. Remedies to be liberally administered.
26-1-1-107. Waiver or renunciation of claim or right after breach.
26-1-1-108. Severability.

SECTION.
26-1-1-109. [Repealed.]

PART 2. GENERAL DEFINITIONS AND PRINCIPLES OF INTERPRETATION

26-1-1-201. General definitions.
26-1-1-202. Prima facie evidence by third party documents.
26-1-1-203. Obligation of good faith.
26-1-1-204. Time — Reasonable time — "Seasonably."
26-1-1-205. Course of dealing and usage of trade.
26-1-1-206. Statute of frauds for kinds of personal property not otherwise covered.
26-1-1-207. Performance or acceptance under reservation of rights.
26-1-1-208. Option to accelerate at will.

Number of section ————

PART 1. SHORT TITLE, CONSTRUCTION, APPLICATION AND SUBJECT MATTER OF THE ACT

Short title ————

26-1-1-101. Short title. — IC 26-1 shall be known and may be cited as Uniform Commercial Code. [Acts 1963, ch. 317, § 1-101, p. 539; P.L.152-1986, § 110.]

Exhibit 3-1 *(Continued)*

Purpose clause ————

26-1-1-102. Purposes — Rules of construction — Variation by agreement. — (1) IC 26-1 shall be liberally construed and applied to promote its underlying purposes and policies.

(2) Underlying purposes and policies of IC 26-1 are:

(a) To simplify, clarify, and modernize the law governing commercial transactions;

(b) To permit the continued expansion of commercial practices through custom, usage, and agreement of the parties;

(c) To make uniform the law among the various jurisdictions.

CHAPTER 2

SALES

Number of ———————
section

PART 1. SHORT TITLE, GENERAL CONSTRUCTION
AND SUBJECT MATTER

Short title ——————

26-1-2-101. Short title. — IC 26-1-2 shall be known and may be cited as Uniform Commercial Code—Sales. [Acts 1963, ch. 317, § 2-101, p. 539; P.L.152-1986, § 119.]

Cross References. Construction against implicit repeal, IC 26-1-1-104.

Rules of construction, IC 26-1-1-102.

Supplementary general principles of law applicable, IC 26-1-1-103.

Indiana Law Journal. The Uniform Commercial Code and Real Estate Law: Problems for Both the Real Estate Lawyer and the Chattel Security Lawyer, 38 Ind. L.J. 535.

Negligence, Economic Loss, and the U.C.C., 61 Ind. L.J. 593 (1986).

Indiana Law Review. The Flammable Fabrics Act and Strict Liability in Tort, 9 Ind. L. Rev. 395.

Survey of Recent Developments in Business and Commercial Law—Vertical Privity and Damages for Breach of Implied Warranty under the U.C.C.: It's Time for Indiana to

Scope ——————

26-1-2-102. Scope — Certain security and other transactions excluded from this chapter. — Unless the context otherwise requires, IC 26-1-2 applies to transactions in goods. It does not apply to any transaction which although in the form of an unconditional contract to sell or present sale is intended to operate only as a security transaction, nor does IC 26-1-2 impair or repeal any statute regulating sales to consumers, farmers, or other specified classes of buyers. IC 26-1-2 does not impair or repeal IC 9-14, IC 9-17, or IC 9-22-5. [Acts 1963, ch. 317, § 2-102, p. 539; P.L.152-1986, § 120; P.L.2-1991, § 86.]

(Continued)

Exhibit 3-1 (Continued)

Definitions

26-1-1-201. General definitions. — Subject to additional definitions contained in IC 26-1-2 through IC 26-1-10 which are applicable to specific provisions, and unless the context otherwise requires, in IC 26-1:

(1) "Action" in the sense of a judicial proceeding includes recoupment, counterclaim, setoff, suit in equity, and any other proceedings in which rights are determined.

(2) "Aggrieved party" means a party entitled to resort to a remedy.

(3) "Agreement" means the bargain of the parties in fact as found in their language or by implication from other circumstances including course of dealing or usage of trade or course of performance as provided in IC 26-1-1-205 and IC 26-1-2-208. Whether an agreement has legal

Substantive provisions

PART 2. FORM, FORMATION AND READJUSTMENT OF CONTRACT

26-1-2-201. Formal requirements — Statute of frauds. — (1) Except as otherwise provided in this section, a contract for the sale of goods for the price of five hundred dollars ($500) or more is not enforceable by way of action or defense unless there is some writing sufficient to indicate that a contract for sale has been made between the parties and signed by the party against whom enforcement is sought or by his authorized agent or broker. A writing is not insufficient because it omits or incorrectly states a term agreed upon, but the contract is not enforceable under this paragraph beyond the quantity of goods shown in such writing.

(2) Between merchants, if within a reasonable time a writing in confirmation of the contract and sufficiently against the sender is received and the party receiving it has reason to know its contents, it satisfies the requirements of subsection (1) against such party unless written notice of objection to its contents is given within ten (10) days after it is received.

(3) A contract which does not satisfy the requirements of subsection (1) but which is valid in other respects is enforceable:

(a) If the goods are to be specially manufactured for the buyer and are not suitable for sale to others in the ordinary course of the seller's business and the seller, before notice of repudiation is received and under circumstances which reasonably indicate that the goods are for the buyer, has made either a substantial beginning of their manufacture or commitments for their procurement; or

(b) If the party against whom enforcement is sought admits in his pleading, testimony, or otherwise in court that a contract for sale was made, but the contract is not enforceable under this provision beyond the quantity of goods admitted; or

(c) With respect to goods for which payment has been made and accepted or which have been received and accepted (IC 26-1-2-606). [Acts 1963, ch. 317, § 2-201, p. 539; P.L.152-1986, § 125.]

Reference information

Cross References. Action. definition. IC 26-1-1-201.

Additional terms in acceptance or confirmation. IC 26-1-2-207.

Between merchants. definition. IC 26-1-2-104.

Buyer and seller. definition. IC 26-1-2-103.

Contract. definition. IC 26-1-1-201.

Exhibit 3-1 (Continued)

Substantive provisions

26-1-2-315. Implied warranty — Fitness for particular purpose. — Where the seller at the time of contracting has reason to know any particular purpose of which the goods are required and that the buyer is relying on the seller's skill or judgment to select or furnish suitable goods, there is, unless excluded or modified under IC 26-1-2-316, an implied warranty that the good shall be fit for such purpose. [Acts 1963, ch. 317, § 2-315, p. 539; P.L.152-1986, § 136.]

Cross References. Buyer and seller, definition, IC 26-1-2-103.

Cumulation and conflict of warranties, IC 26-1-2-317.

Exclusion or modification of warranties, IC 26-1-2-316.

Goods, definition, IC 26-1-2-105.

Implied warranty of merchantability, IC 26-1-2-314.

Product liability actions, IC 33-1-1.5-1 — 33-1-1.5-8.

Indiana Law Journal. Implied and Express Warranties and Disclaimers Under the Uniform Commercial Code, 38 Ind. L.J. 648.

The Private Law Treatment of Defective Products in Sales Situations, 49 Ind. L.J. 8.

Consumer Warranty or Insurance Contract? A View Towards a Rational State Regulatory Policy, 51 Ind. L.J. 1103.

Indiana's Implied Warranty of Fitness for Habitation: Limited Protection for Used Home Buyers, 57 Ind. L.J. 479.

Negligence, Economic Loss, and the U.C.C., 61 Ind. L.J. 593 (1986).

Indiana Law Review. Landlord-Tenant Law: Indiana at the Crossroads, 10 Ind. L. Rev. 591.

and Damages for Breach of Implied Warranty under the U.C.C.: It's Time for Indiana to Abandon the Citadel, 21 Ind. L. Rev. 23 (1988).

Notre Dame Law Review. Economic Institutions and Value Survey — Warranty Representation and Disclaimers, 8 Notre Dame Law. 602.

Merchantability and the Statute of Limitations, 50 Notre Dame Law. 321.

Utility "Services" under the Uniform Commercial Code: Are Public Utilities in for a Shock?, 56 Notre Dame Law. 89.

Lions & Lionesses, Tigers & Tigresses, Bears & ... Other Animals: Sellers' Liability for Dangerous Animals, 58 Notre Dame L. Rev. 537.

Valparaiso University Law Review. An Emerging Concept: Consumer Protection in Statutory Regulation, Products Liability and the Sale of New Homes, 11 Val. U.L. Rev. 335.

Risk of Economic Loss and Implied Warranty Liability in Tripartite Finance Leases, 22 Val. U.L. Rev. 593 (1988).

Reference information

NOTES TO DECISIONS

, ANALYSIS

In general.
Basis for acceleration.
—Encumbrance.
Evidence.
Good faith.
—Erroneous determination of insecurity.

In General.

Acceleration provisions are valid and enforceable in Indiana. Smith v. Union State Bank, 452 N.E.2d 1059 (Ind. App. 1983).

Basis for Acceleration.

—Encumbrance.

The attachment of a superior lien against property subject to security agreement amounted to an encumbrance and was a basis for acceleration under security agreement which provided for acceleration in case of encumbrance. Van Bibber v. Norris, 419 N.E.2d 115 (Ind. 1981).

Evidence.

Where the maker of the note had incurred other financial obligations, had transferred collateral, and secured equipment in which the holder of the note had no superior security interest, the holder could honestly have believed that its chances of payment had

been diminished. Holmes v. Rushville Prod. Credit Ass'n, 170 Ind. App. 509, 353 N.E.2d 509, 54 Ind. Dec. 395 (1976), vacated, 170 Ind. App. 517, 355 N.E.2d 417, reinstated, 170 Ind. App. 509, 357 N.E.2d 734, 55 Ind. Dec. 468 (1977), transfer denied, 267 Ind. 454, 371 N.E.2d 379, 60 Ind. Dec. 413 (1978).

Good Faith.

Where bank had continuing problem of collecting from purchaser of mobile home and such purchaser was delinquent on current payment due and had been arrested and placed in jail and mobile home park had lien on mobile home for rent due, it could not be said that bank did not act in good faith in accelerating payment. Van Bibber v. Norris, 419 N.E.2d 115 (Ind. 1981).

A good faith belief under this section means at least honesty in fact in the conduct or transaction concerned. Smith v. Union State Bank, 452 N.E.2d 1059 (Ind. App. 1983).

—Erroneous Determination of Insecurity.

Assuming a bank was not insecure, even an erroneous determination of insecurity was not necessarily unreasonable or in bad faith. Smith v. Union State Bank, 452 N.E.2d 1059 (Ind. App. 1983).

Exhibit 3-2 *18 U.S.C.A. § 1202 and Accompanying Annotations.* Reprinted from West Group, United States Code Annotated, 18 U.S.C.A. 1201 (2000) pp. 66-68, with permission of Thomson Reuters.

Title

Ch. 55 KIDNAPPING   18 § 1202

Section number

§ 1202. Ransom money

(a) Whoever receives, possesses, or disposes of any money or other property, or any portion thereof, which has at any time been delivered as ransom or reward in connection with a violation of section 1201 of this title, knowing the same to be money or property which has been at any Time delivered as such ransom or reward, shall be fined under this title or imprisoned not more than ten years, or both.

(b) A person who transports, transmits, or transfers in interstate or foreign commerce any proceeds of a kidnapping punishable under State law by imprisonment for more than 1 year, or receives, possesses, conceals, or disposes of any such proceeds after they have crossed a State or United States boundary, knowing the proceeds to have been unlawfully obtained, shall be imprisoned not more than 10 years, fined under this title, or both.

(c) For purposes of this section, the term "State" has the meaning set forth in section 245(d) of this title.

(June 25, 1948, c. 645, 62 Stat. 760; Sept. 13, 1994, Pub.L. 103–322, Title XXXII, § 320601(b), Title XXXIII, § 330016(1)(L), 108 Stat. 2115, 2147.)

History and official comments

─────────────────────── **HISTORICAL AND STATUTORY NOTES** ───────────────────────

Revision Notes and Legislative Reports

1948 Acts. Based on Title 18, U.S.C., 1940 ed., § 408c-1 (June 22, 1932, c. 271, § 4, as added Jan. 24, 1936, c. 29, 49 Stat. 1099).

Words "in the penitentiary" after imprisoned" were omitted in view of section 4082 of this title committing prisoners to the custody of the Attorney General. (See reviser's note under section 1 of this title.)

Minor changes were made in phraseology.

1994 Acts. House Report Nos. 103–324 and 103–489, and House Conference Report No. 103–711, see 1994 U.S. Code Cong. and Adm. News, p. 1801.

Amendments

1994 Amendments. Subsec. (a). Pub.L. 103–322, § 320601(b)(1), designated existing provisions as subsec. (a).

Pub.L. 103–322, § 330016)1)(L), substituted "under this title" for "not more than $10,000".

Subsecs. (b), (c). Pub.L. 102–322 § 320601(b)(2), added subsecs. (b) and (c).

FEDERAL SENTENCING GUIDELINES

See Federal Sentencing Guidelines § 2A4.2, 18 USCA.

AMERICAN LAW REPORTS

What constitutes violation of 18 USCA 1202, prohibiting receipt, possession, or disposition of ransom money, 31 ALR Fed 916.

Exhibit 3-2 *(Continued)*

Library references/ research guides

LIBRARY REFERENCES

American Digest System
    Kidnapping ⚷ 1.
Encyclopedias
    Kidnapping, see C.J.S. §§ 1, 2.
Texts and Treatises
    Character evidence not admissible, see Wright & Graham: Evidence § 5231 et seq.

WESTLAW ELECTRONIC RESEARCH

See WESTLAW guide following the Explanation pages of this volume.

Notes of Decisions

Topics covered in notes to decisions

Case Summary

Delivery   1
Indictment or information   3
Instructions   4
Interstate commerce   2

1. Delivery

Where defendant picked up money which was intended as kidnap ransom but had been left in wrong place and, after learning that it was intended to be ransom money, continued to keep it, defendant was guilty of possession of ransom money, notwithstanding contention that there had been no "delivery," in purview of this section which defined offense as possession of money, "which has at any time been delivered as ransom." U. S. v. Ortega, C.A.3 (N.J.) 1975, 517 F.2d 1006.

2. Interstate commerce

To establish violation of this section prohibiting possession of ransom money there was no requirement that defendant be connected with interstate commerce element of primary kidnapping offense under section 1201 of this title. U. S. v. Ortega, C.A.3 (N.J.) 1975, 517 F.2d 1006.

3. Indictment or information

Indictment charging in several counts conspiracy to commit offenses under this section and sections 875 and 1202 of this title and charging substantive offense of kidnapping and three separate offenses of transmitting communications in interstate commerce demanding ransom money and charging receiving, possessing and disposing of ransom money charged separate offenses and was not duplicitous. Amsler v. U. S., C.A.9 (Cal.) 1967, 381 F.2d 37.

4. Instructions

In prosecution for possession of ransom money and making false statements to grand jury, trial court did not err in refusing to charge that defendant could be acquitted if he had relied upon advice of Federal Bureau of Investigation agents in attempting to return money anonymously, where such advice occurred a week after defendant had made his false statements to grand jury and no attempt was ever made to return money in manner suggested. U. S. v. Ortega, C.A.3 (N.J.) 1975, 517 F.2d 1006.

In prosecution under former section 408c-1 of this title accused could not complain of instruction that receipt of ransom money was criminal offense, where court instructed as to what constituted a conspiracy, and that unless jury found accused became part of conspiracy there should be acquittal, and that if accused entered conspiracy jury should further find that accused accepted ransom money knowing it was such, or aided owners in exchanging it. Laska v. U.S., C.C.A.10 (Okla.) 1936, 82 F.2d 672, certiorari denied 56 S.Ct. 957, 298 U.S. 689, 80 L.Ed. 1407.

A. Numbers

Each statute has numbers assigned for each part of the statute. Every legislative authority—local, state, and federal—follows a different numbering system. Therefore, it is not practical to discuss separately each numbering system. There are some general similarities, however, that can be addressed.

Most laws are usually divided into broad categories, each of which is assigned a **number**. Those broad categories are divided into topics or smaller categories that are also assigned a number. The topics are further divided into subtopics and assigned a number, and so on. The number of categories and divisions depends on the statutory scheme of the particular legislative authority.

> **For Example** The laws of Indiana are divided into broad categories called *titles*. Commercial law is assigned the number 26. (See "Number of Title" at the top of the first page of Exhibit 3-1.) Each title is divided into areas called articles. Commercial law in the Indiana Code is divided into three articles numbered 1, 2, and 3. The Uniform Commercial Code article, that governs commercial transactions, is assigned the number 1. The three articles are listed under "Commercial Law." (See "Number of Article" at the top of the first page of Exhibit 3-1.) Article 1, the Uniform Commercial Code, is divided into 10 chapters. They are listed under "Uniform Commercial Code." (See "Number of Chapter" on the first page of Exhibit 3-1.) The chapter governing the sale of goods is Chapter 2, Sales. Each chapter is divided into sections and each section is assigned a number (see "Number of Section" in Exhibit 3-1). Each section contains the actual law that governs a subject. The section of Chapter 2 (Sales) that establishes when a contract must be in writing is assigned the number 201. This section is called Formal Requirements—Statute of Frauds (see § 26-1-2-201 in Exhibit 3-1).
>
> Therefore, if you want to read the law in the Indiana Code governing when a contract must be written, you refer to Title 26 (Commercial Law), Article 1 (Uniform Commercial Code), Chapter 2 (Sales), Section 201 (Statute of Frauds). This is usually referred to numerically as § 26-1-2-201, Statute of Frauds.

B. Short Title

The **short title** is the name by which the statute is known. It is a name that is easy to use when referring to the statute. Included in the example are two short titles: the short title of Article 1 of the Indiana Code, Uniform Commercial Code (§ 26-1-1-101) and the short title of Chapter 2, Uniform Commercial Code—Sales (§ 26-1-2-101). (See "Short Title" on the first and second pages of Exhibit 3-1.)

C. Purpose Clause

The **purpose clause** includes the purpose the legislative body intended to accomplish when drafting the statute. It is helpful in determining the legislative intent. (See "Purpose Clause" in Exhibit 3-1, § 26-1-1-102.)

D. Scope

Some statutes have sections that state specifically what is covered and not covered by the statute. These are called **scope** sections. A researcher should first review this section when analyzing a statute, because a review of this section may allow a determination at the outset whether the statute applies. (See "Scope" in Exhibit 3-1.)

> **For Example** You are researching a question under Indiana law involving a contract that grants a security interest in goods that are being sold. The scope section of the Uniform Commercial Code (§ 26-1-2-102) provides that the section does not apply to such transactions. You know at the outset that the state Uniform Commercial Code does not apply and need not be considered further.

E. Definitions

Some statutes have **definitions** sections that define terms used in the statute. The definitions are helpful in determining the parties and situations covered by the provisions of the statute. Definitions also help in determining if the legislature gave specific meaning to terms within statutes. (See "Definitions" in Exhibit 3-1, § 26-1-1-301.)

F. Substantive Provisions

The substantive sections set forth the substance of the law. (See "Substantive Provisions" in Exhibit 3-1.) They establish the rights and duties of those governed by the statute: that which is required, prohibited, or allowed. A substantive section of the Indiana Code addresses the question posed at the beginning of this section, "When must a contract for the sale of goods be in writing?" (See § 26-1-2-201 in Exhibit 3-1.)

The substantive sections may include sections that provide remedies, such as fines or imprisonment in criminal cases. There may be sections governing procedure, such as which court has jurisdiction over the matters covered by the statute. The substantive provisions are what you usually refer to when addressing the client's legal problem.

G. Other Provisions

Not included in the example in Exhibit 3-1 are other types of statutory sections that you may encounter.

> **For Example** There may be statutory provisions that:
>
> - State which administrative agency is responsible for administering the act
> - Incorporate by reference sections of other statutes
> - Limit the application of the statute through exceptions
> - Establish when the statute takes effect
> - Repeal other statutes
> - State that the statute is cumulative to the case law and that other remedies still exist

H. Annotations/Reference Information

Following each section of a statute, in small print, are references to various sources of information related to the section. This **reference information**, usually referred to as *annotations*, includes:

- The history of the section, including dates of amendment. It may also include summaries of the amendments and previous statutory numbers if the section number has changed due to a recodification (see the first page of Exhibit 3-2)
- Official comments on the section (see the first page of Exhibit 3-2)

63

- Cross-references to other related statutes (see the last page of Exhibit 3-1)
- Library references/research guides—references to other sources that may be useful when analyzing the statute, such as books, digest key numbers (see Chapter 5), law review and other articles, *ALR* cites, and legal encyclopedia cites (*CJS, Am. Jur. 2d*, etc.) that discuss the section (see the last page of Exhibit 3-1 and the first page of Exhibit 3-2)
- Notes to decisions—the name, citation, and summaries of key court decisions that have discussed, analyzed, or interpreted the statute. When a statute has been interpreted or referred to in a large number of cases, the cases are indexed according to subject and each category assigned a number. If you have a question concerning the interpretation of a statute, by scanning the notes you may immediately locate a case on point. This often saves time in locating a case through other means (see the last pages of Exhibit 3-1 and Exhibit 3-2)

Annotations are sources of information and are not part of the statute. They are not the law and do not have legal authority.

It is easier to work with statutes after you have become familiar with their component parts. The material presented here will help you gain that familiarity, but the greatest familiarity comes with practice. Choose a subject of interest and read the statute in your jurisdiction that governs the area.

III. STATUTORY RESEARCH—LOCATING STATUTES

Statutory research is the process of finding the statutory law that applies to a problem. The first two parts of this section discuss statutory research sources, that is, where statutory law can be found. The third part presents research strategies or techniques, that is, how to conduct statutory research. Locating uniform laws and model acts is covered in Chapter 5. Note that the United States Constitution is included with the *United States Code Annotated (USCA)* and the *United States Code Service (USCS)*, the main research sources for federal law, and most state constitutions are included with the state statutes. The research techniques and strategies that apply to statutory research also apply to constitutional research.

A. Federal Law

1. Publication

Each law passed by Congress is assigned a public law number. The number reflects the order in which the law was passed and the session of Congress. For example, Public Law No. 107-35 was the 35th law passed by the 107th session of Congress. The full text of each law is published separately by the United States Government Printing Office and is referred to as a **slip law**. Slip laws are available at most law libraries and many public libraries. The *United States Code Congressional and Administrative News (USCCAN),* published by West Group, presents the complete text of all public laws passed by Congress. It is available by subscription and through Westlaw. In addition, slip laws may be purchased from the United States Government Printing Office (phone: 1-866-512-1800; Web site: www.gpo.gov) or through your congressional representative(s). The Government Printing Office Web site is provided in the "Internet Resources" section of this chapter. Note that each session of Congress lasts one year. Because there is a new Congress every two years with the election of the House of Representatives, there are two sessions for each Congress.

At the end of each session of Congress, the slip laws are placed in chronological order (according to the date the law was passed) and published in volumes titled the *United States Statutes at Large*. Because the laws are placed in chronological order, it is difficult, if not impossible, to conduct research using the *Statutes at Large*. For example, if you were assigned the task of locating the laws relating to the distribution of drugs, you would have to search every volume of the more than 100 volumes. A further impediment to research is that each volume has a separate index. There is no single index that would inform you which volumes contain laws relating to the distribution of drugs.

In 1925, Congress authorized the preparation of the *United States Code (USC)*. Here the laws contained in the *Statutes at Large* are organized (codified) by subject into 50 categories called titles, with each title covering a different area of law. A citation to a *USC* statute refers to the title number, the name of the code, the section, and the year. Note that the year is the copyright date and not the year the statute was enacted.

For Example	18	U.S.C.	§	1115	(2000)
	Title	Code	Section Symbol	Section No.	Year

A new edition is published every six years, and cumulative supplements called *pocket parts* are published for each volume during intervening years. The *USC* is the official code of the laws of the United States. A publication of a code of laws is considered official when the government itself publishes the code or arranges for or directs a commercial publisher to publish the code.

A drawback of the *USC* is that it is unannotated; it merely recites the federal statutes. It does not provide the researcher with the valuable information included in the annotations, such as library references and notes to court decisions that have interpreted the statutes.

The two privately published annotated codes are the *USCA*, published by West Group and also available on Westlaw; and the *USCS*, published by LexisNexis, a division of Reed Elsevier, Inc. (referred to in the remainder of this text as LexisNexis). These codes are considered unofficial codes; that is, they are not published at the direction of the government. A discussion of these annotated codes follows.

2. United States Code Annotated

The *USCA* consists of approximately 200 volumes and includes the General Index. In the front of each volume is a list of the 50 titles of the *USC* (see Exhibit 3-3). Each volume has a table of contents listing the chapters and features in the volume and a cite page listing the citation to use for the volume. The first volumes contain the United States Constitution with annotations. The subsequent volumes include the entire text of the 50 titles of the *USC*, arranged according to the 50 titles of the *USC*. Most titles include a title index as well as appendix material, and each volume is periodically supplemented with pocket parts that update the main text. The appendix material may include previous sections of the *Code of Federal Regulations* and other materials such as international conventions. (See Exhibit 3-2 for an example of a *USCA* section.)

a. General Index

The General Index is a softbound, multivolume set that is updated annually. It consists of descriptive words or phrases, arranged alphabetically, with headings and subheadings. Following each subheading is the title and section number(s) of the relevant statutory provision. When the reference to a section number is followed by the abbreviation *et seq.*, it means that the reference is to a group of sections beginning with that section. (See Exhibit 3-4 for an example of an index page.)

b. Pocket Parts and Supplementary Pamphlets

The hardcover volumes of the *USCA* are updated with pocket parts that are placed in a pocket at the back of each volume. The pocket parts include any revisions to a statute and additional

Exhibit 3-3 *Titles of United States Code and United States Code Annotated.* Reprinted from West Group, United States Code Annotated, List of Titles of United States Code and United States Code Annotated, 2000, from Title 18 U.S.C.A. p.II., with permission of Thomson Reuters.

TITLES OF UNITED STATES CODE
AND UNITED STATES CODE ANNOTATED

1. General Provisions
2. The Congress
3. The President
4. Flag and Seal, Seat of Government, and the States
5. Government Organization and Employees
6. Surety Bonds (*See Title 31, Money and Finance*)
7. Agriculture
8. Aliens and Nationality
9. Arbitration
10. Armed Forces
11. Bankruptcy
12. Banks and Banking
13. Census
14. Coast Guard
15. Commerce and Trade
16. Conservation
17. Copyrights
18. Crimes and Criminal Procedure
19. Customs Duties
20. Education
21. Food and Drugs
22. Foreign Relations and Intercourse
23. Highways
24. Hospitals and Asylums
25. Indians
26. Internal Revenue Code

27. Intoxicating Liquors
28. Judiciary and Judicial Procedure
29. Labor
30. Mineral Land and Mining
31. Money and Finance
32. National Guard
33. Navigation and Navigable waters
34. Navy (*See Title 10, Armed Forces*)
35. Patents
36. Patriotic Societies and National Observances, Ceremonies, and Organizations
37. Pay and Allowances of the Uniformed Services
38. Veterans' Benefits
39. Postal service
40. Public Buildings, Property, and Works
41. Public contracts
42. The Public Health and Welfare
43. Public Lands
44. Public Printing and Documents
45. Railroads
46. Shipping
47. Telegraphs, Telephones, and Radiotelegraphs
48. Territories and Insular Possessions
49. Transportation
50. War and National Defense

annotations, such as recent cases interpreting the statute. If a statutory section is not included in the pocket part, the section has not been amended and there are no new annotations. The pocket parts are cumulative—they update the volume from the date of the volume's publication. For example, if the hardbound volume was published in 2004, then the 2009 pocket part will include all the changes, updates, and new cases construing the statutes contained in the volume during 2005, 2006, 2007, and 2008.

If the pocket part is too large to fit in the back of a volume, the publisher will produce a soft-bound supplement that sits next to the volume. Occasionally, a new hardbound volume is printed that includes the information contained in the pocket part or supplements. When this occurs, the publisher places in the pocket the notice: "This Volume Contains No Pocket Part." If there is no pocket part and no notice that the volume does not contain a pocket part, assume that the pocket part is missing and check with the librarian. (See Exhibit 3-5 for an example of a portion of a pocket part.)

Exhibit 3-4 *Excerpt from the U.S.C.A. General Index.* Reprinted from West Group, United States Code Annotated, General Index (2000), p. 787.

KEROSENE

Reference to Title 7 Section 515 and the Sections that follow ——

Reference to Title and —— Section

KEROSENE—Cont'd
Summer Fill and Fuel Budgeting Programs,
    42 § 6283
KERR-MILLS ACT
Medical Assistance, generally, this index
KERR-SMITH TOBACOO CONRTOL ACT
Generally, 7 § 515 et seq.
—KETOBEMIDONE
Controlled Substance, generally, this index
KETTLE RIVER
Wild and scenic rivers, 16 § 1276
KETTLEHOLES
Ice Age National Scientific Reserve, generally,
    this index
KEWEENAW NATIONAL HISTORICAL PARK
Generally, 16 § 410yy et seq.
KEY LARGO CORAL REEF PRESERVE
Genarally, 16 § 461, nt, PN 3339
KEY LARGO NATIONAL MARINE
    SANCTUARY
Designation, 16 § 1433 nt
KEYS
Defense Department, Security, theft,
    forgery, fines, penalties and forfeitures,
    18 § 1386
Internal Revenue Service, proprietors of distilled
    spirits plants to furnish to Secretary,
    26 § 5203
KHMER REPUBLIC
Kampuchca, generally, this index
KIAVAH WILDERNESS
Generally, 16 § 1132 nt
KICK-BACK RACKET ACT
Generally, 40 § 276c
Public Building, Property, and Works, generally,
    this index
KICK-BACKS
Anti-Kickback, generally, this index Health insur-
    ance for aged and disabled,
    42 § 1320a-7b
Income tax, deductions, 26 § 162
Medical assistance programs, grants to States for,
    criminal penalty, 42 § 1320a-7b
Presidential Election Campaign Fund,
    26 § 9012
Presidential primary matching payment account,
    26 § 9042
Public works, 18 § 874
Real Estate Settlement Procedures,
    this index Sentence and punishment,
    18 USSG §2B4.1
KICKAPOO INDIANS
Indians, this index
KIDNAPPING
Generally, 18 § 1201 et seq.
Aircraft, jurisdiction, 18 § 1201
Attempts, 18 § 1201
Attorney General, this index

KIDNAPPING—Cont'd
Banks and banking, robbery, 18 § 2113
Cabinet departments, heads and deputies,
    Interception of wire, oral, or electronic
    communications, 18 § 2516
    Kidnapping, attempts, conspiracy, penalties
    and forfeitures, 18 § 351
Chief Justice of Supreme Court, kidnapping,
    attempts, conspiracy, fines, penalties and
    forfeitures, 18 § 351
Children and Minors, this index
CIA, director, deputy director, fines, penalties and
    forfeitures, 18 § 351
Congress, this index
Conspiracy,
    Against right of inhabitants, fines, penalties
    and forfeitures, 18 § 241
    Fines, penalties and forfeitures, 18 § 1201
    Foreign countries, 18 § 956
Deprivation of rights under color of law, fines,
    penalties and forfeitures, 18 § 242
Domestic violence, parental kidnapping, reports,
    28 § 1738A nt
Employee Retirement Income Security Program,
    protection of employee benefit rights,
    fiduciary responsibility, 29 § 1111
Evidence, congress, cabinet department heads,
    knowledge, 18 § 351
Fair housing, sale or rental, intimidation,
    interference, penalties, 42 § 3631
FBI database, crimes against children,
    registration, 42 § 14072
Federal officials, fines, penalties and forfeitures,
    18 § 1201
Federally protected activities, intimidation, inter-
    ference, fines, penalties and forfeitures,
    18 § 245
Fines, penalties and forfeitures, 18 §1201
    Indian lands and reservations, 18 § 1153
    Ransom money, 18 § 1202
    Transportation, interstate commerce, 18 § 1201
Foreign countries.
Children and minors, 42 § 11608a
Conspiracy, 18 § 956
U.S. citizens, 22 § 2715a
Foreign Diplomatic and Consular Officers, this
    index
Forfeitures. Fines, penalties and forfeitures,
    generally, ante
Indians, this index
Interception of wire, oral, or electronic
    communications, President, congress,
    18 § 2516
International Child Abduction Remedies,
    generally, this index
Interstate and Foreign Commerce, this index
Involuntary servitude, intent to sell, 18 § 1583
Jurisdiction,
    Indian Lands and reservations, 18 § 3242
    Internationally protected persons, victims,
    18 § 1201

Exhibit 3-5 *Pocket Part Update for 17 U.S.C.A § 511. Reprinted from West Group, United States Code Annotated, 2001 Cumulative Annual Pocket, Title 17 § 511, p. 27, with permission of Thomson Reuters.*

Amendment to law

§511. Liability of States, instrumentalities of States, and State official for infringement of copyright

(a) In General.—Any State, any instrumentality of a States, and any officer for employee of a States or instrumentality of a State acting in his or her official capacity, shall not be immune, under the Eleventh Amendment of the Constitution of the United States or under any other doctrine of sovereign immunity, from suit in Federal court by any person, including any governmental or nongovernmental entity, for a violation of any of the exclusive rights of a copyright owner provided by section 106 through 121, for importing copies of phonorecords in violation of section 602, or for any other violation under this title.

[See main volume for text of (b)]

(As amended Pub L. 106-14, § 1(g)(6), Aug. 5, 1999, 113 Stat. 222.)

HISTORICAL AND STATUORY NOTES

Amendments
    1999 Amendments. Subsec. (a). Pub.L.
106-44, § 1(g)(6), substituted "121" for "119."

LIBRARY REFERENCES

Text and Treatises
    Business and Commercial Litigation in Federal Courts §§ 65.2, 65.3, 65.4, 65.10, 65.15 (Robert L. Haig ed.) (West Group & ABA 1998)

7A Fed Proc L Ed, Copyrights § 18:187

NOTES OF DECISIONS

New annotations

Constitutionality 1/2
Immunity 2
Waiver 3

1/2. Constitutionality
    Statute purporting to abrogate states' sovereign immunity in copyright infringement suits was not enacted pursuant to a valid exercise of congressional power to enforce the guarantees of the Fourteenth Amendment's due process clause and thus did not validly waive states' immunity. Rodriguez v. Texas Com'n on the Arts, C.A.5 (Tex.) 2000, 199 F.3d 279, 53 U.S.P.Q.2d 1383.

2. Immunity
    Provisions of Copyright Art and Lanham Act that purported to require states to submit to suit in federal court for violation of those statutes exceeded Congress's constitutional powers. Chavez v. Arte Publico Press, C.A.5

(Tex) 1998.157 F.3d 282, rehearing granted, vacated 178 F.3d 601, 53 U.S.P.Q.2d 2009.
    University employee who allegedly authorized printing of copies of author's book in violation of Copyright Act was entitled to qualified immunity, where contractual provision relating to duration of university's publishing license was ambiguous and was susceptible of interpretation that permitted employee's actions. Chavez v. Arte Publico Press, C A.5 (Tex.) 1995, 59 F.3d 539, 35 U.S.P.Q.2d 1609, vacated 116 S.Ct. 1667, 517 U.S. 1184, 134 L.Ed.3d 772, on remand 139 F.3d 504, 46 U.S.P.Q.2d 1541, on remand 157 F.3d 282, certiorari denied 116 S.Ct. 1672, 517, U.S. 1187, 134 L.E.d.2d 776.

3.Waiver
    University waived its Eleventh Amendment immunity from suit for copyright infringement . . .

Pocket parts are published only once a year. To ensure that the information contained in the *USCA* is current, supplemental pamphlets, titled "Statutory Supplements," are published every three to four months following the publication of the pocket part. Like pocket parts, they include any revisions to a statute and additional annotations. These pamphlets are not cumulative; each one covers a specific time period. This means that you must check each supplement when updating your research. These supplemental pamphlets are usually located at the end of the *USCA* set. *You must always check the pocket parts and supplemental pamphlets to ensure that your research is current and that there have not been changes in the law subsequent to the publication of the main volume.*

c. Popular Name Table

Statutes are often referred to by a popular name, such as the Americans with Disabilities Act or the Freedom of Information Act. If you know a statute's popular name but do not know the citation, a quick way to locate the statute is through the popular name table found in the last volume of the General Index. The table provides you with the public law number, the *Statutes at Large* citation, and the title and section numbers. (See Exhibit 3-6 for a page from the table.)

d. Conversion Tables

If you know the *Statutes at Large* citation, the public law number, or the year and chapter of a law, you can use the conversion tables to find where the law is classified in the *USCA*. The conversion tables are located in the tables volumes. They are published annually, and updates are located at the end of each noncumulative supplement. (See Exhibit 3-7 for an example of a conversion table page.)

3. United States Code Service

LexisNexis publishes the *USCS*. It consists of approximately 150 volumes and contains the wording of the federal statutes published in the *Statutes at Large*. The *USCS* and *USCA* are competitive sets, published by different publishers to accomplish the same basic task: to publish the federal laws and provide the information necessary for researchers to interpret and answer questions concerning federal law. Sample pages from the *USCS* are presented in Exhibit 3-8.

The sets are similar in most respects; therefore, most researchers do not use both sets. Which set you use is often based on availability or personal preference. The similarities and differences between the sets are presented here.

Similarities between the two sets are:

1. They are organized in the same way. The organization is based on the 50 titles of the *USC*. For example, Title 42 Section 1983 will be found at 42 U.S.C.A. § 1983 and 42 U.S.C.S. § 1983.

2. They have general indexes, popular name tables, and conversion tables.

3. They are annotated. In both sets, the annotations provide information on the history of the statute, direct you to other research sources, and briefly summarize cases that have construed the statute.

4. They are similarly updated. Both sets are updated annually with pocket parts for each volume and supplemental pamphlets.

Differences between the two sets are:

1. The *USCA* includes more court decisions in the "Notes of Decisions" section of the annotations. The *USCS* tends to be more selective and reference only the more significant cases.

2. The "Research Guide" section of the *USCS* annotations is more comprehensive than the "Library Reference" section of the *USCA*, in that it includes more references to research sources.

Exhibit 3-6 *U.S.C.A. Popular Name Table Page. Reprinted from West Group, United States Code Annotated, Popular Name Table (2000), p. 787, with permission of Thomson Reuters.*

POPULAR NAME TABLE

Freedom of Information Act (FOIA)
  Pub.L. 89-487, July 4, 1966, 80 Stat. 250 (See 5 § 552)
  Pub.L. 90-23, § 1, June 5, 1967, 81 Stat. 54 (5 § 552)
  Pub.L. 93-502, §§ 1 to 3, Nov. 21, 1974, 88 Stat. 1561 (5 § 552)
Freedom of Information Reform Act of 1986
  Pub.L. 99-570, Title I, Subtitle N, Oct. 27, 1986, 100 Stat. 3204-48 (5 §§ 552, 552 notes)
FREEDOM Support Act
  See Freedom for Russia and Emerging Eurasian Democracies and Open Markets
    Support Act of 1992
Freedom to E-File Actw
  Pub.L. 106-222, June 20, 2000, 114 Stat. 353 (7 §§ 6901 note, 7031 to 7035)
Freedom to Farm Law
  See Emergency Farm Financial Relief Act
French Spoliation Claims Act
  Jan. 20, 1885, ch. 25, 23 Stat 283

U.S.C.A. Citation

Fresh Cut Flowers and Fresh Cut Greens Promotion and Information Act of 1993
  Pub.L. 103-190, Dec. 14, 1993, 107 Stat. 2266 (7 §§ 6801, 6801 note, 6802 to 6814)

Public law number

FRIENDSHIP Act
  See Act For Reform In Emerging New Democracies and Support and Help for
    Improved Partnership with Russia, Ukraine, and other New Independent States

Statutes at Large citation

FRLA
  See Federal Regulation of Lobbying Act
FRRAPA
  See Forest and Rangeland Renewable Resources Planning Act of 1974
FRRRRA
  See Forest and Rangeland Renewable Resource Research Act of 1978
FRSA
  See Federal Railroad Safety Act of 1970
Frye Acts
  See Shipping Acts
FSC Repeal and Extraterritorial Income Exclusion Act of 200 (Foreign Sales Corporation
  Repeal and Extraterritorial Income Exclusion Act of 2000)
  Pub l. 106-519, Nov. 15, 2000. 114 Stat, 2423 (see Tables for classification)
FSIA
  See Foreign Sovereign Immunities Act of 1976
FSLMRA
  See Federal Service Labour-Management Relations Act
FSPA
  See Uniformed Services Former Spouses Protection Act
FTCA
  See Federal Tort Claims Act
FTCPMA
  See Federal Timber Contract Payment Modification Act
Fuel Distribution Act
  Sept. 22, 1922, ch. 413, 42 Stat. 1025
Fugitive Felon Act
  June 22, 1932, ch. 271, § 1, 47 Stat. 326
  May 18, 1934, ch. 301, 48 Stat. 301 (See 18 § 1073)
Fugitive Slave Laws
  Sept. 18, 1850, ch. 60, 9 Stat. 462
  June 28, 1864, ch. 166, 13 Stat. 200

Exhibit 3-7 *U.S.C.A. Excerpt from Conversion Table.* Reprinted from West Group, United States Code Annotated, Conversion Table (2000), p. 1542, with permission of Thomson Reuters.

106-546			**2000**

```
106-546...   § 1 ............. 114 Stat 2726 ............. 42 §13701
             § 2 ............. 114 Stat 2726 ............. 42 §14135
             § 3 ............. 114 Stat 2728 ............. 42 § 14135a
             § 4 ............. 114 Stat 2730 ............. 42 § 14135b
             § 5(a)(1)......... 114 Stat 2731 ............. 10 § 1565
             § 5(a)(2)......... 114 Stat 2732 ............. 10prec. 1561
             § 5(b) ........... 114 Stat 2733 ............. 10 § 1565 nt
             § 5(c) ........... 114 Stat 2733 ............. 10 § 1565 nt
             § 6(a) ........... 114 Stat 2733 ............. 28 § 531 nt
             § 6(b)(1)......... 114 Stat 2733 ............. 42 § 14132
             § 6(b)(2)......... 114 Stat 2733 ............. 42 § 14132
             § 6(b)(3)......... 114 Stat 2733 ............. 42 § 14132
             § 6(b)(4)......... 114 Stat 2733 ............. 42 § 14132
             § 7(a)(1) ........ 114 Stat 2734 ............. 18 § 3563
             § 7(a)(2) ........ 114 Stat 2734 ............. 18 § 3563
             § 7(a)(3) ........ 114 Stat 2734 ............. 18 § 3563
             § 7 (b)........... 114 Stat 2734 ............. 18 § 4209
             § 7(c) ........... 114 Stat 2734 ............. 42 § 14135c
             § 7(d) ........... 114 Stat 2734 ............. 42 § 14135c
             § 8(a) ........... 114 Stat 2734 ............. 42 § 3733
             § 8(b) ........... 114 Stat 2735 ............. 42 § 3796kk-2
             § 8(c) ........... 114 Stat 2735 ............. 42 § 14133
             § 9 ............. 114 Stat 2735 ............. 42 § 14135d
             § 10 ............. 114 Stat 2735 ............. 42 § 14135e
             § 11 ............. 114 Stat 2735 ............. 42 § 14135 nt
106-547...   § 1 ............. 114 Stat 2738 ............. 18 § 700 nt
             § 2(a) ........... 114 Stat 2738 ............. 18 § 1036
             § 2(b) ........... 114 Stat 2738 ............. 18prec. 1001
             § 3(a) ........... 114 Stat 2739 ............. 18 §716
             § 3(b) ........... 114 Stat 2740 ............. 18prec. 700
106-548...—  ................. 114 Stat 2741 ............. – § —........... Uncl.
106-549...—  ................. 114 Stat 2743 ............. – § —........... Uncl.
106-550...   § 1 ............. 114 Stat 2745 ............. 36prec. 101 nt
             § 2 ............. 114 Stat 2745 ............. 36prec. 101 nt
             § 3 ............. 114 Stat 2746 ............. 36prec. 101 nt
             § 4 ............. 114 Stat 2746 ............. 36prec. 101 nt
             § 5 ............. 114 Stat 2747 ............. 36prec. 101 nt
             § 6 ............. 114 Stat 2748 ............. 36prec. 101 nt
             § 7 ............. 114 Stat 2749 ............. 36prec. 101 nt
             § 8 ............. 114 Stat 2749 ............. 36prec. 101 nt
             § 9 ............. 114 Stat 2750 ............. 36prec. 101 nt
             § 10 ............. 114 Stat 2750 ............. 36prec. 101 nt
             § 11 ............. 114 Stat 2751 ............. 36prec. 101 nt
             § 12 ............. 114 Stat 2751 ............. 36prec. 101 nt
Dec. 20, 2000  106-331...  § 1 ............. 114 Stat 2752 ............. 42 § 201 nt
             § 2 ............. 114 Stat 2752 ............. 42 § 287a-3a
             § 3 ............. 114 Stat 2759 ............. 42 § 287-3a nt
```

*Labels on diagram:*
- **Public law number** (pointing to 106-547)
- **Statutes at Large citation** (pointing to 114 Stat column)
- **U.S.C.A. Citation** (pointing to U.S.C.A. column)

Exhibit 3-8 Title 18 U.S.C.S 1202. *Lawyers Cooperative Publishing, United States Code Service, Title 18 Crimes & Criminal Procedure § 1202 (1994), p. 2000. Reprinted with permission of LexisNexis.*

18 USCS § 1201, N 64

64. Appellate review

In prosecution under predecessor to 18 USCS § 1201, objection that letter which codefendant had taken from kidnapped victim and which was later found by police in defendant's apartment was obtained by illegal search could not be raised for first time on appeal from conviction. Eaker v United States (1935, CA.10 Colo) 76 F2d 267.

Defendant who had been convicted of interstate transportation of person who had been unlawfully kidnapped could not by writ of habeas corpus applied for in United States District Court for Western District of Oklahoma affect his sentence for such unlawful interstate transportation rendered in United States District Court for Northern District of Texas, nor cause his trial for kidnapping offense in Western District of Oklahoma, wherein no charge for such offense was pending against

CRIMES & CRIMINAL PROCEDURE

him. Trafford v Yellow Cab Co. (1961, CA3 Pa) 293 F2d 43.

65. Habeas corpus proceedings

Whether defendant was member of conspiracy and did conspire in violation of law raised issue of fact, and where that issue was resolved against him in trial court, it could not be relitigated in habeas corpus proceeding. Hudspeth v McDonald (1941, CA10 Kan) 120 F2d 962, cert den (1941) 314 US 617, 86 L Ed 496, 62 S Ct 110, reh den (1945) 325 US 892, 89 L Ed 2004, 65 S Ct 1181.

Motion to vacate sentence for kidnapping conviction of 30 years will be denied when petitioner was adequately made aware of charge against him and where his plea of guilty was voluntarily entered into without fear of death penalty. Wilson v United States (1969, WD Va) 303 F Supp 1139.

§ 1202. Ransom money

Whoever receives, possesses, or disposes of any money or other property, or any portion thereof, which has at any time been delivered as ransom or reward in connection with a violation of section 1201 of this title, knowing the same to be money or property which has been at any time delivered as such ransom or reward, shall be fined not more than $10,000 or imprisoned not more than ten years, or both.

(June 25, 1948, ch 645, § 1, 62 Stat. 760.)

HISTORY; ANCILLARY LAWS AND DIRECTIVES

Prior law and revision:

This section is based on Act June 22, 1932, ch 271, § 4, as added Jan. 24, 1936, ch 29, 49 Stat. 1099 (former 18 U.S.C. § 408c-1).

The words "in the penitentiary" after "imprisoned" were omitted in view of 18 USCS § 4082 committing prisoners to the custody of the Attorney General.

Minor charges in phraseology were made.

CROSS REFERENCES

Sentencing guidelines, Statutory Index, Sentencing Guidelines for U.S. Courts, 18 USCS Appendix.

RESEARCH GUIDE

Annotations:

What constitutes violation of 18 USCS 1202, Prohibiting receipt, possession, or disposition of ransom money. 31 ALR Fed 916.

INTERPRETIVE NOTES AND DECISIONS

1. Generally
2. Relationship with other laws
3. Delivery of ransom

4. Conspiracy
5. Jurisdiction
6. Indictment

Exhibit 3-8 *(Continued)*

CRIMES   **18 USCS § 1203**

1. Generally

18 USCS § 1202 was intended to extend federal jurisdiction to persons having only indirect connection with actual kidnapping and to discourage any co-operation with those primarily responsible. United States v Ortega (1975, CA3 NJ) 517 F2d 1006, 31 ALR Fed 909.

2. Relationship with other laws

18 USCS § 1202 is not separate, detached violation with regard to primary federal kidnapping statute (18 USCS § 1201) and § 1202 is directed to only portion of larger offense which includes number of components. United States v Ortega (1975, CA3 NJ) 517 F2d 1006, 31 ALR Fed 909.

Establishing violation of 18 USCS § 1202 requires proof of money or property which was delivered as ransom or reward, elements that are clearly not identical to any of elements of USCS § 1201 kidnapping offense, and therefore trial court was correct in refusing to instruct that § 1201. Durns v United States (1977, CA8 Mo) 562 F2d 542, 2 Fed Rules Evid Serv 462, cert den (1977) 434 US 959, 54 L Ed 2d 319, 98 S Ct 490.

3. Delivery of ransom

For ransom to have been "delivered" within meaning of § 1202 does not require transfer of possession to kidnappers; all that is needed is for transferor to have placed ransom at place specified by kidnappers, and fact that transferor may have mistak-

enly placed ransom at wrong location does not vitiate "delivery" for purposes of § 1202; thus, violation thereof occurred where defendant found and appropriated ransom mistakenly delivered and concealed fact after learning that it was ransom United States v Ortega (1975, CA3 NJ) 517 F2d 1006, 31 ALR Fed 909.

4. Conspiracy

Conspiracy to violate predecessor to 18 USCS § 1202 began with plan to abduct and ended when ransom money was changed into unmarked money. Laska v United States (1936, CA10 Okla) 82 F2d 672, cert den (1936) 298 US 689, 80 L Ed 1407, 56 S Ct 957.

5. Jurisdiction

18 USCS § 1202 being prohibition of integral part of kidnapping scheme which concededly is within federal jurisdiction, violation of prohibition is within federal jurisdiction even if interstate commerce is not directly involved. United States v Ortega (1975, CA3 NJ) 517 F2d 1006, 31 ALR Fed 909.

6. Indictment

Indictment charging defendant with three separate offenses of transmitting communications in interstate commerce demanding ransom money under 18 USCS § 875(a) and with receiving, possessing and disposing of ransom money in violation of 18 USCS § 1202, is not duplicative as each count charges separate offense. Amsler v United States (1967, CA9 Cal) 381 F2d 37.

---

3. The supplements to the *USCS*, called the *Cumulative Later Case and Statutory Service*, are cumulative. Therefore, you need check only the latest supplement. The *USCS* also publishes a monthly pamphlet called *U.S.C.S. Advance*, which includes new public laws, presidential proclamations, and executive orders.

4. In the *USCA*, the topics covered in the "Notes to the Decisions" are arranged alphabetically; in the *USCS*, the "Interpretive Notes and Decisions" are arranged according to topic (see Exhibit 3-2 and Exhibit 3-8).

B. State Statutory Law and Codes

The enactment and publication of state legislation varies in detail from state to state, but they are similar in many respects to the federal system. Most states initially publish their laws in pamphlets similar to the federal slip laws. When the legislative session is over, the laws are published in books often referred to as *session laws*. These are similar to the *Statutes at Large* in that the laws are presented in the order in which they were passed.

State laws are then organized according to topic (codified) and published with annotations similar to those in the *USCA* and *USCS*. Most state codes are similar to the *USCA* and *USCS* in the following ways:

- Each set has a general index, and some sets have a separate index following each title.
- Some statutes have popular name tables and conversion tables that allow you to locate statutes that have been renumbered or repealed.
- The statutes are organized by subject, with each subject title being subdivided into chapters and so on. (See Exhibit 3-1 and section II.A in this chapter.)
- The state constitution with annotations is included in the code.
- State codes are usually updated annually by some form of supplement. These may be pocket parts inserted in the statutory volume or separate pamphlets.
- State statutes are annotated. The annotations include the history of the section, cross-references to other statutes, research guides, and notes to court decisions (see Exhibit 3-1).

C. The Research Process—Techniques and Strategies

1. Locate the Statute

Inasmuch as federal and state codifications share similar features, the process for locating and researching federal and state constitutional and statutory law is essentially the same, and thus are discussed together here.

The beginning step of all research, including statutory research, is to identify what you are looking for as precisely and narrowly as possible. Define your research question as specifically, and in as concise terms, as possible. Time spent narrowing the focus of your search will save a great deal of research time later. A tightly focused identification of the research question saves time because the researcher is immediately directed to the specific area of the law in question and does not waste time searching multiple statutes.

> **For Example** The question involves the issue of whether a shareholder of a corporation must attend a meeting in person to vote on an issue. If a researcher thinks, "Oh, this is a corporation question" and immediately looks at corporations in the index to the statutes, the researcher will waste time looking through the entire corporation section. If the research is conducted electronically and the search term is simply *corporations,* all the corporation statutes will come up. If, however, the research is focused to *corporations, shareholders, meetings of corporations, shareholders,* and *voting,* the search is narrowed at the outset and the statute is located more quickly, whether the research is manual or electronic.

Consult Chapter 10 for guidance on how to narrow the focus of your search by narrowly identifying the issue. See Chapter 2, section III.A, for help in identifying search terms.

After you have defined your search as specifically and concisely as possible, you have three main ways to approach locating a statute, as discussed here.

a. General Index

The most common approach to locating statutes is to use the General Index. When using this approach, identify as specifically as possible the words that describe the problem. If the term you initially use is not the term used in the index, the index often will refer you to the correct term. For example, if you are looking for statutes concerning trailers, the index under *trailers* may read, "See Manufactured Homes." (See Exhibit 3-4 for an example of an index page.)

After you have found the correct index entry, the index will list the appropriate title and section. With that information, you can locate statutes in the appropriate statutory volume. Most statutes are arranged by title and the titles covered in each volume are indicated on the spine. For example, the spine may read "Titles 5–7," thus indicating that Titles 5 through 7 of the code are included in that volume. Be sure to check the index pocket part if you cannot find a term in the main index volume. It may be that the term has been recently added to the index.

b. Title Table of Contents

Most statutory codifications include a table of contents at the beginning of each title that lists the name and number of the chapters within the title. At the beginning of each chapter, a table of contents typically lists the statutory section number and name of each section. If you know the number of the title you are looking for, you can go directly to the volume and scan the table to quickly locate a statute. It is not necessary to consult the General Index.

> **For Example** You want to locate the statutory definition of a term in the Indiana Commercial Code and you know from experience that the commercial code is Title 26. You can go directly to Title 26 and scan the table of contents to Chapter 1 and immediately locate the appropriate section, "26-1-1-201 General Definitions." (See the first page of Exhibit 3-1.)

Beginning researchers should be aware that some subjects are covered by more than one set of laws. Therefore, referring to a specific title requires that the researcher be sufficiently familiar with the law to know that the search topic is covered only by that title.

> **For Example** The question being researched involves identifying the statutes that govern a loan. Several statutes may cover loans: the commercial paper chapter of the commercial law title of the code, the state's small loan act, and the federal truth-in-lending statutes.

Always consult the General Index and identify all the possible titles that cover the research topic.

c. Popular Name

Many laws are commonly known by their popular name, such as the Good Samaritan Act or the Truth in Lending Act. Many state statutes and the *USCA* and *USCS* have popular name tables listing in alphabetical order the popular names and citation. The tables are usually located with the table of contents volume(s) or as a separate volume. *Shepard's Acts and Cases by Popular Name: Federal and State* also lists the popular names and citations of federal and state laws. If you know the popular name of the act you are looking for, consult the popular name table, and you will be directed to the appropriate section of the statutes.

2. Update Your Research

After you locate a statute, check the pocket parts and supplementary pamphlets to ensure that the statute published in the main volume has not been amended or repealed. Also check the annotations to locate new case law that may affect the interpretation of the statute. *Shepard's Citations* provides updates to state and federal statutes and is published more frequently than state and federal pocket parts and supplementary pamphlets. The process of updating research through the use of *Shepard's Citations* is called "Shepardizing." *Shepard's* is discussed in Chapter 5.

D. Computer-Aided Research

You may research state and federal statutes online by using Westlaw and LexisNexis. In addition, you may access most federal and state laws without a fee through various sites on the Internet. You may locate many through state and federal government Web sites, college and university Web sites, and http://www.findlaw.com. Some of these sites are located in the "Internet Resources" section of this chapter. Also, many annotated statutes are available on CD-ROM through the publisher. Computer-aided statutory research using Westlaw, LexisNexis, and others is discussed in Chapter 7.

E. Ethics—Competence and Diligence

There are considerations of **ethics** to keep in mind when conducting any type of research, whether it be on enacted law, case law, or secondary authority. Rule 1.1 of the American Bar Association's Model Rules of Professional Conduct requires that a client be provided competent representation. Rule 1.3 provides that a client be represented with diligence and promptness. These rules mean that a researcher must possess sufficient knowledge of the law and legal research to research completely the issues raised by the facts of the client's case. They also mean that all avenues of research must be pursued promptly and explored thoroughly.

IV. ADMINISTRATIVE LAW

As discussed in Chapter 1, federal and state legislatures delegate the task of administering laws to administrative agencies. The legislatures pass enabling legislation that authorizes administrative agencies to carry out the intent of the legislature. This enabling legislation usually includes a grant of authority to create the rules and regulations necessary to carry out the law. These rules and regulations have the authority of law; they are primary authority. The body of law that results from the rules and regulations and the court opinions interpreting them is called **administrative law**. The terms *rules* and *regulations* are often used interchangeably when discussing administrative law. To avoid repetition, the term *regulation*, when used in this section, includes both administrative rules and regulations.

On occasion you may be called upon to research issues involving the interpretation or application of an administrative agency regulation.

> **For Example** The client's business is fined by the Occupational Safety and Health Administration (OSHA) for failure to have fire extinguishers located in the proper places in the business. The client challenges OSHA's interpretation of the agency's regulation governing fire extinguishers. Research would be necessary to locate the regulation and the court opinions that have addressed the regulation.

A. Federal Administrative Law

This section discusses research involving the location and interpretation of federal administrative regulations.

1. Publication

Administrative regulations are published in two sources, the *Federal Register* and the *Code of Federal Regulations*.

a. Federal Register

The *Federal Register* is published daily by the United States Government Printing Office. All proposed new regulations, amended regulations, interim and final regulations are published in the *Federal Register*. It also contains summaries of regulations, effective dates, notices of hearings on proposed regulations, and persons to contact for further information. Presidential documents, such as executive orders, are included in the *Federal Register*.

The *Federal Register* includes a table of contents in the front of each issue, arranged by agency (see Exhibit 3-9). At the end of each issue is a section called "Reader Aids" that includes valuable information such as a list of telephone numbers to obtain information, and a table of "CFR Parts Affected" that lists parts and sections of the *Code of Federal Regulations* affected. The pagination of the *Federal Register* is continuous, beginning with the first issue of a year and ending with the last. Therefore, the first page of the first issue of the year will be page 1 and the last issue of the year will end with a page number somewhere around 90,000. The issues are not cumulative; thus, using the *Federal Register* as a research source is difficult.

In addition, a cumulative *Federal Register Index* is published at the end of each month. This index, which is arranged by agency, references all the information published in the previous months of the year.

b. Code of Federal Regulations

It is much easier to conduct regulatory research using the *Code of Federal Regulations (CFR)* for regulations that were published a year or more ago. The regulations of administrative

Exhibit 3-9 *Screenshot of Electronic Table of Contents of Federal Register. Source: http://www.gpo.gov/fdsys/search/getfrtoc.action*

agencies are codified in this multivolume, softbound set of books. The regulations are published in 50 titles, each of which represents a different subject area. The title numbers often, but not always, correspond to the titles assigned in the *United States Code*. The titles are subdivided into chapters, and each chapter usually covers the regulations of an individual agency. The chapters are divided into parts that consist of regulations governing a specific topic. The parts are divided into sections that are the specific regulations (see Exhibit 3-10). The code is reprinted annually on a quarterly basis; that is, one-fourth of the code is reprinted each quarter. Titles 1 through 16 are issued each January; Titles 17 through 27 are issued each April 1; Titles 28 through 41 are issued each July 1; and Tiles 42 through 50 are issued each October 1.

There is a table of contents for each title, chapter, and part. At the end of each title is an index. In addition, there is an index volume (*CFR Index and Finding Aids*) through which regulations may be located by subject matter or agency (see Exhibit 3-11). The index includes a parallel table that allows you to locate the *CFR* title if you know the citation of the *USC* statute that established the agency. The index also includes a list of the agencies and 50 titles, chapters, and parts.

2. Researching Federal Administrative Law

Due to its organization, it is easier to locate federal rules and regulations through the *Code of Federal Regulations* than the *Federal Register*; therefore, the following guides focus on researching the *CFR*.

a. Indexes and Table of Contents

You may locate regulations in the *CFR* by subject matter or agency by consulting the *CFR Index and Finding Aids* volume. If you know the number of the *USC* enabling statute, you may locate the code title in the *Parallel Table of Authorities and Rules* in the index volume or the electronic version of the parallel table at www.gpo.gov/help/parallel_table.pdf. If you already know the code title or section, you may go directly to the code volume and scan the table of contents for the title to locate the appropriate section. You may also consult the index following the title.

You may also locate regulations through the *Index to the Code of Federal Regulations*. This commercial publication by the Congressional Information Service indexes the *CFR* by subject and geographic information. Another print index is *West's Code of Federal Regulations, General Index*. This index provides access to the C.F.R. by subject matter or geographic location. Both are usually available at a law library.

b. Other Sources for Locating Rules and Regulations

You may be directed to specific *CFR* sections by other publications. If you know the statute that established the administrative agency, the annotations following the statute in the *USCA* or *USCS* may include cross-references to specific *CFR* sections. Other secondary sources, such as law review articles and *ALR* annotations, may reference specific *CFR* sections.

c. Federal Register

Inasmuch as the *CFR* is updated annually and issued in parts, it will be necessary to refer to the *Federal Register* to locate rules and regulations published since the last time the *CFR* volumes were issued. Consult the latest *Federal Register Index*, issued monthly, to locate rules and regulations promulgated after the issuance of the latest *CFR* volumes. Entries in the *Federal Register Index* are alphabetical by agency. There is also a section called "Reader Aids" at the end of each daily *Federal Register* that lists sections of the CFR affected, reminders of effective dates, and other helpful information.

Exhibit 3-10 *Page from the Code of Federal Regulations (C.F.R.). Code of Federal Regulations, Title 16, Part 1000 to End, Commercial Practices (2001), p. 7, National Archives and Records Administration, Washington, DC.*

Subchapter ——————————— **SUBCHAPTER A—GENERAL**

Part ———————— **PART 1000—COMMISSION ORGANIZATION AND FUNCTIONS**

Section

Sec.
1000.1   The Commission.
1000.2   Laws administered.
1000.3   Hotline.
1000.4   Commission address.
1000.5   Petitions.
1000.6   Commission decisions and records.
1000.7   Advisory opinions and interpretations of regulations.
1000.8   Meetings and hearings; public notice.
1000.9   Quorum.
1000.10   The Chairman and Vice Chairman.
1000.11   Delegation of functions.
1000.12   Organizational structure.
1000.13   Directives system.
1000.14   Office of the General Counsel.
1000.15   Office of Congressional Relations.
1000.16   Office of the Secretary.
1000.17   Office of the Inspector General.
1000.18   Office of Equal Employment Opportunity and Minority Enterprise.
1000.19   Office of the Executive Director.
1000.20   Office of the Budget.
1000.21   Office of Hazard Identification and Reduction.
1000.22   Office of Planning and Evaluation.
1000.23   Office of Information and Public Affairs.
1000.24   Office of Compliance.
1000.25   Office of Human Resources Management.
1000.26   Office of Information Services.
1000.27   Directorate for Epidemiology.
1000.28   Directorate for Health Sciences.
1000.29   Directorate for Economic Analysis
1000.30   Directorate for Engineering Sciences.
1000.31   Directorate for Laboratory Sciences.
1000.32   Directorate for Administration.
1000.33   Directorate for Field Operations.

AUTHORITY: 5 U.S.C. 552(a).

SOURCE: 56 FR 30496, July 3, 1991, unless otherwise noted.

§1000.1 The Commission.

(a) The Consumer Product Safety Commission is an independent regulatory agency which was formed on May 14, 1973, under the provisions of the Consumer Product Safety Act (Pub. L. 92-573, 86 Stat. 1207, as amended (1.5 U.S.C. 2051, et seq.)). The purposes of the Commission under the CPSA are:

(1) To protect the public against unreasonable risks of injury associated with consumer products;

(2) To assist consumers in evaluating the comparative safety of consumer products;

(3) To develop uniform safety standards for consumer products and to minimize conflicting State and local regulations; and

(4) To promote research and investigation into the causes and prevention of product-related deaths, illnesses, and injuries.

(b) The Commission is composed of five members appointed by the President, by and with the advice and consent of the Senate, for terms of seven years.

§ 1000.2 Laws administered.
The Commission administers five acts:

(a) The Consumer Product Safety Act (Pub. L. 92-573, 86 Stat. 1207, as amended (15 U.S.C. 2051, et seq.)).

(b) The Flammable Fabrics Act (Pub. L. 90-189, 67 Stat. 111, as amended (15 U.S.C. 1191, et seq.)).

(c) The Federal Hazardous Substances Act (15 U.S.C. 1261, et seq.).

(d) The Poison Prevention Packaging Act of 1970 (Pub. L. 91-601, 84 Stat. 1670, as amended (15 U.S.C. 1471, et seq.)).

(e) The Refrigerator Safety Act of 1956 (Pub. L. 84-930, 70 Stat. 953, (15 U.S.C. 1211, et seq.)).

§ 1000.3 Hotline.

(a) The Commission operates a toll-free telephone Hotline by which the public can communicate with the Commission. The number for use in all 50 states is 1-800-638-CPSC (1-800-638-2772).

(b) The Commission also operates a toll-free Hotline by which hearing or speech-impaired persons can communicate by teletypewriter with the Commission. The teletypewriter number for use in all states is 1-800-638-8270.

(c) The Commission also makes information available to the public product recall information, its public calendar, and other information through its

Exhibit 3-11 *C.F.R. Index and Finding Aids Page. Code of Federal Regulations, Index and Findings Aids (2001), p. 186, National Archives and Records Administration, Washington, DC.*

Emergency medical services   **CFR Index**

Teachers, Christa McAuliffe Fellowship Program,
    34 CFR, 237
Upward bound program, 34 CFR 645
Vocational and applied technology education
Demonstration projects for integration of vocational
    and academic learning program, 34 CFR 425
State-administered tech-prep education program,
34 CFR 406
State programs, 34 CFR 403

Subject

Emergency medical services
Cargo air carriers, special authorization for
    emergency transportation, 14 CFR 206
Medicare, conditions for payment, 42 CFR 424
Private land mobile radio services, 47 CFR 90
Public safety officers' death and disability benefits,
    rescue squad or ambulance crew members,
    28 CFR 32
Special nuclear material, domestic licensing,
    10 CFR 70
Surface coal mines and surface work areas of
    underground coal mines, safety standards,
    30 CFR 77
Underground coal mines, mandatory safety
    standards. 30 CFR 75

Emergency mobilization
See Civil defense

Emergency Oil and Gas Guaranteed Loan Board
Emergency Oil and Gas Guaranteed Loan Program,
    13 CFR 500

Emergency powers
Employment of military resources in event of civil
    disturbance 32 CFR 215
Passport requirement and exceptions, 22 CFR53
Procedures for use and coordination of radio spectrum
    during wartime emergency, 47 CFR 214
Telecommunications emergency preparedness
    Emergency restoration priority procedures for
        telecommunications services, 47 CFR 211
    Executive policy, 47 CFR 201
    Government and public correspondence
        telecommunications precedence system,
        47 CFR 213

Planning and execution, 47 CFR 202
Procedures for obtaining international
    telecommunication service for use during
    wartime emergency, 47 CFR 212

Emergency Steel Guarantee Loan Board
Emergency Steel Guarantee Loan Program,
    13 CFR 400

Employee benefit plans
See also pensions
Age Discrimination in Employment Act, 29
    CFR 1625
Bona fide profit-sharing plans or trusts, requirements
    under Fair Labor Standards Act, 29 CFR 549
Bona fide thrift or savings plans, requirements
    under Fair Labor Standards Act, 29 CFR 547
Consolidated Rail Corporation, certain standards
    relating to Corporation's employee stock
    ownership plan, attainment determination,
    49 CFR 49
Convicted persons, applications for certificates
of exemption from certain laws. 28 CFR 4
Employee Retirement Income Security Act of 1974
    Administration and enforcement, 29 CFR 2560
    Administrative definitions, 29 CFR 2510
    Civil penalties adjustment under Title I,
        29 CFR 2575
    Fiduciary responsibilities, 29 CFR 2550
    Group health plans, health insurance portability
        and renewability, 29 CFR 2590
    Interpretive bulletins, 29 CFR 2509
    Procedural regulations, 29 CFR 2570
    Reporting and disclosure, 29 CFR 2520
    Temporary bonding rules, 29 CFR 2580
Family and Medical Leave Act of 1993,
    29 CFR 825
Form and content of and requirements for financial
    statements, Securities Act of 1933, Securities
    Exchange Act of 1934, Public Utility Holding
    Company Act of 1935, Investment Company
    Act of 1940, Investment Advisers Act of 1940,
    and Energy Policy and Conservation Act of
    1975, 17 CFR 210
Income taxes

---

d. Computer-Aided Research

The *CFR* and the *Federal Register* are available electronically on Westlaw and LexisNexis. Federal administrative rules and regulations may be researched through the Government Printing Office's Federal Digest System (FDsys) site. Proposed and final rules are also available at the government Web site "regulations.gov" (see the "Internet Resources" section at the end of this chapter). You also may obtain information from individual agency Web sites.

e. Court and Administrative Decisions

Your research may require you to consult administrative agency or court decisions for an interpretation of a rule or regulation. Agency decisions may be available through the Government Printing Office and commercial publishers such as Commerce Clearing House (CCH) and the Bureau of National Affairs (BNA). Administrative and court decisions can also be accessed through Westlaw and LexisNexis.

 Shepard's United States Administrative Citations and *Shepard's Code of Federal Regulations Citations* include citations to administrative agency and court decisions. *West's Federal Practice Digest* will direct you to federal cases and secondary sources that have interpreted federal regulations.

f. Updating Administrative Law Research

The *Code of Federal Regulations* is updated by consulting the *List of CFR Sections Affected (LSA)* (see Exhibit 3-12). This softcover, monthly publication lists changes to any *CFR* regulation. It is cumulative; therefore, you need only check the most recent issue. The cover indicates the time period addressed in the pamphlet. The *LSA* is organized by title and part; indicates the nature of the change, such as "revised" or "removed"; and includes a reference to the page number in the *Federal Register* where the revised section is published.

 To locate changes that have occurred since the last *LSA* publication, check the "Reader Aids" at the end of the most recent *Federal Register*. The "Reader Aids" includes a table of "CFR Parts Affected" that lists parts and sections of the *Code of Federal Regulations* affected. The *CFR* can be updated to the current date through reference to the *LSA* and "Reader Aids."

 The *CFR* can also be updated through Westlaw and LexisNexis. If you are updating through the Government Printing Office access Web site, consult both the *LSA* and the "Reader Aids."

 Administrative agency and court decisions can be updated through *Shepard's United States Administrative Citations* and *Shepard's Code of Federal Regulations Citations*.

B. State Administrative Law

The publication of state rules and regulations varies from state to state, and it would require a separate text to cover each state. The publication and research of state administrative law, however, often follows in varying degrees that of federal administrative law. Therefore, an understanding of the federal administrative law discussed in the previous two subsections will help you when researching state administrative law. Some states publish agency rules and regulations in a single code like the *CFR*. In some states the regulations are published by the separate agency. Probably the quickest way to locate where an agency's regulations and administrative decisions are published is to contact the individual agency. Often individual agencies have Web sites, and the information may be available through the agency or state government Web site.

V. COURT RULES

Court rules regulate the conduct of matters brought before the court. They range in the subjects they cover from the technical, such as the format of pleadings, to the substantive, such as grounds for dismissal or when an appeal must be filed. Usually the rules are divided into two categories: rules of civil procedure and rules of criminal procedure. Each jurisdiction has the

Exhibit 3-12 *Page from Electronic List of CFR Sections Affected (LSA). Source: http://www*
.gpo.gov/fdsys/pkg/LSA-2011-10/pdf/LSA-2011-10.pdf

OCTOBER 2011	5

CHANGES JANUARY 3, 2011 THROUGH OCTOBER 31, 2011

TITLE 1—GENERAL PROVISIONS

Chapter I—Administrative Committee of the Federal Register (Parts 1—49)

9 Revised...6312
11.4 Revised...................................6313
12.3 Removed.................................6313

Chapter III—Administrative Conference of the United States (Parts 300—399)

304 Added......................................18636

Proposed Rules:

304 1542

TITLE 2—GRANTS AND AGREEMENTS

Chapter VII—Agency for International Development (Parts 700—799)

Chapter VII Established.................34144
780 Added......................................34144
782 Added......................................34574

Chapter XXIV—Department of Housing and Urban Development (Parts 2400—2499)

2429 Added 45166

Chapter XXX—Department of Homeland Security (Parts 3000—3099)

3001 Added 10207

Proposed Rules:

300—399 (Ch. III) 20568
400—499 (Ch. IV)............................22058
600—699 (Ch. VI)............................26651
1100—1199 (Ch. XI) 16700, 32330
1400—1499 (Ch. XIV)..............10526, 40645
1800—1899 (Ch. XVIII) 31884
2400—2499 (Ch. XXIV) 11395, 31884
2800—2899 (Ch. XXVIII) 11163, 34003
3000—3099 (Ch. XXX)......................20568

TITLE 3—THE PRESIDENT
Presidential Documents

Proclamations

6641 *See* Proc. 8682.........................30499
6867 *See* Notice of Feb. 24, 2011
....11073
7463 *See* Notice of Sep. 9, 2011..........56633
7747 *See* Proc. 8682.........................30499
7757 *See* Notice of Feb. 24, 2011
....11073
8097 *See* Proc. 8682.........................30499
8214 *See* Proc. 8682.........................30499
8271 *See* Notice of Jun. 23, 2011
....37237
8405 *See* Proc. 8682.........................30499
8522 Superseded by Proc. 8681 30497
8536 *See* Proc. 8682.........................30499
8622..2241
8623..3817
8624..3819
8625..6305
8626..6307
8627..6521
8628..11927
8629..11929
8630..11931
8631..11933
8632..11935
8633..12265
8634..12817
8635..12919
8636..12921
8637..15209
8638..16523
8639..17327
8640..17329
8641..18629
8642..18631
8643..18633
8644..19259
8645..19261
8646..19263
8647..19265
8648..19899
8649..20215
8650..20829
8651..20831
8652..20833
8653..21221
8654..21223
8655..21999
8656..22001
8657..23685
8658..24785

authority to promulgate its own set of rules, although many states follow in substantial part the Federal Rules of Civil and Criminal Procedure.

On occasion you may need to research matters involving the rules to determine what a rule requires or how a rule has been interpreted.

> **For Example** Rule 60B of the Federal Rules of Civil and Criminal Procedure provides that a judgment may be set aside on the grounds of "excusable neglect." It may be necessary to research the case law to determine how the courts have defined "excusable neglect."

The Federal Rules of Civil and Criminal Procedure are included in the *United States Code.* By consulting the *USCA* or *USCS*, you will find annotations that direct you to summaries of cases and secondary sources, such as legal encyclopedia sections and *ALR* annotations, that have interpreted the rules. Like the federal rules, state court rules are usually published with the state statutes. Locating the rules in the annotated statutes is usually the starting point when researching court rules.

The state and federal rules are available electronically on Westlaw and LexisNexis, through http://www.findlaw.com, and on the state or individual court Web site. In addition, multivolume treatises, such as *West's Federal Practice and Procedure,* provide exhaustive analysis of the federal rules.

In addition to the rules governing civil and criminal procedure, federal courts and many state courts have so-called **local rules**. You should consult these rules before filing any pleading or other document with the court. These rules are specific to the court and generally govern administrative matters such as the size of papers accepted, the number of copies of pleadings that must be filed with the original, and how to file by facsimile transmission. If the court has a Web site, the local rules may be available there. If not, local rules are available through the clerk of the court.

VI. ANALYSIS—THE PROCESS

The analysis of enacted law and court rules is the process of determining if a law applies, how it applies, and the effect of that application to a specific fact situation. When analyzing a legal problem or addressing an issue governed by constitutional, statutory, or administrative law provision, or a court rule, it is helpful to have an approach—an **analysis process**. This process should allow you to approach the matter in a way that efficiently solves the problem in the least amount of time with the least confusion and greatest accuracy. For the sake of clarity, throughout this section the discussion and examples focus upon laws passed by legislative bodies, or statutory law. Note, however, that the principles presented here apply to the analysis of constitutions, statutes, administrative law, and court rules.

It is recommended that you follow the three-step approach presented in Exhibit 3-13 when addressing a legal problem or issue governed by statutory law. These steps are a helpful approach to statutory analysis, although in some instances a step may be unnecessary (for example, step 1 is unnecessary if you already know that the statute applies) and in other instances, a different approach may be required. Each step in this recommended approach is discussed separately in the following sections.

A. Step 1: Determine if the Statute Applies

The first step in the process is to determine which law, if any, covers the legal issue raised by the client's fact situation. The first task, then, is to determine which statute or statutes govern the question.

This step involves two parts:

1. Locate all possible applicable statutes.
2. Determine which statutes apply.

Exhibit 3-13 *Statutory Analysis Three-Step Approach.*

STEP 1	Determine if the statute applies. ■ Part 1: Locate all possible applicable statutes. ■ Part 2: Determine which statutes apply.
STEP 2	Analyze the statute. ■ Part 1: Read the statute. ■ Part 2: Identify the statutory elements—What does the statute specifically declare, require, or prohibit?
STEP 3	Apply the statute to the legal problem or issue. ■ Chart format ■ Narrative format

1. Locate All Possible Applicable Statutes

Before you can determine if a particular statute applies, you first must locate all statutes that possibly apply. The location of one applicable statute does not mean you should stop your search. Make sure your research is thorough and complete. Continue researching until you are confident that you have explored all areas of law that might govern the problem and have located all potential applicable statutes. Some matters are covered by more than one statute.

> **For Example** The client's case may involve the validity and enforceability of a small loan contract. Several statutes may govern the enforcement of such contracts: the federal Truth in Lending Act, the state's Small Loan Act, and the state's Usury Act.

2. Determine Which Statutes Apply

Determine whether each statute applies by asking yourself, "Does the general area of law covered by this statute apply to the issue or question raised by the facts of my client's case?" You can usually answer this question by referring to the scope of the statute, the definitions section, or case law.

Reference to the scope section of the statute often answers the question of whether the statute applies.

> **For Example** The problem involves the validity of a contract for the sale of a security interest in a car. The scope section of the Commercial Code—Sales statute provides, "This chapter applies to the sale of goods, it does not apply to any transaction which . . . is a sale of a security interest or intended to operate only as a security transaction. . . ." Reference to this section clearly indicates that this statute does not cover such transactions. If the facts involved the sale of the car, rather than the sale of a security interest in the car, the statute might apply.

Often reference to the definitions section of a statute will help you determine whether a statute applies.

> **For Example** The legal problem involves the sale of a farm. The question of whether this sale is governed by the provisions of the Commercial Code—Sales statute is answered by reference to the definitions section of the statute. In that section, goods are defined as "all things that are movable at the time of the contract for sale. . . ." The statute clearly does not apply to the sale of a farm.

In some instances, reference to case law may be necessary to determine if a statute governs a situation.

> **For Example** The client's case involves the lease of goods, and neither the scope nor the definitions sections of the Commercial Code—Sales statute indicates whether the term *sale* includes a lease of goods. Reference to case law may be necessary. Court decisions often define terms not defined in a statute.

Note that you may often locate the relevant case law by looking to the reference information following the section of the statute. It may be that two laws apply and govern a legal question. In this event, two causes of action may be available.

> **For Example** A small loan may violate provisions of both the federal Truth in Lending Act and the state usury law. In this case, there may be a cause of action under the federal law and a cause of action under the state law. If this occurs, steps 2 and 3 would be followed in regard to each statute.

When determining if a statute applies, always check the effective date of the statute to be sure that the statute is in effect. This is usually found in the statute itself or in the historical notes or comments in the reference sections following the statute. Also, *always* check the supplements to the statute to make sure that the statute you are researching is the latest version. Supplementary material published after the publication of the main text is often located immediately following the statute or in a separate section or pamphlet. The supplements include any changes in the statute or reference material that have occurred since the publication of the book containing the statute.

B. Step 2: Analyze the Statute

After you determine that a statute applies, you must carefully read and analyze it to determine how it applies. Some statutes are lengthy and difficult to understand. You may need to check the library references to locate other library sources that explain and interpret the statute. It may be necessary to make a chart to assist you in understanding the specific provisions and operation of a statute.

Step 2 involves two parts:

1. Read the statute.
2. Identify the statutory elements: What does the statute specifically declare, require, or prohibit?

1. Read the Statute

Keep the following points in mind when reading statutory law:

1. Read the statute carefully several times.
2. Does the statute set a standard, or merely provide factors that must be considered?
3. Does the statute set out more than one rule or test? Are other rules or tests available? Are there exceptions to the rule or test?
4. All the words and punctuation have meaning. Always check the definitions section for the meaning of a term. If there is no definitions section, consult case law, a legal dictionary, or *Words and Phrases*. Do not assume you know what a term means. Your assumption may be wrong. A legal term may have several meanings, some of which may be unknown to you.

> **For Example** The word *publication* in tort law means more than presentation in the print or visual media. It means communication to a third party by any means. Under this definition, two neighbors gossiping over a backyard fence can constitute publication.

All punctuation counts. If you cannot understand how to read a statute, consult a secondary source, such as a treatise or legal encyclopedia.

5. Review the entire statute (all sections) to determine if other sections in some way affect or relate to the section you are researching.

> **For Example** Section 611-9 of the statute provides:
>
> a. A will that does not comply with Section 611-8 is valid as a holographic will if the signature and the material provisions are in the handwriting of the testator.
>
> b. If a holographic will does not contain a statement as to the date of its execution and it is established that the testator lacked testamentary capacity at any time during which the will might have been executed, the will is invalid unless it is established that it was executed at a time when the testator had testamentary capacity.
>
> c. Any statement of testamentary intent contained in a holographic will may be set forth either in the testator's own handwriting or as part of a commercially printed form will.
>
> Note that a *holographic will* is a will written entirely by the testator in his or her own handwriting and not witnessed. Subsection (a) sets the standard for when a holographic will is valid. Subsection (b), however, addresses a situation that affects the validity of a holographic will even if the requirements of subsection (a) are met. Subsection (c) establishes how testamentary intent may be set forth.

The preceding example illustrates a point that cannot be overemphasized: Read and consider *all parts* of a statute. Suppose the legal question is, "What is required for a holographic will to be valid?" If you stopped reading the statute at subsection (a) because it appeared to answer your question, you would miss the other provisions that also affect the answer to the question. Always read the entire statute. Also, if the statute refers to another section, read that other section to determine how it affects the statute.

6. Certain common terminology must be understood. Be aware of the meaning of the commonly used terms, such as *shall*, *may*, *and*, and *or*.

The term **shall** makes the duty imposed mandatory—it must be done. The term **may** leaves the duty optional. If **and** is used, all the conditions or listed items are required. If the term **or** is used, only one of the conditions or listed items is required.

> **For Example** Section 24-6-7-9 provides "A person is concerned in the commission of a crime if he:
>
> a. directly commits the crime;
>
> b. intentionally causes some other person to commit the crime; or
>
> c. intentionally aids or abets in the commission of the crime."

The use of *or* means that a person is covered by the statute if he or she does *any* one of the listed acts.

> **For Example** Section 50-9-1 provides that holographic wills are valid if they are:
>
> a. Entirely in the handwriting of the testator, and
> b. Signed by the testator

The use of *and* means that both conditions must be met for the will to be valid.

7. Keep in mind the canons of construction when reading. These are presented in section VII of this chapter.

2. Identify the Statutory Elements

After you carefully read the statute, the next part of step 2 is to analyze the section of the statute in question. What does the statute specifically declare, require, or prohibit? How does the statute apply? Ask yourself, "What specific requirements must be met for the statute to apply? What are the elements?" For a statute to apply, certain conditions established by the statute must be met. These conditions or components of the statute are called **statutory elements**. After the elements are identified, you can determine how the statute applies.

After you have a sufficient understanding of the statute, begin this part of step 2 by breaking the statute down into its elements. Identify and list the elements that must be met for the statute to apply. This is necessary because you must know what the statutory elements are before you can proceed to step 3 and apply them to the legal problem or issue raised by the client's facts.

Identify the elements by reading the entire statute, analyzing each sentence word by word, and listing everything required. This includes listing all the various conditions and exceptions contained in the subsections of the statute in question and the conditions and exceptions included in other statutes that may affect the statute in question.

> **For Example** Consider Section 2-2-315 of the Commercial Code—Sales Act of state X:
>
> Where the seller at the time of contracting has reason to know any particular purpose for which the goods are required and that the buyer is relying on the seller's skill or judgment to select or furnish suitable goods, there is an implied warranty that the goods shall be fit for such purpose.

Read the statute in the preceding example and determine the elements. For the implied warranty of § 2-2-315 to apply, the following requirements must be met:

1. *The person must be a seller of goods.* How do you know "of goods" is required? Section 2-2-315 quoted previously does not read "seller of goods"; it only states "the seller." You know "of goods" is required because in step 1, in order to determine if the statute applied to the issue in the client's case, you reviewed the scope section of the act. It provides that the act applies only to the sale of goods.

   How is the term *goods* defined? Assume the term is defined in the definitions section of the Commercial Code—Sales Act as: "All things movable at the time of sale." The statute also requires the individual to be a seller. How is *seller* defined in the definitions section of the act? Assume the term is defined as anyone who sells goods.

2. *The seller has reason to know the purpose for which the goods are required.* For the act to apply, the seller must have reason to know the purpose for which the buyer wants the goods. The statute does not require actual knowledge on the part of the seller. It uses the phrase, "has reason to know." You may need to refer to case law to determine what "reason to know" means or requires.

3. *The seller has reason to know the buyer is relying on the seller's skill or judgment.* This is usually established by the words or actions of the buyer that indicate to the seller the buyer's reliance on the seller's skill or judgment.

4. *The buyer must actually rely on the seller's skill or judgment in furnishing suitable goods.* This is required because the statute provides that "the seller . . . has reason to know . . . that the buyer is relying."

5. *The seller must have known of the purpose for which the goods were required and the buyer's reliance on the seller's skill or judgment in furnishing the goods at the time the sale was taking place, not later.* This is required because the statute provides, "the seller at the time of contracting. . . ."

Be sure to complete both parts of step 2 before proceeding to step 3.

C. Step 3: Apply the Statute to the Legal Problem or Issue

After you have identified the elements, which are the conditions necessary for the statute to apply, then apply the elements to the legal problem or issue raised by the client's fact situation. This entails applying or matching the facts of the client's case to the elements of the statute, which may be accomplished in several ways. One way is to chart the elements of the statute. Next to the elements, list the facts from the client's case that match or establish each of the elements or requirements of the statute. Another way is to prepare a narrative summary of the elements and how the facts of the case apply to match or establish the elements. The following examples illustrate the performance of step 3 in both chart and narrative summary format.

1. Chart Format

In the following example, a **chart format** is used.

> **For Example** Tom goes to the local hardware store and informs the salesperson that he needs to grind metal with a power metal grinder. He tells the salesperson that he needs goggles to protect his eyes. The salesperson, after looking through his stock, hands Tom a pair of goggles and tells him, "These are what you need." Tom purchases the goggles, and when he uses them, a piece of metal pierces the lens of the goggles and damages Tom's eye.

Can Tom state a claim under the provisions of the implied warranty statute, § 2-2-315, presented in the previous example? How does the statute apply?

STATUTORY ELEMENTS	FACTS OF CLIENT'S CASE
1. Seller of goods	The seller was a salesperson at the local hardware store, a seller within the meaning of the statute. The item sold, goggles, meets the definition of goods (the goggles are "things movable at the time of sale").
2. Has reason to know the buyer's purpose in purchasing the goods	Tom explicitly told the seller the purpose for buying the goggles.

3. Has reason to know of buyer's reliance on seller's judgment	This is implied from Tom's conduct of allowing the seller to select the goods without any input from Tom.
4. Reliance by buyer on seller's skill or judgment	Tom relied on the salesperson's judgment. He indicated the purpose and accepted, without independent judgment or act, what the seller selected.
5. At the time of contracting	The seller knew at the time of the sale, not later, of Tom's purpose and reliance.

After the elements of the statute have been identified and the facts of the client's case compared and matched with the required elements of the statute, you can determine how the statute applies. In this example, you can conclude that the statute covers the conduct of the salesperson and that an implied warranty was created. All the required elements of the statute are established by the facts in Tom's case:

1. The salesperson was a seller within the meaning of the statute, and the item sold meets the definition of goods.

2. At the time of the sale, the buyer informed the seller of the specific purpose for which the goods were being purchased.

3. The seller knew of the buyer's reliance on his skill and judgment.

4. The buyer relied on the expertise and judgment of the seller.

5. The seller knew at the time of sale, not later.

2. Narrative Summary

In the following example, a **narrative summary** is used rather than a chart format.

> **For Example** Section 56-6-1 of the Open Meetings Act provides that "all meetings of two or more members of any board . . . at which any public business is discussed or at which any action may be taken or is taken are declared to be public meetings open to the public." The section further provides:
>
> a. Such meetings shall be held only after full and timely public notice.
>
> b. This section does not apply to chance meetings or social gatherings at which discussion of public business is not the central purpose.
>
> Ida and Dan are members of a three-person state board. They run into each other at a Christmas party and discuss board business.

Is this meeting an open meeting governed by § 56-6-1? The application of step 2 reveals the statute requires an open meeting when the following elements are present:

1. Two or more board members

2. Meet at other than a chance or social gathering where discussion of public business is not the central purpose, and

3. Public business is discussed or action may be or is taken.

A narrative summary of the elements and the application of the statute to the facts illustrates step 3:

1. *Two or more board members.* This element is met. Both Dan and Ida are board members.

2. *Meet at other than a chance or social gathering where discussion of public business is not the central purpose.* It appears that this element is not met by the facts.

This was a social gathering and also possibly a chance meeting. The gathering was a Christmas party. It does not appear that the discussion of public business was the central purpose. If it is discovered that the sole reason they went to the party was to discuss public business, the exclusion in subsection (b) of the statute probably does not apply and the meeting may be covered by the act.

3. *Public business is discussed or action may be or is taken.* This element is met. Public business was discussed.

After performing step 3, it appears that this was not a public meeting within the meaning of the act. Although the requirements of the first and third elements are met (two or more board members met and discussed public business), the requirements of the second element are not met.

When performing step 3, remember to match the client's facts with the required elements of a statute. When this is accomplished, you can determine how the statute applies. In the example concerning the purchase of goggles, all the required statutory elements were met by the facts of the client's case and an implied warranty was created. In the public meetings example, the facts did not meet the requirements of the second element of the statute; therefore, the meeting was not a public meeting within the meaning of the statute.

D. Summary of the Statutory Analysis Process

The three steps presented in this section are a useful approach to statutory analysis. These steps may be summarized as follows:

- Step 1: Determine if the statute applies in any way to the legal problem or issue.
- Step 2: Carefully read the statute and identify the required elements.
- Step 3: Compare or match the required elements to the facts of the problem and determine how the statute applies.

In addition to this three-step approach, there are other general considerations to keep in mind when analyzing statutory law. These considerations are presented in the following section.

VII. GENERAL CONSIDERATIONS

Always keep in mind two major considerations and guidelines when engaged in statutory analysis:

1. Legislative history
2. Canons of construction

These considerations come into play, and are of the greatest importance, when the meaning of the statute is unclear and the meaning has not been determined by a court.

When required to interpret a statute, a court will first look to the plain meaning of the language of the statute. This is called the **plain meaning rule**. The rule mandates that a statute be interpreted according to its plain meaning; that is, words will be interpreted according to their common meanings. The court will render an interpretation that reflects the plain meaning of the language and is consistent with the meaning of all other sections of the act. If the meaning is clear on its face, then no additional inquiries concerning the meaning of a statute are allowed. If there is still an ambiguity in the meaning of a statutory section, the court will then look to the legislative history of the statute and apply canons of construction.

When engaging in statutory analysis, be mindful of the considerations that the court applies when interpreting the meaning of a statute. The reason for this is obvious: You want your interpretation of the meaning of a statute and how it will be applied to coincide with that of the court. Each of these considerations is addressed in this section.

A. Legislative History

To determine the meaning of a statute, a court may look to the legislative history of the statute to discover what the legislature intended it to mean. **Legislative history** is the record of the legislation during the enactment process before it became law. It consists of committee reports, transcripts of hearings, statements of legislators concerning the legislation, and any other material published for legislative use in regard to the legislation.

Legislative history may be of assistance in several ways when interpreting a statute. The history may identify why an ambiguous term was used and what meaning the legislature intended, what the legislature intended the statute to accomplish, the general purpose of the legislation, and so on. Researching legislative history is discussed in Chapter 6.

B. Canons of Construction

Canons of construction are rules and guidelines the courts use when interpreting statutes. A fundamental rule of construction that determines when canons of construction are applied by a court is the plain meaning rule, which governs when the canons of construction apply. If the meaning is clear on its face, there is no room for interpretation and a court will not apply the canons of construction.

The canons of construction are too numerous to be addressed individually in this text. Some well-known canons are presented here.

1. Expressio Unius

The entire Latin phrase is *expressio unius est exclusio alterius*, which translates as "the expression of one excludes all others." If the statute contains a list of what is covered, everything else is excluded.

> **For Example** If a statute governing artists lists potters, glass blowers, painters, poets, writers, and sculptors, but does not include weavers, weavers are not covered by the statute. Only the occupations listed are covered, all other occupations are not covered.

Note, however, that a statute often is written to state that a list is not exclusive. When so written, this canon of construction does not apply, and the statute is not limited to the items listed.

> **For Example** "A 'Building' as used in this statute means a structure on private or commercial property and includes *but is not limited to* a dwelling, an office of fixed location. . . ."

2. Ejusdem Generis

The Latin term *ejusdem generis* means "of the same genus or class." As a canon of construction, it means that whenever a statute contains a specific list followed by a general term, the general term is interpreted to be limited to other things of the same class or kind as those in the list.

> **For Example** A statute regulating self-propelled vehicles lists "bicycles, tricycles, unicycles, and other devices." Here "other devices" is limited to mean devices of the same class or kind as bicycles, tricycles, and unicycles. Motorized vehicles are not "other devices" within the meaning of the statute.

3. Pari Materia

The Latin term *pari materia* translates as "on the same subject matter." This canon means that statutes dealing with the same subject should be interpreted consistently.

> **For Example** A state's Fair Housing Act prohibits discrimination against an individual on the basis of "gender preference." The state's Fair Employment Act also uses the term *gender preference*. The term should be interpreted consistently in both statutes unless each statute has a definitions section that gives a clearly different meaning.

4. Last Antecedent Rule

The last antecedent rule states: Qualifying words and phrases apply to the words or phrase immediately preceding and do not extend to other more remote words or phrases.

> **For Example** A DWI statute provides that "driver means every person who drives or is in actual physical control of a motor vehicle upon a highway. . . ." The phrase "upon a highway" modifies the term *motor vehicle*. It does not modify the term *drives*.

5. Intended Remedy

Intended remedy means that statutes are to be interpreted in a manner that furthers the intended legislative remedy.

6. Entire Context

The words, phrases, and subsections of a statute are to be interpreted in the context of the entire statute.

7. Constitutionality

Statutes are assumed to be constitutional and should be construed in a manner that preserves their constitutionality, if possible.

8. Criminal Statutes

Criminal statutes are to be narrowly interpreted.

It is important to remember that, as with all matters involving case law, when a court interprets a statute, the principle of stare decisis applies. A court will follow the interpretation previously adopted unless the previous interpretation is overruled and a new interpretation is adopted.

VIII. KEY POINTS CHECKLIST: *Working with Statutes*

Keep the following key points in mind when working with statutes:

- ✓ When conducting research, identify the question or research terms as narrowly and concisely as possible.
- ✓ *Always* update your research—check the pocket parts and supplements to make sure that the statute has not been changed or repealed.

✓ When researching federal regulatory law, it is easier to use the *Code of Federal Regulations* than the *Federal Register*.

✓ When reviewing a statute, do not limit your focus to a specific section. Remember, a section is one part of an entire act that usually contains several statutory sections. Read a section in the context of the entire act. Be sure you are familiar with all the sections of the act; there may be another section, such as a definitions section, that affects the interpretation of the statute you are reading.

✓ When you find a statute that appears to apply, do not stop your research. In many instances, more than one statute or legislative act applies to a specific question or fact situation.

✓ Read statutes carefully and slowly. Several readings may be necessary. You may have to make a chart or diagram of the various sections and subsections of a statute to gain an understanding of the operation of the statute.

✓ All the words of a statute have meaning. If a word does not seem necessary or appears repetitive, you may have misread the statute. Read it again. Consult a secondary source that contains a discussion or interpretation of the statute.

✓ Do not assume you know the meaning of a word. Many statutory words are terms of art, loaded with meaning. Check the definitions section of the statute, case law, or a legal dictionary to ensure you give the correct meaning to a term.

✓ The plain meaning of a statute governs its statutory interpretation. If the meaning is clear, the statute is not subject to interpretation.

✓ If the statute is unclear or ambiguous, look to other sources for guidance, such as legislative history or applicable canons of construction. Are there court opinions that interpret the statute? Are there secondary sources, such as law review articles or encyclopedia sections, that discuss the statute?

IX. APPLICATION

The application of the principles of statutory analysis is illustrated in the following examples.

A. Chapter Hypothetical

In the hypothetical situation presented at the beginning of the chapter, Alan's assignment is to determine if Mrs. Jackson has a cause of action against Beauty Care Beauty Salon for breach of warranty under the sales provisions of the state's commercial code. The scope of his research has been narrowed greatly by the assignment. He needs to locate the sales provisions of the commercial code, then identify the statutes that address warranties. Alan can look for various terms in the index of the statutes, such as *sales, commercial code, warranties,* and *contracts*. He may look to the popular name table for commercial code, or sales of goods. If he is conducting research electronically, he may begin with the terms *contracts, sales*, and *warranties*.

His research turns up five sections of the state's Commercial Code Sales Act that may apply:

▪ Section 29-2-102 provides that the act applies to the sale of goods only; services are specifically excluded by the act.

▪ Section 29-2-105 defines *goods* as "all things which are movable at the time of the contract for sale."

▪ Section 29-2-313 provides that an express warranty is created by a seller's affirmation of fact or promise that relates to the quality of the goods.

- Section 29-2-314 states that "a warranty that the goods shall be merchantable is implied in a contract for their sale if the seller is a merchant with respect to goods of that kind."

- Section 29-2-315 provides: "Where the seller at the time of contracting has reason to know any particular purpose for which the goods are required and that the buyer is relying on the seller's skill or judgment to select or furnish suitable goods, there is a warranty that the goods shall be fit for such purpose."

After conducting research on how to analyze statutory law, Alan applies the steps recommended in this chapter.

STEP 1. *Determine If the Statute Applies*

When reviewing the statutes, Alan notes that § 29-2-102 provides that the Commercial Code Sales Act only applies to the sale of goods. If this transaction is not a sale of goods, then neither the statute nor the warranty provisions of the act apply.

Section 29-2-105 defines goods as "all things which are movable. . . ." This definition is of no help. Is a permanent hair treatment movable within the meaning of the act? In this case, both goods and services are involved. The service portion, the beautician applying the permanent, does not appear to be goods within the meaning of the statute, but is clearly a service. The invoice, however, shows that Mrs. Jackson paid $20 for a perm kit. The perm kit is clearly goods under the act. The transaction is a mixed transaction involving both services and goods. Alan's review of the statute indicates that there is no section addressing mixed transactions.

Because the statute does not give guidance concerning mixed transactions, Alan must refer to case law. In the case of *Elie v. American Saloon*, the court provides guidance for determining when a mixed transaction is a sale of goods covered by the Commercial Code Sales Act.

In *Elie*, the court adopted what it called the predominant factor test. Under this test, the nature of the contract will be determined by what predominates. If the transaction involves primarily a service, it is a service contract and not covered by the act. If the transaction involves primarily the sale of goods, it is a sale of goods and is covered by the act. In its discussion of the application of the test, the court stated that the bill or receipt should be examined. If the largest portion of the bill applies to the cost of the goods sold, the transaction is predominately a sale of goods and the act applies. If the majority of the bill applies to the services provided, the transaction is a service transaction, not covered by the act.

Applying this test to Mrs. Jackson's facts, the bill clearly indicates that the largest portion of the transaction applied to the service of giving the permanent. The salon charged $20 for the perm kit (goods) and $80 for giving the permanent (services). Alan concludes that under the predominant factor test, the service predominates the transaction; thus, this appears to be a service contract not covered by the act. After performing step 1, Alan concludes that no warranty relief is available against Beauty Care Beauty Salon because the Commercial Code Sales Act does not apply to the transaction.

Alan's conclusion is based on his interpretation of the law. Because he is new at statutory analysis, however, Alan knows his analysis could be wrong. To be on the safe side, he continues his analysis in order to provide his supervisory attorney a complete review of the law. Alan proceeds to steps 2 and 3.

STEP 2. *Analyze the Statute*

If the act does apply—that is, if the conclusion is that the transaction is a sale of goods rather than a service—which of the warranty remedies, if any, would be available to Mrs. Jackson? Alan carefully reads the statute and determines that the three warranties included in § 29-2-313, § 29-2-314, and § 29-2-315 are the only possible warranties available in the act. Which of these would apply?

Clearly § 29-2-313 and § 29-2-315 would not apply. Section 29-2-313 requires some affirmation or promise by the seller relating to the quality of the goods. In Mrs. Jackson's case, there was no statement by the beautician, either oral or written, concerning the quality of the permanent. Section 29-2-315 also would not apply, as Mrs. Jackson did not communicate any particular purpose for which the goods were required. Also, there are no facts to indicate that she in any way relied on the beautician's expertise in selecting the permanent, although it could be argued that this is implicit in getting a permanent. To be on the safe side, Alan reviews the courts' interpretation of the term *particular purpose*. The case law indicates that the term refers to a unique and specific purpose for which the goods are required that is clearly and specifically communicated by the buyer to the seller. The facts in Mrs. Jackson's case show there was no specific communication.

Alan's last hope is § 29-2-314. He reads the statute and identifies the following as the elements of an implied warranty of merchantability:

1. The transaction must be a contract for the sale of goods.

2. The seller must be a merchant of those goods.

On the face of it, it appears that this statute would apply. Alan proceeds to step 3.

STEP 3. *Apply the Statute to the Legal Problem or Issue*

Alan applies the statute to the problem through the use of a chart.

STATUTORY ELEMENTS	FACTS OF CLIENT'S CASE
1. Contract for sale of goods.	Assuming that the predominant factor test led to the conclusion that this transaction is a sale of goods, not services, then this is a sale-of-goods transaction.
2. Seller is a merchant of those goods.	The act defines *merchant* as a person who deals in goods of the kind sold. If the beauty salon and the beautician routinely sell perm kits, then the seller is a "merchant." In Mrs. Jackson's case, the salon routinely sells perm kits when it charges for them as part of a permanent. Therefore, the seller is a "merchant."

After performing this step, Alan can reach a conclusion as to whether the statute applies and whether Mrs. Jackson has a cause of action for breach of warranty under § 29-2-314. Assuming that the transaction is a sale of goods, *which is doubtful in light of the conclusion reached in step 1*, it appears that the statute would apply: There was a contract for the sale of goods by a merchant of those goods.

Under § 29-2-314, the seller warrants that the goods are merchantable, which is defined in case law as meaning "fit for the ordinary purposes for which such goods are used." In Mrs. Jackson's case, the goods obviously were not fit for their ordinary purpose. Her hair changed color and broke off. If § 29-2-314 applies, Mrs. Jackson clearly has a claim for breach of warranty. Remember, however, the conclusion in step 1 was that § 29-2-314 does not apply because the transaction was probably a sale of a service, not goods. *Note*: Alan went through steps 2 and 3 because he is new at statutory analysis and wanted to make sure his analysis was correct. An experienced researcher would stop at step 1.

B. Will Revocation Statute

Section 50-5 of the state statutes is the applicable statute in this example. It provides as follows:

No will in writing, nor any part thereof, shall be revoked unless, with the intent to revoke, the testator:

a. executes a subsequent will or codicil,

b. prepares a writing declaring an intention to revoke the same which is executed in a manner in which a will is required to be executed, or

c. the testator or some person in the testator's presence and by the testator's direction . . . cancels, or destroys the same with the intent to revoke.

The following facts apply in this example. Before Mary Glenn died, she directed her brother, Tom Glenn, to cancel her will. Because she was too weak to write, she directed her brother to cancel the will by writing across the first page, "I hereby revoke this will. It is my intent that this will be no longer valid. I direct my brother to do this because I can no longer write." Tom took the will to Mary's kitchen, a room adjacent to her bedroom, and wrote what Mary had requested on the first page of the will and added, "This was done at the request of Mary Glenn by me, Tom Glenn."

Was the will validly revoked under the terms of the statute?

STEP 1. *Determine If the Statute Applies*

The statute appears on its face to apply to this fact situation. The statute governs will revocations, and this is an attempted revocation.

STEP 2. *Read and Analyze the Statute*

After a careful reading, the statute can be analyzed and the required elements identified. The statute provides three ways in which a written will can be revoked:

1. By a subsequent will or codicil executed by the testator, with the intent to revoke the prior will

2. By a writing intended to revoke the will, executed in the same manner as a will is required to be executed

3. By the testator or some person in the testator's presence and by the testator's direction canceling or destroying the will with the intent to revoke

STEP 3. *Apply the Statute to the Legal Problem or Issue*

When the statute is applied to the fact situation, it appears that subsections (a) and (b) clearly do not apply. Subsection (a) requires a subsequent will or codicil, neither of which is present in Mary Glenn's case. Subsection (b) requires a writing revoking the will, executed in a manner in which a will must be executed. Assume that research reveals that the state statutes require a will to be witnessed by two witnesses. There were no witnesses in this case. The requirements of this subsection are not met because the writing by Tom was not executed in the required manner.

If there is a valid revocation under the statute, it can have occurred only under the cancellation provisions of subsection (c). For a revocation to occur under subsection (c), the following elements must be met:

1. The testator or some person
   a. In the presence of the testator, and
   b. By the testator's direction
2. Cancels or destroys the will
3. With the intent to revoke

In this example, the required elements of the statute will be applied to the facts of the case in a different way than in the previous example. In the previous example, a chart was used; here a narrative summary is used:

1. *Testator or some person.* The requirements of this element are met. The testator did not cancel the will but "some person," her brother, did.

   a. *In the presence of the testator.* It is questionable whether this element is met. Does "in the testator's presence" mean actual physical presence in the same room? If the person canceling the will is in an adjacent room, is that "in the testator's presence"? If the statute does not define the term *presence*, case law must be consulted. If the courts have not interpreted the term, the legislative history of the act may shed some light.

    b. *By the direction of the testator.* This element is met. Mary Glenn directed her brother to revoke the will.

2. **Cancels or destroys the will.** This element appears to be met. The language clearly revokes the will and appears on the will itself. The statute does not require that the revocation language appear on a specific page of the will such as the signature page. Case law should be consulted to see if the courts have established where the revocation language must be placed.

3. **With the intent to revoke.** This element is met. The intent to revoke is clearly indicated in the language Mary Glenn chose.

The conclusion is that the statute applies, and the will has been revoked if the presence requirement is met and if cancellation language is effective when placed on the first page of a will. By following the three steps recommended, subsections (a) and (b) of the statute were eliminated from consideration, and subsection (c), which could possibly apply, was identified. The application analysis helps focus the attention on what research is needed to reach a final conclusion. Note that the final conclusion cannot be reached in step 3 until research is conducted to determine what "in the testator's presence" requires under the statute. The research should begin with a review of the case annotations following the statute to determine if a court has interpreted "in the testator's presence."

Summary

This chapter focuses on how to research and analyze enacted law and court rules. The principles presented in the chapter apply to the research and analysis of constitutions, statutory law, administrative law, and court rules.

An increasingly expanding source of law in the United States is statutory law. This body of law assumes a greater role because many matters once covered by the case law are now addressed by state and federal legislative bodies. As a result of this growth, researchers are more frequently engaged in analyzing legal problems and issues governed by statutory law.

Statutory research is the process of finding the statutory law that applies to a problem. Most federal and state laws are organized according to topic (codified) and published with annotations. The beginning step of all research, including statutory research, is to identify what you are looking for as precisely and narrowly as possible. Most statutes are located through use of the general index, although they also may be found through use of the table of contents or the popular name table.

Administrative law is the body of law consisting of the rules and regulations of administrative agencies and the court opinions interpreting them. The main research source for locating federal administrative law is the *Code of Federal Regulations*. Court rules regulate the conduct of matters brought before the court.

The analysis of enacted law and court rules is the process of determining if a law applies, how it applies, and the effect of that application. For the sake of clarity, the chapter discussion and examples focus upon the analysis of laws passed by legislative bodies, called statutory law. A prerequisite to analyzing a law is a familiarity with the parts or components of the law.

The most efficient way to address a problem involving a statute is to have a process for or an approach to statutory analysis. This chapter presents a three-step approach.

The first step is to determine whether the statute governs the situation in any way. This step involves locating all the possible statutes that may apply, then deciding which apply to the facts raised by the legal problem.

The second step is to carefully read the statute and identify what is required for the statute to apply. These requirements are usually referred to as the elements of the statute. A careful analysis may require several readings of the statute and reference to interpretative sources such as court opinions, or secondary sources such as treatises and law review articles.

The third step is to apply the elements to the facts of the legal problem. This involves matching the elements of the statute to the facts of the case and determining how the statute applies.

When engaging in statutory analysis, it is important to be mindful of certain guidelines. Most of these come into play when the meaning of a statute is unclear or ambiguous. In addition to court opinions, which give guidance to the interpretation of a statute, legislative history and canons of construction may be consulted. Legislative history is composed of all the legislative material and records concerning a statute before it became law. Canons of construction are guidelines developed by courts for use in interpreting ambiguous statutes. These sources should not be used if the meaning of the statute is clear on its face.

The ease with which you are able to locate and analyze statutes increases with practice. The more you read and analyze statutes, the easier it becomes. The exercises at the end of this chapter may prove helpful in this regard.

Quick References

Internet Resources

http://www.law.cornell.edu

Through this site, maintained by Cornell Law School, you may obtain the *Code of Federal Regulations*, the Federal Rules of Civil and Criminal Procedure, and other court rules. The *United States Code* is also available at this site.

http://www.findlaw.com

FindLaw is an excellent source for locating state statutes. Simply type in the name of the state you are researching. Court rules and some state administrative regulations may also be found at this site.

http://www.lawsonline.com

This site provides links to state and federal law sources.

http://www.gpo.gov

This Government Printing Office site provides access to the *United States Code,* the *Code of Federal Regulations,* the *Federal Register,* and numerous other documents.

http://www.house.gov

This site is the home page for the United States House of Representatives.

http://www.senate.gov

This site is the home page for the United States Senate.

http://www.copyright.gov

This is the site for the Library of Congress.

http://www.regulations.gov

This is an online source for U.S. government regulations from nearly 300 federal agencies.

Statutory Citation

The *Bluebook* and *ALWD Citation Manual* rules governing statutory citation are discussed in Chapter 8. If the document you are working on may be filed in a court, such as a state supreme court, check the court rules for any citation rule that may differ from the *Bluebook* or the *ALWD*. The following are examples of federal and state citations.

A. Constitutions

U.S. Const. Art. IV § 3

N.M. Const. Art. IV § 1

B. Federal Citation

18 U.S.C. § 1112 (1994)	*United States Code*
8 U.S.C.A. § 1112 (West 1996)	*United States Code Annotated*
18 U.S.C.S. § 1112 (Lawyers Co-op. 1994)	*United States Code Service*

C. State Statutes

Ind. Code Ann. § 26-1-2-315 (Michie 1992)

Cal. Com. Code § 2314 (West 1964)

Colo. Rev. Stat. Ann. § 19-2-919 (West 1999)

D. Administrative Law

7 C.F.R. pt. 215 (2001)

66 Fed. Reg. 34636 (2001)

E. Court Rules

The rules are cited according to *Bluebook* format, see Chapter 8 for additional information on citing rules.

Fed. R. Civ. P. 4

Fed. R. Crim. P. 18

Exercises

Additional assignments are available on the CourseMate.

ASSIGNMENT 1

Mary and Tom have lived together for eight years in the state, but they have never married. They are buying a home together and they share a checking and savings account. Do the laws of your state recognize common law marriage? If so, do Tom and Mary have a common law marriage?

ASSIGNMENT 2

Irene has good credit and a good job. She believes that a landlord refused to rent her an apartment because she is a single woman. Refer to either the *USCA* or the *USCS*, and identify the federal law that governs this.

ASSIGNMENT 3

Refer to the *USCA*. What is the definition of a "digital audio recording device" under the copyright law?

ASSIGNMENT 4

Refer to the *USCS*. Cite the title and section of the code that addresses equal opportunity in contract solicitation, housing, and community development by the Federal Home Loan Mortgage Corporation.

ASSIGNMENT 5

What is the authorized term of imprisonment for a Class A felony under Title 18 of the *United States Code*? Cite the title and section.

ASSIGNMENT 6

Refer to the Fifth Amendment to the United States Constitution in the *USCA*. Cite a 1967 United States Supreme Court decision addressing the applicability of the privilege against self-incrimination in the case of juveniles.

ASSIGNMENT 7

Look up a statute in your state and identify the component parts. You may find it on the Web at http://www.findlaw.com (from the home page, locate "Learn More About" and click on "State Laws") or look up the statute at a local law or public library (most public libraries have the state statutes).

The following exercises present a statute followed by questions concerning the statute.

ASSIGNMENT 8

Statute: Criminal Code Section 20-4-102, Arson

　　A person who knowingly sets fire to, burns, causes to be burned, or by use of any explosive, damages or destroys, or causes to be damaged or destroyed, any property of another without his consent commits arson.

Questions

a. What are the required elements of arson?

b. Tom breaks into a neighbor's barn, sets off 20 sticks of dynamite, and blows up the barn. The barn does not catch fire, but it is blown to small bits and completely destroyed. Has Tom committed arson? Why?

c. Lois breaks into a house intending to steal cash and jewelry. She lights a match to locate a safe. She drops the match, it falls in a trashcan, and the house catches fire. Has Lois committed arson? Why?

d. Dai's Diner is losing money and about to go out of business. Dai and Steve own the building where the diner is located. One evening Dai sets the building on fire in order to collect the insurance on the building. Has Dai committed arson? Why?

ASSIGNMENT 9

Answer the questions in assignment 8 using your state law governing arson.

ASSIGNMENT 10

What, if any, federal regulation applies to environmental impact statements for activities in Antarctica?

ASSIGNMENT 11

Refer to the *Federal Register* for 2001. On what page of the *Federal Register* is the Drug Enforcement Administration's proposed rule for schedules of controlled substances distributed by electronic commerce?

ASSIGNMENT 12

Statute: Section 30-1-6, Nuncupative Wills

A. A nuncupative will may be made only by a person in imminent peril of death and shall be valid only if the testator died as a result of the impending peril, and must be:

　　1. Declared to be his last will by the testator before two disinterested witnesses;

　　2. Reduced to writing by or under the direction of one of the witnesses within 30 days after such declaration; and

　　3. Submitted for probate within six months after the death of the testator.

B. The nuncupative will may dispose of personal property only and to an aggregate value not exceeding $1,000.

C. A nuncupative will does not revoke an existing written will. Such written will is changed only to the extent necessary to give effect to the nuncupative will.

Note: A nuncupative is an oral will, a will that is not written.

Questions

a. To what type of will does this statute apply?

b. What requirements must be met for a nuncupative will to be valid, that is, what are the elements?

c. Mr. Lang, on his deathbed, writes his will on a piece of notepaper, signs it, and delivers it to his sister for safekeeping. Does the statute govern the validity of this will?

d. Larry, on his deathbed, declares that it is his will and that all his property should go to his girlfriend, Beth. Three witnesses are present: Beth, Larry's sister Mary, and the next-door neighbor, Tom. Tom is in an adjoining room. The door to the adjoining room is open. Tom hears what Larry is saying. Assume for the purposes of this example that the will is reduced to writing within 30 days and is submitted for probate within 6 months.

   1. Is this a valid will under this statute? What additional information may be necessary?

   2. Assume this is a valid will, and also that Larry had a previous valid written will. What impact does the nuncupative will have on the written will? What is disposed of by the nuncupative will?

ASSIGNMENT 13

Statute: Section 2-201, Statute of Frauds

The following statute is a section of the Commercial Code Sales Act adopted by the state legislature.

> A contract for the sale of goods for the price of five hundred dollars or more is not enforceable by way of action or defense unless there is some writing sufficient to indicate that a contract for sale has been made between the parties and signed by the party against whom enforcement is sought or by the party's authorized agent or broker. A writing is not insufficient because it omits or incorrectly states a term agreed upon, but the contract is not enforceable under this paragraph beyond the quantity of goods shown in such writing.

Assume that the act applies to the sales of goods. *Goods* are defined in § 2-100 as "those things movable" and do not include real property.

Questions

a. Does the statute apply to the lease of goods?

b. What are the required elements of the statute? In other words, for a contract for the sale of goods of $500 or more to be enforceable, what is required?

c. Mary orally contracts to buy 10 car tires at $70 each. The seller prepares a contract and gives it to Mary. Neither party signs the contract.

   1. Who can enforce the contract under the provisions of the statute?

   2. Assume that only Mary signs the contract. Who can enforce the contract?

   3. Assume that both parties sign the contract and the written contract incorrectly provides for 9 tires at $70 each. Is the contract enforceable under the statute? If so, to what extent is it enforceable?

   4. Assume both parties sign the contract and it reads 15 tires at $70 each. Is the contract enforceable under the statute? If so, to what extent is it enforceable?

   5. Assume there is no written contract. The seller hands Mary a slip of paper upon which he has written, "This is to confirm our oral agreement." He and Mary both sign the paper. Is there an enforceable contract under the provisions of the statute? If so, to what extent is it enforceable?

ASSIGNMENT 14

Statute: Section 35-1-4, Privileged Communications— Husband and Wife

In all actions, husband and wife may testify for or against each other, provided that neither may testify as to any communication or admission made by either of them to the other during the marriage, except in actions:

a. between such husband and wife, and,

b. where the custody, support, health or welfare of their children or children in either spouse's custody or control is directly in issue.

Questions

a. Prepare an outline of the statutory elements.

b. When can a husband or wife testify against each other? When are they prohibited from testifying against each other?

c. Husband, while driving under the influence of alcohol, ran a stop sign, and his vehicle collided with a vehicle driven by Mr. Smith. Husband's spouse (Wife) and two children were passengers in the car. The day after the wreck, Husband told Wife that he knew he ran the stop sign because he was drunk. Mr. Smith sues Husband for negligence. When answering the following questions, identify any additional information that may be necessary to fully answer the question.

   1. Can Wife be compelled to testify concerning her conversation with Husband? Why or why not?

2. Can Wife voluntarily testify concerning the conversation? Why or why not?

3. If Husband and Wife are legally separated, can Wife voluntarily testify concerning the conversation? Why or why not?

4. Is the conversation admissible if they are divorced at the time of the lawsuit? Why or why not?

5. Husband and Wife have lived together as husband and wife for the past 20 years. They have never been formally married. Can Wife testify against Husband concerning the conversation? Why or why not?

6. Is the conversation admissible in a divorce action between Husband and Wife? Why or why not?

ASSIGNMENT 15

Go to www.gpo.gov/fdsys/ and link to the United States Code. Select the year 2010 and locate the statute regarding the crime of domestic assault by a habitual offender.

Questions

a. What is the term of imprisonment for this offense?

b. How is "domestic assault" defined in this statute?

ASSIGNMENT 16

Using www.gpo.gov/fdsys, link to the *Code of Federal Regulations.* Select the title "Parks, Forests, and Public Property," select the chapter for "Forest Service, Department of Agriculture," select the part for "Travel Management," and then the subpart for "Designation of Roads, Trails and Areas for Motor Vehicle Use."

Questions

a. What section covers public involvement in decisions?

b. What does that section say about the right of the public to be involved in determining the use of trails and roads?

c. When is absence of public involvement authorized?

The available CourseMate for this text has an interactive eBook and interactive learning tools, including flash cards, quizzes, and more. To learn more about this resource and access free demo CourseMate resources, go to **www.cengagebrain.com**, and search for this book. To access CourseMate materials that you have purchased, go to **login.cengagebrain.com**.

CHAPTER 4

Case Law—Research and Briefing

After obtaining an associate's degree in paralegal studies, Vanessa took time off to be with Josh, the newest addition to her family. Josh was born three days after Vanessa's last final examination. She was glad he waited until finals were over. Vanessa decided it was important to give Josh her full attention for as long as she could. She was financially in a position to take a year off from work.

After the year had passed, a large law firm hired Vanessa and assigned her to the torts section of the paralegal department. Her first assignment was to locate and brief a case that could be used in a response to a motion to dismiss. The client filed a battery complaint against a bystander who encouraged the perpetrator in a fight to hit the client. Egged on by the bystander, the perpetrator attacked the client. The bystander's only action in the fight was to strongly encourage the perpetrator. The bystander's attorney filed a motion to dismiss, claiming that a person who only encourages a battery, but does not otherwise participate, cannot be liable for battery.

Vanessa knew it was important to do a good job on her first assignment. She realized she needed to refresh her memory on how to locate and brief a case. It had been a long time since she had researched and briefed cases. She thought to herself, "How do I find a case that supports our position? How do I brief the case?" (The case Vanessa located is presented in section IV of this chapter; also see Exhibit 4-1. Her method of locating and briefing it is presented in section VIII of this chapter.)

Learning Objectives

After completing this chapter, you should understand:

- The role and importance of court opinions
- The elements of a court opinion
- How to find court opinions
- The role and importance of a case brief
- The elements of a case brief
- How to brief a case

I. INTRODUCTION

The focus of this chapter is on court opinions—their elements, where they are published, how to find them, and how to read and brief them. The chapter addresses the same questions Vanessa faced when undertaking her assignment; that is, what are the elements of court opinions, where are opinions published, how to find them, and how to brief them. Throughout this chapter, a court opinion will be referred to as a *court case* and a brief of a court opinion will be referred to as a *case brief*. Chapter 12 discusses case law analysis. Case law analysis is the process you engage in to determine if a court opinion governs or applies to a client's case, that is, if a case is on point.

II. COURT OPINIONS—IN GENERAL

As discussed in Chapter 1, the two major sources of law are enacted law (e.g., constitutions, laws enacted by legislative bodies, administrative regulations) and case law. **Case law** is the body of law on a particular subject created by court opinions and is commonly referred to as **common law** or *judge-made law*. Case law is the most commonly used term and will be used throughout this chapter. Case law is found in the written opinions of the courts.

Case law consists of the law made by courts when they interpret existing law or create new law. It is composed of the legal rules, doctrines, and principles adopted by the courts. Courts often announce rules of law when interpreting statutory or constitutional provisions or create new law when there is no statutory or constitutional law governing a legal dispute.

> **For Example** *Statutory Interpretation:*
>
> A statute uses the term *publication* but fails to define it. The court, addressing the issue of what constitutes publication, announces a rule of law that the term *publication* as used in the statute means "communication to a third party."

> **For Example** *Creating Law:*
>
> A state has not enacted legislation recognizing strict liability as a cause of action in tort. The highest court in the state, in a case before it, announces a rule of law adopting strict liability as a cause of action in the state.

A **court opinion** is the court's written statement explaining its decision in a case. It is the court's resolution of the legal dispute before the court and the reasons in support of its resolution. It usually includes a statement of facts, points or rules of law, and rationale.

Often the terms *court opinion*, *case*, and *decision* are used interchangeably to refer to a court's resolution of an issue or a decision in a dispute. In this chapter, the terms *court opinion* and *case* are used to refer to the written opinion of a court.

> **For Example** "The case stands for the principle that..."
> "The court opinion holds that flag-burning is protected under the freedom of speech provisions of the First Amendment."

III. COURT OPINIONS—IMPORTANCE

Of the two major sources of law, enacted law and case (common) law, case law constitutes the largest body of law, far larger in volume than constitutional or statutory law. It is essential to acquire a general familiarity with this body of law, as it represents such a large portion of the law. Also, you must study case law because so many areas of law are governed by it.

There are numerous additional reasons why reading and analyzing court opinions and studying case law are important. Overall, the major reasons are as follows:

1. *To learn the case law.* Much of the law is court made. To determine the elements of a cause of action for a court-made law, you must refer to case law. Case law may govern your client's fact situation, and to determine what law applies and the probable outcome, you must analyze case law.

> **For Example** In most states, the cause of action for civil battery is a creation of case law, not statutory law. To identify the elements necessary to state a battery claim, the case law must be researched.

2. *To interpret constitutional or statutory law.* Court opinions often announce rules of law that govern how a statutory or constitutional term or provision is interpreted or applied. Therefore, you must consult case law to understand how to interpret and apply statutes and constitutional provisions.

> **For Example** The United States Supreme Court has issued many opinions on the types of speech protected by the First Amendment. To determine if an individual who burns a state flag in front of the state capital is protected by the First Amendment's freedom of speech provisions, Supreme Court opinions interpreting freedom of speech must be consulted.

3. *To understand the litigation process.* Court opinions often address legal questions that arise in the context of the litigation process—either before, during, or after trial. Court opinions give insight into the process by explaining what conduct is appropriate, which arguments are successful, where errors are made, how procedural rules apply, how trials and motion hearings should proceed, and so on.

4. *To gain insight into legal analysis.* In a court opinion, the court often analyzes the law. The court discusses what law applies, how it applies, the reasons for its application, and how the reasons operate to govern the application of the law to the facts of the case. By studying court opinions, you learn how to assemble a legal argument, how to determine if a law applies, and how to support a legal argument.

5. *To develop legal writing skills.* Judges are usually experienced in legal writing, and most opinions are well written. You may read opinions with an eye to how sentences and paragraphs are structured, how case law and statutory law are referred to and incorporated into legal writing, and how transitions are accomplished. If you have a problem putting some aspect of your research into writing, look at an opinion to see how a court handled a similar matter.

> **For Example** You are preparing a research memorandum. There is no case law in your jurisdiction governing the issue; however, there is strong persuasive precedent from another jurisdiction. You are unsure about how to introduce the persuasive precedent in your memorandum. By reading a court opinion in which the court relied on persuasive precedent, you can study the language the court used to introduce the persuasive precedent and use the court's language as a guide after which to model your introduction.

> **For Example** In *Smith v. Jones,* the court stated, "There is no case law in this jurisdiction interpreting the term 'publication' as used in § 55-5-67A. The state of Texas, however, has an identical statute, and the Supreme Court of Texas, in the case of *Frank v. Inex*, interpreted 'publication' to mean communication to a third party." You can use this language as a guide in your introduction of persuasive precedent.

For these reasons and many others, the study of case law is important. The skill of being able to correctly locate, analyze, and apply case law is essential to legal analysis.

IV. COURT OPINIONS—ELEMENTS

A. In General

The first requirement for proper analysis of a court opinion is to be familiar with the elements of an opinion. A court opinion usually includes some or all of the following components:

1. The facts that gave rise to the legal dispute before the court
2. The procedural history and posture of the case—that is, what happened in the lower court or courts, who appealed the decision, and why
3. The issue or issues addressed and resolved by the court
4. The rule of law that governs the dispute
5. The application of the rule of law to the facts—in other words, the holding
6. The reason or reasons supporting the court's application of the rule of law to the facts, that is, why the court decided as it did
7. The relief granted or denied (e.g., "The judgment of the trial court is upheld.")

B. Elements of a Reported Case

West, a Thomson Reuters business that publishes the regional reporters and most of the federal reporters, follows a uniform format when publishing court opinions. LexisNexis follows a similar format in its publication of *Supreme Court Reports—Lawyer's Edition*. Because the majority of court opinions are published by West, an example of an opinion published by West is presented in Exhibit 4-1. The case, *Rael v. Cadena*, is published in the *New Mexico Reports* and the *Pacific Reporter*. Note that the components of the case are identified in the left margin next to each section of the opinion. These components are summarized in the following text.

1. Citation

The **citation** refers to the volume number, page number, and the name of the reporter where the case may be found. The citation for *Rael v. Cadena* is 93 N.M. 684, 604 P.2d 822. That means the printed opinion of this case is published and may be found in two reporters: volume 93 of the *New Mexico Reports* at page 684, and volume 604 of the *Pacific Reporter*, second series, at page 822. (See "Citation" in Exhibit 4-1.) When an opinion may be found in more than one set of books, the citations are referred to as **parallel citations**.

Court decisions are increasingly available through court Web sites or other publications. Thus, public domain citations, also referred to as *neutral citations* or *vendor-neutral citations,* are often included. Therefore, an additional citation number may be present.

Exhibit 4-1 *Court Opinion*—Rael v. Cadena. *Reprinted from 604 Pacific Reporter 2d 822, (1979), with permission from Thomson Reuters.*

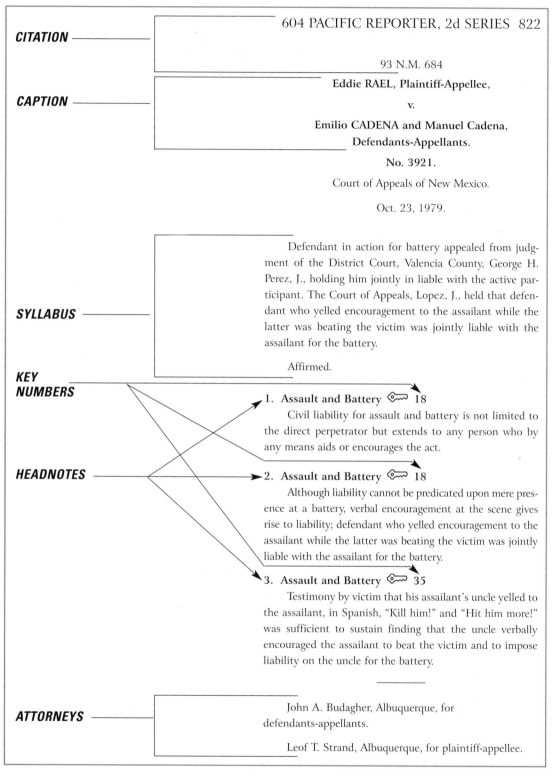

CITATION

604 PACIFIC REPORTER, 2d SERIES 822

93 N.M. 684

CAPTION

Eddie RAEL, Plaintiff-Appellee,

v.

Emilio CADENA and Manuel Cadena,
Defendants-Appellants.

No. 3921.

Court of Appeals of New Mexico.

Oct. 23, 1979.

SYLLABUS

Defendant in action for battery appealed from judgment of the District Court, Valencia County, George H. Perez, J., holding him jointly in liable with the active participant. The Court of Appeals, Lopez, J., held that defendant who yelled encouragement to the assailant while the latter was beating the victim was jointly liable with the assailant for the battery.

Affirmed.

KEY NUMBERS

HEADNOTES

1. Assault and Battery ⚷ 18
   Civil liability for assault and battery is not limited to the direct perpetrator but extends to any person who by any means aids or encourages the act.

2. Assault and Battery ⚷ 18
   Although liability cannot be predicated upon mere presence at a battery, verbal encouragement at the scene gives rise to liability; defendant who yelled encouragement to the assailant while the latter was beating the victim was jointly liable with the assailant for the battery.

3. Assault and Battery ⚷ 35
   Testimony by victim that his assailant's uncle yelled to the assailant, in Spanish, "Kill him!" and "Hit him more!" was sufficient to sustain finding that the uncle verbally encouraged the assailant to beat the victim and to impose liability on the uncle for the battery.

ATTORNEYS

John A. Budagher, Albuquerque, for defendants-appellants.

Leof T. Strand, Albuquerque, for plaintiff-appellee.

(Continued)

Exhibit 4-1 (Continued)

JUDGE

BODY OF THE OPINION

OPINION

LOPEZ, Judge.

Defendant Emilio Cadena, a non-active participant in the battery of plaintiff Eddie Rael, appeals the judgment of the trial court finding him, along with the active participant, jointly and severally liable for the battery. We affirm.

The issue on appeal is whether a person present at a battery who verbally encourages the assailant, but does not physically assist him, is civilly liable for the battery.

On a visit in Emilio Cadena's home, Eddie Rael was severely beaten on the head and torso by Emilio's nephew, Manuel Cadena. As a result of the beating, he suffered a fractured rib and was hospitalized. Eddie Rael testified that once the attack had started, Emilio yelled to Manuel in Spanish, "Kill him!" and "Hit him more!" The trial court sitting without a jury found that Emilio encouraged Manuel while Manuel was beating Eddie. Based on this finding, the court held the Cadenas jointly and severally liable for the battery.

Emilio urges that in order for the trial court to have held him jointly liable for the battery, it had to find either that he and Manuel acted in concert, or that Manuel beat and injured Eddie as a result of Emilio's encouragement. This is a misstatement of the law.

[1] This is an issue of first impression in New Mexico. It is clear, however, that in the United States, civil liability for assault and battery is not limited to the direct perpetrator, but extends to any person who by any means aids or encourages the act. *Hargis v. Herrine*, 230 Ark. 502, 323 S.W.2d 917 (1959); *Ayer v. Robinson*, 163 Cal. App.2d 424, 329 P.2d 546 (1958); *Guilbeau v. Guilbeau*, 326 So.2d 654 (La.App.1976); *Duke v. Feldman*, 245 Md. 454, 226 A.2d 345 (1967); *Brink v. Purnell*, 162 Mich. 147, 127 N.W. 322 (1910); 6 Am.Jur.2d *Assault and Battery* § 128 (1963); 6A C.J.S. *Assault and Battery* § 11 (1975); Annot., 72 A.L.R.2d 1229 (1960). According to the Restatement:

[f]or harm resulting to a third person from the tortious conduct of another, one is subject to liability if he

* * * * * *

(b) knows that the other's conduct constitutes a breach of duty and gives substantial assistance or encouragement to the other so to conduct himself. * * *

Restatement (Second) of Torts § 876 (1979).

[2] Although liability cannot be predicated upon mere presence at a battery, *Duke, supra;* 6 Am.Jur., *supra,* verbal encouragement at the scene gives rise to liability. *Hargis, supra; Ayer, supra; Brink, supra.*

[A] person may be held liable for the tort of assault and battery if he *encouraged* or incited *by words* the act of the direct perpetrator. * * * (Emphasis added.)

6 Am.Jur., *supra* at 108. Because he yelled encouragement to his nephew while the latter was beating Eddie Rael, Emilio Cadena is jointly liable with his nephew for the battery.

[3] Contradictory evidence was offered as to whether Emilio Cadena did yell anything during the beating. Eddie Rael claimed that Emilio urged Manuel to beat him; Emilio denied that he said anything; and Manuel testified that he never heard Emilio. However, the trial court found that Emilio did verbally encourage Manuel to beat Eddie. Although the evidence was in conflict, the court could conclude from the testimony of Eddie Rael that Emilio Cadena verbally encouraged his nephew to attack. This testimony, if believed, is substantial evidence to support the trial court's finding. It is not the function of the appellate court to weigh the evidence or its credibility, or to substitute its judgment for that of the trial court. So long as the findings are supported by substantial evidence, they will stand. *Getz v. Equitable Life Assur. Soc. of U.S.,* 90 N.M. 195, 561 P.2d 468, *cert. denied,* 434 U.S. 834, 98 S.Ct. 121, 54 L.Ed.2d 95 (1977).

The judgment of the trial court is affirmed.

IT IS SO ORDERED.

SUTIN and ANDREWS, JJ., concur.

> **For Example** *State v. Foster*, 1998-NMCA-163, 126 N.M. 177, 976 P.2d 852. 1998-NMCA-163
> is the public domain or vendor-neutral citation. The year published is 1998.
> NMCA is the court—the New Mexico Court of Appeals. The last number, 163, is the case
> number. In this example there are three parallel citations.

The format for neutral citations is discussed in greater detail in Chapter 8.

2. Caption

The **caption** includes the names of the **parties** to the lawsuit and their court status. Eddie Rael was the plaintiff at the trial court level, and he is the appellee on appeal. (The *appellee* is the person against whom the appeal is filed, the person who won at the trial court level.) Emilio Cadena was the defendant at the trial court level and is the appellant on appeal. (The *appellant* is the person who lost at the trial court level and who filed the appeal.) Manuel Cadena is listed as a defendant-appellant, but he is not involved in the appeal. The caption of the case used on appeal is usually the same as the caption used in the trial court. The caption of the case in the trial court includes both Cadenas as defendants, and therefore, the caption on appeal is the same. Note that the plaintiff's and the defendant's last names are printed in all capitals. (See "Caption" in Exhibit 4-1.) Often when referring to or citing the case, only the names in all capitals are used. However, you should always consult the appropriate citation manual to determine which names to present in a citation.

> **For Example** When citing this case, the citation should read: *Rael v. Cadena,* 93 N.M.
> 684, 604 P.2d 822 (Ct. App. 1979).

Note that below the caption is "No. 3921." This is the docket number of the case assigned by the court of appeals. Below the docket number is the name of the court that decided the case and the date of the decision. This is indicated in the citation as: (Ct. App. 1979). If the decision had been rendered by the highest court in the jurisdiction, such as the supreme court of New Mexico, only the year of the decision would appear in the parentheses: (1979). If the citation does not include a state reporter citation, a reference to the state is included in the parentheses.

> **For Example** *Smith v. Jones*, 292 S.W.2d 425 (Tex. 1980).

3. Syllabus

The **syllabus** is a brief summary of the opinion. It is an editorial enhancement written by West, not the court, and cannot be relied upon as the holding of the court. It is presented as a useful aid in providing the reader with a brief overview of the opinion. (See "Syllabus" in Exhibit 4-1.)

4. Headnotes

The **headnotes** are summaries of the points of law discussed in the case. Headnotes follow, in sequential order, the relevant paragraphs of the opinion. The number to the left of the headnote corresponds to the bracketed number in the body of the opinion. (See "Headnotes" in Exhibit 4-1.)

> **For Example** In *Rael v. Cadena*, headnote 1 contains a summary of the point of law
> discussed in the body of the opinion between [1] and [2]. Headnote 2 is a
> summary of the point of law discussed in the opinion between [2] and [3]. Headnote 3 is
> a summary of the law discussed in the opinion between [3] and the end of the opinion.

Note that headnotes are prepared by West and are not part of the case. They are prepared for the convenience of individuals researching the case and are useful in providing a quick overview of the law and legal principles addressed in the opinion. They are not the opinion of the court and have no authority of law. Any reference to or quote from an opinion must be taken from the opinion itself, not from the headnotes.

5. Key Numbers

In bold print next to the headnote number are a few words indicating the area of law addressed in the headnote. Next to this bold-print description of the area of law is a small key symbol and a number. (See "Key Numbers" in Exhibit 4-1.) West has divided all areas of American law into various topics and subtopics. Each area is identified by a topic name (the bold print), and each specific topic or subtopic is assigned a **key number**. West publishes separate volumes called *digests* that contain summaries of court opinions organized by topic and subtopic.

For Example Next to headnote 1 in *Rael v. Cadena* is "Assault and Battery," followed by a key symbol and the number 18. The key symbol and the number 18 refer to a specific subtopic of assault and battery. The subject of this subtopic can be determined by consulting the index to "assault and battery" in the digest (the use of a digest is discussed in Chapter 5). In the body of the opinion between [1] and [2], the area of law covered is assault and battery in general. A reference to the digest reveals that key number 18 is the specific subtopic of assault and battery concerning the liability of persons who aid or encourage an assault or battery. If you want to read other court opinions in which liability for battery was based upon the conduct of aiding or encouraging a batterer at the scene of a battery, refer to the volume of the digest containing the topic "assault and battery." Look to the subtopic key number 18. Under that key number is a summary of all court opinions that have addressed this subtopic and the citations of those opinions.

Through this system, you have easy access to all court opinions dealing with the question you are considering. The key number system is an invaluable research tool.

6. Attorneys

This section provides the names and cities of the attorneys in the case and the parties they represent. (See "Attorneys" in Exhibit 4-1.)

7. Judge

At the beginning of the opinion is the name of the judge who wrote it. (See "Judge" in Exhibit 4-1.)

8. Body of the Opinion

The **body of the opinion** usually includes the facts of the case, the prior proceedings, the issue or issues addressed by the court, the rule or rules of law governing the dispute, the holding, the reasoning in support of the holding, and the relief granted. (See "Body of the Opinion" in Exhibit 4-1.) There are no hard-and-fast rules dictating what must be contained in a court opinion, and often one or more of the components listed here may be missing. Each of the components of the body are discussed separately here.

a. Facts

Opinions usually include the facts that gave rise to the legal dispute. Often the opinion may include very few facts or more facts than appear relevant to the matter decided.

b. Prior Proceedings

In this part of the opinion, the court presents a summary of what happened in the lower court and who appealed. This may be a very brief summary, as in *Rael v. Cadena*, or it may be extensive and detailed.

c. Issue or Issues

The *issue* is the legal question addressed by the court in the opinion. The court may present the issue narrowly in the context of the facts.

> **For Example** Under New Mexico tort law, does a battery occur when an individual, present at a battery, verbally encourages the assailant by yelling, "Kill him!" and "Hit him more!" but does not in any other way participate in the battery?

The court may state the issue broadly, merely phrasing the issue in the context of the area of law.

> **For Example** Did the defendant commit a civil battery?

In many instances, a case addresses more than one legal issue. Also, the court may not present a statement of the issue or issues at all, and it may be difficult to determine what they are.

Identifying and understanding the issue make up the most important task of reading an opinion. If the issue is not understood, then the rule of law applied by the court may not be understood, and the opinion consequently may be misanalyzed and misapplied.

d. Rule of Law

The rule of law is the law that governs the issue. It may be a statutory or constitutional provision or a case law doctrine, rule, principle, and so on. In *Rael v. Cadena*, case law governs the law of civil assault and battery.

e. Holding

The holding is the court's application of the rule of law to the facts of the case. It is the court's answer to the issue(s) in the case. The holding is usually presented immediately after the rule of law in the opinion or after the reasoning at the end of the opinion.

f. Reasoning

The **reasoning** is the court's explanation of how or why the rule of law applies to the dispute. On occasion, the reasoning is difficult to follow. Often, it is helpful to read the holding first and determine how the court ruled, then read the reasoning. By first understanding what decision was reached, you may be better able to understand the reasoning in support of the decision.

g. Disposition/Relief Granted

The relief granted is usually a one-sentence statement by the court that includes the order of the court as a result of the holding.

> **For Example** In *Rael v. Cadena*, next to the last sentence where the court states, "The judgment of the trial court is affirmed," the court presents the relief granted.

A court has several options when granting relief:

- It may agree with the trial court and *affirm* the trial court's decision.
- It may disagree with the trial court and *reverse* the trial court's decision. If it reverses the decision, it will *remand*, that is, send the case back to the trial court. When a case is remanded, the appellate court may order the trial court to:
  1. Enter a judgment or order in accordance with the appellate court decision
  2. Retry the case (conduct a new trial)
  3. Conduct further proceedings in accordance with the appellate court decision
- If there are several issues, it may affirm the trial court on some of the issues and reverse the trial court on other issues.

h. Concurring Opinion

In some instances, a judge may agree with the majority holding but for different or additional reasons than those presented by the majority. The judge may then set out his or her reasons in support of the majority in what is called a *concurring opinion*. There may be more than one concurring opinion if other judges also agree with the majority conclusion but for different or additional reasons.

i. Dissenting Opinion

If a judge disagrees with the majority decision, the judge may present his or her reasons in what is called a *dissenting opinion*. Because a dissenting opinion does not agree with the majority view, it does not have the force of law. It is valuable, however, because it may help a reader understand the majority opinion.

> **For Example** The dissent may summarize what the court stated in the majority opinion. Note, however, that because the dissent disagrees with the majority view, it may mischaracterize the majority opinion.

The dissenting opinion is also important because it may become the majority view in the future when the composition of the court changes or there is a shift in the court's position. The dissent may provide the basis for future arguments in support of overruling outdated precedent. Remember, at one time the United States Supreme Court ruled that segregation on the basis of race was legal, *Plessey v. Ferguson*, 163 U.S. 537, 16 S. Ct. 1138, 41 L. Ed. 256 (1896). Now, segregation on the basis of race is illegal, *Brown v. Board of Education of Topeka*, 347 U.S. 483, 74 S. Ct. 686, 98 L. Ed. 873 (1954).

V. COURT OPINIONS—RESEARCHING

Researching case law is the process of finding a court opinion that answers a question being researched. Usually the search is for case law that governs or guides the resolution of an issue in a client's case. Such a court opinion is often referred to as being *on point*. Chapter 12 indicates how to determine whether a case is on point. This section focuses on how to find court opinions. The first part of this section discusses case law research sources, that is, where federal and state court opinions are published. The second part presents research strategies or techniques, that is, how to conduct case law research.

A. Publication of Court Opinions

1. In General

Not all court opinions are published in the national or state reporters as discussed later in this section (see subsection A.3). Most federal and state trial court decisions are not published, as they are generally only persuasive authority and not binding precedent. Due to the large number of cases, many but not all federal and state appellate court decisions are published. Sometimes an appellate court will choose not to publish a decision because the decision does not have value as precedent. The opinion may address a question already well settled in the law, or it may merely reflect the court's correction of a trial court error. Publication is limited primarily to cases establishing a new rule of law or changing existing law, criticizing existing law, involving matters of public interest, or resolving conflicts of authority.

Do not assume that because a decision is not published that it is not available. All cases are public records, unless a case is sealed, such as for national security reasons or to protect a minor. By virtue of being a public record, all records within a file are accessible at the courthouse, including the opinion of the court. Court opinions not designated for publication are often referred to as *unpublished* decisions. Prior to the widespread use of court Web sites, unpublished court opinions could be obtained only by going to the court-house, requesting the file, and copying the opinion. Today, many courts produce opinions not meant for publication in the hardbound volumes of reporters either by making them available on the court Web site or by releasing them to online resources such as Westlaw and Lexis. In addition, West created the *Federal Appendix*, a reporter that collects unpublished federal circuit court decisions.

In the past, unpublished opinions could not be used as precedent or cited; however, there is an increasing trend toward allowing unpublished cases to be used in this manner. Research-ers should consult their local rules of appellate procedure and the federal rules of appellate procedure to determine whether use of and citation to unpublished cases are allowed in a particular jurisdiction. Even when use of unpublished cases is permitted, be aware that they are often regarded only as being persuasive and have little or no binding precedential effect.

Just as there are so-called official and unofficial publications of statutory law, there are official and unofficial publications of case law as well. The official publications of case law are those published at the direction of the government. Court opinions that are not published at the direction of the government are considered unofficial publications. Both official and unofficial publications include, at a minimum, the full text of court opinions.

2. Forms of Publication

Most court opinions are published three times in three formats: slip opinions, advance sheets, and bound volumes called reports or reporters.

a. Slip Opinion

Most court decisions are first published by the court in the form of a slip opinion. Where there is a court Web site, the opinions may also be published on that site. The **slip opinion** is usually in the form of a pamphlet that contains the full text of the court's opinion in a single case. It includes any concurring or dissenting opinion in the case. It is individually paginated and includes the case name, date of the decision, and attorneys' names. If a state has adopted public domain or vendor-neutral citation, that citation may also be included.

Slip opinions do not usually include a syllabus (synopsis or summary of the facts, issues, and holding of a case), nor do they include headnotes. They are not organized by legal topic. All slip opinions are distributed to the parties involved in the lawsuit. In some jurisdictions they are also available by subscription.

b. Advance Sheets

The permanent hardbound volumes of court decisions are published when there are a large number of court decisions sufficient to fill an entire volume. Therefore, many opinions may not appear in a bound volume until up to a year after the decision is rendered. **Advance sheets** are temporary pamphlets (often softcover books) that contain the full text of a number of recent court decisions. They are designed to provide quick access to recent court decisions. The publishers of the permanent volumes publish advance sheets frequently, often weekly. They are placed next to the last hardbound volume and are discarded when a permanent volume is published that contains the opinions printed in the advance sheets.

The decisions are presented chronologically and are sequentially paginated; that is, the volume and page number in the advance sheet will be the same as the page and volume number of the bound volume when the bound volume is published.

> **For Example** An opinion that appears in volume 525, page 756 of the advance sheet will appear in volume 525, page 756 of the permanent bound volume.

The advance sheets usually contain a case synopsis and headnotes for each case and an index and tables that appear in the permanent volume. They include a Key Number Digest section that arranges the cases by digest topic and subtopic.

c. Reporter

Court opinions are permanently published in hardbound volumes usually referred to as a **reporter** or a *report*. A reporter volume is published when there are a sufficient number of advance sheets to fill a bound volume. The cases are presented chronologically and paginated with the same page numbers as the advance sheets. Each bound volume usually includes a subject index and an alphabetical list of the opinions reported in the volume. The volumes are numbered consecutively so that the highest numbered volume will contain the most recent cases. Often, when there are a large number of volumes in a series, a second or even third series will be started. The new series will begin at volume 1.

> **For Example** West's *Pacific Reporter* publishes the state court opinions for the western states. When the number of volumes of the *Pacific Reporter* (cited as P.) reached 300, a second series, *Pacific Reporter, Second Series* (cited as P.2d), beginning at volume 1, was started. When the second series reached 999 volumes, the *Pacific Reporter, Third Series* (cited as P.3d), beginning at volume 1, was started. The series number is indicated in the citation. The P.2d in the citation "662 P.2d 646" indicates that the decision is found in *Pacific Reporter, Second Series*. The volume number is 662, and the page number is 646.

3. National Reporter System

Most court decisions, both federal and state, are published by West in multivolume sets called *reporters*. These sets are available from the publisher in hardbound volumes and many are available on CD-ROM.

> **For Example** The decisions of the United States Supreme Court are published in the *Supreme Court Reporter*, the decisions of the United States Courts of Appeals are published in the *Federal Reporters*, and the decisions of the various state appellate courts are published in regional or state-specific reporters.

The following sections discuss the various reporters. The features common to all these reporters are presented here rather than repeated in the discussion of each reporter. Most reporter volumes include:

- A table of cases, which lists in alphabetical order the opinions presented in the volume. Most sets have an additional table of cases in which the cases are arranged by state or by circuit.

> **For Example** Each volume of the *Federal Reporter* has a table of cases listing all the cases alphabetically and a table that arranges the cases alphabetically by circuit. All the cases from the First Circuit, Second Circuit, and so on are arranged alphabetically by circuit. The *South Western Reporter* includes a table of cases that lists the cases alphabetically and a table that arranges the cases alphabetically by state so that all the cases from each state are listed separately.

- A table of statutes listing the various statutes, constitutional provisions, and often rules interpreted or reviewed, and listing the relevant court opinions.

> **For Example** If you are researching cases that have interpreted the First Amendment to the United States Constitution, the table will direct you to all the cases in the volume that have interpreted the First Amendment.

- A table of words and phrases listing alphabetically words and phrases judicially defined and indicating the page number in the volume where they are defined.
- A Key Number Digest in the back of each volume, which provides a summary of each case in the volume arranged by topic and key number.
- A case syllabus (a synopsis case summary), headnotes, and key numbers, which are located at the beginning of each case presented in the volume. This allows a researcher quick access to all related cases through West's Digest System. (See the first page of Exhibit 4-1.)

4. Publication of Federal Court Decisions

a. United States Supreme Court

Three different sets publish the decisions of the United States Supreme Court: *United States Reports*, *Supreme Court Reporter*, and *United States Supreme Court Reports, Lawyers' Edition*.

(1) United States Reports The *United States Reports* (cited as U.S.) is the official reporter for the Supreme Court of the United States. It is published by the United States Government Printing Office and contains the full text of all the decisions of the Supreme Court. The decisions are initially published as slip opinions, followed by advance sheets and then, finally, hardbound volumes. The reports are indexed but do not include headnotes or key numbers.

(2) Supreme Court Reporter The *Supreme Court Reporter* (cited as S. Ct.) is an unofficial publication of the decisions of the United States Supreme Court published by West and is

part of West's **National Reporter System**. It includes the decisions of the Supreme Court since 1882. It is published more quickly than the *United States Reports*. Advance sheets are published at least twice a month.

The headnotes with links to the key numbers make the *Supreme Court Reporter* a valuable research tool. The key numbers, through their link to West's Digest System, allow a researcher to research a point of law discussed in a Supreme Court opinion in all reported decisions—both federal and state (see Exhibit 4-2).

Exhibit 4-2 *Opinion from* Supreme Court Reporter. *Reprinted from In Re Kennedy, 525 U.S. 153, 119 S.Ct. 635, 142 L.Ed.2d 573 (1999), with permission from Thomson Reuters.*

---

525 U.S. 154   **IN RE KENNEDY**   635
Cite as 119 S.Ct. 635 (1999)

525 U.S. 153, 142 L.Ed.2d 573
|₁₅₃In re Michael KENNEDY
No. 98-6945.
Decided Jan. 11, 1999

Pro se petitioner sought extraordinary writ in noncriminal matter. On petitioner's motion to proceed in forma pauperis, the Supreme Court held that, because petition was petitioner's twelfth frivolous filing with Supreme Court in a noncriminal matter, he would not be allowed to proceed in forma pauperis, and would be barred prospectively from bringing further petitions for certiorari or for extraordinary writs in noncriminal matters without paying fee and complying with rule governing document preparation.

So ordered.

Justice Stevens dissented with statement.

Federal Courts ⬤⇀ 453

Because pro se petitioner's petition for extraordinary writ was his twelfth frivolous filing with Supreme Court in a noncriminal matter, he would not be allowed to proceed in forma pauperis, and would be barred prospectively from bringing further petitions for certiorari or petitions for extraordinary writs in noncriminal matters without paying docketing fee and complying with rule governing document preparation. U.S.Sup.Ct.Rules 33.1, 38, 39, 39.8, 28 U.S.C.A.

PER CURIAM.

Pro se petitioner Kennedy seeks leave to proceed *in forma pauperis* under Rule 39 of this court. We deny this request Pursuant to Rule 39.8, Kennedy is allowed until February 1, 1999, within which to pay the docketing fee required by Rule 38 and to submit his petition in compliance with this Court's Rule 33.1. We also direct the Clerk of the Court not to accept any further petitions for certio-

rari nor petitions for extraordinary writs from Kennedy in noncriminal matters unless he pays the docketing fee required by Rule 38 and submits his petition in compliance with Rule 33.1.

Kennedy has abused this Court's certiorari and extraordinary writ processes. In October 1998, we invoked Rule 39.8 to deny Kennedy *in forma pauperis* status. See *In re Kennedy*, 525 U.S. 807, 119 S.Ct. 38, 142 L.Ed.2d 30 (1998). At this time, Kennedy had filed four petitions for extraordinary writs and six petitions for certiorari, all of which were both patently frivolous and had been denied without recorded dissent. The instant petition for an extraordinary writ thus constitutes Kennedy's 12th frivolous filing with this Court.

We enter the order barring prospective filings for the reasons discussed in *Martin v. District of Columbia Court* ₁₅₄*of Appeals*, 506 U.S. 1, 113 S. Ct. 397, 121 L.Ed.2d 305 (1992) (*per curiam*). Kennedy's abuse of the writ of certiorari and of the extraordinary writ has been in noncriminal cases, and so we limit our sanction accordingly. The order therefore will not prevent Kennedy from petitioning to challenge criminal sanctions which might be imposed on him. The order, however, will allow this Court to devote its limited resources to the claims of petitioners who have not abused our process.

It is so ordered.

Justice STEVENS, dissenting.

For reasons previously stated, see *Martin v. District of Columbia Court of Appeals*, 506 U.S. 1, 4, 113 S.Ct. 397, 121 L.Ed.2d 305 (1992) (STEVENS, J., dissenting), and cases cited, I respectfully dissent.

---

(3) United States Supreme Court Reports, Lawyers' Edition The *United States Supreme Court Reports, Lawyers' Edition* (cited as L. Ed. or L. Ed. 2d for volumes since 1956) is an unofficial publication of the decisions of the United States Supreme Court published by LexisNexis. It includes all the decisions of the Supreme Court since 1789. Advance sheets are published at least twice a month.

Like the *Supreme Court Reporter,* a summary of the case and headnotes precedes each opinion. Each headnote is assigned a topic and section number (see Exhibit 4-3). The topics are printed in *United States Supreme Court Digest, Lawyers' Edition.* This allows researchers to locate other cases addressing the same topic. In addition, there are summaries of the briefs of counsel and, for some cases, annotations that analyze important points of law covered in the cases are presented.

Exhibit 4-3 *Page Showing Headnote from Opinion Published in* United States Supreme Court Reports, Lawyers' Edition. *Geissal v. Moore Medical Corp., 524 U.S. 74, 118 S.Ct. 1869, 141 L.Ed.2d 64 (1998), page 65. Reprinted with the permission of LexisNexis.*

GEISSAL V MOORE MEDICAL CORP.
(1998) 524 US 74,141 L Ed 2d 64,118 S Ct 1869

defendants (1) had violated COBRA by renouncing an obligation to provide continuing coverage, and (2) were estopped to deny him COBRA continuation coverage. The parties agreed to have a magistrate judge conduct all proceedings. The individual (1) moved for partial summary judgment on the first two counts, and (2) included an argument that the defendants' reliance upon § 1162(2)(D)(i) to deny him continuation coverage was misplaced, as he had first been covered under his wife's plan before he had elected continuation coverage. While the motion was pending, the individual died and his wife, who was also the personal representative of his estate, replaced him as plaintiff. The magistrate judge granted partial summary judgment in favor of the defendants on the two counts, as the magistrate judge expressed the view that under § 1162(2)(D)(I), an employee with coverage under another group health plan as of the date on which the employee elected COBRA continuation coverage was ineligible for such coverage (927 F Supp 352, 1996 US Dist LEXIS 7145). On appeal, the United States Court of Appeals for the Eighth Circuit, in affirming, expressed the view that (1) under § 1162(2)(D)(i), it was within the defendants' rights to cancel the individual's COBRA benefits unless there was a "significant gap" between the coverage afforded under the corporation's plan and that afforded under his wife's plan; and (2) the wife had failed to carry her burden of showing that such a significant gap existed (114 F3d 1458, 1997 US App LEXIS 13589).

On certiorari, the United States Supreme Court vacated the Court of Appeals' judgment and remanded the case for further proceedings. In an opinion by SOUTER, J., expressing the unanimous view of the court, it was held that § 1162(2)(D)(i) did not allow an employer to deny COBRA continuation coverage to a qualified beneficiary who was covered under another group health plan at the time that the beneficiary made a COBRA election, as (1) under the plain meaning of § 1162(2)(D)(i) as it read at the time pertinent to the case at hand, the medical corporation could not cut off the individual's COBRA continuation coverage, where the individual (a) was covered under his wife's plan before he made his COBRA election, and (b) so did not first become covered under his wife's plan after the date of election; and (2) there was no justification for disparaging the clarity of § 1162(2)(D)(i).

HEADNOTE

Classified to United States Supreme Court Digest, Lawyers' Edition

Pensions and Retirement Funds § 1—Employee Retirement Income Security Act—group health plan—continuation coverage

For purposes of some provisions (29 USCS §§ 1161 et seq.) of the Employee Retirement Income Security Act of 1974 as amended by the Consolidated Omnibus Budget Reconciliation Act of 1985 (COBRA)-which provisions authorize a qualified beneficiary of an employer's group health plan to obtain continued coverage under the plan when the beneficiary might otherwise lose that benefit for certain reasons, such as the termination of employment-29 USCS § 1162(2)(D)(i) (later amended) does not allow an employer to deny COBRA continuation coverage to qualified beneficiary who is covered

---

Note that the publisher prepares the case summaries, headnotes, and so on presented in both the *Supreme Court Reporter* and the *United States Supreme Court Reports, Lawyers' Edition;* they are not part of the actual court opinion. They are valuable research tools, but they are not the law. Any reference or quote in research should be to the court opinion itself and not to the material prepared by the publisher.

(4) Loose-Leaf Services and Newspapers There are various sources to obtain quick access to the decisions of the Supreme Court of the United States. The *United States Law Week*, published by the Bureau of National Affairs, is a loose-leaf service that publishes weekly decisions of the Supreme Court. The service includes additional information, such as summaries of cases pending before the court and reports on oral arguments. Often, law firms and law libraries subscribe to legal newspapers that print the decisions of the United States Supreme Court and other federal courts.

(5) Computer and Internet Resources Note that access to most federal court opinions is available through Westlaw and LexisNexis. In addition, court opinions are often available through the official court Web site and other Internet resources (see Internet Resources at the end of this chapter). Many federal reporters are also available from the publisher on CD-ROM. Chapter 7 covers computer-aided research in detail.

b. United States Courts of Appeals

West publishes the decisions of the United States Circuit Courts of Appeals in the *Federal Reporter* (cited as F.), the *Federal Reporter, Second Series* (cited as F.2d), and the *Federal Reporter, Third Series* (cited as F.3d). Like the *Supreme Court Reporter*, it is part of West's National Reporter System. The cases are initially published in advance sheets, which are later compiled in hardbound volumes. The *Federal Reporter* is an unofficial reporter, but it is the only reporter that publishes the decisions of the United States Circuit Courts of Appeals. Therefore, there are no parallel citations for these decisions.

Over the years, the *Federal Reporter* has included decisions of courts other than the United States Circuit Courts of Appeals, such as decisions of the United States District Courts up to 1932 and the United States Court of Claims from 1960 to 1982. As mentioned at the beginning of this section, due to the large number of cases, not all decisions are published.

c. United States District Courts

West publishes selected decisions of the United States District Courts since 1932 in the *Federal Supplement* (cited as F. Supp.). This reporter set includes the decisions of the United States Court of International Trade since 1956 and the Judicial Panel on Multidistrict Litigation since 1932. Like the *Federal Reporter*, it is an unofficial reporter, but it is the only reporter that publishes the decisions of the United States District Courts. Therefore, there are no parallel citations for these decisions. It is part of the National Reporter System. Like the other reporters, the cases are initially published in advance sheets, which are later compiled in hardbound volumes.

d. West's Other Federal Reporters

West publishes the following specialized federal reporter sets.

(1) Federal Rules Decisions (cited as F.R.D.) This set includes selected opinions of the United States District Courts concerning the Federal Rules of Civil and Criminal Procedure. Some cases involving court rules will appear in the *Federal Supplement*. However, if a decision is published in one set, such as the *Federal Rules Decisions*, it generally will not be published in the other set.

(2) West's Bankruptcy Reporter This reporter publishes selected decisions of the United States Bankruptcy Courts and District Courts involving bankruptcy. It includes bankruptcy opinions from the United States Supreme Court and the Courts of Appeals.

(3) United States Claims Court Reporter This set publishes selected trial court decisions of the Claims Court and relevant opinions from the Supreme Court and the Courts of Appeals.

(4) West's Military Justice Reporter This set includes the decisions from the United States Court of Military Appeals and Courts of Military Review.

(5) West's Veterans Appeals Reporter This reporter publishes decisions of the United States Court of Veterans Appeals.

5. Publication of State Court Decisions

a. Regional Reporters

In addition to the reporters that publish the federal court decisions (discussed in the previous subsection), West's National Reporter System includes sets of reports and reporters that publish selected decisions of the state appellate courts. Each reporter volume includes the features discussed in section V.B, such as a table of cases reported and words and phrases defined. The National Reporter System publishes state court decisions by geographic region in reporters called **regional reporters**. These reporters are: *Pacific Reporter, North Western Reporter, South Western Reporter, North Eastern Reporter, Atlantic Reporter, South Eastern Reporter*, and *Southern Reporter*. West created the geographic grouping of regions, and there is no particular significance to the organization of the regions. The map in Exhibit 4-4 shows the reporter regions and the states in each region.

Due to the large number of cases from California, New York, and Illinois, West created separate reporters for these states. The *California Reporter* publishes the decisions of the California Supreme Court and appellate courts. The Supreme Court decisions are published in both the *Pacific Reporter* and the *California Reporter*; the appellate court decisions are published in

Exhibit 4-4 *West's National Reporter System Map. Reprinted from West Group, copyright 2002. Reprinted with permission of Thomson Reuters.*

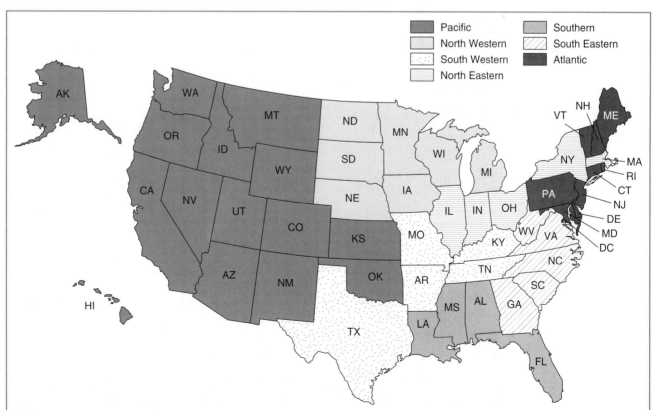

the *California Reporter* only. The *New York Supplement* publishes the decisions of the New York Court of Appeals and the intermediate appellate decisions. The New York Court of Appeals decisions are also printed in the *North Eastern Reporter*; the intermediate appellate decisions are not printed in the *North Eastern Reporter*. The *Illinois Decisions* publishes decisions of the Illinois Supreme Court and appellate courts.

West also publishes individual reporters for many states that are limited to the supreme and appellate court decisions of the state. These reporters are designed for attorneys who are mostly interested in the decisions of the state in which they practice. These decisions are also published in the regional reporter.

> **For Example** A practitioner in New Mexico may need ready access to New Mexico case law for 90 percent of her work and only occasionally need access to case law from other states. It may be worthwhile to purchase a set of the *New Mexico Reports*, which consists of less than 175 volumes, whereas it may be cost prohibitive to purchase the *Pacific Reporter,* which consists of several hundred volumes.

Advance sheets are published for each regional reporter and the advance sheets include the features discussed previously in section V.A.2.b.

Many states have discontinued the official publication of state appellate court decisions. In those states, the court decisions are published only in the regional reporter, and the only citation is to the regional reporter.

> **For Example** Colorado discontinued its official publication of cases in 1980. The only citation to Colorado decisions is to the *Pacific Reporter* cite, for example, *People v. J.D.*, 989 P.2d 762 (Colo. 1999).

Some states have an official publication as well as a public domain citation (also referred to as *medium-neutral citations* or *vendor-neutral citations*). When this is the case three citation numbers will be required.

> **For Example** *State v. Foster*, 1998-NMCA-163, 126 N.M. 177, 976 P.2d 852. The public domain citation is 1998-NMCA-163. The official publication citation is 126 N.M. 177 (volume 126 of the *New Mexico Reports)*. The unofficial *Pacific Reporter* citation is 976 P.2d 852. In this instance, there are three parallel citations, and the opinion may be found in three publications.

b. Computer and Internet Resources

Note that access to most state court opinions is available through Westlaw and LexisNexis. In addition, court opinions are increasingly available through the official court Web site and other Internet sites (see Internet Resources at the end of this chapter). Many state and regional reporters are also available from the publisher on CD-ROM.

6. Attorney General Opinions

The chief attorney for the federal or state government is usually referred to as the **attorney general**. Upon the request of legislators or other government officials, an attorney general may issue a written opinion interpreting how the law applies. This usually occurs when there is no court opinion interpreting how a specific law applies or there are conflicting court opinions.

These opinions are **secondary authority**; they are not enacted law or the opinion of a court. They are not primary authority and do not have to be followed by a court. Nevertheless, because they are written by the attorney general, they are often relied on in the absence of a law or court opinion addressing a specific question.

Attorney general opinions are available through Westlaw and LexisNexis. In addition, they are often available through federal or state government Web sites and other Internet resources. The opinions are also individually available, in slip form, through the attorney general's office. Bound volumes of all the opinions are usually available at law libraries.

B. Researching Court Opinions—Locating Case Law

After you know where the various court opinions are published, the next step is to become familiar with the many research sources and techniques for locating cases (see Exhibit 4-5). Whenever you conduct case law research, *remember to check the advance sheets, pocket parts, or whatever is used to update the source you are researching to ensure that you locate the most recent court decision that answers your question.* Where and how you conduct research depend on the amount and type of information you have at the outset. The main ways to locate case law are discussed here.

Exhibit 4-5 *Research Sources and Techniques for Locating Cases.*

Statutory Annotations	If your research involves a situation that requires the interpretation of a statute, read the statute and look to the case annotations following the statute.
Digest	If the question being researched does not involve a statute or the annotations do not direct you to a relevant case, look to a digest.
Other Case Law Research Sources	If you need to locate additional court opinions, then use other research sources such as legal encyclopedias, treatises, *ALRs*, and law review articles.
Shepard's Citations and Updating Research	If you know the citation of a case and you are looking for other cases that have referred to the case or if you want to know whether the case has been reversed or modified, refer to the appropriate *Shepard's* citator.
Computer-Aided Research	Research sources and court opinions may be located through Westlaw and LexisNexis.

© Cengage Learning 2014

1. Statutory Annotations

If your research involves a situation that requires the interpretation of a statute, the *first step is to read the statute and look to the case annotations following the statute.* Often the annotations to the key court decisions following the statute will include a case that is on point. This saves time spent using another research source such as a digest.

For Example The client robbed a bank with a toy handgun that looked exactly like a real handgun. The client is charged with bank robbery with a dangerous weapon under 18 U.S.C. § 2113(a) & (d). The question is whether a toy handgun is a dangerous weapon under the statute. Referring to the annotations to the statute in the *United States*

Code Annotated or the *United States Code Service,* you will find cases that address the question of whether a toy gun is considered a dangerous weapon. Other than checking to determine if the case has been reversed or modified or there are no recent cases also on point, no further search may be necessary. A digest does not need to be consulted.

If the case located is not exactly the case you are looking for, that is, it is not quite on point, the opinion may reference other cases that are on point or provide you with a key number that will lead you to the proper case. Always read the statute first, because the answer may be in the statute itself or in the annotations.

2. Digest

If the question being researched does not involve a statute or the annotations do not direct you to a relevant case, the next step is to look to a digest. West publishes sets of volumes called *digests* for the various reporters. There is a digest for each regional and state reporter, such as the *Pacific Digest* for the *Pacific Reporter,* and a *Federal Practice Digest.* As discussed previously in section IV.B.5, West has divided the areas of law into various topics and subtopics. Each area is identified by a topic name, such as "Assault and Battery," and each topic is divided into subtopics and assigned a key number. The digests contain summaries of all the court opinions under each key number subtopic.

If you know a case name, you can quickly locate it in a digest's table of cases. If you don't have a particular case in mind but are looking for a case that addresses the question you are researching, scan the topic area, locate the relevant key number, and scan the case summaries to locate the case on point. If there is no case under a particular key number, the digest will refer you to other research sources, such as to a legal encyclopedia cite.

3. Computer-Aided Research

Court opinions may be located through Westlaw and LexisNexis. Also, court opinions are often found through other Internet sources, including the court's official Web site.

4. Other Case Law Research Sources

You may also locate court opinions through other research sources, such as legal encyclopedias, treatises, *ALRs,* and law review articles. These and other secondary authority research sources for locating case law are discussed in Chapters 5 and 6. Usually, however, there are quicker ways of locating cases than through these sources.

For Example The question you are researching is similar to the question raised in *Rael v. Cadena* (presented in Exhibit 4-1): When may a person present at a battery be liable for a battery when the person does not physically participate in the battery? You can look under "assault and battery" in an encyclopedia and eventually find a section that addresses this question and be directed to specific cases. You may, however, spend a lot of time reading before you locate the specific topic you are looking for and spend even more time checking the numerous cases listed before you find the case on point. Through the use of a digest or Westlaw or LexisNexis, your search is more focused and you will usually find cases quicker.

If there is an *ALR* annotation on the question you are researching, it will provide an in-depth analysis of a specific question and reference to key cases addressing the question. First, however, follow the steps mentioned earlier in this section in B.1 and B.2, because if you find a case on point you may not need the in-depth analysis, or the case you find may mention a relevant *ALR* annotation and save you the time locating it.

5. *Shepard's* Citations and Updating Research

If you know the citation of a case and you are looking for other cases that have referred to the case, or if you want to know whether the case has been reversed or modified, refer to the appropriate **Shepard's** citator in print, *Shepard's* online, or (if you are using Westlaw online) refer to Westlaw KeyCite. The use of *Shepard's* and Westlaw's KeyCite is discussed in Chapter 5.

You must always check to determine if the case you have located is good law, that is, whether the court opinion or part of the opinion you are relying on has been reversed or modified by a subsequent court decision. This may be accomplished through the use of the appropriate *Shepard's* in print or electronically through Westlaw or LexisNexis. Increasingly, public and school law libraries are discontinuing their subscription to *Shepard's* citator in print and instead providing at least one computer with public access to *Shepard's* online.

VI. COURT OPINIONS—BRIEFING (CASE BRIEF)
A. Introduction

As a researcher, you may be assigned the task of reading and briefing court opinions. A court opinion is usually called a *case*, and a brief of a court opinion is usually called a *case brief* or a *case abstract*. A **case brief** is a written summary identifying the essential components of a court opinion.

B. Importance of Briefing

The process of briefing a case serves the following purposes and functions:

1. *Analysis/learning.* Writing a summary of the essential elements of an opinion in an organized format leads to better understanding of the case and the reasoning of the court. Opinions are often complex, and the reasoning is hard to identify, difficult to follow, or spread throughout the opinion. The preparation of a case brief requires study of the opinion, identification of what is essential, and elimination of the nonessential. This process of studying a case and analyzing it helps the reader gain a better understanding of it. The analytical process of focusing on the structure of the case helps you gain an understanding of the reasoning, thereby assisting your analysis of the law.

2. *Research/reference.* A case brief is a timesaving research tool. It provides a summary of the essentials of a case that can be quickly referred to when reviewing the case. This saves the time that would be spent rereading and reanalyzing the entire case in order to remember what the court decided and why. When working on a complex legal problem involving several court opinions, or when time has passed since a case was read, the availability of case briefs can result in a considerable saving of time, because it is often difficult to remember which opinion said what.

   A case brief is a valuable tool for the attorney assigned to the case. The attorney may not need to read all the cases related to an issue. The attorney can read the case briefs prepared by the researcher and quickly weed out those cases that are not key and identify and focus on the cases that should be read.

3. *Writing.* The process of briefing a case is a valuable writing tool. It provides you with an exercise in which you learn to sift through a court opinion, identify the essential elements, and assemble your analysis into a concise written summary.

C. How to Read a Case

Before you can brief a case, you must first read it carefully. Sometimes it is necessary to read the entire opinion or parts of it several times to gain an understanding of the decision and the court's reasoning. You cannot expect to skim or quickly read an opinion and hope to understand it. It cannot be read like a newspaper or novel for several reasons:

1. Judges write opinions with the assumption that the reader has an understanding of the law, legal terminology, and the legal system. If you are a beginner, you are slowed by having to look up the meaning of legal terms and become familiar with the style of legal writing.

> **For Example** In the first sentence of *Rael v. Cadena*, the court uses the phrase "jointly and severally liable." Without a legal background, a novice would have to stop reading and look up these terms before continuing to read the case.

Do not get discouraged if at first it takes a long time to read and understand case law. It is normal to "crawl through" court opinions when you are a novice at reading them. As you become familiar with the terminology and style of legal opinions, you will read them faster and with greater understanding. The process, however, is gradual and usually takes months rather than days to learn. No matter your skill level, you must read cases carefully to acquire a full understanding.

2. Some opinions are difficult to read and take time because they involve complex, abstract, or unfamiliar subjects with multiple issues. In such instances, you may have to read the entire case or portions of it several times. You may have to prepare outlines or charts as you read to help you follow and understand the court's reasoning. You may have to refer to a treatise, encyclopedia, or other research tool to obtain an understanding of the area of law involved in the case.

3. Some opinions are difficult to read because they are poorly written. Not all judges are great writers. The reasoning may be scattered throughout the case or not completely presented.

4. Some opinions are difficult to read and understand because the court may have incorrectly interpreted or applied the law. You may be surprised when you read the holding that the court reached a conclusion that is the opposite of the outcome you expected. Remember that some decisions are overruled because a higher or subsequent court determined that the earlier opinion was incorrect. Therefore, *it is important to read each case with a critical eye.*

The difficulty in reading and understanding an opinion may have nothing to do with your ability to read the case.

The purpose of reading a court opinion is to obtain an understanding of the law or principle addressed by the court. To gain this understanding, cases *must* be read and analyzed with *close scrutiny*. The ability to read cases with greater understanding and speed comes with experience.

Several chapters in this text present specific guidelines to assist the reader in reading, interpreting, and analyzing court opinions:

1. Identification of the key facts of a court opinion is discussed in Chapter 9, section VII.

2. Identification of the issue in a court opinion is addressed in Chapter 10, section V.

3. How to determine if a court opinion is on point and may be used as precedent is covered in Chapter 12, section IV.

4. Counteranalysis in case law is discussed in Chapter 13, section VI.C.

D. Case Brief—Elements

There is no standard form for a brief of a court opinion, nor are there any hard-and-fast rules governing format. Some texts recommend that case briefs contain as few as five parts, some as many as sixteen. The style of a case brief may vary from individual to individual and office to office. Be prepared to adapt to different styles.

The goal of a good case brief is a concise summary of the essentials of the court opinion that may be used as a quick reference in the future. Therefore, the brief should be concise. It certainly should not be as long or longer than the case. Do not fill the brief with excessive quotes from the case or long summaries. Spend more time thinking than writing. Reduce the opinion to its essence.

A recommended outline for a case-brief format is presented in Exhibit 4-6. This format should be viewed as a basic outline of the essential parts of a case brief. It can be adapted as necessary to meet your needs. A discussion of each section of the outline follows.

Exhibit 4-6 *Case-Brief Format.*

Citation:	Name of case and where it can be found
Parties:	Names and legal status of the parties
Facts:	A summary of those facts that describe the history of events that caused the parties to be in court (background facts) and those facts to which the law applies and are essential to the decision reached by the court (key facts)
Prior Proceedings:	What happened in the lower court or courts
Issue:	The specific question(s) addressed and answered by the court (State the issue as narrowly and concretely as possible in the context of the case facts. The issue statement should include the rule of law and the key facts.)
Holding:	The court's answer to the issue
Reasoning:	Why the court ruled as it did; the court's application of the case or statutory law to the facts of the case. It should include: a. The rule of law that applies b. How the court applied the rule of law to the facts
Disposition:	What order was entered as a result of the holding (e.g., "The judgment of the trial court is reversed.")
Comments:	Observations concerning the opinion

© Cengage Learning 2014

1. Citation

The citation includes the name of the parties, where the case can be found, the court that issued the opinion, and the year of the opinion.

> **For Example** In *Rael v. Cadena*, the citation is *Rael v. Cadena*, 93 N.M. 684, 604 P.2d 822 (Ct. App. 1979).
>
> - *Rael v. Cadena*—name of the case
> - 93 N.M. 684, 604 P.2d 822—the volume and page numbers of the books where the case can be found. This case can be found in volume 93 of the *New Mexico Reports* at page 684 and in volume 604 of the *Pacific Reporter,* second series, at page 822.
> - (Ct. App. 1979)—The court that rendered the opinion and the year of the opinion. The New Mexico Court of Appeals rendered the opinion in 1979. If the date alone appears in parentheses—(1979)— the highest court of the state wrote the opinion. If there is no reference to a state reporter, a reference to the state would also be included with the date: (N.M. Ct. App. 1979).

2. Parties

The caption at the beginning of the opinion gives the full name and legal status of each party.

> **For Example**
> - Eddie Rael, Plaintiff-Appellee
> - Emilio Cadena, Defendant-Appellant
> - Manuel Cadena, Defendant-Appellant

The legal status refers to the litigation status of the parties. This includes the status at the trial and appellate court levels. The status is usually indicated in the caption. The *plaintiff* is the person who brought the lawsuit, and the *defendant* is the party against whom the suit is brought. Often terminology other than plaintiff and defendant is used.

> **For Example** *Petitioner* and *respondent* are often used in divorce cases. The petitioner is the party who filed the divorce petition, and the respondent is the person against whom the divorce petition is filed.

The appeal status of the parties immediately follows the trial court status in the caption.

> **For Example** In *Rael v. Cadena*, Eddie Rael was the plaintiff at trial (he filed the lawsuit), and he is the party against whom the appeal was filed (he won at the trial level).

3. Facts

The facts section of a case brief includes a summary of those facts that describe the history of the events giving rise to the litigation. The facts section should include key and background facts.

a. Key Facts

The key facts are those facts in the opinion to which the law applies and that are essential to the decision reached by the court. They are those facts upon which the outcome of the case is determined. If the key facts were different, the outcome of the case would probably be different.

b. Background Facts

Background facts are those facts that put the key facts in context. They are facts necessary to make sense of the story and thereby provide the reader with an overall context within which the key facts occur, an overall picture of the events of the case.

> **For Example** In an automobile collision case, where the impact took place on a country road, the fact that the collision took place on a country road may not be a key fact, but its inclusion in the fact section of the brief helps provide the reader with an overview of the context and scene of the collision.

In some texts, the case-brief format presents the prior proceedings before the facts. It is recommended that the facts section precede the prior proceedings section of the brief. Since the facts of the case are the events that led to the litigation and, therefore, occurred prior to the litigation, it is logical that in the case-brief format they should precede the court events (the prior proceedings). Also, it is easier, from a briefing standpoint, to identify what happened before the matter went to the trial court, then identify what happened in court.

4. Prior Proceedings/Procedural History

Prior proceedings are those events that occurred in each court before the case reached the court whose opinion you are briefing. Most opinions are not written by trial courts; they are written by courts of appeals reviewing the decision(s) of a trial court—either:

- An intermediary court of appeals, such as the United States Court of Appeals, or
- The highest court of the jurisdiction, such as the United States Supreme Court

Therefore, there are usually prior proceedings. If you are briefing an opinion of a trial court, there may be no prior proceedings because the trial court was the first court to hear the case.

The prior proceedings should include:

1. The party initiating the proceeding and the cause of action
2. The court before which the proceeding was brought
3. The result of the proceeding
4. The party appealing and what is being appealed

> **For Example** "The plaintiff sued the defendant claiming medical malpractice. The trial court granted the defendant's motion to dismiss, ruling that the statute of limitations had run. The plaintiff appealed the trial court's ruling that the statute had run."

5. Issue(s)

The **issue** is the legal question addressed and answered by the court. It is the precise legal question raised by the specific facts of the case. The issue should be stated as narrowly and concisely as possible in the context of the facts of the case. A court opinion may address several issues. Identify each issue separately in the case brief unless you are instructed to brief only one issue.

> **For Example** In an opinion involving an automobile collision case, the court addresses several issues, some involving insurance, some involving evidence, some involving negligence, and some involving battery. The attorney working on a client's case is interested only in the court's resolution of an evidentiary question raised by the facts in the court case. The client's case involves an evidentiary question and fact situation similar to that addressed in the court opinion. Therefore, a researcher may be instructed to provide a case brief of only the portion of the opinion that addresses the evidentiary question. Although the opinion involves several issues, the case brief will address only one issue.

6. Holding

The **holding** is the court's resolution of the issue. It is the decision of the court, the answer to the issue. There should be a separate holding for each issue identified in the issue section of the case brief. In some brief formats the holding is a simple, one-word, yes-or-no response to the issue. The holding should be presented as a complete response to the issue, which means that the presentation of the holding should include all the elements of the issue and should be in the form of a statement.

> **For Example** The issue in the case is, "Under Indiana's probate code, Ind. Code § 29-1-5-2, is a will valid if the witnesses are brothers of the testator?" If the court ruled that the will was valid, the holding should be presented as follows: "Under Indiana's probate code, Ind. Code § 29-1-5-2, a will is valid if the witnesses are brothers of the testator as long as there is no evidence of undue influence."

7. Reasoning

Usually the largest part of an opinion is the court's presentation of the reasons in support of the holding. Just as for each issue there is a holding, for each holding there should be reasons explaining why the holding was reached.

The reasoning portion of an opinion usually consists of two parts:

1. The rule of law that governs the facts of the dispute (it may be constitutional, legislative, or case law, and it may consist of any legal principle, doctrine, or rule of law that applies to the issue in the case).

2. The court's application of the rule to the facts of the case.

> **For Example** The issue in the case is, "Under state tort law, does a battery occur when law enforcement officers, while making a lawful arrest, encounter resistance, use force to overcome that resistance, and continue to use force after the resistance ceases?"
>
> The reasoning presented in the opinion is as follows:
>
> ■ Rule of law—"In *Smith v. Jones*, the Supreme Court ruled that a civil battery occurs whenever unauthorized harmful contact occurs."
>
> ■ Application of this rule to the facts of the case—"The defendants argue that inasmuch as they were making a lawful arrest, they were authorized to use force; therefore, their conduct was not unauthorized within the meaning of *Smith v. Jones*. In this case, however, although the officers were making a lawful arrest, their conduct ceased to be lawful when they continued to use force against plaintiff after plaintiff ceased resisting. Law enforcement officers are authorized to use the amount of force necessary to overcome resistance. After resistance ceases, any continued use of force is unauthorized within the meaning of *Smith v. Jones* and constitutes a civil battery."

In some instances, it is difficult to identify the reasoning in a court opinion because it is scattered throughout the opinion. A helpful approach is to work backward from the holding. Look to the holding first, and keep it in mind while reading the case. It may be easier to see how the court assembled the reasons in support of the holding if you know the holding or outcome while reading the case.

Also, the rule of law or legal principle governing the issue is usually clearly stated by the court and is easy to identify. The reasons for the application of the rule or principle to the facts of the case usually follow the presentation of the governing law. Therefore, identification of the governing law may also help you locate the reasoning.

The reasoning section of the case brief should include the rule of law and a summary of the court's application of the rule of law to the facts—how the rule of law applies to the facts of the case. Lengthy quotes from the case should be avoided. The reasoning should be summarized.

> **For Example** In the excessive force situation presented in the previous example, the reasoning section of the case brief is as follows: "A civil battery occurs whenever unauthorized harmful contact occurs. *Smith v. Jones*. Law enforcement officers are authorized to overcome resistance. After resistance ceases, any continued use of force is unauthorized and constitutes a civil battery."

Also included in the reasoning section is a summary of the reasoning of any concurring opinion.

8. Disposition

The **disposition** includes the relief granted by the court, which is the order entered by the court. This section is usually located at the very end of the opinion.

> **For Example** The judgment of the trial court was affirmed.

9. Comments

Include in this section of the case brief any observations you may have concerning the court opinion. This could include any of the following:

1. Why you agree or disagree with the decision.

2. A summary of any dissenting opinions. Does the dissenting opinion contain information that is useful in understanding the majority opinion? Does the dissenting opinion contain valuable legal arguments that may be useful in arguing against use of the case as precedent? This is especially helpful if the holding of the court goes against your client's position. *Note*: Some case-brief formats have a separate section for dissenting opinions.

3. Why the case may or may not be on point.

> **For Example** Referring to the excessive force example, assume that in the client's case there is evidence that the client never ceased resisting. You might include the following comment in the comment section of the brief: "It is questionable whether this case can be relied on as precedent due to the differences between the facts of the case and our client's facts. In the court case, force continued after resistance ceased, and the court held that the continued use of force constituted a battery. Inasmuch as in our case there is evidence that resistance never ceased, the court opinion may not be applicable."

4. References to the opinion in subsequent cases or secondary sources, such as a law review article.

5. Any information updating the case, that is, concerning whether the case is still good law (see next section).

E. Case Brief—Updating

Whenever an assignment requires you to brief a case, you should determine if the case is still good law, which means you must check to determine if the opinion has been reversed, modified, or in any way affected by a later court decision. The primary method of accomplishing this is through the use of the appropriate *Shepard's* citator. *Shepard's* citators are published by Lexis-Nexis. A researcher must be familiar with *Shepard's Citations* in order to update a court opinion. Instructions on how to use a *Shepard's* citator are included in the beginning of each volume.

In addition, certain computerized services provide online citators that are usually more up to date than the *Shepard's* printed citators. These online services include:

- LexCite—includes a list of the recent cases citing a case (available through Lexis-Nexis) (see Chapter 7)

- Insta-Cite—provides a summary of the prior and subsequent history of a case and includes references to the case in *Corpus Juris Secundum* (available through Westlaw)

- KeyCite—Westlaw's citator service that includes information on whether a case has been reversed, modified, or in any way affected by later court decisions, as well as a list of all cases citing a case

- *Shepard's Citator Services*—presents information not yet included in the *Shepard's* printed volumes (see Chapter 5)

VII. KEY POINTS CHECKLIST: *Locating, Reading, and Briefing Court Opinion*

- ✓ If the research question involves a statute, look to the statute and the statutory annotations first to locate case law. If the statutory annotations do not provide help, next look to a digest.

- ✓ Read opinions carefully and slowly. You cannot speed-read case law. Often you may have to take notes as you read a case.

- ✓ If you have a problem identifying the key facts, refer to Chapter 9.

- ✓ Watch for the court's statement of the issue. The court may state the issue in a broad or procedural context. If you have a problem identifying or stating the issue, refer to Chapters 10 and 11.

- ✓ If you have trouble understanding the majority opinion, often the concurring or dissenting opinion will summarize and clarify the arguments and reasoning adopted by the majority. Be aware that the dissenting opinion may mischaracterize the majority opinion in support of its own position.

- ✓ If you have trouble understanding the opinion, Shepardize the case to determine if there are any other cases, law review articles, *ALR* citations, or other secondary sources of information concerning the case. Consult a treatise that discusses the area of law involved in the opinion. Refer to the digest for other cases addressing the same area of law.

- ✓ Do not be discouraged if you have trouble reading and understanding opinions. It takes time and experience. The more you read opinions, the easier it becomes. Your skill improves only through doing. Therefore, read as many cases as possible.

✓ Read opinions with a critical eye. Court opinions are just that—opinions. On occasion, courts are wrong. Do not read with unquestioning faith. Read critically. Question! Ask yourself, "Does the reasoning support the conclusion?"

VIII. APPLICATION

This section first discusses Vanessa's assignment to locate a case that could be used in a response to a motion to dismiss. This is followed by a brief of the case (*Rael v. Cadena*). The text and brief of *Sterling Computer Systems of Texas, Inc. v. Texas Pipe Bending Company* follow the brief of *Rael v. Cadena*. The brief of the *Sterling* case is included to provide another example of a case brief.

A. Locating *Rael v. Cadena*

Vanessa begins her search for an appropriate case by looking for a statute that establishes a civil cause of action for battery. Civil battery is tort law, and in most states the majority of tort law is case law (established by court decision) rather than statutory law. If there is a statute, Vanessa looks to the statutory annotations to see if there is a case on point, that is, a case in which the court addressed the question of whether an individual present at the scene of a battery, who did nothing more that strongly encourage the perpetrator, could be liable for civil battery.

If there is no statute or a case on point in the annotations, then Vanessa looks to the regional or state reporter digest under the term *battery*. Assume that Vanessa resides in New Mexico. She refers to the index of either the *New Mexico Reports* or the *Pacific Digest* to locate the volume number for battery. Battery is indexed under "assault and battery," and by scanning the topic key numbers she locates Key 18—Persons Liable. She looks under "persons liable" because that key is closest to the facts identified in the issue: Is a bystander liable when he encouraged the perpetrator to hit the client? Looking at the case summaries under Key 18, Vanessa finds *Rael v. Cadena*, 93 N.M. 684, 604 P.2d 822 (Ct. App. 1979), a case which is on point (see Exhibit 4-1). She continues her search to locate any other cases that may be on point. She checks to determine if the *Rael* case has been overruled or otherwise modified by subsequent court decisions.

If there is no case under Key 18, the digest will refer to a legal encyclopedia cite that addresses the topic and provides reference to cases. At this point, Vanessa could also look for an *ALR* annotation that discusses the question. She could also perform this search electronically using Westlaw or LexisNexis.

B. Brief of *Rael v. Cadena*

The sample brief is presented first, followed by comments on the brief.

Citation:	*Rael v. Cadena*, 93 N.M. 684, 604 P.2d 822 (Ct. App. 1979)
Parties:	Eddie Rael, Plaintiff-Appellee
	Emilio Cadena and Manuel Cadena, Defendants-Appellants
Facts:	While visiting Emilio Cadena's home, Eddie Rael was beaten by Emilio's nephew, Manuel Cadena. After the attack began, Emilio yelled to Manuel, "Kill him!" and "Hit him more!" Emilio never actually struck Rael nor physically participated in the battery. Rael was hospitalized as a result of the beating.
Prior Proceeding:	Eddie Rael sued Emilio and Manuel Cadena for battery. The trial court, sitting without a jury, found Emilio jointly liable with Manuel for the battery. Emilio appealed the judgment of the trial court.

Issue:	Under New Mexico tort law, does a battery occur when an individual, present at a battery, encourages the perpetrator of the battery by yelling "Kill him!" and "Hit him more!" but does not in any other way participate in the battery?
Holding:	Yes. An individual may be liable for battery by encouraging or inciting the perpetrator by words or acts.
Reasoning:	The rule of law in the United States is that civil liability for assault and battery is not limited to the direct perpetrator but extends to any person who by any means aids or encourages the act. The act of verbal encouragement at the scene may give rise to liability. The trial court found that Emilio Cadena yelled encouragement to his nephew while the nephew was beating Rael and, therefore, under the rule of law, is jointly liable for the battery.
Disposition:	The judgment of the trial court was affirmed.
Comments:	If, in the client's case, less aggressive language was used, it may be valuable to review other cases to determine the type of encouragement necessary to constitute a battery. Here, Emilio's comments were very aggressive. Would he have been liable for battery had he merely said, "Go ahead, Manuel"?

C. Comments on the Case Brief

Note that the brief includes the essential information of the case:

1. The name of the case and where it can be found
2. The names of the parties and their status before the court
3. The facts that gave rise to the dispute
4. What the trial court did
5. The issue, or legal question
6. The holding
7. The law governing the issue and the application of that law to the facts of the dispute
8. The disposition
9. Relevant comments

You may include in the comments section a notation that the issue in the case was a matter of first impression in New Mexico; that is, the issue addressed in the case had never been decided by New Mexico courts. That is why the reasoning refers to non–New Mexico law and secondary authority rather than to New Mexico law. See the reasoning section of the brief.

D. Brief of *Sterling Computer Systems of Texas, Inc. v. Texas Pipe Bending Company*

A second example of the application of the principles presented in this chapter is illustrated with the brief of the *Sterling Computer Systems* case. The case is presented in the following text. Comments concerning the case brief follow the brief.

CASE

STERLING COMPUTER SYSTEMS OF TEXAS, INC.,
Appellant,

v.

TEXAS PIPE BENDING COMPANY, Appellee.,
No. 965.

OPINION
Court of Civil Appeals of Texas.

Houston (14th Dist.).

March 20, 1974.

Rehearing Denied April 10, 1974.

507 S.W.2d 282 (Tex. Ct. App. 1974)

Action for breach of contract for data-processing service. The District Court, Harris County, Paul Pressler, J., granted summary judgment for defendant, and plaintiff appealed. The Court of Civil Appeals, Tunks, C. J., held that contract, which contained an express provision that plaintiff would not be liable for an outright refusal to perform data-processing services for defendant, and which contained no requirements that plaintiff make a reasonable effort to perform, failed for want of mutuality and was unenforceable.

Affirmed.

Contracts 10(2)

Contract, which contained an express provision that plaintiff would not be liable for an outright refusal to perform data-processing services for defendant, and which contained no requirement that plaintiff make a reasonable effort to perform, failed for want of mutuality and was unenforceable.

Alvin L. Zimmerman, Houston, for appellant.

Robert H. Singleton, Percy D. Williams, Houston, for appellee.

TUNKS, Chief Justice.

The issue in this case is the propriety of a summary judgment for the defendant in a breach of contract suit, which was granted on the theory that the contract lacked mutuality.

The appellant, Sterling Computer Systems of Texas, Inc., brought suit for breach of contract against the appellee, Texas Pipe Bending Company. In essence, the contract in question provided that Texas Pipe Bending was to provide Sterling with digitized cards and computer programs each month, with which Sterling was to perform data processing services for Texas Pipe Bending. Certain prices were quoted in the agreement, which were "based on a minimum of 20,000 digitized cards per month." The term of the agreement was to have been for one year, but after providing cards and paying in full for eight months, Texas Pipe Bending refused to further provide Sterling with digitized cards. The trial court granted Texas Pipe Bending's motion for summary judgment. Although the judgment does not so recite, it was apparently based on the argument proposed by Texas Pipe Bending that the contract was unenforceable because of the lack of mutuality. Sterling has appealed.

The relevant portion of the contract is found in a clause denominated as "LIMITATION OF LIABILITY." This clause provides in part as follows:

> SCS [Sterling] shall not be liable for its failure to profide [sic] the services herein and shall not be liable for any losses resulting to the client [Texas Pipe Bending] or anyone else by reason of such failure.

The general rule as stated in *Texas Farm Bureau Cotton Ass'n v. Stovall,* 113 Tex. 273, 253 S.W. 1101, 1105 (1923), is:

> [A] contract must be based upon a valid consideration, and … a contract in which there is no consideration moving from one party, or no obligation upon him, lacks mutuality, is unilateral, and unenforceable.

Under the express terms of the contract in question Sterling would not be liable for an outright refusal to perform the data processing services. This fact renders its obligation a nullity.

Sterling cites various cases which purportedly support its position that the trial court erred in granting summary judgment for Texas Pipe Bending. The gist of these cases is that although a contract may not expressly obligate a party to perform, such an obligation may be implied by its terms. In Texas Gas Utilities Company v. Barrett, 460 S.W.2d 409 (Tex. Sup. 1970), the Texas Supreme Court held, under a similar contention, that there was a mutuality of obligation. In that case the contract provided that the Gas Company would not be liable for failure to deliver when such failure was "caused by conditions beyond its reasonable control," and then enumerated certain situations which exemplified the above phrase (over none of which would the Gas Company have control). The Court noted, "It [Gas Company] was bound, however, to supply available natural gas to respondents …" Texas Gas Utilities Company v. Barrett, supra 460 S.W.2d at 413. In the present case there existed no requirement that Sterling make a reasonable effort to perform. The exculpatory clause allowed Sterling to refuse to perform with impunity.

(Continued)

Clement v. Producers' Refining Co., 277 S.W. 634 (Tex. Comm'n App. 1925, jdgmt adopted), was another case in which mutuality was found. That case involved a contract for an agent's commission. By the terms of the agreement the principal was to pay the agent a commission on goods which "may be supplied" by the principal. Notwithstanding this provision the Commission of Appeals held that the contract impliedly obligated the principal to supply goods to the agent. However, the Court stated:

[A]s there is no language used which would clearly indicate that the company was not obligated to furnish goods and products, the courts are not warranted in holding that no such obligation was imposed … by its terms. Clement v. Producers' Refining Co., supra at 635.

The case at bar is distinguishable because the contract contained an express provision that Sterling would not be liable if it did not perform. Various other cases cited by appellant are similarly distinguishable because in those cases contracts were involved which did not expressly provide that one of the contracting parties could fail to perform without incurring liability.

As a matter of law the contract in question fails for want of mutuality. The trial court correctly granted summary judgment for the defendant, Texas Pipe Bending Company.

Affirmed.

CITATION:

Sterling Computer Systems of Texas, Inc. v. Texas Pipe Bending Company, 507 S.W.2d 282 (Tex. Ct. App. 1974).

PARTIES:

Sterling Computer Systems of Texas, Inc., Plaintiff-Appellant
Texas Pipe Bending Company, Defendant-Appellee

FACTS:

Sterling Computer Systems (Sterling) entered into a contract with Texas Pipe Bending (Texas Pipe) under which Texas Pipe was to provide Sterling with digitized cards and computer programs each month with which Sterling was to perform data-processing services for Texas Pipe. After complying for eight months, Texas Pipe refused to provide Sterling with the cards. The contract contained the following provision, "SCS [Sterling] shall not be liable for its failure to profide [sic] the services herein and shall not be liable for any

losses resulting to the client [Texas Pipe] or anyone else by reason of such failure."

PRIOR PROCEEDINGS:

Sterling sued Texas Pipe for breach of contract. Texas Pipe moved for summary judgment, arguing that the contract was unenforceable because it lacked mutuality. The trial court granted the motion. Sterling appealed.

ISSUE:

Under Texas contract law, does a contract lack consideration and is, therefore, unenforceable if it contains a limitation of liability clause that provides that a party "shall not be liable for its failure to provide the services herein and shall not be liable for any losses resulting … by reason of such failure"?

HOLDING:

Yes. Under Texas contract law, a contract lacks consideration and is unenforceable if it contains a limitation of liability clause that provides that a party "shall not be liable for its failure to provide the services herein and shall not be liable for any losses resulting … by reason of such failure."

REASONING:

The rule of law presented in *Texas Farm Bureau Cotton Association v. Stovall*, 113 Tex. 273, 253 S.W. 1101 (1923), is that where there is no obligation upon a party to a contract, the contract lacks mutuality, is unilateral, and is unenforceable. Under the limitation clause, Sterling is not liable for its refusal to perform. Therefore, as a matter of law, the contract fails for want of mutuality.

DISPOSITION:

The trial court's granting of the motion for summary judgment was affirmed.

COMMENTS:

The court did not address any potential avenues of relief that may be available to Sterling in equity, such as equitable restitution or reliance. Such avenues may be available in our case and should be explored. Also, does Sterling have a claim against the drafters of the contract for legal malpractice?

E. Comments on the Case Brief—Procedural versus Substantive Issues

Note that the court identifies the issue as: "The issue in this case is the propriety of a summary judgment for the defendant in a breach of contract suit… ." The actual issue in the case, however, is whether a contract is enforceable when it contains a clause that allows a party to escape liability when it fails to perform. Often a court will state the issue in the procedural context of how the matter came before the court.

> **For Example** "The issue in this case is whether the motion for summary judgment was properly granted by the trial court." This is how the matter came before the court procedurally: An appeal was taken from the trial court's ruling on the motion for summary judgment. The real issue involves a question of whether, in light of the facts and the applicable law, there was a sufficient basis for the court to rule as it did.

In answering the procedural question, the court actually addresses the substantive question raised by the facts of the case. *The substantive question is what the case is actually about.* In this case, summary judgment was granted because, as a matter of law, the contract failed for want of mutuality (lack of consideration) due to the limitation of liability clause. Therefore, Sterling could not enforce the contract because it was not valid. The substantive issue addressed by the court was whether the clause rendered the contract unenforceable due to the lack of consideration. *Always look for the substantive issue when the court states the issue in a procedural context.*

Summary

A court opinion, often referred to as a case, is the court's resolution of a legal dispute and the reasons in support of its resolution. When resolving disputes, courts often interpret constitutional or statutory provisions or create law when there is no governing law. The body of law that emerges from court opinions is called the common or case law. It constitutes the largest body of law in the United States, far larger than constitutional, legislative, or other sources of law.

Because you must read court opinions to learn the case law, it is necessary to become familiar with and proficient at reading and analyzing case law. There are several additional reasons, however, for reading opinions. A court opinion:

1. Helps you understand and interpret constitutional provisions and statutory law
2. Helps you understand the litigation process
3. Provides insight into the structure of legal analysis and legal argument
4. Provides a guide to proper legal writing

Most court opinions consist of the facts of the case, the procedural history of the case (what happened in the lower court), the legal questions (issues) addressed by the court, the decision or holding of the court, the reasons for the decision reached, and the disposition (the relief granted).

Federal and state court opinions are published in books called reports and reporters and are available through Westlaw and LexisNexis. In addition, court opinions are often available through official court Web sites and other Internet resources. If the question involves a statute, the search for case law should begin with a review of the annotations following the statute. If the question does not involve a statutory law, the search usually begins with a digest. Computer-assisted research is discussed in Chapter 7.

A case brief is a written summary of a court opinion that presents, in an organized format, all the essential information of the opinion. A researcher may be assigned the task of briefing a case. A case brief is valuable because it:

1. Saves an attorney the time required to read the case
2. Serves as a valuable learning tool
3. Is a reference tool
4. Is a writing tool

The first and possibly most important step in briefing a case is to read it carefully and slowly. Reading case law is often a difficult process, especially for the beginner. It becomes easier as more opinions are read.

Chapter 9 through Chapter 11 provide guidelines that are helpful in identifying many of the elements of a case brief.

The importance of case law cannot be overemphasized. The difficulties you encounter in reading and briefing court opinions can be lessened through the use of the guidelines presented in this chapter.

Quick References

Internet Resources

http://www.lawschool.cornell.edu

   Opinions of the United States Supreme Court may be located at this site.

http://www.oyez.org

   You may hear the oral arguments or read the court briefs of United States Supreme Court cases at this site. The oral arguments are available for cases from 1960 to present.

http://www.supremecourt.gov

   This official page of the United States Supreme Court features court opinions, orders, rules, calendars and schedules, news releases, and general information.

http://www.law.emory.edu

   This site provides access to United States federal court cases.

http://www.uscourts.gov

   This site is the home page for all federal courts.

http://www.findlaw.com

   Through FindLaw, you can locate court cases in general.

http://www.courts.net

   This site provides access to Web sites maintained by courts nationwide.

http://www.usdoj.gov

   United States Attorney General opinions are available at this United States Department of Justice Web site.

http://www.naag.org

   Many state attorney general opinions are available at this National Association of Attorneys General Web site.

CASE LAW CITATION

The *Bluebook* and *ALWD Citation Manual* rules governing case law citation are discussed in Chapter 8. Some brief notes and examples are presented here. If the document you are working on may be filed in a court, such as a state supreme court, check the court rules for any citation rule that may differ from the *Bluebook*.

A. Federal Courts

1. United States Supreme Court. The *Bluebook* provides that cases from the United States Supreme Court require citation to the official reporter, the *United States Reports: Stone v. Powell*, 428 U.S. 465 (1976)

    Citations may be to all three reporters: *In re Kennedy*, 525 U.S. 807, 119 S. Ct. 38, 142 L. Ed. 2d 30 (1998)

2. United States Court of Appeals. Cite to the *Federal Reporter: Essex Ins. Co. v. Davidson*, 248 F.3d 716 (8th Cir. 2001)

3. United States District Court. Cite to the *Federal Supplement* or the *Federal Rules Decisions: McCollum v. McDaniel*, 136 F. Supp. 2d 472 (D. Md. 2001)

B. State Courts

According to the *Bluebook*, in documents submitted to a state court, all citations to opinions decided by that state's courts must include citation to the official state reporter and any other parallel citation: *Ford v. Revlon, Inc.*, 153 Ariz. 38, 734 P.2d 580 (1987)

   If the state has a public domain citation, citation should be to that citation, and citation to the regional reporter may be added.

   In all other documents, the citation is to the regional reporter: *Ford v. Revlon, Inc.*, 734 P.2d 580 (Ariz. 1987)

Exercises

Additional assignments are available on the CourseMate.

ASSIGNMENT 1
List and describe the elements of a case brief.

ASSIGNMENT 2
Why are court opinions important?

ASSIGNMENT 3
Consult West's *General Digest*, Tenth Series.

A. Give the name and citation of a 2001 Minnesota case which listing the elements of battery.

B. Referring to the Minnesota case, does battery require the intent to injure?

C. Cite a Kentucky case providing that fourth-degree assault can be proved only if the result of the assault is physical injury, not death.

D. You are researching a question concerning the admissibility of evidence in an arson case. To what key number would you refer?

E. You are looking for the case *Adams v. Noble*. What is the *Federal Supplement* citation? What United States District Court rendered the decision? Under what key numbers may the case be found?

ASSIGNMENT 4
Refer to the regional digest for your state (see Exhibit 4-4) or to your state court digest. Give the name and citation of a decision from your state that discusses the elements of assault or battery. Refer to the case. What are the elements of assault and battery? If there is no decision from your state, what legal encyclopedia reference is listed?

ASSIGNMENT 5
The client has been charged with bank robbery with a dangerous weapon in federal court. Refer to the *United States Code Annotated* and answer the following questions:

A. Give the *ALR* cite that addresses the question of how the use of an unloaded gun affects criminal responsibility.

B. Give the name and citation of the 1986 United States Supreme Court case that addresses the question of when an unloaded handgun is a "dangerous weapon."

C. Give the name and citation of a 1993 Eleventh Circuit case that answers the question of whether a toy gun is a "dangerous weapon."

ASSIGNMENT 6
Look to your state statute concerning aggravated or armed robbery and the annotations that follow the statute.

A. Give the legal encyclopedia reference(s) that refers to aggravated or armed robbery.

B. Give the *ALR* cite (if any) that addresses the question of how the use of an unloaded gun affects criminal responsibility.

C. Give the name and citation of any case that answers the question of whether a toy or fake gun is a "dangerous weapon."

ASSIGNMENT 7
Describe the importance of briefing a case.

ASSIGNMENT 8
Refer to *Morgan v. Greenwaldt* at the end of Chapter 10. Identify the citation, holding, and disposition.

ASSIGNMENT 9
Refer to *People v. Sanders* and *United States v. Martinez-Jimenez* in Appendix A. For each of these cases, identify the parties, citation, holding, and disposition.

ASSIGNMENT 10
Following the format presented in this chapter, read and brief the following court opinions.

A. *United States v. Leon* (see Appendix A)

B. *Acacia Mutual v. American General Life* (see Chapter 10)

C. *Commonwealth v. Shea* (see Appendix A)—brief only the issue of whether the ocean can be considered a deadly weapon

D. *Atlantic Beach Casino, Inc. v. Marenzoni* (see Chapter 17)—brief only the issue concerning the constitutionality of the municipal ordinances

E. *Cardwell v. Gwaltney* (see Appendix A)

F. *State v. Benner* (see Appendix A)—brief only the issue of the sufficiency of the evidence to support the conviction

G. *McClain v. Adams* (see Appendix A)

H. *Cooper v. Austin* (see Appendix A)— brief only the issue of the validity of the codicil

ASSIGNMENT 11

Access the U.S. Supreme Court Web site and locate the Opinions link. Under the Opinions link, go to the link for Sliplists.

A. What information is provided in each Sliplist?

B. What happens to each Sliplist as new bound volumes are produced?

ASSIGNMENT 12

Access the U.S. Supreme Court Web site and locate the Opinions link, specifically the 2010 Term Opinions of the Court. Specifically locate the case with the docket number 09-10876. In what volume of the *United States Reports* will the opinion be published?

ASSIGNMENT 13

Access the New Mexico Supreme Court Web site and locate the Opinions link. Specifically, go to the Unpublished Opinions link.

A. How many unpublished opinions are there for the current year?

B. What New Mexico Rule of Appellate Procedure controls whether these unpublished opinions may be cited?

ASSIGNMENT 14

Access the New Mexico Supreme Court Web site and locate the Opinions link. Specifically, go to the Prior Year Opinions link.

A. How are the opinions organized?

B. Locate the link to search New Mexico Court of Appeals and Supreme Court opinions. What online source does that link take you to for conducting the search?

ASSIGNMENT 15

Access the Tenth Circuit Court of Appeals Web site. Locate the link to Opinions. What ways does this Web site provide for researchers to search for cases?

CourseMate

The available CourseMate for this text has an interactive eBook and interactive learning tools, including flash cards, quizzes, and more. To learn more about this resource and access free demo CourseMate resources, go to **www.cengagebrain.com**, and search for this book. To access CourseMate materials that you have purchased, go to **login.cengagebrain.com**.

Secondary Authority and Other Research Sources—Encyclopedias, Treatises, American Law Reports, Digests, Shepard's

Learning Objectives

After completing this chapter, you should understand:

- The role of secondary authority in general

- The role of encyclopedias, treatises, annotated law reports, digests, and citators in research

- How to locate and conduct research using encyclopedias, treatises, annotated law reports, digests, *Shepard's,* and KeyCite.

In early May, Melissa was accepted to law school for the term beginning the following fall. In June, after attending a party where there was a lot of drinking, she left with Damon, a young man she had known since high school. Both of them had been drinking, and rather than take her home as she expected, Damon took her to Lookout Point to "talk." He had something other than talk on his mind, however, and when Melissa resisted his advances, he slapped her, cutting her lip and loosening two of her teeth. As she exited the car, he grabbed for her and tore her blouse. Fortunately, there were other cars parked at Lookout Point, and Damon drove off rather than pursue her.

Melissa was furious; she had never been treated like that. She talked to the police and they informed her that she could file assault and battery charges and she should consult an attorney about obtaining civil relief by filing a battery tort claim. She didn't even know what the officer meant by "battery tort claim." She had assumed that the only thing she could do was file criminal charges. She decided that since she was going to law school, she might as well find out for herself what the officer was talking about. The research sources Melissa would consult to learn about the tort law of battery are discussed in the Application section of this chapter.

I. INTRODUCTION

Chapters 3 and 4 cover primary authority, the law itself: constitutions, enacted law (statutes), and case law. Courts refer to and rely on primary authority first when resolving legal problems. In many instances, a court may be bound to follow the primary authority.

> **For Example** Courts are bound to follow the provisions of the United States Constitution, and lower courts are bound to follow the decisions of the higher courts in the jurisdiction.

Therefore, locating the primary authority that may apply to a problem is *always* the first step of legal research.

This and Chapter 6 address **secondary authority** and other sources a court may rely on that are not the law, that is, not primary authority. Secondary authority consists of sources that summarize, compile, explain, comment on, interpret, or in some other way address the law. As mentioned in Chapter 1, secondary authority is used for several purposes:

- To obtain a background or overall understanding of a specific area of the law if you are unfamiliar with an area of law. Legal encyclopedias, treatises, and periodicals are useful for these purposes.

> **For Example** If the researcher is unfamiliar with a specific area of law, such as defamation, a treatise on tort law or a legal encyclopedia will provide an overview of the area. If the researcher seeks an organized summary of the case law on the topic, the *Restatement (Second) of Torts* would be consulted.

- To locate primary authority (the law) on a question being researched. Secondary authority usually guides the researcher by providing references to statutory and case law. **American Law Reports (ALR)** and digests are particularly useful for this purpose. This chapter discusses these sources, *Shepard's Citations*, and Westlaw's KeyCite. Cases may also be located through reference to legal encyclopedias, treatises, periodicals, *Restatements of the Law*, and uniform laws.

- To be relied upon by the court when reaching a decision. This usually occurs only when there is no primary authority governing a legal question, or it is unclear how the primary authority applies. Treatises, law reviews, and *Restatements* are some secondary sources relied on by courts.

There are literally hundreds of secondary sources. This chapter covers the more frequently used secondary sources. It addresses sources that provide the researcher with either an overview or a detailed treatment of specific areas of law: legal encyclopedias, treatises, and *American Law Reports*. The chapter also discusses other research sources that are of great assistance in locating case law: digests, *Shepard's,* and KeyCite. Exhibit 5-1 shows the primary use of the secondary and other research sources discussed in this chapter.

NOTE: As discussed in Chapter 1, secondary authority is not the law. It is persuasive authority, not binding on the courts, but courts may rely on and follow it. Therefore, secondary authority is usually consulted after primary authority. Most legal research focuses on primary authority with little reference to secondary authority. If there is primary authority that answers a question being researched, such as statutory or case law, then secondary authority is not necessary. If the secondary authority describes and refers to primary authority on a subject, locate and refer to the primary authority when analyzing the law.

Exhibit 5-1 *Secondary Authority—Primary Use as a Research Tool.*

AUTHORITY	PRIMARY USE AS A RESEARCH TOOL
Legal Encyclopedias	Use to obtain an overview of a specific area of the law and to locate case law in that area.
Treatises	Use when you are seeking more than the general summary of the law available in a legal encyclopedia. Treatises provide in-depth discussion of legal topics and explain, analyze, and criticize the law.
American Law Reports	Use to obtain a comprehensive analysis of individual legal issues. *ALR* provides a greater in-depth discussion of specific legal issues than available in a treatise. Legal issues are analyzed through synthesis and discussion of cases from every jurisdiction.
Digests	Use to locate case law that addresses specific point(s) of law. Digests are helpful in two situations: ■ You know the name of a case that addresses the point of law being researched and are looking for other cases that address the same point. ■ You do not know of any cases that address the point of law being researched.
Shepard's Citators	Use to determine whether a case or other authority is good law. *Shepard's* indicates whether a case has been reversed, modified, or overruled. It also refer to any case law or secondary sources that have discussed the primary authority being researched.

© Cengage Learning 2014

II. LEGAL ENCYCLOPEDIAS

Legal encyclopedias are designed to provide an overview of all the areas of law. They do not provide the in-depth coverage that is available in a treatise or periodical article.

> **For Example** In the hypothetical presented at the beginning of the chapter, reference to assault and battery in an encyclopedia would be a good starting point for Melissa to begin her research because it would provide her with an overview of the law.

Legal encyclopedias provide a summary of the law; they do not criticize or analyze it. They summarize the law primarily through a summary of case holdings. For that reason, they are valuable for locating cases on a subject. However, due to the large number of cases on any subject, one-half or less of a page of the encyclopedia may be text, with the remainder of the page listing citations in support of the narrative. The problem becomes one of too many cases. Also, in legal encyclopedias there is less emphasis on statutes and statutory law than on case law. Because of their general treatment of topics, legal encyclopedias are not frequently cited in court opinions or documents filed in court.

Legal encyclopedias are similar to other encyclopedias in that the subject matter is arranged alphabetically, and there is a table of contents for each topic and a detailed general index.

The two types of legal encyclopedias are national and local or state.

A. National Encyclopedias

The two national encyclopedias are *American Jurisprudence Second*, commonly known as *Am. Jur. 2d*, and *Corpus Juris Secundum,* or *CJS*. Both of these encyclopedias are national in scope; that is, they present a general overview of federal and state law. Both *American Jurisprudence Second* and *Corpus Juris Secundum* are preceded by earlier sets: *American Jurisprudence* and *Corpus Juris*. Many law libraries do not retain the earlier sets due to space constraints. In addition, it is increasingly common for law libraries to carry only one of the two national encyclopedias in print format.

Each encyclopedia covers more than 400 legal topics. Originally, they were published by different publishers and were competitive sets. Today, West publishes them both. Inasmuch as they are similar in most respects and share many features, a researcher will use one set or the other, not both.

1. Features

The similar and dissimilar features of *American Jurisprudence Second* and *Corpus Juris Secundum* are discussed here.

a. Similarities

Both sets share the following:

- **Topic presentation.** Topics are arranged alphabetically, with each topic beginning with a table of contents (see Exhibit 5-2). The presentation of topics is in the form of a narrative summary, with the narrative and citations presented on each page (see Exhibit 5-3 and Exhibit 5-4).

- **General index.** A comprehensive general index accompanies each set, and each volume has indexes for the topics covered in that volume.

- **Topic summary.** At the beginning of each topic is a summary of what is covered, what topics are treated elsewhere, and West's key number references. This allows you to use the West's digests to locate other cases on the same topic (see Exhibit 5-4). Both sets will refer you to other research sources.

- **Updates.** Pocket parts are used to update each volume and replacement volumes are provided as necessary (see Exhibit 5-5).

- **Tables.** Each set has a table of statutes, rules, and regulations that lists the title and section where specific statutes, rules, and regulations are cited (see Exhibit 5-6). Neither set has a table of cases.

b. Dissimilarities

The sets are different in the following ways:

- **Size.** *Corpus Juris Secundum* is larger than *American Jurisprudence Second,* with more than 100 volumes compared with 80 volumes. This fact does not indicate that *CJS* provides a more comprehensive coverage of topics than *Am. Jur. 2d*. Rather, *CJS* attempts to include every case reported in its discussion of topics, resulting in many pages having one or two sentences of narrative, with the rest of the page consisting of footnotes to cases, which largely accounts for the additional number of volumes.

  Am. Jur. 2d is more selective in its inclusion of cases, presenting a cross-section of leading cases, and includes citations in its footnotes and other research references (see Exhibit 5-4).

- **Emphasis.** *Am. Jur. 2d* emphasizes statutory law somewhat more than *CJS*. Neither set, however, focuses on statutory analysis.

Exhibit 5-2 *C.J.S. Table of Contents for Assault and Battery. Reprinted from West Group, Corpus Juris Secundum, Vol. 6A (1975), p. 309. Reprinted with permission from Thomson Reuters.*

6A C. J. S.

ASSAULT AND BATTERY

Analysis

Sub-Analysis

See also descriptive word index in the back of this Volume

Exhibit 5-3 *C.J.S. Main Volume Entry for Assault and Battery.* Reprinted from West Group, Corpus Juris Secundum, *Vol. 6A (1975), p. 316. Reprinted with permission from Thomas Reuters.*

§§ 1–2 ASSAULT & BATTERY

I. IN GENERAL

§ 1. Scope of Title

Main text →

This title discusses and includes acts of violence towards the person of another, either with or without any actual touching or striking, which do not constitute an element in or an attempt to commit any other specific injury or offense. Defenses, justification, and excuse for such acts are covered, as well as circumstances of aggravation. Liabilities and remedies therefor, both civil or criminal, are likewise treated.

Subjects which are covered in other titles and not treated in this title include civil liability for assault resulting in death,[1] assaults in connection with unlawful arrest,[2] assaults by operation of motor vehicles,[3] and assaults committed in obstructing process or resisting an officer.[4]

The commission of an assault with intent to, or in an attempt to, perpetrate other offenses, is discussed in connection with the particular offense, in C.J.S. titles Homicide, Rape, and Robbery. Convictions of assault in prosecutions for other offenses are treated in C.J.S. Indictments and Informations.

§ 2. Definitions

    a. Assault

    b. Battery or assault and battery

a. Assault

An assault is any unlawful offer or attempt to injure another with apparent present ability to effectuate the attempt under circumstances creating a fear of imminent peril.

Quoted in: Fla.—Motley v. State, 20 So.2d 798, 800, 155 Fla. 545.

Library References
Assault and Battery ☞ 1, 2, 48. — References to West's key numbers

An assault may be defined as any intentional, unlawful offer of corporal injury to another by force, or force unlawfully directed toward the person of another, under such circumstances as create a well founded fear of imminent peril, coupled with the apparent present ability to effectuate the attempt if not prevented.[5] Also, the

Citations to case law →

1. C.J.S. Death.
2. C.J.S. False Imprisonment.
3. See C.J.S. Motor Vehicles.
4. See C.J.S. Obstructing Justice.
5. Ala.—Western Union Telegraph Co. v. Hill, 150 So. 709, 25 Ala.App. 540, certiorari denied 150 So. 711, 227 Ala. 469.
Fla.—Motley v. State, 20 So.2d 798, 155 Fla. 545.
  McDonald v. Ford, App., 223 So.2d 553—Albright v. State, App., 214 So.2d 887.
Ill.—People v. Allen, 254 N.E.2d 103, 117 Ill.App.2d 20.
Kan.—Corpus Juris Secundum cited in State v. Hazen, 165 P.2d 234, 239, 160 Kan. 733.
Ky.—Jenkins v. Kentucky Hotel, 87 S.W. 2d 951, 261 Ky. 419—Smith v. Gowdy, 244 S.W. 678, 196 Ky. 281, 29 A.L.R. 1353.
La.—Osborne v. People's Benev. Industrial Life Ins. Co. of Louisiana, 139 So. 733, 735, 19 La.App. 667.
Mich.—Corpus Juris Secundum quoted in Tinkler v. Richter, 295 N.W. 201, 203, 295 Mich. 396.
Mo.—Corpus Juris Secundum cited in Adler v. Ewing, App., 347 S.W.2d 396, 402—State v. Higgins, App., 252 S.W.2d 641.
N.C.—State v. Roberts, 155 S.E.2d 303, 270 N.C. 655—State v. Johnson, 142 S.E.2d 151, 264 N.C. 598.
Okl.—Dunbar v. State, 131 P.2d 116, 75 Okl.Cr. 275.

Or.—State v. Carroll, 62 P.2d 830, 155 Or. 85.
S.C.—Kirven v. Kirven, 160 S.E. 432, 435, 162 S.C. 162.
Tenn.—Thomasson v. Western Union Tel. Co., 5 Tenn.Civ.App. 640.
Wash.—Corpus Juris Secundum cited in Peasley v. Puget Sound Tug & Barge Co., 125 P.2d 681, 691, 13 Wash.2d 485—Howell v. Winters, 108 P. 1077, 58 Wash. 436.
5 C.J. p 615 note 5.
Other definitions
  (1) In general.
U.S.—Anderson v. Crawford, C.C.A.Kan., 265 F. 504.
  Ransom v. Matson Navigation Co., D.C.Wash., 1 F.Supp. 244.
  U. S. v. Hand, Pa., 26 F.Cas.No. 15,-297, 2 Wash.C.C. 435.
Ala.—Republic Iron & Steel Co. v. Self, 68 So. 328, 192 Ala. 403, L.R.A.1915F 516.
  Taylor v. State, 175 So. 698, 27 Ala. App. 538.
Cal.—People v. Yslas, 27 Cal. 630.
Del.—Marker v. Hanratty, 97 A. 904, 6 Boyce 217.
Ga.—Copeland v. Dunehoo, 138 S.E. 267, 36 Ga.App. 817.
Iowa.—Holdorf v. Holdorf, 169 N.W. 737, 185 Iowa 838.
Ky.—Commonwealth v. Remley, 77 S.W. 2d 784, 257 Ky. 209.
Mich.—Warmelink v. Tissue, 241 N.W. 203, 257 Mich. 228—People v. Doud, 193 N.W. 884, 223 Mich. 120—Drew

  v. Comstock, 23 L.W. 721, 57 Mich. 176.
Minn.—State v. Intihar, 152 N.W.2d 315, 277 Minn. 223.
Miss.—Cittadino v. State, 24 So.2d 93, 199 Miss. 235.
N.J.—State v. Staw, 116 A. 425, 97 N.J. Law 349.
N.Y.—People v. Wood, 199 N.Y.S.2d 342, 10 A.D.2d 231.
Ohio.—State v. Hetzel, 112 N.E.2d 369, 159 Ohio St. 350.
  State v. Theisen, 115 N.E.2d 863, 94 Ohio App. 461.
Or.—Cook v. Kinzua Pine Mills Co., 293 P.2d 717.
Va.—The Hardy Case, 17 Gratt. 592. 5 C.J. p 712 note 82a.
  (2) Assault is threat of injury.
U.S.—Daly v. Pedersen, D.C.Minn., 278 F.Supp. 88.
  (3) An offer or attempt to inflict bodily harm on another person.
R.I.—Liu v. Sugarman, 254 A.2d 753, 105 R.I . 727.
  (4) Act which is legal cause of contact with another person and which is offensive to reasonable sense of personal dignity if act is done with intention of inflicting harmful or offensive contact upon the other.
Pa.—Esmond v. Liscio, 224 A.2d 793, 209 Pa.Super. 200.
  (5) An intentional attempt by violence to injure the person of another.
Fla.—Bailey v. State, 79 So. 639, 76 Fla. 230.

Exhibit 5-4 Am. Jur. 2d *Main Volume Entry for Assault and Battery.* *Reprinted from West Group, American Jurisprudence, 2d Ed., Vol. 6 (1999), p. 10 with permission of Thomson Reuters.*

§ 1   ASSAULT AND BATTERY   6 Am Jur 2d

I. INTRODUCTION [§§ 1-9]

Research references —

Research References

18 USCA § 113

ALR Digest: Assault and Battery §§ 1, 3, 25

ALR Index: Assault and Battery

2 Am Jur Proof of Facts 81, Assault and Battery; 1 Am Jur POF3d 613, Assault and Battery

36 Am Jur Trials 241, Defending Assault and Battery Cases

West Digest, Assault and Battery ☜ 1-7, 47-53

Topic Summary   _____

§ 1. Generally; assault

Topic summary —

Generally speaking, an assault is a demonstration of an unlawful intent by one person to inflict immediate injury or offensive contact on the person of another then present.[1] Although physical contact is not an essential element, violence or offensive contact—threatened or offered—is.[2] The threat must be to cause immediate injury, not injury in the future.[3]

- *Definition:* Assault is frequently defined as an intentional attempt by a person, by force or violence, to do an injury to the person of another, or as any attempt to commit a battery, or any threatening gesture showing in itself or by words accompanying it an immediate intention, coupled with a present ability, to commit a battery.[4]

Citations to case law —

1. Yale v. Town of Allenstown, 969 F. Supp. 798, 12 I.E.R. Cas. (BNA) 1209, 72 Empl. Prac. Dec. (CCH) ¶; 45184 (D.N.H. 1997) (applying New Hampshire law); Mount Vernon Fire Ins. Co. v. DLRH Associates, 967 F. Supp. 105 (S.D.N.Y. 1997), judgment aff'd, 152 F.3d 919 (2d Cir. 1998) (applying New York law); Billado v. Parry, 937 F. Supp. 337 (D. Vt. 1996) (applying Vermont law); Rivera ex rel. Rivera v. City of Nappanee, 704 N.E.2d 131 (Ind. Ct. App. 1998); Bacon on Behalf of Bacon v. Bacon, 567 N.W.2d 414 (Iowa 1997); City of Greenville v. Haywood, 130 N.C. App. 271, 502 S.E.2d 430 (1998), review denied, 349 N.C. 354, 1998 WL 1014898 (1998); Epps v. Com., 28 Va. App. 58, 502 S.E.2d 140 (1998), reh'g en banc granted, 28 Va. App. 270, 503 S.E.2d 813 (1998) and opinion withdrawn and vacated on reh'g en banc, 29 Va. App. 169, 510 S.E.2d 279 (1999).

As to the liability of accessories or participants in an assault and battery, see 21 Am Jur 2d, Criminal Law §§ 186 et seq.

As to the need for intent, see § 8.

Practice references —

Practice References: 1 Am Jur POF3d 631, Assault and Battery.

2. Yanez v. City of New York, 29 F. Supp. 2d 100 (E.D.N.Y. 1998) (applying New York law); U.S. v. LeCompte, 108 F.3d 948, 46 Fed. R. Evid. Serv. (LCP) 833 (8th Cir. 1997) (applying 18 USCA § 113(a)(3)); Wilson v. Meeks, 98 F.3d 1247 (10th Cir. 1996) (called into doubt on other grounds by, Ensminger v. Terminix Intern. Co., 102 F.3d 1571 (10th Cir. 1996)) (applying Kansas law); Jense v. Runyon, 990 F. Supp. 1320 (D. Utah 1998); People v. Aguilar, 16 Cal. 4th 1023, 68 Cal. Rptr. 2d 655, 945 P.2d 1204 (1997); Dickens v. Puryear, 302 N.C. 437, 276 S.E.2d 325 (1981) (distinguished on other grounds by, Bryant v. Thalhimer Bros., Inc., 113 N.C. App. 1, 437 S.E.2d 519 (1993)); Epps v. Com., 28 Va. App. 58, 502 S.E.2d 140 (1998), reh'g en banc granted, 28 Va. App. 270, 503 S.E.2d 813 (1998) and opinion withdrawn and vacated on reh'g en banc, 29 Va. App. 169, 510 S.E.2d 279 (1999).

3. City of Seattle v. Allen, 80 Wash. App. 824, 911 P.2d 1354 (Div. 1 1996) (distinguished by, State v. Aguilar, 1999 WL 261752 (Wash. Ct. App. Div. 1 1999)).

4. Abraham v. Raso, 15 F. Supp. 2d 433 (D.N.J. 1998) (applying New Jersey law); McVay v. Delchamps, Inc., 707 So. 2d 90 (La. Ct. App. 5th Cir. 1998); Thompson v. Williamson County, Tenn., 965 F. Supp. 1026, 23 A.D.D. 381 (M.D. Tenn. 1997) (applying Tennessee law); Waag v. Thomas Pontiac, Buick, GMC, Inc., 930 F. Supp. 393, 74 Fair Empl. Prac. Cas. (BNA) 12, 69 Empl. Prac. Dec. (CCH) ¶; 44507 (D. Minn. 1996) (disagreed with on other grounds by, Torres v. National Precision Blanking, a Div. of Nat. Material L.P., 943 F. Supp. 952, 73 Fair Empl. Prac. Cas. (BNA) 1843, 70

Exhibit 5-5 Am. Jur. 2d *Pocket Part Page.* *Reprinted from West Group, American Jurisprudence, 2d Ed., Vol. 6 (2001), p. 3. Reprinted with permission from Thomson Reuters/West.*

ASSAULT AND BATTERY

KeyCite®: Cases and other legal materials listed in KeyCite Scope can be researched through West Group's KeyCite service on Westlaw®. Use KeyCite to check citations for form, parallel references, prior and later history, and comprehensive citator information, including citations to other decisions and secondary materials.

I. INTRODUCTION [§§ 1–9]

§ 3 Battery

§ 4 — Need for bodily injury

Research References

Apprehending the weapon within: The case for criminalizing the intentional transmission of HIV, 36 Am Crim LR 2:313 (1999).

§ 9 Relationship between assault and battery

Cases

Defendant was guilty of assault in the third degree, where defendant choked victim, his wife, by placing his hands around her throat, causing her to lose consciousness for brief period of time. C.G.S.A. § 53a-61(a)(2). State v. Atkinson, 46 Conn. Supp. 130, 741 A.2d 991 (Super. Ct. 1999).

II. CRIMINAL LIABILITY [§§ 10–93]

A. IN GENERAL [§§ 10–15]

§ 10 Generally; constitutionality of statutes

Cases

Stalking statute, as narrowly construed to supply requirements of genuine threat and intent to carry out the threat, is not facially overbroad under First Amendment, though statute does not contain express exemption for all forms of constitutionally protected speech. U.S.C.A. Amend. 1; ORS 163.732. State v. Rangel, 328 Or. 294, 977 P.2d 379 (1999).

D. EFFECT OF FAMILY RELATIONSHIP OR POSITION OF AUTHORITY [§§ 29–33]

§ 29 Generally; husband and wife; domestic partners

Research References

The domestic violence dilemma: How our ineffective and varied responses reflect our conflicted views of the problem, 71 S Cal LR 3:641 (1999).

Cases

Statute making a parent guilty of permitting sexual abuse of a child, if parent knowingly allowed act of criminal sexual abuse or criminal sexual assault upon his or her child and failed to take "reasonable steps" to prevent commission or future occurrences of such an act, was unconstitutionally vague under Due Process Clause; it was unclear what reasonable steps were required in order to comply with statute, and statute provided no guidelines for authorities in determining what constituted reasonable steps. U.S.C.A. Amend. 14; S.H.A. Const. Art. 1, § 2; S.H.A. 720 ILCS 150/5 .1. People v. Maness, 191 Ill. 2d 478, 247 Ill. Dec. 490, 732 N.E.2d 545 (2000).

§ 30 Peace officer

Cases

Off-duty, uniformed police officer who was engaged in secondary employment as store security guard for private employer was acting in his "official capacity" as police officer when he investigated confrontation between store employee and defendant, and thus, defendant's ensuing assault on officer warranted convictions for assault on police officer and obstructing police officer; even though officer received compensation from store, duties officer performed as security guard were supplemental to his primary duties as law enforcement officer. Code, 61-2-10b(d, e), 61-5-17(a). State v. Phillips, 205 W. Va. 673, 520 S.E.2d 670 (1999).

§ 32 Parents and persons vested with quasi-parental authority

Research References

Spanking and other corporal punishment of children by parents: Overvaluing pain, undervaluing children, 35 Houston LR 1:147 (1999).

§ 33 —Domestic violence statutes

Research References

Domestic violence and mediation: A tragic combination for victims in California Family Court, 35 Cal West LR 2:355 (1999).

The Lautenberg Amendment: Congress hit the mark by banning firearms from domestic violence offenders, 30 St Mary's LJ 3:801 (1999).

Cases

Standard form for Domestic Violence Protective Order (DVPO), Form AOC-CV-306, is disapproved; form combines several possible find . . .

© West Group, 5/2001   3

(margin annotations:)

No new information on Sections 5 through 8

New cases

New research references

Exhibit 5-6 Am. Jur. 2d *Table of Statutes and Rules Cited.* Reprinted from West Group, American Jurisprudence, 2d Ed., Vol 6 (2001), p. xxiii. Reprinted with permission from Thomson Reuters.

TABLE OF STATUTES AND RULES CITED
UNITED STATES CODE ANNOTATED

Title and Section	Am Jur 2d title and section	Title and Section	Am Jur 2d title and section
5 USCA		**28 USCA**	
8130	Assign § 95	1450	Attach § 29
11 USCA		2405	Attach § 66
365(a)	Assist § 23	2710 et seq	Attach § 261
12 USCA		2710-2717	Attach § 67
91	Attach § 70, 87	2710	Attach § 187
15 USCA		2710(b)	Attach § 314
61	Asso § 2	2711	Attach § 273
714b(c)	Attach § 84	2713	Attach § 444, 614
1671-1677	Attach § 178	2717	Attach § 540
1671(b)	Attach § 178	3001-3308	Attach § 239
1672(c)	Attach § 2, 178	3101	Attach § 265
1673(a)	Attach § 178	3101(b)	Attach § 223
1673(b)(1)	Attach § 178	3101(c)(1)	Attach § 267
1673(b)(2)	Attach § 178	**29 USCA**	
1673(c)	Attach § 178	206(a)(1)	Attach § 178
1674(a)	Attach § 11	**31 USCA**	
16 USCA		192	Assign for Crs § 115
3	Assign § 95	3713	Assign for Crs § 115
18 USCA		3713(a)(1)(A)(I)	Assign for Crs § 115
111	Asslt & B § 2, 15, 18, 63	3713(b)	Assign for Crs § 115
112	Asslt & B § 14	3727(a)	Assign § 95
113	Asslt & B § 9, 14	3727(b)	Assign § 95
113(a)(3)	Asslt & B § 1	3727(c)	Assign § 95
113(a)(4)	Asslt & B § 14	**40 USCA**	
113(f)	Asslt & B § 17	308	Attach § 184
115	Asslt & B § 14	309	Attach § 184
116	Asslt & B § 14	**41 USCA**	
1114	Asslt & B § 15	15	Assign § 95
1501	Asslt & B § 14	15(a)	Assign § 95
2114	Asslt & B § 14	15(b)	Assign § 95
26 USCA		**42 USCA**	
501(i)	Asso § 4	1983	Asso § 5

- **New Topic Service.** *Am. Jur. 2d* includes a New Topic Service binder that introduces new topics. New topics are retained in the binder until they are incorporated in revised volumes in the main set.

- **Desk Book.** *Am. Jur. 2d* includes the *Am. Jur. 2d Desk Book,* which includes general information such as statistical charts, tables, data, and diagrams. It includes, for example, a diagram of various federal agencies, the text of the United States Constitution, and the addresses and telephone numbers of the federal courts.

2. Research Techniques—National Encyclopedias

You use a legal encyclopedia to obtain an overview of a specific area of the law and to locate case law in that area. The following techniques are helpful for locating legal topics.

a. General Index Usually one begins research by consulting the general index that accompanies each set.

> **For Example** If you are interested in aggravated assault with a dangerous weapon, you would look in the index under "assault and battery" and would be directed to the appropriate topic and section.

b. Table of Contents If you know the area of law that covers the subject you are researching, you can refer to the volume that covers the topic and scan the table of contents for the specific topic.

> **For Example** If you are interested in who is entitled to sue for an assault, you could retrieve the volume that covers the topic and scan the table of contents to locate the appropriate section (see Exhibit 5-2).

Note that the spine of each volume identifies the range of subjects covered, such as "Private Franchise Contracts to Process."

c. Statute, Rules, and Regulations If you are looking for a specific statute, rule, or regulation, the Table of Statutes and Rules Cited will direct you to the sections where it is discussed (see Exhibit 5-6).

Always consult the pocket part to update your research, to ensure that the narrative summary in the main text has not changed and to locate the most recent cases.

3. Computer-Aided Research

American Jurisprudence Second and *Corpus Juris Secundum* are available on Westlaw. *Am. Jur. 2d* is also available on LexisNexis and CD-ROM. Neither set is available on nonfee-based Web sites. Note that copyrighted secondary sources are generally not available for free on the Internet. In many law libraries where only one of the national encyclopedias is available in print, the encyclopedia not available in print can often be accessed electronically at a public computer. Check with a research librarian for availability. Computer-aided research is discussed in Chapter 7.

B. State Encyclopedias

Some legal encyclopedias are published for individual states. These encyclopedias are organized like the national encyclopedias and include many of the same features, such as a table of contents for each section, a general index, and pocket part supplements. Some sets have tables of cases, statutes, and regulations. They provide a narrative summary of the laws of the state with citations to state and federal case law that have interpreted state law. Research is conducted in the same manner as when using a national encyclopedia. State encyclopedias are most valuable when conducting research on questions involving state law. Note that most states do not have state encyclopedias. Consult your local law library to determine if one is published for your state.

III. TREATISES

Treatises are texts that provide a comprehensive analysis of a single area of law, such as torts or criminal law. Where a legal encyclopedia presents a broad overview of an area of law, a treatise does much more. It provides a much more in-depth discussion of the law in which it explains, analyzes, and criticizes the law. Some treatises include guidance for the legal practitioner, such as practice tips, checklists, and legal forms. Legal experts in the field write treatises; therefore, courts rely on and cite treatises more often than legal encyclopedias. Treatises, however, are still secondary authority; they are not the law, and courts do not have to follow a position or adopt an interpretation advocated by the author. However, there are a few treatises that are authored by well-known scholars who are highly regarded by the courts. Those particular treatises are often cited by the courts even though the treatise is secondary authority and the court is not required to follow it.

> **For Example** *Search and Seizure: A Treatise on the Fourth Amendment* by Wayne LaFave is a multivolume treatise often cited by the courts when deciding a case involving Fourth Amendment issues because it has comprehensive coverage of federal and state search and seizure laws.

A. Types and Features of Treatises

There are several types of treatises, ranging from single-volume texts to multivolume sets. There are single-volume treatises on hundreds of legal topics, and the topics covered may be very specific (such as the *First Amendment Law Handbook* by James L. Swanson), or they may cover an entire area of law (such as *The Law of Torts* by Dan B. Dobbs). The broader the topic covered by the single-volume text, the less detailed the coverage.

There are multivolume treatises for most major areas of law. A multivolume treatise is like an expanded version of a single-text treatise. Due to its size, it provides more extensive and more in-depth treatment of a legal topic than a single-text treatise can.

> **For Example** *Fletcher Cyclopedia Corporations* consists of 33 hardbound and loose-leaf volumes. It analyzes corporate law and addresses in detail the legal issues corporations may face. Obviously, this publication covers the area of corporate law in much greater detail than a single-volume treatise.

The multivolume sets are more likely to include aids for the practitioner, such as forms, checklists, and practice guides.

Most treatises have the following features:

- **Narrative presentation.** The subject matter is presented in a narrative format similar to that of a legal encyclopedia. Documentation supporting the narrative text, including case citations and references to other sources, is presented in footnotes (see Exhibit 5-7).

- **Index.** An index is included at the end of the single-volume treatise or as a separate volume(s) in multivolume sets.

- **Table of cases.** Most treatises include a table of cases arranged alphabetically and a table of contents for each subject area.

- **Updates.** Most multivolume treatises are updated annually or semiannually through the use of pocket parts for each volume or separate supplements. Most single-volume treatises are updated through the publication of a new edition. Some single-volume treatises, such as the softbound *Corporate Communications Handbook* by Walton and Seghetti, are published annually rather than updated. Always check the pocket part or supplement to ensure your research is up to date.

Exhibit 5-7 *Sample Treatise Page. Reprinted from West Group, Dan B. Dobbs, The Law of Torts (2000), p. 63 . Reprinted with permission from Thomson Reuters.*

§ 33   SIMPLE ASSULT   63

attacker would not be liable for a battery if he merely failed to prevent the attacker from hitting the plaintiff.

Duty to protect the plaintiff from others' batteries? On the other hand, the defendant might be under a duty to protect the plaintiff. Employers, for example, are under a duty to protect employees from sexual batteries (and other forms of sexual harassment). If an employer knows that an employee is being sexually battered by another employee, it is not implausible to say that the employer is also guilty of a battery, though he has not committed any "act" and in some instances the battery claim might be advantageous.[5] Similarly, a hospital is under a duty to protect patients from attack, and a knowing failure to do so might be thought of as a battery by inaction. In practice, however, courts are likely to think of both kinds of claims as negligence claims turning on reasonableness rather than battery claims turning upon intent.[6] That is not necessarily the plaintiff's loss, since the defendant's liability insurance may cover negligence but not battery. The upshot is that an affirmative act is at least ordinarily if not invariably required to establish a battery.

Vicarious liability for battery. Liability may, of course, be imposed upon one who instigates a battery or other trespassory tort by another. That is not a case of inaction[7] but a case of liability of one person for the actions of another.[8] It may also be imposed upon employers and persons in analogous roles for the actions of their employees committed within the scope of employment.

TOPIC D. ASSAULT

§ 33. Simple Assault

Text ———— *Nature of the tort.* Newspapers and even judges and lawyers sometimes use the term assault to mean a battery. More technically, assault is a quite different tort, although it often precedes a battery. An assault is an act that is intended to and does place the plaintiff in apprehension of an immediate unconsented-to touching that would amount to a battery.[1] The plaintiff's subjective recognition or apprehension that she is about to be touched in an impermissible way is at the core of the assault claim.

Intent and transferred intent. As in other cases, intent may be based either on the defendant's purpose or on his substantial certainty that a

5. Because employers are generally protected from negligence claims under workers' compensation laws, but sometimes not for intentional tort claims. See generally, Jean Love, Actions for Nonphysical Harm: The Relationship Between the Tort System and No-Fault Compensation (With an Emphasis on Workers' Compensation), 73 CAL. L. REV. 857 (1985).

References to cases ———— **6.** *Employers liable for negligence:* E.g., Ford v. Revlon, Inc., 153 Ariz. 38, 734 P. 2.d 580 (1987). *Hospital liable for negligence:* Sumblin v. Craven

County Hospital Corp., 86 N.C. App. 358, 357 S.E. 2d 376 (1987) (viewing claim against hospital for failure to protect psychiatric patient from molestation as a negligence case).

7. E.g., West v. LTV Steel Co., 839 F. Supp. 559 (N.D.Ind. 1993).

8. See Chapter 22 on vicarious liability generally.

§ 33

1. Restatement §§ 21 & 32.

Reference to secondary source

B. Research Using Treatises

Most law libraries have a treatise section where both the single-volume and multivolume treatises are arranged alphabetically by legal topic (e.g., treatises on criminal law will follow treatises on contracts). Some public libraries may have single-volume treatises located in the legal section. Check the catalog or with the librarian to determine which treatises are available.

1. Use as a Research Tool

Use a treatise when you are seeking more than the general summary of the law provided by a legal encyclopedia. The issue you are researching may not be covered in sufficient detail in an encyclopedia. Also, the analysis or criticism of the law provided in a treatise may be necessary when seeking information on how to counter an opponent's interpretation of or reliance on a law.

> **For Example** The research question involves a majority shareholder in a family corporation whose actions harm the minority shareholders. The majority shareholder controls the board of directors and refuses to issue dividends or allow the minority shareholders to benefit from the corporation in any way. The minority shareholders want to know what remedies are available to them. A legal encyclopedia may not address the subject in sufficient detail to be of assistance. *Fletcher Cyclopedia Corporations* will certainly cover the topic in greater detail and likely provide the answer. The two-volume treatise, *O'Neal's Oppression of Minority Shareholders*, will provide an even greater in-depth discussion of the subject, along with citations to cases that discuss various types of oppressive conduct.

Treatises are also extremely valuable in locating cases. In the previous example, both *Fletcher Cyclopedia Corporations* and *O'Neal's Oppression of Minority Shareholders* will provide numerous case citations to instances of oppressive conduct, one of which may match the fact situation being researched. A legal encyclopedia usually will not address as many specific fact situations as a treatise.

2. Research Techniques—Treatises

The following techniques are helpful for locating specific topics in treatises.

a. General Index

Usually research begins by consulting the index at the end of the text or the set.

> **For Example** If you are interested in oppressive conduct by majority shareholders, look in the index under "shareholders," "majority shareholders," or "oppressive conduct."

b. Table of Contents/Table of Cases

If you know where the topic you are researching is covered in the treatise, go to the section or volume that covers the subject and scan the table of contents for the specific subtopic. If you are looking for the treatment of a specific case in a treatise, consult the table of cases.

c. Reference from Other Sources

Often another source, such as a citation in a case or legal encyclopedia, will direct you to a specific treatise section.

> **For Example** A court opinion may read, "For an exhaustive treatment of derivative actions see 4 Alan R. Bromberg & Larry E. Ribstein, *Partnership* § 15.059."

As with a legal encyclopedia, *always* consult the pocket part or supplement to update your research, to locate the most recent cases, and to ensure that the narrative summary in the main text has not changed. If the treatise is a single volume that is not updated, check the case citations through *Shepard's* or Westlaw's KeyCite to make sure the cases are still good law. *Shepard's Citations* and KeyCite are discussed in section VI of this chapter.

3. Computer-Aided Research

Many treatises are available on Westlaw or LexisNexis.

> **For Example** Wright and Miller, *Federal Practice and Procedure*, is available on Westlaw.

Many treatises are available on CD-ROM. Treatises, like other copyrighted secondary sources, usually are not available on nonfee-based Web sites.

IV. AMERICAN LAW REPORTS

One approach to reporting and analyzing the case law is that taken by the *American Law Reports (ALR)*. The *ALR* publishes the text of leading state and federal court opinions addressing specific issues. Following the opinion is an analysis (referred to as *annotations*) of the legal issues raised in the opinion and a summary of the cases from every jurisdiction that have addressed the same or similar issues. The case summaries are arranged by jurisdiction and provide the researcher with a view of the treatment of the legal issue or issues raised in the case.

> **For Example** Assume the *ALR* annotation analyzes the question: "When is a worker entitled to compensation for injuries suffered after termination of employment when there is some connection between the injury and the employment?" The annotation organizes and presents the cases according to how the courts have answered the question. The cases that have allowed compensation are presented together by state. The cases that have not allowed compensation are also presented together.

In addition to the case summaries, the annotations provide references to various other research sources. Lawyers with expertise in the area of law select the cases and prepare the annotations.

The annotations following the text of the court opinion are thoroughly researched and may range in length from a few pages to more than 100 pages. A single *ALR* volume may run to more than 1,000 pages and provide annotations to fewer than 15 cases. The annotations cover only selected legal issues. If the issue you are researching is addressed by an annotation, the annotation is a research shortcut. It will often provide, in one place, all your research: a comprehensive analysis of the issue, references to and summaries of the case law on point, and references to other research sources.

ALR began publication in 1919 and for years was published by Lawyers' Co-op. Today, West publishes *ALR*. It is composed of the following multivolume series:

ALR (First Series)	Federal and state cases from 1919 to 1948—175 volumes
ALR.2d (Second Series)	Federal and state cases from 1948 to 1965—100 volumes
ALR.3d (Third Series)	Federal cases from 1965 to 1969 and state cases from 1965 to 1980—100 volumes
ALR.4th (Fourth Series)	State cases from 1980 to 1991—100 volumes
ALR.5th (Fifth Series)	State cases from 1991 to June 2005—125 volumes
ALR.6th (Sixth Series)	State cases from June 2005 to present

| *ALR Federal* | Federal cases from 1969 to 2005—200 volumes |
| *ALR Federal* (Second Series) | Federal cases from 2005 to present |

A. ALR Components

There were changes in organization and updating when the second series was published and again with the publication of the third series. The annotations in the third, fourth, fifth, sixth, and federal series are generally similar in format and updating and share the following components:

- **Prefatory statement.** An annotation begins with a statement that briefly describes the topic of the annotation and cites the case used to illustrate the legal issue discussed in the annotation. At the end of the statement is a reference to the page where the case is printed in the *ALR* volume (see Exhibit 5-8).

- **Table of contents.** Following the prefatory statement is a detailed table of contents for the annotation (see Exhibit 5-9).

- **Research references and sources.** A research section follows which lists references related to the annotation. This section includes references to related *ALR* annotations, encyclopedia sections, texts, West key numbers, law review articles, and other publications, practice aids, and computer-assisted research sources.

- **Article index.** Next is an index that lists the subjects and where each subject is covered in the annotation.

- **Jurisdictional tables.** Following the index is a table that lists all the cases cited in the annotation by jurisdiction and the statutes relevant to the annotation (see Exhibit 5-10).

Exhibit 5-8 A.L.R. *Annotation. Reprinted from Lawyers Cooperative Publishing, American Law Reports, 5th Ser., Vol. 10 (1993), p. 337. Reprinted with permission from Thomson Reuters/West.*

10 ALR5th 337

WHAT PROJECTS INVOLVE WORK SUBJECT TO STATE STATUTES REQUIRING PAYMENT OF PREVAILING WAGES ON PUBLIC WORKS PROJECTS

Prefatory Statement

In some cases involving state statutes requiring the payment of prevailing wages to employees on public works projects, issues arise as to whether the activity in question should be considered a project subject to the statute. Focusing on the type of work that the project calls for, some courts have examined the statutory description of covered work and the type of work called for by the contract. In C & C Teletronics, Inc. v U. S. West Information Systems, Inc. (1987, Minn App). 414 NW2d 758, 10 ALR5th 980, for example, the court held that a general contract for the installation of a new telephone system in the state's university buildings was not subject to prevailing wage requirements, where it did not constitute a "project," "construction," or "repair," for purposes of M.S.A. §§ 177.42 subd. 2 and 177.43 subd. 1, the prevailing wage law. This annotation collects and analyzes such cases, dealing with various types of work.

C & C Teletronics, Inc. v U. S. West Information Systems, Inc. is fully reported at page 980, infra.

Exhibit 5-9 A.L.R. *Annotation—Table of Contents. Reprinted from Lawyers Cooperative Publishing, American Law Reports, 5th Ser., Vol. 10 (1993), p. 338. Reprinted with permission from Thomson Reuters.*

PREVAILING WAGES LAWS—PROJECTS   10 ALR5th
10 ALR5th 337

Table of Contents

Reseach References

Index

Jurisdictional Table of Cited Statutes and Cases

ARTICLE OUTLINE

- **Scope.** The body of the annotation begins with a scope section that identifies what is and what is not covered in the annotation (see Exhibit 5-11).

- **Related annotations.** Next is a reference to related *ALR* annotations (see Exhibit 5-11).

- **Summary and comment.** This section presents a summary of the topic that includes background and other information helpful in understanding the topic.

- **Practice pointers.** The next section of the body presents case preparation and other guidelines for practitioners.

Exhibit 5-10 A.L.R. *Annotation—Jurisdictional Tables.* Reprinted from Lawyers Cooperative Publishing, *American Law Reports, 5th Ser., Vol. 10 (1993), p. 341. Reprinted with permission from Thomson Reuters/West.*

---

10 ALR5th   PREVAILING WAGES LAWS—PROJECTS
                                  10 ALR5th 337

Scope of annotation, § 1[a]   Telecommunications system, §§ 3[a], 4[b], 5[b],
Sewers, §§ 3, 9   6[b]
Shrubbery removal, §§ 3[a], 10[a]   Train service, § 3[b]
Sidewalk removal, § 7   Transmission lines, § 10[a]
Streets, § 3   Tree removal or maintenance, §§ 3[a], 10[a]
Summary, § 2   University campus, §§ 3[a], 4[b], 5[b], 6[b]
Sweeping of streets, § 3[a]   Warranty work, § 3[a]

═══

Jurisdictional Table of Cited Statutes and Cases*

CALIFORNIA

Cal Lab Code § 1720 (Deering). See §§ 3[a, b], 5[a], 7
Cal Lab Code §§ 1771, 1773 (Deering). See § 10[a]

Franklin v Riverside (1962) 58 Cal 2d 114, 23 Cal Rptr 401, 373 P2d 465, 45 CCH LC ¶ 50591—§ 10[a]
International Brotherhood of Electrical Workers v Harbor Comrs., Board of (1977, 2nd Dist) 68 Cal App
    3d 556, 137 Cal Rptr 372, 82 CCH LC ¶ 55083, 57 OGR 329—§ 3[b]
Priest v Housing Authority of Oxnard (1969, 2nd Dist) 275 Cal App 2d 751, 80 Cal Rptr 145—§§ 3[a],
    5[a], 7

ILLINOIS

Ill Ann Stat ch 48 para 39s-1 et seq., 39s-2, 39s-3 (Smith-Hurd). See § 10[a]
Ill Rev Stat ch 48 para 39s-1 et seq. (1987). See § 3[a]
Ill Rev Stat ch 48 para 39s-2 (1975). See § 10[a]
Ill Rev Stat ch 48 para 39s-2 (1989). See § 8

Beaver Glass & Mirror Co. v Education, Board of (1978, 2d Dist) 59 Ill App 3d 880, 17 Ill Dec 378, 376
    NE2d 377, 84 CCH LC ¶ 55143—§ 10[a]
Frye v Iroquois, County of (1986, 3d Dist) 140 Ill App 3d 749, 95 Ill Dec 185, 489 NE2d 406, 27 BNA WH
    Cas 979—§ 10[a]

---

* Statutes, rules, regulations, and constitutional provisions bearing on the subject of the annotation are included in this table only to the extent, and in the form, that they are reflected in the court opinions discussed in this annotation. The reader should consult the appropriate statutory or regulatory compilations to ascertain the current status of relevant statutes, rules, regulations, and constitutional provisions.

For federal cases involving state law, see state headings.

***Exhibit* 5-11** *A.L.R. Annotation—Body of Annotation. Reprinted from Lawyers Cooperative Publishing, American Law Reports, 5th Ser., Vol. 10 (1993), p. 344. Reprinted with permission from Thomson Reuters.*

---

§ 1 [a]   PREVAILING WAGES LAWS—PROJECTS   10 ALR5th

10 ALR5th 337

I. Preliminary Matters

Scope

§ 1. Introduction

[a] Scope

This annotation[1] collects and analyzes the cases discussing whether a project involves work of a nature rendering the project subject to a state statute requiring nongovernmental employers to pay prevailing wages to workers on public works projects.[2]

A number of jurisdictions have rules, regulations, constitutional provisions, or legislative enactments directly bearing on this subject. These provisions, including prevailing wage statutes, are discussed herein only to the extent and in the form that they are reflected in the court opinions that fall within the scope of the annotation. The reader is consequently advised to consult the appropriate statutory or regulatory compilations to ascertain the current status of all statutes discussed herein, including those listed in the Jurisdictional Table of Cited Statutes and Cases.

Related annotations

[b] Related annotations

Employees' private right of action to enforce state statute requiring payment of prevailing wages on public works projects. 10 ALR5th 360.

What employers are subject to prevailing wage requirement of state statutes requiring payment of prevailing wages on public works projects. 7 ALR5th 444.

What are "prevailing wages," or the like, for purposes of state statute requiring payment of prevailing wages on public works projects. 7 ALR5th 400.

Who is "employee," "workman," or the like, of contractor subject to state statute requiring payment of prevailing wages on public works projects. 5 ALR5th 513.

What entities or projects are "public" for purposes of state statutes requiring payment of prevailing wages on public works projects. 5 ALR5th 470.

Validity, construction, and effect of state and local laws requiring governmental units to give "purchase preference" to goods manufactured or services performed in state. 84 ALR4th 419.

What constitutes "public work" within statute relating to contractor's bond. 48 ALR4th 1170.

Validity of state statute or local ordinance requiring, or giving

---

1. This annotation, together with 5 ALR5th 470, 5 ALR5th 513, 7 ALR5th 400, 7 ALR5th 444, and 10 ALR5th 360, supersedes the annotation at 93 ALR 1249.

2. As to the question whether a project is of a "public" nature so as to render the project subject

to a state prevailing wage statute, see 5 ALR5th 470. As to the question whether a particular employer involved in a public works project is covered by a state prevailing wage statute, see 7 ALR5th 444.

- **Substantive provisions.** The bulk of the body of an annotation is composed of the substantive sections that organize, summarize, analyze, and evaluate the case law on the topic of the annotation. For each case discussed in the annotation, there is a presentation of the facts and issue(s) before the court related to the topic of the annotation, the court's conclusions on the issue(s), and the court's reasons for its conclusions.

In addition to the components of each annotation, the *ALR* series has the following general features:

- **ALR Index.** The *ALR* General Index lists terms and phrases alphabetically with references to all related annotations. The index is comprehensive with extensive cross-references (see Exhibit 5-12).

| For Example | If you are looking for annotations on "asphyxiation," the index will direct you to "suffocation." |

Exhibit 5-12 A.L.R. *Index. Reprinted from West Group, American Law Reports, Index A-B (1999), p. 324. Reprinted with permission from Thomson Reuters.*

ALR INDEX

Reference

ASPHALT AND ASPHALT PRODUCTS—Cont'd
frauds exception in UCC § 2-201(3)(a), **45 ALR4th 1126, § 10**

ASPHYXIATION
Suffocation (this index)

ASPIRIN
Drugstores and druggists, liability of pharmacist who accurately fills prescription for harm resulting to user, **44 ALR5th 393, § 15, 20[a], 42[b]**
Malpractice, negligence in diagnosing or treating aspirin poisoning, liability for, **36 ALR3d 1358**

ASPORTATION
Interstate or foreign shipments, what constitutes offense under provisions of 18 U.S.C.A. § 659 penalizing theft from interstate or foreign shipments, **8 ALR Fed 938**
Motor vehicle, asportation of motor vehicle as necessary element to support charge of larceny, 70 ALR3d 1202
Pawning, taking, and pledging or pawning, another's property as larceny, **82 ALR2d 863**
Privacy, false light invasion of, accusation or innuendo as to criminal acts, **58 ALR4th 902, § 11**
Separate offense
  seizure or detention for purpose of committing rape, robbery, or other offense as constituting separate crime of kidnapping, **39 ALR5th 283**
  shoplifting, validity, construction, and effect of statutes establishing shop-lifting or its equivalent as a separate criminal offense, **64 ALR4th 1088**

ASSASSINATION
Alien's entitlement, due to threat to life or freedom, to withholding of deportation under § 243(h) of Immigration and Nationality Act of 1952 (8 U.S.C.A. § 1253(h)), **83 ALR Fed 16, § 8[a, c], 10[c], 11[i], 13[b]**
Contact with attorney, denial or interference with accused's right to or request

ASSASSINATION—Cont'd
for initial contact with attorney, **18 ALR4th 669, § 3[a]; 18 ALR4th 743, § 3**

Topic

ASSAULT AND BATTERY
For related topics, see Abuse of Persons; **Fighting**

Related topic

Admiralty, what constitutes assault resulting in serious bodily injury within the special maritime or territorial jurisdiction of the United States for purposes of 18 U.S.C.A. § 113(f), providing punishment for such act, **55 ALR Fed 895**
Agents and agency
  employer's liability to employee or agent for injury or death resulting from assault or criminal attack by third person, **40 ALR5th 1**
  franchisor's tort liability for injuries allegedly caused by assault or other criminal activity on or near franchise premises, 2 **ALR5th 369**
Aggravated assault
  kicking as aggravated assault, or assault with dangerous or deadly weapon, **19 ALR5th 823**

Stationary object

  stationary object or attached fixture as deadly or dangerous weapon for purposes of statute aggravating offenses such as assault, robbery, or homicide, **8 ALR5th 775**

Annotation

  sufficiency of bodily injury to support charge of aggravated assault, **5 ALR5th 243**
Aggravation of damages, see group Mitigation or aggravation of damages in this topic
AIDS, transmission or risk of transmission of human immunodeficiency virus (HIV) or acquired immunodeficiency syndrome (AIDS) as basis for prosecuting or sentencing defendant for criminal offense, **13 ALR5th 628**
Amusements and exhibitions
  employee, liability of amusement operator for a personal assault by employee upon customer, patron, or other invitee, **34 ALR2d 422**
  patron, liability of owner or operator of theater or other amusement to patron

Consult POCKET PART for Later Annotations

The index is a multivolume set that provides references to annotations in *ALR.2d, ALR.3d, ALR.4th, ALR.5th, ALR.6th,* and *ALR Federal, ALR Federal 2d.*

▪ **Quick Index.** The one-volume softbound index provides references to *ALR.3d, ALR.4th, ALR.5th, ALR.6th, ALR Federal,* and *ALR Federal.2d.* There is also an *ALR Federal Quick Index* providing references to the *ALR Federal* and *ALR Federal.2d.* The *Quick Indexes* are not as detailed as the *General Index.*

▪ **Table of Laws, Rules, and Regulations.** The index includes a table that indicates where statutes, rules, regulations, and so on are cited in annotations.

▪ **Annotation History Table.** The last volume of the *ALR General Index* includes a history table that indicates if an annotation has been supplemented in or superseded by a later annotation (see Exhibit 5-13).

▪ **ALR Digests.** There are multivolume *ALR* digests similar to the West digests (discussed in section V). In the digests, the law is divided into more than 400 topics and arranged alphabetically. Each topic is divided into numerical subsections. The sections include a summary of the annotations and references to other sources, such as encyclopedia references and practice references. There are separate digests for *ALR* and *ALR.2d* and a combined digest for *ALR.3d, ALR.4th, ALR.5th, ALR.6th, ALR Federal,* and *ALR Federal.2d.*

▪ **Updates.** *ALR* and *ALR.2d* are updated differently than the other *ALR* series.

  ▪ **ALR.** The *ALR* is updated by checking the *ALR Bluebook of Supplemental Decisions.* This is a noncumulative multivolume set, meaning that each volume covers supplemental cases for a set period of years—volume 3 covers supplemental decisions from 1952 to 1958. There is an annual paperback pamphlet for decisions subsequent to the last hardbound volume. This means that each volume and supplement must be checked to locate all the supplemental cases. Fortunately, because *ALR* only covers cases through 1948, it is not frequently used. The *Bluebook* lists the *ALR* citation (e.g., 121 A.L.R. 616-627) followed by a list of cases decided after the citation was published. The *Bluebook* also indicates if an annotation has been supplemented or superseded by another annotation.

  ▪ **ALR.2d.** The *ALR.2d* is updated by reference to the multivolume *ALR.2d Later Case Service.* Each volume is updated with a pocket part, so you must check the pocket part as well as the main volume. The *Later Case Service* lists the *ALR.2d* citation followed by a summary of the new cases and lists supplemental or superseding annotations.

  ▪ **ALR.3d, ALR.4th, ALR.5th, ALR.6th,** and *ALR Federal.* The *ALR.3d, ALR.4th, ALR.5th, ALR.6th,* and *ALR Federal* are updated through the use of annual cumulative pocket part supplements inserted in the back of each volume. The pocket part lists the *ALR* citation followed by a list of new sections and subsections, a list of new research references, and summary of the new cases. It also indicates if an annotation has been supplemented or superseded by another annotation.

  ▪ **Latest Case Service Hotline.** In the front of each pocket part supplement of *ALR.3d, ALR.4th, ALR.5th, ALR.6th,* and *ALR Federal* is a toll-free number for obtaining cites to cases decided since the publication of the pocket part.

  ▪ **LexisNexis and Westlaw.** The *ALR Series* are available on LexisNexis (Lexis) and Westlaw. The *ALRs* online are up to date, as supplementation is integrated into the annotation.

Exhibit 5-13 A.L.R. *Annotation History Table.* Reprinted from West Group, American Law Reports, General Index (1999), p. 1325. Reprinted with permission from Thomson Reuters.

ANNOTATION HISTORY TABLE

This table lists annotations in ALR (First Series), ALR2d, ALR3d, ALR4th, ALR5th through Volume 69, ALR Fed through Volume 155, which have been superseded or supplemented by later annotations. Consult the pocket part in this volume for later history.

ALR (First Series)

1 ALR 148
Superseded 74 ALR2d 828

1 ALR 222
Subdiv VIII Superseded 71 ALR2d 1140

1 ALR 329
Superseded 36 ALR2d 861

1 ALR 343
Superseded 51 ALR2d 1404

1 ALR 383
Superseded 13 ALR4th 1153

1 ALR 449
Superseded 28 ALR2d 662

1 ALR 528
Superseded 87 ALR4th 11

1 ALR 546
Superseded 50 ALR2d 1324

1 ALR 834
Superseded 91 ALR2d 1344

1 ALR 861
Superseded 41 ALR2d 1213

1 ALR 884
Superseded, as to private easements 25 ALR2d 1265

1 ALR 1163
Superseded 28 ALR4th 482

1 ALR 1267
Superseded 87 ALR2d 271

1 ALR 1368
Superseded 46 ALR2d 1140

1 ALR 1528
Superseded 13 ALR3d 42

1 ALR 1632
Superseded 53 ALR2d 572

1 ALR 1688
Superseded 99 ALR2d 7

2 ALR 6
Supplemented 49 ALR2d 982

2 ALR 61
Superseded 14 ALR3d 783

2 ALR 225
Supplemented 41 ALR2d 1263

2 ALR 287
Superseded 11 ALR4th 345

2 ALR 345
Superseded 44 ALR2d 1242

2 ALR 545
Superseded 54 ALR3d 9

2 ALR 579
Superseded 50 ALR2d 1161

2 ALR 592
Superseded 12 ALR3d 933

2 ALR 867
Superseded 25 ALR3d 941

2 ALR 1008
Superseded 90 ALR2d 1210

2 ALR 1068
Superseded 6 ALR3d 1457

2 ALR 1368
Superseded 56 ALR3d 1182

2 ALR 1376
Superseded 45 ALR2d 1296

2 ALR 1389
Superseded 28 ALR3d 1344

2 ALR 1428
Superseded 61 ALR5th 739

2 ALR 1522
Superseded 157 ALR 1359

2 ALR 1576
Superseded 77 ALR2d 1182

3 ALR 242
Superseded 72 ALR2d 342

3 ALR 312
Superseded 24 ALR2d 194

3 ALR 610
Superseded 12 ALR2d 611

3 ALR 664
Superseded 48 ALR2d 894
74 ALR4th 90

3 ALR 824
Superseded 13 ALR3d 848

3 ALR 833
Superseded 22 ALR3d 1346

3 ALR 902
Superseded 57 ALR3d 1083

3 ALR 1003
Superseded 98 ALR3d 605

3 ALR 1096
Superseded 89 ALR3d 551

3 ALR 1104
Superseded 8 ALR4th 886

3 ALR 1109
Superseded 92 ALR2d 1009

3 ALR 1130
Supplemented 41 ALR2d 739

3 ALR 1279
Subdiv II Superseded 100 ALR2d 227

3 ALR 1304
Superseded 82 ALR2d 611

Consult POCKET PART for Later Entries

B. Research Using *ALR*

1. Use as a Research Tool

The focus of legal research is usually on a specific issue raised by the facts of a client's case. The value of *ALR* as a research tool lies in its comprehensive analysis of specific legal issues. If there is an annotation that addresses the legal issue you are researching, most of your research is done.

The issue is analyzed through the discussion and synthesis of cases from every jurisdiction. Secondary sources, such as treatises, West digest key numbers, and practice aids are identified.

> **For Example** The question being researched involves the admissibility of polygraph evidence by the defendant in a malicious prosecution case. This is a specific question that could require a great deal of research. There is an *ALR* cite that directly addresses this topic: "Steven J. Gaynor, Annotation, *Admissibility of Evidence of Polygraph Test Results or Offer or Refusal to Take Test, in Action for Malicious Prosecution*, 10 A.L.R. 5th 663 (1993)." Reference to this *ALR* annotation saves the researcher an immense amount of time because all the research to the year of the publication is consolidated in one source.

2. Research Techniques

Certain research techniques will help you locate specific *ALR* annotations, as described here.

a. Index to Annotations

Probably the most frequently used approach to locating annotations is to consult the multi-volume index. If you know the general area of law, the index will direct you to the appropriate annotation.

> **For Example** The question is whether a stationary object can be a deadly weapon under a criminal statute enhancing the penalty for assault with a deadly weapon. By looking in the index under "assault and battery," the researcher will be quickly directed to the appropriate annotation (see Exhibit 5-14).

b. *ALR* Digest

As with the index, annotations can be located by looking up the topic in the general area of law in the digest. In addition to references to annotations, the digest summarizes relevant cases printed in *ALR*.

c. Table of Laws, Rules, and Regulations

If you know the statute that governs the issue being researched, you can refer to the table and be directed to the annotations that discuss the statute.

d. Reference from Other Sources

Often you may be directed to a specific *ALR* annotation from another source, such as a citation in a case, article, or *Shepard's Citations*. In such cases you could go directly to the volume and section cited.

Always consult the pocket part and supplement to update your research and to locate the most recent cases. In addition, *always* consult the appendix volume to ensure that you have located all the case summaries. Note that the appendix volumes are not cumulative; each must be checked.

3. Computer-Aided Research

The *ALR* is available on CD-ROM and Westlaw. Computer-aided research is discussed in Chapter 7.

V. DIGESTS

As discussed in Chapter 4, court opinions are printed in reporters in chronological order; they are not organized by topic. If you are attempting to locate a case that addresses a specific issue, that is, a case on point, it would take you forever to find it by randomly looking through

Exhibit 5-14 *Assault and Battery Key Number Outline. Reprinted from West Group, Eleventh Decennial Digest, Vol. 5 (2001). Reprinted with permission from Thomson Reuters.*

Topic ⎯

ASSAULT AND BATTERY

Subjects included ⎯⎯⎯⎯⎯⎯⎯⎯⎯⎯⎯⎯ **SUBJECTS INCLUDED**

Acts of violence towards the person of another, with or without actual touching or striking, not constituting an element in, or attempt to commit, any other specific injury or offense

Justification or excuse for such acts, and circumstances of aggravation

Liabilities and remedies therefor, civil or criminal

SUBJECTS EXCLUDED AND COVERED BY OTHER TOPICS

Death, assault resulting in civil liability, see DEATH

Subjects covered elsewhere

Motor vehicles, assaults by operation of, see AUTOMOBILES

Obstructing process or resisting officer, assaults committed in, see OBSTRUCTING JUSTICE

Other offenses—

    Commission of assault with intent to, or in attempt to, perpetrate, see HOMICIDE, RAPE, ROBBERY

    Convictions of assault in prosecutions for, see INDICTMENT AND INFORMATION

Unlawful arrest, assaults in connection with, see FALSE IMPRISONMENT

For detailed references to other topics, see Descriptive-Word Index

⎯⎯⎯⎯⎯⎯⎯⎯⎯

Analysis

II. **CIVIL LIABILITY,** ☞ **1–46.**
    (A) ACTS CONSTITUTING ASSAULT OR BATTERY AND LIABILITY THEREFOR, ☞ 1-18.
    (B) ACTIONS, ☞ 19-46.

II. **CRIMINAL RESPONSIBILITY,** ☞ **47–100.**
    (A) OFFENSES, ☞ 47-71.
    (B) PROSECUTION, ☞ 72-99.
    (C) SENTENCE AND PUNISHMENT, ☞ 100.

⎯⎯⎯⎯⎯⎯⎯⎯⎯

I. CIVIL LIABILITY.

(A) ACTS CONSTITUTING ASSAULT OR BATTERY AND LIABILITY THEREFOR.

Key numbers

☞1. Nature and elements of assault and battery.
2. —— In general.
3. —— Intent and malice.
4. —— Ability to execute intent.
5. —— Overt act in general.
6. —— Unlawful act.
7. —— Excessive force in doing lawful act.
8. Defenses.
9. —— In general.
10. —— Exercise of authority or duty.
11. —— Consent.
12. —— Provocation.
13. —— Self-defense.
14. —— Defense of another.
15. —— Defense of property.

16. —— Accident.
17. Persons entitled to sue.
18. Persons liable.

(B) ACTIONS.

☞19. Grounds and conditions precedent.
20. Jurisdiction and venue.
21. Time to sue and limitations.
22. Parties.
23. Process.
24. Pleading.
    (5). In general.
    (1). Declaration, petition, or complaint.
    (2). Plea or answer and replication.
    (3). Issues, proof, and variance.
25. Evidence.
25.1. —— In general.

case after case in the reporters. A digest is not secondary authority; that is, it is not a source a court will rely on to interpret the law. Rather, it is a source designed to allow researchers to locate cases easily.

A **digest** is a set of books that organize the law by topic, such as corporations or torts, and divide each topic into subtopics. The digest provides the citation to and a brief summary, or digest, of all the court opinions that have addressed the subtopics. The ability to review the case summaries allows the researcher to select the case most similar to the client's case, that is, the case most on point. Thus, a digest serves as a tool for locating cases on specific questions being researched.

A. West's Key Number Digest System

The most comprehensive and frequently used digests are those published by West. As discussed in Chapter 4, the appellate court decisions in the United States are published in the various West's reporters. West developed its digest system to facilitate access to those decisions. An understanding of how the system is organized is helpful when learning how to use it.

West organizes the law into the following main categories: persons, property, contracts, torts, crimes, remedies, and government. These broad categories are divided into subcategories, and the subcategories are subdivided into more than 400 topics. The list of every digest topic is located at the beginning of every West digest volume. Each topic is listed in alphabetical order in the digest. Each topic is subdivided into subtopics and each subtopic is assigned a number called a *key number* (see Exhibit 5-14). Each subtopic is referred to by both its topic and key number.

| For Example | Assault and Battery 7 refers to key number 7 of the topic of "assault and battery"; Constitutional Law 7 refers to key number 7 of the topic of "constitutional law." |

To determine the subtopic title of a key number, look to the table of contents of the topic in the digest (see Exhibit 5-14).

| For Example | If you want to know the title of the subtopic Assault and Battery 7, you would look up "assault and battery" in the digest, then look to key number 7 and find that key number 7 is "excessive force in doing lawful act." (See Exhibit 5-14.) |

Following the topic table of contents is the body of the digest that lists the key number followed by a summary (digest) of all the court opinions that have in some way discussed the topic (see Exhibit 5-15).

| For Example | Assume the client wants to sue the police for beating him up when he was arrested for a DUI. To find cases that addressed that topic, you would look to the digest under "assault and battery." In the body of the digest under key number 7, "excessive force in doing a lawful act," is a summary of all the cases that have addressed the topic. |

Every court opinion published in the West's reporters is linked to the digests through the use of headnotes. As you will recall from Chapter 4, *headnotes* are summaries of all the points of law discussed in the opinion. The headnotes follow in sequential order the relevant paragraphs of the opinion. Each headnote is assigned a topic and subtopic key number from the West classification system according to the area of law discussed in the case.

Exhibit 5-15 *Body of Digest for Assault and Battery—Case Summaries.* Reprinted from West Publishing, Federal Practice Digest 4th, Vol. 3A (1994), p. 766. Reprinted with permission from Thomson Reuters.

No cases under key number

Key number

Library reference

Case summary

☞ 1 ASSAULT & BATTERY

3A F P D 4th—766

For later cases see same Topic and Key Number in Pocket Part

I. CIVIL LIABILITY.

(A) ACTS CONSTITUTING ASSAULT
OR BATTERY AND LIABILITY
THEREFOR.

☞ **1. Nature and elements of assault and battery.**

Library references

C.J.S. Assault and Battery § 2.

☞ 2. —— In general.

C.A.D.C. 1988. Under District of Columbia law, surgeon who performs operation on minor patient without consent of minor's parents commits assault for which he is liable in damages, absent exceptional circumstances, such as when there is bona fide medical emergency, patient is "mature minor," parents are not readily accessible, or parents have given their implied consent.

> Kozup v. Georgetown University, 851 F.2d 437, 271 U.S.App.D.C. 182, on remand 1989 WL 39006, appeal after remand 906 F.2d 783, 285 U.S.App.D.C. 89.

C.A.9 (Ariz.) 1987. Person commits tort of "assault" if he acts with intent to cause another harmful or offensive contact or apprehension thereof, and other person apprehends imminent contact.

> Garcia v. U.S., 826 F.2d 806.

Person commits tort of "battery" if he acts with intent to cause harmful or offensive contact, or apprehension thereof, and contact occurs.

> Garcia v. U.S., 826 F.2d 806.

C.A.9 (Cal.) 1991. Employee union steward's state law battery claim against management employee arose from right created by independent state common law and not by collective bargaining agreements and, thus, state law claim was not preempted by Labor Management Relations Act; whatever parties' rights and duties under collective bargaining agreement, they could not possibly have negotiated infringement of employee union steward's state law right to be free from battery. Labor Management Relations Act, 1947, § 301, 29 U.S.C.A. § 185.

> Hayden v. Reickerd, 957 F.2d 1506.

Employee's state law right to be free from battery, continuing infliction of stress, and verbal abuse he alleged was retaliation for his union activities did not turn on interpretation of any term of collective bargaining agreement and were not preempted by Labor Management Relations Act. Labor Management Relations Act, 1947, § 301, 29 U.S.C.A. § 185.

> Hayden v. Reickerd, 957 F.2d 1506.

C.A.9 (Cal.) 1991. An employee's state law assault and battery claim against his supervisor was not preempted by the Labor Management Relations Act, as the acts alleged would violate state law irrespective of the identity of the wrongdoer or his victim and did not require interpretation of collective bargaining agreement provisions. Labor Management Relations Act, 1947, § 301, 29 U.S.C.A. § 185; West's Ann.Cal.Penal Code §§ 240, 242.

> Galvez v. Kuhn, 933 F.2d 773.

Allegation that supervisor's conduct was motivated by desire to find reason to fire employee was too tenuous a connection to collective bargaining agreement discharge provisions to preempt employee's state law claims of assault and battery against supervisor. Labor Management Relations Act, 1947, § 301, 29 U.S.C.A. § 185.

> Galvez v. Kuhn, 933 F.2d 773.

C.A.10 (Colo.) 1979. Hackbart v. Cincinnati Bengals, Inc., 601 F.2d 516, certiorari denied 100 S.Ct. 275, 444 U.S. 931, 62 L.Ed.2d 188.

C.A.11 (Ga.) 1990. In absence of consent, surgery constitutes battery.

> Bendiburg v. Dempsey, 909 F.2d 463, certiorari denied 111 S.Ct. 2053, 500 U.S. 932, 114 L.Ed.2d 459, appeal after remand 19 F.3d 557.

C.A.6 (Mich.) 1986. Prison guard's waving of knife in front of paraplegic prisoner constituted common-law assault, from which general damages were presumed to flow, and thus, prisoner was entitled to general damages for that conduct.

> Parrish v. Johnson, 800 F.2d 600.

C.A.5 (Miss.) 1983. Under Mississippi law, mere words, without threat of physical violence, are insufficient to support finding of civil assault.

> Hart v. Walker, 720 F.2d 1436.

Where county supervisor displayed firearm in purporting to arrest plaintiff, finding that supervisor committed civil assault upon plaintiff under Mississippi law was not clearly erroneous.

> Hart v. Walker, 720 F.2d 1436.

C.A.2 (N.Y.) 1993. "Assault" is intentional placing of another person in fear of imminent harmful or offensive contact.

> United Nat. Ins. Co. v. Waterfront New York Realty Corp., 994 F.2d 105.

"Battery" is an intentional wrongful physical contact with another person without consent.

> United Nat. Ins. Co. v. Waterfront New York Realty Corp., 994 F.2d 105.

For cited U.S.C.A. sections and legislative history, see United States Code Annotated

> **For Example** Refer back to Exhibit 4-1. In *Rael v. Cadena*, headnote 1 contains a summary
> of the point of law discussed in the body of the opinion between [1] and
> [2]. The topic is Assault and Battery, and the subtopic is key number 18 (Persons Liable).
> Headnote 2 is a summary of the point of law discussed in the opinion between [2] and [3],
> also Assault and Battery key number 18. Headnote 3 is a summary of the law discussed
> in the opinion between [3] and the end of the opinion, Assault and Battery key number
> 35 (Weight and Sufficiency of Evidence).

The beauty of the classification system is that the same numbering system is used for all the decisions published by West, essentially all the published federal and state appellate court decisions in the United States. All reported decisions are summarized (provided headnotes) using the same key number classification system, and all cases are linked through the same system to digests that identify all other cases that address the same topic.

> **For Example** If you are interested in any reported case anywhere in the United States, state
> or federal, that discusses when persons may be liable for an assault or battery,
> you can refer to any West digest under Assault and Battery key number 18 and find the other
> cases. Assault and Battery key number 18 is the same in all the headnotes and all the digests.

B. Components of West's Digests

The numerous digests prepared by West are discussed in section V.C. These digests follow the same format and share several components. Each topic presented in a digest begins with the name of the topic title, such as "Assault and Battery." After each topic title is the following:

- **Subjects included and excluded.** This section lists the areas covered in the topic and the areas not covered. For the subjects excluded, there are references to the topics where the subjects are covered (see Exhibit 5-14).
- **Table of contents.** Next is a table of contents listing the title and key number of all the subtopics (see Exhibit 5-14).
- **Case summaries.** Following the table of contents is the body of the digest that presents a summary by key number of every case reported that has addressed a specific subtopic. The digest presents a summary of only that portion of the case that addressed the specific key number.

> **For Example** In the body of the digest under Assault and Battery key number 18 (Persons
> Liable) will be a summary of only that portion of each case which discussed
> the topic of when a person is liable for an assault or battery.

This saves you from having to read a summary of the entire case and allows you to focus on the specific question being researched. If there are no cases that address a key number subtopic, the digest will list an encyclopedia reference where the topic is covered. (See Exhibit 5-15.)

In addition to the components of each annotation, each digest set includes the following:

- **Outline of the law and list of topics.** At the beginning of each digest volume is West's outline of the law and a list of digest topics.
- **Topics covered.** Indicated on the spine are the topics covered in the volume, such as "Gas to Habeas Corpus." This allows you to locate the volume you are looking for without having to look in the book. In addition, inside each volume is a list of topics covered in the volume and the page number where the topic begins, such as "Gas … 1" or "Gifts … 249."

- **Descriptive word index.** A comprehensive descriptive word index accompanies each set. The index is a multivolume set that lists words or phrases in alphabetical order. Following the word or phrase is a reference to the topic and key number where it is discussed (see Exhibit 5-16).

- **Table of cases.** Each digest has a table of cases listing cases alphabetically by the names of the plaintiffs (see Exhibit 5-17). Some digests also have a table of cases listing cases alphabetically by the name of the defendant followed by the plaintiff's name.

- **Words and phrases.** Most federal and state digests include a table that lists, in alphabetical order, words and phrases that have been interpreted or defined in court opinions and the citation to the opinions.

- **Updates.** Digests are updated through use of the following:

  - **Pocket parts.** Each digest volume is updated through the use of an annual pocket part placed at the back of the volume. The pocket part presents by key number the summaries of new cases that address the key number topic. If there are no new cases for a key number, there will be no reference to the key number.

  - **Supplementary pamphlets.** Supplementary pamphlets with further updates are published between annual pocket parts.

  - **Later cases.** Both the pocket parts and supplementary pamphlets include a "Closing" table that lists the names of all the reporters covered in the digest. If there is a reporter volume subsequent to the last one listed, it must be checked to determine if there are cases published after the ones in the supplement. As mentioned in Chapter 4, there is a key number digest in the back of each reporter volume for the cases presented in the volume.

> **For Example** If the closing table reads, "Closing with cases reported in 243 F.3d 713," then check the key number digest in the back of any *Federal Reporter 3d Series* volume subsequent to volume 243, page 713 for later cases.

C. Types of Digests

West publishes several different digests, each of which fulfills a specific need. Each of these digests includes the components discussed in the previous section. A brief description of the digests and their function is presented here.

1. *American Digest System*

The most comprehensive and inclusive digest is the **American Digest System**. This digest presents summaries of all the reported state and federal court decisions. Due to the large number of cases covered, the digest consists of several multivolume sets with each set covering a specific time period. The *General Digest* covers five-year periods of time and the *Decennial Digest* covers ten-year periods of time. The sets are not cumulative; therefore, if you want to find all cases for a specific key number, you would need to check the most recent *General Digests* and move backward through the *Decennial Digests*.

> **For Example** If you want to locate the cases addressing Assault and Battery key number 18, you would have to consult the *General Digest* for cases from 1996 to present, the *Tenth Decennial Digest* for cases from 1986 to 1996, for 1976 to 1986 the *Ninth Decennial Digest*, for 1966 to 1976 the *Eighth Decennial Digest*, and so on.

Exhibit 5-16 *Descriptive-Word Index. Reprinted from West Group, West's General Digest, Vol. 6 (2001), p. 929. Reprinted with permission from Thomson Reuters.*

DESCRIPTIVE - WORD INDEX

Volume 1 General Digest, Tenth Series

References are to Digest Topics and Key Numbers

Topic

Age discrimination

Key number

Range of key numbers

ABANDONMENT
AUTOMOBILES. Autos 12
BANKRUPTCY, abandonment of
  property, see this index Bankruptcy
DEFENSE to criminal charge. Crim Law
  31.10

ABORIGINAL PEOPLES
See generally, this index Indians

ABORTION
FAMILY planning—
  Government grants and grantees.
    Social S 4.6

ABSENCE AND ABSENTEES
BALLOTS, see this index Absent Voters
LIMITATION of actions—
  Guarantors, effect as to. Lim of
    Act 94
  Jointly or severally liable parties,
    effect as to. Lim of Act 94
  Sureties, effect as to. Lim of Act 94

ABUSE OF PROCESS
BANKRUPTCY. Bankr 2253, 3502

ABUSED CHILDREN
EVIDENCE—
  Expert testimony. Crim Law 474.4(4)

ACCESS
CABLE television systems—
  Access rules. Tel 449(10)

ACCOMPLICES AND ACCESSORIES
RACKETEERING. RICO 21

ACCOUNTANTS
BANKRUPTCY—
  Compensation. Bankr 3161
RACKETEERING—
  Enterprise, accounting firm as.
    RICO 42
SECURITIES regulation—
  Federal regulation, see this index
    Securities Regulation
  State regulation, see this index Blue
    Sky Law

ACTIONS AND OTHER
  PROCEEDINGS
COMMENCEMENT of actions—
  Bankruptcy case. Bankr 2202
INJUNCTIONS—
  Preliminary injunction—
    Grounds and objections. Inj
      138.27
    Proceedings. Inj 139–159.5

ADDITUR
LEGAL or equitable, see this index Legal
  or Equitable Nature of Proceedings

ADEQUATE PROTECTION
BANKRUPTCY, see this index
  Bankruptcy

ADMINISTRATIVE LAW
  AND PROCEDURE
APPEAL and error—
  Ripeness. Admin Law 704
COMMODITY futures trading
  regulation—
  Administrative agencies, sanctions
    and proceedings. Com Fut 51–61
DISCOVERY. Admin Law 466
DOUBLE jeopardy, proceedings affected.
  Double J 24
REVIEW, see Appeal and error, ante

ADMIRALTY
INTEREST—
  Prejudgment. Interest 39(2.25)

ADOPTION
HABEAS CORPUS—
  Grounds for relief. Hab Corp 534

ADOPTION OF CHILDREN
HOMOSEXUALS, ability to adopt.
  Adop 4

ADVERTISEMENT
ATTORNEYS, see this index Attorney
  and Client
CONTRACTS—
  United States, advertisement for
    proposals or bids. U S 64.25
EMPLOYMENT, discrimination. Civil
  R 156
FREEDOM of speech and press. Const
  Law 90.3

ADVICE OF COUNSEL
DEFENSE—
Criminal charge. Crim Law 37.20

ADVISORS
COMMODITY futures trading regulation,
  see this index Commodity Futures
  Trading regulation, passim

AFFIRATIVE ACTION
EMPLOYMENT discrimination. Civil R
  154
  Relief in equal employment
    opportunities actions. Civil R 392
EMPLOYMENT discrimination suit,
  relief in, see this index Civil Rights

AFFIRMATIVE DEFENSES
BANKRUPTCY, relief from stay,
  proceedings. Bankr 2436

AGE
DISCRIMINATION. Civil R 106
  Employment—
    Generally. Civil R 168–172
  Presumptions and burden of proof.
    Civil R 380
  Relief in age discrimination in
    employment actions. Civil R
    406, 407
  Remedies and proceedings. Civil
    R 331–431
  Weight and sufficiency of evidence.
    Civil R 388

AGGRAVATION OF DAMAGES
RELIEF in equal employment
  opportunities actions. Civil R 402

AGRICULTURAL COMPOSITIONS
  AND EXTENSIONS
FAMILY farmers, see this index Family
  Farmer Debt Adjustment

AIDERS AND ABETTORS JURORS—
  Representation of community. Jury
    33(1.4)
  Waiver—
    Challenge based on age of
      prospective juror. Jury 110(4)

AIR
POLLUTION, see this index Air
  Pollution

AIR POLLUTION
  Generally. Health & E 25.6
ENVIRONMENTAL impact statement.
    Health & E 25.10
  Judicial review or intervention—
    Scope of inquiry or review. Health
      & E 25.15(10)
JUDICIAL review of regulations or
    intervention. Health & E 25.15
  Scope of inquiry or review. Health &
    E 25.15(9)
MUNICIPAL regulation. Mun Corp 606
NUISANCES—
  Health & E 28
  Nuis 3(3)

AIRPORTS AND LANDING FIELDS
SEARCHES and seizures. Searches 72
  Drug searches. Drugs & N 183.5

Exhibit 5-17 *Table of Cases. Reprinted from West Publishing, Tenth Decennial Digest, Vol. 40 (1993), p. 10th D Pt 1-4. Reprinted with permission from Thomson Reuters.*

A.A.

For Later Case History Information, see INSTA-CITE on WESTLAW

AA Ambulance Co., Inc. v. Multnomah County, OrApp, 794 P2d 813, 102 Or-App 398.—Records 54, 57, 63, 68.

AA Ambulance Co., Inc. v. Multnomah County, OrApp, 777 P2d 997, 97 OrApp 618. See Care Ambulance Co. v. Multnomah County.

AA, Charles, Matter of, NYAD 3 Dept, 550 NYS2d 180. See Charles AA, Matter of.

AA, Faith, Matter of, NYAD 3 Dept, 530 NYS2d 318, 139 AD2d 22. See Faith AA, Matter of.

AA. on behalf of A.A. v. Cooperman, NJSuperAD, 526 A2d 1103, 218 NJSuper 32.—Const Law 278.5(7); Schools 159½(4).

A.A. Poultry Farms, Inc. v. Rose Acre Farms. Inc., CA7 (Ind), 881 F2d 1396, cert den 110 SCt 1326, 494 US 1019, 108 LEd2d 501.—Fed Civ Proc 630; Monop 17(1.8); Trade Reg 918.

A.A. Poultry Farms, Inc. v. Rose Acre Farms, Inc., SDInd. 683 FSupp 680, aff 881 F2d 1396, cert den 110 SCt 1326, 494 US 1019, 108 LEd2d 501.—Fed Civ Proc 2333, 2339, 2608; Fed Cts 660, 660.20; Monop 12(1), 12(1.2), 12(16.5); Trade Reg 911, 913, 914, 920, 929, 931.

A.A. Profiles, Inc. v. City of Ft. Lauderdale, CA11 (Fla), 850 F2d 1483, reh den 861 F2d 727, cert den 109 SCt 1743, 490 US 1020, 104 LEd2d 180.—Civil R 209; Em Dom 2(1.2), 277; Zoning 167, 196.

A.A. Quality Const. v. Thomas, Mont, 728 P2d 416, 224 Mont 108.—Damag 189; Mech Liens 154(2).

AA, Ricky, Matter of, NYAD 3 Dept, 541 NYS2d 264, 146 AD2d 433. See Ricky AA, Matter of.

AAA Bail Bonding Co. v. State, Ga. 383 SE2d 125, 259 Ga 411.—Bail 80.

AAA Bonding Co. v. State, GaApp, 386 SE2d 50, 192 GaApp 684.—Bail 77(1).

AAA Crane Service, Inc. v. Omnibank University Hills, N.A., ColoApp, 723 P2d 156.—Costs 2; Courts 85(1); Mech Liens 272, 281(1); Pretrial Proc 746.

AAA Distributors and Associates, In re, CA4 (NC), 922 F2d 1146. See Raynor, In re.

AAA Elec. Service v. Farmers Home Mut. Ins. Co., Utah App, 763 P2d 814. See American Bonding Co. v. Nelson.

AAA Guaranteed Mortg., Inc. v. State, Dept. of Banking and Finance, Div. of Finance, FlaApp 2 Dist, 517 So2d 761.—Brok 3.

AAA Sod, Inc. v. Weitzer Corp., FlaApp 4 Dist, 513 So2d 750.—Mech Liens 281(1), 304(1), 310(3).

AAA Van Services, Inc. v. Willis, GaApp, 354 SE2d 631, 182 GaApp 46.—App & E 358; Costs 260(5).

AAA Van Services, Inc. v. Willis, GaApp, 348 SE2d 475, 180 GaApp 18.—App & E 215(1); Bailm 33.

AAAA Enterprises, Inc. v. River Place Community Urban Redevelopment Corp., Ohio, 553 NE2d 597, 50 Ohio St3d 157, appeal after remand 598 NE2d 711, 74 Ohio App3d 170, jurisdictional motion overr 579 NE2d 214, 62 Ohio St3d 1441.—Em Dom 18.5; Judgm 181(15), 185(2), 185(6).

AAAA Enterprises, Inc. v. U.S., ClCt, 10 ClCt 191.—Fed Cts 1104, 1105, 1109, 1111, 1139.

AAAction Plumbing Co. v. Stewart, Tex-App-Hous |1 Dist|, 792 SW2d 501, error den.—Time 10(9).

Aaberg By and Through Aaberg v. Aaberg, Ala, 512 So2d 1375.—Marriage 13, 50(1).

Aagaard-Juergensen, Inc. v. Lettelier, FlaApp 5 Dist, 579 So2d 404.—Damag 227.

Aagaard-Juergensen, Inc. v. Lettelier, FlaApp 5 Dist, 540 So2d 224.—App & E 79(2); Corp 363; Judgm 185(2), 185(5).

AAI Corp. v. U.S., ClCt, 22 ClCt 541.—Fed Cts 1078; U S 73(9).

Aaker v. Aaker, MinnApp, 447 NW2d 607, review den.—Divorce 224, 240(1), 240(2), 245(2), 247, 286(1), 308, 310, 312.6(1); Parent & C 3.3(6).

Aakjer v. Spagnoli, SCApp, 352 SE2d 503, 291 SC 165.—App & E 1048(7), 1058(1), 1067; Autos 242(1), 246(39), 246(55); Jury 149; New Tr 30; Trial 18, 30, 115(5), 260(8); Witn 208(1), 275(6), 379(1), 405(1).

A.A.L., In Interest of, WisApp, 448 NW2d 239, 152 Wis2d 159.—App & E 945; Const Law 82(10), 274(5); Counties 138; Courts 1; Infants 212, 243, 252; States 111.

A.A.L., Matter of Adoption of, WisApp, 448 NW2d 239, 152 Wis2d 159. See A.A.L., In Interest of.

Aalbers v. Iowa Dept. of Job Service, Iowa, 431 NW2d 330.—Social S 437, 589.

Aalco-Barney Co. v. Harry Sander Realty Co., Inc., MoApp, 771 SW2d 922. See Shockley v. Harry Sander Realty Co., Inc.

Aalgaard v. Merchants Nat. Bank, Inc., CalApp 3 Dist, 274 CalRptr 81, 224 CA3d 674, review den, cert den 112 SCt 278, 116 LEd2d 230.—Banks 251; Civil R 449; Consp 11; Mast & S 9.5, 34; States 18.23, 18.45.

Aalund v. Williams County, ND, 442 NW2d 900.—Em Dom 187, 238(4).

A.A.M., State in Interest of, NJSuperCh. 548 A2d 524, 228 NJSuper 9.—Drugs & N 107; Infants 68.7(2), 68.7(3).

Aamco Transmissions v. General Cas. Co. of Wisconsin, WisApp. 422 NW2d 154, 143 Wis2d 661. See Silverton Enterprises, Inc. v. General Cas. Co. of Wisconsin.

AAMCO Transmissions, Inc. v. Harris, EDPa, 759 FSupp 1141.—Contracts 168; Fed Civ Proc 2492; Fraud 7; Lim of Act 2(1); Trade Reg 871.3.

Aamco Transmissions, Inc. v. Smith, EDPa, 756 FSupp 225.—Fed Cts 31, 214, 217.

Aamodt v. U.S., ClCt, 22 ClCt 716, aff 976 F2d 691.—Labor 416.1.

A & A Acoustics, Inc. v. Valinsky, IllApp 1 Dist, 147 IllDec 840, 559 NE2d 1180, 202 IllApp3d 516, appeal den 151 IllDec 379, 564 NE2d 834, 135 Ill2d 553.—App & E 984(5); Atty & C 24, 32(11); Costs 2; Mech Liens 249.

A & A Cake Decorating Supplies Inc. v. Ramos, LaApp 3 Cir, 502 So2d 1171.—App & E 1106(1).

A & A Grocery v. State Liquor Authority, NYAD 1 Dist, 556 NYS2d 330. See Mohsin v. State Liquor Authority.

A & A Intern., Inc. v. U.S., CIT, 676 FSupp 263.—Cust Dut 17, 18, 19, 26(1), 26(3), 84(7).

A & A Invalid Van Service v. Medevac Midamerica of Kansas, Inc., DKan, 719 FSupp 1014. See Freeman v. Medevac Midamerica of Kansas, Inc.

A & B Cattle Co. of Nevada, Inc. v. City of Escondido, CalApp 4 Dist, 238 CalRptr 580, 192 CA3d 1032.—Mun Corp 65, 592(1).

A & B Heating & Air Conditioning, Matter of, CA11 (Fla), 861 F2d 1538.—Bankr 3781.

A & B Heating & Air Conditioning, Matter of, CA11 (Fla), 823 F2d 462, cert gr and vac US v. A & B Heating and Air Conditioning, Inc, 108 SCt 1724, 486 US 1002, 100 LEd2d 189, on remand 861 F2d 1538.—Int Rev 4832.

A & B Homes, Ltd., In re, Bkrtcy EDVa, 98 BR 243.—Bankr 2678, 3064; Sec Tran 10, 89.

A & B Horse Farms v. U.S., ClCt, 18 ClCt 302. See Haberman v. U.S.

A & B Pipe and Supply Co. v. Turnberry Towers Corp., FlaApp 3 Dist, 500 So2d 261.—Judgm 188.

A & B Restaurant Equipment, Inc. v. Homeseekers Sav. and Loan, LaApp 4 Cir, 506 So2d 137, writ den 512 So2d 852, reconsideration den 513 So2d 1195.—Brok 106; Refer 100(6); Ven & Pur 34, 113, 143, 334(1), 341(3).

A & C Bldg. and Indus. Maintenance Corp. v. U.S., ClCt, 11 ClCt 385.—Fed Cts 1077.

A & D Care, Inc., In re, BkrtcyMDPa, 86 BR 43.—Bankr 2084.5, 2085, 2102.

A & D Care, Inc., In re, BkrtcyWDPa, 90 BR 138.—Bankr 2045; Fed Cts 47.

A & D Supermarkets, Inc., No. 2 v. United Food and Commercial Workers. Local Union 880, NDOhio. 732 FSupp 770.—Monop 12(9), 17(1.7), 28(1.7), 28(5), 28(6.2); States 18.33.

A & E Pacific Const. Co. v. Saipan Stevedore Co., Inc., CA9 (NMariana Islands), 888 F2d 68.—Civil R 181; Fed Cts 776; Monop 16(1), 24(7), 28(1.6); Ship 103; Territories 18; Treaties 8.

A & E Supply Co., Inc. v. Nationwide Mut. Fire Ins. Co., CA4 (Va), 798 F2d 669, cert den 107 SCt 1302, 479 US 1091, 94 LEd2d 158.—Damag 184; Fraud 58(4); Insurance 11, 602.1; Trover 40(4).

A & H, Inc., In re, BkrtcyWDWis, 122 BR 84.—Bankr 2828, 3544.

A & H Vending Service, Inc. v. Village of Schaumburg, IllApp 1 Dist, 118 IllDec 733, 522 NE2d 188, 168 IllApp3d 61, appeal den 125 IllDec 210, 530 NE2d 238, 122 Ill2d 569.—Licens 7(1), 7(9).

A & J Auto Body, In re, BkrtcyDMass, 63 BR 335. See Russo, In re.

A & J Gifts Shop v. Chu, NYAD 3 Dept, 536 NYS2d 209, 145 AD2d 377, appeal den 542 NYS2d 518, 74 NY2d 603, 540 NE2d 713.—Tax 1311, 1316.

A & J Tie Beam Service v. Kendle. FlaApp 1 Dist, 511 So2d 653.—Work Comp 853, 1861.

A & K Produce, In re, BkrtcySDNY, 106 BR 42. See New York Produce American & Korean Auction Corp., In re.

For Later Case History Information, see INSTA-CITE on WESTLAW

The weakness of the digest is its strength, that is, it covers all the cases. You may be interested only in federal cases, cases from your region of the United States, or cases from your state. With the *American Digest*, you may have to wade through a lot of case summaries to find the case you want. Fortunately, West also publishes other, more focused digests.

2. Digests of Federal Court Opinions

West publishes separate digests for decisions of the federal courts:

- **United States Supreme Court Digest.** The *United States Supreme Court Digest* provides a summary of all the decisions of the Supreme Court of the United States. Thus, if your research is focused on Supreme Court decisions that have addressed a specific topic, you could consult this digest to find the cases.

- **Federal Court System.** West publishes several digests that cover the decisions of the United States Supreme Court, the United States Courts of Appeals, and the United States District Courts. Each digest covers a specific time period.

Federal Digest	1754 to 1938
Modern Federal Practice Digest	1939 to 1961
West's Federal Practice Digest 2d	1961 to 1975
West's Federal Practice Digest 3d	1975 to 1983
West's Federal Practice Digest 4th	1983 to present

The digest summaries of the Supreme Court cases are listed first; the Court of Appeals cases are next, followed by the United States District Courts cases and other federal court cases. There are also specialized federal digests that cover the decisions of other specific federal courts, such as *West's Bankruptcy Digest*.

3. Regional Digests

West publishes digests for four of the regional reporters:

Atlantic Digest for cases reported in the *Atlantic Reporter*

North Western Digest for cases reported in the *North Western Reporter*

Pacific Digest for cases reported in the *Pacific Reporter*

South Eastern Digest for cases reported in the *South Eastern Reporter*

Each **regional digest** includes summaries of the cases presented in the reporter organized by state.

> **For Example** Suppose that you want to locate the cases addressing Assault and Battery key number 18 in the *Pacific Digest*. The digest summaries of the cases from Arizona will be presented together, the digest summaries of the cases from California will be presented together, and so on.

To locate the cases for the states covered in the *North Eastern Reporter*, *South Western Reporter*, and the *Southern Reporter*, you must consult the *American Digest* or the state reporter digest.

4. State Digests

West publishes 46 state digests and a digest for the District of Columbia. No state digests are published for Delaware, Nevada, and Utah. The Delaware decisions are included in the *Atlantic*

Digest, and the Nevada and Utah decisions are included in the *Pacific Digest*. The decisions from Delaware, Nevada, and Utah, along with those from all the other states, are included in the *American Digest System*. The *Dakota Digest* includes both North and South Dakota. The *Virginia and West Virginia Digest* includes both Virginia and West Virginia.

The state digests usually include the reported state court decisions, as well as federal court decisions, arising in the state.

D. Research Using Digests

1. Use as a Research Tool

Digests are used to locate case law that addresses a specific point(s) of law. You use digests in two situations:

- You know the name of a case that addresses the point of law being researched and are looking for other cases that address the same point.

> **For Example** The question being researched is the same as that raised in *Rael v. Cadena*, that is, "When may a bystander be liable for a battery?" (See Exhibit 4-1.) This question is identified in the case headnotes as being covered under the topic Assault and Battery key number 18. You are familiar with the *Rael* case, but the client's facts are somewhat different from those in *Rael*. Checking Assault and Battery key number 18 in a digest will lead you to all the other cases that address the question. A scan of the case summaries may lead you to a case that is factually closer to your client's facts, a case that is on point.

- You do not know of any cases that address the point of law being researched. In most instances a researcher has identified the question being researched but needs to locate court opinions that address the topic.

> **For Example** The client was severely beaten by police when he was arrested for a traffic violation. He wants to sue the police for using excessive force. The question is, "What constitutes excessive force when an arrest is being made?" Consulting the topic "assault and battery" in a digest will lead you to key number 7, "excessive force in doing lawful act," and a summary of all the cases that have addressed the question. One of those cases may be directly on point.

2. Research Techniques

The starting point for conducting digest research is to locate the correct digest set. Refer to the types of digests discussed previously and select the appropriate digest. If you are looking for federal cases, consult a federal digest. If you are looking for cases from a particular state, use the state court digest for that state. For state cases from a particular region, such as the western part of the United States, check the regional digest such as the *Pacific Digest*. If no state or regional digest is available, refer to the *American Digest*.

After selecting a digest, you may use several techniques to locate specific cases.

a. Case Headnotes

If you already know of a case related to the issue being researched, refer to the topic and key number of the relevant headnote from the case and consult that topic and key number in the digest. By going directly to the key number, you avoid other research steps, such as having to refer to the index.

> **For Example** You are researching the issue of who may be liable in a battery. You are familiar with *Rael v. Cadena*, but the client's facts are quite different. Even though *Rael* is not on point, the case headnote, Assault and Battery key number 18, will lead you directly to the cases that have addressed the topic.

This is by far the quickest way to locate other cases. Therefore, it is helpful if you know of a related case when you begin. This is why it is important when conducting statutory research to consult the case summaries in the annotations to the statute. Although there may not be a case directly on point, there may be a related case summarized in the annotations that will provide the digest key number for the point of law being researched.

b. Descriptive Word Index

If you are unaware of a specific case, think of all the areas of law or words and phrases that may be related to the topic being researched and consult the index. The index will refer you to the digest topic and key number.

> **For Example** The question involves the firing of a person because of age. You may look under several index topics, such as "age," "discrimination," "civil rights," or "employment" (see Exhibit 5-16). Identification of search terms is discussed in Chapter 2.

c. Topic Outline

If you know the topic that covers the issue, go directly to the topic in the digest and review the topic outline of all the key numbers under the topic. By scanning the outline, you can identify the relevant key numbers and review the relevant cases in the digest.

d. Table of Cases

If you know the name of a case but do not know the citation, consult the table of cases. The table lists the cases alphabetically, provides the citations, and includes the topic and key numbers for the digest entries (see Exhibit 5-17).

e. Reference from Other Sources

Often, you may be directed to a specific digest topic and key number from another source, such as an *ALR* citation, encyclopedia cite, or an article. In such cases you could go directly to the volume and section cited.

f. Update

Always consult the pocket part and supplement to update your research and to locate the most recent cases.

3. Computer-Aided Research

The digests are not available on nonfee-based Internet sites. However, Westlaw provides a key number service database that provides access to all the key number case summaries. Searching online for cases in general is discussed in Chapter 7.

VI. UPDATING AND VALIDATING RESEARCH

When you locate primary authority that provides an answer to a question being researched, it is necessary to determine if the authority has been reversed or modified by a subsequent law or court decision. That is, you must determine if the authority is still valid, if it is still "good law." The first step to ensuring an authority is "good law" is to use a *citator*. The two most common citators are *Shepard's Citations*, in print or online (Lexis), and Westlaw's **KeyCite**. Traditionally, only *Shepard's Citations* in print was available for validating primary authority. In recent years, however, Westlaw has also developed a citator service, called KeyCite. The process of consulting a *Shepard's* source to determine the current validity of an authority is called **Shepardizing**. You Shepardize a case or statute when you check it in *Shepard's Citations*. However, today that term is used whether you are using *Shepard's* or you are using Westlaw's KeyCite.

A. Using *Shepard's* in Print

Shepard's Citations is a set of books that consist of citations to legal authorities, such as a court opinion, followed by a list of citations to cases and other authorities that discuss, analyze, or in some way affect the legal authority. *Shepard's* will not only tell you whether a case or other authority has been reversed, modified, or overruled, but will also refer you to any other case or authority that has discussed the case. Although it is increasingly common to validate research electronically using *Shepard's* online, understanding the layout and functionality of *Shepard's* in print enhances understanding of online updating. You will find in the front of each volume instructions on how to use *Shepard's*. Because a researcher more frequently uses a *Shepard's* for updating case research, the process of using a *Shepard's* in that context is discussed in detail here,.

A *Shepard's* citator page is covered with numbers and may look incomprehensible at first glance. After you understand the format and components, however, a citator is easy to use. There are various types of *Shepard's* citators and they all share the same basic format and components. The various types of *Shepard's* citators and the common components of them all are discussed here.

1. *Shepard's* Case Law Citators

Shepard's publishes a set of citators for each case reporter. Usually the citators are located next to the case reporters in the law library. Some of the citators and the courts they cover are as follows:

- ▪ United States Supreme Court cases—*Shepard's United States Citations*
- ▪ Lower federal courts, that is, cases from the *Federal Reporter, Federal Supplement, Federal Rules Decisions, Court of Claims Reports,* and *United States Claims Court Reporter—Shepard's Federal Citations*
- ▪ State court decisions. There is a separate set of *Shepard's* covering the decisions of each state and Puerto Rico. In addition, there is a set of *Shepard's* for each of the regional reporters.

> **For Example** The cases published in the *New Mexico Reporter* are covered in *Shepard's New Mexico Citations*. The cases published in the *Pacific Reporter* are covered in *Shepard's Pacific Reporter Citations*.

An advantage of a state citator is that it will direct you to more research sources, such as law review articles and Attorney General opinions. A disadvantage of a state citator is that while it includes citations to state and federal cases, it does not include citations from other states.

Case law citators share the following features:

- **Abbreviations—analysis and introductory material.** At the front of the citator is a table of abbreviations page that identifies all of the abbreviations used in the citator (see Exhibit 5-18). Following this page are instructions on how to use the citator. These instructions usually include an illustration interpreting a sample citation. If you need guidance on how to use the citator, these pages are invaluable.

- **Case location.** The reporter volume number is printed in the upper right or left corner of each page of the citator (see Exhibit 5-19). The case page number is printed in bold on the page (e.g., —1055—). The name of the case and year follow the page number (see Exhibit 5-19).

> **For Example** Assume you are looking for the citations to *Young v. Wyoming*, 695 P.2d 1055 (Wyo. 1985). You would look to the *Shepard's Pacific Reporter Citations*, locate the page with volume 695 at the top of the page, then look for —*1055*— (see Exhibit 5-19).

- **Parallel citations.** Following the case name and year are the parallel citations (if any) in parentheses (see Exhibit 5-19). When a case is printed in more than one reporter, the citation to each reporter is called a parallel citation, for example: *Commonwealth v. DeMichael*, 442 Pa. 553, 277 A.2d 159 (1971). The parallel citations are included in the first *Shepard's* volume published after the parallel citation is available. They are not included in the supplements. If the state court opinions are only published in the regional reporter, no parallel citation is listed.

- **History of the case.** Following the parallel citation are citations to cases that involve the same case. This is the most important section of the case citations because any subsequent decision dismissing, modifying, or reversing the Shepardized case will be indicated here. A letter before the citation will indicate the action taken.

> **For Example** Refer to the citations following 695 P.2d 1010 in Exhibit 5-19. The citation reference "r 713P2d98" means that the case at 695 P.2d 1010 was reversed by the decision found at 713 P.2d 98.

As discussed previously, the list of what the *r* and other abbreviations stand for is presented in the abbreviations page at the front of the citator.

- **Later case treatment.** Following the history of the case are citations to every other case that has mentioned the cited case and references to secondary authorities. The cases are arranged in chronological order with the earlier cases mentioned first. The case citation is to the page in the case where the Shepardized case is discussed. Thus, if a case citation is to "746 P.2d 875," 875 is the page in the case where the Shepardized case is discussed rather than the beginning page of the case. The case citations include treatment codes that indicate how the Shepardized case was treated in the cited case. These treatment code abbreviations are presented in the abbreviations page at the front of the citator.

Exhibit 5-18 *Abbreviations for Case History and Treatment. LexisNexis, Shepard's Federal Citations, 8th Ed., Vol. 15 (1995), inside cover of text. Reprinted with the permission of LexisNexis.*

HISTORY AND TREATMENT ABBREVIATIONS

Abbreviations have been assigned, where applicable, to each citing case to indicate the effect the citing case had on the case you are Shepardizing. The resulting "history" (affirmed, reversed, modified, etc.) or "treatment" (followed, criticized, explained, etc.) of the case you are Shepardizing is indicated by abbreviations preceding the citing case reference. For example, the reference "f434F2d872" means that there is language on page 872 of volume 434 of the *Federal Reporter,* Second Series, that indicates the court is "following" the case you are Shepardizing. Instances in which the citing reference occurs in a dissenting opinion are indicated in the same manner. The abbreviations used to reflect both history and treatment are as follows.

History of Case

a	(affirmed)	The decision in the case you are Shepardizing was affirmed or adhered to on appeal.
cc	(connected case)	Identifies a different case from the case you are Shepardizing, but one rising out of the same subject matter or in some manner intimately connected therewith.
D	(dismissed)	An appeal from the case you are Shepardizing was dismissed.
m	(modified)	The decision in the case you are Shepardizing was changed in some way.
p	(parallel)	The citing case is substantially alike or on all fours, either in law or facts, with the case you are Shepardizing.
r	(reversed)	The decision in the case you are Shepardizing was reversed on appeal.
s	(same case)	The case you are Shepardizing involves the same litigation as the citing case, although at a different stage in the proceedings.
S	(superseded)	The citing case decision has been substituted for the decision in the case you are Shepardizing.
US cert den		Certiorari was denied by the U.S. Supreme Court.
US cert dis		Certiorari was dimissed by the U.S. Supreme Court.
US cert gran		Certiorari was granted by the U.S. Supreme Court.
US reh den		Rehearing was denied by the U.S. Supreme Court.
US reh dis		Rehearing was dismissed by the U.S. Supreme Court.
v	(vacated)	The decision in the case you are Shepardizing has been vacated.

Treatment of Case

c	(criticized)	The citing case disagrees with the reasoning/decision of the case you are Shepardizing.
d	(distinguished)	The citing case is different either in law or fact, for reasons given, from the case you are Shepardizing.
e	(explained)	The case you are Shepardizing is interpreted in some significant way. Not merely a restatement of facts.
Ex	(Examiner's decision)	The case you are Shepardizing was cited in an Administrative Agency Examiner's Decision.
f	(followed)	The citing case refers to the case you are Shepardizing as controlling authority.
h	(harmonized)	An apparent inconsistency between the citing case and the case you are Shepardizing is explained and shown not to exist.
j	(dissenting opinion)	The case is cited in a dissenting opinion.
L	(limited)	The citing case refuses to extend the holding of the case you are Shepardizing beyond the precise issues involved.
o	(overruled)	The ruling in the case you are Shepardizing is expressly overruled.
q	(questioned)	The citing case questions the continuing validity or precedential value of the case you are Shepardizing.

Exhibit 5-19 *Case Citation Page from the* Shepard's Pacific Reporter Citations. LexisNexis, Shepard's Pacific Reporter Citations, 1994 Bound Volume, Vol. 2, p. 13. Reprinted with the permission of LexisNexis.

Case Page Number

Reporter Volume Number — Vol. 695

PACIFIC REPORTER, 2d SERIES

Case name

Cited in dissenting opinion

Point of law discussed in Headnote 7 of the Shepardized case

Secondary authority

Distinguished from Shepardized case

695 P.2d 1010' V reversed

Parallel citation

Young v. Wyoming

Col 1	Col 2	Col 3	Col 4	Col 5	Col 6
791P2d²911	—1014—	707P2d¹⁶164	—1058—	770P2d¹740	—1076—
d 791P2d³912	Washington v	756P2d⁵775	Case 1	776P2d¹244	Keltner v
815P2d¹793	Sellers 1985	767P2d168	City National	e 782P2d²592	Curtis 1985
815P2d²794	(39WAp799)	769P2d⁵889	Bank v Crocker	786P2d¹355	(AKSAS2913)
815P2d³795	cc 628P2d522	773P2d¹³924	National Bank	f 789P2d²1034	f 732P2d³192
847P2d³967	721P2d⁵548	j 789P2d862	1984	791P2d316	784P2d²657
Mont	722P2d²1352	816P2d871	(211 CaR517)	796P2d³1333	j 854P2d739
710P2d³40	734P2d⁹974	j 817P2d450	s 197CaR721	801P2d402	—1081—
—996—	741P2d³593	j 820P2d993	Ala	802P2d¹990	Hall v Add-
Pioneer	741P2d⁴593	848P2d¹⁵818	551So2d977	238CaR¹776	Ventures Ltd.
National Title	763P2d⁸472	Cir. 5	—1058—	239CaR¹117	1985
Insurance Co. v	780P2d⁷879	918F2d¹³1250	Case 2	239CaR¹716	(AKSAS2912)
Washington	789P2d81	Cir. 8	Johnson &	242CaR¹198	727P2d⁷305
1985	f 789P2d¹³82	91BRW¹⁶537	Johnson v	243CaR¹220	774P2d⁶197
(39WAp758)	f 789P2d¹⁴83	Cir. 10	Superior Court	244CaR¹452	779P2d⁷314
cc 765P2d36	813P2d¹⁵1293	901F2d²⁰853	of San Francisco	245CaR¹401	j 791P2d1018
739P2d²706	Nebr	938F2d⁵1112	1985	245CaR¹406	835P2d1207
739P2d³706	492NW47	Utah	(38C3d243)	253CaR¹578	j 835P2d1211
741P2d¹14	—1021—	757P2d¹⁰471	(211CaR517)	254CaR¹797	—1090—
741P2d²15	Amin v	Tenn	s 200CaR812	254CaR¹807	Norton v
741P2d⁴15	Wyoming 1985	728SW755	j 710P2d265	255CaR¹849	Alcoholic
822P2d³1230	cc 694P2d119	87Æ178n	746P2d875	256CaR⁹4	Beverage
—999—	cc 774P2d597	—1042—	j 221CaR465	257CaR¹328	e 264Ca
Evergreen	cc 811P2d255	Hogan v Postin	d 221CaR⁵771	260CaR¹542	266Ca
School District	706P2d⁴256	1985	224CaR422	e 264Ca	268Ca
No. 114 v	715P2d²³240	721P2d²578	j 224CaR424	266Ca	269CaR
Human Rights	715P2d²³249	743P2d⁵865	226CaR30	268Ca	273CaR³328
Commission	d 719P2d²¹230	—1048—	232CaR658	269CaR	276CaR159
1985	d 719P2d²²230	Bauer v	242CaR736	273CaR³328	277CaR¹206
(39WAp763)	719P2d¹⁶234	Wyoming ex rel	d 253CaR¹761	276CaR159	65Æ51n
—1007—	719P2d¹⁷234	Worker's	d 253CaR⁷761	277CaR¹206	67Æ443n
	721P2d1034	Compensation	280CaR⁷539	65Æ51n	740P2d946
	721P2d¹⁸1035	Division 1985	284CaR653	67Æ443n	754P2d¹244
Distinguished from	735P2d²¹442	703P2d1081	14CaR2d56	—1071—	759P2d1297
Sheppardized case	j 743P2d300	j 703P2d1082	Cir. 9	Van Gulik v	786P2d¹386
	752P2d¹⁷414	711P2d399	671FS⁴1543	Resource	787P2d¹030
742P2d³132	768P2d¹⁷1048	719P2d³239	—1066—	Development	791P2d¹618
e 746P2d⁴843	778P2d¹⁶1102	d 719P2d⁷240	Trousil v	Council for	824P2d³711
d 746P2d²845	792P2d¹1358	e 722P2d⁷168	California Bar	Alaska Inc. 1985	824P2d¹1366
746P2d²1222	792P2d⁸1358	d 774P2d591	1985	(AKSAS2910)	850P2d¹631
746P2d⁴1222	f 808P2d⁴203	783P2d166	(38C3d337)	Mass	N M
754P2d²1271	j 820P2d120	783P2d⁵167	(211CaR525)	489NE1024	808P2d66
695 P.2d 1010' V	835P2d¹²310	789P2d869	727P2d¹755	S D	808P2d⁴67
reversed	j 835P2d313	f 795P2d³764	738P2d¹738	504NW597	—1094—
	842P2d⁸522	f 796P2d⁷450	739P2d¹136	64Æ1073n	Winter v Coor
/88	j 842P2d525	—1055—	739P2d¹1284	—1074—	1985
Ariz	Ariz	Young v	741P2d¹213	Spendlove v	(144Az56)
—1010—	720P2d²⁰106	Wyoming	745P2d¹919	Anchorage	708P2d¹1340
Mott v Endicott	720P2d²¹106	1985	747P2d¹1148	Municipal	710P2d1047
School District	—1031—	s 678P2d880	749P2d¹1307	Zoning Board of	736P2d¹822
No. 308 1985	United States	706P2d272	751P2d¹460	Examiners &	d 771P2d¹1381
(39WAp792)	acting Through	707P2d²155	751P2d¹464	Appeals 1985	d 771P2d²1381
r 713P2d98	Farmers Home	707P2d²184	764P2d¹706	(AKSAS2914)	809P2d¹431
704P2d⁴656	Administration v	715P2d²249	766P2d¹563	D 474US895	839P2d⁶467
	Redland 1985			D 88LE217	Cir. 9
	699P2d¹³307			D 106SC216	806F2d²1371
	707P2d¹⁵164				

> **For Example** There are several citations following 695 P.2d 1048 (see Exhibit 5-19) which show different ways the case was treated by subsequent courts: in "j 703P2d1082," the treatment code *j* means the Shepardized case (695 P.2d 1048) was cited in the dissenting opinion in 703 P.2d at page 1082; in "d 774P2d591," the *d* means that the court distinguished the case from the Shepardized case in 774 P.2d at page 591.

◼ The treatment codes are included in the table of abbreviations at the beginning of each *Shepard's* citator.

In addition to the treatment codes, the citations include references to specific points of law discussed in the Shepardized case that are also addressed in the cited case. This is accomplished through the use of small, raised-numeral references following the reporter abbreviation in the citation. These numbers correspond to the headnote number of the Shepardized case.

> **For Example** The case being Shepardized appears at 695 P.2d 1081. One of the case citations is "779P2d^{7}314." The raised 7 means that the point of law discussed in headnote 7 of the Shepardized case (695 P.2d 1081) is discussed in 779 P.2d at page 314 (see Exhibit 5-19).

◼ These reference numbers are invaluable during research because they allow you to compare the treatment of a specific point of law in both cases. If there is no raised number in a citation, then the case discusses the Shepardized case in general or does not summarize a point of law from the case.

◼ **Secondary sources.** Following the case citations are references to secondary sources, such as *ALR* annotations, that in some way reference the Shepardized case (see Exhibit 5-19).

2. *Shepard's* Statutory, Constitutional, and Other Enacted Law Citators

Just as you must Shepardize case law to determine if it is "good law," you must also Shepardize statutory and constitutional provisions, administrative regulations, and court rules. *Shepard's* publishes various citators that allow you to Shepardize these types of laws to determine their history, current status, and how the courts have interpreted them. Some of these citators are:

◼ **Statutory, constitutional, and court rules.** The *Shepard's* citator for a state's statutes is either included with the *Shepard's* state case citator or published as a separate volume. Citations to state constitutions and state court rules are included with the *Shepard's* citations to the state statutes. *Shepard's Federal Statute Citations* covers the federal statutes and includes the citations to the United States Constitution and federal court rules.

◼ **Federal and state regulations.** You may Shepardize the regulations of the federal agencies published in the *Code of Federal Regulations* by using *Shepard's Code of Federal Regulations Citations*. Some state administrative agency regulations citations are included in the *Shepard's* state citations.

Shepard's citators to enacted law are similar to the case law citators in many respects:

◼ **Abbreviations—analysis and introductory material.** At the front of the citator is a table of abbreviations page that identifies all of the abbreviations used in the citator. Following this page are instructions on how to use the citator.

■ **Statute location.** Printed in the upper corner of each page of the citatory is the statute title, volume, or chapter number. As discussed in Chapter 3, statutory or code numbering systems vary from state to state. When more than one title is covered on a page, the title number is usually included in a box. The separate section numbers are printed in bold (see Exhibit 5-20).

■ **History.** The first entries under a section indicate any legislative action taken that affects the statute.

> **For Example** If it has been amended, an *A* followed by the citation to the amendment will be presented (see Exhibit 5-20).

■ **Case treatment.** After the history of the statute are citations to cases that have mentioned the statute. Preceding the case citations are treatment codes that indicate how the statute was treated in the cited case (see Exhibit 5-20).

> **For Example** A *C* preceding a case citation indicates the statute was held constitutional.

If there is no letter preceding the citation, then the case merely discusses the statute generally.

■ **Secondary sources.** Following the case citations are references to secondary sources, such as *ALR* annotations, that in some way reference the statute (see Exhibit 5-20).

3. Updating *Shepard's Citations* in Print

Most sets of *Shepard's Citations* consist of one or more hardbound volumes accompanied by one or more supplement pamphlets. For most citators, advance sheets are published between publication of the pamphlets. The pamphlets and advance sheets update the hardbound volumes. On the cover of each pamphlet is a "what your library should contain" section listing all the hardbound volumes and supplements for the set. Check this list to ensure that your research is complete. If one of the *Shepard's* is missing, check with the librarian.

B. Computerized Updating Using *Shepard's* Online

Traditionally, the only way to update and validate your research was through *Shepard's Citations* in print. Computerized updating is faster and more efficient, and eliminates the need to know what books from each *Shepard's* set are required. Computerized updating and validating is more up to date because electronic references are available much more quickly that those in print. In addition, law libraries or law professionals with a subscription to Lexis have *Shepard's* online, obviating the need for the print versions and saving space and money. Significantly, computerized updating with *Shepard's* online eliminates the need to learn or refer to the list of abbreviations for case treatments, case history, and other references. The online service presents treatment of cases, case history, and the like using regular terminology rather than the abbreviations used in the *Shepard's* print versions.

Exhibit 5-20 *Citation page from* Shepard's Federal Statute Citations. LexisNexis, Shepard's Federal Statute Citations, 1996 Bound Volume, Vol. 1, p. 65. Reprinted with the permission of LexisNexis.

Title

UNITED STATES CODE 1988 and 1994 Eds.   TITLE 33 § 910

Section

Amended

Secondary
source

Held
constitutional

§ 908 (j)	Cir. 1	785F2d1318	**§ 909 (b)**	Cir. 4	Cir. 11
Ad 98St1646	91F2d130	790F2d420	A 86St1251	37FS717	672F2d848
Cir. 1	599F2d468	797F2d213	440US33	Cir. 5	**§ 909 (f)**
11F3d254	646F2d712	818F2d398	461US626	601F2d1319	Cir. DC
Cir. 5	688F2d863	820F2d1411	59LE122	Cir. 9	75F2d236
957F2d1205	851F2d4	958F2d1300	76LE197	567F2d1387	160F2d254
20F3d661	885F2d984	65F3d461	99SC904	**§ 909 (d)**	Cir. 1
23F3d109	885F2d986	29FS377	103SC2047	A 86St1251	91F2d133
Cir. 9	Cir. 2	344FS325	Cir. DC	436US601	136F2d657
953F2d557	93F2d663	391FS1360	57F2d440	56LE568	Cir. 2
§ 908 (j) (3)	209F2d914	662FS99	131F2d234	98SC2001	56F2d1052
Cir. 5	241F2d766	Cir. 6	135F2d258	Cir. DC	60F2d896
17F3d786	272F2d15	600F2d1221	218F2d860	160F2d253	Cir. 4
§ 909 et seq.	C 548F2d1113	850F2d285	545F2d211	545F2d211	154F2d560
Cir. 7	607F2d1039	Cir. 7	548F2d1049	Cir. 2	47FS566
702FS722	702F2d412	554F2d310	352FS195	135F2d152	Cir. 5
§ 909	19FS907	647F2d719	Cir. 1	304FS321	150F2d79
A 86St1251	96FS95	46FRD34	585F2d1169	Cir. 4	818F2d399
A 98St1647	192FS564	Cir. 8	885F2d985	53F2d300	Cir. 6
285US38	202FS859	583F2d877	Cir. 2	198F2d237	138FS834
287US537	411FS1181	58F3d1236	963F2d542	475FS10	Cir. 9
317US391	822FS949	Cir. 9	160FS784	Cir. 5	175F2d912
386US736	Cir. 3	31F2d153	Cir. 3	62F2d122	188F2d455
398US407	98F2d1016	328F2d877	183F2d937	150F2d79	**§ 909 (g)**
440US31	183F2d936	496F2d1249	267F2d60	319FS1376	Cir. 2
461US633	209F2d200	567F2d1385	545F2d338	Cir. 9	192FS569
76LE605	545F2d338	C 596F2d900	16FS677	175F2d911	**§ 910**
77LE480	C 577F2d852	708F2d415	24FS245	567F2d1387	285US38
87LE353	24FS245	717F2d1284	56FS62	**§ 909 (e)**	317US390
18LE492	C 117FS605	882F2d1437	166FS909	A 86St1251	76LE605
26LE360	225FS461	938F2d983	354FS330	A 98St1647	87LE353
59LE123	336FS800	14FS159	Cir. 5	440US29	52SC287
76LE202	Cir. 4	98FS1021	110F2d269	461US626	63SC289
52SC287	43F2d983	313FS314	150F2d79	59LE122	Cir. DC
53SC232	154F2d560	Cir. 11	168F2d873	76LE197	85F2d411
63SC289	184F2d79	766F2d1517	601F2d1308	99SC904	183F2d819
87SC1423	C 539F2d378	CtCl	322FS1232	103SC2047	233F2d701
90SC1791	591F2d985	305F2d378	Cir. 7	Cir. DC	290F2d358
99SC906	594F2d407	16ARF689n	46FRD34	545F2d211	628F2d89
103SC2050	9FS315	**§ 909 (a to g)**	Cir. 9	Cir. 1	793F2d321
Cir. DC	9FS745	Cir. DC	169F2d988	885F2d984	173FS381
77F2d543	47FS568	749F2d75	188F2d457	Cir. 3	Cir. 1
101F2d255	186FS805	**§ 909 (a)**	567F2d1385	183F2d937	489F2d1041
107F2d264	245FS234	A 86St1251	60FS806	545F2d338	646F2d711
131F2d233	475FS10	A 98St1647	Cir. 11	Cir. 4	851F2d4
147F2d563	Cir. 5	Cir. DC	672F2d848	56F2d216	885F2d991
190F2d30	35F2d346	670F2d211	766F2d1514	Cir. 5	942F2d819
512F2d941	49F2d807	Cir. 1	**§ 909 (c)**	322FS1232	11F3d250
545F2d210	54F2d212	885F2d993	A 86St1251	Cir. 6	Cir. 2
607F2d1381	57F2d257	Cir. 3	Cir. DC	850F2d285	769F2d67
607F2d1386	57F2d263	183F2d937	545F2d211	Cir. 9	884F2d57
670F2d210	68F2d56	24FS245	548F2d1049	41F2d154	969F2d1408
749F2d68	133F2d305	Cir. 5	Cir. 1	46F2d541	244FS112
834F2d1030	204F2d173	601F2d1308	885F2d985	567F2d1385	329FS697
929F2d737	519F2d536	Cir. 6	Cir. 3		
173FS381	601F2d1307	850F2d294	183F2d937		
	C 634F2d844				
	681F2d288				

1. How to Use *Shepard's* Online

▓ If you are using Lexis to do case research and you are viewing a case on the screen in the top left toolbar, click the *Shepard's* link. The next page will require you to choose *Shepard's* for validation (KWIC) or *Shepard's* for research (FULL). Make your choice and click "Check." The results are presented in the next screen.

> **For Example** You are viewing *Young v. Wyoming*, 695 P.2d 1055 (Wyo. 1995), in Lexis. Click on the *Shepardize* icon. A separate screen will open, displaying all of the Shepardized results (see Exhibit 5-21). Here there is no negative (subsequent) history and no citing references (see the gray area of the screen shot in Exhibit 5-21).

▓ If you have the citation of a case that you want to Shepardize, log on to Lexis and click on the *Shepard's* icon. Type in your citation (148 N.M. 330) in the blank field provided and select *Shepard's* for validation (KWIC). The results will be provided in plain language, indicating the history and/or treatment of the case, depending upon which option you chose. One of the best features of Shepardizing online is that if you are interested in accessing a reference listed in the Shepardized result, you simply click on it and a new window opens showing that reference in its entirety (see Exhibit 5-22).

> **For Example** You want to Shepardize a case to see what other cases have cited it and whether it is still good law. Log in to Lexis and click on the *Shepard's* link. Enter the citation 148 N.M. 330 and select "*Shepard's* for research" (FULL) and then click on "Check." The results show there is one distinguishing case, three cases following the decision, and two explaining the decision (see Exhibit 5-22).

Exhibit 5-21 *Screen shot of results after using "Shepardize" for a case.* Copyright 2012 LexisNexis, a division of Reed Elsevier Inc. All Rights Reserved. LexisNexis and the Knowledge Burst logo are registered trademarks of Reed Elsevier Properties Inc. and are used with the permission of LexisNexis.

Exhibit 5-22 *Screen shot of results: State v. Sims, 2010-NMSC-027, 148 N.M. 330, 236 P.3d 642 **Shepard's** for validation (KWIC).* Copyright 2012 LexisNexis, a division of Reed Elsevier Inc. All Rights Reserved. LexisNexis and the Knowledge Burst logo are registered trademarks of Reed Elsevier Properties Inc. and are used with the permission of LexisNexis.

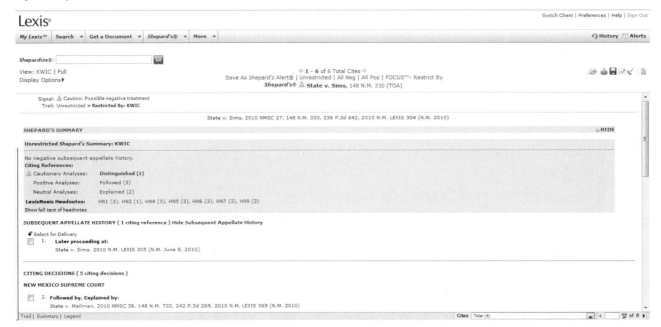

2. Characteristics of *Shepard's* Online

- *Shepard's* for Validation (KWIC)—provides a list of subsequent history and citing references with analysis, which means negative history only. This is used when you only want to determine if the law is still valid.

- *Shepard's* for Research (FULL)—provides prior and subsequent history as well as all citing references, including secondary sources. This method provides a list of all authorities referencing the law being Shepardized.

- *Shepard's* Summary—provides an overview of the entire report at a glance. You can quickly see the signal indicator of whether the law is still valid and a listing of the number of references that have positive, negative, and neutral analysis, as well as other citing references. If you click any of the items, you will be taken to the first item in that portion of the report (see gray areas of Exhibit 5-21 and Exhibit 5-22).

- Navigation Bar Menu (located at the bottom right of the results page)—allows you to jump to particular jurisdictions or sources, such as a particular circuit (10th Circuit) or particular source (A.L.R. Annotation) (see Exhibit 5-21 and Exhibit 5-22).

- *Shepard's* Alerts—allows you to set regularly scheduled updates for certain laws. If you set an alert, you will be e-mailed on the schedule you choose as to whether there has been a change in the validity of the law. This is particularly helpful when you are using a case from an intermediate appellate court that you know still faces review by the highest court.

- Customization—There are numerous ways to customize the report. The "Display Options" link and the "Preferences" link are just a few ways to customize the appearance of a report. There is a tutorial link that will guide you through use of each of the methods of customization.

▨ Table of Authorities—analyzes the cases cited by a case you are relying on. The Table of Authorities feature not only shows the cases your case relied upon, but also the status of those cases. This allows you to discover if the foundation upon which your case rests is weakened in any way, which ultimately may weaken your case.

3. *Shepard's* Signals

▨ **Red Stop Sign.** Warns that there is significant negative history or treatment, such as reversal of the case on at least one point of law.

▨ **Yellow Triangle.** Warns of some negative history or treatment, such as being distinguished from another case (see Exhibit 5-22).

▨ **Green Plus.** Reveals positive history, such as being followed by another case.

▨ **Letter "Q" in Orange Square.** Warns that the validity of the case has been questioned by another jurisdiction.

▨ **Letter "A" in Blue Circle.** Reveals that the case has been analyzed by another case in a neutral manner.

▨ **Letter "I" in Blue Circle.** Indicates other sources have referred to your case.

▨ **Red Exclamation Point.** Warns that there is a case that negatively interprets a statute.

C. Other Lexis Validation Products

There are several other tools that complement Lexis' *Shepard's* service. They include:

▨ **BriefCheck.** This is a separate software program which will scan your document (memorandum, brief, etc.) and collect citations from it automatically. Each authority in your document is Shepardized using either the "FULL" or "KWIC" options, and results can be either displayed on the screen or printed out in a separate document.

▨ *Shepard's* **Link.** This is another software application which identifies citations in a document. This tool adds *Shepard's* signals so that you can see whether there is any weak authority in your document.

▨ **FullAuthority.** This tool will create a table of authorities for your document. This is an alternative to manually creating a table of authorities using a word processing program; however, you must carefully check the accuracy of the table before submitting any document to your supervising attorney or to the courts.

D. Using Westlaw's KeyCite

1. How to KeyCite Cases

KeyCite is Westlaw's online citator. When using Westlaw you will use KeyCite to validate and update your research. KeyCite is obviously a different citator than *Shepard's*, but you will find they are similar in the ways they are most often used. KeyCiting cases, statutes, and other primary sources of law is similar to Sheparding those sources. Because a researcher more frequently KeyCites case citations, the process of KeyCiting in that context is discussed here.

▨ If you are using Westlaw to do a search and you are viewing a case on the screen, clicking on the KeyCite signal for the case will take you to the KeyCite results. Alternatively, from the left margin you can choose one of the KeyCite characteristics of Full History, Direct History (Graphical Review), or Citing References to go directly to particular characteristics of KeyCite.

> **For Example** You do a search for cases in New Mexico involving whether a person was in actual physical control of a vehicle for purposes of being convicted of driving while intoxicated. Your results lead you to *State v. Sims*, 2010-NMSC-027, 148 N.M. 330, 236 P.3d 642. You see a yellow flag in the top left of the case; when you click on it, you are taken to KeyCite and the case that caused the yellow flag signal, *State v. Cotton*, is presented (see Exhibit 5-23). If you want to view the Full History or Direct History, you can click either icon in the left margin

▨ If you have the citation of a case that you want to KeyCite, log on to Westlaw and click the KeyCite icon in the top toolbar. Type in your citation (148 N.M. 330) and click "Go." The results will be provided. If you are interested in accessing any case or reference listed, simply click on it; a new window will open, showing the reference in its entirety.

2. How to KeyCite Statutes, Constitutions, and Other Enacted Law

Just as you must validate case law, you must validate any other primary source of law, such as statutes, constitutional provisions, or administrative regulations. The process of KeyCiting these other sources of law is almost identical to that for KeyCiting case law.

To KeyCite a statute, click on the KeyCite icon in the top toolbar. Type in your citation (NM Stat. Ann. 66-8-102) and click "Go." If you are looking at a statute on the screen as the result of a search, either use the KeyCite box to the left of the screen or click on the signal for the statute.

KeyCite signals for statutes include:

▨ A *red flag* warns that a statute has been amended, repealed, or held unconstitutional.

▨ A *yellow flag* warns that there is some negative history, such as case law limiting the application of the statute or pending legislation.

▨ A *green "C"* indicates that other sources have cited your statute.

Exhibit 5-23 *Screen shot of KeyCite Results After Clicking on a Yellow Flag Signal in a Case. Reprinted with permisison of Thomson Reuters.*

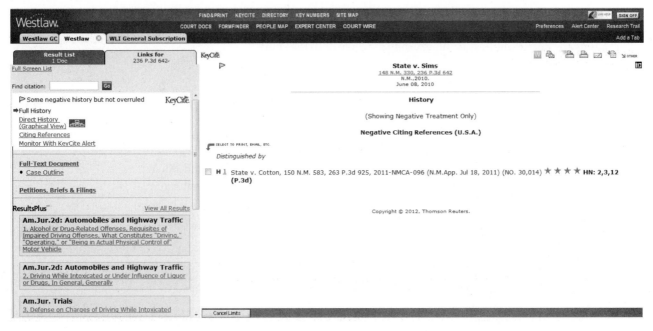

3. Characteristics of KeyCite

Although discussed here in reference to cases, KeyCite for other sources of law has the same characteristics as for KeyCiting cases:

- **Full history.** Provides a full history of the KeyCited case. This includes direct history, citing references, and other materials such as court documents that include citations to the case or the briefs filed in relation to that particular case.

- **Graphical display of direct history.** Shows in a flowchart the progression of the case from trial through the appellate court system.

- **Citing references.** Reveals other sources that have cited the case. This includes levels of treatment such as negative treatment, positive treatment, and secondary sources that have referenced the case (see Exhibit 5-24).

- **Depth of treatment stars.** The list of citing references includes green stars to indicate the level of treatment (see Exhibit 5-24).

> **For Example** Click on the KeyCite link in the top toolbar menu. Enter 148 N.M. 330 (*State v. Sims*) and click "Go." Next click "Citing References" in the left navigation bar. You will see that the case that is *Distinguished* from *State v. Sims* thoroughly examines *Sims* because there are four stars (see Exhibit 5-24).

- **Limit KeyCite Display.** Use the Limit KeyCite Display icon at the bottom left of the results page to narrow the results by document type, date, jurisdiction, headnote, depth of treatment, and so on.

- **Quotation marks.** If quotation marks are included in a listing, the case or other source includes direct quotes from the KeyCited case (see Exhibit 5-24).

Exhibit 5-24 *Screen Shot of Results From Using KeyCite "Citing References"* Reprinted with permisison of Thomson Reuters.

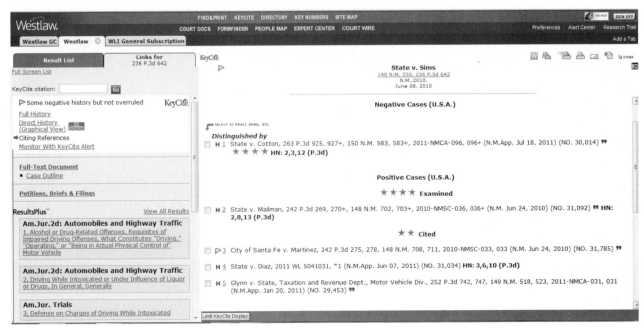

> **For Example** The entry for *State v. Cotton,* which distinguished itself from *Sims,* has purple quotation marks in the listing. *Cotton* will have direct quotations from *Sims* in the opinion (see Exhibit 5-24).

- ▪ **Headnote references.** References to specific headnotes from *Sims* are noted. **HN: 2, 3, 13 (P.3d)** indicates that *Cotton* discusses the point of law related to headnotes 2, 3, and 13 in *Sims* (see Exhibit 5-24).
- ▪ **KeyCite alert.** KeyCite Alert lets you set regularly scheduled alerts for certain laws. If you set up an alert, you will be e-mailed on the schedule you choose when there has been any change to the validity of the law or if there are new citing references.
- ▪ **Table of authorities.** This tool analyzes the cases cited by the case you are KeyCiting. This allows you to determine if the law is weakened by subsequent cases or other laws.

4. KeyCite Signals

- ▪ **Red flag.** Warns that there is significant negative history, such as reversal or the case being overruled on at least one point of law.
- ▪ **Yellow flag.** Warns of some negative history or treatment, such as being distinguished from another later case.
- ▪ **Green "C."** Indicates that the case has been cited by some other sources, but reveals no negative citing references and no direct history.
- ▪ **Blue "H."** Reveals that the source being KeyCited has some history. The history can be direct, such as certiorari being granted; or indirect, such as another case further explaining the source.

VII. RESEARCH USING CITATORS

Shepard's Citations and KeyCite are used for two purposes:

1. To determine if the authority you have located is still "good law." This is the most important use of a citator.
2. To locate case law or secondary sources that have discussed primary authority being researched. Even though a court opinion has not been reversed, it is important to determine how other courts have analyzed it.

> **For Example** If later courts have uniformly criticized the holding and reasoning of a court opinion, or it has been limited in some way, you may not want to rely on it.

You may also wish to locate additional authority to support and add weight to the case being relied on. It is also possible that the reasoning in the case being researched is not clear, and other cases or secondary authority are necessary to help clarify it.

A. Research Using *Shepard's* Citations

The steps presented here are guidelines for using *Shepard's Citations* to conduct research.

1. *Select the appropriate Shepard's citator (in print) or select the Shepard's link in Lexis (online).*

2. *Locate and review the entry for the authority being Shepardized (in print) or review the results of an electronically Shepardized authority (online).* Keep the following in mind:

   a. Carefully review the history for subsequent cases or legislative actions that have reversed, overturned, repealed, amended, modified, or in any way affected the authority being Shepardized. Any such action may mean that the authority is no longer reliable; that is, it is no longer "good law."

   b. Carefully review the treatment of the authority in subsequent court opinions. Even though the authority being Shepardized may not have been reversed, repealed, and so on, reliance on it may be problematic if it has received any negative treatment by the courts.

   > **For Example** If many of the citations to the Shepardized case involve negative letters, such as *c* (criticized) or *q* (questioned), it may indicate that the case, although not overruled or reversed, is not being treated as good authority by subsequent courts.

   You must read the cases that treat the Shepardized case negatively. It is possible that your Shepardized case is being criticized for the treatment of an issue different from the one you are researching. For instance, you may be researching a negligence issue raised in the case being Shepardized, whereas the negative treatment in the subsequent cases involves a different issue such as an improper jury instruction.

   c. If you are concerned with one issue in the Shepardized case, it may only be necessary to review those cited cases addressing that same issue.

   > **For Example** Assume you are researching headnote 7 of the case being Shepardized. Your research would focus on those cited cases addressing headnote 7, that is, cases with the raised 7 following the reporter name (e.g., 779P2d^{7}314).

   d. If a case does not appear in a *Shepard's* volume (in print), or the inquiry results state "No Results Found," it may mean that no court opinion has discussed your case. Always check the citation to be sure it is correct.

3. *Update your research (in print only).* Check the supplementary pamphlets and advance sheets and perform the research steps previously mentioned.

B. Research Using KeyCite

The steps presented here are guidelines for using KeyCite to conduct research.

1. *Once you have identified a case, statute, or other primary source of law that you will rely upon in your document, click the KeyCite icon.*

2. *Enter the citation and click "Go." Choose Citing References in the left margin to review the results.*

a. Review the results for subsequent cases or legislative actions that have reversed, overturned, repealed, amended, modified, or in any way affected the authority being KeyCited. Any such action may mean that the authority is no longer reliable; that is, it is no longer "good law.

b. Review the positive and negative treatment of the authority in subsequent court opinions. Even though the authority being KeyCited may have not been reversed, repealed, and so on, reliance on it may be problematic if it has received any negative treatment by the courts.

VIII. KEY POINTS CHECKLIST: *Secondary Authority*

✓ The first step of legal research is to locate primary authority (the law), because courts look to primary authority first when resolving legal problems. Secondary authority is used when there is no primary authority on a topic in a jurisdiction, in support of the existing primary authority, to help you understand the primary authority, or to locate court opinions and other research sources interpreting the primary authority.

✓ None of the research sources discussed in this chapter are primary authority (the law). A court may refer to and rely on the secondary authorities mentioned in this chapter, but it is not bound to follow them.

✓ Legal encyclopedias and treatises are primarily used to obtain a familiarity with or understanding of a specific area of the law.

✓ Use an *ALR* if you are looking for a comprehensive analysis and synthesis of cases from every jurisdiction on specific legal issues.

✓ Refer to a digest when you need to locate cases that have addressed a specific legal question or when you already have a case and wish to locate other cases that address the same legal question(s).

✓ Always validate and update the primary authority you are relying on, by using *Shepard's* or KeyCite, to ensure that the authority has not been overturned, reversed, repealed, or amended.

✓ With all research sources, you must check the pocket parts, supplements, or whatever is used to update the source to ensure that your research is current.

IX. APPLICATION

This section explores the avenues of research Melissa may pursue to learn about the tort law of battery. Melissa could begin her search by consulting a legal encyclopedia, such as *American Jurisprudence Second* or *Corpus Juris Secundum,* at the local law library. By consulting the General Index, she would be directed to the volume that addresses assault and battery. If she knows that the topic she is looking for is "assault and battery," she can go directly to the volumes on the shelf. The spine of each book will indicate the range of coverage of the volume, such as "Assault and Battery to Attachment and Garnishment." She would pull the appropriate volume and read about assault and battery. The encyclopedia will give her a general overview of the topic. She can also access *American Jurisprudence Second* through both Westlaw and LexisNexis.

If Melissa wants a more in-depth summary or analysis of the law of civil assault and battery, she could consult a treatise such as *Prosser and Keeton on the Law of Torts* or *The Law of Torts* by Dobbs. She would locate these books by going to the local law library and asking for the treatise section. The treatises are usually arranged alphabetically by topic. Therefore, the tort treatises will be shelved together. Melissa is interested in assault and battery in situations such as hers, where the attack took place in a date situation. The treatise will provide a discussion of the topic in greater analytical detail than an encyclopedia. If she has access to Westlaw or LexisNexis, she could check to see if a tort treatise is available.

For a more detailed analysis of the subject specifically regarding date situations, she could look for an *ALR* annotation. If she were to locate an annotation that addresses the question in a situation similar to hers, it will provide, in one place, a comprehensive analysis of the issue, references to and summaries of the case law on point, and references to other research sources.

If Melissa is unable to locate such an annotation, she could refer to a West digest and look under the topic "assault and battery." There she would locate summaries of specific court opinions that discuss assaults and batteries that took place during a date. She would then select the case or cases most factually similar to her situation and read how the law applies.

Through these sources, Melissa could explore the subject in detail and determine what the officer meant when he said she could file a battery tort claim. She could also determine what remedies are available to her.

Summary

The focus of this chapter is secondary authority, that is, sources regarding law that a court may rely on but that are not themselves the law, that is, not primary authority. Secondary authority consists of legal research sources that summarize, compile, explain, comment on, interpret, or in some other way address the law. Secondary authority is used for several purposes, including:

- To obtain a background or overall understanding of a specific area of the law. Legal encyclopedias, treatises, and periodicals are useful for these purposes.

- To locate primary authority (the law) on a question being researched. *American Law Reports (ALR)* and digests are particularly useful for this purpose.

- To be relied upon by the court when reaching a decision. This usually occurs only when there is no primary authority governing a legal question, or when it is unclear how the primary authority applies to the question at hand.

There are literally hundreds of secondary sources. This chapter covers those secondary sources that provide the researcher with treatment of the law that ranges from the general to the specific. These sources are legal encyclopedias and treatises.

Legal encyclopedias provide an overview of all the areas of law. They do not provide in-depth coverage, and they are similar to other encyclopedias in their general treatment of topics.

Treatises are single-volume or multivolume texts that provide a comprehensive analysis of a single area of law such as torts or criminal law. Whereas a legal encyclopedia presents a broad overview of an area of law, a treatise provides an in-depth discussion and explains, analyzes, and criticizes the law.

This chapter also focuses on sources that help a researcher locate and analyze case law: *American Law Reports (ALR)* and digests. *ALR* exhaustively covers specific legal issues. A digest organizes the law by topic and provides a summary or "digest" of all the court opinions that have addressed the topic. It is an excellent case finder when a researcher needs to locate court opinions on specific topics.

Before relying on any primary authority, the researcher must determine if it is still "good law"; that is, the researcher must determine that it has not been reversed, modified, or otherwise negatively affected by some subsequent opinion or statute. The use of *Shepard's Citations* or Westlaw's KeyCite allows a researcher to determine if primary authority is still "good law" and also to locate other cases and secondary authorities that discuss a specific court opinion.

Quick References

Internet Resources

Most of the secondary authority and other research sources discussed in this chapter are available on Westlaw or LexisNexis. Most of the sources are not available on nonfee-based Web sites.

CITATION

The *Bluebook* and *ALWD Citation Manual* rules governing citation to the various secondary authority sources are discussed in Chapter 8. Some examples of citations to the secondary authority sources discussed in this chapter are presented here.

A. Legal Encyclopedias

6 Am. Jur. 2d *Assault and Battery* § 2 (1999)

6A C.J.S. *Assault and Battery* § 11 (1975)

B. Treatises

Dan B. Dobbs, *The Law of Torts* § 23 (West Group 2000)

C. *ALR* Annotations

Jeffrey F. Ghent, Annotation, *Modern Status of Sudden Emergency Doctrine*, 10 A.L.R. 5th 680 (1993)

D. Digests, *Shepard's*

The cases you locate through digests and *Shepard's* are cited according to the *Bluebook*. The digests themselves are not cited.

Exercises

Additional assignments are available on the CourseMate.

ASSIGNMENT 1

What are the uses of secondary authority?

ASSIGNMENT 2

The client seeks advice concerning the actions of the majority stockholder in a small corporation. The majority stockholder owns 58 percent of the stock, and the client and another shareholder together own 42 percent. The majority stockholder controls the board of directors and is president of the corporation. He refuses to allow the corporation to issue any stock dividends. Until recently, the client and the other minority stockholder worked for the corporation. Last month, the majority stockholder fired the client and the minority stockholder.

What sections of *Am. Jur. 2d* discuss this topic?

ASSIGNMENT 3

Which *Am. Jur. 2d* title and sections address 18 U.S.C.S. § 204?

ASSIGNMENT 4

The client's brother was killed in an automobile collision. Family members disagree about whether viewing of the deceased should be allowed, due to the degree of damage to the body. What section of *Am. Jur. 2d* discusses this topic?

ASSIGNMENT 5

Refer to *Corpus Juris Secundum*. What section defines the term *name*, and what is the definition?

ASSIGNMENT 6

The client, a shareholder in a corporation, believes that the corporation exceeded its authority when it expanded the corporation's business from the repair of automobiles to the sale of automobile parts. What section of *Fletcher Cyclopedia of the Law of Private Corporations* addresses this topic? What is the term for the action of a corporation that exceeds its power?

ASSIGNMENT 7

The clients' son belongs to a religious cult. The clients believe the cult used improper means to indoctrinate their son and keep him in the cult. The son has given all his goods to the cult and refuses to see or talk to his parents. Is there an *ALR* annotation that addresses the liability of a cult for improper activities?

ASSIGNMENT 8

Has 2 A.L.R. Fed. 347. been replaced or superseded? By what annotation has this been done?

ASSIGNMENT 9

Your assignment is to obtain general information on the criminal aspects of causing or procuring the termination of a human pregnancy. Consult the *ALR.3d, ALR.4th, ALR.5th, ALR.6th,* and *ALR Federal* digests. Under the "Practice References," what is the reference to the "Defense of Paternity Charges" in *Am. Jur. Proof of Facts 2d*? What is the citation of a 1999 Nebraska case involving the state's partial-birth abortion statute?

ASSIGNMENT 10

What *ALR* annotation discusses 42 U.S.C.A. § 740?

ASSIGNMENT 11

The client's husband attacked her so severely that she was hospitalized. They are now separated, and the client wants to sue her husband. The husband still lives on the military base where they lived at the time of the incident. Refer to the *Federal Practice Digest* and locate the digest topic and key number that address this topic.

ASSIGNMENT 12

Give the name and citation of a 1994 Nevada case holding that the use of a toy gun to carry out a kidnapping is not a defense to a kidnapping charge. Refer to the *Tenth Decennial Digest*.

ASSIGNMENT 13

Your supervising attorney asks you to locate the digest topic and key numbers for the *Glover v. Lockheed Corp.* case listing. He remembers it is a *Federal Supplement* case, but he cannot remember the citation.

ASSIGNMENT 14

The assignment requires reference to a *Shepard's* citator. In regard to 18 U.S.C. § 1201(a), what is the citation of the *United States Reports* decision that held the provision unconstitutional in part? What Sixth Circuit case found the provision constitutional? What Second Circuit case, in 2001, discussed section 1201(a)(1)?

ASSIGNMENT 15

The assignment requires access to Westlaw online. Choose the KeyCite icon and enter the citation for *Bullcoming v.*

New Mexico, 131 S. Ct. 2705 (2011). What is the citation for the 2011 Illinois Court of Appeals, First District, case that *Bullcoming* is distinguished by?

ASSIGNMENT 16

This assignment requires access to *Shepard's* online. Click on *Shepard's* and enter the citation for *Crawford*

v. Washington, 541 U.S. 36 (2004); select FULL and click "Check."

A. What is the *Shepard's* signal for *Crawford*?

B. What types of *cautionary analysis* are there? Provide both the type and the number of references for each.

The available CourseMate for this text has an interactive eBook and interactive learning tools, including flash cards, quizzes, and more. To learn more about this resource and access free demo CourseMate resources, go to **www.cengagebrain.com**, and search for this book. To access CourseMate materials that you have purchased, go to **login.cengagebrain.com**.

CHAPTER 6

Secondary Authority—Periodicals, Restatements, Uniform Laws, Dictionaries, *Legislative History,* and Other Secondary Authorities

Assistant City Attorney Genevieve Gray said to her intern, Luis Sisneros, "Luis, the city council is considering drafting a zoning ordinance restricting the location of adult entertainment businesses. I need some preliminary research on First Amendment and other constitutional limitations on such ordinances. How would you like to take a crack at this?" Luis had just started his internship with the city attorney's office. The city provided three internships for paralegal students. "Yes, I'll start right away," Luis responded, and thinking to himself, "This is great. I expected some go-fer type assignments like locating and copying statutes and cases."

The steps Luis follows when performing this assignment and the results of his search are discussed in the Application section of this chapter.

Learning Objectives

After completing this chapter, you should understand:

- The role of periodicals, *Restatements,* uniform laws and dictionaries, and miscellaneous secondary sources in legal research

- How to conduct research using periodicals, *Restatements,* uniform laws and dictionaries, and other secondary sources

I. INTRODUCTION

Chapter 5 addressed the more frequently used research sources that help a researcher summarize, explain, interpret, locate, or update the law. This chapter presents other frequently used secondary authority sources. The chapter discusses legal periodicals that may be used when seeking an analysis and critique of a specific legal topic that is more in-depth or narrower in focus than that provided by a legal encyclopedia or a treatise. It also covers secondary sources that present definitions or uniform statements of the law, such as dictionaries, *Restatements of the Law*, and uniform laws. In addition, the chapter covers legislative history and practice aids such as form books. Exhibit 6-1 shows the primary use of the secondary sources discussed in this chapter.

Exhibit 6-1 *Secondary Authority—Primary Use as a Research Tool.*

AUTHORITY	PRIMARY USE AS A RESEARCH TOOL
Periodicals	Use when you are seeking an analysis and critique of a specific legal topic that is more in-depth or narrower in focus than that provided by a legal encyclopedia or treatise.
Restatements of the Law	Use to locate a standardized definition or statement of the law, reasons in support of the definition or statement of the law, and citations to related cases, treatises, and other secondary authority.
Uniform Laws and Model Acts	Use to locate a model text from which a law may be crafted, arguments in support of the law, and citations to cases, treatises, and articles interpreting the law.
Dictionaries	Use to obtain the spelling, pronunciation, and legal meaning of terms used in the law.
Legislative History	Use to determine the meaning or application of a law. This may be helpful when the meaning of a law that governs a fact situation is unclear or when the law is written so broadly that its application to a specific fact situation is unclear.

© Cengage Learning 2014

II. LEGAL PERIODICALS

Legal periodicals publish articles on legal topics; through these various publications, articles are available on literally every legal topic. The articles are usually authored by individuals who have expertise in the area, such as law professors and expert practitioners in the field, or by law students who have conducted extensive research on a topic. The articles are valuable for their depth of research; citation to numerous primary and secondary sources; and in-depth analysis of current legal issues, recently emerging areas of the law, or specific topics.

For Example S. K. Hom, *Lexicon Dreams and Chinese Rock and Roll: Thoughts on Culture, Language, and Translation Strategies of Resistance and Reconstruction,* 53 U. Miami L. Rev. 1003 (1999) is an example of a law review article addressing a very specific topic.

Publications in legal periodicals are secondary authority. They are not primary authority, but courts on occasion cite them when there is no primary authority on a topic or when interpreting primary authority such as a statute.

> **For Example** "The courts of this state have not addressed the question of the liability of a majority shareholder in a situation such as the one presented in this case. Guidance, however, is provided in [name of law review article] where the question has been thoroughly analyzed."

A. Types of Legal Periodicals

Legal periodicals can be classified into four distinct categories.

1. Law Reviews

Law reviews are scholarly periodicals published by law schools. They contain articles written by law professors, judges, practitioners, and law students and are usually published four times a year. Most accredited law schools in the United States publish at least one law review. Law students edit law reviews under the guidance of the law school faculty and administration. Rigorous standards are employed to ensure high quality. Due to their scholarly nature, they are often cited by courts.

Law reviews are valuable for their detailed analysis of current legal issues, recently emerging areas of the law, and specific topics (see Exhibit 6-2). Law reviews usually include:

- **Articles.** Articles are written by scholars, judges, or practitioners and usually present a comprehensive analysis of specific topics such as the *Lexicon Dreams* article mentioned previously. The articles are thoroughly researched with footnotes citing numerous cases, studies, and other sources. They often criticize the law and recommend changes or alternative legal solutions.

- **Notes and comments.** These are shorter pieces written by students. They are like the articles in that they are narrow in focus, thoroughly researched, and extensively footnoted. Inasmuch as students and not experts in the field write them, they have less authority and are less frequently cited.

- **Recent developments and cases.** This section discusses recent cases and developments in the law such as new statutes. Students author this section.

- **Book reviews.** Most law reviews include book reviews of recent legal publications.

2. Bar Association and Other Association Publications

Every state has a bar association whose members are attorneys licensed to practice law in the state. There are national bar associations open to practitioners nationally, the largest and best known being the American Bar Association. Most of these associations publish journals that are similar in many respects to law reviews. The journals include articles on specific legal subjects, recent developments in the case and statutory law, and tips and guides for practitioners. They also include book reviews, news about the association, and technology updates. Like law reviews, the articles are thoroughly researched, with footnotes citing cases and other sources. **State bar association journals** tend to publish articles that are local in nature and of interest primarily to practitioners of that jurisdiction. The American Bar Association publishes the *American Bar Association Journal*, which includes articles concerning national legal developments.

Exhibit 6-2 *Sample Law Review Page.* *University of New Mexico School of Law, Toni Lester,* Protecting the Gender Nonconformist from the Gender Police—Why the Harassment of Gays and Other Gender Nonconformists Is a Form of Sex Discrimination in Light of the Supreme Court's Decision in *Oncale v. Sundowner. 29 New Mexico L. Rev. (1999) p. 89. Reprinted with permission from the New Mexico Law Review.*

PROTECTING THE GENDER NONCONFORMIST FROM THE GENDER POLICE—WHY THE HARASSMENT OF GAYS AND OTHER GENDER NONCONFORMISTS IS A FORM OF SEX DISCRIMINATION IN LIGHT OF THE SUPREME COURT'S DECISION IN *ONCALE V. SUNDOWNER*

TONI LESTER[*]

INTRODUCTION—THE SILENCE SURROUNDING HARASSMENT BASED ON HOMOPHOBIA

Traditionally, people who are harassed at work because they are gay[1] have found that they have not been granted the same kind of legal protections that their heterosexual counterparts have received.[2] This is true despite the fact that the sexual harassment of gays is motivated by homophobia, which in turn is motivated in large part by misogyny. Since misogyny in all its many manifestations is one of the things that Title VII's prohibition against sex discrimination is supposed to attack,[3] the failure of the courts to recognize that harassment against gays is a kind of sex discrimination is at best misguided and at worst very dangerous.

---

[*] Affiliated Research Scholar Wellesley Centers for Women; former Visiting Law Scholar, Institute for Research on Women and Gender, Stanford University; Associate Professor of Law, and Johnson Research Chair, Babson College; B.S., J.D., Georgetown University.

[1] I use the term "gay" here broadly to mean those who identify themselves as homosexual men, lesbians, bisexuals, and transsexuals. I recognize that the term is the subject of great debate today, however. I will talk about the debate and explain my use of the term in greater detail in Part I.

[2] *See* Ulane v. Eastern Airlines, Inc., 742 F.2d 1081, 1084–86 (7th Cir. 1984) (stating that Title VII does not protect transsexuals, homosexuals or transvestites); Desantis v. Pacific Tel. & Tel. Co., 608 F.2d 327, 329–30 (9th Cir. 1979) (stating that "Title VII's prohibition of "sex" discrimination . . . should not be judicially extended to include sexual preference"); *see also* Regina L. Stone-Harris, *Same-Sex Harassment—The Next Step in the Evolution of Sexual Harassment Law Under Title VII,* 28 ST. MARY'S L.J. 269, 289 (1996) (stating that in dealing with "hostile or abusive work environment claims" brought by a male victim against a male offender "who believed the victim was homosexual," courts have "rule[d] against the plaintiff," with the author finding it "notable . . . how closely the offensive conduct [in these cases] parallels other conduct which courts have found to be discriminatory").

[3] *See, e.g.,* Price Waterhouse v. Hopkins, 490 U.S. 228, 251 (1989) ("An employer who objects to aggressiveness in women but whose positions require this trait places women in an intolerable and impermissible catch 22: out of a job if they behave aggressively and out of a job if they do not. Title VII lifts women out of this bind."); Meritor v. Vinson, 477 U.S. 57, 67 (1986) ("Sexual harassment which creates a hostile or offensive environment for members of one sex is every bit the arbitrary barrier to sexual equality at the workplace that racial harassment is to racial equality." (citing Henson v. Dundee, 682 F.2d 897, 902 (11th Cir. 1982))); Ellison v. Brady, 924 F.2d 872, 881 (9th Cir. 1991) ("Congress designed Title VII to prevent the perpetuation of stereotypes and a sense of degradation which serve to close or discourage employment opportunities for women." (citing Andrews v. Philadelphia, 895 F.2d 1469, 1483 (3d Cir. 1990))); Barnes v. Costle, 561 F.2d 983, 987 (D.C. Cir. 1977) (noting that "[n]umerous studies have shown that women are placed in the less challenging, the less responsible and the less remunerative positions on the basis of their sex alone," and finding "such blatantly disparate treatment . . . particularly objectionable in view of the fact that Title VII has specifically prohibited sex discrimination since its enactment in 1964."); Torres v. Nat'l Precision Blanking, 943 F. Supp. 952, 954 (N.D. Ill. 1996) (stating that "the principal purpose of including the term 'sex' in the Act was to 'do some good for the minority sex.'" (citing 110 CONG. REC. 2577 (1964).

Some have argued that Title VII's prohibition against sex discrimination was the result of a fluke, in which Congressman Howard Smith of Virginia hoped to stymie the bill's passage by adding the word, "sex" to the bill, never expecting it to be approved. *See* CHARLES & BARBARA WHALEN, THE LONGEST DEBATE—A LEGISLATIVE HISTORY OF THE CIVIL RIGHTS ACT 115-118 (1985).

In addition to bar associations, there are associations for paralegals and legal assistants. Some of these associations publish newsletters that include articles of interest to paralegals and legal assistants.

3. Commercial Publications

There are numerous **commercial journals** and periodicals that focus on specific areas of law, such as the *Journal of Taxation*. Individuals interested in a specific area of law may subscribe to such a publication. The articles are similar to bar journal articles in that they are well researched. They often include book reviews, practitioner guides and tips, and technology updates.

4. Legal Newspapers and Newsletters

A number of **legal newspapers** are available by subscription, such as the *National Law Journal* and the *Legal Times*. The *National Law Journal* and *Legal Times* are published weekly and include articles and features on trends in litigation, developments in the law, information on attorneys and the legal profession, and book reviews. There are many subject-specific newspapers, such as the *Corporate Legal Times*. In many cities, there are local newspapers that publish legal notices, court docket information, and articles of local interest.

In addition to newspapers, there are thousands of **newsletters** published by commercial and public interest groups. These newsletters are usually issued weekly or monthly and focus on current information in specific areas of the law.

Many legal newspapers and newsletters may be accessed online. See the Internet Resources section of this chapter.

B. Research Using Legal Periodicals

1. Use as a Research Tool

Refer to a legal periodical when you are seeking an analysis and critique of a specific legal topic that is more in-depth or narrower in focus than that provided by a legal encyclopedia or a treatise. In many instances, an article in a legal periodical will go into much greater depth than a treatise and provide more case citations, statistical information, and references to other sources. You may also refer to a periodical when seeking information on a recently emerging legal issue that is not yet addressed in treatises.

2. Research Techniques—Legal Periodicals

As is apparent from the previous section, hundreds of periodicals exist, making it impractical to research each publication for articles on a specific topic. The research tools mentioned here are designed to help you locate specific articles.

a. Index to Legal Periodicals

The **Index to Legal Periodicals (ILP)** provides an index to the contents of most legal periodicals in the United States, the United Kingdom, and most Commonwealth countries. (See Exhibit 6-3 for a sample index page.) Hardbound volumes are published annually with monthly soft-cover updates. The volumes and updates are not cumulative. Therefore, if you are looking for an article published in the current year, start with the current soft-cover monthly volume and work your way backward.

For Example	If you are interested in an article published sometime in the past five years, check the hardbound volume for each year and each update.

Exhibit 6-3 *Page from the Index to Legal Periodicals and Books.* The H.W. Wilson Company, Index to Legal Periodicals and Books *(2000), p. 68. Reprinted with permission from The H.W. Wilson Company, a division of EBSCO Publishing.*

INDEX TO LEGAL PERIODICALS & BOOKS

Ashton, Bruce L.—*cont.*
New safe harbors for employers in the Service's qualified plan
correction examples; by C. F. Reish, B. L. Ashton, N. J. White. 91
no6 *J. Tax'n* 349-57 D 1999

Ashton, Roger D.
Consolidation in the financial services sector: tax implications to
stakeholders. 49 *Rep. Proc. Ann. Tax Conf. Convened by Can. Tax
Found.* 21.1-.58 1997

Ashworth, Andrew
Article 6 and the fairness of trials. 1999 *Crim. L. Rev.* 261-72 Ap 1999
Restorative justice and victims' rights. 2000 *N.Z. L.J.* 84-8 Mr 2000

Asia-Pacific Economic Cooperation (Organization)
The role of APEC in the achievement of regional cooperation in
Southeast Asia. L. C. Cardenas, A. Buranakanits. 5 no1 *Ann. Surv.
Int'l & Comp. L.* 49-80 Spr 1999

Asia-Pacific legal development; edited by Douglas M. Johnston and Gerry
Ferguson. University of B.C. Press 1998 611p ISBN 0-7748-0673-7 LC
99-183418

Asiain, Jorge Hugo
Financing of real estate projects in Argentina. 4 no1 *NAFTA Rev.* 96-104
Wint 1998

Asian Americans
All the themes but one. E. L. Muller. 66 no4 *U. Chi. L. Rev.* 1395-33
Fall 1999
Are Asians black?: The Asian-American civil rights agenda and the
contemporary significance of the black/white paradigm. J. Y. Kim,
student author. 108 no8 *Yale L.J.* 2385-412 Je 1999
Asian Americans, the law, and illegal immigration in post-civil rights
America: a review of three books. H. Gee. 77 no1 *U. Det. Mercy L.
Rev.* 71-81 Fall 1999
Beyond black and white: selected writings by Asian Americans within
the critical race theory movement. H. Gee. 30 no3 *St. Mary's L.J.*
759-99 1999
Emerging from the margins of historical consciousness: Chinese
immigrants and the history of American law. R. P. Cole, G. J. Chin.
17 no2 *Law & Hist. Rev.* 325-64 Summ 1999
Justice held hostage: U.S. disregard for international law in the World
War II internment of Japanese Peruvians—a case study. N. T. Saito.
40 no1 *B. C. L. Rev.* 275-348 D 1998
Lexicon dreams and Chinese rock and roll: thoughts on culture,
language, and translation as strategies of resistance and
reconstruction. S. K. Hom. 53 no4 *U. Miami L. Rev.* 1003-17 H 1999
Lochner [Lochner v. New York, 25 S. Ct. 539 (1905)], parity, and the
Chinese laundry cases [Yick Wo v. Hopkins, 6 S. Ct. 1064 (1886)]
D. E. Bernstein. 41 no1 *Wm. & Mary L. Rev.* 211-94 D 1999
McCarthyism, the internment and the contradictions of power. M. J.
Matsuda. 40 no1 *B.C. L. Rev.* 9-36 D 1998
No right to own?: The early twentieth-century "Alien Land Laws" as a
prelude to internment. K. Aoki. 40 no1 *B.C. L. Rev.* 37-72 D 1998
Out of the shadow: marking intersections in and between Asian Pacific
American critical legal scholarship and Latina/o critical legal theory.
E. M. Iglesias. 40 no1 *B. C. L. Rev.* 349-83 D 1998
Praising with faint damnation—the troubling rehabilitation of
Korematsu [Korematsu v. United States, 63 S. Ct. 1124 (1944)] A. C.
Yen. 40 no1 *B.C. L. Rev.* 1-7 D 1998
Race, rights, and the Asian American experience: a review essay.
H. Gee. 13 no4 *Geo. Immigr. L.J.* 635-51 Summ 1999
Racial reparations: Japanese American redress and African American
claims. E. K. Yamamoto. 40 no1 *B.C. L. Rev.* 477-523 D 1998
Reparations and the "model minority" ideology of acquiescence: the
necessity to refuse the return to original humiliation. C. K. Iijima. 40
no1 *B.C. L. Rev.* 385-427 D 1998
The stranger who resides with you: ironies of Asian-American and
American Indian legal history. J. W. Singer. 40 no1 *B.C. L. Rev.*
171-7 D 1998
Symposium: the long shadow of Korematsu [Korematsu v. United
States, 63 S. Ct. 1124 (1944)] 40 no1 *B.C. L. Rev.* 1-535 D 1998
A tale of new precedents: Japanese American internment as foreign
affairs law. G. Gott. 40 no1 *B.C. L. Rev.* 179-274 D 1998
Using DSM-IV to diagnose mental illness in Asian Americans. T. B.
Tran, student author. 10 *J. Contemp. Legal Issues* 335-57 1999

See/See also the following book(s):
Chang, R. S. Disoriented; Asian Americans, law, and the nation-state.
New York University Press 1999 x, 180p

California
The Chinese American challenge to court-mandated quotas in San
Francisco's public schools: notes from a (partisan) participant-
observer. D. I. Levine. 16 *Harv. BlackLetter L.J.* 39-145 Spr 2000
Redeeming whiteness in the shadow of internment: Earl Warren,
Brown, [Brown v. Board of Education, 74 S. Ct. 686 (1954)] and a
theory of racial redemption. S. Cho. 40 no1 *B. C. L. Rev.* 73-170 D
1998

Asian Pacific Economic Cooperation (Organization) *See* Asia-Pacific
Economic Cooperation (Organization)

Asimow, Michael
Bad lawyers in the movies. 24 no2 *Nova L. Rev.* 533-91 Wint 2000
Interim-final rules: making haste slowly. 51 no3 *Admin. L. Rev.* 703-55
Summ 1999
"Justice with an attitude": Judge Judy and the daytime television bunch.
38 no4 *Judges' J.* 24-8+ Fall 1999

Askin, Frank, 1932-
A law school where students don't just learn the law; they help make
the law. 51 no4 *Rutgers L. Rev.* 855-74 1999

Askin, Kelly Dawn
Crimes within the jurisdiction of the International Criminal Court. 10
no1 *Crim. L.F.* 33-59 1999
Issues surrounding the creation of a regional human rights system for
the Asia-Pacific. 4 no2 *ILSA J. Int'l & Comp. L.* 599-601 Spr 1998
Sexual violence in decisions and indictments of the Yugoslav and
Rwandan tribunals: current status. 93 no1 *Am. J. Int'l L.* 92-123 Ja
1999

Åslund, Anders, 1952- ———————————————— *Entry by author*
Law in Russia. 8 no4 *E. Eur. Const. Rev.* 96-101 Fall 1999

Asmus, Daniel G.
Service provider liability: Australian High Court gives the world a
first—should the United States follow suit? 17 no1 *Dick. J. Int'l L.*
189-228 Fall 1998

Asouzu, Amazu A.
The adoption of the UNCITRAL model law in Nigeria: implications on
the recognition and enforcement of arbitral awards. 1999 *J. Bus. L.*
185-204 Mr 1999

Aspen, Marvin E., 1934-
about
It's how you play the game. L. Leshne. 34 no7 *Trial* 28-32 J1 1998

Aspin, Larry
Trends in judicial retention elections, 1964-1998. 83 no2 *Judicature*
79-81 S/O 1999

Asplen, Christopher H.
Integrating DNA technology into the criminal justice system. 83 no3
Judicature 144-9 N/D 1999

*Entry by topic
Assault and Battery*

Assafa Endeshaw *See* Endeshaw, Assafa, 1950-

Assault and battery
See also
Battered women
Child abuse
A jurisprudence in disarray: on battery, wrongful living, and the right to
bodily integrity. M. P. Strasser. 36 no4 *San Diego L. Rev.* 997-1041
Fall 1999
Score and pierce: crimes of fashion? Body alteration and consent to
assault. A. J. Watkins, student author. 28 no2 *Vict. U. Wellington L.
Rev.* 371-98 My 1998

Canada
Fraud, HIV and unprotected sex: R. v. Cuerrier [[1998] 2 S.C.R. 371]
R. K. Yamada, student author. 6 no1 *Sw. J.L. & Trade Am.* 157-76
Spr 1999
Secrets and lives—the public safety exception to solicitor-client
privilege: Smith v. Jones [[1999] 169 D.L.R.4th 385] W. N. Renke.
37 no4 *Alta. L. Rev.* 1045-70 D 1999

Great Britain
Assault, battery and indirect violence. M. Hirst. 1999 *Crim. L. Rev.*
557-60 J1 1999
Consent, threats and deception in criminal law. J. Horder. 10 no1
King's C. L.J. 104-8 1999
Corporal punishment of children: a caning for the United Kingdom.
A. Bainham. 58 pt2 *Cambridge L.J.* 291-3 J1 1999
Theorising the limits of the 'sadomasochistic homosexual' identity in
R v Brown [[1994] 1 A.C. 212] S. Chandra-Shekeran, student author.
21 no2 *Melb. U. L. Rev.* 584-600 D 1997

The index includes the following features:

1. *Subject/author index.* Articles are indexed alphabetically by both subject and author in the subject/author index. If you know the name of the author or you know the subject, such as "assault and battery," you can use this index to locate articles. The index includes the title of the article, the name of the author, and the name and date of the publication (see Exhibit 6-3).

2. *Table of cases.* Cases that have been noted or discussed in articles are indexed alphabetically by the names of both plaintiff and defendant. Following the case name are citations to the articles.

3. *Table of statutes.* If you know the name of a statute, this index will direct you to articles that have discussed the statute.

4. *Book reviews.* The book review index lists by book title the periodicals that have reviewed the title.

b. Current Law Index

The **Current Law Index (CLI)** is a periodical index similar to *ILP*. It provides an index of articles of several hundred periodicals. (See Exhibit 6-4 for a sample index page.) Hardbound volumes are published annually with monthly updates. Like the *ILP*, the volumes and updates are noncumulative. The *CLI* includes articles beginning in 1980; it does not reference articles published prior to 1980. The index includes the following features:

1. *Subject index.* The *CLI* has a separate subject index where articles are indexed alphabetically by subject. If you know the name of the subject, such as "assault and battery," you can use this index to locate articles. The index includes the title of the article, the name of the author, and the name and date of the publication (see Exhibit 6-4).

2. *Author/title index.* There is a separate index where articles are indexed alphabetically by author and title. This index also includes book reviews indexed by author and title.

3. *Table of cases.* Cases that have been noted or discussed in articles are indexed alphabetically by the names of both plaintiff and defendant. Following the names are citations to the articles.

4. *Table of statutes.* If you know the name of a statute, this index will direct you to articles that have discussed the statute.

c. Other Periodical Indexes

In addition to the major indexes discussed previously, there are several other indexes.

> **For Example** *Index to Foreign Legal Periodicals.* This index focuses on journals published outside the United States and the British Commonwealth.
>
> *Current Index to Legal Periodicals.* This index, published weekly, provides access to articles not yet indexed in the *ILP* or the *CLI*.

Check with a law library for specific indexes.

d. Reference from Other Sources

Another source, such as a citation in a court opinion, legal encyclopedia, or treatise, may direct you to a legal periodical article. Often references to law review articles that have analyzed a statute are included in the annotations to the statute. In such instances, you would go directly to the periodical; you would not need to use an index.

Exhibit 6-4 *Sample Subject Page from the* Current Law Index. *The Gale Group,* Current Law Index, *Vol. 21 (2000), p. 51. Reprinted with permission from the Gale Group.*

| SUBJECT INDEX | | ASSETS, FROZEN |

The role of philanthropy in the inter-section between culture and commerce. by Cora Mirikitani
29 Journal of Arts Management, Law and Society 128 Summer, 1999

-Cases

The death of a subsidy and the birth of the entitlement in funding of the arts. (Case Note) Brooklyn Institute of Arts & Sciences v. City of New York by Danielle E. Caminiti
10 Fordham Intellectual Property, Media & Entertainment Law Journal 875-904 Spring, 2000

ARTS, Useful *see*
perspective (electronic commerce) (Interview) by Richard Stavros
238 Public Utilities Fortnightly (1994) 28 April 15, 2000

ASARIOTIS, Regina
Proposed amendments to the U.S. Carriage of Goods by Sea Act: a response to English criticisms (response to article by Regina Asariotis and Michael N. Tsimplis in previous issue of this journal, 1999) by Michael F. Sturley
Hoyds Maritime and Commercial Law Quarterly 519-529 Nov, 1999

United we stand (solicitor Ken Beruldsen diagnosed with mesothelioma from working in a pipe factory and solicitor Jim Taylor handled his case) (Victoria) by Kevin Childs
74 Law Institute Journal 10(2) August, 2000
see also
Asbestos industry
Asbestos removal

-Cases

The Louisiana long-arm statute stretches beyond its reach. (Case Note) Ruckstuhl v. Owens Corning Fiberglas Corp. by Kelly Elizabeth Grieshaber
45 Loyola Law Review 765-781 Winter, 1999
ASBESTOS abatement *see*
removal
Reference to author ——abatement industry *see*
industry
ASBESTOS industry
Asbestos legislation: Could it be the end? by Kristin Loiacono *36 Trial 11 June, 2000*
In the Beltway; Federal Claims Court may quench asbestos fires; DOJ still in hot seat. by Terry Carter
86 ABA Journal 32(1) April, 2000
ASBESTOS mines and mining *see*
Mining industry
ASBESTOS removal
Asbestos fines give warning to construction clients. (United Kingdom) by Lucinda Ponting
Health and Safety Bulletin 8(1) Dec, 1999
see also
Asbestos industry
ASBESTOS removal industry *see*
Asbestos industry
Reference to subject servicing industry *see*
industry
ASEAN *see*
Association of South East Asian Nations
ASH disposal
Trash, ash, and the phoenix: a fifth anniversary review of the Supreme Court's City of Chicago waste-to-energy combustion ash decision. City of Chicago v. Environmental Defense Fund, Inc. by Markus G. Puder
26 Boston College Environmental Affairs Law Review 473-518 Spring, 1999

ASHES, Removal of *see*
Ash disposal
ASHURST Morris Crisp
Merger waves. (law firms) by Sean Farrell
22 American Lawyer 24 August, 2000
ASIA, Southwest *see*
Middle East
ASIA, Western *see*
Middle East
ASIAN Americans
Comparative racialization: racial profiling and the case of Wen Ho Lee. (Race and the Law at the Turn of the Century) by Neil Gotanda
47 UCLA Law Review 1689-1703 August, 2000
The interrelationship between anti-Asian violence and Asian America. (Hate Crimes 2000: A Symposium and Community Forum on Hate in America) by Victor M. Hwang
21 Chicano Latino Law Review 17-37 Spring, 2000
Long struggle for justice; Asian Pacific Americans have played a key role in this country's civil rights struggles. Their fight is not yet over. by Rockwell Chin, William G. Paul, Robert S. Chang, Kristin Choo, Frank H. Wu, Laura Kingsley Hong and Peter M. Suzuki
85 ABA Journal 66(8) Nov, 1999
Finding the me in LatCrit theory: thoughts on language acquisition and loss. (Substantive Self-Determination: Democracy, Communicative Power and Inter/national Labor Rights) (LatCrit III Symposium) by John Hayakawa Torok
53 University of Miami Law Review 1019-1036 July, 1999
Using DSM-IV to diagnose mental illness in Asian Americans. (Diagnostic and Statistical Manual of Mental Disorders) (Rethinking Mental Disability Law: Resolving Old Issues in a New Millennium.) by Tam B. Tran
10 The Journal of Contemporary Legal Issues 335-357 Spring, 1999
ASIAN refugees *see*
Refugees, Asian
ASKA, Gail
Is workfare working? (government programs requiring welfare recipients to work) (New York) (Panel Discussion)
8 Journal of Law and Policy 107-177 Fall, 1999
ASPHALT cement
Paving contractor was not required to use accrual method. by Nicholas J. Fiore
31 The Tax Adviser 748 Oct, 2000
ASPHALTIC cement *see*
Asphalt cement
ASPHYXIA
Fatal suffocation by rubber ballons in children: mechanism and prevention. by H.A. Abdel-Rahman *108 Forensic Science International 97-105 Feb 14, 2000*
see also
Drowning
Strangling
ASSAULT and battery
Costs - defendant's costs order - Prosecution of Offences Act 1985, s. 16 - proceedings discontinued - whether costs order appropriate. (United Kingdom) R. v. South West Surrey Magistrates' Court (ex parte James) by D.C. Ormerod and Tom Rees
Criminal Law Review 690-692 August, 2000

Liability of partnership for a partner's assault. (United Kingdom) Flynn v. Thompson & Partners by J.A. Coutts
64 Journal of Criminal Law 368-370 August, 2000
Recalcitrant HIV-positive persons: the problem of people who are unwilling or unable to prevent the transmission of communicable diseases. (Canada) R. v. Cuerrier by Timothy Christie
20 Health Law in Canada 53-57 May, 2000
Offences against the Person Act 1861, s. 20 - inflicting grievous bodily harm - whether reasonable man foreseeing injury must be taken to have the same age and sex as defendant. (United Kingdom) R. v. Marjoram by Clare Barsby and J.C. Smith
Criminal Law Review 372-374 May, 2000
Racially aggravated assault occasioning actual bodily harm - approach to sentence. (United Kingdom) R. v. Saunders by D.A. Thomas
Criminal Law Review 314-315 April, 2000
Racist assaults - sentencing guidelines. (United Kingdom) R. v. Saunders by Philip Plowden
64 Journal of Criminal Law 158-160 April, 2000
Enforcement of the assault and battery exclusion in Louisiana: Hickey v. Centenary Oyster House. Hickey v. Centenary Oyster House by David A. Szwak
60 Louisiana Law Review 793-807 Spring, 2000
Treating spousal violence 'differently'. (Special Issue on Domestic Violence) by Kathy Laster and Roger Douglas
7 International Review of Victimology 115-139 Spring-Fall, 2000
Paved with good intentions: mandatory arrest and decreasing the threshold for assault. (Women, Children and Domestic Violence: Current Tensions and Emerging Issues) (Panel Discussion)
27 Fordham Urban Law Journal 629-671 Feb, 2000
Crown Court's power to make a restriction order. (United Kingdom) R. v. Avbunudje
64 Journal of Criminal Law 30-32 Feb, 2000
Joint enterprise - withdrawal. (United Kingdom) R. v. Mitchell
63 Journal of Criminal Law 538-539 Dec, 1999
Finding clarity in a Gray option: a critique of Pennsylvania's informed consent doctrine. Gray v. Grunnagle by Nathan A. Kottkamp
61 University of Pittsburgh Law Review 241-285 Fall, 1999
A jurisprudence in disarray: on battery, wrongful living, and the right to bodily integrity. by Mark Strasser
36 San Diego Law Review 997-1041 Fall, 1999
see also
Affray
Indecent assault
Poisoning
ASSAULT, Criminal *see*
Rape
ASSAULT, Sexual *see*
Rape
ASSAULT weapons

3. Computer-Aided Research

The *Index to Legal Periodicals* and *Current Law Index* are available in CD-ROM form. The *ILP* and *CLI* are available on Westlaw and LexisNexis. Both are the most comprehensive indexes and their online versions include all updates. The *ILP* is also available online; this version is called *Index to Legal Periodicals Full Text* and is updated monthly. The *CLI* online, as well as on CD-ROM, is called *LegalTrac* and is available on the Internet by subscription. *LegalTrac* includes sources in addition to those listed in the *CLI*.

Many law reviews, periodicals, and legal newspapers are available on both Westlaw and LexisNexis. Some law reviews are available through law school Web sites, and some periodical articles are available through the publisher's Web site. See Chapter 7 for further discussion of computers and legal research.

III. RESTATEMENTS OF THE LAW

The American Law Institute (ALI) was founded in 1923 to address two major defects in American law: uncertainty and complexity. Uncertainty existed because of a lack of agreement among members of the profession on fundamental principles of the common law. Also, there was a lack of precision in the use of legal terms, and statutes were often poorly drafted. Complexity arose because of numerous differences in the law in the various jurisdictions in the United States.

The primary goal of the ALI is to promote clarification and simplification of the law. The founders decided that this goal could be accomplished through a restatement of the law defining what the law is for basic legal subjects. To accomplish this task, the ALI recruited nationally known scholars to draft the Restatements. From 1923 to 1944, **Restatements of the Law** were published for agency, conflict of laws, contracts, judgments, property restitution, security, torts, and trusts. In 1952, the original Restatements were republished with updates, expanded comments, and analysis. New Restatements were published in such areas as landlord–tenant and foreign relations law. This second set of publications is called *Restatement Second*. In 1987, the ALI began *Restatement Third*. It includes revisions and updates of the *Restatements* and new subjects, such as unfair competition, and suretyship and guarantee.

Restatements are the product of highly competent scholars in each area of the law and are a highly respected and valuable research tool. Due to the authoritativeness of the *Restatements,* they are frequently cited by the courts and often accorded a recognition greater than that accorded to treatises.

> **For Example** Most of the law of torts is not statutory law; that is, it is established in court opinions. Assume a state court has not defined a term such as *superseding cause* in negligence law. An appellate court of the state, when faced with a case that requires the term to be defined, may refer to the *Restatement of the Law of Torts* § 440 and adopt its definition of the term.

Note that the *Restatements of the Law* are secondary authority and used to support primary authority or when there is no primary authority.

Restatement sections currently exist for the following areas of the law:

Agency	Restitution and unjust enrichment
Conflicts of law	Security
Contracts	Suretyship and guaranty
Foreign relations law of the United States	Torts

Judgments   Trusts

Law governing lawyers   Unfair competition

Property

A. Restatement Features

The *Restatements of the Law* have the following features:

■ **Organization.** Each *Restatement* is divided into chapters that cover major areas. The chapters are then divided into broader topics, and the topics are divided into individual sections that present a general principle of law.

> **For Example** One chapter of the *Restatement of the Law of Torts, Products Liability* is titled, "Liability of Commercial Product Sellers Based on Product Defects at Time of Sale." This chapter is divided into topics. Topic 1 is "Liability Rules Applicable to Products Generally." This topic is divided into four sections. Section 1 presents the general principle of law governing the "Liability of Commercial Seller or Distributor for Harm Caused by Defective Products."

At the beginning of each volume and each chapter is a table of contents listing the topic and sections covered in the chapter (see Exhibit 6-5).

■ **Restatement of the Law.** Each *Restatement* section begins with a statement of the principle of law or a rule of law, summarizing and defining the American law on the topic (see Exhibit 6-5).

■ **Comments and Illustrations.** Following the rule of law is a comment section that includes an analytical discussion of the rule and may present hypothetical illustrations of application of the rule (see Exhibit 6-5). The authority who drafted the *Restatement* prepares the comments and reporters' notes (see "Reporters' Note" next). As the work product of a well-known authority, they add value to the *Restatement.*

■ **Reporters' Note.** Following the comments are reporters' notes that include general information concerning the *Restatement* and citations to cases, treatises, articles, and other secondary sources in support of and opposition to the *Restatement* (see Exhibit 6-6).

■ **Cross-references.** Cross-references to the West's digest key numbers and *ALR* annotations accompany each *Restatement.*

■ **Appendix volumes.** Beginning with the *Restatement Second,* there are noncumulative appendix volumes that categorize and summarize decisions of courts from different jurisdictions that have cited *Restatements.*

■ **Updates.** Each *Restatement* is updated with pocket parts for each hardbound volume and supplements that are placed beside the appropriate hardbound volume. The title page of the pocket part or supplement provides the dates of the cases reported and instructions for locating earlier citations (see Exhibit 6-7). Semiannually, interim case citations pamphlets are published that are used in conjunction with the pocket parts and supplements.

■ **Index.** A comprehensive index accompanies each *Restatement* that references sections, comments, and reporters' notes.

Exhibit 6-5 Restatement (Third) of Torts, *Products Liability § 1. American Law Institute*, Restatement (Third) of Torts, *3d ed., Vol. 1 (1998), p. 5. © 1998 by the American Law Institute. All rights reserved. Reprinted with permission.*

CHAPTER 1

LIABILITY OF COMMERCIAL PRODUCT SELLERS BASED ON PRODUCT DEFECTS AT TIME OF SALE

TOPIC 1. LIABILITY RULES APPLICABLE TO PRODUCTS GENERALLY

Contents

Section
1. Liability of Commercial Seller or Distributor for Harm Caused by Defective Products
2. Categories of Product Defect
3. Circumstantial Evidence Supporting Inference of Product Defect
4. Noncompliance and Compliance with Product Safety Statutes or Regulations

TOPIC 2. LIABILITY RULES APPLICABLE TO SPECIAL PRODUCTS OR PRODUCT MARKETS

5. Liability of Commercial Seller or Distributor of Product Components for Harm Caused by Products Into Which Components Are Integrated
6. Liability of Commercial Seller or Distributor for Harm Caused by Defective Prescription Drugs and Medical Devices
7. Liability of Commercial Seller or Distributor for Harm Caused by Defective Food Products
8. Liability of Commercial Seller or Distributor of Defective Used Products

---

TOPIC 1. LIABILITY RULES APPLICABLE TO PRODUCTS GENERALLY

§ 1. Liability of Commercial Seller or Distributor for Harm Caused by Defective Products

Rule

One engaged in the business of selling or otherwise distributing products who sells or distributes a defective product is subject to liability for harm to persons or property caused by the defect.

Comment

Comment:

a. History. This Section states a general rule of tort liability applicable to commercial sellers and other distributors of products generally. Rules of liability applicable to special products

201

Exhibit 6-6 Restatement (Third) of Torts, *Products Liability Notes*. American Law Institute, Restatement (Third) of Torts, *3d ed., Vol. 1 (1998), p. 9.* © 1998 by the American Law Institute. All rights reserved. Reprinted with permission.

Ch. 1   LIABILITY BASED ON TIME-OF-SALE DEFECTS   § 1

nonmanufacturing sellers or distributors do not themselves render the products defective and regardless of whether they are in a position to prevent defects from occurring. See § 2, Comment *o*. Legislation has been enacted in many jurisdictions that, to some extent, immunizes nonmanufacturing sellers or distributors from strict liability. The legislation is premised on the belief that bringing nonmanufacturing sellers or distributors into products liability litigation generates wasteful legal costs. Although liability in most cases is ultimately passed on to the manufacturer who is responsible for creating the product defect, nonmanufacturing sellers or distributors must devote resources to protect their interests. In most situations, therefore, immunizing nonmanufacturers from strict liability saves those resources without jeopardizing the plaintiffs interests. To assure plaintiffs access to a responsible and solvent product seller or distributor, the statutes generally provide that the nonmanufacturing seller or distributor is immunized from strict liability only if: (1) the manufacturer is subject to the jurisdiction of the court of plaintiff's domicile; and (2) the manufacturer is not, nor is likely to become, insolvent.

In connection with these statutes, two problems may need to be resolved to assure fairness to plaintiffs. First, as currently structured, the statutes typically impose upon the plaintiff the risk of insolvency of the manufacturer between the time an action is brought and the time a judgment can be enforced. If a nonmanufacturing seller or distributor is dismissed from an action at the outset when it appears that the manufacturer will be able to pay a judgment, and the manufacturer subsequently becomes insolvent and is unable to pay the judgment, the plaintiff may be left to suffer the loss uncompensated. One possible solution could be to toll the statute of limitations against nonmanufacturers so that they may be brought in if necessary. Second, a nonmanufacturing seller or distributor occasionally will be responsible for the introduction of a defect in a product even though it exercised reasonable care in handling or supervising the product in its control. In such instances, liability for a § 2(a) defect should be imposed on the nonmanufacturing seller or distributor. See § 2, Illustration 2.

REPORTERS' NOTE

Comment a. History.

1. Abundant authority recognizes the division of product defects into manufacturing defects, design defects, and defects based on inadequate instructions or warnings. See, e.g., Caterpillar Tractor Co. v. Beck, 593 P.2d 871, 881–82 (Alaska 1979) (Accord, Shanks v. Upjohn Co., 835 P.2d 1189, 1194 (Alaska 1992)); Dart v. Wiebe Mfg., Inc., 709 P.2d 876, 878–79 (Ariz.1985) (en banc); Barker v. Lull Eng'g Co., 573 P.2d 443, 454 (Cal.1978) (recognizing that different

Exhibit 6-7 Restatement (Third) of Torts, *Pocket Part Cover Page*. *American Law Institute*, Restatement (Third) of Torts, *3d ed., Cumulative Annual Pocket Part for Use in 2000 (2000), p. 26. © 2000 by the American Law Institute. All rights reserved. Reprinted with permission.*

Insert this Pocket Part in the back of the Restatement
of the Law Third, Torts: Products Liability (1998)

CASE CITATIONS TO THE
RESTATEMENT OF THE LAW

Cumulative Annual Pocket Part
For Use In 2000

Dates of the cases reported ———————————— Reporting Cases From July 1984
Through June 1999 That Cite

Restatement of the Law Second,
Torts 2d, §§ 402A and 402B
and
Restatement of the Law Third,
Torts: Products Liability §§ 1 to End

Instructions for locating
earlier and subsequent —— This Pocket Part contains all citations to the Restatement of the Law Third,
citations Torts: Products Liability, as well as citations, for the period from July 1984
through June 1999, to §§ 402A–402B of the Restatement Second of Torts. For
earlier citations to §§ 402A–402B, see the Volume titled "Torts 2d Appendix
§§ 402A to 402B Reporting All Cases through June 1984." For subsequent
citations see also the *Interim Case Citations to the Restatements of the Law*
pamphlets designated for use with the 2000 Pocket Parts and Supplements.

Editor: Marianne McGettigan Walker
The American Law Institute
4025 Chestnut Street
Philadelphia, PA 19104

ST. PAUL, MN
AMERICAN LAW INSTITUTE PUBLISHERS
2000

B. Research Using *Restatements of the Law*

1. Use as a Research Tool

Restatements of the Law have several uses as a research tool. You may refer to a *Restatement* when a specific legal term, principle, or rule has not been defined in your jurisdiction. In such situations, a court may refer to and adopt the *Restatement* as the law in the jurisdiction. The *Restatement* provides guidance as to how the law should be defined or stated; reasons in support of the definition or statement of the law; and citations to cases, treatises, and other secondary authority.

When a *Restatement* has been adopted, the comments and reporters' notes are invaluable aids in locating cases from other jurisdictions and other secondary sources interpreting the *Restatement*. A *Restatement* may also be used to locate authority to challenge an existing law.

> **For Example** The client's case requires the challenge of a rule or statement of the law adopted by a state that differs from the one recommended by the *Restatement*. The *Restatement* may provide reasons and persuasive authority that can be used to challenge the existing rule or statement of the law.

2. Research Techniques—*Restatements*

The following research techniques help you locate specific *Restatement* topics.

a. Index

You may locate *Restatement* topics by consulting the alphabetical index usually located at the end of each *Restatement*.

> **For Example** If you are interested in the definition of *superseding cause* in a negligence case, you would refer to the index to the *Restatement of the Law of Torts, Second*.

b. Table of Contents

If you are familiar with the area and topic, you can scan the table of contents of the *Restatement* volume for the specific section.

> **For Example** You are researching strict liability in a torts case involving manufacturing defects. Look in the table of contents to the *Restatement of the Law of Torts, Products Liability* volume.

c. Table of Cases

More recent *Restatements* have a "Table of Cases" in the index volume for the *Restatement*. If you look up a case name cited in the *Restatement,* this table will lead you to the relevant section.

d. Appendix Volumes

Refer to the noncumulative appendix volumes for summaries of court opinions addressing the *Restatement* section you are researching.

e. Reference from Other Sources

Often you may be directed to a specific *Restatement* section from another source, such as a citation in a case, article, and *Shepard's Restatement of the Law Citations.* You could go directly to the volume and section cited rather than consult the index.

Always check the pocket part and supplement to update your research and to locate the most recent cases. In addition, *always* consult the appendix volume to ensure that you have located all the case summaries. Note that the appendix volumes are noncumulative, so each must be checked.

3. Computer-Aided Research

The *Restatements of the Law* are available on CD-ROM, as well as Westlaw and LexisNexis.

IV. UNIFORM LAWS AND MODEL ACTS

The National Conference of Commissioners on Uniform State Laws (NCCUSL) was formed to draft and promote uniform laws. The members include judges, attorneys, law professors, and legal scholars. The goal of the NCCUSL is to make available for adoption by states **uniform laws** and **model acts** in areas of the law where uniformity would be beneficial to the states.

> **For Example** For commerce to take place smoothly and efficiently between states, it is beneficial if the laws governing commerce, such as the sale of goods, are uniform among the states. To this end, the National Conference of Commissioners on Uniform State Laws and the American Law Institute drafted the Uniform Commercial Code. Every state has adopted the code in whole or in part.

Model acts are drafted for those situations in which a state does not intend to adopt an entire law, but rather intends to modify a uniform law to meet the state's requirements. The American Law Institute has drafted several model codes. These include the Model Penal Code, the Model Code of Evidence, the Model Land Development Code, and the Model Business Corporations Act.

The uniform laws and model acts are secondary authority. They become primary authority only when they are adopted by a state's legislature. When adopted, they will be assigned statutory numbers that fit within the state's statutory numbering scheme.

> **For Example** The first two sections of Article 2, Sales, of the Uniform Commercial Code are numbered and titled Section 2-101, Short Title, and Section 2-102, Scope. When the state of Colorado adopted these sections, the numbers were amended to fit within the state's statutory numbering system—Section 2-101 is Section 4-2-101, Short Title; Section 2-102 is Section 4-2-102, Scope.

A. Features of Uniform Laws and Model Acts

The Uniform Laws Annotated (U.L.A.) have the following features:

- **Organization.** Each law or act is divided into topics and subtopics by articles and sections.
- **Uniform law.** Each section presents a statement of the uniform law (see Exhibit 6-8).
- **Commissioners' notes.** The law may be followed by the commissioners' comments on the law, which include, among other things, the purpose of the law, a discussion of the variations adopted by the states, references to law review articles, and a list of the states that have adopted the law.
- **Library references.** Following the law are library references or guides to other research sources, such as digest key numbers and encyclopedia cites (see Exhibit 6-8).
- **Notes to decisions.** Each law includes a summary of court decisions interpreting the law from all adopting states (see Exhibit 6-9).

■ **Tables.** Each volume has tables listing states that have adopted the law.

■ **Index.** Each uniform law has an index in the back of the volume.

■ **Updates.** Pocket parts update each volume (see Exhibit 6-9).

B. Research Using Uniform and Model Laws

1. Use as a Research Tool

If a researcher is proposing or drafting legislation, uniform laws and model acts are invaluable guides. Not only do they provide a model text from which a law may be crafted, but they also provide access to arguments in support of the law and citations to cases, treatises, and articles interpreting the law.

Exhibit 6-8 *Sample U.L.A. Assault Page. West Group,* Uniform Laws Annotated, *Model Penal Code, Vol. 10, 1975, p. 538. © 1975 by the American Law Institute. All rights reserved. Reprinted with permission.*

§ 211.0   **MODEL PENAL CODE**

ARTICLE 211

ASSAULT; RECKLESS ENDANGERING; THREATS

§ 211.0. Definitions

In this Article, the definitions given in Section 210.0 apply unless a different meaning plainly is required.

§ 211.1. Assault

Text ———— **(1) Simple Assault.** A person is guilty of assault if he:

(a) attempts to cause or purposely, knowingly or recklessly causes bodily injury to another; or

(b) negligently causes bodily injury to another with a deadly weapon; or

(c) attempts by physical menace to put another in fear of imminent serious bodily injury.

Simple assault is a misdemeanor unless committed in a fight or scuffle entered into by mutual consent, in which case it is a petty misdemeanor.

(2) Aggravated Assault. A person is guilty of aggravated assault if he:

(a) attempts to cause serious bodily injury to another, or causes such injury purposely, knowingly or recklessly under circumstances manifesting extreme indifference to the value of human life; or

(b) attempts to cause or purposely or knowingly causes bodily injury to another with a deadly weapon.

Aggravated assault under paragraph (a) is a felony of the second degree; aggravated assault under paragraph (b) is a felony of the third degree.

Library references ———————— **Library References**

Assault and Battery ☞48 to 58.   C.J.S. Assault and Battery §§ 51, 57 et seq., 69, 73 et seq.

§ 211.2. Recklessly Endangering Another Person

A person commits a misdemeanor if he recklessly engages in conduct which places or may place another person in danger of death or serious bodily injury. Recklessness and danger shall be presumed where a person knowingly points

Exhibit 6-9 U.L.A. Cumulative Annual Pocket Part Page. *West Group,* Uniform Laws Annotated, *Model Penal Code, Vol. 10 (1975), Cumulative Annual Pocket Part (2001) p. 191–192. Reprinted with permission from West Group.*

PENAL CODE   § 211.1

Caldwell, Pa.1987, 532 A.2d 813, 516 Pa. 441, reargument denied 550 A.2d 785, 520 Pa. 69.

In all cases charged under the Code's murder provisions, in order for the death penalty to be imposed, State must prove beyond a reasonable doubt that aggravating factors outweighed the mitigating factors. State v. Biegenwald, N.J.1987, 524 A.2d 130, 106 N.J. 13.

To support aggravating factor under N.J.S.A. 2C:11–3, subd. e(4)(f), for murder committed for purpose of escaping detection, apprehension, trial, punishment or confinement for another offense committed by defendant or another, there must be evidence from which jury could infer that at least one reason for killing was to prevent victim from informing police and testifying against defendants. State v. Moore, N.J.Super.L.1985, 504 A.2d 804, 207 N.J.Super. 561.

14. Indictment

Defendant may not be subject to possible imposition of death penalty unless indictment contains allegation that homicidal act was committed by defendant's own conduct or that defendant procured commission of offense by payment or promise of payment of anything of pecuniary value. State v. Moore, N.J.Super.L.1985, 504 A.2d 804, 207 N.J.Super. 561.

15. Prosecution witness

Defendant's admission that he killed victims because of his concern that they could later identify defendant or his accomplices was not sufficient to establish, as aggravating circumstance, for purposes of determining whether death sentence could be imposed, that one victim was prosecution witness killed to prevent his testimony against defendant. Com. v. Caldwell, Pa.1987, 532 A.2d 813, 516 Pa. 441, reargument denied 550 A.2d 785, 520 Pa. 69.

16. Nature and extent of punishment

Sentence of death imposed on defendant for murder of his mother was neither excessive nor disproportionate to penalty

Case summaries interpreting law →

d in similar cases. Com. v. Jermyn, Pa.1987, 533 A.2d 74. 460, denial of post-conviction relief affirmed 620 A.2d 533 Pa. 194, reargument denied, certiorari denied 114 S.Ct. 703, 510 U.S. 1049, 126 L.Ed.2d 669, denial of post-conviction relief affirmed 652 A.2d 821, 539 Pa. 371, certiorari denied 115 S.Ct. 2285, 132 L.Ed.2d 287.

17. Vacated sentence

Death sentence was properly vacated and sentence of life imprisonment imposed upon defendant convicted of murder, based on improper submission to jury, as aggravating circumstance, of aggravated assault conviction subsequently overturned by virtue of grant of defendant's motion to withdraw his guilty plea to aggravated assault charge, which was pending at time of sentencing, notwithstanding defendant's subsequent conviction for aggravated assault, where although jury was properly presented with other aggravating circumstance, that defendant was serving life sentence for murder at time of commission of second

murder, there was no way of determining whether jury would have found one proper aggravating circumstance outweighed any mitigating circumstances, without additional aggravated assault conviction. Com. v. Karabin, Pa.Super.1987, 524 A.2d 516, 362 Pa. Super. 300, appeal granted 531 A.2d 1119, 516 Pa. 617, affirmed 559 A.2d 19, 521 Pa. 543.

Sentence of death could not be allowed to stand where half of jury heard that defendant was wanted on other murder charges prior to verdict on defendant's penalty. Com. v. Williams, Pa.1987, 522 A.2d 1058, 514 Pa. 62.

17a. Resentencing

Admission of murder conviction that was entered after capital murder conviction, but before resentencing phase, and that was to be considered as aggravating factor at resentencing phase did not violate double jeopardy clauses of State and Federal Constitutions. State v. Biegenwald, N.J.1988, 542 A.2d 442, 110 N.J. 521.

18. Intent

Mere fact that murder is preceded by warning to victim would not fulfill requirement that murderer intends to, or has explicit purpose to, inflict severe psychological or physical pain prior to death for purpose of provision in death penalty statute listing as aggravating circumstance fact that murder was outrageously or wantonly vile, horrible, or inhuman and that it involved depravity of mind. State v. Ramseur, N.J.1987, 524 A.2d 188, 106 N.J. 123, denial of habeas corpus affirmed 983 F.2d 1215, certiorari denied 113 S.Ct. 2433, 508 U.S. 947, 124 L.Ed.2d 653.

19. Depravity of mind

Facts that murderer committed murder because he liked it or it made him feel better, that he killed bystanders without reason, that he killed children or others whose helplessness would indicate that there was no reason to murder, or that murderer intentionally mutilated body he believed was no longer a live human being, evidence "depravity of mind" for purposes of provision in death penalty statute listing as aggravating circumstance fact that murder was outrageously or wantonly vile, horrible, or inhuman in that it involved depravity of mind. State v. Ramseur, N.J.1987, 524 A.2d 188, 106 N.J. 123, denial of habeas corpus affirmed 983 F.2d 1215, certiorari denied 113 S.Ct. 2433, 508 U.S. 947, 124 L.Ed.2d 653.

20. State of mind

In determining whether murder was outrageously or wantonly vile, horrible, or inhuman in that it involved torture or aggravated battery to victim for purposes of aggravating circumstance in death penalty statute, court must look at defendant's state of mind, and not mere fact that victim actually suffered as result of attack, and extreme physical or mental suffering must be precisely what defendant wanted to occur in addition to death. State v. Ramseur, N.J.1987, 524 A.2d 188, 106 N.J. 123, denial of habeas corpus affirmed 983 F.2d 1215, certiorari denied 113 S.Ct. 2433, 508 U.S. 947, 124 L.Ed.2d 653.

ARTICLE 211
ASSAULT; RECKLESS ENDANGERING; THREATS

Note to decisions topics →

§ 211.1. Assault.

Notes of Decisions

Generally 1
Adequacy of counsel 9a
Admissibility of evidence
   Generally 16

Excited utterances 18a
Motive and intent 18b
Photographs 18

When a jurisdiction has adopted a uniform law, the commissioners' comments and notes to decisions are invaluable aids in locating cases from other jurisdictions and other secondary sources interpreting the law. This is especially helpful when the state courts have not interpreted the law. The commissioners' comments and notes to decisions may also be helpful in locating persuasive authority to challenge an existing law.

> **For Example** The client's case requires challenging the applicable state statute, which differs from the uniform law. The annotations to the uniform law may provide reasons and persuasive authority that can be used to challenge the existing statute.

2. Research Techniques—Uniform Laws

The following research techniques will help you locate specific uniform laws and model acts.

a. Uniform Laws Annotated, Master Edition

The **Uniform Laws Annotated, Master Edition (ULA),** published by Thomson West, includes the uniform laws and annotations to all uniform laws that have been adopted by one or more states. Exhibit 6-8 and Exhibit 6-9 are from the *ULA*. The annotations include the features listed in subsection A and are invaluable research tools. The set includes uniform laws and model acts. A pamphlet, entitled "Directory of Uniform Acts and Codes: Tables and Codes," is published with the set. The "Directory" lists the uniform laws and model laws by name, subject, and adopting jurisdiction.

b. Reference from Other Sources

Often you may be directed to a specific uniform law section from another source, such as a citation in a case, article, or the *ALR Index to Annotations*.

3. Computer-Aided Research

Uniform laws and model acts are available on Westlaw and LexisNexis.

V. DICTIONARIES AND WORDS AND PHRASES

A. Legal Dictionaries

Words often have a more complex or different meaning when used in a legal context than in everyday use.

> **For Example** Most people think the word *publication* means "to make something known to the public in general," such as through publication in a newspaper. When used in conjunction with the law of defamation, the term means "communicating information to one or more persons." In this context, telling defamatory information about an individual to one other person is "publication."

Legal dictionaries provide the spelling, pronunciation, and legal meaning assigned to terms used in the law. Legal or "law" dictionaries are similar to other dictionaries in that the terms are arranged alphabetically. They differ from other dictionaries in that they cite the source of the definition, such as a treatise or court opinion.

For Example Following the definition of a term such as *salesman* will be a citation to the court opinion or a secondary authority source where the term is defined.

Legal dictionaries, therefore, are valuable not only for their definitions, but also for the citations that are a research source for both primary and secondary authority.

The two best-known law dictionaries are *Black's Law Dictionary* published by Thomson West and *Oren's Dictionary of the Law* published by Thomson Delmar Publishing. The dictionaries are similar. Both dictionaries arrange the terms alphabetically, provide citations to the definitions, and consist of a single volume. *Black's* is available on Westlaw.

B. Words and Phrases

Words and Phrases is a multivolume set, published by Thomson West, that provides the judicial definition of words and phrases. It includes only terms that have been defined in federal and state court opinions. If a term has not been defined in an opinion, it will not appear in *Words and Phrases*. It provides every court definition of a term and a brief summary of the opinion. A term will usually have multiple definitions, sometimes covering several pages. The set is kept up to date with annual pocket parts for each volume. It is available on Westlaw, usually as a separate database. However, court definitions of specific terms are available on both Westlaw and LexisNexis.

Words and Phrases is a valuable case finder, especially in situations when you are looking for a unique definition of a term or phrase (see Exhibit 6-10).

Exhibit 6-10 *Screen Shot of Results from Words and Phrases Search for Cases Providing the Definition of "Actual Physical Control." Reprinted with permission of Thomson Reuters.*

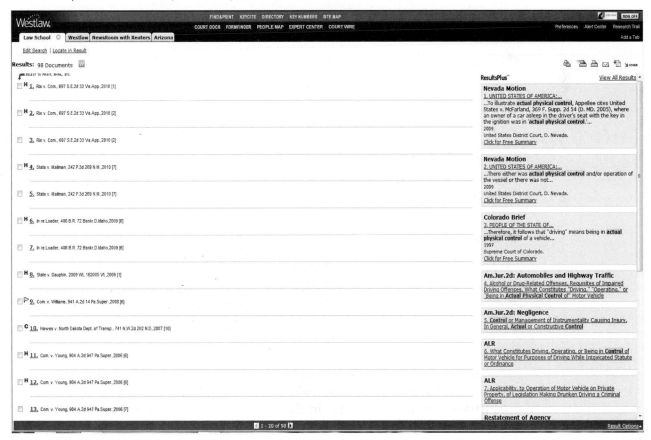

> **For Example** You are looking for how state courts have defined the phrase "actual physical control" as used in driving while intoxicated or driving under the influence statutes. *Black's* does not define the phrase, but a search in Westlaw using *Words and Phrases* yields results of cases with a definition of the phrase (see Exhibit 6-10).

VI. LEGISLATIVE HISTORY

Legislative history is the record of the legislation during the enactment process before it became law. It is composed of committee reports, transcripts of hearings, statements of legislators concerning the legislation, and any other material published for legislative use in regard to the legislation. It is a secondary authority source sometimes relied on by the courts when interpreting laws.

There are several different sources of legislative history for federal statutes. The research sources for locating the legislative history for state statutes may be similar to some or all of the federal legislative history sources. Therefore, the research sources for locating federal legislative history are discussed here. The state sources vary from state to state and may be limited or nonexistent, depending on the state. Consult the appropriate state legislative records or service office for the availability of legislative history.

It is important to note that legislative history is considered only if the plain meaning of a statute is not clear or sections of a statute are internally inconsistent. If the meaning is clear, that meaning will be applied by the court even if the legislative history indicates the legislature intended a different meaning.

A. Federal Legislative History Sources

The following are the main sources of legislative history. Usually, information from more than one of these sources is necessary to determine legislative intent.

1. Congressional Bills

Each bill goes through several versions before it is passed. An examination of the terms or provisions deleted or added in the various versions of the bill may reveal the legislative intent.

> **For Example** An early version of the Housing Discrimination Act may have used the term *citizen* rather than *person*. The substitution of the more expansive term *person* in a later version may support an argument that the legislature intended that the act have an expansive application rather than a limited one.

Information gained through this source concerning legislative intent is based on the *researcher's interpretation* of what the legislature intended when it adopted different versions of a bill. Therefore, other legislative history sources are necessary to obtain additional support for a particular interpretation of legislative intent.

2. Committee Hearings

Congressional committees hold hearings to receive public input and expert testimony concerning proposed legislation. The records of the hearing are composed of transcripts of the legislators' questions and witness testimony along with exhibits and documents submitted. Some of the information may help explain how the legislation applies or the reason certain terms or phrases were used. The hearing records, however, include all arguments and information submitted by individuals and groups both in support of and opposition to some or all of the legislation. It is difficult to determine on which testimony and information the committee relied. Therefore, the information from this source is usually used in support of other legislative history sources.

3. Committee Reports

A committee report on a bill usually includes the text of the bill, the majority's reasons for recommending the bill, an analysis of the contents of the bill, and the minority's reasons for opposing the bill. Because the report clearly states the legislators' intent and is prepared by those who worked with the bill, the report is usually considered the most authoritative source of legislative history by the courts.

4. Congressional Debates

Congress may hold debates on a bill, and the records of the debates are published in the *Congressional Record*. During the debates, members of Congress present arguments for and against a bill and amendments to a bill. The debates often include explanations of provisions of the bill, its purpose, or how it applies. Many different, and often contradictory, reasons may be presented in support of a bill. For this reason, it may be difficult to determine legislative intent from the debates.

B. Researching Federal Legislative History

1. Use of Legislative History

On some occasions, a law that governs a client's fact situation may be written in such a manner that its meaning is unclear. The lack of clarity may be due to the use of an ambiguous term or phrase, or the law may be written so broadly that it is unclear how it is supposed to apply in a specific fact situation. The courts may resolve the matter by looking to the legislative history of the law to determine the legislature's intended meaning of a term or phrase or intention as to when or how the law applies. Legislative history may be of assistance in several ways. The history may identify why an ambiguous term was used and what meaning the legislature intended, what the legislature intended the statute to accomplish, what the general purpose of the legislation is, and so on.

> **For Example** Section A(9) of the Housing Discrimination Act provides that no person shall deny an individual housing on the basis of gender preference. The court is called upon to interpret the term *person*. Does it include corporations and businesses such as partnerships? In the case before the court, a closely held corporation that owned an apartment complex refused to rent an apartment to a couple because of the couple's gender preference. The corporation argued that a corporation is not a person within the meaning of the statute. Included in the legislative history of the statute is a committee report recommending passage of the legislation. The report contains the following language: "the intent of the legislation is to eliminate any and all forms of gender discrimination in housing. The term 'person' is intended to include all individuals and business entities, including corporations." The legislative history in this example provides the court guidance in interpreting the statute.

2. Sources for Locating and Compiling Federal Legislative History

There are several avenues to pursue when you compile the legislative history of a federal statute. The starting point of your research is to locate the statute in the *USC, USCA,* or the *USCS* and review the history of the statute in the annotations. This will provide you with several pieces of information necessary to locate the legislative history: the public law number, the date the law was enacted, the Statutes at Large number, and where the law is published in the ***United States Code Congressional and Administrative News (USCCAN).*** The legislative history may include the Senate report number, the House conference report number, and the popular name.

> **For Example** Following the text of 42 U.S.C.A. § 2000aa is the following information: Pub. L. 96-440, Title I § 101, Oct 13, 1980, 94 Stat. 1879, Senate Report No. 96-874, House Conference Report No. 96-1411, 1980 *United States Code Congressional and Administrative News Service*, page 3950.

The public law number is most important because most of the following sources index laws by the public law number. If you do not know the public law number, some of the sources listed in the following subsections include subject indexes. The following are the main sources for locating and compiling legislative history.

a. *Compiled Legislative Histories*

A starting point for researching legislative history is to determine if the legislative history has already been compiled. For many laws, the government agency charged with regulating the legislation, a commercial publisher, or other groups have already compiled the legislative history. If there is a compiled legislative history, then your research may be done and there is no need to look further. Several publications list compiled legislative histories; check the catalogue listings at a law library. Some of the sources for locating compiled legislative histories include:

■ *Public Laws Legislative Histories on Microfiche,* published by Commerce Clearing House (CCH)

■ *Sources of Compiled Legislative Histories,* sponsored by the American Association of Law Libraries and published by Fred B. Rothman Publications (see Exhibit 6-11)

■ Federal agencies responsible for administering the legislation

b. *Congressional Information Service*

The **Congressional Information Service (CIS)** is a commercial publication that is considered one of the most comprehensive publications of legislative history documents. Pamphlets, which are published monthly, are assembled into annual bound volumes. The *CIS* includes summaries of the law; committee reports, documents, and hearing testimony; and references to debates published in the *Congressional Record*. The *CIS* makes the documents summarized available on microfiche. The *CIS* includes a comprehensive index volume that allows you to locate documents in several ways, such as bill number, subject, and popular name (see Exhibit 6-12).

c. USCCAN *Service*

The *USCCAN* service publishes the texts of federal statutes and committee reports. It is published by Thomson West and is available at most law libraries. West publishes an edition for each session of Congress in monthly pamphlets that are subsequently assembled in bound volumes. In each pamphlet and bound volume is a legislative history table that lists information relating to the law, such as the public law number, date of approval, bill number, the House and Senate report number, and dates the House and Senate considered the bill. With the text of each act is a legislative history section that provides references to all reports related

Exhibit 6-11 *Page from* Sources of Compiled Legislative Histories. *Sources of Compiled Legislative Histories: A Bibliography of Government Documents, Periodical Articles, and Books, by Nancy P. Johnson,* AALL Publ Series No. 14, *Fred B. Rothman Publications, a division of William S. Hein & Co., Inc., Buffalo, New York, 2000, p. B 124. Reprinted with permission from William S. Hein & Co., Inc.*

PUBLIC LAW BILL NUMBER	STATUTE	ACT ENTRY	ACTUAL DOCS.			CITES TO DOCS.			
			REPORTS	HEARINGS	DEBATES	INDEX	DISCUSSION	LISTS	CITES
96-487 H.R. 39	94 Stat. 2371	ALASKA NATIONAL INTEREST LANDS CONSERVATION ACT							
		IHS Legislative Histories Microfiche Program.							
		Quarles, Steven P. "The Alaska Lands Act's Innovations in the Law of Access Across Federal Lands: You Can Get There from Here." 4 Alaska Law Review 1 (1987).						X	X
96-502 H.R. 8117	94 Stat. 2737	SAFE DRINKING WATER ACT AMENDMENTS OF 1980							
		U.S. Congress. Senate. Committee on Environment and Public Works. A Legislative History of the Safe Drinking Water Act. Wash., D.C.: GPO, 1982. SuDoc: Y4.P96/10:97-9 Microfiche: CIS, 82-S322-5	X		X	X			
96-510 H.R. 7020	94 Stat. 2767	COMPREHENSIVE ENVIRONMENTAL RESPONSE, COMPENSATION, AND LIABILITY ACT OF 1980							
		Grad, Frank P. "A Legislative History of the Comprehensive Environmental Response, Compensation and Liability ("Superfund") Act of 1980." 8 Columbia Journal of Environmental Law 1 (1982).						X	X
		IHS Legislative Histories Microfiche Program.							
		Needham, Helen and Cohn, Menefee, ed. Superfund: A Legislative History. Wash., D.C: Environmental Law Institute, 1984.	X		X	X			
96-517 H.R. 6933	94 Stat. 3015	PATENT AND TRADEMARK LAW AMENDMENT OF 1980							
		Chisum, Donald S. Patents: A Treatise on the Law of Patentability, Validity, and Infringement. New York: Matthew Bender, 1978-, vol.6, app.28. LC.: KF3114.C47	X						
96-561 S. 2163	94 Stat. 3296	AMERICAN FISHERIES PROMOTION ACT OF 1980							
		Stanley, Stephen. "Mare Clausum: The American Fisheries Promotion Act of 1980." 9 Syracuse Journal of International Law and Commerce 403 (1982).						X	X

Rev 2-88

Exhibit 6-12 *CIS Index of Bill Numbers. Congressional Information Service, CIS Four-Year Cumulative Index 1979–1982,* Index of Subjects and Names R–Z Supplementary Indexes *(1982), p. 3481. Reprinted with the permission of LexisNexis.*

INDEX OF BILL NUMBERS

This index lists all the Public Bills that were the subjects of publications abstracted in the 1979 through 1982 CIS/Annuals.

The bills are referenced to CIS accession numbers, as well as to Public Law numbers where appropriate. In each case the referenced number begins with a bold face year number indicating the particular CIS/Annual in which that abstract will be found.

This index contains bills from the 91st through the 95th Congresses. All bills are preceded by (91), (92), (93), (94), (95), (96), or (97) identifying the Congress in which they were considered.

Separate lists are provided for each Congress. Within Congresses, House and Senate bills are listed separately arranged by bill type.

91st CONGRESS
House Bills

(91) H. Res. 108	**82** H523–35
(91) H.R. 10351	**81** H343–5
(91) H.R. 17070	**79** H623–4
(91) H.R. 17968	**82** H523–35

91st CONGRESS
Senate Bills

(91) S.J. Res. 1	**79** S523–5
(91) S. 2007	**81** H343–5
(91) S. 3842	**79** H623–4

92nd CONGRESS
House Bills

(92) H. Con. Res. 243	**82** H703–14
(92) H. Con. Res. 296	**82** H703–14
(92) H.R. 850	**81** PL97–34
(92) H.R. 9265	**79** PL96–22
(92) H.R. 12350	**81** H343–5
(92) H.R. 13076	**80** PL96–283
(92) H.R. 13416	**79** H563–2
(92) H.R. 13416	**80** PL96–487
(92) H.R. 13904	**80** PL96–283
(92) H.R. 14100	**81** PL97–34
(92) H.R. 14121	**81** PL97–34
(92) H.R. 14193	**81** PL97–34
(92) H.R. 14918	**80** PL96–283
(92) H.R. 16188	**82** S523–15
(92) H.R. 16932	**80** H343–7

92nd CONGRESS
Senate Bills

(92) S. 215	**81** S521–4
(92) S. 343	**79** PL95–521
(92) S. 344	**79** PL95–521
(92) S. 643	**80** PL96–517
(92) S. 643	**81** PL96–517
(92) S. 1255	**80** PL96–517
(92) S. 1255	**81** PL96–517
(92) S. 1876	**80** PL96–486
(92) S. 2087	**80** H343–7
(92) S. 2108	**79** S763–2
(92) S. 2108	**79** PL96–22
(92) S. 2657	**82** S521–65.4
(92) S. 2801	**79** S313–21
(92) S. 2801	**80** PL96–283
(92) S. 3010	**81** H343–5
(92) S. 3040	**80** PL96–308

(92) S. 3040	**81** PL96–308
(92) S. 3116	**80** PL96–308
(92) S. 3116	**81** PL96–308
(92) S. 3133	**80** S523–8
(92) S. 3133	**80** PL96–308
(92) S. 3133	**81** PL96–308
(92) S. 3145	**80** PL96–308
(92) S. 3145	**81** PL96–308
(92) S. 3587	**80** PL96–308
(92) S. 3587	**81** PL96–308

93rd CONGRESS
House Bills

(93) H. Con. Res. 40	**82** H703–14
(93) H. Con. Res. 152	**82** H703–14
(93) H. Con. Res. 292	**82** H703–14
(93) H. Con. Res. 340	**82** H703–14
(93) H. Con. Res. 404	**82** H703–14
(93) H.J. Res. 784	**79** PL95–521
(93) H.R. 9	**80** PL96–283
(93) H.R. 12	**80** H343–7
(93) H.R. 122	**80** PL96–308
(93) H.R. 122	**81** PL96–308
(93) H.R. 982	**82** S523–15
(93) H.R. 1858	**81** PL97–34
(93) H.R. 2295	**79** H563–2
(93) H.R. 2295	**80** PL96–487
(93) H.R. 6265	**80** H343–6
(93) H.R. 7732	**80** PL96–283
(93) H.R. 9298	**80** H343–6
(93) H.R. 10014	**80** PL96–308
(93) H.R. 10014	**81** PL96–308
(93) H.R. 10792	**79** PL95–598
(93) H.R. 11067	**79** PL95–521
(93) H.R. 11081	**79** PL95–521
(93) H.R. 11135	**79** PL95–521
(93) H.R. 11145	**79** PL95–521
(93) H.R. 11321	**80** H343–7
(93) H.R. 11401	**79** PL95–521
(93) H.R. 11555	**79** PL95–521
(93) H.R. 11754	**82** PL97–446
(93) H.R. 11838	**79** PL95–511
(93) H.R. 12233	**80** PL96–283
(93) H.R. 12993	**80** S263–47
(93) H.R. 14027	**79** PL95–572
(93) H.R. 14212	**79** PL96–122
(93) H.R. 14212	**80** PL96–122
(93) H.R. 14449	**81** H343–5
(93) H.R. 15002	**80** S961–11.3
(93) H.R. 15139	**79** H303–6
(93) H.R. 15139	**79** PL96–122
(93) H.R. 15139	**80** PL96–122
(93) H.R. 15276	**80** H343–6
(93) H.R. 15856	**79** H563–2

(93) H.R. 15856	**80** PL96–487
(93) H.R. 16643	**79** PL95–598

93rd CONGRESS
Senate Bills

(93) S.J. Res. 1	**79** S523–5
(93) S. Res. 71	**79** S381–5
(93) S. 1	**80** H523–42
(93) S. 1	**80** S521–14
(93) S. 1	**82** S523–1
(93) S. 15	**80** H343–7
(93) S. 284	**79** S763–2
(93) S. 284	**79** PL96–22
(93) S. 500	**79** PL95–572
(93) S. 590	**80** S381–28
(93) S. 798	**79** S523–31
(93) S. 978	**80** S523–8
(93) S. 978	**80** PL96–308
(93) S. 978	**81** PL96–308
(93) S. 1040	**80** S313–19
(93) S. 1134	**79** S313–21
(93) S. 1134	**80** PL96–283
(93) S. 1270	**79** PL95–625
(93) S. 1321	**80** PL96–517
(93) S. 1321	**81** PL96–517
(93) S. 1400	**82** S523–1
(93) S. 1401	**80** S523–2
(93) S. 1401	**81** S523–8
(93) S. 1724	**80** H523–6
(93) S. 2504	**82** PL97–247
(93) S. 2575	**79** PL95–483
(93) S. 2576	**79** PL95–483
(93) S. 2600	**79** PL95–521
(93) S. 2603	**79** PL95–521
(93) S. 2611	**79** PL95–521
(93) S. 2615	**79** PL95–521
(93) S. 2616	**79** PL95–521
(93) S. 2631	**79** PL95–521
(93) S. 2642	**79** PL95–521
(93) S. 2733	**79** PL95–521
(93) S. 2878	**80** PL96–283
(93) S. 2879	**82** S313–35
(93) S. 2994	**81** S543–4
(93) S. 3265	**79** PL95–572
(93) S. 3368	**80** S961–11.3
(93) S. 3440	**79** PL95–511
(93) S. 3776	**79** PL95–572
(93) S. 4026	**79** PL95–598
(93) S. 4051	**80** PL96–479
(93) S. 4062	**79** PL95–511
(93) S. 4153	**80** PL96–458
(93) S. 4178	**81** H343–5
(93) S. 4227	**79** PL95–521
(93) S. 4259	**80** S523–5

to the act. Although *USCCAN* does not publish all committee reports, it is a good source for committee and conference report references and an overview of the legislative history of the law. Through this source you can identify the reports and other sources from which you can assemble the legislative history.

d. *Congressional Record*

The *Congressional Record* is a record of the debates on the floor of the Senate and House. It is useful if you are interested in reviewing the floor debates on a bill. It includes an index that references such things as debates, committee reports, and passage information. Information is indexed by subject matter and history. For information in the history section, you must know the House and Senate bill numbers of the legislation.

e. *Congressional Index*

The *Congressional Index* is a loose-leaf service published by Commerce Clearing House. It includes various information on bills, such as indexes of bills by subject and sponsor, a summary of each bill, tables of actions taken on a bill, companion bills, and voting records on a bill. It does not include the text of the bill, debates, committee reports, and so on, but it is a valuable aid in locating documents.

f. *Congressional and Other Sources*

Copies of legislative history documents, such as bills and committee reports, usually are available through your congressional representatives. You can also Shepardize a statute and locate law review articles and *ALR* annotations that have analyzed the statute. Often the analysis will include a summary of the legislative history.

g. *Computer-Aided Research*

There are several online services that may be used to locate and compile legislative history. It is helpful and often necessary to have the public law number of the law or the Senate or House bill numbers.

- Westlaw and LexisNexis. Both of these services have databases that allow you to access the full text of bills, selected legislative history documents such as committee reports, and the *Congressional Record*. Both have bill-tracking services. *CIS* is available on LexisNexis.

- Federal Digest System and Thomas. The federal government maintains the Federal Digest System and Thomas Web sites. They provide access to legislative history documents. The Federal Digest System includes links to legislative history maintained by the Government Printing Office. Thomas is a legislative history site maintained by the Library of Congress. The Web site addresses are listed in the Internet Resources section of this chapter.

C. State Legislative History

Just as courts may look to federal legislative history to resolve an ambiguity in a federal law, state courts may look to state legislative history as a guide to interpret state law. The research sources and processes for locating the legislative history for state statutes are similar to those for federal law. State legislative history and its location vary from state to state and may be limited. Consult the appropriate state legislative records or service office for the availability of legislative history. Information on state legislation may be available from the state legislature's Web site, and Westlaw and LexisNexis both offer state databases. In addition, the local law librarian should be able to guide you to the sources for state legislative history.

VII. JURY INSTRUCTIONS—OTHER RESEARCH SOURCES

In addition to the research authorities mentioned in Chapter 5 and in this chapter, there are other sources, which are briefly discussed in this section.

A. Jury Instructions

Following the presentation of the evidence in a trial, the jury is instructed on the law that applies to the case, such as how terms are defined and what must be proved for a party to prevail (see Exhibit 6-13). Most states adopt uniform or model jury instructions for the courts to follow when instructing the jury. These **jury instructions** are often published with the annotated statutes. If not, check at the local law library or with the court. If there is no approved set of jury instructions, there are several texts that include model jury instructions, such as *Am. Jur. Pleading and Practice Forms*.

It is important to know how to locate jury instructions because you may be called on to prepare them for a case. In addition, the instructions provide the definitions of terms, the elements of a cause of action that must be proved, and so on, which the state has adopted. The instructions also often provide annotations referencing court opinions that discuss the instruction.

> **For Example** If you want to determine what your state requires to establish a negligence claim, consult the state's approved jury instructions. The annotations to the instructions reference court opinions that have discussed the topic.

B. Practice and Form Books

There are many types of single-volume and multivolume texts designed to assist practitioners. They range from **form books** to texts that provide detailed litigation guides and strategy.

> **For Example** If you are called upon to prepare a legal document, such as a contract for the sale of a business, be sure to check a form book to avoid omitting anything.

Check the treatise section of your library or with the librarian. Some of the better known texts are:

- *West's Federal Forms*
- *West's Legal Forms, 2d*—model practice forms such as contracts and real estate forms
- *Fletcher Corporation Forms Annotated*—corporation law forms
- *Am. Jur. Pleading and Practice Forms*—model litigation documents such as complaints and interrogatories
- *Am. Jur. Legal Forms, 2d*—model practice forms such as contracts and wills
- *Am. Jur. Proof of Facts*—information ranging from interviews and discovery to what must be proved in a case
- *Am. Jur. Trials*—information on conducting a trial, such as opening arguments and trial strategy

Many of the form and practice books are also available on Westlaw and LexisNexis.

C. Loose-Leaf Services

Loose-leaf services are publications that focus on a specific area of law and include primary authority such as statutes, regulations, and summaries of court and administrative decisions. Also, they usually include an analysis of the law and references to secondary sources. Each publication includes indexes and finding aids that differ according to the subject matter and

Exhibit 6-13 *Sample Jury Instruction.* West Group, Manual of Model Civil Jury Instructions for the District Courts of the Eighth Circuit, *by Committee on Model Civil Jury Instructions within the Eighth Circuit, 1999, p. 28. Reprinted with permission from West Group.*

2.09 CIVIL INSTRUCTIONS

2.09 IMPEACHMENT OF WITNESS, PRIOR CONVICTION

Jury instruction

You have heard evidence that witness[1] _____ has been convicted of [a crime] [crimes]. You may use that evidence only to help you decide whether to believe the witness and how much weight to give his [her] testimony.

Committee Comments

The admissibility of prior convictions to impeach a witness' credibility is governed by Fed. R. Evid. 609. In civil cases tried before December 1, 1990, the trial judge had no discretion to balance the probative value against the prejudicial effect. The conviction had to be admitted if it came within the rule. *Green v. Bock Laundry Machine Co.,* 490 U.S. 504 (1989); *Jones v. Board of Police Comm'rs,* 844 F.2d 500, 504–05 (8th Cir.1988). Effective December 1, 1990, Rule 609 reinstates the balancing feature. If the conviction involves dishonesty or false statements, it may be admitted even if not a felony. Fed. R. Evid. 609. There is substantial dispute about how much information may be injected concerning the prior conviction. Some judges do not even allow evidence of what crime, or what punishment was involved. The judge may allow evidence of the specific crime committed and the sentence. *Ross v. Jones,* 888 F.2d 548, 551 (8th Cir.1989). Fed. R. Evid. 105 gives a party the right to require a limiting instruction explaining that the use of this evidence is limited to credibility.

See Manual of Model Criminal Jury Instructions for the Eighth Circuit, 2.18; 3 Edward J. Devitt, et al., FEDERAL JURY PRACTICE AND INSTRUCTIONS: Civil § 73.05 (4th ed. 1987); F.J.C.C. Instruction 30; *Fifth Circuit Pattern Jury Instructions—Civil,* Instruction 2.17 (West 1998); *Ninth Circuit Manual of Model Jury Instructions—Criminal,* Instruction 4.8 (West 1997). *See generally* Fed. R. Evid. 609, 105; West Key #"Witnesses" 344(1–5), 345 (1–4).

Notes on Use

1. If the party in a civil case has a conviction which is introduced in evidence, it would be appropriate to modify Eighth Cir. Crim. Inst. 2.16 and give the following instruction, unless the evidence is admitted under Fed. R. Evid. 404(b) to prove motive, intent, plan, etc. Crim, Inst. 2.16, modified for civil cases is as follows:

the publisher. They are not updated by pocket parts; rather, the pages are individually placed in binders and updated by replacement pages. Several different publishers publish loose-leaf services that cover many subjects, such as labor law, environmental law, family law, and tax law. Some of the major publishers are Commerce Clearing House (CCH), Bureau of National Affairs (BNA), and Matthew Bender (MB).

D. Presidential Materials

Presidential materials are directives issued by the president. The two main types are proclamations and executive orders. Proclamations are announcements that have no legal effect, such as declaring a week, for example, "National Bicyclers Week." Executive orders cover a wide range of topics and are usually directives to agencies. These directives have the force of law. Presidential proclamations and executive orders are published in the *Federal Register*, *CFR*, *USCCAN*, and the *Weekly Compilation of Presidential Documents* (published by the Office of the Federal Register). They are also available on Westlaw and LexisNexis, and on the Government Printing Office Web site.

E. Martindale-Hubbell Law Directory

The **Martindale-Hubbell Law Directory**, published by LexisNexis, is a comprehensive directory of attorneys. The multivolume set, arranged alphabetically by state, provides attorneys' names and biographical information, such as date of admission to the bar, law school attended, and publications. There is a multivolume *International Law Directory* listing attorneys from foreign countries. *Martindale-Hubbell* is available on CD-ROM, LexisNexis, and the directory Web site (see Internet Resources at the end of this chapter).

Included with the law directory set is a *Martindale-Hubbell Law Digest,* which contains brief summaries of some (but not all) of the laws of the states and many foreign countries. The set also includes some uniform laws and model acts and the American Bar Association's Model Rules of Professional Conduct.

VIII. KEY POINTS CHECKLIST: *Periodicals, Restatements, Uniform Laws, Dictionaries, Legislative History, and Other Secondary Authorities*

- ✓ Use periodicals primarily to obtain analysis and critique of a specific legal topic that is more in-depth or narrower in focus than that provided by a legal encyclopedia or a treatise.

- ✓ *Restatements of the Law,* uniform laws, and model acts provide a model text from which a law may be crafted. They provide access to reasons supporting a recommended statement of the law and citations to cases, treatises, and articles interpreting the law.

- ✓ Consult the legislative history of a law when the meaning or application of that law is unclear. If the meaning or application of a law is clear, a court will not refer to legislative history.

- ✓ Do not try to draft legal documents or pleadings from scratch. Refer to the forms or samples available in the law office or consult a form book, such as *Am. Jur. Legal Forms, 2d* or *Am. Jur. Pleading and Practice Forms.*

- ✓ Like all research sources, you must check the pocket parts, supplements, or whatever is used to update the source to ensure that your research is current.

IX. APPLICATION

Luis thinks to himself, "The issue here in the broadest sense is, 'What are the constitutional limitations on the city restrictively zoning adult entertainment businesses?' I remember from my constitutional law class that the First Amendment's freedom of speech guarantees are involved. So I could start by looking at the annotations to the First Amendment in the *United States Code Annotated* and locate the section dealing with adult entertainment. This would lead me to case law on the subject. The problem with this is it would take me a while to find the section, then I would have to wade through all the cases. I could look through a treatise on the First Amendment; but again, I may have to wade through a lot of material before I find what I need. I need a source focused on my specific topic that has addressed the question, such as a law review article."

Luis has performed the important first step in his quest. He has identified the question he needs to research and weighed the research avenues available. He could look for a law review article on the topic by consulting the *Index to Legal Periodicals* or the *Current Law Index*, where he will find several articles that address the topic. Both the *ILP* and *CLI* are available on Westlaw and LexisNexis, on the Internet for a subscription, and may be available in the local law library on CD-ROM. A law review article will thoroughly analyze the topic through a discussion of the constitutional issues and synthesis of cases that have addressed such ordinances. It will include references to other research sources.

Luis could consult the *Uniform Laws Annotated, Master Edition* to determine if there is a uniform law or model zoning ordinance restricting the location of adult entertainment businesses. If there is, Luis will be presented not only with the uniform law but also with references to states that have adopted the act, discussion of variations adopted by the states, references to law review articles, research references such as digest key numbers and encyclopedia cites, and summaries of court decisions that have interpreted the law.

Summary

This chapter discusses research authority sources that are frequently used to locate, interpret, and analyze statutory and case law: legal periodicals, *Restatements of the Law,* uniform and model laws, legislative history, and other sources.

Legal periodicals publish articles on legal topics in every area of the law. Periodical articles are valuable for their detailed analysis of current legal issues, recently emerging areas of the law, or very specific topics; depth of research; and citation to primary and secondary sources.

Restatements of the Law present a uniform statement of the law for areas of case law such as torts and contracts. Each *Restatement* provides guidance as to how the law should be defined or stated; reasons in support of the definition or statement of the law; and citations to cases, treatises, and other secondary sources.

Uniform laws and model acts provide uniform statements of the law that are available for adoption by states. They are invaluable guides when drafting or interpreting legislation.

The chapter also covers other topics, such as legislative history, and other research sources, such as form books. The legislative history is the record of the legislation during the enactment process. It often includes guidance as to the meaning or application of the statute.

The chapter briefly covers other research sources that may be valuable to a researcher:

Jury instructions—provide the definition of terms, elements of a cause of action, and so on that a jurisdiction has adopted

Practice and form books—provide guidance when drafting legal documents or pleadings

Loose-leaf services—publications that focus on specific areas of law and compile primary authority such as statutes and summaries of court and administrative decisions

Presidential materials—proclamations and executive orders by the president

Martindale-Hubbell Law Directory—a comprehensive directory of attorneys

Quick References

Internet Resources

The *Index to Legal Periodicals, Current Law Index, Restatements of the Law,* uniform laws, and model acts are available on Westlaw and LexisNexis. *LegalTrac* is available on the Internet by subscription. Both Westlaw and LexisNexis have databases that allow you to access the full text of bills, selected legislative history documents such as committee reports, and the *Congressional Record. Black's* is available on Westlaw. *CIS* is available on LexisNexis.

Some law reviews and periodicals are available on the publisher's Web site. You can check the law school Web site to determine if a law review is published there.

Using "legal newspaper" or "legal newsletters" as a search topic, you can find thousands of Web sites that provide access to legal newspapers, law journals, and newsletters.

http://www.washlaw.edu

This site from Washburn University School of Law provides links to legal newspapers, newsletters, and magazines.

http://thomas.loc.gov

Legislative history is available at this site maintained by the Library of Congress.

http://www.gpo.gov/fdsys

Legislative history is available at this site maintained by the Government Printing Office; access is available to legislative history, presidential documents, the *United States Code*, the *Code of Regulations, Federal Register*, and numerous other documents.

http://www.whitehouse.gov/

The White House virtual library Web site provides access to presidential material.

http://www.house.gov/

This site is the home page of the United States House of Representatives.

http://www.senate.gov/

This site is the home page of the United States Senate.

http://www.martindale.com

The *Martindale-Hubbell* locator site provides links to numerous legal topics.

http://www.cch.com

Commerce Clearing House is a major publisher of loose-leaf services.

http://www.bna.com

The Bureau of National Affairs is a major publisher of loose-leaf services.

http://www.ilrg.com

The Internet Legal Resource Guide site provides links to form sources.

Citation

Chapter 8 discusses the *Bluebook* and *ALWD Citation Manual* rules governing citation to the various secondary authority sources. Some examples of citations to the primary and secondary authority sources discussed in this chapter are presented here.

A. Legal Periodicals

Michael Asimow, *Bad Lawyers in the Movies*. 24 Nova L. Rev. 533 (2000)

B. Restatements

Restatement (Second) of Torts § 21 (1965)

C. Uniform Laws

U.C.C. § 2-315, 1 U.L.A. 111 (1997)

Model Penal Code § 210 (1974)

D. Dictionaries

Black's Law Dictionary 361 (7th ed. 1999)

E. Legislative History

1. Bill—S. 201, 107th Cong. § 2 (2001)

   H.R. 60, 106th Cong. § 8 (1999)

2. Committee Hearing—*The Freedom to E-File Act: Hearings on H.R. 852. Before the Subcomm. on Department Operations, Oversight, Nutrition, and Forestry*, 106th Cong. 56-77 (2000)

3. Committee Report—H. R. Rep. No. 106-986, at 17 (2000)

4. Committee Report—H. R. Rep. No. 101-665, at 279, *reprinted in* 1990 USCCAN at 3004 (1990)

F. Presidential Proclamations and Executive Orders

Rule 14.7 of the *Bluebook* provides that the citation should be to the *CFR* cite with a parallel citation to *USC*. If the material is not in the *CFR*, then the material is cited in the *Federal Register*.

1. Proclamation: Proclamation No. 6642, 58 Fed. Reg. 67625 (1993)

2. Executive Order: Exec. Order No. 13202, 66 Fed. Reg. 11225 (2001)

G. Loose-Leaf Services

Brito v. County of Palm Beach, Florida, [1999 Transfer Binder] Prod. Liab. Rep. (CCH) 15403 (Fla. Dist. Ct. App. Nov. 9, 1998)

Exercises

Additional assignments are available on the CourseMate.

ASSIGNMENT 1

Refer to the *Index to Legal Periodicals*. What 1998 article distinguishes between euthanasia and the withdrawal of life-sustaining treatment?

ASSIGNMENT 2

The supervising attorney is interested in online patent searching. Refer to the *Current Law Index*. What 1997 law review addresses this topic?

ASSIGNMENT 3

Refer to the *Current Law Index*. What *Illinois Bar Journal* law review article addresses *Ward v. KMART Corp.*, 554 N.E.2d 233 (Ill. 1990)?

ASSIGNMENT 4

Refer to *Restatement (Second) of Torts*. What section sets out the elements of false imprisonment? What are the elements of false imprisonment? Is a person liable if he or she unintentionally causes the confinement of another? What section addresses confinement caused indirectly by the institution of criminal proceedings?

ASSIGNMENT 5

Refer to *Restatement (Third) of Unfair Competition*. What section defines a trade secret? What is the definition? What is the reason for providing protection to trade secrets? What Rhode Island law addresses trade secrets? What 1998 case from the United States District Court for the Southern District of Indiana discussed trade secrets?

ASSIGNMENT 6

The client owns a clothing store. She has questions concerning what constitutes an offer and an acceptance. Refer to the *Uniform Laws Annotated, Master Edition*. What uniform law governs this question? What section of that law addresses offer and acceptance? What *CJS* reference is included in the "Library References" section? What 1998 case held that a fax stating that an electric utility was willing to accept shipments of coal from a coal company on a probationary basis if specific conditions were accepted by the coal company constituted an offer?

ASSIGNMENT 7

The supervising attorney's son was able to log on to a Web site that showed children how to torture cats. She seems to remember that some legislation was introduced in the 106th Congress that dealt with online protection of children. Consult the *United States Code Congressional and Administrative News* and locate what, if any, legislation was introduced.

ASSIGNMENT 8

While crossing an intersection, the client was struck by a vehicle driven by a minor. The minor's parents owned the vehicle, and the minor was driving with their knowledge and consent. The minor has been cited twice for speeding in the past three years. Refer to *Am. Jur. Pleading and Practice Forms* and locate the proper negligence complaint form for suit against the parents.

CHAPTER 7

Computers and Legal Research

James Redhorse was born and raised in Window Rock, Arizona, on the Navajo Reservation. His parents insisted that all their children graduate from high school and encouraged them to go to college. After graduating from paralegal school five years ago, James got a job at a law firm in Winslow, Arizona. His dream is to save enough money to go to law school. Over the past five years, James has become quite skilled at legal research and is routinely assigned research projects. Last month, the firm subscribed to Westlaw. The partners are learning to use Westlaw, but because James took a Westlaw course in school, he has become the "Westlaw person."

The senior partner called James into his office and said, "I just had an interview with Mrs. Burgess. She is 80 years old, and since her husband died five years ago, her closest companion is her cat, Alice. Her next-door neighbor hates cats and repeatedly warned Mrs. Burgess that if Alice continued to use his rose garden as a bathroom he would 'get rid of her.' Last week, he set a cat trap for Alice. She was caught in the trap and died. The next day, when Mrs. Burgess asked the neighbor if he had seen Alice, he replied, 'I told you I would take care of her and I did.' He then showed her the trap with Alice still in it. She became so upset over the incident that she went to her doctor. Mrs. Burgess is extremely distraught over the actions of the neighbor and the loss of her cat. She feels that she is now all alone and has lost her best friend. She wants to sue. I want you to get on Westlaw and do some research into what type of damages may be recovered for loss of a pet. I'm especially interested if she can recover for the distress this has caused her."

The answer to this question and the research steps James follows are discussed in the Application section of this chapter.

Outline

I. Introduction
II. Commercial Internet Research
III. Nonfee-Based Law-Related Web Sites and Other Computer-Based Resources
IV. Key Points Checklist: Computers and Legal Research
V. Application

Learning Objectives

After completing this chapter, you should understand:

- The role of computers in legal research

- How to conduct basic legal research using the most frequently used commercial services, Westlaw and LexisNexis

- The role and types of nonfee-based law-related Web sites

- The role of CD-ROMs in legal research

I. INTRODUCTION

A. In General

The earlier chapters of this text focus on the techniques for conducting research using print resources, such as treatises and bound volume sets. Even as technology develops and research is increasingly conducted using electronic resources, it is still important to know how to research using print resources, for at least four reasons:

1. The organization and elements of the electronic databases are based on the structure of the print material. Therefore, a familiarity with the print source makes it much easier to understand the structure of the electronic database and conduct electronic research.

2. The material you are looking for may not be on an electronic database. This is especially true in the case of treatises. Experienced researchers recognize that a research project may require knowledge of and reference to print resources. They do not rely exclusively on computer-assisted legal research.

3. On occasion, access to electronic research sources may be unavailable, such as when the local server is down. In such situations you are helpless if you do not know how to conduct research using print materials.

4. Cost concerns may limit the amount of time you can spend using commercial electronic services. Some firms use electronic services only to double-check what they have located in print sources or to update their research. This limits the time spent on electronic resources and thus reduces costs.

Chapter 3 through Chapter 6 mention if and where the print resources are available on electronic databases such as Westlaw or LexisNexis, but they do not discuss how to conduct electronic research. This chapter presents an overview of legal research using the most frequently used commercial (fee-based) services, Westlaw and LexisNexis, and a review of nonfee-based (free) Internet and other computer-based legal research sources.

B. Search Terms

The initial steps for conducting a search, discussed in Chapter 2, apply to the conduct of a computer-assisted search as well: analyze the assignment, do preliminary preparation, identify the key facts, and identify the issue. Computer searches are usually conducted using key words or terms from the issue (often referred to as **Boolean searches**, or *terms and connectors searches*). Section II.A.1.a(2)-(3) in this chapter describes searches using key terms. The basic steps for determining the search terms are:

1. State the issue you are researching as specifically as possible in the context of the facts.

2. Formulate the search query. Review the issue and select the significant terms. Ask yourself, "What terms in the issue are likely to be included in the constitutional provision, statute, or case I am researching?" To save costs, formulate the search query before you sign on.

After you identify the terms, type them in the search query box and execute the search by clicking on the appropriate command, such as Search or Submit. Most Web sites that allow you to search using key words also include instructions on how to conduct a search; look for a Help icon or a View Tutorial icon near the search query box. Increasingly, Web sites are using simple searches such as those offered by Google rather than using traditional Boolean searches (see Exhibit 7-1).

Exhibit 7-1 United States Government Printing Office Search Query. From *http://www.gpo.gov/fdsys/search/home.action*

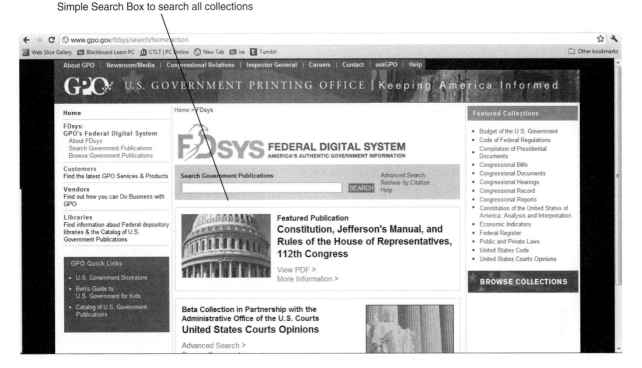

Simple Search Box to search all collections

If you are conducting a broad search for general information on a topic, think of all the terms under which the topic may be categorized and conduct the search using any combination of these terms.

> **For Example** The question involves child custody and the researcher wishes to gain familiarity with this area of law. The first step is to list all of the terms under which "child custody" might be indexed, such as *divorce, marriage, custody, parent and child, child custody, children,* and *domestic relations.* The topic will be found under at least one of those search terms.

II. COMMERCIAL INTERNET RESEARCH

This section presents an overview of legal research using the two most frequently used commercial (fee-based) services: Westlaw (and WestlawNext) and LexisNexis. It also includes a discussion of smaller and somewhat less frequently used services. Although other commercial electronic research services are available, becoming familiar with Westlaw, WestlawNext, and LexisNexis will give you the information you need to use other services. This section is limited to an overview of what information is available and how to conduct basic research, for two reasons:

■ Inasmuch as there are entire texts devoted to how to use Westlaw and LexisNexis, a detailed discussion is beyond the scope of this text. See Judy A. Long, *Legal Research Using Westlaw* (Delmar Cengage Learning, 2001). Westlaw, LexisNexis, Loislaw, VersusLaw, and other fee-based sources update and modify their services frequently, rendering a detailed discussion outdat*ed by the time a text is publi*shed.

Westlaw and LexisNexis each have thousands of databases that include primary and secondary authority research sources and numerous other sources. There are databases for all areas of federal and state law, including statutory and case law. Materials are available on specific practice areas; these services also give you access to public records of all types, news sources, business materials, periodicals, legal treatises, litigation materials, forms, legal and other statistical information sources, directories of all types, law reviews, and international materials. The databases are not limited to law-related information and are too extensive to list here; for example, the Lexis Web site indicates that it has more than 50,000 sources.

A. Westlaw

Westlaw, by Thomson Reuters, provides access to thousands of primary and secondary research sources. It is available directly on the Internet at www.westlaw.com. This section discusses locating primary and secondary authorities, viewing search results, updating research, and printing search results.

1. Finding Primary Authority

As mentioned in Chapter 1, primary authority is the law itself—constitutional law, enacted law (statutes), and case law. This section focuses on locating statutory and constitutional law (note that constitutions are usually located with the statutes) and case law.

a. Finding Statutory Laws and Constitutional Provisions

There are four primary ways to locate a statute or constitutional provision, depending on the amount of information you have.

(1) Search by Citation When you know the citation of a statute or constitutional provision, you can locate it by performing the following steps:

▣ On the Westlaw Welcome page, type the citation in the "Find this document by citation" box and click Go. The document will come up (see Exhibit 7-2).

Exhibit 7-2 *Westlaw Welcome Page. Reprinted with permission of Thomson Reuters.*

Find by Citation   KeyCite   Directory

Database Wizard

> **For Example** If you want to find 18 U.S.C.S. § 2113, type "18 uscs 2113."

▪ If you are not at the Welcome page, click on Find & Print at the top of the page. Find a Document will appear (see Exhibit 7-3), as well as the Find & Print multiple citations box. To access a single citation, type the citation in the "Find this document by citation" box and click Go. To find multiple citations at once, type all of the citations separated by a semicolon or hard return in the "Enter Citation(s)" box and click Send Request.

(2) Search by Issue—Natural Language In most instances, you will not know the citation of the statute that governs the issue being researched. Therefore, you must locate the statute using the information from the issue you have identified. *The most critical step in the research process is framing the issue in the context of the specific facts of the case.* A well-framed issue, stated in the context of the facts, provides a researcher with the information necessary to frame the research query using the two most common research methods: natural language and terms and connectors (see next subsection). For help in identifying and stating issues, see Chapters 10 and 11.

Natural language is a search method that allows you to research by stating the search query (the issue) using plain English. To conduct a natural language search, perform the following steps:

a. State the issue you are researching as specifically as possible in the context of the facts.

> **For Example** The facts of the case are that an individual robbed a bank using a toy gun. The question is whether, under federal law, a "dangerous weapon" was used in the robbery. The assignment is to locate the federal statute governing this question. The issue may be stated as follows: "Under federal statutory law, does bank robbery with a dangerous weapon occur when the weapon is a toy gun?"

Exhibit 7-3 Westlaw Find & Print page. *Reprinted with permission of Thomson Reuters.*

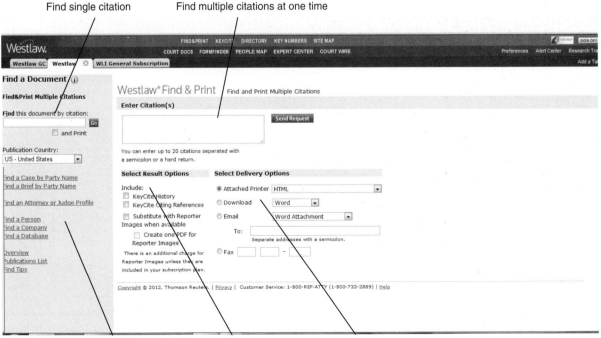

b. Locate the appropriate database. As with any search, narrow it to the sources that contain the material involved in your search, such as the *USCA* for federal law and the state statutes for state law. Just as you would look in different sets of books for different laws, Westlaw has different databases for different research areas (see Exhibit 7-2). To locate databases, use either the Directory link or the Find a Database Wizard (see Exhibit 7-2).

> **For Example** When you are looking for federal statutory law, click on Directory on the Welcome page. On the Directory page, click on U.S. federal materials, then click on Statutes, then United States Code.

c. Enter the natural language description. Once the Database page comes up, on the left side of the page click Natural Language and type the natural language description of the issue in the natural language "Search" box. Next, click on Search Westlaw (see Exhibit 7-4). The search results will then appear.

(3) Search by Issue—Terms and Connectors Another way to find the statute that governs the issue is through the use of **terms and connectors**. This type of search (often referred to as a *Boolean search*) allows you to conduct a search using key words of the issue and symbols (connectors). The connectors specify the relationships between the key terms, and the search retrieves documents based on the relationship between the terms.

> **For Example** In the search query -deadly /p weapon /p bank /p robbery-, the connector "/p" locates all of the documents in which the words *deadly, weapon, bank,* and *robbery* appear in the same paragraph of a document.

Exhibit 7-4 *Westlaw Terms & Connectors Search page. Reprinted with permission of Thomson Reuters.*

To perform a terms and connectors search, you must be familiar with the following information:

- **Plurals and possessives.** Westlaw automatically retrieves plurals and possessives of terms. If you type *robber,* Westlaw will search for *robber, robbers, robbers',* and *robber's.* It will not retrieve the singular forms if you type the plural.

- **Root expander (!).** To search for all forms of a word, place the root expander "!" at the end of the root of the word.

> **For Example** The query -work!- retrieves the various forms of the word (e.g., *worker, working, works*).

- **Universal character (*).** To search for all variations of a word, insert an asterisk (*), the universal character, in place of the variable character.

> **For Example** The query -r*ng- retrieves all the documents with *ring, rang,* and *rung.*

- **Connectors.** Connectors specify the relationship between the search terms. They govern the scope of the search. Always use a space to separate the connector from the search term. The list of connectors can be found at the bottom of the terms and connectors search page (see Exhibit 7-4). Following is a list of the connectors and an explanation of how they are used.

CONNECTOR RULES GOVERNING USE OF CONNECTOR

& (and)	An ampersand (&) between the terms retrieves all documents that contain both terms. Thus, the search query -bank & robber- retrieves all documents with both terms: *bank* and *robber.*
space (or)	A space between words retrieves all documents that contain either search term. Thus, the search query -bank robber- retrieves all documents that contain either the word *bank* or the word *robber.*
/s	An "/s" between the terms retrieves all documents that contain both terms in the same sentence. Thus, the search query -bank /s robber- retrieves all documents in which *bank* and *robber* appear in the same sentence.
/p	A "/p" between the terms retrieves all documents that contain both terms in the same paragraph. Thus, the search query -bank /p robber- retrieves all documents in which *bank* and *robber* appear in the same paragraph.
/n	An "/n" between the terms retrieves all documents in which the terms appear within a certain number of words of each other. The *n* is the specified number of words. Thus, the search query -bank /5 robber- retrieves all documents in which *bank* and *robber* appear within five words of each other.

(continues)

CONNECTOR RULES GOVERNING USE OF CONNECTOR (*continued*)

" "   Place terms in quotation marks when you want to locate documents in which the terms appear in the same order as they appear within the quotation marks. Thus, the search query -"bank robbery"- locates all documents in which the terms *bank* and *robbery* appear together and *bank* precedes *robbery*.

%   To exclude a term from a search query, place the % symbol before the term. Thus, the search query -bank & robber % weapon- retrieves all documents that contain the words *bank* and *robber* but not the word *weapon*.

Following are examples of search queries using connectors. The queries are shown in bold:

- **bank robbery dangerous weapon** The search retrieves all documents that contain *any one of the terms*. This is not a proper terms and connectors search because it does not utilize connectors; it will thus result in a very large number of results that are poorly matched to your desired results.

- **bank & robbery & dangerous & weapon** The search retrieves only the documents that contain all of these terms.

- **bank /p robbery /p dangerous /p weapon** The search retrieves only the documents that contain all of the terms in the same paragraph.

- **"dangerous weapon" & bank & robbery** The search retrieves only those documents that include the terms *bank, robbery, dangerous,* and *weapon* where the terms *dangerous* and *weapon* appear together.

To conduct a terms and connectors search, perform the following steps:

a. State the issue you are researching as specifically as possible in the context of the facts. This step is the same for both natural language and terms and connectors searches.

b. Formulate the terms and connectors search query. Review the issue and select the key terms that are significant to the issue being researched. Ask yourself, "What terms in the issue are likely to be included in the constitutional provision or statute being researched?"

> **For Example** The issue is as follows: "Under federal statutory law, does bank robbery with a dangerous weapon occur when the weapon is a toy gun?" The assignment is to locate the federal law that governs a bank robbery with a dangerous weapon. You are looking for a statute that includes the terms *bank, robbery, dangerous,* and *weapon.*

After you have identified the terms, formulate the query using the appropriate connectors.

> **For Example** Referring to the previous example, the search is for a statute that includes the terms *bank, robbery, dangerous,* and *weapon.* The terms *dangerous* and *weapon* probably appear in the same order, so they are placed in quotations in the query. The query is -"dangerous weapon" & bank & robbery-. Using the *United States Code Annotated* as a database, your search will retrieve all statutes that include the terms *bank, robbery,* and *dangerous weapon.* The search will retrieve only those statutes in which the terms *dangerous* and *weapon* appear together. To narrow the search, the query could read -"dangerous weapon" /p bank /p robbery-. This formulation of the search will retrieve only those statutes where the terms appear in the same paragraph.

    c. Locate the appropriate database. This step is the same as that used for a natural language search.

    d. Enter the terms and connectors. Once the database search page comes up, on the left side of the page click Terms and connectors. In this box, type the terms and connectors for the issue you are searching, then click Search Westlaw (see Exhibit 7-4). The search results will then appear.

When comparing natural language and terms and connectors searches, you will see certain advantages and disadvantages for both. A terms and connectors search has the disadvantage of requiring a familiarity with the use of the connectors. It has the advantage of allowing the researcher to tailor the search.

> **For Example** A terms and connectors search using the "/p" connector retrieves only those documents in which the terms appear in the same paragraph. A natural language search retrieves all the documents that contain the search terms.

Although it takes some practice to become familiar with terms and connectors searches, most researchers prefer them because of the ability to limit the search.

(4) Search by Table of Contents In some instances, you may be able to locate a statute or constitutional provision by reviewing the table of contents of the laws you are searching.

> **For Example** You are looking for the federal law that governs bank robbery. Rather than construct a natural language or terms and connectors search, you may be able to locate the statute simply by looking at the criminal law section of the table of contents of the *United States Code* or the *United States Code Annotated*.

To conduct a table of contents search, perform the following steps:

    a. Select Directory from the navigation bar at the top of the page.

    b. Select the appropriate database. The search query box will open.

    c. From the search page, select Tables of Contents located at the top right. Click on the table of contents you want to view.

    d. To preview the contents of the topic, click on it. To search within the topic, click the box next to it and click Search at the bottom of the page.

b. Finding Case Law

There are several ways to locate court opinions on Westlaw. Most of the search methods and steps are similar to those used to search for statutory and constitutional law.

(1) Search by Citation If you know the citation of a case, you can locate the case by using either of the following steps:

    a. On the Westlaw Welcome page, type the citation in the "Find this document by citation" box and click Go (see Exhibit 7-2). The document will come up.

> **For Example** If the citation is 713 F. Supp. 1296, type "713 fs 1296" and click Go.

    b. If you are not at the Welcome page, click on Find & Print at the top of the page. As when searching statutory law, the Find a document box and the Find & Print multiple citations box will appear. To access a single citation, type the citation in the "Find this document by citation" box and click Go. To find multiple citations at once, type all of the citations, separated by a semicolon or hard return, in the "Enter Citation(s)" box and click Send Request.

(2) Search by Issue—Natural Language In most instances, when you are trying to find the case law that governs the issue being researched, you do not know its name or citation (as is often the case when you are searching for statutes). Therefore, you must locate the case law using the information from the issue. The steps for performing a natural language search for statutory and case law are the same. See section II.A.1.a(2) in this chapter. The most critical step in the research process is framing the issue in the context of the specific facts of the case.

To conduct a natural language search for case law, perform the following steps:

a. State the issue you are researching as specifically as possible in the context of the facts.

> **For Example** Under federal statutory law, does bank robbery with a dangerous weapon occur when the weapon is a toy gun?

b. Locate the appropriate case law database.

c. Enter the natural language description. Once the database page comes up, type the natural language description of the issue in the Natural language description box and click Search. The search results will then appear (see Exhibit 7-4).

(3) Search by Issue—Terms and Connectors The steps for performing a terms and connectors search for statutory and case law are the same. The same terms and connectors are used for all searches. See section II.A.1.a(3) in this chapter.

Following is a summary of the steps for conducting a terms and connectors search for case law.

a. State the issue you are researching as specifically as possible in the context of the facts. This first step is the same for both natural language and terms and connectors searches.

b. Formulate the terms and connectors search query. Review the issue and select the key terms that are significant to the issue being researched. Ask yourself, "What terms in the issue are likely to be included in a court opinion?" After you have identified the terms, formulate the query using the appropriate connectors.

> **For Example** Referring to the previous example, the search is for court opinions that include the terms *bank, robbery, dangerous weapon,* and *toy gun.* The terms *dangerous* and *weapon* and *toy gun* probably appear in the same order, so they are placed in quotations in the query. The query is -"dangerous weapon" & bank & robbery & "toy gun"-. If you want to narrow the search, the query could read-"dangerous weapon" /p bank /p robbery /p "toy gun"-. The search would retrieve only cases in which the specified terms appear in the same paragraph.

c. Locate the appropriate database. This step is the same as that for a natural language search. See section II.A.1.a(2) in this chapter.

d. Enter the terms and connectors. Once the database page comes up, type the terms and connectors for the issue being searched in the Terms and Connectors box and click Search (see Exhibit 7-4). The search results will then appear.

(4) Search by Title/Name If you know the name of one or more of the parties in a case, you can locate the case by performing the following steps:

    a. Click Find & Print. On the left side of the screen, select the method with you would like to search, such as by a party's name.

    b. Find document by the title. On the search screen, type the name of at least one of the parties, select a topic or jurisdiction, and click Go.

(5) Search by Digest—Topic and Key Numbers If you are searching for case law that addresses an issue, you can perform a digest search on Westlaw. As discussed in Chapter 5, West's digests organize the law by topic and subtopics and each subtopic is assigned a key number. The Westlaw Custom Digest allows you to access the digests online. To use the digest, perform the following steps:

    a. Access the Custom Digest page. On the Welcome page, click Key Numbers, then click West Key Number Digest Outline.

    b. Select a topic and key number. At the West Key Number Digest page, review the topics and select the key number for the subject you are researching. To see all of the key numbers under a topic, click the plus sign (+) next to the topic number. Check the box next to the key number you want to search; or, if you already know the key number, type it in the box at the top of the page and click Search Selected at the bottom left of the page. The Key Number Search page with your key number selection will appear.

    c. Select the jurisdiction. Select the federal or state jurisdiction you want to search, and add more search terms in the terms and connectors box (optional). When you click on Search at the bottom of the page, the case summaries will appear on the right side of the page.

c. Field Restrictions

When researching case law, Westlaw allows you to limit your search to specific portions of documents or documents published on certain dates, through the use of **field restrictions**. You can access the list of field restrictions by clicking on the "Fields" box on the Search page (see Exhibit 7-4). Type the field restriction initials before the terms and connectors, which are placed in parentheses.

> **For Example** To locate the federal law governing bank robbery, your query may be -bank & robbery-. To narrow your search to only those documents in which the terms *bank* and *robbery* appear in the caption of the statute, your query would be -TI (bank & robbery)-. The search then would only retrieve statutes in which the terms *bank* and *robbery* appeared in the title. It would not retrieve all of the other statutes where the terms appear in other places, such as in the text or annotations, and thus significantly narrow the search.

d. Search Results

The search results are displayed on a split screen. The text of the document retrieved is on the right-hand frame, and the left frame contains information links concerning the search.

(1) Document Text In the document text, the search terms are highlighted in yellow. In a natural language search, the portion of the document most closely related to the query is in red.

    KeyCite flags, which were discussed in Chapter 5, appear at the beginning of the document. Clicking hyperlinks allows you to immediately view a case or a statute cited in the document.

(2) Information The left frame of the screen allows access to information relevant to the document, including KeyCite results, headnotes for cases, tables of authorities, annotations for statutes, and constitutional provisions. The left frame also lists the number of documents retrieved. The "Results List" allows you to view the list of documents selected; click the link to retrieve documents from the list (see Exhibit 7-5). When there are KeyCite flags, they appear in the citations list.

e. Updating Research—KeyCite

It is essential to determine whether the statute or case you have found is still "good law." **KeyCite** is Westlaw's online citator. How to use KeyCite is discussed in detail in Chapter 5.

2. Finding Secondary Authority

Westlaw provides access to thousands of secondary sources. There are databases for *Am. Jur. 2d, ALR,* legal periodicals including law reviews, treatises, legislative history, and legal forms. To view the available databases, click Directory on the home page. At the Westlaw directory page, be sure to select All Databases; then select the appropriate secondary authority database category, such as "Treatises, CLEs, Practice Guides." Then, click on the appropriate secondary authority database.

Alternatively, you may select the "Find a Database Wizard" link on the Westlaw Welcome page (see Exhibit 7-2). Follow the steps to navigate to the secondary authority databases and select the appropriate one.

The steps for performing a secondary authority search are generally the same as those used for a primary authority search; that is, you may search by citation, terms and connectors, natural language, and so forth. See section II.A.1 in this chapter.

3. Print and Save

Westlaw provides several options for printing and saving. You can download documents to a disk, have them sent to an e-mail address or a fax number, or print them. If you want documents to be printed as they appear in print, select one of the print options, either "composed

Exhibit 7-5 *Case retrieved from a Westlaw search. Reprinted with permission of Thomson Reuters.*

single" or "dual column." Documents can also be printed as they appear on the computer screen. Documents can be printed either immediately or upon exiting Westlaw. On the top of the document being researched are print options (see Exhibit 7-5).

B. WestlawNext

1. Searching WestlawNext

WestlawNext was designed in response to customer feedback seeking a cleaner, less cluttered, and simpler way to search. The result is what Westlaw refers to as WestSearch technology, which eliminates the need to choose a database and provides a single search query box for all searches. Researchers choose a jurisdiction, enter their search query in either natural language or terms and connectors, or enter a citation (see Exhibit 7-6). When you click Search, WestlawNext searches all databases. The list of results includes primary and secondary authority ranked according to relevance and document type.

There are still several ways to search for the law in WestlawNext:

a. Use the single search box. Choose a jurisdiction, then enter your search query in natural language or terms and connectors, or enter a citation and click Search (see Exhibit 7-6). The results will be presented in a list on the left organized by relevance and document type (see Exhibit 7-7). If you wish to narrow the results, use the filters below the "View" list of content categories.

b. Browse databases. On the WestlawNext homepage you can browse the databases, which have been organized under content tabs (see Exhibit 7-8). Simply click through the links to get to the database, enter your search terms in the single search box, and choose a jurisdiction. You may also start typing the name of the database, such as New Mexico Statutes, in the single search box and select the appropriate link that drops down. Additionally, if you recall the database identifier from Westlaw, you may type it into the single search box to access that database.

Exhibit 7-6 *WestlawNext Search Query page. Reprinted with permission of Thomson Reuters.*

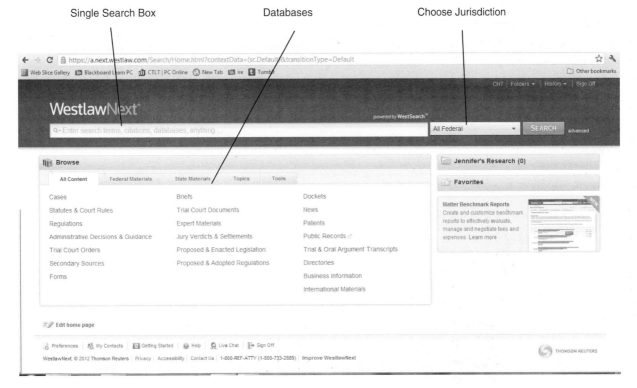

Exhibit 7-7 *Results of WestlawNext search. Reprinted with permission of Thomson Reuters.*

View of Results in List Format   Search Query   Jurisdiction   Print Options

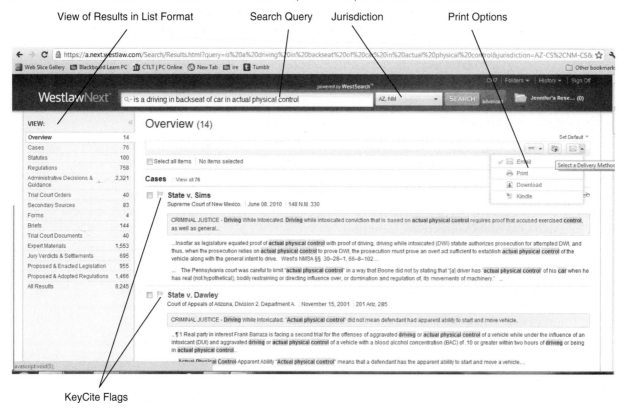

KeyCite Flags

Exhibit 7-8 *List of Databases. Reprinted with permission of Thomson Reuters.*

Databases   Tab Showing Database Category   Search and Jurisdiction boxes

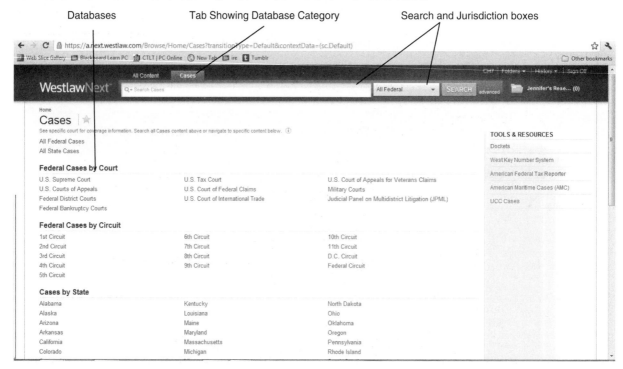

c. Find & Print. This feature of Westlaw is simpler in WestlawNext. If you are seeking a single citation, type it into the single search box and click Search. If you are seeking multiple documents, type all of the citations, separated by semicolons, in the single search box and click Search. Check the box next to each item, or click Select all on the results page and choose your print option. As with Westlaw, you may print, e-mail, or download the documents (see Exhibit 7-7).

2. Reviewing Search Results

Research results from a WestlawNext search include documents from all databases presented in order of relevance. A list of the types of documents and the number of documents for each type appears on the left of the screen in the "View" box (see Exhibit 7-7). The documents themselves, in the order of the list provided, is presented in the center of the screen. On the home page, to the right of the list of documents is a list of additional sources that may be useful. There are several key features to the results page:

- The most relevant results over a variety of content categories (databases) are presented in the overview category in the "View" list (see Exhibit 7-7).

- The researcher controls the amount of content that is visible for reviewing results by selecting more or less detail from a drop-down menu located just above the documents.

- KeyCite Flags for most negative history are included in the results list (see Exhibit 7-7). When a document is selected and opened for review, the KeyCite Flag also includes a description of the negative history, and a short citation to the most negative citation is provided above the document. Other KeyCite information is available from the KeyCite tab at the top of the document (see Exhibit 7-9).

Exhibit 7-9 *Westlaw Next Key Cite results. Reprinted with permission of Thomson Reuters.*

Negative KeyCite Explanation and Citation

Other KeyCite History

Headnotes

Highlighting of Text and Options

- Filters for search results allow the search to be narrowed by categories such as jurisdiction, date, topic, or whether the document was reported or unreported.

- Once a document has been viewed, an eyeglasses icon appears to alert you that you have already viewed that document.

- Relevant portions of search results can be highlighted. The highlighted portion can be copied with the citation, a note can be added, or the text can be saved to a folder (see Exhibit 7-9).

3. Organizing Search Results

WestlawNext offers the ability to organize search results in folders. Results can be dragged and dropped into folders. Highlighted text can be saved with citation to folders (see Exhibit 7-9). You can even organize the content within the folder.

4. Validating Research

KeyCite continues to be the method of validating research. To KeyCite a case, statute, constitutional provision, or other primary source of law, simply type the citation into the single search box and click Search. Once the result page opens, any negative KeyCite flag will be presented at the top of the document. To see the full KeyCite history, click on the KeyCite tab above the document (see Exhibit 7-9).

C. LexisNexis

LexisNexis (Lexis), like Westlaw, is a commercial legal research service that provides access to thousands of primary and secondary research sources. The Lexis research service is operated by LexisNexis, a division of Reed Elsevier Inc. It is available directly on the Internet at http://www.LexisNexis.com. There are differences between Lexis and Westlaw, but the basic organization and research principles are the same. Lexis recently changed its interface to be cleaner and more like WestlawNext.

Rather than repeat the information that applies to searches on both LexisNexis and Westlaw, you will find reference here to the appropriate subsections of the previous Westlaw discussion. The first section addresses finding primary and secondary authority, followed by viewing search results, updating your research, and printing search results.

1. Finding Primary Authority by Citation

This section focuses on locating primary authority.

a. My Lexis Tab

From the My Lexis tab, type in the citation in the "Get Citation" box. Choose Get a Document and click Go.

b. Search Tab

Type the citation into the "Quick Tools" box and click Get a Doc.

c. Get a Document Tab

Type the citation into the search box and click Get. This tab also provides a link to citation formats if you are unsure of or unfamiliar with the proper citation form. In addition, you can search for a document by party name or docket number: Select the appropriate link and type in any party's name or the docket number of a case (see Exhibit 7-10).

Exhibit 7-10 *Search by Citation from the Get a Document tab.* Copyright 2012 LexisNexis, a division of Reed Elsevier Inc. All Rights Reserved. LexisNexis and the Knowledge Burst logo are registered trademarks of Reed Elsevier Properties Inc. and are used with the permission of LexisNexis.

2. Search by Issue—Natural Language or Terms and Connectors

a. From the My Lexis Tab

There are three ways to search under the My Lexis tab: terms and connectors, natural language, and easy search. The steps for performing a terms and connectors search for primary authority are the same. The same terms and connectors are used for all searches. See section II.A.1.a(3) and Exhibit 7-11. You can also search using natural language. As with all natural language searches, the key is framing the issue in the context of the specific facts or terms of the issue. Easy Search allows you to enter your search terms with less precision and is meant to be like a Google search. Enter your terms in accord with the search method you have selected.

You will then need to choose a search type. "Recent Sources" provides a drop-down menu of sources you have searched recently. If you choose "Source Type," you will need to choose a jurisdiction, practice area, and source category (see Exhibit 7-11). Once you have chosen all the appropriate boxes, click Next. Choose the database you want and click Search.

b. From the Search Tab

The Search tab provides several ways to obtain documents.

(1) Browse Sources In Lexis, Sources are similar to Westlaw's Directory categories (see Exhibit 7-12). To search in this manner, choose a source and then choose a specific file. In Lexis, files are similar to Westlaw's databases. Choose a file and click Search Selected. This will take you to the search query box. As with all searches in Lexis, you may search by terms and connectors, natural language, or Easy Search.

(2) Recently Used Sources Choose the recently visited source and click Go. You will be taken to the search query box, where you can search by terms and connectors, natural language, or Easy Search (see Exhibit 7-12).

c. Search by Topic or Headnote

Lexis provides a mode for searching by topic and headnote (see Exhibit 7-12). Under the Search tab, use the View More icon to open the list of topics. As you move through the layers of topics, you will end at a search page where you can search by headnote, or search across sources

Exhibit 7-11 Search from My Lexis tab. *Copyright 2012 LexisNexis, a division of Reed Elsevier Inc. All Rights Reserved. LexisNexis and the Knowledge Burst logo are registered trademarks of Reed Elsevier Properties Inc. and are used with the permission of LexisNexis.*

Search Query   Find by Citation   Choosing Jurisdiction and Practice Area

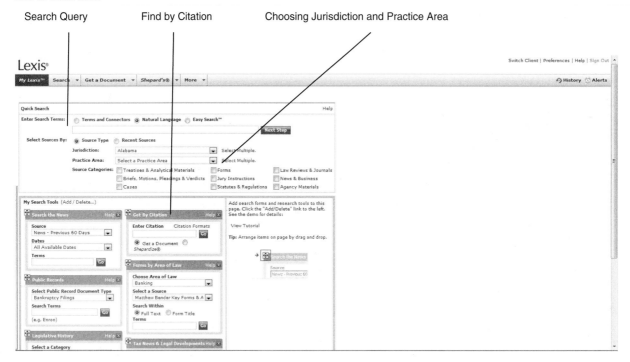

Exhibit 7-12 Using the Search tab. *Copyright 2012 LexisNexis, a division of Reed Elsevier Inc. All Rights Reserved. LexisNexis and the Knowledge Burst logo are registered trademarks of Reed Elsevier Properties Inc. and are used with the permission of LexisNexis.*

Tabs   Sources   Quick Tools

Search by Headnote or Topic

Exhibit 7-13 *Screen shot of Lexis search results.* Copyright 2012 LexisNexis, a division of Reed Elsevier Inc. All Rights Reserved. LexisNexis and the Knowledge Burst logo are registered trademarks of Reed Elsevier Properties Inc. and are used with the permission of LexisNexis.

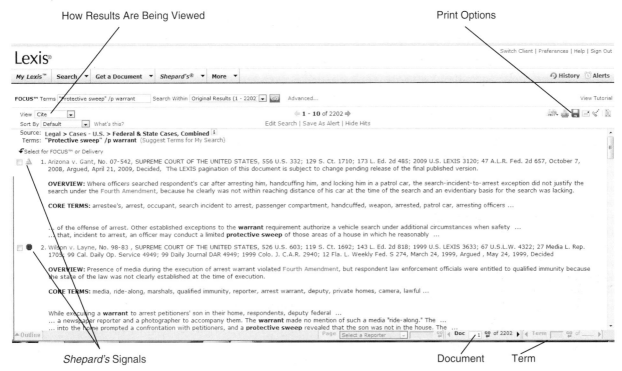

using terms and connectors or natural language. Searching using terms and connectors and natural language is the same as with the other search options.

The steps for performing a terms and connectors search for primary authority are the same. The same terms and connectors are used for all searches. See section II.A.1.a(3) and Exhibit 7-11. As with Westlaw and WestlawNext, you can also search using natural language. In all natural language searches, the key is framing the issue in the context of the specific facts or terms of the issue.

3. Search Results

The search results will list all the documents that match your search (see Exhibit 7-13 for a specific search result). You have several options for viewing any document listed:

1. *Cite.* To view the citations or bibliographic references of a document, click on Cite in the upper left corner of the screen.

2. *KWIC.* If you want to view only the portions of the document surrounding the included search terms, click on KWIC in the upper left corner of the screen. KWIC (key words in context) displays a window of 15 to 25 words on each side of the search words.

3. *Full.* To view the complete text of a document the search has retrieved, click on Full in the upper left corner of the screen.

4. *Custom.* To view only a portion of a document, such as the dissent in a court opinion or an annotation of a statute, click on Custom. Select the segment of the field that you want to view.

5. *FOCUS.* The FOCUS feature allows you to further narrow your search within your retrieved documents. Click FOCUS above the retrieved document, type in the additional search terms, and click FOCUS again.

6. *Term.* To move to any of your search terms while viewing a document in KWIC, click on the arrow next to the number in the bottom right lower navigation bar.

7. *Document.* To move to the next document, click on the arrow next to the number in the lower right navigation bar.

4. Finding Secondary Authority

LexisNexis, like Westlaw, provides access to thousands of secondary sources, including databases for *Am. Jur. 2d, ALR,* legal periodicals such as law reviews, treatises, legislative history, and legal forms. Most of these databases are listed under Secondary Legal.

The steps for performing a secondary authority search are generally the same as those used to conduct a primary authority search. That is, you can search by citation, terms and connectors, natural language, or Easy Search.

Following are the basic steps for conducting a secondary authority search when you do not know the citation:

1. State the issue or research question as specifically as possible in the context of the facts.

2. Formulate the terms and connectors or natural language search.

3. Locate and click on the appropriate database.

4. Perform the search once the database page comes up, using terms and connectors, natural language, or Easy Search.

5. Print and Save

LexisNexis provides several options for printing and saving documents (see Exhibit 7-13). You may download documents, have them sent to an e-mail address, or print them. Documents can be printed in single or dual column, with the search terms in bold or italics, among other options. In the upper right corner of the document, click on Print, Download, or Email. A drop-down list will appear; select your preferences from that list. Once you have selected the desired options, click Print in the lower right corner to transfer the documents to the word processor you have selected and print them from there.

6. Validating Research.

Shepardizing continues to be the method of validating research in Lexis. See Chapter 5 for a detailed description on how to validate research.

D. Other Commercial Internet Research Sources

Loislaw and VersusLaw are commonly used commercial legal research services. Their databases are not as extensive as those of Westlaw and LexisNexis.

1. Loislaw

Loislaw databases include federal and state case, statutory, constitutional, and administrative law, as well as other authority. The secondary authority databases include treatises, practical tools, and forms from Wolters Kluwer companies, Aspen Publishers, CCH, state bar partners, and other sources. The databases cover a wide variety of practice areas. A list of Loislaw services and prices is available on its Web site: http://www.loislaw.com. Searches are conducted in a terms and connectors format similar to the one used in both Westlaw and LexisNexis. Loislaw also has a validation tool, called GlobalCite, and an alert tool, called LawWatch. GlobalCite is not as comprehensive as either Westlaw's KeyCite or Lexis's *Shepard's,* so researchers should be sure to validate using one of the more comprehensive citators.

2. VersusLaw

VersusLaw provides access to the *United States Code;* state statutes; full-text appellate decisions from 50 states, the United States Supreme Court (since 1900), 13 federal circuits from 1930, federal district courts, and specialty practice collections. Searches are conducted using a terms and connectors format. A list of VersusLaw services and prices is available on its Web site: http://versuslaw.com.

3. Fastcase

Fastcase primarily allows access to federal and state cases and statutes. Many state bar associations provide access to Fastcase for their members. Fastcase has Authority Check as a validation tool. Authority Check, like VersusLaw's GlobalCite, is more limited than *Shepard's* or KeyCite, but it does provide a list of other cases citing your case.

4. Casemaker

Casemaker is similar to Fastcase in that numerous state bar associations provide access to it for their members. Casemaker allows access to state and federal primary sources as well as legal forms. Casemaker is expanding to include secondary sources as well.

III. NONFEE-BASED LAW-RELATED WEB SITES AND OTHER COMPUTER-BASED RESOURCES

This section presents an overview of the various nonfee-based (free) Internet and other computer-based legal research sources.

A. Ethics

The Internet hosts literally thousands of nonfee-based Web sites. Note that a nonfee-based service does not involve a contractual relationship with the consumer of its information. No laws or regulations govern the accuracy of the content of nonfee-based Web sites. Such sites do not have a legal duty to provide information that is accurate or up to date. From an **ethics** standpoint, you have an obligation to provide the client with competent representation. Therefore, it is vital that you verify the accuracy of information you obtain from such sites and determine whether it is up to date.

There are no hard-and-fast rules for determining what makes a nonfee-based site "good." Sites maintained by law schools are usually accurate and well maintained. Always consider the author and publisher and the content of the information; and check the site to determine how frequently the information is updated. Be aware that advocacy groups publish some sites, and that information may be limited or slanted in favor of the position advocated by the sponsoring group. You may obtain aids to evaluate Web sites at the Evaluation of Information Sources site: http://www.vuw.ac.nz/~agsmith/evaln/evaln.htm; from "Evaluating Internet Resources: A Selective Bibliography," http://www.lib.auburn.edu and The Virtual Chase, http://www.virtualchase.justia.com.

B. Limitations

Another disadvantage of nonfee-based Internet research is the limited amount of information available. On many Web sites, when you search for statutory law, *only* the statute is available, not the annotations. Therefore, none of the valuable research information, such as *ALR* annotations, law review articles, and case references, is included.

> **For Example** If you are using http://www.lawschool.cornell.edu/ to search the *United States Code* for the bank robbery statute, you will be able to retrieve the statute but not the annotations.

When you are looking for case law, many nonfee-based sites require that you know the name or citation of the case. If you are trying to find any case that answers the question raised by the issue, you may not be able to conduct the search based on search terms. In many sites that do allow Boolean searching, the search capabilities are not as sophisticated as those of commercial (fee-based) services such as Westlaw and LexisNexis or even sites like Loislaw, Versuslaw, and Fastcase. Importantly, most nonfee-based sites do not enable you to update research.

> **For Example** If you locate a case that is on point, most nonfee-based sites do not allow you to check the history or treatment of the case to determine if it has been overturned or affected by a subsequent case. The sites also have no mechanism such as *Shepard's* to identify cases, articles, and other secondary sources that have cited the case.

C. Nonfee-Based Law-Related Web Sites

The address of a Web site is referred to as a **uniform resource locator (URL)**. The addresses provided in this text are current as of the date of publication. If a Web site is not at the address listed, it does not mean that the site no longer exists. The site could be down temporarily due to technical problems, or the address may have changed. To determine whether an address has changed, do an online search for a key term in the address using a search engine.

> **For Example** If you are looking for Legal-Pad and the site does not come up at http://www.legal-pad.com, then perform a search using the keywords *legal pad*. If you are looking for a school's law library, search under the name of the school and *law library*.

You may have a specific Web page address, such as a page from the Willamette College of Law Web site, http://www.willamette.edu/wucl, which provides summaries of recent United States Supreme Court opinions. Often specific page addresses change. If you are unable to retrieve a specific page, go to the home page. In this example, the home page is http://www.willamette.edu/wucl. The directory of information on the home page will lead you to the information you want. In this case, the home page directory includes links to Supreme Court opinions.

D. Legal Search Engines

1. General Access

Several sites provide **general access** and links to legal research sites. The links are to Web sites that access statutory law, case law, and other research sources. Some of the most comprehensive sites are as follows:

- http://www.findlaw.com/—FindLaw is considered one of the best and most comprehensive sites providing links to sources for federal and state statutory law, case law, government directories, law firms, legal organizations, law schools, legal practice materials, and numerous other sources.

- http://lawcrawler.findlaw.com/—LawCrawler uses simple search terms and phrases to search the Internet for legal information sites. FindLaw is the parent site of LawCrawler.

- http://www.jflax.com/law.htm/—Jeff Flax's Law Related Resources includes a comprehensive list of links to law-related Web sites.

- http://law.gsu.edu/—This Georgia State University College of Law site provides links to federal resources. It includes information on major topics such as judicial opinions, federal regulations, and federal legislation (House and Senate bills and the *Congressional Record*). At the home page, click on "Law library."

- http://www.abanet.org/—This American Bar Association (ABA) site includes links to legal research sources, law school libraries, branches of government, courts, and numerous other sources.

- http://www.legal-pad.com/—This site includes legal clip art and a large number of links to law-related sites.

- http://www.loc.gov/—Through this Library of Congress Web site, you can locate any book that has been published and has an ISBN.

- http://www.legaldocs.com/—This site provides templates for legal documents in many areas, such as wills, trusts, sales, and real estate, many of which are free. Check the law of the state where the document is to be used to ensure that the template document complies with state law.

- http://www.lawguru.com/—Lawguru provides links to Web sites for hundreds of legal resources.

- http://www.ilrg.com/—Internet Legal Resource Group provides links to forms and other research sources.

- http://www.lectlaw.com/—This site provides links to numerous research sources.

2. Law Schools

Most **law schools** have a Web site, and each site provides a link to the school's law library. The list of every law school Web site is too extensive to include here. To locate the site of a school of interest, use a search engine and insert the name of the law school, such as "Yale Law School."

You can conduct research through many law school library Web sites. Following is a list of law school sites that provide legal research links, resources, and information:

- http://www.law.indiana.edu/—This Indiana University Virtual Law Library includes links to sites of specialty areas of law, government resources, search engines, and law journals.

- http://library.lawschool.cornell.edu/—This Cornell University Law School site provides extensive resource guides and access to different legal topics.

- http://www.washlaw.edu/—In addition to providing links to numerous law-related and legal research–related Web sites, this Washburn University School of Law site provides links to state and federal court and government sites.

- http://www.law.utexas.edu/—This University of Texas School of Law site includes a legal resource guide on different legal topics.

- http://www.kentlaw.edu/—Information on how to find online legal materials on the Internet is available at this Chicago-Kent College of Law site. Included are lists governing various areas, such as the federal government, computer law, and health law.

> ▤ http://www.law.emory.edu/—This Emory University School of Law site provides access to many federal circuit court decisions and other research material.
>
> ▤ http://www.law.villanova.edu/—At this site, you can use locators to find official Web sites for federal and state courts and federal government information resources.

E. Federal Government Sources

1. General Access Sources

The following sites are helpful in locating **federal government online resources**:

> ▤ http://www.usa.gov/—FirstGov is the United States government's official Web portal. The site provides information and access links to various federal government online resources.
>
> ▤ http://www.fedworld.gov/—FedWorld allows you to search for government reports, and locate United States government Web sites, government documents, government studies, and other materials.
>
> ▤ http://www.uscourts.gov/—This site is the home page for the federal courts.
>
> ▤ http://www.gpo.gov/fdsys/—This is the link for the Government Printing Office (see Exhibit 7-1). The site provides information on the executive branch, including the *Code of Federal Regulations,* the *Federal Register,* the *Congressional Record,* government reports, and other materials.

2. Federal Courts Opinions

The following sites provide access to the United States Supreme Court, the United States Circuit Courts of Appeal, and the Federal District Court resources.

a. United States Supreme Court

Access to United States Supreme Court materials is available at the following sites, among others:

> ▤ http://www.supremecourt.gov/—This official page of the United States Supreme Court features court opinions, orders, rules, calendars and schedules, news releases, and general information.
>
> ▤ http://www.findlaw.com/casecode/supreme.html/—This FindLaw site includes Supreme Court cases and the *United States Code.*
>
> ▤ http://www.oyez.org/—You can hear the oral arguments or read the court briefs of United States Supreme Court cases at this multimedia Web site.
>
> ▤ http://www.lawschool.cornell.edu/—At this Cornell University Law School site, on the home page, click on Court opinions and in the drop-down box type "US Supreme Court" to access Supreme Court transcripts, orders, and decisions.
>
> ▤ http://www.fedworld.gov/—The FedWorld site allows you to locate opinions from 1937 to 1975 if you know the names of the parties. (You do not need to know the citation.)
>
> ▤ http://www.willamette.edu/wucl/—Summaries of recent Supreme Court opinions and the text of the opinions are available at Willamette College of Law. Cases from 2002 to present are available.

b. United States Circuit Courts of Appeal

Access to federal circuit court cases is available through several sources, including the ones listed here:

- http://www.findlaw.com/—Through the FindLaw site, you can locate all types of court cases.
- http://www.law.villanova.edu/—This Villanova University School of Law site includes circuit court opinions and rules.
- http://www.law.emory.edu/—You can access circuit court opinions through this Emory University School of Law site.

c. United States District Courts

As discussed in Chapter 1, the United States District Courts are the primary trial courts in the federal system. Most federal district courts list their opinions on the court Web page. The home page for the federal courts is http://www.uscourts.gov/, which provides information about the courts and links to the district court Web sites.

d. Attorney General Opinions

United States Attorney General opinions are available at http://www.usdoj.gov, the Web site for the United States Department of Justice. Many state Attorney General offices now also make their opinions available online. To locate a state Attorney General's office, use a search engine. Most state government Web sites now have a search query box allowing you to enter a query such as "attorney general opinions" or even "opinions."

3. Federal Statutes, Court Rules, and Regulations

The *United States Code,* federal court rules, and the *Code of Federal Regulations* are available at the following sites.

a. United States Code

The Cornell University Law School site, http://library.lawschool.cornell.edu/, provides access to the *USC.* You can search by title and chapter, popular name, title of individual sections, and table of contents. The *USC* is also available through FindLaw (http://www.findlaw.com/) and the Government Printing Office Web site (http://www.gpo.gov/fdsys).

b. Federal Court Rules

The federal court rules are included in the *USC,* as discussed in the previous section. Local court rules are usually available through the specific federal court's Web site, which may be accessed at http://www.uscourts.gov/. The federal court rules are also available at many law school Web sites, such as http://www.lawschool.cornell.edu/. At the Cornell University Law School site, you can search the Federal Rules of Civil Procedure and Evidence by key word search.

c. State and Federal Law

The Web site http://www.lawsonline.com provides links to state and federal law sources. Many states now provide state law sources on their supreme court Web sites, or provide a link to a Web page where the state's laws can be accessed for free.

d. Code of Federal Regulations

You may conduct *CFR* searches at the following sites:

- http://www.lawschool.cornell.edu/—This Cornell University Law School site allows you to search by title and section, index of section headings, the GPO search engine, or the *CFR* table of contents.

- http://www.gpo.gov/fdsys/—This GPO site includes the *CFR* and a search engine for finding code sections.

e. Federal Register

The *Federal Register* is available at the Government Printing Office Web site, http://www .gpo.gov/fdsys.

4. Legislation

Information on federal legislation, including legislative history, is available at http://thomas. loc.gov, a site maintained by the Library of Congress. It includes information on legislation, the full text of the *Congressional Record,* and committee information.

Legislative history and presidential documents are also available at the site maintained by the Government Printing Office, http://www.access.gpo.gov.

5. Congress and Federal Agencies

The following is a partial list of URLs for Congress and various federal agencies. The URLs for Web sites of agencies not listed here may be accessed through the Library of Congress Web site, http://www.loc.gov/index.html.

- http://www.census.gov/—United States Census Bureau
- https://www.cia.gov/—Central Intelligence Agency
- http://www.cpsc.gov/—United States Consumer Product Safety Commission
- http://www.uspto.gov/—United States Department of Commerce/Patent and Trademark Office
- http://www.usdoj.gov/—United States Department of Justice
- http://www.dol.gov/—United States Department of Labor
- http://www.dot.gov/—United States Department of Transportation
- http://www.epa.gov/—United States Environmental Protection Agency
- http://www.faa.gov/—Federal Aviation Administration
- http://www.fbi.gov/—Federal Bureau of Investigation
- http://uscis.gov/—United States Citizenship and Immigration Services
- http://www.irs.ustreas.gov/—Internal Revenue Service
- http://www.loc.gov/—Library of Congress
- http://www.nhtsa.dot.gov/—National Highway Traffic Safety Administration
- http://www.sec.gov/—United States Securities and Exchange Commission
- http://www.ssa.gov/—Social Security Administration
- http://www.state.gov/index.html/—United States Department of State
- http://www.house.gov/—United States House of Representatives
- http://www.senate.gov/—United States Senate
- http://www.whitehouse.gov/—The White House

6. Presidential Materials

Presidential proclamations and executive orders are available on Westlaw and LexisNexis, as well as the Government Printing Office Web site, http://www.gpo.gov/fdsys. The site of The White House's virtual library is http://www.whitehouse.gov.

F. State Sources

The amount of state legal research material available through the Internet varies from state to state, as does the availability of **state sources**. Increasingly, states are providing primary authority (such as cases, statutes, constitutions, and administrative regulations) on or through the Web site of the highest state court.

Law-related material is usually available through Web sites of state courts, state governments, local law schools, and state bar associations. Consider accessing those sites when conducting a search within your state. The legal materials most commonly available are state statutes, court opinions, law reviews, and agency regulations. Space limitations prevent the listing of all Web sites for all the states. Following is a list of the Web addresses for sites that provide links to state sources:

- http://www.findlaw.com/—Through FindLaw, you can access state statutes, case law, administrative law, law schools, professional legal organizations, and some law reviews.
- http://www.lawsonline.com/—Laws Online provides links to state sources, including state codes.
- http://www.law.villanova.edu/—This Villanova University School of Law site provides links to state courts and court opinions.
- http://www.law.indiana.edu/—At the Indiana University Virtual Law Library, you can find information on many state sources and links to different specialty areas of law, such as family law.
- http://www.kentlaw.edu/—Access to instructions on finding online legal materials are available at this Chicago-Kent College of Law site. The site provides lists of state government and specialty areas such as health law.
- http://www.ncsc.org/—The National Center for State Courts Web site includes a list of state courts. You also can find other law-related Internet sites here.
- http://www.hg.org/—The site provides access to state and local government information on uniform laws, online journals, and other topics.
- http://www.courts.net/—This site provides access to Web sites maintained by courts nationwide.
- http://www.washlaw.edu/—Specifically for state statutes, this site includes links to state laws.
- http://www.statelocalgov.net/—Links to state government sources are available at this Piper Resources site.
- http://www.naag.org/—This site of the National Association of Attorneys General provides many state attorney general opinions.

G. Secondary Authority and Specialty Areas

Many secondary authority and other sources such as *ALR,* West's digests, and treatises are available only at commercial (fee-based) Web sites such as Westlaw and LexisNexis. Many secondary sources such as ***Shepard's*** are available on commercial Web sites and CD-ROM (see section III.J). However, many secondary and other materials in **specialty areas** are available on the Internet at no charge. These specialty area and secondary source materials are discussed here. A good source site for information and links to numerous sources for the specialty areas listed below may be found at the Rominger Legal Web site, http://www.romingerlegal.com. Another site for accessing information and research sources in numerous specialty areas is the LawyerExpress site at http://www.lawyerexpress.com.

1. Specialty Area Sources

Following is a list of legal topics, accompanied by Web sites where you can find information on each specific topic.

a. Administrative Law

The FindLaw site, http://www.findlaw.com/, provides access to federal administrative codes, regulations, orders, and agency rulings. State and local administrative laws are available through the Municipal Code Corporation site, http://www.municode.com. Administrative law research may be conducted through the American Bar Association's Administrative Procedure Database at http://www.law.fsu.edu/ (go to "Research Center," then "Research Resources," then "Legal Research Databases"). The GPO site, http://www.gpo.gov/fdsys, provides access to the *USC*, the *Code of Regulations,* the *Federal Register,* and numerous other documents. The *LSA: List of CFR Sections Affected* (the monthly pamphlet accompanying the *CFR*) is also available at the GPO site.

b. Arbitration and Mediation

At the FirstGov Web site, http://www.gpo.gov, you can locate numerous sources of information on arbitration and mediation. Type in either "arbitration" or "mediation" in the Search box on the home page.

c. Bankruptcy

At http://www.findlaw.com/, you may access information on the various types of bankruptcy and bankruptcy law and links to bankruptcy courts. InternNet Bankruptcy Library, http://bankrupt.com, provides access to publications and resource materials, and links to bankruptcy resources.

d. Civil Litigation

A directory of expert witnesses is available at http://www.jurispro.com/. A site that provides links to experts is http://www.expertpages.com. A site that includes information on damages is http://www.lawcatalog.com; type "damages" in the Search box for information sources concerning damages.

e. Civil Rights

The civil rights provisions of the *USC* may be found through FindLaw, http://www.findlaw.com. The Web site of the American Civil Liberties Union (ACLU), http://www.aclu.org/, provides extensive information on issues concerning civil rights.

f. Consumer Law

The site of the National Consumer Law Center, http://www.nclc.org, includes comprehensive information on consumer law.

g. Corporate Law

General information about corporate law is available through the LawyerExpress site, http:// www.lawyerexpress.com. State business and professional codes are available through the Cornell University Law School Web site, http://www.lawschool.cornell.edu. Information on thousands of companies is available at http://www.learnwebskills.com/company. Each state's office of the secretary of state has information on incorporating in a state. Forms and documents usually are available there as well. Secretary of state offices can be contacted through the state government Web site.

h. Criminal Law

Florida State University's College of Criminology and Criminal Justice site, http://www .criminology.fsu.edu, provides extensive information on criminal law. You can find links to criminal justice sites at the Institute for Law and Justice, http://www.ilj.org/.

i. Elder Law

Information concerning Medicare, Medicaid, rights of the elderly, and so on, may be researched at http://www.seniorlaw.com.

j. Environmental Law

The Web site of the Environmental Protection Agency is http://www.epa.gov. You can find links to environmental law resources at the WWW Virtual Library site, http://www.vlib.org.

k. Estate Planning

Consult state probate statutes when a research question involves estate planning. Those statutes are available through FindLaw, http://www.findlaw.com.

l. Family Law

The DivorceNet site, http://www.divorcenet.com, provides information on state divorce laws. Information on numerous family law matters, such as property issues, custody, and tax planning, is available at http://www.nolo.com/.

m. Immigration

The Citizenship and Immigration Services Web site is http://uscis.gov. Links to all types of material on immigration are available at http://www.immigrationdirect.com/. Immigration procedures, forms books, and other materials are available at http://www.us-immigration.com.

n. International Law

International legal resources are available at the site of the Cornell University Law School Legal Information Institute, http://www.lawschool.cornell.edu/, and at the United Nations System of Organizations site, http://www.unsystem.org/. Also see the American Society of International Law's *ASIL Guide to Electronic Resources for International Law* at http://www.asil.org/.

o. Intellectual Property and Copyright

The Web site of the United States Copyright Office is http://www.loc.gov/index.html. The United States Patent and Trademark Office site is http://www.uspto.gov. Information about copyrights is also available at the Copyright Clearance Center site, http://www .copyright.com.

p. Legal Documents and Forms

You may find legal documents and forms at several sites. Two popular sites are the 'Lectric Law Library, http://www.lectlaw.com/, and Legaldocs, http://www.legaldocs.com/. Links to form sources are provided at the sites of the Internet Legal Resource Group, http://www.ilrg .com/, and FindLaw, http://www.findlaw.com.

q. Legal Ethics

You can find links to sites providing information on legal ethics at http://www.lawschool .cornell.edu and http://www.legalethics.com.

r. Personal Injury

The National Highway Traffic Safety Administration (http://www.nhtsa.dot.gov) provides information on traffic safety, consumer complaints, and other facts. Data on consumer products are available at the United States Consumer Product Safety Commission, http://www .cpsc.gov. The Americans with Disabilities Act Document Center is located at http://www.jan .wvu.edu/. Medical information is available at the Virtual Medical Law Center, http://www .martindalecenter.com.

s. Real Property and Landlord Tenant Law

The National Association of Realtors site is http://www.realtor.com. The site provides links to a wide variety of sources on real estate matters. Nolo Press maintains a landlord and tenant site at http://www.nolo.com/.

t. Tax Law

The Web site of the Internal Revenue Service is http://www.irs.ustreas.gov/. Links to numerous tax law resources are available through The Tax Prophet Web site at http://www.taxprophet.com.

u. Uniform Commercial Code

Comprehensive information on the Uniform Commercial Code is available at the Cornell University Law School Legal Information site, http://www.lawschool.cornell.edu/. At the home page on the left side of the screen, select "Law about . . ."; then select "Commercial transactions" in the drop-down menu. In addition to the Uniform Commercial Code, the site provides links to state commercial code statutes and links to information about the UCC.

2. Secondary Authority and Other Sources

This section provides a list of some secondary authority and other source material sites that are available at nonfee-based Web sites.

a. Law Reviews, Journals, and Periodicals

Numerous law reviews, journals, and periodicals are available online. Many law schools publish their law reviews and journals. Some examples are the *Harvard Law Review,* at http://www.harvardlawreview.org; and the *Cornell Law Review,* at http://www.lawschool .cornell.edu.

Directories that provide links to law reviews and law journals include FindLaw at http://stu.findlaw.com/ and The University of Chicago D'Angelo Law Library at http://www .lib.uchicago.edu/. The University Law Review Project, http://www.lawreview.org, provides information on the availability of law reviews on the Internet. Also see Anderson's Directory of Law Reviews and Scholarly Legal Publications at http://www.lexisnexis.com/.

b. Legal Dictionaries

Links to legal dictionaries are available at http://www.duhaime.org/. Recently legal dictionaries have become available by wireless application for personal digital assistants (PDAs), smartphones, and tablets.

c. Legal Newspapers and Newsletters

You can access legal newspapers and newsletters online by using the name as a search term. Many can also be accessed through FindLaw at http://www.findlaw.com. Both the Washburn University School of Law Web site, http://www.washlaw.edu; and the Law News Network, http://www.law.com, provide links to legal newspapers, newsletters, and magazines.

d. Law Firms

Information on law firms and attorney locators is available through FindLaw at http://www.findlaw.com and Martindale-Hubbell at http://www.martindale.com.

e. Statistical Information

You can find statistical information about the federal courts online at http://www.uscourts.gov/publications.html. The Federal Bureau of Investigation's *Uniform Crime Reports* is available at http://www.fbi.gov. The Bureau of Justice Statistics provides information at http://www.ojp.usdoj.gov/bjs/.

f. Treaties

An extensive collection of treaties is available through the Treaties & International Agreements Researchers' Archive. It is available through subscription at http://www.oceanalaw.com.

g. Uniform State Laws and Model Acts

Uniform state laws and model acts are available at the National Conference of Commissioners on Uniform State Laws (NCCUSL) Web site, http://www.uniformlaws.org/. Access to information on uniform laws is also available through the University of Pennsylvania Law School Web site, http://www.law.upenn.edu/.

H. Listservs

A **listserv** is an e-mail discussion group that links people with common interests so they can share information on a topic or an area of expertise. To participate, you must subscribe to or join the group. Once you have joined a listserv discussion group, you can send (post) messages and receive messages from group members. When you post a message, it is available to all members who subscribe to the group. In essence, the information is public; it is not like private e-mail.

There are hundreds of discussion groups on various legal topics. Listservs are valuable because they allow you to receive the input of colleagues who are interested in and often experts on a certain legal topic. If you have difficulty in finding an answer to a legal question, you can post the question on a listserv and obtain an answer or guidance from other members of the group. However, you must always verify the information you receive.

There are two types of listservs: *unmoderated*, in which all messages by group members are sent to everyone in the group; and *moderated*, in which a message is sent to a moderator, who reviews the message and decides whether to return it to the sender, edit it and send it on to the group, or send it on to the group as is. The rules established by the group usually govern the activities of the moderator.

Two Web sites that provide information on legal listservs are the Washburn University School of Law site, http://washlaw.edu/; and the Westchester Library System site, http://www.westchesterlibraries.org/. E-mailing lists are also available through the Lyonette Louis-Jacques's Law Lists, http://www2.lib.uchicago.edu/.

I. Organizations

Following is a list of law-related **organizations** and associations. Additional organizations may be accessed through FindLaw.

- http://www.aallnet.org/—American Association of Law Libraries
- http://www.abanet.org/—American Bar Association
- http://www.aclu.org/—American Civil Liberties Union
- http://www.alanet.org/—Association of Legal Administrators
- http://www.aafpe.org/—American Association for Paralegal Education
- http://www.nala.org/—The National Association of Legal Assistants
- http://www.nals.org/—National Association of Legal Secretaries
- http://www.nass.org/—National Association of Secretaries of State
- http://www.paralegals.org/—National Federation of Paralegal Associations

1. State Bar Organizations

You can access state bar organizations by using a search engine and typing in the name of the state bar, such as "New York State Bar."

2. International Organizations

Following is a list of prominent international organizations:

- http://www.europa.eu/—European Union
- http://www.icj-cij.org/—International Court of Justice (World Court)
- http://www.oas.org/—Organization of American States
- http://www.un.org/—United Nations
- http://www.wto.org/—World Trade Organization

J. CD-ROM

Many legal research sources are still available on **CD-ROM** (compact disk, read-only memory). They include *American Jurisprudence 2d*, *ALR*, the *USCA, Shepard's*, state statutory and case law, treatises such as Wright and Miller's *Federal Practice and Procedure,* and practice aids such as *American Jurisprudence Legal Forms,* to name just a few. For obvious space-saving reasons, many law firms now purchase legal materials in CD-ROM form rather than as paper texts.

CD-ROMs are used with a computer like any compact disk. They have the advantage of allowing a researcher to conduct research at home, at court, or while on the road traveling, through the use of a laptop computer. Publishers usually update their CD-ROMs with replacement disks at regular intervals, such as monthly or quarterly. A disadvantage of CD-ROMs is that the material is only as current as the update. Many law libraries have research sources on CD-ROM, and as long as you are familiar with computerized research, it may be easier to perform your a search using a CD-ROM rather than a text if you are familiar with computerized research.

CD-ROMs, like texts, vary in their organization and search features. However, performing a search on most CD-ROMs is similar to performing a search on Westlaw or LexisNexis.

That is, a search may be conducted by citation, natural language, terms and connectors, and so forth. If the material is updated only monthly or quarterly, it may be necessary to update your research using Westlaw or LexisNexis for more timely information. For a list of law-related CD-ROM products, see the *Directory of Law-Related CD-ROMs,* a subscription service by Infosources Publishing, at http://www.infosourcespub.com. A reference book that includes a law-related CD-ROM product list is *Directory of Law-Related CD-ROMs* by Arelene L. Eis (Infosources Publishing).

K. WIRELESS APPLICATIONS

Some resources are becoming available through applications (apps) for wireless devices such as personal digital assistants, smartphones such as the iPhone, and tablets. Both Westlaw and Lexis have wireless applications that enable users to research cases, statutes, and validation tools. *Black's Law Dictionary* is also available through a wireless application. This accessibility is allowing legal practitioners to validate a case or get a statute, rule, or document quickly at a court proceeding recess or in the middle of settlement conferences or depositions.

IV. KEY POINTS CHECKLIST: *Computers and Legal Research*

✓ It is important to know how to research using print resources because electronic resources may not be available or may be too expensive. Electronic research systems are based on print resources, and a familiarity with print resources makes it easier to understand electronic research.

✓ The most frequently used commercial services are Westlaw and LexisNexis. A familiarity with either of these two services will provide you with sufficient information to use other services.

✓ The most critical step in the research process is framing the issue in the context of the specific facts of the case (see Chapters 10 and 11). A well-framed issue, stated in the context of the facts, provides a researcher with the information necessary to conduct research using natural language or terms and connectors.

✓ As with any research, it is essential to determine if the results of electronic research are still good law. Both Westlaw and LexisNexis include services that allow you to update your research.

✓ Nonfee-based online research sources do not have a contractual duty to provide information that is accurate or up to date. Verify the accuracy of any information you obtain from such sites and check to determine if the information is current.

✓ When using a CD-ROM, always check to see that the disk is current. It may be necessary to use another source to update the material.

V. APPLICATION

As James Redhorse learned in his legal research course, the first step of any research project is to identify the issue as concretely as possible in the context of the facts. He knows a concise statement of the issue will allow him to focus his search and identify the search terms. After considering the facts of the case and several drafts, his preliminary formulation of the issue is: "Under Arizona law, may damages for emotional distress be recovered when an individual traps and kills a neighbor's pet and shows the dead pet to the owner, causing the owner severe distress?" James knows the issue may become more refined as he conducts his research.

The next step is to determine where to look. Will he look for statutory law, case law, or secondary authority? Although research normally begins with a search for a governing statute, James knows that recovery for emotional distress is usually governed by tort law, and most torts are not statutory. He decides to check Arizona case law for a court opinion that has addressed this question.

Reviewing the issue, James concludes that a terms and connectors search should include *emotional distress, damages,* and *pet.* He chooses the Westlaw Arizona courts database and formulates his search query as -"emotional distress" & damages & pet-. The search results reveal no cases on point. This doesn't surprise James, because Arizona doesn't have a large body of case law. This means he will have to look to the law from other jurisdictions.

Rather than search state by state, James decides to look for an *ALR* article that addresses the subject. If there is one, it will provide an analysis of the question and include relevant state statutory law, case law, and secondary authority. He selects the *ALR* database and enters the query: "emotional distress" & damages & pet. The results show more than 180 documents.

James doesn't want to wade through that many annotations, so he decides to edit his query by restricting the search to the titles of those *ALR* annotations that include his search terms. He clicks on "edit query," and (using field restrictions) limits the search to titles that include the search terms. The query reads: TI ("emotional distress" & damages & pet). The search results in one annotation: *"Recovery of Damages for Emotional Distress Due to Treatment of Pets and Animals"* by Jay M. Zitter, 91 A.L.R.5th 545.

This annotation answers the question. It summarizes all the case and statutory law that has addressed this question. It reveals that some states allow damages for emotional distress for the loss of a pet and some do not. With this information, James can review the cases that are factually close to Mrs. Burgess's case and prepare a memorandum to the senior partner summarizing the law.

Summary

The earlier chapters of the text focus on the techniques for conducting research using print resources such as texts and bound volumes. This chapter discusses research using electronic resources. It is important, however, to know how to research using print resources for at least four reasons:

1. A familiarity with the print source makes it much easier to understand the structure of the electronic database and conduct electronic research.

2. The material you are looking for may not be in an electronic database.

3. On occasion, access to electronic research is unavailable, such as when the local server is down.

4. Cost concerns may limit the amount of time you can spend using commercial electronic services.

Experienced researchers do not rely exclusively on computer-assisted legal research.

This chapter presents an overview of legal research done through the most frequently used commercial services: Westlaw and LexisNexis. Although many other electronic research services are available, a familiarity with either of these two provides sufficient information to use the other services.

Despite the differences between LexisNexis and Westlaw, the basic organization and research principles are the same. Both services share the following features:

- Documents may be located by name, title, or citation.

- Documents may be located by natural language, a search method that allows you to state the search query using plain English.

- Documents may be located by using terms and connectors.

- Searches may be conducted through reference to the table of contents of research sources.

- Documents may be located by focusing research on specific areas of law through Westlaw's Key Number and KeySearch services, and LexisNexis's Search Advisor.
- Research may be updated through the use of Westlaw's KeyCite or LexisNexis's *Shepard's* services.

In addition to Westlaw and LexisNexis, there are other commercial Web-based legal research services. Two services with less comprehensive databases are Loislaw and VersusLaw.

Thousands of nonfee-based Web sites provide access to various types of legal information online. There are no laws or regulations governing the accuracy of the content of nonfee-based Web sites; therefore, they do not have a legal duty to provide information that is accurate or up to date. You must verify the accuracy and determine if any information you obtain from such sites is current. When selecting a nonfee-based site, always consider the author and publisher and the content of the information, and check the site to determine how frequently the information is updated.

A limitation of most nonfee-based Internet sources is that they do not have databases as extensive as those offered by the commercial sources. Many sites that provide statutory law do not include the annotations. Many sites that provide access to case law do not allow searches based on search words or terms (Boolean searches).

This chapter discusses and lists the Web addresses (URLs) for many nonfee-based Web sites that provide access to various types of legal information. Included are federal and state government Web sites, secondary authority and specialty area sources, and e-mail discussion groups (listservs). The chapter closes with a discussion of CD-ROMs.

Quick References

Citation

The 18th edition of *The Bluebook* and the current edition of the *ALWD Citation Manual: A Professional System of Citation* provide that if the authority is readily available in print, you should cite to the print source. It is not necessary to reference the electronic source, such as Westlaw or LexisNexis. This rule applies unless the documents are not available in a printed source or are difficult to obtain, such as unpublished cases. See the discussion of citation to electronic sources in Chapter 8.

Exercises

Additional assignments are available on the CourseMate.
For assignments 1 through 4, use Westlaw.

ASSIGNMENT 1

The client is the chairman of the board of directors of an Ohio corporation. The board of directors has decided to merge the corporation with another Ohio corporation. The client wishes to know if shareholder approval is required for the merger. Identify the Ohio statute that governs this question and what it provides concerning shareholder approval.

ASSIGNMENT 2

Perform assignment 1 using your own state's law.

ASSIGNMENT 3

Your supervising attorney recalls that there was a 1989 Arkansas case in which a county court judge was convicted in federal court of vote buying. After the United States Court of Appeals denied the appeal, the state circuit court declared the judge ineligible to hold public office. The judge claimed that he had received insufficient notice of the state court hearing because he had less than a 24-hour notice to appear at the hearing. What is the name and citation of the case? Under the holding of the case, when is a person "convicted" for purposes of removal of a public official from office?

ASSIGNMENT 4

What is the citation of a 1993 *ALR* annotation that discusses the admissibility of polygraph test results in an action for malicious prosecution? What *Am. Jur. 2d* evidence research references are listed? To what malicious prosecution key numbers does the citation refer?
For assignments 5 through 7, use LexisNexis.

ASSIGNMENT 5

While the client was walking her dog in a city park, the client's dog was attacked by another dog. Before the dogs could be separated, the client's dog was severely injured, and it died later that day. The client's dog was on a leash, and the other dog was not leashed. The client was very close to her pet, and she wants to sue the owner of the other dog for the emotional distress she suffered as a result of witnessing the attack and death of her pet. Your supervisory attorney remembers that there was an Arizona case, with similar facts, in which recovery was denied. Find the Arizona case.

ASSIGNMENT 6

There is a question in the client's negligence case as to whether an intervening force may cut off the client's right to recover. What *Restatement 2d* sections define *intervening force* and *superseding cause?* How are the terms defined?

ASSIGNMENT 7

The client and her husband are residents of the state of Georgia. She wants to sue for divorce claiming adultery. She does not want to file a no-fault divorce. Is adultery a ground for divorce in Georgia? If so, what is the statute and what does it provide? What law review article presents a survey of Georgia cases dealing with domestic relations?
For assignments 8 through 15, use nonfee-based Internet sites.

ASSIGNMENT 8

The client is a shareholder of a corporation in Tennessee. What is required for an action to be taken by shareholders without a meeting?

ASSIGNMENT 9

Perform assignment 8 using your state's law.

ASSIGNMENT 10

Using the Cornell Law School Web site, locate a 1998 United States Supreme Court case from the state of Minnesota that involved a warrantless search.

ASSIGNMENT 11

The Hobbes Bridge Act is included in which section of the *United States Code?*

ASSIGNMENT 12

What is the fee charged by the United States District Courts for a search of the court records?

ASSIGNMENT 13

Under the Federal Rules of Civil Procedure, must leave of the court be obtained to take the deposition of a person detained in prison? Include the rule citation.

ASSIGNMENT 14

How is "claim" defined in National Park Services regulations dealing with minerals management? Include the *CFR* citation.

ASSIGNMENT 15

What was the topic of the Federal Reserve notice issued on January 2, 2004 (published in the *Federal Register*)?

The available CourseMate for this text has an interactive eBook and interactive learning tools, including flash cards, quizzes, and more. To learn more about this resource and access free demo CourseMate resources, go to **www.cengagebrain.com,** and search for this book. To access CourseMate materials that you have purchased, go to **login.cengagebrain.com.**

CHAPTER 8

Legal Citation

Learning Objectives

After completing this chapter, you should understand:

- The specific citation rules that apply when citing primary authority—that is, case, constitutional, and enacted (statutory) law

- The specific citation rules that apply when citing secondary authority

- The general citation rules that apply when citing most types of legal sources

Mike Myers is a second-semester paralegal student enrolled in an introductory research and writing class. Following a six-week introduction to basic research, the class assignment is to draft a simple, one-issue legal research memorandum. The assignment involves the question of when a mother can lose her parental rights due to drug use and other misconduct. Students must include parallel citations in the case citations in the memo. The instructor divides the class into groups, and the assignment for Mike's group is to answer the question using Georgia law. Based on two Georgia cases and one statute, Mike prepares the rough draft of the memo. For the final draft, he ensures his citations are correctly formatted. Mike's authorities and the steps he takes to ensure the citation formats are correct are discussed in the Application section of this chapter.

I. INTRODUCTION

A. In General

The discussions in Chapter 3 through Chapter 7 address how to find primary and secondary authority. This chapter discusses how to present authority once you find it. Whenever a reference is made in legal writing to the law (primary authority) or to a nonlaw source upon which a court may rely (secondary authority), you must identify the source of the reference. As the writer, you cannot simply say, "This is what the law provides," without referencing the legal authority that supports the statement. Thus, when making an argument that a certain legal principle governs a particular set of facts or a legal question, you must reference the source of the principle. This reference is called a **citation**.

A citation provides the information necessary for the reader to locate the reference (the specific statute, court opinion, law review, encyclopedia, etc.) in order to check its content. Citations are usually required in office legal memoranda, court briefs, and scholarly writings such as law review articles. They may also be included in general legal correspondence or other documents when there is reference to legal authority.

It is essential that the information included in a citation be correct. The writer serves no purpose by referring a reader to a source of information and incorrectly identifying the location of that source. The reader will not be pleased if he or she takes the time to look up the authority and finds that the authority is not located at the page or volume indicated in the citation. There are several additional reasons why it is important that your citations be correct:

- A citation that is incorrect in form or content sends the message that the drafter either is not careful or lacks education. If there are errors in citation, the reader may wonder if there are also errors in the substance of the research.

- Errors in documents submitted to a court may cause the judge to question the competence of the attorney and the quality and content of the research and analysis. Court rules require proper form, and improper citation exhibits a disregard for those rules and disrespect for the court.

- Opposing counsel may question the attorney's ability to mount an effective opposition and be less inclined to settle a case.

- The writer's research and analysis skills may become suspect if research sources are not properly presented. Professional reputation is often determined by the quality of one's work product.

B. The *Bluebook* and the *ALWD Citation Manual*

Unfortunately, no standard set of rules governing citation form has been adopted by all the jurisdictions in the United States. The main guide and source of authority on legal citations for the past 75 years has been *The Bluebook: A Uniform System of Citation (Bluebook)* published by the Harvard Law Review Association. It presents the rules and proper format for citing constitutions, statutes, regulations, rules, cases, and other legal sources such as legal encyclopedias and law reviews. Some states have adopted the *Bluebook* in whole or in part as the official citation reference for pleadings and papers filed in the state courts. Most states, though, have adopted at least some citation rules that differ from the *Bluebook*, especially in the area of citation to state court opinions and statutes. Therefore, *it is necessary to check the state rules whenever you are preparing a document to be submitted to a court.*

The *Bluebook* is not designed as a teaching tool; and many students, instructors, and practitioners find it difficult to use. As an alternative to the *Bluebook*, the Association of Legal Writing Directors created the *ALWD Citation Manual: A Professional System of Citation (ALWD)*. The association's members are professors from nearly all American law schools.

An authority on American legal citation, Professor and Associate Dean Darby Dickerson, of the Stetson University College of Law, drafted the *ALWD*. Aspen Publishers published the first edition in 2000. It is designed to be easy to understand and use by providing a single set of rules for all forms of legal writing. Within three months of its publication, the manual was adopted by 80 law schools and more than 35 paralegal schools.

At the time of this publication, the *Bluebook* and the *ALWD* are the primary sources for rules on citation used by law and paralegal schools. Inasmuch as the *Bluebook* is composed of 512 pages and the *ALWD* 661 pages, a detailed discussion of the citation rules of either text is beyond the scope of this chapter. The following discussion presents a brief review of the main rules of citation with references to rules from both the *ALWD* and the *Bluebook*. The goal of the chapter is to provide you with quick access to the main rules of citation in either authority. The discussion and examples are based on *The Bluebook: A Uniform System of Citation* (19th ed., 2010) and the *ALWD Citation Manual: A Professional System of Citation* (4th ed., 2010).

The format of both texts begins with an introduction, followed by the basic rules of citation, then citation form for primary sources (cases, constitutions, and statutes) and secondary sources. Because researchers most frequently refer to the citation rules for primary and secondary authority, the chapter presents those rules first, followed by the general rules of citation.

The *Bluebook* notes differences between the citation format used when citing authorities in court documents and legal memoranda and the citation format used in scholarly pieces such as law review articles. Most of the differences involve the use of different typefaces. In the *ALWD*, the same format is used for all types of documents. The type of formal legal writing usually engaged in by practitioners, law students, and paralegals involves court documents and legal memoranda rather than law review articles. Therefore, this chapter focuses on the citation format used in court documents and legal memoranda, and the examples are to citation forms used in those types of legal writing.

Most of the examples provided in the white pages of the *Bluebook* are for citation when writing a law review. The light blue pages of the *Bluebook*, called "Bluepages," provide guidance on how to adapt the examples found throughout the body of the *Bluebook* to the drafting of legal memoranda and court documents. There are cross-references to the Bluepages in the margins of the *Bluebook* rules and tables. Also, at the end of the *Bluebook* is a "Quick Reference" section that provides examples of citation forms commonly used in court documents and legal memoranda.

II. PRIMARY AUTHORITY

This section presents an overview of rules of citation to be used when citing primary authority, that is, case, constitutional, and enacted (statutory) law. The citation format for rules, such as procedural and evidentiary rules, is also included in this section. The examples are to citation forms used in court documents and legal memoranda rather than law review articles. See Exhibit 8-1 for a list of the primary authority sources and the citation rule references.

The rules discussed in this section and in the following sections are referenced as follows: References to *The Bluebook: A Uniform System of Citation* are Bluebook R-___ (rule number) or Bluebook B-___ (Bluepages number); references to the *ALWD Citation Manual: A Professional System of Citation* are ALWD-___ (rule number).

For Example   Bluebook R-2 refers to rule 2 of the *Bluebook*. Bluebook B-1 refers to number 1 of the *Bluebook's* Bluepages. ALWD-1 refers to rule 1 of the *ALWD*.

Exhibit 8-1 *Primary and Secondary Authority Citation Rule References.*

Primary Authority Citation Rules		
Authority	*Bluebook* Rules and Bluepages Notes	ALWD Rules
Case Law	R-10 and B-5	ALWD-12
Constitutions	R-11 and B-7	ALWD-13
Statutory Law	R-12 and B-5	ALWD-14
Rules of Evidence and Procedure	R-12.8.3	ALWD-17
Administrative Law	R-14	ALWD-19
Secondary Authority Citation Rules		
American Law Reports (ALR)	R-16.6.5	ALWD-24
Dictionaries	R-15.7	ALWD-25
Legal Encyclopedias	R-15.7	ALWD-26
Periodicals (Law Reviews, etc.)	R-16	ALWD-23
Restatements	R-12.8.5	ALWD-27
Treatises/Books	R-15	ALWD-22

© Cengage Learning 2014

Note that although most of the citation conventions are the same in both manuals, there are differences between *Bluebook* and *ALWD*. Do not assume that you can substitute one for the other.

The general rules governing each type of primary authority are listed following the subsection title. A detailed discussion of each rule is beyond the scope of this text.

If the citation rules of the jurisdiction where you are filing a brief or other court document require the use of the *Bluebook*, then you must cite according to the *Bluebook* rules. Do not substitute the *ALWD* format if it differs from the *Bluebook*.

A. Case Law—Bluebook R-10, B-2, B-5; ALWD-12

Following is a list of the components of case citations with examples and a summary of the applicable rules. Citations to federal and state cases are similar in form.

1. Citation Components—Bluebook R-10.1; ALWD-12.1

The components of a case citation are as follows:

1. Case name
2. Reporter in which the case is published (volume number, abbreviation of the reporter, and page number on which the case begins)
3. Pinpoint page if the citation is to a specific page
4. Parallel (unofficial) publication, if any (volume number, abbreviation of the publication, and page number on which the case begins)
5. Abbreviation for the court issuing the opinion, unless the issuing court is included in the reporter abbreviation

6. Year of the decision (in parentheses)

7. Subsequent history of the case, if any

Some examples are presented first with a space (^) symbol indicating where spaces are placed, followed by the example without the space symbol.

For Example | *Federal Court Decisions*

United States Supreme Court

United ^ States ^ v. ^ Matlock, ^ 415 ^ U.S. ^ 164 ^ (1974)

United States v. Matlock, 415 U.S. 164 (1974)

1. *United States v. Matlock* is the case name.

2. 415 U.S. 164 is the reporter in which the case is published: 415 is the volume number, 164 is the page number, and U.S. is the abbreviation of the case reporter.

3. No parallel publication is included in this citation.

4. The court issuing the opinion is not identified because it is apparent from the citation. *U.S. Reports* contains the opinions of the United States Supreme Court. Notice that in the next two examples, the identity of the court issuing the opinion is included: 9th Cir. and N.D. Ill.

5. The year 1974 is the year the decision was issued.

United States Court of Appeals

United ^ States ^ v. ^ Martinez-Jiminez, ^ 864 ^ F.2d ^ 664 ^ (9th ^ Cir. ^ 1989)

United States v. Martinez-Jiminez, 864 F.2d 664 (9th Cir. 1989)

United States District Court

United ^ States ^ v. ^ Central ^ R.R., ^ 436 ^ F. ^ Supp. ^ 739 ^ (N.D. ^ Ill. ^ 1990)

United States v. Central R.R., 436 F. Supp. 739 (N.D. Ill. 1990)

State Court Decisions

Britton ^ v. ^ Britton, ^ 100 ^ N.M. ^ 424, ^ 671 ^ P.2d ^ 1135 ^ (1983)

Britton v. Britton, 100 N.M. 424, 671 P.2d 1135 (1983)

Burnon ^ v. ^ State, ^ 55 ^ S.W.3d ^ 752 ^ (Tex. ^ Crim. ^ App. ^ 2001)

Burnon v. State, 55 S.W.3d 752 (Tex. Crim. App. 2001)

1. *Britton v. Britton* and *Burnon v. State* are the case names.

2. 100 N.M. 424 is the state reporter in which the case is published: 100 is the volume number, 424 is the page number, and N.M. is the abbreviation of the case reporter; 55 S.W.3d 752 is the regional reporter in which the Texas cases are published. Texas does not have a state reporter; therefore, there is no parallel citation.

3. 671 P.2d 1135 is the parallel (unofficial) publication: 671 is the volume number, 1135 is the page number, and P.2d is the abbreviation of the parallel publication.

4. The New Mexico court issuing the opinion is not identified because it is apparent from the citation. The decision was rendered by the New Mexico Supreme Court. If a court other than the New Mexico Supreme Court issued the decision, the abbreviation for that court would be included with the year of the opinion; for example: (Ct. App. 1983). Tex. Crim. App. is the Texas court that rendered the decision.

5. The years 1983 and 2001 are the dates of the decisions.

2. Case Names—Bluebook R-10.2; ALWD-12.2

The *Bluebook's* rules for abbreviating case names have more exceptions than those of the *ALWD,* but both books have numerous detailed rules governing case names. *Always check the rules when preparing case citations.* Following is a summary of the rules on case names. The case names may be italicized or underscored. The names are italicized in most of the examples in this chapter. (The *ALWD* states that case names should be printed [styled] the same in court documents as in other documents.)

a. Individual Names

Cite the last names of the individuals, not the first names.

For Example	Correct: *Clothier v. Guillez*
	Incorrect: *Daniel J. Clothier v. Mary Guillez*

b. Organization and Business Names

Include an organization's full name. When a business has more than one legal designation (e.g., Co., Ltd. Corp., or Inc.), use the first designation and omit the others.

For Example	Correct: *Clothier v. David Johnson Packing Co.*
	Incorrect: *Clothier v. Johnson*
Correct: *Davis v. Sally Smits Co.*	
Incorrect: *Davis v. Sally Smits Co., Inc.*	

When an organization or a business is commonly known by its initials, you may substitute the initials for the name. Do not use periods with the initials.

For Example	Correct: *ACLU v. Houseman*
	Incorrect: *A.C.L.U. v. Houseman*

c. Abbreviations

The abbreviations used in party names are presented in Table T.6 of the *Bluebook* and in Appendix 3 of the *ALWD.* Do not abbreviate names that are not listed.

For Example	Corporation—Corp.; Market—Mkt.

d. Multiple Parties

When there are multiple plaintiffs or defendants, include only the first party on each side of the case. Do not use *et al.* or *et ux.* to indicate additional parties.

For Example	Correct: *Pugh v. Holmes*
	Incorrect: *Pugh, Smith, Reasoner v. Holmes, Taylor, Johnson*
Incorrect: *Pugh, et al. v. Holmes, et al.*	

e. Consolidated Cases

When a case consists of more than one case consolidated together, list only the first case.

> **For Example** Correct: *Davis v. Outland*
>
> Incorrect: *Davis v. Outland, McCray v. Whensal*

f. United States

When the United States is a party, both the *Bluebook* and the *ALWD* state that *"of America"* should be omitted. The *Bluebook* requires that *United States* be spelled out. The *ALWD* states that it should be abbreviated.

> **For Example** *Bluebook* format: *United States v. Leon*
>
> *ALWD* format: *U.S. v. Leon*

g. State or Commonwealth

When citing a decision of a court of your state in which the state or commonwealth is a party, refer only to the state, commonwealth, or people. Do not add the state name, such as *State of Colorado* or *Commonwealth of Massachusetts.*

> **For Example** Correct: *State v. Benner*
>
> Incorrect: *State of Maine v. Benner*
>
> Correct: *Commonwealth v. Shae*
>
> Incorrect: *Commonwealth of Massachusetts v. Shae*

When you are referring to the decision of another state in which the state or commonwealth is a party, refer to the party by state name and do not include *State of* or *Commonwealth of.*

> **For Example** Correct: *Maine v. Benner*
>
> Incorrect: *State v. Benner*
>
> Correct: *Massachusetts v. Shae*
>
> Incorrect: *Commonwealth of Massachusetts v. Shae*

h. Geographical Terms

Include in the citation only the first geographical location in a party's name.

> **For Example** Correct: *Smith v. City of Boston*
>
> Incorrect: *Smith v. City of Boston, Massachusetts*
>
> Correct: *Smith v. County Commission*
>
> Incorrect: *Smith v. County Commission of Johnson County*

i. Procedural Phrases—*In re*, *Ex parte*, and *Ex rel.*

In re refers to an action that does not involve adversarial parties, but something such as an estate. *Ex parte* refers to an action on behalf of one party without contest by the other side, such as a divorce in which one party does not participate. *Ex rel.* refers to an action by one person on behalf of another, such as a parent on behalf of a child. When using *ex rel.,* include the names of both parties. These phrases are included when they appear in case names.

For Example	*In re Estate of Jones; Ex parte Turner; New York ex rel. Smith v. Hardworth; Johnson ex rel. Casey v. Carrington*

j. The

Do not include *the* in a citation when it is the first word of a party name.

For Example	Correct: *Los Angeles Times v. Jones*
	Incorrect: *The Los Angeles Times v. Jones*

k. Property

When property is a party, such as when the government is seizing property, include only the first-listed piece of property.

For Example	Correct: *Maine v. One 1998 Cadillac Seville*
	Incorrect: *Maine v. One 1998 Cadillac Seville, Serial No. 134998, and One 2001 Toyota Corolla, Serial No. 77564432*

l. Punctuation

The case name is followed by a comma (then the reporter information); the comma is not italicized or underscored.

For Example	Correct: *Smith v. Jones,* or <u>Smith v. Jones</u>,
	Incorrect: *Smith v. Jones,* or <u>Smith v. Jones,</u>

m. Citations as Part of a Sentence

See section IV.D.2.f in this chapter.

3. Volume, Reporter, and Page—Bluebook R-10.3; ALWD-12.3 to ALWD-12.5

Following the case name in a citation is the reference to the reporter in which the case is printed. This reference includes the volume number of the reporter and the page on which the case begins. The volume number precedes the abbreviation for the reporter, followed by the page number of the case. Following is a summary of the rules governing citation to reporters. Note that local court rules may require differences in citation; therefore, always check the rules.

a. Abbreviations

Do not assume you know the abbreviations for the various reporters. Always consult *Bluebook* Table T.1 or *ALWD* Chart 12.1 and Appendix 2. Also refer to the general rules governing abbreviations presented in section IV.D in this chapter.

b. Spacing

Refer to the general rules governing spacing presented in section IV.D.2 in this chapter.

c. United States Supreme Court

Unless required by local rule, citation to decisions of the United States Supreme Court should be to the official reporter only, the *United States Reports*. A parallel citation to another reporter, such as the *Supreme Court Reporter* or *United States Supreme Court Reports, Lawyers' Edition*, should not be included.

> **For Example**   Correct: *United States v. Matlock,* 415 U.S. 164 (1974)
>
> Incorrect: *United States v. Matlock,* 415 U.S. 164, 94 S. Ct. 988, 39 L. Ed. 2d 242 (1974)
>
> Note that the second example would be correct if the court rule required or allowed parallel citations.

When the *United States Reports* citation is not available, then cite to another reporter, such as the *Supreme Court Reporter* (S. Ct.). The preference is to cite to the *Supreme Court Reporter;* when it is not available, cite to *United States Supreme Court Reports, Lawyers' Edition*.

> **For Example**   If the opinion in the previous example was not yet available in the *United States Reports,* a proper citation would be *United States v. Matlock,* __U.S.__, 94 S. Ct. 988 (1974).

d. United States Court of Appeals

Decisions of the United States Court of Appeals are cited to the *Federal Reporter*. Note that the circuit that rendered the decision is included in parentheses in the citation.

> **For Example**   *United States v. Martinez-Jiminez,* 864 F.2d 664 (9th Cir. 1989)

e. United States District Courts

Decisions of the United States District Courts are cited to the *Federal Supplement*. Note that the district that rendered the decision is included in parentheses in the citation.

> **For Example**   *United States v. Central R.R.,* 436 F. Supp. 739 (N.D. Ill. 1990)

f. State Court and Parallel Citations

The format and abbreviations for citing state court decisions are presented in Table T.1 of the *Bluebook* and in Appendix 1 of the *ALWD*. Again, make sure you check local rules. The general rule for state court decisions is to cite to the relevant regional reporter.

> **For Example** | *Guilbear v. Guilbear,* 326 So. 2d 654 (La. Ct. App. 1976)

Many state court decisions are published in both a regional reporter and a state reporter. When a citation includes a reference to more than one reporter, it is called a *parallel citation*. Generally, a parallel citation is used only when a citation to a state court case is used in a document submitted to a court in that state. Check the state court citation rules to determine when parallel citations are required.

When a parallel citation is required, cite the official reporter before the unofficial reporter and separate each citation with a comma and one space.

> **For Example** | *Race Fork Coal v. Turner,* 5 Va. App. 350, 363 S.E.2d 423 (1985)

g. Page Numbers

The page number on which the case begins follows the reporter abbreviation. When the reference is to a specific page within the case, the reference to the specific page (*pinpoint citation*) follows the initial page reference. See section IV.G in this chapter.

> **For Example** | *Guilbear v. Guilbear,* 326 So. 2d 654, 658 (La. Ct. App. 1976)
>
> *Race Fork Coal v. Turner*, 5 Va. App. 350, 352, 363 S.E.2d 423, 425 (1985)
> Note that in the second example, the pinpoint citation is included with both the state and parallel regional reporter citations.

Some of the West reporters, such as the *Supreme Court Reports,* include throughout the text of reported cases cross-references to the pages in the official reporter. This cross-reference system is called **star paging**. It saves you time looking up a case in more than one reporter when citing page numbers in parallel citations. The cross-reference appears as an upside-down *T* with the page number (⊥234) and is inserted in the text to indicate the beginning of a page in an official reporter.

> **For Example** | "Thus, the tolling provision does ⊥234 not apply, and count two is subject to the two-year statute of limitations and was properly dismissed."
> Page 234 of the official reporter begins with "not apply."

h. Cases Not Yet Reported—Slip Opinions

A case may be unreported or not yet published in a reporter and may be available only as a separate slip opinion or in loose-leaf form. In this situation, the citation should include the case name, docket number, court abbreviation, and date of disposition.

> **For Example** | *Jason v. Kelly,* No. 22-231 (Colo. App. Aug. 15, 2002)

4. Date and Court Abbreviation—Bluebook R-10.4, R-10.5; ALWD-12.5, ALWD-12.6

In parentheses following the reporter and page citation are the court abbreviation (if necessary) and the date on which the case was decided. When the decision is by the United States Supreme Court or highest court of a state, you do not have to insert the court abbreviation.

The date appears by itself in parentheses. The fact that only the date appears in parentheses tells the reader that the opinion is from the highest court. The information in parentheses is separated from the reporter page by a space. No comma is used.

For Example	*United States v. Matlock,* 415 U.S. 164 (1974)
	Kline v. Angle, 216 Kan. 328, 532 P.2d 1093 (1975)

For any other court decision, include the court abbreviation. The abbreviations are in *Bluebook* Table T.1, Table T.7, and Table T.10, and in *ALWD* Appendix 1 and Appendix 4.

For Example	*United States v. Central R.R.,* 436 F. Supp. 739 (N.D. III. 1990)
	Burnon v. State, 55 S.W.3d 752 (Tex. Crim. App. 2001)

The court abbreviation is not required when the court that decided the case is apparent from the name of the reporter.

For Example	*Race Fork Coal v. Turner,* 5 Va. App. 350, 353, 363 S.E.2d 423, 425 (1985). It is apparent from the citation (Va. App.) that the court is the Virginia Court of Appeals.

5. Subsequent History—Bluebook R-10.7; ALWD-12.8

The *Bluebook* and the *ALWD* state that the subsequent history should be included in the citation unless it refers to the history on remand, a denial of rehearing, or a denial of certiorari or similar discretionary appeals (where the cited case is more than two years old). ALWD-12.8(a) includes an exhaustive list of subsequent history actions that should be included. The subsequent history is placed after the full citation. Place a comma after the court and date parenthetical; then include the italicized history designation, a comma, and the citation.

For Example	*Jackson v. State,* 225 Ga. 790, 167 S.E.2d 628 (1969), *rev'd, Furman v. Georgia,* 408 U.S. 238 (1972)

6. Prior History—Bluebook R-10.7; ALWD-12.9

The prior history of a case is not required and should be included in a citation only when it is significant to a point presented in your writing. Place the prior history after the full citation.

For Example	*Furman v. Georgia,* 408 U.S. 238 (1972), *rev'g Jackson v. State,* 225 Ga. 790, 167 S.E.2d 628 (1969)

7. Parenthetical Information: Concurring, Dissenting, and Plurality Opinion—Bluebook R-10.6; ALWD-12.11

If the reference in your writing is to part of an opinion other than the majority opinion, you must so indicate in a parenthetical following the full citation. You also may include, within parentheses, information about the weight of the case, such as the size of the majority. Insert one space, without a comma, between the court and date parenthetical of the full citation and the parenthetical containing the additional information. When the information in the parenthetical is not a full sentence, do not include final punctuation, such as a period in the parenthetical.

> **For Example**   *United States v. Leon,* 468 U.S. 897 (1984) (Powell, J., dissenting); *United States v. Leon,* 468 U.S. 897 (1984) (5-4 decision)

8. Short Citation Format—Bluebook B-5.2; ALWD-12.21

Once a case has been cited in full, several short citation formats may be used depending on the situation. Do not include subsequent or prior history with a short citation. When the use of *id.* is appropriate (see section IV.I in this chapter), use it as the preferred short citation format.

> **For Example**   *Id.* at 755

When *id.* cannot be used and the case name or part of the case name is *not* included in the sentence, use one party's name, the volume number, the reporter, and the page reference. Use the first party's name unless doing so would be confusing.

> **For Example**   Full citation: *Burnon v. State,* 55 S.W.3d 752 (Tex. Crim. App. 2001)
> Short citation: *Burnon,* 55 S.W.3d at 755

When making a reference to the case in general rather than to a specific page, do not use *at.*

> **For Example**   Full citation: *Burnon v. State,* 55 S.W.3d 752 (Tex. Crim. App. 2001)
> Short citation: *Burnon,* 55 S.W.3d 752

When the case name or part of the case name *is* included in the sentence, use only the volume number, reporter, and page reference.

> **For Example**   In *Burnon,* the court held that the defendant had the required intent. 55 S.W.3d at 755 (or 55 S.W.3d 752 when the reference is to the case in general).

When the case has a parallel citation, the short citation includes the parallel citations.

> **For Example**   Full citation: *Race Fork Coal v. Turner,* 5 Va. App. 350, 363 S.E.2d 423 (1985)
> Short citation: *Race Fork Coal,* 5 Va. App. at 355, 363 S.E.2d at 427
> The *ALWD* also allows reference to the regional reporter only: *Race Fork Coal,* 363 S.E.2d at 427.

Bluepages B-5.2 allows the use of *id.* as a short form with parallel citations. ALWD-12.21(f) states that the use of *id.* is not appropriate with parallel citations.

> **For Example** Full citation: *Race Fork Coal v. Turner,* 5 Va. App. 350, 363 S.E.2d 423 (1985)
>
> Short citation: *Bluebook: Id.* at 355, 363 S.E.2d at 427

9. Neutral/Public Domain Citations—Bluebook R-10.3.3; ALWD-12.16

Increasingly, court decisions are available through court Web sites and other sources, such as public domain citations (also referred to as *neutral* or *vendor-neutral citations*). These citations do not refer to a particular vendor source, such as a West reporter. When such citations are available in a jurisdiction, check the local rule to determine what the citation format is and whether the neutral citation is required. See *Bluebook* Table T.1 and *ALWD* Appendix 2. The standard neutral citation includes the case name, year of the decision, court abbreviation, case number, and citation to a reporter or online source.

> **For Example** *State v. Foster,* 1998-NMCA-163, 976 P.2d 852. The year published is 1998. NMCA is the court, the New Mexico Court of Appeals. The last number, 163, is the case number. The reporter citation is 976 P.2d 852.

10. Cases—Electronic Sources

See section IV.M in this chapter for citations to electronic sources.

B. Constitutions—Bluebook R-11; ALWD-13

Constitutions usually are composed of articles and amendments. According to the *Bluebook,* the citation form for a constitution consists of the abbreviated name of the constitution, the article or amendment number, and the section number. The *ALWD* requires the abbreviated name of the constitution and a pinpoint reference (the article or amendment number and the section number). Regardless of those descriptive differences, the citation format is the same in both the *Bluebook* and the *ALWD.* The *Bluebook* states that constitutional subdivisions should be abbreviated according to Table T.16; the *ALWD* states that the jurisdictional and subdivision abbreviations in Appendix 3 should be used. Each example is presented first with a space (^) symbol indicating where spaces are placed, followed by the example without the space symbol.

> **For Example** U.S. ^ Const. ^ art. ^ IV ^ § ^ 3
>
> U.S. Const. art. IV § 3
>
> Conn. ^ Const. ^ art ^ XII ^ § ^ 1
>
> Conn. Const. art. XII § 1

In the examples, the elements of the citation are as follows:

1. U.S. Const. and Conn. Const. are the abbreviated names.
2. art. IV and art. XII are the article numbers.
3. § 3 and § 1 indicate the section numbers (pinpoint references).

Include in parentheses information about an article or amendment when the provision has been repealed or superseded.

> **For Example** U.S. Const. amend XVIII (repealed 1933 by U.S. Const. amend. XXI)

The only short-form citation appropriate for use with constitutional citations is *id.* When the use of *id.* is not appropriate (see section IV.I in this chapter), the full citation must be given.

C. Statutory Law—Bluebook R-12, B-6; ALWD-14

Statutes may be cited to the official or unofficial code, session law, or secondary sources. The preference is to cite to the official code, then to the unofficial code if the citation is not available in the official code. When the citation is not available in either the official or unofficial codes, cite to the session law. The abbreviations and formats for codes and session laws are presented in *Bluebook* Table T.1 and *ALWD* Appendix 1.

1. General Rules When Citing Statutes

The following rules apply when citing both federal and state statutes.

a. Main Text and Supplements

When the cited material is taken from the main text, the year of the volume of the text is placed in parentheses at the end of the citation (the year the volume was published, which usually appears on the spine of the volume). When the cited material appears only in the supplement, you must so indicate in parentheses with the date. When the cited material is taken from the main text and the supplement, it must be indicated with the date.

For Example	Citation from main text: 15 U.S.C. § 7 (1988)

Citation from supplement only: 15 U.S.C. § 7 (Supp. 2002)

Citation from main text and supplement: 15 U.S.C. § 7 (1988 & Supp. 2002)

Citation from main text and supplement, unofficial commercial publisher: 15 U.S.C.A. § 7 (West 1988 & Supp. 2002)

b. Section Symbol (§) and Multiple Sections

The section symbol (§) is used to indicate a section of a statute. Note, however, that you may not use the symbol to start a sentence. In such cases, the word *Section* is used.

For Example	Correct: Section 2253 of the Act provides . . .

Incorrect: § 2253 of the Act provides . . .

Refer to section IV.L in the chapter for the rules on citing multiple sections.

c. Name of Act

Although it is not required, the name of the act may be included in the citation. According to both the *Bluebook* and the *ALWD*, the name should be in regular type.

For Example	*Bluebook* format: Robinson-Patman Act, 15 U.S.C. § 7 (1988)

2. Federal Statutes—Bluebook R-12; ALWD-14.2

The federal statutes of general public interest are printed in three separate publications:

- *United States Code (USC)*—the official code
- *United States Code Annotated (USCA)*—Thomson West
- *United States Code Service (USCS)*—LexisNexis

The citation format for federal statutes consists of the following elements:

1. Title number
2. Code abbreviation
3. Section symbol (§)
4. Section number
5. Publisher in parentheses when it is a commercial publication
6. Year of the publication or supplement (year the volume was published, which usually appears on the spine of the volume), in parentheses

---

For Example Official code: 15 ^ U.S.C. ^ § ^ 7 ^ (1988)

15 U.S.C. § 7 (1988)

Unofficial codes: 15 U.S.C.A. § 7 (West 1984)

15 U.S.C.S. § 7 (LexisNexis 1984).

1. The number 15 is the title number.
2. U.S.C., U.S.C.A, and U.S.C.S. are the abbreviated names of the codes.
3. Section (§) 7 is the section symbol and number.
4. The dates (1988), (West 1984), and (LexisNexis 1984) mark the years of publication and the publishers for unofficial codes.

When citing to the *Internal Revenue Code,* substitute I.R.C. for U.S.C. and omit the title number.

For Example Correct: I.R.C. § 100 (1994)

Incorrect: 26 U.S.C. § 100 (1994)

---

3. Short Citation Format for State and Federal Statutes—Bluebook R-12.9; ALWD-14.5

When the use of *id.* is appropriate (see section IV.I in the chapter), it is the preferred short citation format. Otherwise, the short citation is the full citation format without the parenthetical information.

For Example Full citations: 15 U.S.C. § 7 (1988 & Supp. 2002); Minn. Stat. § 519 (1990)

Short citations: 15 U.S.C. § 7; *Id.* § 7; Minn. Stat. § 519; *Id.* § 519

---

4. State Statutes—Bluebook R-12; ALWD-14.4

The citation form for state statutes varies from state to state. *Bluebook* Table T.1 and *ALWD* Appendix 1 present the abbreviations and formats for state statutes. Also note that some states have local citation rules that require a citation format different from that presented in the *Bluebook* and the *ALWD*. The local court rules should be consulted for the proper citation format. The local rules are included in Appendix 2 of the *ALWD*.

The citation format for state statutes usually includes the following elements:

1. Name of the code

2. Section symbol (§)

3. Chapter/title/section number

4. Publisher in parentheses when it is a commercial publication

5. Year of the publication or supplement (year the volume was published, which usually appears on the spine of the volume), in parentheses

> **For Example** Official code: Minn. ^ Stat. ^ § ^ 519 ^ (1990)
>
> Minn. Stat. § 519 (1990)
>
> Unofficial code: Minn. Stat. Ann. § 519 (West 1991)
>
> 1. Minn. Stat. is the name of the code.
>
> 2. The § is the section symbol.
>
> 3. Number 519 is the section number.
>
> 4. West is the publisher of the unofficial code (in the second example).
>
> 5. The dates 1990 and 1991 mark the years of publication.

Some states, such as California, identify portions of their codes by subject matter rather than by title. For those states, the subject matter code is included in the citation.

> **For Example** Cal. Corp. Code § 200 (West 1986); Tex. Fam. Code Ann. § 2.101 (Vernon 1993)

5. Session Laws—Bluebook R-12.4; ALWD-14.6 to ALWD-14.8

When a citation is not available in the official or unofficial codes, it is appropriate to cite to the session law. You may have to do this when a recently passed law has not yet been published in the official or unofficial codes. As with state statutes, the citation form for session laws varies from state to state. The abbreviations and formats for state session laws are presented in *Bluebook* Table T.1 and *ALWD* Appendix 1.

The basic elements of a federal session law citation are:

1. Name or title of the act (optional)—in the *ALWD* example, the name/title is italicized; in the *Bluebook* Quick Reference examples, the name/title is neither italicized nor underscored

2. Law abbreviation and number

3. Pinpoint reference when citing a specific section

4. Volume, statute, and initial page number

5. Pinpoint page reference when referring to a specific page

6. Date (year in parentheses) of the cited volume of the *Statutes at Large*

> **For Example** Uniformed Services Former Spouses Protection Act, Pub. L. No. 101–510, § 554, 104 Stat. 1569, 1572 (1993)
>
> 1. Uniformed Services Former Spouses Protection Act is the name or title of the act (roman for *Bluebook* style; italicized or underscored for *ALWD* style).
> 2. Pub. L. No. 101–510 is the law abbreviation and number.
> 3. Section (§) 554 is the pinpoint reference to a specific section.
> 4. 104 Stat. 1569 is the volume, statute, and initial page number.
> 5. The number 1572 is the pinpoint page reference to a specific page.
> 6. The year of enactment (1993).

D. Rules of Evidence and Procedure—Bluebook R-12.8.3; ALWD-17

The *Bluebook* rule governing citations to evidentiary and procedural rules differs from the *ALWD* rule. The *Bluebook* states that the citation should include the abbreviated name of the rule and the number of the rule.

> **For Example** Fed. R. Civ. P. 4   Rule 4 of the Federal Rules of Civil Procedure
> Fed. R. Evid. 407   Rule 407 of the Federal Rules of Evidence
> Fed. R. Crim. P. 18 Rule 18 of the Federal Rules of Criminal Procedure

The *ALWD* rule states that the citation should include, in addition to the abbreviated name and rule number, the name of the publisher when the source is other than an official code and the year of publication, both in parentheses.

> **For Example** Fed. R. Civ. P. 4 (2001)   Rule 4 of the Federal Rules of Civil Procedure
> Fed. R. Evid. 407   Rule 407 of the Federal Rules of Evidence,
> (West 2002)   published by Thomson West
> Fed. R. Crim. P. 18 (2001)   Rule 18 of the Federal Rules of Criminal Procedure

E. Administrative Law—Bluebook R-14; ALWD-19

The components of citations to administrative rules or regulations are:

1. Title (topic or agency) number in the code publication
2. Abbreviated name of the publication (e.g., *Code of Federal Regulations—CFR; Federal Register—Fed. Reg.*)
3. Section number or page number of the rule or regulation
4. Year of publication

> **For Example** 27 C.F.R. § 20.235 (1988)
> 48 Fed. Reg. 37,315 (1983)
>
> 1. The numbers 27 and 48 are the title (topic or agency) numbers.
> 2. C.F.R. and Fed. Reg. are the abbreviated names of the publications.
> 3. Section (§) 20.235 and 37,315 are the section numbers or page numbers.
> 4. The dates 1988 and 1983 mark the years of publication.

III. SECONDARY AUTHORITY

This section presents an overview of the rules of citation to be used when citing secondary authority—sources a court may rely on that are not the law, that is, not primary authority. The examples are to citation forms used in court documents and legal memoranda rather than law review articles. See Exhibit 8-1 for a list of the secondary authority sources and the citation rule references.

A detailed discussion of the citation rules for each type of secondary authority is beyond the scope of this text. Therefore, this section presents the citation format for the most commonly used secondary authorities. As with the previous sections, *there are differences between the* Bluebook *and the* ALWD. *Do not assume you can substitute one for the other.*

A. Annotated Law Reports—Bluebook R-16.6.5; ALWD-24

1. Full Citation Format

The components of an *ALR* citation are:

1. Full name of the author
2. Word *Annotation* (note that the *ALWD* omits the use of *Annotation* following the author name)
3. Title (italicized or underscored)
4. Volume number
5. Abbreviated name of the publication
6. Page number on which the annotation begins (followed by the pinpoint page when a specific page is referred to, for example, 852, 860)
7. Year of publication

> **For Example** Michael J. Weber, Annotation, *Application of Statute of Limitations to Actions for Breach of Duty in Performing Services of Public Accountant,* 7 A.L.R.5th 852 (1992)
>
> 1. Michael J. Weber is the full name of the author.
> 2. The word *Annotation* is included when using *Bluebook,* but not when using *ALWD.*
> 3. *Application of Statute of Limitations to Actions for Breach of Duty in Performing Services of Public Accountant* is the title (italicized or underscored).
> 4. The number 7 is the volume number.
> 5. A.L.R.5th is the abbreviated name of the publication with no spaces.
> 6. The number 852 is the page number on which the annotation begins.
> 7. The year 1992 is the year of publication.

2. Short Citation Format

Use *id.* when appropriate (see section IV.I.1 in this chapter). When *id.* is not appropriate, include the author's last name, volume number, *ALR* series, *at,* and the pinpoint reference.

> **For Example** *Id.* at 861; Weber, 7 A.L.R.5th at 861

B. Legal Dictionary—Bluebook R-15.7; ALWD-25

1. Full Citation Format

A legal dictionary citation should include:

1. Author (if any)
2. Full name of the dictionary (underscored or italicized)
3. Page containing the definition (no comma after the name of the dictionary and the page)
4. Editor (required only in the *ALWD* format)—begin parenthesis
5. Edition
6. Publisher (required only in the *ALWD* format)
7. Year of publication—end parenthesis

> **For Example** *Bluebook* format: *Black's Law Dictionary* 451 (7th ed. 1992)
>
> 1. *Black's Law Dictionary* is the full name of the dictionary (in italics or underscored).
> 2. The number 451 is the page number of the definition.
> 3. (7th ed. 1992) is the edition and the year of publication.

> **For Example** *ALWD* format: *Black's Law Dictionary* 451 (Bryan A. Garner ed., 7th ed., West 1992)
>
> 1. *Black's Law Dictionary* is the full name of the dictionary (in italics or underscored).
> 2. The number 451 is the page number of the definition.
> 3. Bryan A. Garner ed. is the name of the editor.
> 4. 7th ed. is the edition number.
> 5. West is the publisher.
> 6. The year 1992 is the year of publication.

2. Short Citation Format

Use *id.* when appropriate (see section IV.I.1 in this chapter). When *id.* is not appropriate, repeat the name and the page number.

> **For Example** *Id.* at 451; *Black's Law Dictionary* at 45

C. Legal Encyclopedia—Bluebook R-15.7; ALWD-26

1. Full Citation Format

A full citation to a legal encyclopedia should contain:

1. Volume number of the encyclopedia
2. Abbreviated name of the encyclopedia, usually either Am. Jur. 2d or CJS (no underscore or italics)
3. Title or topic name (italicized or underscored)

4. Section symbol (§) and section number within the article

5. Year of publication in parentheses

> **For Example** 88 C.J.S. *Trial* § 105 (1980)
>
> 59A Am. Jur. 2d *Partnership* § 925 (Supp. 1995)
>
> 1. The numbers 88 and 59A are the volume numbers of the encyclopedias.
> 2. C.J.S. and Am. Jur. 2d are the abbreviated names of the encyclopedias.
> 3. *Trial* and *Partnership* are the topic names (italicized).
> 4. Section (§) 105 and § 925 are the section symbols and section numbers within the article.
> 5. The dates (1980) and (Supp. 1995) indicate the year(s) of publication.

2. Short Citation Format

Use *id.* when appropriate (see section IV.I.1 in the chapter). When *id.* is not appropriate, repeat the full citation without the date.

> **For Example** *Id.* § 925; *Id.* § 105; 59A Am. Jur. 2d *Partnership* § 925; 88 C.J.S. *Trial* § 105

D. Periodicals—Law Review/Journal Citations—Bluebook R-16; ALWD-23

1. Full Citation Format

Following are the components of a law review, journal, or another periodical citation:

1. Full name of the author

2. Title of the article (italicized or underscored)

3. Volume number

4. Abbreviated title of the periodical

5. Page number on which the article begins (followed by the pinpoint page when a specific page is referred to, for example, 159, 165)

6. Year of publication in parentheses

> **For Example** Patricia W. Bennett, *After* White v. Illinois: *Fundamental Guarantees to a Hollow Right to Confront Witnesses,* 40 Wayne L. Rev. 159 (1993)
>
> 1. Patricia W. Bennett is the full name of the author.
> 2. *After* White v. Illinois: *Fundamental Guarantees to a Hollow Right to Confront Witnesses* is the title of the article (note that the case name, normally italicized, is in roman to distinguish it from the italicized article title).
> 3. The number 40 is the volume number.
> 4. Wayne L. Rev. is the abbreviated title of the periodical.
> 5. The number 159 is the page number on which the article begins.
> 6. The date (1993) is the year of publication.

2. Short Citation Format

Use *id.* when appropriate (see section IV.I.1 in this chapter). When *id.* is not appropriate, include the author's last name, the volume number, the periodical abbreviation, *at,* and the pinpoint reference.

For Example	*Id.* at 165; Bennett, 40 Wayne L. Rev. at 165

E. Restatements—Bluebook R-12.85; ALWD-27

1. Full Citation Format

A citation to a *Restatement* should include:

1. Full name and edition of the *Restatement* (in the *ALWD,* the full name and edition is in italics or underscored, including a subtitle when the reference is to a subtitle)
2. Section symbol (§) and number of the *Restatement*
3. Year of publication in parentheses

For Example	*Bluebook* format: Restatement (Second) of Judgments § 28 (1982)
	ALWD format: *Restatement (Second) of Judgments* § 28 (1982)

Bluebook format: Restatement (Second) of Torts: Products Liability § 52 (1989)

ALWD format: *Restatement (Second) of Torts: Products Liability* § 52 (1989)

1. Restatement (Second) of Judgments is the full name of the *Restatement* and the edition; Restatement (Second) of Torts: Products Liability is the full name of the *Restatement,* edition, and subtitle.
2. Section (§) 28 and § 52 are the section numbers.
3. The dates (1982) and (1989) indicate the year of publication.

---

2. Short Citation Format

Use *id.* when appropriate (see section IV.I.1 in this chapter). Otherwise, repeat the full citation without the date.

For Example	*Id.* § 28; *Restatement (Second) of Judgments* § 28

F. Treatises/Books—Bluebook R-15; ALWD-22

1. Full Citation Format

Treatise and book citations should include:

1. Volume number when there is more than one volume
2. Full name of the author or editor when a name is given
3. Full title of the publication as it appears on the title page (italicized or underscored)

4. Number of the section, paragraph, or page when you are referring to a specific number, paragraph, or page

5. Editor when there is one, the edition or series number of the book when it is not the first edition, and the publisher (the *Bluebook* does not require the inclusion of the publisher)—begin parenthesis

6. Year of publication—end parenthesis

For Example	*ALWD* format: 6A Richard R. Powell, *Powell on Real Property* ¶ 899 (Patrick J. Rohan ed., Matthew Bender 1994)

1. The number 6A is the volume number.

2. Richard R. Powell is the full name of the author.

3. *Powell on Real Property* is the full title of the publication as it appears on the title page.

4. ¶ 899 is the number of the paragraph.

5. (Patrick J. Rohan ed., Matthew Bender 1994) is the editor, publisher, and year of publication. This is the first edition; therefore, no edition number, such as "3d ed.," is used.

2. Short Citation Format

Use *id.* when appropriate (see section IV.I.1 in this chapter). When *id.* is not appropriate, include the author's last name, the title, *at,* and the pinpoint reference.

For Example	*Id.* ¶ 899; Powell, *Powell on Real Property* ¶ 899

IV. GENERAL RULES OF CITATION

This section presents an overview of basic rules of citation for citing most legal sources. The general rule(s) governing each area are listed after the subsection title. See Exhibit 8-2 for a list of the general rules of citation and the citation rule references. A detailed discussion of each rule is beyond the scope of this text.

A. Typeface—Bluebook R-2, B-2; ALWD-1.1

Bluebook R-2 requires different typeface conventions and the use of large and small capital letters for citations in law reviews and other writings such as books. Bluepages B-2 covers the use of italics/underscores in court documents and legal memoranda. ALWD-1.1 does not distinguish between types of documents and states that ordinary type and italics or underscores should be used in all legal writing. The use of italics or underscores is discussed in the next subsection.

B. Italics and Underscores—Bluebook B-2; ALWD-1.3

These rules present a summary of the items that should be underscored or italicized. The rules governing each type of item should be checked for other provisions that may govern the use of underscores or italics.

Exhibit 8-2 *Rule References to General Rules of Citation.*

General Rules of Citation		
Topic	***Bluebook* Rules and Bluepages Notes**	*ALWD* **Rules**
Abbreviations	R-6 Tables T.5 to T.16 and B-T1	ALWD-2 Appendices 3, 4, 5
Capitalization	R-8 and B-10.6	ALWD-3
Electronic Sources	R-18	ALWD-38 to ALWD-42
Internal Cross-References (*supra* and *infra*)	R-3.6	ALWD-10
Italics and Underscoring	B-2	ALWD-1.3
Page Numbers (Pinpoint Citations)	R-3.3, R-3.4, R-3.5	ALWD-5.2, ALWD-5.3, ALWD-5.4
Placement of Citations in Sentences and Clauses	B-2	ALWD-3.1
Quotations	R-5	ALWD-47 to ALWD-49
Sections (§) and Paragraphs (¶)	R-3.4	ALWD-6
Short Citations (*id., supra,* hereinafter)	R-4, B-5.2, B-6.2, B-8.2, B-9.2, B-10.5	ALWD-11.2, ALWD-11.3, LWD-11.4
Signals (*eg, see, accord,* etc.)	R-1.2, R-1.3, R-1.4, R-1.5	ALWD-44 to ALWD-46
String Citations	R-1.2	ALWD-43.3(a)

© Cengage Learning 2014

> **For Example** When citing cases, in addition to these rules, check the separate rules governing case names for other requirements, such as what names are used.

The rules are referenced next to the subject below.

The following items should be *italicized* or underscored:

1. Case names—Bluebook R-10.2; ALWD-12.2 and ALWD-12.21
2. Titles of publications and most documents—Bluebook R-13, R-15, R-16; ALWD-15.7(c), ALWD-22.1(b), ALWD-23.1(b), ALWD-26.1(c)
3. Introductory signals, such as *See* and *Contra*—Bluebook R-1.2; ALWD-45
4. Internal cross-references and short forms, such as *supra*—Bluebook R-4; ALWD-10, ALWD-11
5. Phrases indicating subsequent or prior history, such as *aff'd* and *rev'd*—Bluebook R-10.7.1; ALWD-12.8, ALWD-12.9

6. Words or phrases introducing related authority, such as *available at*—Bluebook R-1.6, R-15.5, R-18.2, R-18.6, R-20.1.5

7. Names of Internet sites—ALWD-40.1(b)

8. Words used for emphasis, words italicized in the matter quoted, and foreign words that are not common—Bluebook R-5, R-7

C. Citation Placement in Sentences and Clauses—Bluebook B-2; ALWD-43.1

Citations are placed in legal documents by including them as separate citation sentences or clauses or by incorporating them within a sentence.

1. Citation Sentence

When a statement about the law is a complete sentence, the citation immediately follows the statement as a separate sentence that begins with a capital letter and ends with a period. In this situation, placement of the citation indicates that the citation supports the entire statement about the law included in the sentence.

> **For Example** It is well established that a defendant has a right to counsel at a preliminary hearing. *Coleman v. Alabama,* 399 U.S. 1 (1970).

2. Citation Clause

When the citation supports only part of a sentence, the citation is placed as a clause immediately after the statement it supports and is set off by commas.

> **For Example** Although the "good faith" exception to the exclusionary rule has been adopted by the United States Supreme Court, *United States v. Leon,* 468 U.S. 897 (1984), it has not been adopted by all of the states, *State v. Gutierrez,* 116 N.M. 431, 863 P.2d 1052 (1993).

In this example, the first citation supports the first clause of the sentence and the second citation supports the second clause.

3. Embedded Citations

When the authority is mentioned in the sentence, the citation may be incorporated within the sentence.

> **For Example** In the case of *Coleman v. Alabama,* 399 U.S. 1 (1970), the Supreme Court held that a defendant has a right to counsel at a preliminary hearing.

Placing the citation in the sentence adds variety to the writing. Note that the citation is not repeated at the end of the sentence.

D. Abbreviations—Bluebook R-6, Tables T.5 to T.16, B-T.1, B-T.2; ALWD-2, Appendix 3 to Appendix 5

1. In General

Various terms and sources, such as court names, legal periodicals, and case names, are abbreviated in legal citations.

For Example	Term	Abbreviation
	Southern Reporter	So.
	United States Supreme Court	U.S.
	Cumberland Law Review	Cumb. L. Rev.
	Case name—Corporation	Corp.

The lists of abbreviations are included in the *Bluebook* tables and the *ALWD* appendices referenced at the beginning of this subsection.

2. Spacing

In the *Bluebook* section, "Typical Legal Citations Analyzed" (pages 5–9), dots (•) are inserted in the example to indicate a single space in the citation. In the *ALWD*, a green triangle (▲) indicates a single space. Following is a summary of the rules governing spacing.

a. Single Capital Letters and Ordinals

Do not place a space between single capital letters or single capital letters and an ordinal. An *ordinal* is a number used to designate a position in a series, such as 10th Circuit. Ordinals such as 2d and 10th are treated as a single capital letter.

For Example	F.R.D.—Federal Rules Decisions; P.2d—Pacific Reporter Second Series. There are no spaces between the single capital letters or between the single capital letter(s) and the ordinal.

b. Single Capital Letters and Nonsingle Capital Letters

When an abbreviation includes one or more capital letters and when an abbreviation does not include a single capital letter, include a space between the single capital letter and the other abbreviation.

For Example	F. Supp.—Federal Supplement. There is a space between *F.* and *Supp.* because *Supp.* is not a single capital letter. N.D. Miss.—Northern District of Mississippi. There is a space between *D.* and *Miss.* because *Miss.* is not a single capital letter. There is no space between *N.* and *D.* because each is a single capital letter.

c. Abbreviated and Nonabbreviated Words

When an abbreviated word is combined with a nonabbreviated word, place a space on each side of the nonabbreviated word.

> **For Example** J. Real Est. Tax'n—Journal of Real Estate Taxation. There is a space on each side of *Real* because it is a nonabbreviated word combined with abbreviated words.

d. Legal Periodicals

In a legal periodical, use a space to separate the institutional or geographic abbreviation from the other parts of the abbreviation.

> **For Example** U.S.F. L. Rev.—University of San Francisco Law Review. *U.S.F.* is separated with a space from the *L.* because *U.S.F.* is the institutional abbreviation. *L.* is set off by a space from *Rev.* because *Rev.* is not a single capital letter.

e. Section Symbol (§), Paragraph Symbol (¶), and Ampersand (&)

Place a space after the section and paragraph symbols and the ampersand.

> **For Example** 18 U.S.C. § 2113—A space is placed on each side of the section symbol.

f. Authorities Included in the Text of a Sentence

The name of an authority is not abbreviated when it is used in a sentence. According to *Bluebook* R-10.2.1, widely known abbreviations such as *Co.* and *Inc.* continue to be used.

> **For Example** The case citation is *Bachman Chocolate Mktg. Co. v. Leigh Warehouse & Transp. Co.,* 1 N.J. 239, 62 A.2d 806 (1949). When used in a sentence, *Marketing,* and *Transportation* are not abbreviated: The court ruled against the manufacturer in *Bachman Chocolate Marketing Co. v. Leigh Warehouse & Transportation Co.,* 1 N.J. 239, 62 A.2d 806 (1949).

E. Capitalization—Bluebook R-8, B-10.6; ALWD-3

1. General Rule

In a heading, title, or subtitle, capitalize the initial letter of the first word, the first word following a colon, hyphen, or dash, and all other words except articles, prepositions, and conjunctions.

> **For Example** Michael Asimow, *Bad Lawyers in the Movies,* 24 Nova L. Rev. 533 (2000)

2. Court and Party Designations

Bluepages B-10.6 states that in addition to capitalizing the word *Court* when referring to a specific court (such as the California Supreme Court), also capitalize *Court* when the court receiving the document is referred to in the document.

> **For Example** This Court has already denied defendant's petition on two previous occasions.

Bluepages B-10.6 also states that the party designations (plaintiff, defendant, appellant, etc.) should be capitalized when referring to the parties in a matter before the court.

> **For Example** The Appellant claims that the letter should not have been admitted at trial.
>
> On six occasions, Plaintiff attempted to contact Defendant regarding Defendant's failure to answer the interrogatories.

3. Specific Words

Rule 8 of the *Bluebook* includes a page-and-a-half list of specific words and rules governing capitalization.

> **For Example** Capitalize *Act* only when referring to a specific act; capitalize *Code* only when referring to a specific code, such as the 1990 Code; capitalize *Judge* only when it is the name of a specific judge or a justice of the United States Supreme Court.

4. All Other Capitalizations

Both manuals refer to the *U.S. Government Printing Office Style Manual* for the capitalization of other words. The *ALWD* also refers to *The Chicago Manual of Style*.

F. Quotations—Bluebook R-5; ALWD-47 to ALWD-49

Quotations are stronger than summaries or paraphrases. Too many quotations, however, may cause the writing to become disjointed and lead the reader to question whether the writer has analyzed the material or understands the material well enough to analyze it. Use quotations for emphasis. Use quotes primarily for statutory language, the law or legal principle presented by a court, or key portions of a court's reasoning.

1. Quotation Marks

Quotations of fewer than 50 words should be placed in quotation marks (" "); the quotations are not indented or otherwise set off. The citation is usually placed after the sentence that contains the quotation.

> **For Example** The United States Supreme Court gave the following guidance when interpreting treaties: "In construing a treaty, as in construing a statute, we first look to its terms to determine its meaning." *United States v. Alvarez-Machain,* 504 U.S. 655, 663 (1992).
>
> The court noted that the text of the treaty must be "interpreted in good faith in accordance with the ordinary meaning to be given to the terms of the treaty in their context in light of its object and purpose." *Kreimerman v. Casa Veerkamp, S.A. de C.V.,* 22 F.3d 634, 638 (5th Cir. 1994).

Place periods and commas inside the closing quotation marks. Other punctuation marks, such as semicolons, colons, question marks, and exclamation points, are placed outside the closing quotation marks unless they are a part of the quotation.

> **For Example** The court defined *publication* as "communication to a third party"; therefore. . . .
>
> The victim then shouted, "I've been hit!" [The exclamation point is part of the quote; therefore, it belongs within the quotation marks.]

2. Indented Quotations

Quotations of 50 words or more (called *block quotations*) are set off from the rest of the text by a five-space indentation (one tab) from the left and right margins and are single spaced. They are not set off by quotation marks. Place the citation at the left margin of the line of text following the quotation. Do not place the citation with the block quotation. The block quotation should be set off from the rest of the text with a double space.

> **For Example** In regard to the individual rights of tenants in common, the court noted the following:
>
> However, numerous other elements of control do follow the percentage of ownership. For example, if a cotenant obtains a loan and mortgages the property, he is able to mortgage only his percentage of ownership interest. If one cotenant rents the whole property to a third party, he must share the proceeds with his cotenants in accordance with their respective percentages of ownership. . . .
>
> *Garcia v. Andrus,* 692 F.2d 89, 92 (9th Cir. 1982).

Block quotations are punctuated as they appear in the original quote.

3. Quote Within a Quote

Enclose quotations within a block quotation in double quotation marks (" "). As mentioned in the previous subsection, block quotations are punctuated as they appear in the original quote. Enclose quotations within a short quotation in single quotation marks.

> **For Example** "The statute requires that the annual statement 'must be filed within thirty (30) days of the end of the fiscal year.'"

4. Citing a Quote Within a Quote

When the source of a quote within a quote is included within the quotation, do not repeat it in the citation.

> **For Example** "The state corporation statute, section 57-9-21, requires that the annual statement 'must be filed within thirty (30) days of the end of the fiscal year.'"
> In this situation, you do not cite section 57-9-21 at the end of the quotation.

When the source of a quote within a quote is not cited within the quotation, place the citation in a parenthetical that follows the citation for the entire quotation.

> **For Example** In discussing the time limits for appeal, the court in *El Dorado* noted "'[j]urisdiction of the matters in dispute does not lie in the courts until the statutorily required administrative procedures are fully complied with.'" *El Dorado Utils., Inc. v. Gallisteo Domestic Water Users Ass'n,* 120 N.M. 165, 167, 899 P.2d 608, 610 (Ct. App. 1995) (quoting *In re Application of Angel Fire Corp.,* 96 N.M. 651, 652, 634 P.2d 202, 203 (1981)).

5. Altering Quotations

The reader must be alerted to any changes made to a quotation. Following are the rules governing alterations.

a. Altering a Letter Case

When you change the case of a letter from uppercase to lowercase or vice versa, enclose the letter in brackets.

> **For Example** Original quote: The court does not have jurisdiction until the administrative procedures are complied with.
>
> Alteration: The Supreme Court noted that "[t]he court does not have jurisdiction until the administrative procedures are complied with."

b. Adding, Deleting, or Changing Letters

Enclose the added, deleted, or changed letter(s) in brackets.

> **For Example** Original quote: Jurisdiction of the matter in dispute does not lie in the court.
>
> Alteration: Jurisdiction of the matter[s] in dispute does not lie in the court.

c. Substituting or Adding Words

Place substituted or added words in brackets.

> **For Example** Original quote: Jurisdiction of the matters in dispute does not lie in the courts until the administrative procedures are fully complied with.
>
> Alteration: Jurisdiction of the matters in dispute does not lie in the courts until the [statutorily required] administrative procedures are fully complied with.

d. Mistakes in Original Quote

Indicate a mistake in quoted material by placing *[sic]* after the mistake.

> **For Example** The preliminary hearing is a stage at which the defendant have *[sic]* a right to counsel.

e. Adding Emphasis

Any change in the typeface of the quotation, such as when adding emphasis, should be noted in parentheses following the citation.

> **For Example** Original quote: "If one cotenant rents the whole property to a third party, he must share the proceeds...." *Garcia v. Andrus,* 692 F.2d 89, 92 (9th Cir. 1982).
>
> Alteration: "If one cotenant rents the whole property to a third party, *he must share* the proceeds...." *Garcia v. Andrus,* 692 F.2d 89, 92 (9th Cir. 1982) (emphasis added).

6. Omitting Words or Citations

On occasion, you may want to quote only the parts of a quoted passage relevant to the issue being discussed rather than the entire passage. When you are omitting one or more words, the following rules apply.

a. Omission of One or More Words—Ellipsis (...)

An *ellipsis* is three periods placed together to indicate the omission of material from the middle of a quotation.

> **For Example** "No will ... shall be revoked, unless ... by subsequent will or codicil."

To indicate the omission of words at the end of a quotation, use an ellipsis and the final punctuation of the quote.

> **For Example** The statute provides that a will may be revoked by "cutting, tearing, burning, obliterating, canceling...."

Do not use an ellipsis to indicate the omission of words at the beginning of a quotation when the quotation is part of a sentence.

> **For Example** Correct omission: The court noted that a testator may revoke a will by "cutting, tearing, or cancellation with the intent to revoke."
>
> Incorrect omission: The court noted that a testator may revoke a will by "... cutting, tearing, or cancellation with the intent to revoke."

When language at the beginning of a quotation is omitted, capitalize the first letter and place it in brackets if the quoted material begins your sentence.

> **For Example** Original quote: "This court has held in several cases that a defendant need not brandish the firearm in a threatening manner."
>
> Correct omission: "[D]efendant need not brandish the firearm in a threatening manner."

To indicate the omission of one or more paragraphs from a block quote, place an ellipsis on a line by itself. Also, to indicate the omission of language from the beginning of a subsequent paragraph, use an ellipsis.

FOR EXAMPLE However, numerous other elements of control do follow the percentage of ownership. For example, if a cotenant obtains a loan and mortgages the property, he is able to mortgage only his percentage of ownership interest.

… If one cotenant rents the whole property to a third party, he must share the proceeds with his cotenants in accordance with their respective percentages of ownership.

In this example, the ellipsis on a separate line indicates the omission of a paragraph from the block quotation. The ellipsis at the beginning of the second paragraph indicates the omission of language from the beginning of the second paragraph.

b. Omission of Citations or Footnotes

A quotation may contain numerous citations or footnotes that you do not want to include in your writing. Indicate the omission of a citation or footnote in a parenthetical.

For Example "It is clear, however, that in the United States, civil liability for assault and battery is not limited to the direct perpetrator, but extends to any person who by any means aids or encourages the act." *Rael v. Cadena,* 934 N.M. 684, 684, 604 P.2d 822, 823 (Ct. App. 1979) (citations omitted).

---

7. Paragraph Structure

When a quotation of fewer than 50 words is the first sentence of a paragraph from the quoted text, the paragraph is enclosed in quotation marks but is not indented. When the quotation is 50 words or more (a block quotation) and the quotation begins with the first sentence of a paragraph from the quoted text, indent a second tab on the left side of the block quotation. All subsequent paragraphs are likewise indented as they appear in the quoted text. In other words, indent the rest of a block quote like the paragraph or paragraphs from the quoted text.

For Example In regard to the individual rights of tenants in common, the court noted the following:

However, numerous other elements of control do follow the percentage of ownership. For example, if a cotenant obtains a loan and mortgages the property, he is able to mortgage only his percentage of ownership interest. If one cotenant rents the whole property to a third party, he must share the proceeds with his cotenants in accordance with their respective percentages of ownership. ....

In this example, the first word, *However,* is indented in the block quote because it is the beginning of a paragraph in the quoted text.

G. Page Numbers (Pinpoint Citations)—Bluebook R-3.3, R-3.4, R-3.5; ALWD-5.2, ALWD-5.3, ALWD-5.4

Whenever you quote material from a source, you must include a reference to the exact page or location of the information. Also, when you paraphrase or otherwise refer to specific information rather than quote it, you should include a reference to the exact page or location. That reference is called a *pinpoint cite* or a *jump cite*. It allows the reader to go to the exact page on which the quotation appears rather than search through the entire source to find the quote. That rule applies to all reference sources, and information on how to cite specific sources is scattered throughout the rules regarding primary and secondary sources. The rules covering pinpoint citations in general are discussed here.

Place the page number on which the quote or reference appears immediately after the page on which the source begins.

> **For Example** "[I]t is not a search by a federal officer if evidence secured by state authorities is turned over to federal authorities on a silver platter." *Lustig v. United States,* 338 U.S. 74, 79 (1949). [Page 79 is the page on which the quote appears.]
>
> The Eighth Circuit addressed the derivative nature of proceedings brought on behalf of limited partnerships. *Allright Mo., Inc. v. Billeter,* 829 F.2d 631, 638 (8th Cir. 1987). [Page 638 is the page on which the Eighth Circuit addressed the matter.]
>
> It has been noted that those trained in the law are confused by the topic. Terry Christlieb, Note, *Why Superseding Cause Analysis Should Be Abandoned,* 72 Tex. L. Rev. 161, 162. [Page 162 is the reference page.]

When the citation includes a parallel citation, you must include a reference to the page in the parallel citation. Parallel citations are discussed in section II.A.3.f in this chapter.

> **For Example** *Commonwealth v. Appleby,* 380 Mass. 296, 300, 402 N.E.2d 1051, 1054 (1980)

When the quotation or reference is from the first page of the reference source, repeat the initial page number.

> **For Example** *Lustig v. United States,* 338 U.S. 74, 74 (1949)

When the quotation or reference covers more than one page, separate the pages by a hyphen, en dash, or *to*.

> **For Example** *Lustig v. United States,* 338 U.S. 74, 74-79 (1949)
> *Lustig v. United States,* 338 U.S. 74, 74–79 (1949)
> *Lustig v. United States,* 338 U.S. 74, 74 to 79 (1949)

Always retain at least the last two digits of the second number.

> **For Example** | Correct: 74–79
> Incorrect: 74–9
> Correct: 104–09
> Incorrect: 104–9

When the quotation or reference is from multiple pages that are not consecutive, list each page separated by a comma and one space. Do not use *and* or *&* before the final page.

> **For Example** | *Lustig v. United States,* 338 U.S. 74, 74, 76, 79 (1949)

When the quotation or reference is from a public domain format (also referred to as *vendor-neutral format*), the pinpoint citation may be to a specific paragraph rather than a page.

> **For Example** | *State v. Anaya,* 1997-NMSC-010, ¶ 28, 123 N.M. 14, 20, 933 P.2d 223, 229.
> [The quote is located in paragraph 28.]

Consult the rule of the jurisdiction governing neutral citations. Both the *Bluebook* and the *ALWD* have tables/appendices that set out each state's citation rules and formats.

H. String Citations—Bluebook R-1.1, R-1.2; ALWD-43.3(a)

When a proposition is supported by more than one authority in a citation clause or sentence, the citation is referred to as a *string citation*. Use a semicolon to separate each authority cited.

> **For Example** | The sudden emergency doctrine tends to elevate its principles above what is required to be proven in a negligence action. *Knapp v. Stanford,* 392 So. 2d 196 (Miss. 1980); *Simonson v. White,* 220 Mont. 14, 713 P.2d 938 (1986).

The use of string citations in court documents and legal memoranda is generally disfavored, but their use is not prohibited. The preference is to present only the strongest authority in support of a proposition. String citations are seen more frequently in periodical publications such as law review articles.

I. Short Citation Forms (*Id., Supra,* and *Hereinafter*)—Bluebook R-4, B-5.2, B-6.2, B-8.2, B-9.2, B-10.5; ALWD-11.2 to ALWD-11.4

Once the full citation to an authority is presented in a document, subsequent citations to the authority may be shortened. Those shortened citations usually are referred to as *short citations* or *short-form citations*. Short citations are used primarily because they save space and are less disruptive to the flow of the text. *Bluebook* B-5.2 states that short citations may be used when it is clear from the short form what is being referenced, the earlier full citation is in the same general discussion, and the reader can easily locate the full citation.

The rules included in the title to this subsection are the general rules governing short citations. The rules for each type of citation have sections on short citations; for instance, the rule governing case citations has a section on short citations and the rule governing book citation has a section on short citations. The discussion of each type of citation in sections II and III of this chapter includes the short citation format. This subsection addresses general rules governing all short citations and provides some examples.

1. *Id.* as a Short Citation

Id. means "the same" and is used the same way *ibid.* is used. You use *id.*, not *ibid.*, in legal writing. It is italicized or underscored. When it is underscored, the period is underscored as well (id.). *Id.* is used in court documents and legal memoranda when you are referring the reader to the immediately preceding citation. In other words, you must be referring to the same citation as the last citation presented.

> **For Example** Numerous other elements of control follow the percentage of ownership. *Garcia v. Andrus,* 692 F.2d 89, 92 (9th Cir. 1982). For example, if a cotenant obtains a loan and mortgages the property, he is able to mortgage only his percentage of ownership interest. If one cotenant rents the whole property to a third party, he must share the proceeds with his cotenants in accordance with their respective percentages of ownership. *Id.* at 94.

The use of *id.* indicates that the source of the statement is the preceding citation, *Garcia v. Andrus.* If the source is on the same page as the previous citation (page 92), just *Id.* is used, not *Id. at 94.* If another citation followed *Garcia v. Andrus,* the use of *id.* following that citation to refer to *Garcia v. Andrus* would be improper.

> **For Example** Incorrect use of *Id.*: Numerous other elements of control follow the percentage of ownership. *Garcia v. Andrus,* 692 F.2d 89, 92 (9th Cir. 1982). For example, if a cotenant obtains a loan and mortgages the property, he is able to mortgage only his percentage of ownership interest. *Appeal of Schramm,* 414 N.W.2d 31, 32 (S.D. 1987). If one cotenant rents the whole property to a third party, he must share the proceeds with his cotenants in accordance with their respective percentages of ownership. *Id.* at 94.

The use of *Id. at 94* to refer to *Garcia v. Andrus* is improper. Note that when *id.* is used with statutory or paragraph citations, the word *at* is not included when referring to a different statutory section.

> **For Example** The full citation of the statute referred to is 18 U.S.C. § 1112 (1994). When the reference is to § 1113, the short citation is *Id.* § 1113, not *Id.* at § 1113.

Id. may be used for any legal authority except internal cross-references. Internal cross-references are discussed in section IV.J.

2. *Supra* as a Short Citation

Supra as a short citation means "above" and is used to refer to a reference source that was previously fully cited in a document. It cannot be used in place of *id*. In other words, *supra* is not used when referring to an immediately preceding cited source. It is used to refer to a previously cited source in a document when there have been other intervening cited sources. *Supra* cannot be used to refer to cases, statutes, session laws, ordinances, legislative materials (other than hearings), constitutions, and administrative regulations. It is italicized or underscored; when it is underscored, do not underscore any accompanying punctuation. When using *supra*, put the author's last name first (or the title when the name is not available) followed by a comma, then *supra*. When the reference is to a page other than the page in the earlier citation, follow *supra* with a comma, then *at* and the page number.

> **For Example** It is clear that a mixed motive does not invalidate zoning restrictions on adult entertainment as long as the predominant concern of the zoning body is legitimate. *See* Alfred C. Yen, *Judicial Review of the Zoning of Adult Entertainment: A Search for the Purposeful Suppression of Protected Speech,* 12 Pepp. L. Rev. 651, 655 (1985). Courts have noted that respect must be given to the community's need to preserve the quality of life. *Las Vegas v. Nevada Industries, Inc.,* 105 Nev. 174, 772 P.2d 1275 (1989). The key question is what is the predominant concern of the zoning body. Yen, *supra*, at 657.

In this example, *supra* is used because a different citation appears between the Yen citation and the second reference to the Yen article. If the second Yen reference immediately followed the first full citation, *Id.* would be used.

> **For Example** It is clear that a mixed motive does not invalidate zoning restrictions on adult entertainment as long as the predominant concern of the zoning body is legitimate. *See* Alfred C. Yen, *Judicial Review of the Zoning of Adult Entertainment: A Search for the Purposeful Suppression of Protected Speech,* 12 Pepp. L. Rev. 651, 655 (1985). The key question is what is the predominant concern of the zoning body. *Id.* at 657.

3. *Hereinafter* as a Short Citation

Hereinafter may be used in certain circumstances to shorten a long title that is cumbersome to cite repeatedly, such as when the source has no author and the title is long. *Hereinafter* is also used when two or more authorities appear in a footnote and the use of *supra* would be confusing. Place the hereinafter designation in ordinary type in brackets ([ ]) immediately following the end of the first full citation to the authority. The shortened form should clearly identify the authority.

> **For Example** *Assume here that the article in the previous example does not have an author:* It is clear that a mixed motive does not invalidate zoning restrictions on adult entertainment as long as the predominant concern of the zoning body is legitimate. *See Judicial Review of the Zoning of Adult Entertainment: A Search for the Purposeful Suppression of Protected Speech,* 12 Pepp. L. Rev. 651 (1985) [hereinafter *Adult Entertainment Zoning*].

J. Internal Cross-References (*Supra* and *Infra*)—Bluebook R-3.5; ALWD-10

Often, especially when a document is long or includes many footnotes, you will want to refer the reader to source material on a specific page, section, or footnote of the document. For that purpose, *supra* is used to refer to material that appears earlier in the document and *infra* is used to refer to material that appears later. When used in this context, *supra* has a different function from its use as a short citation. When used as a short citation, *supra* refers to a specific source, such as a law review article. As internal cross-references, *supra* and *infra* refer to parts of the document, not specific sources. The terms are either italicized or underscored, and it may be necessary to add an explanatory parenthetical to identify the reference.

For Example	*See supra* pp. 9–11 (discussing the rights of third parties)

Supra n. 7 (cases supporting third-party claims)

Supra Section III.B–F

Infra notes 8–9 and accompanying text

Infra pp. 23–25 and note 16

Infra Part II. A and B (discussing interrogatory questions)

K. Signals—Bluebook R-1.2 to R-1.5; ALWD-44 to ALWD-46

Signals are terms or words used to indicate the manner in which the cited authority supports or contradicts the text. A signal is not used when the citation identifies the source of a quotation, directly supports a statement, or identifies the authority in reference.

For Example	The United States Supreme Court has adopted the "good faith" exception to the exclusionary rule. *United States v. Leon*, 468 U.S. 897 (1984).

1. Types of Signals

Following is a list of citation signals with examples of their use:

E.g.—Indicates that the cited authority is representative of (or an example of) many other authorities that stand for the same proposition. It may be used with other signals, such as *see, e.g.* and *but see, e.g.*

See—Used to indicate that the cited authority clearly supports a proposition but does not directly state the proposition.

See also—Used to show additional authority that supports a proposition.

See generally—Used to identify authority that presents helpful background information related to the stated proposition.

Accord—Used to indicate other cases that state or support a proposition. It is placed after the citation given in support of the proposition.

Cf.—Indicates authority that supports a proposition different from but analogous to the proposition stated.

Compare ... with—Used to compare authorities that may illustrate or reach a result different from the stated proposition. The *Bluebook* and the *ALWD* differ somewhat in their use of *compare*.

But see—Used to identify authority that contradicts the stated proposition.

But cf.—Identifies authority that supports a proposition analogous to the contrary of the stated proposition.

Contra—Used to identify authority that directly contradicts the stated proposition.

2. Presentation

Capitalize the first letter of a signal that begins a sentence. Italicize or underscore signals and separate them from the rest of the citation with a space. Use a semicolon to separate each authority within a signal. Both the *Bluebook* and the *ALWD* strongly recommend the use of parenthetical explanations to describe the relevance of the cited authority. Some examples of the use of signals are presented here.

> **For Example** *See, e.g., Renton v. Playtime Theatres, Inc.,* 475 U.S. 41, 55 (1986); *Young v. American Mini Theatres, Inc.,* 427 U.S. 50, 59 (1976).
>
> *Goldstar (Panama) S.A. v. United States,* 967 F.2d 965, 968 (4th Cir. 1992); *accord Argentine Republic v. Amerada Hess Shipping Corp.,* 488 U.S. 428, 442 (1989) (Supreme Court determining that the convention set forth only substantive rules of conduct and did not create a private right).
>
> *Contra Knapp v. Stanford,* 392 So. 2d 196, 198 (Miss. 1981) (sudden emergency doctrine confuses the principle of comparative negligence).

3. Order of Presentation

Following is a summary of the order of presentation of authorities. For a detailed list, refer to the *Bluebook* and the *ALWD*. Present citations in the following order:

a. Constitutions—federal constitution, followed by state constitutions (alphabetically by state), then foreign constitutions (alphabetically by country)

b. Statutes—federal statutes (chronologically by title number), followed by state statutes (alphabetically by state), then foreign statutes (alphabetically by country)

c. Cases—federal cases (starting with the highest court to the lowest court), followed by state cases (alphabetically by state from the highest to the lowest courts), then foreign cases (alphabetically by country)

d. Administrative and executive materials—such as the *CFR* or executive orders

e. Legislative materials—such as bills and legislative history

f. Secondary authority—see Bluebook R-1.3 or ALWD-46.4(c) for the order of presentation of secondary authority

L. Sections (§) and Paragraphs (¶)—Bluebook R-3.4; ALWD-6

Following is a summary of citation rules when an authority is organized by sections or paragraphs.

Insert a space before and after the section or paragraph symbol—18 U.S.C. § 2111 (1994). Do not use *at* when referring to a paragraph or section.

> **For Example** Correct: *Id.* § 2111
>
> Incorrect: *Id.* at § 2111

When the authority is divided into subsections or subparagraphs, use the punctuation of the original source to separate sections and subsections. When the source does not have any punctuation, place the subdivisions in parentheses—18 U.S.C. § 842(a)(1). Note that there is no space between the main section 842 and the subsections (a)(1).

A section may include a letter as part of the designation. In that case, the letter does not refer to a subsection. Therefore, do not separate it with punctuation; for example, 42 U.S.C. § 2000e-1(a) (1994), not 42 U.S.C. § 2000(e)(1)(a) (1994). The *e* is part of the section designation and does not refer to a subsection.

When citing consecutive sections or paragraphs, include the first and last sections and separate the sections with a hyphen, a en dash, or *to*. Retain all digits on both sides of the span. Use consecutive section or paragraph symbols to reference multiple sections or paragraphs.

> **For Example** Correct: ¶¶ 115–123; §§ 15 to 17
>
> Incorrect: ¶¶ 115-23; §§ 15 to 7

When citing multiple sections or paragraphs that are not consecutive, place a comma between the sections or paragraphs and do not place *and* or *&* before the final section or paragraph.

> **For Example** Correct: ¶¶ 115, 123, 129; §§ 15, 17, 19
>
> Incorrect: ¶¶ 115, 123, and 129; §§ 15, 17, & 19

When citing multiple subsections or subparagraphs of a single section or paragraph, use one section or paragraph symbol.

> **For Example** § 231(a)–(f); ¶ 22(g)-(k) (multiple consecutive subsections and subparagraphs)
>
> § 231(a), (f), (k); ¶ 22(a), (g), (k) (multiple nonconsecutive subsections and subparagraphs)

M. Electronic Sources—Bluebook R-18; ALWD-38 to ALWD-42

Both the *Bluebook* and the *ALWD* state that if the authority is readily available in print, the citation should be to the print source. It is not necessary to reference the electronic source, such as Westlaw or LexisNexis. That rule applies unless the documents are not available as printed sources or are difficult to obtain, such as unpublished cases. The *Bluebook* and the *ALWD* differ as to electronic citation details; therefore, you should check the rules when citing those sources. For example, in the *ALWD,* citations to Westlaw and LexisNexis are placed in parentheses with the words *available in WL* or *available in LexisNexis,* that is, available in LexisNexis in the Legal News database. In the *Bluebook*, Westlaw and LexisNexis citations are not placed in parentheses and are not preceded by *available in*. The examples in this subsection follow the *Bluebook* format.

In general, a citation to an authority should include information that clearly indicates the source. The rules governing electronic sources are quite detailed, and it is beyond the scope of this text to present a discussion of each rule. Therefore, this section contains a brief summary of the key points for citing electronic sources.

1. Commercial Sources

Due to the reliability of databases, *Bluebook* R-18.1 recommends the use of commercial electronic databases over other Internet sources. In addition to the usual information given in a citation, such as a case name or statute number, the database identifier must be included in the citation. The identifier usually includes the database name "LEXIS" (*Bluebook*) and "Lexis" (*ALWD*) for LexisNexis and WL for Westlaw; year; and document number. Some examples of citations to Westlaw and LexisNexis are presented here.

> **For Example** Unpublished cases: *Christians v. Stafford,* No. 14-99-00038-CV, 2000 Tex. App. LEXIS 6423 (Tex. Ct. App. Oct. 26, 2000)
>
> *Devji v. Keller,* No. 03-99-00436-CV, 2000 Tex. App. WL 1862819, at *2 (Tex. Ct. App. Dec. 21, 2000)

Note: When you are referring to a specific screen or page number, place an asterisk before the number (*at *2* in the preceding example). When the reference is to a specific paragraph number, precede the number with the paragraph symbol and do not use *at* (¶ 15). The previous example references a specific screen page number.

Congressional bills: H.R. 1167, 106th Cong. (1999) WL 1999 CQ US HR 1167; H.R. 301, 107th Cong. (2001) LEXIS Archived Bill Text and Tracking Library, 106th Congress file

Newsletter: Kim Biello, Susan Beck, Andrew Longstreth, *Bar Talk,* The American Lawyer, Sept. 2001, available in LEXIS Legal News Library, The American Lawyer file

Law review: Alfred C. Yen, *Judicial Review of the Zoning of Adult Entertainment: A Search for the Purposeful Suppression of Protected Speech,* 12 Pepp. L. Rev. 651 (1985), WL 12 PEPLR 651

2. World Wide Web Sources

An online citation should include: the full name of the author or owner; the title in italics; pinpoint references such as paragraph numbers, if any; the URL (Web address); and the date enclosed in parentheses.

> **For Example** MSNBC, *MSNBC Home News, Oil Prices Sink after OPEC Dithers,* <http://www.msnbc.com/news/657546.asp> (Nov 15, 2001).

ALWD-12.5 states that if a case is available in a reporter or through an online database such as Westlaw, other Internet sources should not be cited.

V. KEY POINTS CHECKLIST: *Legal Citation*

✓ When checking citations, always consult an authority, such as the *Bluebook* or the *ALWD Citation Manual.*

✓ Make sure the appropriate words in a citation, such as case names and article titles, are properly italicized or underlined.

✓ Check the rules and tables or appendices to ensure that words, such as *Incorporated* and *South Eastern Reporter,* are properly capitalized, abbreviated, and spaced.

✓ When signals, such as *See also*, are included in a citation, check to ensure that you are using them properly.

✓ Check the use of *id*. and other short citations. Is the use of a short citation proper? If so, is the citation format proper?

✓ Check case citations to ensure that all the elements are present—case name, reporter volume, and page, pinpoint page if the citation is to a specific page, parallel citation (if any), court abbreviation if necessary, year of the decision in parentheses, and subsequent history, if any.

✓ Make sure all the elements of statutory citations are present. Statutory citations usually include the name of the code or code abbreviation; the section symbol (§); title, chapter, or section numbers; and, in parentheses, the publisher if it is a commercial publication and the year the volume was published.

✓ For any other citation, such as a secondary citation, check the rules to ensure that all the elements of the citation are present and properly used.

VI. APPLICATION

Mike's research memo is based on two cases and a Georgia statute. As he researched, he wrote them down as follows: In the Interest of M.N.L. vol. 221 Georgia Appeals Court page 123 and volume 470 South Eastern Reporter 2d page 753, 1996; In the Interest of G.L.H. vol. 209 Georgia Appeals Court page 146 and volume 433 South Eastern Reporter 2d page 357, 1993; Section 15-11-94 of the Georgia Code Annotated 2000. By referring either to *Bluebook* Rule 10, Practitioners' Note P.1 and Table T.1, or to *ALWD* Rule 12 and Appendix 1, Mike would convert his case notes to the following citations: *In the Interest of M.N.L.*, 221 Ga. App. 123, 470 S.E.2d 753 (1996); *In the Interest of G.L.H.*, 209 Ga. App. 146, 433 S.E.2d 357 (1993). After consulting *Bluebook* Rule 12 and Table T.1 or *ALWD* Rule 14 and Appendix 1, he would properly cite the statute as Ga. Code Ann. § 15-11-94 (2000).

Summary

Whenever a reference is made in legal writing to a primary or secondary legal authority, the source of the reference must be identified. This reference is called a citation. A citation provides the information necessary to allow the reader to locate the reference, thus allowing the reader to check its content. Citations are usually required in most legal writing, such as office legal memoranda, and may be included in general legal correspondence or other documents when there is reference to a legal authority.

It is essential that the information included in a citation be correct. It is useless to refer a reader to a source of information and incorrectly identify the location of the source.

The main guides and sources of authority on legal citations are *The Bluebook: A Uniform System of Citation* (Bluebook) and the *ALWD Citation Manual: A Professional System of Citation*. This chapter presents a brief review of the main rules of citation.

The chapter begins with an overview of the numerous rules of citation used when citing primary authority, that is, case, constitutional, and enacted (statutory) law. The next section summarizes the citation format for major secondary sources such as legal encyclopedias, *Annotated Law Reports* (ALR), law reviews, *Restatements,* and treatises.

The chapter concludes with an overview of basic rules of citation to be followed when citing most legal sources. Among other topics, the section covers the use of italics, abbreviations, capitalization, quotations, pinpoint citations, short citations, signals, and citations to electronic sources.

Inasmuch as both *Bluebook* and *ALWD* consist of hundreds of pages, a detailed discussion of the citation rules of either text is beyond the scope of this chapter. This chapter includes references to rules from both *ALWD* and *Bluebook* with the goal of providing quick access to the main rules of citation in either authority.

Quick References

Internet Resources

http://www.alwd.org

This Web site for the *ALWD Citation Manual* includes many features such as additional material, examples, and updates.

http://www.legalbluebook.com

This Web site includes information on the nineteenth edition of the *Bluebook*.

Exercises

Additional assignments are available on the CourseMate.

For the following exercises, use either *Bluebook* or *ALWD*.

ASSIGNMENT 1

Provide the correct citation name for the following cases:

The United States of America v. Thomas Terry

Mary Kay Kraft, Mark Johnson, and Vanessa Hays v. Joseph Beazley and the City of Chicago

Kerry Handle et al v. The Jamestown Cooperative

Kalley Institute v. Carrington Insurance Company, Incorporated

The American Civil Liberties Union v. Micron Management Corporation dba Taylor Management

ASSIGNMENT 2

Give the correct citation for the following case, include the parallel citations: The United States of America versus Matlock, volume 94, page 988 of the *Supreme Court Reporter*, volume 39, page 242 of the *United States Supreme Court Reports, Lawyer's Edition*, volume 415, page 164 of the *United States Reports*, decided February 20, 1974.

ASSIGNMENT 3

Give the correct citation for the following case, include the parallel citations: Douglas D. Robberts versus Carroll E.

Swain, volume 487 *South Eastern Reporter* page 760, North Carolina Appeals Court 1997. The citation is to page 766.

ASSIGNMENT 4

Correct the following citation: Hoang Nguyen v. Fasano 84 F. Supp.2d 1099,(S.D.Cal.2000).

ASSIGNMENT 5

Correct the following citation: Lynda Herndon v. Jackie Barrell, 101 N.C.App. 636; 400 S.E. 2d 769 (N.C.App. 1991).

ASSIGNMENT 6

Give the correct citation for the following statutes: Title eighteen of the *United States Code* section 1112 the 1999 edition. Title eighteen of the *United States Code Annotated* section 1112 by West Group 2000 and title eighteen of the *United States Code Service* by LexisNexis 2000.

ASSIGNMENT 7

Give the correct citation for the following: the fifth Amendment to the United States Constitution; article four section three of the United States Constitution.

ASSIGNMENT 8

Correct the following citations: 26 U. S. C. §112; U. S. Const. Amend 4.

ASSIGNMENT 9

Correct the following citation: Vol. 6 American Jur. (second), *Assault and Battery*, §2(1999).

ASSIGNMENT 10

Give the correct citation to section 40 of the treatise *The Law of Torts* by Dan B. Dobbs published by West Group in 2000.

ASSIGNMENT 11

Give the correct citation for the following law journal article: An article by Douglas J. Gunn entitled Torts—Negligence—The Sudden Emergency Doctrine is abolished in Mississippi, volume 51, page 301 of the Mississippi Law Journal published in 1980.

What is the short citation?

ASSIGNMENT 12

Give the correct citation to the Restatement of the Law of Torts Third, Apportionment of Liability Sections 8 through 10, 1999.

ASSIGNMENT 13

Give the citation to an American Law Reports Federal annotation published in 1999 in the 155 volume at page 535. The annotation is entitled "Effect of Use, or Alleged Use, of Internet on Personal Jurisdiction in, or Venue of, Federal Court Case" by Jason H. Eaton.

ASSIGNMENT 14

What is the short citation format for assignments 12 and 13?

PART III

The Specifics of Legal Analysis

OVERVIEW

Part III covers matters essential to the analysis of a legal problem. It begins with a chapter on a principal component of a legal question (legal issue), the key facts—facts critical to the outcome of the case.

Next are two chapters on identifying and writing legal issues:

1. Identifying the legal issue presented by a fact situation or in a court opinion

2. Stating or presenting the issue

Part III concludes with two chapters on topics fundamental to legal analysis:

1. Case law analysis—the analytical process used to determine if a court opinion applies to a legal question

2. Counteranalysis—the process of discovering and considering the counterargument to a legal position or argument

CHAPTER 9

Legal Analysis—Key Facts

Alice was recently hired by Kinsey Law Firm and placed under the guidance and supervision of Karen, a 15-year veteran paralegal. Karen did an initial interview with a client, Mr. Aper, and Alice sat in on the interview to observe the process and gain experience. After the interview, Karen told Alice, "I'm going to prepare a summary of the interview, then prepare a list of the potential issues. I want you to identify the key facts that should be included in the statement of the issues."

Alice's notes of the interview indicate that Mr. Aper owns a 1,000-acre farm on the outskirts of town. He has lived on the farm for the past 20 years. About 200 acres of the property are forested, and deer frequent the forest. Mr. Aper refuses to allow hunting on his property and, to discourage hunting, has fenced and posted the property.

One day, two weeks ago, Mr. Aper noticed a new path entering the forested portion of the farm. Someone had removed part of the wood fence surrounding the forest and apparently entered the property several times. He followed the trail and found several small pine trees cut down and a crude lean-to constructed from the trees. In front of the lean-to was a small fire pit where there had been a fire quite recently; the coals were still warm. Some of the wood removed from the fence was still smoldering in the fire. Mr. Aper got up early the next morning, before dawn, and watched the lean-to from a hidden spot in the bushes. Shortly after sunrise, he saw his neighbor, Eric Rascon, an avid bow hunter, come down the trail carrying a hatchet and loaded down with bow-hunting gear.

Eric proceeded to set up camp. He started a fire with wood from the fence and some old tree branches and cut down another small tree and added it to the lean-to. Mr. Aper stepped out from behind the bushes and confronted Eric. "What are you doing here? You know you can't hunt here. Who told you it's okay to cut down my trees? Get off my property!" Eric angrily replied, "You stingy old man. These deer should be hunted; it's nature's way. I'll leave, but I'll be back and start again; you can't watch this forest every hour of every day." Eric then left.

Mr. Aper wants to take whatever legal action he can against Eric. Alice's assignment is to identify the key facts in the case. The Application section of this chapter addresses how Alice performs her assignment. The chapter discusses facts in general and emphasizes the critical role of the key facts in a case.

Outline

Learning Objectives

After completing this chapter, you should understand:

- What key facts are
- What background and irrelevant facts are
- The role and importance of key facts
- How to identify key facts in a client's case
- How to identify key facts in a court opinion

I. INTRODUCTION

Most, if not all, attorney–client relationships begin with the initial interview with the client. During the interview, the client presents information concerning a situation the client believes requires a legal solution. If a lawsuit is ultimately filed, the process begins here. The role of the attorney, often performed by the paralegal or law clerk, is to sift through the facts and determine what relief, if any, the law may provide for the problem raised by the facts. Any legal solution to a client's problem involves the application of the law to the facts of the client's case.

Usually, some of the factual information the client provides in an interview is not relevant to the outcome of the case. Sometimes important factual information is left out. Before a legal solution to the client's problem can be found or a determination made as to whether a lawsuit should be filed, it is necessary to identify the facts critical to the outcome of the case—the key facts. To ensure that all the key facts are identified—that is, to make sure none are missed—all the factual information concerning the problem must be identified at the outset. This is accomplished by a thorough and comprehensive initial interview.

Often the importance of certain facts may not be determined until the legal issues and the governing law are identified.

> **For Example** In regard to the hypothetical at the beginning of the chapter, assume that the researcher, based on her experience, concludes that the burning of the fence may give rise to a cause of action for conversion (an improper act that deprives an individual of the rightful possession of the individual's property). Upon conducting subsequent research, she learns that conversion requires that the person suing be in possession of the property.
>
> It is an important fact, therefore, that Mr. Aper not only owns the land but also was in possession of the land when the events took place. If the land were rented out to a tenant, the tenant would be in possession of the land. The tenant, being the person in possession of the land, would have the right to sue for conversion. The landlord, Mr. Aper, would not be in possession of the land and, therefore, would not have a right to sue Eric Rascon for conversion. The importance of the fact that Mr. Aper not only owned the land but was also in possession of it may not become apparent until the legal question and governing law are identified.

This example illustrates another important point concerning facts. When a lawsuit proceeds to trial, the facts presented at trial are those facts identified and considered important prior to trial. Identifying and gathering the facts depend entirely on the thoroughness and quality of the pretrial preparation. If the researcher performs a sloppy job, that is, fails to gather and examine all the facts, then a poor outcome and a lost case may be the result.

> **For Example** Referring to the previous example, assume that the land was leased. Mr. Aper did not reveal this fact during the interview because, being the owner of the land, he did not think it mattered who was in possession. The interview was not thorough because Mr. Aper was not asked who was in possession of the land. Assume also that the researcher believed that the "possession" requirement of conversion is met if the party suing owns the property. The researcher did a sloppy job of research and did not thoroughly research what constitutes "possession" under the law.
>
> If a lawsuit alleging conversion against Mr. Rascon went to trial and this key fact was not identified, Mr. Aper would lose because he was not in possession of the land and did not have a right to sue. The key fact of who was in possession of the land was not identified prior to trial and, therefore, would not be presented at trial. The poor quality of the interview and subsequent research resulted in a poor outcome.

Ethics

This may appear to be an extreme example, but it illustrates an important point: The facts presented at trial and the outcome of the trial depend entirely on the quality of work prior to trial. As noted in Chapter 2, Rule 1.1 of the American Bar Association's Model Rules of Professional Conduct requires that a client be provided competent representation. Failure to conduct a proper interview and identify the key facts denies the client competent representation.

The focus of this chapter, and the task assigned to many paralegals and law clerks, is to identify the facts that give rise to the legal dispute in either a client's case or a court opinion. The facts that give rise to the legal dispute are often referred to as *significant, material,* or *key facts*. In this chapter, and throughout the text, these facts are referred to as *key facts*.

As noted in Chapters 10 and 11, key facts and issues are integrally related. The key facts are an essential element of the issue. They are essential in identifying and stating the issue because they give rise to the legal dispute. Disputes arise and take place in the context of facts.

II. FACTS IN GENERAL—DEFINITION

A fact is something that is real, that actually exists, an actual event as opposed to an opinion or someone's interpretation of what took place. In a lawsuit, a **fact** is information present in a case concerning some thing, action, event, or circumstance.

> **For Example** In the hypothetical at the beginning of the chapter, the presence of the lean-to, Mr. Rascon's actions of entering the property, and Mr. Rascon's statements are all facts.

Facts should not be confused with a **rule of law**. A rule of law is a standard, established by a governing authority, that prescribes or directs action or forbearance. It may be a constitutional provision, statute, ordinance, regulation, or case law doctrine. Its application determines the outcome of the question raised by the facts of a dispute.

> **For Example** Title 23, section 1991, of the state statutes provides that the maximum speed limit in a school zone is 10 mph while school is in session. When an individual proceeds through a school zone at 12 mph, this statute governs the question of whether the individual is speeding, that is, the outcome of the question raised by the facts.

Before defining and discussing key facts, it is helpful to consider the importance of facts in general and to identify and distinguish the various types of facts present in a client's case and a court opinion.

III. IMPORTANCE OF FACTS

The importance of giving due consideration to the facts of a dispute cannot be overemphasized. Often minimal attention is given to the facts. This is surprising, since our legal system revolves around resolving disputes by applying the rules of law to the facts of a case. Notice the two major factors here: *rules of law* and *facts of the case*. Both are equally important. Novice researchers, however, often focus primarily on the rules of law.

The *issue* is the precise question raised by the specific facts of the client's case. Therefore, the facts are an essential element of the issue. Rules of law are general principles designed to apply to multiple fact situations, and a determination of which law governs the issue is controlled primarily by the facts of the client's case. Consequently, facts play a role of primary importance in determining what is in dispute in a case and which law applies. Clients often have little knowledge or concern about general legal principles, but they are very concerned with how the law applies to the facts of their case.

Facts are also important because determining how or if a law applies to the client's case often depends on the presence or absence of certain facts.

> **For Example** Tom is stopped at a light at a four-way intersection in the city, waiting for the light to change. Mary, stopped behind him, accidentally lets her foot slip off the brake, and her vehicle bumps into Tom's vehicle. After exiting their vehicles and examining them, they discover that there is no visible damage to either vehicle. Tom, however, complains of neck pain from whiplash.
>
> Tom sues Mary for negligence. The researcher working for Mary's attorney knows that the elements of negligence are duty, breach of duty, proximate cause, and damages. Based on her research and education, she also knows that to state a claim, Tom must present facts establishing each of the elements of negligence. Although there are facts to support the first three elements, there was no damage to the vehicle; thus, it is questionable whether the impact was severe enough to cause whiplash neck injuries. Also, if the impact did not cause whiplash injuries and there is no damage to Tom's vehicle, there are no facts that establish the element of damages.
>
> This hypothetical is referred to as the "minor impact" example throughout this chapter.

In the minor impact example, as in every case, there are two equally important factors—the law and the facts. The law establishes the conditions that must be met to state a claim for negligence, that is, the elements of negligence. The outcome of the application of the law depends on the existence of facts, and on one fact in particular in the case: Was Tom's injury caused by the impact? Like this example, all legal problems are fact sensitive; that is, the outcome depends on the existence or nonexistence of a particular fact or facts.

Another reason facts are important is that the determination of whether a court opinion is on point is largely governed by the similarity between the facts of the court opinion and the facts of the client's case. There must be a sufficient similarity between the key facts of the court opinion and those of the client's case before the court opinion can be considered on point and apply as precedent in the client's case.

IV. TYPES OF FACTS IN GENERAL

In either a client's case or a court opinion, there may be hundreds of facts, some of which are critically important, some not. To identify the legal issue, the researcher must sort through the facts and determine which facts give rise to the legal question and are essential to its resolution. Helpful to this process is an understanding of the basic categories of facts present in a case. The facts of a case may be placed within the three broad categories presented in Exhibit 9-1.

Exhibit 9-1 Types of Facts.

Irrelevant Facts	Facts coincidental to the event but not of significant legal importance in the case
Background Facts	Facts presented in a court opinion, case brief, or legal memorandum that put the key facts in context; facts that give an overview of a factual event and provide the reader with the overall context within which the facts occurred
Key Facts	The legally significant facts of a case that raise the legal question of how or whether the law governing the dispute applies; the facts that establish or satisfy the elements of a cause of action and are necessary to prove or disprove a claim; a fact so essential that, if it were changed, the outcome of the case would be affected or changed

© Cengage Learning 2014

A. Irrelevant Facts

Irrelevant facts are facts coincidental to the event that are not of legal significance in the case.

> **For Example** In the minor impact example, the race or gender of the parties, the day of the week, and whether Mary's car was insured are all irrelevant facts. They are irrelevant because they are facts that are not necessary to establish or satisfy the elements of the cause of action in the case. They are not necessary to prove or disprove the claim. The race or gender of the parties is irrelevant to the question of whether Mary was negligent. Whether it was Sunday or Wednesday when the accident occurred does not affect the outcome of the case. Mary's insurance status will not affect a determination of whether she is liable.

Beware! Certain facts may be relevant in one situation and not relevant in another.

> **For Example** In the minor impact example, whether it was snowing is probably not a relevant fact. Both vehicles were stopped at a light, and the existence of snow should not affect Mary's duty to keep her foot from slipping off the brake pedal. If the facts, however, were that she was approaching the stoplight and failed to apply the brakes in a timely fashion, the existence of snow conditions becomes a relevant fact. The nature of her duty to exercise care while driving varies with the weather conditions, and the existence of snow conditions requires her to exercise greater care when braking.

B. Background Facts

Background facts are those irrelevant facts that put the key facts in context. They give an overview of the factual event and provide the reader with the overall context within which the key facts occurred. They are not key facts because they are not essential to a determination of the issues in the case, but they are usually necessary and often helpful because they provide information that helps the reader gain an overall picture of the environment within which the key facts occurred.

> **For Example** In the minor impact example, the location and type of intersection are background facts that provide the reader with an overview of the context and scene of the collision. The reader is aware that the impact took place at an intersection in the city, rather than in the country. This information is not essential, but it may be helpful for many reasons. The reader, for example, may want to visit the scene at a later date to investigate and determine if individuals working in the area witnessed the accident.

C. Key Facts

Key facts are often referred to as *significant, material,* or *ultimate facts.* They are facts that are critical to the outcome of the case. The following section discusses the definition and types of key facts.

V. KEY FACTS—DEFINITION AND TYPES
A. Definition

Key facts are the legally significant facts of a case that raise the legal question of how or whether the law governing the dispute applies. They are those facts upon which the outcome of the case is determined—the facts that establish or satisfy the elements of a cause of action and are necessary to prove or disprove a claim. A key fact is a fact so essential that, if it were changed, the outcome of the case would probably change. In fact, a useful test in determining whether a fact is key is to ask the question, "If this fact is changed, would the outcome of the application of the law be affected or changed?"

> **For Example** Law enforcement officers are sued for battery based on the following facts. Law enforcement officers pursued a suspect on foot for five blocks after observing him snatch a woman's purse. While making the arrest, the officers encountered resistance, used force to overcome that resistance, and continued to use force for more than a minute after the resistance ceased. The law provides that law enforcement officers may use the amount of force necessary to overcome resistance when making a legal arrest. This hypothetical is referred to in this chapter as the "resisting arrest" example.

What are the key facts in the resisting arrest example? Which of the facts, if changed, would change the outcome in this case? If the suspect had never resisted, the use of force would clearly have been improper. If the suspect never ceased resisting, the officers' continued use of force would have been proper. If the officers stopped using force when the resistance ceased, the use of force probably would have been proper. If the arrest was illegal, the use of force would have been improper. The key facts follow:

- A lawful arrest was being made.
- There was resistance to the arrest.
- Force was used to overcome the resistance.
- The resistance ceased.
- The use of force continued for more than a minute after the resistance ceased.

Each of these facts is a key fact. Each fact, if changed, would affect the outcome of the case.

Other facts, however, are not key facts. How far the officers pursued the suspect or the fact that the pursuit was on foot are not key facts. These facts, if changed, would not change the outcome of the case.

> **For Example** In the minor impact example, the lack of damage to Tom's automobile is a key fact. It is a fact that, if changed, would affect the outcome of the case. If there had been damage to Tom's vehicle, he clearly would have a claim. Damage is an element of negligence, and the existence of damage is a fact that is essential to establishing a negligence claim.

B. Types of Key Facts

There are two categories of key facts:

- Individual key facts
- Facts considered as a group—groups of facts

1. Individual Key Facts

Often an individual or several **individual facts** are key facts in a case. A key fact is an individual key fact if it meets the following test: If the fact is changed, the outcome of the case will be affected or changed.

> **For Example** 1. In the resisting arrest example, all the facts identified as key facts are individual key facts: A lawful arrest was being made, there was resistance to the arrest, force was used to overcome the resistance, resistance ceased, and the use of force continued after the resistance ceased. Each of these individual facts, if changed, would change or affect the outcome of the case.
>
> 2. Consider a breach-of-contract case in which the claim of breach is founded on the fact that payment was received nine days late, and the contract specifically provided that late payments constituted a breach of contract. The lateness of the payment is a key fact. This individual fact, if changed, would change the outcome of the case.

2. Groups of Facts

In some fact situations, no individual fact standing alone is a key fact—that is, no single fact is so significant that, if changed, it would change the outcome.

> **For Example** An inmate is challenging the conditions of his confinement as cruel and unusual punishment. He alleges the following: There are cockroaches in his jail cell, the recreational periods are too short, his mail is improperly censored, his visitation rights are too restricted, and the temperature in his cell is too low in the winter and too high in the summer. It may be that no single fact by itself meets the test of a key fact, that is, no single fact is so critical that, if changed, the outcome of the case would change. The fact that there are cockroaches in his cell may not be sufficient, by itself, to constitute cruel and unusual punishment; the fact that the recreational periods are too short, by itself, may not constitute cruel and unusual punishment; and so on.
>
> All the individual facts, however, when considered as a group, may determine the outcome of the case and, if changed as a group, would change the outcome. This may be identified in a court opinion when the court states, "No single fact of plaintiff's allegations constitutes cruel and unusual punishment. When taken as a whole, however, the individual allegations combine to establish a violation of the Eighth Amendment's prohibition against cruel and unusual punishment."

Recognizing **groups of facts** is important because, when analyzing a case, you must be aware that individual facts that seem to be insignificant may be key facts when considered and weighed as a group. When addressing a problem that involves key facts as a group, first review the facts individually to determine whether any individual fact, standing alone, is a key fact. If there is no individual fact that, if changed, would change the outcome of the case, look to the facts as a group.

There is no magic formula for determining how many or what types of facts are required for facts to be considered as a group, or what is necessary for a group of facts to be considered a key fact. Usually, it is necessary to consult case law and locate a case in which the court addressed a similar legal problem involving a group of facts.

The next step, after defining and categorizing key facts, is to determine how to locate them in both a client's case and a court opinion. Because the key facts are an element of the issue, the steps involved in identifying and stating the issue necessarily include, in part, some of the steps necessary for locating key facts. Therefore, the information from this chapter through Chapter 11 overlaps somewhat regarding the identification of key facts.

VI. KEY FACTS IDENTIFICATION—CLIENT'S CASE

A client's fact situation usually includes a mix of facts—some irrelevant, some background, and some key. A researcher's assignment may be to identify the key facts in the case. The four-step process presented in Exhibit 9-2 is recommended for determining which of the client's facts are key facts.

Exhibit 9-2 *Steps in Key Fact Identification—Client's Case.*

STEP 1	Identify each cause of action possibly raised by the facts.
STEP 2	Determine the elements of each cause of action identified in step 1.
STEP 3	List all the facts possibly related to the elements of the causes of action identified in step 2.
STEP 4	Determine which of the client's facts apply to establish or satisfy the elements of each cause of action—the key facts.

The following example is referred to in this section's discussion of the operation of this four-step process.

For Example The researcher is assigned the task of identifying the key facts in a case. A review of the file reveals the following facts. Jerry and Ann are neighbors. They have lived on adjoining half-acre lots in a rural subdivision for the past 15 years. Their children are close friends and ride the school bus together. Four years ago, Jerry put in a hedge and planted several trees along his property line with Ann. Every year since then, Jerry rakes the leaves from the hedge and trees into a big pile close to the shared property line and burns it. The prevailing wind carries the smoke and soot across Ann's property, preventing her from working in her garden and usually soiling the clothes that are drying on Ann's clothesline. Every year she asks him not to burn the leaves, and every year he ignores her request and burns the leaves.

Ann wants Jerry to stop burning the leaves and pay her for the clothes that have been "ruined" by the smoke. This hypothetical is referred to as the "trespass" example in this chapter.

A. Step 1: Identify Each Cause of Action

The first step requires determining the possible cause(s) of action raised by the facts. Depending on the education and legal experience of the researcher, this initial step may not require any research.

In the trespass example, upon reviewing the facts, the researcher may come to a preliminary conclusion that the possible causes of action include trespass to land, private nuisance, and negligence.

B. Step 2: Determine the Elements of Each Cause of Action

The second step, determining the elements of each cause of action, usually requires some research. Such research may be necessary either to determine the elements of the possible cause of action or to ensure that the law has not changed since the last time research was conducted. This step is necessary because, to state a claim and thereby obtain relief, the plaintiff must present facts that establish or prove the existence of each element of the cause of action. These facts are the key facts of the case.

> **For Example** The paralegal's research reveals that the elements of trespass to land are as follows:
>
> 1. An act
> 2. Intrusion on land
> 3. In possession of another
> 4. Intent to intrude
> 5. Causation of the intrusion

The researcher also would identify the elements of each of the other potential causes of action identified in step 1.

C. Step 3: List All Facts Related to the Elements

The third step is to list all the facts possibly related to the elements of the causes of action identified in step 2. This includes gathering the facts from the client interview, and any interviews that have been conducted with witnesses, and reviewing any documents in the case file that may contain factual information. The client files must be checked to ensure that they are complete. At the initial stages of a case, the client interview may be the only available source of information.

When listing the facts, include all facts that may possibly be related to any of the causes of action. Err on the side of listing too many facts. You want to have all possibly related facts at hand when you proceed to step 4, the step in which the irrelevant facts are eliminated and the key facts are identified.

> **For Example** The fact that the children ride the school bus probably is not related to any of the potential causes of action. The nature of what is being burned may be related. The number of years Jerry has burned the leaves may be related. The weather conditions when the leaves are burned may be related.

Consider the elements of each cause of action individually when performing this task.

> **For Example** Using trespass to land as a cause of action, take each element and determine what facts from the client's case possibly establish or are related to that element. Which of the facts relate to intrusion? Which of the facts relate to "in possession of another"? Which of the facts relate to the intent to intrude? Which of the facts relate to causation of the intrusion? After completing this process for the elements of trespass, do the same for each potential cause of action identified in the previous steps.

Note that some facts may establish or relate to more than one cause of action. Some causes of action overlap. Therefore, all the facts must be reviewed when considering the elements of each cause of action.

> **For Example** The fact that smoke from the burning leaves crosses onto Ann's property may establish or relate to both trespass to land and private nuisance. The smoke crossing to Ann's land may be the act of trespass, and the crossing coupled with the interference to Ann's enjoyment of her gardening may relate to nuisance. The fact that smoke crosses the property line relates to elements of both of these causes of action.

D. Step 4: Determine Which Facts Apply

The fourth step is to determine which of the client's facts apply to establish or satisfy the elements of each cause of action. The facts identified in this step are the key facts. Be sure to consider each fact listed in step 3 and determine if it is essential to establish or satisfy an element of any potential cause of action. It is important to consider all the facts identified in step 3. Step 4 consists primarily of the process of eliminating those facts listed in step 3 that are not essential or key facts. This is accomplished by taking each element of each cause of action and identifying the facts essential to establish or satisfy that element.

> **For Example** Referring to the trespass-to-land cause of action, the key facts follow:
>
> 1. Act—the burning of the leaves produces smoke.
> 2. Intrusion on land—the smoke crosses over Ann's land.
> 3. In possession of another—Ann owns and lives on the land.
> 4. Intent—Jerry built the fires (they were not caused by lightning or the acts of another), and he continued to build fires after he was notified of the problem.
> 5. Causation of the intrusion—the fire produced the smoke that passed over Ann's property, and there is no evidence that it came from another source.

When determining which facts identified in step 3 establish or satisfy an element, apply the following test:

- ◼ "Which of these facts, if changed, would change the outcome of the application of that element?" In other words,
- ◼ "Which of these facts, if changed, would affect the determination of whether there is present a fact or facts that establish or satisfy that element?"

> **For Example** Referring to the trespass-to-land cause of action, if the smoke did not pass over Ann's land, there would be no facts to support the element of intrusion. If the smoke crossing her land came from a source other than Jerry's land, Jerry would not be responsible for the causation of the trespass.

Other facts identified in step 3 as related to an element, but that do not establish or satisfy an element, are not key facts.

> **For Example** In step 3, the facts of what was being burned, the weather conditions when the burning took place, and the number of years Jerry had burned the leaves were considered as possibly related to the trespass cause of action. If it is determined that these facts, if changed, would not tend to establish or satisfy an element of trespass, they are not key facts and can be eliminated from further consideration.

All the facts identified in step 4 are the key facts. They are essential to the outcome of the case.

E. Multiple Issues

Steps 2 through 4 should be applied to each potential cause of action identified in step 1. Some causes of action may be eliminated because there no facts are present that support the existence of an element.

> **For Example** If the smoke passes harmlessly over Ann's land and does not interfere with her use or enjoyment of the land, there may be no cause of action for private nuisance.

Additional causes of action may be identified as research and investigation continue. Be sure to address each element of each possible cause of action and determine if there is any fact in the case that tends to establish or satisfy the element.

NOTE: These steps are useful tools and helpful guides when identifying key facts. They will usually help you quickly identify the key facts. Nothing, however, is foolproof. You may not be certain about whether a fact meets the standard required or is necessary to support the existence of an element. In some instances, that determination may not be made until trial.

> **For Example** The court may rule that the smoke crossing Ann's land is not a sufficient intrusion to constitute trespass.

Just make sure that there is some fact that arguably meets the requirements of each element of the cause of action.

VII. KEY FACTS IDENTIFICATION—CASE LAW

Every court opinion involves the court's application of the law to the facts of the case. The key facts are those facts in the case that the law applies to and that are essential to the decision reached by the court. If the key facts had been different, the outcome of the case probably would have been different.

Situations in which the court clearly points out the key facts are not addressed in this chapter.

> **For Example** The court states, "The critical facts in the resolution of this dispute are...."

The focus here is on those situations in which the key facts are not so easily determined, such as in cases where the court opinion intersperses many irrelevant and background facts with the key facts.

The steps recommended in Chapter 10 for identifying the issue in a court decision are similar, in part, to the steps for identifying the key facts presented here. As with determining the key facts in a client's case, there is no magic formula for identifying key facts in a court opinion. The three-step process presented in Exhibit 9-3 is recommended, however, and may prove helpful.

In this section, the following example is referred to when discussing the application of these steps. Notice that the example is factually similar to the case of *Rael v. Cadena*, presented in Exhibit 4-1.

Exhibit 9-3 *Steps in Key Fact Identification—Case Law.*

STEP 1	Read the entire case with the following general question in mind: What was decided about which facts?
STEP 2	Look to the holding. What is the court's answer to the legal question? How does the court apply the rule of law to the legal question raised?
STEP 3	Identify the facts necessary to the holding—the key facts. Part 1: List all facts in any way related to the holding. Part 2: Identify which of the listed facts are key facts and determine the key facts.

© Cengage Learning 2014

> **For Example** In the case of *Joins v. Stevens*, the court summarized the facts as follows:
> Jason Stevens and his nephew Allen Stevens have known Mark Joins for several years. The three occasionally engaged in recreational activities, such as attending baseball games and going on fishing trips. On these outings, they usually drank alcoholic beverages, often to excess. On some occasions, their spouses joined in the activities.
> On one of the fishing trips, on a Sunday afternoon in July, they were standing under a tree, drinking beer, and waiting for the rain to stop so they could resume fishing. They had been drinking since morning and were a little drunk. Mark was the only one who had caught any fish earlier in the day. Mark had an annoying habit of bragging, especially when he drank. Jason and Allen became increasingly angry as Mark claimed that he was the only "real fisherman" of the group. He continued bragging for an irritatingly long period. When he claimed that he was actually the "only real man" of the three, Allen lost control and beat him up. While the beating was going on, Jason yelled to Allen, "Hit him harder! Kick him! Kick him!"
> Mark suffered two broken ribs and was hospitalized. He sued Jason and Allen for the tort of battery. In deciding that Jason had committed a battery, the court stated, "Although liability cannot be based upon one's mere presence at a battery, a person may be held liable for the tort of battery if he encourages or incites by words the act of the direct perpetrator. Because he yelled encouragement to his nephew while the latter was beating Mark Joins, Jason Stevens is jointly liable with his nephew for the battery."

A. Step 1: Read the Entire Case

The first step is to read the entire case with the following general question in mind: "What was decided about which facts?" Because the key facts in a court opinion are those facts necessary to the decision reached by the court, you must have a general overview of the case before you can focus on determining which of the facts are key facts. You must read the entire case to determine the legal question addressed and the decision reached by the court, keeping in mind the question: "What was decided about which facts in this case?"

- "What was decided . . ." keeps the mind focused on the holding or decision reached.

- "About which facts . . ." keeps the mind focused on specific facts, those specific facts necessary to the resolution of the legal question—the key facts.

By the time you finish reading the entire case, you usually realize that the decision rests on only some of the facts mentioned in the opinion. If at this point you have not clearly identified which of the facts are key facts, proceed to step 2.

B. Step 2: Look to the Holding

The *holding* is the court's application of the rule of law to the legal question raised by the facts of the case. It is the court's answer to the legal question. Ask the following questions to help identify the holding:

- "What is the court's answer to the legal question?"
- "How does the court apply the rule of law to the legal question raised?"

In this example, the last two sentences are the court's presentation of the rule of law and the holding—the application of the rule of law to the facts:

- Rule of law—"Although liability cannot be based upon one's mere presence at a battery, a person may be held liable for the tort of battery if he encourages or incites by words the act of the direct perpetrator."

- Holding—"Because he yelled encouragement to his nephew while the latter was beating Mark Joins, Jason Stevens is jointly liable with his nephew for the battery."

C. Step 3: Identify the Key Facts

Identify the facts necessary to the holding. This step is composed of two parts:

1. List all facts in any way related to the holding.
2. Identify which of the listed facts are key facts.

1. List All Facts Related to the Holding

List all the facts presented in the case related to the holding. This may require going through the case and listing all the facts presented by the court. The court may present a multitude of background and irrelevant facts that in no way affect the outcome of the case. If that is the situation, identify and list only the facts that are possibly related or necessary to the decision reached.

In the preceding example, it is not necessary to list all the facts presented by the court. Some facts, such as the fact that the spouses sometimes accompanied the men, clearly are not relevant. Some facts—for example, it was a Sunday in July—are merely background facts that provide the reader with the time context of the event. All the facts relating to the argument should be included, such as the location of the argument, the fact the participants had been drinking, and what was said.

2. Determine the Key Facts

From the facts listed, determine the key facts by identifying those facts necessary or essential to the decision reached. Which facts determine the outcome of the case? There are several ways to identify these facts.

1. One test to determine the outcome is to ask yourself whether the decision would have been the same if a fact had not occurred, or if the fact had occurred differently. If Jason had merely stood by and watched, would he be liable for battery? In the previous resisting arrest example, if the individual had never ceased active resistance, would the police be liable for battery? Apply this test to each fact listed.

2. If this test is applied to each fact and no single fact, when changed or omitted, would affect or change the decision, ask whether the decision was governed by the court's consideration of the facts as a group.

> **For Example** The court may state, "No single act of the defendant is sufficient to constitute breach of contract. The defendant's various acts, however, when taken as a whole, are sufficient to establish breach."

3. If the court lists in its reasoning the elements of a cause of action, ask yourself which of the facts apply to establish the elements. In the battery example, the court stated that an individual may be liable if that individual "incites by words" the acts of the perpetrator. Jason's inciting words are the facts that relate to this element.

4. Ask yourself whether the court indicates that a certain fact is a key fact:

   a. Does the court describe a fact as "essential," "key," or "important"?

   b. Is a fact repeated throughout the opinion, especially in the reasoning supporting the decision?

   c. Does the court agree with a party's description of a fact as critical or key?

> **For Example** The court may state, "We agree with plaintiff's position that the failure to make timely payment is key to a determination of whether a breach of contract occurred."

5. Does a concurring or dissenting opinion identify the key facts? Be aware, however, that the concurring or dissenting judge may have a different view of which facts are key facts and may identify as key facts some facts the majority did not consider key.

D. Multiple Issues

The foregoing discussion focuses upon locating the key facts related to a single issue and holding in a case. Often, there are several issues and holdings in a court opinion. Apply the steps presented to determine the key facts related to each issue and holding. Follow each step completely for each issue and holding.

NOTE: The steps presented in this section are useful tools and guidelines. Following them helps you identify the key facts of a case. In some instances, however, the court may omit key facts. Also, as you read more cases and become more familiar with case law, you may automatically focus on the key facts without using any of the steps presented here.

VIII. KEY POINTS CHECKLIST: *Key Facts*

✓ Do not overlook the importance of the facts. Facts give rise to the legal dispute and, therefore, are an integral part of it. Disputes have little meaning outside the context of the facts. How many court opinions have you read that did not have any facts?

✓ Key facts are those facts that establish or satisfy the elements of a cause of action and are necessary to prove or disprove a claim. Therefore, the nature and presence or absence of certain facts determine the outcome of a case.

✓ A useful test for determining whether a fact is a key fact is to ask the question, "If this fact is changed or omitted, would the outcome of the application of the law be changed?"

✓ Follow the steps recommended for the determination of key facts in a client's case. Be aware that the importance of certain facts may not become apparent until legal research is conducted and the elements of a cause of action are determined.

✓ When identifying key facts in a court opinion, keep in mind the question, "What was decided about which facts in this case?"

✓ Do not get discouraged. The process of identifying key facts becomes easier with practice, and parts of the process become intuitive.

IX. APPLICATION

This section presents examples of key fact identification in a client's case and in a court opinion. Each example illustrates the application of the principles discussed in this chapter.

A. Client's Fact Situation

The following example illustrates the application of the principles to the hypothetical presented at the beginning of this chapter.

1. Identify Each Cause of Action

The first step is to identify each cause of action possibly raised by the facts. Based on Alice's recently completed education and limited job experience, she identifies three potential causes of action Mr. Aper may have against Mr. Rascon: trespass to land, trespass to chattels, and conversion. This preliminary identification may be expanded or reduced upon additional research.

> **For Example** Case law may reveal that Mr. Rascon's conduct also constitutes a private nuisance.

Step 1 provides a starting point for identification of the key facts in the case.

2. Determine the Elements

The second step is to determine the elements of each cause of action identified in step 1. For each potential cause of action, identify the elements necessary to state a claim. Research is usually required to determine the elements. Facts must be present that establish or satisfy each element of each cause of action. These facts are the key facts of the case. For illustration purposes, we will apply step 2 to the conversion cause of action.

Alice's research reveals that the elements of conversion are as follows:

■ Personal property

■ Plaintiff is in possession of the property or is entitled to immediate possession

▨ Intent to exercise dominion or control over the property by the defendant

▨ Serious interference with plaintiff's possession

▨ Causation of the serious interference

3. List All Facts Related to the Elements

Issue
Rule

The third step is to list all the facts possibly related to the elements of the causes of action identified in step 2. List all facts that might relate in some way to each of the elements of each cause of action. In this fact situation, the facts include:

1. Mr. Aper owns a farm with a 200-acre area that is forested and inhabited by deer.

2. The property is fenced and posted.

3. Mr. Aper discovered a newly traveled path through the property.

4. Part of the fence had been removed, several small trees had been cut down, and a lean-to had been constructed from the trees.

5. A fire had been built, and some of the wood from the fence was still smoldering in the fire.

6. Mr. Aper observed Eric Rascon, a neighbor, entering the property with his hunting gear, building a fire, and cutting a tree.

7. Mr. Aper saw Mr. Rascon add a tree to the lean-to.

Note that some of the facts included may not be related to any element, such as the fact that deer inhabit the forest or that Mr. Rascon is a neighbor. In this step, however, it is better to include all potentially related facts rather than omit them. Later research may demonstrate the importance of a fact initially thought to be insignificant.

4. Determine Which Facts Apply

Procedural Facts
Issue
Holding
Reasoning

The fourth step is to determine which of the client's facts apply to establish or satisfy the elements of each cause of action. The facts identified in this step are the key facts. Using the conversion cause of action as an illustration, the key facts are as follows:

▨ Personal property—the wood from the fence and the trees that were cut are Mr. Aper's personal property. Research may reveal that things growing on the land are real property and, therefore, are not covered by this tort. It may be though, that once cut down, a tree becomes personal property. This fact should be included until research determines the status of this property.

▨ Plaintiff is in possession of the property or is entitled to immediate possession—Mr. Aper owns and occupies the land.

▨ Intent to exercise dominion and control over the property—Mr. Rascon's actions include adding the fence wood and trees to the fire and cutting down the trees for the lean-to.

▨ Serious interference with plaintiff's possession—the cutting of trees and the burning of wood seriously interfere with Mr. Aper's rights of possession.

▨ Causation of serious interference—Mr. Rascon's actions of cutting and burning are clearly the cause of the interference. No other factual cause is present.

Note that this step results in the identification of those facts related to the elements of the cause of action and the elimination of all facts that are not necessary to establish a claim. You must apply this step to identify the key facts for each potential cause of action identified in step 1. Once this is done, all the key facts for each claim are identified. Note that the relationship between key facts, issue identification, and stating the issue is discussed in the next two chapters, Chapter 10 and Chapter 11.

B. Court Opinion

This example illustrates the operation of the principles for identifying the key facts in a court opinion. Read the *Flowers v. Campbell* case presented in the following text and apply the steps discussed in this chapter to determine the key facts of the collateral estoppel issue.

issues

Note that the doctrine of collateral estoppel is discussed in the case. The doctrine of collateral estoppel prevents a party in a lawsuit from relitigating an issue that was decided in a previous lawsuit. In the case, the trial court ruled that the question of whether the defendant, Campbell, used excessive force in resisting the assault of Flowers had already been litigated in an earlier criminal case. Based upon this ruling, the trial court determined that the doctrine of collateral estoppel applied and dismissed Flowers's claim that Campbell used excessive force. The appeal in *Flowers v. Campbell* is from this ruling by the trial court.

CASE

FLOWERS v. CAMPBELL

725 P.2d 01295 (Or. Ct. App. 1986)

ROSSMAN, Judge.

Plaintiff brought this assault and battery action to recover damages for injuries allegedly sustained in a skirmish with defendant Campbell (defendant), who was, at the time, an employee of defendant Montgomery Ward & Company. Plaintiff alleges that defendant used excessive force to repel his own aggressive behavior, for which plaintiff was convicted of assault in the fourth degree and harassment. The trial court dismissed the action after ruling, on defendant's motion for a directed verdict, that all material issues of fact were decided against plaintiff at his criminal trial and that he was precluded from relitigating those issues. We reverse.

The violence erupted after plaintiff accused defendant of charging him $12.99 for a lock that had been advertised for $9.97.[1] Plaintiff admits that he became involved in a verbal exchange with defendant immediately before the fight and that he "threw the first punch." He also concedes both that the jury at his criminal trial necessarily found that his use of force was not justified and that he is collaterally estopped from relitigating that issue. See Roshak v. Leathers, 277 Or. 207, 560 P.2d

275 (1977). He contends, however, that the dispositive issue in this civil action is whether defendant responded to his own admitted aggression with excessive force. He contends that that issue was not litigated at his criminal trial.

Under the doctrine of collateral estoppel, a party to an action may be prevented from relitigating issues that were actually decided and necessary to the judgment in a previous action. State Farm v. Century Home, 275 Or. 97, 550 P.2d 1185 (1976); Bahler v. Fletcher, 257 Or. 1, 474 P.2d 329 (1970). Plaintiff was convicted in the criminal action of assault and harassment. The victim's use of more force than was justified to repel the attacker's criminal acts is not a defense to either of those crimes. It follows that defendant's response to plaintiff's actions could not have been an issue that was necessarily decided in plaintiff's criminal trial. Accordingly, because an aggressor may recover in an action for battery if he proves that the defendant used more force than was justified in repelling the aggression, Linkhart v. Savely, 190 Or. 484, 497, 227 P.2d 187 (1951), the trial court erred in holding that plaintiff was precluded from litigating all issues "essential" to his recovery by reason of the judgment entered in his criminal trial.

Reversed and remanded.

[1] Plaintiff was 62 years old at fight time; defendant was 33. Plaintiff allegedly sustained a broken arm and a detached retina. Defendant's jaw was broken.

---

1. Read the Entire Case

The first step is to read the entire case with the following general question in mind: "What was decided about which facts?" This step helps you keep the facts in mind while obtaining an overview of what legal questions were addressed and answered.

2. Look to the Holding

The *holding* is the court's application of the rule of law to the legal question raised by the facts of the case. "What is the court's answer to the legal question? How did the court apply the rule of law to the legal question(s) raised?" These are questions to ask when looking to the holding.

In this case, the court stated that the doctrine of collateral estoppel prevents a party from relitigating issues that were actually decided in a previous action. The court noted that the victim's use of more force than was justified to repel the attacker's criminal acts is not a defense to assault or harassment. Therefore, the issue of the victim's use of excessive force to repel the plaintiff's attack was not litigated in the plaintiff's criminal trial. The court concluded that the trial court erred in applying the doctrine of collateral estoppel to preclude the plaintiff from litigating the question of the victim's use of excessive force to repel the plaintiff's aggression.

3. Identify the Key Facts

The third step is to identify the facts necessary to the holding—the key facts.

a. Part 1: List All Facts Related to the Holding

What facts are possibly related to the holding? The plaintiff filed an assault and battery civil action against the defendant to recover damages for injuries sustained in a skirmish with the defendant. The plaintiff and the defendant became involved in a fight as a result of a dispute over an amount the plaintiff was charged for an item. The plaintiff threw the first punch. He claims that the defendant responded with excessive force to the plaintiff's aggression. The plaintiff was tried in a separate criminal action and convicted of assaulting and harassing the defendant. The trial court ruled that "all material issues of fact were decided against plaintiff at his criminal trial and he was precluded from relitigating those issues." All of these facts are possibly related to the holding. Some of the facts of the case, such as what they were fighting about, are clearly not related and are eliminated in this part of step 3.

The trial court in this action ruled that the plaintiff was precluded from relitigating his claim in this action because the issues of fact regarding the fight were decided in the criminal action. The trial court, therefore, dismissed his claim.

b. Part 2: Determine the Key Facts

Which of the facts listed in part 1 are necessary or essential to the decision reached? Which of the facts, if changed, would change the outcome of the case?

- The trial court's ruling that the issue of the victim's response was litigated in the criminal case is clearly a key fact. Had the trial court ruled otherwise, the case would not have been dismissed and the appeal filed. Note that a "fact" in this instance is how the trial court ruled.

- The fact that the plaintiff was convicted of assault and harassment in an earlier criminal case is clearly a key fact. Had there been no criminal trial, the civil trial court could not have applied the doctrine of collateral estoppel.

- The fact that the defendant (victim) used force in response to the plaintiff's aggression is a key fact. The plaintiff's lawsuit rests upon the nature of the defendant's response.

- The fact that the victim's alleged use of excessive force to repel an attacker's acts of assault or harassment is not a defense to those acts in a criminal case is also key. Had this been a defense to those acts, the question of the victim's use of excessive force would have been litigated in the criminal case, and the trial court's ruling would have been correct.

Note that in this case, a key fact is a rule of law: The victim's use of force in response to assault and harassment is not a defense to either crime.

- The fact that the plaintiff threw the first punch in his fight with the defendant is probably not a key fact. It is not necessary to establish or satisfy any element of the collateral estoppel issue.

This case is somewhat different from some other cases because the key facts on appeal involve the facts of what occurred between the plaintiff and the defendant, the actions of the trial court, and the law governing defenses to assault and harassment.

Summary

All lawsuits arise as a result of disputes involving facts. Our legal system revolves around resolving disputes through the application of rules of law to the facts of a case. Therefore, the two major components of the dispute resolution process are the applicable law and the facts of the dispute. Each component deserves appropriate attention.

Some facts are more important than others, and the most important facts are the key facts—those facts upon which the outcome of the case depends. Key facts are those facts necessary to prove or disprove a claim. A key fact is so essential that if it were changed, the outcome of the case would be different. Key facts are an element of a legal issue, and that role is discussed in Chapters 10 and 11.

The four recommended steps to follow when determining the key facts of a client's case are:

- Step 1: Identify each cause of action possibly raised by the facts.
- Step 2: Determine the elements of each cause of action identified in step 1.
- Step 3: List all the facts possibly related to the elements of the causes of action identified in step 2.
- Step 4: Determine which of the client's facts apply to establish or satisfy the elements of each cause of action—the key facts.

The three recommended steps for identifying the key facts in a court opinion are:

- Step 1: Read the entire case with the following general question in mind: "What was decided about which facts?"
- Step 2: Look to the holding.
- Step 3: Identify the facts necessary to the holding—the key facts.

These recommended steps are usually helpful in identifying the key facts. You may develop shortcuts or different methods as you become more proficient in analyzing a client's case or a court opinion.

Quick References

Background facts	309	Irrelevant facts	309
Ethics	307	Key facts	310
Fact	307	Key facts—case law	315
Groups of facts	312	Key facts—client's case	312
Individual facts	311	Rule of law	307

Internet Resources

As of the date of publication of this text, there are no Web sites dedicated specifically to key facts. However, using a search engine such as http://www.google.com and "IRAC key facts" or "legal analysis and key facts" as a topic, you will find a wide range of Web sites related to the topic of legal analysis and key facts. Most of these sites provide information without charge. As noted in Chapter 7, the two major fee-based online research services are Westlaw and LexisNexis. The publishers closely monitor these services. Information you obtain free from other sites may not be closely monitored and may not be as accurate or have the same quality of material as that obtained from fee-based services. Therefore, exercise care when using freely obtained material.

Exercises

Additional assignments are available on the CourseMate.

ASSIGNMENT 1

Detail the steps for determining the key facts in a client's case.

ASSIGNMENT 2

Detail the steps for determining the key facts in a court opinion.

ASSIGNMENT 3

Identify the background facts in the following cases:
Flowers v. Campbell (presented in this chapter)
United States v. Leon (see Appendix A)

ASSIGNMENT 4

Identify the key facts in assignments 5 and 6 in the Exercises section of Chapter 10.

ASSIGNMENT 5

Identify the key facts in each of the hypotheticals presented at the beginning of Chapters 10, 11, and 12.

ASSIGNMENT 6

Identify the key facts in the cases listed in A, B, C, and E of assignment 10 in the Exercises section of Chapter 4.

ASSIGNMENT 7

Identify the key facts in assignments 5, 6, and 7 in the Exercises section of Chapter 17.

ASSIGNMENT 8

Facts: Terry, a bill collector, has been attempting to collect a bill from Client. Every other evening for the past two weeks, he has called Client at home after 8:30 p.m. and threatened to call her employer and inform him that she refuses to pay her bills. On every Monday, Wednesday, and Friday during the two-week period, he has called Client at work. She repeatedly requested that he quit calling her at work. On the past two Saturdays, he has come by her home and threatened to sue her and throw her in jail.

Rule of Law: Infliction of emotional distress—extreme or outrageous conduct that causes severe emotional distress.

Assignment: The researcher's assignment is to determine if the actions of the bill collector constitute "extreme or outrageous conduct." Discuss the assignment from the perspective of individual key facts and from the perspective of a group of facts.

ASSIGNMENT 9

Identify the key facts in assignments 16 and 17 in the Exercises section of Chapter 17.

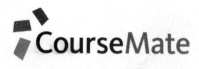

CourseMate

CHAPTER 10

Legal Analysis: Issue Identification—Spotting the Issue

It was the late afternoon of an already long day when Kevin realized he still had a lot of work to finish before he could go home. Kevin has been Randi McGuire's paralegal for the past five years. He admires her for her tenacity and appreciates the responsibility and independence she gives him in the performance of his assignments. Kevin's primary role is to conduct the initial interview with the client, prepare a summary of the interview, and assemble a legal memorandum containing an identification of the legal issues and an analysis of the applicable law.

Identifying the legal issue is often the trickiest part of Kevin's job. It did not seem, however, that it would be too much of a problem in Ida Carry's case. He had just finished his interview with Ms. Carry, whose home is across the street from Roosevelt Elementary School. Ms. Carry's best friend, Karen, lives a block away. Karen's 7-year-old son attends school at Roosevelt.

Last month, on April 14, Ida was in her front yard planting tulips. It was lunchtime, and children were playing on the playground. She heard the crossing guard's whistle blow and tires squealing. She looked up and saw a car approaching a curve in the school zone at a very high rate of speed. It jumped the curb, crashed through the chain-link fence surrounding the playground, and hit the seesaw. The first thing she recognized was the car—it was Bob Barton's hot-rod Camaro. It looked like he was going too fast, lost control on the curve in the school zone, and crashed through the fence.

Bob, a local teen, continually raced in the neighborhood. Several teachers complained to his parents, who did nothing. Bob had received several speeding tickets.

The second thing Ida noticed was that two children playing on the seesaw were injured. One of them was Karen's son, Tim. When Ida realized it was Tim who was injured, she became extremely upset.

Since the wreck, Ida has had severe insomnia and extreme anxiety. When she can sleep, she has nightmares. Her doctor prescribed medication for her nerves and to help her sleep, and he recently referred her to a psychologist. Ida came to Ms. McGuire's office seeking to recover the expenses she has incurred.

After summarizing the interview, Kevin focuses on the next task and asks himself, "What is the legal issue in this case?" The process of identifying the issue is the subject of this chapter. The Application section of this chapter discusses the answer to Kevin's question.

Learning Objectives

After completing this chapter, you should understand:

- What a legal issue is and the various types of issues
- The elements of an issue
- How to identify (spot) the issue in a client's case
- How to identify the issue in a court case

I. INTRODUCTION

The most important task a researcher faces when engaging in legal analysis is to correctly identify the legal issue. Identifying the issue, commonly referred to as "spotting the issue," is the first step of the legal analysis process. Identifying the legal issue(s) presented by the fact situation is the foundation and key to effective legal analysis. It guides the researcher to the specific legal problem raised by the unique facts of the client's case. You must know what the precise legal problem is before you can begin to solve it. Identifying the issue determines which direction the research will take. It is like selecting a road: If you choose the wrong road, you will waste a lot of time before you get to your destination, or you may get lost and never get there. Half the battle of legal research and analysis is knowing what you are looking for; that is, *what is the issue?*

If you misidentify the issue (ask the wrong legal question), you waste time and commit legal error. If you ask the wrong question, you will get the wrong answer to the client's problem.

> **For Example** If you incorrectly identify the issue as a contract law issue when it is really a corporation law issue, you will waste time researching contract law, and the answer you find will not apply to the client's case.

The client does not retain counsel to find the answer to the wrong question. The client pays to have a problem solved. If the issue is misidentified, the problem remains unsolved, time is wasted, and you are no better off than when you started. If the error is not caught, you may have committed malpractice because the client is billed for a service that was not requested.

Not only is identifying the issue the most important step in the analytical process, it is often the most difficult. When you ask a professional how to spot an issue, the response often is, "I just know" or "After a while it becomes intuitive." Indeed, it does become intuitive after one has read and worked on hundreds of cases. This, however, does not help the beginner. Although no simple rule or magic formula exists, certain techniques and steps are helpful when identifying the issue in a client's fact situation or a court opinion. The starting point is to know what an issue is—how it is defined.

II. DEFINITION AND TYPES

In the broadest sense, the **issue** is a question: the legal question raised by the dispute. It is the legal question that must be answered before a case can be resolved. It occurs whenever there is disagreement or uncertainty about whether or how a rule of law applies to a client's facts. In a narrower sense, it is the precise legal question raised by the specific facts of a dispute.

Issues may be broken into three broad categories:

1. A question of which law applies

> **For Example** Do the traffic code provisions of Municipal Code § 2254 or state statute § 35-6-7-28 apply when an individual is stopped in a municipality for driving under the influence of intoxicants?

2. A question of how a law applies

> **For Example** Under the provisions of Colorado battery law, does an individual commit a battery when the individual, present at the scene of a battery, encourages others to commit the battery but does not actively participate in the actual battering of the victim?

3. A question of whether a law applies at all

For Example	Does Municipal Code § 2100, Public Sales/Auctions, govern garage sales held on private property?

Regardless of the type of legal question raised by a dispute, the definition is the same: The issue is the precise legal question raised by the specific facts of the dispute.

Now that you know what an issue is, the next step is to determine what it is composed of—the elements. Every issue is composed of elements, and these elements must be determined to identify the issue. Identifying the elements is key to the process of identifying the issue. In fact, once you have determined the elements, you can identify the issue quite easily.

III. ELEMENTS

A client enters the law office with a unique fact situation that may or may not have a legal remedy. The attorney's role is to identify the question raised by the facts and determine if a legal remedy is available and, if so, what legal remedy is available. Because the issue is defined as the precise legal question raised by the specific facts of the client's case, a correctly identified issue is composed of three elements: the applicable law, the legal question, and the key facts (see Exhibit 10-1).

A. Applicable Law

Applicable law is the specific law that governs the dispute. This may be a constitutional provision, statute, ordinance, regulation, or case law doctrine, principle, rule, test, or guide.

For Example	Under Indiana Code § 35-42-3-2, kidnapping . . .
	According to Florida's law governing breach of contract, . . .

B. Legal Question

This portion of the inquiry refers to the **legal question** concerning the law governing the dispute, raised by the facts of the dispute.

Exhibit 10-1 *Elements of an Issue.*

Applicable Law	The specific law that governs the dispute. (e.g., a constitutional provision, statute, regulation, ordinance, or case law doctrine, principle, rule, test, or guide)
Legal Question	The question concerning the law governing the dispute raised by the facts of the dispute
Key Facts	The legally significant facts that raise the legal question of how or whether the law governing the dispute applies; facts that, if changed, would change or affect the outcome of the application of the law

© Cengage Learning 2014

For Example	. . . does kidnapping occur when . . .
	. . . is a contract breached when . . .

C. Key Facts

Key facts are the key or legally significant facts that raise the legal question of how or whether the law governing the dispute applies.

For Example	. . . when the individual is held against her will but is not held for ransom?
	. . . when the product delivered is grade A– and the contract calls for grade A?

D. Examples

The three elements of the issue—the applicable law, the legal question concerning the law, and the key facts that raise the legal question—are referred to in this text as a comprehensive, **narrow (specific) statement of the issue**. An issue including these elements is comprehensive because it includes the specific law and key facts. It is a narrow statement of the issue because the more facts you include, the more specific (or narrow) the legal question becomes. Identify each element as precisely and completely as possible. The following are examples of statements of issues containing the three elements:

- Under the holographic will statute, Colo. Rev. **(Applicable Law)**
  Stat. § 15-11-503, is a holographic valid if it is **(Legal Question)**
  handwritten by a neighbor at the direction of the
  testator, but not written in the testator's handwriting? **(Key Facts)**

- Under Arizona tort law, does a battery occur when **(Applicable Law)**
  law enforcement officers, while making a lawful **(Legal Question)**
  arrest, encounter resistance, use force to overcome
  that resistance, and continue to use force after
  resistance ceases? **(Key Facts)**

- Does Municipal Code § 3362 permit the **(Applicable Law)**
  installation of a sign that is 20 feet high by 40 feet **(Legal Question)**
  wide, is more than 15 feet from the property line,
  and does not block the view of traffic? **(Key Facts)**

Each of these examples contains the precise law, legal question, and the key facts essential to resolution of the dispute. Note that the issue is narrowly focused upon the law and specific facts of the client's case.

Failure to include these elements results in an abstract question, a **broad statement of the issue** that is missing the legal (applicable law) and factual context.

For Example	If the three previous examples were stated broadly, and did not include the specific elements discussed in this section, they would appear, respectively, as follows:

- Was the will valid?
- Did the police commit a battery?
- Is the sign in violation of the municipal ordinance?

Each broad statement of the issue in this example could apply to a multitude of cases involving wills, batteries, or sign ordinance violations. Each issue fails to inform the researcher of the specific factual context of the dispute, the precise law involved, and the question that must be resolved to determine if a remedy is available to the client (and if so, what remedy). A broadly stated issue is not appropriate in legal research and writing for several reasons:

1. It is not helpful or useful for the reader who is not familiar with the facts of the case. This may be a judge in the instance of a brief in support of a motion, or an attorney in the office who is referring to an old memorandum from the office files.

2. It does not guide the reader to the specific law in question. In the previous examples, what specific wills or battery statutes are we talking about? What municipal ordinance does the sign violate? What is the precise legal context of this dispute?

3. It is not useful to the individual drafting and researching the issue.

> **For Example** The question, "Did Mr. Smith commit a battery?" is such a broad formulation of the issue that it is of little value. Stated this way, the issue applies to all battery cases. So stated, it is useless. It fails to focus the researcher's inquiry or guide the researcher to the specific area of battery law in dispute.

In West's digests, which are used to help locate case law, legal topics are identified by key numbers. There are more than 100 key numbers under the topic "assault and battery." A broad statement of the issue forces the researcher to scan all the subtopics looking for the one that applies. If research is conducted electronically, as with Westlaw, the search will locate hundreds (if not thousands) of cases—far too many for the researcher to review. By stating the issue comprehensively, or narrowly, the researcher narrows the inquiry.

> **For Example** "Under California's tort law, is a battery committed when a bystander encourages and convinces a perpetrator to beat another individual, and that individual is beaten as a result of the encouragement?" This narrow statement of the issue directs the researcher's attention to that specific area of the digest involving individuals liable for battery, that is, Assault and Battery—Key Number 18, Persons Liable. If electronic research is conducted, the search is focused enough so that only cases involving the liability of individuals encouraging a battery will be located.

As the preceding example illustrates, a comprehensive statement focuses the researcher's inquiry on a specific subtopic in the digest, and thereby saves research time. Also, the question is not abstract. The reader does not have to refer to the facts in some other document or file to understand what is in dispute.

In summary, a shorthand/broad statement of the issue fails to inform. It produces an abstract question that forces the reader to engage in further inquiry to determine what specifically is in dispute in the case. It is useless except in casual conversation or conversations in which the participants are familiar with the case. In short, an issue broadly identified is an issue not truly identified at all.

A paralegal or an attorney becomes involved in issue identification in two different but related situations:

1. Identifying the issue(s) in a client's case
2. Identifying the issue(s) in a court opinion

In each situation, it is necessary to determine the three elements of the issue to correctly identify the issue. The next two sections recommend steps for identifying the issue in a client's case and in a court opinion.

IV. ISSUE IDENTIFICATION—CLIENT'S CASE

The client's fact situation presents a legal question (issue) or set of questions that must be identified before the case can be resolved. A helpful question to keep in mind from the outset is, "What must be decided about which facts?" or, "What question concerning which law is raised by these facts?" This questioning keeps you focused on the elements of the issue—the law, question, and key facts of the case. It helps you avoid being sidetracked by related or interesting questions raised by the facts that are not necessary to resolve the legal question(s) of the case. The value of keeping these questions in mind will be illustrated throughout this section.

Identifying the legal issue(s) in a client's case is primarily a four-step process (see Exhibit 10-2). Note that steps 1 through 3 are essentially the same as steps 1 through 4 in Chapter 9, section VI. They are summarized here with different examples so that you will not have to refer to that chapter.

Exhibit 10-2 *Steps in the Identification or Spotting of the Issue in a Client's Case.*

STEP 1	Identify each type of cause of action and area of law possibly involved.
STEP 2	Determine the elements of each cause of action identified in step 1.
STEP 3	Determine which of the facts of the client's case apply to establish or satisfy the elements of each cause of action—the key facts.
STEP 4	Assemble the issue from the law and key facts identified in steps 2 and 3. Follow the format presented in Chapter 11: relevent law + legal question + key facts.

© Cengage Learning 2014

A. Step 1: Identify Each Type of Cause of Action

The first step is to identify each type of cause of action and area of law possibly involved. This means to identify the potential cause(s) of action and area(s) of law raised by the client's fact situation, including a broad identification of potential issues, the general areas of law, and the client's facts related to each area of law. This preliminary identification is based upon education and experience and usually does not require research.

For Example Mary is stopped at a stoplight waiting for the light to change. She is drinking a soft drink. She has been stopped for about 10 seconds when a pickup, driven by Sam, slams into the back of her vehicle. Her automobile is knocked into the intersection and narrowly misses being struck by a vehicle passing through the intersection. Sam jumps out of his pickup, runs to Mary's vehicle, and screams at her that she should not have been stopped and she caused the wreck. Mary thinks he is either crazy or drugged. She is afraid he might hit her. He yanks open her vehicle door and pulls her out of the automobile, screaming, "It's all your fault, it's all your fault." He pulls out a knife and waves it around. A couple of pedestrians approach, and Sam runs back to his pickup.

As a result of the incident, Mary suffered whiplash injuries and bruises on her arm, she experiences anxiety whenever she is stopped at a light, and she has developed severe insomnia. This hypothetical is referred to as the "rear-end collision" example throughout this chapter.

Based upon experience and tort classes, the researcher identifies four possible causes of action involving four broad areas of law: Did Sam's failure to stop constitute negligence? Did he commit an assault? Did he commit a battery? Did his actions constitute intentional infliction of emotional distress?

This initial identification of the broad issues and areas of law may be expanded or reduced following subsequent research. The purpose is twofold:

- To identify in general terms the issues involved
- To provide a starting point for the identification and clarification of each specific issue that must be resolved in the case

B. Step 2: Determine the Elements of Each Cause of Action

The second step is to determine the elements of each cause of action identified in step 1. Apply steps 2, 3, and 4 separately to each potential issue or cause of action identified in step 1. In other words:

- Choose one potential issue identified in step 1.
- Apply steps 2, 3, and 4 to that issue.
- Complete the identification of that issue before addressing the next potential issue.

> **For Example** In the rear-end collision example, four broad issues and areas of law are involved: negligence, assault, battery, and emotional distress. Choose one area, such as negligence, and complete steps 2 through 4. Be careful to identify and finish with that issue before addressing the next issue.

Focusing on one issue at a time avoids the confusion that may occur when dealing with multiple causes of action that often have overlapping elements. In this example, some of Sam's conduct may constitute elements of both assault and intentional infliction of emotional distress. Researching both issues at the same time could cause confusion.

Step 2 requires researching the area of law to determine the elements necessary to establish a cause of action. To know whether the law provides relief for the client, it is necessary to determine what the law requires to be established (the elements) in order to obtain that relief. Locate the elements by researching primary authority, such as the statutory or case law. If there is no primary authority in the jurisdiction, refer to secondary authority, such as the *Restatement of the Law*, governing the topic.

> **For Example** Using the rear-end collision example, suppose the researcher begins with the issue involving intentional infliction of emotional distress. Research reveals that the following elements must be established to prevail:
>
> 1. The defendant's conduct must be intentional.
> 2. The conduct must be extreme and outrageous.

> 3. There must be a causal connection between the defendant's conduct and the plaintiff's mental distress.
>
> 4. The plaintiff's mental distress must be extreme or severe.

NOTE: To help you locate the law at this stage of the process, you may roughly identify the issue with the facts you think are important.

> **For Example** The assignment is to determine if a will was validly revoked when the testator wrote, in pencil, across the top of the first page of the will: "I hereby revoke this will." To help guide the research for the relevant statute (primary authority) that applies, a rough formulation of the issue can be drafted: Under the wills statutes, is a will revoked when the testator writes in pencil across the top of the first page of the will, "I hereby revoke this will."? This rough formulation guides the researcher to look for the specific wills statute that addresses revocation. After locating the statute and identifying the requirements of the statute (elements), the researcher applies step 3 to determine which facts are key facts. The researcher then formulates a complete statement of the issue that includes the specific rule of law, after locating the law and performing steps 3 and 4.

After identifying the elements, proceed to step 3.

C. Step 3: Determine the Key Facts

The third step is to determine which of the facts of the client's case apply to establish or satisfy the elements of each cause of action—the key facts. Steps 1 and 2 identify the law that must be included in the issue, and step 3 identifies the facts that must be included in the issue—the key facts.

Identify the key facts by determining which facts of the client's case apply to establish or satisfy the requirements of each element of the cause of action. This step is necessary because, in order to state a claim and thereby obtain relief, facts must be presented that establish or satisfy the requirements of each element.

> **For Example** Using the rear-end collision example, apply the client's facts to the elements:
>
> 1. ***Defendant's conduct must be intentional.*** In this case, the defendant's running toward the client screaming, opening her car, pulling her out, and waving his knife are the facts showing intentional conduct that satisfy or apply to establish this element. This conduct is clearly intentional.
>
> 2. ***The conduct must be extreme and outrageous.*** The acts identified in number 1 are the facts showing extreme and outrageous conduct that establish this element.
>
> 3. ***There must be a causal connection between the defendant's conduct and the plaintiff's mental distress.*** Since the accident, the client has been unable to sleep and is anxious when stopped at a light. These facts satisfy the third element.
>
> 4. ***Plaintiff's distress must be extreme or severe.*** Experiencing anxiety whenever stopped at a light and severe insomnia are facts showing extreme or severe distress and are the facts that establish the fourth element.

By matching the facts with the required elements, the key facts of the emotional distress issue are identified. Because the question is, How does the law apply to the facts, these facts become part of the issue and must be included. After step 3 is completed, all the elements necessary to identify the issue are in place. All that is left is to proceed to step 4 and assemble the issue.

NOTE: You may not be certain whether a fact meets the standard established for an element. Often that determination is not made until trial. Ensure that some fact arguably meets the requirements of each of the elements of the cause of action.

> **For Example** A determination of whether Mary's insomnia and anxiety are extreme or severe enough to warrant relief may not be made until trial. Her symptoms, however, are arguably sufficient to meet the requirement of the fourth element. If research reveals that this harm is not sufficiently extreme for the requirements of emotional distress, however, then there is no emotional distress issue.

If there are no facts that satisfy or establish an element, there probably is no cause of action or issue. In this example, if Mary did not suffer anxiety or insomnia, there would be no facts to meet the requirements of the fourth element, and there most likely would be no emotional distress issue.

D. Step 4: Assemble the Issue

The last step is the easiest: Gather and assemble the elements of the issue from the law and key facts identified in steps 2 and 3. The law is emotional distress, the legal question is whether emotional distress occurred, and the key facts are the facts identified in step 3. Putting it all together, the issue is as follows:

> Under [name of state] law of emotional distress, does emotional distress occur when the driver of the rear vehicle in a rear-end collision runs screaming toward the other driver, opens her car door, pulls her out, and waves a knife, and the other driver suffers anxiety and insomnia as a result of the conduct?

E. Summary of the Four-Step Process

The four steps presented here simplify the issue identification process by breaking it down into workable steps. It may not be necessary to go through all the steps. The issue may be apparent in step 1 or at some other point. This process, however, takes some of the mystery out of issue identification and provides a useful tool when the issues are not clear or easy to identify. It allows you to answer the question, "What question concerning which law is raised by the client's facts?"

The answer to the emotional distress issue identified in the preceding example may be determined by reference to case law. The important thing to remember is that by concisely identifying the issue in the context of the key facts, the key facts are less likely to be overlooked. By including the key facts in the issue, the researcher's focus is narrowed, and the researcher is less likely to omit a critical fact and thereby ignore a crucial line of inquiry, or misidentify the issue entirely. In the rear-end collision example, it may be that Sam's actions are not sufficiently outrageous to constitute emotional distress—maybe there is not sufficient evidence to connect the anxiety and insomnia to the acts, or maybe the harm is not the type of harm for which relief is granted in emotional distress cases.

NOTE: At the outset, you may only know the general area of law that applies and not the specific statute. By going through the steps and identifying the key facts or terms and the question components of the issue, you narrow your search. After locating the law, you can make a complete statement of the issue that includes the specific rule of law.

> **For Example** An individual is arrested by the Federal Bureau of Investigation while robbing a bank with a toy gun. He is informed that he will be charged with robbing the bank with a deadly weapon. By including the known facts, the issue can be stated as, "Under the federal bank robbery statute, is there sufficient evidence to support charges of bank robbery with a dangerous weapon when the weapon is a toy gun?" By identifying this much of the issue, a researcher is guided to search for the specific bank robbery statute that addresses bank robbery with a dangerous weapon.

As mentioned, steps 2 through 4 are applied to each of the issues broadly identified in step 1. Certain possible issues may be eliminated as the other steps are followed, such as when research reveals that there are not sufficient facts present to support a cause of action. It may also be that additional issues are identified as research proceeds.

> **For Example** In the "armed" robbery example, it may be that emotional distress was not considered until research on another issue, such as assault, revealed a case with similar facts that included a discussion of emotional distress.

F. Multiple Issues

Often there are **multiple issues** in a case. In the rear-end collision example, there were four possible causes of action, each one involving a separate issue. Be sure to list all the facts in the client's case and examine each one to determine if it relates to any identified issue or in any way raises a new issue. In the rear-end collision example, the fact that Mary was drinking a soda may not be important. The fact that Sam ran from his car rather than walked may be critical. It is important to ensure that all the facts are considered and nothing is overlooked. All potential issues should be identified, and the four-step process helps ensure that nothing is missed.

Note also that a single issue may have multiple parts or subissues.

> **For Example** In the rear-end collision example, the intentional infliction of emotional distress issue may have separate subissues:
> - Was Sam's conduct sufficiently extreme and outrageous?
> - Are anxiety and severe insomnia "extreme or severe distress" within the meaning of the law?
> - Did Sam's conduct cause the insomnia?

Each part or subissue should be separately considered and addressed.

NOTE: The steps presented in this section are useful tools and guides. These steps will usually help you quickly identify the issue. Remember that the process gets easier with experience.

V. ISSUE IDENTIFICATION—CASE LAW

This section focuses on identifying, or spotting, the issue(s) in a court opinion. The issue is the legal question addressed and answered by the court. It is what the case is about. If you do not know what question the court addressed, it is possible to misunderstand the rule of law applied or adopted in the opinion. As a result, it is likely that you will misunderstand how or if the rule of law applies in your client's case.

This section does not address situations in which the issue is easily identified because somewhere in the opinion the court clearly states the issue.

> **For Example** "In this case we decide whether an individual's Fourth Amendment right to be free from unreasonable searches is violated when officers, executing a search warrant for a stolen television, search the individual's pockets and discover drugs."

This section covers those situations in which identifying the issue is difficult because the court does not identify the issue, states the issue in such broad terms that it is not helpful, or states the issue in terms of the procedural context in which the case was brought before the court:

- Issue not stated—In some opinions, the court never clearly discusses what the issue is in the case.

- Broad statement of the issue—"The issue in this case is whether the defendant breached the contract."

  Comment: This is a broad statement of the issue. It fails to inform the reader what the case is about. In the ultimate sense, the court decided whether the defendant breached the contract. In reality, however, it reached that conclusion by making a substantive decision concerning the specific facts of the defendant's conduct.

  > **For Example** The court may have concluded that the defendant's timely delivery of the order, 95 percent of the time, was substantial compliance with the contract and, therefore, not a breach.

- Issue stated in the procedural context—"The issue in this case is whether the trial court erred when it granted the motion to suppress the evidence."

  Comment: The court stated the issue in the context of how the case came before the court procedurally, namely an appeal of a trial court order granting a motion to suppress. To answer this question, the court actually addressed a substantive question raised by the facts of the case, and the substantive issue is what the case is actually about.

  > **For Example** The substantive issue decided was, "Under the provisions of the exclusionary rule, should evidence be suppressed when law enforcement officers obtained the evidence as a result of requiring the defendant to allow them to inspect the glove box when they were making a routine stop for speeding?"

Beginning students often make the mistake of identifying the issue in the procedural context stated by the court when, in reality, the issue involves a substantive determination of the application of the law to the facts of the case.

The goal when reading a case should be to identify the substantive issue(s) in the case. Ask yourself when reading the case, "What was decided about which facts in this case?" or "What question concerning which law and key facts was decided by the court?" Like a client's case, a court case is about a dispute concerning how the law applies to the facts. Had there been no dispute involving how the law applied to the facts, the case would not have gone to trial. If your identification of the issue in a court opinion fails to include the rule of law applied and the key facts, you have failed to identify the issue correctly.

How, then, is issue identification in a court opinion accomplished? Again, there is no magic formula. The three-step process presented in Exhibit 10-3 is suggested as a useful tool.

Steps 1 and 2 include the requirements of steps 1 through 3 in Chapter 9, section VII. They are summarized here with a focus on the issue-identification aspect of each step.

Exhibit 10-3 *Steps in the Identification or Spotting of the Issue in a Court Opinion.*

STEP 1: General Question	Read the entire opinion before attempting to identify the issue. While reading, keep in mind the question, "What was decided about which facts in this case?"
STEP 2: Look to the Holding	Focus on the holding and ask the following questions: ■ To identify the law applied ask, "What statute, rule of law, or principle did the court apply to reach its decision?" ■ To identify the question addressed by the court ask, "What legal question was addressed and answered by the holding?" ■ To identify the key facts ask, "Which of the facts presented in the case, if changed, would alter or affect the question addressed in the holding?"
STEP 3: Assemble the Issue	Assemble the issue from the answers to the questions in step 2. Structure the issue in the format presented in Chapter 11: Rule of law + legal question + key facts.

A. Step 1: General Question

The first part of this step is to read the entire court opinion before attempting to identify the issue. Important information concerning an issue may be scattered throughout the opinion. An initial reading of the entire case provides the researcher with an awareness of where information is located in the opinion and an overview of the case. This is helpful when you begin to analyze specific portions of the opinion. Read the entire opinion at the outset, even if the court clearly identifies the issue.

While reading the case, keep in mind the question, "What was decided about which facts in this case?" This question helps keep your mind focused on what you need to look for while reading the case in order to identify the elements of the issue:

■ The first part of the question, "What was decided?" keeps the mind focused on searching for the legal issue that was resolved and the law necessary for its resolution.

■ The second part of the question, "about which facts?" keeps the mind focused on looking for the facts essential to the resolution of the legal question.

If you keep this question in mind as you read the case, you remain focused on the essence of the case: the court's application of a rule of law to the legal question raised by the facts. Asking this question forces you to keep the facts in mind as you read because you are aware that you must decide which of the facts relate to the holding. When you get to the end of the opinion, you may realize that the holding relates to only a few of the facts presented.

Do not identify the issue(s) from the syllabus or headnotes of the opinion. As noted in Chapter 4, these are prepared by the publisher of the opinion. They are not part of the court opinion and are not intended to be used to identify the issue(s) addressed in the opinion. Headnotes may, however, be relied on to help you locate the issue within the opinion.

If you have not identified the issue by the time you have finished reading the case, proceed to step 2.

B. Step 2: Look to the Holding

As noted in Chapter 4, the *holding* is the court's application of the rule of law to the legal issue raised by the facts of the case. It is the court's answer to the issue. In a court opinion, the key facts, legal question, and holding are all related. Finding one will help you find the others. Therefore, often the fastest way to track down the issue is to focus on the holding and ask the following questions:

1. "What was decided in the holding?" In other words, "What issue was addressed and answered by the holding?" This identifies the second element of the issue, the legal question addressed by the court.

2. "What statute, rule of law, principle, and so on did the court apply to reach this holding?" This question helps identify the relevant rule of law, the first element of the issue.

3. "Which of the facts presented in this case are related and necessary to the determination of the question identified as addressed in the holding?" or "Which of the facts, if changed, would change the outcome of the holding?" These questions help identify the third element of the issue, the key facts.

By answering these questions you identify the elements of the issue: the rule of law, question, and key facts. You can state the issue by adding the rule of law and key facts to the holding and reformulating the holding in question form. It sounds complicated, but it is not.

For Example In a workers' compensation case, the court presents several facts concerning the plaintiff before and after she joined a monastery, including the following:

1. Her duties as a monastic
2. Her written application for admission as a volunteer to the service of God
3. The written invitation from the monastery, which included an offer of spiritual guidance and room and board in exchange for volunteer service
4. Information concerning her previous career
5. The fact that she did not receive a paycheck
6. Her spiritual motivation
7. Her daily duties
8. The fact that she was injured while mopping the floor
9. Her family relationships
10. The fact that there was no contract of employment

(Continued)

The plaintiff appealed the trial court's decision granting the defendant's motion to dismiss for failure to state a claim. The issue is not stated in the opinion. The holding in the case was: "Plaintiff rendered services out of religious devotion as indicated by her application as a volunteer, lack of employment agreement, and lack of a paycheck; therefore, she was not an employee within the meaning of the law, and the trial court's dismissal of the complaint is affirmed." This example is referred to in this chapter as "the monastery" example.

A quick way to identify the issue in the monastery example is to focus on the holding and keep in mind the question, "What was decided about which facts to reach this holding?" Then, identify the elements of the issue by asking:

1. "What question was decided in this holding?" The question decided is whether the plaintiff was an employee. The answer to this question provides the legal question element of the issue.

2. "What rule of law or principle did the court apply to reach this holding?" The answer to this question provides the rule of law element of the issue. It may be a statute, case law principle, doctrine, and so on. Assume here that it is the Workers' Compensation Act § 36-9-7.

3. "Which facts mentioned in the opinion are related and necessary to the determination of the question of whether the plaintiff is an employee?" The answer to this question provides the key facts element of the issue. In this case, the court focused on the written application as a volunteer, the absence of an employment agreement, and the lack of a paycheck. These facts, if changed, would probably change the outcome. If treated as a group, the changing of all these facts would change the outcome.

C. Step 3: Assemble the Issue

Assemble the identified elements in the relevant law + legal question + key facts format presented in Chapter 11. The rule of law is the Workers' Compensation Act § 36-9-7. The question is whether the plaintiff was an employee. The key facts are the written application for admission to the monastery as a volunteer, the absence of an employment agreement, and the lack of a paycheck. The issue, when assembled, is: "Under the provisions of Workers' Compensation Act § 36-9-7, is an individual an employee when the individual is admitted to a monastery upon a written application as a volunteer, does not receive a paycheck, and does not have an agreement of employment?"

D. Other Aids—Case Law Issue Identification

1. Concurring or Dissenting Opinion

In a concurring or dissenting opinion, the issue may be set out more clearly than in the majority opinion. Therefore, do not overlook these opinions when identifying the issue. Be aware, however, that the concurring or dissenting judge may have a different view of what the issue is, especially in the case of a dissent. Nevertheless, even if the formulation is different, the discussion of the issue by the concurring or dissenting judge may be helpful in determining the issue in the majority opinion.

2. Other Opinions

Reading other opinions cited in the case may provide guidance concerning the issue in the case at hand. Also, reading a later court's discussion of the case may prove helpful, as it may summarize and clarify the issue in the case you are reading. *Shepard's Citations* will guide you to subsequent cases.

E. Multiple Issues

The foregoing discussion focuses on locating a single issue. Often there are multiple issues in a court opinion. Apply the steps presented in Exhibit 10-3 to all the issues in the case, one at a time. Be sure to follow all the steps presented in this section completely when identifying an issue before proceeding to identify the next issue. Remember, for each issue, you must identify the relevant rule of law, specific question, and key facts.

You may read a case to find the answer to a single question relevant to your client's fact situation, or you may be looking for a specific legal principle, doctrine, or rule of law addressed by the court.

> **For Example** You are researching a court opinion that involves several torts, but you are only interested in the court's discussion of the emotional distress issue. Follow the steps presented in Exhibit 10-3 to identify the emotional distress issue, but ensure that the court's resolution of the other issues does not in some way affect its treatment of the emotional distress issue. You can accomplish this by reading the entire opinion and checking for any overlap of the issues or interconnectedness of the reasoning.

NOTE: As in section IV, consider the steps presented in this section as useful tools and helpful guidelines. When followed, they will usually help you to quickly identify the issue in a court opinion. In certain instances, the opinion may be so obscure that you are unable to identify the issue. Also, as you read more and more cases, a sort of intuition develops, and you may immediately spot the issue without going through any of the steps.

VI. KEY POINTS CHECKLIST: *Spotting the Issue*

- ✓ When determining the issue(s) in a client's case, it is helpful to keep in mind the question, "What must be decided about which facts in this case?" This question helps keep the mind focused on the rule of law in conjunction with the facts.

- ✓ When identifying the issue(s) in a court opinion, as you read, keep asking the question, "What was decided about which facts in this opinion?" All cases are about how the law applies to facts. By keeping focused on the law and facts of the case, you are less likely to be sidetracked by issues and questions that need not be addressed.

- ✓ Address one issue at a time. For each issue under consideration, follow each of the steps presented in this chapter before proceeding to the next issue. In multiple-issue cases, separate the issues and identify one completely before addressing the next one.

- ✓ When reading a court opinion or working on a client's case, keep in mind the three elements of the issue: rule of law, question, and key facts. This helps you stay focused on what you need to determine to identify the issue.

- ✓ Do not be concerned if you cannot immediately identify the issue(s) in a client's case. The complete identification of the issue may not take place until you conduct the research, read laws and cases, and identify the required elements of the cause of action. Likewise, the existence of additional issues may not be known until research reveals their presence.

- ✓ Do not stop when you have identified one issue. Most cases involve more than one legal question. Separate areas of law, such as torts and contracts, may bear on one fact situation. Always look for all possible causes of action that could arise from a fact situation.

- ✓ Use any technique that works for you. The steps suggested here are designed as guidelines to assist you. Use any or all of them and anything else that works.

VII. APPLICATION

This section presents two examples of issue identification. Each example illustrates the principles discussed throughout this chapter and includes a discussion of the application of those principles.

A. Client's Fact Situation

The following example involves the application of the principles to the hypothetical presented at the beginning of the chapter.

1. Identify Each Possible Cause of Action and Area of Law Involved

The first step is to identify each type of cause of action and area of law that may be raised by the client's fact situation. Kevin, based upon his training, realizes that this is a civil, not a criminal, matter. No crime has been committed against Ms. Carry. He also knows that the applicable area of civil law is tort. By a process of elimination, based upon experience, he focuses on infliction of emotional distress. There is no assault or battery claim because there was no act directly or indirectly aimed at the client. Step 1 may require no research. Kevin may arrive at this point based solely on his education and experience, although he may realize, as he conducts research into the emotional distress issue, that other causes of action are present as well. If more than one claim is identified, steps 2 through 4 should be followed separately for each.

> **For Example** If a part from the car flew off and hit Ms. Carry, there are potential battery or negligence issues, and Kevin would follow steps 2 through 4 for each issue.

2. Determine the Elements of Each Cause of Action Identified in Step 1

Kevin's research reveals that emotional distress is a case law doctrine. The legislature has not adopted a statute concerning emotional distress. The state's highest court has recognized the tort of intentional infliction of emotional distress. The court requires that the following elements be established to state a claim:

1. The defendant's conduct must be either intentional or grossly or recklessly negligent.
2. The conduct must be extreme and outrageous.
3. There must be a causal connection between the defendant's conduct and the plaintiff's mental distress.
4. The plaintiff's mental distress must be extreme or severe.

3. Determine Which of the Facts Apply

The third step is to determine which of the facts of the client's case apply to establish or satisfy the elements of each cause of action—the key facts.

1. Defendant's conduct of driving at a very high rate of speed, crashing through the fence, hitting the seesaw, and injuring the son of the plaintiff's friend are the facts that apply to satisfy the first element of intentional or grossly negligent conduct.
2. Driving through a school zone at an extremely high rate of speed is the fact that satisfies the second element of extreme or outrageous conduct.

3. Ms. Carry's insomnia and anxiety immediately after the event are facts that apply to the third element of causation.

4. Ms. Carry's anxiety and insomnia are extreme and apply to establish the fourth element.

If Kevin could not find a fact that would arguably apply to each element, there would be no issue involving that area of law, and that cause of action would have to be abandoned as a potential avenue of redress for Ms. Carry.

> **For Example** If Ms. Carry did not suffer any anxiety or insomnia, there probably would be no cause of action for emotional distress.

NOTE: As discussed in section IV of this chapter, you may not be certain whether a fact meets the established standard for an element. Often that determination cannot be made until trial. Your task is to ensure that some fact arguably meets the requirements of each of the elements of the cause of action.

> **For Example** A determination of whether Ms. Carry's insomnia and anxiety are extreme enough to warrant relief may not be made until trial; however, her symptoms are arguably sufficient to meet the requirements of the fourth element. If research reveals that this harm is not sufficiently extreme to meet the requirements of emotional distress, then there is no emotional distress issue.

4. Assemble the Issue

Assemble the elements and state the issue. Kevin now has all the elements necessary to identify and state the issue: the area of law, the legal question, and the key facts. He identifies the issue as: "Under [name of state] tort law, does intentional infliction of emotional distress occur when a person suffers severe insomnia and anxiety as a result of witnessing a friend's child being injured by a vehicle that is out of control due to being driven at a high rate of speed through a school zone?"

By following the four steps, moving from a broad identification of the possible causes of action to the specific elements of and facts involved in each cause of action, Kevin has identified an issue. He knows what must be decided about which facts for this cause of action. His research is focused on cases in which the conduct involved accidents in school zones where witnesses suffered harm similar to that experience by Ms. Carry.

If other possible causes of action were identified in step 1, then steps 2 through 4 would be followed for each potential cause.

B. Court Opinion

The following example illustrates the application of the principles to the identification of the issues in a court opinion. The three steps to follow are:

- Step 1: General Question—While reading the case, keep in mind the general question, "What was decided about which facts in the case?"

- Step 2: Look to the Holding—Identify the rule of law and key facts relevant to the holding.

- Step 3: Assemble the Issue

Read the following case of *Acacia Mutual Life Insurance Company v. American General Life Insurance Company.*

CASE

ACACIA MUTUAL LIFE INSURANCE COMPANY,
et al., Plaintiffs,

v.

AMERICAN GENERAL LIFE INSURANCE
COMPANY, et al.,

Involuntary Plaintiff,

111 N.M. 106, 802 P.2d 11 (1990)

OPINION

BACA, Justice

Appellant David Silver was the general partner of the Santa Fe Private Equity Fund II, L.P. (SFPEF II), a limited partnership. He appeals from a court order that affirms a settlement agreement arrived upon by the limited partners through their receiver, John Clark, appellee. The order distributes the assets of the limited partnership in order of priority mandated by the legislature in Section 54-2-23 of the Uniform Limited Partnership Act. See NMSA 1978, §§ 54-2-1 to -30 (Repl. Pamp. 1988). Silver claims that this order unjustly bars his contractual indemnification claim as set out in the partnership agreement. The right to contract is jealously guarded by this court, but if a contractual clause clearly contravenes a positive rule of law, it cannot be enforced, *General Electric Credit Corp. v. Tidenberg*, 78 N.M. 59, 428 P.2d 33 (1967). The indemnification clause clearly contravenes the order of priority in the distribution of assets of a dissolved limited partnership as set out by the legislature. We, therefore, affirm.

FACTS

In February 1987 the limited partners unanimously voted to terminate their failing partnership, which had shown a loss from the outset, and filed in district court for a confirmation of the dissolution of SFPEF II. They also voted to remove Silver as general partner, but allowed him to resign. Clark was named as receiver and published a notice of dissolution of the partnership in *The Santa Fe New Mexican* on March 23, 1987. This notice requested creditors to respond with claims against the partnership within fourteen days. Silver wrote a letter within this time, asserting his claim under the partnership agreement for indemnification and reimbursement from the partnership for any partnership debts he paid.

After the notification of dissolution, Clark began negotiations with known creditors of the limited partnership and a determination of the status of the SFPEF II. In analyzing the assets and liabilities of SFPEF II, Clark determined that the limited partners had contributed in excess of $7 million, but he could document only $2.4 million in investments. The

estimated value of SFPEF II was eventually determined to be negative $1.4 million, equaling a loss to the limited partners of $8.4 million. Aside from checks written to the general partners in excess of $1 million, the balance of the limited partners' contributions remains unaccounted for.

Clark determined the amount necessary to settle all creditors' claims and on that basis made a third, partial capital call to limited partners to wind up affairs and terminate the partnership. At this point some of the limited partners refused to pay a third partial capital call, claiming other limited partners had not yet paid on the second call.

Approximately a year after the request for confirmation of dissolution was filed, the dispute finally was settled. Clark arrived upon a global settlement agreement that allowed creditors to be paid and the receivership to be terminated. Under the settlement the limited partners were to contribute a final $1.3 million. The settlement agreement also provided for payment of creditors, distribution of any remaining liquid assets to the limited partners, and assignment of all of the partnership's claims against the general partners to one limited partner. Approval of the settlement by the court would bar all claims of creditors who had not asserted a claim. The motion for confirmation was served on Silver, who objected and asserted his indemnification claim from SFPEF II. This was over a year after notification of dissolution and the letter written by Silver to the receiver in March of 1987—the only notice of Silver's indemnification claim. The district court held that Silver's claim was untimely and approved the settlement that foreclosed Silver's indemnification claim. This appeal is taken from that order.

ISSUES—AND NON-ISSUES

Silver phrases the six points of his appeal in terms of his timely notice of a claim against the partnership and of an improper "bar" to this claim for indemnification, along with related claims of procedural due process, equal protection violations, and laches. We identify the issues differently.

We are dealing here with the time-worn principles underlying limited partnerships that restrict the potential liability of a "limited" partner and hold a "general" partner to general, personal liability. "[L]imited partners * * * take no part in management, share profits and *do not share losses beyond their capital contributions to the firm.*" A. Bromberg, *Crane & Bromberg on Partnership*, § 26 at 143 (1968) (emphasis added).

Indemnifying a general partner for partnership debts by essentially forcing limited partners to pay for them violates the general public policy of limited partnership law. However, it is not necessary to decide this case on general policy grounds alone because such grounds are incorporated into specific statutory provisions that control the order of priority of distribution of assets in these circumstances, and the general partner is statutorily the last in priority. A court cannot depart from the express language of an act, but can only say what the legislature intended. *Security Escrow Corp. v. Taxation & Revenue Dep't*, 107 N.M. 540, 760 P.2d 1306 (Ct.App.1988); *State v. Michael R.*, 107 N.M. 794, 765 P.2d 767 (Ct.App.1988).

The partnership agreement itself supports our interpretation. Silver argues that in the partnership agreement a clause existed, 13(b), which provides that the "Partnership * * * shall indemnify * * * the General Partner [and] its partners * * * against all claims * * * incurred by them in connection with their activities on behalf of the Partnership * * *." This clause, however, is subject to paragraph 6(f) of the partnership agreement, which deals with liability of limited partners and states in pertinent part: "No limited Partner shall be liable for any debts or obligations of the Partnership, including obligations in respect of indemnification provided in paragraph 13, in excess of its unpaid Capital Contribution * * *."

The partnership was terminated, pursuant to its requirements, when the limited partners unanimously voted to terminate. At this point the partnership, along with potential remaining capital calls, went into receivership and dissolution, and this dissolution came under the New Mexico Limited Partnership Act. NMSA 1978, Section 54-2-23(Repl. Pamp.1988) sets out the order of priority for the distribution of assets:

A. In settling accounts after dissolution the liabilities of the partnership shall be entitled to payment in the following order:

(1) those to creditors, in the order of priority as provided by law, except those to limited partners on account of their contributions, and to general partners;

(2) those to *limited partners* in respect to their share of the profits and other compensation by way of income on their contributions;

(3) those to *limited partners* in respect to the capital of their contributions;

(4) those to *general partners* other than for capital and profits;

(5) those to general partners in respect to profits;

(6) those to general partners in respect to capital. (Emphasis added.)

The law of New Mexico mandates that in a dissolution of a limited partnership, the limited partners are to be paid off before the general partners. The interpretation of the indemnification clause in the contract urged by Silver would have the general partners paid off by the limited partners. Since there are no assets left in this terminated partnership, to indemnify the general partner would require the limited partners to contribute even more funds to a dead entity. The clear language of a statute must be given its full meaning. *Schoonover v. Caudill*, 65 N.M. 335, 337 P.2d 402 (1959); *Weiser v. Albuquerque Oil & Gasoline Co.*, 64 N.M. 137, 325 P.2d 720 (1958). To indemnify the general partners would contravene this statute and is therefore unenforceable. We AFFIRM.

IT IS SO ORDERED.

1. General Question

Read the entire case. While reading the case, ask yourself, "What did the court decide about which facts?" To answer this question, it is necessary to keep in mind the elements of the issue—the rule of law, legal question, and key facts. Keeping this question in mind helps you focus on these elements.

2. Look to the Holding

You probably cannot identify the issue after completing step 1. The court did not specifically state the issue, nor is the issue clear from a simple reading of the case. Follow step 2 and find the holding. Here, the holding is presented in the next-to-last sentence: "To indemnify the general partners would contravene this statute and is therefore unenforceable." Once identified, locate the elements of the issue relevant to this holding. Ask the following questions:

■ "What was decided in the holding?" In other words, "What legal question or issue was addressed and answered by the court?" Determine the answer to this question by looking to the holding and deciding what question was answered by the holding.

Here, Silver, a general partner and an appellant in the case, argued that section 13(b) of the partnership agreement allowed him to be reimbursed, by additional contributions from the limited partners, for partnership debts he paid. In other words, section 13(b) would require limited partners to share losses beyond their capital contributions to the partnership and require limited partners to pay off general partners. The court held that the section, so interpreted, would clearly contravene the provisions of the statute. The legal question, then, is whether an interpretation of the section of the agreement that would require such payments by limited partners is enforceable.

In this case, it is difficult to identify the issue without this step because the opinion includes information that tends to mislead the reader.

> **For Example** The last two sentences in the "Facts" section of the opinion indicate that the appeal was taken from a trial court ruling that Silver's claim was untimely. Based upon those statements, the reader is led to believe that the case involves a timeliness issue and looks for the court's discussion of that question. The court, however, never mentions timeliness in the rest of the opinion. By looking to the holding and following this step, the reader is directed to the issue actually decided by the court.

- "What statute, rule of law, or principle did the court apply when it reached this holding?" In this case, the court looked to § 54-2-23 of the New Mexico Limited Partnership Act.

- "Which facts mentioned in the opinion are related and necessary to the determination of the question addressed in the holding?" What are the key facts? In this case, as in many cases, the court presents several facts that have nothing to do with the holding. Usually these facts are presented to give the reader the background and context of the holding. The presentation of too many background facts, however, may mislead the reader and make it difficult to determine what the case is actually about.

  This is especially true in this case. The opinion contains several paragraphs discussing the financial status of the partnership and the details of the global settlement agreement arranged by the receiver. So much is presented concerning these facts that the reader tends to focus on them, and not on the key facts that involve the provisions of the partnership agreement.

  When the holding, however, is referred to and the question is asked, "Which facts are necessary or related to this holding?" it is clear that the facts relevant to the holding are the facts concerning section 13(b) of the partnership agreement and Silver's interpretation of that section. The key facts are the section of the partnership agreement providing that the partnership shall indemnify the general partner against all claims, and Silver's interpretation of that section to require limited partners, upon dissolution of the partnership, to reimburse general partners with contributions beyond their capital contributions.

3. Assemble the Issue

The final step is to assemble the issue. All the elements have been identified in step 2:

- The rule of law is § 54-2-23 of the New Mexico Limited Partnership Act.

- The question is whether an indemnification provision of the partnership agreement is enforceable.

- The key fact is an interpretation of the indemnification provision that requires limited partners, upon dissolution of the partnership, to reimburse general partners with additional contributions beyond their capital contributions.

The assembled issue is: "Under the provisions of § 54-2-23 of the New Mexico Limited Partnership Act, is an indemnification provision of a partnership agreement enforceable when it is interpreted to require limited partners, upon dissolution of the partnership, to reimburse general partners with additional contributions beyond their capital contributions?"

Summary

The most important task in either analyzing a client's case or reading a court opinion is to correctly identify the issue(s). You must identify the problem before it can be solved. A mis-identified issue can result not only in wasted time but also in malpractice.

The issue is the precise legal question raised by the facts of the dispute. Therefore, each issue is unique because the facts of each case are different, and each issue must be narrowly stated within the context of the facts of that case. The issue is composed of the applicable law, the legal question relevant to the law, and the facts that raise the question. These elements must be precisely identified to determine the issue.

There is no magic formula, but this chapter includes steps that help in issue identification. When working on a client's case, four steps are recommended:

1. Identify each area of law that may possibly be involved.

2. Identify the elements necessary for a cause of action under each law identified in the first step.

3. Apply the elements of the law to the client's facts to determine the key facts.

4. Assemble the issue from the law, elements, and key facts identified in the first three steps.

There are three steps to follow to identify the issue(s) in a court opinion:

1. General question—while reading the case, keep in mind the question, "What was decided about which facts?"

2. Look to the holding to identify the rule of law, legal question, and key facts of the case.

3. Assemble the issue.

These are the recommended steps. They usually work when correctly followed and are always helpful in focusing the practitioner's attention on that which is essential: the rule of law, legal question, and facts.

Quick References

Applicable law	327	Key facts	328
Broad statement of issue	328	Legal question	327
Elements of issue	327	Multiple issues	334
Issue	326	Narrow statement of issue	328
Issue statement—procedural	335		

Internet Resources

As of the date of publication of this text, there are no Web sites dedicated specifically to issue identification. However, using a search engine and "legal analysis spotting issues" as a topic will return a wide range of Web sites that address some aspect of legal analysis and issue spotting. Some sites discuss identifying legal issues in specific areas of the law, such as labor law, whereas others discuss the topic in relation to taking exams. There are numerous other related sites.

Exercises

Additional assignments are available on the CourseMate.

ASSIGNMENT 1

Detail the steps for identifying the issue(s) in a client's case.

ASSIGNMENT 2

Detail the steps for identifying the issue(s) in a court opinion.

ASSIGNMENT 3

Statutes: *Criminal Code Section 18-760, Robbery.* A person who knowingly takes anything of value from the person or presence of another by use of force, threats, or intimidation commits robbery.

Criminal Code Section 18-773, Larceny. Any person who wrongfully takes, obtains, or withholds, by any means, from the possession of the owner or of any other person any money, personal property, or article of value of any kind, with intent permanently to deprive another person of the use and benefit of property is guilty of larceny.

Facts: Over the years, Larry borrowed several tools from his next-door neighbor. Usually he returned the items, but on occasion he forgot. One of the tools he did not return is a drill. The neighbor goes to Larry's house and tells him that if he doesn't return the drill the neighbor will file criminal charges. Larry says, "I'm keeping your drill and if you try to come get it or file charges I'll beat you up."

Question: Identify the issue(s) involving criminal law raised by this fact situation.

ASSIGNMENT 4

Perform assignment 3 using your state's larceny and robbery statutes.

ASSIGNMENT 5

Identify the issue in the following two fact situations.
Part A Beth loaned Allen $5,000. The agreement was oral. Allen commutes to a nearby city to work. Beth needs to go to the city three times in May. Allen told her he would give her three free rides to the city to help repay the loan. On one of the trips, Allen was not paying attention, lost control of the car, and wrecked it. Beth suffered severe injuries and wants to sue Allen to recover damages.

The state automobile guest statute bars suits against drivers by automobile guests. The statute does not apply if the passenger confers a substantial benefit on the driver and that is the reason the driver provided the ride.

Part B Tom and Alex are next-door neighbors. While arguing with Tom, Alex breaks Tom's lawn chair, and as Alex begins to break more lawn furniture, Tom makes a citizen's arrest of Alex. Tom's sons help Tom, and after Alex is subdued, they continue to hit and kick him for a few moments. Alex wants to sue Tom.

The state's case law defines battery as unauthorized harmful contact; it also allows a citizen's arrest when the purpose is to prevent the destruction of property.

ASSIGNMENT 6

Part A Read *Dean v. Dickey* in Appendix A. Identify the issue regarding the validity of the will.
Part B Read *United States v. Martinez-Jimenez* in Appendix A. Identify the issue concerning whether the weapon was a dangerous weapon.
Part C Read *Wolcott v. Wolcott* in Appendix A. Identify the issue concerning the modification of child support due to change of circumstances.
Part D Read *People v. Sanders* in Appendix A. Identify the issue concerning the existence of spousal privilege for communications made in the presence of the children.

ASSIGNMENT 7

Read the following case of *Metropolitan Life Insurance Company v. Syntek Finance Corporation.* The procedural issue is whether the trial court properly denied Syntek's motion for disqualification of counsel. What issue concerning the substantive disqualification of counsel is raised by the facts of the case?

CASE

METROPOLITAN LIFE INSURANCE COMPANY,
Petitioner

v.

SYNTEK FINANCE CORPORATION,
Respondent.

881 S.W.2d 319 (Tex. 1994) PER CURIAM.

This case turns on the application of the "substantial relationship" test for attorney disqualification based on prior representation of the same or a related client. Following a lengthy hearing, the trial court overruled a motion to disqualify counsel filed by Syntek Finance Corporation. After a jury trial, a judgment for approximately $6.7 million was rendered in favor of Metropolitan Life Insurance Company. The court of appeals reversed that judgment and remanded the case for a new trial, holding that the trial court abused its discretion when it denied Syntek's motion for disqualification of counsel. 880 S.W.2d 26. We reverse the judgment of the court of appeals and remand the case to that court for consideration of points of error not previously addressed.

Gene Phillips owns a controlling interest in Syntek and several other related companies. In 1986, the law firm of Hughes & Luce represented Phillips in a divorce and subsequently drafted a prenuptial agreement. In the course of that representation, Phillips disclosed his personal financial status to Hughes & Luce, including the intricate structure of his various companies. This suit, filed by Syntek in April 1989, arises out of a hotel Syntek purchased from Metropolitan. Hughes & Luce attorney Richard Nelson represented Metropolitan. Nelson made an initial conflicts check and determined to his satisfaction that there was no conflict of interest due to the firm's previous representation of Phillips.

After nearly two years of pretrial activity, Nelson acquired information about Phillips' possible involvement in Syntek's decision to stop loan payments to Metropolitan. Nelson again reviewed the circumstances of his firm's former representation of Phillips and once more satisfied himself that there was no substantial relationship between the two representations. Nelson then amended Metropolitan's pleadings to include new allegations concerning Phillips' involvement. In response, Syntek and Phillips filed a motion to disqualify Hughes & Luce. The trial court denied the motion.

[1] Rule 1.09 of the Texas Disciplinary Rules of Professional Conduct provides that a lawyer shall not take a representation that is adverse to a former client if the new matter "is the same or a substantially related matter." Tex. Disciplinary R. Prof. Conduct 1.09(a)(3)(1989), *reprinted in* Tex. Gov't Code Ann., tit. 2, subtit. G. app. (Vernon Supp.1993) (State Bar Rules art. X, § 9). In NCNB Tex. Nat'l Bank v. Coker, 765 S.W.2d 398, 400 (Tex.1989), we stated that to satisfy the substantial relationship test as a basis for disqualification a movant must prove that the facts of the previous representation *321 are so related to the facts in the pending litigation that a genuine threat exists that confidences revealed to former counsel will be divulged to a present adversary. Id.

[2] The disqualification hearing consumed five days. The trial court heard live and deposition testimony from fourteen fact witnesses concerning the previous and pending representations, and from five expert witnesses concerning the Coker standard. There was testimony that the information at issue was both available in the public domain and provided to Metropolitan by Syntek through discovery. There was also testimony that the information used in the amended pleadings was available to the public through an examiners' report from a bankruptcy proceeding against one of the companies controlled by Phillips. The trial court also conducted an in camera review of documents from the former representation.

The test for abuse of discretion is whether the trial court acted without reference to any guiding rules or principles, or acted in an arbitrary or unreasonable manner. *See* Downer v. Aquamarine Operators, Inc., 701 S.W.2d 238, 241-42 (Tex.1985), *cert. denied*, 476 U.S. 1159, 106 S.Ct. 2279, 90 L.Ed.2d 721 (1986). We hold that on the evidence presented, based on the Coker standard, it was not an abuse of discretion for the trial court to conclude that no substantial relationship existed between the former and current representations and to deny the motion to disqualify.

We therefore conclude that the court of appeals improperly substituted its judgment for that of the trial court. *See* Flores v. Fourth Court of Appeals, 777 S.W.2d 38, 41-42 (Tex.1989). Accordingly, a majority of the court grants Metropolitan's application for writ of error, and without hearing oral argument, reverses the judgment of the court of appeals and remands the case to that court for consideration of Syntek's other points of error which it did not previously address. Tex. R. App. P. 170.

ASSIGNMENT 8

Read the following case of *Morgan v. Greenwaldt*. The procedural issue is whether the trial court properly granted a directed verdict on the false imprisonment claim. What issue regarding the substantive false imprisonment is raised by the facts of the case?

CASE

MORGAN v. GREENWALDT

786 So. 2d 1037 (Miss. 2001)

Direct Verdict in favor of defendants

SMITH, Justice, for the Court:

1. Genia A. Morgan ("Morgan") sued St. Dominic-Jackson Memorial Hospital ("Hospital"), and two of the Hospital's nurses, Brenda Greenwaldt and Susan Brotherton, and a psychiatric technician, Melinda Leah Lewis, over an incident that occurred in June 1996. Morgan alleged that she had been assaulted and battered, falsely imprisoned, and treated negligently while she was a patient. She also sued for intentional infliction of emotional distress. The trial court granted a directed verdict for all the defendants on the issues of assault and battery, false imprisonment, gross negligence, and intentional infliction of emotional distress, but allowed the jury *1040 to determine if the defendants were negligent in their treatment of Morgan. After four days of trial, the jury returned a verdict in favor of the defendants, and the trial court entered judgment accordingly. Morgan's motion for a new trial was denied January 4, 2000, and thereafter she appealed to this Court. We find no reversible error and affirm the judgment of the trial court.

FACTS

2. Genia Morgan started seeing a psychiatrist in 1990 for depression. In early June 1996, Morgan's psychiatrist, Dr. Barbara Goff, suggested that Morgan voluntarily check into the psychiatric unit of the Hospital due to her severe depression and sleep disorder. Dr. Goff wanted Morgan in a monitored environment while she worked on adjusting Morgan's medication. At the time of her admission, Morgan was having suicidal thoughts, and her depression had advanced to the stage where she had given up her job. Also, Morgan was experiencing hallucinations and trances which required an adjustment in her anti-psychotic medication. During her admission assessment, Morgan reported having a metaphysical experience. Morgan described this experience to the admitting nurse as one where "[she] was lying in bed when something grabbed [her] neck and then it let go when [she] started to pray." Upon her admittance into the Hospital, Morgan signed a Consent to Treatment Form authorizing the Hospital to treat her for illness. She was placed on the intermediate ward where patients were free to walk around the floor and mingle with other patients.

3. On June 18, 1996, Morgan went to the nurses' station and asked for a bottle of hydrogen peroxide that she said she had brought to the Hospital with her. She claimed that it was her practice to brush her teeth with hydrogen peroxide. Nurse Susan Brotherton looked for the hydrogen peroxide but could not locate it. Melinda Leah Lewis, a psychiatric technician, and Brotherton checked Morgan's personal belongings checklist, which is filled out upon a patient's admittance to the Hospital. The hydrogen peroxide was not listed on the sheet as one of the items brought in by Morgan. Brotherton told Morgan that she would call Dr. Goff to get an order for the hydrogen peroxide. Brotherton called Dr. Goff's office and left a message regarding the peroxide and its intended use by Morgan as a mouth rinse. Dr. Goff stated that Morgan could not have the peroxide but could have Cepacol mouthwash instead. Brotherton informed Morgan of the doctor's orders. Morgan became upset and left the unit. Thereafter, she retreated to her room crying.

4. Brotherton, Lewis, and technician Jeannie Smith walked toward Morgan's room to see what was wrong. Brotherton and Lewis entered Morgan's room. Morgan was lying across the bed crying. In an effort to calm her down, Brotherton told Morgan that even though there was no record of her bringing the hydrogen peroxide into the Hospital, the Hospital could reimburse her if she believed the Hospital was responsible for the loss. According to Brotherton's testimony, Morgan began yelling profanity and ordered the nurses out of her room. The nurses returned to their station.

5. Shortly thereafter, Morgan came out of her room and approached the nurses' station. According to Brotherton and Lewis, Morgan yelled, used profanity, and demanded her hydrogen peroxide. She walked to the nurse manager's door and began pounding her fist on the door. At this point, Dr. Goff was again called, and Brotherton left a message with the doctor's secretary that Morgan was out of *1041 control and was acting in a hostile manner. Due to the escalating situation, Brotherton called the nursing supervisor, Brenda Greenwaldt. When Greenwaldt arrived and introduced herself, Morgan started ranting and raving that she demanded an apology. Morgan then proceeded to pound her fist on the nurses' station desk and point her finger in nurse Greenwaldt's face. According to Greenwaldt, Brotherton, and Lewis, the patient appeared totally out of control and became a threat to the safety of herself and others.

6. . . . . [G]reenwaldt wrote an order that stated "[p]lace in seclusion for threatening staff for four to six hours until calm and nonthreatening."

7. Several witnesses testified that Morgan was escorted, without any physical contact, to the seclusion area. Even Morgan stated in her testimony that she walked to seclusion on her own accord. According to Morgan, she was strip searched and forced to change into a Hospital gown in front of several people. However, various staff members of the Hospital testified that it was standard procedure for someone in seclusion

to be searched for dangerous instrumentalities and to change into a Hospital gown. Further, according to Hospital personnel, Leah Lewis stood in front of the window to the seclusion door so there would be privacy. Morgan was left in seclusion for about two hours, from 4:30 P.M. until 6:45 P.M.

§ 8. Morgan raises the following issues on appeal:

I. WHETHER THE TRIAL COURT PROPERLY DIRECTED A VERDICT ON ALL COUNTS OF INTENTIONAL INFLICTION OF EMOTIONAL DISTRESS, FALSE IMPRISONMENT, GROSS NEGLIGENCE, AND ASSAULT AND BATTERY?

***

ANALYSIS

I.

§ 9. At the close of the testimony, the defendants moved for a directed verdict on all counts except the medical malpractice negligence claim. The trial court granted the motion, thereby taking from the jury the claims of intentional infliction of emotional distress, false imprisonment, gross negligence, and assault and battery. Morgan argues that there was sufficient evidence to make out a jury question on all of these claims, and thus, the directed verdict for the defendants was reversible error.

[1][2][3] § 10. This Court conducts a de novo review of a motion for directed verdict. _Northern Elec. Co. v. Phillips_, 660 So.2d 1278, 1281 (Miss.1995). If we find that the evidence favorable to the non-moving party and the reasonable inferences drawn therefrom present a question for the jury, the motion should not be *1042 granted. _Id._ (citing _Pittman v. Home Indem. Co._, 411 So.2d 87, 89 (Miss.1982)). This Court has also held that an issue should only be presented to the jury when the evidence creates a question of fact on which reasonable jurors could disagree. _Herrington v. Spell_, 692 So.2d 93, 97 (Miss.1997).

A. False Imprisonment

[4] § 11. False imprisonment has only two elements: "detention of the plaintiff and the unlawfulness of such detention." _Lee v. Alexander_, 607 So.2d 30, 35 (Miss.1992) (citing _Page v. Wiggins_, 595 So.2d 1291 (Miss.1992); _Thornhill v. Wilson_, 504 So.2d 1205, 1208 (Miss.1987) (citing _State ex rel. Powell v. Moore_, 252 Miss. 471, 174 So.2d 352, 354 (1965); _Hart v. Walker_, 720 F.2d 1436, 1439 (5th Cir.1983))).

[5] § 12. Morgan contends that the trial court erred in granting a directed verdict because she was locked up against her will, and the determination of whether her detainment was a reasonable one should have been a question of fact for the jury. This Court finds that such an argument lacks merit. Morgan consented to the treatment at the Hospital, and such treatment includes placing patients who are out of control in a secure environment for the protection of both the patient and the others at the Hospital.

§ 13. The evidence indicates that prior to the 1996 incident in question, Morgan had undergone a psychological evaluation that concluded she was suffering from personality disorders. She had a history of mental illness dating back to 1990 and was diagnosed as having been severely depressed upon her admittance to the Hospital in June of 1996. She also suffered from hallucinations and crying episodes. Moreover, on the morning of the alleged incident, Morgan's doctor noted in the medical records that she was experiencing trances that lasted up to fifteen minutes.

§ 14. Morgan argues that the mere fact that she was undergoing treatment in a Hospital does not mean that the Hospital is justified in performing any medical procedures it deems warranted. Although such an argument is a valid one, it is not warranted in the case sub judice. The cases Morgan cites as support for such an argument are not applicable to the case at bar. Such cases deal with situations where the appellant did not consent to the treatment or was detained upon a request or attempt of the patient to leave the Hospital. _Felton v. Coyle_, 95 Ill.App.2d 202, 238 N.E.2d 191 (1968); _Fox v. Smith_, 594 So.2d 596 (Miss.1992). Genia Morgan voluntarily signed an Authorization for Treatment form when she was admitted to the Hospital. Moreover, there was substantial testimony to support the fact that Morgan was out of control and was posing a threat to the environment, including herself. Confinement in a secured environment is a common method of treatment in psychiatric wards and Hospitals. The Hospital is charged with the duty of maintaining a safe and secure environment for all patients. The evidence showed that Morgan was acting in a way that clearly conveyed the possibility of violence.

§ 15. Morgan relies on _Fox v. Smith_, 594 So.2d 596 (Miss.1992), to bolster her argument that the mere fact that she was undergoing treatment in a Hospital does not mean that the Hospital is justified in performing any medical procedure it deems warranted. In _Fox_, the patient was admitted to the Hospital for a laparoscopy and alleged that the removal of an intrauterine device was done without her consent. _Id._ at 596. This case can clearly be distinguished from the case at bar since the patient in _Fox_ initially refused to sign the consent form because she objected to a *1043 clause in the form which authorized the Hospital to dispose of severed tissues or specimens. _Id._ at 599. The Court stated that _Fox_ turned on the issue of consent, or not, for the removal of the patient's intrauterine device. _Id._ at 597. This Court made clear that a patient's informed consent to treatment is a prerequisite to treatment, and because a material dispute existed on important facts concerning the patient's consent, the question should have been presented to the jury. _Id._ at 604.

§ 16. In comparison, Morgan clearly consented to treatment by the doctors and personnel at the Hospital by signing the consent form. Moreover, Morgan never retracted her consent to receive treatment. She never informed the nurses that she refused their treatment or that she wanted to leave the Hospital. Indeed, she even voluntarily walked to the isolation room.

§ 17. Morgan also relies upon _Felton v. Coyle_, 95 Ill. App.2d 202, 238 N.E.2d 191 (1968), for her argument that she was falsely imprisoned. This case is not only factually distinguishable from the case at bar, but is also from another jurisdiction and, therefore, not controlling on this Court. In _Felton_, the patient suffered a broken clavicle and was taken to a Chicago Hospital for treatment. _Id._ at 192. After an altercation between the patient and Hospital personnel, patient's doctor ordered him out of the Hospital. _Id_. When the patient attempted to leave the Hospital, the doctor grabbed the patient by the shoulders and told him he was going to call the police. _Id._ at 193. The doctor then sent the patient to a psychiatric Hospital. _Id_. The trial court issued a directed verdict in favor of the defendant, and on appeal the patient argued that he was entitled to a directed verdict. _Id._ at 194. The appellate court disagreed, holding that under the facts and circumstances of the case, it was properly presented to the trier of fact to determine whether the patient was improperly detained. _Id_.

§ 18. Unlike _Felton_, here there were no efforts by the Hospital to prevent Morgan from leaving the Hospital at her will. Morgan did not leave the Hospital until two days after the alleged incident. Even after that time, she continued to attend classes at the Hospital.

§ 19. The trial court properly directed a verdict on the issue of false imprisonment. There is simply no proof in the record of the unlawfulness of Morgan's detention. She voluntarily signed an authorization for treatment form. She had a history of psychological problems, and there was substantial testimony to support the fact that she was out of control and was posing a threat to herself and to others.

CONCLUSION

§ 29. In sum, the trial court did not err in granting a directed verdict on the issues of assault and battery, false imprisonment, gross negligence and intentional infliction of emotional distress. Genia A. Morgan simply failed to meet her burden of proof in showing the necessary elements of these causes of action. . . . For these reasons, we affirm the judgment of the Hinds County Circuit Court.

§ 30. AFFIRMED.

PITTMAN, C.J., BANKS, P.J., MILLS, WALLER, COBB AND DIAZ, JJ., CONCUR. McRAE, P.J., CONCURS IN RESULT ONLY. EASLEY, J., DISSENTS WITHOUT SEPARATE WRITTEN OPINION.

ASSIGNMENT 9

Identify the issue in assignments 16 and 17 of Chapter 17.

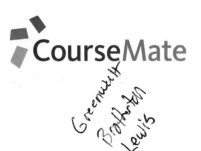

CHAPTER 11

Legal Analysis: Stating the Issue

"Mary, I want you to determine if we can get the evidence suppressed in this case. I need a memo on this by the day after tomorrow, if possible." Jan handed Mary the case file as she gave these instructions. Mary Strate is a legal assistant working in an Oregon law firm that specializes in criminal defense. Jan Brite is her supervising attorney, and according to Jan, Mary is her "right hand."

After reviewing the case and conducting some research, Mary's focus turns to the significant facts relevant to the suppression-of-evidence issue. She determines that there are several key facts. The state police seized the evidence during the execution of a search warrant. A state court judge improperly issued the warrant. The warrant was improperly issued, and therefore defective, because the state police did not present the court sufficient probable cause to justify the search. The opposing side, the state, concedes that the warrant was improperly issued. The officers did not know the warrant was defective and executed it in the good-faith belief that it was valid.

Mary's research indicates that the resolution of the issue is governed by Oregon's exclusionary rule, which provides that evidence illegally seized may not be admitted at trial. The rule was adopted by the state supreme court and is not statutory. As Mary begins the assignment, her first question is how to phrase the issue. "What is the proper format? What is the best way to effectively communicate precisely what is in dispute in this case?" The Application section of this chapter presents the answer to the latter question. The material discussed in this chapter prior to the Application section addresses Mary's other questions.

Learning Objectives

After completing this chapter, you should understand:

- The elements of a well-crafted issue

- The value and importance of phrasing the issue narrowly and comprehensively

- The best way to assemble the elements to effectively communicate the issue

- The importance of stating the issue objectively

I. INTRODUCTION

Chapter 10 points out that the most important step in the case analysis process is correctly identifying the issue. If the issue is misidentified, time is wasted researching and writing about the wrong question. Once the issue is identified, it is equally important to correctly state it. Of what value is it to correctly identify the question, then fail to accurately communicate what you have identified? Therefore, how Mary states the issue is of critical importance, because the issue governs the direction of the research and communicates the nature of the dispute.

A well-crafted issue informs the reader of the scope of the memo by identifying in a sentence the precise legal question raised by the key facts of the case. It informs the reader of the relevant law, the key facts of the case, and the legal question raised by the law. The exactness and the degree of specificity with which the question is posed determine its usefulness to the reader and researcher.

The goal is to inform the reader of what you have identified as the legal question raised by the dispute. This goal is achieved by focusing your attention on drafting the issue clearly, concisely, and completely. Because so much hinges on correct presentation of the issue, several drafts may be required. Do not get discouraged. The final draft may not emerge until well into the process, and often not until after extensive research and writing.

Chapter 10 identifies the issue as being composed of the law, the question, and the key facts. The focus of that chapter was on how to identify these elements in a client's situation and a court opinion. Here the focus is on how to present these elements when framing the issue: how to write the issue to ensure that the reader knows the precise legal question at the core of the dispute; and how to present the law, question, and key facts to effectively communicate that question.

Ultimately, the issue is the legal question raised by the facts of the dispute. Because it is a question, it should be drafted as a question rather than a statement.

Although there are no established rules governing what the issue must contain or how to assemble it, the law, question, and key fact **elements** should be included to achieve the goal of clearly, concisely, and completely communicating the nature of the dispute. A simple test to determine if the statement of the issue is complete (whether it does its job) is the following: If someone reads the issue alone—if the rest of the memorandum or brief is lost or not referred to—would the reader know what specific legal question, concerning what law, and involving what facts is in dispute in this case? Given this test, there are two ways to state the issue, one effective and one not:

 ■ Shorthand, or broad, statement
 ■ Comprehensive, or narrow, statement

II. SHORTHAND OR BROAD STATEMENT OF THE ISSUE

A **shorthand statement** is a broad formulation of the issue that usually does not include the specific facts or law.

For Example	■ Did Mr. Smith commit a battery?
	■ Can Mr. Jones recover damages for negligence?
■ Did the court err when it granted the motion to dismiss?	
■ Did the chair of the board violate his fiduciary duty?	

A **broad statement of issue** is often used in conversation or oral communications when the participants are familiar with the facts and know the law that applies to the case. It is appropriate in this informal context. It may also be appropriate initially in the analytical process by helping to focus attention on the general area of the law to be researched; for example, in the preceding list, the first two illustrations focus the researcher's attention on the general areas of battery and negligence. As noted in section III of Chapter 10, a broadly stated issue may be proper in such situations, but it is not appropriate in legal research and writing.

III. COMPREHENSIVE OR NARROW STATEMENT OF THE ISSUE

The most effective formulation of the issue is a comprehensive, **narrow statement of issue**. In one sentence, the specific law, legal question, and key facts are presented. This form communicates the specific law that may have been violated in a specific fact situation, or whether and how that law applies in a specific situation. It conveys, in the terms and circumstances of the case, the precise law and question in dispute.

> **For Example** ■ Under the requirements of Florida tort law, can a claim for negligent infliction of emotional distress be made by a witness, not related to the victim, who witnesses a severe beating of the victim?
>
> ■ According to New Washington's probate code, N. Wash. Code § 29-1-5, is a will valid if the witnesses are brothers of the testator?
>
> Note that the specific law and question involved in the dispute are presented in the context of the facts of the dispute.

The value and importance of phrasing the issue comprehensively cannot be overemphasized.

1. For a researcher, it directs the research to the specific area of the law that controls the question raised by the facts of the dispute. This narrowing of focus saves research time because the researcher is immediately directed to the specific area of the law, and need only read cases with similar key facts.

2. In an interoffice memorandum or a court brief, a comprehensive, or narrow, formulation of the issue sets the scope of the memo by informing the reader at the outset what precisely is in dispute. It does not force the reader to try to determine what the question is from the analysis section. It thereby makes it less likely that the reader will misunderstand what is in dispute.

3. In a law-office setting, a narrowly framed issue saves time. Future researchers, by merely reading the issue, will know precisely what law and facts a memorandum addresses. They are not forced to read the analysis section to determine if the memo is related or may apply to the case at hand.

With this in mind, the issue should include the following elements, as presented in Exhibit 11-1:

1. The specific law or rule that controls the dispute (the *relevant law*)
2. The *legal question* regarding the law raised by the facts
3. The *key facts* that determine whether or how the law or principle applies

The challenge is to include all three elements in one sentence; therefore, focus on:

1. Completeness—Include the precise law, question, and key facts.
2. Conciseness—Include no more than is absolutely necessary to guarantee completeness.
3. Clarity—Craft the complete and concisely assembled material in the most effective manner.

There are several ways to meet this challenge:

1. Present the facts first, followed by the legal question and the law.

> **For Example** "Can a witness, not related to the victim, who witnesses a severe beating of the victim, establish a claim for negligent infliction of emotional distress under Florida tort law?"
>
> "If the brothers of the testator witness the will, is the will valid under the provisions of the California wills attestation statute?"

2. Present the law first, followed by the facts, and then the legal question.

> **For Example** "Under Florida's tort law, can a witness, not related to the victim, who witnesses a severe beating of the victim, establish a claim for negligent infliction of emotional distress?"
>
> "Under the California wills attestation statute, if the brothers of the testator witness the will, is the will valid?"

3. Present the legal question first, followed by the law and the facts.

> **For Example** "Can a claim for negligent infliction of emotional distress be established under Florida tort law when a witness, not related to the victim, witnesses a severe beating of the victim?"
>
> "Is a will valid under the California wills attestation statute if the brothers of the testator witness the will?"

4. Present the rule of law first, followed by the legal question and the facts.

> **For Example** "Under Florida's tort law, can a claim for negligent infliction of emotional distress be established when a witness, not related to the victim, witnesses a severe beating of the victim?"
>
> "Under the California wills attestation statute, is a will valid if the brothers of the testator witness the will?"

Any of these structures may be used. There are no hard-and-fast rules that mandate the selection of one form over another. However, the format presented in number 4 in the preceding list is recommended. The formula for this format is presented in Exhibit 11-1.

In sentence form, the formula in Exhibit 11-1 is, "Under this law, what legal question is raised by these facts?" There are several reasons for recommending this format:

1. It follows the standard legal analysis format, which proceeds from the general to the specific—the general law followed by application of the law to the specific facts.

> **For Example** In a court brief or an interoffice legal research memorandum, the applicable law is presented first, followed by the application of the law to the specific facts.

Exhibit 11-1 *Relevant Law + Legal Question + Key Facts.*

Relevant Law	The specific law that governs the dispute (e.g., "Under Ind. Code § 29-1-5-5, legal execution of a will . . .")
Legal Question	The question concerning the application of the law governing the dispute to the facts of the dispute (e.g., "Is a will validly executed . . .")
Key Facts	The legally significant facts that raise the legal question of how or whether the law governing the dispute applies; facts that, if changed, would change or affect the outcome of the application of the law (e.g., "When one of the witnesses is the brother of the deceased.")

© Cengage Learning 2014

The suggested format for formulation of the issue presented in Exhibit 11-1 follows the same format: The general legal context is presented first, followed by the specific facts of the dispute.

2. Present the rule first for readability purposes. A reader understands the importance of the facts in a dispute in the context of the law. If the facts are presented first and the law last, the reader must reread the facts to put them in the proper legal context because the legal context (the law that applies) is not known until the end of the issue.

3. The last and probably most important reason is that it is usually *easier to write the issue following this format*. It is a most effective tool when confronting the complex challenges presented by multiple-fact issues. Multiple facts are generally easier to write and read when placed at the end of a sentence. Try it. Once the specific law and significant or key facts are identified, it is much easier to craft the issue in the sequence of relevant law + legal question + key facts.

For these reasons, the examples used throughout this chapter and the text follow the relevant law + legal question + key facts format.

IV. ISSUE—LAW COMPONENT

Obviously you must include the relevant law in the statement of the issue, because every case involves whether or how a law applies in a specific fact situation. If the law is not included, you are asking the reader to either guess or infer what law applies or conduct research to find the applicable law. To avoid possible confusion and save extra work, establish the relevant legal context at the beginning of the issue.

You may present the law in a broad context, such as "corporations," or a narrow one, such as a specific section of a statute. Include the specific jurisdiction and the area of law.

For Example	*(jurisdiction)*	*(area)*
▪ Under	New Washington	Contract law
▪ Under	N. Wash. Code § 35-42-7	Kidnapping law

The law component of the issue consists of either enacted law or case law. As defined in Chapter 1, the term *enacted law* includes any constitutional law or rule or enactment of a legislative body, such as a statute, ordinance, or regulation. *Case law* refers to any court-made doctrine, law, rule, principle, test, or guide.

A. Issue Based on Case Law

When an issue is based on case law, do not cite only a single case, because the case law is usually based on a group or body of cases, and generally, no single case encompasses the relevant law. It is sufficient to present the law with a short introductory phrase that includes the jurisdiction and the area of the law. The easiest format follows:

	(jurisdiction)	*(area)*
Under	New Mexico	Corporation law
Applying	Utah's	Emotional distress law
According to	Indiana's	Doctrine of res ipsa loquitur
In light of	California's	Definition of confinement in false imprisonment actions

However you state it, the description should be as focused and specific as possible. The goal is to inform the reader, as precisely as possible, of the area of law involved in the dispute. Therefore, such broad statements as, "According to the Colorado case law . . ." or "Under the case law . . ." are generally not acceptable. Such statements are so broad as to be meaningless. The reader is given no direction about which area of the law is involved in the dispute.

Along these same lines, a specific description is preferable to a broad one.

> **For Example** ■ "Under Wyoming's definition of oppressive conduct by majority share-holders . . ." is preferable to "Under Wyoming corporation law. . . ."
>
> ■ "Applying Georgia's definition of consideration . . ." is preferable to "Applying Georgia contract law. . . ."
>
> ■ "Under California's law of trespass to chattels . . ." is preferable to "Under California tort law. . . ."

Again, the key is to be as specific and focused as possible when describing the area of the law. The greater the specificity of the legal description, the better the reader understands what precisely is at issue in the dispute. If you are using a broad description, such as "torts," reexamine the issue to determine if a narrower focus, such as false imprisonment, battery, and so on, can be applied.

B. Issue Based on Enacted Law

You may present an issue based on enacted law, such as a constitutional provision or statute, in several ways. The various ways may include a specific citation, a title, and/or a description.

> **For Example**
>
> *(citation)* *(title)*
> ■ "According to N. Wash. Code § 20-40-1, kidnapping. . . ."
>
> *(title paraphrased)* *(description)*
> ■ "Under the New Washington kidnapping statute, which includes intent to confine as an element of kidnapping. . . ."
>
> *(title paraphrased)*
> ■ "In light of the provisions of the involuntary dissolution of corporations . . ."
>
> *(citation)*
> ■ ". . . statute, N. Wash. Corp. Code § 56-7-14, . . ."

The goal of clearly, completely, and concisely communicating the issue governs the choice or combination of choices selected. This, in turn, is governed by the complexity of the issue and the degree to which the description conveys the necessary information.

1. Enacted Law—Citations

Is it necessary or advisable to include the **citation** in the statement of the issue? Some believe the inclusion of the citation clutters the issue, arguing that it is not necessary because the citation can be determined by referring to the analysis section of the memorandum. Others believe the inclusion of the citation is, if not required, at least advisable. It focuses the reader on the exact section of the law in dispute, allowing the reader to immediately refer to that section if necessary. In a law office, a subsequent researcher who is reviewing a memo from the memo files can, by referring to the issue, tell what specific law is discussed in the memo. By merely referring to the issue, the researcher knows if the memo involves the same law as the law being researched.

> **For Example** A researcher is checking the office memorandum files to determine if any research has been conducted on section 956.05(b) of the state's corporation statutes. If the citation is included in the issue, a mere glance at the issue tells the researcher if the memo involves the same statute. The researcher's time is saved by not having to read the body of the memo to determine if it is on point.

In some instances, the firm may require or prefer the inclusion or exclusion of the citation in the issue. In the case of a court brief, the court rules may determine the answer to that question. If the choice is yours, do what works. If the length or complexity of the issue precludes use of the citation, then leave it out.

Keep in mind the following rules when using a citation:

1. Use the proper citation form. A summary of citation form is presented in Chapter 8.

2. Do not use a citation alone. In addition to a citation, a title or description is necessary to adequately inform the reader of the legal context of the issue.

> **For Example** *Incorrect:* "Under Ind. Code § 29-1-5-5, does. . . ." Without a description or title, one does not know which area of the law is being considered. The reader will be forced to stop and look up the citation unless he or she is familiar with that particular section.
>
> *Correct:* "Under Ind. Code § 29-1-5-5, legal execution of a will, . . ." The specific area of law covered in the citation is provided.

2. Enacted Law—Titles and Descriptions

Whereas citations should not be used without a title or description, you can use a title or description without a citation when describing enacted law. **Titles** and **descriptions** provide the amount of information sufficient to inform the reader of the legal context of the issue. Although the citation is not required, its inclusion may be advisable for the reasons discussed in section IV.B.1.

A title of a constitutional section, statute, and so on, is a heading that provides the name by which an act or section is individually known. A description is a brief summary of the relevant portions of the act and may include part of the title.

> **For Example** *Examples of titles:*
>
> - Ind. Code § 29-1-5-2. Writing required—witnesses, competency, interest
> - Cal. Corp. Code § 1800. Verified complaint; plaintiffs; grounds; intervention by shareholder or creditor; exempt corporations
>
> *Examples of descriptions:*
>
> - "Under the Indiana statute that governs the writing and witnessing of wills, . . ."
> - "In light of the provisions of the California corporation statute that applies to lawsuits against corporations and intervention by shareholders, . . ."

When using a title or description of enacted law, the guiding principle is whether it provides the reader with enough information to know the legal context of the issue. The title alone may provide sufficient information. The terms from the titles in the following example are in italic.

> **For Example**
> - "Applying the provisions of Maryland's *kidnapping* statute, . . ."
> - "Under California's *holographic wills* statute, . . ."

Occasionally, the title may require modification. You may need to add or delete words to enhance clarity and readability. In the following examples, the title is presented followed by the modified statement of the issue containing additional language.

> **For Example**
> - Limitation of actions. (Title of N.M. Stat. Ann. § 41-1-2.) "Under the limitation-of-action provisions of New Mexico's wrongful death statute, . . ."
> - Holographic wills; requirements. (Title of Cal. Prob. Code § 6111.) "According to the requirements of the holographic wills section of the California statutes, . . ."

Sometimes it is necessary to delete language from the title because it is not relevant to the issue or needed to enhance clarity. In the following examples, the title is presented first, followed by the modification containing fewer words.

> **For Example**
> - Verified complaint; plaintiffs; grounds; intervention by shareholder or creditor; exempt corporations. (Title of Cal. Corp. Code § 1800.) "Under the California corporation statute that allows shareholder intervention in dissolution actions, . . ."
> - Writing required—witnesses, competency, interest. (Title of Ind. Code § 29-1-5-2.) "In light of the requirements of the Indiana wills statute that governs witness competency, . . ."
>
> *Comment:* In these examples, "exempt corporations, interest" and other words were deleted because these terms, although included in the title, are not relevant to the issue in the case.

If the title of a statute or law does not provide the required information, or if it is necessary to emphasize a particular aspect or element of the statute or law, the use of a description may be appropriate. In the following examples, the title is presented first, followed by an example.

For Example
- Nuncupative wills. (Title of Ind. Code § 29-1-5-4.) "Under the Indiana statute providing that an oral will does not revoke an existing written will, . . ."
- Limitations of actions. (Title of N.M. Stat. Ann. § 41-1-2.) "Under New Mexico's wrongful death statute, which requires that an action be brought within three years of the date of death, . . ."
- Ski area sign requirements. (Title of Wash. Rev. Code § 70.117.010.) "Under the Washington statute that requires a resort to post a notice at the top of closed trails, . . ."

As mentioned, there are no rules mandating use of a particular format when composing the legal component of the issue. The unwritten rule, however, is to keep focused on the goal:

- Is the information included sufficient to provide the reader with the specific legal context of the issue?
- Is the legal component of the issue stated narrowly enough that the reader will not have to look elsewhere (in the analysis portion of the memorandum or in the statutes) to determine what precise area of the law is in dispute?

C. Format of the Law Component

There are two basic formats to choose from when presenting the **law component of the issue**:

1. The jurisdiction or citation followed by the title or description
2. The title or description followed by the jurisdiction or citation

---

For Example Jurisdiction or citation followed by title or description:

      (jurisdiction)   *(title)*
- "Under the New Mexico wrongful death statutes, . . ."

      (jurisdiction)   *(description)*
- "Under the Washington statute that requires a resort to post a notice at the top of closed trails, . . ."

      (citation)   *(title)*
- "According to Ind. Code § 35-42-3-3, kidnapping, . . ."

      (citation)   *(description)*
- "Under Cal. Civ. Proc. Code § 340, which establishes a one-year statute of limitations in slander cases, . . ."

> **For Example** Title or description followed by jurisdiction or citation:
>
> *(title)*   *(jurisdiction)*
> ▫ "According to the wrongful death provisions of the Colorado statutes, . . ."
>
> *(description)*
> ▫ "In light of the requirement that drivers carry proof of insurance under. . . ."
>
> *(jurisdiction)*
> ▫ ". . . California law, . . ."
>
> *(title)*   *(citation)*
> ▫ Under the kidnapping statute, Ind. Code § 35-42-3-3, . . ."
>
> *(description)*
> ▫ "Under the statute that requires skiers to ski within the range of their ability. . . ."
>
> *(citation)*
> ▫ ". . . ability, Wash. Rev. Code § 70.117.020, . . ."

V. ISSUE—QUESTION COMPONENT

The question component is really what the issue is about. What legal question is being raised by the facts? In the formula adopted in this chapter, the **question component** follows the law component. It must do the following:

1. Relate to or concern the specific law included in the law component
2. Present the specific legal question raised by the facts
3. Link the law with the facts

In the following examples, the question component is italicized. The linking verbs are boldfaced.

> **For Example** ▫ Under New York landlord-tenant law, ***does** a landlord **breach** his duty to provide a habitable residence* when he fails to provide air conditioning?
>
> ▫ Under Cal. Civ. Proc. Code § 340, which establishes a one-year statute of limitations in slander cases, ***did** the statute of limitations **begin** to run* when the newsletter was printed or when the newsletter was distributed to the customers?
>
> ▫ According to the statute governing oppressive conduct, Cal. Corp. Code § 1800, ***does** a majority shareholder **engage** in oppressive conduct* when he refuses to issue dividends while providing himself with bonuses equal to twice his salary?
>
> ▫ Under the Colorado law governing ski resorts, ***is** a resort **responsible** for warning* skiers of hazardous areas between ski runs?

Note that in all the preceding examples, the question specifically relates to the law included in the issue. Note, also, that the question links the law to the facts. This connection may be created through the use of **linking verbs**. There are many possible linking verbs, such as *constitute*, *establish*, and various forms of *to be* (e.g., *is*, *was*). In drafting this component of the issue, the main focus is to ensure that the legal question raised by the facts is included. In other words, under the law included in the issue, is the precise legal question raised by the facts clearly presented?

VI. ISSUE—SIGNIFICANT OR KEY FACTS COMPONENT

The last section of the formula for writing an issue is the presentation of the significant or key facts. It is especially important to keep in mind the goals of clarity, completeness, and conciseness, because cases with multiple or complex facts often make these goals difficult to achieve. The **facts component of the issue** must do the following:

1. Be readable
2. Include key facts legally relevant to the law component
3. Set the factual scope of the legal question

The facts component should not be so complex that the reader has trouble understanding the issue.

It is always preferable to include all key facts. However, when there are multiple key facts, it may be necessary for the sake of clarity to take other steps, such as categorizing, condensing, or listing the facts. Examples of the key fact component follow.

For Example All key facts included:

■ According to the provisions of Washington's ski safety act, does a resort have a duty to warn skiers of ice hazards on expert runs?

■ Under the holographic will statute, Colo. Rev. Stat. § 15-11-503, is a holographic will valid if it is handwritten by a neighbor at the direction of the testator, but not written in the testator's handwriting?

Comment: Note that the facts are presented clearly and in a logical sequence.

For Example Key facts condensed—some included and some referred to generally:

■ Under Ohio's corporation law governing oppressive conduct, does oppressive conduct occur when a majority shareholder of a closely held corporation engages in several acts that may be harmful to a minority shareholder, such as refusing to issue dividends and firing the minority shareholder from her position in the corporation without a stated cause?

■ Under New York's constitutional provision prohibiting cruel and unusual punishment, are conditions of confinement cruel and unusual when the confinement may be unhealthy in several ways, such as the total calories served each inmate daily being less than the recommended minimum and the jail cells being kept at a temperature under 60 degrees in the winter?

For Example Key facts presented in general categories:

■ Under Indiana corporation law, does oppressive conduct occur when a majority shareholder engages in several actions that are beneficial solely to the majority shareholder and detrimental to the interests of the minority shareholders?

■ Under Arizona's constitutional provision prohibiting cruel and unusual punishment, are conditions of confinement cruel and unusual when they are unsanitary, unsafe, and in violation of various health codes?

Comment: Take care to avoid distorting or misstating the issue when condensing or categorizing the key facts. In the previous two examples, assumptions are contained in the categorizations. As stated, the first issue formulation assumes the actions of the majority shareholder are solely beneficial to the majority shareholder, and the second assumes the conditions of confinement are unsanitary. To avoid these problems, present multiple or complex facts in the form of a list.

For Example Key facts listed:

- According to the provisions of California corporation law, Cal. Corp. Code § 1800, does oppressive conduct occur when a majority shareholder:
  1. Fires a minority shareholder from her job without stating a reason;
  2. Refuses to issue dividends when the corporation has a cash surplus of more than $1,000,000 and there are no plans for use of the money by the business;
  3. Triples his salary three times within one year and his salary already was twice the amount of similarly situated employees when the raises were given; and
  4. Gives himself a $100,000 cash bonus without a stated reason for the bonus?
- Under the United States Constitution's prohibitions against cruel and unusual punishment, are conditions of confinement cruel and unusual when:
  1. The food is nutritionally deficient in that the total calories per meal are less than the recommended minimum;
  2. Jail cells designed for one inmate currently house three inmates;
  3. Jail cell temperatures are routinely kept below 60 degrees in the winter; and
  4. Jail cells are roach- and ant-infested?

Remember, it is always best to include all key or significant facts in the fact component of the issue. If doing so would make the issue unreadable or lacking in clarity, however, employ one of the options presented in the preceding examples instead.

VII. ETHICS—OBJECTIVELY STATING THE ISSUE

The preceding sections discuss the structure of the issue. An additional matter to keep in mind when composing the issue is to state the issue objectively. To **state objectively** means to construct or write the issue in a manner that fairly and completely presents all the key facts without favoring an outcome.

Rule 3.3(a)(1) of the Model Rules of Professional Conduct provides that a lawyer should not make false statements of law or fact to a tribunal. Broadly interpreted, this means that matters should not be presented in a manner that may mislead the court. Therefore, when writing for the client, for the supervising attorney, and often for the court, state the issue objectively so that a conclusion is not suggested, and the reader is not misled. The purpose of legal analysis, whether in a letter to the client, an office legal memorandum, or a court brief, is to inform the reader how the law applies to a particular legal problem, not to prejudge or distort the law and its application.

There are several additional reasons why you should state the issue objectively:

1. A one-sided presentation of the facts or elimination of some unfavorable key facts can mislead the reader—and may result in disaster. Either the opposing side or the court will discover and point out the misrepresentation or omission.

2. Ultimately, the law will govern the issue, and usually no amount of creative phrasing will change the outcome. Provide the reader with an objective presentation of the facts, and let your legal argument do the persuading.

3. If the issue is presented in a biased or slanted manner, the reader may question the author's ability and credibility and discount the legal argument that follows.

For Example "Applying Colorado's law of conversion, does conversion occur when an individual, with a known reputation as a thief and a burglary conviction, takes and uses his neighbor's electric saw without permission?"

Comment: The statement is not objective. The facts relating to the individual's reputation and conviction are prejudicial and nonrelevant. Readers will conclude either that you do not know what the relevant facts are or that you are trying to influence them.

Restated objectively: "Applying Colorado's law of conversion, does conversion occur when an individual takes and uses his neighbor's electric saw without permission?"

For Example "Under the Colorado ski act, does a resort have a duty to warn of an obviously dangerous ice hazard?"

Comment: In this example, assume these additional facts are left out: The skier was a novice skier using an expert ski run, and the nature and degree of the ice hazard have, not has determined. The issue is not stated objectively for two reasons:

1. The ice condition is described in such a way as to lead the reader to a conclusion that it was dangerous.

2. A key fact is omitted: A novice skier was on an expert ski run. This fact could very well govern the outcome of the case. It may be that the ice condition is hazardous only to novice skiers, and since the run is an expert run, the resort does not have a duty to warn. Omission of this fact, which will come to light as the case progresses, only serves to mislead. The reader will conclude either that you are misstating the question with the intent to mislead or that you do not understand the law.

Restated objectively: "Under the Colorado Ski act, does a resort have a duty to warn a novice skier of ice conditions on an expert ski run?"

For Example "Under the United States Constitution's prohibitions against cruel and unusual punishment, are conditions of confinement cruel and unusual when the conditions are unsanitary and unhealthy?"

Comment: The issue is stated both prejudicially and too broadly. It is prejudicial because it assumes that conditions are unsanitary and unhealthy. Whether the conditions are unsanitary and unhealthy is in dispute and has yet to be decided. The statement is too broad because the facts concerning the conditions are not included; instead, readers are just given conclusions about the facts. What are the factual conditions that are allegedly unsanitary and unhealthy? Are the jail cells unclean? Is the water unsafe to drink?

Restated objectively: "Under the United States Constitution's prohibitions against cruel and unusual punishment, are conditions of confinement cruel and unusual when a jail cell is cleaned once a month, its toilet overflows daily, and its tap water is not potable?"

Always state the issue objectively. When in doubt, err on the side of completeness. If condensing or categorizing key facts results in a biased or distorted statement of the question, do not condense or categorize. It is better to have a long or complicated issue statement than a loss of credibility or misleading formulation of the issue.

In many instances, when the question is to be presented to a court in a court brief, it may be desirable to state the issue in a persuasive manner. This may be advantageous when you are trying to persuade the court to adopt a legal position or concept that is favorable to the client. In light of the provisions of Model Rule 3.3(a)(1), great care must be taken when constructing an issue persuasively to avoid misleading the court or misrepresenting the issue. The examples presented in this section point out some of the hazards.

Persuasive issue writing is generally applicable in the courtroom in oral argument or in trial and appellate briefs. It usually is not applicable in research and writing projects such as the preparation of an interoffice legal memorandum. The considerations involved in persuasive issue writing and persuasive writing in general are addressed in Chapter 18.

VIII. GENERAL CONSIDERATIONS

There are several general considerations to keep in mind when drafting an issue.

A. Name

Do not identify people or events specifically by name. Specific names have no meaning to readers unless they are familiar with the case or unless they have read the body of the memorandum. A reader who retrieves a research memo from the office memo files probably will not be familiar with the names of the people or events.

For Example *Incorrect:* Under . . . , did oppressive conduct occur when Tom Hardin refused to issue a $3 dividend and gave himself a $20,000 bonus?

Correct: Under . . . , does oppressive conduct occur when a majority shareholder refuses to issue dividends and grants himself a $20,000 bonus?

B. Approach

Write the issue several times. Have an issue page in your research outline or material, and keep that page nearby. When you think of a way to state the issue (regardless of how broadly or poorly phrased), write it down on the issue page so your ideas are not lost.

Even your poorly drafted constructions of the issue may contain something valuable. You may ultimately have a page full of various formulations of the issue. The final draft may require a combination of the various initial drafts, and having them all in one place may help you put together that combination. See Chapter 15 for a discussion of the use of an outline when drafting the issue.

The following is a basic approach to drafting an issue:

1. State the question in the context of the general area of law, for example, "Was there false imprisonment?"
2. Identify the specific law that applies.
3. List all the key facts.
4. Put the elements in the sequence recommended in this chapter.

LAW	QUESTION		FACTS
Under	is		when
In light of	did	exist	when
According to	does	constitute	when
Applying	was	required	when
Under	does	establish	when

C. Multiple Issues

Separate the issues. If the research involves several related or complex questions—**multiple issues**—break the questions into individual issues. Address them one at a time, applying the principles presented in this chapter. The law and facts may become confused if you attempt to work on more than one issue at a time.

IX. KEY POINTS CHECKLIST: *Stating the Issue*

✓ Do not expect to accurately state the issue on the first draft or early in the research and analysis process. A broad statement may be all you can develop until you research and study statutory and case law. The key facts may not emerge until you have studied the case in depth.

✓ Always prepare a comprehensive or narrow presentation of the issue. Include in the statement of the issue the specific law, the legal question, and the key facts.

✓ Remember the format recommended in this chapter for presenting the issue: relevant law + legal question + key facts. It is easier to draft the issue in this format.

✓ If you get stuck, *start*. If you cannot seem to get started writing, just write anything about the issue on the issue page—that is, just start.

✓ Sometimes when you are stuck, it may be that you need to *stop*. Often the brain needs time to assimilate information. Take a break. Sleep on it. The brain will continue to work while you rest, and after you wake, it may all fall into place.

✓ Remember, the issue is the legal question in dispute in the case and should be phrased as a question, not a statement, even though what you are drafting is frequently called an issue statement.

X. APPLICATION

The following are two examples that illustrate the principles discussed in this chapter. Each example includes a discussion of the application of those principles.

A. Chapter Hypothetical

This example is based on the memorandum assignment introduced at the beginning of the chapter. In the assignment, Mary Strate, the legal assistant, has determined that the following are the key facts:

1. The state police were acting in good faith when they relied on the validity of the search warrant.

2. The evidence was seized pursuant to the execution of the warrant.

3. The warrant was improperly issued due to judicial error.

Mary's research reveals that the law governing the issue is the state court's adoption of the exclusionary rule.

There are several ways to frame the issue:

a. "Should the evidence be suppressed?"

b. "Does Oregon's exclusionary rule require the suppression of the evidence?"

Comment: Both issues (a) and (b) are too broad. They are examples of a shorthand statement of the issue. Issue (a) is so broadly phrased that it is of little value to the reader. What law is involved? What facts? This statement of the issue could apply to any case involving the suppression of evidence. Issue (b) informs the reader of the applicable law but omits the facts necessary for resolution of the question. Both issues require additional reading and research to determine the law and facts involved in the dispute in the case.

> c. "Does Oregon's exclusionary rule require the suppression of evidence seized by officials acting upon a warrant improperly issued due to judicial error?"

Comment: This construction of the issue is neither objective nor complete. It leaves out a key fact: The officers were acting in good faith when they relied on the validity of the warrant. This key fact is critical if the state's exclusionary rule has an exception that allows the admission of evidence when officers execute a warrant in the good-faith belief that it is valid. Failure to include this key fact misleads the reader and slants the question in favor of suppression.

> d. "Under Oregon's exclusionary rule, must evidence be suppressed when it is seized by law enforcement officers acting in the good-faith belief in the validity of a warrant that was invalid due to judicial error?"

Comment: This statement of the issue is complete. It identifies the law in question, includes all the significant or key facts necessary for resolution of the issue, and informs the reader of what legal question must be resolved. It meets the test presented at the beginning of the chapter: Does the reader, by reading the issue alone, know what specific factual dispute concerning which law is involved in this case?

B. False Imprisonment

The client, Steve, has a history of respiratory problems. Tom is an acquaintance of Steve who is secretly jealous of him. Both Steve and Tom vie for the affections of Karen. One cold winter evening, before leaving for a party at Tom's house, Steve took some cough medicine for a cold he had been fighting. After a few drinks at the party, he told Tom he did not feel well and wanted to lie down for a minute. Tom directed him to a back bedroom. Steve went to the room and promptly fell into a deep sleep.

The bedroom had recently been converted from a storage room. It had no windows, and Tom shut the heat off when he did not have guests. The door to the room was usually kept open, so the room stayed reasonably warm. It quickly became very cold, however, when the door was shut. Tom, knowing Karen was coming to the party, checked on Steve. When he saw that Steve was asleep, he closed and locked the bedroom door and did not turn on the heat.

Three hours later, after Karen left, he unlocked the bedroom door. Steve woke up shortly thereafter and left. He was not aware that he had been locked in the room until Tom told him several days later. As a result of being in the cold room, Steve's cold got worse and he incurred medical expenses. Steve wants to know if he can sue Tom for false imprisonment. Assume this took place in Montana. Some of the ways the issue can be framed are as follows:

> a. "Can Steve recover his medical expenses?"
> b. "Under Montana law, did false imprisonment occur?"

Comment: These issues are incomplete and too broadly framed. Issue (a) is of little value, as it provides the reader with no information or guidance as to the facts of the case. Stated this way, the issue could apply to a thousand cases. Issue (b) provides the law but no facts; it too could apply to any false imprisonment case. Neither issue communicates the specific law or facts in dispute in this case.

> c. "Under Montana law, does false imprisonment occur when an individual maliciously locks another in a room and turns off the heat, intending to cause the person harm?"

Comment: This issue is incomplete, inaccurate, and not objective. It leaves out the critical key facts that Steve was unaware of the confinement and was harmed. It is inaccurate because it states that Tom intended to cause Steve harm, and there are no facts to support this. It is not objective because it characterizes Tom as malicious and intending to cause harm. It is a prejudicial formulation of the issue that misleads the reader and is slanted against Tom.

    d. "Under Montana tort law, does false imprisonment occur when an individual, suffering from a cold, is locked in a room while asleep and is unaware of the confinement, but suffers physical harm as a result of a worsening of the cold due to the confinement?"

Comment: Issue (d) is complete. The reader is provided with the question, the law, and all the key facts necessary to determine what must be decided under the law. Without any additional reading or research, the reader is informed of the specific legal and factual context of the dispute.

Summary

Writing the issue is one of the most critical tasks in the legal research and writing process. It should communicate what is in dispute. To accomplish this task, it is necessary to completely, concisely, and clearly identify the question to be resolved. A poorly crafted issue either fails to inform because it is too broad, or misleads because it adds improper information or omits critical information.

There are two ways to state an issue:

1. A shorthand or broad statement presents the question in the context of the general area of the law.

2. A comprehensive or narrow statement presents the specific question in the context of the relevant law and specific facts.

A broad statement may be appropriate when the readers are thoroughly familiar with the case. A comprehensive, or narrow, statement is the appropriate form for use in research and writing. It specifically identifies all the essential information necessary to understand and resolve the dispute.

Several different formats may be followed when crafting the issue, but the recommended format is as follows:

relevant law + question + key facts

There are several reasons for this recommendation. First, it follows the standard legal analysis format in which the presentation of the law is followed by the application of the law to the specific facts. Second, it is easier to draft an issue when the facts are inserted at the end.

When drafting the issue, always include the jurisdiction and area of the law in the law component. The question portion must introduce the specific law presented in the law component. The fact section should present all key facts if possible, although it may sometimes be necessary to categorize or condense the key facts.

Present the issue objectively and do not phrase it so as to mislead the reader or misrepresent the nature of the dispute. A well-crafted issue meets the following test: Does the reader, by reading the issue alone, know what specific legal question, concerning what law, involving what facts, is in dispute in the case?

Quick References

Susp act on ph r get new one

Return this one

Internet Resources

As of the date of publication of this text, there were no Web sites dedicated specifically to stating the issue. However, because the topic of how to state the issue is often discussed along with issue identification, the sites mentioned in the Internet Resources section of Chapter 10 may prove helpful. Also, the law school Web sites listed in Chapter 7, section III.D, often have material on legal writing topics such as stating the issue.

Exercises

Additional assignments are available on the CourseMate.

ASSIGNMENT 1

Distinguish between a broad and narrow formulation of an issue. Describe the elements of a narrow statement of an issue. Why is it important to phrase an issue narrowly when engaged in legal writing?

ASSIGNMENT 2

The statute is Cal. Corp. Code § 1800. The title of the statute is, "Verified complaint; plaintiff; grounds; intervention by shareholder or creditor; exempt corporations." The statute applies in dissolution cases and includes the grounds for dissolving a corporation. The dispute involving this corporation statute is whether there are grounds for dissolution of the corporation.

Part A Draft the law component of the issue, including the relevant portion of the title.

Part B Draft the law component of the issue and include the relevant portion of the title and the citation.

Part C Draft the law component of the issue using a description that focuses on an element of the statute. The element in question is the requirement of shareholder deadlock. Assume the statute provides that a court may dissolve a corporation in the event of a dispute among the shareholders only if there is shareholder deadlock.

Part D To the answer in part C, add the statutory citation.

ASSIGNMENT 3

The statute is Georgia Code Ann. § 11-2-314. The title of the statute is "Implied warranty: merchantability; usage of trade." The question is whether there is an implied warranty of merchantability. In the following problems, draft a comprehensive or narrow statement of the issue in the relevant law + legal question + key facts format; for the law component, use the Georgia statute. When drafting the law component, include the citation and a relevant portion of the title.

Part A Alice purchases a new toaster from a booth at the flea market. The market is open year round and the same products are always sold at the booth.

Part B Alice purchases a new toaster at a garage sale.

Part C Alice becomes ill from a soft drink purchased at a local fast-food restaurant.

Part D Alice, while shopping at the flea market, purchases a soft drink from a vendor at the market. She becomes sick from the drink.

ASSIGNMENT 4

Perform assignment 3 using a description of the title when drafting the law component, rather than a relevant portion of the title.

ASSIGNMENT 5

Perform assignment 3 using your state commercial code statute governing the warranty of merchantability and the sale of goods.

ASSIGNMENT 6

In the following problems:

- Draft a shorthand or broad statement of the issue.

- Draft a comprehensive or narrow statement of the issue in the relevant law + legal question + key facts format. For the law component in problems A through C, use either the relevant section of your state's probate code or New Wash. Prob. Code § 60, Exception Pertaining to Holographic Wills. Assume this statute applies to all the fact situations presented in problems A through C. For each problem, draft the issue twice. One draft should contain the title or a description of the title. One draft should contain the title or description and the citation.

Part A
Key Facts: A will is handwritten. One-half is in the testator's handwriting, and the other half is in the handwriting of a witness. The will is properly witnessed.
Question: Is the will valid?

Part B
Key Facts: A will is handwritten. One-half is in the testator's handwriting, and the other half is in the handwriting of a witness. It is witnessed by three witnesses, two of whom will inherit under the will.
Question: Is the will valid?

Part C
Key Facts: A will is handwritten. One-half is in the testator's handwriting, and the other half is in the handwriting of a witness. A witness, at the direction of the testator, signed the testator's name. The will was properly witnessed.
Question: Is the will valid?

ASSIGNMENT 7

In the following problems:

- Draft a shorthand or broad statement of the issue.

- Draft a comprehensive or narrow statement of the issue in the relevant law + legal question + key facts format.

Part A
Key Facts: An individual on a radio talk show states that all the town's psychiatrists are frauds.
Question: Is the statement "concerning" the plaintiff (a local psychiatrist)?
Law: Assume the law of slander in your jurisdiction is case law (court made) and one of the elements is that the statement must concern the plaintiff.

Part B
Key Facts: Use the same facts as in the preceding problem, with the additional fact that the plaintiff is the only psychiatrist in the town.
Question: Same as in part A.
Law: Same as in part A.

ASSIGNMENT 8

Redraft the following issues in the format presented in this chapter.

Part A Can a bystander who witnesses the death of a victim from three blocks away recover for negligent infliction of emotional distress under Ohio law?

Part B Does oppressive conduct occur, according to the provisions of the Texas Corporation Code, when a majority shareholder refuses to issue dividends, triples his salary, and grants himself excessive bonuses?

Part C The issue is whether a newspaper that publishes an article indicating that Tom Smith has criminal connections has committed libel according to Florida tort law.

Part D Do law enforcement officers commit a battery when, while making a lawful arrest, they encounter resistance, use force to overcome that resistance, and continue to use force after the resistance ceases?

FOR FURTHER READING

Ray, Mary Barnard, and Barbara J. Cox. *Beyond the Basics.* St. Paul, MN: West, 1991.

This text presents an excellent and expanded discussion of the relevant law + legal question + key facts format recommended in this chapter.

Case Law Analysis—Is a Case On Point?

"That bum has cheated us for the last time," David Simms said as he walked out the office door. David Simms and his brother, Don, had just finished their initial interview with Ms. Booth, the attorney who would handle their case. Their tale was one of financial abuse by their older brother, Steve.

Their father, Dilbert Simms, died in December 1997 and left his plumbing business, Simms Plumbing, Inc., to his three sons—Steve, Don, and David. Steve, who had been running the business since 1995, was left 52 percent of the stock. David and Don, who had never worked at Simms Plumbing and were employed in other occupations, were each left 24 percent.

As the majority shareholder, Steve completely controls the business. To date, he refuses to issue stock dividends even though the corporation has an accumulated cash surplus of $500,000. He has given himself three very large salary increases and several cash bonuses since his father's death. When questioned by David and Don about stock dividends, he tells them, "You don't work in the business. You don't deserve any money out of it. If you want any money, you're going to have to work at the store, every day, just like I do."

After this conversation, David and Don consulted the supervising attorney, Ms. Booth. They seek redress for the wrong they feel their brother has committed in refusing to issue dividends.

The paralegal task, assigned by Ms. Booth, is to find the applicable statute and the leading case on point in the jurisdiction. The statute, § 96-25-16 of the Business Corporation Act, provides that a court may order the liquidation of a corporation when a majority shareholder has engaged in oppressive conduct. The statute, however, does not define what constitutes oppressive conduct.

The hard part of the assignment is locating a case on point in the jurisdiction that defines or provides the elements of oppressive conduct. After an extensive search, the paralegal locates only one case dealing with oppressive conduct, *Karl v. Herald*. In this case, a husband and wife owned a small corporation in which the husband owned 75 percent of the stock and the wife owned 25 percent. When they divorced, he fired her from her salaried position of bookkeeper, took away her company car, and refused to issue stock dividends. The company was very profitable, had a large cash surplus, and was clearly in a financial position to issue dividends. After the divorce, the husband gave himself a hefty salary increase. The court held that he had engaged in oppressive conduct in freezing his wife out of the corporation. It defined *oppressive conduct* as "any unfair or fraudulent act by a majority shareholder that inures to the benefit of the majority and to the detriment of the minority."

Upon finding this case, several questions run through the paralegal's mind. Is this case on point? How does one determine if a case is on point? Why does it matter?

Learning Objectives

After completing this chapter, you should understand:

- What *on point* means in relation to case law
- The role and importance of a case being on point in legal analysis
- How to determine if a case is on point

I. INTRODUCTION

Legal research, analysis, and writing are all related and are often part of a single process. Research locates the law, analysis determines how the law applies, and legal writing assembles and integrates the results into a usable form.

The focus of this chapter is on the application of case law to a legal question. It covers **case law analysis**—the analytical process you engage in to determine if and how the decision in a court opinion either governs or affects the outcome of a client's case. A case that governs or affects the outcome of a client's case is commonly referred to as being "on point."

Throughout this chapter, reference is made to single issues and single rules of law or legal principles when discussing court opinions and clients' cases. The focus is on how to determine if a single issue, addressed in a court opinion, is on point and, therefore, may affect or govern an issue in a client's case. Always be aware that there are often multiple issues and legal rules or principles involved in court opinions, some of which may be on point and, therefore, govern the outcome of an issue in the client's case, and some of which may not be on point. When determining if an opinion is on point, follow the steps discussed in this chapter separately for each issue in a client's case.

The chapter opens with a definition of the term *on point*, followed by a discussion of the importance of locating a case on point and the process of determining if a case is on point.

II. DEFINITION—ON POINT

Throughout this chapter, the term *on point* is used to describe a court opinion that applies to the client's case. What do "on point" and "applies to the client's case" mean? A case is **on point** if the similarity between the key facts and the rule of law or legal principle of the court opinion and those of the client's case is sufficient for the court opinion to govern or provide guidance to a later court in deciding the outcome of the client's case. In other words, does the court opinion govern or guide the resolution of an issue in the client's case? Is the court opinion precedent? If a case is on point, it is precedent. The terms *on point* and *precedent* are often used interchangeably.

III. ON POINT—IMPORTANCE

Before discussing the process involved in determining if a case is on point, it is helpful to understand why you must engage in the process of finding past court decisions that affect the client's case. Why is it important?

As discussed in Chapter 1, case law is a major source of law in the legal system. Through case law, courts create law and interpret the language of constitutions, legislative acts, and regulations. The determination of whether a case is on point is important because of two doctrines covered in Chapter 1: precedent and stare decisis. The doctrines of precedent and stare decisis govern and guide the application of case law and thereby provide uniformity and consistency in the case law system. They help make the law more predictable. A brief revisiting of these doctrines is helpful in obtaining an understanding of the process involved in determining whether a case is on point.

A. Precedent

Precedent is an earlier court decision on an issue that governs or guides a subsequent court in its determination of an identical or similar issue based on identical or similar key facts. This chapter identifies the steps involved in determining when a case may be either mandatory or persuasive precedent. A case is precedent (on point) if there is a sufficient similarity between the key facts and rule of law or legal principle of the court opinion and the matter before the subsequent court.

For Example The state collections statute provides that efforts to collect payment for a debt must be made in a reasonable manner. The statute does not define "reasonable." In the case of *Mark v. Collections, Inc.*, the supreme court of the state held that it is not reasonable, within the meaning of the collection statute, for a bill collector to make more than one telephone call a day to a debtor's residence, nor is it reasonable to make calls before sunrise or after sunset.

The facts of the case were that the collector was making seven calls a day, some of which were after sunset.

The facts of the client's case are that a bill collector is calling the client six times a day between the hours of 9:00 a.m. and 5:00 p.m. The ruling in *Mark v. Collections, Inc.* applies as precedent to the issue of whether the frequency of the collector's calls is unreasonable and, therefore, in violation of the act. The *Mark* case is sufficiently similar to the current case to apply as precedent. Both cases involve:

- The same law—the collections statute
- The same question—a determination of when the frequency of the telephone calls constitutes unreasonable conduct within the meaning of the act
- Similar key facts—six telephone calls per day and seven calls per day

The application of *Mark* as precedent guides the court in its resolution of the question, presented in the client's case, of whether six calls a day constitute a violation of the act. The court in *Mark* held that more than one call a day is unreasonable. Therefore, the six calls a day in the client's case are unreasonable in light of the holding in the *Mark* case. This example is referred to as the "collections" example in this chapter.

B. Mandatory Precedent

Mandatory precedent is precedent from a higher court in a jurisdiction. If a court opinion is on point—that is, if it is precedent—the doctrine of stare decisis mandates that the lower courts in the jurisdiction follow it. In the previous example, if the decision in *Mark v. Collections, Inc.* is the ruling of the highest court in the jurisdiction, the lower courts in the jurisdiction must follow it.

C. Persuasive Precedent

Persuasive precedent is precedent that a court may look to for guidance when reaching a decision but is not bound to follow. In the collections example, courts in other jurisdictions are not bound to follow the *Mark* decision. Also, if the decision was by a lower court in the jurisdiction, such as a trial court, then a higher court, such as a court of appeals, is not bound to follow the decision. A higher court may, however, choose to refer to and use a lower court decision as guidance when deciding a similar case.

D. Stare Decisis

The doctrine of **stare decisis** is a basic principle of the case law system that requires a court to follow a previous decision of that court or a higher court in the jurisdiction when the current decision involves issues and key facts similar to those involved in the previous decision. In other words, the doctrine of stare decisis requires that similar cases be decided in the same way; it mandates that cases that are precedent should be followed. The doctrine applies unless there is good reason not to follow it.

> **For Example** In regard to the *Mark* case discussed in the collections example, stare decisis is the doctrine holding that once it is determined that the *Mark* case is precedent, the lower courts in the jurisdiction must follow it unless good cause is shown for not doing so. It is mandatory precedent.

E. The Role of Precedent

Without the doctrines of stare decisis and precedent, there would most likely be chaos in the court decisionmaking process. Judges and attorneys would not have guidance about how matters should be decided. Similar cases could be decided differently based upon the whims and diverse beliefs of judges and juries. These doctrines provide stability, predictability, and guidance for courts and attorneys. An individual can rely on a future court to reach the same decision on an issue as an earlier court when the cases are sufficiently similar.

With this in mind, it becomes clear why determining whether a case is on point is important and why a researcher needs to find a case that is on point:

1. The determination must be made before the case may apply as precedent and be used and relied on by a court in its determination of how an issue will be decided. Note that if the court is unaware of the case, it may be necessary to bring it to the court's attention.

2. Inasmuch as the court will consider precedent in reaching its decision, a researcher needs to find cases that are on point to guide the attorney as to how the issue in the client's case may be decided. Cases that are on point must be located and analyzed to determine what impact they may have on the decision in the client's case. Also, they must be analyzed to help the attorney determine what course of action to take. If a case that is on point indicates that the decision will most likely be against the client, it may be appropriate to pursue settlement or other options.

IV. DETERMINING IF A CASE IS ON POINT

The process of deciding if a court opinion is on point involves determining how similar the opinion is to the client's case. The more similar the court opinion is to the client's case, the more likely it is to be considered precedent; that is, the more likely it is that the rule or principle applied in the opinion will govern or apply to the client's case.

In section II of this chapter, a case is defined as being on point if there is a sufficient similarity between the key facts and rule of law or legal principle of the court opinion and those of the client's case. Therefore, for a case to be on point and apply as precedent, there are two requirements:

1. The significant or key facts of the court opinion must be sufficiently similar to the key facts of the client's case; or, if the facts are not similar, the rule of law or legal principle applied in the court opinion must be so broad that it applies to many diverse fact situations.

2. The rule of law or legal principle applied in the court opinion must be the same or sufficiently similar to the rule of law or legal principle that applies in the client's case. *Rule of law* and *legal principle*, as used here, include any constitutional, legislative, or case law provision, act, doctrine, principle, or test relied on by the court in reaching its decision.

If these two criteria are not met, the court opinion is not on point and may not be used as precedent for the client's case. The two-step process presented in Exhibit 12-1 is recommended for determining if the two requirements are met.

Exhibit 12-1 *Steps in Determining if a Case Is On Point.*

For a court opinion to be on point and apply as precedent, the following requirements must be met:	
STEP 1	**Are the key facts sufficiently similar for the case to apply as precedent?** The key facts of the court opinion must be sufficiently similar to the key facts of the client's case. If the facts are not similar, the opinion will serve as precedent only if the rule of law or legal principle is broad enough to apply to other fact situations, including the client's.
STEP 2	**Are the rules or principles of law sufficiently similar for the case to apply as precedent?** The rule of law or legal principle applied in the court opinion must be the same or sufficiently similar to the rule of law or legal principle that applies in the client's case.

© Cengage Learning 2014

A. Step 1: Are the Key Facts Sufficiently Similar?

The first step in the analysis process is to determine if the significant or key facts in the court opinion are sufficiently similar to the key facts in the client's case for the court opinion to apply as precedent. This is accomplished by comparing the key facts of the court opinion with those of the client's case. A key fact is so essential that it affects the outcome of the case. You must identify the key facts before you can determine if a case is on point. If there is not a sufficient similarity between the key facts of the client's case and the court opinion, the opinion usually cannot be used as precedent—that is, it is not on point.

You may encounter two situations when comparing the key facts of a client's case and a court opinion:

1. The key facts are directly on point—that is, they are identical or nearly identical.

2. The key facts are different.

1. Identical or Nearly Identical Key Facts

When the **key facts** in a given court opinion and the client's case are **identical** (or nearly identical), the opinion is on point factually and can be a precedent that applies to the client's case if the requirements of step 2 are met. The phrase **on all fours** is often used to describe such opinions: those in which the facts of the opinion and of the client's case, and the rule of law that applies, are identical or so similar that the court opinion is clearly on point. When such an opinion is the opinion of a higher court in a jurisdiction, it is mandatory precedent that the lower courts in the jurisdiction must follow.

> **For Example** In the case of *Davis v. Davis*, Ms. Davis had sole custody of her two daughters, ages 8 and 10 years. Ms. Davis had a boyfriend who occasionally stayed overnight at her home. The children were aware of the overnight visits. Mr. Davis, her former husband, filed a motion with the court asking for a change of custody. He based his claim solely upon his ex-wife's alleged "immoral conduct." No evidence was presented indicating how the overnight visits affected the children. The trial court granted a change of custody.

The court of appeals overturned the trial court, ruling that "mere allegations of immoral conduct are not sufficient grounds to award a change of custody." The court required the presentation of evidence showing that the alleged immoral conduct harmed the children.

Assume, for the sake of this example, that the client was divorced one year ago and granted sole custody of his two minor daughters, ages 8 and 12 years. On occasion, his girlfriend stays overnight, and the children are aware of the overnight visits. The client's former spouse has filed a motion for change of custody alleging that his immoral conduct is grounds for a change of custody. She does not have evidence that the children have been harmed or affected negatively.

Clearly, the requirements of step 1 are met. *Davis v. Davis* is factually on point, and is therefore a precedent that applies to the client's case. Note that the requirements of step 2 are also met. The same legal principle is being applied in the court opinion and the client's case: Mere allegations of immorality are not sufficient grounds for granting a change of custody. Step 2 addresses the requirement that the legal principles be sufficiently similar.

Although some of the facts are different—in the client's case, it is the father who has custody and his girlfriend who stays overnight, whereas in *Davis v. Davis* it was the mother who had custody and her boyfriend who stayed overnight—these facts are not key facts. The gender of the custodial parent and the gender of the person staying overnight are not key facts. The key facts are identical: occasional overnight visits, the children are aware of the visits, the children are preteen (the age of the children is always an important consideration), and no evidence was presented that the children are harmed by the visits. This example is referred to as the "custody" example throughout the remainder of this chapter.

It is rare to find instances in which the key facts are identical. Usually there is at least some difference in the key facts. When you find a case with identical facts that you determine is mandatory precedent, be thankful if the holding supports your client's position. It is difficult for a lower court not to follow the higher court's decision when it is so clearly on point.

2. Different Key Facts

When the key facts of the court opinion and the key facts of the client's case are not identical, the opinion *may* be on point and *may* apply as precedent. It depends on the degree of the difference. When you have **different key facts**, you must determine whether the differences are of such a nature or degree that they render the court opinion unusable as precedent. Use the following three-part process when making this determination. (See Exhibit 12-2.)

Part 1: Identify the similarities between the key facts.

Part 2: Identify the differences between the key facts.

Part 3: Determine if the differences are of such a significant degree that the opinion cannot apply as precedent.

Throughout this discussion of different key facts, assume that the requirements of step 2 have been met—that is, the rule of law applied in the court opinion is the same or sufficiently similar to the rule of law that applies in the client's case.

For Example The client's case is the same as the custody example except that instead of occasional overnight visits by the girlfriend, the girlfriend has moved in with the client. Is the case of *Davis v. Davis* on point?

Exhibit 12-2 *Three-Part Process for Addressing Different Key Facts.*

Three-part process for determining if a case is on point when the key facts of the court opinion differ from the key facts of the client's case	
PART 1	Identify the similarities between the key facts.
PART 2	Identify the differences between the key facts.
PART 3	Determine if the differences are of such a significant degree that the opinion cannot apply as precedent.

© Cengage Learning 2014

To answer this question, perform the following steps:

a. Part 1: Identify the similarities between the key facts. In both the client's case and the *Davis* case:

- The minor children are under the age of 12 years.
- Someone of the opposite sex is staying overnight with the custodial parent.
- There is no showing that the children have been harmed by the conduct.

b. Part 2: Identify the differences between the key facts. The difference in the key facts is that in *Davis v. Davis*, the overnight visits were occasional. In the client's case, there is cohabitation rather than occasional overnight visits.

c. Part 3: Determine if the differences are of such a significant degree that the opinion cannot apply as precedent. To determine the significance of the differences, substitute the client's key facts for those of the court opinion. If the substitution of the key facts would result in a change in the outcome of the case, the court opinion cannot be used as precedent.

In this example, would the court in *Davis v. Davis* have reached the same conclusion if Ms. Davis's boyfriend had moved in with her? The answer is probably, because the same legal principle applies: Allegations of immoral conduct alone are not sufficient grounds to award a change of custody; there must be a showing that the conduct harmed the children.

As indicated in *Davis v. Davis*, an essential element necessary before a change of custody is granted is a showing of harm to the children. A key fact in the *Davis* decision was the lack of any showing of harm to the children. Both the court opinion and the client's case lack a showing of harm to the children; therefore, the principle applied in *Davis* should apply to the client's case even though the *Davis* opinion involved overnight visits and the client's case involves cohabitation.

You must be careful, however. There may be another statute or case law doctrine providing that cohabitation is per se harmful to children; that is, in cohabitation cases such as the client's case, the law presumes that cohabitation is harmful to the children. If this were the situation, the plaintiff would not need to establish harm in cohabitation cases such as the client's, and the *Davis* opinion would not be on point and could not be used as precedent. The difference in the key facts would be so significant that the substitution of the client's cohabitation fact for the *Davis* opinion's occasional overnight visits fact would change the decision reached by the court because a different statute would apply.

Four variations may be encountered when dealing with different key facts. These variations are summarized in Exhibit 12-3.

1. Minor differences in key facts—Some key facts are so insignificantly different that they clearly do not affect the use of a court decision as precedent.

Exhibit 12-3 *Different Key Fact Variations.*

Variations that may be encountered when dealing with different key facts
1. Minor differences in key facts—case on point
2. Major difference in key facts—case not on point
3. Major difference in key facts—case on point
4. Major difference in key facts—case on point, broad legal principle

© Cengage Learning 2014

> **For Example** If, in the custody example, the client's children were ages 9 and 11 years as opposed to 8 and 10 years, *Davis v. Davis* would still clearly apply as precedent. Although the age of the children is a key fact, a minor difference of one year in the ages of the children is not a significant difference in the key facts. If the client's children were several years older than the children in *Davis v. Davis*, such as ages 17 and 18, the age difference could be a major difference in the key facts, because a different standard might apply if the children were in their late teens.

2. Major difference in key facts, and the case is not on point—The following example presents a situation where the key facts of the court opinion and the key facts of the client's case are sufficiently different that the opinion is not on point and does not apply as precedent. The following example is referred to in this chapter as the "arrest" example.

> **For Example** In the court case of *State v. Thomas*, Mr. Thomas was handcuffed and taken to the police station after officers broke up a fistfight. Thomas was not read his rights at the scene of the fight. He was read his rights and formally arrested at the police station 30 minutes later. The court, ruling that he was under arrest when handcuffed at the scene, stated, "An arrest takes place when a reasonable person does not believe he is free to leave."
>
> In the client's case, the client explains that the police handcuffed him and told him to stay in the hallway of the house while they executed a search warrant. He was not allowed to leave. It appears that the key facts regarding whether an arrest has taken place are nearly the same. In both the court opinion and the client's case, the individual was handcuffed and not free to leave. The critical difference in the facts is the context of the seizure of the individual. In *Thomas*, the seizure took place at the scene of a fight. No warrants were involved. In the client's case, the seizure took place during the execution of a search warrant.
>
> In regard to the question of whether the client was under arrest when handcuffed and detained in the hallway, is *State v. Thomas* on point? The answer is no. Although the facts of the detention are similar, the difference in the context of the seizure is a critical key fact difference. There is other case law holding that a seizure during the execution of a search warrant is an exception to the rule stated in *Thomas*, and that such seizures do not constitute an arrest.
>
> The other case law provides that a search warrant implicitly carries with it the authority to detain an individual for the purposes of the officer's safety and to determine if there is cause to make an arrest. Therefore, such detentions do not constitute an arrest within the meaning of the law. Because of this authority, the difference between the key facts of *Thomas* and the client's case is critical, and the case is not on point.

3. Major difference in key facts, but case is on point—A major difference in the key facts does not necessarily result in a determination that the case is not on point. The opinion may still be on point, but the outcome may be different. The legal principle applied by the court may still apply to the client's case, although its application may lead to a different result.

> **For Example** Suppose that in the custody example, there were an additional key fact in the client's case that the spouse seeking custody had evidence showing that the children were being harmed by exposure to the overnight visits. *Davis v. Davis* could still be on point, even though no evidence of harm to the children was presented in the *Davis* case. Although there is now a major difference between the key facts of the court opinion and the client's case, the court opinion may still apply as precedent and govern the outcome of the change-of-custody question.
>
> The court in the *Davis* case concluded that there were not sufficient grounds to award a change of custody because *no evidence* was presented showing harm to the children. The same principle governing *Davis* governs the facts here: that is, allegations of immorality, *standing alone*, are not sufficient for an award of a change of custody; there must be a showing of harm to the children.
>
> A corollary of the rule, however, is that if there is a *showing of harm* to the children, there may be sufficient grounds for a change of custody. It can be argued that when the key fact of evidence of harm is present, the corollary of the rule applies. Even though the facts of the court opinion and the client's case are different, the corollary applies to support a change of the custody award—a result different from the result reached in the court opinion.

4. Major difference in key facts, but case is on point, broad legal principle—Generally, if key facts are significantly different, it is highly probable that a different rule or principle applies and a court case will not apply as precedent. There are, however, instances in which the key facts are different, but the court opinion is on point because the rule of law or legal principle is so broad that it applies to many different fact situations. This situation is addressed in greater detail in section IV.B, step 2.

> **For Example** The client was detained as part of a group of exotic dancers in a bar. The officers who detained the client were not executing a search or arrest warrant. Before informing the dancers they were under arrest, or in any way informing them what was taking place, the officers moved them to a separate room where they were detained for more than an hour. They were clearly not free to leave. They were formally arrested two hours later, then taken to jail.

> **For Example** In regard to the question of whether the client was under arrest when detained in the room prior to arrest, *State v. Thomas* (presented in the arrest example) is probably on point. The definition of *arrest* presented in *Thomas* applies to the client's case even though the factual context of the seizure is different (handcuffing at a fist fight versus detention with a group of exotic dancers at a bar). Applying that definition to the client's case results in the conclusion that an arrest occurred when the client was moved to a separate room and detained for more than an hour. A reasonable person in the client's situation would not believe she was free to leave. The definition of *arrest* presented in *Thomas* is so broad that it applies to a wide range of detention situations.

NOTE: Be careful. It is always preferable to locate an opinion that is as factually similar to the client's case as possible. The more dissimilar the key facts, the easier it is for the other side to argue that the differences are critical, the opinion is not on point, and thus does not apply as precedent to the case at hand.

A difference in key facts should alert you to be careful and cause you to explore all potential legal avenues that may open due to the fact differences. Focus on the differences. Ask yourself, "Are they important?" Engage in counteranalysis (see Chapter 13). Conduct further research and Shepardize the case to determine if there are other cases more on point.

In summary, if the key facts are the same and the same rule of law applies (step 2), the court opinion is usually on point and can be considered precedent that applies to your client's case. If the key facts are different, either in part or totally, you must perform careful analysis to ensure that the factual differences are not so significant that they are fatal to use of the court opinion as precedent.

B. Step 2: Are the Rules or Principles of Law Sufficiently Similar?

By applying the techniques presented in step 1, you determine whether the key facts of the court opinion are sufficiently similar to the key facts of the client's case for the opinion to apply as precedent factually. Once this is accomplished, half of the task is completed. Note that this is a two-step process, and you must complete both steps before you can determine whether a case is on point and apply it as precedent.

The second step is to determine whether the rule of law or legal principle applied in the court opinion is the same rule of law or legal principle that applies in the client's case. If it is not the same rule of law, is it sufficiently similar to the rule that applies in the client's case for the opinion still to apply as precedent? You may encounter two situations when performing step 2:

1. The rule or principle applied in the court opinion is the same rule or principle that applies in the client's case.

2. The rule or principle applied in the court opinion is different from the rule or principle that applies in the client's case.

1. Same Rule or Principle

If you determine that the key facts are sufficiently similar so that the court opinion can apply as precedent and the same rule of law is involved in both the opinion and the client's case, then the requirements of step 2 are met, and the case is on point. The rule of law comparison is simple. The rule of law applies in the client's case in the same way as it was applied in the court's opinion.

> **For Example** In the custody example, if the client's case involves the situation of the client having occasional overnight visits by his girlfriend, the same rule of law governs the court opinion and the client's facts—that is, allegations of immorality without evidence of harm to the children are not sufficient grounds to support a change of custody. The rule applies in the same way in the client's case as in the court opinion: A change of custody will not be granted where there is no showing of harm to the children.

> **For Example** The client is charged with erecting a sign too close to the street in violation of § 19(b) of the Municipal Code, which prohibits the erection of a sign "unreasonably close" to any property line abutting a street. In your research, you come across the case of *City v. Guess*, which interprets "unreasonably close" as within 10 feet of the property line. If the key facts of the court opinion are sufficiently similar to the client's key facts, then the rule of law analytical process is simple. The same rule of law applied in the opinion applies to the client's case, in the same way: If the client's sign is within 10 feet of the property line abutting the street, it is in violation of the statute.

NOTE: Even when the same rule of law applies, its application in the client's case may result in an outcome different from the outcome in the court case. See the example presented in the list in section IV.A.2 (Major difference in key facts, but case is on point). In that example, the same legal principle applied in both the client's case and the court opinion, but the result was different.

2. Different Rule or Principle

What if there is no court decision in your jurisdiction applying or interpreting the rule or legal principle that applies to your client's case? What if the rule or principle applied in the closest court opinion you can find is different from the rule or principle that applies in the client's case? Can the court opinion apply as precedent? The general rule is no. Usually this is obvious. For example, a child custody opinion can rarely be precedent for a murder case.

Again, there are exceptions. The court's interpretation of a provision of a legislative act or case law rule or principle may be so broad in scope that it applies to the different law or rule that governs the client's case. Keep in mind, though, that because the law or rule applied in the court opinion is different from that which applies to the client's case, the court opinion is at best *persuasive* precedent. The court hearing the client's case does not have to follow it—it is not *mandatory* precedent. The court has discretion and must be persuaded.

There are two areas to explore when considering these exceptions: legislative acts and case law rules or principles. In regard to these two areas, it is important to remember that the discussion involves only those situations in which there is *no court opinion* in the jurisdiction directly interpreting the same legislative act or case law rule that applies to the client's case.

a. Legislative Acts

A court opinion interpreting one legislative act may be used as precedent for a client's case that involves the application of a different legislative act when there is similarity in the following (see Exhibit 12-4):

1. The language used in the legislative acts
2. The function of the legislative acts

Exhibit 12-4 *Requirements When Different Legislative Acts Apply.*

Requirements that must be met for a case to be on point when the legislative act applied in the court opinion differs from the legislative act that applies in the client's case
1. There is a similarity in the language used in the legislative acts.
2. There is a similarity in the function of the legislative acts.

For Example Three statutes have been adopted in the jurisdiction:

- Section 56 provides that an individual must be a resident of the county to be eligible to run for the position of county animal control officer.
- Section 3105 provides that an individual must be a resident of the county to be eligible to run for a seat on the county school board.
- Section 4175 provides that an individual must be a resident of the state to be eligible to run for the office of governor.

The term *resident* is not defined in any of the statutes, and none of the statutes establishes a length of residency requirement. The only case in the jurisdiction that defines the term is *Frank v. Teague*, a case involving § 3105. In this case, the court ruled that to be eligible to run for a seat on the school board, the candidate must have been a resident of the county of the school board district for a minimum of three months immediately prior to the election. This example is referred to in this chapter as the "residence" example.

The client, a resident of the county for three and one-half months, wants to run for the office of governor. Does the *Frank* opinion apply as precedent and support the client's claim of eligibility to run for the office of governor? The answer is probably not.

Although there is a similarity in the language of the statutes, in that both use the term *resident,* there is not a similarity in their function. The considerations involved in determining the length of residence required as a prerequisite for eligibility to run for each office are quite different. The court's decision in *Frank*, imposing a three-month residency requirement for the school board position, may be based upon the court's determination that this is the amount of time an individual needs to become sufficiently familiar with the county to perform the duties of a school board member. The position of governor, however, involves different considerations. The office is statewide, and the court could conclude that a longer residency period is necessary for an individual to become sufficiently familiar with the state to adequately perform the duties of governor.

For Example The client wants to run for the position of animal control officer. He has been a resident of the county for four months. In this situation, it is more likely that *Frank* will apply as precedent—that it is on point and supports the position that the client is eligible to run for animal control officer.

Again, both statutes use the same language, *resident*. They are more closely related in function, however, than the school board and governor statutes. Both involve countywide positions wherein the duties are focused on county concerns. It can be argued that no more time is required to become familiar with the county to perform the duties of animal control officer than is required to perform the duties of a school board member.

The court, following this line of reasoning, could conclude that the residency requirement for the position of animal control officer should not exceed the minimum residency set for a seat on the school board. It could, therefore, adopt the three-month standard established in the *Frank* case as the standard for the animal control officer statute.

Because the statutes are different, you are always open to a counterargument pointing out some critical difference in function between the statutes.

In this example, you could argue that the duties of animal control officer are much different from those of a school board member. The duties of the animal control officer require a great degree of familiarity with the geography of the county; therefore, a longer period of residency should be required to ensure that a candidate has sufficient time to become familiar with the county.

In every situation in which the statutes differ in function, even if they have some similarities, you can argue that the difference, no matter how slight, dictates that a court's interpretation of one statute in one case cannot apply to another statute in a different case.

The preceding examples involve statutes from the same state. All the statutes were passed by the same state legislature, and the court opinion came from a court in that state. What if, in the residency example, there is no case law in the state interpreting the term *resident*, and the *Frank v. Teague* opinion is a decision from another state interpreting a statute of that state that is identical or very similar to § 3105? Can *Frank* apply as precedent?

The answer is the same as the answer discussed in the previous examples. If there is sufficient similarity in language and function of the statutes, the opinion can apply as persuasive precedent. If there is not sufficient similarity, it cannot apply as precedent. As long as the court is convinced that the similarity is sufficient, it can apply.

Bear in mind that a decision from another jurisdiction is only persuasive precedent, and a court is more likely to adopt persuasive precedent from a court within the jurisdiction than from a court without. It is best to locate authority within your jurisdiction. Look out of state only if there is no opinion that could apply as persuasive precedent within your jurisdiction.

Realistically, it is always risky to argue that a court's interpretation of a provision of one statute applies as precedent for the interpretation of a provision of a different statute. You are always open to, and will probably have to fend off, counterarguments that the statutes are functionally different and that reliance on a particular court opinion is misplaced. Your position in such a situation is never solid. Always try to find another opinion or pursue other avenues of research.

b. Case Law Rule or Principle

The same principles discussed in the preceding section apply when attempting to use as precedent a court opinion interpreting a case law rule or principle. Can a court opinion interpreting a case law rule or principle apply as precedent for a client's case that requires the application of a different case law rule or principle? The requirements are similar to those mentioned in the preceding section. Are the case law rules or principles similar in language and function? A court opinion interpreting one case law rule or principle may be used as precedent for a client's case that involves the application of a different case law rule or principle when there is similarity in the following (see Exhibit 12-5):

1. The language used in the case law rules or principles
2. The function of the case law rules or principles

Exhibit 12-5 *Requirements When Different Common Law Rules/Principles Apply.*

Requirements that must be met for a case to be on point when the case law rule or principle applied in the court opinion differs from the case law rule or principle that applies in the client's case
1. There is a similarity in the language used in the case law rules or principles, and
2. There is a similarity in the function used in the case law rules or principles.

© Cengage Learning 2014

For Example The jurisdiction recognizes the torts of intrusion and public disclosure of a private fact. Intrusion protects against the act of prying or probing into the private affairs of an individual, and public disclosure of a private fact protects against the act of publishing information concerning the private affairs of an individual. Both of these torts have been established by the highest court in the jurisdiction. There is no statutory law defining or governing the torts. One of the elements of the tort of *intrusion* is an act of prying or probing into the private affairs of the plaintiff. One of the elements of the tort of *public disclosure of a private fact* is the public disclosure of a fact concerning the *private affairs* of the plaintiff.

In the client's case, the client was having an affair with the wife of a city council member. A campaign rival of the client disclosed the existence of the relationship at a campaign rally. The campaign rival acquired the information from a campaign aide who obtained the information by peeking through the client's bedroom window. The client wants to sue for public disclosure of a private fact. The question is whether the affair is a private fact.

The only case in the jurisdiction is *Claron v. Clark*, an intrusion case in which a private investigator, by means of a wiretap, discovered that the plaintiff was engaged in an affair. The court ruled that the term *private affairs* includes any sexual activity that takes place within the confines of an individual's residence.

Is the *Clark* opinion an intrusion case on point? Can it be precedent in the client's case, which involves a different tort (public disclosure of a private fact)? May it be used as precedent in the client's case to guide the court in its interpretation of the meaning of the term *private affairs*? There is a similarity in the elements of the torts; both use the term *private affairs*. Both torts are similar in function, in that they are designed to protect the private affairs and lives of individuals.

If the court is convinced that the similarities are sufficient, then the case may apply as precedent. It can always be argued, however, that because the torts are different, there is a difference in function, no matter how slight, that dictates that a court's interpretation of the one tort cannot apply to a different tort. In this case, it can be argued that prying is different from publication; therefore, the difference in the interest being protected in the torts is sufficient to prevent an interpretation of a term in intrusion from being used to interpret the same term in public disclosure of a private fact.

Again, be careful. The same pitfalls exist here as when different legislative acts apply. A court opinion within the jurisdiction interpreting a different rule of law is only persuasive precedent. It is not mandatory precedent that must be followed. It is very easy to present a counterargument that the functions of the two doctrines are clearly different, so the court opinion cannot apply as precedent. Also, keep in mind that when the decision is from another jurisdiction, it is still only persuasive precedent, and a court is more likely to adopt persuasive precedent from within the jurisdiction than from without.

NOTE: It is always preferable to locate an opinion that applies a rule or legal principle that is the same as the rule or principle that applies in the client's case. If different rules or principles are involved, it is easier for the other side to argue that the opinion is not on point and, therefore, does not apply as precedent for the case at hand.

When different rules or principles are involved, you should conduct further research and Shepardize the case to determine if there are other cases more on point.

V. KEY POINTS CHECKLIST: *Is a Case On Point?*

✓ Focus on the key facts and the rule of law or legal principle of both the court opinion and client's case.

✓ When there are differences between the key facts of the court opinion and the client's case, carefully determine whether the differences are significant. Be aware, however, that different key facts may lead to the application of an entirely different law or principle despite other key fact similarities. The rule of law or legal principle, however, may be so broad that it applies to many different fact situations.

✓ Clearly identify the rule of law or legal principle that applies in the court opinion and in the client's case.

✓ When the rule of law applied in the court opinion is different from the rule that applies in the client's case, consider using the court opinion as precedent *only when there is no authority* interpreting or applying the rule or principle that applies in the client's case.

✓ Consider authority from another jurisdiction *only* when there is no authority from the jurisdiction in which the client's case arose.

✓ If in doubt about whether a fact is a key fact, continue your analysis until you are certain. Refer to the steps presented in Chapter 9.

✓ Follow your instincts. If an opinion does not appear to be on point but your intuition tells you it is on point, continue your analysis until you are certain. If you never reach the point of feeling certain, search elsewhere.

VI. APPLICATION

This section presents two examples illustrating the application of the principles presented in this chapter for determining when a case is on point.

A. Chapter Hypothetical

This example is based on the fact pattern presented at the beginning of this chapter. Returning to that problem, is the case of *Karl v. Herald* on point so that it applies as precedent for the client's case?

1. Are the Key Facts Sufficiently Similar?

The first step is to determine whether the key facts of *Karl v. Herald* are sufficiently similar to the client's case for *Herald* to apply as precedent—to be on point. Although the facts in *Herald* are somewhat different, they are sufficiently similar. In both cases, the corporation was in a position to pay dividends. In both cases, while refusing to pay dividends, the majority shareholder allegedly enriched himself through excessive raises and bonuses. In both cases, the minority shareholders were effectively prevented from benefiting by the corporation's success.

A difference in *Herald* is the plaintiff worked in the business. In the client's case, the brothers did not work in the business. This difference in the cases is not a key fact difference. The fact that the plaintiff in *Herald* worked in the business relates to her status as an employee, but does not relate to her status as a shareholder. In *Herald*, the court defined oppressive conduct as conduct against shareholders, not employees. The plaintiff's status as an employee may give rise to employee rights, but it is not related to her rights as a shareholder, and thus is not a key fact.

2. Are the Rules or Principles Sufficiently Similar?

Is there a sufficient similarity between the law that applies in *Karl v. Herald* and that which applies in the client's case for the case to be considered on point and apply as precedent?

The same statute, § 96-25-16 of the Business Corporation Act, applies to both the court opinion and the client's case. Both cases involve allegations of oppressive conduct by a majority shareholder against a minority shareholder and are governed by the same section of the statute.

In the *Herald* opinion, *oppressive conduct* was defined as "any unfair or fraudulent act by a majority shareholder that inures to the benefit of the majority and to the detriment of the minority." The client's case also involves questions of oppressive conduct by the majority shareholder and is governed by the same definition. Just as in *Herald*, there is alleged unfair conduct by the majority shareholder that inures to the benefit of the majority and to the detriment of the minority. There are no major differences between *Herald* and the client's case that restrict the application of *Herald* as precedent.

NOTE: What if you concluded that *Herald* was not on point, but it was the only case in the jurisdiction that discusses oppressive conduct? You would need to be sure to analyze the case in the memorandum to your supervisor and explain why the case is not on point.

B. Libel Case

The following fact situation and court opinion illustrate another example of the use of the steps discussed in this chapter.

> **For Example** Jerry lives in an apartment building. He often sees couples, and sometimes individuals, entering and leaving Eve's apartment in the late evening and early morning. Convinced that Eve is engaged in immoral behavior, he prepares a petition requesting that Eve be kicked out of the building. He intends to present copies of the petition to the other tenants of the building and submit the signed petitions to the landlord. In the petition, he refers to Eve as an immoral person.
>
> Early one evening, he decides to confront Eve. In the ensuing conversation, he discovers that Eve is a marriage counselor employed by a local business. The couples he has seen visiting her apartment are workers at the business who, due to their schedule, can come to counseling only during the late evening. She has an agreement with her employer that allows her to counsel couples and individuals in her apartment.
>
> Jerry, realizing he is mistaken about Eve, decides to destroy the petitions. On the way to the incinerator, he unknowingly drops a copy of the petition. Another tenant finds it and ultimately circulates it among the tenants of the building. Eve hears about the petition and decides to sue Jerry for libel.
>
> The state's libel statute defines *libel* as "the intentional publication, in writing, of false statements about a person." A leading libel case in the jurisdiction is *Cox v. Redd*. In this case, Redd wrote a letter, which he intended to mail to Cox, wherein he called Cox a crook and a thief. The statements were not true. Redd intended for Cox, and no one else, to read the letter. The day before he planned to mail the letter, he invited several friends over to spend the evening. He forgot to put the letter away. He left it open on the dining room table, and some of the guests read it. Redd was not aware that his guests had read the letter. Cox heard about it and sued Redd for libel.
>
> The court, interpreting the libel statute, ruled that "intentional publication" means either the actual intent to publish or, where there is no intent to publish, "reckless or grossly negligent conduct that results in publication." The court held that Redd's conduct of leaving the letter open where he knew his guests might see it was grossly negligent conduct and that he had therefore intentionally published the letter and had committed libel. The court commented that Redd knew company was coming to his house, and his failure to exercise care in securing the letter in light of that knowledge was gross negligence.

In this example, is *Cox v. Redd* on point so that it applies as precedent in Jerry's case?

1. Are the Key Facts Sufficiently Similar?

Both cases involve false written statements that were published. In both cases, there is the question of intentional publication. In the *Cox* case, even though he may not have intended to publish the letter, Redd's carelessness in leaving it out resulted in its publication.

Are the facts concerning intentional publication in Eve's case sufficiently similar? It is questionable. In the *Cox* case, Redd was careless and took no steps to secure the letter. In Eve's case, Jerry was taking steps to avoid publication and accidentally dropped a copy of the petition. It could be argued that some key facts are clearly different—that his conduct was simple negligence and not gross negligence—and that the *Cox* case is therefore not on point. It could also be argued that due to the extreme sensitivity of the contents of the petition, Jerry should have taken great care to ensure that all the copies of the petition were burned, and the failure to exercise that care constitutes gross negligence. Under this argument, the *Cox* case can apply as precedent.

It is important to note that the difference in the key facts makes it questionable whether the case is on point. To remove doubt, additional research must be conducted to determine what constitutes gross negligence and whether Jerry's conduct rises to the level of gross negligence.

2. Are the Rules or Principles Sufficiently Similar?

If it is decided that there is a sufficient similarity in the facts, then is there a sufficient similarity between the law that applies in the *Cox* opinion and that which applies in the client's case for the opinion to be considered on point and apply as precedent? Both cases are libel cases that apply the same libel statute. Both cases involve the element of intent to publish. Both cases are concerned with an aspect of that element: whether there is "intentional publication" when the conduct that results in publication is unintentional.

Therefore, there is little question that *Cox* is on point with regard to step 2. If it is determined that Jerry's conduct is gross negligence, under the rule of law applied in *Cox*, Jerry's conduct is intentional publication.

Summary

Court opinions are important because under the doctrines of precedent and stare decisis, judges reach decisions according to principles laid down in similar cases. Therefore, a researcher should find a case that is precedent (on point) because it guides the attorney as to how the issue in the client's case may be decided. An opinion is on point, and may be considered as precedent, if there is a sufficient similarity between the key facts and the rule of law or legal principle that governs both the court opinion and the client's case.

When considering the key facts, the heart of the process is the identification of the similarities and differences between them. The more pronounced the differences between the facts of the court opinion and those of the client's case, the greater the likelihood that the opinion is not on point. Be very critical in your analysis when there are differences. Always pursue other avenues of research when the key facts are different.

When the key facts are sufficiently similar for the opinion to be considered on point, look to the rule of law that governs the court opinion and the client's case. If the same rule applies in the same way, the opinion is usually on point. If a different rule applies, a court opinion usually cannot apply as precedent. When the language and function of the applicable rules or principles are sufficiently similar, however, it can be argued that an opinion is on point and can be used as precedent.

Reliance on a court opinion that applies a different rule or principle than that which applies in the client's case is risky and should be attempted only when there is no case that interprets the rule or principle governing the client's case.

Quick References

Case law analysis	372	On point	372
Different key facts	376	Persuasive precedent	373
Different rule or legal principle	381	Precedent	372
Identical key facts	375	Same rule or legal principle	380
Mandatory precedent	373	Stare decisis	373
On all fours	375		

Internet Resources

Various Web sites discuss the subject of cases on point. Most sites discuss specific cases and topics. These sites may be accessed by using "case law on all fours" or "cases on all fours" as a topic in a search engine. As mentioned in Chapter 9, most sites provide information without charge. Information you obtain free may not be closely monitored and may not be as accurate or have the same quality of material as that obtained from fee-based services. Therefore, exercise care when using freely obtained material.

Exercises

Additional assignments are available on the CourseMate.

ASSIGNMENT 1

What does it mean when a case is on point? When is a case on point?

ASSIGNMENT 2

Describe the two-step process for determining when a case is on point.

ASSIGNMENT 3

Describe the three-part process for determining if a case is on point when there are different key facts.

ASSIGNMENT 4

Describe the two steps to follow when the doctrine or rule applied by the court is different from the doctrine that applies in the client's case.

ASSIGNMENT 5

Why is it important for a researcher to find a case on point?

ASSIGNMENT 6

In the following examples, use the statutory and case law presented in the hypothetical at the beginning of the chapter, that is, § 96-25-16 and *Karl v. Herald*. The client seeks redress for the other party's refusal to issue dividends. In each example, determine if *Karl v. Herald* is on point.

Example 1

Client and his sister, Janice, are shareholders in a corporation. Janice is the majority shareholder, the sole member of the board of directors, and the manager of the corporation. For the past five years, she has paid herself a lucrative salary, twice that paid to managers of similar corporations. The corporation has a $400,000 cash surplus that Janice claims is necessary for emergencies. No emergency has occurred in the past five years that would require expenditure of more than $50,000.

Example 2

Client and Claire own a fabric store. The business is a corporation, and Claire holds 80 percent of the stock and makes all the business decisions. Client, an employee of the business, owns 20 percent of the stock. The business has a large cash surplus, but Claire has never issued dividends. Claire's salary is three times Client's. When Client asks that dividends be issued, Claire responds, "Your dividend from this corporation is your job."

Example 3

Client and Don are partners in a business. Don owns 70 percent of the partnership and Client owns 30 percent. Client does not work for the business. Don runs the business and pays himself a large salary that always seems to equal the profits. Client thinks this is fishy and that Don should have a set salary and the profit above Don's salary should be shared 70/30. There is no partnership case law in the jurisdiction addressing this question.

ASSIGNMENT 7

Each of the following examples presents a brief summary of the court opinion, followed by a client's fact situation. For each client fact situation, parts A through G, determine the following:

1. What are the fact similarities and differences between the court opinion and the client's situation?

2. Is the court opinion on point? Why or why not?

3. If the opinion is on point, what will the probable decision be in regard to the question raised by the client's facts?

Example 1

Court Opinion: *State v. Jones.* Mr. Jones, a first-time applicant for general relief funds, was denied relief without a hearing. The denial was based on information in Mr. Jones's application indicating that his income was above the threshold maximum set by the agency regulations. The regulation provides that when an applicant's income, or the financial support provided to an applicant plus income, exceeds $12,000 a year, the individual may be denied general relief funds. The regulation is silent about the right to a hearing.

Mr. Jones's application reflected that the gross income from his two part-time jobs exceeded by $2,000 the maximum allowable income for eligibility. He believed there were special circumstances that would allow him to be eligible for general relief. His demand for an appeal hearing to explain his special circumstances was denied.

The court held that the due process clause of the state constitution entitles a first-time applicant for general relief funds to a hearing when special circumstances are alleged. The question in the following three fact situations is whether the client is entitled to a hearing.

Part A

Client's Facts: Tom lives at home with his parents. He has a part-time job. He does not pay rent or utilities. He uses the money from his job to attend school, and he has very little left over. His application for general relief was denied. The written denial stated that the combination of the support provided by his parents and his part-time income exceeded the maximum allowable income. His application for an appeal hearing was denied.

Part B

Client's Facts: In the last session of the state legislature, the legislature passed legislation providing that when applicants for general relief are denied relief based on information provided in the application, they are not entitled to an appeal hearing. The purpose of the legislation is to cut costs.

Mr. Taylor, a first-time applicant for general relief funds, was denied benefits based solely on his application. He believes that he has special circumstances that entitle him to benefits. His request for an appeal hearing was denied.

Part C

Client's Facts: Client has been receiving general relief funds for the past year. Last week, he received notice that his relief would be terminated due to information received from his employer indicating that he had received a raise, and his income is now over the statutory maximum. His request for an appeal hearing on the termination of relief was denied.

Example 2

Court Opinion: *Rex v. Ireland.* Mr. Rex, the landlord, filed an eviction suit against his tenant, Mr. Ireland. Mr. Rex served notice of default upon Mr. Ireland by rolling up the notice of default and placing it in Mr. Ireland's mailbox. The mailbox was situated next to the street. Mr. Ireland retrieved the notice the next day. Mr. Ireland, in his defense to the eviction suit, stated that he was not given proper notice of default under the provisions of § 55-67-9 of the Landlord/Tenant Act; therefore, the case should be dismissed. The statute provides that notice of default may be accomplished in one of three ways:

1. Delivery by certified mail

2. Hand delivery to the individual to be evicted

3. Posting at the most public part of the residence

The statute further provides that the court may enter an order of eviction if the notice of default is not responded to within 30 days.

The court, denying the request for dismissal, ruled that the intent of the statute was to ensure that tenants receive notice of default. The court noted that although the method of delivery used by Mr. Rex did not comply with the statute, the intent of the act was accomplished, inasmuch as Mr. Ireland had actual notice of default and was not prejudiced by the improper notice.

The question in the following four fact situations is whether the notice of default is effective.

Part D

Client's Facts: The client is a tenant. The landlord told the client's daughter to inform the tenant that he was in default and, under the terms of the lease, would be evicted if he did not pay or otherwise respond within 30 days. The daughter informed the tenant the next day. Would it make any difference if the daughter informed the tenant after 30 days but before the eviction suit was filed?

Part E

Client's Facts: Client, the tenant, was on vacation when the landlord posted the notice of default on the front door.

Client did not return from vacation and learn of the default until after the 30-day default period had passed.

Part F

Client's Facts: Landlord sent the notice of default by regular mail, and the tenant received it.

Part G

Client's Facts: The landlord sent the notice by certified mail, but the client refused to accept it.

 CourseMate

The available CourseMate for this text has an interactive eBook and interactive learning tools, including flash cards, quizzes, and more. To learn more about this resource and access free demo CourseMate resources, go to **www.cengagebrain.com**, and search for this book. To access CourseMate materials that you have purchased, go to **login.cengagebrain.com**.

CHAPTER 13

Counteranalysis

On a frigid Saturday in December, Mr. Henry "Hot Dog" Thomas, an inexperienced skier, was skiing an expert run at a local resort. As he came over a hill, he encountered a patch of ice, lost control, crashed into a tree, and was severely injured. The ski resort did not post a warning sign indicating the presence of the ice patch. Mr. Thomas consulted with Ms. Booth, a local attorney, and retained her to represent him. Shortly thereafter, Ms. Booth filed a negligence suit against the resort. She sent her paralegal a memo indicating that the resort's attorney had filed a Rule 12(b)(6) motion to dismiss for failure to state a claim. The memo directed the paralegal to prepare a legal research memo assessing the likelihood of the motion being granted.

The Ski Safety Act, which governs the rights and liabilities of skiers and ski resorts, provides that:

■ The resort has a duty to warn of hazardous conditions.

■ The skier has the duty and the responsibility to be aware of snow and ice conditions.

The act also provides that skiers have a duty to refrain from skiing beyond the range of their ability. One of the questions to be addressed by the paralegal is which of the duties apply in the client's case.

The memo the paralegal prepared focused on the resort's duty to warn and the skier's duty in regard to snow and ice conditions. Based on this focus and the relevant case law, the paralegal concluded that the resort had the duty to warn of the ice patch that the client encountered. Therefore, the 12(b)(6) motion would probably not be granted.

At the motion hearing, the resort's counsel did not focus on the issue of the resort's duty to warn, but rather argued the issue in the context of probable cause. The resort's counsel contended that the cause of the accident was the skier's admitted violation of his statutory duty to refrain from skiing beyond the range of his ability. As an admitted inexperienced skier, his skiing an expert run violated the statute and, therefore, was the cause of the accident as a matter of law. The skier's attorney, relying on the paralegal's memo, which did not address the proximate cause issue, was unprepared to counter this argument. Consequently, the motion was granted and the case dismissed.

Learning Objectives

After completing this chapter, you should understand:

• What counteranalysis is

• Why counteranalysis is important

• The techniques of counteranalysis

• Where to place counteranalysis in an interoffice research memorandum or a court brief

I. INTRODUCTION

What went wrong in the preceding hypothetical? Of course, the supervising attorney should have more carefully reviewed the paralegal's memo, noticed that the assistant had not addressed the proximate cause issue, and engaged in additional research. Often an attorney is too busy and, based on past excellent and reliable performance by a paralegal or law clerk, may rely fully on the individual's work product and not sufficiently review what has been submitted.

What went wrong with the paralegal's research? The paralegal failed to anticipate the legal argument the opposing side was likely to make. He failed to analyze the position from the other side's point of view. In other words, he failed to provide a complete counteranalysis in the memo. A paralegal or law clerk's role in conducting legal research, or in any situation that requires legal analysis, includes determining the potential weaknesses of a legal argument and the counterarguments the other side may present.

The purpose of legal research is not only to discover how the law applies to the client's case but also to determine the strength of that case. To accomplish this, the strength of the opponent's case must be analyzed as well. The case must be looked at in its entirety to determine its strengths and weaknesses.

The focus of this chapter is the process of identifying the strengths and weaknesses of a client's case through an analysis of the case from the perspective of the opposition. That is, the focus is on counteranalysis. Thorough research must be conducted and all applicable law identified prior to beginning the process.

II. COUNTERANALYSIS—DEFINITION

If analysis is the application of the law to the facts of a case, what is **counteranalysis**? At one level, it is an exploration of how and why a specific law does or does not apply to the facts of a case. It is the process of anticipating the argument the opponent is likely to raise in response to your analysis of an issue—the **counterargument**. In essence, it is the process of discovering and considering the counterargument to a legal position or argument. It involves an identification and objective evaluation of the strengths and weaknesses of each legal argument you intend to raise.

III. COUNTERANALYSIS—WHY?

The role of the attorney, paralegal, or law clerk is to represent the client in the best way possible and to pursue a course of action that is in the best interest of the client. This is accomplished by engaging in research and analysis that thoroughly examines all the aspects of the case. One of those aspects, counteranalysis, is important for several reasons:

1. Under Rule 3.3(a)(3) of the American Bar Association's Model Rules of Professional Conduct, an attorney has an **ethical** duty to disclose legal authority adverse to the position of the client that is not disclosed by opposing counsel.

   The goal of the adversary system is that justice be served. The ends of justice require the discovery and presentation of all relevant authority so that a just resolution of the issues may be achieved. Therefore, a legal researcher, to properly inform the attorney, must locate and provide the attorney with all relevant authority, including that which is adverse to the client.

2. The attorney, paralegal, and law clerk have an ethical duty to do a complete and competent job. See Model Rule 1.1. Research and analysis are not complete unless all sides of an issue and all legal arguments have been considered. Failure to completely analyze a problem can constitute malpractice.

To represent the client competently, you must be prepared to respond to any legal argument raised by the other side. The identification of opposing arguments allows you to consider what the other side's position is likely to be. It allows you to answer the questions:

- "What will they do?"
- "How can we counter their arguments?"
- "What preparation is necessary to respond?"

In essence, counteranalysis allows you to anticipate opposing arguments and prepare to counter them. The last thing you want is to be responsible for the supervisory attorney being unprepared to respond to an argument.

3. Counteranalysis aids in the proper evaluation of the merits of a case and can assist in selection of the appropriate course of action.

> **For Example** Counteranalysis may reveal a weakness in the client's case that leads to the conclusion that settlement should be pursued. Without conducting a thorough counteranalysis, an improper course of action could be followed, such as taking the matter to trial rather than pursuing settlement options.

4. It is important to locate and disclose adverse authority to maintain credibility with your supervisor. You may not be considered reliable, and the credibility, accuracy, and thoroughness of your research may be questioned, if you ignore or fail to identify and disclose adverse authority. The opposition or the court, if the issue comes before a court, most likely will discover the opposing authority. Your failure to do so indicates lack of ability, sloppiness, or intentional concealment. Your credibility and trustworthiness will be enhanced if you candidly reveal and meet head on unfavorable authority.

5. When a legal brief is submitted to a court, if you identify and address adverse authority in the brief, you have an opportunity to soften its impact by discrediting or distinguishing it. You have an opportunity to provide reasons why the adverse authority does not apply, and your credibility is thereby enhanced. This allows the reader to consider the adverse authority in the context of your response to it. This opportunity is missed if you fail to include the adverse authority.

Weaknesses in your position or analysis will not go away if you ignore them. No matter how strongly you feel you are right, you can count on the other side to raise some counterargument, and if you have not considered and prepared for the counterarguments, you may very well lose in court.

IV. COUNTERANALYSIS—WHEN?

Employ counteranalysis whenever legal research is conducted or the strengths and weaknesses of a case are considered—in other words, *always*. When addressing a legal problem, look for all potential counterarguments to any position taken. Use counteranalysis when preparing an interoffice legal memorandum or conducting any research on an issue in a case. It is certainly necessary when you are assisting in the preparation of a response to a brief filed by the opposing party. Engage in the process even when you are considering the legal issues in the client's case. Counteranalysis may be required even in the initial stages of a case.

> **For Example** Some paralegals and law clerks conduct the initial interview with a client and provide the supervisory attorney with a summary of the interview and the applicable statutory and case law. The summary of the applicable law should include a counteranalysis section that points out any apparent weaknesses in the client's case.

V. COUNTERANALYSIS—RESEARCH SOURCES

When conducting legal research, counteranalysis means looking for legal authority that supports the argument the opponent is likely to raise in response to your analysis of the issue. There are several things to keep in mind and sources to look to when conducting counteranalysis and legal research.

When researching statutory law, Shepardize the statute or check the annotations for cases analyzing or interpreting the statute. The cases may present counterarguments to a position you are taking in regard to the interpretation of the statute.

When researching case law, if you find a case that supports the client's position, then Shepardize the case to determine if another case analyzes the law differently. Cases that distinguish, criticize, and limit the case you are researching are identified in *Shepard's*. Be sure to check all these cases.

> **For Example** Under the case you are Shepardizing is the reference "c746P2d845." The "c" means that the court opinion at 746 P.2d 845 disagrees with the reasoning/decision of the case you are Shepardizing. Be sure to check this opinion, because it may present a counterargument to the legal argument in support of the client's position.

In addition to Shepardizing the case that supports the client's position, also check the digest for other cases that may analyze the law differently. *Shepard's* will only identify those cases that specifically mention the case you are researching. There may be other cases that analyze the same question, but do not mention the same case. Check the headnote of the case you are researching, identify the key number for the issue in question, and then check the appropriate digest for other cases on the topic.

When reading a case that supports the client's position, always check for a dissent. If there is a dissent, it will present the counterargument to the position taken in the majority opinion and often include references to cases and other sources in support of the counterargument. It is possible that the facts of the client's case are sufficiently different from the court opinion that the dissenter's position may apply.

There are several other sources to check when conducting counteranalysis. A treatise usually presents an analysis of legal issues that includes arguments and counterarguments. If the question being researched has an *ALR* annotation, the annotation will include a thorough analysis of the issue. It will discuss the various ways the courts have decided the issue and the arguments and counterarguments in support of those decisions. The annotation will also include references to numerous cases on the question and other research sources.

Another helpful source when conducting counteranalysis is a law review article. If there is a law review article that discusses the question being researched, it will provide a comprehensive analysis and critique of the legal position(s) the courts have taken. Like an *ALR* annotation, it will include reference to numerous cases that address the question and other research sources.

VI. COUNTERANALYSIS—TECHNIQUES

A. In General

Before counteranalysis can begin, a prerequisite is that you must analyze and thoroughly research the issue or legal position being addressed. You must know the law before you can respond to it. Thorough research should reveal the weaknesses of a legal position and the counterarguments to it.

> **For Example** Mary Kay, a door-to-door sales representative for Ace Brush, sold Ella Smith a set of brushes at Ms. Smith's residence. Ms. Smith signed a contract to purchase the brushes. The contract provided for three monthly payments. Ms. Smith called two days later and canceled the contract. When Ace Brush attempted to deliver the goods, Ms. Smith refused to accept the delivery. Ace Brush sued Ms. Smith for breach of contract.
>
> Tom, a law clerk with the firm representing Ace Brush, was assigned the task of determining whether Ms. Smith could legally cancel the contract after it was signed. He determined that article II of the state Commercial Code governed the transaction. His research indicated that the code had no provision allowing a cooling-off period for door-to-door sales; therefore, he concluded that Ms. Smith's rejection of the goods was a breach of the contract.
>
> Tom, however, committed a major error. He failed to thoroughly research the question. The state had another statute, called the Consumer Sales Act, which provided that in the event of a credit transaction involving a home solicitation sale, the buyer had a right to cancel the sale within three days of the transaction.

Had Tom's research been thorough, he would have located the weakness in his legal position based upon the Commercial Code and identified the counterargument to the conclusion that the contract was breached.

When embarking on counteranalysis, always assume that there is a counterargument to the position you have taken. Put yourself in the opponent's place and ask yourself:

- "How do I respond to this argument?"
- "What is the argument in response to this position?"

Remember, counteranalysis consists of identifying any possible counterargument the opponent may use to challenge your legal position or argument.

To determine what the counterarguments to an argument or position are likely to be, it is necessary to consider the ways a legal argument is attacked. After you are familiar with the techniques used to challenge an argument, use those techniques to seek out the weaknesses in your own argument and to anticipate the likely counterarguments.

A legal argument or legal position is usually based on enacted law or case law, or both. The various approaches that you may use to attack or challenge an argument based on enacted law or case law are explored separately in the following two sections.

B. Enacted Law

Ways to challenge or attack a legal position or argument based on an enacted law are discussed here. **Enacted law**, as defined in Chapter 1, includes any law passed or adopted by the people through a representative body, such as Congress or a state legislature, city council, and so on. Throughout this section and the remainder of the chapter, the term *statute* is used when discussing legal arguments or positions based on enacted law.

There are several approaches to consider when attacking a legal position based on a statute. Some of these approaches are listed in Exhibit 13-1. Consider all of them when analyzing an argument based on a statute to identify every possible weakness and counterargument.

Exhibit 13-1 *Counteranalysis Approaches to a Legal Position Based on a Statute.*

1. The elements of the statute are not met.

2. The statute is sufficiently broad to permit a construction or application different from that urged by the opposition.

3. The statute has been misconstrued or does not apply.

4. The statute relied upon as a guide to interpret another statute does not apply and, therefore, cannot be used as a guide in interpreting the other statute.

5. The statute relied on has not been adopted in your jurisdiction.

6. The interpretation of the statute urged by the opposition is unconstitutional or violates another legislative act.

7. The statute relied on is unconstitutional.

1. Elements of the Statute Are Not Met

Every statute is composed of elements (see Chapter 3) that must be met before the statute can apply. When a client's case is based on a statute, facts must be present in the case that establish or satisfy each of the elements of the statute.

For Example Criminal Code § 1000 defines *burglary* as the breaking and entering of the residence of another with the intent to commit a crime. The elements are:

1. Breaking and entering
2. The residence
3. Of another
4. With the intent to commit a crime

Facts must be present that establish each of these elements before an individual can be convicted of burglary.

One way to attack a legal position based on a statute is to argue that the elements of the statute have not been met—that is, facts present in the case fail to establish each element of the statute.

For Example Mary is charged under Criminal Code § 1000 with burglary of Steve's house. Steve is a friend of Mary, and Mary often stays at Steve's house. On the date of the alleged burglary, Steve's house was unlocked. Mary came over to see Steve, entered the house, saw money on the kitchen table, took it, and left.

The counterargument to the prosecution's reliance on the statute is that there are no facts present in the case to establish two elements of the law:

1. Mary did not break into the house; it was unlocked.
2. Mary did not enter with the intent to commit a crime. She entered with the intent to visit Steve. The intent to commit a crime was not formed until after entry had taken place.

When conducting counteranalysis of an argument based on a statute, closely examine the facts relied on to establish *each* of the required elements. Ask yourself, "Have the elements of the statute been met?" Look for any possible argument that the facts do not establish or satisfy an element or elements.

2. Statute Is Sufficiently Broad to Permit Different Construction

In many situations, a statute may be sufficiently broad to allow an interpretation or application different from that relied on by the opposing side.

> **For Example** Section 54-9-91 of the state domestic relations statute provides that custody shall be determined in the best interest of the children. Gerald contends that he should be granted custody of the children because he lives in a small town, and his former spouse lives in a large city. He argues that a small town is a better environment because it is safer and free from the pressures of gang violence and drug use.
>
> A counterargument can be made that the benefits of the city, such as greater access to the arts, museums, and universities, offset the alleged disadvantages of a large city. The phrase "best interest of the children" can be interpreted in a manner different from that urged by the opposing side.

When the language relied on in a statute is broadly crafted, such as in the previous example, look for the counterargument that a different interpretation is permissible because of the broadness of the language. Ask the question, "Is the statute sufficiently broad to permit a construction or application different from that urged by the opposition?"

3. Statute Misconstrued or Does Not Apply

Explore the possibility of a counterargument that the statute is being misconstrued or misapplied.

> **For Example** Section 9(A) of the Deceptive Trade Practices Act provides a remedy in tort for "deceptive practices in negotiation or performance" of a contract for the sale of goods. Tom and Larry have a contract for the delivery of goods. Under the contract, Tom is to deliver the goods on the fifth of each month. Every month, Tom comes up with some excuse for not delivering the goods on the fifth, and the goods are always delivered between the seventh and fifteenth of the month. Finally, Larry gets fed up and sues Tom for violation of the Deceptive Trade Practices Act, claiming that Tom is engaging in deceptive practices in violation of § (9)A of the act.
>
> A review of the legislative history and case law clearly indicates that the Deceptive Trade Practices Act is not designed to apply to simple breach-of-contract cases. The Sale of Goods provisions of the Commercial Code statutes govern breach-of-contract situations. The courts have consistently held that when there is an adequate remedy in contract law, the tort remedy available under the act does not apply. Therefore, a counterargument can be raised that the statute has been misconstrued and does not apply in a simple breach-of-contract case such as that of Tom and Larry.

When a legal position or argument is based on a statute, engage in counteranalysis to ensure that the statute is not being misconstrued or applied in a situation to which it clearly does not apply. Always consult case law to determine if the courts have interpreted or applied the statute in a manner different from that relied on. Ask the following questions: "Has the statute been misconstrued or does not apply?" "Does another statute apply?"

4. Statute Relied on as a Guide Does Not Apply

In some situations, the statute that governs does not have a provision addressing a specific question raised by the facts of a client's case. In such instances, there may be an argument that a different statute, which has a section governing a similar fact situation, can be used as guidance in interpreting the applicable statute. It is usually argued that the different statute can be used as guidance because the language and functions of the statutes are similar.

When this occurs, you can make the counterargument that the statute relied on to interpret another statute is not intended to govern or apply to the type of situation presented by the client's case and, therefore, cannot be used as a guide. The argument usually is that the statute governs or applies only to those limited fact situations covered by the language of the statute and cannot be used as a guide for the interpretation of another statute.

> **For Example** The jurisdiction has adopted the following statutes:
>
> - § 59-1 provides that an individual must be a resident of the county to be eligible to run for the position of animal control officer.
> - § 200-1 provides that an individual must be a resident of the county for three months to run for a position on the county school board.
>
> Erin, a resident of the county for three months, wants to run for the position of animal control officer. She argues that since § 59-1 is silent on the length of residency necessary to be eligible to run for the position of animal control officer, the three-month residency requirement established in § 200-1 should be used as a guide to determine the length of residency required under § 59-1. She reasons that because both statutes are similar in language (both use the word *resident*) and both involve county elective offices, they are sufficiently similar for the residency requirement of § 200-1 to be used as the standard for § 59-1.
>
> Because the statutes are different, however, a possible counterargument is the duties of an animal control officer are much different from those of a school board member. The duties of the animal control officer require a degree of familiarity with the geography of the county that cannot be acquired in three months. Therefore, the differences in the requirements of the positions represent a factual difference that renders § 200-1 inappropriate for use as a guide to interpret § 59-1.

In every situation in which it is argued that a provision of one statute may apply or be used to interpret a provision of a different statute, a counterargument can always be made that no matter how similar in language and function, the statutes differ functionally in some way. Therefore, the provisions of one statute cannot be relied on or applied to interpret or govern the other statute.

When your legal position or argument is based on the use of one statute as a guide to interpret another statute, consider the counterargument that focuses on the differences in the statutes. Keep in mind the question, "Is it possible that the statute relied on as a guide is so functionally different that it cannot be used as a guide to interpret the statute being analyzed?

5. Statute Relied on Has Not Been Adopted in Jurisdiction

The jurisdiction has no law or statute governing a fact situation, and your legal position is based on an argument that advocates the adoption of the language of, or principles embodied in, a statute from another jurisdiction. In such situations, you are attempting to persuade the court to adopt the law, or the principles embodied in the law, of another jurisdiction.

A counterargument can be made that a statute, or principles that apply to facts in another jurisdiction, should not be adopted to apply to similar facts in your jurisdiction. It is usually possible to point out some difference between the jurisdictions or difference in the public policy of the jurisdictions and argue that the difference precludes the adoption of the language or principles of the statute.

> **For Example** Ida, a resident of state A, borrows her next-door neighbor's lawn mower. Due to a defect in the mower, Ida is injured. Ida sues the manufacturer, a local company, for breach of warranty. The manufacturer moves for dismissal, claiming that the warranty does not extend to nonpurchasers. The commercial code adopted in state A does not address the question, nor is there any case law on point. Ida argues that the court should adopt the language of the law of state B, a neighboring state. Section 2-389 of state B's commercial code provides that warranties extend to the buyer and any person who may be reasonably expected to use the goods, which includes a neighbor.
>
> The manufacturer's counterargument could be that the law of state B should not be looked to because of policy differences between the states. State A, to encourage and protect the growth of local industry, has traditionally adopted a policy that narrowly limits manufacturer liability. State B's position represents an expansive view that broadly extends manufacturer liability, a position contrary to state A's traditional view.

When conducting counteranalysis, look for the argument that the statute relied on has not been adopted and should not apply. Ask the question, "Where a legal position is based upon an argument that advocates the adoption of the language or principles embodied in a statute of another jurisdiction, are there differences in the jurisdictions that preclude the adoption of the language or principles of the other jurisdiction's statute?" Note that there is always the additional counterargument that such matters are of legislative concern and should be addressed by the legislature, not the courts.

6. Interpretation of Statute Is Unconstitutional or Violates Another Legislative Act

Be alert for an argument that the application or interpretation of the statute advocated is unconstitutional or violates another statute.

> **For Example** Section 22 of the state's Secured Transaction Code allows a creditor to repossess collateral after providing the debtor with notice of default and allowing the debtor 60 days to cure the default. A car dealer, after providing notice of default and waiting more than 60 days for the customer to cure the default, repossessed the customer's car from the customer's residence while the customer was at work. The car dealer interpreted the statute as not requiring prior court approval, and therefore did not seek a court order authorizing the repossession.
>
> The customer sued the car dealer, claiming that the dealer illegally seized the car because the due process clause of the state constitution requires a court order before property can be seized. The dealer claimed that the seizure was legal because he complied with the statute: he provided notice of default and waited 60 days.
>
> The counterargument is that the interpretation of the statute urged by the dealer is unconstitutional because it allows for prejudgment seizure—that is, it allows the seizure of property without prior court approval.

Always counteranalyze a legal position or argument based on an interpretation of a law for the possibility that the interpretation violates a constitutional or statutory provision.

Ask yourself, "Is the interpretation of the statute urged by the opposition unconstitutional or does it violate another legislative act?"

7. Statute Relied on Is Unconstitutional

Although statutes are not usually unconstitutional and, therefore, are not likely to be vulnerable to constitutional attack, consider the constitutionality of the statute on which a legal position is based. Has the constitutionality of the statute been questioned in scholarly journals, law reviews, and so on? Try to anticipate any argument based on a constitutional challenge.

> **For Example** Ellen is prosecuted under a local ordinance prohibiting the sale of any material that "shows genitalia or excites a prurient interest." Such a statute may be subject to challenge as being unconstitutional because the term *prurient interest* is too vague.

When working with statutes, consider a counterargument based on a challenge to the constitutionality of the statute. Consider the question, "Is the statute unconstitutional?"

NOTE: When a legal position or argument is based on a statute, conduct thorough research to ensure that some other law, provision, or court decision does not apply that affects your reliance on the statute.

C. Case Law

To understand how to counteranalyze a legal position or argument based on or relying on **case law**, it is necessary to understand the process involved in determining if a court opinion is on point. Therefore, it is helpful to review Chapter 12 before beginning this section. When used in this section, the terms *rule of law* and *legal principle* include any constitutional, legislative, or case law provision, act, doctrine, principle, or test relied on by the court in reaching its decision.

There are several approaches for challenging a legal position based on a court opinion. Some of these approaches are listed in Exhibit 13-2. Consider each of them when conducting counteranalysis.

Exhibit 13-2 *Counteranalysis Approaches to a Legal Position Based on Case Law.*

1. Reliance on the court opinion is misplaced because the key facts in the opinion and the key facts of the client's case are different to such a nature or degree that they render the court opinion unusable as precedent.

2. Reliance on the court opinion is misplaced because the rule of law or legal principle applied in the court opinion does not apply.

3. The court opinion is subject to an interpretation different from that relied on in support of a legal position.

4. The rule or principle adopted in the opinion relied on is not universally followed.

5. The opinion relied on presents several possible solutions to the problem, and the one urged by the opposition is not mandatory and is not the best choice.

6. The position relied on no longer represents sound public policy and should not be followed.

7. There are other equally relevant cases that do not support the position adopted in the case relied on.

1. Reliance on Court Opinion Is Misplaced Because Key Facts Differ

Apply the test from Chapter 12, section IV. Substitute the client's key facts for those of the court opinion. If the substitution of the key facts would result in changing the outcome of the case, the court opinion cannot be used as precedent.

> **For Example** The plaintiff requests that a psychologist's records be admitted into evidence. The plaintiff bases his argument on the holding in the case of *Smith v. Jones*, which allowed the admission of a psychologist's records into evidence. In that case, the evidence was admitted because no claim was raised that the evidence was privileged. The decision turned on the key fact that privilege was not claimed.
>
> In the plaintiff's case, privilege is vigorously claimed. Therefore, *Jones* cannot be relied on as precedent to support the argument for admission of the records, because *Jones* is not on point. There is such a significant difference in the key facts that the case cannot be relied upon as precedent. In *Jones*, privilege was not claimed, but in the plaintiff's case, it is claimed.

Be cautious when your legal argument relies on a court opinion that has key facts different from those of your case. Conduct counteranalysis to identify a possible counterargument that the court opinion relied on does not apply because of differences in the key facts. Ask the question, "Is the opinion relied on not on point because of key fact differences?"

2. Reliance on Court Opinion Is Misplaced Because Rule of Law or Legal Principle Does Not Apply

When conducting counteranalysis, look for a counterargument that the legal principle applied in the court opinion does not apply in the case at hand. Refer to Chapter 12, section IV, when considering this approach.

> **For Example** In the case of *Davis v. Davis*, Ms. Davis had sole custody of her two daughters. Ms. Davis's boyfriend occasionally stayed overnight at her home, and the daughters were aware of the overnight visits. Mr. Davis, her former husband, filed a motion with the court asking for a change of custody. He based his claim solely on his wife's alleged "immoral conduct." He presented no evidence indicating how the overnight visits affected the children.
>
> The trial court granted a change of custody. In overturning the trial court, the court of appeals ruled that "mere allegations of immoral conduct are not sufficient grounds to award a change of custody." The court stated that evidence must be presented showing that the alleged immoral conduct harmed the children.
>
> In the client's case, the facts are the same as those in *Davis v. Davis* except that instead of occasional overnight visits, the custodial spouse is cohabiting with another person. There is a statute in the jurisdiction providing that cohabitation is per se harmful to children—that is, in cohabitation cases, evidence of harm to the children need not be presented because cohabitation is presumed to be harmful to them.
>
> If the custodial spouse relies on *Davis* for the proposition that the noncustodial spouse's request for change of custody must be denied because he has failed to present evidence of harm to the children, the reliance is misplaced. The reliance is misplaced because the cohabitation statute does not require the presentation of evidence of harm to the children. Therefore, the rule of law presented in *Davis* is not applicable in the client's case, and the case is not on point.

When a court opinion is used to support a legal position, ask the question, "Is reliance on the opinion misplaced because the principle applied does not apply to the case at hand?"

3. Court Opinion Is Subject to a Different Interpretation

The court may have interpreted a term in a manner that is subject to an interpretation different from that relied on in support of a legal position.

> **For Example** Mr. Johns is charged with violating Municipal Code § 982, which prohibits nude dancing. Mr. Johns was dancing in see-through bikini briefs. In prosecuting Mr. Johns, the city relied on the court opinion of *City v. Dew*. In that case, the court, in interpreting the term *nude dancing*, ruled that a dancer is nude when the breast or genitalia are exposed. In *Dew*, the dancer was completely nude.
>
> In Mr. Johns's case, the city contends that Mr. Johns was dancing nude because his genitalia were exposed by his see-through bikini briefs. A counterargument could be made that the term *exposed*, as used in the opinion, should be interpreted to mean "uncovered." Therefore, a dancer is not nude under the definition adopted in *Dew* when he is covered by any fabric, no matter how sheer. The counterargument is that the language of the opinion is subject to an interpretation different from that relied on by the opposition.

Closely scrutinize the language of the court opinion to determine if it is subject to another interpretation. Be aware that the interpretation you adopt may not be the only possible interpretation. Ask the question, "Is the court opinion subject to a different interpretation from that relied upon?"

4. Rule or Principle Adopted in Opinion Relied on Is Not Universally Followed

This counterargument should be a consideration when the opinion relied on is not mandatory precedent—that is, when there is no court opinion directly on point, and a party is urging the court to follow a rule or principle adopted by another court ruling in a similar case in either the same or a different jurisdiction.

> **For Example** The counterargument could be, "Although the plaintiff relies on and urges the adoption of the principle presented in *Smith v. Jones*, and that opinion is followed by the Ninth, Fifth, and Seventh Circuits, several other circuits have chosen not to follow it. The better position, presented in the case of *Grape v. Vine*, is followed by the Fourth, Sixth, and Eleventh Circuits. The principle adopted in *Vine* more accurately reflects the policies of this jurisdiction."

Identify other rules or legal principles that may apply by reading the opinions of courts that have adopted other positions in similar cases. Keep in mind the question, "Is the rule or principle of the case relied on universally followed?"

5. Opinion Presents Several Possible Solutions; One Urged by Opposition Is Not Mandatory and Is Not Best Choice

Check the court opinion relied on in support of a legal position to determine if the opinion includes other solutions in addition to the one relied on. Also, check other court opinions to identify different solutions that may have been adopted in other cases. If it is not mandatory to follow a single solution or position, conduct counteranalysis to identify the other possible solutions and anticipate counterarguments that may be based on one of these other solutions. Ask yourself, "If the opinion relied on is not mandatory precedent, does the opinion or another court opinion allow for other possible positions?"

> **For Example** A counterargument could be, "In the case of *Smith v. Harris*, the court stated that the plaintiff could pursue several avenues of relief, including injunction and damages. The defendant argues that *Harris* mandates the pursuit of injunctive relief when, in fact, the court allowed the pursuit of several avenues of relief in addition to injunction."

6. Position Relied on No Longer Represents Sound Public Policy and Should Not Be Followed

If the court opinion is mandatory precedent and thus must be followed, explore the possibility that it no longer represents sound public policy and should be overruled. This approach is available only if the court considering the question has the authority to overrule the precedent. A trial court does not have the power to overrule a higher court decision. If an intermediate court of appeal set the precedent, that court has the power to overturn it. If the highest court in the jurisdiction set the precedent, only that court has the power to overturn it.

This approach is always risky because a court will not lightly choose to ignore precedent. A court usually requires a strong argument to support a decision to abandon or not follow precedent. Nevertheless, when a position is based on a court opinion, consider the possibility that the rule or principle adopted in the opinion should no longer be followed due to some change in policy or other change. In such situations, it can be argued that fairness demands that the court reexamine the law.

> **For Example** Mr. Clark wishes to move into an apartment complex that has restrictions based on parental status. The restrictions provide that no individual or couple may rent an apartment if they have children. The restrictions also provide that if tenants have children after they rent an apartment, they must vacate the premises within three months of the birth of a child. The only case on point is the 1935 case of *Edwards v. Frank*. In that case, the court ruled that restrictions based on parental status did not violate the constitution and, therefore, were enforceable.
>
> A counterargument is current public policy strongly favors families with children; current policy dictates that rental restrictions based on parental status are no longer acceptable or desirable; and, therefore, *Frank* should no longer be followed.

Consider the question, "Does the court opinion relied on no longer represent sound public policy and, therefore, should not be followed?"

7. Other Equally Relevant Cases Do Not Support Position Adopted in Case Relied On

In some instances, a matter has not been clearly settled by the highest court in the jurisdiction, or the opinions of the highest court appear to conflict. Look for other opinions that may take a position different from the one taken in the court opinion relied on to support a legal position or argument. Ask yourself, "Are there equally relevant cases that do not support the position adopted in the case relied on?"

For Example The client is seeking punitive damages in a negligence case. There are three court opinions from the highest court in the jurisdiction. In the case of *Yaws v. Allen*, the court held that punitive damages may be recovered in a negligence case when there is a showing of gross negligence on the part of the tortfeasor. In the case of *X-ray v. Carrie*, the court ruled that before punitive damages can be awarded in a negligence case, there must be some demonstration that the tortfeasor had a culpable state of mind. In the case of *Casy v. Cox*, the court held that the establishment of gross negligence by itself does not indicate the existence of a culpable state of mind; it is also necessary to demonstrate willful and wanton misconduct by the tortfeasor.

Reliance on *Yaws v. Allen*, in support of a legal position that the establishment of gross negligence on the part of the tortfeasor is sufficient to obtain punitive damages, is subject to challenge. A counterargument is that the *Carrie* and *Cox* cases, also from the highest court in the jurisdiction, require more than gross negligence.

NOTE: When a legal position or argument is based on a court opinion, be sure to conduct thorough research to find any other law, provision, or court decision that may affect your reliance on the opinion. The research should identify all court opinions presenting possible solutions and approaches to the problem being analyzed.

VII. COUNTERANALYSIS TECHNIQUES—COMMENTS

When engaging in legal research or analysis, review all the approaches presented in the preceding sections and determine if the legal position or argument may be challenged through any of them. Be aware, however, that the techniques and considerations presented here do not constitute all of the available ways to attack or challenge a legal position or argument based on a legislative act or court opinion. In addition to using the techniques listed, use any other approach that comes to mind. Also, combinations of methods may be utilized. The particular circumstances of the case will determine which, if any, of the suggested approaches are applicable or helpful. It is most important to remember that when your position or argument is based on a legislative act or court opinion, you must engage in thorough counteranalysis to locate any weaknesses, anticipate any counterarguments, and prepare a responses to each.

VIII. COUNTERANALYSIS—WHERE?

Where does counteranalysis fit in an interoffice research memorandum or court brief? Because counteranalysis involves analysis, it obviously fits in the analysis section. But where in the analysis section does it belong? There are no established guidelines or formal rules for the placement of counteranalysis. The following are recommendations and considerations.

A. Court Brief

In a **court brief**, inasmuch as counteranalysis involves discussing potential counterarguments to or weaknesses in your analysis, it is recommended that counteranalysis be presented in the middle of the analysis, that is, immediately after the analysis but before the conclusion. Present your argument and analysis first. Then present the other side's position after your argument, in the middle of the analysis.

Presenting counteranalysis in the middle of the analysis keeps the focus on your position rather than on your opponent's position. A reader tends to remember the beginning and end of a presentation more than the middle. Because you believe your analysis or legal argument is correct and should prevail, you want the memory of your analysis to be foremost in the reader's mind. Therefore, you do not want to place the counterargument in a location where it is more likely to be remembered or emphasized, such as at the beginning or end. Hence, put it after your own analysis and before the conclusion (i.e., in the middle).

> **For Example** "It is appropriate for the court to allow the admission of DNA test results based on the IMAK test. In this state, in the case of *State v. Diago*, the supreme court ruled that the results of scientific tests are admissible when the test's reliability and scientific basis are recognized by competent authorities. The IMAK test, developed in 1992, is universally accepted by all competent authorities as scientifically valid.
>
> Defendant's reliance on the state case of *Arc v. Arc* is misplaced. In that case, the court's refusal to allow the admission of DNA evidence was based on the disagreement among experts about the reliability of the test being administered at the time, the ITAK test. The ITAK test was not universally accepted and was not as accurate as the current IMAK test. Indeed, IMAK test results have been admitted into evidence in all cases where they have been submitted. For the reasons of universal scientific acceptance, reliability, and court acceptance, the results of IMAK DNA testing should be admitted in this case."

B. Interoffice Research Memorandum

In an **interoffice research memorandum**, it is recommended that counteranalysis be placed after the analysis of each issue. It logically follows the analysis, and this placement ensures that the supervising attorney will review it before proceeding to the next issue(s). It may be useful, for the purpose of making certain that it is not overlooked, to include a separate counteranalysis subsection for each issue addressed in the memo. One possible outline of the analysis portion of a legal research memorandum is as follows:

Analysis Section—The legal analysis of the issue(s)

Issue I

   A. *Introductory sentence.*

   B. *Rule of law.* State the rule of law that governs the issue. This may be a constitutional provision, statutory provision, court doctrine, principle, and so on.

   C. *Case(s).* Present the case or cases that are on point and illustrate the application of the rule of law to the facts.

   D. *Counteranalysis*

   E. *Conclusion*

Assume the information included in the previous example is presented in an interoffice memorandum. A portion of the analysis and counteranalysis section of the memo might appear as follows:

Analysis

It is likely the court will allow the admission of DNA test results based on the IMAK test. The state supreme court, in the case of *State v. Diago*, ruled that the results of scientific tests are admissible when the test's reliability and scientific basis are recognized by competent authorities. The IMAK test, developed in 1992, is universally accepted by all competent authorities as scientifically valid.

Although the courts of this state have not addressed the question of the admission of DNA evidence based on the IMAK test, the United States Court of Appeals for the Fifth Circuit has considered the matter. In *Eric v. Eric*, the court of appeals stated, "The time has arrived to admit the results of DNA testing into evidence. The IMAK test meets the requirements established by this court for the admission of scientific evidence." IMAK test results have been admitted into evidence in all cases where they have been submitted. For the reasons of universal scientific acceptance, reliability, and court acceptance, the results of IMAK DNA testing should be admitted in this case.

Counteranalysis

Defendant may rely on the state case of *Arc v. Arc* and argue that the results of the test should not be admitted. In *Arc*, the court refused to allow the admission of DNA test results from the ITAK test. The court's refusal was based on the disagreement among experts about the reliability of the test. The ITAK test was not universally accepted and was not as accurate as the current IMAK test. Because the *Arc* opinion involved a different test that was neither as universally accepted nor as accurate as the IMAK test, the opinion is not on point and cannot be relied on as precedent in this case.

For an in-depth discussion of the analysis section of an interoffice legal research memorandum, see Chapter 17.

IX. KEY POINTS CHECKLIST: *Counteranalysis*

✓ A weakness in an argument will not go away if you ignore it. You can count on either the other side or the court to bring it to light. It is much better for you to raise the counterargument and diffuse it.

✓ For every issue presented in a legal research memorandum, consider how the other side is likely to respond.

✓ Put yourself in your opponent's position. Assume you are the opponent and consider all possible counterarguments, no matter how ridiculous—be ruthless.

✓ The more strongly you believe in the correctness of your analysis, the greater the likelihood that you will miss or overlook the counteranalysis to that analysis. Beware: When you feel extremely confident or sure, take extra precautions. Overconfidence can seriously mislead you.

✓ Do not let your emotions, preconceived notions, or stubbornness interfere with an objective counteranalysis of your position.

✓ When analyzing court opinions, a counteranalysis of the majority opinion may be found in the dissenting opinion or other opinions that criticize or distinguish the majority opinion.

✓ When conducting counteranalysis, always consider each of the approaches listed in this chapter. Remember, more than one approach may apply, and approaches other than those listed may be available.

✓ Even if you find a case on point, always research thoroughly. Look for other laws or court opinions that may also apply.

X. APPLICATION

This section explores the application of the principles discussed in this chapter. Three situations are explored in the following examples.

A. Chapter Hypothetical

Review the example presented at the beginning of the chapter. In the hypothetical, the paralegal failed to conduct a thorough counteranalysis. The assignment was to assess the likelihood that a Rule 12(b)(6) motion to dismiss for failure to state a claim would be granted. In a 12(b)(6) motion, the movant is basically arguing that under the facts of the case, the plaintiff cannot state a claim. To state a claim in a negligence case, facts must be present that establish or satisfy each of the elements of negligence: duty, breach of duty, proximate cause, and damages. In the example, the paralegal focused on duty, that is, on which duty applied. In light of the provisions of the applicable statute, the Ski Safety Act, and the facts of the case, there appeared to be a conflict of duties. The paralegal focused on which duty applied:

- The resort's duty to warn of hazards, or
- The skier's duty to know of and be responsible in snow and ice conditions

The paralegal's mistake was in failing to conduct a complete counteranalysis. A proper counteranalysis would have led the paralegal to consider the opponent's possible challenge involving the other areas of negligence—breach of duty, proximate cause, and damages. Had this been done, the paralegal would have recognized that the opposing side could raise a proximate cause argument: The cause of the accident was the skier's breach of duty by skiing beyond the range of his ability, not the resort's failure to warn. Had the paralegal considered this argument, a response could have been prepared, and the motion might not have been granted.

This example illustrates one of the most important considerations in counteranalysis: When analyzing a legal position, always conduct thorough and complete research that considers every possible attack, no matter how remote.

B. Counteranalysis—Reliance on Legislative Act

Section 35-6-6A of the Construction Industries Licensing Act provides that contractors must be licensed. The section requires all licensed general contractors to take reasonable steps to ensure that the subcontractors they hire are licensed. The section also provides that licensed general contractors who hire unlicensed subcontractors are vicariously liable in breach-of-contract suits filed against the unlicensed subcontractors.

In the client's case, the client (Plaintiff) is acting as his own general contractor; the subcontractor (SC) is unlicensed. Tom's, Inc. (TI), a licensed general contractor, has used SC on projects in the past and has acted as an agent for SC, often helping SC obtain jobs with other general contractors. Plaintiff, a private individual building his own home, contacted TI seeking assistance in locating a subcontractor. TI arranged the contract between SC and Plaintiff. TI recommended that SC be hired and fully disclosed to Plaintiff that TI was merely an agent for SC. TI was not party to the contract. SC breached its contract with Plaintiff, and Plaintiff sued both SC and TI.

In the lawsuit, Plaintiff argues that § 35-6-6A allows a cause of action for breach of contract against a general contractor who is not a party to the contract. This cause of action exists when the general contractor is acting as an agent for an unlicensed contractor who is a party to the contract. Plaintiff also contends that § 35-6-6A imposes an implied duty on licensed general contractors to protect third parties against all unlicensed contractors, not just unlicensed subcontractors. Plaintiff reasons that the implied duty arises because the intent of the statute is to place a duty on licensed general contractors to assist in the elimination of use of unlicensed contractors on construction projects.

The counterargument is that the statute is being too broadly interpreted. The statute, by its language, applies only to subcontractors hired by general contractors. In the case at hand, TI was merely a disclosed agent. TI did not hire SC, SC was not a subcontractor of TI, and TI was not a party to the contract. Therefore, the statute does not apply.

Further counteranalysis may reveal an additional counterargument: The law of agency governs the case rather than the contractor statute. Agency law provides that disclosed agents who are not parties to a contract are not liable for breach of contract. In this case, TI fully disclosed that it was acting only as an agent for SC and, therefore, under the law of agency, it is not liable.

This example illustrates the application of two counteranalysis approaches:

■ The legal position is based on a misinterpretation of the legislative act.

■ Another legal principle governs rather than the act relied on.

C. Counteranalysis—Reliance on Court Opinion

Customer is suing Bank, claiming that Bank's debt collection calls to his place of employment constitute intentional infliction of emotional distress. The calls were placed daily for a two-week period between 11:00 a.m. and noon. The issue is whether Bank's conduct is "outrageous conduct"—an essential element of intentional infliction of emotional distress.

There are no cases in the jurisdiction addressing the question of whether contact with a debtor at the debtor's place of employment constitutes outrageous conduct. In the case of *Tyron v. Bell*, a bill collector made daily telephone calls for three weeks to a debtor's residence. In that case, the highest court in the jurisdiction ruled that daily calls to a debtor's residence do not constitute outrageous conduct as long as only one telephone call per day is made and the call is placed at a reasonable time—between 8:00 a.m. and 7:00 p.m.

Bank argues that *Bell* is analogous and on point because both cases involve daily telephone calls to a debtor, made at a reasonable time. Relying on this reasoning, Bank contends that its conduct, like the conduct in *Bell*, cannot be considered outrageous.

The counterargument is that the court opinion is clearly distinguishable and, therefore, cannot apply as precedent. Telephone calls to an individual's place of employment are much more threatening than telephone calls to the individual's residence. Telephone calls to the place of employment disrupt the individual's work, interfere with job performance, and disrupt the work of others who have to answer the calls. Such persistent work interruptions can cause the employer to fire the employee. Calls to the workplace are outrageous because they pose a threat to the individual's livelihood. No such threat exists when the calls are to a residence. Therefore, calls to the workplace are clearly distinguishable, and the court opinion is not analogous, is not on point, and does not apply as precedent.

In this example, the counteranalysis challenges reliance on a court opinion by focusing on differences in the key facts of the opinion and the case. The counterargument is based on a common sense comparison of the facts of *Bell* and the facts of the client's case. This comparison leads to the conclusion that the key facts are so different that *Bell* cannot apply as precedent. Whenever your legal position or argument is based on a court opinion, be sure to conduct a counteranalysis of the position using all the approaches presented in this chapter, as well as any other approach that comes to mind.

Summary

Counteranalysis is the process of discovering and presenting the counterarguments to a legal position or argument. It is important because to adequately address a legal problem, you must consider all aspects of the problem. This includes identifying all the potential weaknesses in a legal position and being prepared to respond to all challenges to the position.

Employ counteranalysis whenever you research a legal issue or address a legal problem. Always be alert and look for counterarguments.

A prerequisite to engaging in counteranalysis is thorough research of the question or legal argument. This may help you identify some counterarguments and give credence to or dismiss those already identified. Once the research is complete, you can choose from many approaches to assist in counteranalysis.

Because most legal arguments are based on either enacted or case law, this chapter focuses on various counterarguments that may be raised when attacking reliance on an enacted law or case law. The list of approaches presented in this chapter is by no means inclusive of all the available ways to challenge a legal argument or position. It is important to make sure that you engage in counteranalysis using *all* the avenues listed (and any other possible approaches) when looking for potential weaknesses in or counterarguments to a legal position. You can count on the opposing side to discover weaknesses in your position and use them against you. Remember, whenever you are reviewing your client's case, you are negligent if you fail to engage in counteranalysis.

Quick References

Internet Resources

As of the date of publication of this text, there are no Web sites dedicated specifically to counteranalysis. However, using a search engine and "law counteranalysis" as a topic, you may find a limited range of sites (21 sites when this text was drafted) that address some aspect of law and counteranalysis. Some sites involve counteranalysis in specific areas of the law, such as military law, whereas others discuss the topic in relation to taking law school exams. Although some sites briefly mention the role of counteranalysis in the analysis process, no site addresses the topic in depth.

When using "law counterargument" as the topic, you may find a much larger range of sites (more than 2,000 sites when this text was drafted). Most of these sites involve counterarguments in specific cases or do not discuss the role of counterargument in the legal analysis process.

Exercises

Additional assignments are available on the CourseMate.

ASSIGNMENT 1

What is counteranalysis? When should counteranalysis be conducted?

ASSIGNMENT 2

Why is counteranalysis important?

ASSIGNMENT 3

Counteranalysis—Legal Position or Argument Based on a Statute

Legislative Acts: Section 359-23A of the state statutes provides that to be eligible to run for the state senate, an individual must have been a resident of the state for three years.

Local ordinance § 2231 provides that an individual must be a resident of the municipality to run for a position on the city council. The ordinance does not define *resident* or *residency*.

Facts: Jerrie wishes to run for the city council. She has been a resident of the state for two years and nine months. The city clerk informs her that she is not eligible to run for city council because she has not been a resident of the state for three years. The clerk says that the city relies on the residency requirement established in § 359-23A.

Assignment: What is the counterargument to the clerk's position?

ASSIGNMENT 4

Counteranalysis—Legal Position or Argument Based on a Court Opinion

Case Law: In the case of *Baldonado v. State*, the plaintiff sued the state for false arrest. In *Baldonado*, a police officer received information from the dispatcher concerning a violent domestic dispute that specifically described the plaintiff and his vehicle. The dispatcher reported that the plaintiff had been drinking and was leaving the residence with his two minor children. When the officer arrived at the residence, he saw the plaintiff and the two children in the described car. At the scene, the plaintiff's spouse and neighbors corroborated the dispatcher's information that a violent dispute had taken place. When the officer requested the plaintiff to shut off the engine and stay at the scene, the plaintiff attempted to leave. The officer stopped the plaintiff from leaving. The court noted that detention by a police officer is allowable only when there is reasonable suspicion that a crime has been committed. The court concluded that there was reasonable suspicion that a crime had been committed, and that the officer's detention of the defendant was lawful.

Facts: The officer was dispatched to the plaintiff's residence to investigate a domestic dispute. When the officer arrived, he saw a red vehicle driving away from the residence. A neighbor who was standing on the sidewalk informed the officer that he thought a domestic dispute had taken place at his neighbor's house and the plaintiff had just left in the red vehicle. The officer pursued the plaintiff and required him to return to the residence. The plaintiff is suing the officer for illegally detaining him.

Assignment: The state argues that *Baldonado v. State* supports the position that the detention was proper. What is the counterargument?

ASSIGNMENT 5

List seven ways to challenge an argument based on an enacted law.

ASSIGNMENT 6

List seven ways to challenge an argument based on case law.

ASSIGNMENT 7

Counteranalysis—Legal Position or Argument Based on a Statute

Legislative Act: Section 40-3-6-9A of the state criminal code provides that a noncustodial parent may be convicted of custodial interference when the noncustodial parent "maliciously takes, detains, conceals, entices away, or fails to return the child, without good cause, for a protracted period of time."

Assume there is no case law on point in the jurisdiction relevant to the following fact situation.

Facts: Mary has primary custody of her son. The father, Tom, has legal custody for two months in the summer. Tom takes the son for two months in the summer but fails to tell Mary where the son is and does not allow her to communicate with him. Before he leaves with the son, Tom tells Mary, "I'm going to punish you for the way you've treated me."

Assignment: Mary presents the following arguments in support of her claim that Tom is in violation of the statute. What are the counterarguments to each argument?

Part A Tom's actions constitute concealment within the meaning of the statute.

Part B Same facts, but when Tom is leaving, he says, "Since you wouldn't allow me to communicate with him when you had custody, I'm going to do the same." Mary argues that Tom's actions constitute concealment.

Part C Same facts except that Tom says nothing when he picks up the son.

Part D Tom allows the son to communicate with Mary, but he returns the son one day late. Mary argues that this constitutes failing to return the child without good cause for a protracted period of time.

Part E Same facts as in part D except that Tom returns the son two weeks late.

Part F Same facts as in part E except that Tom explains that he was unable to return the son on time because his car engine blew up, and it took two weeks to fix it.

ASSIGNMENT 8

Counteranalysis—Legal Position or Argument Based on Case Law

In the following example, assume that the only court opinion on point is *United States v. Leon* (see Appendix A).

Facts: Officer Jones submits to Judge Bean a request for a search warrant for the search of Steve's apartment. Officer Jones knows that there is not sufficient probable cause for issuance of the warrant, but he also knows that Judge Bean favors law enforcement and will most likely issue the warrant anyway. Judge Bean issues the warrant. Officer Jones gives the warrant to other officers and instructs them to execute it. He does not tell them that he knows it is defective because of the lack of probable cause for its issuance. The other officers execute the warrant in the good-faith belief that it is valid. The officers find drugs, and charge Steve with possession.

Steve moves for suppression of the evidence, claiming that the search was illegal and the evidence must be excluded under the exclusionary rule. What is the counterargument to the prosecution's position in each of the following situations?

Part A The prosecution argues that because the officers executing the warrant were acting in the good-faith belief that the warrant was valid, *United States v. Leon* governs the case. The good-faith exception to the exclusionary rule applies, and therefore the evidence should not be suppressed.

Part B Same facts except that Officer Jones delivers the warrant to members of the Citizens Protection Association, a private group of citizens trained by the police to assist in the performance of minor police functions. The group volunteers its services and is not employed by the police. They execute the warrant and make a citizen's arrest of Steve. The prosecution argues that *United States v. Leon* governs, and that case holds that the exclusionary rule is designed only to protect against police misconduct, not misconduct by private citizens.

ASSIGNMENT 9

Legislative Act: Section 41-1-6-9 of the state statutes defines *defamation* as the intentional publication of a false statement about a person. The statute defines *publication* as communication to a third person.

Case Law: *Ender v. Gault* is an opinion of the highest court in the state. In the case, Gault wrote a letter to Ender accusing Ender of defrauding his clients. Gault intended to hand-deliver the letter to Ender at a party at Ender's house. Gault became intoxicated at the party and left the letter on Ender's kitchen table. The letter was in an unsealed envelope with Ender's name on it. A business competitor of Ender, who was at the party, opened and read the letter.

Ender sued Gault for defamation. In its ruling in favor of Ender, the court stated that "*intentional publication* as used in the statute includes publication that occurs as a result of the gross negligence of the defendant." The court held that Gault's act of leaving the envelope unsealed on the kitchen table during a party constituted gross negligence.

Facts: Tom is a business associate of Allen. He believes Allen is stealing from their clients. Tom writes a letter to Allen stating that he knows Allen is stealing and that he intends to file criminal charges.

Tom, intending to hand-deliver the letter to Allen, goes to a restaurant where Allen usually has lunch. After waiting an hour for Allen, one of Allen's friends enters the restaurant. Tom folds the letter and seals it with tape. He gives the letter to the friend and asks him to deliver it to Allen. He does not tell the friend not to open the letter. The friend peels back the tape, reads the letter, reseals it, and delivers it to Allen. Allen finds out that the friend read the letter and sues Tom for defamation under § 41-1-6-9.

Assignment: Take into consideration the statute, the court opinion, and the facts when doing the following.

Part A Prepare an argument in support of the position that Tom defamed Allen.

Part B Prepare a counterargument to the argument prepared in part A.

PART IV

LEGAL WRITING

OVERVIEW

The focus of Part IV is on legal writing and the legal writing process. It covers the application of the principles presented in the previous chapters to the drafting of legal research memoranda, court briefs, and legal correspondence, with chapters on the following topics:

- Fundamentals of writing

- The legal writing process in general

- Office legal memoranda (two chapters)

- Court briefs

- Correspondence

Fundamentals of Writing

Learning Objectives

After completing this chapter, you should understand:

- Sentences and paragraphs
- Word selection and usage
- Grammar and punctuation
- Formal writing conventions

Your professional reputation and job performance evaluations are determined by the quality of your work. If the job involves legal writing, your reputation as a paralegal or law clerk is primarily based upon the quality of your writing. The value of the finished product depends not only on the accuracy and thoroughness of legal research and analysis, but also on the manner of its presentation. Excellent research and analysis skills are undermined if you cannot present the results of your research and analysis clearly and free of mechanical errors. Therefore, good writing skills are equally as important as good research and analysis skills.

Writing skills are also important because a poorly written product affects more than the paralegal's or law clerk's reputation. It also affects the reputation of the law firm. A law firm's reputation is affected, either positively or negatively, when a written product is directed to an audience outside the law firm, such as the client. A writing that contains grammatical or other mechanical errors reflects poorly on the firm. The client may wonder if the errors extend to the quality of the research and question the firm's capability to handle the case. Opposing counsel may conclude that the firm is not capable of mounting an effective opposition and be less inclined to settle a case they otherwise would have settled.

The creation of a professionally written product requires knowledge of the fundamentals of writing. This chapter summarizes some of these fundamentals and highlights areas where writing errors commonly occur. In this regard, the chapter presents general information concerning sentences, paragraphs, word selection and usage, grammar, punctuation, and some formal writing conventions. The chapter does not provide a comprehensive, in-depth exploration of these topics. Sources you may refer to for additional guidance are listed at the end of the chapter.

I. SENTENCES

The **sentence** is the fundamental building block of writing. It is usually a statement that conveys an idea or ideas. Good writing skills include an understanding of the basics of proper sentence construction.

A. Sentence Structure or Pattern

A sentence is usually a statement in which the actor (the subject) performs some action or describes a state of being (the predicate).

For Example	**Subject**	**Predicate**
	John	wrecked the car.
	John	is ill.

The predicate is composed of the verb and object of the verb, such as a direct object (if necessary). An object of the verb may be required to receive the action of the verb.

For Example	**Subject**	**Predicate**
	John	wrecked the car.

The *car* is a direct object that receives the action of the verb *wrecked*.

At a minimum, a sentence must have a subject and a predicate. In its simplest form, a sentence requires a noun and a verb.

For Example	Judges rule.
	Make sure your sentences have a subject and a predicate.

B. Basic Rules in Sentence Writing

The following subsections introduce basic rules involving sentences and sentence structure. Exhibit 14-1 lists the topics covered by these rules. Keep this list in mind when drafting or reviewing sentences.

1. Subject–Verb Distance

Keep the subject and verb as close together as possible. A sentence is easier to understand if the subject and verb are close together. Intervening words, clauses, or phrases disrupt the action and make the sentence difficult to understand.

For Example	**Intervening words in italics:** John, *apparently upset and in a bad mood*, hit James.
	Revision: Apparently upset and in a bad mood, John hit James.
	Intervening clause in italics: The argument that the good faith exception applies *because the officers were acting in good faith and the warrant was defective due to magistrate error* is supported by the facts.
	Revision: The argument that the good-faith exception applies is supported by the facts. The officers were acting in good faith and the warrant was defective due to magistrate error.

Exhibit 14-1 *Topics to Keep in Mind When Drafting Sentences.*

Subject–Verb Distance	Keep the subject and verb as close together as possible.
Sentence Length	A short sentence is easy to understand and concise. A suggested average sentence length is 15 to 25 words.
Active/Passive Voice	The general rule is to draft sentences using active voice. Active voice is easier to understand and more powerful than passive voice. Active: Steve keeps the records. Passive: The records are kept by Steve.
Action Verbs	Select verbs that are active rather than verbs that show a state of being or are passive. Action: Mary keeps the books. State of being: The bookkeeper is Mary. Action: Mary concluded that Tom was guilty. Passive: The conclusion that Mary reached was that Tom was guilty.
Transitions	Use transitional words and phrases to connect sentences and to establish the relationship between the subjects of sentences.

© Cengage Learning 2014

2. Sentence Length

Although there is no hard-and-fast rule governing sentence length, shorter sentences are easier to understand. The length of a sentence will vary according to the nature of the information it must convey. A good average for sentence length is 15 to 25 words. If you find that your sentences are too long, eliminate extra words or break the sentence into shorter sentences.

> **For Example** **Sentence too long:** The evidence should be suppressed because the warrant did not authorize unannounced entry, and there were no exigent circumstances at the scene that provided justification for the officers' actions of entering the residence unannounced.
>
> **Revision:** The evidence should be suppressed because the warrant did not authorize unannounced entry. In addition, the circumstances at the scene did not provide justification for unannounced entry.

Watch out for run-on sentences. Each sentence should contain one main idea. It is often tempting to pack more than one idea into a sentence. This usually occurs when the ideas being conveyed are related. If the sentence you are reviewing is very long, it may be that it is a run-on sentence, and you are attempting to convey too many ideas in one sentence.

> **For Example** **Run-on sentence:** Thomas does not dispute the fact that the court properly resorted to estimating a plant quantity for the 1991 grow, his dispute concerns the basis for the court's estimation.
>
> Note that this sentence conveys two related ideas: what he does not dispute and what he does dispute. Each idea should be presented in separate sentences.
>
> **Revision:** Thomas does not dispute the fact that the court properly resorted to estimating a plant quantity for the 1991 grow. His dispute concerns the basis for the court's estimation.

3. Active and Passive Voice

a. Active Voice

The general rule is that you should draft sentences using **active voice**. When you adopt active voice, the subject of the sentence becomes the actor. When you use passive voice, the subject of the sentence is acted upon.

For Example	**Active voice:**	The automobile hit the child.
		The construction workers built the dam.
Passive voice:	The child was hit by the automobile.	
	The dam was built by the construction workers.	

Active voice is easier to understand and is more powerful. It is easier to understand because the doer of the action is mentioned at the beginning of the sentence prior to the action. Readers do not have to read the entire sentence before they are informed who is performing the action. Active voice is more powerful because, at the outset, it identifies the actor as the performer of the action. This focuses attention on the actor and emphasizes the actor's actions. When passive voice is used, the actor is removed from the action or not identified at all.

> **For Example** **Active voice:** The defendant breached the contract when he failed to deliver the goods on time.
>
> **Passive voice:** The contract was breached when the goods were not delivered on time. (The actor is not identified.)

b. Passive Voice

In certain situations it is appropriate to use **passive voice.** You may use passive voice when the actor is unknown or unimportant or when you do not want to emphasize the actor's conduct. See Chapter 18 for a discussion of the appropriate use of passive voice in court briefs.

> **For Example** **Actor unknown:** A portion of the transcript was lost.
>
> **Actor unimportant:** The bank deposit was found by a passerby.
>
> **Actor deemphasized:** The vase was broken and the plaintiff injured when the vase slipped from the defendant's hand.

4. Action Verbs

When possible, select **action (active) verbs** rather than passive verbs that show a state of being.

> **For Example** **Passive:** Mary reached the conclusion that Tom was guilty.
>
> **Revision:** Mary concluded that Tom was guilty.
>
> **State of being:** The record keeper is Steve Jones.
>
> **Revision:** Steve Jones keeps the records.

5. Transitions

Transitional words and phrases connect sentences and establish the relationship between the subjects of the sentences. **Transitions** are important because they guide the reader and make the writing cohesive.

For Example	**No transition:** The statute requires that fences exceeding 5 feet in height must be located no closer than 10 feet from the property line. Your fence will be 6 feet high; you must build it at least 10 feet from the property line.

With transition—transition in italics: The statute requires that fences exceeding 5 feet in height must be located no closer than 10 feet from the property line. *Therefore, because your fence will exceed 5 feet,* you must locate it at least 10 feet from the property line.

· The following are examples of transitional words and phrases: ·

however	even so	but	still
furthermore	nevertheless	so	and
although	simply put	for	on the other hand
conversely	moreover	that is	in other words
contrary to	above all	clearly	more importantly
initially	meanwhile	finally	all the same
specifically	therefore	thus	consequently
arguably	in contrast	instead	to illustrate
likewise	allegedly	unlike	subsequently
undoubtedly	in addition	likewise	in conclusion
in summary	nonetheless	since	without question

II. PARAGRAPHS

A **paragraph** is a group of sentences that address the same topic. Paragraphs are important because they organize the writing according to topic. They make it easier for the reader to understand the material by separating it into manageable units. A reader may encounter difficulty understanding the subject matter when it is not divided into paragraphs. Start a new paragraph when addressing a new idea or topic. Use transitional phrases or sentences to link new paragraphs.

A paragraph usually consists of the following elements:

- A topic sentence
- The body
- A closing sentence

Every paragraph does not require each of these elements. A short paragraph, for example, may not have a closing sentence. The following subsections discuss the elements of a paragraph and other considerations to keep in mind when writing paragraphs (see Exhibit 14-2).

Exhibit 14-2 *Topics to Keep in Mind When Drafting Paragraphs.*

Topic Sentence	Use a topic sentence to introduce the subject and provide the focus of the paragraph.
Body	The body of the paragraph should support or develop the subject introduced by the topic sentence. Generally, a paragraph should address a single idea or topic rather than several different topics.
Closing Sentence	End with a closing sentence that summarizes or applies the topic addressed in the paragraph.
Transition Sentence	Include transitional words, phrases, or sentences to connect the subjects discussed in the different paragraphs.

A. Topic Sentence of a Paragraph

The **topic sentence** identifies the subject of the paragraph. It introduces the subject and provides the focus of the paragraph for the reader. The topic sentence is usually placed at the beginning of the paragraph.

> **For Example** ◾ Topic sentence of a paragraph that discusses why the exclusionary rule is necessary: "The Supreme Court has identified several reasons why the exclusionary rule is necessary."
>
> ◾ Topic sentence of a paragraph that discusses Mr. Smith's actions: "Mr. Smith's actions do not constitute a breach of contract."
>
> ◾ Topic sentence of a paragraph that addresses required conditions: "A warranty of fitness for a particular purpose is created when the following conditions are present."

B. Paragraph Body

The body of a paragraph consists of sentences that support or develop the subject introduced by the topic sentence. The sentence(s) should develop the subject clearly and logically.

> **For Example** The topic sentence in this example is printed in italics to separate it from the body:
>
> *To support a negligence claim against Mrs. Jones, four elements must be proven.* First, we must establish that she had a duty to keep the tree on her property trimmed. Next, we must show that she failed to properly trim the tree. Then it is necessary to prove that, as a result of her failure to trim the tree, a branch fell and struck Mr. Thompson. Finally, we must establish that Mr. Thompson's injuries resulted from the branch striking him.

Notice in this example that the sentences in the body are presented clearly and in logical order. Remember, when preparing the body of a paragraph, the goal is to draft it clearly, concisely, and logically.

C. Closing Sentence of a Paragraph

A paragraph should end with a **closing sentence**. The content of the sentence varies according to the subject matter covered in the paragraph. It should summarize the topic addressed in the body or apply the subject discussed to the facts of the case.

> **For Example** **Summary:** Therefore, to establish a claim for negligence, we must show that Mrs. Jones had a duty, the duty was breached, the breach caused the accident, and the accident caused the harm that resulted.
>
> **Application of subject to the facts of the case:** The rule of law adopted in the *Craig* case clearly applies in this case because Mr. Smith failed to warn Mr. Jones that the brakes were defective.

D. Transition Sentences

Transition sentences (or words, phrases) connect the subjects discussed in different paragraphs. They guide the reader by linking the paragraphs, thereby providing coherence to the overall writing. The topic or closing sentence of a paragraph may include the transitional language. Transitional words, phrases, and sentences are usually placed at either the beginning or the end of the paragraph.

For Example | *Transitions at the Beginning of a Paragraph:*

The following transitional language is in italics:

- If the *above mentioned* requirements are not met, breach of contract may not be claimed.
- There are, *however*, exceptions to this rule.
- *In addition* to a cause of action for negligence, Mr. Smith may allege ... (Note: Use when the body of the paragraph addresses the other possible causes of action, and the previous paragraph discusses the negligence cause of action.)
- The *second* element of the statute requires ... (Note: Use when separate paragraphs discuss separate elements.)

Transitions at the End of the Paragraph:

The following transitional language is in italics:

- The statute, *however*, does not define "publication"; therefore, case law must be consulted. (Note: Use when the next paragraph introduces the case law.)
- *In addition* to this case, other cases also discuss the requirements of the statute. (Note: Use when the following paragraph discusses the other cases.)

E. Paragraph Length

As with sentences, there is no rule that establishes a standard length for paragraphs. Paragraphs usually are three to six sentences in length. Most paragraph topics can be covered comfortably in six to seven sentences, although a paragraph may be as short as one sentence or as long as ten. Determine the length by keeping in mind the goal of clearly and completely covering the topic of the paragraph. The reader may have difficulty understanding or become confused by extremely long paragraphs. A series of extremely short paragraphs may lack transition and distract the reader. Therefore, extremely long and short paragraphs should be the exception in legal writing. The following are examples of short paragraphs.

For Example | **One-sentence paragraph:** The second element of the/rule requires that the witness be present at the signing.

Two-sentence paragraph: Section 2(b) of the statute addresses the requirement of the number and presence of witnesses. It requires that there be a minimum of two witnesses and both must be present at the signing.

Notice that the preceding examples lack transition language or sentences that connect the paragraphs to the paragraphs that follow.

III. WORD SELECTION AND USAGE

Not only is it necessary to be skilled in sentence and paragraph construction, you must also be skilled in selecting and using words. This section presents some guidelines on word selection and usage.

A. Excessive or Redundant Words

Avoid the use of excessive or redundant words. Check each sentence for words that can be eliminated. Simplify the finished product.

> **For Example**   **Excessive words:** The statute provides individuals protection against the use of evidence obtained by warrantless wiretaps.
>
> **Revision:** The statute prohibits the use of evidence obtained by warrantless wiretaps.
>
> **Redundant words:** The sole and exclusive remedy provided by the statute is criminal prosecution.
>
> **Revision:** The exclusive remedy provided by the statute is criminal prosecution. OR
>
> **Revision:** The statute establishes criminal prosecution as the exclusive remedy.

The following lists commonly used redundant pairs. Any one of the terms can be used; the use of both terms is not required or appropriate.

full/complete	merged/together	cease/desist
each/every	join/together	null/void
true/correct	due/owing	exact/same
end/result	alter/change	descend/down
and/moreover	sole/exclusive	specific/example

Other unnecessary words occur in phrases such as "few in number," "green in color," "continue on," and "five a.m. in the morning." If omission of a word does not change the intended meaning of the sentence, leave it out.

B. Noun–Verb Strings

A **noun–verb string** is a group of related words used to convey information. It is a form of redundancy that should be avoided when a single descriptive word will accomplish the same end.

> **For Example**   *Noun–Verb Strings:*
>
> The distributor is not responsible for failures to perform due to *riots, floods, earthquakes, and acts of God.*
>
> A stockholder may not *grant, give, sell, or assign* her interest in the stock without the consent of the other shareholders.
>
> *Revisions:*
>
> The distributor is not responsible for failure to perform caused by events beyond the distributor's control.
>
> A stockholder may not transfer her interest in the stock without the consent of the other shareholders.

C. Nominalizations

A **nominalization** is a noun created from a verb.

For Example	Verb	Noun
	determine	determination
	realize	realization
	possess	possession
	important	importance

Nominalizations weaken a sentence by taking the action away from the actor. They make the sentence passive and less forceful.

For Example *Nominalizations:*

> He came to the realization that the assignment required more work.
> The importance of the opinion is that. . . .

Revisions:

> He realized that the assignment required more work.
> The opinion is important because. . . .

D. Legalese

Legalese, as used here, refers to terms of art used in the legal profession that are not generally known outside the profession. The goal of legal writing is to effectively communicate information. Writing in plain English usually accomplishes this goal, and plain English should be used when possible.

The audience governs the extent to which you incorporate legal terminology in legal writing. Legal terms are appropriate when communicating with others in the field. If the reader is trained in the law, the use of legal terms or phrases, such as *res ipsa loquitur*, is much easier than providing a definition or explanation. When the recipient is a nonlawyer, however, you should avoid using legal terms. Be sure to define legal terms when communicating with nonlawyers if the meaning of the term is not obvious.

For Example **Legalese in italics:** The constitution requires *probable cause* before the police can conduct a search of your residence.

Revision: The constitution requires the police to have a valid reason before they can search a house. An example of a valid reason would be if reliable persons informed the police that they saw illegal drugs in the house.

E. Archaic Terms

Archaic terms are words or phrases frequently used in the past that are being phased out of legal writing. Do not include such terms in your writing. Such terms include *saith, party of the first part, aforesaid, hereinbefore, hereinafter, henceforth,* and *the said party.*

> **For Example** **Archaic and excess verbiage in italics:** Upon the signing of the Agreement, *the party of the first part* will *hereinafter cease and desist* from attending hearings where *the party of the second part* acts as chairperson.
>
> **Revision:** Upon the signing of the Agreement, Mr. Smith will *not* attend hearings where Ms. Carson acts as chairperson. (Assume that names, Mr. Smith and Ms. Carson, are mentioned earlier in the agreement. Rather than use the phrase *party of the first part* and *party of the second part*, simply repeat the names of the parties or use a pronoun such as *he* or *she* when it is clear which party is being referenced.)

F. Sexist Language

In any form of writing, using gender-specific language is prejudicial and inappropriate unless it refers to a specific person whose gender is known. **Sexist language** has no place in legal writing. The following guidelines will help ensure gender-neutral writing.

1. Words

Change gender-specific terms to gender-neutral terms.

> **For Example**
>
> | Gender-Specific | Gender-Neutral |
> | --- | --- |
> | chairman | chairperson |
> | wife/husband | spouse |
> | draftsman | drafter |
> | forefathers | forebearers |
> | housewife | homemaker |
> | mankind | people, human beings, humanity |
> | workman | worker |
> | anchorman | anchor |
> | congressman | congressperson, representative |

2. Restructuring Sentences with *He* and *She*

You can use *he or she* in place of *he* to render a sentence gender-neutral. The result, however, may be awkward.

> **For Example** The rule requires the plaintiff to file his or her response within 15 days.

You may adopt several alternatives to avoid the use of *his or her*, *he/she*, and so forth.

a. Restate the sentence so the antecedent is plural.

> **For Example** The rule requires the plaintiff to file his pleadings. . . .
>
> **Revision:** The rule requires plaintiffs to file their pleadings. . . .

b. Eliminate use of the pronoun; substitute the definite article.

> **For Example** The officer is responsible for the actions of his troops.
>
> **Revision:** The officer is responsible for the actions of the troops.

c. Repeat the name.

> **For Example** Before the client may liquidate the assets of the company, he must. . . .
>
> **Revision:** Before the client may liquidate the assets of the company, the client must. . . .

d. Use *one*, *you*, or *your* when possible.

> **For Example** Everyone has a right to his personal preferences.
>
> **Revisions:** Everyone has a right to personal preferences. You have a right to your personal preferences.

e. Rephrase the sentence.

> **For Example** A legal assistant should not communicate with the litigants he knows we do not represent.
>
> **Revision:** A legal assistant should not communicate with litigants we do not represent.

3. Appropriate Reference to Gender

Reference to gender is appropriate only when you intend to refer to a specific sex.

> **For Example** Each member of the women's basketball team had her name printed on the back of her uniform.

G. Specific Words—Problem Areas

Some words are commonly misused. You can avoid problems of misuse by following some basic rules.

1. Affect/Effect

Affect is a verb meaning "to influence." *Effect* is either a verb or noun. As a verb, it means "to bring about or cause"; as a noun, it means "result."

> **For Example** "His actions will not *affect* [not *effect*] the outcome of the case." The meaning of *affect* is "to influence."
>
> "He tried to *effect* [not *affect*] an agreement." Here, the meaning of *effect* is "to bring about."
>
> "The test did not bring about the desired *effect* [not *affect*]." The meaning of *effect* (used as a noun) is "result."

2. Among/Between

Use *among* when referring to three or more things, *between* when referring to two.

> **For Example** The jury award was divided *among* the six plaintiffs.
>
> The jury award was divided between Tom and Grace.

3. And/Or

When the word *and* is used in regard to a list of words, all the items listed are included and required.

> **For Example** "The case law requires the plaintiff to prove duty, breach of duty, proximate cause, *and* damages." The use of *and* means that all four elements must be proved. All the listed items are included in the requirement.

When *or* is used, all the items listed are not required to be included. Any one or all of the items are included.

> **For Example** "The case law requires the corporate president to provide notice orally, by mail, *or* by facsimile." All the listed items are not required. Only one of the items is required. The president has the choice of giving notice by one or all of the means listed.

The use of *and/or* creates an ambiguity and is not proper.

> **For Example** "The statute requires that the notice be given orally, by mail, *and/or* by facsimile." What does the statute require? Are all the listed items required? If so, *and* should be used. If only one of the items is required, *or* should be used.

4. Council/Counsel

A *council* is a deliberative or administrative body. A *councilor* is a member of such a body. *Counsel,* when used as a verb, means to give advice or guidance. *Counsel,* when used as a noun, is advice. A *counselor* (*counsel*) is a person, such as a lawyer, who gives advice or guidance.

> **For Example** She presented the resolution to the city council.
> The city councilor received the petition.
> The school guidance officer provided counsel to the new student.
> The counselor informed the shareholders of their legal rights.

5. Each Other/One Another

When referring to two nouns, use *each other*. When referring to more than two nouns, use *one another*.

> **For Example** Bob and Mary supported each other during the trial.
> The members of the team supported one another during the tournament.

6. Good/Well

Good is an adjective (adjectives modify nouns and pronouns). It cannot be used as an adverb (adverbs modify verbs, adjectives, and adverbs). *Well* can act as an adverb or an adjective.

> **For Example** **Incorrect:** "She worked good."
>
> **Correct:** "She worked well." *Well* is an adverb that modifies the verb *worked*. The use of *good* is inappropriate, because *good* is an adjective and should not be used to modify a verb.
>
> **Correct:** "She did good work." In this sentence, *good* is used as an adjective modifying the noun *work*.

7. Lie/Lay

Lie is an intransitive verb that means "to rest or recline." (An *intransitive verb* is a verb that does not take a direct object.) Its forms are *lie, lay, lain, lying*.

> **For Example** I think I will *lie* [not *lay*] down.
>
> He was so tired he *lay* [not *laid*] down.
>
> She has been *lying* [not *laying*] around all day.

Lay is a transitive verb that means "to put or place." (A *transitive verb* takes a direct object.) Its forms are *lay, laid, laid,* and *laying*.

> **For Example** I think I will *lay* [not *lie*] the paper down.
>
> He *laid* [not *lay*] the paper down.
>
> He has been *laying* [not *lying*] brick all day.

8. Like/As

Like should be used as a preposition; it should be followed by a noun or noun phrase. *As* may act as a conjunction or a preposition in a sentence.

> **For Example** "In this contract he used the same technique as [not like] he did in the other agreement." The use of *like* would not be appropriate because here *as* functions as a conjunction, not a preposition.
>
> "The legal assistant, *like* all the other participants, was on time." This use of *like* is appropriate because *like* functions as a preposition in the sentence.

9. Shall and May

The word *shall* is used to impose a duty that is mandatory. The performance of the duty is not optional.

> **For Example** "Mr. Smith *shall* terminate all contact with Mrs. Black." The duty to terminate all communication is mandatory. Mr. Smith has no option.

The word *may* indicates that the performance of an act is not mandatory. The performance of the act is optional.

> **For Example** "Mr. Smith *may* terminate all communication with Mr. Black." The act of terminating all communication is optional for Mr. Smith. He has a choice as to whether to terminate communication.

10. That/Which

Use *that* to introduce restrictive clauses and *which* to introduce nonrestrictive clauses. A *restrictive clause* is necessary to the meaning of the sentence.

> **For Example** "You must perform all the steps *that are listed in the statute.*" The italicized clause is a restrictive clause. It informs the reader that the required steps are the steps listed in the statute. It is necessary to an understanding of the steps that must be taken.

A *nonrestrictive clause* is not necessary to the meaning of the sentence. It can be set off from the rest of the sentence with commas without changing the meaning of the sentence.

> **For Example** "I always buy his products, which *usually are of high quality.*" The italicized clause is a nonrestrictive clause. It is not necessary to the main meaning of the sentence.

IV. GRAMMAR

The rules of **grammar** govern the construction of sentences. This section introduces basic rules of grammar to keep in mind when performing a writing assignment.

A. Subject–Verb Agreement

The subject and verb should agree in person and number. This means that singular subjects require singular verbs and plural subjects require plural verbs.

> **For Example** **Incorrect:** The decision in the case *require* the defendant to give notice to the plaintiff. (This sentence has a singular subject, *decision*, and a plural verb, *require*.)
>
> **Correct:** The decision in the case *requires* the defendant to give notice to the plaintiff. (The singular subject *decision* agrees with the singular verb *requires*.)

The following basic rules concern **subject–verb agreement:**

1. Two or more subjects joined by *and* usually require a plural verb.

> **For Example** Mary and Joan *were* present.
>
> The president, secretary, and treasurer *are* going to the conference.

2. Two or more subjects joined by *or* or *nor* require a verb that agrees with the subject closest to the verb.

> **For Example** Tom or his brothers *are* going to attend.
>
> Either the brothers or Tom *is* the responsible party.
>
> Neither Tom nor his brother *is* going to attend.
>
> To accept the contract or to draft a new one *is* your option.

3. Most indefinite pronouns require singular verbs. Indefinite pronouns are pronouns that do not refer to a specific person or thing, such as *anyone, everybody, nobody, someone, each,* and *something.*

> **For Example** Everybody *is* responsible.
>
> Each of the members has a specific task.

4. Some indefinite pronouns require a verb that matches the noun to which they refer. Some of these pronouns are *all, none, most, some,* and *any.*

> **For Example** All of the property *is* distributed.
>
> All of the items *are* missing.

5. Plural indefinite pronouns such as *both, few, many, several,* and *others* require a plural verb.

> **For Example** Few *are* selected.
>
> Although there were multiple presentations, several *were* not in attendance.
>
> The others *are* not required to be present.

6. Collective nouns usually require a singular verb. A *collective noun* is a noun that refers to a group (e.g., *jury, family, crowd, majority*).

> **For Example** The jury *was* deadlocked.
>
> The family *is* present.

7. Nouns that are plural in form but have a singular meaning require a singular verb (e.g., *politics, news, mathematics*).

> **For Example** The news *is* bad.
>
> The politics of the party *is* corrupt.
>
> Mathematics is her strength.

8. The title of a work takes a singular verb.

> **For Example** Military tactics *is* wonderful reading.

9. A relative pronoun requires a verb that agrees with its antecedent. A *relative pronoun* is one that refers to another noun in the sentence (e.g., *which, who,* and *that*). The *antecedent* is the noun to which the relative pronoun refers. If the antecedent is singular, the verb should be singular. If the antecedent is plural, the verb should be plural.

> **For Example** Our *client* is one of the persons *who* has been indicted in the case. (*Who* is the relative pronoun, and *client* is the antecedent.)

> **For Example** **Singular:** Our *client, who* was present at the scene, *has* been indicted.
> The antecedent (*client*) of the relative pronoun (*who*) is singular; therefore, *who* takes a singular verb (*has*).
>
> **Plural:** The *clients, who* were present at the scene, *have* been indicted.
> The antecedent (*clients*) of the relative pronoun (*who*) is plural; therefore, *who* takes a plural verb (*have*).

B. Verb Tense

Verb tense is the time in which a verb's action occurs. Events happening in the present use the present tense, events that occurred in the past use the past tense, and events that will take place in the future use the future tense. Usually, sentences and paragraphs are written in the same tense. Check to ensure that your writing does not have inappropriate changes in verb tense.

> **For Example** **Inappropriate change in verb tense:** The complaint *was* filed on
> January 1, 2003. The defendants *move* to dismiss the complaint. The motion *was* denied. (Notice that the verb tense in this sentence moves from past, to present, then back to past tense.)
>
> **Revision:** The complaint *was* filed on January 1, 2003. The defendants *moved* to dismiss the complaint. The motion *was* denied. (Notice that all the verbs are in past tense.)

Guidelines concerning correct verb tense follow:

1. When presenting your position or legal analysis, use present tense.

   > **For Example** Plaintiff contends that the rule requires 30 days' notice.

2. When addressing a court opinion that has already been decided, use past tense.

   > **For Example** In *Smith v. Jones*, the court held that the rule does not require 30 days' notice.

3. When discussing a law or rule still in effect, use present tense.

   > **For Example** The provisions of § 44-556 require a contractor to give 30 days' notice.

C. Parallel Construction

Parallel construction means that items in a list are similar in grammatical structure. The rule requires that in sentences including a list, a group of activities, and so on, each of the items must use the same grammatical form; that is, all the items or members of the group should agree in verb tense, number, and so on.

| For Example | **Lack parallel construction:** |

- The defendant is a trained officer with 15 years' experience who has won several service medals.

- The goals of the association are the following:
  a. educating the public about crime,
  b. to provide support for the police, and
  c. improvement of local neighborhood watch groups.

- Most states have passed uniform laws for corporations, partnerships, and that allow limited liability companies.

- The client gave consideration not only *to the* exclusion term but also *the* waiver clause.

Revisions with parallel construction:

- The defendant is a trained officer *who* has 15 years' experience and *who* has won several service medals.

- The goals of the association are the following:
  a. *to educate* the public about crime,
  b. *to provide* support for the police, and
  c. *to improve* local neighborhood watch groups.

- Most states have passed uniform laws for corporations, partnerships, and limited liability companies.

- The client gave consideration not only *to the* exclusion term but also *to the* waiver clause.

D. Superfluous Verbs

Avoid the use of verb constructions that are unnecessarily wordy.

| For Example | **Superfluous verbs in italics:** |

- He decided to *perform an investigation* into the matter.
- The arbitrator *decided to give consideration* to the argument.
- The judge *reached a decision* on the question.
- The contractor *made an attempt* to complete the contract on time.

Revisions without superfluous verbs:

- He decided to investigate the matter.
- The arbitrator considered the argument.
- The judge decided the question.
- The contractor attempted to complete the contract on time.

E. Modifiers and Infinitives

Modifiers are words or phrases that describe the subject, verb, or object in a sentence. Exhibit 14-3 presents the four types of common problems involving modifiers.

Exhibit 14-3 *Problem Modifiers.*

Misplaced Modifiers	Words or phrases that are placed in the wrong location in a sentence and may create ambiguity or cause a loss of clarity. "If we contend that the contract applies, it will be attacked by the defense." (What will be attacked, our contention or the contract?)
Dangling Modifiers	Modifiers that do not modify any other part of the sentence. "*To determine whether the contract was breached*, the provisions of the statute must be referred to." (The italicized modifier does not refer to or modify any part of the sentence.)
Squinting Modifiers	A modifier located in a position in the sentence that makes it unclear whether it modifies the word that precedes it or the word that follows it. "The report that was prepared routinely indicates that the structure was unsafe." (Was the report prepared routinely, or did the report routinely indicate the structure was unsafe?)
Split Infinitives	An adverb is placed in an infinitive after *to* and before the verb. "Stephanie began to rapidly climb." (The adverb *rapidly* is placed between the infinitive *to* and the verb *climb*.) Correct: "Stephanie began to climb rapidly."

© Cengage Learning 2014

1. Misplaced Modifiers

A *misplaced modifier* is a word or phrase that is placed in the wrong location in a sentence. Because of its placement, it appears to modify one word or phrase when it is intended to modify another. You may create an ambiguity or cause a loss of clarity by misplacing a modifier. The solution is to rephrase the sentence or to move the modifier to ensure clarity. Usually this means placing the modifier before or after the word or phrase it modifies.

For Example **Misplaced modifiers:**

- If we contend that the contract applies, it will be attacked by the defense. (What will be attacked, our contention or the contract?)
- Present the client's counterargument only in the third section of the brief. (Does this mean the counterargument should be presented in the third section and no other section, or does it mean that the third section should consist only of the counterargument?)

Revision—sentence rephrased:

- If we contend that the contract applies, the defense will attack the contention.

Revision—modifier moved:

- In the third section of the brief, present only the client's counterargument.

2. Dangling Modifiers

Modifiers that do not modify any other part of the sentence are *dangling modifiers*.

> **For Example** **Dangling modifier in italics:** *To determine whether the contract was breached*, the provisions of the statute must be referred to.

The italicized modifier does not refer to or modify any part of the sentence. It refers to a contract mentioned in another sentence. The problem may be corrected by rewriting the sentence to make sure modifiers refer to a noun or nouns in the sentence.

> **For Example** **Dangling modifier eliminated:** To determine whether the terms of the contract violate the statute, the statutory provisions must be referred to.

3. Squinting Modifiers

A *squinting modifier* is a modifier located in a position in the sentence that makes it unclear whether it modifies the word that precedes it or the word that follows it. Eliminate squinting modifiers when you edit your writing.

> **For Example** **Squinting modifier in italics:** The report that was prepared *routinely* indicated that the structure was unsafe. (Was the report prepared routinely, or did the report routinely indicate the structure was unsafe?)
> **Revision:** The report that was routinely prepared indicated that the structure was unsafe.

Limiting modifiers such as *only, even, almost, nearly,* and *just* are often misplaced. These modifiers should be placed in front of the word they modify.

> **For Example** **Incorrect:** The lawyer only prepared the document.
> As the sentence reads, the lawyer prepared the document and nothing else. If the sentence is intended to mean that the lawyer and no one else prepared the document, *only* is misplaced.
> **Correction:** Only the lawyer prepared the document.

4. Split Infinitives

An *infinitive* is a verb form that functions as a noun or as an auxiliary verb, such as *to argue, to understand,* and *to consider.* The general rule is that infinitives should not be split; that is, an adverb should not be placed after the *to* and before the verb.

> **For Example** **Split infinitives:** In each of the following examples, the infinitive is split: "to completely understand," "to rapidly climb," "to thoroughly test." An adverb is placed between the *to* and the verb.
> **Revisions:** "to understand completely," "to climb rapidly," "to test thoroughly."

This general rule is not invariable; technically, split infinitives are not wrong even though they are not preferred. Sometimes an infinitive may be split to emphasize the modification of the verb (e.g., "to better understand") or to avoid an awkward placement of the modifier far from the verb it is modifying (e.g., "to best convey one's actual meaning" rather than "to convey one's actual meaning best").

F. Noun–Pronoun Agreement

Pronouns must agree in number (singular/plural) and gender (feminine/masculine/neuter) with the nouns to which they refer—their antecedents. Pronouns include *I, me, mine, my, we, us, our, you, yours, your, he, him, his, she, her, hers, it, its, they, them, their,* and *theirs*.

There are several guidelines to follow to ensure noun–pronoun agreement.

1. Pronouns must agree with their antecedents (the noun to which the pronoun refers).

> **For Example** The *workers* put on *their* helmets when *they* entered the building.
>
> The pronouns *their* and *they* agree in number (plural) with the antecedent *workers* (plural).
>
> *Mary* was required to wear *her* helmet.
>
> The pronoun *her* agrees in number and gender with the antecedent *Mary*.

2. Pronouns that do not refer to a definite person or thing are *indefinite pronouns*. Some examples of indefinite pronouns are *all, anyone, anybody, each, everyone, someone, somebody, everything, something,* and *none*. Indefinite pronouns are usually singular.

> **For Example** Everyone has the freedom to select *his* or *her* candidate.

3. Antecedents joined by *and* require a plural pronoun.

> **For Example** Tom and Mary are separating *their* property.
>
> Tom, Jon, and Mary are going *their* separate ways.

4. Antecedents joined by *or* or *nor* require a pronoun that agrees in number and gender with the antecedent closest to the pronoun.

> **For Example** Mary or the other defendants must conduct *their* investigation.
>
> The defendants or Mary must conduct *her* investigation.

When a construction appears awkward, as the second sentence does, consider rephrasing the sentence.

> **For Example** Mary or the defendants must conduct an investigation.

5. The number of a pronoun that refers to a collective noun is determined by the function of the collective noun. A *collective noun* is a noun that refers to a group. If the collective noun functions as a unit, the pronoun is singular.

> **For Example** The *committee*, after reviewing the matter, presented *its* conclusion. (In this sentence, the collective noun, *committee*, functions as a unit; the review is the act of the committee as a whole and therefore the pronoun *its* is singular.)

If the collective noun does not function as a unit, that is, the members of the collective noun are acting separately and not as a unit, then a plural pronoun is required.

> **For Example** The team have stated *their* various positions on the question of whether *they* should wear the new helmets. (In this example, the collective noun, *team*, does not function as a unit. The reference is to the team as individual members; therefore, the sentence takes the plural pronoun *they*.)

G. Adverbs, Adjectives, and Conjunctions

An *adjective* is a word used to modify a noun or pronoun.

> **For Example** She wore a *red* dress to the party.
> The *race* car had *vinyl* seats.

An *adverb* is a word used to modify a verb, adjective, or another adverb.

> **For Example** John ran *quickly* into the house.

A *conjunction* is a word that connects words, phrases, clauses, or sentences.

> **For Example** We can select the first clause *or* the entire second paragraph.
> All of the participants had heard of the agreement, *but* none had seen it.

1. Forming Adverbs and Improper Use of Adjectives

Many, but not all, adverbs are formed by adding *-ly* to a word. A common problem occurs when an adjective is used incorrectly to modify a verb.

> **For Example** **Incorrect:** The plant supervisor must see that the factory machinery runs *efficient*.
>
> **Correct:** The plant supervisor must see that the factory machinery runs *efficiently*.
>
> **Incorrect:** John behaves *conservative* around his parents.
>
> **Correct:** "John behaves *conservatively* around his parents." In this sentence, *conservatively* is an adverb; it modifies the verb *behaves*.
>
> "John's *conservative* behavior pleases his parents." In this sentence, *conservative* is an adjective; it modifies the noun *behavior*.

2. Adjectives, Adverbs, and Linking Verbs

In some situations it is difficult to determine if the correct word to use is an adjective or an adverb. This often occurs with words that follow linking verbs, such as *feel, look, believe, become, grow, smell, taste,* and *appear*. The linking verb does not show physical or emotional action; rather, it suggest a state of being. Use an adjective if the word following the verb describes the subject of the sentence; use an adverb if the word refers to the verb.

> **For Example** "The inspector felt *careful*." The adjective *careful* is used because it describes the inspector (the subject).
>
> "The inspector felt *carefully* when he searched the table." The adverb *carefully* is used because it modifies the verb *felt* and thus shows action (that is, how the inspector searched the table).
>
> "John looked *sad*." *Looked* describes John. *Looked* is a linking verb because it does not show action. The adjective *sad* is used because it modifies the noun *John*.
>
> "John looked *quickly* around the room." In this sentence, the verb *looked* shows action and is therefore not a linking verb. The adverb *quickly* is used because it modifies (describes) the verb *looked*.

3. Comparatives and Superlatives

Use a comparative to indicate a comparison between two things (e.g., *better, older, easier, faster, worse*). Use a superlative to indicate a comparison of three or more things (e.g., *best, oldest, easiest, fastest, worst*).

> **For Example** **Incorrect:** He is the *best* of the two applicants.
>
> Mary is the *fastest* of the two runners.
>
> **Correct:** He is the *better* of the two applicants.
>
> Mary is the *faster* of the two runners.
>
> The comparatives *better* and *faster* are used because two things are being compared.
>
> **Incorrect:** He is the *better* of the three applicants.
>
> Mary is the *faster* of all the runners.
>
> **Correct:** He is the *best* of the three applicants.
>
> Mary is the *fastest* of all the runners.
>
> The comparatives *best* and *fastest* are used because more than two things are being compared.

To form the comparative and superlative of most one- and two-syllable adjectives, add -er or -est: *big, bigger, biggest; old, older, oldest; funny, funnier; funniest.*

For some two-syllable adjectives and long adjectives, form the comparative by using *more* and the superlative by using *most*: *more outrageous, most outrageous; more entertaining, most entertaining.*

To form the comparative and superlative of some one-syllable adverbs, use -er and -est: *faster, fastest; sooner, soonest.* To form the comparative and superlative of longer adverbs and those ending in -ly, use *more/less* for the comparative and *most/least* for the superlative: *more acutely, most acutely; more likely, most likely.*

Comparatives are not used with concepts that are absolute, such as *perfect, unique, empty, impossible,* and *excellent.*

> **For Example** **Incorrect:** It was a most perfect story.
>
> **Correct:** It was a perfect story.
>
> **Incorrect:** His viewpoint was very unique.
>
> **Correct:** His viewpoint was unique.

4. Adverbs Used for Emphasis

Place adverbs used for emphasis immediately before the word or phrase they modify. Some examples of words of emphasis are *only, so, very,* and *quite.*

> **For Example** John intended only to influence the outcome of the meeting." *Only* modifies the phrase that follows: "to influence the outcome of the meeting."

5. Coordinating Conjunctions

Use a coordinating conjunction when joining clauses and words of equal rank. Some coordinating conjunctions are *and, or, but, for, so, yet, nor.*

> **For Example** We have three selections available: section a, section b, *or* section c." *Or* joins equal words.
>
> "The landlord had the option to seek restitution, *but* he did not choose this option." *But* joins equal clauses.

6. Correlative Conjunctions

Correlative conjunctions are also used to link items of equal rank. Correlative conjunctions are used in pairs. Some correlative conjunctions are *either/or, neither/nor, if/then, both/and, since/therefore, on the one hand/on the other hand.*

> **For Example** *Either* they will sign the agreement, *or* we will select another vendor.
>
> *If* we are forced to pursue that option, *then* we will require additional funds.
>
> *Both* Thomson *and* Haynes are present.

V. PUNCTUATION

Punctuation is designed to make writing clear and easy to understand. Poor punctuation may cause the reader to misunderstand the context or be distracted by the errors and not focus on the context. Poor punctuation usually causes the reader to question the author's competence. A comprehensive discussion of all the rules governing punctuation would require an entire text. This section discusses the major elements of punctuation and summarizes rules that apply to commonly encountered problems.

A. Comma (,)

The function of a comma is to separate the parts of a sentence so that the meaning is clear. It is the most frequently used punctuation mark. Basic rules that apply to commas follow:

1. Use a comma before a coordinating conjunction that joins two main or independent clauses. An independent clause can stand alone as a complete sentence.

> **For Example** The statute provides that the contract must be witnessed, but it does not require that the contract be in writing. (Note that each clause of the sentence could be a complete sentence: The statute provides that the contract must be witnessed. It does not require that the contract be in writing.)

2. Set off introductory phrases or clauses with a comma.

> **For Example** **Introductory phrase in italics:** *After the prosecutor concluded his opening statement*, the court declared a recess.

3. Use a comma after each item in a series of three or more items, and place a comma before *and* or *or* at the end of the series.

> **For Example** The defendant had no identification, money, or other possessions.
>
> Bicycles, tricycles, unicycles, and other nonmotorized vehicles are covered by the statute.

4. Use a comma to avoid a misreading of the subject.

> **For Example** Instead of rule A, rule B applies in this situation.

5. Separate coordinate adjectives with a comma. Coordinate adjectives independently modify the same noun. To determine if the modifiers are coordinate, reverse their order or insert *and* between them. If the meaning is not changed, they are coordinate.

> **For Example** ***Coordinating Adjectives in Italics:***
>
> The *correct, concise* interpretation is that. . . .
>
> The *concise, correct* interpretation is that. . . .

6. Set off transitional or interpretive words or phrases with a comma. These are words or phrases that provide qualification or clarification but are not essential to the meaning of a sentence.

> **For Example** *The plaintiffs, however, have failed to comply.*
> *The correct course, therefore,* is to settle the case.

7. Set off nonrestrictive clauses with a comma. A nonrestrictive clause is one that is not necessary to the meaning of the sentence.

> **For Example** **Nonrestrictive clause in italics:** The court of appeals denied the appeal, *finding that the evidence was properly admitted.*

8. Use a comma to set off appositives. An *appositive* is a noun or noun phrase that further identifies another noun or noun phrase.

> **For Example** *Appositives in Italics:*
>
> The client, *Ms. Smith,* was elected to the position.
> The plaintiffs, *Mr. Evans and Ms. Thompson,* were present at the hearing.

9. Set off contrasting phrases with a comma or commas.

> **For Example** **Contrasting phrase in italics:** Mr. Jones, *not Ms. Smith,* was the guilty party.

10. Use commas when required to set off quotations. Place the comma between the quotation and the attribution.

> **For Example** He said, "I did not do it."

11. Place a comma inside the closing quotation mark, not outside the quotation mark.

> **For Example** "Witnessing is not required," he said.

12. Place a comma before and after descriptive titles, such as M.D., Ph.D., and Esq.

> **For Example** The doctor in this case is Mary Place, M.D., who attended medical school at Yale Medical School.

NOTE: Do not use a comma before Jr. II, and so on, after a personal name.

> **For Example** Mr. Steven Jones Jr. and Arthur Cleaver II delivered the closing address.

13. Do not use a comma before parentheses.

> **For Example** All employees (executives and assistants) shall arrive at work at 8:00 a.m.

14. In general do not use a comma after short prepositional phrases. A prepositional phrase consists of, at minimum, a preposition and a noun that is the object of the preposition. If the phrase is short (usually three words or less) and the meaning of the sentence is clear, the comma *may* be omitted.

> **For Example** *Not Necessary—The Prepositional Phrase is in Italics:*
>
> *In every situation*, you should read the contract.
> *After the test,* I'm going to sleep.
>
> **Better:**
>
> In every situation you should read the contract.
> After the test I'm going to sleep.

15. Place a comma between the day and year if the full date is written.

> **For Example** The hearing will be held on November 16, 2005.

When only the month and year are used, no comma is used.

> **For Example** There will be no hearings during November 2005.

16. Use a comma when a word or group of words is omitted but the meaning of the sentence is clear.

> **For Example** Mary represents the northern and eastern districts; Arthur, the southern district.
> Mary prepared the opening and analysis; Jane, the closing.

B. Semicolon (;)

A semicolon is used primarily in two situations:

- To separate major elements of complex sentences
- To separate items in a series if the items are long or if one of the items has internal commas

In regard to these situations, note the following rules:

1. Use a semicolon to separate main or independent clauses in a sentence that are *not* joined by a coordinating conjunction. Both main and independent clauses have a subject and a verb. Each could be a separate sentence. A *conjunction* is a word that is used to connect words and phrases. A *coordinating conjunction*, such as *and*, *but*, and *or*, is a conjunction that connects like elements.

> **For Example** **Incorrect:** The shareholders held their meeting at noon, the board of directors met immediately thereafter. (The use of the comma is incorrect because there is no coordinating conjunction, such as *and*, connecting the two clauses. The coordinating conjunction is in italics in the following sentence.)
>
> **Correct — coordinating conjunction used:** The shareholders held their meeting at noon, and the board of directors met immediately thereafter.
>
> **Correct — semicolon used:** The shareholders held their meeting at noon; the board of directors met immediately thereafter.

2. Use a semicolon when independent clauses are joined by a conjunctive adverb. Some examples of conjunctive adverbs are *therefore, however, furthermore, consequently, likewise,* and *nevertheless.*

> **For Example** The rule requires that the will must be witnessed in writing; *however,* there are three exceptions.

3. When a series of items is long or commas are already used in some of the items in the series, use a semicolon to separate the items.

> **For Example** **Long items:** The plaintiffs must prove the following to establish that the will was validly witnessed:
>
> a. there were two witnesses to the will;
>
> b. the witnesses were present in the room when the will was signed; and
>
> c. the witnesses were not related to the testator or were not bequeathed anything in the will.
>
> **List of items with internal commas:** The stockholders present were Mary Hart, the president; Tom Jones, the secretary; and Monica Murton, the treasurer.

4. At the end of a sentence, use a semicolon to separate an appositive introduced by such terms as *that is, for example,* and *namely.*

> **For Example** The plaintiff has not shown that the defendant violated all the statutory requirements; for example, the requirements that a firearm be used, that the firearm be in plain sight, and that the firearm be loaded.

C. Colon (:)

Use a colon when you want to introduce or call attention to information that follows, such as lists, conclusions, explanations, and quotations. The function of a colon is to introduce what follows.

1. When you use a colon to introduce a list or series, it must be preceded by a main clause that is a complete sentence.

> **For Example** **Incorrect:** The statutory requirements are: the will must be witnessed by two witnesses, the witnesses must be present when the testator signs the will, and the witnesses must sign the will. (The sentence is incorrect because the colon is not preceded by a main clause that is grammatically complete; the clause lacks an object.)
>
> **Correct:** The statutory requirements are the following: the will must be witnessed by two witnesses, . . .

> **For Example** The statute provides that three steps must be performed before the water right is established: (1) a permit must be obtained from the state engineer; (2) the water must be applied to a beneficial use; and (3) the beneficial use must be continuous for a period of three years.

2. A colon may be used to introduce quotations, or to introduce a short quotation introduced by an independent clause.

> **For Example** **Introduce short quotation:** Standing in open court, Smith loudly entered his plea: "I am not guilty."

A colon may be used to emphasize a quotation.

> **For Example** **Emphasize a quotation:** The senator concluded his remarks with the following statement: "I do not choose to run for reelection."

A colon is usually used to introduce block quotations, transcripts, statutes, and so on.

> **For Example** After reviewing the matter at length, the court adopted the following rule:
>
> (Block Quotation)

3. A colon may be used to join two separate but related clauses. In this instance, the colon is used to emphasize the information that follows.

> **For Example** The client made a major mistake: he failed to file the annual report.

D. Apostrophe (')

An apostrophe indicates possession or forms a contraction. Some of the basic rules governing the use of apostrophes to indicate possession follow:

1. Make singular nouns possessive by adding an apostrophe and an *s*.

> **For Example** the officer's car
>
> Mr. Jones's house

Singular nouns ending in *s* take an apostrophe and an *s* just like any other singular noun. Note the possessive of "Mr. Jones" in the preceding example.

2. Make plural nouns possessive by adding an apostrophe after the *s*.

> **For Example** the players' uniforms
>
> the workers' organization

3. Use an apostrophe and an *s* after the last word of a compound word or word group.

> **For Example** attorney general's office
>
> Fred and Tom's car (where Fred and Tom own the same car)
>
> Fred's and Tom's cars (where Fred and Tom own separate cars)

4. The possessives of personal pronouns do not require an apostrophe.

> **For Example** *yours, his, hers, ours, its* (possessive of *it*), *whose* (possessive of *who*)

An apostrophe is also used to form contractions. Contractions are generally not used in formal writing. To make a contraction, use an apostrophe in place of the omitted letter or letters.

> **For Example** *they're* (they are), *can't* (cannot), *don't* (do not), *who's* (who is), *it's* (it is)

Note the difference between it's and its. It's is the contraction for "it is." Its is the possessive pronoun form for it.

E. Quotation Marks (" ")

Use quotation marks to identify and set off quoted material. Note the following guidelines when quoting material:

1. Long quotations are not set off by quotation marks. Instead, they are set off from the rest of the text by a five-space indentation (0.5 inch indentation) from the left and right margins. They are also single spaced. These quotations are called *block quotations* and, according to *Bluebook* and *ALWD*, should be used for quotations of 50 words or more.

> **For Example** The court made the following statements in regard to the requirement of the presence of the witness:
>
> The statute requires the witnesses to be present when the testator signs the will. The witnesses must be in the same room with the testator, not in a separate room from which they can see the testator. The witnesses also must actually see the testator sign the will. Their presence in the room is not sufficient if they do not actually see the testator sign the will.

Because readers tend to skip over or skim long quotations, use them sparingly and only when the entire language, verbatim, is essential.

2. Place periods and commas inside the quotation marks.

> **For Example** He was described as "a dangerous individual."

Other punctuation, such as semicolons, colons, question marks, and exclamation marks, are placed outside the quotation marks unless they are a part of the quotation.

> **For Example** The court defined publication as "communication to a third party"; therefore. . . .
>
> The victim then shouted, "I've been hit!" (The exclamation mark is part of the quotation; therefore, it belongs within the quotation marks.)

3. You may use quotation marks to indicate that a word is used in a special way or is a special term. (Note, though, that a term being defined, or a "word used as a word" is usually indicated by setting in italics.) In legal writing, particularly material that uses many quotations, a proliferation of quotation marks can be confusing and visually irritating; therefore, use such marks sparingly to set off special terms.

> **For Example** The attorney acted as a "hired gun" in the case.
>
> The term "oppressive conduct" has a special meaning in corporation law.

4. When quoting a quote within a quote, use single quotation marks.

> **For Example** The court held that "the term 'oppressive conduct' requires that the shareholder engage in some wrongful conduct."

When the quote within a quote is part of a block quotation, use double quotation marks to set off the internal quote.

> **For Example** The court made the following statements in regard to the requirement of the presence of the witness:
>
> The statute requires the witnesses to be present when the testator signs the will. The witnesses must be in the same room with the testator, not in a separate room from which they can see the testator. The witnesses also must "actually see" the testator sign the will. Their presence in the room is not sufficient if they do not actually see the testator sign the will.

5. Quotation marks may also be used to indicate that a term is informal or questionable.

> **For Example** William "Wild Bill" James.
>
> The only "injury" sustained in this lawsuit was the cost of the litigation.

F. Ellipses (three spaced dots: ...)

The function of an ellipsis is to indicate the omission of part of a quotation.

> **For Example** The statute provides that skiers are "responsible for ... snow and ice conditions. . . ."

Note the following rules in regard to the use of ellipses:

1. When the omission occurs inside a quotation, use three ellipsis dots (created either by insertion of the three-dot ellipsis symbol on your computer, or by typing three periods in a row). Use hard spaces after the last quoted word, between each ellipsis dot, and the next quoted word.

   > **For Example** When I went on my trip, I first went to the tower ... and saw the mountains on the horizon.

   Retain any punctuation that appears before or after the omitted material if it is grammatically necessary for the restructured sentence.

   > **For Example** When we went on the tour of the villa, . . . we also visited the famous gardens.

2. When the end of a quoted sentence is omitted, add a period for the punctuation to end the sentence. Follow the last word with a space, the three ellipsis dots, a space, and a period. Place a hard space between the last ellipsis dot and the period.

   > **For Example** The statute requires that "the majority shareholder must refrain from engaging in oppressive conduct. . . ."

3. When the omission is at the beginning of a quote, do not use an ellipsis; merely indicate where the quoted material begins with the opening quotation marks. In legal writing, a bracketed first letter signals that you have changed the case of the initial letter of the quotation.

   > **For Example** **Incorrect:** In this case, the court stated that ". . . the act does not require specific intent."
   > **Correct:** In this case, the court stated that "the act does not require specific intent."
   > **Incorrect:** The court noted that "Ignorance of the law is no excuse."
   > **Correct:** The court noted that "[i]gnorance of the law is no excuse."

4. If the quote is a phrase or clause, no ellipsis is required.

   > **For Example** **Incorrect:** The state must establish "... specific intent."
   > **Correct:** The state must establish "specific intent."

G. Brackets ([ ])

Brackets are used to perform three separate functions:

- To show changes in or add information to quotations, usually for the purpose of providing clarification to the quotation
- To indicate an error in the original quotation
- To indicate a change of case in the first letter of a quotation.

> **For Example** **To show changes in a quotation:** "The privilege [against self-incrimination] allows an individual to remain silent."
>
> **To indicate an error in the original quoted material:** "The bord [*sic*] of directors voted against the proposal."
>
> **To show a change of case:** According to this court, "[i]gnorance of the law is no excuse."

In legal writing, do not use brackets to indicate parentheses that fall within parentheses.

> **For Example** **Incorrect:** (When the annual meeting was held [June of 2004], the board decided to call for a vote of the members.)
>
> **Correct:** (When the annual meeting was held (June of 2004), the board decided to call for a vote of the members.)

H. Parentheses ( )

Use parentheses to add supplementary information to the sentence that is outside the main idea of the sentence or of lesser importance.

> **For Example** The cost of the paper (only $2) was not included in the invoice.

When referring the reader to other cases, attached material, or an appendix, or when providing summary information following a case citation, you may use parentheses.

> **For Example** **Reference to an appendix:** (See Appendix A.)
>
> **Reference to other cases:** See also *Smith v. Jones,* 981 N.E.2d 441 (N. Wash. 1993) (where the court required specific intent in a similar situation).

I. Hyphen (-)

A hyphen is required to form compound modifiers and compound nouns. There are numerous words that may or may not require hyphenation.

> **For Example** ex-judge
>
> well-known personality
>
> self-defense

Consult a dictionary when you are unsure whether a word must be hyphenated. Be sure to consult a recently published dictionary. This area of the English language changes frequently.

J. Dash (—)

The true dash is often referred to as the em dash or long dash. Use a dash in the following situations:

- To emphasize something
- To set off lists or briefly summarize materials containing commas
- To show an abrupt change of thought or direction, or an interjection

> **For Example** **To emphasize:** The child—only eight years old—was clearly not capable of understanding what he was doing.
>
> **To set off a list:** The items found at the scene—the knife, the drugs, and the scarf—have disappeared from the evidence room.
>
> **To show a sudden break:** Basel Corporation—primarily known for its herbs—is involved in the manufacture of glassware.

K. Slash (/)

The slash is not frequently used in legal writing. Note the following when using slashes:

1. Use a slash to separate one option from another or indicate alternatives.

> **For Example** The either/or option is not acceptable.
>
> The course was offered on a pass/fail basis.
>
> Ms. Darling was the writer/producer.

2. Use a slash when writing dates informally.

> **For Example** His birthday is 9/6/86.

3. Use a slash to separate line breaks in poetry.

> **For Example** Yes! We can turn the tide / Break the waves that rush to the shore / And undo the way of things.

L. Period (.)

The period is probably the most commonly used punctuation mark. It is used to mark the end of a sentence, in abbreviations, as a decimal point in numbers, and after letters and numbers in an outline or list.

1. Use a period to indicate the end of a sentence that is not a question or exclamation.

> **For Example** It is clear that the client is not telling the entire story.
>
> Please tell us what you want.

2. Use a period with letters and numbers in an outline or list.

> **For Example** **Outline:**
>
>   I. Introduction
>
>   A. Introduction
>
>   B. Body
>
>   1. Introductory sentence
>
>   2. Body
>
> **Lists:** In a list, the number or letter is placed in parentheses or is followed by a period, but not both parentheses and a period.
>
> **Incorrect:**   (1) Creditors
>
>   (2) Investors
>
>   (3) Debtors
>
> **Correct:**   (1) Creditors   **or**   1. Creditors
>
>   (2) Investors   **or**   2. Investors
>
>   (3) Debtors   **or**   3. Debtors

3. Use a period after a heading if the heading is a complete sentence or runs in with the text.

> **For Example** **Complete sentence:** I. The position relied on no longer represents sound public policy and should not be relied on.
>
> **Heading runs in with text:** 1. *The prewriting stage.* The prewriting stage begins with a review of the assignment.

4. Use a period in most abbreviations.

> **For Example** Mr. (for Mister)
>
>   Sept. (for September)
>
> Co. (for Company)

Do not add a second period if a period falls at the end of a sentence.

> **For Example** The meeting will begin promptly at 8:00 a.m.

Abbreviations of corporations, government agencies, scientific and technical terms, or those composed of all capital letters do not take periods unless the initials stand for a person's name or a different style is specified.

> **For Example** NASA, DNA, FBI, CD-ROM
>
>   J. R. Smith (in a person's name, periods are used)

M. Question Mark (?)

A question mark is used at the end of a sentence that asks a direct question.

> **For Example** Has the client made a follow-up appointment?
>
> You filed the deed even when we told you not to, didn't you?

In regard to the use of question marks, note the following guidelines:

1. In a compound sentence, use a question mark if the ending clause is a question.

> **For Example** Although we discussed this several times, do you still maintain your innocence?

2. If there are multiple endings to a question, use a question mark after each ending word or phrase.

> **For Example** Is the person responsible for this the president? the secretary? the treasurer?
>
> **NOTE:** The first word of the ending phrases (*the*) is not capitalized.

3. Place a question mark in parentheses following a term (usually a number or date) to indicate uncertainty.

> **For Example** Mr. Thompson left his home town in 1988 (?), and moved to New Orleans.
>
> It appears that only one state, Mississippi (?), has adopted this position.

N. Exclamation Point (!)

An exclamation mark is used to indicate the end of a sentence that expresses emotion or deserves special emphasis.

NOTE: Exclamation points are rarely used in legal writing unless they are part of a quotation. Keep in mind the following when using exclamation points:

1. Use an exclamation point to express a demand, surprise, emotion, and so on.

> **For Example** Hurry up, he's coming!
>
> Come here right now!
>
> You must pay me immediately!

2. Use an exclamation point to emphasize an interjection or command.

> **For Example** No! Don't touch that!
>
> Oh, my goodness! How could I have done that?

VI. GENERAL CONSIDERATIONS

Three additional matters that require attention when you are performing a writing assignment are spelling, use of numbers, and formal writing conventions. These matters are addressed in the following subsections.

A. Spelling

Obviously, you must correctly spell all the words you use. If you are in doubt about the spelling of a word, use a dictionary. Legal writing requires the use of both a regular and a legal dictionary; therefore, you must have both of these dictionaries.

If you use a computer that checks spelling, you still must carefully check for word usage errors. The computer may catch a spelling error, but generally it will not catch the use of the wrong word or typographical errors that result in the use of a wrong word.

> **For Example** **Use of a wrong word:** You used the word *to* when you intended to use *too*. A computer spell-check function will not catch the use of the wrong word.
>
> **Typographical error that results in the use of a wrong word:** You typed *cast* when you meant to type *case*. *Cast* is a word, and spell-check will not consider this an error.

B. Numbers

The following rules govern the presentation of numbers in legal writing:

1. In text, the general rule is to spell out numbers from one to ninety-nine (that is, numbers that can be spelled out in one or two words). Note that a different style convention, which requires that numbers from one to nine be spelled out, is also very commonly used.

> **For Example** one
>
> twenty-seven
>
> ninety-nine
>
> The contract has twenty-seven clauses.

Use numerals for numbers that are more than two words long.

> **For Example** 379
>
> 1,300
>
> 145,378
>
> The contract has 379 clauses.

There is one exception: if you have a list of numbers and one of the items on the list should be written with numerals, use numerals for all the items listed.

> **For Example** The numbers in the code are 16, 44, 397, and 1,001. (The numbers sixteen and forty-four are not spelled out.)

As a general rule, do not spell out the following numbers: dates, statute numbers, section numbers, volume numbers, exact times, sums of money, addresses, percentages, scores, identification numbers, ratios, statistics, decimals and fractions, and measurements with symbols or abbreviations.

> **For Example** Date: May 6, 2005
>
> Statute: Title 18 of the code
>
> Section: Section 3212, § 3212
>
> Percentage: 75 percent, 75%
>
> Score: The final score was 2 to 1.
>
> Exact sum of money: $34.21
>
> Decimal: 9.38
>
> Fraction: 9¼
>
> Measurement with symbol: 9°
>
> Exact time: 5:45 A.M., 7:23 p.m.

NOTE: Hours are spelled out when the time is accompanied by *o'clock.*

> **For Example** **Incorrect:** 11 o'clock
>
> **Correct:** eleven o'clock

2. Spell out numbers that begin a sentence.

> **For Example** **Incorrect:** 506 paralegals were present.
>
> **Correct:** Five hundred six paralegals were present.

3. Use hyphens for fractions and numbers from twenty-one to ninety-nine.

> **For Example** Fifty-six of the stockholders were present. The thirty-seven shareholders represented three-fourths of the outstanding shares.

Do not use *and* when writing whole numbers.

> **For Example** **Incorrect:** Two hundred *and* seventy-five dollars was needed to pay the debt.
>
> **Correct:** Two hundred seventy-five dollars was needed to pay the debt.

Hyphenate fractions that are spelled out.

> **For Example** One-fifth of the student body attended the meeting.

4. To make a number plural, add *s* (without an apostrophe).

> **For Example** 1990s
>
> There were three 190s in the paragraph.

Possessive numbers are not frequently encountered. If you have to form the possessive of a number, add an apostrophe and *s*.

> **For Example** The instructor illustrated his point by referring to the 1920's Black Friday.

5. When two numbers appear together that are not of the same kind, spell out the first number.

> **For Example** **Incorrect:** There were 190 $50 bills.
> **Correct:** There were one hundred ninety $50 bills.

C. Formal Writing Conventions

Most legal writing is considered formal, and formal **writing conventions** apply, especially to legal briefs and memorandums. Two of these conventions concern the use of contractions and personal pronouns.

As mentioned in the subsection addressing the use of apostrophes, the use of contractions is not considered acceptable in formal writing. Do not use contractions unless instructed to do so.

The general rule is that you should draft legal memoranda or briefs in the third person. Also, unless instructed otherwise, use the third person in correspondence to clients.

> **For Example** **Incorrect:** It is my position that the court should grant the motion.
> We feel that the contract has been broken.
> **Correct:** The court should grant the motion.
> It is Mr. Black's position that the contract has been broken.

When presenting your position or legal analysis, use present tense.

> **For Example** Plaintiff *contends* that the rule requires thirty days' notice. It *is* the defendant's position that the contract is void.

When addressing a court opinion that has already been decided, use past tense.

> **For Example** In *Smith v. Jones,* the court *held* that the rule does not require thirty days' notice. The court *listed* three possible solutions to the problem.

When discussing a law or rule still in effect, use present tense.

> **For Example** The provisions of section 44-556 *require* a contractor to give thirty days' notice. The statute *provides* that the notice must be signed by the owner of the property.

VII. KEY POINTS CHECKLIST: *Fundamentals of Writing*

✓ The goal of legal writing is to prepare a professional product—one that is free of substantive and mechanical error. Perform the number of edits and redrafts necessary to attain this goal.

✓ Use short, clear sentences when possible. Fifteen to twenty-five words is a good average length for sentences. Excessively long sentences are difficult to understand.

✓ A paragraph should address one topic and should usually range from three to six sentences.

✓ Keep the reader in mind when drafting. Avoid legalese when possible, especially when the reader is a person not trained in the law.

✓ Make sure the writing is grammatically correct. Check for subject–verb agreement, parallel construction, and so on.

✓ Check the punctuation. Use commas and other punctuation devices correctly.

✓ Check the spelling to ensure that all words are spelled correctly.

VIII. APPLICATION

Checklist

The checklist presented in Exhibit 14-4 may be used as a guide to help you proofread and correct your legal writing.

Exhibit 14-4 *Proofreading Checklist.*

Checklist to be used when Proofreading Legal Writing	
General Considerations	**Grammar**
▢ Spelling	▢ Subject/verb agreement
▢ Numbers	▢ Verb tense
▢ Formal writing conventions	▢ Parallel construction
Sentence Structure/Pattern	▢ Superfluous verbs
▢ Subject/verb distance	▢ Modifiers and infinitives
▢ Sentence length	▢ Noun/pronoun agreement
▢ Active/passive voice	**Paragraphs**
▢ Action verbs	▢ Topic sentence
▢ Transitions	▢ Body
Punctuation	▢ Closing
▢ Commas	▢ Transition sentence
▢ Semicolons	▢ Paragraph length
▢ Colons	**Word Selection and Usage**
▢ Apostrophes	▢ Excessive/redundant words
▢ Quotations	▢ Noun/verb string
▢ Ellipses	▢ Nominalizations
▢ Brackets	▢ Legalese
▢ Parentheses	▢ Archaic words
▢ Hyphens	▢ Sexist language
▢ Dashes	▢ Specific words—problem areas

Summary

One requirement of a legal writing assignment is the preparation of a final product that is free from mechanical errors. The value of quality research and analysis is undermined if the written presentation is poorly assembled. This chapter presents an overview of some of the fundamental writing skills essential for good writing. The chapter addresses sentence and paragraph structure, word selection and usage, grammar, punctuation, and other general considerations regarding the mechanics of good writing.

A sentence is the fundamental building block of writing. It is usually a statement; at a minimum, it must have a subject and a predicate.

The second fundamental component of writing is the paragraph. A paragraph is a group of sentences that address the same topic. Paragraphs are usually composed of a topic sentence, a sentence or sentences discussing the topic, and a closing sentence.

The proper selection and use of words are critical elements of good writing. The improper use of words or the use of sexist language or legalese detracts from the quality of the writing.

Rules of grammar guide the drafting of legal writing. Subject–verb agreement, parallel construction, proper verb tense, noun–pronoun agreement, and other rules are necessary to good writing.

Spelling and punctuation are the final subjects addressed in this chapter. Proper spelling is always required. In like manner, proper punctuation is a basic requirement of proper writing. The correct uses of commas, semicolons, apostrophes, and other punctuation devices are summarized in the chapter.

All of the rules and guidelines discussed in the chapter are essential to good writing skills. You must learn and employ them when engaged in legal writing. The chapter only briefly addresses the rules and guidelines that apply to legal writing; you should refer to other resources for detailed coverage of each topic.

Quick References

Internet Resources

Using grammar, punctuation, word selection, sentences, and other topics, you will find various Web sites (literally thousands of sites) that refer to writing fundamentals. Some sites refer to books; some provide self-help handouts; some present tips, guidelines, and examples; some are materials from various English courses; some are articles on specific writing topics; some are tutorials or workshops; and some advertise writing services and courses. As with most topics on the Web, the problem is not the lack of sites but the abundance of sites. Probably the best strategy is to narrow your search to a specific writing topic such as "parentheses." If you are going to do a lot of writing, another strategy would be to purchase a comprehensive text such as *The Chicago Manual of Style* (listed in "For Further Reading" at the end of this chapter).

Exercises

Additional assignments are available on the CourseMate.

ASSIGNMENT 1

Discuss the essential requirements of a well-crafted sentence.

ASSIGNMENT 2

Discuss the elements and requirements of a well-crafted paragraph.

ASSIGNMENT 3

What is the difference between active voice and passive voice?

ASSIGNMENT 4

Draft the following sentences in active voice.

- The defendant was attacked by the plaintiff at the beginning of the argument.
- It is a requirement of good writing skills that active voice be used.
- Payment must be made by Mr. Smith no later than May 15, 1997.

ASSIGNMENT 5

What is a nominalization? What are some examples of nominalizations?

ASSIGNMENT 6

What is legalese? Give three examples of legalese.

ASSIGNMENT 7

Rephrase the following sentences using nonsexist language.

- A paralegal may draft a letter to the client informing him of an upcoming hearing.
- The lawyer must file his response within 30 days.
- The chairman of the committee conducted a private hearing.
- Each person must bring his records to the conference.
- Everyone must bring his records to the hearing.

ASSIGNMENT 8

Discuss the proper use of *shall/may*, *and/or*, and *that/which*.

ASSIGNMENT 9

What are the basic rules concerning subject–verb agreement, proper verb tense, and noun–pronoun agreement?

ASSIGNMENT 10

What is parallel construction?

ASSIGNMENT 11

What are squinting modifiers? Give some examples of squinting modifiers.

ASSIGNMENT 12

What are the rules concerning the proper use of commas, colons, semicolons, and apostrophes?

ASSIGNMENT 13

Correct the following sentences and identify why they are incorrect.

1. The statute requires the witnesses to be present when the testator signs the will, and the witnesses must be in the same room with the testator, not in a separate room, and watch the testator sign the will.

2. Mary reached the conclusion that she had made a mistake.

3. A relative pronoun requires a verb which agrees with its antecedent.

4. Either the cousins or Darryl are going to the party.

5. Sara, after giving careful consideration to the matter, reached the conclusion that she should buy the business.

6. He decided to thoroughly and completely test the theory.

7. Neither the members of the board nor Steve had reached their conclusion.

8. The statute requires stockholder approval for merger but it does not require approval for multiple real estate purchases.

9. The key executives, (president, secretary, and treasurer) are required to attend the board meeting.

10. The corporation statute requires: an annual board of directors meeting, an annual shareholder meeting, and the filing of an annual report.

11. Tom and Pam decided there going to buy stock in the corporation.

12. The law requires a partner to ". . . share partnership profits equally with the other partners. . . ."

13. Joseph and Claire decided they were going too there cabin for two weeks.

14. Fifty five of the partners attended the partnership meeting.

15. The law provides that profits should be shared equally, however, the law allows the partners to provide otherwise in the partnership agreement.

ASSIGNMENT 14

Correct the following sentences by properly using colons and semicolons.

▪ The court's instructions to the respondent are: to refrain from contacting the plaintiff in person, by telephone, or by mail; to pay monthly child support, and to perform one hundred hours of community service.

▪ The following statutes govern the issue, section 29-9-516, section 29-9-517, and section 29-9-544.

ASSIGNMENT 15

Summarize the rules governing the use of quotations, ellipses, brackets, parentheses, hyphens, and dashes.

ASSIGNMENT 16

Correct the paragraphs presented in part A and part B. Use the proofreading checklist presented in Exhibit 14-4.

Part A

The governments' first witness at Bean's sentencing were the DEA Task Force Officer Tony Silva. He testifies that in his debriefing Luiz had told him about four seperate marijuana "grows" in which Luiz had participated. The first was in 1986 In Tress, Texas: this "grow" produced 700 marijuana plants. The second was in 1987 in the Tonto wilderness; and it produced approximatly 1500 marijuana plants. The third "grow" was in 1988 in Sies Colorado and they produced approximately 900 marijuana plants.

The final "grow" was in 1991, also at the Sies site.

Before the plants in this grow had been harveted, a Colorado State Police aircraft was spotted doing a "flyover" of the property. This prompted Luiz to completely destroy the crop, only fifty two plants were seized. As they were seized the officers noted that two or three plants were in a single grow site. Approximately 1,000 "grow holes," with sprinkler heads connected to an extensive irritation system, were found another one thousand uninstalled sprinkler heads, two water tanks and fertilizer also was found on the property.

Part B

The trial court sentenced Smith well within the statutory limits. Therefore the sentence is legal.

The record thoroughly, clearly and positively shows that Smith and his attorney have ample time to thoroughly review Smiths' sentence report prior to sentencing. They did so and had: "no problems with it." It is shown by the record that Smith never appealed his conviction or sentence. His section 2255 Motion were his first and only attempt to challenge his sentence. Any objections to the sentence report as submitted were clearly waived by Smith. The defendant have the responsibility to advise the Court of any claimed errors in the sentence report. His failure to voice any objections waive any issue not properly presented. It has been long held by this court that "Section 2255 is not available to test the legality of matters which should have been raised on appeal." Unless good cause can be shown why a defendant did not appeal or raise a particular issue on appeal; the defendant is barred from raising that issue in a section 2255 Motion.

For Further Reading

Block, Gertrude. *Effective Legal Writing*. 4th ed. Westbury, NY: Foundation Press, 1992.

The Chicago Manual of Style. 15th ed. Chicago and London: University of Chicago Press, 2003.

Good, Edward. *Mightier Than the Sword*. Charlottesville, VA: Blue Jeans Press, 1989.

Putman, William H. *Pocket Guide to Legal Writing*. Clifton Park, NY: Thomson/Delmar Learning, 2006.

Strunk, William, Jr., and E. B. White. *The Elements of Style*. 3rd ed. New York: Macmillan, 1972.

Tepper, Pamela R. *Basic Legal Writing*. Lake Forrest, IL: Glenco, 1992.

 CourseMate

The available CourseMate for this text has an interactive eBook and interactive learning tools, including flash cards, quizzes, and more. To learn more about this resource and access free demo CourseMate resources, go to **www.cengagebrain.com**, and search for this book. To access CourseMate materials that you have purchased, go to **login.cengagebrain.com**.

The Writing Process for Effective Legal Writing

For the past five years, Rick Strong has been the paralegal for Sara Fletcher, a criminal defense attorney. He started law school last year. Rick now works part time during the school year and full time in the summer. He performs a wide range of law clerk and paralegal tasks for Sara. He interviews clients and witnesses, conducts legal investigations, arranges and maintains client files, conducts legal research, and occasionally prepares legal memoranda.

Rick enjoys legal research and determining the answers to legal questions. He dreads the actual writing process—the assembly of the research and analysis into a written format.

Carol Beck recently retained Sara to represent her in the case of *State v. Beck*. In the case, police officers obtained a search warrant from a magistrate court judge authorizing a search of Ms. Beck's house for drugs. On the bottom of the warrant, the judge wrote, "Unannounced entry is authorized to ensure officer safety." When the officers obtained the warrant, they told the judge that in other drug search cases, if the officers announced their presence prior to entry, the persons occupying the premises being searched often posed a threat to the officers. Based on this statement, the judge authorized the officers to enter Ms. Beck's house unannounced. When the officers executed the warrant, they did not announce their presence and purpose prior to entry. Their search recovered a plastic bag containing an ounce of cocaine. Carol Beck was charged with possession with intent to distribute.

Sara and Rick have just begun the preliminary stages of preparing Ms. Beck's defense. Rick's assignment is to prepare a legal memorandum addressing the possibility of obtaining suppression of the evidence on the basis that the search was illegal. Sara tells Rick that any suppression motion must be filed in 30 days. What process should Rick follow when preparing the memorandum? The legal writing process is presented in this chapter. The answer to Rick's question is discussed in the Application section of this chapter.

Learning Objectives

After completing this chapter, you should understand:

- The importance of writing skills

- What a legal writing process is and its importance in legal writing

- The three stages of the legal writing process

- The importance and use of an expanded outline in the legal writing process

I. INTRODUCTION

This chapter presents a collection of general considerations involved in legal analysis and writing, including an approach to the writing process and guidelines to follow when engaging in the process.

The legal issue raised by the facts of a client's case must be researched and analyzed and the results communicated, usually in written form. Legal research, analysis, and writing are all related. Each is a step in a process designed to answer legal questions and lead to the resolution of disputes. Legal analysis usually takes place when the research is converted into a written product and is part of the writing process. Therefore, legal analysis is included here in the discussion of legal writing. Legal writing is the step where the research and analysis are assembled in a written form designed to concisely record and communicate the answer to a legal question or questions.

For various reasons, many people believe that most legal communication is oral and takes place either in the courtroom or in a law office. This is not the case, however. The bulk of legal communication is written. The vast majority of cases never go to trial. They are settled, and the settlements are reduced to writing. When cases do go to trial, much of the trial work involves writing: written motions, trial briefs, jury instructions, and so on. In many instances, the law firm's practice rarely involves litigation, but instead focuses on the preparation of contracts, wills, corporation instruments, and other legal documents. A great deal of time is spent in research and in communicating the findings of that research in the form of legal memoranda and legal instruments.

II. IMPORTANCE OF WRITING SKILLS

There are several reasons why it is critically important for a paralegal or law clerk to possess good writing skills. This section details some of the major reasons.

In many instances, you may spend most of your time engaged in legal writing in one form or another. If you possess good writing skills, you can produce a finished product in a shorter time than an individual who does not possess such skills. This results in greater productivity, which enhances your value to the law firm.

The quality of a written product depends on writing skill: the greater the skill, the higher the quality of the product. Part of your job evaluation may be based on the quality of your written product. In addition, a written product that leaves the firm, such as correspondence to a client, represents the law firm. A shoddy product reflects poorly on the firm and may damage its reputation.

Legal research and analysis are meaningless if the results cannot be clearly and concisely communicated. The goal of a legal research memorandum is to inform and record information. An individual who does not possess good writing skills may not be able to fulfill this goal.

Poor writing skills may also lead to miscommunication. One may intend the writing to convey a certain meaning when, in fact, it literally conveys a different meaning. This may lead to disaster if the supervising attorney relies on the literal meaning and thereby commits an error. Correspondence to a client may be so unclear that the client does not understand the communication.

> **For Example** The written communication reads, "Individuals who file with the court promptly receive consideration." This is ambiguous. Does it mean that individuals who file promptly with the court receive redress, or does it mean that those who file with the court will receive prompt redress?

III. GOAL OF LEGAL WRITING

Before addressing the considerations involved in the legal writing process, it is important to identify the goal of legal writing. Law offices are busy places, and the reader of a paralegal's or law clerk's work product is usually a busy person who does not have time to wade through flowery prose, extraneous or unclear material, or disorganized material. The primary goal of legal writing, therefore, is to clearly, concisely, and completely convey legal information in a manner that accomplishes both of the following:

- Fully addresses the topic in as few words as possible
- Allows the reader to gain a clear understanding of the information in as little time as possible

You may feel that you do not possess good writing skills or that you do not have the capability of clearly, concisely, and completely conveying information in a written form. Writing may be a struggle for you. Take heart: Writing skills can be developed and writing made easier through practice and the use of a writing process.

IV. LEGAL WRITING PROCESS

A **legal writing process** is a systematic approach to legal writing. It is an organized approach to legal research, analysis, and writing that helps you develop writing skills. It makes legal writing easier and is necessary for the following reasons:

1. Legal writing is highly organized and structured. The organized structure helps ensure that complex subject matter is clearly communicated.

> **For Example** The IRAC (issue, rule, analysis, conclusion) legal analysis process discussed in Chapter 2 is a structured approach to problem solving. The IRAC format, when followed in the preparation of a legal memorandum, helps ensure the clear communication of the complex subject matter of legal issue analysis.

The use of a legal writing process helps you conduct research and analysis within the structure and format of the type of legal writing assigned. A writing process saves time by providing the means to organize your legal analysis and research material as it is gathered.

2. If you do not have a writing process and merely gather research material and immediately begin to write, you will waste a great deal of time. You are not ready to write. If you begin to write without organizing your research and analysis, or without thinking through what you are going to write, you will flounder. If you gather a mountain of research that requires a great deal of analysis, you will waste time in the struggle to determine what goes where and how. Using a writing process forces you to think before you write. It forces you to follow an organized structure from the beginning. By using a process, when you actually begin to write, you will be ready. Your project, then, will be thorough and organized.

3. When you are researching or analyzing an assignment or engaging in legal writing, a writing process helps you capture ideas as they come to you. A process provides a framework within which to capture ideas and record them in their proper place as they occur. Without a process, ideas may be lost. See section IV.A.3 in this chapter for a discussion on creating an outline.

4. A writing process also helps you overcome the difficult areas of legal writing. You may get stuck in a difficult analytical area or encounter writer's block. A writing process helps you avoid these problems by providing a stepped approach. Often you become stuck or blocked because you have missed a step or left something out. A process is a guide that includes all the steps and helps ensure that nothing is left out.

This section presents a general overview of the writing process and discusses matters that you should consider at each stage of the process. There are many different processes and combinations of processes that you may adopt when engaging in legal writing. What works for one person may not work for another. You may ultimately adopt a process that includes steps from various approaches to legal writing, including some of those presented in this chapter. It does not matter which process you ultimately adopt, but it is essential that you adopt some writing process.

The legal writing process consists of the three basic stages presented in Exhibit 15-1. The following sections discuss each of these stages. A prerequisite to the first stage—to the beginning of any writing process—is the assembly of all available information concerning the case.

Exhibit 15-1 *Stages of the Legal Writing Process.*

Prewriting Stage	The stage where the assignment is organized, researched, and analyzed.
Writing Stage	The stage where research, analysis, and ideas are assembled into a written product.
Postwriting Stage	The stage where the assignment is revised, edited, and assembled in final form.

© Cengage Learning 2014

For Example The assignment is to prepare an office legal memorandum addressing the question of when the statute of limitations runs in a client's medical malpractice case. Gather all information concerning the case before you begin. This includes the client's file, depositions, interrogatories, witness interviews, any other discovery information, and so on.

A. Prewriting Stage

The **prewriting stage** is the stage in the legal writing process where an assignment is organized, researched, and analyzed. Novice writers often begin to write without adequate preparation. One of the most important aspects of the writing process is the performance of the steps necessary to become adequately prepared to begin. Drafting becomes much easier if you are fully prepared when you begin to write. This stage of the writing process may be divided into the three sections presented in Exhibit 15-2.

Exhibit 15-2 *Sections of the Prewriting Stage.*

1. Assignment	An identification of the type and purpose of the writing assignment
2. Constraints	A consideration of any constraints placed on the assignment
3. Organization	The organization of the writing assignment

© Cengage Learning 2014

1. Assignment

The writing process begins with an identification of the type and purpose of the **assignment**. Three questions must be considered when reviewing the assignment:

- Is the assignment clearly understood?
- What type of legal writing (document) is required?
- Who is the audience?

a. Is the Assignment Clearly Understood?

You may receive the assignment in the form of a written memorandum or through oral instructions from the supervising attorney. An early and important step in the prewriting stage is to be sure that you understand the task you have been assigned. If you have any questions concerning the general nature or specifics of the assignment, ask.

A misunderstanding of the assignment can result in a great deal of time being wasted in the performance of the wrong task. Most attorneys welcome inquiries and prefer that a paralegal or law clerk ask questions rather than proceed in a wrong direction. In this regard, if the assignment is unclear in any way, summarize the assignment orally with the attorney. Another approach could be to draft a brief recapitulation of the assignment and submit it for the attorney's review and signature.

b. What Type of Legal Writing (Document) Is Required?

The next step is to determine the type of legal writing the assignment requires. This is important because each type of legal writing has a different function and different requirements. Before you begin, you must know what form of legal writing is required.

There are various types of legal writing and numerous ways to categorize the types. The focus of this text is on legal research and analysis and the types of writing related to legal research and analysis, such as the following:

1. Law-office legal research and analysis memoranda. A researcher may be assigned the task of researching and analyzing the law that applies to a client's case. The law-office legal memorandum is designed to inform the reader of the results of the research and analysis. The assignment may be as simple as identification of the statutory or case law that applies to a legal issue or as complex as identification of the issues in a case and analysis of the law that applies. The preparation of a law-office legal memorandum is discussed in Chapters 16 and 17.

2. Correspondence. There are several types of correspondence that a paralegal or law clerk may be required to draft: demand letters, settlement proposals, notices of events such as hearing dates, and so on. The assignment may require preparation of a draft of a letter to be sent to the client informing the client of the law that applies in the client's case and how the law applies. Neither a paralegal nor a law clerk may give legal advice to the client, but they may prepare a draft of the correspondence that the attorney will send to the client. Legal correspondence is addressed in Chapter 19.

3. Court briefs. A **court brief** is a document filed with a court that contains an attorney's legal argument and the legal authority in support of that argument. There are primarily two categories of court briefs: trial court briefs and appellate court briefs.

(1) Trial Court Briefs A court may require an attorney to submit a brief in support of a position the attorney has taken in regard to a legal issue in a case. A **trial court brief** is usually submitted in support of or in opposition to a motion filed with the court.

> **For Example** An attorney files a motion to dismiss a complaint, claiming that the statute of limitations has run. In support of the motion, the attorney files a legal brief containing the legal and factual reasons why the court should grant the motion. The opposing side will also file a brief in opposition to the granting of the motion.

(2) Appellate Court Briefs An **appellate brief** is a document filed with an appellate court. It presents the legal arguments and authorities in support of the client's position on appeal. It is designed to persuade the appellate court to rule in the client's favor.

Court briefs are discussed in detail in Chapter 18.

Each of these types of legal writing is structured differently. The organization and considerations involved in drafting these documents vary. The subsequent stages of the writing process are governed by the type of legal writing the assignment requires. Therefore, an early step in the prewriting stage is the identification of the type of writing required.

Other types of legal writing include the drafting of legal documents such as contracts, wills, and pleadings. Other courses such as contracts and wills cover the specific considerations involved in the drafting of these documents; therefore, they are not covered in this text. You may follow the writing process presented in this chapter, however, when preparing such documents.

c. Who Is the Audience?

An important step when assessing the requirements of an assignment is to identify the intended audience. Inasmuch as the goal of legal writing is to clearly communicate information to the reader, you must ensure that the writing is crafted in a manner suited to meet the needs of that reader.

Legal writing assignments are designed to reach a number of different audiences. The intended reader may be a judge, an attorney, a client, or some other person. The reader's ability to understand the writing will depend on the reader's legal sophistication and how the document is written. A legal writing designed to inform a client or other layperson of the legal analysis of an issue is drafted differently than a writing designed to convey the same information to an attorney. The use of fundamental legal terminology may be appropriate when the writing is to be read by a person trained in the law. In contrast, if the reader has little or no legal training, it may be necessary to use nonlegal terms to convey the same information clearly.

> **For Example** Communication to the supervising attorney:
>
> The motion to suppress the evidence should be granted. Exigent circumstances that would have justified an unannounced entry were not present at the time the officers executed the warrant, and the judge who issued the search warrant did not authorize unannounced entry.
>
> Communication of the same information to the client:
>
> The court may not allow the prosecution to use at trial the evidence seized when the officers searched your house. The law requires officers to announce their presence before they enter your house to conduct a search. They are required to do this unless a judge gives them permission to enter without first announcing their presence. They may also enter unannounced if, when they arrive at your house, they believe that you are destroying evidence or present a danger to them. In your case, the judge did not authorize the officers to enter unannounced and nothing occurred when they arrived at your house to indicate that you were destroying drugs or you were a threat to them.

Another factor to consider is whether the writing is intended solely for internal office use. A writing that will be read only by individuals working in the office may contain information, comments, or assessments that would not be included in a writing intended to be read outside the office.

> **For Example** After analyzing the facts of the client's case and the applicable law, it may be necessary to convince the client to reconsider the amount of damages he believes he is entitled to recover and the possibility of settling this case. He needs to be informed about the amount of damages he can realistically expect to receive. He is adamant in his belief that he is entitled to more than $1 million, and he is not willing to consider settling for less. The range of recovery is more likely between $10,000 and $100,000.

Exhibit 15-3 *Constraints on the Writing Process.*

Time	If the performance of the assignment is governed by a deadline, allocate a specific amount of time to each stage of the writing process.
Length	If the assignment is limited to a set number of pages, organize the writing to ensure that each section is allotted sufficient space.
Format/Organization	If the assignment is governed by a specific format or style established by office guidelines or court rule, identify the proper format and be sure you follow it.

© Cengage Learning 2014

Identify the audience to ensure that the legal communication is crafted in a manner commensurate with the reader's ability to understand the contents.

2. Constraints

The next step in the prewriting process is to consider any possible **constraints** that may affect performance of the assignment. Three major constraints that should be considered are presented in Exhibit 15-3.

a. *Time*

A time constraint may govern the performance of an assignment. Most assignments have a deadline. You must determine the deadline, and then allocate a specific amount of time to each stage of the writing process to meet that deadline.

> **For Example** You have 15 days to write a legal research memorandum on an issue in a case. You should allocate your time among the prewriting, writing, and postwriting stages of the writing process. A possible allocation could be six days for prewriting, five days for drafting, and four days for postwriting.

If you fail to allocate your time properly or fail to stick to the allocation, you may become absorbed or stuck in one stage and fail to leave enough time to properly complete the assignment. It does no good to completely research and analyze an issue if you do not have time to translate the research and analysis into a good written form.

> **For Example** You have 15 days to prepare an office memorandum. You become absorbed in the intricacies of the research and leave only two days to write the memo. This is not sufficient time to prepare a well-crafted product. The memorandum will either not be turned in on time or be poorly written. Either way, your professional reputation is harmed.

b. *Length*

The assignment may have a length constraint. The supervising attorney may require that it not exceed a certain number of pages. If this is so, keep the length limitation in mind from the start. The amount of research material you gather is affected by this limitation. Of course, you must gather all the applicable law. You must, however, screen the research to ensure that you do not gather excessive information. With the space limitation in mind, consider how much of the material you are gathering can be included in the writing. Also, organize the writing to make sure that each section is allotted sufficient space.

> **For Example** The assignment is to prepare a legal research memorandum that does not exceed 15 pages. The organization must allocate sufficient space for each section of the memorandum. If the analysis ends up consisting of 14 pages, there will not be sufficient space for the statement of the facts, the issue, or the conclusion.

c. *Format*

Most law offices have rules or guidelines governing the organization and format of most types of legal writing, such as case briefs, office memoranda, and correspondence. Courts have formal rules governing the format and style of briefs and other documents submitted for filing.

> **For Example** Many courts have rules governing the size of the paper, the size of the margins, the length of briefs, and so on. If you do not conform to these rules, your submission may be rejected.

Inasmuch as you must draft the assignment within the constraints of the required format, you must identify that format at the beginning of the prewriting process.

3. Organization (Format)

Organization in the prewriting stage is the key to successful legal writing. You must be organized when conducting research and analysis in the prewriting stage, and the assignment must be organized when it is written. This may be accomplished through the development and use of an outline. An **outline** is the skeletal structure and organizational framework of the legal writing. Three aspects of outlines follow:

- The value of an outline
- The creation of an outline
- The use of an outline

a. *Value of an Outline*

An outline is considered useful in the writing stage. It makes writing easier by providing an organized framework for the presentation of research and analysis. An outline, however, is of greatest value when properly used in the prewriting stage. There are several reasons for this:

- The act of creating an outline causes you to organize ideas and prepare an approach to the assignment at the beginning of the process. This helps you to think through all the aspects of the assignment and take a global view, thereby avoiding gaps and weaknesses in your approach. You focus your attention and organize your thinking before you jump into the assignment.
- The use of an outline saves time. When used properly, all the information from a research source is placed in the outline when research is being performed. Time is often wasted having to retrieve a research source for a second or subsequent time to

gather information that you either thought was not important or forgot to retrieve. If an outline is used properly, you should not have to retrieve any research source more than once.

■ An outline provides an organized framework for the structure of the assignment and for conducting research and analysis. It provides a context within which to place research and ideas. This is discussed in detail in section IV.A.3.c of this chapter.

■ An outline breaks complex problems into manageable components. It provides an organized framework from which to approach complex problems.

b. *Creation of an Outline*

The goal when creating an outline is to prepare the skeletal framework of the document you are going to draft. The outline should provide an overall picture of how all the pieces of the assignment relate to each other and fit together. The form of the outline is not important. Whether you use Roman numerals (I and II), capital letters (A and B), narrative sentences, fragments of sentences, or single words does not matter. Use whatever form or style works for you. You should use indentations to separate main topics from subtopics.

For Example	I. Introduction

II. Issue

III. Analysis

    a. Rule of law

    b. Case law

        1. Name of case

        2. Facts of case

The outline of the legal writing is governed by the type of writing you are preparing. Locate the standard format used in the office for the type of legal writing you are drafting. In the case of an office legal memorandum or correspondence, the law office may have a special format that must be followed. Use that format as the basis for the outline. If the writing is to be filed in court, such as an appellate brief, follow the format set out in the court rules. Whatever the basic format is, it may be necessary to make additions and expand the outline.

For Example The firm's format for an office legal memorandum is the following:

1. Description of assignment
2. Issue
3. Facts
4. Analysis
5. Conclusion

This is a broad format and takes a lot of filling in to be useful. It may be necessary to fill in details for each section. The outline is a perfect place to do this.

For Example An expansion of the analysis section may be as follows:

1. Analysis
   1. Introduction
   2. Rule of law
   3. Case interpreting the rule of law
      a. Name of case/citation
      b. Facts of case
      c. Rule of law or legal principle presented in the case that applies to the client's facts
      d. Application of rule/principle from the case to the client's facts

This outline example is referred to in this chapter as the "analysis" outline example.

When developing an outline, keep the following points in mind:

1. Keep the facts and issues of the assignment in mind while developing the outline. It may be necessary to expand the outline to accommodate additional facts and issues.

   For Example The standard office outline may accommodate only one issue, whereas your assignment involves more than one issue. Expand the outline to apply the standard office outline to each issue.

2. Be flexible when creating and working with an outline. Realize that it may be necessary to change the outline as you conduct research.

   For Example The assignment involves the drafting of a simple office legal memorandum that addresses one issue. The outline you decide to follow is the analysis outline example presented previously. When research is conducted, it becomes apparent that two aspects of the rule of law apply to the issue, so two court opinions must be included in the analysis. The memo outline must now be expanded:

   1. Analysis
      1. Introduction
      2. Rule of law
      3. Case interpreting the meaning of *publication* as used in the rule of law
         a. Name of case/citation
         b. Facts of case
         c. Interpretation of term
         d. Application of the interpretation to the client's facts
      4. Case interpreting the meaning of *written* as used in the rule of law
         a. Name of case/citation
         b. Facts of case
         c. Interpretation of term
         d. Application of the interpretation to the client's facts

3. Do not be surprised if it is necessary to reorganize the outline as a result of your research. Research may provide a clearer picture of the relationship between issues and necessitate a rethinking of the organization of the outline.

> **For Example** As a result of your research, you realize that the sequence in which you plan to address the issues should be changed. The issue you thought should be discussed first should come second.

4. The basic organizational format for most legal writing that requires legal analysis is the IRAC format. That is, first state the question or issue, next identify the rule of law that governs the issue, then analyze how and why the rule applies, and end with a conclusion summarizing the analysis. You may follow this format when addressing each issue and subissue. If for some reason you are at a loss for a format to follow, use the IRAC format.

5. Include in the outline a reference to or some notation for transition sentences. **Transition sentences** connect the major sections of the writing and lead the reader smoothly through the legal analysis. They make the document more readable. It is easy to become so focused on the law, cases, and analysis that you forget the transitions.

> **For Example** "The rule of law that governs this issue is § 36-6-6, which prohibits oppressive conduct by majority shareholders. In the case of *Jones v. Thomas*, the court held. . . ."
>
> There should be a transition sentence linking the case to the rule of law: "The rule of law that governs this issue is § 36-6-6, which prohibits oppressive conduct by majority shareholders. *Because the statute does not provide a definition of the term oppressive* conduct, *case law must be referred to. A case on point is Jones v. Thomas*, where the court held. . . ."

Outline formats for correspondence, office legal memoranda, and court briefs are presented in Chapter 16 through Chapter 19.

c. Use of an Outline

The value of an outline is determined by its use. If you prepare an outline and then set it aside while you are researching and analyzing the assignment, it is of limited value. Its only value when used in this manner is to help organize your thinking and provide the organizational framework for the writing that follows. An outline is of greatest value when it is actively integrated into the prewriting stage. It can serve as an *invaluable guide* during the research and analysis process.

> **For Example** Follow the outline format when researching and analyzing: First identify the issue, next locate the rule of law that governs the issue, then identify the case law that interprets the rule of law in a fact situation similar to the client's case, and so on.

When integrated in the research and analysis process, an outline provides an organized context within which to place research and ideas. When so used, it will result in the development of a rough draft while research and analysis are being conducted. The result is

Exhibit 15-4 *Two-Step Approach for Use of an Outline in the Prewriting Stage.*

STEP 1	Convert the outline to a usable form—an expanded outline.	Use several sheets of three-holed or binder paper, or create separate pages if you are using a computer. Write the name of each section and subsection of the outline at the top of a separate page (e.g., at the top of one page write "Issue," at the top of another page "Facts," and so on).
STEP 2	Integrate all research, analysis, and ideas into the outline while conducting research and analysis.	As you conduct the research and develop ideas concerning any aspect of the case, enter them on the appropriate page of the expanded outline.

© Cengage Learning 2014

a tremendous savings of time and effort. The integrated use of an outline in the prewriting stage simplifies the writing stage and makes it much easier.

How, then, do you integrate an outline into the research and analysis process in the prewriting stage? There are several ways to accomplish this. The practical approach suggested here is to use an **expanded outline**. This approach is composed of the two steps presented in Exhibit 15-4.

For illustration purposes, assume the assignment is to prepare an office legal memorandum addressing a single issue in a client's case. The cause of action is a slander tort claim. The broad issue is whether there was publication within the meaning of the law. Section 20-2-2 of the state statutes provides that civil slander is "the oral publication of a false statement of fact concerning an individual. . . ." The statute does not define *publication*. The facts of the case are that neighbor A, while visiting neighbor B's house, communicated to neighbor B a false statement of fact concerning the client. This example is referred to in this chapter as the "slander" example.

The format for the body of an office legal memorandum adopted in the office is as follows:

I. Issue

II. Statement of facts

III. Analysis/application

    1. Rule of law—the rule of law that governs the issue—enacted/case law

    2. Case(s)—court interpretation of rule if necessary

        A. Name and citation

        B. Brief summary of facts showing case is on point

        C. Rule/principle/reasoning applied by the court that applies to client's case

        D. Application—discussion of how the rule of law presented in the court decision applies in the client's case

    3. Counteranalysis

IV. Conclusion—a summary of the analysis

(1) Convert the Outline to a Usable Form The memorandum format used in the office is typed on one page of paper and is not very useful in this form. The first step in the use of the outline is to convert it to a usable form—to expand the outline. This is accomplished by taking several sheets of three-holed or binder paper, or creating separate pages if you are using a computer, and writing the name of each section and subsection of the outline at the top of a separate page.

For Example At the top of one sheet of paper or computer page, write "Issue." At the top of another page, write "Statement of facts." At the top of another page, write "Analysis—rule of law." Continue with a new page for each of the following: "Analysis—case," "Analysis—application of case to client's facts," "Counteranalysis," and "Conclusion."

Some sections of the outline may require more than one page.

For Example The "Analysis—case" section may require two pages: one page for "Analysis—case—citation and facts of case" and one page for "Analysis—case—rule/principle/reasoning." Two or more pages may be required for a case because, in many instances, a great deal of information may be taken from a case, such as lengthy quotes from the court's reasoning.

If more than one rule of law applies, there should be a separate page for each rule of law. If several cases apply, there are separate pages for each case. If there are separate issues, research and analyze each issue separately, and prepare a separate expanded outline for each issue.

When completed, there should be a separate page for each section and subsection of the outline. Place the pages in a loose-leaf binder or enter them in the computer in the order of the outline. In other words, the first page will be the "Issue" page, followed by the "Statement of facts" page, then the "Analysis—rule of law" page, and so on. If you are using binder paper, insert blank sheets of paper between each section. This allows for the expansion of each section to accommodate additional notes, comments, ideas, and other information. The end result is a greatly expanded outline that is usable in the prewriting stage.

(2) Integrate Research, Analysis, and Ideas into the Outline As you conduct research and develop ideas concerning any aspect of the case, enter them on the appropriate page of the expanded outline.

(i) *Ideas* When any idea occurs concerning the case, enter it on the page of the expanded outline relating to that idea.

For Example In the slander example, you may begin with a broad definition of the issue, such as "Was there publication?" As you conduct research and give more thought to the case, more refined formulations of the issue will become apparent, such as: "Under § 20-2-2, does slander occur when one person orally communicates to a third party false statements of fact concerning an individual?" As soon as this formulation of the issue comes to you, write it on the issue page. When it is time to write the memorandum, you will have multiple versions of the issue listed on the issue page. When all the ideas concerning the issue are in one place, it is easier to assemble the final statement of the issue.

The term *ideas* as used here includes all thoughts relating to the writing of the assignment, including how to compose transition sentences.

For Example While researching a case, an idea may come to you about how the transition sentence linking the case to the rule of law should be written. Write the sentence in the beginning of the case section of the expanded outline or at the end of the rule of law page.

Keep the expanded outline with you. Often the mind will work on an aspect of a case during sleep. You may wake up in the middle of the night or in the morning with an idea concerning the assignment or the answer to a problem. If the expanded outline is handy, you can immediately enter the idea or answer in the appropriate section. If it is not convenient to keep the outline with you, then carry a notepad. Enter ideas on the notepad as they come to you and place them in the outline later.

The value of the ability to immediately place ideas where they belong in the structure of the writing cannot be overemphasized. The following are some of the benefits:

▪ Ideas are not lost. When researching, you often may have an idea and say to yourself, "I'll remember to include this when I write the ___ section." Five minutes later, the idea is lost. If you can immediately write the idea down where it belongs, it will not be lost.

▪ You can avoid confusion if you record ideas in the section where they will appear in the writing. If you keep the binder with the expanded outline with you throughout the prewriting stage, and you place all ideas where they belong as they come to you, you will avoid confusion and time lost figuring out which ideas go where.

> **For Example** While you are reading a case that interprets the rule of law, an idea may occur that relates to another aspect of the assignment, such as, "This gives me an idea about the counteranalysis of this issue." You may jot the idea down on a separate piece of paper or think you will remember it. You say to yourself, "I'll remember to include this when I write the counteranalysis."
>
> By the time you get down to writing, time has passed, and you cannot remember what the idea was or, if you jotted it down, where the idea fits into the assignment. There are several pieces of paper with notes and ideas, and you have forgotten what many of them relate to or why.

▪ Writing becomes easier. When you sit down to write, all ideas are there, each in its proper place. You do not waste time in performing the additional step of organizing ideas. *Ideas are immediately organized as they come to you.*

> **For Example** If the "Issue" page of the expanded outline contains all the ideas concerning the ways the issue may be stated, it is easier to craft the final draft of the issue. You have every possible variation at hand. Drafting the issue is just a matter of assembling the issue from the best of the variations.

(ii) *Research* Just as you add ideas in the proper place in the expanded outline as they occur, enter all the relevant data on the appropriate page as you conduct your research.

> **For Example** Referring to the slander example, when you locate the slander statute, § 20-2-2, place it on the "rule of law" page. Include the proper citation and a copy of the statute. Include on the outline page all the information concerning the statute that you may need when writing. This avoids having to look up the statute more than once.

> **For Example** When you find a case or cases on point, enter the information concerning the case on the appropriate case page of the outline. This should include information such as the full citation, pertinent quotes concerning the rule of law or legal principle applied by the court, and the legal reasoning.

When researching case law, retrieve everything you may need from the case and include it in the expanded outline as you read the case. Why waste time looking up the same case twice? Place a copy of the case in the outline if necessary.

> **For Example** First, read through the entire case. Then, on the second reading, as you come upon a statement of the legal principle or legal reasoning that may apply to the client's case, stop reading. Enter the information from the case in the appropriate page of the expanded outline. Indicate the page of the case from which it was taken and, if appropriate, quote the information.

All too often, when reading a case, the tendency is to tell yourself that you will come back later and note the pertinent information. If there is any possibility that you will use information from a case, *retrieve it as you find it* and place on the appropriate case page of the outline. You will save time by not having to reread portions of the case.

Often the reasoning or rule you want to use is not where you remembered, and then you waste time wading through the case trying to relocate it. If it turns out that information retrieved will not be used in the legal writing, it is simply not used. It is much better to have everything concerning the case in your expanded outline when you begin to write than to have to stop, retrieve, and reread the case.

If you use an expanded outline as suggested here, you are ready to write. All your research and ideas are assembled and organized. In effect, you have prepared a rough draft, so the writing task is made much simpler: The organization is finished, ideas are captured, research is assembled in the proper place, and many transition sentences are already crafted and in place. The writing task is reduced to simply converting the outline to paragraph and sentence form.

B. Writing Stage

The second stage in the writing process is the actual drafting of the legal writing. In the **writing stage** you assemble the research, analysis, and ideas into a written product. Many individuals find it difficult to go from the research stage to the drafting stage, from the prewriting stage to the writing stage. This is often called "writer's block." Some of the obstacles that can make it difficult to begin writing are organizing the research and determining what goes where and how it relates and is connected. If you use an expanded outline in the prewriting stage, it is much easier to begin writing. The research and analysis are already organized, the relationship of the material is already established by the outline, and many introductory and transitional sentences have already been written.

Chapter 16 through Chapter 19 present a detailed discussion of what must be included when writing an office legal memorandum, court brief, or legal correspondence. The rules and guidelines in Exhibit 15-5 will help with the writing process in general.

Exhibit 15-5 Rules and Guidelines—Writing Stage.

1. Prepare the writing location.
2. Write during the time of day when you do your best work.
3. Limit interruptions.
4. Begin writing; do not procrastinate.
5. Begin with a part of the assignment you feel most confident about.
6. Do not try to make the first draft the final draft.
7. Do not begin to write until you are prepared.
8. If you become stuck, move to another part of the assignment.
9. Establish a timetable.

1. Prepare the writing location. Make sure the work environment is pleasant and comfortable. Have at hand all the resources you need, such as paper, computer, and research materials.

2. Write during the time of day when you do your best work.

> **For Example** If you are a "morning person," write in the morning and save other tasks for later in the day.

3. Limit interruptions. Legal writing requires focus and concentration. Therefore, select a writing time and environment that allow you to be as free from interruptions and distractions as possible.

4. Begin writing; do not procrastinate. One of the most difficult steps is beginning. Do not put it off. The longer you put it off, the harder beginning will become. Start writing anything that has to do with the project. Do not expect what you start with to be great, just start. Once you begin writing, it will get easier.

5. Begin with a part of the assignment you feel most confident about. You do not have to write in the sequence of the outline. Write the easiest material first, especially if you are having trouble starting.

6. Do not try to make the first draft the final draft. The goal of the first draft is to translate the research and analysis into organized paragraphs and sentences, not to produce a finished product. Just write the information in rough form. It is much easier to polish a rough draft than to make the first draft a finished product.

7. Do not begin to write until you are prepared. Do all the research and analysis before beginning. It is much easier to write a rough draft if the prewriting stage is thoroughly completed.

8. If you become stuck, move to another part of the assignment. If you are stuck on a particular section, leave it. The mind continues to work on a problem subconsciously. That is why solutions to problems often seem to appear in the morning. Let the subconscious work on the problem while you move on. The solution to the difficulty may become apparent when you return to the problem.

9. Establish a timetable. Break the project into logical units and allocate your time accordingly. This helps you avoid spending too much time on one section of the writing and running out of time. Do not become fanatical about the time schedule, however. You created the timetable, and you can break it. It is there as a guide to keep you on track and alert you to the overall time constraints.

C. Postwriting Stage

The **postwriting stage** is the stage of the legal writing process where an assignment is revised, edited, and assembled in final form.

1. Revising

The first draft will not be the final draft. Revise all initial drafts with the idea of improving quality and clarity. Do not be surprised if the initial draft requires several **revisions**. Do not set a limit on the number of drafts that may be required. The goal is that the final product clearly, concisely, and completely conveys the information it is designed to convey. The number of drafts should be governed by this goal. Develop a checklist for use when revising a draft (see Exhibit 15-6). Some items that you may wish to include in the checklist follow:

1. Is the writing well organized? Is it organized in a logical manner? Does each section logically follow the previous section?

Exhibit 15-6 *Reviewing a Draft Checklist.*

1. Is the writing well organized?
2. Is it written in a manner the audience will understand?
3. Is the writing clear? Does it make sense?
4. Is the writing concise? Are there extra words that can be eliminated?
5. Is the writing complete? Are all the aspects of the assignment covered?
6. Are the legal authorities correctly cited?

© Cengage Learning 2014

2. Is it written in a manner the audience will understand? If the writing is addressed to a layperson, is the draft written in plain language the reader will understand?

3. Is the writing clear? Does it make sense? Are the sections connected with transition sentences that clearly link the sections and guide the reader from one section to the next?

4. Is the writing concise? Are there extra words that can be eliminated? Is it repetitive? If multiple examples are included to illustrate a single point, are all the examples necessary?

5. Is the writing complete? Are all the aspects of the assignment covered? If there are multiple issues, is each issue and subissue thoroughly analyzed?

6. Are the legal authorities correctly cited? Are all legal citations in the correct form? All legal research sources must be correctly cited. The rules and resources for ensuring your citations are correct are discussed in Chapter 8.

When reviewing a draft, allow time to elapse between drafting and revising. This allows the mind to clear. You will then be able to approach the revision with a fresh perspective and are more likely to catch errors and inconsistencies.

2. Editing

Editing is actually part of the revision process. The revision process discussed in the previous section addresses the broad intellectual and structural content of the legal writing, such as overall organization, clarity, and conciseness. Editing focuses on technical writing issues, such as punctuation, spelling, grammar, phrasing, typographical errors, and citation errors. Many of these specific areas are discussed in Chapter 16. A few general editing tips to keep in mind, however, follow:

1. Be prepared to edit a legal writing several times. It may be necessary to edit a revision several times to catch all the errors.

2. Read the document aloud. When you silently read your own draft, the mind may automatically fill in a missing word or correct an error without your knowing it, and you will not catch the error. If possible, have a colleague read it to you.

3. Have a colleague whose writing skills you respect edit the document.

4. Do not rely on computer spell-check or grammar-check functions.

V. GENERAL RESEARCH SUGGESTIONS

Research is a major part of the prewriting stage of the writing process. The steps involved in legal research are discussed in Chapter 2 through Chapter 7; some general suggestions and guidelines concerning legal research as it relates to the prewriting stage are included in Exhibit 15-7.

Exhibit 15-7 *Suggestions and Guidelines—Legal Research and the Prewriting Stage.*

1. Prepare and use an expanded outline when conducting research.
2. Identify the issue first.
3. Research issues one at a time.
4. Become familiar with the area of law.
5. Locate the enacted law that governs the question.
6. Locate the case law that may apply.
7. Make sure that the research is current.
8. If you reach a dead end, reanalyze the issue.

1. Prepare and use an expanded outline when conducting research.

2. Identify the issue first, as you cannot begin to look for an answer until you know the question. The preliminary identification may be very broad, such as "Did negligence occur?" or "Was there a breach of contract when the goods were delivered 10 days late?" This preliminary identification of the issue will usually identify the general area of law to be researched, such as contracts, negligence, and so on.

3. Thoroughly research each issue to its conclusion before proceeding to the next issue. If you find material on another issue, note a reference to it on the page in the expanded outline for that issue. Researching several issues at once only leads to frustration and confusion.

4. Become familiar with the area of law. If you are unfamiliar with the area of law that applies to the issue, obtain a general overview. Legal encyclopedias and treatises are examples of sources to consult to obtain an overview of an area of law.

5. Locate first the enacted law that governs the question, such as a statute or constitutional provision.

6. Locate the relevant case law if there is no enacted law that governs or if the enacted law is so broadly drafted that case law is required to interpret the enacted law. Attempt to locate mandatory precedent first, then persuasive precedent and secondary authority.

7. Make sure that the research is current. Check supplements and Shepardize cases to be sure that the authority located is current.

8. If you reach a dead end, reanalyze the issue. If you cannot find any authority, either primary or secondary, chances are the issue is too broadly or too narrowly stated. Restate the issue. If the issue is too broadly stated, restate it in narrower terms. Return to a basic research source for guidance, such as a legal encyclopedia. If the issue is too narrowly framed, restate it in broader terms.

VI. KEY POINTS CHECKLIST: *The Writing Process*

✔ Adopt a writing process. An organized approach is essential for legal writing. Develop a process that works for you. Follow the process recommended in this chapter or create your own.

✔ Work from an expanded outline in the prewriting stage. An expanded outline provides a framework for organizing your research and capturing your ideas.

✔ Consider the audience. Always identify the audience early in the process. The type of audience influences the style, depth, and complexity of the finished product.

✔ Consider time, length, and format constraints. Identify any constraints that affect the assignment, and design the approach to the assignment with these constraints in mind.

✔ Do not procrastinate. If you have trouble beginning to write, start with the easiest section. Sit down and begin. Do not worry about quality—just start.

✔ Break large assignments into manageable sections. Do not become overwhelmed by the complexity of an assignment.

✔ Do not try to make the first draft the final draft. Be prepared to compose several drafts. The goal is a quality product. Let the number of drafts be determined by this goal.

✔ Update your research. Check all authority to ensure that it is current.

VII. APPLICATION

This section presents an overview of the writing process by applying the process to the hypothetical presented at the beginning of the chapter. After gathering and reviewing all the information available in the office concerning Ms. Beck's case, Rick follows the process recommended in this chapter. An outline of Rick's application of the process follows.

A. Prewriting Stage

I. *Assignment.* Rick first reviews the assignment.

    A. *Is the assignment clear?* He reviews the assignment to be sure he understands what is required. Rick has no question in this regard. The assignment is to research and analyze the question of whether the evidence seized in the case can be suppressed.

    B. *What type of legal writing is required?* The assignment is to draft an office legal memorandum. Rick retrieves the office memorandum outline form used by the firm. The body of the outline is presented here.

       I. Issue

      II. Statement of facts

     III. Analysis/application

         1. Rule of law—the rule of law that governs the issue—enacted/case law

         2. Case(s)—court interpretation of the rule of law if necessary

            A. Name and citation

            B. Brief summary of facts showing the case is on point

            C. Rule/principle/reasoning applied by the court that applies to client's case

            D. Application—discussion of how the rule of law presented in the court decision applies in the client's case

         3. Counteranalysis

      IV. Conclusion—a summary of the analysis

    C. *Who is the audience?* The memorandum is for office use. Rick knows he does not have to write it in layperson's terms.

II. *Constraints.* What are the constraints on the assignment? Rick has a time constraint. Any motion to suppress the evidence must be filed within 30 days. He must finish the memorandum sufficiently in advance of the 30 days to allow Ms. Fletcher time to review it and prepare the appropriate motion. Based on past experience, he knows Ms. Fletcher prefers to have 10 days to review the memorandum and prepare the motion. This leaves him 20 days to complete the assignment.

Rick also knows that Ms. Fletcher prefers shorter memos. She has told him that a single-issue memo should not exceed seven pages. He knows he must budget his time and research to meet these constraints.

III. *Organization.* Rick organizes the assignment around the outline.

   A. *Creation of expanded outline.* Rick expands the outline as suggested in section IV.A.3 of this chapter. The initial expanded outline is composed of eight pages of paper or computer pages. He labels the pages as follows: Issue; Facts; Analysis—rule of law; Analysis—case name, facts, and citation; Analysis—case rule/principle and reasoning; Analysis—application of case to facts; Counter-analysis; and Conclusion.

   B. *Use of expanded outline.* Rick begins his research with the expanded outline at hand. He studies the facts and begins to formulate the issue. Every time he thinks of a way to state the issue, he writes it on the "Issue" page.

> **For Example** The first formulation of the issue is, "Can the evidence be suppressed?" Later formulations are, "Can evidence be suppressed when officers execute a warrant unannounced based on the warrant's authorization of unannounced entry?" and "Under the state's exclusionary rule, can evidence be suppressed when officers conduct a search unannounced, pursuant to a warrant authorizing unannounced entry to ensure officer safety, and the authorization is based upon an affidavit that gives no particularized facts regarding threats to officer safety?"

As he researches, Rick finds article II, section 5, of the state constitution, which prohibits illegal searches and seizures. He copies article II, section 5, and places it on the "Analysis—rule of law" page. He realizes this provision is so broadly formulated that he must locate case law for an interpretation of how it applies in an unannounced entry situation.

> **For Example** Article II, section 5, does not provide guidance as to what constitutes an illegal search when law enforcement officers enter a residence unannounced; therefore, case law must be consulted.

While looking for a case on point, he thinks of a transition sentence that will connect the rule of law section of the memo to the case law section. Rick immediately writes this sentence at the end of the "Analysis—rule of law" page of the outline.

Rick locates the court opinion of *State v. Brick*. Addressing a fact situation almost identical to Ms. Beck's, the court held that a warrant may authorize unannounced entry. The court went on to state, however, that the authorization must be based on a "particularized showing that the individuals whose residence is being searched have in the past represented a threat to officer safety. Any authorization based upon a generalized statement, such as 'Drug offenders often present a threat to officers' safety during the execution of search warrants,' violates article II, section 5, and the exclusionary rule requires the suppression of any evidence seized."

Rick enters all the relevant information from the case in the appropriate "Analysis—case" pages of the outline. He includes the full citation, any relevant quotations from the case, and the page-number references for the quotations. He does not have to reread the case when he writes the memorandum. All the key information is in the expanded outline.

While analyzing the case, he thinks of a sentence he will use when discussing how the case applies to the client's facts. He enters this sentence in the "Analysis—application of case to facts" page of the outline.

| **For Example** | "In our case, just as in *State v. Brick*, the officers executed a warrant unannounced, based on the authorization contained in the warrant. In our case, as in *Brick*, the authorization was based upon a generalized statement that drug offenders often pose a threat to officer safety when the officers announce their presence prior to entry. In *Brick*, the court ruled that such searches violate the state constitution and the evidence seized must be suppressed. If the trial court follows the rule of law presented in *State v. Brick*, the evidence should be suppressed." |

If there are more cases that should be included in the memo, Rick will insert additional pages in the outline for each case and enter the pertinent information on the appropriate page.

Rick identifies any counterargument, such as that contained in conflicting case law, and enters it in the "Counteranalysis" section of the outline. If Rick has any thoughts concerning the conclusion while conducting the research and analysis, he enters them in the "Conclusion" section of the outline.

While working on the assignment, Rick keeps the outline or a notepad with him. He takes it home after work. He writes any idea concerning the assignment on the appropriate page when the idea occurs. Nothing is lost, and all his ideas and research are organized in the outline. Transition sentences and other parts of the writing, such as how the issue should be written, are already drafted and in the proper place. If more than one issue must be addressed, Rick prepares a separate section of the outline for that issue and the rule of law and case law that apply to it.

B. Writing Stage

After completing the research and analysis, Rick prepares a rough draft. He simplifies the task by using the expanded outline. All the research, analysis, and ideas are already organized, and many of the sentences are written and in place. All Rick has to do is to convert the outline into sentence and paragraph form and fill in the gaps. When drafting, Rick keeps in mind the guidelines presented in section IV.B of this chapter, such as not procrastinating and preparing a comfortable writing location.

C. Postwriting Stage

The final step is to revise and edit the memorandum. Focusing on conciseness, clarity, and completeness, Rick uses a checklist similar to the one presented in section IV.C of this chapter. Rick may need to create several drafts and spend considerable time revising. Because his work is judged by the finished product, Rick takes care during this stage of the writing process.

Note that this chapter places a great deal of emphasis on the prewriting stage of the writing process. Organization here is the key to simplicity, taking care in this part of the process and using an expanded outline. It may seem like a lot of work to prepare an expanded outline, but its use will actually save time in the long run.

Summary

Contrary to popular belief, the bulk of the practice of law involves writing in one form or another. Legal writing includes the preparation of documents, such as office legal memoranda; legal correspondence to clients and other individuals; litigation documents that will be filed with a court; and transaction documents prepared for clients' use, such as contracts.

Legal writing is often complex, requiring in-depth research and detailed analysis. The complexities of an assignment, time constraints, and heavy workloads dictate the necessity of following a writing process when engaging in legal writing. There is no standard writing process. Each individual should adopt or create a process that works for them. The chapter presents a process that focuses on the three stages of the writing process: prewriting, writing, and postwriting.

The prewriting stage has three sections: the assignment, constraints affecting the assignment, and the organization of the assignment. When approaching an assignment, you should first review the assignment and consider any constraints that affect the assignment, such as time, length, and format.

After you address these matters, prepare an expanded outline and use it when engaging in the research and analysis of the assignment. An expanded outline consists of a separate notebook page or computer-generated page for each topic and subtopic of the outline. Enter research and analysis in the expanded outline throughout the prewriting stage as you gather material and conduct analysis. The end result is a rough draft developed during the prewriting stage.

Adopting a prewriting process simplifies the writing stage. In the writing stage, the rough draft represented by the expanded outline is converted to the finished product (for example, a legal memorandum).

All drafts must be revised and edited. A revision focuses on ensuring clarity, completeness, and conciseness. Editing focuses on narrower concerns involving accuracy, such as punctuation and grammar.

The chapter concludes with reminders concerning legal research as it relates to the prewriting stage of the writing process. These suggestions include starting with the identification of the issue and making sure to update all research.

Quick References

Internet Resources

Using "legal writing for paralegals" or "legal research memorandum" as a topic, you will find various Web sites (literally thousands of sites) that concern legal writing. Some sites refer to legal writing textbooks, some focus on legal research and analysis, others focus on legal writing for law school students, some advertise research and writing services, some are Web sites for specific classes taught at schools, some advertise courses and seminars on legal writing, and some sites discuss legal memoranda in specific areas such as environment law. A Chicago-Kent College of Law site, http://www.kentlaw.edu, presents a sample legal memorandum (in the Search box, type "sample memo"). Another Web site, the Georgetown University Law Library, http://www.ll.georgetown.edu, provides links to research and writing resources and related materials useful to legal writers.

As with most topics on the Web, the problem is not the lack of sites but the presence of too many sites. Probably the best strategy is to narrow your search to a specific type of legal writing and topic, such as "legal memorandum, public service contracts." The following sites may provide useful support information when you engage in projects requiring legal research.

http://www.nala.org

> This is the site for the National Association of Legal Assistants (NALA). The association site provides a wealth of information ranging from articles on the profession to education and certification programs for paralegals. It includes information on court decisions affecting paralegals and links to other related sites.

http://www.paralegals.org

> This is the Web page for the National Federation of Paralegal Associations (NFPA), another national paralegal organization. Its Web page provides links to a wide range of sites of interest to paralegals, such as research sources, publications, and products.

http://www.paralegaltoday.com

> *Paralegal Today* is a magazine geared toward the needs of paralegals. It often includes helpful articles on legal research and writing.

Exercises

Additional assignments are available on the CourseMate.

> The following exercises are helpful in developing an understanding of and familiarity with the use of a writing process.

ASSIGNMENT 1

Describe the stages of the legal writing process.

ASSIGNMENT 2

Describe the steps of the prewriting stage.

ASSIGNMENT 3

Describe the types of legal writing discussed in this chapter.

ASSIGNMENT 4

Why is the type of audience important?

ASSIGNMENT 5

What are some of the constraints that may affect your performance of an assignment? How do they affect your performance of an assignment?

ASSIGNMENT 6

What is an expanded outline? Describe the creation and elements of the body of an expanded outline for an office legal memorandum.

ASSIGNMENT 7

Describe the use of an expanded outline in the preparation of an office legal memorandum.

ASSIGNMENT 8

What are some of the rules to keep in mind during the writing stage?

ASSIGNMENT 9

Prepare a checklist for revising and editing.

ASSIGNMENT 10

What are the general factors to keep in mind when engaging in research?

ASSIGNMENT 11

The paralegal is assigned the task of preparing an office legal memorandum. The memorandum is due in 10 days, and there is a 5-page limit. The facts and law are as follows:

Facts: Mary was Tom's stockbroker and financial advisor. Tom owned five acres of property. Mary advised Tom to sell the property to Ana at a price slightly below the market value. She recommended that Tom buy stock with the proceeds. Tom sold the property to Ana and now wants to have the transaction set aside because he believes Mary unduly and improperly influenced his decision. Mary and Ana are very close friends.

Law: Statutory law (§ 96-4-4-1 of the state statutes) provides that a contract for the sale of land may be set aside if it is entered into under undue influence.

Case law: *Lorn v. Bell*. In a fact situation similar to Tom's, the court ruled that under § 96-4-4-1, undue influence occurs when:

1. The person influenced is susceptible to undue influence.

2. The person influenced is influenced to enter the contract.

3. The opportunity to influence is present.

4. Undue influence is present.

5. The person exercising the undue influence benefits from the undue influence.

Part A
Detail the application of each step of the prewriting stage to this assignment.

Part B
For the organization step of the prewriting stage, prepare an expanded outline based on the outline presented in section IV.A.3.c(ii) in this chapter.

Part C
Based only on the preceding information, fill in the expanded outline. Include a statement of the issue, analysis, counteranalysis, conclusion, and recommendations.

ASSIGNMENT 12
The following assignment is based on assignment 8 in Chapter 17. Use the assignment memo, statutory law, and case law from that assignment. The memo is due in seven days, and there is a five-page limit.

1. Describe in detail the application of each step of the prewriting stage to the assignment.

2. For the organization step of the prewriting stage, prepare an expanded outline based on the outline presented in section IV.A.3.c of this chapter. Using the information presented in the assignment, fill in the expanded outline. Include in the "Issue" section of the outline a broad statement of the issue and at least one narrow statement of the issue.

 CourseMate

The available CourseMate for this text has an interactive eBook and interactive learning tools, including flash cards, quizzes, and more. To learn more about this resource and access free demo CourseMate resources, go to **www.cengagebrain.com**, and search for this book. To access CourseMate materials that you have purchased, go to **login.cengagebrain.com**.

CHAPTER 16

Office Legal Memorandum: Issues and Facts

Jeff Lyons, a paralegal with Berdwin and Associates, received the following memo:

To:	Jeff Lyons, Paralegal
From:	Rita Berdwin, Attorney
Date:	April 20, 2013
Office File No:	Cr. 13-136
Re:	*State of Illinois v. Meril Findo*, Cr. 13-378, privileged communication

We have been retained to represent Meril Findo in the above-referenced case. He is charged with assault with a deadly weapon. Mr. Findo allegedly assaulted his neighbor Joseph Markham with a hammer. Mr. Findo and Mr. Markham were arguing over the location of a fence Mr. Markham was building. According to Mr. Findo, Mr. Markham became angry and attempted to hit him with a brick. A struggle ensued, and the brick fell and hit Mr. Markham on the head. Mr. Markham claims that Mr. Findo became increasingly angry as the argument progressed; Mr. Findo grabbed a hammer and struck him repeatedly on the head and arms. Mr. Markham claims he never assaulted Mr. Findo with a brick. There were no witnesses to the argument. Mrs. Findo is currently separated from Mr. Findo and has agreed to testify against him. Her testimony is that before the confrontation, Mr. Findo stated, "Markham is out there building that damn fence again. I'll put a stop to this once and for all." He grabbed a hammer and went out the door. The Findos' children, Tomas, age 16, and Alice, age 10, were present and heard the conversation. Neither Mrs. Findo nor the children saw the confrontation.

Prepare a memorandum addressing the question of whether the conversation between Mr. and Mrs. Findo is a privileged spousal communication and, therefore, not admissible in the trial of Mr. Findo. I need the memo within two weeks. You can probably cover this in three to five pages.

Outline

Learning Objectives

After completing this chapter, you should understand:

- The importance of an office legal memorandum

- The purposes and uses of an office legal memorandum

- The sections of a basic office legal memorandum

- How to draft the sections of an office legal memorandum: heading, statement of assignment, issue, brief answer, and facts

Exhibit 16-1 *Sections of an Office Legal Memorandum.*

Heading
Statements of Assignment
Issue
Brief Answer
Statement of Facts
Analysis
Conclusion
Recommendations

This chapter and Chapter 17 address the *process and considerations* involved in preparing an office legal memorandum. The office legal memorandum is usually composed of some or all of the sections presented in Exhibit 16-1.

The Application section of this chapter addresses the first half of Jeff's assignment—the heading through the facts sections. The Application section of Chapter 17 covers the remainder of the assignment—the analysis through the recommendations sections.

I. INTRODUCTION

The office legal memorandum is the type of legal writing a paralegal or law clerk engaged in legal research and analysis most frequently prepares. The role of most paralegals and law clerks is to provide assistance and support to an attorney. When this support function involves legal research, it usually focuses on research and analysis of the legal issues in a client's case. The results of this research and analysis are communicated to the attorney in the form of an office legal memorandum. It is one of the most effective and valuable ways paralegals and law clerks can support an attorney.

This chapter and the next are devoted to the preparation of office legal memoranda. Two chapters are devoted to this topic for the following reasons:

- Most law-office analytical legal writing involves the preparation of office legal memoranda.

- The considerations involved in the preparation of office legal memoranda also apply to the preparation of legal analysis documents designed for external use.

This chapter focuses on the basic format for the office legal memorandum and the preparation of the first half of the memorandum: the heading through the statement of facts sections. Chapter 17 focuses on the heart of the memo: the legal analysis through the recommendations sections.

The preparation of an office legal memorandum is a multistep process involving the integration of legal research, analysis, and writing. This chapter and Chapter 17 cannot be read in a vacuum. They require you to integrate the material presented in Chapter 1 through Chapter 15. Although it is assumed that you are familiar with those chapters, cross-references to specific chapters are included to help you correlate and integrate the material.

As mentioned previously, the majority of the legal research and writing prepared by paralegals and law clerks is designed for the use of the supervising attorney rather than for use outside the office. The basic format and analytical process that are followed are fundamentally the same for both an office legal memorandum and a legal analysis document designed for external use. Therefore, consider the information presented here and in Chapter 17 when reading Chapters 18 and 19. External-use documents usually involve:

- Correspondence to clients or other individuals informing them of the law or the analysis of a legal problem
- Briefs submitted to a trial court or court of appeals

II. DEFINITION

An **office legal memorandum** provides an objective, critical analysis of a legal problem. It is an informative document that summarizes the research and analysis of the legal issue or issues raised by the facts of a client's case. It contains a summary of the law and how the law applies to the facts of the case. It presents an objective legal analysis and includes the arguments in favor of and in opposition to the client's position.

A legal memorandum prepared for office use is referred to by many different names: interoffice legal research memorandum, interoffice memorandum of law, office legal memorandum, office research memorandum, objective memorandum, and legal memo. Here and in Chapter 17, the term *office memo* is used when referring to an office legal memorandum.

III. PURPOSES, USES, AND IMPORTANCE

The major purposes and functions of an office memo are as follows:

1. An office memo identifies and records the law that applies to a specific issue or issues raised by the client's facts.
2. An office memo analyzes and explains how the law applies to the issue.
3. An offices memo assesses the strengths and weaknesses of the client's case.
4. An office memo presents a conclusion and proposed solution based on the analysis.

A well-crafted office memo may be put to a variety of uses in a law office:

- It may be used as a guide to determine whether a claim exists.

> **For Example** One of the client's potential causes of action involves a breach of the implied warranty of merchantability. In the client's case, the purchase took place at a garage sale. The office memo reveals that under the applicable statute, the warranty applies only if the seller is a merchant. The case on point provides that individuals holding garage sales are not merchants within the meaning of the statute. The office memo reveals that no cause of action exists for a breach of implied warranty of merchantability.

- It may be used as a guide to the course of action to be pursued.

> **For Example** The case involves a question of whether the client had a duty to discover and disclose information in a real estate transaction. The client was unaware that his house had termites, and consequently, the buyer was not informed of this problem. The office memo reveals that the case law requires the seller to inspect for termites and disclose the results of the inspection to the buyer. This information may lead the attorney to recommend that settlement be pursued.

- It may inform subsequent researchers in the law office, working on other cases with similar issues and facts, how the law applies. Future researchers do not have to spend time reinventing the wheel.

- It may refresh the memory of the attorney assigned to the case on how the law applies to an issue. This is especially true in complex cases. It is also true when the memo is prepared early in the case, and the attorney does not review it until months later when the matter is addressed by the court.

- It may be used as a guide by the attorney preparing a document to be filed with the court or correspondence for the client. The office memo may contain the statutory law, case law, and legal analysis that are the basis for the preparation of the document.

> **For Example** The office memo addresses the question of whether a search warrant was improperly issued due to the insufficiency of the affidavit in support of the warrant. The standards required for a warrant to be sufficient are spelled out in the office memo. The attorney may use the office memo as a basis for preparing a brief in support of, or opposition to, a motion to suppress the evidence seized when the warrant was executed.

Office memos are of primary importance because they provide the answer to legal questions. Their importance is evidenced by the fact that office memos are required at every stage of the litigation process:

- Early in the case, they identify the required elements of the cause of action and what is required to state a claim.

- They are used to determine whether the client has a defense or a cause of action.

- Throughout the litigation they help determine what is required to support or oppose a motion.

- In the discovery process, legal memos address discovery issues, such as what constitutes an attorney's work product.

- At the trial stage, office memos often analyze evidentiary issues, such as whether evidence is admissible.

- At the posttrial stage, office memos may address issues raised on appeal, such as whether the court properly ruled on a matter during the trial.

Ethics. Regardless of the purpose of the memo or at what point in the litigation process it is prepared, the actions of the supervisory attorney and the outcome of the case may largely depend upon the quality of the office memo. Also, as mentioned in Chapter 2, Rule 1.1 of the Model Rules of Professional Conduct requires that a client be provided competent representation. It is critical, therefore, that the performance of research, analysis, and drafting of the memo be thorough, careful, and complete.

As discussed in Chapter 15, legal writing is easier if you use a writing process. In this chapter, you can take that information and use it as the framework for preparing an office memo. Recall the three stages of the writing process: prewriting, writing, and postwriting.

IV. PREWRITING STAGE

The **prewriting stage** consists of three sections:

1. Nature of the assignment—an identification of the type and purpose of the writing assignment

2. Constraints on the assignment—a consideration of any constraints placed on the assignment

3. Organization—the organization of the writing assignment

A prerequisite to beginning the prewriting stage is to assemble all available files and information concerning the client's case. All the relevant files and information must be complete. After this is accomplished, you are able to address the three sections.

A. Nature of the Assignment

The first section of the prewriting stage requires a review of the assignment in which you determine the following:

- Is the assignment clearly understood?
- What type of legal writing is required?
- Who is the audience?

1. Is the Assignment Clearly Understood?

Review the assignment and make a list of all the questions you have concerning the nature or specifics of the assignment. Review the questions with the attorney; take thorough notes when discussing the matter. Most attorneys would prefer that you seek clarification rather than misunderstand the assignment and waste time addressing the wrong question.

> **For Example** The assignment is to analyze the client's case. You may need to seek clarification on which aspects of the case the supervisory attorney wants you to analyze or the specific questions or areas of law you should address.

The assignment may appear simple and clear at first, but as research and analysis progress, multiple issues or separate causes of action may become apparent. It may be necessary to have a brief follow-up meeting with the supervising attorney to determine if the focus should be narrowed.

> **For Example** A case that involves what appears to be a car-wreck situation with a simple negligence issue may blossom into a case involving multiple issues, such as negligence, battery, and negligent infliction of emotional distress. It may be necessary to consult with the supervisory attorney to determine if you should pursue each issue or if some of the issues should be assigned to other paralegals or law clerks. If there are time constraints, it may be necessary for others to address the newly identified issues.

An additional concern when you address this question is whether the assignment requires skills you have not yet acquired.

> **For Example** You have just begun working as a paralegal or law clerk for a solo practitioner, and you are assigned the task of analyzing a complex products liability issue. The research and analysis skills required for the assignment may be beyond your current ability. If this occurs, discuss the matter with the attorney. More harm may occur if you try and fail than if you communicate your concerns up front. The attorney may divide the task into manageable sections and reassign parts of it to other paralegals or law clerks or assign you to work with others to gain experience.

2. What Type of Legal Writing Is Required?

This question is easy to answer; the assignment usually identifies the type of writing required. In the example at the beginning of the chapter, the assignment calls for the preparation of a law office memorandum. The organization, format, and elements of the office memo are discussed in section IV.C in this chapter.

3. Who Is the Audience?

An office memo is usually designed for office use only. Therefore, the reader of the memo (the audience) will be familiar with the law, and the use of legal terminology is appropriate. Determine the writing preferences of the person for whom the office memo is being prepared, such as preferences regarding style.

> **For Example** Some attorneys prefer that the paralegal or law clerk summarize the requirements of the statutory or case law. Some prefer that the law be quoted.

If the memo may be read outside the office, be sure to exclude any comments, recommendations, or other material intended only for office use, such as: "The client's expectations are unreasonable."

B. Constraints on the Assignment

The next section of the prewriting stage requires you to identify any constraint that may affect the preparation of the office memo. Ask yourself if there are any time or page limitations. These matters should be taken into consideration at the beginning. Time constraints govern the allocation of time for research, analysis, and drafting. Length constraints may limit the depth of research and analysis.

> **For Example** If you are limited to five pages and one week, you may want to focus your research on the lead case or cases. There may not be sufficient time or space to address additional cases or secondary authority.

C. Organization of the Assignment

The most important section of the prewriting stage is the organization of the memo. In this section, the format or outline of the office memo is identified, and an expanded outline is created and used.

Most attorneys have a preferred format for an office memo. This format serves as a basic outline and starting point for the organization of the assignment. The creation and use of an expanded outline from the office format is discussed in Chapter 15, section IV.A. In this chapter, the focus is on the format and outline of an office memo and the requirements and considerations involved in the preparation of each section of the outline. This chapter and Chapter 17 include a discussion of the use of an expanded outline when preparing each section of the office memo.

There is no standard format for an office memo. Formats vary from office to office, and attorneys within an office may have different preferences. Follow the format preferred by your supervisor. The format presented in Exhibit 16-2 is recommended for a basic office memo. It includes the standard sections of most office memos that you may encounter. Exhibit 16-3 presents the recommended format for a complex office memo. Following presentation of these formats, discussion turns to the requirements and considerations involved in the preparation of each section.

Exhibit 16-2 *Basic Office Legal Memorandum Format.*

Heading
Statements of Assignment
Issue
Brief Answer
Statement of Facts
Analysis
    Rule of law
    Case law (if necessary) interpretation of rule of law
    Application of law to facts of case
    Counteranalysis
Conclusion

© Cengage Learning 2014

Exhibit 16-3 *Recommended Format for a Complex Office Legal Memorandum Format.*

The recommended format for a complex office legal memorandum

Heading
Statement of Assignment
Issue I
Issue II
Issue III
Brief Answer Issue I
Brief Answer Issue II
Brief Answer Issue III
Statement of Facts
Analysis Issue I
    Rule of Law
    Case law (if necessary)—interpretation of rule of law
    Application of law to facts of case
    Counteranalysis
    Conclusion Issue I
Analysis Issue II
    Rule of Law
    Case law (if necessary)—interpretation of rule of law
    Application of law to facts of case
    Counteranalysis
    Conclusion Issue II
Analysis Issue III
    Rule of Law
    Case law (if necessary)—interpretation of rule of law
    Application of law to facts of case
    Counteranalysis
    Conclusion Issue III
Recommendations (Separate recommendation sections may follow conclusion of each issue.)

© Cengage Learning 2014

Certain sections, such as statements of assignment and brief answers, are not included in all formats and may not be included in the format preferred by your supervising attorney. They are included here so that you will be familiar with them in the event they are part of the format used in your workplace. Other sections, such as issue and analysis, are required in all office memos. In addition, note that the organization of the format may vary among offices.

> **For Example** Usually, the issue section follows the statement of assignment section and precedes the facts section. Some offices, however, may prefer that the facts section precede the issue section.

There is no definition of what constitutes a complex office legal memorandum. Generally, however, it consists of more than one issue and is relatively long (more than 10 pages). The formal outline of a complex office memo is merely an expansion of the basic office memo format. The components and considerations involved in the preparation of a complex office memo are the same as those for a basic office memo. The sections are the same in basic content, but greater in number.

> **For Example** A complex memo may cover three issues. The procedures recommended for identifying, stating, and analyzing each issue are the same as those for the preparation of a basic single-issue memo. Each issue is addressed separately, and the process for addressing each issue is the same as that followed when addressing the single issue in a basic office memo.

See Exhibit 16-3 for a complex office legal memorandum format.

The office memo format may require the inclusion of a table of authorities or a table of contents. These usually follow the statement of the assignment.

> **For Example**
>
> ## TABLE OF CONTENTS
>
> | | | Page |
> |---|---|:---:|
> | ▪ | Issues | 2 |
> | ▪ | Facts | 3 |
> | ▪ | Analysis Issue I | 5 |
> | ▪ | Analysis Issue II | 10 |
> | ▪ | Recommendations | 18 |
>
> ## TABLE OF AUTHORITIES
>
> | CASES | Page |
> |---|:---:|
> | *Smith v. Jones*, 354 F.2d 786 (9th Cir. 1970) | 7 |
> | *Tod v. Doe*, 559 N.E.2d 31 (Ind. Ct. App. 1988) | 13 |
> | CONSTITUTIONAL PROVISIONS | |
> | Art. 3 Ind. Constitution | 6 |
> | STATUTES | |
> | Ind. Code § 35-42-3-2 | 6 |
> | Ind. Code § 35-42-3-8 | 13 |

V. SECTIONS OF THE OFFICE MEMORANDUM

This section discusses the heading, statement of assignment, issue, brief answer, and facts sections of the office memo. Chapter 17 addresses the analysis, conclusion, and recommendations sections.

A. Heading

Most office memos begin with a heading. The **heading** is usually brief and at a minimum contains:

- A heading in all capitals indicating the type of document (e.g., MEMORANDUM OF LAW).
- The name of the person to whom the memo is addressed.
- The name of the person who prepared the memo.
- The date.
- Information identifying the subject of the memo. This may include the case name, client's name, case number, office file number, and subject matter of the memo. It usually follows "Re:".

There are various styles for the heading, as shown in the following example.

For Example

MEMORANDUM OF LAW

To:	Susan Day, Attorney
From:	Tom Clug, Paralegal
Date:	December 1, 2013
Case:	*Smith v. Garage Doors, Inc.*
Office File No.:	Civ. 013-1136
Docket No.:	Civ. 13-378
Re:	Whether a contract for the sale and installation of a garage door is a sale of goods covered by the commercial code or is a sale of a service.

OFFICE LEGAL MEMORANDUM—CONTRACTS

Title:	*Smith v. Garage Doors, Inc.*, Civ. 013-378
Office File:	Civ. 013-1136
Requested by:	Susan Day, Attorney
Submitted by:	Tom Clug, Paralegal
Date Submitted:	12/1/13
Re:	Contract law, Commercial Code § 42-2-205 Sale of goods/sale of service

OFFICE LEGAL MEMORANDUM

To:	Susan Day, Attorney
From:	Tom Clug, Paralegal
Date:	Dec. 1, 2013
Re:	Smith v. Garage Doors, Inc., Civ. 013-378. Whether a contract for the sale and installation of a garage door is a sale of goods or a sale of a service; Commercial Code § 42-2-205.

B. Statement of Assignment

The **statement of assignment** section may also be referred to as a *background* or *purpose section*. Some offices require a section that discusses what the writer has been assigned to do. This section usually follows the heading and may include some background information. The purpose of this section is to provide the reader with a description of the topic covered and the parameters of the assignment.

> **For Example** STATEMENT OF ASSIGNMENT. You have asked me to prepare a legal memorandum on the question of whether the sale and installation of a garage door by Garage Doors, Inc., is a sale of a service or a sale of goods covered by Commercial Code § 42-2-205.

> **For Example** STATEMENT OF ASSIGNMENT. You have asked me to research the question of whether the search of our client's automobile was an illegal search when she was stopped for a minor traffic offense and did not consent to the officer's request for permission to search the back seat of her vehicle. Pursuant to your request, this memo includes an analysis of the relevant state and federal law.

C. Issue

In an office legal memo, present the issue(s) at the beginning of the memo following the heading and the statement of assignment. Doing so establishes the focus of the memo. A well-crafted issue informs the reader, at the outset, of:

- The law that applies
- The precise legal question
- The significant facts of the case

In other words, it identifies the specific question to be addressed and places it in the context of the applicable law and the facts of the case. It sets the scope of the memo, thereby saving the reader from having to determine the issue by reading the analysis section.

Keep in mind the following when preparing the issue section of the memo:

- The issue should be correctly identified.
- The issue should be completely and correctly stated.
- An expanded outline should be used when preparing the section.
- Issues should be addressed separately when preparing complex office memos.

1. Identify the Issue

The **issue** is the precise legal question raised by the facts of the client's case. One of the most important tasks in the legal analysis process is to correctly identify the legal issue. Chapter 10 presents the analytical process that will help you identify the issue when preparing a memo.

2. Correctly State the Issue

Present the issue completely and correctly. When stated correctly, the reader is informed of the focus of the memo at the outset.

For Example The issue involves a question of whether a will is valid if one of the witnesses does not actually see the testator sign the will. If the issue were stated, "Was the will validly executed?" the reader would have to read the analysis section of the memo to determine why it may not have been validly executed. There could be several reasons why the will may not have been validly executed: It may not have been witnessed correctly, there may not have been enough witnesses, or it may have been signed improperly. If the issue is stated, "Under Probate Code § 29-5-7, is the execution of a will valid if one of the witnesses is present in the room when the testator signs but does not actually see the testator sign?" the issue is correctly and completely stated. The reader knows the precise question being addressed, the key facts, and the applicable law. The reader is not forced to obtain this information from the analysis section of the memo.

3. Use the Expanded Outline

As discussed in Chapter 15, the use of an **expanded outline** can greatly simplify the identification and drafting of the issue. On the issue page of the expanded outline, write every formulation of the issue as it comes to mind. The initial draft may be as simple as, "Was the will valid?" As you conduct research and gain a greater understanding of the applicable law, more complete formulations will become apparent.

For Example "Under the state probate code, is a will validly executed if a witness is merely present in the room when the testator signs?" "Under the probate code, is the execution of a will valid if one of the witnesses is present in the room when the testator signs but does not actually see the testator sign?"

When you begin to write the issue section of the memo, all your ideas concerning the issue and drafts of the possible ways it may be stated are before you in one place. The crafting of the final statement of the issue becomes merely a matter of selecting and combining the necessary elements from the various drafts. The Application section of this chapter illustrates the use of an expanded outline in regard to the preparation of an office memo.

4. Address Issues Separately

Office memo assignments, such as a complex memorandum, often involve more than one issue. When performing such assignments, it is preferable to list each issue sequentially in the issue section of the memo. In the analysis section of the format, address each issue separately and completely (this is discussed in Chapter 17). Exhibit 16-4 presents an outline of the format for the analysis section.

When there are multiple issues, list them in the issue section in the order they are discussed in the analysis section. The issue listed as "Issue I" in the issue section should be the first issue addressed in the analysis section. "Issue II" in the issue section should be the second issue addressed in the analysis section, and so on. Also, list the issues in logical order. If the analysis of one issue is dependent on or affected by the analysis of another issue, then present the issue that affects the other issue first. For example, if the analysis of issue B is in some way affected by the analysis of issue A, then address issue A first in the memo.

Exhibit 16-4 Complex Memorandum—Analysis Section Format.

Analysis Issue I
  Rule of law
  Case law (if necessary) interpretation of rule of law
  Application of law to facts of case
  Counteranalysis
  Conclusion issue I
Analysis Issue II
  Rule of law
  Case law (if necessary) interpretation of rule of law
  Application of law to facts of case
  Counteranalysis
  Conclusion issue II
Analysis Issue III, and so on

© Cengage Learning 2014

For Example The client alleges that she entered into a contract to purchase dresses from a dressmaker, and the dressmaker installed defective zippers in the dresses. The dressmaker claims that the contract between them was not a valid contract, and even if there was a valid contract, the zippers were not defective. There are two separate issues. Present and discuss the issue of whether there is a valid contract first, because if there is no contract, there can be no breach. The issue section would appear as follows:

Issue I: Existence of contract

Issue II: Breach of contract

If the issues are not dependent on or affected by other issues, present them in chronological order.

For Example The client was involved in an automobile accident. The defendant ran a red light and hit the client's car. After the wreck, the defendant approached the client's car screaming and threatening the client. The defendant then pushed the client. At least four possible causes of action are present. They should be presented in the order in which they occurred:

Issue I: Negligence—the car wreck

Issue II: Assault—approaching client's car threatening and screaming

Issue III: Battery—pushing the client

Issue IV: Infliction of emotional distress—arising from the combined acts of assault and battery

Exhibit 16-5 presents a checklist for the issue section.

Exhibit 16-5 *Checklist—Issue Section.*

- Is the issue correctly identified?
- Is the applicable rule of law included in the issue?
- Is the citation of the rule correct?
- Is the legal question clearly stated in the issue?
- Are the key facts included in the issue?
- If there are multiple issues, are they presented in the proper order, such as logical or chronological?

© Cengage Learning 2014

D. Brief Answer

The **brief answer** section of the office memo consists of a brief, precise answer to the issue(s). In one or two sentences, it informs the attorney of the answer to the question and briefly summarizes the reasons in support of the answer. Its purpose is to provide a quick answer to the issue. It should not include information that is not discussed in the analysis section of the memo.

Usually, this section begins with a one- or two-word answer, such as "Yes," "No," "Maybe," or "Probably not." The brief answer is followed by a brief statement of the facts and reasoning in support of the answer.

For Example

Issue:	According to the provisions of the Ski Safety Act § 679-33, does a resort have a duty to warn skiers of ice hazards on expert runs?
Brief Answer:	No. The act provides that resorts have the duty to warn of hazards, and that skiers are responsible for snow and ice conditions. The state supreme court has ruled that resorts have a duty to warn of snow and ice hazards only on intermediate and novice ski runs. The court specifically held that there is no duty to warn of any ice hazard on an expert run.
Issue I:	Under the holographic will statute, Colo. Rev. Stat. § 15-11-503, is a holographic will valid if it is handwritten by a neighbor at the direction of the testator, but not written in the testator's handwriting?
Issue II:	Under the holographic will statute, Colo. Rev. Stat. § 15-11-503, is a holographic will valid if one of the witnesses to the testator's signature is a beneficiary of the will?
Brief Answer Issue I:	Yes. The statute requires a holographic will to be handwritten by the testator. The state court of appeals has held that the statute should be interpreted liberally to effect the intent of the testator. If there is clear and convincing evidence that the writing took place at the direction of the testator, the will is valid even if it is not written in the testator's handwriting.
Brief Answer Issue II:	No. The statute requires that the testator's signature be witnessed by two disinterested witnesses.

Exhibit 16-6 presents a checklist for the brief answer section.

Exhibit 16-6 *Checklist—Brief Answer Section.*

> ▪ Does the brief answer follow the office format (e.g., a one- or two- word answer followed by a short statement of the reasons)?
> ▪ Is it brief? Does it summarize the reasons in one or two clear sentences?
> ▪ Is there a separate answer for each issue?

E. Statement of Facts

Following the brief answer section is the presentation of the facts of the case. The purpose of this section is to inform the attorney of the factual context of the issue. There are four considerations to keep in mind when preparing the statement of facts (see Exhibit 16-7).

Exhibit 16-7 *Checklist—Considerations for Statement of Facts Section.*

Importance of the facts	Don't underemphasize the importance of the facts. The law is always applied in the context of the facts of the dispute.
Contents of the section	Include the key and background facts.
Organization of the section	Organize the facts chronologically, topically, or a combination of the two.
Manner of the presentation of the facts	Present the facts accurately, objectively, and free of legal conclusions.

1. Facts Section—Importance

Some writers underemphasize the facts section of an office memorandum because they fail to understand the importance of the facts. The facts and, therefore, the facts section of the memo, are important for several reasons:

> ▪ Every legal dispute involves a question of how the law applies to the facts of the case. Legal questions are not decided in a vacuum. The law is always applied in the context of a dispute raised by the facts of the case. The rule of law selected is determined by identification of the law that applies to the facts.

> ▪ The facts section may refresh the attorney's memory. The attorney may be working on other issues in the case or on several other cases and may not recollect the specific factual context of the issues addressed in the assignment. The facts section saves the supervising attorney from having to review the file to determine the facts.

> ▪ In many law offices, office memos are kept in research files, categorized by areas of law. They are available for reference and use in other cases involving similar issues. Subsequent researchers may not be familiar with the facts of the case. A subsequent reader should be able to obtain all the facts necessary to understand the analysis from the facts section. It should not be necessary to review the case file.

> ▪ The facts section protects you from possible criticism. If additional facts come to light after preparation of the memo that affect the analysis of the issue and lead to a different conclusion, a well-drafted facts section provides a record of the factual basis of your conclusion. It protects you from the criticism that you misanalyzed or misapplied the law.

2. Facts Section—Content

The **statement of facts** of the office memorandum should not simply repeat the facts included in the memo assignment; it should include only a brief statement of the background and key facts. The preparation of this section requires you to identify those facts necessary to provide the reader with a complete understanding of the factual context of the issues analyzed in the memo. It may require fewer facts than those included in the memo assignment, or it may require additional facts.

Include in the facts section all facts referenced or included in the analysis section of the memo. The goal is to provide, as briefly as possible, enough facts to make the memo a self-contained document; that is, it should be sufficiently complete so that any reader who is not familiar with the facts of the case need not refer to the case file. To accomplish this end, the facts section should include background and key facts.

- Background facts are necessary because they put the key facts in context. They provide the reader with the information necessary for an overall understanding of the context within which the key facts occurred.

- *Key facts* are those facts upon which the outcome of the case is determined. The key facts are so essential that if they were changed, the outcome of the case would probably be different.

When preparing the facts section of the office memo, refer to Chapter 9 for assistance in identifying key and background facts.

3. Facts Section—Organization

Organize the statement of facts in a manner that enables the reader to clearly understand the events relating to the issue(s) addressed in the memo. There are basically three organizational formats for presenting the facts:

- Chronological
- Topical
- A combination of chronological and topical

The format selected is usually governed by the nature of the facts.

a. Chronological Order

A **chronological organization** of the facts usually is adopted when the facts are a series of events related by time or date.

For Example The memo involves the following fact situation: On December 1, the client, Mr. Smith, was driving in the 600 block of First Street when the defendant, Mr. Doe, ran a red light at the intersection of First and Rose Streets. As a result, Mr. Doe's vehicle collided with Mr. Smith's vehicle. Mr. Smith suffered a broken leg, and his wallet was stolen at the scene. On the way to the hospital, the ambulance was involved in a collision when it yielded at a stop sign. Mr. Smith suffered additional injuries, including a separated shoulder, in this collision. At the emergency room, his back was sprained when he was being helped onto the examining table by the hospital staff. Mr. Smith wants to know who he can sue for his various injuries and whether he can recover from Mr. Doe for the loss of his wallet. This example is referred to as the "auto collision" example in the remainder of this chapter.

The best way to present the facts of the case in the preceding example is chronologically. The facts that give rise to the various causes of action occurred in a linear sequence, and they are most clearly understood when narrated chronologically.

b. Topical Order

Some fact situations do not lend themselves to a chronological presentation. In such situations, the facts are related more by **topical organization** than by time sequence.

> **For Example** The memo involves the following divorce situation. The client, Mrs. Jones, is the petitioner in a divorce action. Mr. and Mrs. Jones disagree on the property distribution. They own three pieces of real property, parcels A, B, and C. All three parcels are held in both their names as joint tenants.
>
> Parcel A includes the family home. The property is paid for. Forty percent of the mortgage was paid from an inheritance Mrs. Jones received from her father. The remainder was paid by both Mr. and Mrs. Jones from income from their respective employments. The assessed value is $150,000.
>
> Parcel B is a rental property. They purchased the property shortly after the marriage. The mortgage on the property is being paid from the rent payment and contributions from the income of both Mr. and Mrs. Jones. Their current equity is $100,000. Part of the equity ($10,000) was a contribution by Mr. Jones from his separate property.
>
> Parcel C is recreational property. It was purchased five years after the marriage. It includes a small cabin and a storage shed. Their equity in the cabin and shed is $75,000. Mrs. Jones contributed $12,000 of the equity from lottery ticket winnings. The balance of the equity represents equal contributions from Mr. and Mrs. Jones.

In this example, a presentation of the facts by topic is most appropriate. The dates of purchase and the dates payments were made on the various parcels may be available, but presenting these facts by date would not lead to the clearest presentation of the facts. In the statement of facts, all the facts relating to each parcel should be presented separately, by parcel, regardless of the time sequence. All the facts relating to parcel A should be presented together; all the facts relating to parcel B should be presented together; and all the facts relating to parcel C should be presented together. The facts are more clearly understood when all the facts relating to each parcel are presented together; therefore, each parcel should be addressed separately in the facts section of the memo.

c. Combination of Chronological and Topical Order

It may be appropriate to present the facts both chronologically and topically.

> **For Example** In the previous example, assume that parcel B was purchased by the husband three years prior to the marriage, parcel A immediately after the marriage, and parcel C five years later. Assume also that there is personal property: an automobile purchased two years after the marriage and a boat purchased three years after the marriage.
>
> In addition to the issues concerning the three parcels, there are other issues in the divorce involving the other property. The appropriate presentation of the facts is a combination of the chronological and topical schemes.

In this situation, the real and personal property should be presented in the facts section in a chronological sequence according to the order of purchase, such as parcel B first, then parcel A, followed by the automobile, the boat, and finally parcel C. Note that all the information concerning each parcel of property is included when the parcel is discussed even though some factual events concerning the parcel may have occurred after the purchase of another parcel.

> **For Example** All the information concerning parcel B is included in the discussion of parcel B even though some of that information concerns occurrences taking place after the purchase of parcel A. Mr. Jones's $10,000 contribution of separate property may have taken place after parcel A, the automobile, and the boat were purchased.

It would be confusing to present all the facts in this example in chronological order only. It is much clearer to present the property in chronological order and, within the discussion of each piece of property, present all the facts relating to that piece of property regardless of when they occurred.

The goal in the organization of the statement of facts is clear presentation of the facts. Select the organizational format that best meets this goal.

4. Facts Section—Presentation and Ethics

As mentioned in Chapter 11, Rule 3.3(a)(1) of the Model Rules of Professional Conduct provides that a lawyer should not make false statements of law or fact to a tribunal. Therefore, when drafting the facts section of the memo, present the facts accurately and objectively, and avoid legal conclusions.

a. Accuracy

Accuracy in presenting the facts means that all the facts are presented, including those unfavorable to the client.

> **For Example** If, in the auto collision example, Mr. Smith was speeding when the defendant ran the red light, this fact should be included. Although it may not be a key fact that affects the outcome of the negligence claim, it is at minimum a background fact that should be included.

Accuracy also means not adding or changing facts. It is not proper to add a fact even if the existence of the fact seems obvious.

> **For Example** In the auto collision example, it is not proper to state that the defendant knew she was running a red light if there are no facts indicating her awareness of that fact. It is improper to add such a fact even if it seems obvious.

b. Objectivity

State the facts objectively. This means you should present the facts in a neutral manner that is neither slanted nor biased.

> **For Example** **Slanted presentation:** Mr. Banker obviously knew what he was doing when he advised Mrs. Widow to buy a risky stock when the market was at its peak. Mrs. Widow, unfortunately, relied on his bad advice to her detriment.

The use of the words *obviously, unfortunately, detriment, bad,* and *risky* slant the presentation of the facts in favor of Mrs. Widow. The facts should be stated neutrally.

> **For Example** **Neutral presentation:** The market was at its peak when Mr. Banker advised Mrs. Widow to buy the stock. Mrs. Widow relied on his advice and purchased the stock. The value of the stock subsequently fell, and Mrs. Widow suffered a loss of $1,000.

c. Legal Conclusions

When composing the facts section, avoid legal conclusions.

> **For Example** Mrs. Roe was driving negligently through the school zone. (The phrase *driving negligently* is a legal conclusion.)

State the facts without legal conclusions.

> **For Example** Mrs. Roe was driving 35 miles per hour through the school zone. The posted speed is 15 miles per hour.

Exhibit 16-8 presents a checklist for the facts section of an office memo.

Exhibit 16-8 *Checklist—Facts Section.*

- Are sufficient background facts presented to inform the reader of the factual context of the assignment? Will the reader be required to refer to the case file to understand the analysis of the issues?
- Are all the key facts included? Will the reader have to refer to the case file to obtain key facts?
- Are the facts organized chronologically, topically, or chronologically and topically combined?
- Are the facts presented accurately and objectively?
- Are legal conclusions excluded from the fact presentation?
- Is the facts section complete?

© Cengage Learning 2014

VI. KEY POINTS CHECKLIST: *Office Legal Memorandum—Issues and Facts*

✔ An office memo should be a self-contained document. Include in the memo all the information necessary to understand the context of the legal analysis. Subsequent readers should not need to refer to the case file to understand the issue, facts, or analysis.

✔ To achieve the goal of properly presenting the issue, include the rule of law, legal question, and key facts in the issue. Refer to Chapters 10 and 11 when identifying and stating the issue.

✔ Present the fact situation objectively, and include both background and key facts.

✔ Follow the format adopted by your workplace when preparing the office memo. You may be familiar with or prefer a different format; if appropriate, recommend changes to the office format. If your suggestions are not adopted, be sure to follow the approved format used in the office.

✔ Be sure you understand the assignment. If you are unclear about any aspect of the assignment, ask the supervising attorney. Do not waste time pursuing answers to the wrong question or performing the wrong task.

✔ If the complexity of the task requires skills beyond your ability, communicate your concerns.

VII. APPLICATION

This section illustrates the principles and guidelines discussed in the previous sections through their application to the hypothetical assignment presented at the beginning of the chapter. Jeff Lyons's assignment is to research a question involving privileged spousal communications. He performs the assignment by adopting and following the writing process presented in Chapter 15. The brief summary in this section explains the steps Jeff follows when applying the writing process.

The first step of the prewriting stage of the writing process is to review the assignment. After reviewing the assignment, Jeff has no questions concerning the nature of the task ahead and the constraints on performance of the task. The assignment is to prepare an office memo for Rita Berdwin, his supervisory attorney; the memo should not exceed five pages; and he must complete the memo within two weeks.

The next step of the prewriting stage is to organize the approach to the research, analysis, and writing of the assignment. To accomplish this, Jeff retrieves the office memo format preferred by Ms. Berdwin. Assume that the format preferred by Ms. Berdwin is the recommended office memo format presented in Exhibit 16-1. From this format, Jeff prepares an expanded outline. Using three-hole paper or a computer, he creates a separate page for each section of the outline. Jeff titles one page "Statement of Assignment," one page "Issue," one page "Brief Answer," one page "Statement of Facts," and so on. He continues in this manner until he has a separate page for each section and subsection of the outline.

After completing the expanded outline, Jeff begins the prewriting process. As he brainstorms ideas concerning the assignment, Jeff enters each idea on the appropriate page of the outline.

> **For Example** Assume that, at the outset, Jeff has an idea about how the issue should be stated. "Is the conversation between Mr. and Mrs. Findo a privileged interspousal communication that cannot be admitted at trial?" He immediately enters this possible formulation of the issue on the "Issue" page of the expanded outline.

Jeff locates the statute governing privileged spousal communications, 735 ILCS 5/8-801 (West 1992). The relevant portion of this statute provides: "In all actions, husband and wife may testify for or against each other, provided that neither may testify as to any communication or admission made by either of them to the other or as to any conversation between them during marriage. . . ." He places a copy of this statute in the "Rule of Law" section of the outline.

Jeff's research locates the lead case on point, *People v. Sanders*, 99 Ill. 2d 262, 457 N.E.2d 1241 (1983). He places the relevant portions of the case in the "Case Law" section of the expanded outline. These portions follow:

- The defendant's murder conviction was based in part upon the testimony of his wife.

- She was allowed to testify about two conversations she had with the defendant that took place in the presence of their three children, ages 13, 10, and 8 years.

- The conversations implicated the husband in the murder.

- The defendant appealed the conviction, claiming the trial court erred when it allowed the testimony.

- The defendant argued that under the statute the conversations were privileged spousal communications and, therefore, were not admissible.

- The state supreme court, upholding the court of appeals, stated, "The appellate court appears to have exhaustively researched the subject and concluded, as we do, that the great weight of authority is that the presence of children of the spouses de-stroys confidentiality unless they are too young to understand what is being said (citations omitted). Nothing in the record indicates that Robert, then 13 years old, was not old enough or sufficiently bright to understand the conversation he heard, particularly inasmuch as the wife's testimony indicates that some of it was directed to him. In these circumstances, under the rule followed in this State, his presence rendered the conversation ineligible for the protection of the statutory privilege."

Jeff may place the entire case in the outline or include only the relevant parts. If only the relevant quotations are included in the outline, he notes the page numbers of the quotations.

Upon reviewing the information at hand, Jeff concludes that he has sufficient informa-tion to complete the assignment. He continues researching, however, to make sure he has thoroughly explored the question, and he updates his research to ensure that it represents the current law.

While researching and thinking about the case, whenever Jeff has an idea about how something should be written or where something should be placed in the memo, he enters the idea in the expanded outline.

> **For Example** A reading of the statute reveals that the privilege applies only to conversa-tions between spouses during the marriage; therefore, a key fact is that the conversation took place during the marriage. While reading the case, he discovers that the presence of children of the spouses destroys confidentiality unless the children are too young to understand. Therefore, the fact that the children in the client's case, pres-ent during the conversation, were 16 and 10 years old is also a key fact. As he becomes aware of this information, Jeff notes these key facts on the fact and issue pages of the expanded outline.

By the time Jeff completes the prewriting stage of the writing process, the expanded outline contains all the information necessary to write the memo. Each section of the ex-panded outline contains:

- The research relevant to the section
- Any draft sentences, sentence fragments, and ideas relevant to the section, such as transition sentences
- Notes concerning the drafting of each section, such as order of presentation and what must be included

A brief summary of each section of the expanded outline follows:

- On the statement of assignment page, Jeff has noted all of his thoughts regarding how this section should be written.
- The issue page includes a reference to the statute, key facts, and every formulation of the issue that has occurred to Jeff as he worked on the assignment.
- The brief answer page includes draft sentences on how the brief answer should be phrased. Ideas for this section may have come to him while he was preparing the analysis, conclusion, or other sections of the memo.
- Included on the facts page is a list of all the key and background facts he has identi-fied as he conducted research. Jeff also has noted any drafts of sentences he might use in composing this section.

■ On the rule of law page of the analysis section, he has included the applicable statute with the correct citation. He has listed here any ideas he had on drafting this section, such as transition sentences.

> **For Example** "The statute does not provide guidance concerning what effect the presence of children during the communication has on the privilege. Therefore, case law must be consulted."

■ The case law page of the analysis section contains the case citation and a copy of the case or relevant sections of the case. Also included here are any notes Jeff has made concerning the discussion or presentation of the case in the memo.
■ On the application page of the analysis section, Jeff has included any information, ideas, or sentences regarding how the rule of law from the case and statute will be applied to the facts.
■ The counteranalysis page of the analysis section includes any information concerning the counteranalysis, such as opposing case law.
■ On the conclusion and recommendations pages of the outline, just as on the other pages of the expanded outline, Jeff has included notes, ideas, draft sentences, and anything that may be used when drafting these sections.

After Jeff completes the research and analysis, and the expanded outline, he begins the writing process. The use of the expanded outline greatly simplifies his work.

> **For Example** Included on the issue page of the expanded outline are all the various ways the issue may be stated: "Is the communication between Mr. and Mrs. Findo privileged?" "Is the conversation between Mr. and Mrs. Findo a privileged interspousal communication that cannot be admitted at trial?" "Does the presence of children of the spouses during a conversation render the communication nonprivileged?" "Is the interspousal communication privilege destroyed if the communication takes place in the presence of children of the spouses?" "Under Illinois law, is the interspousal communication privilege destroyed when the conversation takes place in the presence of children (ages 16 and 10) of the spouses?"
>
> When Jeff begins to draft the issue section of the memo, his task becomes easier because all the various formulations of the issue are in one place. Jeff has only to compose the issue by selecting and combining the best language from the various formulations on the issue page of the expanded outline.

Using the writing process presented in Chapter 15, the writing tips presented in Chapter 14, and the guidelines presented in the other chapters of this text, Jeff completes the assignment. The completed portions of Jeff's assignment that involve the sections of the office memo discussed in this chapter, the heading through the facts sections, are presented in the following office memo. Because the remaining portions of an office memo—the analysis through recommendations sections—are discussed in Chapter 17, those sections of Jeff's completed office memo are presented in the Application section of that chapter.

OFFICE MEMORANDUM OF LAW

To: Rita Berdwin, Attorney

From: Jeff Lyons, Paralegal

Date: April 30, 2013

Case: *State v. Findo*

Office File No.:   Cr. 13-136

Docket No.:   Cr. 13-378

Re: Privileged spousal communications

STATEMENT OF ASSIGNMENT

You have asked me to prepare a memorandum of law addressing the question of whether the conversation between Mr. Findo (our client) and Mrs. Findo, which took place in the presence of their children, ages 16 and 10 years old, is a privileged spousal communication and, therefore, is not admissible in the criminal trial of Mr. Findo.

ISSUE

Under the Illinois privileged spousal communication statute, 735 ILCS 5/8-801 (West 1992), is a spousal conversation privileged and not admissible into evidence if it takes place in the presence of the spouses' children, ages 16 and 10 years old?

BRIEF ANSWER

No. The communication is not a privileged communication protected by the provisions of the statute. The state supreme court has ruled that the privilege is destroyed when the conversation takes place in the presence of children of the spouses who are old enough to understand the content of the communication.

STATEMENT OF FACTS

Mr. Findo is charged with assaulting his neighbor, Mr. Markham, with a deadly weapon, a hammer. Mr. Markham claims that Mr. Findo attacked him and struck him several times with a hammer. Mr. Findo claims he did not attack Mr. Markham with a hammer; he claims that Mr. Markham attacked him with a brick, and during the struggle, the brick fell and hit Mr. Markham on the head. Mrs. Findo, currently separated from her husband, has agreed to testify that before the confrontation Mr. Findo stated, "Markham is out there building that damn fence again. I'll put a stop to this once and for all." This conversation took place in the presence of the Findos' children, Tomas, age 16, and Alice, age 10. There were no witnesses to the argument. Neither Mrs. Findo nor the children saw the confrontation.

Summary

The drafting of an office legal memorandum is one of the most important and often most difficult types of legal writing assignments a paralegal or law clerk may perform. It requires integration of the research, analysis, and writing skills discussed throughout this text.

An office memo is designed for office use and is usually drafted for the supervising attorney. It involves the legal analysis of issues raised by the facts of a client's case. The writing process presented in Chapter 15 is recommended when preparing an office memo.

This chapter presents the considerations involved in preparing the heading, statement of assignment, issue, brief answer, and statement of facts sections of the office memo. Chapter 17 discusses the considerations involved in preparing the analysis through recommendations sections.

The heading section contains information describing who the memo is from and to, the name of the case, and the nature of the issue. The statement of assignment section describes the topic covered and the parameters of the assignment.

The issue section follows the statement of assignment. It is one of the most important parts of the memo. It informs the reader of the precise legal question addressed in the analysis section of the memo. The brief answer section provides a brief and precise answer to the issue and a brief summary of the reasons in support of the answer.

The statement of facts section provides the facts of the client's case that gave rise to the issue addressed in the memo. It includes the background and key facts of the dispute and should provide sufficient factual information to allow the reader to understand the analysis without having to refer to the case file or any other source outside the memo.

Many of the procedures and steps involved in preparing an office memo apply to the preparation of legal writing designed for external use, such as correspondence to clients and documents to be filed with a court, including trial court and appellate court briefs.

Quick References

Internet Resources

The Internet resources for this chapter are the same as those listed in Chapter 15. Due to the large number of sites, the best strategy is to narrow your search to a specific type of legal writing and topic, such as "issues, legal memorandum, public service contracts."

EXERCISE

ASSIGNMENT

For each of the memo and Web assignments presented at the end of Chapter 17, prepare the following sections of an office memo: heading, statement of assignment, issue, brief answer, and statement of facts. Use the format and guidelines presented in this chapter when performing this assignment.

The available CourseMate for this text has an interactive eBook and interactive learning tools, including flash cards, quizzes, and more. To learn more about this resource and access free demo CourseMate resources, go to **www.cengagebrain.com**, and search for this book. To access CourseMate materials that you have purchased, go to **login.cengagebrain.com**.

Office Legal Memorandum: Analysis to Conclusion

Outline

Learning Objectives

After completing this chapter, you should understand:

- The elements and format of the analysis, conclusion, and recommendations sections of an office legal research memorandum

- How to draft the analysis, conclusion, and recommendations sections of an office legal research memorandum

- General considerations to keep in mind when drafting a legal research memorandum

Ellen Taylor is a law clerk working in a district attorney's office in the hypothetical state of New Washington. Ms. Taylor recently received the following assignment.

To:	Ellen Taylor, Intern
From:	Carl Pine, Assistant District Attorney
Re:	*State v. Kent*. Arrest during execution of search warrant and constructive possession
Case:	Cr. 13-404

On January 7, police officers executed a search warrant authorizing the search of the apartment of David Kent for narcotics. Mr. Kent's apartment is located on the third floor of a four-story apartment complex. Upon entering the apartment, the officers found Mr. Kent lying on the bed in the bedroom. The officers secured the apartment and, after frisking Mr. Kent for weapons, handcuffed him and moved him into the kitchen for the stated purpose of "his and our safety." They did not read him his rights or officially place him under arrest at this time.

The search of the apartment did not reveal any narcotics. The police, however, discovered an "eight-inch hole" in the only window in the bedroom, and the window screen was pushed out. The police went downstairs and searched the area below the window. The bedroom window faces the rear of the apartment complex, and below the window is a parking lot. In the parking lot, three stories below Mr. Kent's bedroom window, the officers found a plastic bag containing one ounce of rock cocaine. The parking lot is a common area of the complex, accessible to the public and all apartment dwellers. No witnesses have been located who saw the defendant throw the cocaine out the window. There were no fingerprints on the bag or other evidence linking Mr. Kent to the cocaine. After locating the bag, the police read the defendant his rights and placed him under arrest. The charge is possession of a controlled substance.

Please prepare an office legal memorandum addressing the following questions:

1. Was the defendant under arrest when he was handcuffed and moved into the kitchen?

2. Is the connection between the defendant and the cocaine sufficient to support charges of possession of a controlled substance?

The office legal memorandum prepared by Ms. Taylor is presented in the Application section of this chapter.

I. INTRODUCTION

Chapter 16 focuses on preparing the first half of an office legal memo: the heading, statement of assignment, issue, brief answer, and statement of facts sections. This chapter addresses preparation of the second half of the office legal memo: the analysis, conclusion, and recommendations sections. In this chapter, as in Chapter 16, an office legal research memorandum is referred to as an *office memo.*

The discussion in Chapter 16 addressing the adoption of a writing process and the use of an expanded outline also applies to the preparation of the second half of an office memo. The guidelines presented in that chapter in regard to the writing process and the use of an expanded outline should be followed when preparing the analysis, conclusion, and recommendations sections of the office memo. The examples in this chapter refer to the enacted and case law of the hypothetical state of New Washington.

II. ANALYSIS SECTION

The purpose of an office memo is to provide a legal analysis of the issue(s) in a case. The **analysis section** is the part of the memo where the law is presented, analyzed, and applied to the issue(s). It connects the issue with the conclusion. It is the heart of an office memo assignment.

The analysis section is often referred to as the *discussion* section. The conventional analytical format, and the most efficient way to approach a legal question, is the IRAC format (issue, rule, analysis, conclusion). Under the IRAC approach and the office memo format introduced in Chapter 16, the issue is presented at the beginning of the memo; the analysis section covers the rule of law, analysis, and application of the rule of law to the facts; and the conclusion summarizes the analysis. The reasons for following this approach are obvious:

■ The reader must know the question to know the context in which the rule is analyzed.

■ The rule that applies to the question must be identified before the rule can be analyzed and applied to the facts of the case.

■ The rule must be applied to the facts; this must take place before a conclusion can be reached.

Although IRAC is the basic format for addressing legal issues, it is only a broad outline of the format. It is necessary to have a more detailed outline of the analysis section to effectively approach an office memo assignment and prepare an office memo.

A. Analysis Format

Exhibit 17-1 presents the recommended format of the analysis section.

Exhibit 17-1 *Basic Four-Part Format—Analysis Section.*

Part A	Rule of law
Part B	Case law (if necessary) interpretation of rule of law 1. Name of case 2. Facts of case sufficient to demonstrate case is on point 3. Rule or legal principle from case that applies to the client's case
Part C	Application of law to facts of case
Part D	Counteranalysis

© Cengage Learning 2014

In the prewriting stage of the writing process, assign each subsection of the analysis section at least one page in the expanded outline: a page for the rule of law, a page for each case, at least one page for the application of the law to the facts, and at least one page for the counteranalysis.

If the memo is a complex memo involving multiple issues, follow the same basic format for each issue (see Exhibit 17-2).

Exhibit 17-2 *Complex Memo—Analysis Section Format.*

Issue I	Analysis
Part A	Rule of law
Part B	Case law (if necessary) interpretation of rule of law 1. Name of case 2. Facts of case sufficient to demonstrate case is on point 3. Rule or legal principle from case that applies to the client's case
Part C	Application of law to facts of case
Part D	Counteranalysis
Issue II	Analysis
Part A	Rule of law
Part B	Case law (if necessary) interpretation of rule of law 1. Name of case 2. Facts of case sufficient to demonstrate case is on point 3. Rule or legal principle from case that applies to the client's case
Part C	Application of law to facts of case
Part D	Counteranalysis
Issue III	Analysis (same format as issues I and II)

© Cengage Learning 2014

If more than one rule of law applies to a specific issue, include a reference to each rule in the outline.

For Example Issue I Analysis

Part A Rule of law

1. Section 59-703 of the commercial code
2. Section 45-211 of the usury statute

If more than one case is required to interpret the rule of law, such as when more than one element of the rule requires case law interpretation, include a reference to each case in the outline.

For Example Issue I Analysis

Part A Rule of law—section 59-703 of the commercial code

Part B Case law

    1. Case 1: *Smith v. Jones*—interpreting the term *sale* as used in § 59-703

      a. Facts of case—sufficient to demonstrate case is on point

      b. Rule or legal principle from case that applies to the client's case

Part C Application of the law to the facts of the client's case

Part D Counteranalysis

    2. Case 2: *Row v. Downs*—interpreting the term *merchant* as used in § 59-703

      a. Facts of case—sufficient to demonstrate case is on point

      b. Rule or legal principle from case that applies to the client's case

Part C Application of the law to the facts of the client's case

Part D Counteranalysis

Part A Rule of law—§ 45-211 of the usury statute

Part B Case law

    1. *Doe v. Dean*—interpreting the term *loan* as used in § 45-211

      a. Facts of case—sufficient to demonstrate case is on point

      b. Rule or legal principle from case that applies to the client's case

Part C Application of the law to the facts of the client's case

Part D Counteranalysis

[handwritten margin note: How to include more than one case if needed to interpret case law.]

The remainder of this section discusses the elements of the basic format for the analysis section of an office memo. After you master the considerations involved in preparing the analysis of a single issue, you can approach complex memo assignments that address multiple issues or separate subissues by applying the basic process to the analysis of each issue or subissue.

B. Analysis Part A: Rule of Law

Inasmuch as the analysis section of an office memo addresses how the law applies to the issue(s) and facts of the client's case, the starting point is a presentation of the rule of law or legal principle that applies. Simply put, you must present the law before it can be applied.

The governing law may be enacted law, such as a constitutional provision or a legislative act; or case law, such as a court-adopted rule of law. Exhibit 17-3 lists some considerations to keep in mind when preparing the rule of law portion of the analysis section.

Exhibit 17-3 *Part A—Rule of Law—Considerations.*

Introduction	Use introductory language to introduce the rule of law (e.g., "The law governing the witnessing of wills is . . .").
What to include	Paraphrase or quote only the relevant portions of the law.
Multiple rules of law	Use introductory language and present the relevant portion of each rule.
Citation	Provide the citation for the rule of law. If it is enacted law, cite the statute, ordinance, rule, and so forth; if it is case law, cite the court opinion.

1. Rule of Law—Introduction

The analysis section begins with a presentation of the rule of law. Do not start immediately with the rule itself; use introductory language. The introductory language is italicized in the following examples.

> **For Example** *The rule of law governing the sale of securities* is section 59-903 of the New Washington Commercial Code. The section provides. . . .
>
> *In New Washington, the doctrine of strict liability was established in the case of Elton v. All Faiths Hospital,* 931 N. Wash. 395, 396 (1976), where the court stated. . . .

2. Rule of Law—What to Include

When presenting the rule of law, paraphrase or quote only the relevant portions of the law. In some instances, the rule of law is very lengthy, and only portions of the law apply to the issue being addressed. This is often true when the applicable law is statutory law, the statute is composed of many subsections, and only one subsection applies. If this is so, include only the relevant portion of the law.

> **For Example** Statutory law:
>
> The rule of law governing oppressive conduct is § 50-14-5, which provides:
>
> A. The district courts may liquidate the assets and business of a corporation:
>
>   1. in an action by a shareholder when it is established that:. . . .
>
>   (b) the acts of the directors . . . are illegal, oppressive, or fraudulent. . . .
>
> *Note:* Subsection (a) is omitted because its provisions do not apply to the issue being discussed.

> **For Example** Case law:
>
> The rule of law governing a ski resort's duty to warn of snow and ice conditions was established in the case of *Jones v. Mountain Ski Resort,* 943 N. Wash. 857, 877 (1988), where the court stated, "Resorts have a duty to warn of snow and ice conditions in the following situations: . . . when the snow or ice condition is a latent hazard. . . ."
>
> *Note:* Portions of the opinion are omitted because they do not apply to the issue being discussed. The omission is indicated by the three-dot ellipsis.

3. Rule of Law—Multiple Rules

The analysis may require consideration of more than one rule of law. If this is so, use a format similar to that discussed in the preceding text. Use introductory language, and present the relevant portions of each rule.

> **For Example** The New Washington Commercial Code section 50-101 establishes which contracts must be in writing. In our case, two subsections of that section apply: section 50-101B, which requires that "[a]n agreement which is not to be performed within one year from the making" must be in writing, and section 50-101C, which provides that "[c]ontracts for the sale of goods in the amount of $500 or more" must be in writing.

When the rule of law involves both general and specific sections of a statute, present the relevant general portion of the statute first, followed by the specific portion of the statute.

> **For Example** Section 50-501 creates an implied warranty of merchantability if the seller is a merchant with respect to goods of that kind. The term *merchant* is defined in section 50-401 as "A person who deals in goods of that kind. . . ."

4. Rule of Law—Citation

Whenever the reference is to a rule of law or legal principle, you must present the authority in support of your statement of the rule. If the source for the rule is enacted law, cite the enacted law; if it is case law, cite the case. Note that in the previous four examples, the reference includes the source for the rule of law, either statutory or case law. Without a reference to the authority, it is merely your word that the rule of law presented in the memo is actually what the law states. Readers need to know the source so they can check for accuracy and answer any questions concerning the law.

C. Analysis Part B: Rule of Law Interpretation—Case Law

Exhibit 17-4 presents three considerations to keep in mind when addressing the interpretation of the rule of law discussed in the memo.

Exhibit 17-4 *Rule of Law Interpretation—Considerations.*

Is interpretation required?	Does the rule of law require interpretation? Can the law be applied directly to the facts without interpretation?
What is the role of case law?	Is the rule of law so broadly stated that case law must be consulted to determine how it applies?
What is the process for presenting case law?	If case law is required, use a format like the one laid out in Exhibit 17-5 when presenting each case.

© Cengage Learning 2014

1. Rule of Law Interpretation—No Interpretation Required

In some instances, the rule of law, whether it is statutory or case law, applies directly to the facts of the client's case. Further case law is not required to determine how the rule applies.

> **For Example** The rule of law establishes a 15 mph speed limit in school zones, and the client was ticketed for driving 30 mph in a school zone. In this situation, case law is not needed to determine how the law applies. The law can be applied directly to the facts: driving 30 mph in the school zone is a violation of the law.

In such instances, proceed to section II.D of this chapter for guidance.
Note, however, that you should always perform at least a cursory check of the case law. This is necessary to ensure that there is not some special interpretation of the rule or a term used in the rule that is not apparent from a plain reading of it.

2. Rule of Law Interpretation—Role of Case Law

Usually the rule of law that governs the issue being analyzed has some unexpected quirk or is so broadly stated that you must refer to case law to determine how it applies. Case law, in effect, provides the link between the rule of law and the issue raised by the facts of the client's case. Court opinions determine and explain how the law is interpreted and applied in specific fact situations.

> **For Example** The First Amendment protects freedom of speech. The amendment does not define what constitutes speech. If the client's case involves the question of whether a symbolic act, such as burning a state flag, is protected under the First Amendment's freedom-of-speech provisions, you must consult case law. The Supreme Court has interpreted how the First Amendment applies in this specific fact situation. Acts such as burning a state flag are considered symbolic speech and are protected under the First Amendment.

> **For Example** A statute prohibits oppressive conduct by majority shareholders against minority shareholders, but *oppressive conduct* is not defined in the statute. Court decisions may define what constitutes oppressive conduct in specific fact situations, and reference to court decisions is necessary to determine how the law applies.

3. Rule of Law Interpretation—Process for Presenting Case Law

When presenting the case law that interprets how the law applies to a fact situation such as the client's, the recommended format is to present the name and citation of the case first, then the facts of the case, followed by the rule of law or legal principle applied by the court (see Exhibit 17-5).

Exhibit 17-5 Format for Presenting Case Law.

Name and citation of court opinion	First, provide the name and citation of the case.
Facts of the case	Next, provide those facts from the case sufficient to demonstrate that the case is on point.
Rule of law	Then, identify the rule of law or legal principle adopted by the court that applies to the issue addressed in the memo.

© Cengage Learning 2014

a. Name and Citation of Court Opinion

When presenting the case, first identify the case name and citation. The reader should know the name of the case at the beginning of the discussion. This eliminates any possible confusion that may arise concerning which case is being discussed.

> **For Example** The case that defines the term *publication* as used in the statute is *Smith v. Jones*, 956 N. Wash. 441, 881 N.E.2d 897 (1995).

b. Facts of the Case

The next step is to provide sufficient information concerning the facts and rule of law applied in the case to demonstrate that the case is on point. To accomplish this, you must include enough information about the court opinion to demonstrate that the similarity between the key facts and rule of law of the opinion and those of the client's case is sufficient for the court opinion to govern or provide guidance in deciding how the law applies.

For Example The client's case involves the question of whether a majority shareholder in a closely held corporation engaged in oppressive conduct when he refused to issue dividends while granting himself, as CEO of the corporation, semiannual bonuses in an amount triple his annual salary. Section 90-9-4 of the state corporation statutes prohibits oppressive conduct by majority shareholders against minority shareholders. The statute does not define *oppressive*. The case on point is *Cedrik v. Ely*, 956 N. Wash. 776, 881 N.E.2d 451 (1995).

The introduction of the case might read as follows:

The case that defines what constitutes "oppressive" conduct in a fact situation such as that presented in our case is *Cedrik v. Ely*, 956 N. Wash. 776, 881 N.E.2d 451 (1995). In that case, just as in our case, a majority shareholder of a closely held corporation granted himself bonuses in excess of triple his salary. In *Cedrik*, the majority shareholder also refused to issue dividends. In defining what constitutes "oppressive conduct" under 90-9-4, the court stated. . . . *Id.* at 778.

Chapter 12 presents a comprehensive discussion of the steps and considerations involved in determining if a case is on point. Refer to that chapter for assistance in deciding what must be included in the presentation of a case to demonstrate that the case is on point. Note that the presentation of a case in a case brief is different from the presentation of a case in an office memo. When presenting a case in an office memo, it is not necessary to include all the information that you would include in a case brief. In an office memo, present only the facts sufficient to show the case is on point. A case brief should include more detail, such as background facts and other information.

c. Rule of Law

The last step when discussing a case that is on point is to identify the rule of law or legal principle adopted by the court that applies to the issue being addressed in the office memo.

For Example The state collections statute provides that efforts to collect payment for a debt must be made in a "reasonable manner." *Reasonable manner* is not defined in the statute. In the client's case, the collector called the client three times a day, often after 9:00 p.m. The case on point is *Cerro v. Collectors, Inc.*, 955 N. Wash. 641, 880 N.E.2d 401 (1994). The presentation of the rule of law applied by the court would read as follows: "In the *Cerro* case, the court stated that 'reasonable contact' as used in the collections statute means no more than one telephone call a day to the debtor's residence. The court went on to state that no calls should be placed before 6:00 a.m. or after 7:00 p.m. *Id.* at 645."

Keep in mind two considerations when presenting the rule of law from the case:

1. Quote the language of the court whenever practical. Quotations are stronger than paraphrases. Sometimes the language does not lend itself to quotation, such as when the rule is composed of several parts or steps that are presented in more than one paragraph of the opinion.

   Do not use too many quotations. Use quotations to set forth the law or legal principle presented by the court and key portions of the court's reasoning. They should not be used as a substitute for or in place of your own analysis. You have failed to properly analyze the case law if your analysis consists almost entirely of quotations of a court's presentation of the law and its reasoning.

2. When presenting the law, always cite the page of the court opinion where the rule is discussed.

> **For Example** In defining what constitutes "oppressive conduct" under § 90-9-4, the court stated, "Oppressive conduct occurs when a majority shareholder engages in wrongful conduct which inures to the benefit of the majority and the detriment of the minority." *Id.* at 778.

In summary, the sequence when presenting a case is as follows:

- Case name and case citation
- Relevant facts from the case demonstrating the case is on point
- The rule of law or principle adopted by the court that applies to the issue in the client's case

[handwritten margin note: 1) case name + citation. 2) Relevant facts from it. 3) apply to facts of this case]

This sequence is recommended because it is logical to discuss a case using this format for the following reasons:

- It is more readable if the reader first knows the name of the case; then what happened, the facts; then the rule of law applied by the court.
- It is logical to discuss the rule of law last because the next step in the memo is application of the rule to the issue(s) and facts of the client's case. The memo flows more smoothly if the *application* of the rule immediately follows the *presentation* of the rule.

This is only a recommended sequence, however, not a hard-and-fast rule. In some instances, it may be better to address the rule of law from the opinion first, then present the case name and facts from the case. Follow a sequence that works best for the memo you are drafting.

D. Analysis Part C: Application of Rule of Law to Client's Case

The purpose of the office memo is to determine how the law applies. Therefore, a critical element of the analysis section is the application of the law to the issue(s) raised by the facts of the client's case. You will encounter two situations when applying the rule of law to the facts of the case:

- The rule does not require interpretation through the use of case law
- The rule requires interpretation through the use of case law

1. Application of Rule That Does Not Require Case Law Interpretation

As discussed in section II.B, in certain instances case law is not required to interpret how the rule of law applies to the issue being analyzed, because it is clear from the face of the rule how it applies. In such instances, simply apply the rule directly to the issue being addressed in the office memo.

> **For Example** Municipal ordinance 91-1 establishes 25 mph as the maximum speed in residential areas of the municipality. The client was ticketed for driving 55 mph in a residential neighborhood. The application of the ordinance is clear. The client violated the ordinance.

2. Application of Rule That Requires Case Law Interpretation

Most instances involve the question of how the rule of law applies to the issue(s) being analyzed. In such cases, it is necessary to refer to case law for guidance as to how the law applies. After the case on point is discussed, you must apply the rule of law or legal principle adopted by the court to the facts of the client's case. This is the next step of the analysis process. It immediately follows the presentation of the rule of law from the case on point.

> **For Example** In this case, the court defined *oppressive conduct* as "wrongful conduct that inures to the benefit of the majority and the detriment of the minority." *Id.* at 675. The court ruled that the majority shareholder's act of granting himself a bonus triple his annual salary while refusing to allow dividends was wrongful, inured to his benefit and the detriment of the minority shareholders, and was, therefore, "oppressive conduct" within the meaning of the statute.
>
> In our case, just as in the *Cedrik* case, the defendant (the majority shareholder) gave himself bonuses in excess of triple his salary while refusing to allow the issuance of dividends. If the court follows the definition of "oppressive conduct" established in the *Cedrik* case, the defendant engaged in oppressive conduct.

> **For Example** In the *Cerro* case, the court held that "reasonable contact" as used in the collections statute means no more than one telephone call a day to the debtor's residence, and no call should be placed before 6:00 a.m. or after 7:00 p.m. *Id.* at 645.
>
> The collection agency contacted our client more than three times a day for seven straight days, and several of the calls were made after 9:00 p.m. If the trial court follows the rule adopted in *Cerro*, the outcome should be in our favor. The collections statute has clearly been violated.

Remember to include in the analysis a discussion of how the law applies to the issue(s) and facts of the client's case. It is useless to introduce the rule of law and discuss how the rule is interpreted through the presentation of a case on point, then fail to apply the law to the facts of the client's case. The purpose of the office memo is to demonstrate how the rule of law and the case law apply to guide or govern the determination of the issue(s) addressed in the memo.

E. Analysis Part D: Counteranalysis

The next part of the analysis section is the counteranalysis. The analysis of a legal issue is not complete unless counterarguments to the analysis are explored. Refer to Chapter 13 when conducting counteranalysis and drafting the counteranalysis portion of the analysis. Note the following when preparing a counteranalysis:

- In the analysis section, the counteranalysis should follow part C, the application of the law to the issue and facts of the client's case. By doing so you immediately apprise readers of any counterargument so they can easily compare and contrast the arguments and counterarguments and evaluate the merits of each.

- If rebuttal is necessary, it should follow the counteranalysis. Rebuttal may be required if it is necessary to explain why the counterargument does not apply, or if you want to evaluate the merits of the counterargument.

> **For Example** The opposing side may argue that oppressive conduct did not occur, and the *Cedrik* case does not apply, because the majority shareholder in our case earned the triple bonuses by working long hours and weekends. In *Cedrik*, just as in our case, the majority shareholder worked long hours, and the court noted, "Even though the majority shareholder is entitled to receive extra compensation, he is not entitled to receive an amount of compensation that results in the total denial of benefits to the minority shareholders." *Id.* at 778.

Exhibit 17-6 presents a checklist for the analysis section.

Exhibit 17-6 *Checklist—Analysis Section.*

- Does the analysis section follow the proper format? The format is rule of law ± case interpreting the rule of law (if necessary) + application + counteranalysis.
- If the application of the rule of law is not clear, is case law presented that is on point and interprets how the rule of law applies?
- Is the proper citation presented for each rule of law and authority included in the analysis?
- Is there a separate analysis section for each issue addressed in the memo?
- Is the rule of law, presented in the analysis, applied to the issue raised by the facts of the client's case?
- Is there a counteranalysis and rebuttal to the counteranalysis if necessary?

© Cengage Learning 2014

They squashed me somehow

III. CONCLUSION

Part C of the analysis section, the application of the rule of law to the client's case, is a discussion of how the law applies to the issue. This application of the law to the issue is really a mini-conclusion, because it concludes how the law applies. In effect, the analysis section includes a conclusion. Because the analysis section includes a brief conclusion, some law firms do not require a separate conclusion section. It is recommended, however, that you include a separate conclusion section that summarizes the entire memo.

The conclusion section should not introduce new information or authorities, nor should it merely repeat the brief answer. It should summarize the conclusions reached in the analysis section. It is recommended that the conclusion be crafted to include a reference to and summary of all the law discussed in the analysis section, both the enacted and case law. It requires, however, fewer introductory and transitional sentences. Ideally, the **conclusion** should briefly inform the reader of all the law that applies and how it applies. The reader should be able to obtain from the conclusion a general understanding of the law and its application without having to read the entire memo.

The advantage of this type of conclusion is that researchers working on similar cases can determine from the conclusion whether a memo from the office memo files applies to their case. They should be able to obtain all the essential information merely by reading the conclusion. The researcher saves time by not having to read the entire memo if all that is needed is a summary of the law and analysis.

> **For Example** Section 30-3-9 of the criminal code prohibits the possession of proscribed drugs. The case of *Smith v. Jones* provides that when an individual does not have actual possession, he may be in constructive possession if there is either direct or circumstantial evidence establishing that the defendant had both knowledge and control of the drugs. In our case, there is no evidence, either direct or circumstantial, that the client had either knowledge or control of the drugs he was charged with possessing. If *Smith v. Jones* is followed, there is not sufficient evidence to support charges of possession under § 30-3-9.

> **For Example** Article II, section 7, of the state constitution prohibits illegal searches and seizures. In the case of *State v. Idle*, the court held that an individual is seized within the meaning of the law when the actions of the law enforcement officers are such that a reasonable person would not believe that he was free to leave. In our case, the client was handcuffed and ordered to sit in the back seat of a police car. He was not placed under arrest. A reasonable person would not believe he was free to leave in this situation; therefore, if in our case the court follows the test adopted in *State v. Idle*, our client was under arrest.

Note that in these examples, the reader is able to obtain all the essential information concerning the applicable law by merely reading the conclusion. Note also that introductory sentences are not used to introduce the law, and that transition sentences are not used to connect the statutory and case law. The importance and use of introductory and transition sentences in the other sections of an office memo are discussed in section V of this chapter.

When there are multiple issues, a conclusion is usually presented immediately after the analysis of each issue. When there are only two issues and the analysis is not complex, you may present at the end of the memo one conclusion that summarizes the analysis of both issues.

Exhibit 17-7 presents a checklist for the conclusion section.

Exhibit 17-7 *Checklist—Conclusion Section.*

- ▪ Does the conclusion include a brief summary of the analysis of each issue?
- ▪ Is all the law discussed in the analysis section, both enacted and case law, summarized in the conclusion?
- ▪ Is new information or authority excluded from the conclusion?

© Cengage Learning 2014

IV. RECOMMENDATIONS

Not all law firms include a recommendations section as part of the basic format of an office memo. Also, in some formats, recommendations are included in the conclusion section. Generally, a separate section for any comments or recommendations should follow the conclusion section. **Recommendations** are not really part of the analysis or conclusion sections; they frequently address matters to be considered and steps to be taken as a result of the conclusions reached in the analysis section. Include in the recommendations section any comments or suggestions you have concerning the client's case or matters discussed in the memo.

Some areas you may address in the recommendations section include:

1. What the next step should be

> **For Example** Based on the analysis of the issues, it is apparent that the risk of liability is great. It may be advisable to seek a settlement in this case.

2. The identification of additional information that may be necessary due to questions raised in the analysis of the issue

> **For Example** It appears from the case file that the neighbors were not asked if they heard any strange noises. Inasmuch as the analysis of this issue reveals that this information is critical, it is recommended the neighbors be reinterviewed.

3. The identification of additional research that may be necessary on the issue

> **For Example** Additional research may be required because the necessary research sources are not locally available, the analysis is preliminary due to time constraints, or the factual investigation of the case has not been completed.

4. The identification of related issues or concerns that became apparent as a result of the research and analysis

> **For Example** The memo addresses a negligence issue concerning an automobile accident. If the analysis of the negligence issue reveals other possible causes of action in the case, such as assault or negligent infliction of emotional distress, the attorney should be advised of the existence of these additional causes of action.

V. GENERAL CONSIDERATIONS

The following are some general considerations when preparing an office research memorandum. A separate section is devoted to these matters because they often apply to more than one section of a memo and you should keep them in mind when approaching any memo assignment.

A. Heading

Although an office memo is written in paragraph form, use headings for each section. **Headings** provide the overall structure of the assignment, guide the reader, and apprise the reader of what is covered in each section. The reader may desire to read a specific section, such as the analysis, in which case a heading allows the reader to quickly locate that section. Headings also guide the preparation of the table of contents if a table is needed. Use the format presented in Chapter 16 as a guide for the appropriate headings (see Exhibit 16-1). Refer to the Application section of this chapter and Chapter 16 for examples.

B. Introductory Sentences

Use **introductory (topic) sentences** to inform the reader of what is to follow. Avoid immediately jumping into a discussion of a topic, such as the presentation of the law.

> **For Example** No introduction: Section 59-3-2 of the criminal code provides that possession of cocaine is illegal. In *Smith v. Jones*, the defendant. . . .

Provide an introduction when discussing a topic. The introductions are italicized in the following example.

> **For Example** Includes an introduction: *The rule of law prohibiting the possession of cocaine* is criminal code § 59-3-2, which states that possession of cocaine is illegal. The statute does not define "possession"; therefore, case law must be referred to. *The case that provides guidance as to what constitutes possession in a fact situation such as ours* is *Smith v. Jones*. In the *Smith* case, ...

C. Transition Sentences

Use **transition sentences** to connect sections, subsections, and related topics. The following example lacks a transition.

> **For Example** The rule of law governing possession of drugs is § 59-3-2. Section 59-3-2c makes it illegal to possess cocaine. *Smith v. Jones* provides that possession occurs when. . . .

A transition should have been used in this example to connect the statutory law with the case law. The reader should be informed why case law is being presented.

The following example uses a transition sentence. The transition sentence is italicized in the example.

> **For Example** The rule of law governing possession of drugs is § 59-3-2. Section 59-3-2c makes it illegal to possess cocaine. *The statute does not define what constitutes possession; therefore, it is necessary to refer to case law for guidance.* A case that defines what constitutes possession in a fact situation such as ours is *Smith v. Jones*. In the *Smith case*, . . .

D. Paragraphs

Paragraphs add coherence and make the memo more readable. Address each area or topic in a separate paragraph.

> **For Example** In the analysis section of the memo, address in a separate paragraph or paragraphs the discussion of the rule of law, the case that serves as a guide to interpretation of the rule of law, the application of the rule to the issue, the counteranalysis, and the rebuttal to the counteranalysis.

E. Persuasive Precedent

When presenting persuasive authority, indicate the reason you are relying on this type of authority and lay a proper foundation for its use.

> **For Example** Section 90-9-6 prohibits oppressive conduct by a majority shareholder. The statute does not define what constitutes oppressive conduct, and the courts of this state have not addressed the question.
>
> The state of New Washington, however, has a statute identical to our statute, and the New Washington courts have addressed the question of what constitutes oppressive conduct under the statute. In the case of *Darren v. Darren*, . . .

In the preceding example, the reader is informed why the out-of-state law (**persuasive precedent**) is referenced: The statute does not define the term, and the state courts have not addressed the question. A foundation for presentation of the persuasive precedent is thus set: "The statute of the state referred to is identical to our state statute, and the other state's courts have addressed the question." In the following example, a foundation is set for use of a court's interpretation of one statute to interpret another statute.

> **For Example** Our courts have not defined the term *oppressive conduct* as used in § 90-9-6. Section 45-5-6C of the Small Loan Act prohibits "oppressive conduct" in small loan transactions. The state court of appeals, in the case of *Irons v. Fast Loans, Inc.*, has defined what constitutes oppressive conduct under the Small Loan Act, and we can look to that definition for guidance in interpreting § 90-9-6.

Refer to Chapter 2 and Chapter 18 when relying on persuasive precedent.

F. Conclusions

In many instances, after researching and analyzing a legal problem, you may not be able to provide a definite yes or no answer as to how it may be resolved.

> **For Example** If there is no mandatory precedent, and persuasive precedent or secondary authority is relied on, you may not be able to provide an answer as to how the court is likely to resolve the issue. If the case law that applies is very old and policies have changed, it may be questionable if the case law will be followed.

In such instances, present your conclusions and explain your reservations.

> **For Example** In conclusion, the courts of this state have not addressed this question. The majority of states that have addressed this issue follow the rule adopted by the New Washington Supreme Court in the case of *Tyler v. Tyler*. As stated in the analysis of this issue, the progressive approach of the New Washington court reflects the approach our supreme court has taken in resolving similar issues and will likely be adopted by the court.

G. Revisions and Drafts

When preparing an office memo, it is essential to produce a professional product. This demands thorough research and analysis of all issues assigned and all aspects of each issue. It also requires assembly of the research and analysis into an organized, error-free final product. Be prepared to compose a number of drafts.

H. Additional Authority

If there are several cases on point, it is not necessary to thoroughly discuss each case. Present and discuss thoroughly the most recent case on point, and refer briefly to the other cases.

> **For Example** The case that defines what constitutes "oppressive" conduct in a fact situation such as that presented in our case is *Cedrik v. Ely*, 956 N. Wash. 776, 881 N.E.2d 451 (1995). In this case, the majority shareholder gave himself three bonuses that were triple his salary. At the same time, he refused to allow dividends to be issued. In defining what constitutes "oppressive conduct" under § 90-9-4, the court stated, "Oppressive conduct occurs when a majority shareholder engages in wrongful conduct which inures to the benefit of the majority and the detriment of the minority." *Id.* at 778. See also *Tyre v. Casey*, 953 N. Wash. 431, 878 N.E.2d 49 (1993) (oppressive conduct found when no dividends were issued and majority shareholder received several bonuses and was provided an extravagant expense account); *Ireland v. Ireland*, 952 N. Wash. 288, 873 N.E.2d 553 (1992) (oppressive conduct found when no dividends were issued and majority shareholder was given a house as a bonus).

VI. KEY POINTS CHECKLIST: *Office Legal Memorandum—Analysis to Conclusion*

✔ Follow the standard format for the analysis section of a memo: rule + case law (interpretation of the rule) + application of rule + counteranalysis. This format is based on the standard IRAC model.

✔ The presentation of a case in a case brief is different from the presentation of a case in an office memo. When introducing a case in the analysis section of a memo, it is not necessary to include all the information you would include in a case brief.

✔ In the analysis section, discuss how the rule of law applies to the issue and facts of the client's case.

✔ Always conduct a counteranalysis. If there is no counterargument, mention the fact that no counterargument or different position is supported by the case law.

✔ Provide enough information in the conclusion to inform the reader of all the applicable enacted and case law.

✔ Use introductory and transition sentences. Do not jump from one topic to another. Provide a smooth transition between subjects.

✔ Before presenting persuasive precedent or secondary authority, indicate why you are not relying on mandatory authority.

✔ Do not be disturbed if you do not reach a definite conclusion as to how the law applies. There are many gray areas and issues that have not been ruled upon. Your job is to inform the reader of the existing law and provide a well-reasoned analysis of its application. Predicting the legal outcome always involves some measure of uncertainty.

✔ As mentioned in Chapter 15, do not try to make the first draft the final draft. Just write the information in rough form. It is easier to polish a rough draft than to try to make the first draft the finished product.

VII. APPLICATION

The first example in this section illustrates the application of the principles to the analysis, conclusion, and recommendations sections of the office memo assignment introduced at the beginning of Chapter 16. Recall that the Application section of that chapter only addressed the first half of the memo assignment presented at the beginning of that chapter, that is, the heading, assignment, issue, brief answer, and facts sections of the memo. The second example in this section illustrates the application of the principles discussed in this chapter and the previous chapter to the office memo assignment presented at the beginning of this chapter.

Both Chapter 15 and Chapter 16 discuss the use of an expanded outline and present examples that illustrate the use of an expanded outline when drafting an office memo. Inasmuch as the use of an expanded outline is illustrated in those chapters, a detailed discussion of its use is not included in the two examples explored in this section. The examples in this section present the completed office memoranda.

A. Example 1

The first example illustrates the completion of the memorandum assignment introduced at the beginning of Chapter 16. The heading through facts sections of the assignment are included in the Application section of that chapter. The remainder of the memorandum follows.

Analysis

The rule of law governing privileged communications between spouses is 735 ILCS 5/8-801, which provides, "In all actions, husband and wife may testify for or against each other, provided that neither may testify as to any communication or admission made by either of them to the other or as to any conversation between them during marriage. . . ." The statute does not include any sections that address waiver of the privilege. There is, however, Illinois case law that discusses the question of when the privilege is waived.

A state supreme court case that addresses the question of waiver of the privilege when children are present during the spousal communication is *People v. Sanders*, 99 Ill. 2d 262, 457 N.E.2d 1241 (1983). In this case, the trial court admitted into evidence conversations between the defendant and his spouse. The conversations took place in front of their children, ages eight through thirteen years old; the conversations implicated the defendant in a murder. When addressing the question of whether the communications were privileged, the supreme court stated that the rule followed in the state is that the presence of children of the spouses destroys confidentiality unless the children are too young to understand what is being said.

In our case, just as in *People v. Sanders*, the conversation between the spouses involved incriminating statements made in the presence of children. In our case, just as in *Sanders*, the children were old enough to understand the conversation. If the trial court follows the rule of law presented in *Sanders*, the conversation between Mr. Findo and Mrs. Findo is not a privileged communication under the statute and is admissible into evidence in the trial of Mr. Findo.

No case law in this jurisdiction establishes an exception to the rule presented in *Sanders*. The only possible counterargument is that the children, although present, did not hear the conversation. The *Sanders* opinion does not directly state that the children must actually hear the conversation, but this is implied by the requirement that the children must be old enough to understand what is being said. See the Recommendations section in regard to taking steps to determine if the children heard and understood the conversation.

Conclusion

The rule of law governing privileged spousal communications is 735 ILCS 5/8-801. It provides that communications between spouses during the marriage are privileged. In *People v. Sanders*, the court held that the privilege is waived if it takes place in front of children old enough to understand what is being said. In our case, because the conversation took place in the presence of children old enough to understand, it appears that the privilege does not apply, and the conversation is admissible into evidence.

Recommendations

1. We should conduct further investigation to determine if the children heard and understood the conversation.
2. Additional research should be conducted to determine if there are any cases addressing the question of whether, in addition to being present, the children must actually hear the conversation.

B. Example 2

The second example illustrates the completion of the office memo assignment presented in the hypothetical at the beginning of this chapter. Assume that Ellen Taylor's expanded outline includes the following law from the state of New Washington that applies to the assignment.

- **Article II, section 4,** of the state constitution. "The right of the people to be secure in their persons, houses, papers and effects against unreasonable searches and seizures shall not be violated. . . ."

- **Section 95-21-14** of the state criminal code provides that "[i]t is unlawful for any person intentionally to possess a controlled substance . . . ." Cocaine is listed as a controlled substance under the act.

- *State v. Ikard,* **945 N. Wash. 745, 853 N.E.2d 652 (1989).** In this case, law enforcement officers were looking for a suspect in an armed robbery. The officers recognized a friend of the suspect walking down a street. They stopped him, handcuffed him, and asked him where the suspect was. When he refused to answer the question, the officers searched him and found marijuana in his shirt pocket. The officers then arrested him for possession of narcotics.

  In regard to the initial stop and handcuffing of the defendant, the court held that a person is seized (arrested) within the meaning of Article II, section 4, of the state constitution when a reasonable person would believe he was not free to leave. The court held that a reasonable person in the defendant's position would not believe he was free to leave; therefore, the defendant was under arrest when the officers stopped and handcuffed him.

- *State v. Wilson,* **953 N. Wash. 111, 878 N.E.2d 431 (1993).** In this case, law enforcement officers were executing a search warrant. Upon entering the premises, an officer held the defendant by the arm and refused to allow him to leave. In addressing the question of whether the defendant was under arrest when the officer held him by the arm and refused to allow him to leave, the court held that "[n]ot all detentions constitute a seizure within the meaning of Article II, section 4 of the Constitution. A warrant to search for contraband founded on probable cause implicitly carries with it the limited authority to detain the occupants of the premises while a proper search is conducted. Such a detention does not constitute a seizure within the meaning of the Constitution." *Id.* at 121.

- *State v. Bragg,* **955 N. Wash. 221, 880 N.E.2d 998 (1994).** In this case, the police searched an apartment where Bragg and several other people resided. Narcotics were found in a drawer in the kitchen. There was no evidence linking Bragg to the drugs. Only Bragg was charged with possession. The court noted that possession may be either actual or constructive.

  In overturning his conviction, the court ruled that in a situation where several individuals have access to the location where the drugs are found, and there is no evidence indicating that the defendant has actual possession of the drugs, a conviction can still take place if there is evidence that the defendant is in constructive possession of the drugs. The court stated that to convict the defendant of constructive possession, either direct or circumstantial evidence must be presented that he had knowledge of the presence of the drugs and control over the drugs. In this case, there was no such evidence.

The following is the memorandum prepared by Ellen Taylor.

OFFICE RESEARCH MEMORANDUM

To: Carl Pine, Assistant District Attorney

From: Ellen Taylor, Intern

Re: *State v. Kent*

Case: Cr. 13-404

Re: Arrest during the execution of a search warrant and constructive possession of drugs

STATEMENT OF ASSIGNMENT

You have asked me to prepare a memorandum addressing the following questions: Was Mr. Kent under arrest when he was handcuffed and held in the kitchen while his apartment was searched? Is there sufficient evidence to support charges of possession in this case?

ISSUES

Issue I: Under Article II, section 4, of the state constitution, is an individual seized (under arrest) when police officers handcuff and detain him in the kitchen during the execution of a search warrant?

Issue II: Under § 95-21-14 of the criminal code, is there sufficient evidence to support charges of possession when the defendant is located in the bedroom of a third-story apartment and the drugs are located below a broken window of the bedroom in a parking lot?

BRIEF ANSWER

Issue I: No. The state supreme court has held that detentions during the execution of a search warrant do not constitute seizures within the meaning of Article II, section 4, of the state constitution.

Issue II: No. When drugs are found in a common area accessible to multiple individuals and there is no evidence that the defendant has actual possession, the defendant may constructively possess the drugs. The state supreme court has ruled that constructive possession requires evidence that the defendant had knowledge and control of the drugs. In our case, there is no evidence that the defendant had knowledge and control of the drugs found in the parking lot.

FACTS

On January 7, police officers executed a search warrant for the apartment of the defendant, David Kent. The apartment is located on the third floor of an apartment complex. When the police entered the apartment, Mr. Kent was lying on the bed in the bedroom. He was frisked for weapons, handcuffed, moved to the kitchen, and detained while the search was conducted. He was not placed under arrest or read his rights. The police found a broken window in the bedroom, and the window screen was pushed out. In the parking lot three stories below the bedroom window, the officers found a bag containing cocaine. There were no witnesses who saw the defendant throw anything out of the apartment window. No fingerprints were found on the bag, nor was there any other evidence linking Mr. Kent to the cocaine. Mr. Kent has been charged with possession of a controlled substance.

ANALYSIS

Issue I

The rule of law governing arrest in New Washington is Article II, section 4, of the state constitution which provides, in part, "The right of the people to be secure in their person, . . . against unreasonable searches and seizures shall not be violated. . . ." Neither the constitution nor the state statutes define the term *seizure*. There is, however, New Washington case law that defines the term.

The New Washington case that establishes the standard for what constitutes a seizure is *State v. Ikard*, 945 N. Wash. 745, 853 N.E.2d 652 (1989). In this case, law enforcement officers were looking for a suspect in an armed robbery. The officers recognized a friend of the suspect walking down a street. They stopped him, handcuffed him, and asked him where the suspect was. When he refused to answer the question, the officers searched him and found marijuana in his shirt pocket. The officers then arrested him for possession of narcotics. In ruling that the defendant was under arrest when he was stopped and handcuffed, the court held that a person is seized (arrested) within the meaning of Article II, section 4, of the state constitution when a reasonable person would believe he was not free to leave. *Id.* at 750.

The rule of law defining seizure adopted in *State v. Ikard* is so broadly stated that it can apply to a number of seizure situations, including the situation presented in our case. In our case, a reasonable person would not believe he was free to leave when handcuffed and moved to the kitchen during the execution of a warrant. It appears, therefore, that Mr. Kent was seized (under arrest) within the meaning of *Ikard*.

Not all detentions, however, constitute a seizure. There are exceptions. One exception is when the detention takes place while officers are executing a search warrant. This exception was announced by the supreme court in the case of *State v. Wilson*, 953 N. Wash. 111, 878 N.E.2d 431 (1993). In *Wilson*, after entering the premises during the execution of a search warrant, an officer held the defendant by the arm and refused to allow him to leave. In regard to whether the seizure constituted an arrest, the court held, "Not all detentions constitute a seizure within the meaning of Article II, section 4 of the constitution. A warrant to search for contraband founded on probable cause implicitly carries with it the limited authority to detain the occupants of the premises while a proper search is conducted. Such a detention does not constitute a seizure within the meaning of the constitution." *Id.* at 121.

In our case, just as in *Wilson*, the police were executing a search warrant and the defendant was detained while the search was being conducted. None of our facts indicates the warrant was issued without probable cause. If it was based on probable cause, under *Wilson*, the police had the authority to detain the defendant, and the detention was not a seizure within the meaning of the constitution.

No case or statutory law in New Washington contradicts or limits the *Wilson* ruling in regard to detention during the execution of a warrant. The only possible counterargument is that the warrant was issued without probable cause, and therefore, the police did not have authority to detain Mr. Kent. There is no evidence in the case file indicating a problem in this regard. See the Recommendations section below.

Issue II

The rule of law governing the possession of cocaine is section 95-21-14 of the state criminal code, which provides that "[i]t is unlawful for any person intentionally to possess a controlled substance . . . ." Cocaine is listed as a controlled substance under the statute. The statute does not define what constitutes possession; therefore, it is necessary to refer to case law for guidance.

A case in which the supreme court has defined possession is *State v. Bragg*, 955 N. Wash. 221, 880 N.E.2d 998 (1994). In this case, the police searched an apartment where Bragg and several other individuals resided. Narcotics were found in a drawer in the kitchen. There was no evidence linking Bragg to the drugs. Only Bragg was charged with possession. The court noted that possession may be either actual or constructive. In overturning Bragg's conviction, the court ruled that in a situation where several individuals have access to the location where the drugs are found, and there is no evidence indicating that the defendant has actual possession of the drugs, a conviction can still take place if there is evidence that the defendant is in constructive possession of the

drugs. The court stated that in order to convict for constructive possession, "there must be either direct or circumstantial evidence presented that the defendant had knowledge of the presence of the drugs and control over them." *Id.* at 225.

In our case, just as in *Bragg*, there is no evidence indicating that the defendant actually possessed the drugs. Also, there is no evidence, either direct or circumstantial, of constructive possession. There is no evidence that the defendant had knowledge of the presence of the drugs in the parking lot. Also, there is no evidence that he had control of the drugs. The drugs were found three stories below his apartment in a parking lot. There is no evidence linking the defendant to the drugs. If the rule of law presented in *Bragg* is followed, it appears that there is not sufficient evidence to support charges of possession.

There is no New Washington case law contradicting *Bragg* or establishing a different definition of *constructive possession*. A possible counterargument is that the fact the drugs were found below the defendant's broken apartment window is sufficient to link him to the drugs. There is no case law to support this position. It may be necessary to look for additional evidence that links the defendant to the drugs. See the Recommendations section below.

CONCLUSION

Article II, section 4, of the state constitution prohibits the unreasonable seizure (arrest) of individuals. The case of *State v. Ikard* states that an arrest takes place if a reasonable person would not believe he was free to leave. The case of *State v. Wilson* provides that a detention that takes place during the execution of a search warrant does not constitute a seizure within the meaning of the constitution. In our case, the defendant was detained during the execution of a search warrant. Therefore, under the ruling in *Wilson*, it appears the detention of the defendant was not a seizure (arrest).

Section 95-21-14 of the state criminal code provides that it is illegal to possess cocaine. In *State v. Bragg*, the court held that to establish constructive possession, evidence must be presented showing that the defendant had knowledge of the presence of the drugs and control over them. In our case, the defendant did not actually possess the drugs, and there is no evidence indicating he had knowledge of or control over them. Therefore, it appears that there is not sufficient evidence to support charges of possession.

RECOMMENDATIONS

1. We should determine whether the issuance of the search warrant was supported by probable cause or if there is any other matter that affects the legality of the search. If the issuance of the warrant or the

execution of the search was in some way defective, the detention exception established in *State v. Wilson* may not apply.

2. We need to conduct further investigation to determine if there is any evidence linking the defendant

to the drugs found in the parking lot. For example, was glass from the window embedded in the bag? Were there any individuals in the apartment complex who heard a window being broken?

C. Comments on Examples

Note that the analysis section of both memos follows the same analytical format: rule of law + case law interpreting the rule of law + application of the law to the issue and facts of the client's case + counteranalysis. There are transition sentences linking the presentation of the rule of law to the case law. No extra or superfluous material is presented; the reader is not required to wade through related but unnecessary case law or analysis. The applicable law is introduced, explained, and applied. The reader is clearly and concisely informed of the law and how it applies.

In both examples, there is one conclusion that includes a reference to the applicable law and summarizes the analysis of the issues. The conclusion summarizes all the applicable enacted and case law. If the reader desires a detailed analysis and discussion of the law, the analysis section can be referenced. When the memo is more complex and involves multiple issues, it may be appropriate to provide a conclusion section at the end of the analysis of each issue.

Summary

This chapter addresses considerations involved in preparing the second half of an office memorandum: the analysis, conclusion, and recommendations sections. The focus of the chapter is on the analysis section.

The heart of an office memorandum is the analysis section. The purpose of a memorandum is to inform the reader of the law that governs the issue and how the law applies in the client's case. This information is conveyed in the analysis section of the office memo. In this section, the reader is informed through:

- A presentation of the law that governs the issue
- An explanation of how the law applies through reference to court opinions that applied the law in similar situations
- A discussion of how the law applies to the issue(s) in the client's case

Included in the analysis is a discussion of any counterargument the opposing side may raise.

Following the analysis section is the conclusion. Because the application of the law to the issue is discussed in the analysis section, the conclusion should contain a summary of the law and analysis already presented. It should inform the reader of all the applicable law and how it applies.

The recommendations section is the last section of the office memo. It includes any suggestions or recommendations concerning the next steps to be taken or further research or investigation that should be conducted.

The format discussed in this chapter is a recommended format. There is no standard office memo format. Different law offices have different preferences. Use the format presented in this chapter if appropriate; modify it according to your needs.

Quick References

Internet Resources

The online resources for this chapter are the same as those listed in Chapter 15. Due to the large number of sites, the best strategy is to narrow your search to a specific type of legal writing and topic, such as "analysis, legal memorandum, public service contracts" or "application of law, legal memorandum, highway construction."

Exercises

Additional assignments are available on the CourseMate.

ASSIGNMENT 1

Detail the process for presenting a case in the analysis section of an office memo.

ASSIGNMENT 2

Detail the format of the analysis section of an office memo.

ASSIGNMENT 3

Describe what should and should not be included in the conclusion section of an office memo.

ASSIGNMENT 4

Perform assignments 5, 6, 7, 9, 10, or 11 using your state's statutory and case law.

In each of the following exercises, the assignment is to prepare an office memo. Each assignment contains an assignment memo from the supervising attorney that includes all the available facts of the case. Complete the memo based on these facts. If additional facts are needed, note this in the recommendations section of the memo. When preparing the heading of each assignment, use "Supervising Attorney" in the "To" line, and put your name after the "From."

Following each assignment is a reference to the applicable enacted and case law. In some assignments, the case citation includes a reference only to the regional reporter citation; the state reporter citation is not included. Use only the citation presented in the assignment. The cases are presented in Appendix A.

The first time you cite the opinion, use the citation format you are given for the opinion in the assignment.

> **For Example** *Britton v. Britton* is cited in assignment 5 as 100 N.M. 424, 671 P.2d 1135 (1983).

This is how you should cite this opinion the first time it is used in the memorandum. When you need to quote from an opinion in the memo, use a blank line to indicate the page number from which the quotation is taken.

> **For Example** *Britton,* 100 N.M. at ___, 671 P.2d at ___, or *Id.* at ___, 671 P.2d at ___.

Do not conduct additional research. Complete the assignment using the facts, enacted law, and case law contained in each assignment. For the purposes of the assignments, assume that the cases have not been overturned or modified by subsequent court decisions.

ASSIGNMENT 5

> To: [Your name]
> From: Supervising Attorney
> Re: *Dixon v. Cary;* probate of holographic will

We represent Holly Dixon, the widow of Thomas Dixon, in the case of *Dixon v. Cary*. She wishes to challenge the probate of the holographic will of Thomas Dixon. Mary Cary, the sister of Thomas Dixon and personal representative of his estate, has submitted for probate a holographic will prepared by Mr. Dixon.

The first half of the will is in the handwriting of Mr. Dixon. The second half is typewritten. It was typed by the next-door neighbor, Edgar Mae. Mr. Mae states that Mr. Dixon asked him to finish the will because Mr. Dixon was too weak to continue. The will is signed by Mr. Dixon. There are no subscribing witnesses to the will, but it includes a self-proving affidavit that meets the requirements of the statute.

Is the will admissible to probate under Texas law?

Statutory Law: Tex. Prob. Code. Ann. § 59, Requisites of a Will (Vernon 1980), provides: "Every last will and testament . . . shall be in writing . . . , and shall, if not wholly in the handwriting of the testator, be attested by two (2) or more credible witnesses . . . ."

Tex. Prob. Code. Ann. § 60, Exception Pertaining to Holographic Wills (Vernon 1980), provides: "Where the will is written wholly in the handwriting of the testator, the attestation of the subscribing witnesses may be dispensed with. Such a will may be made self-proved at any time during the testator's lifetime by the attachment or annexation thereto of an affidavit by the testator to the effect that the instrument is his last will; that he was at least eighteen years of age when he executed it . . . ; that he was of sound mind; and that he has not revoked such instrument."

Case Law: *Dean v. Dickey*, 225 S.W.2d 999 (Tex. Civ. App. 1949) (see Appendix A).

ASSIGNMENT 6

To: [Your name]

From: Supervising Attorney

Re: *Eldridge v. Eldridge;* modification of child support

We represent Gwen Eldridge in the case of *Eldridge v. Eldridge*. The Eldridges were divorced in 2010. Mrs. Eldridge was awarded custody of their two minor children. Mr. Eldridge was ordered to make child support payments in the amount of $700 per month. He lost his job in January of 2011 and was unemployed from that date through October of 2011. He then obtained employment as an electrician.

Mr. Eldridge did not make child support payments for the months he was unemployed. In January of 2012, Mrs. Eldridge filed a motion with the court that entered the divorce decree, seeking an order forcing Mr. Eldridge to pay the child support payments due for the months he did not make payments; the amount totaled $7,000. Mr. Eldridge countered with a petition to modify his child support obligation. The petition requested that he be excused from having to pay the obligations that accrued during the 10 months he was unemployed. The court ordered Mr. Eldridge to pay one-half of the amount due, $3,500, and excused him from paying the remaining $3,500. The court stated that Mr. Eldridge did not have to pay the full amount because he was unemployed during the months the child support accrued. The attorney that represented Mrs. Eldridge in the trial court told her that there is no basis for an appeal of the court order.

Please check the statutory and case law to determine if the trial court acted properly when it excused Mr. Eldridge from paying $3,500 of the back child support.

Statutory Law: Ind. Code § 31-2-11-12, Modification of delinquent support payment, provides:

(a)   Except as provided in subsection (b) . . . , a court may not retroactively modify an obligor's duty to pay a delinquent support payment.

(b)   A court with jurisdiction over a support order may modify an obligor's duty to pay a support payment that becomes due:

(1) After notice of a petition to modify the support order has been given . . . to the obligee . . . and

(2) Before a final order concerning the petition for modification is entered.

Case Law: *Cardwell v. Gwaltney*, 556 N.E.2d 953 (Ind. Ct. App. 1990) (see Appendix A).

ASSIGNMENT 7

To: [Your name]

From: Supervising Attorney

Re: *Commonwealth v. Jones;* assault by means of a dangerous weapon—lightning

This is a bizarre case to say the least. We have been appointed by the court to represent Sedrick Jones in the case of *Commonwealth v. Jones*. Mr. Jones is charged with attempted murder, battery, false imprisonment, and assault with a dangerous weapon. Mr. Jones has had a stormy 10-year relationship with Elizabeth Steward. The relationship has been marked by multiple instances of domestic violence. They live in a cottage located on a bluff overlooking the Atlantic Ocean. On April 5 of this year, after an extended bout of drinking and arguing, Mr. Jones dragged

Ms. Steward outside and tied her to the lightning rod attached to the cottage. This took place during a violent electrical storm. When he tied her to the pole, he said, "I'll fix you, you're gonna fry." Lightning did not strike the pole. This act is the basis of the assault by means of a dangerous weapon charge. The state claims that the dangerous weapon is lightning.

Please prepare a memo addressing the question of whether there is a sufficient basis to support the charge of assault by means of a dangerous weapons.

Statutory Law: G.L. c. 265, § 15A, Assault and Battery with Dangerous Weapon (state of Massachusetts), provides: "(b) Whoever, by means of a dangerous weapon, commits assault and battery upon another shall be punished by imprisonment in the state prison for not more than five years. . . ."

Case Law: *Commonwealth v. Shea*, 38 Mass. App. Ct. 7, 644 N.W.2d 244 (1995) (see Appendix A).

ASSIGNMENT 8

To: [Your name]

From: Supervising Attorney

Re: *United States v. Canter;* armed bank robbery with a dangerous weapon

We have been appointed to represent Eldon Canter in the case of *United States v. Canter*. Mr. Canter is charged with one count of armed bank robbery, in violation of 18 U.S.C. § 2113(a) and (d).

On January 5 of this year, Mr. Canter robbed the First State Bank. After he entered the bank, he approached a teller and pulled from his pocket a crudely carved wooden replica of a 9 mm Beretta handgun. He had carved the replica from a block of pine wood and stained it with dark walnut wood stain to make it look black. He drilled a hole in the barrel end in an attempt to make it look like a real Beretta.

The teller was so frightened that he only glanced at the wooden gun. He believed it was real. The teller at the next window looked at the replica and afterward stated that she was fairly certain at the time that it was fake. No one else noticed whether the wooden replica was real.

Please determine whether, in light of the facts of this case, there is sufficient evidence to support the charge that Mr. Canter committed bank robbery by use of a "dangerous weapon."

Statutory Law: 18 U.S.C. § 2113(a) & (d), Bank robbery and incidental crimes, provides:

(a) Whoever, by force and violence, or by intimidation, takes, or attempts to take, from the person or presence of another . . . any property or money or any other thing of value belonging to, or in the care, custody, control, management, or possession of, a bank. . . .

Shall be fined under this title or imprisoned not more than 20 years, or both.

(d) Whoever, in committing, or in attempting to commit, any offense defined in subsections (a) and (b) of this section, assaults any person, or puts in jeopardy the life of any person by use of a dangerous weapon or device, shall be fined under this title or imprisoned not more than 25 years, or both.

Case Law: *United States v. Martinez-Jimenez*, 864 F.2d 664 (9th Cir. 1989) (see Appendix A).

ASSIGNMENT 9

To: [Your name]

From: Supervising Attorney

Re: Mr. Arturo Garcia; child support modification

After 15 years of marriage, Arturo Garcia and Mary Chavez were granted a divorce in May 2001. There are three children from the marriage. Mr. Garcia was awarded primary custody of the children. Ms. Chavez, a brain surgeon at the time of the divorce, was ordered to pay monthly child support in the amount of $3,000 per month. The terms of the divorce order were undivided in that it did not specify a "per child" amount.

Ms. Chavez always resented the amount of child support she was ordered to pay; her frustration over this led her recently to quit her medical practice and enroll in the paralegal program at the community college. This career change resulted in a substantial reduction in her income. She told several individuals that she quit her practice because she "can't stand to pay that much money to my ex-husband."

Four months ago, the oldest child turned 18 and moved out of Mr. Garcia's house. As soon as the oldest child moved out, Ms. Chavez reduced by one-third the amount of child support she was paying. She neither sought nor obtained a court order granting a modification of her support obligation. She told Mr. Garcia that she did not have to pay the full amount because the oldest child had turned 18. Two months ago, she unilaterally reduced her child support payments to $500 per month. She told Mr. Garcia, "That's all I can afford to pay now that I'm going to school."

Mr. Garcia has come to us seeking legal advice. With the above facts in mind, prepare a memo addressing the following questions:

1. Was it permissible for Ms. Chavez to unilaterally reduce support when the oldest child reached the age of majority?

2. What is the likelihood of the court granting a modification of child support due to Ms. Chavez's change of occupation?

Statutory Law: NMSA § 28-6-1 (Repl. Pamp. 1991) (state of New Mexico) provides that the age of majority is reached when an individual turns 18 years old.

NMSA § 40-4-7 (Repl. Pamp. 1994)—Proceedings; spousal support; support of children; division of property—(state of New Mexico), section F, provides: "The court may modify and change any order in respect to . . . care, custody, maintenance . . . of the children whenever circumstances render such change proper. The district court shall have exclusive jurisdiction of all matters pertaining to the . . . care, custody, maintenance . . . of the children so long as the children remain minors."

NMSA § 40-4-11.4(A) (Repl. Pamp. 1994)—Modification of child support orders; exchange of financial information—the relevant portion of section A provides: " A court may modify a child support obligation upon a showing of material and substantial changes in circumstances subsequent to the adjudication of the preexisting order."

Case Law: *Britton v. Britton*, 100 N.M. 424, 671 P.2d 1135 (1983) (see Appendix A).

Wolcott v. Wolcott, 105 N.M. 608, 735 P.2d 326 (Ct. App. 1987) (see Appendix A).

ASSIGNMENT 10

> To: [Your name]
>
> From: Supervising Attorney
>
> Re: *Kells v. Simns;* implied warranty of fitness for a particular purpose

Our client, Mr. Merril Simns, is being sued by Tom Kells for breach of an implied warranty of fitness for a particular purpose in the case of *Kells v. Simns*. Mr. Simns placed an ad in the *Daily Post* offering to sell a Ryder 1000 riding lawn mower for $400. Mr. Kells responded to the ad and came to Mr. Simns's house to purchase the mower. Mr. Kells told Mr. Simns that he needed a good riding mower because he had two and one-half acres that had to be mowed once a week. Mr. Simns responded that, although he had never needed to mow more than an acre, the mower had always

done a good job for him. After discussing the terms, Mr. Kells purchased the mower for $300.

One week later, Mr. Kells called Mr. Simns and informed him that the mower was too small and underpowered for his needs, and he wanted his money back. Mr. Simns refused, and Mr. Kells has filed suit in small claims court, claiming breach of an implied warranty of fitness for a particular purpose. Mr. Simns's only experience with riding mowers is based on his use of the Ryder 1000. He does not have any special expertise concerning riding mowers.

Please assess the likelihood of Mr. Kells prevailing on an implied warranty of fitness for a particular purpose claim.

Statutory Law: ORS 72.3150, Implied warranty: fitness for particular purpose (state of Oregon), provides: "Where the seller at the time of contracting has reason to know any particular purpose for which the goods are required and that the buyer is relying on the seller's skill or judgment to select or furnish suitable goods, there is unless excluded or modified under ORS 72.3610 an implied warranty that the goods shall be fit for such purpose."

Case Law: *Beam v. Cullett*, 48 Or. App. 47, 615 P.2d 1196 (1980) (see Appendix A).

ASSIGNMENT 11

> To: [Your name]
>
> From: Supervising Attorney
>
> Re: *Commonwealth v. Clavel;* execution of search warrant—unannounced entry

We represent Darren Clavel in the case of *Commonwealth v. Clavel*. In this case, police officers executed a search warrant that authorized the search of the client's home for drugs. When the police arrived at Mr. Clavel's house, they knocked on the door, shouted "Police, open up," waited 15 seconds, kicked the door open, and searched the premises. Mr. Clavel, who is hard of hearing, heard some noise and was approaching the door to open it when it was kicked open. Upon searching the house, the police found a pound of marijuana in the bedroom closet. Mr. Clavel was charged with intent to distribute narcotics.

Please prepare a memo assessing the likelihood of having the evidence suppressed because of the manner in which the officers executed the warrant.

Statutory Law: The Fourth Amendment to the United States Constitution (U.S. Const. Amend. IV).

Case Law: *Commonwealth v. DeMichel*, 442 Pa. 553, 277 A.2d 159 (1971) (see Appendix A).

ЁЁЁ

ЁЁЁ

ASSIGNMENT 12

> To: [Your name]
> From: Supervising Attorney
> Re: Mrs. Joyce Helger; probate of copy of lost original will

We represent Mrs. Helger in the probate of her husband's estate. Mr. Helger died four weeks ago after a sudden heart attack. Mrs. Helger has been unable to locate the original of Mr. Helger's will. She knows that he had prepared a will, and she has a conformed copy of the will executed December 1, 2002. She also has a conformed copy of a codicil executed on May 6, 2007. She does not have the original of the codicil. Mrs. Helger thought the law firm that prepared the will kept the original, but she was informed that the firm could not locate the original. The senior partner at the firm told her that they do not keep the original of wills or codicils.

Please assess the likelihood of the probate court granting a petition for administration of the conformed copy of the will and codicil.

Rule of Law: The rule of law governing this question is case law rather than statutory law—*In the Estate of Parson*, 416 So. 2d 513, 515 (Fla. Dist. Ct. App. 1982): The court held that there is a "presumption that a will which was in the possession of the testator prior to death and which cannot be located subsequent to death was destroyed by the testator with the intention of revoking it."

Case Law: The court opinion that interprets the application of the rule stated in the previous case is the following case: *In re Estate of Kuszmaul*, 491 So. 2d 287 (Fla. Dist. Ct. App. 1986) (see Appendix A).

ASSIGNMENT 13

> To: [Your name]
> From: Supervising Attorney
> Re: *Mad Dog Review v. Jonesville*; First Amendment—freedom of expression

We represent Mad Dog Review, a local rap band. As you know, this is a controversial group. The lyrics of one of their songs, "Mad Dog City Council," describes our city council in explicit terms using "dirty" words and language generally considered obscene. Based upon the language in their songs, and specifically that in "Mad Dog City Council," the city council of Jonesville (a neighboring municipality) has banned the group from performing in their community.

The Jonesville city council based its authority to enact the ban on Municipal Ordinance section 355-20. The ordinance provides: "The City Council, upon majority vote, may prohibit the public performance of any type of entertainment that does not comport with local standards of decency or acceptability." The ordinance does not define "local standards of decency or acceptability" or provide any standards or guidelines that the city council must follow.

Mad Dog Review wants to challenge the authority of the Jonesville city council to ban its performance. Please prepare an office memorandum addressing the question of whether the municipal ordinance violates the group's right to freedom of expression.

Rule of Law: First Amendment to the United States Constitution (U.S. Const. Amend. I).

Case Law: Assume that the only case law governing this question is *Atlantic Beach Casino, Inc. v. Morenzoni*, 749 F. Supp. 38 (D.R.I. 1990). The relevant portions of the case are presented at the end of this chapter.

ASSIGNMENT 14

Note: Assignments 14 and 15 were prepared by Mary Kubichek, JD, director of Paralegal Studies at Casper College in Casper, Wyoming. The initial draft of the model answer to each assignment included in the Instructor's Manual was prepared by Ms. Kubichek's students.

> To: [Your name]
> From: Supervising Attorney
> Re: *Wright v. State*; liability of State University for battery of student

We represent Joe and Ann Wright, parents of Bob Wright, a freshman at State University of Generic who was living 400 miles from home. Bob lived in Smith Hall, a freshman dormitory. Bob wanted to be involved in school activities. The university supported intramural sports activities where dorm students competed against other dorm students. Bob was not very athletic and his dorm lost games because of his lack of skill and he often got in the way of his team. After a 0–4 record, Bob's teammates threatened him and told him to quit. Bob notified a counselor at the university. Bob did not quit, and after two more losing games, he was beaten by three teammates. Bob, who is a diabetic, suffered a broken arm, had a fifth of alcohol poured down his throat, and required 40 stitches to his torso. Bob withdrew from the university. Bob's parents and Bob want to sue the college under the following sections of the state statute.

You are only to consider the following statutes. Do not bring in any outside facts or law.

Statutes:

(a) **Hazing** is defined as follows:

(1) Any willful action taken or situation created, whether on or off any school, college, university, or other educational premises, which recklessly or intentionally endangers the mental or physical health of any student, or

(2) Any willful act on or off any school, college, university, or other educational premises by any person alone or acting with others in striking, beating, bruising, or maiming; or seriously offering, threatening, or attempting to strike, beat, bruise, or maim, or to do or seriously offer, threaten, or attempt to do physical violence to any student of any such educational institution or any assault upon any such students made for the purpose of committing any of the acts, or producing any of the results to such student as defined in this section.

(3) The term hazing as defined in this section does not include customary athletic events or similar contests or competitions, and is limited to those actions taken and situations created in connection with initiation into or affiliation with any organization.

(4) The academic institution, college, university, etc. is liable for hazing if:

(i) it occurred by members of a campus group;

(ii) it had notice.

Please draft an interoffice memorandum. Include the following:

> To:
> From:
> Re:
> Facts: (Remember to include parties and what the clients want.)
> Issue(s): (Remember that the issue or issues must include jurisdiction, key facts, and be in question form.)
> Analysis:
> Conclusion:

ASSIGNMENT 15

> To: [Your name]
> From: Supervising Attorney
> Re: *Martin v. City Airport*; 42 U.S.C. § 2000e

We represent Jake Martin. Jake is a 25-year-old American citizen. He is olive skinned, 6 feet 3 inches, 220 pounds with thick dark hair and a full beard. Jake applied for an airport security position. He stated that he has filled out all forms. He was informed that he will not be hired. Jake's mother lives on an Indian reservation within five miles of the airport security position. Jake argues that he is being discriminated against under 42 U.S.C. § 2000e-2(a)(1). Jake wants a job with airport security.

You are to consider only the following statutes. Do not bring in any outside facts or law.

Statutes:

42 U.S.C. § 2000e-2

(a) Employer practices

It shall be an unlawful employment practice for an employer . . .

(1) To fail or refuse to hire or to discharge any individual, or otherwise to discriminate against any individual with respect to his compensation, terms, conditions, or privileges of employment, because of such individual's race, color, religion, sex, or national origin; . . . .

(g) National security

Notwithstanding any other provision of this subchapter, it shall not be an unlawful employment practice for an employer to fail or refuse to hire and employ any individual for any position, for an employer to discharge an individual from any position, or for an employment agency to fail or refuse to refer any individual for employment in any position, or for a labor organization to fail or refuse to refer any individual for employment in any position, if. . . .

(1) the occupancy of such position, or access to the premises in or upon which any part of the duties of such position is performed or is to be performed, is subject to any requirement imposed in the interest of the national security of the United States under any security program in effect pursuant to or administered under any statute of the United States or any Executive order of the President; and

(i) Businesses or enterprises extending preferential treatment to Indians

Nothing contained in this subchapter (regarding national security) shall apply to any business or enterprise on or near an Indian reservation with respect to any publicly announced employment practice of such business or enterprise under which a preferential treatment is given to any individual because he is an Indian living on or near a reservation.

Please draft an interoffice memorandum. Include the following:

To:

From:

Re:

Facts: (Remember to include parties and what the clients want.)

Issue(s): (Remember that the issue or issues must include jurisdiction, key facts, and be in question form.)

Analysis:

Conclusion:

ASSIGNMENT 16

To: [Your name]

From: Supervising Attorney

Re: *Espinosa v. Capital Insurance;* contract breach

We represent Emilio Espinosa. On May 2nd of this year, Mr. Espinosa purchased a home from First City Bank. On that date he purchased homeowner insurance from Capital Insurance Company. The Bank had foreclosed on the home on March 15, forty-eight days prior to Mr. Espinosa's purchase. Mr. Espinosa did not plan to move into the home until July 1st. On June 5, thirty-four days after Mr. Espinosa purchased the home and signed the homeowner insurance contract with Capital Insurance, copper thieves broke into the home, tore into the walls and ceiling, and stole the copper water pipes. There was extensive damage to the walls and ceiling and water damage to the carpet. The estimated repair costs were $19,000.

The house was vacant from March 15, the date of the foreclosure until the date of the damage; a period of eighty-two days. Paragraph 20 of the insurance contract Mr. Espinosa signed with Capital Insurance excludes from coverage loss caused by "theft or attempted theft, damage by burglars, . . . if the described location: is held as a residence and has not been occupied as a residence for more than 60 consecutive days immediately before the loss."

Capital Insurance is denying coverage based upon this section of the contract.

Please check the statutory and case law to determine whether Capital Insurance can deny coverage based upon this section.

Statutory Law: For the purposes of this assignment, there is no statutory law that applies.

Case Law: *Pappas Enterprises, Inc. v. Commerce & Industry Insurance Co.,* 422 Mass. 80, 661 N.E.2d 81 (1996) (see Appendix A).

ASSIGNMENT 17

To: [Your name]

From: Supervising Assistant District Attorney

Re: *State v. James Young;* burglary

On August 7, Mr. Young went to Coronado Mall. He took a coat hanger which he planned to use to break into cars parked at the mall. The mall parking lot was full and Mr. Young went unobserved. As he approached Karl Wilson's vehicle, he noticed that the windows were open about an inch. He also observed Mr. Wilson's wallet on the front seat. Unknown to Mr. Wilson, the wallet fell out of his pocket when he exited the car.

Mr. Young was unable to unlock Mr. Wilson's vehicle. However, after fashioning a hook, he was able to pull the wallet through the open window. The wallet contained $300 and two credit cards, all of which Mr. Young took.

I would like to charge Mr. Young with burglary under our burglary statute. Does Mr. Young's use of the coat hanger to retrieve the wallet constitute entry within the meaning of the statute? Please prepare a memo addressing this question.

Statutory Law: New Mexico Statute § 30-16-3. Burglary

Burglary consists of the unauthorized entry of any vehicle, watercraft, aircraft, dwelling or other structure, movable or immovable, with the intent to commit any felony or theft therein.

Case Law: *State v. Muqqdin,* 2010 NMCA 69, ___ NMCA ___, ___ P.3d ___ (see Appendix A).

CASE

ATLANTIC BEACH CASINO, INC.
d/b/a the Windjammer,
et al., Plaintiffs,

v.

Edward T. MARENZONI,
et al., Defendants.
Civ. A. No. 90-0471.
United States District Court,
D. Rhode Island.
Sept. 28, 1990.
749 F. Supp. 38 (D.R.I. 1990)

OPINION AND ORDER

PETTINE, Senior District Judge.

In the last few years legislators and citizens have paid increasing attention to the lyrical content of popular music. The interest is not entirely new, for "rulers have long known [music's] capacity to appeal to the intellect and to the emotions and have censored musical compositions to serve the needs of the state." *Ward v. Rock Against Racism*, ___ U.S. ___, 109 S.Ct. 2746, 2753, 105 L.Ed.2d 661 (1989). The controversy some groups have ignited is not, in itself, any reason to take such speech outside the First Amendment. Indeed, expression may "best serve its high purpose when it induces a condition of unrest, creates dissatisfaction with conditions as they are, or even stirs people to anger." *Terminiello v. Chicago*, 337 U.S. 1, 4, 69 S.Ct. 894, 96, 893 L.Ed. 1131 (1949). The message and reputation of the rap music group 2 Live Crew evidently came to the attention of the Westerly Town Council, for they have taken steps toward possibly preventing the group from playing a scheduled concert. It is in this way that 2 Live Crew became the subject of, though not a party to, the present litigation.

On September 19, 1990, plaintiffs, who have contracted to present the 2 Live Crew concert, moved for a temporary restraining order prohibiting the defendants, members of the Westerly Town Council, from holding a show cause hearing on September 24, 1990, concerning the revocation of plaintiffs' entertainment license; from revoking the plaintiffs' entertainment license; from prohibiting the 2 Live Crew concert scheduled for October 6, 1990; and from imposing any special requirements on plaintiffs relative to the October 6 presentation. On September 21, 1990, the parties and this Court agreed that the matter would be considered as an application for a preliminary injunction and that the show cause hearing would be continued until October 1, 1990, subject to and dependent upon this Court's ruling. Based on the September 21 conference and my review of the parties' briefs, this Court has determined that the central issue in this case is plaintiffs' facial challenge to the town of Westerly's licensing ordinances on First Amendment grounds. Because I find, for the reasons set out below, that the ordinances as written are unconstitutional under the First and Fourteenth Amendments, defendants are enjoined from conducting a show cause hearing and from revoking plaintiff's entertainment license. I also enjoin the defendants from prohibiting the concert for failing to allege sufficient harm to overcome plaintiffs' First Amendment rights.

III. INJUNCTIVE RELIEF

In order for plaintiffs to prevail in their request for a preliminary injunction, they must meet the following standards: the plaintiff must demonstrate a likelihood of success on the merits, immediate and irreparable harm, that the injury outweighs any harm engendered by the grant of injunctive relief and that the public interest will not be adversely affected by such grant. *LeBeau v. Spirito*, 703 F.2d 639, 642 (1st Cir. 1983). I shall address each of these standards in turn.

A. Likelihood of Success on the Merits

Rather than allow 2 Live Crew to perform and then prosecute for any illegal activity that could occur, the Town Council wishes to review and decide in advance whether to allow the performance to go forward. This is a prior restraint. See *Southeastern Promotions, Ltd. v. Conrad*, 420 U.S. 546, 554–55, 95 S.Ct. 1239, 1244–45, 43 L.Ed.2d 448 (1975). "Any system of prior restraints of expression comes to this Court bearing a heavy presumption against its constitutional validity." *Bantam Books, Inc. v. Sullivan*, 372 U.S. 58, 70, 83 S.Ct. 631, 639, 9 L.Ed.2d 584 (1963). A licensing scheme involving such prior restraint survives constitutional scrutiny only when the law contains "narrow, objective and definite standards to guide the licensing authority." *Shuttlesworth v. Birmingham*, 394 U.S. 147, 150–51, 89 S.Ct. 935, 938–39, 22 L.Ed.2d 162 (1969); see *Lakewood*, 486 U.S. 760, *Southeastern Promotions*, 420 U.S. at 553, 95 S.Ct. at 1243–44, *Cox v. State of Louisiana*, 379 U.S. 536, 557–58, 85 S.Ct. 453, 465–66, 13 L.Ed.2d 471 (1965), *Irish Subcommittee v. R.I. Heritage Commission*, 646 F.Supp. 347, 359 (D.R.I.1986).

The Westerly Ordinance, see *supra* note 3, provides even less guidance than the law struck down in *Shuttlesworth*. *Id.* 394 U.S. at 149, 89 S.Ct. at 937–38 (permit could be denied if demanded by the "public welfare, peace, safety, health, decency, good order, morals or convenience"). For example, Section 17–87 merely states, "Any license granted under Section 17–84 and 17–88 may be revoked by the Town Council after public hearing for cause shown." As in *Venuti*, the Westerly ordinance is utterly devoid of standards. See 521 F.Supp. at

1030–31 (striking down entertainment license ordinance). It leaves the issuance and revocation of licenses to the unbridled discretion of the Town Council. Our cases have long noted that "the danger of censorship and of abridgement of our precious First Amendment freedoms is too great where officials have unbridled discretion over a forum's use." *Toward a Gayer Bicentennial Committee v. Rhode Island Bicentennial Foundation*, 417 F.Supp. 632, 641 (D.R.I.1976) (quoting *Southeastern Promotions*, 420 U.S. at 553, 95 S.Ct. at 1242–44).

The defendants assert that they are guided by specific concerns for public safety, as outlined in their notice to plaintiffs, and not by the message of 2 Live Crew's lyrics. When dealing with the First Amendment, however, the law does not allow us to presume good intentions on the part of the reviewing body. *Lakewood*, 486 U.S. at 770, 108 S.Ct. at 1243–44. The standards must be explicitly set out in the ordinance itself, a judicial construction or a well-established practice. *Id.* Without standards there is a grave danger that a licensing scheme "will serve only as a mask behind which the government hides as it excludes speakers from the . . . forum solely because of what they intend to say." *Irish Subcommittee*, 646 F.Supp. at 357. Such exclusion is repugnant to the First Amendment.

This Court recognizes that the Westerly Town Council has a valid interest in regulating entertainment establishments. It is well established that time, place and manner restrictions on expressive activity are permissible, but even then the regulations must be "narrowly and precisely tailored to their legitimate objectives." *Toward a Gayer Bicentennial*, 427 F.Supp. at 638; *see* Shuttlesworth, 394 U.S. at 153, 89 S.Ct. at 940; Cox, 379 U.S. at 558, 85 S.Ct. at 466. The Westerly licensing ordinances do not even approach the necessary level of specificity constitutionally mandated. Given the complete lack of standards in the ordinances and the long and clear line of precedent, plaintiffs' likelihood of success is overwhelming.

ORDER

Because Westerly Code of Ordinances, Sections 17-84 and 17-87 are facially unconstitutional, because the plaintiffs have met the other requirements for a preliminary injunction, and because defendants have failed to allege sufficient harm. IT IS ORDERED that defendants are enjoined from conducting a show cause hearing, revoking plaintiffs' license pursuant to these ordinances or from otherwise prohibiting the scheduled concert.

External Memoranda: Court Briefs

Learning Objectives

After completing this chapter, you should understand:

- The similarities and differences between court briefs and office memoranda

- Techniques of persuasive writing

- The elements of trial and appellate court briefs

- How to draft trial and appellate court briefs

Pam Hayes, a paralegal living in the hypothetical state of New Washington, received the following assignment from her supervisor.

To: Pam Hayes, Paralegal

From: Alice Black, Attorney

Case: Civil 013-601, *Nick Shine v. Blue Sky Ski Resort*

Re: Motion to dismiss for failure to state a claim

On December 5, 2012, Nick Shine, an expert skier, was skiing Bright Light, an intermediate ski run, at Blue Sky Ski Resort. At the midway point, the run takes a sharp, slightly uphill turn to the south, then plunges steeply downhill. When Mr. Shine encountered the turn, the sun was shining directly in his eyes; he did not see that the run was completely covered with ice. Due to the sun's glare, he could not see the ice hazard until it was too late to avoid it. He immediately lost control and hit a tree, breaking his left arm and leg. There was no warning sign posted to indicate the presence of the ice hazard.

We filed Mr. Shine's complaint against the resort on April 6, 2013. In the complaint, we allege that the resort was negligent in failing to post a warning indicating the presence of the unavoidable and latent ice hazard.

On April 20, Blue Sky Ski Resort filed a motion to dismiss under Rule 12(b)(6) of the Rules of Civil Procedure for failure to state a claim. In the motion, Resort argues that under the Ski Safety Act, the resort does not have a duty to warn of ice hazards. They argue that ice conditions are the responsibility of the skier under the act; therefore, we cannot, as a matter of law, state a claim in regard to duty.

Please prepare a response to their motion for my review.

Note that this assignment is a variation of the assignment presented at the beginning of Chapter 13. The following sections of this chapter introduce the guidelines that Ms. Hayes will follow when performing her assignment. The completed assignment is presented in the Application section.

I. INTRODUCTION

The focus of this text is on legal analysis and the main type of writing related to legal analysis: the legal research memorandum. Chapters 16 and 17 address the type of legal writing most frequently performed by paralegals and law clerks engaged in legal analysis: the office legal memorandum. As discussed in those chapters, the office legal memorandum is designed for use within the law office and is drafted primarily as an objective research and analysis tool. This chapter and Chapter 19 discuss the preparation of documents using legal analysis that are designed for use outside the law office:

- Documents submitted to a court, such as briefs in support of motions
- Documents designed for other external use, such as correspondence to clients and opposing attorneys

Paralegals and law clerks are less frequently involved in the preparation of external-use documents than those designed for use within the law office; however, experienced paralegals and law clerks may be called upon to prepare the initial drafts of documents intended for external use—referred to here as *external memoranda*.

The focus of this chapter is on the considerations involved in the preparation of legal analysis documents designed for submission to a court: trial court and appellate court legal memorandum briefs. A trial court brief is often referred to as a *memorandum of law* or a *memorandum of points and authorities*. In this chapter, a legal memorandum brief submitted to a trial court is referred to as a **trial court brief** or **trial brief**, and a brief submitted to a court of appeals is referred to as an **appellate court brief**. The Application section of this chapter provides an example of a trial court brief; Appendix B includes an example of an appellate court brief.

II. GENERAL CONSIDERATIONS

Both trial and appellate court briefs are similar in many respects to office legal memoranda, and the fundamental principles that apply to the preparation of office memos also apply to the preparation of court briefs. The similarities are outlined here.

A. Similarities—Court Briefs and Office Memoranda

1. Legal Writing Process

Just as it is necessary when preparing an office memo to adopt and use a legal writing process, it is also necessary to do so when preparing a court brief. The basic writing process is the same for both court briefs and office memoranda:

Prewriting Stage

    Assignment—type of brief, audience, and so on

    Constraints—time, length, format (court rules)

    Organization—creation of an expanded outline

      Use of an expanded outline

Writing Stage

Postwriting Stage

    Revising

    Editing

2. Basic Format

Court briefs follow the same basic format as office memos. Both include a presentation of the issue(s), the relevant facts, a legal analysis, and a conclusion. Refer to Chapters 16 and 17 for information and guidelines concerning the preparation of these components of a brief.

3. Analysis Approach

Court briefs follow the same basic organizational approach to the legal analysis of an issue as office memoranda: the rule of law is presented first, then the interpretation of the rule of law through the case law (if interpretation is necessary), the application of the law to the issues presented by the facts of the case, followed by the conclusion. Exhibit 18-1 presents the basic format of this approach.

Exhibit 18-1 *Legal Analysis—Court Brief Organizational Approach.*

Rule of law—present the rule of law or legal principle that applies.

Case law (if necessary)—follow the rule of law with the presentation of the case law that interprets how the rule of law applies:

1. Name of case
2. Facts of case sufficient to demonstrate case is on point
3. Rule or legal principle from case that applies to the client's case

Application of law to facts of case after the presentation of the case law— apply the law or principle in the case to the facts of the client's case.
    Include an explanation of why the opposing position does not apply.

Conclusion—provide a summary of the legal analysis.

© Cengage Learning 2014

B. Dissimilarities—Court Briefs and Office Memoranda

As noted previously, both trial and appellate court briefs are similar in many respects to office legal memos in basic format and content. The major difference is in the presentation of the format and content. An office memo is designed to present an objective analysis of the law. The goal is to provide a neutral analysis that thoroughly addresses all sides of an issue and provides the attorney with guidance on how the court may resolve the issue.

Whereas an office memo is designed to objectively inform, a court brief is designed to convince. A court brief is an advocacy document designed to persuade the court to adopt a position or take an action favorable to the client. Therefore, although the elements of an office memo and court brief are basically the same, court briefs are different in that they are drafted to advocate a position and persuade the reader.

The following subsections address the guidelines, factors, and considerations involved in the preparation of persuasive court briefs. To avoid repetition, this section addresses the factors involved in the persuasive presentation of both trial and appellate court briefs. Therefore, the detailed discussion of court briefs presented in sections III and IV does not include information on elements and techniques of persuasive writing. The information presented here applies to the preparation of both trial and appellate court briefs and should be kept in mind when preparing those briefs.

Ethics. As discussed in Chapter 11, Rule 3.3(a)(1) of the Model Rules of Professional Conduct provides that a lawyer should not make false statements of law or fact to a tribunal. Broadly interpreted, this means that matters should not be presented in a manner that may mislead the court. Also, under Rule 3.3(a)(3) of the Model Rules, an attorney has an ethical duty as an officer of the court to disclose legal authority adverse to the client's position that is not disclosed by opposing counsel. Therefore, when preparing a persuasive presentation of a legal position or argument, you must keep in mind the importance of the rules of professional conduct and intellectual honesty as discussed in Chapter 2. Although designed to persuade, a court brief must present the issue(s), facts statement, and analysis accurately, clearly, and concisely. It should not mislead, distort, or hide the truth. The guidelines for how this is accomplished are presented in the following subsections.

1. Issues—Persuasive Presentation

After you identify the issue, introduce each of its elements—the law, the question, and the key facts—in a persuasive manner.

a. Law Component of the Issue

State the law component of the issue persuasively.

> **For Example** The case involves oppressive conduct by a majority shareholder against the minority shareholders in the hypothetical state of New Washington. The corporation consists of three shareholders. The majority shareholder holds 60 percent of the stock and is employed as president of the corporation. The minority shareholders are not employed by the corporation.
>
> In the case, the defendant, the majority shareholder, controlled the board of directors and has refused to allow the issuance of dividends for a 10-year period. During this period, he gave himself an annual 40 percent raise each year and an annual bonus equal to 50 percent of his salary. The minority shareholders filed a suit claiming that the majority shareholder's actions constitute oppressive conduct.
>
> Section 53-6 of the New Washington statutes authorizes the court to dissolve a corporation when the majority shareholder engages in oppressive conduct. This example is referred to in this chapter as the "corporation" example.

In an office memo, the law component of the issue in this example is stated objectively: "Under the New Washington corporation statute, NWSA § 53-6, did oppressive conduct occur when . . . ?" In a court brief, however, the law is presented persuasively. The persuasive language is italicized: "Under the New Washington corporation statute, NWSA § 53-6, *which prohibits oppressive* conduct, did . . . ?"

Note that the persuasive presentation of the law component emphasizes the prohibitory nature of the statute.

> **For Example** If your position is that the statute has limited application, present the law in a manner that focuses on that limitation: "Under NWSA § 51-7, which *limits the requirement of a written contract to. . . .*"
>
> If you want to emphasize the applicability of the statute, present the law in a manner that focuses on applicability: "Under NWSA § 51-7, *which requires that a contract be in writing when. . . .*"

b. Question Component of the Issue

Present the question component of the issue in a persuasive manner that suggests a result.

> **For Example** *Objective presentation:* "did oppressive conduct occur when . . . ?"
>
> *Persuasive presentation:* "was the majority shareholder's conduct oppressive when . . . ?" or "did the majority shareholder engage in oppressive conduct when . . . ?"
>
> Note that in the objective presentation, the focus is on the conduct. In the **persuasive presentation**, the statement immediately links the conduct to the majority shareholder.

The language used should focus on the result desired.

> **For Example** The key language is italicized: "does the statute *allow* oral contracts for . . . ?" or "does the statute *require* oral contracts for . . . ?" or "does the statute *prohibit* oral contracts for . . . ?"

c. Fact Component of the Issue

State the key facts of the issue in a manner designed to focus the reader on the facts favorable to the client and persuade the reader to favor the client's position.

> **For Example** *Objective presentation:* "did oppressive conduct occur when dividends were not issued for a 10-year period and the majority shareholder received annual salary increases and bonuses?"
>
> *Persuasive presentation:* "did the majority shareholder engage in oppressive conduct when he refused to issue dividends for a 10-year period while giving himself large annual salary increases and bonuses?"

> **For Example** *Objective presentation:* "when the defendant entered the property after being advised not to enter?"
>
> *Persuasive presentation:* "when the defendant intentionally entered the property even though he was warned not to enter?"

Note that in both examples, the persuasive presentation focuses on the defendant and links the defendant directly to the improper conduct.

Exhibit 18-2 presents a checklist for use in the persuasive presentation of the issues.

Exhibit 18-2 *Checklist: Issues—Persuasive Presentation.*

- Law component: Is the law correctly presented, stated persuasively, and accurately cited?
- Question component: Are the law, question, and key facts included and stated persuasively?
- Fact component: Are the key and background facts included and stated persuasively?

2. Statement of Facts—Persuasive Presentation

The **statement of facts** section of a court brief presents the facts of the case. This section is often called the *statement of the case*. In a court brief, just as in an office memo, the statement of facts should include both the background and the key facts. In a court brief, introduce the facts credibly, persuasively, and in a light most favorable to the client's position. This is accomplished by emphasizing favorable facts and deemphasizing or neutralizing unfavorable facts.

There are several techniques you may use to emphasize favorable facts and neutralize unfavorable facts. Some of these are discussed in the following subsections.

a. Placement

Readers tend to remember information presented at the beginning and end of a section, and usually give most attention to opening and closing sentences. Therefore, introduce the facts favorable to the client's position at the beginning and the end of the factual statement.

Present the facts unfavorable to the client's position—the ones you wish to deemphasize—in the middle of the section.

> **For Example** Referring to the corporation example, "The defendant is the majority share-holder and controlling member of the board of directors of XYZ Corporation. He has refused to authorize the issuance of dividends for 10 years. During this time, the defendant has been the president of the corporation. As president, he has granted himself a 40 percent raise each year. In addition, he has given himself an annual bonus equal to 50 percent of his salary. It is claimed by the defendant that he is entitled to the salary increases and bonuses because he works long hours, is underpaid, and is the person in charge. The defendant has rebuffed the plaintiff's repeated requests to discuss the defendant's grants to himself of salary increases and bonuses and failure to issue dividends. The defendant has informed the plaintiff that he does not intend to issue dividends."

In this example, the facts least favorable to the defendant—his failure to issue dividends and receipt of salary increases and bonuses—are presented at the beginning. His conduct immediately captures the reader's attention. His conduct is also mentioned again at the end of the presentation. The reader's first and last impressions are focused on the acts least favorable to the defendant. The facts favorable to the defendant—that he is entitled to the salary increases and bonuses—are deemphasized by their placement in the middle of the fact statement.

If the facts statement consists of several paragraphs, place the favorable material at the beginning of the presentation and close with a summary or rephrasing of the favorable key facts. Place the unfavorable facts in the middle of the presentation and mention them only once or as few times as possible.

Note that the goal is a persuasive presentation of the facts. This goal should not be so rigidly pursued as to lose clarity.

> **For Example** It may not be practical to state the favorable facts at the beginning of a paragraph. To ensure clarity, you may need to present transition or introductory sentences first, then follow them with the presentation of the favorable facts.

b. Sentence Length

Use short sentences to emphasize favorable information and long sentences to deemphasize unfavorable information. Shorter sentences generally draw the reader's attention, and are easier to understand and remember; therefore, they are more powerful.

> **For Example** The defendant is the majority shareholder and controlling member of the board of directors of XYZ Corporation. He has refused to authorize the issuance of dividends for 10 years. During this time, the defendant has been the president of the corporation. As president, he has granted himself a 40 percent raise each year.

The sentences in this example are short and clear, drawing the reader's attention. Longer sentences that string together several facts tend to downplay and reduce the impact of each fact.

> **For Example** It is claimed by the defendant that he is entitled to the salary increases and bonuses because he works long hours, is underpaid, and is the person in charge.

In this example, if each of the defendant's actions were presented in separate sentences, they would stand out and be clear.

c. Active Voice

Use **active voice** to emphasize favorable information and passive voice to deemphasize unfavorable information. When active voice is used, the subject of the sentence is the actor. When passive voice is used, the subject is acted upon. Active voice draws attention to and emphasizes the actor. It thus lends power to the statement. **Passive voice** draws attention away from and deemphasizes the actor.

> **For Example** *Passive voice:* "It is claimed by the defendant that he is entitled to the bonuses . . ." draws attention away from the actor, the defendant.
>
> *Active voice:* "The defendant claims he is entitled . . ." is less wordy and focuses the attention on the actor.

d. Word Choice

Ideally, the words you choose should introduce the client's facts in the most favorable light and the opponent's facts in the least favorable light. Present the client's position in the most affirmative manner and the opponent's position in the least favorable manner.

> **For Example** The plaintiff states that. . . .
>
> The defendant alleges. . . .

In this example, notice that the plaintiff's presentation sounds stronger because it is presented as a statement. The defendant's position is presented as a charge—an "allegation" rather than a statement of fact. There are numerous ways to present positions in a strong or weak manner. Be sure to check your word choice.

It is easy, however, to get carried away and state the facts in such a slanted way that your bias is painfully obvious.

> **For Example** The defendant stubbornly and unreasonably refuses to issue dividends.

In this example, the presentation of the facts is clearly biased and heavy handed. It is better just to note that the defendant has refused to issue dividends. When in doubt, avoid inflammatory language and exercise restraint.

Refer to the techniques presented in this section when preparing a persuasive presentation of the facts. Exhibit 18-3 presents a checklist for use in conjunction with the guidelines for the persuasive presentation of the statement of facts.

Exhibit 18-3 Checklist: Statement of Facts—Persuasive Presentation.

- Placement of favorable and unfavorable facts: Are the facts favorable to the client's position placed at the beginning and end of the factual statement?
- Sentence length: Are short sentences used to emphasize favorable information and long sentences used to deemphasize unfavorable information?
- Active and passive voice: Is active voice used to emphasize favorable information and passive voice used to deemphasize unfavorable information?
- Word choice: Are words chosen that introduce the client's facts in the most favorable light and the opponent's facts in the least favorable light?

Chapter 9 is helpful when identifying key and background facts. Many of the considerations involved in preparing the statement of facts section of an office legal memo are the same as those involved in preparing the statement of facts section of a court brief. Chapter 16, section V.E, therefore, will prove helpful when preparing this section.

3. Argument—Persuasive Presentation

The persuasive tone of the court brief is initially established in the issue and facts statements. The persuasive techniques discussed in the previous sections of this text, such as word choice, sentence length, and active and passive voice, also apply and should be employed when crafting the argument section of a court brief.

The **argument** section is the heart of the court brief. It is the equivalent of the analysis section of an office legal memorandum. Unlike the analysis section of an office memo, however, the argument section of a court brief is not an objective presentation of the law. Because the goal of the argument section is to persuade the court that your position is valid, be sure to craft it by drafting the following in a persuasive manner:

- The law in support of your position
- The analysis of the law
- The argument that your analysis is valid and the opposition's analysis is invalid

The following text presents a summary of the techniques you may use to ensure that you present the argument component of a court brief in a persuasive manner. Several helpful guidelines apply to both trial and appellate court briefs. Sections III and IV of this chapter introduce additional information concerning the format and content of the argument section. Those sections focus on the differences between trial and appellate court briefs.

Organization. The organization of the argument section is similar to that of the analysis section of the office memo: The rule of law is introduced, followed by an interpretation of the law (usually through case law), then an application of the law to the issue raised by the facts of the case. The opposing position is included in the presentation of the argument rather than in a separate counteranalysis section.

1. Issue presentation. When there is more than one issue or when there are issues and subissues, discuss the issue supported by the strongest argument first. There are several reasons for this:

   - First impressions are lasting. The tone of the argument is set at the beginning. By presenting the strongest argument first, you set a tone of strength and credibility.

   - If you introduce the strongest argument first, the court is more likely to be persuaded that your position is correct and look more favorably on your weaker arguments.

   - Judges are often very busy. On some occasions a judge may not read or give equal attention to all the sections of a brief, especially if the brief is long. In such instances, the judge may not read your strongest argument if you do not present it first or near the beginning of the brief. For this reason, if there are several arguments in support of a position, omit the weak arguments. Weak arguments or positions that have little supporting authority detract and divert attention from the stronger arguments.

2. Rule of law presentation. Present the rule of law, whether it is enacted or case law, in a manner that supports your argument.

> **For Example** *Objective presentation:* The statute that *governs oppressive conduct* is. . . .
>
> *Persuasive presentation:* The statute that *prohibits* oppressive conduct by a majority shareholder is. . . .
>
> The first example merely indicates that the statute governs the area. The second example persuasively emphasizes the prohibitory nature of the statute.
>
> *Objective presentation:* The courts of other states are split on what constitutes oppressive conduct. Most courts follow *Smith v. Jones*, which provides. . . . A minority of courts follow *Dave v. Roe*. . . . The majority view is based on the premise that the conduct must be either wrongful or improper. . . .
>
> *Persuasive presentation:* The majority of courts follow the definition of *oppressive conduct* presented in *Smith v. Jones*. In this case, the court defined *oppressive conduct* as. . . . This definition is based on the well-reasoned view that the conduct need only be wrongful or improper. A minority of courts follow. . . .

In this example, the persuasive presentation more forcefully introduces the majority view in a manner indicating that it is preferable. The objective view is passive and treats both the majority and minority views equally. It does not emphasize one view as favorable. Refer to section II.B.1 in the chapter for the discussion on persuasive presentation of issues when drafting the rule of law component of the argument section of a brief.

3. Case presentation. When introducing case law, discuss the favorable case law first; follow with the unfavorable or opposing case law, then include a response or rebuttal that emphasizes why the favorable case law should be followed. This is similar to the format followed in the facts statement: The placement of the unfavorable material in the middle of the presentation following the favorable material tends to minimize its importance.

The discussion of the case law should emphasize the similarities and applicability of the case you rely on and the dissimilarities and inapplicability of the case relied on by the opposition.

> **For Example** The term *oppressive conduct* is defined in the case of *Tyrone v. Blatt*. In *Tyrone*, the majority shareholder refused to authorize the issuance of dividends. He granted himself four major pay increases, quadrupling his salary during the period dividends were not issued. In the holding, the court noted that there was no justification for the salary increases and ruled that his conduct was oppressive. The court stated that "oppressive conduct" occurs when there is wrongful conduct that inures to the benefit of the majority shareholder and to the detriment of the minority shareholders.
>
> In our case, just as in *Tyrone*, the *majority* shareholder refused to issue dividends. In our case, like *Tyrone*, the majority shareholder gave himself large salary increases. In both cases, there was no justification for the increases. Therefore, the court should apply the standard established in *Tyrone* and find that the defendant engaged in oppressive conduct.
>
> It is argued by the defendant that the court should apply the holding reached in *Wise v. Wind* and find that the defendant's conduct was not oppressive. The defendant's reliance on *Wise* is misplaced. In *Wise*, there was evidence that the salary increases were justified.

> Our situation is distinguishable. There is no evidence that the salary increases the defendant awarded himself and his refusal to issue dividends were justified. Therefore, the *Wise* opinion is not on point and is not applicable. The *Tyrone* opinion is on point and should be followed.

4. Argument order. When interpreting and applying a rule of law, always introduce your arguments first, address the counterargument, then present your response. In addition, spend more time affirmatively stating your position than responding to the opponent's counterargument. There are several reasons for this:

- As with the presentation of the facts statement and organization of the argument, the reader tends to remember and emphasize information presented at the beginning and end of a section or paragraph. You want to draw attention to and emphasize your argument; therefore, address it first.

- By introducing your argument first, you have the opportunity to soften the impact of the opposing argument through the strong presentation of your position.

- In a busy court, if you discuss your position or argument after the opponent's, you run the risk of it not being read or given equal attention by the court.

- By following the counterargument with a response or rebuttal that sums up your position, you move the counterargument further from the reader's attention. It is buried in the middle of the argument where its significance is downplayed and deemphasized. The defendant's position is italicized in the following example.

For Example It is appropriate for the court to allow admission of the INDM test results. The court of appeals in *State v. Digo* ruled that scientific tests are admissible when the reliability and scientific basis of the test are recognized by competent authorities. The INDM test, developed in 1985, is universally accepted by all competent authorities as scientifically valid. *It is argued by the defendant that the test results should not be relied on by the court. Defendant relies on the case of Ard v. State to support this argument. Defendant's reliance on Ard v. State is misplaced. In this 1985 case, the court of appeals did not allow the admission of the INDM test results because the INDM was a new test not universally accepted.* The ruling in *Ard* is no longer applicable. The INDM test is no longer a new test and is universally used and accepted.

5. Word choice. Careful **word choice** is an invaluable aid when crafting a persuasive argument. You can significantly enhance the argument by the use of forceful, positive, and confident language.

For Example *Ineffective:* We believe that the defendant engaged in oppressive conduct.

Effective: The defendant engaged in oppressive conduct.

Ineffective: It is the defendant's position that the search was illegal. . . .

Effective: The search was illegal. . . .

Present the opposing position in a manner that deemphasizes its importance or credibility.

For Example *Ineffective:* The defendant states. . . .

Effective: The defendant alleges. . . .

Ineffective: The defendant's position is. . . .

Effective: The defendant claims. . . .

6. Point headings. **Point headings** are a summary of the position advocated in the argument. They are presented at the beginning of each argument. Section III of this chapter addresses the details of format, content, and presentation of point headings. This section discusses the persuasive nature and presentation of point headings.

The persuasive role of a point heading is to focus the reader on the position advocated in the argument. Therefore, draft a point heading in a manner that provides a positive presentation of that position.

For Example	*Not persuasive:* The court should not grant the motion to suppress. . . . The photos of the victim were inflammatory and should not have been admitted into evidence by the trial court.
	Persuasive: The court should deny the motion to suppress. . . . The inflammatory nature of the photographs of the victim outweighs their probative value, and their admission was highly prejudicial to the defendant and was improper.

The difference in the two presentations in this example is that the persuasive presentation more affirmatively and positively characterizes the position argued. The discussions in the previous section concerning word choice and active voice apply to point headings.

Exhibit 18-4 presents a checklist for use in the persuasive presentation of the argument in a court brief.

Exhibit 18-4 *Checklist: Argument—Persuasive Presentation.*

Argument organization:	Follow the standard organizational format: rule of law, followed by the interpretation of the law through case law, followed by the application of the law to the issue.
Issue presentation:	If there is more than one issue, discuss the issue supported by the strongest argument first.
Rule of law presentation:	Present the rule of law in a manner that supports your argument.
Case presentation:	Discuss favorable cases first, followed by unfavorable cases, then a rebuttal emphasizing why the favorable cases should be followed.
Argument order:	When applying the rule of law, introduce your argument first, then the counterarguments, and conclude with your response.
Argument word choice:	Present your argument with forceful, positive, and confident language.
Argument point heading:	Draft point headings persuasively.

© Cengage Learning 2014

III. TRIAL COURT BRIEFS

In many instances, when a trial court is in the process of ruling on a motion or an issue in a case, the judge requires the attorneys to submit a memorandum of law. This memorandum of law is often referred to as a *memorandum of points and authorities* or a *trial brief.*

The trial brief presents the legal authority and argument in support of the position advocated by the attorney.

A trial brief is similar to an office memo in many respects. Both are designed to inform the reader how the law applies to the issues raised by the facts of the case. Most of the considerations involved in the preparation of an office memo also apply to the preparation of a trial brief. Therefore, when preparing a trial brief, in addition to this chapter, refer to Chapters 16 and 17 for guidance.

The guidelines for preparing a persuasive trial brief are discussed in the previous section. This section addresses other considerations involved in preparing a trial brief, such as the writing process.

A. Audience

The audience for the trial brief is the judge assigned to the case. Trial court judges are usually busy people, with heavy caseloads, who may rule on several motions a day. They may not have time to carefully read lengthy briefs. Therefore, a judge usually appreciates a well-organized, concise presentation of the law.

B. Constraints

Court rules are procedural rules that govern the litigation process. Many trial courts have local rules that govern various aspects of a trial brief, such as format and style. The major constraints on a trial brief are usually imposed by the local court rules.

> **For Example** A local rule may establish a maximum length of a trial brief and require the court's permission before that length can be exceeded.

Always consult the local rules when preparing a trial brief.

Usually there is a time constraint. The court or the local rules often require that the brief be submitted within a certain number of days. Know the time deadline and allocate your time accordingly. Usually, but not always, the court may grant extensions of time upon request.

C. Format or Content

The format of a trial brief varies among courts and among jurisdictions. In many instances, the local court rules establish a required format. Generally, a trial court brief includes some or all of the components presented in Exhibit 18-5.

Exhibit 18-5 *Components of Trial Court Brief.*

Caption
Table of contents
Table of authorities
Preliminary statements
Question(s) presented/issue(s)
Statement of the case (fact statement)
Argument
Conclusion

© Cengage Learning 2014

If the brief is short, such as in the case of a single-issue brief, then a table of contents, table of authorities, or preliminary statement may not be required. In many instances it is clear from the motion what the issue is, and the brief will consist of only a short facts statement, argument, and conclusion. Often trial court briefs are informal in such situations.

> **For Example** A motion to dismiss a complaint is filed for failure to include an indispensable party. The issue is clear from the motion, and the memorandum in support of the motion may simply consist of a brief summary of the facts, the legal argument, and a conclusion.

Each of the components in Exhibit 18-5 is briefly discussed in the following subsections. For examples of these components, refer to the Application section of this chapter and Appendix B.

1. Caption

Every brief submitted to a trial court requires a caption. The format varies from court to court, but the caption usually includes:

- The name of the court
- The names and status of the parties
- The file number and type of case—civil or criminal
- The title of the document, such as BRIEF IN SUPPORT OF MOTION TO DISMISS

Refer to the Application section of this chapter for an example of a caption.

2. Table of Contents

If a **table of contents** is required, it follows the caption page. The table of contents allows the reader to locate the various components of the brief and their respective page numbers. If point headings are used in the argument section, they are stated in full in the table of contents. For an example of a table of contents, see the appellate brief presented in Appendix B.

3. Table of Authorities

If a **table of authorities** is required, it is presented after the table of contents page. A table of authorities lists all the law used in the brief and the page on which the law is cited in the brief. This allows the reader to quickly locate where the authority is discussed in the brief. Present the case law and enacted law in separate sections. List the case law in alphabetical order by case name. For an example of a table of authorities, see the appellate brief presented in Appendix B.

4. Preliminary Statement

The **preliminary statement** introduces the procedural posture of the case. It usually includes:

- An identification of the parties
- The procedural events in the case relevant to the matter the court is addressing
- A description of the matter being addressed by the court, such as "This matter is before the court on a motion to dismiss the complaint."

■ The relief sought, such as "This memorandum is submitted in support of the motion to suppress the evidence seized during the search."

> **For Example** *PRELIMINARY STATEMENT*
>
> Edna and Ida Tule, the plaintiffs, are minority shareholders in Tule, Inc. Their brother, Thomas Tule, is the defendant in this action, the majority shareholder, and president of Tule, Inc. On January 9 of this year, a request for the production of company records relating to salary increases and bonuses granted to Mr. Tule was delivered to him. Mr. Tule refuses to produce the company records. This memorandum is submitted in support of a motion to compel the production of those documents.

5. Question(s) Presented

This section of a brief persuasively presents the legal issue(s) addressed in the brief. The issue should include the rule of law, legal question, and the key facts. When there is more than one issue, list the issues in the order they are discussed in the argument section of the brief. Section II.B.1 of this chapter discusses the techniques for persuasively drafting the issue. Chapter 16 addresses the presentation of the issue(s) in an office memo. Refer to that chapter when preparing the issue.

6. Statement of the Case

This section is often referred to as the *statement of facts*. It corresponds to the statement of facts section of an office memo. Its purpose is to introduce the facts of the case in a light that most favors the client's position. Section II.B.2 of this chapter discusses the persuasive nature of the facts section. That subsection and the Application section of this chapter introduce examples of persuasive statements of facts. The facts section should be accurate and complete and should include background and key facts. For additional guidance when drafting the facts section, refer to Chapter 16, section V.E.

7. Argument Section

The argument section of a trial brief, like the analysis section of an office memo, is the heart of the document. It differs from the analysis section of an office memo in that it is not an objective legal analysis. Rather, it is designed to persuade the court to adopt your interpretation of the law. Section II.B.3 of this chapter discusses the considerations involved in crafting the argument in a persuasive manner. This section addresses the basic organization of the argument and the components. Exhibit 18-6 presents the organization and components of this section.

Exhibit 18-6 *Organization and Components of Argument Section of Trial Brief.*

1. Summary of argument
2. Point headings
3. Argument
   Rule of law
   Case law (if necessary) interpretation of rule of law
   Application of law to the issue being addressed
      Discussion of opposing position (similar to counteranalysis in office legal memorandum)

© Cengage Learning 2014

The format in Exhibit 18-6 is recommended; it is not necessarily followed in every office, and a different format may be required by local court rule. In some instances, a summary of the argument may not be required, and some local court rules and office formats do not require point headings. This is often true when the brief is short and involves a single issue. Nevertheless, all of the components of the argument section are presented here so that you will be familiar with them when they are required.

a. Summary of Argument

The argument section of a trial brief should begin with an introductory paragraph that summarizes the argument. It presents the context of the argument, the issues in the order in which they will be discussed, a summary of the conclusions regarding each issue, and the major reasons supporting each conclusion.

> **For Example** On December 12, 2011, John Jones, the defendant, was arrested for possession of cocaine. On January 1, 2012, he was indicted for possession of 4 ounces of cocaine. The trial commenced on October 25, 2012. On November 11, 2012, he was found guilty by a jury and convicted of possession of 4 ounces of cocaine. This matter is before the court on Mr. Jones's motion for a new trial, filed March 7, 2013. Mr. Jones's motion is based on the claim that new evidence has been uncovered showing that the drugs belonged to a Mr. Tom Smith, a visitor in Mr. Jones's home. For a new trial to be granted on the basis of newly discovered evidence, the defendant must demonstrate that the newly discovered evidence was not available or discoverable at the time of trial. The information concerning Mr. Smith was available at the time of trial. The defense made no effort to interview Mr. Smith or in any way discover whether the drugs belonged to him. The evidence regarding Mr. Smith is not newly discovered evidence, and the motion should be denied.

The use of an argument summary is valuable when you believe the judge may not have time to read the entire brief. It may not be necessary if the brief is short or when a single issue is involved. It should be a complete summary; the reader should not have to refer to the body of the argument to understand the summary.

b. Point Headings

Point headings are summaries of the position you are asking the court to adopt. They should be drafted persuasively. Section II.B.3 of this chapter addresses the guidelines for drafting persuasive point headings in an argument.

Point headings are designed to:

- Organize, define, and emphasize the structure of the argument
- Act as locators that allow the reader to quickly find specific sections of the argument
- Focus the court's attention on the outcome you advocate and provide an outline of your theory

Point headings may not be required in a trial brief, especially when the brief is short or addresses only a single issue. In such instances, they are not needed as an organizational tool, nor are they needed to guide the reader. Check the court rules and office format to determine when they are required.

In regard to point headings, note the following guidelines:

1. Place the point headings at the beginning of each section of the argument and include them in the table of contents.

2. Divide the point headings into major and minor point headings. There should be a major point heading for each issue presented. Use minor headings to introduce significant points supporting the major heading.

> **For Example** ARGUMENT
>
> I. THE TRIAL COURT ERRED WHEN IT RULED THAT MR. SMITH'S CON-DUCT DID NOT CONSTITUTE BREACH OF CONTRACT BECAUSE THE GOODS WERE DEFECTIVE AND DELIVERED LATE.
>   A. <u>Mr. Smith's delivery of the widgets 10 days late constituted a breach of the contract</u>. (text of argument)
>   B. <u>The delivery of the widgets with a 5-pound spring instead of a 10-pound spring constituted a breach of the contract</u>. (text of argument)

3. Each heading and subheading should be a complete sentence.

4. Each heading should identify the legal conclusion you want the court to adopt and the basic reasons supporting the conclusion.

> **For Example** THE TESTIMONY OF DR. SMITH IS PROBATIVE OF THE DEFEN-DANT'S INTENT AND THEREFORE IS ADMISSIBLE.
> THE DISTRICT COURT'S SUPPRESSION OF THE EVIDENCE WAS IMPROPER BECAUSE THE SEARCH WARRANT WAS SUPPORTED BY PROBABLE CAUSE.

5. Use minor headings only if there are two or more. The rules of outlining require more than one subheading when subheadings are used. Minor headings present aspects of a major point heading in the context of the specific facts of the case. Note that the minor point headings in the example in number 2 above present two aspects of the major point heading. State the minor point headings in the specific context of the facts of the case:

   A. <u>Mr. Smith's delivery of the widgets 10 days late constituted a breach of the contract.</u>

   B. <u>The delivery of the widgets with a 5-pound spring instead of a 10-pound spring constituted a breach of the contract.</u>

6. Type major headings in ALL CAPITALS and minor headings in regular upper and lower case. Minor headings may be underlined. Check the court rules for the proper format. The preceding example in number 2 illustrates the format for major and minor point headings.

c. Argument Format

The argument section of the trial brief is similar to the analysis section of an office memo; refer to Chapter 17, section II, when preparing a trial brief. The same basic IRAC format is followed:

Rule of law

Case law (if necessary)—interpretation of rule of law

   1. Name of case

   2. Facts of case—sufficient to demonstrate the case is on point

   3. Rule or legal principle from case that applies to the issue being addressed

Application of law to the issue being addressed

Discussion of opposing position (similar to counteranalysis in office legal memorandum)

The major difference between the argument component of an office memo and that of a trial brief is that the trial brief introduces the argument in a persuasive rather than an objective manner. Refer to section II.B.3 of this chapter for guidance in organizing and preparing a persuasive argument.

8. Conclusion

The **conclusion** section of a trial brief requests the specific relief desired. Depending on the complexity of the brief, it may be a single sentence stating the requested relief or a summary of the entire argument.

For Example	*Single sentence:* For the foregoing reasons, the defendant requests that the motion to dismiss be granted.

A single-sentence conclusion is appropriate when the trial brief is a simple, one- or two-issue brief, and the argument section concludes with a summary of the analysis. When the trial brief is longer and more complicated, the conclusion may include an overall summary of the law presented in the argument section and end with a request for relief. This type of conclusion is similar to the conclusion section of an office memo discussed in Chapter 17, section III. Note that the conclusion should summarize the argument section and reflect the persuasive nature of the argument.

IV. APPELLATE COURT BRIEFS

An individual who disagrees with the decision of a trial or lower court may appeal the decision to a court of appeals. The individual who appeals is called the **appellant**, and the individual who opposes the appeal is called the **appellee**. On appeal, the appellant argues that the lower court made an error, the error affected the outcome of the case, and the appellant is entitled to relief. The appellee argues that the lower court did not commit an error that entitles the appellant to relief.

An appellate court brief is an external memorandum of law submitted to a court of appeals. It presents the legal analysis, authority, and argument in support of a position that the lower court's decision or ruling was either correct or incorrect. The format and style of the appellate brief is strictly governed by appellate court rules, and these rules must be consulted when preparing an appellate brief.

The preparation of an appellate brief is a complex undertaking, and a detailed discussion of this subject is beyond the scope of this chapter. Entire texts (available at the local law library) address the detailed considerations involved in preparing an appellate brief, and you should refer to those texts when assigned the task of preparing an appellate brief.

Paralegals and law clerks are not usually required to draft appellate briefs. They may, however, be called upon to assist in the preparation of the brief and, therefore, should be familiar with its components. This section summarizes considerations regarding the format and basic components of an appellate brief.

An appellate brief, like a trial brief, is designed to advocate a legal position and to persuade the court to adopt the position argued in the brief. Therefore, you should draft the brief in a persuasive manner. The discussion of the persuasive nature of court briefs, presented in section II.B of this chapter, applies to the preparation of appellate briefs; that is, an appellate brief should be crafted in a persuasive manner.

An appellate brief, like a trial brief, is similar to an office memo in many respects. For example, a writing process should be used when preparing both briefs. Therefore, in addition to this chapter, refer to Chapter 15 through Chapter 17 when performing an appellate brief assignment.

A. Audience

A trial court brief is submitted to a single judge, the trial judge assigned to the case. The audience for the appellate brief is usually a panel of three or more judges. In addition, the judge's law clerk usually reads the brief; on many occasions the law clerk is the first to read the brief. Although you are writing to a wider audience, the same basic considerations are involved in the preparation of trial court and appellate court briefs. Appellate court judges, like trial court judges, are usually busy persons with substantial caseloads, so they appreciate an appellate brief that is a well-organized and concise presentation of the law.

B. Constraints

The major constraints on appellate briefs are imposed by the court's rules. The appellate court rules differ from trial court rules in that they are usually much more detailed than trial court rules: The appellate court rules may establish the sections that must be included, the format of each of the sections, the type of paper, the citation form, a maximum length for the briefs and a requirement that permission of the court be obtained before the length can be exceeded, and so on. Always consult the appellate court rules when preparing an appellate brief.

C. Format or Content

The format of an appellate brief varies among jurisdictions. Generally, the basic appellate court brief includes some or all of the components presented in Exhibit 18-7.

Exhibit 18-7 *Components of a Basic Appellate Court Brief.*

```
Cover page/title page
Table of contents/index
Table of authorities
Opinions below/related appeals
Jurisdictional statement
Question/issue(s) presented
Statement of the case/statement of facts
Summary of argument
Argument
Conclusion
```

© Cengage Learning 2014

The following subsections briefly discuss each of the components of the appellate brief. Refer to the appellate brief presented in Appendix B for an example of the components.

1. Cover Page/Title Page

The court rules govern the format of the cover page, often called the *title page*. The cover page usually includes:

- Name of the appellate court
- Number assigned to the appeal
- Parties' names and appellate status (appellant and appellee or petitioner and respondent)
- Name of the lower court from which the appeal is taken
- Names and addresses of the attorney(s) submitting the brief

2. Table of Contents/Index

Sometimes referred to as an *index*, the table of contents lists the major sections of the brief and the page number on which each section begins. The table of contents provides the reader with a reference tool for locating specific information within the brief. The table includes the point headings and subheadings. The point headings, when included in the table of contents, provide the reader with an overview of the legal arguments and allow the reader to easily locate the discussion of the arguments in the brief.

3. Table of Authorities

The table of authorities lists all the law cited in the brief. The authorities are listed by category, such as constitutional law, statutory law, regulations, and case law. The table includes the full citation of each authority and the page number or numbers on which it appears.

4. Opinions Below/Related Appeals

The brief *may* include a section that references any prior opinions on the case or related appeals.

> **For Example** *From a Supreme Court brief:* The opinion of the Court of Appeals is reported at 580 F.2d 501. The order of the District Court is not reported.

5. Jurisdictional Statement

The brief usually includes a separate section that introduces, in a short statement, the subject matter jurisdiction of the appellate court.

> **For Example** This court has jurisdiction under 42 U.S.C. § 1983.

Some appellate rules do not require a **jurisdictional statement**. Some appellate rules require, in addition to the jurisdictional statement, a history of the case and how the matter came before the court.

> **For Example** The judgment of the trial court was entered on October 5, 2012. The notice of appeal was filed on October 26, 2013. The jurisdiction of the court is invoked under 42 U.S.C. § 1983.

6. Question(s) Presented

This section may also be referred to as *legal issues* or *assignment of error*. The section lists the legal issues the party is requesting the court to consider. List the issues in the order they are addressed in the argument section, and write them in a persuasive manner as discussed earlier in this chapter in section II.B.1.

7. Statement of the Case/Statement of Facts

The statement of the case section, often referred to as the *statement of facts*, is generally similar to the statement of facts section of the trial brief, and the same considerations apply when preparing both.

The statement of the case in an appellate brief, however, differs from the statement of facts in a trial brief in that the statement of the case should also include a summary of the prior proceedings (what happened in the lower court) and appropriate references to the record. In the following example, "Tr." refers to the pages in the transcript of the trial record, and "Doc." refers to documents included in the record on appeal.

For Example After the presentation of the key and background facts of the case, the information concerning the prior proceedings might read:

At the hearing on the motion to suppress, held on December 12, 2012, the trial court denied the motion to suppress. (Tr. at 37). At the hearing, Officer Smith, the officer conducting the search, testified . . . (Tr. at 33). The trial court stated that there were sufficient exigent circumstances present at the scene to support the unannounced entry by the officers. (Tr. at 38).

Trial was held on January 15, 2013. (Tr. at 201). On January 18, 2013, the jury found the defendant guilty of possession of an ounce of cocaine. (Tr. at 291). On January 28, 20013, the defendant filed a notice of appeal. (Doc. 44). On March 7, 2013, the defendant was sentenced to a term of imprisonment of five years. (Doc. 49).

8. Summary of Argument

This section may be optional under the appellate court rule. Rule 28 of the Federal Rules of Appellate Procedure states that the argument may be preceded by a summary. The content of an argument summary is discussed in section III.C.7 of this chapter.

9. Argument Section

a. Point Headings

The considerations involved in preparing point headings are the same for appellate and trial court briefs. Refer to the discussion of point headings in section III.C.7 of this chapter when preparing point headings for appellate briefs.

b. Body

The argument section of an appellate brief is similar to the argument section of a trial brief. The format is the same as in a trial brief. Refer to section III.C.7 of this chapter when preparing the argument section of an appellate brief. Remember to present the argument section of an appellate brief in a persuasive manner, as discussed in section II.B.3 of this chapter. Review that subsection when preparing the argument.

10. Conclusion

Prepare the conclusion section of an appellate brief in the same way as the conclusion of a trial brief. The content, structure, and considerations involved are the same for both. Refer to section III.C.8 of this chapter when preparing the conclusion.

V. KEY POINTS CHECKLIST: *External Memoranda—Court Briefs*

✔ Trial and appellate briefs are similar to office memoranda in many fundamental respects. Refer to Chapter 15 through Chapter 17 when preparing them.

✔ The writing fundamentals presented in Chapter 14 apply to all legal writing and should be kept in mind when preparing court briefs.

✔ Remember to craft the brief persuasively. Court briefs are designed to persuade the reader to adopt the position taken or recommended in the analysis. They are not supposed to present a purely objective analysis.

✔ Deemphasize the position taken by the opposition. Part of the persuasive nature of a court brief is to downplay and discredit the opponent's position. This is accomplished through the use of passive voice, long sentences, placement of the opposing argument in the middle of the analysis, and so on.

    ✔ Always check the court rules. The format, length, and so on of court briefs are often governed by the rules of the court. The appellate court rules extensively govern most aspects of appellate briefs.

    ✔ The required components of trial and appellate court briefs may vary among jurisdictions. Some of the components discussed in this chapter may not be required or necessary, such as a table of contents, table of authorities, or argument summary. This is often true when the analysis is brief.

VI. APPLICATION

This section illustrates the guidelines and principles discussed in this chapter by applying them to the hypothetical presented at the beginning of the chapter. The paralegal, Pam Hayes, approaches this assignment through the use of an expanded outline, as discussed in Chapter 15. She also follows the guidelines and principles discussed in Chapters 16 and 17 to the extent they apply to the preparation of a trial brief. What follows is a presentation of the trial brief prepared by Ms. Hayes and comments on the brief.

In regard to the assignment, Ms. Hayes found the following New Washington law on point:

Statutory Law. Chapter 70 of the New Washington Statutes, the Ski Safety Act, governs ski resorts and the sport of skiing. New Washington Statutes Annotated (NWSA) § 70-11-7A provides, "The ski area operator shall have the duty to mark conspicuously with the appropriate symbol or sign those slopes, trails, or areas which are closed or which present an unusual obstacle or hazard." Furthermore, NWSA § 70-11-8B provides, "A person who takes part in the sport of skiing accepts as a matter of law the dangers inherent in that sport, and each skier expressly assumes the risk and legal responsibility for any injury to a person or property which results from . . . surface or subsurface snow or ice conditions. . . ."

Case Law. In *Karen v. High Mountain Pass*, 55 N. Wash. 462, 866 N.E. 995 (Ct. App. 1994), a skier broke his leg after failing to negotiate a series of moguls that were present in the middle of a sharp turn on a ski run. The moguls were unavoidable. The trial court granted the resort's motion to dismiss for failure to state a claim. On appeal, the court of appeals stated that skiers are responsible for snow and ice hazards, and moguls, even though unavoidable, are snow hazards easily observable and routinely present on most ski runs. The court went on to state that under the statute, the skier assumes the risk of snow and ice hazards that are easily observable and routinely encountered on ski runs, and resorts have no duty to warn of such hazards under NWSA § 70-11-7A.

In *Aster v. White Mountain Resort*, 55 N. Wash. 756, 866 N.E. 421 (Ct. App. 1994), a skier was skiing a newly opened intermediate run. Several fairly large rocks had not been removed from the run. Normally, the rocks would have been removed before the run was opened. The rocks were covered by approximately two and one-half feet of new snow and were not visible. The resort did not post a warning that the large rocks were present on the run. Mr. Aster hit a rock with the tip of his ski, lost control, and injured his knee and back. The trial court, in granting the resort's motion to dismiss for failure to state a claim, held that the hazard was a snow hazard for which the skier was responsible under NWSA § 70-11-8B. On appeal, the court of appeals noted that the snow condition was an unavoidable latent hazard. The court ruled that under NWSA § 70-11-7A, a resort has a duty to warn of hazardous snow conditions if they are unavoidable and latent. The court stated, "The statute will not be interpreted to reach an absurd result, and requiring a skier to be responsible for unavoidable latent hazards would lead to an absurd result. Skiers are only responsible for those unavoidable snow or ice conditions which are not latent or unobservable."

Myron v. Cox Inc., 40 N. Wash. 210, 740 N.E. 309 (1989), sets the standard for the granting of a Rule 12(b)(6) motion to dismiss. The court stated, "A Rule 12(b)(6) motion to dismiss is properly granted only if it appears that there is no provable set of facts which entitles the plaintiff to relief."

A. Trial Brief

The following is the trial brief prepared by Ms. Hayes.

LINCOLN COUNTY DISTRICT COURT

STATE OF NEW WASHINGTON
NO. CIV. O13-601
NICK SHINE,
     Plaintiff,

vs.

BLUE SKY SKI RESORT,
     Defendant.

BRIEF IN OPPOSITION TO MOTION TO DISMISS
PRELIMINARY STATEMENT

On December 5, 2012, Nick Shine, the plaintiff, was injured while skiing on a ski run at Blue Sky Ski Resort. He was injured skiing on an ice hazard that the resort admits was not marked with any type of warning sign. Mr. Shine filed a complaint against the resort for negligence in failing to warn of the hazard. The resort has filed a Rule 12(b)(6) motion to dismiss for failure to state a claim, alleging that it does not have a duty to warn of ice hazards. This memorandum is submitted in opposition to that motion.

QUESTION PRESENTED

Under the New Washington Ski Safety Act, sections 70-11-1 et seq., can a negligence claim be stated when a skier is injured on an unmarked ice hazard that is unavoidable and unobservable by the skier due to the sun glare?

STATEMENT OF THE CASE

On December 5, 2012, Mr. Shine, an expert skier, was skiing on an intermediate ski run at Blue Sky Ski Resort. Midway through the run there is a slightly uphill turn to the south. When Mr. Shine encountered the turn, the sun was directly in his eyes, and the glare prevented him from seeing that the trail was entirely covered with ice. Due to the glare, he was unable to avoid the dangerous ice hazard. He hit the ice and immediately lost control. As a result, he slid into a tree and broke his left arm and leg. No signs warning of the ice hazard were present.

On April 6, 2013, Mr. Shine filed a negligence complaint against Blue Sky Ski Resort for the resort's negligent failure to warn of the unavoidable ice hazard. On April 20, 2013, the resort filed a motion to dismiss under Rule 12(b)(6), alleging that they do not have a duty to warn of ice hazards, and therefore, as a matter of law, a claim for negligence cannot be stated.

ARGUMENT

MR. SHINE'S ARGUMENT THAT THE ICE HAZARD IS UNAVOIDABLE AND LATENT IS A SET OF FACTS WHICH, IF PROVEN, WOULD ESTABLISH THE DEFENDANT'S DUTY TO WARN AND, THEREFORE, A CLAIM CAN BE STATED AS TO DUTY.

This matter is before the court on a Rule 12(b)(6) motion to dismiss for failure to state a claim. In the case of *Myron v. Cox, Inc.*, 40 N. Wash. 210, 215, 740 N.E. 309, 314 (1989), the New Washington Supreme Court established the standard for the granting of a 12(b)(6) motion. The court stated, "A Rule 12(b)(6) motion to dismiss is properly granted only if it appears that there is no provable set of facts which entitles the plaintiff to relief." Blue Sky Ski Resort's motion specifically alleges that a claim cannot be stated in this case in regard to duty. To survive this motion, Mr. Shine must demonstrate that there is a provable set of facts that would establish the duty of Blue Sky to warn of the ice hazard in this case.

The Ski Safety Act establishes the duties of ski resorts and skiers. Section 70-11-7A sets out the duties of the resort; it provides, "The ski area operator shall have the duty to mark conspicuously with the appropriate symbol or sign those slopes, trails, or areas which are closed or which present an unusual obstacle or hazard."

Section 70-11-8B sets out the duties and responsibilities of the skier:

> A person who takes part in the sport of skiing accepts as a matter of law the dangers inherent in that sport, and each skier expressly assumes the risk and legal responsibility for any injury to a person or property which results from . . . surface or subsurface snow or ice conditions. . . .

The act does not define the terms "hazard" or "snow and ice conditions." The statute also does not provide guidance as to which duty applies in a fact situation such as the one presented in this case. New Washington case law, however, does provide guidance.

The controlling case is *Aster v. White Mountain Resort*, 55 N. Wash. 756, 866 N.E. 421 (Ct. App. 1994). In the *Aster* case, Mr. Aster was skiing on a newly opened run from which several fairly large rocks had not been removed. Normally, the rocks would have been removed before the run was opened. The rocks were covered by approximately two and one-half feet of new snow and were not visible. The resort did not post a warning that the large rocks were present on the run. Mr. Aster hit a rock with the tip of his ski, lost control, and was injured. The court ruled that under NWSA § 70-11-7A, a resort has a duty to warn of hazardous snow conditions if they are unavoidable and latent. The court stated, "The statute will not be interpreted to reach an absurd result, and requiring a skier to be responsible for unavoidable latent hazards would lead to an absurd result. Skiers are only responsible for those unavoidable snow or ice conditions which are not latent or unobservable." *Id.* at 759.

Mr. Shine's complaint, like the complaint in the *Aster* case, states that the ice condition encountered was an unavoidable latent hazard. Under *Aster*, the resort has the duty under § 70-11-7A to warn of such hazards. Under the rule adopted in *Aster*, Mr. Shine's complaint does present a provable set of facts that establishes a claim as to duty and entitles him to relief. Therefore, the motion to dismiss should be denied.

It is contended by Blue Sky that they do not have a duty to warn of the ice hazard, and in support of this contention, they rely on *Karen v. High Mountain Pass*, 55 N. Wash. 462, 866 N.E. 995 (Ct. App. 1994). In this case, a skier broke his leg after failing to negotiate a series of moguls that were present in the middle of a sharp turn of a ski run. The moguls were obvious to the skier but unavoidable. The trial court granted the resort's motion to dismiss for failure to state a claim. On appeal, the court of appeals, in upholding the trial court, held that under the statute, the skier assumes the risk of snow and ice hazards that are easily observable and routinely present on ski runs.

Blue Sky's reliance on *Karen* is misplaced. The case is clearly distinguishable. The snow condition in *Karen*, though unavoidable, was clearly observable, and moguls are routinely present on ski runs. Skiers are aware that they will encounter moguls and know they must be able to navigate them. Ice conditions also may be encountered on ski runs. The ice condition Mr. Shine encountered, however, was not a routine ice condition. It was unobservable, unavoidable, and extremely dangerous due to the glare of the sun. The *Karen* case involves observable, routine snow hazards. The present case involves unobservable ice hazards that are not routinely encountered. *Karen* is obviously not on point and is not controlling in this case.

The hazard Mr. Shine encountered was identical in nature to the hazard in the *Aster* case: the ice condition was an unavoidable, latent hazard. Under the holding in *Aster*, the resort has a duty under § 70-11-7A to warn of this type of hazard. Mr. Shine's complaint argues that the hazard is an unavoidable and latent hazard. The complaint presents a provable set of facts in regard to duty upon which relief can be granted, and therefore, a claim for duty can be stated and the motion to dismiss should be denied.

CONCLUSION

Blue Sky Ski Resort's motion to dismiss for failure to state a claim should be denied. Mr. Shine's argument that the ice condition constitutes a latent hazard is a provable set of facts that entitles him to relief.

B. Comments

1. Note that the preceding example of a trial brief does not have a table of contents or a table of authorities. When a trial brief is short or involves a single issue and few authorities, these tables may not be required. Be sure to check the local court rule.

2. The preliminary statement presented at the beginning of the brief is often called an *introduction*.

3. A summary of the argument section is not included in this brief. A summary of the argument is usually included in an appellate brief, but not always in a trial brief. It is useful in a trial brief, and may be necessary, when there are several issues or the analysis is complex, but it is not necessary when the analysis involves a single issue or is not complex.

4. Note the persuasive tone of the brief:

   ▪ The statement of the case introduces the facts with language that favors the client: "dangerous hazard," "he immediately lost control."

   ▪ The statement of the case and argument sections state the client's position in short, clear sentences using active voice. The opponent's position is presented in a long sentence using the passive voice: "It is contended by Blue Sky that they do not have a duty to warn of the ice hazard. . . ."

   ▪ The argument section downplays the opposition's position. It is placed in the middle of the argument and is immediately discounted after it is presented.

   ▪ The conclusion is very short. In a brief that is short or does not involve a complex analysis, an abbreviated conclusion is appropriate.

Summary

This chapter focuses on the preparation of documents containing legal analysis that are designed to be submitted to a court. Such a document, usually called a court brief, is often formally referred to as a "memorandum of law" or a "memorandum of points and authorities." The chapter presents an overview of the major considerations, key points, and helpful guidelines involved in the preparation of court briefs.

At the trial court level, these documents are trial court briefs submitted in support of a legal position advocated by an attorney. They are usually submitted in conjunction with a motion that requests some action or relief by the trial court. At the appellate court level, the documents submitted to an appellate court that involve legal analysis are appellate court briefs.

Office legal memoranda and court briefs are similar in many respects. When preparing both office memoranda and court briefs, it is helpful to use a writing process such as that suggested in Chapter 15. Office memoranda and court briefs follow a similar format: presentation of the issue, facts, analysis, and conclusion.

The major difference between an office memo and a court brief is the orientation of the presentation. An office memo is designed to inform and is written in an objective manner. A court brief is designed to advocate a position and persuade the court; therefore, the issue(s), facts, and legal argument are crafted in a persuasive manner designed to convince the court to adopt the position advocated.

A trial court brief is a memorandum of law submitted by an attorney to a trial court. In the memorandum, the attorney introduces the legal authority and analysis that supports a position advocated by the attorney. An appellate court brief is the written legal argument submitted to a court of appeals. In the appellate brief, an attorney presents the legal authority and analysis in support of or in opposition to an argument that a lower court committed reversible error.

Trial and appellate court briefs are similar in many respects. A major difference is that appellate court briefs are usually more formal: the style and format are more strictly governed by the appellate court rules. Both trial and appellate court briefs, however, are governed to some degree by court rules, and these rules must be carefully reviewed when preparing a court brief.

A legal assistant's role in preparing a court brief usually involves conducting legal research and analysis and preparing a rough draft. The final document requires the attorney's signature and is usually prepared by the attorney assigned to the case.

Quick References

Active voice	540	Persuasive presentation	537
Appellee	550	Point headings	544
Appellant	550	Preliminary statement	546
Appellate court briefs	535	Sentence length	539
Argument	541	Statement of facts	538
Conclusion	550	Table of authorities	546
Court rules	545	Table of contents	546
Ethics	536	Trial court briefs	535
Jurisdictional statement	552	Word choice	543
Passive voice	540		

Internet Resources

Using "trial court briefs" or "appellate court briefs" as a topic, you will find a wide range of Web sites (literally thousands of sites) referring to trial and appellate court briefs. The following is a summary of the categories of sites that may prove helpful when working on court briefs:

- Sites of federal and state trial and appellate courts (some of these sites include the court rules and guides and practice tips for preparing briefs)
- Sites that provide the trial or appellate court briefs filed in specific cases, such as the O. J. Simpson case or the Florida presidential election cases
- Sites advertising businesses that assist in the preparation of trial and appellate court briefs
- Sites for schools advertising programs that include as part of the curricula trial and appellate advocacy
- Sites that provide links to appellate court Web sites, court rules, opinions, and resources

As with most topics on the Web, the problem is not the lack of sites but too many sites. You are more likely to avoid the frustration of finding too many sites by narrowing your search to a specific type of trial or appellate court brief.

Exercises

Additional assignments are available on the CourseMate.

ASSIGNMENT 1

Describe how to draft each of the following components of a brief in a persuasive manner. Include the considerations involving organization, word choice, sentence structure, and so on.

A. Issue

B. Fact statement

C. Point heading

D. Argument

ASSIGNMENT 2

Describe in detail the components and format of a trial and appellate court brief.

ASSIGNMENT 3

Restate the following question component of the issue in a persuasive manner.

A. "should the evidence be suppressed when . . . ?" In the case, the police failed to obtain a search warrant prior to searching a vehicle.

B. "did the court err when . . . ?" In the case, the trial court admitted hearsay evidence.

C. "Under the statute of frauds . . . , is an oral contract valid when . . . ?" Rewrite this portion of the issue using language that focuses on a desired result.

D. "Under the sale of goods statutes, . . . is a statute enforceable when . . . ?" Rewrite this portion of the issue using language that focuses on a desired result.

ASSIGNMENT 4

Restate persuasively each of the following issues. Each issue should be redrafted twice—persuasively from the view of the opposing sides.

A. Under the provisions of the exclusionary rule, should evidence be suppressed when law enforcement officers executed a search warrant by unannounced entry because they saw the defendant run into the apartment upon their arrival at the scene?

B. Did the district court improperly exercise its discretion when it admitted into evidence photographs of the murder victim?

C. In light of the provisions of the hearsay rule, did the trial court improperly admit into evidence the defendant's statements to his neighbor that he would kill his wife?

D. Does the privileged communications statute allow the admission into evidence of the defendant's threats of physical harm to his spouse?

ASSIGNMENT 5

Restate the following point headings in a more persuasive manner.

A. THE EVIDENCE WAS INCORRECTLY SUPPRESSED BY THE TRIAL COURT SINCE THERE WERE SUFFICIENT EXIGENT CIRCUMSTANCES AT THE SCENE.

B. THE DENIAL OF THE DEFENDANT'S MOTION FOR MISTRIAL WAS NOT ERROR BY THE TRIAL COURT BECAUSE THE PROSECUTOR'S COMMENT ON THE DEFENDANT'S PRIOR CONVICTION WAS ADMISSIBLE.

C. THE TRIAL COURT'S ALLOWANCE OF THE PEREMPTORY CHALLENGE WAS PROPER. THE CHALLENGE WAS NOT RACIALLY MOTIVATED.

D. THE COURT SHOULD NOT GRANT THE DEFENDANT'S MOTION TO DISMISS. . . .

ASSIGNMENT 6

Restate the following rule of law presentations in a more persuasive manner.

A. In determining whether an individual has constructive possession, the court decides whether the defendant had knowledge of and control over the drugs.

B. Under the first part of the test, it must be shown that the defendant had knowledge of the presence of the drugs.

C. The court has stated that an arrest has taken place when a reasonable person would not feel free to leave.

ASSIGNMENT 7

In the following exercise, the assignment is to prepare a trial court brief. The assignment contains the memo from the supervising attorney, which includes all the available facts of the case. Complete the brief based on these facts. When preparing the heading of each assignment, use your name for the "To" line, and put "Supervising Attorney" after the "From."

Following the assignment is a reference to the applicable enacted and case law.

The first time you cite the opinion, use the citation format you are given for the opinion in the assignment.

> **For Example**   *Melia v. Dillon Cos., Inc.,* 18 Kan. App. 2d 5, 846 P.2d 257 (1993).

This is how you should cite this opinion the first time it is used in the memorandum. If you are using the opinion provided in Appendix A, when you quote from the opinion in the memo, use a blank line to indicate the page number from which the quotation is taken.

For Example	*Melia*, 18 Kan. App. 2d 5 at ___, 846 P.2d at ___.

Do not conduct additional research. Complete the assignment using the facts, enacted law, and case law contained in the assignment. For the purposes of the assignment, assume the cases have not been overturned or modified by subsequent court decisions. In most instances a simple trial court brief such as the one presented in this assignment would not include a table of contents, table of authorities, or preliminary statement. It would be composed of a question presented, statement of the case/facts, and argument sections. For the purposes of this assignment, do not include a table of contents, table of authorities, or preliminary statement section. For the title page, use the format presented in section VI.A of this chapter. The court is the District Court and the state is New Mexico.

Memo:

	To:	[Your name]
	From:	Supervising Attorney
	Re:	*White v. Calkin*, Civ. 03-388

Our client, Sage Rent-A-Car Inc., leased a vehicle to Jeffery Calkin. Mr. Calkin failed to stop at a stop sign and collided with Jane White, the plaintiff. Ms. White filed a negligence suit against both Mr. Calkin and Sage Rent-A-Car. In paragraph 36 of the complaint, plaintiff claims that Sage is required to carry insurance under the provisions of the Mandatory Financial Responsibility Act and therefore, under the act, has a duty to assume responsibility for this accident. When Sage incorporated, it filed a surety bond with the superintendent of insurance and is self-insured under the act. I do not read the act to extend liability to lessors for the damages that result from the negligent use of vehicles by lessees. Therefore, I plan to file a Rule 1-012B(6) motion to dismiss for failure to state a claim.

Please prepare a rough draft of a brief in support of the motion to dismiss.

Statutory Law:

NMRA 1-012B(6)—The rule provides in part, "the following defenses may at the option of the pleader be made by motion:

. . .

(6) failure to state a claim upon which relief can be granted; . . . ."

New Mexico Mandatory Financial Responsibility Act (MFRA), NMSA 1978 § 66-5-201 to 66-5-239.
MFRA, NMSA 1978 § 66-5-205 (1998):

No owner shall permit the operation of an uninsured motor vehicle, or a motor vehicle for which evidence of financial responsibility as was affirmed to the department is not currently valid, upon the streets or highways of New Mexico unless the vehicle is specifically exempted from the provisions of the Mandatory Financial Responsibility Act. . . .

MFRA, NMSA 1978 § 66-5-218 (1998):

Evidence of financial responsibility, when required under the Mandatory Financial Responsibility Act, may be given by filing:

A. evidence of a motor vehicle insurance policy;

B. a surety bond as provided in Section 66-5-225 NMSA 1978; or

C. a certificate of deposit of money as provided in Section 66-5-226 NMSA 1978.

MFRA, NMSA 1978 § 66-5-207 (1998):

The following motor vehicles are exempt from the Mandatory Financial Responsibility Act:

. . .

E. a motor vehicle approved as self-insured by the superintendent of insurance pursuant to Section 66-5-207.1 NMSA 1978; . . .

Case Law: *Las Lumarias of the N.M. Council v. Isengard*, 92 N.M. 297, 300–301 (Ct. App. 1978). The following quote from the case is all that is needed for the assignment. "A motion to dismiss a complaint is properly granted only when it appears that the plaintiff cannot recover or be entitled to relief under any state of facts provable under the claim. . . ."

Cordova v Wolfel, 120 N.M. 557, 903 P.2d 1390 (1995) (see Appendix A).

ASSIGNMENT 8

Perform assignment 7 using the law from your state.

ASSIGNMENT 9

The assignment is to prepare a rough draft of the appellee's brief in opposition to the appellant's appeal of the trial court's denial of the motion to suppress evidence seized from appellant's suitcase. The plaintiff/appellee is the United States; the defendant/appellant is Arnold J. Stewart. The trial court ruled that the suitcase had been abandoned and, therefore, the defendant did not have a reasonable expectation of privacy protected by the Fourth Amendment in the suitcase.

Numerous cases deal with the issue of abandonment of personal property, and an appellate brief usually would include references to at least several cases. This assignment is an exercise in preparing a very simple, single-issue appellate brief and is designed to acquaint students with the basic elements of such a brief. Therefore, when performing this assignment, use only the constitutional and case law presented in the assignment; do not perform additional research. Assume the cases have not been overturned or modified by subsequent court decisions.

Follow the format presented in section IV of this chapter. The caption is presented in the following text. Prepare a separate statement of the case and statement of the facts. Information necessary for preparing the brief follows. Note that the transcript pages (references to the trial court record) and docketing pages are referenced in parentheses. When drafting the brief, include the references to the record in the brief. References to the case and statutory law also follow. When citing the *United States v. Jones* case, use the citation instructions presented in assignment 7.

Facts: On October 15, 2012, Arnold Stewart arrived at the airport an hour and fifteen minutes prior to his scheduled flight. (Tr. at 6). He was going to visit a friend in Chicago. (Tr. at 7). He was carrying one suitcase that he intended to carry on the flight. (Tr. at 7). His flight was scheduled to leave from gate 9, but he decided to wait at gate 8 because it wasn't so crowded. (Tr. at 8). After a few minutes, he decided to get something to eat. (Tr. at 8). He approached Larry Holt, who was also waiting at gate 8, and asked if Holt would watch his suitcase. (Tr. at 8). Stewart did not know Mr. Holt. (Tr. at 8). Holt asked him how long he would be gone and Stewart replied, "Just a few minutes." (Tr. at 9). Holt said, "Well, ok." (Tr. at 9). Stewart then walked off. (Tr. at 9). Across from where they were seated were several coin-operated lockers where Stewart could have placed the suitcase. (Tr. 9–10). Stewart went to the food bar. (Tr. at 10). There was a long line, and he wasn't served for 20 minutes. (Tr. at 10). On the way back to his seat, he ran into an acquaintance and talked to him for several minutes. (Tr. at 10). He didn't return to his seat in the gate area for 45 minutes. (Tr. at 13).

Meanwhile, after 20 minutes, Mr. Holt became concerned. (Tr. at 41). He thought, "Where is that guy? I wonder if this suitcase contains a bomb." (Tr. at 41). The more he thought about it, the more concerned he became. (Tr. at 41–42). He contacted airport security and expressed his concerns. (Tr. at 42). Approximately a minute later, Officer Robert Dwyer arrived. (Tr. at 42). There was no nametag on the suitcase, no airline claim ticket attached, and no evidence of ownership on the exterior. (Tr. at 71). In such situations airport policy is that the suitcase should be immediately inspected, then taken to the security office. (Tr. at 72). Officer Dwyer inspected the suitcase and its contents at the scene. (Tr. at 72). Upon opening the suitcase, he found a large bag that contained 40 smaller bags of a white powdery substance. (Tr. at 73). The substance was later identified as heroin. (Tr. at 122). The suitcase was taken to the security office and federal officers were called. (Tr. at 74).

Approximately 45 minutes after he left, Stewart returned to his seat. (Tr. at 13). Holt informed him that he thought Stewart had abandoned the suitcase so he turned it over to airport security. (Tr. at 44). Stewart left the gate area, went to the ticket counter, and asked for information concerning the next flight. (Tr. at 14). The ticket counter is next to the security office. (Tr. at 75). Stewart never entered the office to inquire about his suitcase. (Tr. at 75). He was arrested when he went to the gate area and attempted to board his flight. (Tr. at 91).

Information for Statement of the Case: On November 21, 2012, Arnold J. Stewart was indicted by a federal grand jury sitting in the District of Utah on charges of possession with intent to distribute more than 100 grams of heroin in violation of 21 U.S.C. §§ 841(a)(1) and 841(b)(1)(B). (Doc. at 5). On January 7, 2013, Stewart filed a motion to suppress the physical evidence. (Doc. at 18). On February 14, 2013, the motion was denied. The trial court found:

> Under the circumstances, for all intents and purposes the suitcase was abandoned. The defendant did not express a possessory interest in the suitcase at any time after he learned its location.
>
> Having been abandoned, the defendant had no expectation of privacy in it or its contents.

(Tr. at 40–41). On March 6, 2013, defendant entered a conditional guilty plea, reserving his right to appeal the suppression ruling. (Doc. at 22). On April 27, 2013, the court sentenced Stewart to imprisonment for 60 months, to be followed by a three-year term of supervised release. (Doc. at 55). Stewart filed his notice of appeal on April 29, 2013.

Constitutional and Case Law: Amendment IV, U.S. Constitution

United States v. Arango, 912 F.2d 441 (10th Cir. 1990). All you need to know for the purposes of this assignment is that the *Arango* case stands for the proposition that one who has the right to possession of personal property has the right to exclude others from searching it.

United States v. Jones, 707 F.2d 1169 (10th Cir. 1983). See Appendix A.

Prior Related Appeals: There are no prior or related appeals in this case.

Caption:

UNITED STATES COURT OF APPEALS

TENTH CIRCUIT

NO. 2009-123

UNITED STATES OF AMERICA

Plaintiff/Appellee,

vs.

ARNOLD J. STEWART,

Defendant/Appellant.

APPEAL FROM THE UNITED
STATES DISTRICT COURT
FOR THE DISTRICT OF UTAH
ANSWER BRIEF OF APPELLEE

Correspondence

In the hypothetical introduced at the beginning of the last chapter, Alice Black, the supervisory attorney, assigned Pam Hayes, the paralegal, the task of preparing a response to a motion to dismiss for failure to state a claim. After Ms. Hayes completed the assignment, she received the following memo.

To:	Pam Hayes, Paralegal
From:	Alice Black, Attorney
Case:	Civil 13-601, *Nick Shine v. Blue Sky Ski Resort*
Re:	Correspondence to client

Please prepare a letter to Mr. Shine advising him of the status of the case. Include in the letter the following:

- Inform Mr. Shine that a motion to dismiss has been filed. Explain to him what a motion is, and tell him how the court will proceed in regard to the motion.

- Summarize the analysis of the law contained in the memorandum brief you prepared in response to the motion.

The Application section of this chapter includes the correspondence prepared by Ms. Hayes and other sample correspondence.

Learning Objectives

After completing this chapter, you should understand:

- The basic components of correspondence

- The types of law office correspondence that communicate the results of legal research and analysis

- The elements of information, opinion, and demand letters

- How to draft information, opinion, and demand letters

I. INTRODUCTION

This chapter and Chapter 18 focus primarily on the preparation of documents that contain legal research and analysis and are designed for an audience outside the law office. This chapter examines the preparation of documents designed for an external audience other than a court. These documents are usually correspondence addressed to a client. A paralegal or law clerk may, however, be called on to draft correspondence to a variety of external audiences, such as witnesses, court personnel, and opposing counsel.

Correspondence is a major form of written communication between the law firm and the outside world. Other than documents submitted to courts and transaction documents, such as contracts, correspondence is the *primary form* of writing designed for an audience outside the law office.

It is essential, therefore, that correspondence be well crafted, because it helps establish and maintain the image and reputation of the law firm. Correspondence that contains grammatical or substantive errors or is difficult to understand reflects poorly on the law firm:

- A client may question the firm's capability to handle the client's case.

- The court may question the competence of the individual who signed the document.

- Opposing counsel may conclude that if the law firm is incapable of preparing quality correspondence, it is not capable of successfully representing its client.

Because most legal correspondence is in letter rather than memo form, the term *letter* is used in this chapter to refer to legal correspondence. A paralegal or law clerk may prepare letters for a variety of purposes. The three main categories of letters that include legal research and analysis to some degree are:

1. Letters that provide information—*informational letters*
2. Letters that provide answers or legal opinions—*opinion letters*
3. Letters that demand action—*demand letters*

Although the focus in this chapter is on letters that contain legal research and analysis, other types of letters are briefly mentioned. Following a discussion of the components common to all three categories mentioned, separate sections of this chapter address each category.

II. BASIC COMPONENTS

Basic conventions apply to the various types of letters prepared in a law office and basic components are usually present in all types of letters. Each of these components may not be necessary or required in every letter you draft. This section, however, introduces all of the possible components so that you will be familiar with them.

The content and manner of presentation of each of the components discussed in the following text may vary from office to office. Compose your letters according to the guidelines adopted in your office. Refer to the Application section of this chapter for examples of the components discussed in the following subsections.

Exhibit 19-1 presents the basic format and components of letters prepared in a law office.

A. Letterhead

The **letterhead** usually consists of the full name, address, telephone number, and facsimile number of the law firm. It is usually preprinted on the firm's stationery and centered at the top of the page. An example of the information in a letterhead follows:

Thomas, Belter and Ryan

751 Main Street

Friendly, New Washington 00065

(200) 444-7778 • FAX 444-7678 • www.thomaslaw.com

Exhibit 19-1 *Basic Format and Components of Law Office Correspondence.*

- Letterhead/heading
- Date
- Method of delivery
- Recipient's address block
- Reference (Re:) line
- Salutation
- Body
- Closing
- Signature and title
- Initials of drafter
- Enclosure notation
- Others receiving copies

© Cengage Learning 2014

Subsequent pages contain an identification of the letter, which is usually called a **header**. These pages do not contain the letterhead. The header includes the name of the addressee, the date, and the page number, and sits at the top left or right margin of the page. An example of a header is as follows:

Jon Jones

May 5, 2013

Page Three

B. Date

The full date is usually below the letterhead at the left or right margin, or centered below the letterhead. The date includes the full date: the day, month, and year. Because most correspondence is filed chronologically, a date is essential for the chronological file. Note that many offices date-stamp correspondence when it is received in the office and file it according to that date.

C. Method of Delivery

At the left margin, below the date, is the **method of delivery**. This is usually required only if the manner of delivery is other than United States mail. Examples are as follows:

Via Federal Express

Via hand delivery

Via facsimile

D. Recipient's Address Block

Below the date and method of delivery is the **address block** of the addressee. Place it at the left margin. The address block includes:

- The name of the person to whom the letter is addressed
- The individual's title (if any)
- The name of the business (if applicable)
- The address

The following is an example of an address block:

Elizabeth Counter

President

Friendly Enterprises

139 Main Street

Friendly, NW 00065

E. Reference (Re:) Line

The **reference line** briefly identifies the topic of the letter. A reference line is usually placed at the left margin following the address block. Some firms require that the reference line include the case name and number if the letter concerns a pending lawsuit. The following is an example of a reference line:

Re: Request for production of documents

Smith v. Jones, Civil Action 13-1001

F. Salutation

Below the reference line is the **salutation** or greeting. Legal correspondence is generally formal in tone, and the greeting is normally formal. An example of a greeting follows:

Dear Ms. Counter:

You may use the first name if you know the addressee well, but this is usually the exception. If in doubt, ask the supervising attorney. If you do not know the name of the addressee, such as may be the case when the letter is addressed to a business, contact the business and ascertain the individual's name. The use of "To whom it may concern:" is impersonal and invites a slow response. A person is likely to respond more quickly when he or she is specifically named.

G. Body

The **body** is the heart of the letter—what the letter is about. The body is usually composed of an introduction, main body, and requests or instructions (see Exhibit 19-2).

Exhibit 19-2 *Components of the Body of a Letter.*

Introduction	Introductory paragraph or sentence summarizing the purpose of the letter
Main body	Detailed explanation of the purpose of the letter
Requests/instructions	Request or instructions for the recipient

© Cengage Learning 2014

1. Introduction

The body of the letter usually begins with an introductory sentence or paragraph (if necessary) that identifies or summarizes the main purpose of the letter.

For Example This letter is to advise you of the filing of a motion for summary judgment by the defendant. The hearing on the motion is scheduled to take place on March 4, 2013.

This letter is to confirm our conversation today in which you stated that you would not be able to attend the hearing scheduled to take place on May 16, 2013.

2. Main Body

The main body of the letter follows the introduction. The main body explains in detail the purpose of the letter. Craft the main body with care to ensure that you communicate the required information clearly and concisely. It may be necessary to use an outline when a letter covers multiple or complex matters. As with an office memorandum or court brief, the body may require several drafts.

You must always consider the audience when drafting the main body. If you are drafting the letter to a layperson, such as the client, avoid the use of legalese; define and clearly explain any legal terms used.

When writing to a layperson, consider the sophistication of the reader. Ask yourself:

- How familiar with legal matters is the reader?
- Does the reader often read material that involves complex subjects?

Although the addressee may not be familiar with the law, the individual may be highly educated or may often deal with complex or technical matters. In such situations, you may be able to craft the letter with greater complexity and present the subject matter with greater legal or technical detail. If the reader does not as a matter of course engage in a lot of complex or technical reading or is not familiar with such matters, then you should avoid including a detailed, complex discussion in the main body.

The content of the body will differ according to the type of letter you are drafting. The subsections of this chapter that address information, opinion, and demand letters discuss the differences in the format and content of the body of these types of correspondence.

3. Requests/Instructions

Include any **requests** or **instructions** for the recipient in the last section of the body.

> **For Example** Please bring with you copies of the contract and any other written material related to the contract.
>
> Please keep a daily diary. Include in it a detailed description of all your daily activities, such as how long you sleep, what physical activities you engage in during the day, and so on.

In some instances, a paralegal or law clerk may draft and sign a letter to the client. A paralegal or law clerk may sign a letter that provides general information. Neither may sign a letter that gives a legal opinion or legal advice. Most state laws and rules of ethics prohibit a paralegal or law clerk from practicing law, and providing a legal opinion or legal advice constitutes the practice of law. Therefore, when preparing a letter that you, another paralegal, or law clerk will sign, be sure not to include a legal opinion or provide legal advice.

H. Closing

The **closing** follows the body of the letter. The closing usually consists of some standard statement. The following are examples of closings:

- Thank you for your prompt consideration of this matter.

  Sincerely,

- Please contact me if you have any questions in regard to this matter.

  Very truly yours,

- Thank you for your assistance.

  Best regards,

I. Signature and Title

The signature and title of the person signing the letter follow the closing. An example follows:

_____

Sarah Smith

Attorney at Law

When the individual signing the letter is a paralegal, the paralegal status should be clearly indicated below the signature line, as in the following examples:

_____

Jon Jones

Paralegal

_____

Sarah Smith

Paralegal

J. Initials of Drafter

The final notation on the letter is a reference to the author of the letter and the typist. Note the **initials of the drafter** in all capitals, and note the typist's initials in lowercase letters (e.g., JDR/mwt).

K. Enclosure Notation

If enclosures, such as contracts and documents, are included with the letter, indicate their presence with an **enclosure notation** by typing "Enc." or "Encs." at the left margin following the signature.

_____

Sarah Smith

Attorney at Law

Encs.

L. Others Receiving Copies

If other individuals are receiving copies of the letter, indicate this by typing "cc:" and the name of the individual(s) after the signature and title. This follows the enclosure notation if an enclosure notation is used. An example is as follows:

cc: Colin Smith

Mae Carrey

If you are uncertain who should receive copies, check with your supervisor.

M. Format Style

The basic format of a letter varies among firms, and is dictated by personal taste and style. Two fundamental styles are full block and modified block. In full block, everything but the letterhead is flush with the left margin. The information letter in the first example in the

Application section is typed in full block format. In modified block, the date is centered, and the signature line may be just to the right of the center of the page or flush left. The first line of each paragraph is indented. The opinion letter in the second example in the Application section is presented in modified block format.

N. General Considerations—All Correspondence

Adopt the highest standards of accuracy, both substantive and stylistic, when drafting legal correspondence. As mentioned in the introduction, correspondence helps determine the image, reputation, and success of the law firm. In many situations, the information provided in the correspondence constitutes the practice of law and subjects the firm to possible liability for claims of legal malpractice. Therefore, the quality of the product is critically important. You should do the following:

- Take the utmost care to ensure that any legal research and analysis are free of error.
- Make sure that the finished product is free from writing errors involving grammar, spelling, and so on.
- Be prepared to perform the number of edits and redrafts necessary to ensure that the final product is professionally prepared.

Draft letters so clearly that they cannot be misinterpreted. A reader may not like the information conveyed in the letter and wish to intentionally misinterpret the contents. The discussion in the following sections is designed to assist in the preparation of letters that clearly convey information and are difficult to misinterpret.

III. TYPES OF CORRESPONDENCE

Although, as discussed in the preceding section, the basic components of legal correspondence are the same, the content of the body of the correspondence varies according to the type of letter being drafted. There are many categories of legal correspondence, and the categorization is based upon the purpose that each category is designed to serve. Inasmuch as this text focuses on legal research and analysis, this section addresses law office correspondence that communicates the results of legal research and analysis. The three basic categories of letters that communicate such information are information letters, opinion letters, and demand letters (see Exhibit 19-3).

Exhibit 19-3 *Types of Letters That Communicate the Results of Legal Research and Analysis.*

Information letters	Letters that provide general legal information or background on a legal issue (e.g., the information may be a summary of the law or the requirements of a particular statute)
Opinion letters	Letters that provide information concerning the law, an analysis of that information, and a legal opinion or legal advice
Demand or advocacy letters	Letters designed to persuade someone to take action favorable to the interest of the client or cease acting in a manner that is detrimental to the client (e.g., a summary of the applicable law in support of the requested action)

© Cengage Learning 2014

This section focuses on the body of these categories of letters and how each differs in the presentation of legal research and analysis. The following subsections address the preparation of letters to nonlawyer recipients, as most of the correspondence a paralegal or law clerk prepares is for that audience.

A. Information Letter

A paralegal or law clerk is often asked to draft a letter that provides information to the client or other layperson. The components of an **information letter** usually include the elements mentioned in section II of this chapter. The body of the information letter, however, varies according to the type of information being conveyed. There are many types of information letters. Some of the types, and examples of parts of the body of these types, follow:

- Letters that confirm an appointment or inform of the date and time of scheduled events

> **For Example** This letter is to advise you that the court hearing on the motion to modify child support will be held on May 6, 2013, in the courtroom of. . . .
> This letter is to confirm our appointment at 9:00 a.m., May 22, 2013. . . .

- Letters that inform the client of the current status of the case

> **For Example** The defendants filed an answer on June 6, 2013. On June 14, 2013, we sent them a request to produce documents concerning the contract and are awaiting their response to that request. We will contact you when we receive their response.

- Letters that present the firm's bill
- Letters that give the results of an investigation

> **For Example** After performing a thorough investigation, we were unable to locate any witness who actually saw the accident. We interviewed the witnesses at the scene, canvassed the neighborhood, and contacted all the store owners in the area. If you happen to remember the license plate of any vehicle that passed by or have any additional information, please let us know. . . .

- Letters that provide general legal information or background on a legal issue (This is the type of information being provided to Mr. Shine in the assignment at the beginning of the chapter.)

    The information may be a summary of the law involved in the client's case or the requirements of a particular statute. This type of information letter is usually the most complex of the information letters and often involves communicating results of legal research and analysis. The body of this type of information letter is discussed in the remainder of this subsection.

    The body of an information letter that provides the results of legal research and analysis usually consists of an introduction/opening, answer/explanation, and a closing (see Exhibit 19-4).

Exhibit 19-4 Body of Information Letter—Recommended Format and Components.

Introduction/opening	A sentence or paragraph explaining the purpose of the letter
Answer/explanation	A detailed presentation of the legal information or background on a legal issue
Closing	A standard closing statement or if the answer/explanation is lengthy, a summary of the answer

© Cengage Learning 2014

1. Introduction/Opening

The introduction states the purpose of the letter.

> **For Example** The purpose of this letter is to inform you of a request that has been filed by the defendant and the law the court will consider when addressing the request.
> The purpose of this letter is to inform you of a recent law that was passed that affects your business.

2. Answer/Explanation

The answer/explanation section presents the results of legal research and analysis.

> **For Example** Section 97-355-21 of the corporation statutes was recently amended. Under the provisions of the amendment, you must file your annual report no later than 20 days after the end of the fiscal year. As you know, the statute prior to the amendment allowed 40 days to file the report.

The body of the letter presented in the first example in the Application section provides a detailed illustration of this component of an information letter.

3. Closing

The closing of the letter is similar to the closing of any legal correspondence, as discussed in section II of this chapter.

> **For Example** Because you prepare the annual report for your corporation, I feel it is important that you be advised of the change in the law. If you have any questions, please contact me.

In some instances, especially when the answer/explanation is lengthy or complex, it may be necessary to include a summary or a conclusion in the closing. See the closing of the information letter in the first example in the Application section.

This type of information letter merely presents a summary of the law or the legal status of a case. It communicates basic information; it does not give a legal opinion on a question or provide legal advice. That role is performed by an opinion letter.

B. Opinion Letter

An **opinion letter** is like an information letter in that it provides information concerning the law. It is different in that it often includes, in addition, an analysis of that information and provides a legal opinion or legal advice. The purpose is to inform the reader how the law applies to the facts. An opinion letter is usually generated in response to a client's question or raised by the facts in a client's case. Therefore, the focus of this section is on opinion letters addressed to the client.

You may be assigned the task of researching, analyzing, and preparing an interoffice memorandum that addresses the question to be answered in an opinion letter. The purpose of the assignment is to provide the attorney with the information necessary to prepare the letter. On occasion, you may be assigned the additional task of preparing a rough draft of the opinion letter. Many of the considerations involved in preparing an opinion letter are the same as those involved in preparing an office memorandum. When you are assigned the task of preparing such a letter, refer to Chapters 16 and 17 in addition to this chapter for guidance.

An opinion letter provides the reader with a legal opinion and legal advice; therefore, it constitutes the practice of law and an attorney must sign it. The attorney is subject to legal liability for harm that occurs as a result of the client acting upon erroneous information contained in the letter. If you are preparing the draft of an opinion letter, take great care to ensure that your research and analysis are accurate.

Because the purpose is to inform the client of the law and provide legal advice, the opinion letter is drafted in the same objective tone as the office memorandum. The difference is that the client is usually a layperson unfamiliar with legal terms and legal writing. When this is so, avoid legalese and keep legal quotations and citations to a minimum. If the reader is familiar with the law and legal writing, you may use more legal terms, quotations, and citations. In some instances, the attorney may direct that the client be provided with the office memorandum rather than an opinion letter.

Although an opinion letter and an office memorandum are similar in many respects, there are differences in format. An opinion letter follows a business format as discussed in section II of this chapter, whereas an office memorandum follows a memo format as discussed in Chapters 16 and 17. The body of the letter includes the basic elements of the office memorandum, but the elements are presented with less technical detail and fewer legal terms.

As with most legal writing, there is no standard format for the body of an opinion letter. The body of most opinion letters, however, follows the format presented in Exhibit 19-5.

Exhibit 19-5 *Body of Opinion Letter—Recommended Format and Components.*

Introduction/opening	A sentence or paragraph identifying the question or questions that will be answered
Facts	A brief presentation of the background and key facts relative to the question(s) being addressed
Answer/conclusion	A brief answer to the question similar to the brief answer section of an office memorandum
Explanation	An explanation of how the law applies to the facts raised by the question, crafted in a manner that the recipient will understand
Closing/conclusion	The last paragraph of the explanation section, containing a standard closing statement (or if the explanation is lengthy, a summary of the explanation); also includes a statement of any action the client should take or what will occur next

1. Introduction/Opening

The introduction establishes the focus of the letter and identifies the question or questions that will be answered. The opening usually begins with a reference to the question and the context within which the client raised the question.

> **For Example** On January 2, 2012, you hired me to represent you in your criminal case. When we met in my office on that date, you asked me to determine whether we could obtain a suppression of the evidence (the heroin) seized when the police officers executed a search warrant by entering your residence unannounced.

Notice that the question is stated in broader terms than it would be in an office memorandum. Draft the question in a manner sufficient for the client to understand the question. You do not have to state it as completely or as formally as discussed in Chapter 11, nor do you necessarily have to follow the law + question + key facts format. In the preceding example, there is no reference to the rule of law.

Include language in the introduction to indicate that the opinion and advice apply only to the addressee and the specific facts included in the letter. You should also mention that the opinion is based on the law as of the date of the opinion.

> **For Example** This opinion is provided for your use and solely for your benefit. It applies only to the facts presented in the facts section of this letter and the law as of the date of the letter.

2. Facts

Present the facts in an opinion letter in the same objective manner as in an office memorandum. Include only the key and background facts to keep the section as short as possible.

3. Answer/Conclusion

The answer/conclusion section presents a brief answer to the question. It is similar to the brief answer section of the office memorandum. By placing the answer near the beginning of the letter, the reader immediately knows the result without having to read the explanation. This is helpful if the reader is busy and may not be able to read the explanation until a later time.

The answer should be clear and as short as possible. Because the answer is usually a legal opinion, you should state it as an opinion.

> **For Example** The court will probably not suppress the evidence based upon the officers' failure to announce their presence prior to entering your residence when they executed the warrant.

Add any needed specifics or limitations after the answer.

> **For Example** The outcome could be different if Officer Galen changes his testimony and states he did not see you holding a rifle in your front room when they approached the house. Officer Kaler stated that he did not see you in the front room as they approached the house. In light of Officer Kaler's statement, Officer Galen could change his statement.

4. Explanation

The explanation section is similar to the analysis section of an office memorandum. The difference is that the explanation must be crafted in a manner that is not so technical that the client has difficulty understanding it. Also, the explanation section is usually not as long or as complex as the analysis section of an office memorandum. When preparing this section, note the following guidelines:

- If there is more than one issue, discuss the issues in the order they are presented in the introduction.

- If possible, limit the letter to as few issues as possible (i.e., two to three). If there are multiple issues, the letter may become too complex or long, and the reader may have difficulty understanding or keeping track of the subject matter. Separate the issues, and prepare more than one letter if necessary.

- Draft the content with the reader's legal sophistication in mind. The client may not be familiar with the law and technical writing, and an explanation that is as detailed as the analysis section of an office memorandum may not be appropriate. Keep quotations and citations to a minimum. Rather than quoting, rephrase the statutory or case law in a manner that a layperson can understand. If you must use a legal term, make sure its meaning is clear. Define the legal terms that you use.

- Provide a complete explanation. The client must be fully informed. Do not omit important information because the client is unsophisticated in the law. Present all the key information in a manner that fully and clearly informs the client.

The following is an example of an explanation section of an opinion letter.

The Fourth Amendment to the United States Constitution and article II, section 9, of the state constitution prohibit "unreasonable searches and seizures." These amendments do not prohibit all searches and seizures, however, just those that are "unreasonable."

The law provides that anything seized as a result of an unreasonable search may not be admitted into evidence in a trial. The state supreme court has ruled that officers must announce their presence before entering a residence when executing a search warrant. The court stated that an unannounced entry is unreasonable and violates the United States and state constitutions.

There are, however, exceptions to the rule that officers must announce their presence before executing a warrant. One exception is when the officers arrive at the place to be searched and there is evidence that the person or persons present at the scene are a danger to the officers. *Smith v. Jones* is a court case remarkably similar to your case. In this case, when the police arrived at the residence to be searched, they saw the defendant enter the house with a rifle in his hands. The state supreme court ruled that this evidence provided the officers with authority to execute the warrant and enter the residence to be searched without first announcing their presence.

Based upon the ruling in the *Smith v. Jones* case and the similarity between the facts of that case and the facts in your case, the trial court probably will not suppress the evidence seized at your residence and will allow its admission at trial.

5. Closing/Conclusion

The closing is usually not a separate section of an opinion letter. Rather, it is usually the last paragraph of the explanation section. It is similar to the closing of any legal correspondence, as discussed in section II of this chapter. In addition, in an opinion letter, the closing should summarize any action the client should take or what will occur next.

For Example I hope this letter answers your questions. Please note that, although the officers may have acted properly when they entered your residence unannounced, there is a question as to whether the warrant was properly issued in the first place. When we complete our investigation into this matter, we anticipate that we will file a motion to suppress the evidence because the warrant should not have been issued at all. We will discuss this at our appointment scheduled on Friday the ninth. Please contact me if you have any questions.

An example of an opinion letter is presented in the second example in the Application section of this chapter.

C. Demand or Advocacy Letter

Another basic type of letter you may be called upon to draft is a **demand letter**, sometimes called an *advocacy letter*. This type of letter is designed to persuade someone to take action favorable to the interests of the client or cease acting in a manner that is detrimental to the client. This may be as simple as demanding payment on a debt or as complex as requesting that a course of conduct be taken, such as rehiring an employee. In many instances, a demand letter will include a summary of the applicable law in support of the requested action. This section addresses the considerations involved when preparing a demand letter that includes a reference to the law and an analysis of the law.

You may be given an assignment to prepare an office memorandum summarizing the law that will be used as the basis for the demand letter and to prepare a draft of the letter. Like the opinion letter, the attorney must sign a demand letter.

The basic format and components of a demand letter are similar to those discussed in section II of this chapter; as with an opinion letter, there is no standard format for the demand letter. A major difference is that a demand letter is not designed to address a legal question, but to encourage action or seek relief. Therefore, it does not contain an answer/conclusion section in the body because it does not address a question that requires a brief answer. The demand letter also differs from an opinion letter in that it is designed to advocate a position and persuade the reader; therefore, it is written in a persuasive manner.

The body of a demand letter follows the same basic format and is composed of elements similar to the body of the opinion letter (see Exhibit 19-6).

Exhibit 19-6 Body of Demand Letter—Recommended Format and Component.

Introduction/opening	An identification of the writer or client followed by the statement of the purpose of the letter
Facts	A brief presentation of the background and key facts relative to the question(s) being addressed
Explanation	A presentation of the legal authority in support of the relief requested, crafted in a manner that the recipient will understand
Closing/conclusion	The last paragraph of the explanation section, containing a standard closing statement (or, if the explanation is lengthy, a summary of the explanation); should restate the relief requested and indicate the next course of action

This section explores the differences between the body of a demand letter and the body of an opinion letter. The discussion focuses on demand letters sent to nonlawyers. The attorney will usually draft a demand letter that will be sent to another attorney.

1. Introduction/Opening

The introduction of a demand letter is somewhat different from the opening of an opinion letter. It begins with the identification of the writer or the client.

> **For Example** Our office represents Mr. Jason Hill in the above-referenced case. Mr. Jason Hill has retained this office in regard to. . . .

A statement of the purpose of the letter follows the identification. It establishes the focus of the letter and identifies the problem addressed and the relief sought.

> **For Example** Your efforts to collect payment from Mr. Hill on his automobile loan are in violation of the Collections Act, and we demand that they cease immediately.

2. Facts

The content of the facts section is the same as in the opinion letter except that you should present the facts in a persuasive manner similar to the persuasive presentation of the facts in a court brief. See Chapter 18, section II.B.2, for additional information on persuasive presentation of facts.

> **For Example** On January 7, 2012, Mr. Hill signed a loan with your company to pay for the purchase of an automobile. From the date of the loan until two months ago, he has paid, on time and in full, every installment on the loan. For the past two months, due to the illness of his oldest child, Mr. Hill has been able to pay only one-half of the required monthly payment. He contacted your office on the fifth of last month and informed the loan officer that for the next three months he would be making reduced payments. He was informed that he should be making full payments.
>
> For the past three weeks, your collections department has telephoned Mr. Hill after 7:00 p.m. six nights a week demanding full payment. In each instance, Mr. Hill has politely informed the caller that he is paying all he can and requested that the calls cease. The calls have not ceased.

3. Explanation

The explanation section presents the legal authority in support of the relief requested. Because the reader is a nonlawyer, draft the section with this in mind. Refer to the explanation subsection of an opinion letter for guidance. This section of a demand letter differs from the explanation section of an opinion letter in that you should draft the section in a persuasive manner.

> **For Example** The Collections Act provides that efforts to collect debts shall be made in a reasonable manner. The state supreme court, in the case of *Irons v. Collections, Inc.,* ruled that telephone calls to a debtor's residence after 7:00 p.m. or more frequently than three times a week are unreasonable and violate the act if the debtor objects to the calls. Your office has contacted Mr. Hill after 7:00 p.m. six nights a week for the past three weeks. The calls have continued despite Mr. Hill's objections and requests that they cease.

4. Closing/Conclusion

Like the closing of an opinion letter, the closing of a demand letter is usually not a separate section. It is usually the last paragraph of the explanation section and is similar to the closing of any legal correspondence, as discussed in section II of this chapter. The closing should restate the relief requested and indicate the next course of action.

For Example	Your calls to Mr. Hill are unreasonable, clearly in violation of the Collections Act, and must cease immediately. If the calls do not cease, we will take the appropriate steps necessary to obtain the relief provided in the act.
	If you have any questions in regard to this matter, please contact me.

IV. KEY POINTS CHECKLIST: *Correspondence*

- ✔ Prepare correspondence accurately and professionally. Letters may affect the reputation of the firm, and poorly drafted letters do not inspire the client's confidence.

- ✔ Draft the correspondence with the reader's legal sophistication in mind. Avoid legalese; if you must use legal terms, define them clearly.

- ✔ Keep legal citations and quotations to a minimum. Use quotations only if they are easy to understand and add clarity to the subject matter. Paraphrase the material if it is written in a manner that is difficult to comprehend.

- ✔ When drafting an opinion letter, be sure to indicate that the letter is limited to the facts of the case, based on the current law, and intended solely for the benefit of the addressee.

- ✔ If there are multiple issues, divide the subject into separate manageable topics. Prepare and send separate letters covering these topics.

- ✔ Do not include legal advice or recommend a course of action if the correspondence is to be signed by someone other than an attorney. Such information constitutes the practice of law and must be signed by an attorney.

- ✔ Keep a file of the letters and other documents you have prepared. Organize the file by topic, such as demand letters and opinion letters. Often, rather than starting a new letter, it is faster and easier to edit an old letter or use it as a guide for the correspondence you are drafting.

V. APPLICATION

This section contains two examples of legal correspondence that illustrate the application of the principles discussed in this chapter. The first example addresses the assignment presented at the beginning of the chapter. This assignment requires the preparation of an information letter by the paralegal, Pam Hayes. The second example illustrates an opinion letter. It is based on the same law used in the first example and on facts that are similar to those of the first example.

A. Example—Information Letter

The assignment introduced at the beginning of the chapter calls for the preparation of an information letter. In this example, the letter is presented in full block style.

Law Offices of Alice Black
2100 Main Street
Friendly, New Washington 00065

(200) 267-7000 • FAX 267-7001 • www.ablacklaw.com

April 29, 2013

Mr. Nick Shine
9100 2nd Street
Friendly, NW 00065

Re: *Shine v. Blue Sky Ski Resort*

Motion to dismiss for failure to state a claim

Dear Mr. Shine:

The purpose of this letter is to inform you of the status of your case and to summarize the law in regard to the motion that will be heard on May 17, 2013.

As you know, on April 6, we filed your complaint against Blue Sky Ski Resort. In the complaint, we claim that the resort was negligent for failing to post a sign warning skiers of the ice hazard you encountered. To prove a claim for negligence, one of the requirements we must establish is that the resort had a duty to warn skiers of the ice hazard.

On April 20, the resort filed a motion with the court asking that the court dismiss the case. A motion is a request submitted to the court asking the court to take some form of action. The court usually holds a hearing on a motion. At the hearing, the parties present their position on whether the request should be granted.

On May 17, 2013, the court will conduct a hearing on the resort's motion to dismiss. At that hearing, we anticipate the resort will claim that under the provisions of the Ski Safety Act, it does not have a duty to warn skiers of ice hazards. The resort will argue that ice hazards are the responsibility of skiers under the act, and therefore, it cannot be sued for negligence, because it had no duty to warn of the ice hazard.

In support of its argument that it does not have a duty to warn of ice hazards, the resort will rely on section 8B of the act. This section states that skiers are responsible for injuries that result from snow and ice conditions. Our position is that the resort does have a duty to warn of this type of hazard under section 7A of the act. That section provides that resorts have a duty to warn skiers of unusual conditions or hazards on ski runs.

It is unclear from the statute which section of the act applies in a situation such as yours. The state court of appeals, in the case of *Aster v. White Mountain Resort*, interpreted the act in a fact situation similar to yours. In this case, a skier, while skiing on a new ski run, hit a rock covered by snow. The court stated that resorts have a duty to warn of snow conditions if they are unavoidable and present an unobvious or latent hazard.

At the motion hearing, we will argue that the resort's motion to dismiss should be denied because the ice condition you encountered was unavoidable and latent, just as the snow condition was in *Aster v. White Mountain Resort*. We will further argue that the rule of law stated in that case provides that resorts have a duty to warn of hazards such as the one you encountered. Therefore, the resort can be sued for its negligence in failing to post a warning of the ice hazard.

The resort will probably argue that the ruling of the court of appeals in *Karen v. High Mountain Pass* should apply. In that case, a skier broke his leg after failing to negotiate a series of moguls that were present in the middle of a turn on a ski run. The court stated that skiers are responsible for snow and ice hazards, and moguls, even though unavoidable, are snow hazards easily observable and routinely present on most ski runs. We believe the court will not apply the ruling in the *Karen* case because that case involved a snow hazard that was observable and routinely encountered by skiers. In your case, the ice hazard was unobservable, unavoidable, and not routinely encountered by skiers.

In conclusion, we are optimistic that the court will rule in our favor and deny the motion. The ice hazard you encountered was unavoidable and latent just like the snow condition in *Aster v. White Mountain Resort*. This being the case, the court should follow the holding in that case and find that Blue Sky Ski Resort had a duty to warn skiers of the hazard. You are not required to attend the hearing, but you may attend if you wish. Please let us know if you plan to attend.

If you have any questions please call.

Sincerely,

_____

Pam Hayes

Paralegal

PAH/wkk

B. Example—Opinion Letter

The example in this section is based on the following fact situation. On January 6, 2013, the client, David Duggan, appeared for an initial interview at the law offices of Alice Black. Pam Hayes, the paralegal, conducted the interview. In the interview, Mr. Duggan stated that he was skiing on December 7, 2012, on an expert ski run at Red Mountain Ski Resort. He encountered a series of moguls near the top of the ski run. The moguls were difficult to ski, and he lost control, fell, and broke his left arm. There was no sign at the top of the run indicating the presence of difficult moguls on the run. He believes the resort should have posted a sign, well in advance of the moguls, warning of their presence. He wants to know if he can sue the resort for its failure to post a warning.

Alice Black assigned Pam Hayes the task of preparing a rough draft of an opinion letter to be sent to Mr. Duggan. The letter should inform him of the likelihood of successfully suing the resort for its failure to post a warning of the presence of the moguls. The governing law is chapter 70 of the New Washington Ski Safety Act. The governing case is *Karen v. High Mountain Pass*, 55 N. Wash. 462, 866 N.E. 995 (Ct. App. 1994). The relevant portions of the statute and case are introduced at the beginning of the Application section of Chapter 18. The opinion letter is presented in modified block format.

Law Offices of Alice Black

2100 Main Street

Friendly, New Washington 00065

(200) 267-7000 • FAX 267-7001 • www.ablacklaw.com

January 18, 2013

Via Facsimile and U.S. Mail

Mr. David Duggan

5501 Glenview Ave.

Friendly, NW 00065

Re: Possibility of a lawsuit against Red Mountain Ski Resort for failure to warn of moguls

Dear Mr. Duggan:

On January 6, 2013, we met in my office to discuss the possibility of suing Red Mountain Ski Resort for the ski injury you suffered on December 7, 2012. This opinion is based on the facts outlined in the facts section of this letter and the applicable law as of the date of the letter. This letter is solely for your benefit and limited to the facts discussed below. Please contact me if any of the facts are misstated or if you have additional information.

FACTS

On December 7, 2012, you were skiing on an expert run at Red Mountain Ski Resort. Near the top of the run, you encountered a series of moguls. The moguls were difficult to ski, and as a result, you lost control and broke your left arm. There were no signs posted on the run that warned skiers of the upcoming moguls.

ANSWER

Based upon the above facts, you probably cannot successfully sue Red Mountain Ski Resort for its failure to warn of the moguls. The only possible theory under which you could sue is negligence. You would claim that the resort was negligent for failing to warn of the upcoming moguls. Under the applicable state statute and the court opinions interpreting that statute, the resort does not have a duty to warn of the presence of moguls.

EXPLANATION

Chapter 70 of the New Washington statutes, the Ski Safety Act, governs the operation of ski resorts and establishes the duties of skiers and resort operators. Section 7A of the act requires resorts to warn of sections of trails "which present an unusual obstacle or hazard." Section 8B of the act states that a skier "expressly assumes the risk and legal responsibility for any injury to a person or property which results from . . . surface or subsurface snow or ice conditions. . . ."

The act does not discuss whether a mogul is a snow condition for which the skier is responsible. The state court of appeals, however, in the case of *Karen v. High Mountain Pass*, addressed the question of whether a resort has a duty to post a warning of the presence of moguls on a ski run. In this case, a skier broke his leg after failing to negotiate a series of moguls that were present in the middle of a turn on a ski run. The court stated that skiers are responsible for snow and ice hazards. The court noted that moguls, even though unavoidable, are snow hazards easily observable and routinely present on most ski runs. The court ruled that under the act, resorts have no duty to warn of snow hazards such as moguls.

The facts in your case are very similar to the facts in *Karen v. High Mountain Pass*. In your case, just as in that case, the injury occurred as a result of an encounter with moguls. It is apparent from section 8B of the statute, and the court's interpretation of that section in *Karen v. High Mountain Pass*, that skiers are responsible for injuries sustained as a result of encountering moguls on a ski run. Therefore, based on the statute and the court opinion in *Karen v. High Mountain Pass*, it is my opinion that it is highly unlikely that a lawsuit against Red Mountain Ski Resort for the injuries you sustained would be successful.

I hope this information answers your question. I regret that I am not able to provide a more favorable answer. If you have additional information concerning the accident, or if you have any other questions, please contact me.

Sincerely,

_____

Alice Black

Attorney at Law

ALB/wkk

C. Comments on Examples

In regard to the preceding examples, note that both letters:

- Present the subject matter clearly through the use of short sentences rather than complex sentences, which are often more difficult to follow and understand.

- Present the law in an objective and professional manner.

◾ Avoid legalese and discuss the material in a simple and clear manner. (Although there are references to statutes and case law, a summary of the law is provided rather than a technical discussion. The legal points are simply phrased in lay terms.)

In addition, the opinion letter clearly states at the outset that the opinion is limited to the current law and the facts provided by the client. Reference is made to the fact that the letter is intended solely for the benefit of the recipient.

Summary

This chapter discusses the preparation of legal correspondence, referred to as letters in the chapter. The focus is on letters that communicate the results of legal research and analysis. Letters are one of the primary forms of written communication directed to an audience outside the law office.

There are several fundamental components of all types of legal correspondence. There is no standard format; the content and style of presentation of these components vary according to personal and local preference. Section II of this chapter discusses the fundamental components of all legal correspondence.

Letters that include the results of legal research and analysis fall into three basic categories based upon the purpose of the communication:

1. To provide information—information letters
2. To provide an opinion—opinion letters
3. To demand action—demand letters

These three types of letters differ primarily in the content of the body.

The body of an information letter presents an objective summary of the research and analysis without the inclusion of any legal opinion or advice. The body of an opinion letter, in addition to a summary of the law, usually provides an objective assessment of the application of the law to the facts and often recommends a course of action. Because it includes a legal opinion or legal advice, an opinion letter constitutes the practice of law and must be signed by an attorney.

A demand letter is designed to persuade the reader to act in a manner that benefits the client, for example, to pay a debt. Like an opinion letter, a demand letter is signed by an attorney. The body of a demand letter is similar to the body of an opinion letter. The major difference is that the law and analysis are drafted in a persuasive manner.

Because the recipient of legal correspondence is an individual outside the law office, the correspondence affects the image and reputation of the law firm. For this reason, and because legal liability attaches to some correspondence, it is of paramount importance that you draft an accurate and professional product.

Quick References

Address block	565	Initials of drafter	568
Body	566	Letterhead	564
Closing	567	Method of delivery	565
Demand letter	575	Opinion letter	571
Enclosure notation	568	Reference line (Re)	566
Header	565	Requests/instructions	567
Information letter	570	Salutation	566

Internet Resources

Using "legal correspondence" as a topic, you will find a wide range of Web sites (thousands) that refer to legal correspondence. The following is a summary of the categories of sites that may prove helpful when working on legal correspondence.

Sites providing legal correspondence in specific cases, such as correspondence of the Association of Trial Lawyers regarding a specific subject. (Through such sites, you may view the examples of legal correspondence in specific areas.)

Sites advertising businesses that prepare or assist in the preparation of correspondence.

School sites advertising programs that include preparation of correspondence as part of the curriculum.

Sites advertising legal forms and templates for legal correspondence.

Sites containing job announcements for jobs that require the preparation of legal correspondence.

Sites advertising texts that cover the preparation of legal correspondence.

As with most topics on the Web, the problem is not the lack of sites but too many sites. You can avoid some of the frustration of finding too many sites by narrowing your search to a topic, such as "preparing legal opinion correspondence" or "legal correspondence, child custody cases."

Exercises

Additional assignments are available on the CourseMate.

ASSIGNMENT 1

Describe the three types of correspondence discussed in this chapter and the purposes of each type.

ASSIGNMENT 2

Describe how the three types of correspondence are different.

ASSIGNMENT 3

Refer to the assignment introduced at the beginning of Chapter 16 and the law relevant to that assignment presented in the Application section of that chapter. The law firm represents Mrs. Findo. Draft an opinion letter informing her whether she can testify against her husband in light of the applicable Illinois statutory and case law.

ASSIGNMENT 4

Refer to the assignment introduced at the beginning of Chapter 17 and the relevant law included in the Application section of that chapter. You work for a law firm that represents the defendant.

A. Draft an information letter informing the defendant of what constitutes an arrest in the state of New Washington and how the law has been interpreted to apply in search warrant situations.

B. Draft an opinion letter advising the defendant whether there is sufficient evidence to support charges of possession.

ASSIGNMENT 5

The client, Mrs. Tatum, purchased a new microwave oven from Inki Appliances Company. No written or oral warranty was given when the sale was made. The microwave stopped working one week after Mrs. Tatum took it home. She returned the microwave three days after it quit working. The owner of Inki Appliances refused to repair or replace the microwave or give Mrs. Tatum her money back. Prepare a demand letter to be sent to Inki Appliances. The letter is to be signed by your supervising attorney, Alice Black. Use the letterhead presented in the Application section of this chapter. Mr. Terry Spear is the president and owner of Inki Appliances Company, and the address is 1001 Maple Drive, Friendly, NW 00065.

Statutory Law: Section 50-102-314 of the New Washington statutes provides that "a warranty that the goods shall be merchantable is implied . . . if the seller is a merchant with respect to the goods of that kind." Mr. Spear is a merchant. Mrs. Tatum did not misuse the microwave or in any other way cause it to quit working.

Case Law: The case on point is *Smith v. Appliance City*, 56 N. Wash. 162, 868 N.E. 997 (1995). In *Smith*, the New

Washington supreme court ruled that the seller has three options when an implied warranty is breached: return the purchase price to the buyer, repair the merchandise, or replace the merchandise.

ASSIGNMENT 6

Refer to Assignment 8 in Chapter 17. Prepare an information letter to Mr. Canter informing him of the results of your research in regard to armed bank robbery.

ASSIGNMENT 7

Refer to Assignment 5 in Chapter 17. Draft an opinion letter to Mrs. Dixon informing her of the results of your research and the likelihood that the holographic will submitted by Mary Cary will be eligible for probate.

ASSIGNMENT 8

Refer to Assignment 9 in Chapter 17. Prepare a demand letter to Ms. Chavez informing her of the law concerning the unilateral reduction of child support when a child reaches the age of majority. Include in the letter a demand that she resume paying the full child support ordered by the court.

ASSIGNMENT 9

The client, Mr. David Keys, would like to know what state law provides concerning the removal of a director from the board of directors of a corporation. Prepare an information letter to Mr. Keys summarizing the requirements of the removal statute. Draft the letter for the signature of your supervisory attorney, Alice Black. Use the letterhead presented in the Application section of this chapter. Mr. Keys's address is 761 South Vine Street, Sunnydale, NW 00066.

Statute: New Washington Statutes Annotated § 77-11-22. Removal of directors: At a meeting of shareholders called expressly for that purpose, directors may be removed in the manner provided in this section. Any director or the entire board of directors may be removed, with or without cause, by a vote of the holders of a majority of the shares then entitled to vote at an election of directors.

ASSIGNMENT 10

Perform Assignment 9 using your state law. Make up local addresses for the law firm and client.

ASSIGNMENT 11

Draft an information letter to the client, Mr. Daniel Hope, Vice President, National Insurance Company. In the letter, summarize the state law concerning National's duty to defend persons it insures under its automobile insurance policies. Draft the letter for the signature of your supervising attorney, Alice Black. Use the letterhead presented in the Application section of this chapter. National Insurance Company's address is 459 Twenty-Second Street, Friendly,

NW, 00065. There is no statutory law governing an insurance company's duty to defend its insured. The relevant case law follows.

Case Law: *Wrickles v. Washington Ins. Co.*, 61 N. Wash. 104 (Ct. App. 2008). Where it is determined that the insurer has unjustifiably failed to defend against claims against its insured, the insurer is liable for any judgment entered against its insured. In addition, the insurer may be liable for any reasonable settlement entered into by the insured.

State Farm Ins. Co. v. Peterson, 56 N. Wash. 38 (1995). The obligation to defend arises out of and must be found in the insuring agreement promising to defend the insured against liability.

Alison v. Lincoln Ins. Co., 60 N. Wash. 677 (Ct. App. 2000). The duty to defend is triggered when an injured party's complaint against the insured states facts that bring the case within the coverage of the policy.

Jamison v. Lincoln Ins. Co., 58 N. Wash. 430 (1998). An insurance company may refuse to defend its insured only when the allegations in the complaint are completely outside the insurance policy coverage.

Wilson v. Washington Ins. Co., 59 N. Wash. 980 (1999). If the allegations in the complaint against the insured may fall within the coverage of the policy but are potentially excluded by any noncoverage provision in the policy, then the insurer is under a duty to defend the insured in the primary action. The duty continues until a court having jurisdiction over the case finds that the insurer is relieved of the liability under the noncoverage provisions of the policy.

ASSIGNMENT 12

In this assignment, draft the letter for the signature of the supervising attorney, Alice Black. Use the letterhead presented in the Application section of this chapter. Mr. Sanders's address is 930 North Hardwood Court, Friendly, NW 00065.

Assignment Memo: We represent Washington Ins. Co. They paid a claim by their insured in the amount of $21,235.00. The claim arose out of an automobile collision between the insured, Deborah Anderson, and Mr. Karl Sanders. Mr. Sanders ran a stop sign, and his vehicle collided with the insured resulting in the damage. Washington Ins. has written to Mr. Sanders requesting that he either provide proof of insurance at the time of the accident or that he pay the claim in full. He has not responded.

Prepare a draft of a demand letter to Mr. Karl Sanders demanding that he pay the $21,235.00 or contact me to see if we can reach an agreement for payment of the debt. Inform him that this is an attempt to collect a debt. Also inform him that if he does not contact us within

33 days of the date of the letter, I will assume that he does not dispute the debt and I will pursue all legal remedies available under the law. Inform him that a lawsuit will be filed in the district court for the full amount of the debt plus interest, and I will request any fees and costs I may incur in pursuit of the litigation.

In addition, inform him that pursuant to New Washington law, once a judgment is obtained I can take action to have his driver's license and vehicle registration suspended under the provisions of the Financial Responsibility Act, NWSA § 45-6-124.

Statutory Law: Section 45-6-124 of the New Washington Financial Responsibility Act allows a judgment creditor to take action to suspend a debtor's driver's license and vehicle registration for nonpayment of any judgment arising from a motor vehicle accident.

ASSIGNMENT 13

Refer to Assignment 16 in Chapter 17 Prepare a demand letter to Capital Insurance Company informing the company of the law regarding the counting of time in exclusionary clauses. Include a demand that the company pay the claim.

The available CourseMate for this text has an interactive eBook and interactive learning tools, including flash cards, quizzes, and more. To learn more about this resource and access free demo CourseMate resources, go to **www.cengagebrain.com**, and search for this book. To access CourseMate materials that you have purchased, go to **login.cengagebrain.com**.

Court Opinions Referred to in the Text

INTRODUCTION

The court opinions in this appendix are presented in alphabetical order rather than in the order in which they are referred to in the text. To save space, portions of some cases that are not relevant to specific assignments or the discussion presented in the text have been omitted. A series of three asterisks indicates that a portion of the opinion has been omitted.

Stephen Craig BEAM and Lori A. Beam, husband and wife, Respondents,

v.

John C. CULLETT, Appellant.

No. 77–1732; CA 15733.

Court of Appeals of Oregon.

Argued and Submitted June 18, 1980.

Decided Sept. 2, 1980.

Reconsideration Denied Oct. 7, 1980.

48 Or. App. 47, 615 P.2d 1196 (1980)

JOSEPH, Presiding Judge.

Plaintiff brought this action for fraud and breach of an implied warranty of fitness for a particular purpose. Plaintiff was in the business of hauling scrap automobile bodies from southern Oregon to a steel plant in McMinnville. He bought a 1969 Ford Diesel truck from defendant to haul the scrap auto bodies. The truck had been used by defendant for approximately two and one-half years until the engine "blew up." Defendant had the engine rebuilt by a diesel engine mechanic. Plaintiff purchased the truck with the rebuilt engine for $10,000; there were no written warranties. After the truck was used for a brief period of time, the engine lost a rod bearing and the intake manifold was broken. This action followed.

The trial court, sitting without a jury, found in favor of defendant on the fraud claim; a judgment was entered against defendant for breach of an implied warranty of fitness for a particular purpose. Plaintiff was awarded damages of $7,000.

Defendant appeals. He claims (1) that the court erred in entering judgment for plaintiff because an implied warranty of fitness for a particular purpose could not arise under the facts of this case and (2) that the court erred in assessing damages at $7,000.[1]

ORS 72.3150 provides for an implied warranty of fitness:

"Where the seller at the time of contracting has reason to know any particular purpose for which the goods are required and that the buyer is relying on the seller's skill or judgment to select or furnish suitable goods, there is unless excluded or modified under ORS 72.3160 an implied warranty that the goods shall be fit for such purpose."

An implied warranty of fitness for a particular purpose arises then when two conditions are met: (1) the buyer relies on the seller's skill and judgment to select or furnish suitable goods; and (2) the seller at the time of contracting has reason to know of the buyer's purpose and that the buyer is relying on his skill and judgment. *Controltek, Inc. v. Kwikee Enterprises, Inc.*, 284 Or. 123, 585 P.2d 670 (1978); *Valley Iron and Steel v. Thorin*, 278 Or. 103, 562 P.2d 1212 (1977).

The trial court found that defendant was advised that plaintiff intended to use the truck to haul scrap auto bodies. There was evidence to support that finding. No finding was made as to whether plaintiff–buyer relied on the defendant–seller's skill and judgment to select the truck or that defendant had

---

1. The first assignment of error was preserved by defendant's motion for non-suit and motion for reconsideration. We need not reach the second assignment of error in light of our determination of the warranty issue.

(continues)

reason to know of any reliance. The evidence was that plaintiff, who runs a junk yard, learned of defendant's truck being for sale from one of his employees. Plaintiff had had some experience with trucks, including driving, although usually not diesel trucks. He inspected the truck and drove it for a short distance. He was told by defendant that the engine had been rebuilt and was given the name of the mechanic who did the work. Defendant leases trucks, but does not drive them. He operates a well-drilling business and owns drilling rigs. He does not have any particular expertise concerning diesel trucks.

There was no evidence that plaintiff relied on defendant's judgment in selecting the truck he purchased. Defendant merely answered plaintiff's inquiries concerning the mechanic's work on the engine. While the needs of plaintiff were known to defendant, there was no showing that defendant offered to fulfill those needs, that plaintiff in fact relied on defendant's judgment or that defendant had reason to know of plaintiff's reliance, if any.

The existence of a warranty of fitness for a particular purpose depends in part on the comparative knowledge and skills of the parties. *Blockhead, Inc. v. Plastic Forming Company, Inc.*, 402 F. Supp. 1017, 1024 (D. Conn. 1975); *Valley Iron and Steel v. Thorin, supra.* There can be no justifiable reliance by a buyer who has equal or superior knowledge and skill with respect to the product purchased by him. White and Summers, Uniform Commercial Code 298, § 9–9 (1972); *Valley Iron and Steel v. Thorin, supra.*

In the instant case, both parties had limited knowledge of diesel trucks. Absent evidence that plaintiff justifiably relied on defendant's judgment in selecting the truck to fulfill his hauling needs, there was no implied warranty of fitness for a particular purpose.

Reversed.

June F. BRITTON, Petitioner–Appellee,

v.

H.R. BRITTON, Respondent–Appellant.

No. 14577.

Supreme Court of New Mexico.

Oct. 17, 1983.

100 N.M. 424, 671 P.2d 1135 (1983)

OPINION

SOSA, Senior Justice.

Petitioner–Appellee, June Britton (Petitioner) filed a petition in the Bernalillo County District Court to reduce accrued and unpaid child support arrearages to judgment. The district court concluded that the divorce decree mandating child support was enforceable and that no statute of limitations period bars action on the arrearages. It did not allow H.R. Britton, Respondent, any offset. The court issued an order setting arrearages and a final judgment in the amount of $7,900.00 without interest and did not award attorney's fees. Respondent appeals from the district court's determination awarding arrearages. Petitioner cross-appeals on the failure of the district court to award her attorney's fees.

The questions presented here are (1) whether the amended final divorce decree was unambiguous and therefore enforceable; (2) whether accrued and unpaid child support installments are deemed final judgments, thereby rendering action on them subject to a statute of limitations period; (3) whether

Respondent should have been allowed an offset against the arrearage judgment; (4) whether laches bars any recovery of the accrued child support installments; and (5) whether Petitioner should have been awarded attorney's fees for her presentation at the district court level. We affirm on all issues except the second.

FACTS

The parties were married on September 4, 1952. Four children issued from the marriage, all requiring specialized care and treatment due to varying degrees of developmental disability. By 1964 both the youngest and oldest child had been made wards of the state and committed to Los Lunas Training School. These two children remained under the direct care and control of the Los Lunas facility at all times relevant to this case. The oldest child attained majority on June 27, 1971, the youngest on January 28, 1977.

The parties were divorced by final decree entered May 26, 1970 by Judge Edwin Swope of the Bernalillo County District Court. On June 28, 1971 a different judge entered an amended final decree which added the phrase "per month" after the one hundred dollar child support figure in the original final decree. The amendment was done *ex parte.* Respondent never moved the district court for a modification of the terms of either decree.

One of the twin children remained intermittently under Petitioner's direct care from the time of the divorce until the child was transferred to a group home in Albuquerque in January 1976. The other twin remained under the direct care of Petitioner through December 1972. Since that time he has voluntarily lived with Respondent.

ASSERTED AMBIGUITY

Respondent initially contends that the original final decree of May 26, 1970 was ambiguous and should not have been amended *ex parte*. The original final decree in relevant part awarded custody of all four children to Petitioner and also awarded her "one hundred dollars ($100)" in child support. The sole change made by the judge in the amended final decree was the addition of the phrase "per month" after the one hundred dollar child support figure.

The omission of the phrase "per month" was clearly a clerical mistake apparent on the face of the record. On Petitioner's timely motion this mistake was properly corrected without resort to extrinsic evidence pursuant to Rule 60(a) of the New Mexico Rules of Civil Procedure NMSA 1953, Section 21-1-1(60)(a) (Repl. Vol. 4, 1970), presently compiled as NMSA 1978, Civ.P.R. 60(a) (Repl. Pamp. 1980). *Telephonic, Inc. v. Montgomery Plaza Co.*, 87 N.M. 407, 534 P.2d 1119 (Ct. App. 1975); *see De Baca v. Sais*, 44 N.M. 105, 99 P.2d 106 (1940).

This simple amendment obviously did not purport to clear up any ambiguity that Respondent alleges existed regarding the exact amount of child support that was to apply to each minor child. Respondent asserts that he should have been afforded an opportunity to present [parol] evidence prior to modification so that the support terms could have been modified to apply to the twins only and to reflect the fact that another child had attained majority. In New Mexico, the duty of a parent to support a child continues until the child reaches the age of majority. NMSA 1978, §§ 28-6-1 and 28-6-6 (Repl. Pamp. 1983); *Phelps v. Phelps*, 85 N.M. 62, 509 P.2d 254 (1973); *Coe's Estate*, 56 N.M. 578, 247 P.2d 162 (1952). The well-established general rule is that an undivided support award directed at more than one child is presumed to continue in force for the full amount until the youngest child reaches majority. Annot., 2 A.L.R.3d 596 (1965). We see no compelling reason to depart from this view.

Respondent's proper remedy, if indeed he though [sic] the final decree ambiguous and/or unjust, would have been to seek prospective modification of the decree on the basis of changed circumstances. We note as to the alleged ambiguity that Respondent at no time petitioned the district court for any modification of either decree. Respondent, having failed to timely petition for possible relief from this asserted ambiguity, cannot now seize upon the mere *ex parte* correction of a clerical error and expand this into an inquiry regarding his interpretation of his obligations under the final decree. We concluded that the decrees were not ambiguous in their terms, and thus were enforceable.

STATUTE OF LIMITATIONS

A hearing was held on Petitioner's December 15, 1981 motion to reduce accrued child support arrearages to judgment. Petitioner was awarded a judgment of $7,900.00. The district court found that Respondent had not made any of the monthly child support payments required by the amended final decree. The $7,900.00 figure was based on the calculation that the monthly payments should have been made during the seventy-nine months that elapsed between the entry of the original May 26, 1970 divorce decree and January 28, 1977, the date that the youngest child reached majority.

Respondent's central contention is that Petitioner's action to collect accrued arrearages at this late date is barred by the statute of limitations. He maintains that over eleven and one-half years had passed between May 1970 entry of the original final decree and Petitioner's December 1981 petition. Respondent primarily maintains that the seven year statute of limitations applicable to judgments in effect in December 1981 (formerly compiled as NMSA 1978, Section 37-1-2) should apply and bar any claim for arrearages that accrued seven years prior to the date Petitioner filed her petition.

Respondent's argument thus presents the question of whether accrued and unpaid periodic child support installments mandated in a New Mexico divorce decree are considered final judgments in New Mexico on the date they become due. This appears to be a case of first impression as the parties have not cited, and our research has not revealed, any New Mexico authority directly on point.

The applicability of any statute of limitations period will depend on the characterization of monthly child support installments as they become due. Both *Corliss v. Corliss*, 89 N.M. 235, 549 P.2d 1070 (1976), and *Slade v. Slade*, 81 N.M. 462, 468 P.2d 627 (1970), involved the characterization and enforcement of monthly child support provisions incorporated in *foreign* divorce decrees. In *Slade* this Court considered whether the New Mexico statute of limitations applicable to judgments applied to bar recovery of accrued child support arrearages under a Kansas divorce decree. Looking to Kansas law to determine the nature of a child support award, we concluded that the child support award was a judgment in installments. We further concluded that the seven year New Mexico statute of limitations then applicable to judgments (formerly compiled as NMSA 1953, Section 23-1-2 (Supp.1969)) applied and began to run on each monthly installment on the date it became due and unpaid. Accordingly, all uncollected installments that accrued more than seven years prior to the initiation of the action to collect the arrearages were deemed subject to the seven year statute of limitations applicable to judgments generally.

In considering the enforceability of a Missouri divorce decree, this Court in *Corliss* looked to Missouri law to determine whether child support awarded by the decree was subject to retroactive modification. This Court concluded that since Missouri courts had no power to modify or forgive accrued child support arrearages under a Missouri decree, New Mexico Courts could not do so.

Both *Slade* and *Corliss* lend support to a characterization of each monthly installment as a final judgment. In both cases, once the installment had become due, the amount payable was essentially deemed liquidated and, as with final judgments, not subject to retroactive modification. *Corliss* in particular concluded that child support arrearages would not be modified once accrued. Although this conclusion arose out of an application of Missouri law to a Missouri decree, the same

(continues)

characterization has obtained regarding New Mexico decrees.

In *Gomez v. Gomez*, 92 N.M. 310, 587 P.2d 963 (1978), *overruled on other grounds, Montoya v. Montoya*, 95 N.M. 189, 619 P.2d 1234 (1980), this Court considered whether weekly child support installment payments mandated in a New Mexico decree were modifiable once accrued. The then controlling New Mexico statute, NMSA 1953, Section 22-7-6(C) (Supp. 1975) was compared with the substantially identical Missouri statute construed in *Corliss*. This Court held that, as with accrued Missouri installments, past due child support payments mandated in a New Mexico divorce decree were deemed not subject to retroactive modification.

Neither the reasoning nor the holding of *Gomez* bear out Petitioner's assertion that applying a statute of limitations to bar recovery of support installments is inconsistent with the proposition that such installments cannot be modified. Retroactive modification of child support awards is an issue distinct from the issue concerning the applicability of a statute of limitations period. Application of a statute of limitations merely bars the remedy on a stale claim without determining the underlying validity of that claim or modifying it in any way. *See Davis v. Savage*, 50 N.M. 30, 168 P.2d 851 (1946).

The fact[s] of *Gomez* presented the question of retroactive modification of child support payments. It did not address the issue of a statute of limitations period as it would apply to the collection of accrued child support installments. As such, the holding is not determinative of the instant statute of limitations question. Furthermore, *Gomez* cites *Catlett v. Catlett*, 412 P.2d 942 (Okla. 1966) for the crucial proposition that accrued child support arrearages cannot be modified. While passing judgment on this question, the *Catlett* court also considered the applicability of the Oklahoma statute of limitations to a collection action for delinquent child support payments. In this regard the court stated:

> This apparently is a new question for the Oklahoma court but the rule appears to be well settled that where a divorce decree provides for the payment of alimony or support in installments the right to enforce payment accrues on each payment as it matures and the statute of limitations begins to run on each installment from the time fixed for its payment.

Id. at 946. The *Catlett* court thus properly viewed the application of a statute of limitations period as being compatible with its conclusion that accrued child support obligations were not modifiable.

Aside from Oklahoma, numerous other jurisdictions consider child support installments final judgments and hold that a statute of limitations begins to run on each installment as it becomes due. See 24 Am.Jur.2d *Divorce and Separation* § 863 (1966). In a number of decisions this construction has barred collection of child support installments accruing beyond the relevant limitations period. *See, e.g., Corbett v. Corbett*, 116 Ariz. 350, 569 P.2d 292 (App. 1977); *Bruce v. Froeb*, 15 Ariz. App. 306, 488 P.2d 662 (1971); *Hauck v. Schuck*, 143 Colo. 324, 353 P.2d 79 (1960); *Turinsky v. Turinsky*, 359 S.W.2d 114 (Tex. Civ. App. 1962); *Seeley v. Park*, 532 P.2d 684 (Utah 1975). Indeed, rendering accrued child support

installments individually subject to a limitations period appears to be the majority rule in the United States. Annot., 70 A.L.R.2d 1250 (1960); *cf.* 27B C.J.S. *Divorce* § 256 (1959) (outlining the analogous majority rule that as to judgments for alimony in installments, the pertinent statute of limitations begins to run on each installment as it falls due).

Since the installment obligations were clearly embodied in a final decree, they were a product of a precise judicial determination of Respondent's obligations. The authority is extensive and well-established that each monthly child support installment mandated in the final decree was a final judgment, not subject to retroactive modification.

Having determined that each installment was a final judgment, we turn to the question of which statute of limitations period should apply. We note at the outset that there is no special statute of limitations specified under child support or the enforcement provisions, respectively, of NMSA 1978, Section 40-4-7 or 40-4-19 (Repl. Pamp. 1983).

In *Coe's Estate*, 56 N.M. 578, 247 P.2d 162, the ex-wife sought a judgment for arrearages pursuant to a divorce decree mandating undivided child support for the minor children under her custody. This Court first held that the child support order was a judgment in monthly installments granted only during the minority of the children, thereby precluding any accrual of liability after the youngest child reached majority. The next holding applied the general judgment statute of limitations then obtaining under former NMSA 1941, Section 27-102 to bar recovery since the claim was filed more than seven years after the youngest child reached majority.

Similarly, in *Slade* this Court considered the applicability of a statute of limitations period to an action on a Kansas decree mandating periodic child support payments. Having concluded, as we do here, that the mandated installments were judgments, we there applied the seven year judgment statute of limitations under former NMSA 1953, Section 23-1-2 (Supp. 1969). *Slade* and *Coe's Estate* together provide clear authority for our application of the judgment statute of limitation. In addition, virtually all of the out-of-state decisions we have cited regarding construction of accrued installments as judgments have applied their statute which limits executions on judgments. *Corbett v. Corbett*, 116 Ariz. 350, 569 P.2d 292 and *Bruce v. Froeb*, 15 Ariz. App. 306, 488 P.2d 662 (both applying the general five-year Arizona statute of limitations applicable to execution on judgments); *Hauck v. Schuck*, 143 Colo. 324, 353 P.2d 79 (applying twenty-year limitations period pertaining to execution on judgments rendered in Colorado); *Turinsky v. Turinsky*, 359 S.W.2d 114 (applying general ten-year Texas statute limiting execution on judgments); *Seeley v. Park*, 532 P.2d 684 (eight-year statute of limitations pertaining to actions on judgments applies to suit for collection of accrued child support arrearages).

The judgment statute here strikes a reasonable balance between the competing interests of enforcing the supporting parent's right to periodic payments on the one hand and protecting the obligor parent from stale claims on the other.

The determination that accrued child support installments are final judgments of record results in the application of the longest possible statute of limitations period available to a collection action by the supporting parent. Application of the catchall four year limitations statute of NMSA 1978 Section 37-1-4 would provide for an inordinately short period in which a custodial parent could assert the child support claim. This would be clearly inimical to the best interests of the child, would place an undue burden on the custodial parent, and might encourage dilatory tactics on the part of obligor parents intent on avoiding their child support duties.

Accordingly, we hold that the judgment statute of limitations that was in effect at the time Petitioner filed her December 15, 1981 petition applies. This was the seven year statute codified at NMSA 1978, Section 37-1-2 (Orig. Pamp.). We note, however, that the judgment statute has since been amended and now provides for a fourteen year limitations period. NMSA 1978, § 37-1-2 (Cum. Supp. 1983).

Applying the relevant seven year judgment statute of the facts of the instant case, we conclude that Petitioner is barred from recovering the installment arrearages that accrued more than seven years prior to her December 15, 1981 petition. The trial court was incorrect in awarding judgment based on a seventy-nine month arrearage period. The only installments which Petitioner may properly collect are those falling due between December 15, 1974, the last payment not barred by the judgment statute, and January 28, 1977, the date that the youngest child attained majority—a period of twenty-five months. The trial court should have awarded judgment to Petitioner in the amount of $2,500.00.

OFFSET

Respondent also asserts that he is entitled to an offset against any arrearages not barred by the statute of limitations. This offset claim is based in large part on the fact that Respondent has made substantial expenditures connected with the care and support of the son that has been living with him since December 1972. While it is entirely commendable that Respondent voluntarily undertook the responsibilities associated with the direct care and treatment of his son, we nevertheless cannot agree that Respondent's actions merit an offset under the circumstances of this case.

As we have previously concluded, the amended final decree clearly set forth Respondent's child support obligations and was fully enforceable at all time[s] relevant herein. Respondent, as the obligor parent, cannot by his actions unilaterally alter the support obligations set forth in the decree. As we stated in our discussion concerning the asserted ambiguity of the decree, Respondent properly should have petitioned to modify the child support terms of the decree in light of this asserted change in circumstances. Modification of support obligations is strictly a matter to be determined by the courts. Not having pursued this avenue, Respondent cannot now claim an offset for his self-imposed expenditures, substantial though they may have been. *See Baures v. Baures*, 13 Ariz. App. 515, 478 P.2d 130 (1970) and authorities cited therein. As stated in *Baures*:

A father who is required to make periodic payments for the support of minor children has an opportunity to relieve himself of that liability by a petition to modify the decree *in futuro* but he cannot remain silent while the installments accrue and then claim credit for his voluntary acts. In view of the mandatory requirements of the divorce decree as to payments of the monthly support installments to appellant, although it is to appellee's credit that he cared for his [child], he was a volunteer and is not thereby relieved from the obligations of the decree.

Id. at 519, 478 P.2d at 134. The district court in the instant case properly disallowed any and all of Respondent's offset claims.

LACHES

Respondent next maintains that he has been prejudiced by Petitioner's delay in pursuing her action and that laches should therefore bar any claim for arrearages not barred by the statute of limitations. We find this contention without merit.

There is sufficient evidence to support the district court's determination that Respondent would not be unduly prejudiced by the judgment for arrearages. The standard review on appeal is whether substantial evidence reasonably supports the factual determinations of the trial court. *Toltec International, Inc. v. Village of Ruidoso*, 95 N.M. 82, 619 P.2d 186 (1980). Resolving all disputes and reasonable inferences in favor of the successful party below and refusing to reweigh the evidence, we conclude that the trial court properly determined that laches does not apply in this case.

ATTORNEY'S FEES

Petitioner contends that she should be awarded attorney's fees related to the instant appeal, and for her presentation at the district court level. The district court in its final order of August 30, 1982 did not include an award of attorney's fees at the level as Petitioner had requested but noted that all findings and awards not specifically included were denied. This should properly be interpreted as a finding against Petitioner on the attorney's fees issue. *See Maynard v. Western Bank*, 99 N.M. 135, 654 P.2d 1035 (1982). We have carefully reviewed the record and conclude that substantial evidence supports the district court's denial of attorney's fees. *Toltec International, Inc. v. Village of Ruidoso*, 95 N.M. 82, 619 P.2d 186; *Cave v. Cave*, 81 N.M. 797, 474 P.2d 480 (1970). Furthermore, we conclude that Petitioner does not merit attorney's fees for her instant cross-appeal.

The trial court is affirmed on all issues except that regarding the application of a statute of limitations period to an action on unpaid child support installments. The cause is remanded to the district court for further proceedings consistent with this opinion.

IT IS SO ORDERED.

RIORDAN and STOWERS, JJ., concur.

Dwonna Gayle Gwaltney CARDWELL, Appellant,

v.

Kenneth Wayne GWALTNEY, Appellee.

No. 87A01–9002–CV–80.

Court of Appeals of Indiana, First District.

July 17, 1990.

556 N.E.2d 953 (Ind. Ct. App. 1990)

OBERTSON, Judge.

The sole issue raised in this appeal is whether an individual should be absolved from paying child support because of his incarceration.

The underlying material facts show that the appellant Cardwell and the appellee Gwaltney were divorced with Gwaltney ordered to pay child support. About a year and one-half later, Gwaltney filed a petition to modify the support order based upon the reason that he had spent a year in jail. Gwaltney sought to be absolved from the support which had accrued during that year and to have future support reduced. Cardwell and Gwaltney reached an agreement that, among other things, excused Gwaltney from paying support for the year he was imprisoned. The trial court approved the agreement; however, that agreement was challenged when the county prosecuting attorney appeared in the matter and sought to set aside the agreement because Cardwell had been a recipient of AFDC funds through the State and had assigned her support rights. The trial court refused to set aside the earlier agreements with this appeal resulting.

Even though the trial judge was prompted by equitable concerns when Gwaltney was excused from paying support[,] the law is that any modification of a support order must act prospectively:

In *Biedron v. Biedron* (1958), 128 Ind. App. 299, 148 N.E.2d 209, the Appellate Court of Indiana said, "in this state after support installments have accrued, the court is without power to reduce, annul or vacate such orders retrospectively, and therefore, the court committed error in attempting to do so." (Citations omitted). Therefore, payments must be made in the manner, amount, and at the times required by the support order embodied in the divorce decree until such order is modified or set aside. *Stitle v. Stitle* (1964), 245 Ind. 168, 197 N.E.2d 174, Indiana does permit cancellation or modification of support orders

as to future payments; but, all modifications operate prospectively. *Kniffen v. Courtney* (1971), 148 Ind. App. 358, 266 N.E.2d 72; *Haycraft v. Haycraft* (1978), Ind. App. [176 Ind. App. 211], 375 N.E.2d 252.

Jahn v. Jahn (1979), 179 Ind. App. 368, 385 N.E.2d 488, 490. See also *O'Neil v. O'Neil* (1988), Ind. App., 517 N.E.2d 433 (transfer granted on other grounds).

Additionally, I.C. 31-2-11-12 provides:

Modification of delinquent support payment.

(a) Except as provided in subsection (b), *a court may not retroactively modify* an obligor's duty to pay a delinquent support payment.

(b) A court with jurisdiction over a support order may modify an obligor's duty to pay a support payment that becomes due:

(1) After notice of a petition to modify the support order has been given to each obligee; and

(2) Before a final order concerning the petition for modification is entered. (Emphasis added.)

Although the Indiana Child Support Guidelines, effective October 1, 1989, were not officially in use at the time of the trial court's decision in this appeal, we are of the opinion that a part of the commentary to Ind. Child Support Guideline 2 takes into consideration existing statutes and case law as heretofore cited. That part of the commentary reads:

Even in situations where the non-custodial parent has no income, Courts have routinely established a child support obligation at some minimum level. An obligor cannot be held in contempt for failure to pay support when he does not have the means to pay, but the obligation accrues and serves as a reimbursement to the custodial parent, or, more likely, to the welfare department if he later acquires the ability to meet his obligation.

We conclude that the trial court erred in retroactively excusing Gwaltney's support obligation for the time he was incarcerated.

Cause reversed and remanded for further action not inconsistent with this opinion.

Reversed and remanded.

RATLIFF, C.J., and CONOVER, J., concur.

COMMONWEALTH of Pennsylvania

v.

Adam DeMICHEL, Appellant.

Supreme Court of Pennsylvania.

April 22, 1971.

Rehearing Denied May 21, 1971.

442 Pa. 553, 277 A.2d 159 (1971)

OPINION OF THE COURT

ROBERTS, Justice.

Upon the basis of various lottery paraphernalia seized pursuant to a search warrant and introduced into evidence at trial, appellant Adam DeMichel was convicted of setting up and maintaining an illegal lottery and sentenced to undergo imprisonment for three to twelve months and to pay a fine of five hundred dollars plus costs. In this appeal from the judgment of sentence, appellant asserts that the evidence that led to his conviction was the fruit of an illegally executed search warrant. Upon reviewing the record we must agree.

Appellant was arrested on January 14, 1967, during a police search of his home at 707 Sears Street in Philadelphia. Also present at the time were appellant's wife and daughter. Upon initial entry into the house, the police observed appellant at a kitchen sink attempting to destroy rice paper, and in the course of the ensuing search they found and seized other sheets of rice paper containing several thousand lottery bets, other blank sheets of rice paper, lists of names, adding machine tape, and other lottery paraphernalia.

Prior to trial appellant filed a timely motion to suppress these items, and an evidentiary hearing was held on March 4, 1968. From testimony elicited at that hearing it appeared that five police officers armed with a search warrant arrived at the front of appellant's two-story row house at 12:40 p.m. on January 14, 1967. All were dressed in plain clothes, and one of their number, Officer Daniel Creden, approached the front door alone carrying a cardboard box in an attempt to create the false impression of a deliveryman.

Corporal Frank Hall, another member of the raiding party, testified as follows concerning the execution of the search warrant:

"Q.   Did * * * [appellant] admit you to the premises?"

"A.   No. We had to gain entrance."

"Q.   How?"

"A.   We broke the door down."

"Q.   With or without prior warning?"

"A.   With."

* * *

"Q.   What type of warning did you give to the occupants of the house before breaking in the door?"

"A.   I told him we were police officers, we had a warrant."

"Q.   How much time elapsed between the time you said that and when you broke in the door, approximately?"

"A.   Approximately ten or fifteen seconds."

Upon cross-examination by appellant's counsel, Hall restated his version of the entry into the house but did not reaffirm that he *personally* gave any warnings to the occupants.[1]

At the conclusion of the hearing, appellant's counsel argued that the affidavit supporting the issuance of the search warrant was defective and that the police's method of entry into appellant's home was illegal. The hearing judge was unpersuaded and the motion for suppression denied.[2]

Appellant thereafter waived a jury, and his case proceeded to trial on May 16, 1968, before a different judge of the Philadelphia Court of Common Pleas. During the Commonwealth's case in chief, new and different evidence came to light concerning the execution of the search warrant. Corporal Hall again described the events surrounding the police's entry into appellant's house but failed to mention that he had given any warnings to the occupants, and Officer Creden, the policeman who actually knocked on appellant's door, gave the following testimony:

"Q.   Now, sir, would you relate to the Court specifically in detail what occurred from the time you arrived at these premises until the time entry was made?"

"A.   Well, I guess we arrived around 12:40 p.m., I walked west on Sears Street, at 7th Street, I went up and knocked on the door. A few seconds, the blind was lifted up, and I announced that we were police. The blinds dropped, and we proceeded to knock the door down."

"Q.   Within what period of time, sir?"

"A.   From the time that the blinds were dropped?"

"Q.   Yes, sir."

"A.   Ten, five, I don't know how many seconds."

"Q.   Seconds, sir?"

---

1. Instead, Hall used the pronoun "we":

    Q.   "And would you describe specifically, sir, the manner in which you attempted to gain entrance to these premises?"

    A.   "We knocked on the door, and after hearing sound coming from inside the house *we* announced ourselves as police officers and that we had a warrant * * *."

277 A.2d 11.

    Q.   "What did you do?"

    A.   "We announced ourselves as police officers and we had a search warrant * * *."

2. The question of the sufficiency of the affidavit is not pressed on this appeal.

(continues)

"A. Well, as soon as the blinds dropped, I called the fellow officer who had the sledge hammer and knocked the door down."

"Q. Just to make the record perfectly clear, when you first knocked, you did not say anything at all, did you?"

"A. No. I just knocked."

"Q. And then, according to your testimony, someone lifted up the blinds?"

"A. Yes, sir."

"Q. Could you tell whether that was male or female, sir?"

"A. I couldn't tell. I believe there were curtains behind the blinds. I couldn't see who it was."

"Q. Then the blinds dropped, sir, is that correct?"

"A. That is correct."

"Q. And then you made an announcement that you were police officers, is that correct, sir?"

"A. No, it is not. While the blinds were up, I said, 'Open up, it is the police.'"

"Q. *And that is all you said, sir?*"

"A. *Yes.*" (Emphasis added.)

Appellant was adjudged guilty, but the trial judge granted his post-trial motion in arrest of judgment on the ground that the evidence at trial demonstrated that the officer who executed the search warrant had not announced their purpose before resorting to forcible entry.

* * *

The Superior Court, reasoning that a trial judge has no power to overrule the decision of a suppression hearing judge, reversed the order granting arrest of judgment and remanded the case for sentencing, 214 Pa. Super. 392, 257 A.2d 608. Following the imposition of sentence, appellant again appealed to the Superior Court. That court affirmed the judgment of sentence, 216 Pa. Super. 804, 263 A.2d 480, and we granted allocatur.

Preliminarily we note our disagreement with the Superior Court's apparent categorical holding that a trial judge is powerless to overrule the decision of a suppression hearing judge. While "[w]e impliedly held in *Commonwealth v. Warfield*, 418 Pa. 301, 211 A.2d 452 (1965) that the trial judge cannot reverse *on the same record* at trial the decision made after the pretrial suppression hearing * * *," *Commonwealth v. Washington*, 428 Pa. 131, 133 n. 2, 236 A.2d 772, 773 n. 2 (1968) (emphasis added), the same does not hold true when the trial judge's different ruling is based upon new and different evidence. When information comes to light after the suppression hearing clearly demonstrating that the evidence sought to be introduced by the Commonwealth is constitutionally tainted, no considertion [sic] of justice or interest of sound judicial administration would be furthered by prohibiting the trial judge from ruling it inadmissible. Although a favorable ruling at the suppression hearing relieves the Commonwealth of the burden of proving a second time at trial that its evidence was constitutionally obtained, the trial judge must exclude evidence previously held admissible at the suppression hearing when the defendant proves by a preponderance of new evidence at trial that the evidence sought to be introduced by the Commonwealth was obtained by unconstitutional means.[3]

Although we thus disagree with the Superior Court, we believe that the trial judge in the instant case erred in granting appellant's motion in arrest of judgment upon the basis of a finding that the police officers executing the search warrant did not properly announce their purpose before entering appellant's house. Officer Creden testified unequivocally at trial that *he* had made no announcement of purpose, but he did not state that his fellow officers were similarly mute or contradict Corporal Hall's suppression hearing testimony that Hall had made such an announcement of purpose. That being so, the record at trial in no way proves the absence of a proper police announcement of purpose.

Despite the foregoing, we are nevertheless persuaded for other reasons that the search of appellant's home was illegally executed. It is settled in this Commonwealth that the Fourth Amendment prohibition against unreasonable searches and seizures demands that before a police officer enters upon private premises to conduct a search or to make an arrest he must, absent exigent circumstances, give notice of his identity and announce his purpose. *Commonwealth v. Newman*, 429 Pa. 441, 240 A.2d 795 (1968); *United States ex rel. Manduchi v. Tracy*, 350 F.2d 658 (3d Cir.), *cert. denied*, 382 U.S. 943, 86 S. Ct. 390, 15 L. Ed. 2d 353 (1965); *United States ex rel. Ametrane v. Gable*, 276 F. Supp. 555 (E.D. Pa. 1967). The purpose of this announcement rule is that "* * * the dignity and privacy protected by the Fourth Amendment demand a certain propriety on the part of policemen even after they have been authorized to invade an individual's privacy. Regardless of how great the probable cause to believe a man guilty of a crime, *he must be given a reasonable opportunity to surrender his privacy voluntarily.*" *United States ex rel. Ametrane v. Gable*, supra, 276 F. Supp. at 559 (emphasis

---

3. At the time of appellant's trial, the method of pretrial litigation of the legality of searches and seizures was governed by Pa. R. Crim. P. 2001, 19 P.S. Appendix, which did not expressly speak to the question [of] whether a trial judge could overrule the decision of the suppression hearing judge. Rule 2001 was superseded by a 1969 amendment to Pa. R. Crim. P. 323, which consolidated and made uniform the procedures relating to pretrial suppression of any evidence alleged to have been obtained in violation of a defendant's constitutional rights. Even this new consolidated rule recognized that there are some circumstances in which the trial judge should be free to exclude evidence previously held admissible.

"If the [suppression hearing] court determines that the evidence is admissible, such determination shall be final, conclusive and binding at trial, *except upon a showing of evidence which was theretofore unavailable.* * * *"

Pa. R. Crim. P. 323(j) (emphasis added).

added). Accordingly, even where the police duly announced their identity and purpose, forcible entry in still unreasonable and hence violative of the Fourth Amendment if the occupants of the premises sought to be entered and searched are not first given an opportunity to surrender the premises voluntarily. See *United States ex rel. Manduchi v. Tracy*, 350 F.2d at 662.

The Commonwealth appears to concede this proposition of constitutional law but argues that the occupants of appellant's house were in fact given an adequate opportunity to open the door voluntarily. Corporal Hall and Officer Creden testified that they and the other officers began to break down the front door of appellant's house five to fifteen seconds after announcing their presence and purpose. We cannot deem this a reasonable sufficient period of time. In *Newman*, supra, for example, this Court stated that "a mere twenty second delay in answering the door cannot constitute support for a belief that evidence was being destroyed * * *." 429 Pa. at 448, 240 A.2d at 798. And in *Ametrane*, supra, the United States District Court for the Eastern District of Pennsylvania noted that "[e]ven if * * *[the occupant] had known the officers to be policemen, he might have had countless legitimate reasons for taking a minute to answer the door." 276 F. Supp. at 559.

In both of the above cases the occupants were known by the police to be on the second floor whereas here Corporal Hall and Officer Creden testified that they saw someone peering at them through the blinds of a first story window located very near the front door. Given the close proximity of this person to the door, we are urged to conclude that a mere five to fifteen second delay was reasonable. But even in these circumstances this might be entirely innocent "for countless legitimate reasons." Appellant's wife, for example, testified that it was she who peered through the window and that her delay in responding was occasioned by her being attired in a nightgown and having to go to the kitchen to put on a robe. Regardless of the truth of her testimony, it serves to illustrate that a five to fifteen second delay was insufficient for the police to have formed a reasonable belief that the occupants of appellant's house did not intend to permit peaceable entry.

Finally, we are not persuaded that this case presents "exigent circumstances" suspending the ordinary requirement that the occupants of premises sought to be searched be given a reasonable opportunity to open the door voluntarily. The police officers involved were seeking to execute a warrant authorizing them to enter, search for and seize lottery paraphernalia, and from their prior experience with this type of mission they reasonably believed that some of the paraphernalia would be in the form of almost instantaneously destructible rice paper. However, as we stated in *Newman*:

"The fact that some lottery paraphernalia is easily destroyed does not justify the suspension of the Fourth Amendment in all lottery prosecutions. One of the prices we have to pay for the security which the Fourth Amendment bestows upon us is the risk that an occasional guilty party will escape."

429 Pa. at 448, 240 A.2d at 798 (citation omitted). To excuse the police's failure to announce their purpose and presence and thereafter to allow a reasonable time for the voluntary surrender of the premises, there " * * * must be more than the presumption that the evidence *would* be destroyed because it *could* be easily done." *State v. Mendoza*, 104 Ariz. 395, 399, 454 P.2d 140, 144 (1969).

The testimony that appellant was found standing by a kitchen sink attempting to destroy rice paper is without significance.

"It goes without saying that in determining the lawfulness of entry and the existence of probable cause we may concern ourselves only with what the officers had reason to believe *at the time of their entry. Johnson v. United States*, 333 U.S. 10, 17, 68 S. Ct. 367, 370–371, 92 L. Ed. 436 (1948). As the [Supreme] Court said in *United States v. Di Re*, 332 U.S. 581, 595, 68 S. Ct. 222, 229, 92 L. Ed. 210 (1948), "a search is not to be made legal by what it turns up. In law it is good *or bad* when it starts and does not change character from what is dug up subsequently. (Emphasis added.)"

Ker v. California, 374 U.S. 23, 40 n. 12, 83 S. Ct. 1623, 1633 n. 12, 10 L. Ed. 2d 726 (1963).

We hold that forcible entry in the circumstances of this case violated the standards of the Fourth Amendment and that the fruits of the ensuing search were improperly admitted at appellant's trial. Accordingly, the order of the Superior Court is reversed. The judgment of sentence is vacated and the case remanded for a new trial.

BELL, C. J., did not participate in the consideration or decision of this case.

* * *

COHEN, J., did not participate in the decision of this case.

* * *

POMEROY, J., filed a dissenting opinion, in which JONES, J., joins.

* * *

EAGEN, J., concurs in the result.

* * *

POMEROY, Justice (dissenting).

* * *

COMMONWEALTH

v.

John J. SHEA.

No. 93–P–1066.

Appeals Court of Massachusetts, Plymouth.

Argued Sept. 12, 1994. Decided Jan. 5, 1995.

Further Appellate Review Denied Feb. 28, 1995.

38 Mass. App. Ct. 7, 644 N.E.2d 244 (1995)

PERRETTA, Justice.

On the afternoon of June 15, 1991, the defendant and his friend invited two women who were sun bathing on the banks of the Charles River to board the defendant's boat and go for a ride. Once the women were aboard, the defendant headed out to the open sea. An hour later and about five miles offshore from Boston, he stopped the boat, disrobed, and made sexual remarks and advances toward the women. He ignored all requests that he dress and stop his offensive behavior. When the women demanded that he return them to Boston, he threw them overboard and drove away without a backward glance. The women were rescued after managing to swim within shouting distance of a sailboat. On evidence of these acts, a jury found the defendant guilty, as to each woman, of kidnapping, attempted murder, assault and battery by means of a dangerous weapon (the ocean), and indecent assault and battery. The defendant argues on appeal that the trial judge erroneously denied (1) his request for a continuance of the trial; (2) his motion in limine by which he sought to preclude the Commonwealth's use of a videotape showing the ocean from the perspective of the women in the water and the defendant on his boat; and (3) his motion for required findings of not guilty on all the indictments. Although we conclude that the ocean is not a dangerous weapon within the meaning of G.L. c. 265, § 15A, we affirm the kidnapping and attempted murder convictions.[1]

1. *The motion for a continuance.* Trial counsel was appointed to represent the defendant on August 29, 1991.[2] On February 21, 1992, he filed a motion seeking funds for a psychiatric evaluation of the defendant. The motion was allowed that same day, and the case was continued to April 21, 1992, "for trial." One week before the scheduled trial date, counsel sought a continuance of at least two months. The

Commonwealth opposed the motion on numerous grounds, not the least of which was the fact that the victims had been receiving threatening mail and telephone calls. The judge denied the request and the defendant claims error. "[A] motion for continuance . . . lies within the sound discretion of the judge, whose action will not be disturbed unless there is a patent abuse of that discretion, which is to be determined in the circumstances of each case." *Commonwealth v. Bettencourt,* 361 Mass. 515, 517–518, 281 N.E.2d 220 (1972). We relate the circumstances of the denial of the defendant's motion.

An affidavit and a letter from a psychiatrist, dated March 17, 1992, were attached to the motion for a continuance. It appears from these documents that the defendant's medical history indicated that he had suffered a series of head injuries from which he might have sustained brain trauma and that, according to the psychiatrist, the "charges now pending against him may reflect behavior caused by those head injuries." As further stated by the psychiatrist: "For a more conclusive answer to the question of the effect of Mr. Shea's head traumas to his alleged criminal acts, it would be necessary for him to undergo independent extensive neuropsychological testing and, in addition, have a BEAM study of the electrical activity of his brain."

As of April 14, 1992, the date of the hearing on the motion for a continuance, the BEAM study had been completed and the results reported to the psychiatrist. A copy of the report which had been submitted to the psychiatrist was also attached to the motion. The report recited the following conclusion of the BEAM study: "Overall this study is quite compatible with a history of multiple head injuries and suggests a generalized encephalopathy with irritable qualities falling just short of being a seizure disorder. The latter diagnosis, of course, should be made on clinical grounds."

It was not until the psychiatrist was called to testify at trial that the defendant's theory of defense took on a clarity: on the afternoon of June 15, 1991, he was experiencing a temporal lobe seizure which prevented him from formulating the specific intent necessary for criminal liability for his actions. At the time of the hearing on the motion, however, the trial judge was informed only that a continuance of two months was necessary so that in addition to the psychiatrist, various other named medical professionals could also review the results of the BEAM study and conduct psychoneurological testing of the defendant. Even were we to conclude that an adequate case for granting the motion had been made at that time, but see *Commonwealth v. Bettencourt,* 361 Mass. at 517–518, 281 N.E.2d 220, the defendant has failed to show that his defense was prejudiced by the denial of his request.

Although the defendant argues that the denial of the continuance prevented psychoneurological testing which would have allowed the psychiatrist to opine whether, at the time in question, the defendant was experiencing a temporal lobe seizure, the psychiatrist's testimony does not support the claim. The psychiatrist testified on voir dire that

1. The defendant was also found guilty on two counts of indecent assault and battery. Because he assented to those convictions being placed on file, they are not before us. See *Commonwealth v. Delgado,* 367 Mass. 432, 438, 326 N.E.2d 716 (1975).

2. Appellate counsel was not trial counsel.

had additional psychoneurological testing been available, he could be more "definitive" or "conclusive" in his opinion concerning the defendant's potential for temporal lobe seizures.[3] The psychiatrist nonetheless could, and did, relate to the jury that it was his opinion, to the requisite degree of medical certainty, that the defendant's "history, test results, and behavior is consistent with a temporal lobe disorder."

As for the more immediate question of whether the defendant was experiencing a seizure at the time of the incident, the psychiatrist testified, on voir dire, that he could not say "with [a] high degree of certainty that at that moment on that boat, that type of episode occurred." Rather, he could state only that "this individual, with his condition, has a high potential for things like that happening." At no time was the psychiatrist asked whether psychoneurological testing could reveal to a reasonable degree of medical certainty whether a person who suffered from temporal lobe disorder had in fact experienced a seizure at a specific time in the past.

In sum, the defendant's temporal lobe disorder was fully presented to the jury. Although the defendant's expert and the expert for the Commonwealth agreed that the defendant's BEAM study indicated a temporal lobe abnormality, they sharply disagreed on the issue of whether the defendant's actions were consistent or inconsistent with a temporal lobe seizure. However, any weaknesses that the jury might have found in the testimony of the defendant's psychiatrist cannot, on the record before us, be attributed to a lack of psychoneurological testing and the denial of the continuance.

2. *The videotapes.* At trial, the Commonwealth was allowed to use two chalks, that is, videotapes, to illustrate to the jury the victims' testimony concerning the condition of the ocean when the defendant threw them into the water and abandoned them. The first videotape depicted the victims' view from the water as they watched the defendant drive away, and the second showed how two people in the water would appear from the vantage point of the back of the boat as it drove away from them. The Commonwealth argued that the tapes were relevant to the defendant's murderous intent. After an *in camera* viewing of the tapes, the trial judge ruled that the videos could be used as chalks. Immediately before the jury viewed the tapes, the trial judge instructed: "This is not offered for your consideration as evidence in this case. It is offered in the nature of what we refer to as a chalk to the extent that it may be of assistance to you in understanding the evidence that you have heard in view of the similarities, if any, and it's for you to determine if there are any similarities

in the circumstances of the events of June 15, 1991." See generally Liacos, Massachusetts Evidence § 11.13.2 (6th ed. 1994) ("Chalks are used to illustrate testimony . . . they are not evidence in the ordinary sense of the word").

The defendant complains that the tapes were a prejudicial recreation of the crime, that they were not based upon the evidence, and that they were inflammatory. We see no abuse of discretion or other error in the trial judge's decision to allow the Commonwealth to use the videotapes as chalks.

"Whether the conditions were sufficiently similar to make the observation [offered by the demonstration] of any value in aiding the jury to pass upon the issue submitted to them [is] primarily for the trial judge to determine as a matter of discretion. [The judge's] decision in this respect will not be interfered with unless plainly wrong." *Commonwealth v. Chipman*, 418 Mass. 262, 270–271, 635 N.E.2d 1204 (1994), quoting from *Field v. Gowdy*, 199 Mass. 568, 574, 85 N.E. 884 (1908). See also *Terrio v. McDonough*, 16 Mass. App. Ct. 163, 173, 450 N.E.2d 190 (1983). To the extent the videotapes do not depict anyone being thrown from the boat into the ocean, they are not a recreation of the crime. The tapes otherwise essentially track the victims' testimony.

State police officers Earle S. Sterling and Leonard Coppengrath testified that at 9:30 a.m. on April 15, 1992, they and a number of their associates boarded a boat and proceeded to the point five miles offshore from Boston where the women had been pulled from the water. They described the weather conditions that day as well as the height of the waves and the temperature of the water. They had video cameras and other equipment with them. When they reached their destination, Sterling and another man, who was holding a camera, jumped overboard. Once in the water, the other man held the camera about two inches (the eye level of the victims) above the water, and filmed the boat as it drove off. Meanwhile, Coppengrath, who remained on the boat, focused a camera on the two men in the water as another one of the men slowly drove away.[4] After proceeding about one-half mile, the men in the water were no longer visible from the boat. Coppengrath then panned the "area from where we had come and to where we were heading and circled across the skyline of Boston towards the point in Hull which is the closest point of land to where we were."

There is no persuasive force to the defendant's argument that the Commonwealth's use of the videotapes was no

---

3. The psychiatrist had reviewed some psychoneurological test results which were in the defendant's medical records. When asked by defense counsel whether he could be more conclusive in his opinion had "more extensive psychoneurological testing" been done, the psychiatrist responded, "[Y]es, everything that enhances helps become more definitive until ultimately, hopefully, you can become almost conclusive about it. I'm only saying I can't be conclusive, I can only render an opinion at this time."

---

4. Although the victims testified that the defendant sped away in the boat, that testimony did not require preclusion of the use of the videotapes, see *Commonwealth v. Chipman*, 418 Mass. at 270–271, 635 N.E.2d 1204 (1994), especially in light of the trial judge's instructions to the jury prior to the viewing of the films.

We also think it inconsequential that there was no evidence to show that the defendant turned to watch the victims as he drove off. The information being illustrated pertained to the water conditions and surroundings, which remained the same irrespective of any particular vantage point, and the defendant's awareness of them.

(continues)

more than a disguised inflammatory appeal to the jurors to put themselves in the place of the victims. See, *for example, Commonwealth v. Sevieri,* 21 Mass. App. Ct. 745, 753–754, 490 N.E.2d 481 (1986). The Commonwealth was entitled to dispel any notion that the defendant's actions were no more than a sunny-day prank gone too far and that he returned for the victims but again departed when he saw them being pulled aboard the sailboat. When the defendant first threw one of the women into the water, she screamed that she did not know how to swim. He then jumped overboard, held her head under the water, and reboarded the boat for the second woman. Before he threw her into the water, she too told him that she could not swim. Having experienced the frigid temperature of the water and the height of the waves and having been told that the victims could not swim, the defendant drove away leaving the women in great peril. The videotapes show what that defendant saw and experienced, and they were relevant to the issue of whether he "did an act designed to result in death with the specific intent that death result." *Commonwealth v. Beattie,* 409 Mass. 458, 459, 567 N.E.2d 206 (1991). See also *Commonwealth v. Hebert,* 373 Mass. 535, 537, 368 N.E.2d 1204 (1977) ("An attempt to commit a crime necessarily involves an intent to commit that crime").[5] We have viewed the videotapes and conclude that the trial judge neither abused his discretion nor committed other error of law in allowing them to be seen by the jury. See *Commonwealth v. Chipman,* 418 Mass. at 271, 635 N.E.2d 1204; *Terrio v. McDonough,* 16 Mass. App. Ct. at 173, 450 N.E.2d 190.

3. *Attempted murder and kidnapping.* It is the defendant's argument that the Commonwealth failed to prove that when he threw the women into the water and drove away, he specifically intended their death. Taking the evidence in the light most favorable to the Commonwealth, we see no error in the trial judge's denial of the defendant's motion for a required finding of not guilty on the indictments charging him with attempted murder by drowning. There was evidence to show that the defendant was five miles offshore with no boats in sight when he threw the women overboard. The water was fifty-two degrees, and the waves were one to two feet high. Because the defendant had jumped into the water to hold one of the woman under, he knew that it was cold and choppy. For all he knew, they could not swim.

This evidence of the defendant's conduct was sufficient to warrant the reasonable inference that he intended that the victims drown. See *Commonwealth v. Henson,* 394 Mass. 584, 591, 476 N.E.2d 947 (1985) ("[An] intent to kill may be inferred from the defendant's conduct"); *Commonwealth v. Dixon,* 34 Mass. App. Ct. 653, 656, 614 N.E.2d 1027 (1993) (attempted murder statute reaches act of throwing someone

who cannot swim from a boat into water).[6]

In arguing that there was no evidence of kidnappings apart from the conduct incidental to the attempted murders, that is, picking the women up and throwing them into the water, the defendant ignores the testimony of the victims. Both women related that after the defendant disrobed and made sexual advances towards them, they demanded that he return them to shore. He refused, continued with his offensive behavior, became angry over their reaction, and then threw them overboard. Moreover, the conduct which the jury reasonably could find as the basis for kidnapping, forcing the women to remain at sea while the defendant committed an indecent assault and battery upon them (see note one, *supra*), would not necessarily be based on the acts that constituted the attempted murders. See *Commonwealth v. Rivera,* 397 Mass. 244, 253–254, 490 N.E.2d 1160 (1986); *Commonwealth v. Sumner,* 18 Mass. App. Ct. 349, 352–353, 465 N.E.2d 1213 (1984).

4. *The dangerous weapon.* General Laws c. 265, § 15A, reads, in pertinent part: "Whoever commits assault and battery upon another by means of a dangerous weapon shall be punished. . . ." The sole argument made by the defendant in respect to the indictments charging him with assault and battery by means of a dangerous weapon is that the ocean is not a dangerous weapon within the meaning of § 15A.

We need not consider whether the specified weapon, the ocean, is dangerous per se or dangerous as used. See *Commonwealth v. Tarrant,* 367 Mass. 411, 416–417, 326 N.E.2d 710 (1975); *Commonwealth v. Appleby,* 380 Mass. 296, 303, 402 N.E.2d 1051 (1980). Although the ocean can be and often is dangerous, it cannot be regarded in its natural state as a weapon within the meaning of § 15A. See *Commonwealth v. Farrell,* 322 Mass. 606, 614–615, 78 N.E.2d 697 (1948), stating that the term "dangerous weapon" comprehends "any *instrument or instrumentality* so constructed or so used as to be likely to produce death or great bodily harm" (emphasis added); *Commonwealth v. Tarrant,* 367 Mass. at 417 n. 6, 326 N.E.2d 710, noting with approval the definition of dangerous weapon adopted in the Proposed Criminal Code of Massachusetts c. 263, § 3(i): "any firearm or other weapon, device, instrument, material or substance, *whether animate or inanimate*, which in the matter [in] which it is used *or is intended to be used* is capable of producing death or serious bodily injury" (emphasis added);[7]

---

5. As the videotapes were illustrative on the issue of the defendant's intent, we need not consider whether, as the Commonwealth argues, they were also helpful to an understanding of the victims' state of mind, an issue of questionable relevancy. See *Commonwealth v. Zagranski,* 408 Mass. 278, 282–283, 558 N.E.2d 933 (1990).

6. In deciding this issue, we need not, contrary to the defendant's argument, consider the testimony of his friend, that he was "eventually" able to persuade the defendant to turn back for the women and that with the aid of binoculars they were able to see the women about three-quarters of a mile away being pulled aboard a sailboat. See Commonwealth v. Lydon, 413 Mass. 309, 312, 597 N.E.2d 36 (1992).

7. This definition tracks that of "deadly weapon" set out in § 210 of the Model Penal Code (1980), which, as noted in comment 5, was "designed to take account of the ingenuity of those who desire to hurt their fellows without encompassing every use of an ordinary object that could cause death or serious injury."

Commonwealth v. Appleby, 380 Mass. at 308, 402 N.E.2d 1051, concluding that the "offense of assault and battery by means of a dangerous weapon under G.L. c. 265, § 15A, requires that the elements of assault be present . . . that there be a touching, however slight . . . that the touching be by means of the weapon . . . and that the battery be accomplished by use of an inherently dangerous weapon, or by use of *some other object* as a weapon, with the intent to *use that object* in a dangerous or potentially dangerous fashion" (emphasis added).

All the cases collected and cited in the discussion of dangerous weapons, per se and as used, in *Commonwealth v. Appleby*, 380 Mass. at 303–304, 402 N.E.2d 1051, share a common fact that is consistent with the definitions of "dangerous weapons" which speak in terms of "objects" or "instrumentalities." The commonality found in those cases is that the object in issue, whether dangerous per se or as used, was an instrumentality which the batterer controlled, either through possession of or authority over it, for use of it in the intentional application of force. Because the ocean in its natural state cannot be possessed or controlled, it is not an object or instrumentality capable of use as a weapon for purposes of § 15A.

Our conclusion should not be construed to mean that there can never be criminal liability for causing physical harm to someone by subjecting them to a force of nature. We conclude only that for purposes of § 15A, the ocean, not being subject to human control, was not, in the instant case, an object or instrumentality which could be found by the jury to be a dangerous weapon. Accordingly, the defendant's motion for required findings of not guilty on the indictments charging him with assault and battery by means of a dangerous weapons should have been allowed.

5. *Conclusion.* It follows from what we have said that the judgments entered on the indictments charging kidnapping and attempted murder are affirmed. The judgments entered on the indictments charging assault and battery by means of a dangerous weapon are reversed, the verdicts are set aside and judgments for the defendant are to enter on those indictments.[8]

SO ORDERED.

---

8. The Commonwealth has not argued that the defendant should, in any event, be resentenced on the lesser offense of assault and battery, presumably for the reason, if no other, that it would make no practical difference. The sentence imposed on the conviction for assault and battery by means of a dangerous weapon was to be served concurrently with that imposed on the attempted murder conviction.

Philip J. COOPER, Administrator Pendente Lite of the Estate of W.A. Bisson, Deceased, Plaintiff-Appellant,

v.

Charles AUSTIN, Defendant-Appellant.

Court of Appeals of Tennessee, Western Section, at Jackson.

Feb. 18, 1992.

Application for Permission to Appeal Denied by Supreme Court May 26, 1992.

837 S.W.2d 606 (Tenn. Ct. App. 1992)

CRAWFORD, Judge.

This is a will contest case involving a codicil to the Last Will and Testament of Wheelock A. Bisson, M.D., deceased. Phillip Cooper, Administrator *pendente lite* of the estate, is a nominal party only; the real parties in interest are the proponent of the codicil, Alois B. Greer, and the contestant, Charles Austin.

Dr. Bisson's will, which is not contested, was executed June 18, 1982. Dr. Bisson died in 1985, and shortly thereafter Greer filed a petition in probate court to admit the June 18,

1982 will and two codicils thereto dated August 20, 1984, and August 6, 1985, respectively, to probate as and for the Last Will and Testament of Wheelock A. Bisson, M.D. By order entered November 26, 1985, the probate court admitted the paper writings to probate as the Last Will and Testament of Dr. Bisson.

On May 20, 1986, Austin filed a petition in probate court to contest the two codicils,[1] and, after answer to the petition by Greer, the probate court certified the contest to circuit court by order entered August 13, 1986.

No action was taken in circuit court until the administrator pendente lite filed a "Complaint to Establish Will and Codicil" on November 9, 1988. Austin's answer to the complaint, *inter alia*, denied that either codicil had been properly executed by the decedent or properly witnessed and further denied that the codicils had any legal validity or effect.

---

1. The codicil dated August 6, 1985, made no property disposition, but merely appointed Greer as executrix of the estate. During the course of the circuit court trial, the proponent withdrew this codicil from evidence. Since it is not involved in this appeal we will omit further reference to it in this Opinion.

(continues)

Greer filed a motion for summary judgment in October, 1990, seeking to have Austin's case dismissed on the grounds that it was barred by T.C.A. § 32-4-108 (1986), because it was brought more than two years from the entry of the order admitting the will to probate. The trial court denied this motion.

On March 26, 1991, a jury trial was held on the issue of *devisavit vel non* as to the 1984 codicil. The 1982 will was introduced into evidence by stipulation, and Greer offered the 1984 codicil through the attesting witnesses.

In his 1982 will, Dr. Bisson left everything to his wife and if she predeceased him he left the majority of his estate to Austin. This disposition was changed by the 1984 codicil which provides:

CODICIL TO MY LAST WILL AND TESTAMENT

I, Wheelock Alexander Bisson, M.D., of 2312 Park Avenue, Memphis, Shelby County, Tennessee, this August 20th, 1984. Bequeath that my adopted daughter, Alois B. Greer, receive a child's share of my estate which will consist of all real property, personal property, household furniture and any and all savings which I might have at the time of my demise.

/s/ Wheelock A. Bisson, M.D.
WHEELOCK ALEXANDER BISSON, M.D.
/s/ Michael E. Harrison
WITNESS
3907 Kerwin Dr. Memphis, Tenn. 38138
ADDRESS
/s/ Charles L. Harrison
WITNESS
4905 Sagewood, Mphs., TN. 38116
ADDRESS
Sworn to and subscribed before me this 20th day of August, 1984.
/s/ Lillie M. Thomas
NOTARY PUBLIC
My Commission Expires:
Jan. 5, 1987

On direct examination, Michael Harrison stated that he signed the codicil in the presence of Dr. Bisson. He then gave the following testimony regarding that signing:

Q. All right. When you got ready to sign did Dr. Bisson indicate to you what you were signing as a witness?

A. Yes. At the time I had no idea what a codicil was.

Q. All right.

A. But I did—I did witness it.

On cross-examination, Michael Harrison gave the following testimony:

Q. All right. You didn't know what this document was now you've got in front of you at the time you signed it. Correct? This is one dated August, 1984.

A. I didn't understand your question.

Q. Well, Dr. Bisson didn't tell you what it was, he just said he needed a paper signed and notarized. Right?

A. He didn't tell me anything. I was asked to witness the document. He told Ms. Thomas. She notarized it, I was asked to witness it.

Q. At the time did you know what the document was—

A. No, sir.

Q. . . . that you were witnessing? Pardon me?

A. No, sir.

Q. And Dr. Bisson didn't tell you what it was?

A. No, sir.

Q. You didn't ask anybody what it was?

A. No, sir.

Charles Harrison, the other witness appearing on the 1984 codicil, testified on direct examination pertinent to the issue before us:

Q. All right. Do you recall the occasion when you signed this document?

A. Yes, sir.

Q. Okay. Will you give us the background as to how you came to be involved with this document at all?

A. On this particular day, the 20th of August, 1984, we were on our way back from Memorial Park—the rotunda at the Memorial Park Cemetery, and Dr. Bisson was seated on the front seat of the limousine with me.

And he said, "When you get back, you know, to my place"—which he referred that was his home—he said, when you get back to my place, he said, I have something I want you all to do for me. And so I said, well, okay, Doc. And that was that. And so the rest of the people that was in the limousine they were just carrying on casual conversation. So when we got back to his residence on Park Avenue we were letting them out of the limousines and he said, don't leave, come on in, I have something, you know, I want you to take care of for me. And so he asked me where was Ms. Thomas. I said, well, she's at the funeral home. He said, well, call her and tell her to come down here, I need her—you know, I need her here, you know, on this too. And so when we got inside—We came through the side entrance and we went up to his front office. And he said, I have this codicil that I want you all to notarize for me and witness, and that's how I came in contact with him.

Q. All right, sir. Now, at the time that this document was signed were you present?

A. Yes, sir.

Q. And did you see Dr. Bisson sign this document?

A. Yes, sir.

Q. Was your brother Michael also present?

A. Yes, sir.

Q. And all three of you were together at the time; is that correct?

A.   Yes, sir.

Q.   Ms. Thomas is on there as a notary. Was she also in the room or was she not?

A.   No, she was in the room. Yes, sir.

Q.   All right. And Dr. Bisson asked you all to sign this; is that correct?

A.   Yes, sir.

Q.   And all three of you signed it in each other's presence?

A.   That's correct.

* * *

The pertinent testimony from Charles Harrison on cross examination is:

Q.   Now, Dr. Bisson didn't tell you what was in the document that you were signing. Correct?

A.   No, he did not.

Q.   And he didn't tell you what the document was?

A.   Yes, sir, he did.

Q.   Well, let me ask you. Do you recall giving a deposition, meaning when you came to my conference room up at my office January 14, 1987 and you swore to tell the truth, and there was a court reporter—it wasn't this woman, but another woman with a machine like that that took down your testimony? Do you recall that?

A.   January the 14th of '87?

Q.   Yes, sir.

A.   I remember coming to your office, yes, sir.

Q.   All right.

A.   I don't remember the exact date, but I do remember coming to your office.

Q.   Have you had a chance to look over this document—this deposition transcript?

A.   No, sir.

Q.   I asked you on page 40 at that time when you were under oath, I said—At line 3 you said, I just glanced over it. I didn't stop, I just glanced over it.

Q.   (Line 5) Did Dr. Bisson tell you what was in it?

A.   No, sir.

Q.   Did he tell you what it was?

A.   No, sir.

Q.   Was that your testimony at that time? Would you agree with me that your memory was probably better about this in January of 1987, which would be, what, four years ago?

A.   I'm not playing with my memory, but I'd say that—well, you know, I—

Q.   Would you accept that as the truth if that's what you said then?

A.   Yes, sir.

Q.   So Dr. Bisson didn't elaborate as to what the document was, he said I want you to witness a document. He had the document already. Right?

A.   Right.

Q.   You didn't give it to him?

A.   No.

Q.   Okay. And then he signed it and he said, okay, now you sign it, and that was it. Correct?

A.   Yes, sir, basically. He didn't say sign it, he said witness it.

Q.   Witness it. And then there wasn't any more conversation about it after you witnessed it, y'all got up and left. Correct?

A.   Right.

On re-direct examination, Charles Harrison testified as follows:

Q.   Mr. Harrison, be very careful now and think regarding both what you said previously and what you just said. Are you absolutely certain that Dr. Bisson told you what it was he wanted you to witness?

A.   MR. MITCHELL: Note my objection to the leading, Your Honor. He never testified he knew what it was.

THE COURT: He did testify, I believe, in his direct-examination. He said that Dr. Bisson said he had a codicil that he wanted witnessing.

MR. MITCHELL: Yes, sir, that's all he said.

Q.   (BY MR. BEATY): Is that what you recall today as to what he said?

A.   Yes, sir.

MR. BEATY: That's all I have.

Charles Harrison's re-cross examination is:

Q.   But that was before you ever went in the room?

A.   I beg your pardon.

Q.   That was before you ever went into the room; that was when you were out in the car?

A.   Right.

Q   When you went in the room he didn't say what it was or what was in it, just like you testified four years ago. Right?

A.   Right.

Lillie Thomas, who appears as a notary public on the 1984 codicil, testified that all Dr. Bisson said in her presence was that he had a paper that he wanted her to notarize and that he said nothing in her presence about the paper being a will, a codicil or anything of that sort. We quote from the testimony:

Q.   All right. And what did Dr. Bisson say about it in your presence?

(continues)

A. He said I have a—he said a paper that I want you to notarize for me.

Q. All right. Did he use any language: will, codicil, anything of that sort?

A. No. He said a paper.

Q. All right. Did he sign it in your presence?

A. Yes, sir.

Q. Did he sign it in the presence of the other witnesses?

A. Yes, sir.

Q. Now Michael Harrison was present?

A. Yes, sir.

Q. And Charles Harrison, also; is that correct?

A. Yes, sir.

Following the testimony of these witnesses, counsel for Austin moved the court to disallow submission of the codicil to the jury on the grounds that the codicil's proponent, Mrs. Greer, had not met her burden of proof pursuant to T.C.A. § 32-1-104, regarding the manner in which a will must be executed.

The trial court granted Austin's motion and directed a verdict on the grounds that Ms. Greer had not proved the proper execution of the codicil. Accordingly, judgment was entered declaring that the Last Will and Testament of Wheelock A. Bisson dated June 18, 1982, be admitted to probate without any codicils.

Greer has appealed and presents two issues for review. The first issue is whether the trial court erred in denying Greer's motion for summary judgment on the grounds that Mr. Austin's will contest was barred by T.C.A. § 32-4-108 (Supp. 1991) which provides:

All **actions** or **proceedings** to set aside the probate of any will or petitions to certify such will for an issue of **devisavit vel non,** must be brought within two (2) years from entry of the order admitting the will to probate, or be forever barred, saving, however, to persons under the age of eighteen (18) years or of unsound mind at the time the cause of action accrues, the rights conferred by § 28-1-106. (Emphasis added.)

Greer contends that this statute bars Austin's action, because the 1984 codicil was admitted to probate by order entered November 26, 1985, and Austin filed no pleading in circuit court until he filed an answer to the complaint on December 2, 1988. Greer argues that the filing of the complaint in circuit court was the commencement of the action pursuant to Rule 3, Tennessee Rules of Civil Procedure, and because it was filed more than two years from the order of probate court admitting the will to probate, the action is barred by the two year statute of limitations in T.C.A. § 32-4-108.

We must respectfully disagree with Greer for several reasons. The statute itself is clear and unambiguous. It is confined to actions to set aside the probate of a will or to petitions

to certify a will for an issue of *devisavit vel non.* Obviously, the proceedings contemplated by this statute are proceedings that take place in the probate court. It is equally clear that the proceeding in the circuit court on the issue of *devisavit vel non* after the case is certified from the probate court to the circuit court is in substance an original proceeding to probate the will, separate and distinct from any proceedings held in probate court. *Bearman v. Camatsos,* 215 Tenn. 231, 385 S.W.2d 91 (1964); *Arnold v. Marcom,* 49 Tenn. App. 161, 352 S.W.2d 936 (1961). In a proceeding of this nature, no particular form of pleading is required. All that is required is that the proponent shall offer it as a will and the contesting party shall deny it. See *Bowman v. Helton,* 7 Tenn. App. 325 (1928).

Finally, it has long been held in this state that the right of a contestant to resist the probate of a will is a preliminary matter and presents a separate and distinct issue from the issue of *devisavit vel non,* and that the order of the probate court sustaining or denying the right to contest the will is an appealable order. See *Winters v. American Trust Co.,* 158 Tenn. 479, 14 S.W.2d 740 (1929). T.C.A. § 32-4-108 clearly applies only to this separate action.

We hold that the statute of limitations set out in T.C.A. § 32-4-108 applies only to the proceeding filed in the probate court seeking to set aside the probate of a will or a certification for a will contest.

The second issue for review is whether the trial court erred in directing a verdict for the contestant Austin by refusing to allow the 1984 codicil to be submitted to the jury.

The rule for determining a motion for directed verdict requires the trial judge and the reviewing court on appeal to look to all of the evidence, taking the strongest legitimate view of it in favor of the opponent of the motion and allowing all reasonable inferences from it in his favor. The court must discard all countervailing evidence, and if there is then any dispute as to any material determinative evidence or any doubt as to the conclusion to be drawn from the whole evidence, the motion must be denied. *Tennessee Farmers Mut. Ins. Co. v. Hinson,* 651 S.W.2d 235 (Tenn. App. 1983).

The court should not direct a verdict if there is any material evidence in the record that would support a verdict for the plaintiff under any of the theories he had advanced. See *Wharton Transport Corp. v. Bridges,* 606 S.W.2d 521 (Tenn.1980).

The formal requirements for the execution of a will are set out in T.C.A. § 32-1-104 (1984), which provides:

Will other than holographic or nuncupative—The execution of a will, other than a holographic or nuncupative will, must be by the signature of the testator and of at least two (2) witnesses as follows:

(1) The testator shall signify to the attesting witnesses that the instrument is his will and either:

(A) Himself sign;

(B) Acknowledge his signature already made; or

(C) At his direction and in his presence have someone else sign his name for him; and

(D) In any of the above cases the act must be done in the presence of two (2) or more attesting witnesses

(2) The attesting witness must sign:

(A) In the presence of the testator; and

(B) In the presence of each other.

Austin contended, and the trial court agreed, that Greer's proof failed to established that Dr. Bisson did "signify to the attesting witnesses that the [1984 codicil] is his will . . ." as required by the statute. Greer argues that the testimony of the attesting witnesses was sufficient to create an issue of fact for the jury as to whether Dr. Bisson so signified.

Austin relies primarily upon the case of *Lawrence v. Lawrence*, 35 Tenn. App. 648, 250 S.W.2d 781 (1951) which involved a will without an attestation clause and where the only surviving attesting witness testified both that the testatrix informed her that the instrument to be witnessed was the testatrix's will and also testified to the contrary by stating that she did not know that the instrument was a will. The Court of Appeals, in directing a verdict against the will, said:

The meaning of this statute is clear, plain and unambiguous. When a testator calls upon persons to witness his will, "the testator shall signify to the attesting witnesses that the instrument in [sic] his will." Surely it cannot be contended that this provision of the statute is doubtful of meaning. It simply means that the testator must state to the witnesses in substance that the paper writing is his will and that he wants them to sign it as witnesses. By the uncontradicted evidence before us that essential requisite of the execution of a valid will is lacking. The testatrix did not signify to the attesting witnesses that the instrument was the will of testatrix.

250 S.W.2d at 784.

Austin contends that the cases relied upon by Greer—*Whitlow v. Weaver*, 63 Tenn. App. 651, 478 S.W.2d 57 (Tenn. App. 1970); *Needham v. Doyle*, 39 Tenn. App. 597, 286 S.W.2d 601 (1955); and *Miller v. Thrasher*, 38 Tenn. App. 88, 251 S.W.2d 446 (1952), and *In re Estate of Bradley*, 817 S.W.2d 320 (Tenn. App. 1991)—all involve wills which contained an attestation clause. He concedes that an attestation clause raises a strong presumption that the recitals therein contained are true and that contrary evidence raises a question for the jury. *Needham*, 286 S.W.2d at 601. We agree that these cases are distinguishable on their facts.

Greer also relies upon *Leathers v. Binkley*, 196 Tenn. 80, 264 S.W.2d 561 (1954). In *Leathers*, the will did not contain an attestation clause and the two attesting witnesses testified that they had signed the will in the presence of the testatrix and in the presence of each other. Neither witness testified specifically that the will had been declared by the testatrix to be her will at the time of the signing. In holding in favor of the will, the Court said:

While it is true that neither Mr. Morrison nor Mrs. Gilmer remembered every detail of the signature and attestation of the will, the important fact in the record is that there was neither from Morrison, Mrs. Gilmer, nor the Notary Public, *a line of positive affirmative testimony that would support the allegations of the petition of contest, nor the verdict of the jury, that the will had not been regularly and legally executed in strict accordance with the requirements of Code, sec. 8089.4.*

"Where, for instance, the subscribing witnesses testify that they do not recollect the circumstances, but do recognize their signatures, and declare that they would not have placed them to the instrument unless they had seen the testator sign it, or heard him acknowledge his signature, the due execution may be presumed." Sizer's Pritchard on Wills, § 336, p. 380.

"In establishing the facts essential to the validity of the will by a preponderance of the evidence, proponents are, however, not obliged in all cases to prove each fact by direct evidence; but they may rely upon presumptions. There is, at the outset, no presumption that the alleged testator executed the will in question or any will; but when a paper propounded as a will is shown to have been signed by the alleged testator and the requisite number of witnesses, **in the absence of any satisfactory evidence to the contrary** the presumption is that all the formalities have been complied with" (Our Emphasis). Page on Wills, Vol. 2, § 755, p. 462.

"The foregoing statement is supported by cases from many jurisdictions, including Georgia, Illinois, Iowa, Missouri, Montana, New Jersey, New Mexico and South Carolina." Compare: Annotations, 47 L.R.A., N.S., 722; 76 A.L.R. 604; 14 L.R.A., N.S., 255; Ann. Cas. 426.

264 S.W.2d at 563 (Emphasis added).

Austin asserts that *Leathers* is not controlling authority for the case at bar because in *Leathers* there was no positive affirmative testimony that the will had not been regularly and legally executed. We agree with Austin [that] *Leathers* turned on that point, so we must examine the testimony in the case at bar to determine if there is uncontroverted positive testimony that Dr. Bisson did not "signify to the attesting witnesses" that the 1984 instrument was his will or codicil.

In examining the testimony of the witnesses, we must look at the testimony in the best light and afford to it all legitimate inferences. With that direction in mind, we will examine the testimony.

Charles Harrison's testimony is to the effect that prior to the gathering of attesting witnesses, notary public and testator, testator told him that he, the testator, had "this codicil that I want you all to notarize for me and witness." He specifically pointed out that this statement by Dr. Bisson was made before the gathering for the signing of the instrument.

Michael Harrison's testimony indicates both that he was told by Dr. Bisson that it was a codicil to be witnessed and that Dr. Bisson did not tell him what it was that he was witnessing. He specifically testified that he did not know what the document was. These contradictory statements effectively eliminate any testimony from this witness on that fact. *Taylor v. Nashville Banner Pub. Co.*, 573 S.W.2d 476 (Tenn. App. 1978), *cert. den.*, 441 U.S. 923, 99 S. Ct. 2032, 60 L. Ed. 2d 396 (1979); *Donaho v. Large*, 25 Tenn. App. 433, 158 S.W.2d 447 (1941).

Lillie Thomas, the notary public, testified that Dr. Bisson said he had a paper to be witnessed and he did not use any language such as will, codicil or anything of that sort. Dr. Bisson's statement was made at the time the parties gathered for the signing.

An examination of the witness[es]' testimony indicates that there is uncontroverted affirmative proof that Dr. Bisson did not signify to at least one attesting witness that the instrument to be witnessed was his will or a codicil thereto. Therefore, the trial court correctly directed a verdict against the admission of the will.

The judgment of the trial court is affirmed and this case is remanded to the trial court for such further proceedings as may be necessary.

Costs of the appeal are assessed against the appellant.

TOMLIN, P.J. (W.S.), and HIGHERS, J., concur.

Michael Anthony CORDOVA, Plaintiff–Appellant,

v.

Frederick WOLFEL, Jr., David Abeyta, James Abeyta, Priscilla Abeyta, and National Car Rentals Systems, Inc., Defendants–Appellees.

Supreme Court of New Mexico.

120 N.M. 557, 903 P.2d 1390 (1995)

MINZNER, Justice.

Cordova appeals from a decision granting summary judgment in favor of National Car Rentals Systems (National). This case raises the issue of whether the Mandatory Financial Responsibility Act (the MFRA), NMSA 1978, §§ 66-5-201 to -239 (Repl. Pamp. 1994), imposes liability upon a self-insured rental car company for the negligence of an unauthorized driver, despite a contrary rental contract provision. We conclude that the MFRA does not impose such liability, and we affirm summary judgment.

I. FACTS

On January 26, 1990, Priscilla Abeyta rented a car from National at the Albuquerque Airport. Her purpose was to drive her son David and his two friends to Reno, Nevada. At the time of renting, she intended to drive the vehicle exclusively herself. There is a factual dispute between the parties about what rental documents Abeyta read and consented to at the time that she entered into the lease. It is clear, however, that Abeyta signed a standard National form wherein she acknowledged that only she had an "additional authorized driver may drive vehicle." A space for the designation of an additional authorized driver appeared next to Abeyta's signature, and that space was blank. Abeyta declined to purchase optional personal accident insurance.

Shortly after picking up the vehicle, Abeyta became ill, and she decided not to make the trip. She gave permission to her son David to drive. There appears to be a factual dispute about whether she also gave David's friends Wolfel and Cordova permission to drive. After the three men started on their trip, they began to drink, and Wolfel took over the driving. There is a factual dispute about whether Wolfel had had anything to drink and whether he was intoxicated at the time of the accident, which occurred on an interstate highway in Arizona.[1] The accident resulted, at least in part, from Wolfel's negligence, and there were no other vehicles involved.

Cordova claims to have sustained injuries in the amount of $650,000. This figure includes medical expenses exceeding $69,000, lost wages, and permanent loss of the sense of smell. Cordova brought suit against Wolfel, National, Mr. and Mrs. Abeyta, their son David, and Travelers Insurance Company, the Abeytas' personal liability insurer. Cordova has settled his claims against the Abeytas and Wolfel. The trial court granted summary judgment in favor of Travelers after it determined that the insurance contract between Travelers and the Abeytas did not extend coverage to the rental car. National is the sole remaining defendant.

---

1. We assume that New Mexico's substantive law applies to this appeal because neither party asserts otherwise.

II. DISCUSSION

A. Summary Judgment

Along with its motion for summary judgment, National submitted the car rental agreement wherein Abeyta acknowledged that she was the only authorized driver of the vehicle. National asserted that because the agreement provided liability coverage only to authorized drivers, National had no obligation to indemnify Wolfel for liability resulting from his negligent operation of the vehicle. National maintains that as the self-insured owner of the rental car, it is not an insurer, and there was no insurance contract between it and Abeyta. National further contends that the MFRA specifically exempts self-insurers from its provisions.

Cordova argues that National's "Certificate of Self-Insurance [issued by the State Superintendent of Insurance] provides liability coverage on [the] vehicle driven by Frederick Wolfel." Cordova does not dispute National's contention that Wolfel was not an authorized driver. Rather, Cordova argues that Wolfel was a permissive driver because he operated the vehicle with Abeyta's express or implied permission. *See United Servs. Auto. Ass'n v. National Farmers Union Property & Casualty*, 119 N.M. 397, 891 P.2d 538 (1995). This contention rests upon the premise that National, as a self-insurer, provided insurance coverage under which Abeyta was the "named insured." Cordova asserts that because the MFRA mandates that liability coverage must extend to persons using the vehicle with the express or implied permission of the named insured, coverage extends to Wolfel by operation of law. *See id.;* § 66-5-221(A)(2).

Cordova argues on appeal that the trial court erred when it determined that, as a matter of law, National is not liable for Wolfel's negligence. We agree with the trial court's interpretation of the rental agreement and its resolution of the purely legal issues presented by this case. Resolving all disputed facts in favor of Cordova, we conclude that National is entitled to judgment, and we affirm. *See Tapia v. Springer Transfer Co.*, 106 N.M. 461, 462-63, 744 P.2d 1264, 1265-66 (Ct. App.), *cert. quashed*, 106 N.M. 405, 744 P.2d 180 (1987).

B. Self-Insurance

* * *

[3] Most authorities agree that self-insurance is not insurance. Insurance is a contract whereby for consideration one party agrees to indemnify or guarantee another party against specified risks. *See New Mexico Life Ins. Guar. Ass'n v. Moore*, 93 N.M. 47, 50, 596 P.2d 260, 263 (1979); NMSA 1978, § 59A-1-5 (Repl. Pamp. 1992). In contrast, self-insurance is a process of risk retention whereby an entity "set[s] aside assets to meet foreseeable future losses." Robert E. Keeton & Alan I. Widiss, *Insurance Law: A Guide to Fundamental Principles, Legal Doctrines and Commercial Practices* § 1.3, at 14 (1988); *see also Levi Strauss & Co. v. New Mexico Property & Casualty Ins. Guar. Ass'n (In re Mission Ins. Co.)*, 112 N.M. 433, 437, 816 P.2d 502, 506 (1991) (holding that a certificate of

self-insurance "cannot be equated with an insurance contract or policy"). A self-insurer protects itself from liability; it does not assume the risk of another. *See Levi Strauss & Co.*, 112 N.M. at 436-37, 816 P.2d at 505-06; *Consolidated Enters., Inc. v. Schwindt*, 172 Ariz. 35, 833 P.2d 706, 709 (1992) (en banc). We note that self-insurance and insurance serve similar purposes and that insurance principles may sometimes apply to self-insurance by way of analogy. Nonetheless, we reject as inaccurate Cordova's theory that self-insurance is a sub-set of insurance.

[4] The relationship between National and its lessees is one of bailment, and there generally is no common law basis for imposing upon a bailor liability for a bailee's negligent operation of a bailed vehicle. *See Stover v. Critchfield*, 510 N.W.2d 681, 683-84 (S.D. 1994). The legislatures of a few states have altered this common law rule through legislation. *See* Ariz. Rev. Stat. Ann. § 28-324 (1994 Cum. Supp.) (requiring owner of rental vehicles to obtain public liability insurance protecting passengers and third parties against negligence of renter; however, owner not liable for damages beyond limits of insurance policy); Conn. Gen. Stat. § 14-154a (1995) (owner of leased vehicle liable for damage caused by operation of leased vehicle to same extent as operator would be held liable if operator were owner); *cf.* Neb. Rev. Stat. § 25-21,239 (1994 Cum. Supp.) (making owner of leased truck jointly and severally liable with lessee for lessee's negligence). Moreover, the court of at least one state has determined that, as a matter of public policy, a vehicle lessor will be liable for the negligence of a lessee, irrespective of contrary contractual language. *See Motor Vehicle Accident Indem. Corp. v. Continental Nat'l Am. Group Co.*, 35 N.Y.2d 260, 360 N.Y.S.2d 859, 861-63, 319 N.E.2d 182, 184-85 (1974). The New Mexico legislature has not enacted legislation that would make vehicle lessors generally liable for injuries that result when lessees negligently use their vehicles, and we decline to take that step in the absence of legislative action. We conclude that a vehicle lessor is liable for the negligence of a lessee or a lessee's permittee only to the extent that a statute, administrative regulation, or agreement of the parties imposes such liability.

[5] Cordova's arguments on appeal largely proceed from the premise that a self-insured entity such as National is subject to the requirements of the MFRA. However, the MFRA itself belies this contention. In unambiguous language, the MFRA exempts from its provisions "motor vehicle[s] approved as self-insured by the superintendent of insurance." Section 66-5-207(E). We recognize that there may be situations where it is appropriate to apply the provisions of the MFRA to self-insurers by analogy. Nonetheless, we cannot ignore the statute's plain language, *see V.P. Clarence Co. v. Colgate*, 115 N.M. 471, 473 853 P.2d 722, 724, (1993), and a literal interpretation of Section 66-5-207(E) does not lead to an absurd result. *Cf. State v. Gutierrez*, 115 N.M. 551, 552, 854 P.2d 878, 879 (Ct. App.) (holding that where literal language of statute leads to absurd result, court may construe statute to avoid such result), *cert. denied*, 115 N.M. 545, 854 P.2d 872 (1993).

* * *

(continues)

III. CONCLUSION

We conclude that the trial court correctly determined that National is exempt from the MFRA, and that, in the absence of a contractual agreement, National is not vicariously liable for Wolfel's negligence. Summary judgment in favor of National is affirmed.

IT IS SO ORDERED.

BACA, C.J., and FROST, J., concur.

DEAN et al.

v.

DICKEY et al.

No. 4662.

Court of Civil Appeals of Texas. El Paso.

Sept. 28, 1949.

Rehearing Denied Oct. 26, 1949.

225 S.W.2d 999 (Tex. Civ. App. 1949)

MCGILL, Justice.

The sole question presented by this appeal is whether a typewritten instrument of testamentary character typed wholly by Trollis Dell Dickey on June 12, 1945, and intended by him to be his last will and testament, and signed by him and one witness in ink, is entitled to probate as the holographic will of the said Trollis Dell Dickey, Deceased. The trial court affirmed the order of the County Court denying probate of the instrument, and this appeal has been duly perfected.

The Statutes applicable on June 12, 1945, are the following: Vernon's Texas Civil Statutes:

Article 8283: "Every last will and testament except where otherwise provided by law, shall be in writing and signed by the testator or by some other person by his direction and in his presence, and shall, if not wholly written by himself, be attested by two or more credible witnesses above the age of fourteen years, subscribing their names thereto in the presence of the testator."

Article 8284: "Where the will is wholly written by the testator the attestation of the subscribing witnesses may be dispensed with."

Article 3344, Section 4: "If the will was wholly written by the testator, by two witnesses to his handwriting, which may be made by affidavit taken in open court and subscribed to by the witnesses, or by deposition."

These Statutes construed together leave no room for doubt that the language employed in Article 8283 "if not wholly written by himself"; in Article 8284 "wholly written by the testator" and in Article 3344, Section 4 "if the will was wholly written by the testator, by two witnesses to his handwriting," require that the words "wholly written" used in these articles be construed to mean wholly written in the handwriting of the testator. Article 8283 prescribes the requisites of a holographic will. Article 8284 provides that when those requisites have been complied with, attestation by subscribing witnesses may be dispensed with, while Article 3344, Section 4 prescribes the character of proof necessary to prove such will. To give the identical language "wholly written" used in these Statutes the meaning for which appellants contend would render Articles 8283 and 3344, Section 4, inconsistent and repugnant, since such interpretation would make it impossible to prove a typewritten will in the manner prescribed by Article 3344, Section 4, that is, by two witnesses to the handwriting of the testator.

Appellants concede that this case is one of first impression in this State, and that the construction for which they contend is contrary to the overwhelming weight of authority in other jurisdictions where similar Statutes have been construed, citing 68 C.J., p. 719, Section 402, and 57 Am.Jur. p. 433, Section 634. The reason for the rule laid down by these authorities is ably stated in *In re Dreyfus' Estate*, 175 Cal. 417, 165 P. 941, L.R.A. 1917F, 391:

"From time immemorial, letters and words have been written with the hand by means of pen and ink or pencil of some description, and it has been a well-known fact that each individual who writes in this manner acquires a style of forming, placing, and spacing the letters and words which is peculiar to himself and which in most cases renders his writing easily distinguishable from that of others by those familiar with it or by experts in chirography who make a study of the subject and who are afforded an opportunity of comparing a disputed specimen with those admitted to be genuine. The provision that a will should be valid if entirely 'written, dated, and signed by the hand of the testator,' is the ancient rule on the subject. There can be no doubt that it owes its origin to the fact that a successful counterfeit of another's handwriting is exceedingly difficult, and that therefore the requirement that it should be in the testator's handwriting would afford protection against a forgery of this character."

See also: *Adams' Ex'x v. Beaumont*, 226 Ky. 311, 10 S.W.2d 1106; and *McNeill v. McNeill*, 261 Ky. 240, 87 S.W.2d 367, where the statutory language "wholly written" under construction is identical with that of ours. However, appellants contend that a different interpretation should be given to Articles 8283 and 8284, supra, for two reasons: First, because of Section 3, Article 23:

"Definitions" of Title 1: "General Provisions" R.C.S., which provides: "'Written' or 'in writing' includes any representation of words, letters or figures, 'whether *by writing, printing or otherwise*'" (Our Emphasis).

Secondly: Because of the emergency clause of S.B. 328, enacted by the 50th Legislature, Acts of 1947, 50th Leg., Reg. Sess., Ch. 170, p. 275, which amended Articles 8283 and 8284 by substituting for the words "wholly written by himself" in Article 8283, the words "wholly in the handwriting of the testator" and for the words "wholly written by the testator" in Article 8284, the words "wholly written in the handwriting of the testator." The relevant portion of the emergency clause is "that under the present interpretation of the statute any form of writing including *typewriting, or printing or otherwise* (our emphasis) is sufficient to constitute a will which leaves a dangerous and unsafe condition not properly protecting widows and orphans of this state." Section 3.

By the very terms of Article 23, the meaning given the words "written or in writing" by Section 3 has no application where "a different meaning is apparent from the context." As

above pointed out, Articles 8283–8284 and 3344, Section 4, construed together leave no room for doubt as to the meaning of the words "wholly written" therein employed. Therefore, Article 23, Section 3 has no application. For like reason, without application is the rule enunciated in *Stanford et al v. Butler*, 142 Tex. 692, 181 S.W.2d 269, *loc. cit.* 274(8, 9), 153 A.L.R. 1054:

"* * * where a later act implies a particular construction of an existing law, and particularly where the existing law is ambiguous or its meaning uncertain, interpretation of the prior act by the Legislature as contained in the later act is persuasive when a court is called upon to interpret the prior law."

Articles 8283 and 8284, when construed with Article 3344, Section 4, are not ambiguous, nor is their meaning uncertain. Furthermore, when S.B. 328 was enacted there had been no decision by any appellate court of this State construing Articles 8283 and 8284 as declared in the emergency clause. From the similarity of the language emphasized it is probable that the Legislature erroneously assumed that Article 23, Section 3 was applicable and controlling in its construction of Articles 8283 and 8284. For this additional reason, the above quoted rule is inapplicable.

The judgment of the trial court is affirmed.

In re ESTATE OF Clifford P. KUSZMAUL, Deceased.

No. 85–647.

District Court of Appeal of Florida, Fourth District.

June 25, 1986.

491 So. 2d. 287 (Fla. Dist. Ct. App. 1986)

ON MOTION FOR REHEARING

LETTS, Judge.

The motion for rehearing is granted. The original opinion filed May 7, 1986, is withdrawn and we substitute the following:

This case involves the disposition of certain estate assets. The distribution hinges on whether a conformed copy of a will, found together with an original executed codicil, will suffice to uphold the provisions of that will and its codicil, despite the absence of the original executed last will and

testament. The trial judge denied the petition for administration. Under the facts here presented, we disagree and reverse.

When the testator died, the interested parties fruitlessly searched for the original executed will, supposedly last seen in the decedent's possession. There is a dispute over where the copy of that will and the codicil were first located. It is conceded, however, that shortly after the testator died, a conformed copy of the will and the original of the executed codicil thereto, were found together among the decedent's personal possessions. The codicil stated in its concluding paragraph:

THIRD. I hereby ratify and confirm my said Last Will and Testament except insofar as any part thereof is modified by this Codicil.

We begin by reaffirming our conclusion in *In the Estate of Parson*, 416 So. 2d 513, 515 (Fla. 4th DCA 1982) that there is a "presumption that a will which was in the possession of the testator prior to death and which cannot be located subsequent to death was destroyed by the testator with the intention of revoking it." We further continue to align ourselves with the proposition, also set forth in *Parson*, that "the

(continues)

presumption may only be overcome by competent and substantial evidence." *Id.* at 515. Unlike the trial judge, however, we are of the opinion that the facts of the case now before us yield competent and substantial evidence to overcome the presumption.

The proponents of the view that the instant will was revoked point to another decision of this court with somewhat similar facts. *See In re Estate of Baird*, 343 So. 2d 41 (Fla. 4th DCA 1977). However, there are important distinctions. In *Baird* the discovered executed codicil was not, so far as we can determine, accompanied by a copy of the will, as it was in the matter now before us. Further, while Mr. Kuszmaul, like Mr. Baird, showed continuing affection for the beneficiaries under the will, the former also wrote a letter to one of the beneficiaries under the will, after its execution, stating that property devised in that will would "someday . . . be yours."

We are of the opinion that the instant cause is more closely allied to the facts in the New York decision of *Will of Herbert*, 89 Misc. 2d 340, 391 N.Y.S.2d 351 (1977) where the court held that the presumption was overcome because a copy of the will and the original codicil "were carefully kept together among [the testator's] personal possessions" and because it would be "unlikely that the testator intentionally revoked his will while retaining the codicil and a copy of the original will." *Id.* at 352.

We would also point to two Florida statutes not considered in *Baird*. The first of these is section 732.5105, Florida Statutes (1983) wherein it is stated that "the execution of a codicil referring to a previous will has the effect of republishing the will as modified by the codicil." True, that section does not set forth whether or not it is applicable if the executed original will cannot be found. However, the ensuing section 732.511, provides that even if a will has been revoked "it may be republished and made valid [by] . . . the execution of a codicil republishing it with the formalities required by this law for the execution of wills." The codicil before us now was executed with requisite formality.

In the sum of all that we have set forth above, we conclude that the presumption was overcome and the trial judge was in error.

REVERSED AND REMANDED IN ACCORDANCE HEREWITH.

DOWNEY and DELL, JJ., concur.

McCLAIN et al. v. ADAMS.

In re DOUGLASS' ESTATE.

No. 2340-7579.

Commission of Appeals of Texas, Section A.

Jan. 15, 1941.

146 S.W.2d 373 (Tex. Civ. App. 1941)

HICKMAN, Commissioner.

The subject matter of this litigation is an alleged nuncupative will. Annie Douglass, deceased, was the alleged testator; Willie Adams, defendant in error, was the proponent in the probate court; and Eliza McClain and others, plaintiffs in error, the next of kin of the deceased, were the contestants. The county court of Jefferson County sustained the contest and denied the probate. On appeal the district court of that county entered judgment admitting the alleged will to probate, which judgment was affirmed by the Court of Civil Appeals. 126 S.W.2d 61.

One of the requisites of a nuncupative will, as prescribed by article 3346, R.C.S., is that, "it be made in the time of the last sickness of the deceased." As we understand the position of plaintiffs in error, they concede that the trial court was warranted in finding that all other statutory requisites of a nuncupative will were met and complied with. Their sole contention here is that, as a matter of law, the words uttered by the deceased which are claimed to constitute her will were not uttered during her "last sickness" within the meaning of those words as used in the article above referred to. The case turns upon our decision of that single question and our statement will therefore be limited to such facts as are thought to be relevant thereto.

Annie Douglass, the alleged testator, died on September 8, 1934, at the age of more than sixty years. During the four years next preceding her death she had "spells." Dr. R. N. Miller, a witness for the proponent, began attending her professionally in June 1934. In his opinion the original cause of her condition was malaria, but the immediate cause of her death was "aortic insufficiency," which he explained to be a weakened condition of the heart and aorta. The "spells" about which the other witnesses testified were in the nature of fainting spells brought about, according to the evidence as we understand it, by the general weakened condition of her heart. The words claimed to constitute a nuncupative will were spoken by the deceased at about 4:30 p.m. on Thursday, September 6, 1934. The proponent and four other witnesses were present in her bedroom at that time. One of the witnesses, Berttrue McDaniel, went to the home of the deceased to pay her some rent. He testified that he stayed there about two hours, and that while he was there she said to him:

"'Mr. McDaniels, I am feeling not very well at this time, and I know that I am going to die,' and says 'I want Willie Adams to have everything that I possess, and land and money.' She says 'She is the only one stood to me in my sick hour at my bedside.' Says, 'I haven't any relatives at all.'"

"She called your name and said that?"

"Yes, sir, said 'Mr. McDaniels.'"

Thereafter, on September 12, 1934, the witness committed the substance of the testimony to writing, his written memorandum being as follows:

"Beaumont, Texas, Sept. 12, 1934.

On the 6 day of September, 1934, I was at Annie duglas home and she told me and others beside that at her death she wanted Willie Adams to have all that she had land and money and every thing else that she new she was going to die that she had no kin and she was the only one that sat at her bed side and waited on her and she wanted her to have all her estate at her death

'Berttrue McDaniel.'"

He testified that when he went to the home of the deceased he found her in bed; that when he paid her the rent she handed him a receipt therefor which she had theretofore written. His testimony with regard to what occurred on the occasion is, in the main, corroborated by the other witnesses who were present at that time. There is practically no testimony concerning the condition of the deceased from Thursday afternoon until about noon on Saturday. The proponent testified that "she had taken the bed on a Thursday. Friday she was in and Thursday she had taken the bed and stayed in bed from Thursday up to Friday." That testimony probably means that deceased did not leave her home on Friday but was in bed at least a part of that day. Shortly before noon on Saturday morning the deceased went to the home of a neighbor, Julia Keegans, to get Julia to pay a water bill for her which amounted to $1. Deceased had only a $5 bill with her and Julia was unable to change it. Deceased next went to a grocery store near by and purchased some bacon and a small sack of flour. She then returned to Julia's home and gave her $1 with which to pay the water bill. At that time she discovered that she had failed to bring the bill with her, whereupon Julia accompanied her home to get it. The deceased carried the bacon and Julia carried the flour. Shortly after reaching home the deceased became sick. Dr. Miller was later called and he came to see her about six o'clock that evening. She died some two hours or more thereafter.

All text-writers and opinions on the subject of what constitutes "last sickness" within the meaning of statutes relating to nuncupative wills seem to agree that the leading authority upon the question is *Prince v. Hazleton*, 20 Johns., N.Y., 502, 11 Am. Dec. 307. Of that case the author of Redfield, *On the Law of Wills, 4th Ed.*, in Vol. 1, ch. VI, Section 17a wrote: "* * * This subject came before the Court of Errors in New York, at an early day, * * * and is most exhaustively discussed by Chancellor Kent, and by Mr. Justice Woodworth. These opinions contain the substance of all the learning upon the subject of nuncupative wills, from the earliest days to that date and very little has occurred since, which could add much to the very full discussion which the subject there receives."

Our investigation has lead [sic] us to the conclusion that the foregoing is still an accurate statement of the situation. Nothing has been written to date, within our knowledge, which adds materially to the discussion contained in the majority and minority opinions in that case. In fact, there have been relatively few cases before the appellate courts in this generation in which a nuncupative will was offered for probate.

In the majority opinion Chancellor Kent announced this conclusion: "Upon the strength of so much authority, I feel myself warranted in concluding, that a nuncupative will is not good, unless it be made by a testator when he is in extremis, or overtaken by sudden and violent sickness, and has not time or opportunity to make a written will."

That has become known generally as the in extremis rule. The minority opinion in that case announced a somewhat more liberal rule of construction. From that decision two lines of decisions have emerged, one based upon the doctrine that the testator must be in extremis, as announced by Chancellor Kent in the majority opinion, and the other based upon the more liberal rule announced by Justice Woodworth in the dissenting opinion, that the testator need not actually be in extremis. The majority of the courts have adopted the Chancellor Kent doctrine. *Schmitz v. Summers*, 179 Miss. 260, 174 So. 569; *O'Neill v. Smith*, 33 Md. 569; *Bellamy v. Peeler*, 96 Ga. 467, 23 S.E. 387; *Page v. Page*, 2 Rob., Va., 424; *Reese v. Hawthorn*, 10 Grat., Va., 548. Annotations: 20 Am. Dec. 45; 9 A.L.R. 464; 13 L.R.A., N.S., 1092; 67 Am. St. Rep. 572.

The Court of Civil Appeals in its opinion in this case recognized the existence of both the rules above referred to, but concluded that Texas had not adopted the majority rule, and upon the theory that the minority rule was the more reasonable, it adopted and applied that rule. We cannot agree with its conclusions.

In the first place, this court has approved the rule of strict construction. While the facts in the cases below cited were not like those before us, still they presented situations calling upon the court to declare the rule of construction which should govern in cases like the instant one, and the court declared it in very clear language.

In *Jones v. Norton*, 10 Tex. 120, will be found the following: "* * * Nuncupative wills had their origin in the suddenness and urgency of the occasion, where there were present no means of making a formal written will, and no time for delay. And, among all civilized nations, where the necessity has been apparent, nuncupative wills have, under some regulations, been allowed. But the danger of fraud, in setting up such wills,

(continues)

has always exacted full and satisfactory proof of the existence of the necessity; and, where we have a statute regulating such wills, there is the same reason why we should require its conditions and requisites to be satisfactorily made out. * * *"

In *Mitchell v. Vickers*, 20 Tex. 377, it is stated: "Nuncupative wills are not favorites of the law. But as they are authorized by the statute, they must, when duly proved, be allowed and established. They are hedged round with numerous restrictions, to guard against the frauds for which oral wills offer so many facilities; and it is a well established rule, that strict proof is required of all the requisites prescribed by the law. ([*Parsons v. Parsons*] 2 Greenl. [Me.], 298; [*In re Yarnall's Will*] 4 Rawle [Pa.], 46 [26 Am. Dec. 115]; 20 Johns. 502; 1 Jarman on Wills, 89; Modern Probate of Wills, 304.) The provision of the statute (Hart. Dig. Art. 1113) is essentially a copy from the statute of frauds of the 29 Ch. 2, Sect. 19-21; and in substance the same provision is found in the codes of most of the other States; and everywhere a strict construction has been applied."

One of the authorities cited above, 20 Johns. 502, is the *Prince-Hazleton* case.

And in *Watts v. Holland*, 56 Tex. 54, Chancellor Kent's opinion in the *Prince-Hazleton* case, was cited in support of the following conclusion announced in the opinion:

"* * * Wills of this kind, by the law, are allowed to exist, on its bare toleration, and under the shadow of its jealously [sic]; and the establishment of them is allowed, subject to exacting restrictions and conditions which correspond in degree with its fears of their dangerous qualities. * * *"

From the foregoing we conclude that early in the jurisprudence of this state the majority rule that the testator must be in extremis was approved by this court.

In the second place, we do not concur in the conclusion of the Court of Civil Appeals that the so-called liberal rule is the more reasonable. In Chancellor Kent's opinion, supra, written in 1822, reference was made to the fact that, in the ages of Henry the Eighth, Elizabeth and James reading and writing had become so widely diffused that nuncupative wills were confined to extreme cases. Under the view there expressed, which is the commonly accepted view, the more widely the ability to read and write becomes diffused, the less justification exists for recognizing nuncupative wills, except in cases of necessity. With the general diffusion of knowledge at this time, we can perceive of no reason why we should depart from or vary the terms of the rule of construction as heretofore pronounced by this court. The instant case appears to be free of the taint of fraud, but to adopt the rule pressed upon us would be to afford opportunity for fraud in many other cases.

Applying the approved rule to the facts of this case, it is obvious that Annie Douglass was not in extremis when she uttered the words claimed to constitute her will. Thereafter she had the time, ability and opportunity to prepare or have prepared a written will. About that there is no dispute in the record. Certain it is that she could have attended to that matter on Saturday morning when she was able to transact business and go in person to a store to purchase groceries. The probate court did not err in refusing to admit the alleged will to probate.

It is therefore ordered that the judgments of the district court and the Court of Civil Appeals both be reversed, and that judgment be here rendered that the alleged will be not admitted to probate. It is further ordered that upon receipt of the mandate of this court the district court certify this court's judgments to the county court for observance.

Opinion adopted by the Supreme Court.

PAPPAS ENTERPRISES, INC., & others[1]

v.

COMMERCE AND INDUSTRY INSURANCE COMPANY.

661 N.E.2d 81

Supreme Judicial Court of Massachusetts, Suffolk.

Argued Dec. 4, 1995. Decided Feb. 14, 1996.

Insured commenced action in the United States District Court for the District of Massachusetts after insurer declined liability for a fire loss under vacancy exclusion in policy. The District Court certified questions of law to the Supreme Judicial Court. The Supreme Judicial Court, Wilkins, J., held that: (1) 60-day vacancy provision does not apply in case where part of 60 days of vacancy occurred prior to day policy came into force, and (2) however, where policy in force at time of fire was renewal of immediately preceding policy, and portion of vacancy beyond 60 days occurred during immediately preceding policy period, exclusion would operate to preclude coverage for loss.

Certified questions answered.

CERTIFICATION of questions of law to the Supreme Judicial Court by the United States District Court for the District of Massachusetts.

---

1. Pappas Management Corp., The 418 Worcester Wareland Realty Trust, and Capital Site Management Associates.

* * *

* * *

Before LIACOS, C.J., and WILKINS, O'CONNOR, GRE-ANEY and FRIED, JJ.

OPINION

WILKINS, Justice.

The plaintiffs, whom we shall refer to collectively as the insured, are beneficiaries of an insurance policy issued by the defendant insurer that provided coverage against fire loss to numerous properties in the Boston area. The policy, which became effective on September 1, 1990, was a renewal of property damage policies that had been issued on September 1, 1988, and September 1, 1989. On October 27, 1990, fifty-seven days after the effective date of the policy then in effect, one of the covered properties was damaged by fire. That property had been vacant since May, 1989, a period of well over a year.

When the insurer declined liability for the fire loss, the insured commenced an action in the United States District Court for the District of Massachusetts. In defense of the claim, the insurer relied in part on policy language, pre-scribed by G.L. c. 175, § 99 [Twelfth] (1994 ed.), that excluded liability for a loss occurring while the described premises "are vacant or unoccupied beyond a period of sixty consecu-tive days." The facts presented the question [of] whether the period of sixty consecutive days of vacancy included only days during the policy period in which the loss occurred or could also include consecutive days of vacancy during the prior policy period.

A District Court judge determined that (1) the policy pro-vision was inherently ambiguous; (2) there was no control-ling Massachusetts authority; (3) cases elsewhere relied on factors not applicable in the circumstances of this case; and (4) the ambiguity is "contained in every fire insurance policy written in Massachusetts." She invoked S.J.C. Rule 1:03, as appearing in 382 Mass. 700 (1981), and certified the follow-ing two questions to this court:

"1. Does the 60-day vacancy provision for fire insurance policies prescribed by M.G.L. ch. 175 § 99—that the insurance company is not liable for losses occurring 'while the described premises, whether intended for occupancy by owner or tenant, are vacant or unoc-cupied beyond a period of sixty consecutive days'— apply in the case where part of the 60 days of vacancy occurred prior to the day the policy came into force?

"2. If the answer to the preceding question is in the nega-tive, would the result be different (that is, would the vacancy provision apply, and thus preclude coverage) where the policy in force at the time of the fire was a renewal of an immediately preceding policy, and a por-tion of the period of vacancy beyond 60 days occurred during the immediately preceding policy period?"

We conclude that consecutive days of vacancy occurring prior to the policy period may be counted toward the sixty days of vacancy, referred to in the vacancy exclusion provi-sion, only if the current policy is a renewal of substantially the same coverage of the damaged property provided in the previous policy period.

1. Today, and since its insertion in the General Laws (by St.1951, c. 478), § 99 [Twelfth] of G.L. c. 175 has required that a policy state that, unless it otherwise provides, the in-surer of premises of the kind involved in this case "shall not be liable for loss occurring . . . (b) while the described prem-ises, whether intended for occupancy by owner or tenant, are vacant or unoccupied beyond a period of sixty consecutive days." Prior to the 1951 amendment, the relevant statute had required that the standard Massachusetts policy provide that the policy was void "if the premises hereby insured shall be-come vacant by the removal of the owner or occupant, and so remain vacant for more than thirty days." In *Wainer v. Mil-ford Mut. Fire Ins. Co.*, 153 Mass. 335, 339, 26 N.E. 877 (1891), the court construed that former language to mean a vacancy of thirty days commencing while the policy was in force. The words "shall become vacant" pointed to a prospective event, a future vacancy. *Id.* The language of the current § 99 concern-ing premises that "are vacant" for more than sixty days is not as clearly prospective in its focus. The 1951 change in the rel-evant language tends to suggest that the Legislature may have no longer intended that the focus should be only on a prospec-tive vacancy.

The Legislature may not, however, have had its eye on the *Wainer* case when it placed the relevant language in § 99. That language came from the New York standard fire insurance policy, which was adopted in most States by statute and was adopted in Massachusetts in part. See Annot. of the 1943 Standard Fire Insurance Policy 3 (ed. ABA Tort and Insurance Practice Section, 2d ed. 1994); Vance on Insurance 807-808 (3d ed. 1951). The old stan-dard form policy used nationally (but not here) and re-placed generally in this country by the New York standard fire insurance policy, provided that, if premises "be or be-come vacant or unoccupied and so remain for ten days," the policy was void. See *Old Colony Ins. Co. v. Garvey*, 253 F.2d 299, 301 (4th Cir.1958); *Thomas v. Industrial Fire & Casu-alty Co.*, 255 So. 2d 486, 488 (La. App. 1971). The abandon-ment of the old form ("be or become vacant") in favor of the less certain "are vacant" provision was a move away from voiding a policy or coverage based on a vacancy existing at the policy's inception.

We decline to interpret language used in a national stan-dard policy to have a special Massachusetts meaning simply because of an implication that could be derived from an un-certain legislative history. The language "are vacant" (which replaced "be or become vacant") has been consistently regarded as referring only to a vacancy occurring after the commencement of coverage. See *Home Mut. Fire Ins. Co. v. Pierce*, 240 Ark. 865, 402 S.W.2d 672, 674-675 (1966); *Kolivera v. Hartford Fire Ins. Co.*, 8 Ill. App. 3d 356, 360-361, 290 N.E.2d 356 (1972); *Thomas v. Industrial Fire & Casualty*

(continues)

Co., 255 So. 2d 486, 488 (La. App. 1971); *Hurst v. Donegal & Conoy Mut. Fire Ins. Co.*, 224 S.C. 188, 78 S.E.2d 189, 191 (1953); *Old Colony Ins. Co. v. Garvey*, 253 F.2d 299, 302 (4th Cir.1958) (North Carolina law); *United States Fidelity & Guar. Co. v. Board of Educ. of Fairfield*, 339 F. Supp. 315, 318 (N.D. Ala. 1972) (Alabama law).

2. Some opinions holding that the entire vacancy must occur during the policy period resolve the policy ambiguity by reliance on the principle that ambiguities should be construed against the insurer. See *Home Mut. Ins. Co. v. Pierce, supra*, 402 S.W.2d at 675; *Old Colony Ins. Co. v. Garvey, supra; United States Fidelity & Guar. v. Board of Educ., supra*. That principle has no proper place in construing policy language that is, as in this case, dictated by statute. See *McNeill v. Metropolitan Property & Liab. Ins. Co.*, 420 Mass. 587, 589, 650 N.E.2d 793 (1995); *Bilodeau v. Lumbermens Mut. Casualty Co.*, 392 Mass. 537, 541, 467 N.E.2d 137 (1984).

We conclude that the period of a vacancy existing prior to the date coverage is first effective should not be counted in determining whether a vacancy that excludes liability has occurred. One factor is our interest in giving § 99 the same treatment that is given to identical language in policies issued in other States. Another consideration is the opportunity an insurer has to determine whether a vacancy exists at the inception of a policy and to choose not to underwrite the risk, to amend the policy provisions (where permitted), or explicitly to provide coverage at an additional premium. See *Commerce Ins. Co. v. Koch*, 25 Mass. App. Ct. 383, 388, 522 N.E.2d 979 (1988). Most important is the understanding that the parties should reasonably have concerning the policy language, applying normal reasoning and analysis. See *Save-Mor Supermarkets, Inc. v. Skelly Detective Serv., Inc.*, 359 Mass. 221, 225-226, 268 N.E.2d 666 (1971). See also *Home Indem. Ins. Co. v. Merchants Distrib., Inc.*, 396 Mass. 103, 107, 483 N.E.2d 1099 (1985). If a vacancy exists at the inception of coverage, it is hardly reasonable to believe that the coverage should terminate earlier than sixty days later when, for the premium paid, the insurer has agreed to assume for sixty days the increased risk of loss that vacant premises present.

We answer the first certified question in the negative because the vacancy exclusion does not apply when the loss occurred within sixty days of the effective date of the policy, assuming that there was no prior coverage of the type we shall describe in answer to the next question.

3. We next consider whether the vacancy exclusion applies where, as here, the fire loss occurred during the first sixty days of the policy renewal and the vacancy had existed for more than sixty days before the date of the fire. We conclude that the vacancy exclusion precludes coverage of the fire loss, assuming that the renewal did not involve any change of significance in the coverage provided for the property damaged by fire. See *Thatcher v. Reliance Ins. Co.*, 226 A.2d 919, 924-925 (Del. Super. 1967). We do not have the circumstances of the renewal before us and, therefore, our comments can only be general.

The rule we state would unquestionably apply when a policy by its terms, unlike the case before us, was automatically renewed on the timely payment of premium. See *State Farm Gen. Ins. Co. of Bloomington v. Chambers*, 260 Ark. 637, 640, 543 S.W.2d 470 (1976) (denying coverage because "[t]he old and only insurance contract was simply extended for an additional year by the payment of the premium for the ensuing year"). The result should not turn, however, formalistically on whether a new policy, substantially identical as to the damaged property, was issued or the old policy was continued by its terms.

The controlling factor should be what the parties reasonably should have understood the policy language to mean. The property had been vacant since May, 1989. Coverage of the vacant premises undeniably ceased under the first policy sometime in July, 1989, pursuant to the vacancy exclusion clause, sixty days after the vacancy began. That exclusion of coverage continued at least to September 1, 1989, when the second policy period began. An exclusion of coverage unquestionably thereafter existed during the second policy period at least from the end of October, 1989, to September 1, 1990, when the third policy period began. No reasonable insured would believe, in those circumstances, with the uncontestable periods of noncoverage defined above, that the vacant premises would annually be provided coverage during the first sixty days of each renewal period. There is no sensible reason why that result should be reached or expected. The insurer agreed to assume the increased risk during a sixty-day period and not during a period of a vacancy lasting more than sixty days.

We answer the second certified question in the affirmative because a period of a vacancy during a prior policy period should be tacked on to the vacancy continuing during the next subsequent policy period, assuming that there was no significant change in the coverage of the premises.

---

3. We answer the first question in the negative (on the assumption that there was no continuation of coverage), and the second question in the affirmative.

The PEOPLE of the State of Illinois, Appellant,

v.

Robert SANDERS, Appellee.

No. 57801.

Supreme Court of Illinois.

Dec. 16, 1983.

99 Ill. 2d 262, 457 N.E.2d 1241 (1983)

SIMON, Justice

The principal issue raised by this appeal is the construction and application to be given to the Illinois statute which prohibits husband and wife from testifying in criminal trials as to any communication or admission made one to the other or as to any conversation between them (Ill. Rev. Stat. 1981, ch. 38, par. 155-1). More precisely, the question is whether the privilege established by the statute is destroyed when the communication, admission or conversation in question is in the presence of children of the spouses (including a child of one of the spouses who is not the child of defendant) who are old enough to understand the content of the conversation. A secondary issue is whether the plain error rule (87 Ill. 2d R. 615) should be applied to the admission of testimony about two conversations between spouses which may not have occurred in the presence of children but where no objection was advanced when all that was said in them was repeated in a third conversation which took place a few hours later and concerning which testimony was admissible.

A murder conviction of the defendant, Robert Sanders, in a jury trial in the circuit court of Cook County based in part upon the testimony of his wife was reversed by the appellate court (111 Ill. App. 3d 1, 66 Ill. Dec. 761, 443 N.E.2d 687). We allowed the State's petition for leave to appeal (87 Ill. 2d R. 315(a)).

During pretrial discovery, the defense filed a motion *in limine* to prevent the defendant's wife, Beverly Sanders, from testifying about conversations she had with her husband, the defendant. Shortly after it was filed, the public defender's office, which had been representing the defendant, was replaced by other appointed counsel, who represented the defendant at trial. Defendant's new attorney did not seek a ruling on the motion *in limine*, and that motion was never ruled upon. Neither did defendant's attorney object at trial to the wife's testimony.

She testified to three conversations with her husband which implicated him in the murder of which he was convicted. In the first conversation, which occurred the day before the murder, she testified the defendant told her while one or more of her children was present that he was going to rob the murder victim. The second conversation occurred in their bedroom in the early morning hours of the next day. During this conversation, at which no one else was present, the defendant gave his wife a ring and a watch which the woman who lived with

the murder victim identified at trial as the victim's. The third conversation took place later that day. The defendant told her, she testified, that he had robbed the murder victim after striking him with a brick and tying him up. He also told her that he got the watch and ring during the robbery. This conversation, she said, was in the presence of their children.

The State argues that communications between spouses are privileged only when intended to be confidential. In this case the State contends the confidentiality of the first and third conversations was destroyed by the presence of their children. It contends that the second conversation was not confidential because the defendant must have expected that his wife would display the watch and ring he gave her by wearing them in public, and that he did not therefore intend his act to be confidential. The defendant argues that the record does not clearly show that their children were in the immediate presence of his wife and himself in a position to hear their first and third conversations, and that during the second communication he acted in reliance upon the expectation that what transpired would be confidential.

The starting point for our decision is the interpretation given in *People v. Palumbo* (1955), 5 Ill. 2d 409, 125 N.E.2d 518, to the statute relating to the admissibility of interspousal communications (Ill. Rev. Stat. 1981, ch. 38, par. 155-1). This court, in *Palumbo*, rejected the argument advanced by the defendant there that the statute covered all conversations between spouses, holding instead that the statutory privilege, like the similar common law privilege, applied only to conversations which were of a confidential character. The problem is to determine under what circumstances conversations between spouses are to be regarded as confidential in character. This court, in *Palumbo*, adopted the standards announced by the Supreme Court in *Wolfle v. United States* (1934), 291 U.S. 7, 14, 54 S. Ct. 279, 280, 78 L. Ed. 617, 620, a holding which the court 41 years later in *Trammel v. United States* (1980), 445 U.S. 40, 100 S. Ct. 906, 63 L. Ed. 2d 186, said remained undisturbed, by adopting language from *Wolfle* which teaches the following: There is a presumption that interspousal communications are intended to be confidential. But if, because of the circumstances under which the communication took place, it appears that confidentiality was not intended, the communication is not to be regarded as privileged. In this regard, communications made in the presence of third persons are usually not regarded as privileged because they are not made in confidence. In *Palumbo* the communication testified to by the wife was regarded as not privileged because the entire conversation took place in the presence of a third person who, according to the wife, was trying to purchase narcotics from the husband, who was the defendant in the case.

We agree with the appellate court's conclusion that the evidence establishes that the third conversation took place in the presence of her sons, Robert who was 13, and two others who were 10 and 8 at the time. On cross-examination the wife repeated her direct testimony, which is quoted at length

(continues)

in the appellate court opinion, that the three children were present during the third conversation when the following exchange took place:

"Q.   Did you know anything about Curtiss Lovelace?

A.   Only what my husband had told me.

Q.   You say he was bragging when he told you this?

A.   Yes.

Q.   He wasn't nervous, was he?

A.   Not until he found out the man was dead.

Q.   When he first told you was he nervous or bragging?

A.   Not nervous.

Q.   Pacing around the room?

A.   No, he wasn't.

Q.   Excited?

A.   No.

Q.   Who was present when this conversation occurred?

A.   Robert, Albert and Pee Wee.

Q.   They were all there?

A.   Yes."

Following this exchange there was another reference during her cross-examination to the presence of the wife's oldest son:

"Q.   And that day of the events that you have testified to, October the 14th, that day you had just finished a fight with your husband, right?

A.   Yes.

Q.   Did he threaten your son, Robert, in any way at that time?

A.   No.

Q.   But during all of these conversations, Robert, your son, was present, right?

A.   Yes, he was."

The question presented in this case is whether the communications fell outside the ambit of the statute's protection because of the presence of the children. We have found no Illinois case holding that the confidentiality of a conversation between a husband and wife is preserved when it takes place in the presence of children. The appellate court appears to have exhaustively researched the subject and concluded, as we do, that the great weight of authority is that the presence of children of the spouses destroys confidentiality unless they are too young to understand what is being said. (See, e.g., *Master v. Master* (1960), 223 Md. 618, 166 A.2d 251; *Freeman v. Freeman* (1921), 238 Mass. 150, 130 N.E. 220; *Fuller v. Fuller* (1925), 100 W. Va. 309, 130 S.E. 270; McCormick, *Evidence* sec. 80, at 166 (2d ed. 1972); 97 C.J.S. *Witnesses* sec. 271, at 777 (1957).) Nothing in the record indicates that Robert, then 13 years old, was not old enough or sufficiently bright to understand the conversation at which he was present, particularly inasmuch as the wife's testimony indicates that some

of it was directed to him. In these circumstances, under the rule followed in this State, his presence rendered the conversation ineligible for the protection of the statutory privilege.

The defendant argues that this court should recognize a privilege, which he concedes does not presently exist in Illinois, between parents and children which would include conversations between spouses at which their children are present. Courts in a few other jurisdictions have cloaked communications between parent and child with a privilege. (*In re Agosto* (D. Nev. 1983), 553 F. Supp. 1298; *People v. Fitzgerald* (1979), 101 Misc. 2d 712, 422 N.Y.S.2d 309.) The source of all privileges currently applicable in Illinois, with the exception of the attorney–client privilege which has a long-standing common law existence, is statutory. (See Ill. Rev. Stat. 1981, ch. 51, par. 5.1, Ill. Rev. Stat. 1981, ch. 38, par. 104-14 (physician–patient); Ill. Rev. Stat. 1981, ch. 51, par. 48.1 (clergymen); Ill. Rev. Stat. 1981, ch. 91fi, par. 810 (therapist–client); Ill. Rev. Stat. 1981, ch. 111, par. 5533 (accountants); Ill. Rev. Stat. 1981, ch. 51, par. 5.2 (rape crisis personnel–victims); Ill. Rev. Stat. 1981, ch. 48, par. 640 (public officers, regarding unemployment compensation).) We decline, therefore, to introduce an additional privilege by judicial authority which would be applicable to communications between parents and children. Even if we were to initiate this type of privilege, to assist the defendant here we would have to extend it to children of only one spouse, for Robert, the oldest and presumably the most discerning of the children and who was privy at least to the third conversation, was the son of the wife and not the defendant. The statute by its terms does not contemplate such a stretch. Were we to recognize such a privilege under our judicial authority, it would be impossible to contain it logically from spreading to conversations with other relatives in whom a person might normally confide, or even to close friends.

Moreover, we are constrained not only by the legislature's lack of interest in extending an interspousal communications privilege to communications between parent and child, but also by the fact that evidentiary privileges of this sort exclude relevant evidence and thus work against the truthseeking function of legal proceedings. In this they are distinct from evidentiary rules, such as the prohibition against hearsay testimony, which promote this function by insuring the quality of the evidence which is presented. The privilege at issue here results not from a policy of safeguarding the quality of evidence at trial but from a policy of promoting family harmony independent of what might occur in a trial at some future date. The Supreme Court in *Trammel v. United States* (1980), 445 U.S. 40, 50, 100 S. Ct. 906, 912, 63 L. Ed. 2d 186, 195, has stated:

"Testimonial exclusionary rules and privileges contravene the fundamental principle that 'the public . . . has a right to every man's evidence.' *United States v. Bryan* [(1950), 339 U.S. 323, 331, 70 S. Ct. 724, 730, 94 L. Ed. 884, 891.] As such, they must be strictly construed and accepted 'only to the very limited extent that permitting a refusal to testify or excluding relevant evidences has a public good transcending the normally predominant principle of utilizing all rational means for ascertaining truth.' *Elkins v. United States* [(1960), 364 U.S. 206, 234, 80 S. Ct. 1437, 1454, 4 L. Ed. 2d 1669, 1695] (Frankfurter, J., dissenting)."

See also 8 J. Wigmore, *Evidence* section 2285, at 527–28 (1961).

The expansion of existing testimonial privileges and acceptance of new ones involves a balancing of public policies which should be left to the legislature. A compelling reason is that while courts, as institutions, find it easy to perceive value in public policies such as those favoring the admission of all relevant and reliable evidence which directly assist the judicial function of ascertaining the truth, it is not their primary function to promote policies aimed at broader social goals more distantly related to the judiciary. This is primarily the responsibility of the legislature. To the extent that such policies conflict with truth seeking or other values central to the judicial task, the balance that courts draw might not reflect the choice the legislature would make.

The defendant argues, however, that inasmuch as the Federal courts have recognized the right of privacy to be of constitutional dimension in the context of certain functions which are intimately associated with the family, we should hold that communications of a confidential nature between a parent and his child enjoy an evidentiary privilege under the Constitution which did not exist under the common law. The defendant points out that in *In re Agosto* (D. Nev. 1983), 553 F. Supp. 1298, and *People v. Fitzgerald* (1979), 101 Misc. 2d 712, 422 N.Y.S.2d 309, courts have recognized the sort of constitutionally based privilege sought to be invoked here.

We need not decide here, and we do not decide, whether the decisions in *In re Agosto* or *People v. Fitzgerald* were sound, for the question in both of these cases was whether a parent or a child could be compelled against his will to testify against the other. (See also *In re A & M* (1978), 61 A.D.2d 426, 403 N.Y.S.2d 375 (same).) The testimony in the instant case, by contrast, was given by the defendant's wife, without protest and apparently of her own free will, after she was approached and requested to give it by an assistant State's Attorney.

We find this difference to be significant. Both *Agosto* and the New York courts, in holding that a constitutional privilege protected the communications there at issue, relied heavily on conjecture that a family member who is forced to testify against her will would face the unpleasant choice of aiding the criminal conviction of a loved one, perjuring herself on the stand, or risking a citation for contempt of court for refusing to testify, and the belief that the harshness of this choice has the effect of sundering the family relationship. (*In re Agosto* (D. Nev. 1983), 553 F. Supp. 1298, 1309–10, 1326; *In re A & M* (1978), 61 A.D.2d 426, 432–33, 403 N.Y.S.2d 375, 380.) Such a fear is without foundation

where, as in this case, the witness who is a family member volunteers her testimony; the voluntariness of the act is strong evidence that the choice the witness faced was an easy one for her to make. We conclude that even if the Constitution bestows a privilege on communications between a parent and a child, an issue which we do not decide here, that privilege may be waived by the testifying witness acting alone. Compare *United States v. Penn* (9th Cir. 1980), 647 F.2d 876, 882 (rejecting a challenge to a child's voluntary testimony based on due process, on which the right to privacy depends).

Although they were the subject of the motion *in limine* which was never ruled upon, no objection was advanced at trial when the wife testified about the first and second conversations. Under *Palumbo* the Illinois statute preventing testimony by either spouse concerning confidential communications between them creates only a privilege, and a privilege may be waived by the holder of it, in this case the husband. (See Comment, *Marital Privileges*, 46 Chi.-Kent L. Rev. 71, 82–83 (1969).) Therefore, in order to affirm the appellate court's reversal of the conviction, we would have to conclude that the court properly applied the plain error doctrine (87 Ill. 2d R. 615) in holding that testimony regarding the first two conversations was improperly admitted. We believe the appellate court erred in reaching that conclusion.

The plain error doctrine is properly applied only when the question of guilt is close and the evidence in question might have significantly affected the outcome of the case (*People v. Jackson* (1981), 84 Ill. 2d 350, 359, 49 Ill. Dec. 719, 418 N.E.2d 739; *People v. Pickett* (1973), 54 Ill. 2d 280, 283, 296 N.E.2d 856), or where the error alleged is so substantial as to reflect on the fairness or impartiality of the trial regardless of how closely balanced the evidence is (*People v. Baynes* (1981), 88 Ill. 2d 225, 233–34, 244, 58 Ill. Dec. 819, 430 N.E.2d 1070; *People v. Roberts* (1979), 75 Ill. 2d 1, 14, 25 Ill. Dec. 675, 387 N.E.2d 331). The third conversation which we conclude, as the appellate court did, was properly admitted, incorporated substantially all of what was said in the first two conversations. The defendant, in the third conversation, discussed the robbery of the murder victim, said he hit him over the head with a brick, displayed several items of clothing taken from the victim, and referred to the watch and ring he had given his wife earlier that day. Thus, even conceding that no one overheard the first two conversations and that they were privileged and should have been excluded had timely objections been made, in practical effect they did no more than duplicate the incriminating content of the third conversation which was properly admitted. For that reason, the testimony which narrated the defendant's conversation and conduct during the first two conversations was not prejudicial. It added nothing to the third conversation that was needed by the prosecutor to implicate the defendant, and after the third conversation was in evidence, the evidence as to the defendant's guilt was no longer closely balanced.

(continues)

Nor do we regard any errors that might have been made concerning the admissibility of the first and second conversations as depriving the accused of the substantial means of enjoying a fair and impartial trial (*People v. Roberts* (1979), 75 Ill. 2d 1, 14, 25 Ill. Dec. 675, 387 N.E.2d 331; citing *People v. Burson* (1957), 11 Ill. 2d 360, 370–71, 143 N.E.2d 237, see *People v. Whitlow* (1982), 89 Ill. 2d 322, 342, 60 Ill. Dec. 587, 433 N.E.2d 629), as the admission of polygraph evidence does (see *People v. Baynes* (1981), 88 Ill. 2d 225, 244, 58 Ill. Dec. 819, 430 N.E.2d 1070). As we have noted, the husband–wife testimonial privilege operates not to purge a trial of unreliable evidence but to withhold relevant and often highly reliable evidence from the trier of fact. The decision whether to apply the plain error doctrine where the evidence is not close is one of grace. (*People v. Roberts* (1979), 75 Ill. 2d 1, 14, 25 Ill. Dec. 675, 387 N.E.2d 331; *People v. Burson* (1957), 11 Ill. 2d 360, 370–71.) We believe it should not have been applied here, for the fairness and impartiality of the *trial* was not substantially compromised by the errors, if any took place. See *People v. Roberts* (1979), 75 Ill. 2d 1, 14–15, 25 Ill. Dec. 675, 387 N.E.2d 331.

The defendant has raised a number of other issues, none of which were considered by the appellate court because of its erroneous reversal of the conviction on the ground of improper use of privileged communications. The judgment of the appellate court is reversed and the cause is remanded to that court for disposition of the issues raised by the defendant but not reached by its original decision. See *People v. Simpson* (1977), 68 Ill. 2d 276, 284, 12 Ill. Dec. 234, 369 N.E.2d 1248.

Reversed and remanded, with directions.

Peter STANLEY, Sr., Petitioner,

v.

State of ILLINOIS.

No. 70–5014.

Argued Oct. 19, 1971.

Decided April 3, 1972.

405 U.S. 645 (1972)

Mr. Justice WHITE delivered the opinion of the Court.

Joan Stanley lived with Peter Stanley intermittently for 18 years, during which time they had three children.[1] When Joan Stanley died, Peter Stanley lost not only her but also his children. Under Illinois law, the children of unwed fathers become wards of the State upon the death of the mother. Accordingly, upon Joan Stanley's death, in a dependency proceeding instituted by the State of Illinois, Stanley's children[2] were declared wards of the State and placed with court-appointed guardians. Stanley appealed, claiming that he had never been shown to be an unfit parent and that since married fathers and unwed mothers could not be deprived of their children without such a showing, he had been deprived of the equal protection of the laws guaranteed him by the Fourteenth Amendment. The Illinois Supreme Court accepted the fact that Stanley's own unfitness had not been established but rejected the equal protection claim, holding that Stanley could properly be separated from his children upon proof of the single fact that he and the dead mother had not been married. Stanley's actual fitness as a father was irrelevant. In re Stanley, 45 Ill. 2d 132, 256 N.E.2d 814 (1970).

Stanley presses his equal protection claim here. The State continues to respond that unwed fathers are presumed unfit to raise their children and that it is unnecessary to hold individualized hearings to determine whether particular fathers are in fact unfit parents before they are separated from their children. We granted certiorari, 400 U.S. 1020, 91 S. Ct. 584, 27 L. Ed. 2d 631 (1971), to determine whether this method of procedure by presumption could be allowed to stand in light of the fact that Illinois allows married fathers—whether divorced, widowed, or separated—and mothers—even if unwed—the benefit of the presumption that they are fit to raise their children.

I

At the outset we reject any suggestion that we need not consider the propriety of the dependency proceeding that separated the Stanleys because Stanley might be able to regain custody of his children as a guardian or through adoption proceedings. The suggestion is that if Stanley has been treated differently from other parents, the difference is immaterial and not legally cognizable for the purposes of the Fourteenth Amendment. This Court has not, however, embraced the general proposition that a wrong may be done if it can be undone. Cf. *Sniadach v. Family Finance Corp. of Bay View*, 395 U.S. 337, 89 S. Ct. 1820, 23 L. Ed. 2d 349 (1969). Surely, in the case before us, if there is delay between the doing and the undoing petitioner suffers from the deprivation of his children, and the children suffer from uncertainty and dislocation.

It is clear, moreover, that Stanley does not have the means at hand promptly to erase the adverse consequences of the

---

1. Uncontradicted testimony of Peter Stanley, App. 22.

2. Only two children are involved in this litigation.

proceeding in the course of which his children were declared wards of the State. It is first urged that Stanley could act to adopt his children. But under Illinois law, Stanley is treated not as a parent but as a stranger to his children, and the dependency proceeding has gone forward on the presumption that he is unfit to exercise parental rights. Insofar as we are informed, Illinois law affords him no priority in adoption proceedings. It would be his burden to establish not only that he would be a suitable parent but also that he would be the most suitable of all who might want custody of the children.

Neither can we ignore that in the proceedings from which this action developed, the "probation officer," see App. 17, the assistant state's attorney, see *id.*, at 29–30, and the judge charged with the case, see *id.*, at 16–18, 23, made it apparent that Stanley, unmarried and impecunious as he is, could not now expect to profit from adoption proceedings.[3] The Illinois Supreme Court apparently recognized some or all of these considerations, because it did not suggest that Stanley's case was undercut by his failure to petition for adoption.

Before us, the State focuses on Stanley's failure to petition for "custody and control"—the second route by which, it is urged, he might regain authority for his children. Passing the obvious issue whether it would be futile or burdensome for an unmarried father—without funds and already once presumed unfit—to petition for custody, this suggestion overlooks the fact that legal custody is not parenthood or adoption. A person appointed guardian in an action for custody and control is subject to removal at any time without such cause as must be shown in a neglect proceeding against a parent. Ill. Rev. Stat., c. 37, § 705–8. He may not take the children out of the jurisdiction without the court's approval. He may be required to report to the court as to his disposition of the children's affairs. Ill. Rev. Stat., c. 37, § 705–8. Obviously then, even if Stanley were a mere step away from "custody and control," to give an unwed father only "custody and control" would still be to leave him seriously prejudiced by reason of his status.

We must therefore examine the question that Illinois would have us avoid: Is a presumption that distinguishes and burdens all unwed fathers constitutionally repugnant? We conclude that, as a matter of due process of law, Stanley was entitled to a hearing on his fitness as a parent before his children were taken from him and that, by denying him a hearing and extending it to all other parents whose custody of their children is challenged, the State denied Stanley the equal protection of the laws guaranteed by the Fourteenth Amendment.

---

3. The Illinois Supreme Court's opinion is not at all contrary to this conclusion. That court said:

"[T]he trial court's comments clearly indicate the court's willingness to consider a *future* request by the father for *custody and guardianship.*" 45 Ill. 2d 132, 135, 256 N.E.2d 814, 816. (Italics added.) See also the comment of Stanley's counsel on oral argument: "If Peter Stanley could have adopted his children, we would not be here today." Tr. of Oral Arg. 7.

II

Illinois has two principal methods of removing nondelinquent children from the homes of their parents. In a dependency proceeding it may demonstrate that the children are wards of the State because they have no surviving parent or guardian. Ill. Rev. Stat., c. 37, §§ 702–1, 702–5. In a neglect proceeding it may show that children should be wards of the State because the present parent(s) or guardian does not provide suitable care. Ill. Rev. Stat., c. 37, §§ 702–1, 702–4.

The State's right—indeed, duty—to protect minor children through a judicial determination of their interests in a neglect proceeding is not challenged here. Rather, we are faced with a dependency statute that empowers state officials to circumvent neglect proceedings on the theory that an unwed father is not a "parent" whose existing relationship with his children must be considered.[4] "Parents," says the State, "means the father and mother of a legitimate child, or the survivor of them, or the natural mother of an illegitimate child, and includes any adoptive parent," Ill. Rev. Stat., c. 37, § 701–14, but the term does not include unwed fathers.

Under Illinois law, therefore, while the children of all parents can be taken from them in neglect proceedings, that is only after notice, hearing, and proof of such unfitness as a parent as amounts to neglect, an unwed father is uniquely subject to the more simplistic dependency proceeding. By use of this proceeding, the State, on showing that the father was not married to the mother, need not prove unfitness in fact, because it is presumed at law. Thus, the unwed father's claim of parental qualification is avoided as "irrelevant."

In considering this procedure under the Due Process Clause, we recognize, as we have in other cases, that due process of law does not require a hearing "in every conceivable case of government impairment of private interest." *Cafeteria and Restaurant Workers Union etc. v. McElroy*, 367 U.S. 886, 894, 81 S. Ct. 1743, 1748, 6 L. Ed. 2d 1230 (1961). That case explained that "[t]he very nature of due process negates any concept of inflexible procedures universally applicable to every imaginable situation" and firmly established that "what procedures due process may require under any given set of circumstances must begin with a determination of the precise nature of the government function involved as well as of the private interest that has been affected by governmental action." *Id.*, at 895, 81 S. Ct., at 1748; *Goldberg v. Kelly*, 397 U.S. 254, 263, 90 S. Ct. 1011, 1018, 25 L. Ed. 2d 287 (1970).

The private interest here, that of a man in the children he has sired and raised, undeniably warrants deference and, absent a powerful countervailing interest, protection. It is plain that the interest of a parent in the companionship, care, custody, and management of his or her children "come[s] to this

---

4. Even while refusing to label him a "legal parent," the State does not deny that Stanley has a special interest in the outcome of these proceedings. It is undisputed that he is the father of these children, that he lived with the two children whose custody is challenged all their lives, and that he has supported them.

(continues)

Court with a momentum for respect lacking when appeal is made to liberties which derive merely from shifting economic arrangements." *Kovacs v. Cooper*, 336 U.S. 77, 95, 69 S. Ct. 448, 458, 93 L. Ed. 513 (1949) (Frankfurter, J., concurring).

The Court has frequently emphasized the importance of the family. The rights to conceive and to raise one's children have been deemed "essential," *Meyer v. Nebraska*, 262 U.S. 390, 399, 43 S. Ct. 625, 626, 67 L. Ed. 1042 (1923), "basic civil rights of man," *Skinner v. Oklahoma*, 316 U.S. 535, 541, 62 S. Ct. 1110, 1113, 86 L. Ed.1655 (1942), and "[r]ights far more precious . . . than property rights," *May v. Anderson*, 345 U.S. 528, 533, 73 S. Ct. 840, 843, 97 L. Ed. 1221 (1953). "It is cardinal with us that the custody, care and nurture of the child reside first in the parents, whose primary function and freedom include preparation for obligations the state can neither supply nor hinder." *Prince v. Massachusetts*, 321 U.S. 158, 166, 64 S. Ct. 438, 442, 88 L. Ed. 645 (1944). The integrity of the family unit has found protection in the Due Process Clause of the Fourteenth Amendment, *Meyer v. Nebraska, supra*, 262 U.S. at 399, 43 S. Ct. at 626, the Equal Protection Clause of the Fourteenth Amendment, *Skinner v. Oklahoma, supra*, 316 U.S., at 541, 62 S. Ct., at 1113, and the Ninth Amendment, *Griswold v. Connecticut*, 381 U.S. 479, 496, 85 S. Ct. 1678, 14 L. Ed. 2d 510 (1965) (Goldberg, J., concurring).

Nor has the law refused to recognize those family relationships unlegitimized by a marriage ceremony. The Court has declared unconstitutional a state statute denying natural, but illegitimate, children a wrongful-death action for the death of their mother, emphasizing that such children cannot be denied the right of other children because familial bonds in such cases were often as warm, enduring, and important as those arising within a more formally organized family unit. *Levy v. Louisiana*, 391 U.S. 68, 71–72, 88 S. Ct. 1509, 1511, 20 L. Ed. 2d 436 (1968). "To say that the test of equal protection should be the 'legal' rather than the biological relationship is to avoid the issue. For the Equal Protection Clause necessarily limits the authority of a State to draw such 'legal' lines as it chooses." *Glona v. American Guarantee & Liability Ins. Co.*, 391 U.S. 73, 75–76, 88 S. Ct. 1515, 1516, 20 L. Ed. 2d 441 (1968).

These authorities make it clear that, at the least, Stanley's interest in retaining custody of his children is cognizable and substantial.

For its part, the State has made its interest quite plain: Illinois has declared that the aim of the Juvenile Court Act is to protect "the moral, emotional, mental, and physical welfare of the minor and the best interests of the community" and to "strengthen the minor's family ties whenever possible, removing him from the custody of his parents only when his welfare or safety or the protection of the public cannot be adequately safeguarded without removal. . . ." Ill. Rev. Stat., c. 37, § 701–2. These are legitimate interests, well within the power of the State to implement. We do not question the assertion that neglectful parents may be separated from their children.

But we are here not asked to evaluate the legitimacy of the state ends, rather, to determine whether the means used to achieve these ends are constitutionally defensible. What is the State interest in separating children from fathers without a hearing designed to determine whether the father is unfit in a particular disputed case? We observe that the State registers no gain towards its declared goals when it separates children from the custody of fit parents. Indeed, if Stanley is a fit father, the State spites its own articulated goals when it needlessly separates him from his family.

In *Bell v. Burson*, 402 U.S. 535, 91 S. Ct. 1586, 29 L. Ed. 2d 90 (1971), we found a scheme repugnant to the Due Process Clause because it deprived a driver of his license without reference to the very factor (there fault in driving, here fitness as a parent) that the State itself deemed fundamental to its statutory scheme. Illinois would avoid the self-contradiction that rendered the Georgia license suspension system invalid by arguing that Stanley and all other unmarried fathers can reasonably be presumed to be unqualified to raise their children.[5]

---

5. Illinois says in its brief, at 21–23, "[T]he only relevant consideration in determining the propriety of governmental intervention in the raising of children is whether the best interests of the child are served by such intervention.

"In effect, Illinois has imposed a statutory presumption that the best interests of a particular group of children necessitates some governmental supervision in certain clearly defined situations. The group of children who are illegitimate are distinguishable from legitimate children not so much by their status at birth as by the factual differences in their upbringing. While a legitimate child usually is raised by both parents with the attendant familial relationships and a firm concept of home and identity, the illegitimate child normally knows only one parent—the mother. . . .

". . . The petitioner has premised his argument upon particular factual circumstances—a lengthy relationship with the mother . . . a familial relationship with the two children, and a general assumption that this relationship approximates that in which the natural parents are married to each other.

". . . Even if this characterization were accurate (the record is insufficient to support it) it would not affect the validity of the statutory definition of parent. . . . The petitioner does not deny that the children are illegitimate. The record reflects their natural mother's death. Given these two factors, grounds exist for the State's intervention to ensure adequate care and protection for these children. This is true whether or not this particular petitioner assimilates all or none of the normal characteristics common to the classification of fathers who are not married to the mothers of their children." See also Illinois' Brief 23 ("The comparison of married and putative fathers involves exclusively factual differences. The most significant of these are the presence or absence of the father from the home on a day-to-day basis and the responsibility imposed upon the relationship"), *id.*, at 24 (to the same effect), *id.*, at 31 (quoted below in n. 6), *id.*, at 24–26 (physiological and other studies are cited in support of the proposition that men are not naturally inclined to childrearing), and Tr. of Oral Arg. 31 ("We submit that both based on history or [sic] culture the very real differences . . . between the married father and the unmarried father, in terms of their interests in children and their legal responsibility for their children, and the statute here fulfills the compelling governmental objective of protecting children . . .").

It may be, as the State insists, that most unmarried fathers are unsuitable and neglectful parents.[6] It may also be that Stanley is such a parent and that his children should be placed in other hands. But all unmarried fathers are not in this category: some are wholly suited to have custody of their children.[7] That much the State readily concedes, and nothing in this record indicates that Stanley is or has been a neglectful father who has not cared for his children. Given the opportunity to make his case, Stanley may have been seen to be deserving of custody of his offspring. Had this been so, the State's statutory policy would have been furthered by leaving custody in him.

Carrington v. Rash, 380 U.S. 89, 85 S. Ct. 775, 13 L. Ed. 2d 675 (1965), dealt with a similar situation. There we recognized that Texas had a powerful interest in restricting its electorate to bona fide residents. It was not disputed that most servicemen stationed in Texas had no intention of remaining in the State; most therefore could be deprived of a vote in state affairs. But we refused to tolerate a blanket exclusion depriving all servicemen of the vote, when some servicemen clearly were bona fide residents and when "more precise tests," *id.*, at 95, 85 S. Ct., at 779, were available to distinguish members of this latter group. "By forbidding a soldier ever to controvert the presumption of nonresidence," *id.*, at 96, 85 S. Ct., at 780, the State, we said, unjustifiably effected a substantial deprivation. It viewed people one-dimensionally (as servicemen) when a finer perception could readily have been achieved by assessing a serviceman's claim to residency on an individualized basis.

6. The State speaks of "the general disinterest of putative fathers in their illegitimate children" (Brief 8) and opines that "[i]n most instances the natural father is a stranger to his children." Brief 31.

7. See In re T., 8 Mich. App. 122, 154 N.W.2d 27 (1967). There a panel of the Michigan Court of Appeals, in unanimously affirming a circuit court's determination that the father of an illegitimate son was best suited to raise the boy, said:

"The appellants' presentation in this case proceeds on the assumption that placing Mark for adoption is inherently preferable to rearing by his father, that uprooting him from the family which he knew from birth until he was a year and a half old, secretly institutionalizing him and later transferring him to strangers is so incontrovertibly better that no court has the power even to consider the matter. Hardly anyone would even suggest such a proposition if we were talking about a child born in wedlock.

"We are not aware of any sociological data justifying the assumption that an illegitimate child reared by his natural father is less likely to receive a proper upbringing than one reared by his natural father who was at one time married to his mother, or that the stigma of illegitimacy is so pervasive it requires adoption by strangers and permanent termination of a subsisting relationship with the child's father." *Id.*, at 146, 154 N.W.2d, at 39.

"We recognize that special problems may be involved in determining whether servicemen have actually acquired a new domicile in a State for franchise purposes. We emphasize that Texas is free to take reasonable and adequate steps, as have other States, to see that all applicants for the vote actually fulfill the requirements of bona fide residence. But [the challenged] provision goes beyond such rules. '[T]he presumption here created is . . . definitely conclusive—incapable of being overcome by proof of the most positive character.'" *Id.*, at 96, 85 S. Ct., at 780.

"All servicemen not residents of Texas before induction," we concluded, "come within the provision's sweep. Not one of them can ever vote in Texas, no matter" what their individual qualifications. *Ibid.* We found such a situation repugnant to the Equal Protection Clause.

Despite *Bell* and *Carrington*, it may be argued that unmarried fathers are so seldom fit that Illinois need not undergo the administrative inconvenience of inquiry in any case, including Stanley's. The establishment of prompt efficacious procedures to achieve legitimate state ends is a proper state interest worthy of cognizance in constitutional adjudication. But the Constitution recognizes higher values than speed and efficiency.[8] Indeed, one might fairly say of the Bill of Rights in general, and the Due Process Clause in particular, that they were designed to protect the fragile values of a vulnerable citizenry from the overbearing concern for efficiency and efficacy that may characterize praiseworthy government officials no less, and perhaps more, than mediocre ones.

Procedure by presumption is always cheaper and easier than individualized determination. But when, as here, the procedure forecloses the determinative issues of competence and care, when it explicitly disdains present realities in deference to past formalities, it needlessly risks running

8. Cf. *Reed v. Reed*, 404 U.S. 71, 76, 92 S. Ct. 251, 254, 30 L. Ed. 2d 225 (1971). "Clearly the objective of reducing the workload on probate courts by eliminating one class of contests is not without some legitimacy. . . . [But to] give a mandatory preference to members of either sex over members of the other, merely to accomplish the elimination of hearings on the merits, is to make the very kind of arbitrary legislative choice forbidden by the Equal Protection Clause of the Fourteenth Amendment." *Carrington v. Rash*, 380 U.S. 89, 96, 85 S. Ct. 775, 780 (1965), teaches the same lesson. ". . . States may not casually deprive a class of individuals of the vote because of some remote administrative benefit to the State. *Oyama v. [State of] California*, 332 U.S. 633, 68 S. Ct. 269, 92 L. Ed. 249. By forbidding a soldier ever to controvert the presumption of nonresidence, the Texas Constitution imposes an invidious discrimination in violation of the Fourteenth Amendment."

(continues)

roughshod over the important interests of both parent and child. It therefore cannot stand.[9]

Bell v. Burson held that the State could not, while purporting to be concerned with fault in suspending a driver's license, deprive a citizen of his license without a hearing that would assess fault. Absent fault, the State's declared interest was so attenuated that administrative convenience was insufficient to excuse a hearing where evidence of fault could be considered. That drivers involved in accidents, as a statistical matter, might be very likely to have been wholly or partially at fault did not foreclose hearing and proof in specific cases before licenses were suspended.

We think that [the] Due Process Clause mandates a similar result here. The State's interest in caring for Stanley's children is *de minimis* if Stanley is shown to be a fit father. It insists on presuming rather than proving Stanley's unfitness solely because it is more convenient to presume than to prove. Under the Due Process Clause that advantage is insufficient to justify refusing a father a hearing when the issue at stake is the dismemberment of his family.

III

The State of Illinois assumes custody of the children of married parents, divorced parents, and unmarried mothers only after a hearing and proof of neglect. The children of unmarried fathers, however, are declared dependent children without a hearing on parental fitness and without proof of neglect. Stanley's claim in the state courts and here is that failure to afford him a hearing on his parental qualifications while extending it to other parents denied him equal protection of the laws. We have concluded that all Illinois parents are constitutionally entitled to a hearing on their fitness before their children are removed from their custody. It follows that denying such a hearing to Stanley and those like him while granting it to other Illinois parents is inescapably contrary to the Equal Protection Clause.[10]

The judgment of the Supreme Court of Illinois is reversed and the case is remanded to that court for proceedings not inconsistent with this opinion. It is so ordered.

Reversed and remanded.

Mr. Justice POWELL and Mr. Justice REHNQUIST took no part in the consideration or decision of this case.

Mr. Justice DOUGLAS joins in Parts I and II of this opinion.

Mr. Chief Justice BURGER, with whom Mr. Justice BLACKMUN concurs, dissenting.

---

9. We note in passing that the incremental cost of offering unwed fathers an opportunity for individualized hearings on fitness appears to be minimal. If unwed fathers, in the main, do not care about the disposition of their children, they will not appear to demand hearings. If they do care, under the scheme here held invalid, Illinois would admittedly at some later time have to afford them a properly focused hearing in a custody or adoption proceeding.

Extending opportunity for hearing to unwed fathers who desire and claim competence to care for their children creates no constitutional or procedural obstacle to foreclosing those unwed fathers who are not so inclined. The Illinois law governing procedure in juvenile cases, Ill. Rev. Stat., c. 37, § 704–1 et seq., provides for personal service, notice by certified mail, or for notice by publication when personal or certified mail service cannot be had or when notice is directed to unknown respondents under the style of "All whom it may Concern." Unwed fathers who do not promptly respond cannot complain if their children are declared wards of the State. Those who do respond retain the burden of proving their fatherhood.

10. Predicating a finding of constitutional invalidity under the Equal Protection Clause of the Fourteenth Amendment on the observation that a State has accorded bedrock procedural rights to some, but not to all similarly situated, is not contradictory to our holding in *Picard v. Connor*, 404 U.S. 270, 92 S. Ct. 509, 30 L. Ed. 2d 438 (1971). In that case a due process, rather than an equal protection, claim was raised in the state courts. The federal courts were, in our opinion, barred from reversing the state conviction on grounds of contravention of the Equal Protection Clause when that clause had not been referred to for consideration by the state authorities. Here, in contrast, we dispose of the case on the constitutional premise raised below, reaching the result by a method of analysis readily available to the state court.

For the same reason the strictures of *Cardinale v. Louisiana*, 394 U.S. 437, 89 S. Ct. 1161, 22 L. Ed. 2d 398 (1969), and *Hill v. California*, 401 U.S. 797, 91 S. Ct. 1106, 28 L. Ed. 2d 484 (1971), have been fully observed.

STATE of Maine

v.

David BENNER.

Supreme Judicial Court of Maine.

Submitted on Briefs Jan. 3, 1995.

Decided Feb. 10, 1995.

654 A.2d 435 (Me. 1995)

CLIFFORD, Justice.

David Benner appeals from a conviction for assault, 17-A M.R.S.A. § 207 (1983 & Supp.1994),[1] following a jury trial in Superior Court (Washington County, *Mills*, J.). On appeal Benner contends, *inter alia*, that the trial court erred in giving a cautionary instruction on how the jury should consider the hearsay testimony of the investigating state trooper, and that there was insufficient evidence to support the jury's verdict. Finding no error, we affirm the conviction.

The evidence at trial revealed the following. The victim testified that Benner is her boyfriend, and at the time of the alleged assault, she was living with him. On the night of September 11, 1993, she was home alone with Benner; they were arguing and she wanted him out of the house. The victim stated that she called the state police and complained that Benner had hit her. She also testified that she told the investigating trooper that Benner had struck her on the hand with either an ax handle or a broom stick. She testified that she had said that Benner had hit her only because she wanted him out of her house and not because he had actually hit her. She further testified that the injury to the back of her hand occurred because she was drunk and had fallen.

State Trooper Raymond Bessette testified that while on patrol on the night of September 11, 1993, he received a call from the dispatcher that the victim called to complain that Benner had struck her. When Bessette arrived at the home, he observed the victim to be visibly distraught, scared, and quite nervous, and that she had an injury to the back of her hand. She also had watery eyes. He did not, however, observe her to be under the influence.

In order to impeach her credibility, and without objection by the defendant,[2] Bessette further testified as to what the victim had told him that night. Before Bessette did so, however,

Benner requested the jury be instructed that the statements "can be used for impeachment value, but not as substantive evidence." The court cautioned the jury as follows:

> [T]he Trooper is now going to testify about statements that were made to him by [the victim], and that testimony is offered to impeach her testimony, the statements that she has testified about. It is not offered for the truth of the matter asserted.

The defendant did not object to the instruction. The jury returned a verdict of guilty and the court accordingly entered a judgment of conviction.

I

Benner contends that the trial court's cautionary instruction to the jury prior to Trooper Bessette's testimony was inadequate. Although he concedes that the court's instruction is a correct statement of the law, and that he failed to object, he avers that the trial court committed reversible error by failing to give a full explanation of the instructions. We disagree.

Because Benner did not object to the instruction when it was given, we review the charge only for obvious error affecting his substantial rights. *State v. McCluskie*, 611 A.2d 975, 978 (Me. 1992); *see* M.R. Crim. P. 30(b). Giving an instruction that is a correct statement of the law does not rise to the level of obvious error. Jurors are presumed to understand the instruction. *See State v. Naoum*, 548 A.2d 120, 123 (Me. 1988). While it would have been more helpful for the trial court to have given a more detailed instruction on the limited purposes for which the hearsay testimony was admitted, *see* D. Alexander, *Maine Jury Instruction Manual* § 6-24 (2d ed. 1990), the cautionary instruction actually given was not obvious error.

II

Benner further contends that the evidence presented at trial was insufficient to support a judgment of conviction. The standard to determine if evidence at trial was sufficient to support the jury's verdict is "whether, based on the evidence viewed in the light most favorable to the prosecution, any trier of fact rationally could find beyond a reasonable doubt every element of the offense charged." *State v. Barry*, 495 A.2d 825, 826 (Me. 1985).

The affirmative evidence supporting a guilty verdict includes the following. The victim was home alone with Benner; the two were having an argument; the victim made a complaint; when the trooper arrived, the victim was distraught, scared, and nervous; the trooper observed the back of the victim's hand to be swollen; Benner was intoxicated; the trooper testified that the victim was sober.

Although the victim testified at the trial that Benner had not hit her and that she sustained her injuries while drunk

---

1. 17-A M.R.S.A. § 207(1) (1983) provides that "[a] person is guilty of assault if he intentionally, knowingly, or recklessly causes bodily injury or offensive physical contact to another."

2. Benner did not argue for the exclusion of the statements because the probative value of Bessette's testimony as to the victim's statement was substantially outweighed by the danger of unfair prejudice. *See* M.R. Evid. 403.

(continues)

by falling into a wall, her testimony was substantially impeached by her own testimony[3] and that of Trooper Bessette. It was reasonable for the jury to disregard her denials. As we have previously stated, "the weight of the evidence and the determination of witness credibility are the exclusive province of the jury." *State v. Glover*, 594 A.2d 1086, 1088 (Me. 1991). Therefore, her testimony alone does not mandate a conclusion that the evidence was insufficient.

Although the conviction in this case was based substantially on circumstantial evidence, a conviction may be grounded on such evidence. *State v. Ingalls*, 554 A.2d 1272, 1276 (Me. 1988). Indeed, a conviction based solely on

---

3. The victim's trial testimony that she told police that Benner hit her was hearsay. It normally would not be admissible for the truth of the matter asserted, but would be admissible to impeach the victim's trial testimony that Benner did not strike her. M.R. Evid. 801, 802. In this case, however, because there was no objection to the victim's statement that she told the police that Benner had hit her, there was no instruction that the testimony could be considered for impeachment only. It is not wholly unreliable and its admission was not obvious error.

circumstantial evidence is not for that reason less conclusive. *State v. LeClair*, 425 A.2d 182, 184 (Me. 1981). The factfinder is allowed to draw all reasonable inferences from the circumstantial evidence. *State v. Crosby*, 456 A.2d 369, 370 (Me. 1983). Viewing the evidence in the light most favorable to the State, the jury could have rationally inferred that Benner had assaulted the victim.[4]

The entry is:

Judgment affirmed.

All concurring.

---

4. Benner also contends that the court's instruction on the elements of assault constituted error. Our review of the instructions, to which Benner did not object, reveals no error. See *State v. Griffin*, 459 A.2d 1086, 1091–92 (Me. 1983); 17-A M.R.S.A. § 2(5) (1983).

STATE of New Mexico, Plaintiff-Appellee,

v.

Abdul MUQQDDIN, Defendant-Appellant.

No. 28,474.

May 5, 2010.

Certiorari Granted, Aug. 2, 2010, No. 32,430.

2010 NMCA 69, __ P.3d __ (Ct. App. 2010)

* * *

OPINION

KENNEDY, Judge.

{1} Abdul Muqqddin (Defendant) used a nail to penetrate the gas tank of a van parked in a dark alley without the permission of the owner. After piercing the tank, Defendant positioned a container below the hole so as to catch the fuel as it drained from the van. The van was in extremely bad condition and had been parked in the alley for as many as six months, though it had not been abandoned. Defendant appeals his convictions for auto burglary under NMSA 1978, Section 30-16-3 (1971), criminal damage to property under NMSA 1978, Section 30-15-1 (1963), and larceny under NMSA 1978, Section 30-16-1 (1987) (amended 2006). Defendant argues that penetrating a gas tank with a nail is

insufficient to constitute an entry under the burglary statute, and because he believed the van to be abandoned, he lacked the requisite intent to commit the crimes of burglary, criminal damage, and larceny. As a result, Defendant claims, his convictions are unsupported by substantial evidence. We hold that entry, under Section 30-16-3, is complete when a defendant penetrates a gas tank with a nail. We also hold that substantial evidence supports Defendant's convictions. We affirm.

FACTS

{2} Neither party disputes what took place in the early morning hours of August 21, 2005. An Albuquerque police officer, responding to an unrelated call, heard loud banging noises coming from an alley. Suspicious of the noise, he stopped his vehicle at the entrance to the alley and cautiously investigated on foot. After proceeding approximately halfway down the alley, the officer saw Defendant lying underneath a van. Next to Defendant was a red plastic container, positioned beneath the van to catch fuel dripping from the tank. The officer detained Defendant, asked him his name, and Defendant falsely identified himself as Edward Edgerton. A routine computer check revealed that Edgerton had an outstanding warrant for his arrest, and at that time, Defendant gave the officer his real name.

{3} When asked what he was doing under the van, Defendant first stated that he was taking gas from the tank with the permission of the owner. Upon further questioning, however, Defendant admitted that he did not have permission to take the gas, but that because the van was abandoned, it was alright [sic] for him to do so. He said he had used a nail to create a hole in the tank so that the gas could escape, and two nails were found in his pocket. At that point, the officer placed Defendant under arrest and called for additional personnel to assist in an investigation of the scene.

{4} Police identified the van's owner as Emil Hanson, the proprietor of a nearby dry cleaning business. Hanson had purchased the van approximately two years prior but stopped driving it when it became too expensive for him to do so. While trying to figure out what to do with it, he purchased a new van and parked the old one in the alley behind his business. He testified that although the van was in bad condition and could have been sitting in the alley for as many as six months, he had neither abandoned it nor given Defendant permission to enter or remove fuel from it.

{5} When the State completed its case in chief, Defendant made a motion for directed verdict on all counts. In pertinent part, Defendant argued that penetration of a gas tank with a nail is insufficient to constitute burglary in New Mexico, and further, that he lacked the requisite intent to commit burglary, criminal damage, and larceny because he thought the van was abandoned. As a result, Defendant contended, substantial evidence did not support the charges against him. These arguments failed to persuade the district court, Defendant's motion was denied, and he was convicted as stated above. Defendant now reasserts the arguments from his motion for directed verdict.

* * *

THE CRIME OF BURGLARY

{7} Section 30-16-3 defines the crime of burglary as "the unauthorized entry of any vehicle, watercraft, aircraft, dwelling or other structure, movable or immovable, with the intent to commit any felony or theft therein." As such, Section 30-16-3 expresses "a radical departure from its common law predecessor," which required "(1) breaking and (2) entering (3) a dwelling house (4) of another (5) in the nighttime (6) with the intent to commit a felony therein." *State v. Rodriguez,* 101 N.M. 192, 193, 679 P.2d 1290, 1291 (Ct. App. 1984); *see State v. Bybee,* 109 N.M. 44, 45, 781 P.2d 316, 317 (Ct. App. 1989). Thus, our Legislature has chosen to keep only the element of entry completely intact. *Rodriguez,* 101 N.M. at 193, 679 P.2d at 1291. As this Court has held, entry contemplates penetration of a space by either a person or an instrument. *State v. Tixier,* 89 N.M. 297, 298-99, 551 P.2d 987, 988-89 (Ct. App. 1976) (holding that a one-half-inch penetration with an instrument is enough to effectuate an entry; "[a]ny penetration, however slight, of the interior space is sufficient").

{8} This Court's opinions in *Rodriguez* and *State v. Reynolds,* 111 N.M. 263, 804 P.2d 1082 (Ct. App. 1990), define the limits of entry in the context of vehicle burglary. In *Rodriguez,* the defendant reached into the uncovered bed of a pickup truck and removed a toolbox with the intent of taking it unlawfully. 101 N.M. at 193, 679 P.2d at 1291. This Court held that such an entry is sufficient to constitute a burglary. "[W]e hold that the bed of a pickup truck, as a part of a vehicle, falls within the statutorily protected area." *Id.* at 194, 679 P.2d at 1292. A similar issue prompted the analysis in *Reynolds.* In that case, like the one before us, police found the defendant on the ground beneath a vehicle. Testimony at trial established that he reached into the engine compartment from underneath in an apparent attempt to remove the vehicle's starter. *Reynolds,* 111 N.M. at 264-65, 804 P.2d at 1083-84. This Court, citing *Tixier,* held that such an act is sufficient to sustain a conviction for burglary. *Reynolds,* 111 N.M. at 270, 804 P.2d at 1089. "In establishing a burglary, [a]ny penetration, however slight, of the interior space is sufficient [to constitute entry]. Since there was no dispute that [the] defendant's hand penetrated the engine compartment of the vehicle, there would have been no rational basis for the jury to find attempted burglary but not burglary itself[.]" *Id.* (second alteration in original) (internal quotation marks and citation omitted). Thus, a jury could reasonably conclude that a burglary had occurred. *Id.*

{9} We are sympathetic to the unique facts of Defendant's case. He was found draining fuel from the tank of a van with no license plate, several broken windows, and four flat tires. The investigating officer testified that the van would have been unsafe to drive, and Hanson, the owner, testified that the van might have been sitting in the alley for as many as six months prior to the incident. In fact, during direct examination, Hanson stated that although the van had not been abandoned, his plan for it was to "just give it to charity or try to sell it for the engine."

{10} Necessary or not, that which might be a prudent measure of justice must bow to that which the State may legally prove. Simply put, Defendant was properly charged. He did not have permission to enter the van, and his actions clearly constitute entry under New Mexico's burglary statute.

{11} By Defendant's own uncontroverted admission to police, he laid down on the ground beneath the van, procured an instrument, and used it to create a hole in the tank. As fuel dripped from the hole, he caught it in a container specifically positioned to do so. He did not own the van or the fuel. Such facts are plainly analogous to this Court's opinions in *Rodriguez* and *Reynolds.* A fuel tank—attached as it is, to a vehicle—is unquestionably *a part of* that vehicle and absolutely necessary for its primary function as a mode of transportation. Any penetration of a vehicle's perimeter is thus a penetration of the vehicle itself. *See Reynolds,* 111 N.M. at 270, 804 P.2d at 1089. Like the defendant's entry of the truck bed in *Rodriguez,* this Defendant reached into the undercarriage of the van and removed fuel from inside the tank located there. *See Rodriguez,* 101 N.M. at 193, 679 P.2d at 1291. In fact, Defendant went even further by puncturing the tank in order to effectuate the theft. But perhaps even more analogous is *Reynolds.* In that case, the defendant reached into the

(continues)

engine compartment from underneath so he could remove the starter. *Reynolds,* 111 N.M. at 265, 270, 804 P.2d at 1084, 1089. Likewise, Defendant in this case reached into the fuel tank, albeit via an instrument, in order to remove fuel, and as this Court has held, "[a]ny penetration, however slight . . . is sufficient." *Id.* at 270, 804 P.2d at 1089.

{12} The facts of the instant case fit cleanly within the conceptual framework established by *Reynolds* and *Rodriguez,* and understandably, Defendant had difficulty distinguishing those opinions. He thus relies heavily upon out-of-state cases to support his argument, but each is readily distinguishable in either law or fact. For instance, in *People v. Davis,* 18 Cal. 4th 712, 76 Cal. Rptr. 2d 770, 958 P.2d 1083, 1090 (1998), the defendant placed a forged check into the deposit window of a check cashing business. The court held that such an act, although technically an entry with the intent to commit a theft, should nevertheless not be considered an entry for purposes of California's burglary statute. *Id.* Likewise, in *R.E.S. v. State,* 396 So. 2d 1219, 1220 (Fla. Dist. Ct. App. 1981), the court analyzed whether, under Florida's burglary statute, siphoning gas from the tank of a vehicle constituted an entry. It held that siphoning did not constitute an entry and based its holding on the notion that Florida's burglary statute contemplates only vehicle compartments "which can be entered either wholly or partially by a person; e.g., engine and passenger compartments, trunks, etc." *Id.* Finally, the Florida Supreme Court reached the same conclusion in *Drew v. State,* 773 So. 2d 46, 47 (Fla. 2000), when it considered whether the removal of tires or hubcaps from a vehicle constituted an entry. In that opinion, the court held that such an act could not constitute a burglary because Florida's common law requires that the theft actually take place "within" the vehicle. Removal of a tire or hubcap, which requires disassembly, thus does not take place within the vehicle as required by the statute. *Id.* at 52.

{13} On the facts and New Mexico law before us, the reasoning of these out-of-state authorities fails to persuade.

The facts of *Davis,* for instance, are readily distinguishable. In that case, the California court held that an entry had not occurred because the chute in which the defendant placed the forged check was regularly used by other patrons who also deposited checks. Such an entry does not violate "the occupant's possessory interest in the building." *Davis,* 76 Cal. Rptr. 2d 770, 958 P.2d at 1089. In the case before us, Hanson's possessory interest in the van was clearly violated when Defendant punctured its tank. Nor are we persuaded by *R.E.S.* and *Drew,* the Florida opinions, which both proceed from interpretations of Florida's case law. In those cases, it is apparent that burglary in Florida contemplates the entry of a vehicle compartment large enough to accommodate at least a part of a person and that the theft actually occurred within the vehicle. *See Drew,* 773 So. 2d at 52; *R.E.S.,* 396 So. 2d at 1220. Not so in New Mexico, where a slight entry by use of an instrument is sufficient. *See, e.g., Reynolds,* 111 N.M. at 264-65, 804 P.2d at 1083-84 (providing that removal of a starter from the engine compartment is sufficient to constitute burglary); *Tixier,* 89 N.M. at 298-99, 551 P.2d at 988-89 (including the use of an instrument in the definition of an entry). We turn now to Defendant's other argument on appeal.

* * *

CONCLUSION

{16} For the reasons stated above, we hold that using a nail to penetrate a vehicle's gas tank constitutes an entry under Section 30-16-3. We also hold that substantial evidence supports each of Defendant's convictions. We affirm.

{17} IT IS SO ORDERED.

WE CONCUR: JONATHAN B. SUTIN and TIMOTHY L. GARCIA, Judges.

UNITED STATES of America, Plaintiff–Appellee,

v.

Carless JONES and Eugene Harvey, Defendants–Appellants.

707 F.2d 1169 (l0th Cir. 1983)

SEYMOUR, CIRCUIT JUDGE.

On December 31, 1981, three armed men robbed a Denver area savings and loan branch. Lisa Dalke, a teller, and Marilyn Gates, the branch manager, were bound and forced to lie on the floor. The robbers removed money orders, traveler's

checks, and $2,024 in cash, triggering a bank surveillance camera. The robbers were seen leaving the bank and walking towards an automobile by a bank customer, Christine Christensen, who had just driven up to the front of the bank. Because the men appeared suspicious, Christensen wrote down the license number of their car. One of the robbers ordered Christensen into the bank, and the men left.

On January 4, 1982, members of the Denver Police Department responded to a family disturbance call at or near 3434 High Street in Denver. While there, the officers saw a car bearing the license number observed by Christensen at the robbery. Denver Police Officer Andrade saw a man carrying a brown satchel emerge from the back of number 3434.

Andrade ordered him to halt, and the man ran. The officers found the man, later identified by Andrade as defendant Jones, hiding in the rear of another building. He no longer had the brown satchel. When questioned about the satchel, Jones replied, "I don't know what you are talking about." Rec., vol. II, at 27.

The police arrested Jones and took him into the residence from which he had fled. He was questioned several times about the location of the brown satchel. Finally, Jones directed a woman who was present, "Show 'em where I put it," pointing towards a closet. *Id.* at 29. The officers searched the closet, but found nothing. Shortly thereafter, however, other police officers found a satchel lying outside the building where Jones had been found hiding, near the spot where he was apprehended. Officer Andrade identified the satchel as the one Jones had been carrying, and opened it. Inside was a handgun, traffic tickets written out in Jones' name, and a small knapsack. The officers asked Jones if the satchel was his, and he again denied owning it.

Appellants Harvey and Jones were jointly indicted and charged with armed robbery of a savings and loan in violation of 18 U.S.C. § 2113(a), (d) (1976). Both defendants filed motions for severance. Jones also filed a motion to suppress the fruits of the search of the satchel. After a lengthy pretrial hearing, these and other motions were denied. Jones and Harvey were tried and found guilty. Both filed motions for a new trial, alleging that adverse prior contact between the jury forewoman and Jones had denied them a fair trial. The trial court denied the motions.

On appeal, Harvey argues that the trial court erred in denying his motion to sever. Jones argues that the warrantless search of the satchel violated his Fourth Amendment rights. Both defendants argue that their Sixth Amendment rights to a fair trial were violated by juror misconduct. For the reasons discussed below, we affirm defendants' convictions.

* * *

II

Abandonment

Jones argues that the warrantless search of the satchel violated his Fourth Amendment rights. The trial court held that the search was permissible on two grounds: that Jones had abandoned the satchel and therefore had no legitimate expectation of privacy in it entitling him to Fourth Amendment protection; and that the search was permissible as incident to a lawful arrest. Because of our resolution of the first ground, we need not address the court's alternative holding that the search was incident to Jones' arrest, and we offer no opinion as to the correctness of that holding.

In *Abel v. United States*, 362 U.S. 217, 241, 80 S. Ct. 683, 698, 4 L. Ed. 2d 668 (1960), the Supreme Court declared that the Government's warrantless seizure of abandoned property did not violate the Fourth Amendment. *Id.* at 241, 80 S. Ct.

at 698. Since *Abel*, the circuit courts have examined the issue, and the following guidelines to the "abandoned property" exception to the Fourth Amendment's warrant requirement have emerged. When individuals voluntarily abandon property, they forfeit any expectation of privacy in it that they might have had. *United States v. Berd*, 634 F.2d 979, 987 (5th Cir. 1981). Therefore, a warrantless search or seizure of abandoned property is not unreasonable under the Fourth Amendment. *For example, United States v. Diggs*, 649 F.2d 731, 735 (9th Cir.), *cert. denied*, 454 U.S. 970, 102 S. Ct. 516, 70 L. Ed. 2d 387 (1981); *Berd*, 634 F.2d at 987; *United States v. D'Avanzo*, 443 F.2d 1224, 1225-26 (2d Cir.), *cert. denied*, 404 U.S. 850, 92 S. Ct. 86, 30 L. Ed. 2d 89 (1971). The existence of police pursuit or investigation at the time of abandonment does not of itself render the abandonment involuntary. *United States v. Colbert*, 474 F.2d 174, 176 (5th Cir. 1973); *see generally, for example, Berd*, 634 F.2d at 987; *United States v. Canady*, 615 F.2d 694 (5th Cir.), *cert. denied*, 449 U.S. 862, 101 S. Ct. 165, 66 L. Ed. 2d 78 (1980); *United States v. Williams*, 569 F.2d 823 (5th Cir. 1978); *D'Avanzo*, 443 F.2d 1224.

The test for abandonment is whether an individual has retained any reasonable expectation of privacy in the object. *Diggs*, 649 F.2d at 735. This determination is to be made by objective standards. *United States v. Kendall*, 655 F.2d 199, 201 (9th Cir. 1981), *cert. denied*, 455 U.S. 941, 102 S. Ct. 1434, 71 L. Ed. 2d 652 (1982). An expectation of privacy is a question of intent, which "may be inferred from words spoken, acts done, and other objective facts." *Kendall*, 655 F.2d at 202 (quoting *Williams*, 569 F.2d at 826). "A finding of abandonment is reviewed under the clearly erroneous standard." *Diggs*, 649 F.2d at 735.

When Jones discarded the satchel, he may have hoped that the police would not find it and that he could later retrieve it. However, his ability to recover the satchel depended entirely upon fate and the absence of inquisitive (and acquisitive) passersby. When questioned by the police, he repeatedly disavowed any knowledge of the satchel. His comment to the woman in the residence to "[s]how 'em where I put it" appears at most to have been a mere ruse to deceive the police as to the existence of a satchel, rather than "words which acknowledged ownership," Brief of Appellants, at 17. Here, the "words spoken" and, more significantly, the "acts done" objectively manifested Jones' clear intent to relinquish his expectation of privacy and abandon the satchel. This is not a case like *United States v. Burnette*, 698 F.2d 1038 (9th Cir. 1983), where, after an initial disclaimer of ownership, the defendant's subsequent conduct "strongly indicated her intent to retain a 'reasonable expectation of privacy in the purse.'" *Id.* at 1048.

We hold that Jones voluntarily abandoned the satchel. Accordingly, the subsequent warrantless search by the police did not violate his Fourth Amendment rights.

* * *

Affirmed.

UNITED STATES, Petitioner

v.

Alberto Antonio LEON et al.
No. 82–1771.
Argued Jan. 17, 1984.
Decided July 5, 1984.

Rehearing Denied Sept. 18, 1984.
468 U.S. 897 (1984)

Justice WHITE delivered the opinion of the Court.

This case presents the question whether the Fourth Amendment exclusionary rule should be modified so as not to bar the use in the prosecution's case in chief of evidence obtained by officers acting in reasonable reliance on a search warrant issued by a detached and neutral magistrate but ultimately found to be unsupported by probable cause. To resolve this question, we must consider once again the tension between the sometimes competing goals of, on the one hand, deterring official misconduct and removing inducements to unreasonable invasions of privacy and, on the other, establishing procedures under which criminal defendants are "acquitted or convicted on the basis of all the evidence which exposes the truth." *Alderman v. United States*, 394 U.S. 165, 175, 89 S. Ct. 961, 967, 22 L. Ed. 2d 176 (1969).

I

In August 1981, a confidential informant of unproven reliability informed an officer of the Burbank Police Department that two persons known to him as "Armando" and "Patsy" were selling large quantities of cocaine and methaqualone from their residence at 620 Price Drive in Burbank, Cal. The informant also indicated that he had witnessed a sale of methaqualone by "Patsy" at the residence approximately five months earlier and had observed at that time a shoebox containing a large amount of cash that belonged to "Patsy." He further declared that "Armando" and "Patsy" generally kept only small quantities of drugs at their residence and stored the remainder at another location in Burbank.

On the basis of this information, the Burbank police initiated an extensive investigation focusing first on the Price Drive residence and later on two other residences as well. Cars parked at the Price Drive residence were determined to belong to respondents Armando Sanchez, who had previously been arrested for possession of marihuana, and Patsy Stewart, who had no criminal record. During the course of the investigation, officers observed an automobile belonging to respondent Richard Del Castillo, who had previously been arrested for possession of fifty pounds of marihuana, arrive at the Price Drive residence. The driver of that car entered the house, exited shortly thereafter carrying a small paper sack, and drove away. A check of Del Castillo's probation records led the officers to respondent Alberto Leon, whose telephone number Del

Castillo had listed as his employer's. Leon had been arrested in 1980 on drug charges, and a companion had informed the police at the time that Leon was heavily involved in the importation of drugs into this country. Before the current investigation began, the Burbank officers had learned that an informant had told a Glendale police officer that Leon stored a large quantity of methaqualone at his residence in Glendale. During the course of this investigation, the Burbank officers learned that Leon was living at 716 South Sunset Canyon in Burbank.

Subsequently, the officers observed several persons, at least one of whom had prior drug involvement, arriving at the Price Drive residence and leaving with small packages; observed a variety of other material activity at the two residences as well as at a condominium at 7902 Via Magdalena; and witnessed a variety of relevant activity involving respondents' automobiles. The officers also observed respondents Sanchez and Stewart board separate flights for Miami. The pair later returned to Los Angeles together, consented to a search of their luggage that revealed only a small amount of marihuana, and left the airport. Based on these and other observations summarized in the affidavit, App. 34, Officer Cyril Rombach of the Burbank Police Department, an experienced and well-trained narcotics investigator, prepared an application for a warrant to search 620 Price Drive, 716 South Sunset Canyon, 7902 Via Magdalena, and automobiles registered to each of the respondents for an extensive list of items believed to be related to respondents' drug-trafficking activities. Officer Rombach's extensive application was reviewed by several Deputy District Attorneys.

A facially valid search warrant was issued in September 1981 by a State Superior Court Judge. The ensuing searches produced large quantities of drugs at the Via Magdalena and Sunset Canyon addresses and a small quantity at the Price Drive residence. Other evidence was discovered at each of the residences and in Stewart's and Del Castillo's automobiles. Respondents were indicted by a grand jury in the District Court for the Central District of California and charged with conspiracy to possess and distribute cocaine and a variety of substantive counts.

The respondents then filed motions to suppress the evidence seized pursuant to the warrant.[1] The District Court

---

1. Respondent Leon moved to suppress the evidence found on his person at the time of his arrest and the evidence seized from his residence at 716 South Sunset Canyon. Respondent Stewart's motion covered the fruits of searches of her residence at 620 Price Drive and the condominium at 7902 Via Magdalena and statements she made during the search of her residence. Respondent Sanchez sought to suppress the evidence discovered during the search of his residence at 620 Price Drive and statements he made shortly thereafter. He also joined Stewart's motion to suppress evidence seized from the condominium.

Respondent Del Castillo apparently sought to suppress all of the evidence seized in the searches. App. 78–80. The respondents also moved to suppress evidence seized in the searches of their automobiles.

held an evidentiary hearing and, while recognizing that the case was a close one, see *id.*, at 131, granted the motions to suppress in part. It concluded that the affidavit was insufficient to establish probable cause,[2] but did not suppress all of the evidence as to all of the respondents because none of the respondents had standing to challenge all of the searches.[3] In response to a request from the Government, the court made clear that Officer Rombach had acted in good faith, but it rejected the Government's suggestion that the Fourth Amendment exclusionary rule should not apply where evidence is seized in reasonable good-faith reliance on a search warrant.[4]

The District Court denied the Government's motion for reconsideration, *id.*, at 147, and a divided panel of the Court of Appeals for the Ninth Circuit affirmed, judgt. order reported at 701 F.2d 187 (1983). The Court of Appeals first concluded that Officer Rombach's affidavit could not establish probable cause to search the Price Drive residence. To the extent that the affidavit set forth facts demonstrating the basis of the informant's knowledge of criminal activity, the information included was fatally stale. The affidavit, moreover, failed to establish the informant's credibility. Accordingly, the Court of Appeals concluded that the information

---

2. "I just cannot find this warrant sufficient for a showing of probable cause.

* * *

"There is no question of the reliability and credibility of the informant as not being established.

"Some details given tended to corroborate, maybe, the reliability of [the informant's] information about the previous transaction, but if it is not a stale transaction, it comes awfully close to it; and all the other material I think is as consistent with innocence as it is with guilt.

"So I just do not think this affidavit can withstand the test. I find, then, that there is no probable cause in this case for the issuance of the search warrant. . . ." *Id.*, at 127.

3. The District Court concluded that Sanchez and Stewart had standing to challenge the search of 620 Price Drive; that Leon had standing to contest the legality of the search of 716 South Sunset Canyon; that none of the respondents has established a legitimate expectation of privacy in the condominium at 7902 Via Magdalena; and that Stewart and Del Castillo each had standing to challenge the searches of their automobiles. The Government indicated that it did not intend to introduce evidence seized from the other respondents' vehicles. *Id.*, at 127–129. Finally, the court suppressed statements given by Sanchez and Stewart. *Id.*, at 129–130.

4. "On the issue of good faith, obviously that is not the law of the Circuit, and I am not going to apply that law.

"I will say certainly in my view, there is not any question about good faith. [Officer Rombach] went to a Superior Court judge and got a warrant; obviously laid a meticulous trail. Had surveilled for a long period of time, and I believe his testimony—I think he said he consulted with three Deputy District Attorneys before proceeding himself, and I certainly have no doubt about the fact that that is true." *Id.*, at 140.

---

provided by the informant was inadequate under both prongs of the two-part test established in *Aguilar v. Texas*, 378 U.S. 108, 84 S. Ct. 1509, 12 L. Ed. 2d 723 (1964), and *Spinelli v. United States*, 393 U.S. 410, 89 S. Ct. 584, 21 L. Ed. 2d 637 (1969).[5]

* * *

We have concluded that, in the Fourth Amendment context, the exclusionary rule can be modified somewhat without jeopardizing its ability to perform its intended functions. Accordingly, we reverse the judgment of the Court of Appeals.

II

Language in opinions of this Court and of individual Justices has sometimes implied that the exclusionary rule is a necessary corollary of the Fourth Amendment, *Mapp v. Ohio*, 367 U.S. 643, 651, 655–657, 81 S. Ct. 1684, 1689, 1691–1692, 6 L. Ed. 2d 1081 (1961); *Olmstead v. United States*, 277 U.S. 488, 462–463, 48 S. Ct. 564, 567, 72 L. Ed. 944 (1928), or that the rule is required by the conjunction of the Fourth and Fifth Amendments. *Mapp v. Ohio, supra*, 367 U.S., at 661–662, 81 S. Ct., at 1694–1695 (Black, J., concurring); *Agnello v. United States*, 269 U.S. 20, 33–34, 46 S. Ct. 4, 6–7, 70 L. Ed. 145 (1925). These implications need not detain us long. The Fifth Amendment theory has not withstood critical analysis or the test of time, see *Andresen v. Maryland*, 427 U.S. 463, 96 S. Ct. 2737, 49 L. Ed. 2d 627 (1976), and the Fourth Amendment "has never been interpreted to proscribe the introduction of illegally seized evidence in all proceedings or against all persons." *Stone v. Powell*, 428 U.S. 465, 486, 96 S. Ct. 3037, 3048, 49 L. Ed. 2d 1067 (1976).

A

The Fourth Amendment contains no provisions expressly precluding the use of evidence obtained in violation of its commands, and an examination of its origin and purposes makes clear that the use of fruits of a part[ly] unlawful search or seizure "work[s] no new Fourth Amendment wrong." *United States v. Calandra*, 414 U.S. 338, 354, 94 S. Ct. 613, 623, 38 L. Ed. 2d 561 (1974). The wrong condemned by the Amendment is "fully accomplished" by the unlawful search or seizure itself, *ibid.*, and the exclusionary rule is neither intended nor able to "cure the invasion of the defendant's rights which he has already suffered." *Stone v. Powell, supra*, 428 U.S., at 540, 96 S. Ct., at 3073 (WHITE, J., dissenting). The rule thus operates as "a judicially created remedy designed to safeguard Fourth Amendment rights generally through its

---

5. In *Illinois v. Gates*, 462 U.S. 213, 103 S. Ct. 2317, 76 L. Ed. 2d 527 (1983), decided last Term, the Court abandoned the two-pronged *Aguilar–Spinelli* test for determining whether an informant's tip suffices to establish probable cause for the issuance of a warrant and substituted in its place a "totality of the circumstances" approach.

(continues)

deterrent effect, rather than a personal constitutional right of the party aggrieved." *United States v. Calandra, supra*, 414 U.S., at 348, 94 S. Ct., at 620.

*   *   *

The substantial social costs exacted by the exclusionary rule for the vindication of Fourth Amendment rights have long been a source of concern. "Our cases have consistently recognized that unbending application of the exclusionary sanction to enforce ideals of governmental rectitude would impede unacceptably the truth-finding functions of judge and jury." *United States v. Payner*, 447 U.S. 727, 734, 100 S. Ct. 2439, 2445, 65 L. Ed. 2d 468 (1980). An objectionable collateral consequence of this interference with the criminal justice system's truth-finding function is that some guilty defendants may go free or receive reduced sentences as a result of favorable plea bargains.[6] Particularly when law enforcement officers have acted in objective good faith or their transgressions have been minor, the magnitude of the benefit conferred on such guilty defendants offends basic concepts of the criminal justice system. *Stone v. Powell*, 428 U.S., at 490, 96 S. Ct., at 3050. Indiscriminate application of the

exclusionary rule, therefore, may well "generat[e] disrespect for the law and administration of justice." *Id.*, at 491, 96 S. Ct., at 3051. Accordingly, "[a]s with any remedial device, the application of the rule has been restricted to those areas where its remedial objectives are thought most efficaciously served." *United States v. Calandra, supra*, 414 U.S., at 348, 94 S. Ct., at 670; see *Stone v. Powell, supra*, 428 U.S., at 486–487, 97 S. Ct., at 3048–3049; *United States v. Janis*, 428 U.S. 433, 447, 96 S. Ct. 3021, 3028, 49 L. Ed. 2d 1046 (1976).

*   *   *

III

A

Because a search warrant "provides the detached scrutiny of a neutral magistrate, which is a more reliable safeguard against improper searches than the hurried judgment of a law enforcement officer 'engaged in the often competitive enterprise of ferreting out crime,'" *United States v. Chadwich*, 433 U.S. 1, 9, 97 S. Ct. 2476, 2482, 53 L. Ed. 2d 538 (1977) (quoting *Johnson v. United States*, 333 U.S. 10, 14, 68 S. Ct. 367, 369, 92 L. Ed. 436 (1948)), we have expressed a strong preference for warrants and declared that "in a doubtful or marginal case a search under a warrant may be sustainable where without one it would fall." *United States v. Ventresca*, 380 U.S. 102, 106, 85 S. Ct. 741, 744, 13 L. Ed. 2d 687 (1965). See *Aguilar v. Texas*, 378 U.S., at 111, 84 S. Ct., at 1512. Reasonable minds frequently may differ on the question [of] whether a particular affidavit establishes probable cause, and we have thus concluded that the preference for warrants is most appropriately effectuated by according "great deference" to a magistrate's determination. *Spinelli v. United States*, 393 U.S., at 419, 89 S. Ct., at 590. See *Illinois v. Gates*, 462 U.S., at 236, 103 S. Ct., at 2331; *United States v. Ventresca, supra*, 380 U.S., at 108–109, 85 S. Ct., at 745–746.

Deference to the magistrate, however, is not boundless. It is clear, first, that the deference accorded to a magistrate's finding of probable cause does not preclude inquiry into the knowing or reckless falsity of the affidavit on which that determination was based. *Franks v. Delaware*, 438 U.S. 154,

---

6. Researchers have only recently begun to study extensively the effects of the exclusionary rule on the disposition of felony arrests. One study suggests that the rule results in the nonprosecution or nonconviction of between 0.6% and 2.35% of individuals arrested for felonies. Davies, A Hard Look at What We Know (and Still Need to Learn) About the "Costs" of the Exclusionary Rule: The NIJ Study and Other Studies of "Lost" Arrests, 1983 A.B.F. Res. J. 611, 621. The estimates are higher for particular crimes the prosecution of which depends heavily on physical evidence. Thus, the cumulative loss due to nonprosecution or nonconviction of individuals arrested on felony drug charges is probably in the range of 2.8% to 7.1%. *Id.*, at 680. Davies' analysis of California data suggests that screening by police and prosecutors results in the release because of illegal searches or seizures of as many as 1.4% of all felony arrestees, *Id.*, at 650, that 0.9% of felony arrestees are released, because of illegal searches or seizures, at the preliminary hearing or after trial, id., at 653, and that roughly 0.5% of all felony arrestees benefit from reversals on appeal because of illegal searches. *id.*, at 654. See also K. Brosi, A Cross-City Comparison of Felony Case Processing 16, 18–19 (1979); U.S. General Accounting Office, Report of the Comptroller General of the United States, Impact of the Exclusionary Rule on Federal Criminal Prosecutions 10–11, 14 (1979); F. Feeney, F. Dill, & A. Weir, Arrests Without Convictions: How Often They Occur and Why 203–206 (National Institute of Justice 1983); National Institute of Justice, The Effects of the Exclusionary Rule: A Study in California 1–2 (1982); Nardulli, The Societal Cost of the Exclusionary Rule: An Empirical Assessment, 1983 A.B.F. Res. J. 585, 600. The exclusionary rule also has been found to affect the plea-bargaining process. S. Schlesinger, Exclusionary Injustice: The Problem of Illegally Obtained Evidence 63 (1977). But see *Davies, supra*, at 668–669; *Nardulli, supra*, at 604–606.

Many of these researchers have concluded that the impact of the exclusionary rule is insubstantial, but the small percentages with which they deal mask a large absolute number of felons who are released because the cases against them were based in part on illegal searches or seizures. "[A]ny rule of evidence that denies the jury access to clearly probative and reliable evidence must bear a heavy burden of justification, and must be carefully limited to the circumstances in which it will pay its way by deterring official unlawlessness." *Illinois v. Gates*, 462 U.S., at 257–258, 103 S. Ct., at 2342 (WHITE, J., concurring in judgment). Because we find that the rule can have no substantial deterrent effect in the sorts of situations under consideration in this case, see *infra*, at 3417–3419, we conclude that it cannot pay its way in those situations.

*   *   *

98 S. Ct. 2674, 57 L. Ed. 2d 667 (1978).[12] Second, the courts must also insist the magistrate purport to "perform his 'neutral and detached' function and not serve merely as a rubber stamp for the police." *Aguilar v. Texas, supra,* 378 U.S., at 111, 84 S. Ct., at 1512. See *Illinois v. Gates, supra,* 462 U.S., at 239, 103 S. Ct., at 2332. A magistrate failing to "manifest that neutrality and detachment demanded of a judicial officer when presented with a warrant application" and who acts instead as "an adjunct law enforcement officer" cannot provide valid authorization for an otherwise unconstitutional search. *Lo-Ji Sales, Inc. v. New York,* 442 U.S. 319, 326–327, 99 S. Ct. 2319, 2324–2325, 60 L. Ed. 2d 920 (1979).

Third, reviewing courts will not defer to a warrant based on an affidavit that does not "provide the magistrate with a substantial basis for determining the existence of probable cause." *Illinois v. Gates,* 462 U.S., at 239, 103 S. Ct., at 2332. "Sufficient information must be presented to the magistrate to allow that official to determine probable cause; his action cannot be a mere ratification of the bare conclusions of others." *Ibid.* See *Aguilar v. Texas, supra,* 378 U.S., at 114–115, 84 S. Ct., at 1513–1514; *Giordenello v. United States,* 357 U.S. 480, 78 S. Ct. 1245, 2 L. Ed. 2d 1503 (1958); *Nathanson v. United States,* 290 U.S. 41, 54 S. Ct. 11, 78 L. Ed. 159 (1933).[13] Even if the warrant application was supported by more than a "bare bones" affidavit, a reviewing court may properly conclude that, notwithstanding the deference that magistrates deserve, the warrant was invalid because the magistrate's probable-cause determination reflected an improper analysis of the totality of the circumstances, *Illinois v. Gates, supra,* 462 U.S., at 238–239, 103 S. Ct., at 2332–2333, or because the form of the warrant was improper in some respect.

Only in the first of these three situations, however, has the Court set forth a rationale for suppressing evidence obtained pursuant to a search warrant; in the other areas, it has simply excluded such evidence without considering whether Fourth Amendment interests will be advanced. To the extent that proponents of exclusion rely on its behavioral effects on judges and magistrates in these areas, their reliance is misplaced. First, the exclusionary rule is designed to deter police misconduct rather than to punish the errors of judges and magistrates. Second, there exists no evidence suggesting that judges and magistrates are inclined to ignore or subvert the Fourth Amendment or that lawlessness among these actors requires application of the extreme sanction of exclusion.[14]

Third, and most important, we discern no basis, and are offered none, for believing that exclusion of evidence seized pursuant to a warrant will have a significant deterrent effect on the issuing judge or magistrate.[15] Many of the factors that indicate that the exclusionary rule cannot provide an effective "special" or "general" deterrent for individual offending law enforcement officers[16] apply as well to judges or magistrates. And, to the extent that the rule is thought to operate

---

12. Indeed, "it would be an unthinkable imposition upon [the magistrate's] authority if a warrant affidavit, revealed after the fact to contain a deliberately or recklessly false statement, were to stand beyond impeachment." 438 U.S., at 165, 98 S. Ct., at 2681.

13. See also *Beck v. Ohio,* 379 U.S. 89, 85 S. Ct. 223, 13 L. Ed. 2d 142 (1964), in which the Court concluded that "the record . . . does not contain a single objective fact to support a belief by the officers that the petitioner was engaged in criminal activity at the time they arrested him." *Id.,* at 95, 85 S. Ct., at 227. Although the Court was willing to assume that the arresting officers acted in good faith, it concluded that:

"'[G]ood faith on the part of the arresting officers is not enough,' *Henry v. United States,* 361 U.S. 98, 102, 80 S. Ct. 168, 171, 4 L. Ed. 2d 134. If subjective good faith alone were the test, the protections of the Fourth Amendment would evaporate, and the people would be 'secure in their persons, houses, papers, and effects,' only in the discretion of the police." (*Id.,* at 97, 85 S. Ct., at 228.)

We adhere to this view and emphasize that nothing in this opinion is intended to suggest a lowering of the probable-cause standard. On the contrary, we deal here with the remedy to be applied to a concededly unconstitutional search.

14. Although there are assertions that some magistrates become rubber stamps for the police and others may be unable effectively to screen police conduct, see, *for example,* 2 W. LaFave, Search and Seizure § 4.1 (1978); Kamisar, Does (Did) (Should) The Exclusionary Rule Rest on a "Principled Basis" Rather than an "Empirical Proposition"?, 16 Creighton L. Rev. 565, 569–571 (1983); Schroeder, Deterring Fourth Amendment Violations: Alternatives to the Exclusionary Rule, 69 Geo. L.J. 1361, 1412 (1981), we are not convinced that this is a problem of major proportions. See L. Tiffany, D. McIntyre, & D. Rotenberg, Detection of Crime 119 (1967); Israel, Criminal Procedure, the Burger Court, and the Legacy of the Warren Court, 75 Mich. L. Rev. 1319, 1414, n. 396 (1977); P. Johnson, New Approaches to Enforcing the Fourth Amendment 8–10 (Working Paper, Sept. 1978), quoted in Y. Kamisar, W. LaFave, & J. Israel, Modern Criminal Procedure 229–230 (5th ed. 1980); R. Van Duizend, L. Sutton, & C. Carter, The Search Warrant Process, ch. 7 (Review Draft, National Center for State Courts, 1983).

15. As the Supreme Judicial Court of Massachusetts recognized in *Commonwealth v. Sheppard,* 387 Mass. 488, 506, 441 N.E.2d 725, 735 (1982):

"The exclusionary rule may not be well tailored to deterring judicial misconduct. If applied to judicial misconduct, the rule would be just as costly as it is when it is applied to police misconduct, but it may be ill-fitted to the job-created motivations of judges. . . . [I]deally a judge is impartial as to whether a particular piece of evidence is admitted or a particular defendant convicted. Hence, in the abstract, suppression of a particular piece of evidence may not be as effective a disincentive to a neutral judge as it would be to the police. It may be that a ruling by an appellate court that a search warrant was unconstitutional would be sufficient to deter similar conduct in the future by magistrates."

But see *United States v. Karathanos,* 531 F.2d 26, 33–34 (CA2), cert. denied, 428 U.S. 910, 96 S. Ct. 3221, 49 L. Ed. 2d 1217 (1976).

16. See, *for example, Stone v. Powell,* 428 U.S., at 498, 96 S. Ct., at 3054 (BURGER, C.J., concurring); Oaks, Studying the Exclusionary Rule in Search and Seizure, 37 U. Chi. L. Rev. 665, 709–710 (1970).

(continues)

as a "systemic" deterrent on a wider audience,[17] it clearly can have no such effect on individuals empowered to issue search warrants. Judges and magistrates are not adjuncts to the law enforcement team; as neutral judicial officers, they have no stake in the outcome of particular criminal prosecutions. The threat of exclusion thus cannot be expected significantly to deter them. Imposition of the exclusionary sanction is not necessary meaningfully to inform judicial officers of their errors, and we cannot conclude that admitting evidence obtained pursuant to a warrant while at the same time declaring that the warrant was somehow defective will in any way reduce judicial officers' professional incentives to comply with the Fourth Amendment, encourage them to repeat their mistakes, or lead to the granting of all colorable warrant requests.[18]

B

If exclusion of evidence obtained pursuant to a subsequently invalidated warrant is to have any deterrent effect, therefore, it must alter the behavior of individual law enforcement officers or the policies of their departments. One could argue that applying the exclusionary rule in cases where the police failed to demonstrate probable cause in the warrant application deters future inadequate presentations or "magistrate shopping" and thus promotes the end of the Fourth Amendment. Suppressing evidence obtained pursuant to a technically defective warrant supported by a probable cause also might encourage officers to scrutinize more closely the form of the warrant and to point out suspected judicial errors. We find such arguments speculative and conclude that suppression of evidence obtained pursuant to a warrant should be ordered only on a case-by-case basis and only in those unusual cases in which exclusion will further the purposes of the exclusionary rule.[19]

We have frequently questioned whether the exclusionary rule can have any deterrent effect when the offending officers acted in the objectively reasonable belief that their conduct did not violate the Fourth Amendment. "No empirical researcher, proponent or opponent of the rule, has yet been able to establish with any assurance whether the rule has a deterrent effect. . . ." *United States v. Janis*, 428 U.S., at 452, n. 22, 96 S. Ct., at 3031, n. 22. But even assuming that the rule effectively deters some police misconduct and provides incentives for the law enforcement profession as a whole to conduct itself in accord with the Fourth Amendment, it cannot be expected, and should not be applied, to deter objectively reasonable law enforcement activity.

As we observed in *Michigan v. Tucker*, 417 U.S. 433, 447, 94 S. Ct. 2357, 2365, 41 L. Ed. 2d 182 (1974), and reiterated in *United States v. Peltier*, 422 U.S., at 539, 95 S. Ct., at 2318:

"The deterrent purpose of the exclusionary rule necessarily assumes that the police have engaged in wilful, or at the very least negligent, conduct which has deprived the defendant of some right. By refusing to admit evidence gained as a result of such conduct, the courts hope to instill in those particular investigating officers, or in their future counterparts, a greater deal of care toward the rights of an accused. Where the official action was pursued in complete good faith, however, the deterrence rationale loses much of its force."

The *Peltier* Court continued, *id.*, at 542, 95 S. Ct., at 2320:

"If the purpose of the exclusionary rule is to deter unlawful police conduct, then evidence obtained from a search should be suppressed only if it can be said that the law enforcement officer had knowledge, or may properly be charged with knowledge, that the search was unconstitutional under the Fourth Amendment."

See also *Illinois v. Gates*, 462 U.S., at 260–261, 103 S. Ct., at 2344 (WHITE, J., concurring in judgment); *United States v. Janis, supra*, 428 U.S., at 459, 96 S. Ct., at 3034; *Brown v. Illinois*, 422 U.S., at 610–611, 95 S. Ct., at 2265–2266 (POWELL,

---

17. See, *e.g., Dunaway v. New York*, 442 U.S. 200, 221, 99 S. Ct. 2248, 2261, 60 L. Ed. 2d 824 (1979) (STEVENS, J., concurring); Mertens & Wasserstrom, The Good Faith Exception to the Exclusionary Rule: Deregulating the Police and Derailing the Law, 70 Geo. L.J. 365, 399–401 (1981).

18. Limiting the application of the exclusionary sanction may well increase the care with which magistrates scrutinize warrant applications. We doubt that magistrates are more desirous of avoiding the exclusion of evidence obtained pursuant to warrants they have issued than of avoiding invasions of privacy.

Federal magistrates, moreover, are subject to the direct supervision of district courts. They may be removed for "incompetency, misconduct, neglect of duty, or physical or mental disability." 28 U.S.C. § 631(i). If a magistrate serves merely as a "rubber stamp" for the police or is unable to exercise mature judgment, closer supervision or removal provides a more effective remedy than the exclusionary rule.

---

19. Our discussion of the deterrent effect of excluding evidence obtained in reasonable reliance on a subsequently invalidated warrant assumes, of course, that the officers properly executed the warrant and searched only those places and for those objects that it was reasonable to believe were covered by the warrant. Cf. *Massachusetts v. Sheppard*, 468 U.S. 981, 989, n. 6, 104 S. Ct. 3424, 3429, n. 6, 82 L. Ed. 2d 737 ("[I]t was not unreasonable for the police in this case to rely on the judge's assurances that the warrant authorized the search they had requested").

J., concurring in part).[20] In short, where the officer's conduct is objectively reasonable,

> "excluding the evidence will not further the ends of the exclusionary rule in any appreciable way; for it is painfully apparent . . . the officer is acting as a reasonable officer would and should act in similar circumstances. Excluding the evidence can in no way affect his future conduct unless it is to make him less willing to do his duty."

Stone v. Powell, 428 U.S., at 539–540, 96 S. Ct., at 3073–3074 (WHITE, J., dissenting).

This is particularly true, we believe, when an officer acting with objective good faith has obtained a search warrant from a judge or magistrate and acted within its scope.[21] In most such cases, there is no police illegality and thus nothing to deter. It is the magistrate's responsibility to determine whether the officer's allegations establish probable cause and, if so, to issue a warrant comporting in form with the requirements of the Fourth Amendment. In the ordinary case, an officer cannot be expected to question the magistrate's probable-cause determination or his judgment that the form of the warrant is technically sufficient. "[O]nce the warrant issues, there is literally nothing more the policeman can do in seeking to comply with the law." *Id.*, 428 U.S., at 498, 96 S. Ct., at 3054 (BURGER, C.J., concurring). Penalizing the officer for the magistrate's error, rather than his own, cannot logically contribute to the deterrence of Fourth Amendment violations.[22]

We conclude that the marginal or nonexistent benefits produced by suppressing evidence obtained in objectively reasonable reliance on a subsequently invalidated search warrant cannot justify the substantial costs of exclusion. We do not suggest, however, that exclusion is always inappropriate in cases where an officer has obtained a warrant and abided by its terms. "[S]earches pursuant to a warrant will rarely require any deep inquiry into reasonableness," *Illinois*

---

20. We emphasize that the standard of reasonableness we adopt is an objective one. Many objections to a good-faith exception assume that the exception will turn on the subjective good faith of individual officers. "Grounding the modification in objective reasonableness, however, retains the value of the exclusionary rule as an incentive for the law enforcement profession as a whole to conduct themselves in accord with the Fourth Amendment." *Illinois v. Gates*, 462 U.S., at 261, n. 15, 103 S. Ct., at 2344, n. 15 (WHITE, J., concurring in judgment); see *Dunaway v. New York*, 442 U.S., at 221, 99 S. Ct., at 2261 (STEVENS, J., concurring). The objective standard we adopted, moreover, requires officers to have a reasonable knowledge of what the law prohibits. *United States v. Peltier*, 442 U.S. 531, 542, 95 S. Ct. 2313, 2320, 45 L. Ed. 2d 374 (1975). As Professor Jerold Israel has observed:

> "The key to the [exclusionary] rule's effectiveness as a deterrent lies, I believe, in the impetus it has provided to police training programs that make officers aware of the limits imposed by the fourth amendment and emphasize the need to operate within those limits. [An objective good-faith exception] is not likely to result in the elimination of such programs, which are now viewed as an important aspect of police professionalism. Neither is it likely to alter the tenor of those programs; the possibility that illegally obtained evidence may be admitted in borderline cases is unlikely to encourage police instructors to pay less attention to fourth amendment limitations. Finally, [it] should not encourage officers to pay less attention to what they are taught, as the requirement that the officer act in 'good faith' is inconsistent with closing one's mind to the possibility of illegality."

Israel, *supra* n. 14, at 1412–1413 (footnotes omitted).

21. According to the Attorney General's Task Force on Violent Crime, Final Report (1981), the situation in which an officer relies on a duly authorized warrant

> "is a particularly compelling example of good faith. A warrant is a judicial mandate to an officer to conduct a search or make an arrest, and the officer has a sworn duty to carry out its provisions. Accordingly, we believe that there should be a rule which states that evidence obtained pursuant to and within the scope of a warrant is prima facie the result of good faith on the part of the officer seizing the evidence."

Id., at 55.

22. To the extent that Justice STEVENS' conclusions concerning the integrity of the courts, *post*, at 3454–3455, rest on a foundation other than his judgment, which we reject, concerning the effects of our decision on the deterrence of police illegality, we find his argument unpersuasive. "Judicial integrity clearly does not mean that the courts must never admit evidence obtained in violation of the Fourth Amendment." *United States v. Janis*, 428 U.S. 433, 458, n. 35, 96 S. Ct. 3021, 3034, n. 35, 49 L. Ed. 2d 1046 (1976). "While courts, of course, must ever be concerned with preserving the integrity of the judicial process, this concern has limited force as a justification for the exclusion of highly probative evidence." *Stone v. Powell*, 428 U.S., at 485, 96 S. Ct., at 3048. Our cases establish that the question whether the use of illegally obtained evidence in judicial proceedings represents judicial participation in a Fourth Amendment violation and offends the integrity of the courts

> "is essentially the same as the inquiry into whether exclusion would serve a deterrent purpose. . . . The analysis showing that exclusion in this case has no demonstrated deterrent effect and is unlikely to have any significant such effect shows, by the same reasoning, that the admission of the evidence is unlikely to encourage violations of the Fourth Amendment."

United States v. Janis, supra, 428 U.S., at 459, n. 35, 96 S. Ct., at 3034, n. 35.

Absent unusual circumstances, when a Fourth Amendment violation has occurred because the police have reasonably relied on a warrant issued by a detached and neutral magistrate but ultimately found to be defective, "the integrity of the courts is not implicated." *Illinois v. Gates, supra*, 462 U.S., at 259, n. 14, 103 S. Ct., at 2343, n. 14 (WHITE, J., concurring in judgment). See *Stone v. Powell*, 428 U.S., at 485, n. 23, 96 S. Ct., at 3048, n. 23; *id.*, at 540, 96 S. Ct., at 3073 (WHITE, J., dissenting); *United States v. Peltier*, 442 U.S. 531, 536–539, 95 S. Ct. 2313, 2317–2318, 45 L. Ed. 2d 374 (1975).

(continues)

v. Gates, 462 U.S., at 267, 103 S. Ct., at 2347 (WHITE, J., concurring in judgment), for "a warrant issued by a magistrate normally suffices to establish" that a law enforcement officer has "acted in good faith in conducting the search." *United States v. Ross*, 456 U.S. 798, 823, n. 32, 102 S. Ct. 2157, 2172, n. 32, 72 L. Ed. 2d 572 (1982). Nevertheless, the officer's reliance on the magistrate's probable-cause determination and on the technical sufficiency of the warrant he issues must be objectively reasonable, cf. *Harlow v. Fitzgerald*, 457 U.S. 800, 815–819, 102 S. Ct., 2727, 2737–2739, 73 L. Ed. 2d 396 (1982),[23] and it is clear that in some circumstances the officer[24] will have no reasonable grounds for believing that the warrant was properly issued.

Suppression therefore remains an appropriate remedy if the magistrate or judge in issuing a warrant was misled by information in an affidavit that the affiant knew was false or would have known was false except for his reckless disregard of the truth. *Franks v. Delaware*, 438 U.S. 154, 98 S. Ct. 2674, 57 L. Ed. 2d 667 (1978). The exception we recognize today will also not apply in cases where the issuing magistrate wholly abandoned his judicial role in the manner condemned in *Lo-Ji Sales, Inc. v. New York*, 442 U.S. 319, 99 S. Ct. 2319, 60 L. Ed. 2d 920 (1979); in such circumstances, no

reasonably well trained officer should rely on the warrant. Nor would an officer manifest objective good faith in relying on a warrant based on an affidavit "so lacking in indicia of probable cause as to render official belief in its existence entirely unreasonable." *Brown v. Illinois*, 422 U.S., at 610–611, 95 S. Ct., at 2265–2266 (POWELL, J., concurring in part); see *Illinois v. Gates, supra*, 462 U.S., at 263–264, 103 S. Ct., at 2345–2346 (WHITE, J., concurring in the judgment). Finally, depending on the circumstances of the particular case, a warrant may be so facially deficient—*that is,* in failing to particularize the place to be searched or the things to be seized—that the executing officers cannot reasonably presume it to be valid. Cf. *Massachusetts v. Sheppard*, 468 U.S., at 988–991, 104 S. Ct. at 3428–3430.

In so limiting the suppression remedy, we leave untouched the probable-cause standard and the various requirements for a valid warrant. Other objections to the modification of the Fourth Amendment exclusionary rule we consider to be insubstantial. The good-faith exception for searches conducted pursuant to warrants is not intended to signal our willingness strictly to enforce the requirements of the Fourth Amendment, and we do not believe that it will have this effect. As we have already suggested, the good-faith exception, turning as it does on objective reasonableness, should not be difficult to apply in practice. When officers have acted pursuant to a warrant, the prosecution should ordinarily be able to establish objective good faith without a substantial expenditure of judicial time.

Nor are we persuaded that application of a good-faith exception to searches conducted pursuant to warrants will preclude review of the constitutionality of the search or seizure, deny needed guidance from the courts, or freeze Fourth Amendment law in its present state.[25] There is no need for courts to adopt the inflexible practice of always deciding whether the officers' conduct manifested objective good faith before turning to the question [of] whether the Fourth Amendment has been violated. Defendants seeking suppression of the fruits of allegedly unconstitutional searches or seizures undoubtedly raise live controversies which Art. III empowers federal courts to adjudicate. As cases addressing questions of good-faith immunity under 42 U.S.C. § 1983, compare *O'Connor v. Donaldson*, 422 U.S. 563, 95 S. Ct. 2486, 45 L. Ed. 2d 396 (1975), with *Procunier v. Navarette*, 434 U.S. 555, 566, n. 14, 98 S. Ct. 855, 862, n. 14, 55 L. Ed. 2d 24 (1978), and cases involving the harmless-error doctrine, compare *Milton v. Wainwright*, 407 U.S. 371, 372, 92 S. Ct. 2174, 2175, 33 L. Ed. 2d 1 (1972), with

---

23. In *Harlow*, we eliminated the subjective component of the qualified immunity public officials enjoy in suits seeking damages for alleged deprivations of constitutional rights. The situations are not perfectly analogous, but we also eschew inquiries into the subjective beliefs of law enforcement officers who seize evidence pursuant to a subsequently invalidated warrant. Although we have suggested that, "[o]n occasion, the motive with which the officer conducts an illegal search may have some relevance in determining the propriety of applying the exclusionary rule," *Scott v. United States*, 436 U.S. 128, 139, n. 13, 98 S. Ct. 1717, 1724, n. 13, 56 L. Ed. 2d 168 (1978), we believe that "sending state and federal courts on an expedition into the minds of police officers would produce a grave and fruitless misallocation of judicial resources." *Massachusetts v. Painten*, 389 U.S. 560, 565, 88 S. Ct. 660, 663, 19 L. Ed. 2d 770 (1968) (WHITE, J., dissenting). Accordingly, our good-faith inquiry is confined to the objectively ascertainable question whether a reasonably well-trained officer would have known that the search was illegal despite the magistrate's authorization. In making this determination, all of the circumstances—including whether the warrant application had previously been rejected by a different magistrate—may be considered.

24. References to "officer" throughout this opinion should not be read too narrowly. It is necessary to consider the objective reasonableness, not only of the officers who eventually executed a warrant, but also of the officers who originally obtained it or who provided information material to the probable-cause determination. Nothing in our opinion suggests, for example, that an officer could obtain a warrant on the basis of a "bare bones" affidavit and then rely on colleagues who are ignorant of the circumstances under which the warrant was obtained to conduct the search. See *Whiteley v. Warden*, 401 U.S. 560, 568, 91 S. Ct. 1031, 1037, 28 L. Ed. 2d 306 (1971).

---

25. The argument that defendants will lose their incentive to litigate meritorious Fourth Amendment claims as a result of the good-faith exception we adopt today is unpersuasive. Although the exception might discourage presentation of insubstantial suppression motions, the magnitude of the benefit conferred on defendants by a successful motion makes it unlikely that litigation of colorable claims will be substantially diminished.

Coleman v. Alabama, 399 U.S. 1, 90 S. Ct. 1999, 26 L. Ed. 2d 387 (1970), make clear, courts have considerable discretion in conforming their decision-making processes to the exigencies of particular cases.

If the resolution of a particular Fourth Amendment question is necessary to guide future action by law enforcement officers and magistrates, nothing will prevent reviewing courts from deciding that question before turning to the good-faith issue.[26] Indeed, it frequently will be difficult to determine whether the officers acted reasonably without resolving the Fourth Amendment issue. Even if the Fourth Amendment question is not one of broad import, reviewing courts could decide in particular cases that magistrates under their supervision need to be informed of their errors and so evaluate the officers' good faith only after finding a violation. In other circumstances, those courts could reject suppression motions posing no important Fourth Amendment questions by turning immediately to a consideration of the officers' good faith. We have no reason to believe that our Fourth Amendment jurisprudence would suffer by allowing reviewing courts to exercise an informed discretion in making this choice.

IV

When the principles we have enunciated today are applied to the facts of this case, it is apparent that the judgment of the Court of Appeals cannot stand. The Court of Appeals applied the prevailing legal standards to Officer Rombach's warrant application and concluded that the application could not support the magistrate's probable-cause determination. In so doing, the court clearly informed the magistrate that he had erred in issuing the challenged warrant. This aspect of the court's judgment is not under attack in this proceeding.

Having determined that the warrant should not have issued, the Court of Appeals understandably declined to adopt a modification of the Fourth Amendment exclusionary rule that this Court had not previously sanctioned. Although the modification finds strong support in our previous cases, the Court of Appeals' commendable self-restraint is not to be criticized. We have now reexamined the purposes of the exclusionary rule and the propriety of its application in cases where officers have relied on a subsequently invalidated search warrant. Our conclusion is that the rule's purposes will only rarely be served by applying it in such circumstances.

In the absence of an allegation that the magistrate abandoned his detached and neutral role, suppression is appropriate only if the officers were dishonest or reckless in preparing their affidavit or could not have harbored an objectively reasonable belief in the existence of probable cause. Only respondent Leon has contended that no reasonably well trained police office could have believed that there existed probable cause to search his house; significantly, the other respondents advance no comparable argument. Officer Rombach's application for a warrant clearly was supported by much more than a "bare bones" affidavit. The affidavit related the results of an extensive investigation and, as the opinions of the divided panel of the Court of Appeals make clear, provided evidence sufficient to create disagreement among thoughtful and competent judges as to the existence of probable cause. Under these circumstances, the officers' reliance on the magistrate's determination of probable cause was objectively reasonable, and application of the extreme sanction of exclusion is inappropriate.

Accordingly, the judgment of the Court of Appeals is *Reversed*.

Justice BLACKMUN, concurring.

The Court today holds that evidence obtained in violation of the Fourth Amendment by officers acting in objectively reasonable reliance on a search warrant issued by a neutral and detached magistrate need not be excluded, as a matter of federal law, from the case in chief of federal and state criminal prosecutions. In so doing, the Court writes another chapter in the volume of Fourth Amendment law opened by *Weeks v. United States*, 232 U.S. 383, 34 S. Ct. 341, 58 L. Ed. 652 (1914). I join the Court's opinion in this case and the one in *Massachusetts v. Sheppard*, 468 U.S. 981, 104 S. Ct. 3424, 82 L. Ed. 2d 737 (1984), because I believe that the rule announced today advances the legitimate interests of the criminal justice system without sacrificing the individual rights protected by the Fourth Amendment. I write separately, however, to underscore what I regard as the unavoidably provisional nature of today's decision.

As the Court's opinion in this case makes clear, the Court has narrowed the scope of the exclusionary rule because of an empirical judgment that the rule has little appreciable effect in cases where officers act in objectively reasonable reliance on search warrants. See *ante*, at 3419–3420. Because I share the view that the exclusionary rule is not a constitutionally compelled corollary of the Fourth Amendment itself, see *ante*, at 3412, I see no way to avoid making an empirical judgment of this sort, and I am satisfied that the Court has made the correct one on the information before it. Like all courts, we face institutional limitations on our ability to gather information about "legislative facts," and the exclusionary rule itself has exacerbated the shortage of hard data concerning the behavior of police officers in the absence of such a rule. See *United States v. Janis*, 428 U.S. 433, 448–453, 96 S. Ct. 3021, 3029–3031, 49 L. Ed. 2d 1046 (1976). Nonetheless, we cannot escape the responsibility to decide the question before us, however imperfect our information may

---

26. It has been suggested, in fact, that "the recognition of a 'penumbral zone,' within which an inadvertent mistake would not call for exclusion, . . . will make it less tempting for judges to bend fourth amendment standards to avoid releasing a possibly dangerous criminal because of a minor and unintentional miscalculation by the police." Schroeder, *supra* n. 14, at 1420–1421 (footnote omitted); see Ashdown, Good Faith, the Exclusionary Remedy, and Rule-Oriented Adjudication in the Criminal Process, 24 Wm. & Mary L. Rev. 335, 383–384 (1983).

(continues)

be, and I am prepared to join the Court on the information now at hand.

What must be stressed, however, is that any empirical judgment about the effect of the exclusionary rule in a particular class of cases necessarily is a provisional one. By their very nature, the assumptions on which we proceed today cannot be cast in stone. To the contrary, they now will be tested in the real world of state and federal law enforcement, and this Court will attend to the results. If it should emerge from experience that, contrary to our expectations, the good-faith exception to the exclusionary rule results in a material change in police compliance with the Fourth Amendment, we shall have to reconsider what we have undertaken here.

The logic of a decision that rests on untested predictions about police conduct demands no less.

If a single principle may be drawn from this Court's exclusionary rule decisions, from *Weeks* through *Mapp v. Ohio*, 367 U.S. 643, 81 S. Ct. 1684, 6 L. Ed. 2d 1081 (1961), to the decisions handed down today, it is that the scope of the exclusionary rule is subject to change in light of changing judicial understanding about the effects of the rule outside the confines of the courtroom. It is incumbent on the Nation's law enforcement officers, who must continue to observe the Fourth Amendment in the wake of today's decisions, to recognize the double-edged nature of that principle.

UNITED STATES of America, Plaintiff–Appellee,

v.

Gilbert MARTINEZ–JIMENEZ, Defendant–Appellant.

No. 87–5305.

United States Court of Appeals, Ninth Circuit.

Submitted Oct. 4, 1988.

Decided Jan. 3, 1989.

864 F.2d 664 (9th Cir. 1989).

NELSON, Circuit Judge.

Gilbert Martinez–Jimenez appeals his conviction following a bench trial on one count of armed bank robbery in violation of 18 U.S.C. § 2113(a) & (d). He contends that the trial court erred in concluding that the toy gun that he held during the bank robbery was a "dangerous weapon" as defined by 18 U.S.C. § 2113(d). We affirm the judgment of the district court.

PROCEDURAL BACKGROUND

On July 14, 1987, a federal grand jury in the Central District of California returned a three-count indictment that charged the appellant and an accomplice, Joe Anthony De La Torre, with armed bank robbery in violation of 18 U.S.C. § 2113(a) & (d) and with carrying a firearm during a crime of violence in violation of 18 U.S.C. § 924(c). At a bench trial the appellant and his accomplice were found guilty of armed bank robbery as charged in count one and not guilty of carrying a firearm during a crime of violence, as charged in counts two and three.

FACTS

On June 19, 1987, at approximately 12:55 p.m., Martinez–Jimenez and De La Torre entered a bank in Bellflower, California. While De La Torre took cash from a customer and two bank drawers, Martinez–Jimenez remained in the lobby and ordered that the people in the bank lie "face down on the floor." During this time Martinez–Jimenez was holding an object that eyewitnesses thought was a handgun. These persons included two bank employees and a customer who was familiar with guns because he owned handguns, had handled weapons while in military service, and occasionally used weapons at firing ranges. The three witnesses testified that the object was a dark revolver about eight or nine inches long and that it caused them to fear for the safety of themselves and of those around them.

At trial, De La Torre testified that neither he nor Martinez–Jimenez had operable firearms when they entered the bank. He testified that Martinez–Jimenez had a toy gun that he and Martinez–Jimenez had purchased at a department store a few hours prior to the robbery. De La Torre also testified that he hid the toy gun in his closet after the robbery, that neither he nor Martinez–Jimenez wanted the bank employees to believe that they had a real gun, and that they did not want the bank employees to be in fear for their lives. Martinez–Jimenez testified that he had carried the toy gun because he felt secure with it and that during the robbery he held it down towards his leg in order to hide it so that people would not see it. The defense introduced into evidence a toy gun. Martinez–Jimenez testified that the gun used in the robbery was the toy gun introduced into evidence. It was stipulated that De La Torre's attorney had received the toy gun offered as the gun used in the robbery from De La Torre's mother.

Based upon observation of the bank robbery photographs and the toy gun, the court concluded that Martinez–Jimenez possessed a toy gun during the course of the bank robbery and that he had kept the toy gun pointed downwards by his side during the course of the bank robbery. On the basis of his display of the toy gun in the course of the robbery, Martinez–Jimenez was convicted under section 2113(d) which provides an enhanced penalty for use of a "dangerous weapon" during a bank robbery.

STANDARD OF REVIEW

The question presented is whether a toy gun is a "dangerous weapon" within the meaning of the federal bank robbery statute. Interpretation of a statute presents a question of law reviewable de novo. *United States v. Wilson*, 720 F.2d 608, 609 n. 2 (9th Cir. 1983), *cert. denied*, 465 U.S. 1034, 104 S. Ct. 1304, 79 L. Ed. 2d 703 (1984); *United States v. Moreno-Pulido*, 695 F.2d 1141, 1143 (9th Cir. 1983).

DISCUSSION

A robber may be guilty of an armed bank robbery under section 2113(d) if he uses a dangerous weapon or device in the commission of the crime. The instrumentality does not have to be a firearm. The use, or unlawful carrying, of a firearm in a bank robbery is a more serious offense punishable separately under section 924(c). In this case, the appellant carried a toy replica of a firearm that simulated the appearance but not the weight of a genuine firearm. The toy gun did not fit the statutory definition of a firearm under 18 U.S.C. § 921(a)(3). However, it did fall within the meaning of a "dangerous weapon or device" under section 2113(d). Section 2113(d) states that

> Whoever, in committing, or in attempting to commit, any offense defined in subsections (a) and (b) of this section, assaults any person, or puts in jeopardy the life of any person by the use of a dangerous weapon or device, shall be fined not more than $10,000 or imprisoned not more than twenty-five years, or both.

In *McLaughlin v. United States*, 476 U.S. 16, 106 S. Ct. 1677, 90 L. Ed. 2d 15 (1986), the Supreme Court found that a defendant who used an unloaded handgun was convicted properly under section 2113(d) because the unloaded handgun was a dangerous weapon under the statute. *Id.* at 17, 106 S. Ct. at 1677–78. Prior to *McLaughlin* this circuit, and other circuits, had assumed that section 2113(d) was violated only by the use of a loaded operable gun. *United States v. Terry*, 760 F.2d 939, 942 (9th Cir. 1985); see also *Parker v. United States*, 801 F.2d 1382, 1384 n. 2 (D.C. Cir. 1986), *cert. denied*, 479 U.S. 1070, 107 S. Ct. 964, 93 L. Ed. 2d 1011 (1987).

The *McLaughlin* opinion stated:

> Three reasons, each independently sufficient, support the conclusion that an unloaded gun is a "dangerous weapon." First, a gun is an article that is typically and characteristically dangerous; the use for which it is manufactured and sold is a dangerous one, and the law reasonably may presume that such an article is always dangerous even though it may not be armed at a particular time or place. *In addition, the display of a gun instills fear in the average citizen; as a consequence, it creates an immediate danger that a violent response will ensue.* Finally, a gun can cause harm when used as a bludgeon.

McLaughlin, 476 U.S. at 17–18, 106 S. Ct. at 1677–78 (footnote omitted) (emphasis added).

The *McLaughlin* opinion recognizes that the dangerousness of a device used in a bank robbery is not simply a function of its potential to injure people directly. Its dangerousness results from the greater burdens that it imposes upon victims and law enforcement officers. Therefore an unloaded gun that only simulates the threat of a loaded gun is a dangerous weapon. The use of a gun that is inoperable and incapable of firing also will support a conviction under section 921(a)(3) and section 2113(d). *United States v. York*, 830 F.2d 885, 891 (8th Cir. 1987), *cert. denied*, ___ U.S. ___, 108 S. Ct. 1047, 98 L. Ed. 2d 1010 (1988); see also *United States v. Goodheim*, 686 F.2d 776, 778 (9th Cir. 1982).

These cases reflect a policy that the robber's creation of even the appearance of dangerousness is sufficient to subject him to enhanced punishment. Other cases have given effect to this policy by holding that the trier of fact may infer that the instrument carried by a bank robber was a firearm based only on witness testimony that it appeared to be genuine. *Parker*, 801 F.2d at 1283–84; *United States v. Harris*, 792 F.2d 866, 868 (9th Cir. 1986). *McLaughlin* validates this policy but eliminates the inefficiencies associated with the inference process.

A robber who carries a toy gun during the commission of a bank robbery creates some of the same risks as those created by one who carries an unloaded or inoperable genuine gun. First, the robber subjects victims to greater apprehension. Second, the robber requires law enforcement agencies to formulate a more deliberate, and less efficient, response in light of the need to counter the apparent direct and immediate threat to human life. Third, the robber creates a likelihood that the reasonable response of police and guards will include the use of deadly force. The increased chance of an armed response creates a greater risk to the physical security of victims, bystanders, and even the perpetrators. Therefore the greater harm that a robber creates by deciding to carry a toy gun is similar to the harm that he creates by deciding to carry an unloaded gun.

The *McLaughlin* opinion examined the floor debate on the provision that became section 2113(d) and concluded that Congress was concerned with the potential of an apparently dangerous article to incite fear. *McLaughlin*, 476 U.S. at 18 n. 3, 106 S. Ct. at 1678 n. 3. The House debate on the provision that became section 2113(d) indicates that an ersatz wooden gun used in a bank robbery would satisfy the statutory

(continues)

meaning of a dangerous weapon or device. *See* 78 Cong. Rec. 8132 (1934). If Congress intended that an ersatz wooden gun would fall within the statute, by analogy an ersatz plastic gun should fall within the statute. Congress' intent focused on the nature of the effect that the robber creates, not the specific nature of the instruments that he utilizes.

Appellant concedes that *McLaughlin* applies to the use of an inherently dangerous weapon such as an unloaded firearm but argues that it does not apply to a harmless instrumentality of a crime, such as a toy gun, unless the defendant used the instrumentality in an assaultive manner. The trial court found that the replica was a "totally plastic and extremely light" toy gun, and that Martinez–Jimenez had held it downward by his side and not towards any of the bank employees or customers. Therefore the defendant urges that his manner of displaying this particular toy gun avoids *McLaughlin's* definition of a dangerous weapon because it would not have instilled fear in an average citizen and would not have created a danger of a violent response.

We disagree. A bank robber's use of a firearm during the commission of the crime is punishable even if he does not make assaultive use of the device. He need not brandish the firearm in a threatening manner. *United States v. Mason*, 658 F.2d 1263, 1270–71 (9th Cir. 1981). His possession of the weapon is an integral part of the crime. *United States v. Moore*, 580 F.2d 360, 362 (9th Cir.), *cert. denied*, 439 U.S. 970, 99 S. Ct. 463, 58 L. Ed. 2d 430 (1978). By analogy, a bank robber's use of a replica or simulated weapon violates section 2113(d) even if he does not make assaultive use of the device. His possession of the instrument during the commission of the crime evidences his apparent ability to commit an assault. The appellant's possession of the toy gun facilitated the crime and increased its likelihood of success. The appellant testified that he carried the toy gun because he "felt secure with it." This suggests that he may not have begun the robbery without it.

Section 2113(d) is not concerned with the way that a robber displays a simulated or replica weapon. The statute focuses on the harms created, not the manner of creating the harm. The record shows substantial evidence that the appellant's possession of the toy gun created fear and apprehension in the victims. Appellant argues that we should put aside this testimony because it was based upon the witnesses' mistaken assessment of the apparent threat. Appellant's argument fails because, during a robbery, people confronted with what they believe is a deadly weapon cannot be expected to maintain a high level of critical perception.[1]

By extension, appellant also argues that the toy gun did not jeopardize the life of any person because it did not increase the police's burden to interdict the crime during its commission or aftermath and could not have provoked the police's use of a deadly response that could have endangered others. This argument fails because the police must formulate a response to an apparently armed robber during the course of the crime, not after it. They must confront the risk that a replica or simulated gun creates before knowing that it presents no actual threat. These confrontations often lead to gunfire and casualties. *See, for example*, L.A. Times, Oct. 18, 1988, § 2, at 3, col. 1 (San Diego County ed.); *id.*, May 13, 1988, § 2, at 2, col. 5 (home ed.).

CONCLUSION

The values of justice, administrability, and deterrence require the rule that a robber's use of a replica or simulated weapon that appears to be a genuine weapon to those present at the scene of the crime, or to those charged with responsibility for responding to the crime, carries the same penalty as the use of a genuine weapon. In this case appellant avoided the harsher penalties associated with use of a firearm in violation of section 924(c) by proving that he only had simulated the use of a firearm. However, the appellant's decision to bluff did not eliminate the harms that Congress intended to address in section 2113(d).

AFFIRMED

---

1. The recent trend in toy and replica manufacturing to duplicate precisely the outward appearance of genuine weaponry compounds the difficulty and risk of making any distinction. *See* N.Y. Times, Oct. 16, 1988, § 4, at 7, col. 1. This trend has led some state and local governments to enact bans on realistic toy guns. *See* N.Y. Times, Aug. 5, 1988, § A, at col. 1; L.A. Times, Apr. 29, 1988, § 1, at 2, col. 6 (home ed.). Congress has held hearings on a federal ban. 134 Cong. Rec. D 1084 (daily ed. Aug. 11, 1988).

Stephen Alan WOLCOTT, Petitioner–Appellant,

v.

Sandra Lee WOLCOTT, Respondent–Appellee.

No. 9308.

Court of Appeals of New Mexico

March 5, 1987.

Certiorari Denied April 9, 1987.

105 N.M. 608, 735 P.2d 326 (Ct. App. 1987)

OPINION

FRUMAN, Judge.

Our opinion, previously filed on February 3, 1987, is withdrawn and the following opinion is substituted therefor.

Husband appeals from the denial of his post-divorce motions to reduce or abate his child support obligations and to terminate or abate his alimony obligation. Husband relied upon his voluntary change of employment, which resulted in a major reduction of his income, as the substantial change of circumstances justifying his motions. In denying these motions, the trial court found that husband had not acted in good faith with regard to his support obligations when he changed employment.

Husband's issues on appeal are: "1. Whether the voluntary career change of a professional never justifies modification of his support obligation, even if undertaken in good faith." and 2. Whether there is substantial evidence to support the trial court's finding that husband was not acting in good faith when he changed specialty.

As the first issue is presented in the abstract, it would require an advisory opinion on review. This court does not give advisory opinions. *In re Bunnell*, 100 N.M. 242, 668 P.2d 1119 (Ct. App. 1983). Although the first issue will not be directly addressed, it will be generally considered in our review of the second issue. We affirm the trial court on the second issue.

FACTS

Following their marriage of thirteen years, the parties were divorced in December 1983. Pursuant to the marital settlement agreement incorporated into the decree of dissolution, husband was to pay $1,500 monthly for the support of the three minor children, and $300 monthly for alimony for a period of five years. At the time of the divorce, husband was a physician specializing in obstetrics and gynecology in Albuquerque.

For a number of years husband had considered changing his specialty to psychiatry. In March 1985, he was accepted in a psychiatric residency program in Washington, D.C.

Husband closed his Albuquerque office in June 1985 and commenced his residency the following month. The duration of the program is three to four years, and during this period, husband's annual gross income will range from approximately $21,000 to $24,000. This salary is approximately one-fourth of his annual gross income during the several years prior to and the year following the divorce.

In June 1985, husband unilaterally reduced his combined monthly child support and alimony payment from $1,800 to $550, contrary to the terms of the marital settlement agreement and without judicial approval or forewarning his former spouse.

DISCUSSION

Husband contends that the denial of his motion for reduction of support payments was erroneously based on the trial court's finding of a lack of good faith in changing his speciality and that there was not substantial evidence to support this finding.

To justify modification in the amount of child support already awarded, there must be evidence of a "substantial change of circumstances which materially affects the existing welfare of the child and which must have occurred since the prior adjudication where child support was originally awarded." *Henderson v. Lekvold*, 95 N.M. 288, 291, 621 P.2d 505, 508 (1980). See *Spingola v. Spingola*, 91 N.M. 737, 580 P.2d 958 (1978). A similar change in circumstances of the supported spouse must be shown before the request may be granted as to alimony. See *Brister v. Brister*, 92 N.M. 711, 594 P.2d 1167 (1979). The recipient's actual need for support is the essential criterion. See *Weaver v. Weaver*, 100 N.M. 165, 667 P.2d 970 (1983); *Brister v. Brister*.

Husband, as the petitioner for the modification, had the burden of proving to the trial court's satisfaction that circumstances had substantially changed and, thereby, justified his requests. See *Smith v. Smith*, 98 N.M. 468, 649 P.2d 1381 (1982); *Spingola v. Spingola*. Any change in support obligations is a matter within the discretion of the trial court, and appellate review is limited to a determination of whether that discretion has been abused. *Henderson v. Lekvold*. If substantial evidence exists to support the trial court's findings, they will be upheld. See *Chavez v. Chavez*, 98 N.M. 678, 652 P.2d 228 (1982). Cf. *Pitcher v. Pitcher*, 91 N.M. 504, 576 P.2d 1135 (1978).

The common trend in various jurisdictions is that a good faith career change, resulting in a decreased income, may constitute a material change in circumstances that warrants a reduction in a spouse's support obligation. See *Thomas v. Thomas*, 281 Ala. 397, 203 So. 2d 118 (1967); *Graham v. Graham*, 21 Ill. App. 3d 1032, 316 N.E.2d 143 (1974); *Schuler v. Schuler*, 382 Mass. 366, 416 N.E.2d 197 (1981); *Giesner v. Giesner*, 319 N.W.2d 718 (Minn. 1982); *Fogel v.*

(continues)

Fogel, 184 Neb. 425, 168 N.W.2d 275 (1969); *Nelson v. Nelson*, 225 Or. 257, 357 P.2d 536 (1960); *Anderson v. Anderson*, 503 S.W.2d 124 (Tex. Civ. App. 1973); *Lambert v. Lambert*, 66 Wash. 2d 503, 403 P.2d 664 (1965). Likewise, where the career change is not made in good faith, a reduction in one's support obligations will not be warranted. See *In re Marriage of Ebert*, 81 Ill. App. 3d 44, 36 Ill. Dec. 415, 400 N.E.2d 995 (1980) (evidence of a desire to evade support responsibilities); *Moncada v. Moncada*, 81 Mich. App. 26, 264 N.W.2d 104 (1978) (no evidence that husband acted in bad faith or with willful disregard for the welfare of his dependents); *Bedford v. Bedford*, 49 Mich. App. 424, 212 N.W.2d 260 (1973) (husband voluntarily avoided re-employment opportunities); *Nelson v. Nelson* (no evidence that the sale of a medical practice and assumption of clinic duties, resulting in a decrease in income, was made to jeopardize the interests of the children); *Commonwealth v. Saul*, 175 Pa. Super. 540, 107 A.2d 182 (1954) (husband literally gave away assets available for support payments). *See generally* Annot., 89 A.L.R.2d 1 at 54 (1963).

Husband challenges the trial court's findings that: (1) at the time husband entered the marital settlement agreement, he had planned to terminate his private practice and return to school, but did not so advise wife; (2) although wife may have had prior knowledge of husband's future employment desires, she had no reason to believe that he would effect a career change upon entering the settlement agreement, if it interfered with the support obligations he was assuming; and (3) husband was not acting in good faith with regard to his child support and alimony obligations when he voluntarily made his career change.

The record contains both direct and reasonably inferred evidence from the testimony of the parties to support the first two challenged findings. The third finding is supported by evidence of husband's disregard for several financial obligations undertaken by him in the marital settlement agreement, by his failure or inability to make a full disclosure of his income and assets to wife and the court, and by his self-indulgence with regard to his own lifestyle and personal necessities without regard to the necessities of his children and his former spouse. We find this evidence sufficient to support the trial court's decision to deny husband's petition for a modification of his child support obligation.

Husband also argues that, during their marriage, wife was willing to make changes in the family's lifestyle as would be necessary to accommodate his career change. Because of this, husband contends that his career change following the divorce does not indicate a lack of good faith. Husband did not, however, request a finding as to this contention, and his failure to do so waives any merit the argument may have. See *Worland v. Worland*, 89 N.M. 291, 551 P.2d 981 (1976).

In the determination of alimony, the recipient's actual need for support is the focal point. See *Brister v. Brister*. While husband did request a finding as to wife's employment and there was testimony as to her employment, there was also testimony indicating her continued need for alimony. We find this evidence sufficient to support the trial court's decision to continue wife's alimony.

Although husband asserts that his voluntary career change was made entirely in good faith, without a disregard of the welfare of his children and former spouse, this change does not automatically mandate a reduction in his support obligation. See *Spingola v. Spingola*. The decision as to reducing or maintaining the support obligation rests within the trial court's discretion. *Id.*

We recognize that the "responsibilities of begetting a family many times raise havoc with dreams. Nevertheless, the duty [to support] persists, with full authority in the State to enforce it." *Romano v. Romano*, 133 Vt. 314, 316, 340 A.2d 63, 63 (1975).

Based upon our review of the record we conclude that the decision of the trial court does not constitute an abuse of its discretion. Its decision is affirmed.

IT IS SO ORDERED.

DONNELLY, C.J., and ALARID, J., concur.

Appellate Court Brief

INTRODUCTION

The brief of the appellee in the case of *Frank Lewis v. U.S. Attorney, U.S. Marshal and New Mexico Department of Corrections* is presented in this appendix. The brief was filed in the United States Court of Appeals for the Tenth Circuit. The legal research, legal analysis, and initial drafts of this brief were performed by Gardner Miller. Mr. Miller, listed in the 1998–1999 edition of *Who's Who in American Law*, received his Associate of Applied Science degree in Paralegal Studies from Central New Mexico Community College in Albuquerque, New Mexico. Mr. Miller was employed as a paralegal in the Criminal Division of the United States Attorney's Office for the District of New Mexico when he worked on this brief.

The Tenth Circuit Court of Appeals decided this case on the briefs submitted to the court (there was no oral argument). The decision was in favor of the appellee (United States government).

UNITED STATES COURT OF APPEALS

TENTH CIRCUIT

NO. 94-2275

FRANK LEWIS,

Petitioner-Appellant,

vs.

U.S. Attorney, U.S. Marshal and

New Mexico Department of Corrections,

Respondents-Appellees.

APPEAL FROM THE UNITED STATES DISTRICT COURT

FOR THE DISTRICT OF NEW MEXICO

BRIEF OF APPELLEE

ORAL ARGUMENT IS NOT REQUESTED

JOHN J. KELLY

United States Attorney

LARRY GÓMEZ

Assistant U.S. Attorney

P.O. Box 607

Albuquerque, New Mexico 87103

(505) 766-3341

Attorneys for Appellee

January, 1995

TABLE OF CONTENTS

POINT I

LEWIS'S HABEAS PETITION SHOULD
HAVE BEEN DISMISSED BY THE DISTRICT COURT
FOR LACK OF JURISDICTION

POINT II

IN DECIDING ON THE MERITS OF LEWIS'S HABEAS
PETITION, THE DISTRICT COURT ACTED PROPERLY IN
DENYING THE PETITION AND DISMISSING IT WITH
PREJUDICE

TABLE OF CASES AND OTHER AUTHORITIES

TABLE OF CASES

TABLE OF CASES cont.

TABLE OF OTHER AUTHORITIES

PRIOR OR RELATED APPEALS

The United States informs this Court, pursuant to *10th Cir. R. 28.2(a)*, that there are no prior or related appeals in this case.

STATEMENT OF ISSUES PRESENTED FOR REVIEW

This appeal is a review of the District Court's denial of Appellant's Habeas Petition, and presents the following issues for review:

POINT I:

WHETHER THE DISTRICT COURT SHOULD HAVE DISMISSED APPELLANT'S HABEAS PETITION FOR LACK OF JURISDICTION?

POINT II:

WHETHER THE DISTRICT COURT ACTED PROPERLY IN DENYING APPELLANT'S HABEAS PETITION ON THE MERITS AND DISMISSING THE PETITION WITH PREJUDICE?

STATEMENT OF THE CASE

On March 15, 1993, Petitioner-Appellant Frank Lewis (hereinafter referred to as Lewis) filed a pro se Petition for Writ of Habeas Corpus under 28 U.S.C. § 2254 for a person in state custody.[1] (Doc. 1). On March 25, 1993, United States Magistrate Judge William Deaton issued an Order appointing Tova Indritz, the Federal Public Defender, to represent Lewis. (Doc. 4).

On May 25, 1993, Lewis filed an Amended Petition (Doc. 5) with numerous exhibits. The government filed its Answer on July 20, 1993, requesting that Lewis's Amended Petition be dismissed for lack of jurisdiction. (Doc. 8). Lewis then filed a Memorandum Brief in support of his Amended Petition on September 27, 1993. (Doc. 12). Because this Memorandum Brief restructured Lewis's habeas petition under 28 U.S.C. § 2241 and § 2255, revamped old arguments, requested new remedies and introduced new exhibits, it was, for all practical purposes, a new habeas petition. Without being ordered to do so, the government responded to Lewis's Memorandum Brief on December 13, 1993. (Doc. 14).

On October 4, 1994, United States Magistrate Judge Lorenzo Garcia issued his proposed findings and recommended disposition of Lewis's habeas petition. (Doc. 17). Lewis filed his objections to Judge Garcia's findings and recommended disposition on October 17, 1994. (Doc. 18).

On November 8, 1994, Senior United States District Judge Juan Burciaga adopted Judge Garcia's proposed findings and recommended disposition and ordered that Lewis's action be dismissed with prejudice. (Doc. 19). Lewis timely filed a notice of appeal of Judge Burciaga's Order on November 22, 1994. (Doc. 20).

---

[1] The following day, March 16, 1993, the New Mexico Department of Corrections transferred Lewis into Federal custody.

STATEMENT OF THE FACTS

The facts underlying Lewis's habeas petition are not in dispute. They are summarized from the record as follows:

On February 27, 1985, Lewis pled guilty in New Mexico State District Court for the Second Judicial District (Bernalillo County) to two crimes he committed on December 22, 1983. One was the felony offense of heroin possession and the other was the misdemeanor offense of possession of drug paraphernalia. (Doc. 5, Petitioner's Exhibit 1).

As a result of these convictions, on May 17, 1985, State District Judge Burt Cosgrove sentenced Lewis to the custody of the New Mexico Department of Corrections for a term of 6-1/2 years. The court also ordered Lewis to turn himself in to authorities at 9:00 A.M. on May 21, 1985 to begin serving his sentence. On June 4, 1985, about two weeks after Lewis started serving his sentence, a federal grand jury indicted him on four counts of heroin trafficking. The first two counts charged Lewis with possession with intent to distribute heroin and distribution of heroin on or about August 18, 1983. The other two counts charged that Lewis committed the same offenses on or about August 25, 1983. (Doc. 5, Petitioner's Exhibit 2).

On April 29, 1986, as a consequence of the federal indictment, United States District Judge Juan Burciaga issued a Writ of Habeas Corpus Ad Prosequendum commanding the Warden of the New Mexico State Penitentiary to deliver Lewis into federal custody so that he could be prosecuted on the federal drug charges. (Doc. 5, Petitioner's Exhibit 5).

On May 23, 1986, pursuant to a plea agreement, Lewis pled guilty to Count IV of the Indictment (heroin distribution). In return, the government agreed to dismiss the other three counts against him and not seek a sentence enhancement under 21 U.S.C. § 851, based on his prior state drug conviction. The agreement also stated there was no agreement that "a specific sentence is the appropriate disposition of this case." (Doc. 5, Petitioner's Exhibit 3).

Judge Burciaga accepted Lewis's guilty plea and, on July 18, 1986, sentenced Lewis to eight years imprisonment to be followed by a special parole term of three years. After imposing the sentence, the court dismissed the remaining counts against Lewis. The Judgment was entered on the docket on July 28, 1986. (Doc. 5, Petitioner's Exhibit 4).

Lewis was returned to the state's custody on July 23, 1986. (Doc. 12, Petitioner's Exhibit 16 at 3).

Five months later, on December 22, 1986, Lewis escaped from the New Mexico State Penitentiary and also kidnapped someone. The record does not show when he was apprehended. However, on January 12, 1988, Lewis was convicted in state district court (Thirteenth Judicial District, Valencia County) for the felony offenses of Escape from the penitentiary and Kidnapping. On April 11, 1988, the state district court sentenced Lewis to the custody of the New Mexico Corrections Department for 19 years for these convictions. The court then suspended eight years of the sentence and ordered the remaining eleven years to be served in the state penitentiary, "consecutive to any other state or federal time that he is now serving or served." (Doc. 5, Petitioner's Exhibit 6). According to an affidavit from Lewis's attorney at this sentencing, State District Court Judge Mayo T. Boucher actually wanted the new eleven-year sentence to be concurrent with Lewis's existing state and federal sentences. (Doc. 5, Petitioner's Exhibit 9).

Consequently, the state district court for Valencia County issued a series of Amended Judgments regarding Lewis's latest state sentence. The first, filed August 27, 1990, ordered the sentence to run concurrently with the eight-year federal sentence, but consecutively to the original state sentence of 6-1/2 years. (Doc. 5, Petitioner's Exhibit 7). The second, filed October 31, 1990, made Lewis's latest sentence run concurrently with both his original state sentence and his federal sentence. (Doc 5, Petitioner's Exhibit 8). The Third Amended Judgement, filed September 10, 1992, retained the basic nineteen-year sentence, but suspended half of it (9-1/2 years) instead of the eight years that had been previously suspended. It again ordered the state sentence to be served concurrently with the federal sentence, this time specifying the underlying case number, and ordered Lewis to be remanded to the custody of the U.S. Marshal's Office for transfer to a federal prison to serve his federal sentence. (Doc. 5, Petitioner's Exhibit 10). A year earlier, New Mexico prison officials had given Lewis written notification that the U.S. Marshal's Office, on the advice of the U.S. Attorney's Office, would not take him into federal custody until he had been paroled or discharged from the state. (Doc. 5, Petitioner's Exhibit 12). The Fourth (and final) Amended Judgment was filed on January 7, 1993. It again specified that Lewis's state sentence for escape and kidnapping run concurrently with his federal sentence to be served and ordered Lewis's immediate transfer to federal custody. (Doc. 5, Petitioner's Exhibit 11).

As a result of his federal sentence, a federal detainer had been lodged against Lewis while he was incarcerated at the New Mexico State Penitentiary. However, despite the state court judgment ordering his transfer to federal custody, the U.S. Marshal's Office refused to take him into custody until he had been released from all his state sentences. (Doc. 12, Petitioner's Exhibit 17 at 2).

Upon being paroled from his final state sentence, Lewis was transferred to federal custody on March 16, 1993 and began serving his federal sentence. (Doc. 12, Petitioner's

Exhibit 15 at 2). On April 30, 1993, Lewis arrived at his present place of incarceration, the Federal Correctional Institution (FCI) at Florence, Colorado. (Doc. 12, Petitioner's Exhibit 16 at 3).

After his arrival at FCI Florence, Lewis sought to receive credit against his sentence through a Request for Administrative Remedy. His request was denied, as was his appeal of that denial. (Doc. 12, Petitioner's Exhibits 14 and 15). Lewis then pursued the habeas petition which was denied by the federal district court.

POINT I

LEWIS'S HABEAS PETITION SHOULD HAVE BEEN DISMISSED BY THE DISTRICT COURT FOR LACK OF JURISDICTION.

STANDARD OF REVIEW: Jurisdictional issues are reviewed *de novo. United States v. 51 Pieces of Real Property*, 17 F.3d 1306, 1309 (10th Cir. 1994).

It is well settled that jurisdictional issues are important enough that they may be raised at any time during the proceedings. *McGrath v. Kristensen*, 340 U.S. 162, 167 (1950); *United States v. Siviglia*, 686 F.2d 832, 835 (10th Cir. 1981), *cert. denied,* 461 U.S. 918 (1983); *Bledsoe v. Wirtz*, 384 F.2d 767, 769 (10th Cir. 1967).

28 U.S.C. § 2242 provides that a habeas petition shall state "the name of the person who has custody over him" (i.e., the petitioner). Likewise, 28 U.S.C. § 2243 states: "The writ, or order to show cause shall be directed to the person having custody of the person detained." As the Supreme Court noted: "The writ of habeas corpus does not act upon the prisoner who seeks relief, but upon the person who holds him in what is alleged to be unlawful custody." *Braden v. 30th Judicial Circuit Court of Kentucky*, 410 U.S. 484, 494-5 (1973). The *Braden* Court then quoted from *In the Matter of Jackson*, 15 Mich. 417, 439-440 (1867), characterizing the quotation as a "classic statement":

> The important fact to be observed in regard to the mode of procedure upon this writ is, that it is directed to, and served upon, not the person confined but his jailer. The officer or person who serves it does not unbar the prison doors and set the prisoner free, but the court relieves him by compelling the oppressor to release his constraint. The whole force of the writ is spent upon the respondent.

410 U.S. at 495.

When the habeas petitioner is incarcerated, the only appropriate respondent to his habeas petition is the warden of the facility where he is incarcerated. *Guerra v. Meese*, 786 F.2d 414, 417 (D.C. Cir. 1986) ("Until they are paroled . . . the proper respondents are the wardens of the federal facilities at which the prisoners are confined."). *Guerra* was expressly reaffirmed in *Chatman-Bey v. Thornburgh*, 864 F.2d 804, 810–11 (D.C. Cir. 1988) ("[T]he proper defendant in federal habeas cases is the warden."). *See also Joyner v. Henman*, 755 F. Supp. 982, 984 (D. Kan. 1991) (proper respondent for petitioner's habeas action is the warden at USP Leavenworth because he is the petitioner's present custodian). The "custodian," for habeas corpus purposes, is the person having day-to-day control of the prisoner and is the only one who can produce "the body" of the habeas petitioner. *Guerra, supra* at 416.

The record clearly shows that Lewis was delivered to FCI Florence on April 30, 1993. (Doc. 12, Petitioner's Exhibit 16 at 3). On May 25, 1993, Lewis (through his appointed counsel) filed his Amended Petition. (Doc. 5). In this Amended Petition, Lewis acknowledged that "he is currently in the custody of the Bureau of Prisons at Florence, Colorado." (Doc. 5 at 4). Yet, the respondent to his Amended Petition was not his present custodian, the warden of FCI Florence. Instead, Lewis named as respondents: the U.S. Attorney (for the District of New Mexico), the U.S. Marshal (for the same District), and the New Mexico Department of Corrections.

A similar situation occurred in *Billiteri v. United States Board of Parole*, 541 F.2d 938 (2d Cir. 1976). There, instead of naming as respondent the Warden of USP Lewisburg, Pennsylvania, where he was confined, the petitioner named the parole board which had denied his release. In dismissing his petition, the *Billiteri* Court declared:

It would have imposed no great hardship on Billiteri to have brought his action against the Warden in the Middle District of Pennsylvania, as he should have done. As he did not, the present case must be dismissed for lack of jurisdiction over an application for a writ of habeas corpus . . .

541 F.2d at 948-49.

Recently, the Ninth Circuit in *Stanley v. California Supreme Court*, 21 F.3d 359 (9th Cir. 1994), addressed the same situation as here where there were two habeas petitions with multiple respondents, but none of them were the petitioner's custodian:

> A petitioner for habeas corpus relief must name the state officer having custody of him or her as the respondent to the petition . . . . Failure to name the petitioner's custodian as a respondent deprives federal courts of personal jurisdiction. (Citations omitted). . . . Neither of Stanley's two petitions named his custodian as a respondent and *therefore* the district lacked jurisdiction. (Emphasis added).

21 F.3d at 360.

In its initial Answer to Lewis's Amended Petition, the government sought to have the petition dismissed for lack of jurisdiction. (Doc. 8). The district court never ruled on this request, but impliedly rejected it by addressing the merits of Lewis's Amended Petition as presented in his Memorandum Brief.

For the reasons stated herein, this Court, as a matter of law, should remand the case with instructions to dismiss for lack of jurisdiction.

IN DECIDING ON THE MERITS OF LEWIS'S HABEAS
PETITION, THE DISTRICT COURT ACTED PROPERLY IN
DENYING THE PETITION AND DISMISSING IT WITH
PREJUDICE.

STANDARD OF REVIEW: This Court reviews *de novo* a district court's decision to deny habeas relief. *Sinclair v. Herman*, 986 F.2d 407, 408 (10th Cir.), *cert. denied*, ___ U.S. ___, 114 S. Ct. 129 (1993).

As an introductory note, it is recognized that, should this court indeed remand the case with instructions to dismiss for lack of jurisdiction, Lewis may be tempted to file another habeas petition under 28 U.S.C. § 2241 in perhaps a different forum. In that event, an opinion from this Court which also discusses the merits of Lewis's contentions would prove very useful.

The thrust of Lewis's habeas petition was that he was entitled to receive credit against his federal sentence because the U.S. Marshal's Service, on advice from the U.S. Attorney, ignored the custody transfer orders issued by a New Mexico district court. In his Memorandum Brief (Doc. 12), Lewis introduced a second stratagem under 28 U.S.C. § 2255 for obtaining the credit he sought. It was to request that Judge Burciaga (who had imposed his federal sentence) recommend *nunc pro tunc* that New Mexico State Correctional Facilities be designated as the location for serving his federal sentence. In his Order Adopting the Magistrate's Findings and Dismissing Action with Prejudice, Judge Burciaga expressly declined to make such a recommendation. (Doc. 19). Because the decision was clearly within Judge Burciaga's discretion, this avenue for obtaining the desired credit is permanently blocked.

As previously stated, Lewis's main complaint centers around the conduct of the U.S. Marshals. By ignoring the repeated custody transfer orders of a state district judge, they ensured that Lewis would not start serving his federal sentence until he had been paroled from his second state sentence. This also defied the state district court's Orders that Lewis's second state sentence be served concurrently with his imposed but unserved federal sentence.

A somewhat similar situation existed in *Del Guzzi v. United States*, 980 F.2d 1269 (9th Cir. 1992). The federal marshals in that case also created a consecutive sentence by refusing to accept custody of the defendant until he had completed his state sentence. In *Del Guzzi*, however, the expectation of concurrent sentences was shared by all parties concerned *before* the state sentence was imposed and may have even contributed to its length (the statutory maximum). Nonetheless, the court upheld the marshal's actions, stating it had "no authority to violate the statutory mandate that federal authorities need only accept prisoners upon completion of their state sentence and need not credit prisoners with time spent in state custody." *Del Guzzi*, 980 F.2d at 1271.

In his proposed findings and recommended disposition, Magistrate Judge Garcia found the following guidance from Judge Norris's concurring opinion in *Del Guzzi* to be "highly instructive." (Doc. 17 at 9).

> While Del Guzzi will get no relief from this court, I hope his case will serve as a lesson to those who are in a position to guard against future cases of this sort. State sentencing judges and defense attorneys in state proceedings should be put on notice. Federal prison officials are under no obligation to, and may well refuse to, follow the recommendation of state sen-

tencing judges that a prisoner be transported to a federal facility. Moreover, concurrent sentences imposed by state judges are nothing more than recommendations to federal officials. Those officials remain free to turn those concurrent sentences into consecutive sentences by refusing to accept the state prisoner until completion of the state sentence and refusing to credit the time the prisoner spent is state custody.

980 F.2d at 1272-73.

To counter this harsh reality, Lewis contends that a prisoner should not be made to suffer because ministerial officers, such as federal marshals, failed to execute a court order. Among the cases Lewis relies upon to support this contention are: *Kiendra v. Hadden*, 763 F.2d 69 (2d Cir. 1985); *United States v. Croft*, 450 F.2d 1094 (6th Cir. 1971); and *Smith v. Swope*, 91 F.2d 260 (9th Cir. 1937). As Magistrate Judge Garcia noted, these cases are easily distinguishable because they involved federal marshals failing to execute orders issued by federal courts, not state courts. (Doc. 17 at 7-9).

Lewis also attempts to find support in Tenth Circuit case law. He cites *Bloomgren v. Belaski*, 948 F.2d 688, 690 (10th Cir. 1991), for the proposition that a "federal prisoner is entitled to credit for time spent in state prison on an unrelated charge 'if the continued state confinement was exclusively the product of such action by federal law enforcement officials as to justify treating the state jail as the practical equivalent of the federal one.'" (Appellant's Brief-in-Chief at 9, 20).

What Lewis fails to mention is that this exception was being applied to the pretrial state time served by Bloomgren on bailable offenses; Bloomgren had been denied bail in accordance with a federal arrest warrant that had

been lodged against him after his arrest by state officials. *Bloomgren*, 948 F.2d at 689-90. In contrast, all
of Lewis's state prison time was the direct result of
his convictions and sentences imposed by state district
courts.

In fact, *Bloomgren* supports the government's case.
Bloomgren had committed his bailable state offenses while
on a federal appeal bond from an earlier federal conviction. That conviction became final while Bloomgren
was serving a state sentence from yet another set of
offenses. Although the state sentencing judge had ordered
Bloomgren's state sentence to be concurrent with his
unserved federal sentence, the federal marshals refused
to take him into custody until he had been paroled from
his state sentence. *Bloomgren*, 948 F.2d at 290-91. The
Bloomgren court held:

> Bloomgren thus served his federal sentence after his
> state sentence, rather than serving them concurrently as
> anticipated by the state court. Nonetheless, Bloomgren is
> not entitled to credit on his federal sentence from time
> spent incarcerated on state charges. The federal govern-
> ment has no duty to take one in Bloomgren's situation
> into custody. See *Smith v. United States Parole Comm'n*,
> 875 F.2d 1361, 1364 (9th Cir. 1989).

948 F.2d at 691.

If the federal government did have such a duty, then
merely by ordering concurrent sentences and custody transfers, state courts could require the federal government to
assume the costs of incarcerating any state prisoner facing
a previously imposed federal sentence.

In imposing Lewis's federal sentence, by not recommending that New Mexico corrections facilities be designated as
Lewis's place of federal confinement, Judge Burciaga made

it clear that he intended for Lewis's federal sentence to be consecutive to his first state sentence.[2] The *Bloomgren* Court declared:

> The determination by federal authorities that Bloomgren's federal sentence would run consecutively to his state sentence is a federal matter which cannot be overridden by a state court provision for concurrent sentencing on a subsequently-obtained state conviction.

948 F.2d at 691.

Also, in *Salley v. United States*, 786 F.2d 546, 548 (2d Cir. 1986), another federal circuit court observed: "There is no reason why the (United States) district court's sentence, which was prior in time, must give way to that of the State court." (Citations omitted).

Another case in which U.S. Marshals ignored a state judge's order for concurrent sentences was *Lionel v. Day*, 430 F. Supp. 384 (W.D. Okla. 1976). In *Lionel*, as here, consecutive sentences resulted and federal prison officials refused to grant the petitioner credit for time spent in state custody. In upholding their decision, the Lionel court declared: "Obviously no comment or order by a state judge can control the service of a federal sentence." 430 F. Supp. at 386.

As established by these cases, the comment by U.S. Marshal John Sanchez that "state court judges cannot dictate when a federal sentence begins" is a correct statement of the law. (Affidavit of Cathleen M. Catanach, Doc. 12, Petitioner's Exhibit 17 at 2). The portions of the Amended Judgments which directed Lewis to be transferred into fed-

---

[2] In his Memorandum Brief, Lewis acknowledged that Judge Burciaga intended that Lewis serve his federal sentence after his existing state sentence. (Doc. 12 at 19).

eral custody (and thus begin serving his federal sentence) were invalid; therefore, the marshals were free to ignore such orders.

A crucial part of Lewis's claim is the theory that, once Lewis was paroled from his first state sentence on December 9, 1989, the state lost its jurisdiction over Lewis and Lewis was now subject to federal jurisdiction by virtue of his federal arrest and conviction that occurred "before the Valencia County case even arose." (Appellant's Brief-in-Chief at 10).

The government's position is based on the fact that Lewis's first state sentence was clearly still in force on April 11, 1988, when his second state sentence was imposed. Therefore, Lewis's second state sentence merely extended the time the State had jurisdiction over Lewis. This also was the conclusion reached by Magistrate Judge Garcia. (Doc. 17 at 6).

The authority for this proposition lies in another Tenth Circuit case, *McIntosh v. Looney*, 249 F.2d 62 (10th Cir. 1957), *cert. denied*, 355 U.S. 935 (1958), which the appellant has relied upon for support.[3] McIntosh was serving a six-month sentence in a Missouri county jail when, pursuant to a Writ of Habeas Corpus Ad Prosequendum, he was sentenced in federal district court for violation of the federal kidnapping statute. He received a five-year sentence, to begin upon completion of his misdemeanor sentence. He was returned to the county jail and, while still serving his six-month sentence, he assaulted a jailer there.

---

[3] *McIntosh* agreed with the "ministerial officer malfeasance" exception propounded by *Smith*, calling it the "academic premise" for the claims in its case. *McIntosh*, 249 F.2d at 64. However, the Court then described why the marshal's actions in its case were proper. (*Id.*)

McIntosh's misdemeanor sentence was still in force when he was indicted in state court for the assault, pled guilty, and received a five-year sentence. It also was to begin when he completed his misdemeanor sentence. When McIntosh finally completed his six-month sentence, he was taken from the county jail to the Missouri penitentiary to serve his second state sentence. Only after his second state sentence was completed on October 11, 1956, was McIntosh transferred into federal custody to begin serving his federal sentence. *McIntosh*, 249 F.2d at 63.

Like Lewis, McIntosh claimed the State had lost its jurisdiction over him upon completion of his first state sentence and that the federal marshals had a duty to take him into custody at that time to begin serving his federal sentence. *Id.* at 64. In rejecting his claim, the *McIntosh* Court declared:

> The State of Missouri . . . had continuous jurisdiction and custody of appellant until October 11, 1956, at which time state jurisdiction and the right to custody were terminated. . . . Appellant's incarceration was continuous and under a single and proper authority, that of the State of Missouri. *(Id.)*.

The Court then compared its case to *Harrell v. Shuttleworth*, 200 F.2d 490 (5th Cir. 1952). There, while serving a state sentence, a federal court sentenced the prisoner to a federal sentence to begin upon completion of his state sentence. Before completion of the state sentence, the prisoner received an additional state sentence for an offense committed at the state prison. The *Harrell* Court held that [the] federal sentence did not begin to run upon completion of the first state sentence. The comparison which the *McIntosh* Court made was as follows:

> In *Harrell*, the state sentences overlapped. In the instant case they were consecutive. The effect was the

same—*continuous jurisdiction* and custody under a single sovereign authority. (Emphasis added).

249 F.2d at 64.

In recognition of the State of New Mexico's jurisdiction over Lewis and Judge Burciaga's intent that Lewis's federal sentence be consecutive, a federal detainer was lodged against Lewis at the New Mexico State Penitentiary. It was not linked to a specific conviction or sentence and it could be executed only after New Mexico had released Lewis from all his state sentences, thereby relinquishing its jurisdiction over him. This occurred on March 16, 1993, and Lewis was transferred into federal custody on that date.

In his Appeal Brief, Lewis acknowledges that 18 U.S.C. § 3568 (since repealed)[4] governed the calculation of federal sentences imposed for crimes committed prior to November 1, 1987. (Appellant's Brief-in-Chief at 12).

This statute clearly stated "The sentence of imprisonment . . . shall commence to run from the date on which such person is received at the penitentiary, reformatory, or jail for service of such sentence."

Although Lewis decries applying § 3568 "mechanistically," there is no other way to apply it. Federal courts have uniformly interpreted the plain language of § 3568 as precluding the calculation of the time served on a federal sentence from any date other than the one on which the prisoner was delivered into federal custody. See, e.g., *Thomas v. Whalen*, 962 F.2d 358, 363 (4th Cir. 1992); *Meagher v. Clark*, 943 F.2d 1277, 1282

---

[4] 18 U.S.C. § 3568 (1982) (repealed effective November 1, 1987) by P.L. 98-473, Title II § 212(a)(2), 98 Stat. 1987, 2031 (1984), *reenacted in part*, 18 U.S.C. § 3585 (1988).

(11th Cir. 1991); *Thomas v. Brewer*, 923 F.2d 1361, 1367 (9th Cir. 1991); *Scott v. United States*, 434 F.2d 11, 21 (5th Cir. 1970).

Title 18 U.S.C. § 3568 also stated that, in order to receive credit against a federal sentence for state time served, the offense underlying the state sentence must be "in connection with the offense or acts for which (the federal) sentence was imposed." Lewis' federal sentence was for drug trafficking while his second state sentence (for which he seeks credit against his federal sentence) was for escape and kidnapping. Thus, the statute itself precludes the credit Lewis seeks. See *Bloomgren*, *supra* at 690, citing to *Goode v. McCune*, 543 F.2d 751, 753 (10th Cir. 1976) (no credit for time spent in state custody where state time was attributable to state charges only).

In effect, Lewis's pleadings are an attempt to obtain double credit for much of the time he was incarcerated by the State of New Mexico. In *Bruss v. Harris*, 479 F.2d 392, 394 (10th Cir. 1973), the court addressed a similar claim:

> We attach no significance to the fact that the state sentence ran concurrently with the previously imposed federal sentence. Petitioner owed a debt to two sovereigns, and each had a right to exact its debt independently of the other. The petitioner's claim is that after having received credit from one sovereign he is entitled to double credit.

Lastly, Lewis decries the perceived unfairness and unjustness of his plight resulting from federal marshals' actions. Lewis was convicted of five distinct crimes for which he was sentenced to a total of more than 33 years imprisonment. Even if he serves every day of his federal sentence, his total time of incarceration (even counting the time he was a fugitive) will be less than 16 years.

CONCLUSION AND STATEMENT CONCERNING ORAL ARGUMENT

For the reasons stated above, Lewis's habeas petition was properly denied. Oral argument is not necessary in this case and the matter should be submitted on the briefs of the parties.

Respectfully submitted,
JOHN J. KELLY
United States Attorney
LARRY GÓMEZ
Assistant U.S. Attorney
P.O. Box 607
Albuquerque, NM 87103
(505) 766-3341

CERTIFICATE OF SERVICE

I HEREBY CERTIFY that the Brief of Appellee was served upon Defendant-Appellant, Frank Lewis, by mailing two true and correct copies to his Attorney of record, Tova Indritz, at her address of record, Post Office Box 449, Albuquerque, New Mexico, 87102, this <u>27th</u> day of January, 1995.

LARRY GÓMEZ
Assistant U.S. Attorney
P.O. Box 607
Albuquerque, NM 87103
(505) 766-3341

Web Sites

The following is a list of the Web sites presented in the Internet Resources sections of the text. The addresses are current as of the date of publication of this text. If a Web site is not at the address listed, it does not mean that the site no longer exists. The site could be down temporarily due to technical problems, or the address may have changed. To determine if the address has changed, search for a key term in the address using a search engine. Note that section III of Chapter 7 includes comprehensive coverage of additional nonfee-based Web sites.

> **For Example** If you are searching for Legal Pad and the site does not come up at the address listed in this appendix, perform a search using "Legal Pad" as the search term. If you are looking for a school's law library, search under the name of the school and "law library."

Links to documents that help you evaluate Web sites can be found at the site "Evaluation of Information Sources" by Alastair Smith at http://www.vuw.ac.nz/~agsmith/evaln/evaln.htm.

A. General Access and Links to Case and Statutory Law and Other Sources

Several sites provide links to Web sites that allow access to statutory law, case law, and other research sources. Some of the most comprehensive sites follow:

http://www.findlaw.com
> Findlaw is one of the most comprehensive sites providing links to sources for federal and state statutory and case law, law firms, legal organizations, law schools, legal practice materials, and numerous other sources.

http://www.law.indiana.edu
> This virtual law library includes links to sites of specialty areas of law, government resources, and law journals.

http://www.law.cornell.edu
> This Cornell University site provides resource guides to many different legal topics, including United States Supreme Court opinions, *United States Code,* and others.

http://www.washlaw.edu
> In addition to links to numerous law and legal research–related Web sites, legal newspapers, newsletters, and magazines, this Washburn University School of Law site provides links to state and federal court and government sites.

http://www.abanet.org/lawlink/home.html
> This American Bar Association site includes links to legal research sources, branches of government, and courts.

http://www.lawsonline.com/

This site provides quick access to state statutes, case law, and administrative law.

http://www.oyez.org

You may hear the oral arguments or read the court briefs of the United States Supreme Court cases at this site. The oral arguments are available for cases from 1960 to present.

http://law.gsu.edu/

Provides an index to legal sites on the Web, including links.

http://www.law.villanova.edu

This Villanova Law School site is a state court locator.

B. Government Sources

http://www.loc.gov/index.html

This is the Library of Congress site. You may search by title, key words, or author for any book that has an ISBN.

http://thomas.loc.gov

Legislative history is available at this site maintained by the Library of Congress.

http://www.access.gpo.gov

The Government Printing Office Web site provides access to congressional, presidential, and various other government documents, such as the *United States Code*.

http://www.whitehouse.gov/

The White House Virtual Library at this Web site provides access to presidential material.

http://www.house.gov/

This is the home page of the United States House of Representatives.

http://www.senate.gov/

This is the home page of the United States Senate.

http://www.usdoj.gov

United States attorney general opinions are available at this United States Department of Justice Web site.

http://www.uscourts.gov

This Web site is the home page for the federal courts.

http://www.courts.net

This site provides access to Web sites maintained by courts nationwide.

http://www.supremecourt.gov

This official page of the United States Supreme Court features court opinions, orders, rules, calendars and schedules, news releases, and general information.

http://www.naag.org

Many state attorney general opinions are available at this National Association of Attorneys General Web site.

http://www.regulations.gov

This is an online source for U.S. government regulations from nearly 300 federal agencies.

C. Law School Web Sites

Every law school has a Web site, and most sites provide links to the school's law library. A list of all the law school Web sites is too large to include here. To locate the site of a school of interest, use a search engine and insert the name of the law school. Research may be conducted through many law school library Web sites. Some of the more frequently used sites follow:

http://www.lawschool.cornell.edu/
Cornell University Law School

http://www.law.emory.edu/LAW/law.html
Emory University Law School

http://www.law.harvard.edu/library
Harvard Law School

http://www.law.indiana.edu/
Indiana University Law School

http://www.law.villanova.edu/
Villanova University School of Law

http://www.ll.georgetown.edu/
Georgetown University E.B. Williams Law Library

http://www.washlaw.edu
Washburn University School of Law

D. Miscellaneous

http://www.abanet.org/
American Bar Association

http://www.nala.org
National Association of Legal Assistants

http://www.paralegals.org
National Federation of Paralegal Associations

http://www.paralegaltoday.com
Paralegal Today magazine

http://www.martindale.com
Martindale-Hubbell locator site

http://www.alwd.org
The Web site for the *ALWD Citation Manual*. The site includes many features, such as additional material, examples, and updates.

http://www.legalbluebook.com
This Web site includes information on the 18th edition of *The Bluebook*.

http://www.ilrg.com
Links to form sources are provided at this Internet Legal Resource Guide site.

Active voice   *See* voice.

Adjective   A word that modifies a noun or pronoun. An adjective usually describes a noun or pronoun (a *red* car).

Administrative law   Rules, regulations, orders, and decisions adopted by administrative agencies that have the authority of law.

Advocacy   To support or urge the adoption of a position through the use of an argument.

Advocacy letter   *See* demand/advocacy letter.

Affirm   A decision of an appellate court that upholds the decision of the trial court.

Agreement   Words that are related must agree in number (singular/plural) and gender (feminine/masculine/neuter) (e.g., *Workers* must wear *their* helmets. *Mary* must wear *her* helmet.).

Antecedent   A word, clause, or phrase referred to by a pronoun. In the following sentence, the word *workers* is the antecedent for the pronoun *their*: The *workers* put on *their* helmets.

Apostrophe (')   A mark that indicates possession (Mary's hat) or forms a contraction (can't).

Appeals court   A court that reviews the decision of a trial court or other lower court to determine and correct any error that may have been made.

Appellant   The party who files an appeal. On appeal, the appellant argues that the lower court made an error that entitles the appellant to relief.

Appellate brief   An external memorandum of law submitted to a court of appeals. It presents the legal analysis, authority, and argument in support of a position that the lower court's decision or ruling was either correct or incorrect. It is often referred to as an appellate brief.

Appellee   The party who opposes the appeal. On appeal, the appellee usually argues that the lower court did not make an error that entitles the appellant to relief.

Authority   Anything a court may rely on when deciding an issue. It includes the law, such as constitutions and statutes, and nonlaw sources, such as legal encyclopedias and treatises.

Background facts   Facts presented in a court opinion, case brief, or legal memorandum that put the key facts in context. They give an overview of a factual event and provide the reader with the overall context within which the key facts occurred.

brackets ([ ])   Marks used to show changes in or additions to quotations, usually for the purpose of providing clarification to the quotation or indicating an error in the original quotations. (The privilege [against self-incrimination] allows an individual to remain silent.)

brief   *See* appellate court brief, case brief, and trial court brief.

brief answer   A section of a memorandum of law that presents a brief, precise answer to the issue(s) addressed in the memo.

canons of construction   The rules and guidelines courts use when interpreting statutes.

caption   In an opinion, the caption consists of the names of the parties to a lawsuit and their court status (e.g., Eddie RAEL, Plaintiff-Appellee v. Emillio CADENA and Manuel Cadena, Defendants-Appellants).

case brief   A written summary identifying the essential components of a court opinion.

case law   *See* common law/case law.

case law analysis   The analytical process engaged in to determine if and how a decision in a court opinion either governs or affects the outcome of a client's case.

cause of action   The legal basis upon which a lawsuit is based (e.g., negligence). To state a claim in a lawsuit means to allege facts in support of each element of the cause of action (e.g., in a negligence case, there must be facts alleged in support of each of the elements of negligence duty, breach of duty, proximate cause, and damages).

certiorari   *See* writ of certiorari.

citation   Information that allows the reader to locate where a reference can be found. In case law, the term refers to the volume number, page number, and name of the reporter where a case may be found.

cite   *See* citation.

collateral estoppel, doctrine of   The doctrine prevents a party in a lawsuit from relitigating an issue that has been decided in a previous lawsuit.

colon (:)   A punctuation mark used to introduce or call attention to information that follows. (The statutory requirements are the following: the will must be witnessed by two witnesses . . .).

comma (,)   The most frequently used punctuation mark. It is used to separate parts of a sentence.

common law/case law   The body of law created by courts. It is composed of the general legal rules, doctrines, and principles adopted by courts when interpreting existing law or when creating law in the absence of controlling enacted law.

concurring opinion   A judicial opinion that agrees with the majority holding in a case but for different or additional reasons than those presented by the majority.

constitution   A governing document adopted by the people that establishes the framework for the operation of the government, defines the powers of the government, and guarantees the fundamental rights of the people.

contraction   A word formed by combining two words: *can't* (cannot), *isn't* (is not).

counteranalysis   The process of discovering and considering the counterargument to a legal position or argument; the process of anticipating the argument the opponent is likely to raise in response to the analysis of an issue. It is the identification and objective evaluation of the strengths and weaknesses of a legal argument.

counterargument   The argument in opposition to a legal argument or position. The argument the opponent is likely to raise in response to the analysis of an issue.

court opinion   The statement of a court of its decision reached in a case, the rule that applies, and the reasons for the court's decision.

court rules   Procedural rules adopted by a court that govern the litigation process. Court rules often govern the format and style of documents submitted to the court.

dangling modifier   A modifier that does not modify any other part of a sentence.

dash (—)   A mark used in a sentence to emphasize something, set off lists, briefly summarize materials containing commas, or show an abrupt change of thought or direction. (The items located at the scene—the knife, the drugs, and the scarf—have disappeared from the evidence room.)

defendant   The party against whom a lawsuit is brought.

demand/advocacy letter   Correspondence designed to persuade someone to take action favorable to the interests of the client or cease acting in a manner that is detrimental to the client.

dissenting opinion   A judicial opinion in a case that disagrees with the majority opinion.

district court   In many states, the district court is the trial court of general jurisdiction. *See also* United States District Court.

ejusdem generis   A cannon of construction that provides that whenever a statute contains a specific list followed by a general term, the general term is interpreted to be limited to other things of the same class or kind as the list.

element   An essential component of a law, rule, principle, or doctrine. In order for a law, rule, and so on to apply, the requirements of each element must be met. (The elements of negligence are duty, breach of duty, proximate cause, and damages. For a claim of negligence to prevail, the plaintiff must establish that the defendant had a duty, the defendant breached the duty, the breach of duty was the cause of the incident, and the plaintiff was damaged as a result of the breach.)

ellipsis (. . .)   The use of three dots to indicate the omission of part of a quotation (e.g., The statute provides that contractors are responsible for . . . the preparation of work orders . . .).

enacted law   The body of law adopted by the people or legislative bodies, including constitutions, statutes, ordinances, and administrative rules and regulations.

expanded outline   *See* outline, expanded.

expressio unius   A canon of construction that provides that if a statute contains a list of items covered by the statute, everything else is excluded.

external memorandum   A memorandum of law designed for use outside the law office (e.g., memoranda submitted to a court, such as briefs in support of motions; memoranda designed for other external use, such as for clients or opposing attorneys).

fact   Information concerning some thing, action, event, or circumstance.

general jurisdiction   A court of general jurisdiction has the power, with few exceptions, to hear and decide any matter brought before it.

headnotes   Summaries of the points of law discussed in a court opinion prepared by the publisher of the opinion.

holding   The court's application of the rule of law to the legal question raised by the facts of a case; the court's answer to the legal issue in a case.

hyphen (-)   A mark used to form compound modifiers and compound nouns (e.g., *well-known*, *ex-judge*).

infinitive   A verb form that functions as a noun or as an auxiliary verb (e.g., to argue, to leave). A *split infinitive* refers to the placement of an adverb between *to* and the verb in an infinitive (e.g., to *completely* understand).

information letter   Correspondence that provides general legal information or background on a legal issue. It usually involves the communication of the results of legal research and analysis to a client or a third party.

in personam jurisdiction   *See* personal jurisdiction.

intellectual honesty   In the context of legal analysis, to research and analyze a problem objectively. This includes analyzing all aspects of a problem free of preconceived notions, personal views, and emotions.

interoffice memorandum of law   *See* office legal memorandum.

IRAC   An acronym commonly used in reference to the legal analysis process. It is composed of the first letter of the descriptive term for each step of the process—*issue, rule, analysis/application, conclusion.* The standard legal analysis process is the identification of the issue, followed by the presentation of the governing rule of law, the analysis/application of the rule of law, and the conclusion.

irrelevant facts   Those facts that are coincidental to an event but are not of significant legal importance in a case.

issue   The precise legal question raised by the specific facts of a dispute.

issue comprehensive/narrow statement   A complete statement of the issue that includes the specific law, legal question, and key facts.

issue short/broad statement   A broad formulation of the issue that usually does not include reference to the specific facts of the case or the applicable law.

Jurisdiction   The court's authority to hear and resolve specific disputes. Jurisdiction is usually composed of *personal jurisdiction* (authority over persons) and *subject matter jurisdiction* (authority over the types of cases a court may hear and decide).

key fact(s)   The legally significant facts of a case that raise the legal question of how or whether the law governing the dispute applies; the facts upon which the outcome of the case is determined. They are the facts that establish or satisfy the elements of a cause of action and are necessary to prove or disprove a claim. A key fact is so essential that, if it were changed, the outcome of the case would probably change.

key facts groups   Individual facts that, when considered as a group, are key facts. Individual facts, when treated as a group, may determine the outcome of a case.

key facts individual   A key fact that, if it were changed, the outcome of the case would be affected or changed.

key numbers   West Group has divided all areas of American law into various topics and subtopics. Each area is identified by a topic name, and each specific topic or subtopic is assigned a number called a key number.

law   The enforceable rules that govern individual and group conduct in a society. The law establishes standards of conduct, the procedures governing standards of conduct, and the remedies available when the standards are not followed.

legal analysis   The process of identifying the issue or issues presented by a client's facts and determining what law applies and how it applies; the process of applying the law to the facts of a case. It is an exploration of how and why a specific law does or does not apply.

legal issue   *See* issue.

legal research   The process of identifying the law or legal authority that applies to the issue.

legal writing process   A systematic approach to legal writing; an organized approach to legal research, analysis, and writing. It is composed of three stages: prewriting, writing, and postwriting.

legislative history   The record of legislation during the enactment process. It is composed of committee reports, transcripts of hearings, statements of legislators concerning the legislation, and any other material published for legislative use in regard to the legislation.

limited jurisdiction   This type of court is limited in the kinds of cases it may hear and decide.

majority opinion   The opinion in a court decision of the majority of judges.

mandatory authority   Any authority or source of law that a court must rely on or follow when reaching a decision (e.g., a decision of a higher court in the jurisdiction on the same or a similar issue).

memorandum of law   A written analysis of a legal problem. It is an informative document that summarizes the research and analysis of the legal issue or issues raised by the facts of a case. It contains a summary of the law and how the law applies in the case.

modifier   A word or phrase that provides a description of the subject, verb, or object in a sentence.

nominalization   A noun created from a verb (e.g., *realization* from the verb *realize*).

nouns   Words that refer to persons, places, things, or qualities.

office legal memorandum   A legal memorandum prepared for office use. It presents an objective legal analysis of the issue(s) raised by the facts of the client's case and usually includes the arguments in favor of and in opposition to the client's position. It is often referred to by other names, such as interoffice legal research memorandum, office research memorandum, and interoffice memorandum of law.

on all fours   A prior court opinion in which the key facts and applicable rule of law are identical or nearly identical with those of the client's case or the case before a court.

on point   A term used to refer to a prior court opinion in which the facts are sufficiently similar to the facts of the client's case or the case before the court for the prior court opinion to apply as precedent. A case is on point if the similarity between the key facts and rule of law or legal principle of the court opinion and those of the client's case is sufficient for the court opinion to govern or provide guidance to a later court in deciding the outcome of the client's case.

opinion   The written statement by the court expressing how it ruled in a case and the reasons for its ruling.

opinion letter   Correspondence, usually written to a client, that in addition to informing the reader of how the law applies to a specific question, provides legal advice. It informs the reader how the law applies and advises which steps should be taken.

outline   The skeletal structure and organizational framework of a writing.

outline, expanded   An outline that has been expanded so that it may be used in the prewriting stage. The use of an expanded outline allows the integration of all research, analysis, and ideas into an organized outline structure while research and analysis are being conducted. It facilitates the preparation of a rough draft.

paragraph   A group of sentences that address the same topic.

parallel citation   When a court opinion is printed in more than one reporter, each citation is a parallel citation to the other citation or citations, for example, "*Britton v. Britton*, **100 N.M. 424, 671 P.2d 1135** (1983)." The parallel citations are in bold.

parentheses ( )   Marks used to add to a sentence information that is outside the main idea of the sentence or of lesser importance.

pari materia   A canon of construction that provides that statutes dealing with the same subject should be interpreted consistently.

party   A plaintiff or defendant in a lawsuit.

passive voice   *See* voice.

personal jurisdiction   The authority of the court over the parties to resolve a legal dispute involving the parties.

persuasive authority   Any authority a court is not bound to consider or follow but may consider or follow when reaching a decision (e.g., a decision of a court in another state on the same or a similar issue, secondary authority, and so on).

plain meaning rule   A canon of construction that provides that if the meaning of a statute is clear on its face, it will be interpreted according to its plain meaning and the other canons of construction will not be applied by the court.

plaintiff   The party who starts (files) a lawsuit.

point heading   A summary of the position advocated in the argument section of a trial or appellate brief.

postwriting stage   The stage in the legal writing process where an assignment is revised, edited, and assembled in final form.

precedent   An earlier court decision on an issue that applies to govern or guide a subsequent court in its determination of an identical or similar issue based upon identical or similar facts. A court opinion is precedent if there is a sufficient similarity between the key facts and rule of law or legal principle of the court's opinion and the matter before the subsequent court.

predicate   A verb, its modifiers, and the object of the verb, such as a direct object (if necessary). The predicate of a sentence provides information concerning the subject of a sentence (e.g., Tom *ran to the store.*). The predicate of the sentence is in italic.

prewriting stage   The stage in the legal writing process where the assignment is organized, researched, and analyzed.

primary authority   Authority that is composed of the law (e.g., constitutions, statutes, and court opinions).

prior proceedings   The events that occurred in the litigation in a lower court or administrative hearing.

punctuation   Marks or characters used in writing to make the meaning clear and easy to understand, such as period (.), comma (,), semicolon (;), and colon (:).

purpose clause   A statutory section that includes the purpose the legislative body intended to accomplish when drafting the statute.

quotation   Marks used to identify and set off quoted material. (Mary said, "I do not believe it is true.")

Re   A term that means, "in the matter of, about, or concerning." It is usually placed at the beginning of the reference line in a memo or correspondence.

remand   A decision of an appellate court that sends the case back to the trial court for further action.

reverse   A decision of an appellate court that disagrees with the decision of the trial court.

salutation   The part of a letter that presents the greeting (Dear Ms. Jones).

scope   A statutory section that states what is specifically covered and not covered by the statute.

secondary authority   Any source of law a court may rely on that is not the law (e.g., legal treatises, restatements of the law, and legal encyclopedias).

semicolon (;)   A punctuation mark used to separate major elements of complex sentences, or to separate items in a series if the items are long or if one of the items has internal commas. (The shareholders held their meeting at noon; the board of directors met immediately thereafter.)

sentence   The fundamental building block of writing. It is composed of a group of words that convey a single thought. It is usually a statement in which the actor (subject) performs some action or describes a state of being (the predicate).

short title   The name by which a statute is known (e.g., Uniform Commercial Code Sales).

split infinitive   *See* infinitive.

squinting modifier   A modifier located in a position in a sentence that makes it unclear whether it modifies the word that precedes it or the word that follows it. (For example, "The report that was prepared *routinely* indicated that the structure was unsafe." It is unclear whether *routinely* refers to the report being prepared routinely or the report routinely indicated the structure was unsafe.)

stare decisis   A basic principle of the common law system that requires a court to follow a previous decision of that court or a higher court when the current decision involves issues and facts similar to those involved in the previous decision; the doctrine that provides that precedent should be followed.

statement of facts   The section of a memorandum of law that presents the factual context of the issue(s) addressed in the memorandum.

statutes   Laws passed by legislative bodies that declare rights and duties, or command or prohibit certain conduct.

statutory analysis   The interpretation and application of statutory law; the process of determining if a statute applies to a specific fact situation, how it applies, and the effect of that application.

statutory elements   The specific conditions or components of a statute that must be met for the statute to apply.

statutory law   The body of law composed of laws passed by legislative bodies. The term includes laws or ordinances passed by any legislative body.

subject   A noun or pronoun that is the actor in a sentence (e.g., *Tom* ran to the store.). The subject of the sentence is in italic.

subject matter jurisdiction   The types or kinds of cases the court has the authority to hear and decide.

topic sentence   The sentence that identifies the subject of a paragraph. It introduces the subject and provides the focus of a paragraph.

trial court   The court where the matter is heard and decided. In the trial court testimony is heard, evidence is taken, and a decision is reached.

trial court brief   An external memorandum of law submitted to a trial court. It presents the legal authority and argument in support of a position advocated by an attorney, usually in regard to a motion or issue being addressed by the court. It is often referred to as a trial brief.

United States District Court   The trial court of general jurisdiction in the federal judicial system.

United States Supreme Court   The final court of appeals in the federal system and the highest court in the United States.

verbs   Words that express action, a state of being or feeling, or a relation between two things (e.g., Tom *ran* to the store.). The verb in this sentence is in italic.

voice   The relationship of the subject to the action of the sentence.
   Active voice: the subject of the sentence is performing the action in the sentence. (The automobile hit the child.)
   Passive voice: the subject of the sentence is acted upon. (The child was hit by the automobile.)

writing stage   The stage in the legal writing process where research, analysis, and ideas are assembled into a written product.

writ of certiorari   A writ from a higher court asking a lower court for the record of a case. A petition for a writ of certiorari is a request filed by a party in a lawsuit that a higher court is to review the decision of a lower court.

INDEX